Medieval Britain
1300-1500
SCOTLAND
WALES
Glasgow
Lindisfarne
Bamborough
Alnwick
Melrose
I. OF ARRAN
TYNE
Carlisle
Finchale
TEES
Whitby
Rievaulx
ISLE OF MAN
Fountains
York
HUMBER
TRENT
Beaumaris
Conway
Bangor
Caernarvon
Valle Crucis
Darley
Lincoln
Tattershall
Nottingham
Sempringham
Walsingham
Castle Rising
Harlech
SEVERN
Crowland
Norwich
Caister
Carrow
Lichfield
Thorney
Peterborough
Bungay
Maxstoke
Ramsey
Ludlow
Ely
Bury St. Edmunds
WYE
Catesby
Worcester
Evesham
Elstow
Gt. Malvern
Hereford
Deerhurst
Hayles
Woburn
Flamstead
St. Davids
Tewkesbury
Gloucester
Godstow
St. Albans
Thame
Abingdon
Dorchester
Tintern
Chepstow
LONDON
Barking
Llandaff
Malmesbury
Goring
Westminster
Rochester
Reading
Windsor
Tower of London
Lacock
Bath
East Sheen
Canterbury
Cleeve
Farleigh Hungerford
Wells
Glastonbury
Salisbury
Bodiam
Athelney
Bruton
Winchester
Battle
Romsey
Herstmonceux
Portchester
Forde
Chichester
Pevensey
Crediton
Portsmouth
Exeter
Corfe
I. OF WIGHT
ENGLISH CHANNEL
- Castle
- Cathedral or Religious Institution
CELTIC SPEAKING
NORTHERN ENGLISH
WEST MIDLAND ENGLISH
EAST MIDLAND ENGLISH
KENTISH ENGLISH
SOUTHERN ENGLISH

Regions and Towns associated with Writers
Bannockburn
Edinburgh
LAMMERMUIR HILLS
Berwick
Lindisfarne
TWEED
ETTRICK
SOUTHERN UPLANDS
Flodden and Halidon Hill
ISLE OF ARRAN
Ayr
Auchinleck
LIDDESDALE
CHEVIOTS
Otterbourne
Gretna Green
HADRIAN'S WALL
Newcastle
Carlisle
PENNINES
Cockermouth
Grasmere
Hawkshead
NORTH YORK MOOR
Marston Moor
Lancaster
York
Haworth
Hull
Preston
Wakefield
Manchester
Liverpool
GWYNEDD
Knutsford
SHERWOOD FOREST
Lincoln
Chester
Stoke
Nottingham
Boston
Norwich
Shrewsbury
Lichfield
CAMBRIAN MTS.
Bosworth
Little Gidding
Huntingdon
FENS
Birmingham
Coventry
Ely
Bury St. Edmunds
Ludlow
Rugby
Naseby
Aldeburgh
Warwick
Cambridge
FOREST OF ARDEN
Stratford
Bedford
Worcester
Gt. Malvern
Banbury
Buckingham
SILURES
VERULAMIUM
COTSWOLD HILLS
CHILTERN HILLS
St. Albans
Monmouth
Oxford
Tintern
FOREST OF DEAN
Eton
Harrow
Malmesbury
Westminster
LONDON
Swansea
Bristol
Windsor
Greenwich
Newbury
Southwark
Rochester
Bath
SALISBURY PLAIN
Canterbury
MENDIP HILLS
Stonehenge
Steventon
NORTH DOWNS
Dover
EXMOOR
Sedgemoor
Glastonbury
Wilton
Salisbury
Winchester
QUANTOCK HILLS
Southampton
SOUTH DOWNS
Portchester
NEW FOREST
Portsmouth
Exeter
ISLE OF WIGHT
Tintagel
Dorchester
Widdecombe
DARTMOOR
Plymouth
ENGLISH CHANNEL
Lands End
ST. MICHAEL'S MOUNT
LYONESSE ISLAND
Extinct names: LYONESSE ISLAND
Thomas Hardy's Wessex
D.H. Lawrence: Nottinghamshire
Arnold Bennett The 5 Towns
Chaucer: Canterbury Pilgrimage
The Brontës: Yorkshire W. Riding
W. Langland: Malvern Hills
J. Clare: Northamptonshire
G. Crabbe: Suffolk Coast
Burns & Scott: Scott. Lowlands
George Eliot: Warwickshire
W. Wordsworth: Lake District
Balladists: Anglo-Scott. Border

A Companion to British Literature

Christopher Gillie

GRAND RIVER BOOKS · 1249 WASHINGTON BLVD ·
DETROIT, MICHIGAN 48226

US ISBN 0-8103-2022-3
UK ISBN 0 582 55706 2

To Cecilia and in memory of Darsie

Contents

Symbols

References:

* The asterisk is used in two ways:

1 Following an item, it means that further information is available in the *Reference Section*, *eg*

T. S. Eliot* – refers to the entry 'Eliot, Thomas Stearns'

*Bleak House** – refers to the entry '*Bleak House*' (under B)

2 *a* Before a word or words, it means 'See (also) the entry in the *Reference Section*. . .', *eg*

*Morality Plays – See the *Reference Section* entry 'Morality Plays' (under M)

b Before figures, it means 'See (also) the *Essay Section*. . .', *eg*

*1.2.4 – See Essay 1, section 2.4

Dates:

'Forster, E. M. (1879–1970)' – dates of birth and death

'Elizabeth I (1558–1603)' – dates of the beginning and end of a sovereign's reign

Symbols used to indicate the usual British-English pronunciation of the names:

CONSONANT SOUNDS	ʃ as in *sh*ip	ʒ as in mea*s*ure
	tʃ – *ch*in	dʒ – *j*u*dg*e
	θ – *th*in	ð – *th*is
	j – *y*es	ŋ – lo*ng*
VOWEL SOUNDS	a as in c*a*t	a: as in f*ar*
	i – w*i*n	i: – s*ee*
	u – p*u*t	u: – t*oo*
	o – l*o*t	o: – s*aw*
	ə – comm*a*	ə: – g*ir*l
	e – b*e*g	ʌ – f*u*n
DIPHTHONGS	ai as in b*uy*	au as in h*ow*
	ei – d*ay*	əu – ag*o*
	oi – b*oy*	
	iə as in h*ere*	
	eə – f*air*	
	uə – s*ure*	
STRESS	(ˈ) is placed before a stressed syllable, e.g. /ˈsi:zə/ (*Cae*sar), /əˈθeləu/ (O*the*llo)	

Preface to the New Edition

The function of a Companion is to provide information needed in study. The purpose of this Preface is to make clear, first, the kinds of reader to whom this information is particularly addressed; secondly, the kinds of information that the book seeks to provide; and thirdly, the plan of the book – that is to say, the ways in which the information is provided.

Readers. The book is intended for two categories: on the one hand for readers who are studying English Literature in other countries, whether or not their first language is English. It is meant for general readers as well as students, but the kind of reader kept specially in mind is the student whose knowledge of the language is good, and who is approaching or actually engaged in university studies. At the same time, it is felt that readers in Britain will also find a use for the book. Such readers may well feel that some of the information offered is already known to them, but the majority of it is of the sort that every serious reader above a superficial level will require.

Information. Because the book is addressed also to foreign readers, it contains more information about the background to literature than is usual in such works of reference. This is the obvious reason for the three essays on English history, society and thought, and for articles in the alphabetical reference section on such subjects as politics, education and places.

In regard to the reference section, it has been assumed that readers will need at least the bare biographical facts about writers, in so far as these are relevant to the character of their works, and an outline of the contents of their main works. However, no Companion can include all writers, still less articles on, or even mention of, all their works. Consequently some principle of selection is required. The principle adopted has been to choose for more extended account those subjects, writers and works which have attracted most interest during the last fifty years of scholastic and critical study. A partial exception has been made in the choice of contemporary writers: many readers have a natural preference for writers of their own day, and consequently the names of living writers have been included more liberally than those of past periods. A very brief bibliography is usually offered at the end of an article on a writer. These bibliographies are not, of course, comprehensive, but give some guidance to the reader who needs extended information.

Dates after the names of people indicate their life spans, except when they follow the names of kings, when they show the length of the reign. Dates after the titles of works indicate the time of writing, and also of publication when these nearly coincide.

Information about American and Commonwealth literature has not been included except when writers such as Henry James and T. S. Eliot have adopted Britain as their place of work, or, as in the instance of Ezra Pound, where a writer has made a strong impact on English literature. The literatures of Commonwealth countries and of the United States proceed from cultures of distinct growth; to include them in English literature merely because they happen to be in the same language would be misleading. However, brief accounts are included of those foreign writers and literatures which have had a marked influence on English writing.

Plan. The disadvantage of a work of reference in which all the information is arranged alphabetically is that the reader is not able to see this information in proper perspective; each subject has the appearance of existing independently of its context in contemporary society, and of being isolated from its context in history. To counteract this disadvantage, the following expedients have been used.

1. One quarter of the book consists of essays, divided into sections so that the reader need not feel obliged to read an entire essay to find the information he needs. The essays are intended to present English literature as a unity, and to enable the reader to feel it as constantly related to other aspects of English life and thought.

2. A liberal use of cross-reference has been made. In the essays, names, titles, and topics are frequently marked with an asterisk (*) to guide the reader to the appropriate article in the reference section for clearer or more detailed explanation. Similarly, many of the articles in the reference section have references to those sections of the essays which deal with the topic, as well as to articles on related topics elsewhere in the reference section.

For this second edition twenty-six entries have been added to the Reference Section and twenty-eight others have been amended or expanded. There are two additional maps, and titles of works by living authors have been updated. Entries referring fictional characters to the works in which they occur have been omitted, unless they contain additional information.

Acknowledgments. No work of reference on so large and complex a subject as English Literature can be altogether adequate in the information it provides, particularly when it is the work of a single writer. The present Companion would be much more inadequate than it is without the generous and helpful assistance of the following advisers: Professor J. C. Maxwell, who made many suggestions and corrections; L. G. Alexander, S. H. Burton, A. G. Eyre, Dr Bernard Lott, and D. K. Swan, who gave general advice throughout; and, in their own special fields, J. C. Alldridge, B. A. Richards, D. G. Richards, A. E. Rodway and Dr. A. Ross.

Christopher Gillie

Acknowledgments

We are grateful to the following for permission to reproduce copyright material:

J. M. Dent & Sons Ltd. and Oxford University Press, New York for extracts from *Piers Plowman* modernized by Coghill; J. M. Dent & Sons Ltd. and New Directions Publishing Corporation for 'The Force that Through the Green Fuse' by Dylan Thomas: *Dylan Thomas Collected Poems*, Copyright 1939 by New Directions Publishing Corporation; Faber & Faber Ltd. and Harper & Row for 'The Thought Fox' by Ted Hughes, Copyright 1957 by Ted Hughes. By permission of Harper & Row, Publishers Inc.; Faber & Faber Ltd. and Harcourt Brace Jovanovich Inc. for the first twenty-four lines of 'The Waste Land' by T. S. Eliot from *Collected Poems 1909–1962* by T. S. Eliot, Copyright 1936 by Harcourt Brace Jovanovich, Inc., Copyright 1963, 1964 by T. S. Eliot. Reprinted by permission of the publisher; The Trustees of the Hardy Estate, The Macmillan Company of Canada, Macmillan London and Basingstoke and The Macmillan Company of New York for 'At Day-Close in November' by Thomas Hardy; Oxford University Press on behalf of the Society of Jesus for 'Spring and Fall' by G. M. Hopkins; Penguin Books Ltd. for an extract from 'Sir Gawain and the Green Knight', II, iii, translated by Brian Stone, Copyright Brian Stone, 1959; and Routledge & Kegan Paul Ltd. for 'On the Death of a Child' from *The Laughing Hyena and Other Poems* by D. J. Enright (1953).

We are grateful to the following for permission to reproduce the illustrations:

Aerofilms Limited for pages 86 below, 87 below, 89 above, 108 above, 494, 769, 828; B. T. Batsford for pages 88 centre, 88 below, 578; City of Birmingham Corporation for page 473; Bodleian Library, Oxford for pages 637, 643; The Bodley Head for page 405 right; The Trustees of the British Museum for pages 90 below, 91 below, 105 below, 107 above, 108 below, 257, 390, 410, 425, 427, 469, 472, 489, 493, 501, 515, 540, 543, 561, 571, 663, 695, 696, 702, 717, 741, 746, 755, 756, 786, 796, 799, 832, 850, 881; Browns of Liverpool for pages 443, 790; Cambridge University Library for pages 95 above, 95 centre left, 104, 105 above, 109 below, 417, 692, 778, 848; The trustees of the Chatsworth Settlement for page 641; Corpus Christi College, Cambridge for page 268; *Country Life* for pages 89 below, 861; William Gordon Davis for page 93; John R. Freeman for pages 95 centre right, 106 below; The Guildhall Library for pages 513, 548; pages 107 below, 463 below right and 761 are reproduced by gracious permission of Her Majesty the Queen; *Illustrated London News* for page 110 below; A. F. Kersting for pages 87 above, 89 centre; London Museum for page 525; Magdalene College, Cambridge for page 708; Manchester City Art Gallery for page 42; The Mansell Collection for facing page 1, pages 92 above, 97, 109 above, 122, 182, 258, 322, 419, 431, 464 above, 464 below right, 465 above, 465 below left, 466, 467, 474, 510, 512, 584, 615, 659, 660, 713, 719, 780, 853; Mermaid Theatre for page 264; National Gallery for page 95 below; National Monuments Record for pages 86 above, 88 above, 552, 621, 676, 820, 870, 872;

National Portrait Gallery for pages 463 below left, 464 below left, 465 below centre, 465 below right, 619, 751, 781; *Punch* for page 735; R. A. (Postcards) Limited for page 234; Radio Times Hulton Picture Library for pages 393, 404 left, 464 below centre, 492, 671, 699, 796; His Grace the Duke of Richmond and Gordon for page 106 above; Science Museum for page 98; Scottish National Portrait Gallery for page 604; Edwin Smith for pages 90 above, 91 above, 705, 809; Society of Antiquaries for page 92 below; The Tate Gallery for pages 407, 439, 728; *The Times* for page 110 above; Trinity College, Cambridge for page 657; Rodney Todd-White and Son for page 92 centre; University Library, Utrecht for page 235; Victoria and Albert Museum for pages 222, 461, 462, 463 above; The Walker Art Gallery, Liverpool for page 537.

The essay section

The Election at Eatanswill. Elections of M.P.s to Parliament were often like very disorderly popular festivals, since candidates were inclined to attract support by distributing large supplies of free drink, and factions supporting rival candidates were apt to come to blows, as in the illustration, taken from Dickens's first novel, *Pickwick Papers*.

I Political history and institutions of England: 1066 – *present day*

1.1 1066–1485
Introduction
1.1.1 Judicial and political institutions
1.1.2 Relationship with France
1.1.3 Relationships with Scotland, Ireland, Wales

1.2 1485–1603
Introduction
1.2.1 Tudor government
1.2.2 The English Reformation
1.2.3 Political aspects of the English Renaissance

1.3 1603–1714
Introduction
1.3.1 Puritanism, the Civil War, and the Protectorate
1.3.2 Republican interlude: the Protectorate
1.3.3 The Restoration and the beginning of party politics
1.3.4 The Revolution of 1688 and the Act of Settlement (1701)
1.3.5 England into Great Britain: the relationship with Ireland and Scotland

1.4 1714–1815
Introduction
1.4.1. The Whig oligarchy
1.4.2. The revival of Toryism
1.4.3 The French Revolution: the Industrial Revolution: the Napoleonic War

1.5 1815–present day
Introduction
1.5.1 Political change
1.5.2 The British Empire
1.5.3 Relationship with Ireland
1.5.4 Britain today: the Welfare State

I.I

1066—1485

Introduction

English people think of their history as having an unusually distinct beginning: the Battle of Hastings, 1066. This was the victory of William*, Duke of Normandy, Norse by descent and French by culture, over the Anglo-Saxon king, Harold; William went on to conquer the whole of England, though not the rest of Britain (i.e. Scotland*, Wales* and Ireland*). Such a view of the beginning of English history is of course a simplified one; it is not true that all Anglo-Saxon political habits of thought and institutions were extinguished by the Conquest, nor is it true that Anglo-Saxon art and literature, which had been notable, simply expired.

Nonetheless, the Norman Conquest made a profound break in English political and cultural history. Politically, William I and his successors were able, because of the completeness of the Conquest, to reorganize governing institutions, giving them a pattern which is still visible as the basis of those of the present day. Socially, he removed most of the Anglo-Saxon ruling class, replacing it by his own Norman-French followers, bound together by a Norman-French system of relationships. Culturally, this immense social change meant that England became a three-language nation for at least two centuries: the upper class spoke French, and English was the tongue of the lower classes, while the educated class (the churchmen or 'clerks') used Latin – as elsewhere in Europe – for official business and scholarship.

Another important consequence of the Conquest was that, since the royal families and the nobility were Norman-French or French, England was closely involved in French politics and wars against the kings of France until the middle of the 15th century. In the second half of the period this conflict with France led the Norman-French nobility of England to think of themselves as English rather than French, and in the 14th century they took to English instead of French as their normal speech. Henry IV* (1399–1413) is reputed to have been the first of the kings since the Conquest to use English as his native tongue; Chaucer* (1340?–1400) was the first poet of a royal court to write in English.

The period 1066–1485 is what we think of as 'the English Middle Ages' linguistically, as the 'Middle English' period between the Old English of the pre-Conquest Anglo-Saxons and the Modern English speech and writing of the 16th century. It shaped many of the most important political institutions of our own day, and an English culture which is almost as different from the culture of the

***Indicates mention in the reference section**

Anglo-Saxons as it is from the Norman-French culture that succeeded it. Above all, it shaped a sense of nationhood and civilization among the English, a sense of identity which intensified their awareness of the identity of the larger civilization of Europe in which they participated.

1.1.1. *Judicial and political institutions*

BECKET: *You forget the barons. Who will not forget*
Constant curbing of petty privilege.
TEMPTER: *Against the barons*
Is King's cause, churl's cause, Chancellor's cause.

T. S. Eliot* – *Murder in the Cathedral*

1.1.1.1 *Feudalism*

The social organization which William the Conqueror established in England was the one known to most of western Europe in the 11th century; historians call it 'the feudal system'. This kind of society had grown up under the later Roman Empire of the West, when organization was breaking down and social order had to be maintained by an appeal to self-interest. By this 'system', a landholder held his land as a 'feudum' or 'fee' from a superior lord; in return for protection by this superior, the landholder rendered him some service, such as work on the superior's land or military service. Feudal relationship had grown up spontaneously as a method by which the relatively weak could find defence against forces of disorder, but in few regions besides England after the Conquest was it in any sense systematic. Even in England, the king's government needed its own centralizing institutions for efficient rule; the barons (i.e. the nobility) recognized no interests except their own, evaded service of the king when they could, and regarded themselves as independent rulers within their own territories.

1.1.1.2 *The King's Council and the Chancellor*

Thus the King's Council (Curia Regis) became a central body of professional officials, who, under efficient kings such as Henry I (1100–35) and Henry II (1154–89), worked equally as administrators and as judges ensuring that 'the King's Peace' was kept uniformly throughout the country. The king needed educated men for such tasks, and until the 14th century he found them only among men bred to the Church, such as Thomas à Becket*, Henry II's Chancellor, and later Archbishop and the king's enemy. The king's Chancellor was his secretary, and the office was at first overshadowed by that of Justiciar, i.e. chief judge. After 1231, however, the office of Justiciar died out, and the Chancellorship became the most important office of state. The Chancellor came to control not only the administrative machine but also the judicial system, since it was he who handled petitions to the king. The modern Lord Chancellor* is the historical descendant of the medieval chancellors; he is the head of the judicial system (equivalent to a Minister of

Justice) and, though his political importance diminished greatly after the reign of Henry VIII* (1509–47), he still has high political status as president of the upper house of Parliament, the House of Lords.

1.1.1.3 *The Great Council and Parliament*

When he needed the support of his nobles, the king expanded his Curia Regis into the Magnum Concilium (Great Council), of which the modern House of Lords* is the historical descendant. Now, as then, the reigning king or queen composes it by summoning to it the lords, lay and spiritual,– i.e. the hereditary nobility and the bishops – though the House of Lords also contains other components.

In 1295 Edward I*, following the example of Simon de Montfort, who had ruled England during part of the previous reign of Henry III*, expanded the Great Council by adding to it the Commons*, i.e. elected representatives of the towns and Knights of the Shire* from the provincial districts now known as counties. The king was not making a very early experiment in liberal democracy when he formed this Model Parliament; he was merely continuing the policy of previous Norman* and Plantagenet* kings of extending the effectiveness of their central administration. The great administrative problem for governments in the 12th and 13th centuries, when communications were bad, administrators few, and the nobility had not learned public spirit, was to establish effective relationships with the people. When the king needed to raise money by taxation, he could not rely on his officials to collect it against the wishes of local interests, until he found means to deal directly with these interests through their elected representatives. Thus the system of government through elected representatives, which by the end of the 19th century was the main instrument of democracy, was in the 14th century an instrument of monarchy, exercised by kings who never imagined that one day the people would take possession of it and use it against monarchical rule. The process by which this came about was gradual: already in the 14th century the Commons presented 'petitions' to the king, which he often found it expedient to grant in order to secure their agreement to taxation more readily; in the 15th century this petition became a 'bill' which, when accepted by the king, was called an 'act' or 'statute' and became a law of the land; in the 17th century Parliament secured that laws were made in no other way, and in the 18th century the king's assent was becoming what it is today – a mere formality concluding a procedure initiated by Parliament*.

1.1.1.4 *Trial by jury*

The use of elected representatives to assist government did not originate with the transformation of the Great Council into Parliament by the addition of the Commons. It was already a habit of the Curia Regis to send for representative Knights of the Shire to give evidence in difficult cases that came before it, and the annual shire courts, presided over by sheriffs ('shire reeves'), were attended by representatives from the subdivisions ('hundreds') of the shires. More important, because it was as central to the development of justice as representatives of the Commons were to the development of government, was the election of 'sworn men' or 'juries'* (from French *juré*) to meet judges (Justices of Assize) sent out from the Curia Regis to the shires. These judges tried cases which were too serious for the powers of the local shire courts. In criminal cases, it was at first the main function of the juries to present to the royal judges such men as were accused of serious crimes; the actual trial of criminal cases in the 11th and 12th centuries was often conducted by some sort of 'ordeal' undergone by the accused man, who was judged guilty or otherwise in accordance with his ability to survive it. 'Trial by ordeal' was supposed to reveal the judgement of Heaven which would not allow an innocent man to perish; not until the 13th century did public opinion come to accept the judgement of a jury, selected from among neighbours, as a superior means of arriving at the truth. In 'civil cases' of disputes between neighbours, the jury was at first a panel of witnesses who declared the facts (e.g. about the ownership of land) as they knew them. But like the elected representatives of the Commons summoned by the kings to Parliament, the jury began as an instrument to secure efficient government, and by the 17th century it was being used by opponents of the king's government as a safeguard to private liberty.

1.1.1.5 *Local government: Sheriffs and Justices of the Peace*

The office of Sheriff, who stood for the king's interests in every shire, was important in the Middle Ages and still survives, but it began to lose most of its importance in the 16th century. He was the principal local authority for law and order; however, he was not a professional official like the members of the king's court, but a local landholder of importance, who occasionally succeeded in making the office hereditary in his family. Justices of the Peace (first known as Guardians of the Peace and nowadays called Magistrates*) began obscurely in the 12th and 13th centuries and only became supremely important in the 16th century. Like the sheriff, they have never been professional, but were until the 19th century members of the middle range of landowner. Nowadays they are commonly drawn from all classes, trades and professions, and their authority is restricted to trial (without jury, but with a professional lawyer called the Clerk to advise them) of petty offences and the examination of more serious charges. At the height of their power (16th–19th centuries) they were the principal local authorities. Sometimes, like Justice Shallow in Shakespeare's *Henry IV**, they held office more because of their status in their localities than because of their competence for the work; equally often, they were responsible men who constituted a very important link between the government and society. The 18th-century novelist, Henry Fielding*, himself an admirable representative of the class of magistrates, depicts a worthy and an unworthy example in Squire Allworthy and Squire Western, characters in his novel, *Tom Jones**.

1.1.1.6 *Common Law; Magna Carta*

The history of England in the Middle Ages is partly the political and legal shaping of a society; the chief shaping force was the monarchy, which enforced through its officials a Common Law* (i.e. a law which was the same for all members of society) based on custom and precedent. The Common Law was a great force for social liberation, because it freed common men from tyranny by the self-interested nobility. However, the kings sometimes attempted to advance their personal interests against those of society, and it is often difficult to decide when they were in fact doing this and when they were really resisting the self-interest of the nobles. An outstanding example of this difficulty is the reign of King John* (1199–1216), who is traditionally regarded as a bad, self-interested king, on whom the barons, in alliance with the Church, were able to impose a charter of rights – the famous Magna Carta* (Great Charter) of 1215. This charter was first given importance as an assertion of human rights against arbitrary government in the 17th century, when Parliament came into open conflict with the king, and used it to provide its members with legal support and protection; clauses in it can be interpreted as a basis for the right of trial by jury and for protection against imprisonment without trial. In other respects, modern historians are inclined to interpret Magna Carta as principally a defence of the interests of the barons and of the Church. The truth is, perhaps, that in defending their class the barons created a precedent for the defence of more general liberties later.

1.1.2. *Relationship with France*

KING HENRY: *For he today that sheds his blood with me*
Shall be my brother; be he ne'er so vile,
This day shall gentle his condition:
And gentlemen in England now a-bed
Shall think themselves accurst they were not here;
And hold their manhoods cheap whiles any speaks
That fought with us upon Saint Crispin's day.

Shakespeare – *Henry V** (before the Battle of Agincourt)

The Norman* and Plantagenet* kings of England were also French nobles; Henry II* (1154–89) indeed controlled more land in France than did the King of France himself; all of it was acquired by inheritance and by marriage. Such preponderance of power in France naturally led to rivalry with the French king, and to intermittent war throughout the 12th and 13th centuries; at the end of this period, the French possessions of the kings of England were greatly reduced.

The second and more important phase of medieval Anglo-French hostility began in 1337 and ended in 1453; it is known as the Hundred Years' War*, and ostensibly it was caused by the claim of Edward III (1327–77) to be the rightful King of France. The real causes were deeper and more complex; amongst them was the fact that the English national identity had taken shape faster than that of France, and the mood of this new national consciousness was consequently self-reliant and aggressive, particularly among the rich and ambitious nobility. 'The English', wrote the 14th-century French chronicler Froissart*, 'will never love or honour their king, unless he be victorious and a lover of arms and war against their neighbours. . . . The king of England must needs obey his people and do their will.' Between 1307 and 1460, the kings who did not engage in successful war in France all had serious trouble with their nobility at home: Edward II* (1307–27), Richard II* (1377–99), Henry IV* (1399–1413) and especially Henry VI* (1422–61). The prosperous reigns were those of successful warriors: Edward III* (1327–77, especially until 1360) and Henry V* (1413–22). Shakespeare makes the dying Henry IV give this advice to his son:

> *Therefore, my Harry,*
> *Be it thy course to busy giddy minds*
> *With foreign quarrels; that action, hence borne out,*
> *May waste the memory of the former days.*
>
> *2 Henry IV* IV.v

According to modern ideas, the Hundred Years' War was an inexcusable war of aggression, but it had the effect of further strengthening the English sense of national unity, as well as creating – by the end – such a feeling among the French. The few great battles (Crécy* 1346, Poitiers 1356, and Agincourt* 1415) were victories of English common soldiers (archers, using the long bow) over French aristocratic cavalry; the fact indicates radical historical change, since it means that this was the first major European war to be fought (at first only on the English side, but in the end on both sides) by national armies, and not by feudal ones loosely kept together by ties with the feudal lords.

The final defeat of the English was in the long run a blessing not only for the French. The English royalty and nobility awoke from the distraction of their French dreams. If they had been realized, England, as the smaller and poorer country, would have become a mere appendage to France; instead she became free to shape her own very individual course in the newly arising comity of self-conscious European nations. But the immediate effect on England was disastrous; failure in the foreign war led to extensive civil war amongst the English nobility.

The Wars of the Roses*, which opened in 1455 and were only finally closed by by the victory of Henry Tudor over Richard III* at the battle of Bosworth in 1485, were remembered as a warning of the hell of national disunity. Shakespeare's first four history plays (*1, 2,* & *3 Henry VI** and *Richard III**) are a tragic epic on the culmination of this disunity, just as his second historical tetralogy (*Richard II**, *1* & *2 Henry IV**, *Henry V**) celebrates the rescue of a nation from civil wars into brotherhood.

1.1.3. *Relationships with Scotland, Ireland, Wales*

We are discussing English history, since we are concerned with the political background to English literature. It is still important to remember that England is not Britain, though in modern times the names are so often used interchangeably. In 1485 there was, as yet, no Britain. Politically, Ireland* was overrun by Anglo-Norman barons in the 12th century, and Henry II took the title of Lord of Ireland, but English rule was not effective beyond a strip on the eastern coastline known as the Pale*; Wales* was conquered by Edward I in the 13th century, but it was not properly assimilated into the English political system until the 16th; Scotland* defeated English attempts to conquer it early in the 14th century, and during the Hundred Years' War it allied itself to France. Both Ireland and Wales had Celtic spoken languages with literatures in those languages, and Scotland was divided between Celtic and a variety of English. Only Scotland made a contribution to literature in English during the Middle Ages – see the item in the reference section, Scottish Literature.

1.2

1485–1603

Introduction

England was one of the first countries in Europe to feel its nationhood. It had behaved in the 14th and 15th centuries like Europe's turbulent boy. In the 16th century England was like a boy flanked by giant men; France and Spain had also achieved unity and nationhood. They towered above England almost as the U.S.A. and the U.S.S.R. do today, and constituted a potential – at times an actual – threat to its very existence. Fortunately, they were not often friendly to each other.

Yet this was not a period of decline for England; its relative inferiority was due to the increase in stature of its neighbours, not to its own diminution. On the contrary, the 16th century was that in which the nation grew up, consolidated its energies, and found its true use for them overseas in seafaring adventure. The century was indeed more fortunate for England than for France and Spain, for at the end of it England, unlike Spain, was still advancing economically, and unlike France it had lost none of the representative political institutions which France had sacrificed.

All this was thanks partly to the reigning family of the Tudors*, the most gifted of the dynasties which have reigned over England. National solidarity elsewhere in Europe had been gained by the consolidation of monarchic power, and in this England was no exception; the period is in fact sometimes described as that of the 'Tudor despotism'. Yet Henry VIII* (1509–47), the most apparently despotic of English sovereigns, has also been described by an English historian as 'the greatest parliamentarian ever to occupy the English throne'. This seeming paradox is explained by the fact that, whereas the other sovereigns of Europe relied on their professional armies for their authority, and abandoned, as forces for disunity, their representative institutions, the Tudors had no such armies, and, realizing that they could achieve little if they did not carry the nation with them, they found it necessary to keep Parliament alive. So it happened that the political institutions that eventually made for popular government survived in England while they decayed elsewhere; their survival in this period accounts for the difference between the later history of England and that of the other larger nations of Europe.

1.2.1. *Tudor government*

1.2.1.1 *The Privy Council and the Prerogative Courts*

SHALLOW: *I will make a Star-Chamber* matter of it; if he were twenty Sir John Falstaffs, he shall not abuse Robert Shallow, esquire.... Knight, you have beaten my men, killed my deer, and broke open my lodge.*
FALSTAFF: *But not kiss'd your keeper's daughter?*
SHALLOW: *Tut, a pin! this shall be answered.*
FALSTAFF: *I will answer it straight; I have done all this.—That is now answered.*
SHALLOW: *The Council shall know this.*

Shakespeare – *The Merry Wives of Windsor** I.i

Although they found it wiser to respect and use Parliament while other European monarchs found it more convenient to relinquish equivalent institutions, the Tudors nonetheless required other institutions of government which were more strengthening to their power.

In the 15th century, Parliament, though it had by no means yet become the channel of national feeling, was already an instrument of opposition to the monarchy. The House of Lords was the meeting-place of the great nobles who tore England apart in the Wars of the Roses, and they were able to use the House of Commons as their tool, for the townsmen and smaller landowners who composed it were not yet able to find an independent voice and leadership. To manage so dangerous a body, the Tudors relied upon the old Curia Regis (King's Council), which by this time was known as the Privy Council. The Privy Council had the acknowledged right to issue ordinances which had the force of law, and when the matter affected the nation too gravely for this to be a wise procedure, the Councillors took their seats in Parliament, much as modern ministers do, and directed the needed Bills through both Houses.

But the Privy Council was put to other purposes as well; subcommittees of it were used to expand the king's administration and justice, just as Henry II in the 12th century had used the Curia Regis to expand his system of justice by imposing on the feudal nobles the rule of Common Law. The weaknesses of the Common Law courts in the 16th century were that their procedure was often slow, and that the juries employed in them could be bribed or intimidated by powerful influences, especially in the wild districts of the north, where the old feudal nobility was still strong, and in Wales. Thus new courts were shaped out of the Privy Council, such as the Council of the North, the Council of Wales, and, most famous of all, the Court of the Star Chamber, so called from the pattern of stars on the ceiling of the room in which it met. These new courts did not supersede the courts of Common Law; they even revived the prestige of the Common Law courts by restoring public faith in and respect for justice.

However, these new courts had two characteristics which eventually turned public opinion against them: they based their authority on royal prerogative, i.e. powers peculiar to the king; and they worked without juries. Hence when Parliament once more set itself against the king in the 17th century, it saw them no longer as instruments of justice but of tyranny, and it abolished them. The Privy Council, on the other hand, survives today; it is no longer the central instrument of executive power (since the Cabinet is that), but a body which serves a variety of consultative purposes in this scientific and technological age.

1.2.1.2 *Tudor political society*

The time was well past when the kings depended on churchmen as the only men educated enough to be capable of the art of government; Cardinal Wolsey* was the last priest–statesman in the tradition of Thomas à Becket*. Country gentlemen, lawyers, and merchants of the towns were now plentiful in the educated classes, and it was from among these that the Tudors chose their Privy Councillors and Ministers of State. This policy renewed the English aristocracy; not only were the new men of power different in kind from their predecessors, and from different families, but they used their power in a different way. They were politicians and administrators in the modern sense, and they established traditions within their families such that the descendants of some of them, for instance the Cecils, the Russells, the Cavendishes, continue to play an important part in politics at the present day.

The former feudal nobility had battered itself into relative weakness during the 15th-century Wars of the Roses, and the first Tudor, Henry VII, eliminated their private armies by fining heavily any nobleman who tried to keep one. The strongholds of this old nobility were in the economically backward north and west, and they did not give way without a struggle; the Pilgrimage of Grace* in 1536 and the rebellion of the northern earls in 1569 were their principal endeavours to re-establish their prestige and the interests of their more conservative society. But the advancing society of the south-east was more numerous, and its interests were strengthened by the inter-relationship of the classes: landed gentry apprenticed* their younger sons to merchants of London – at the end of the century already the largest city in Europe – and both intermarried with the great aristocracy.

The landed gentleman, high in prestige among his lesser farming neighbours who were often bound to him, not by feudal obligations, but as rent-paying tenants, was the successor to the medieval baron, and exerted comparable but very different power as Justice of the Peace. As such he was responsible for the law and order of his neighbourhood, and if in this he was sometimes unduly mindful of his interests – especially the protection of his 'game', i.e. animals reserved for hunting on his land – he was too much in awe of the Privy Council which commissioned his authority to carry tyranny far. The Justices of the Peace, settled men in the upper-middle ranges of society, carried ideas of government and order from the professional administrators of the Privy Council into the intimate world of the village parishes, making justice and politics human, if not always humane.

1.2.2. *The English Reformation*

The daughter of debate, that eke discord doth sow,
Shall reap no gain where former rule hath taught still peace to grow.
No foreign banished wight shall anchor in this port;
Our realm it brooks no stranger's force, let them elsewhere resort.
Our rusty sword with rest shall first his edge employ
To poll their tops that seek such change and gape for joy.

Queen Elizabeth I*

Since 1066, the English have never had a reigning family of purely English origins; the Tudors* were a Welsh family, which in the 15th century connected itself with the Lancastrian* branch of the originally French Plantagenets*. However, no other reigning family related itself so closely to English ways of thinking and feeling, and this is most apparent in their handling of the great crisis of the century – the crisis that absorbed into itself so many other crises of domestic and foreign concern – that of the religious Reformation*. This movement, which divided Europe in ways that were to prove permanent, was common to most of the northern countries, but in England it took a peculiar form. As elsewhere, the English Reformation had two aspects, political and doctrinal; it also had three phases, corresponding to the reigns of Henry VIII* (1509–47), of his son Edward VI* (1547–53), and of his younger daughter Elizabeth I* (1558–1603).

The strictly religious aspect must wait for another essay; our task here is to identify its political aspect. The Church of the Middle Ages had been not only a religious body; it had been a political and legal power as well. Its bishops and greater abbots owned extensive property, which gave them material importance in an age when ownership of land was the measure of influence. Their interests involved them in political games, the prizes of which rewarded the international Catholic Church as well as the English clergy. The Church had its own courts of law, which sometimes competed for authority with those of the Common Law. Taxes, often resented throughout society, were paid to the head of the Church – the Pope in Rome. Nor was the Pope the only international authority of the Church; the heads of the great monastic orders often lived in France or Italy, and the abbots of English monasteries owed obedience and financial contributions to them as well as to the English king. Thus the medieval kings were never full masters of their country, but it often suited them to accept the special position of the Church for the sake of its support against their own barons or some foreign prince, or because they needed churchmen in the running of their governments.

These circumstances which made the Church partly acceptable to the medieval kings no longer applied to the 16th-century monarchy. Henry VIII felt only exasperation at the Church's exercise of authority within the English frontiers, at the draining away of money to Church authorities abroad, at the lack of practical value of such institutions as monasteries which had lost many of their social functions and (often) their spiritual vocations. He knew that public opinion was mainly behind him, and his 'Reformation Parliament' (1529–36) supported him in passing the necessary laws to separate the Church of England from Rome, and place it under the supremacy of the King himself. Yet Henry – whom the Pope had rewarded with the title 'Defender of the Faith' for writing against the German reformer Martin Luther* – was conservative in his beliefs, and the Act of Six Articles (1539) reaffirmed the Catholic dogma of Transubstantiation, and such conservative practices as the celibacy of the clergy and the duty of regular confession to and absolution by a priest.

'There are many opinions in England concerning religion', a Venetian ambassador had written early in the century; in the 14th century, John Wycliffe* had been a radical reformer of doctrine, and he had died peacefully in his bed instead of being put to death like his contemporary, the Bohemian John Huss. Some of Henry's subjects were more Protestant than himself, and some were more Catholic; his Archbishop of Canterbury, Thomas Cranmer*, was amongst the former. Cranmer led the Protestant movement in the next reign (Edward VI*) with his noble Book of Common Prayer* for use in all English churches; in the reign after he was burnt alive in accordance with the counter-reformation policy of Henry's Catholic daughter, Mary I* (1553–8), who brought England back to allegiance to Rome. Neither reign was popular with the English, perhaps as much for reasons of political feelings as for religious ones. The Protestant reign of the boy King Edward let loose upon the country the more rapaciously self-seeking of the new style of nobleman, and it upset conservative sentiment by the unnecessary destruction of time-honoured religious images in the churches. Mary I was, however, much worse hated for her public burnings of Protestants, and for opening the way to detested foreign influences by marrying 'His Most Catholic Majesty' Philip II of Spain – a much fiercer persecutor of Protestantism in his own dominions. Foxe's* *Book of Martyrs* was revered next to the Bible in many English households for generations later.

So Elizabeth I*, last and greatest of the Tudors, re-established the Anglican* Church – again by Act of Parliament – in 1559, but characteristically she chose 'a middle way'. Her Settlement was so cautiously worded as to admit the possibility that good Catholics might feel that they could combine their loyalty to the Pope with that to the Queen, and their faith in Catholic dogmas with membership of the Anglican Church. It was not until 1571 that the Pope could bring himself to excommunicate Elizabeth, and the Anglican opinion was that the Church of Rome 'seceded' from the Church of England, not the other way round.

The Elizabethan Settlement established the Church of England* durably; it has remained largely what she meant it to be – a religious body elastic enough to include, to this day, Christians who are Catholic in all points except acknowledgement of the Pope, and Christians who are Protestant enough to resent all but the austerest religious ritual – the High Church and the Low Church as the two extremes came to be called in the 19th century. It did not, indeed, do all that she meant: the Roman Catholics did not join it, and the extremer Protestants, first called in her reign Puritans*, remained discontented with it, until they were cast out a century later to make up those numerous dissenting denominations which caused the French writer Voltaire to describe England as the land of 'many religions and only one sauce'. It is often called the 'Elizabethan Compromise', but it was no mere compromise, as was to be testified by the thinkers of great spiritual dignity which it was to produce in the next hundred years: Richard Hooker*, Lancelot Andrewes*, Jeremy Taylor*. Nor did they testify alone, for we have the great Anglican poets of the same period: Herbert*, Donne*, and Vaughan*.

1.2.3. *Political aspects of the English Renaissance*

KING HENRY VI (on the future Henry VII):

Come hither, England's hope. – If secret powers
Suggest but truth to my divining thoughts,
This pretty lad will prove our country's bliss.
His looks are full of peaceful majesty;
His head by nature framed to wear a crown,
His hand to wield a sceptre: and himself
Likely in time to bless a regal throne.
Make much of him, my lords, for this is he
Must help you more than you are hurt by me.

Shakespeare – *3 Henry VI* IV.vi

CRANMER (on the future Elizabeth I):

She shall be lov'd and fear'd: her own shall bless her;
Her foes shake like a field of beaten corn,
And hang their heads with sorrow; good grows with her.
In her days every man shall eat in safety

Under his own vine what he plants; and sing
The merry songs of peace to all his neighbours.
God shall be truly known; and those about her
From her shall read the perfect ways of honour,
And by those claim their greatness, not by blood.

Fletcher and Shakespeare – *Henry VIII* V.v

The Renaissance* was Rebirth – Europe recovering its origins in the cultures of ancient Greece and Rome. The Reformation was a product of it: men first became critical of the unexamined assumptions of the Middle Ages, and then – in northern Europe – turned against the Church that seemed to embody them. They were disintegrating movements, but also liberating ones, and they were consistently related, by cause and by effect, to liberating movements in politics, commerce, and society in every country.

The liberation of English national energies at the end of the century – in trade, seafaring, literature, music – was new; never before had the people cohered in the many-sided activities of a distinctive nation as they did then. But the English were only partly fanciful in their feeling that they were experiencing *rebirth* as a nation. The glorious myth of King Arthur* gave them an image of an ancient British golden age, with which the Tudors were dimly but impressively connected. King Arthur had been an ancient Briton; the descendants of those Britons were the Welsh; the Tudors were Welsh – Henry VII* had called his eldest son Arthur – and like King Arthur, Henry rescued the country from the darkness of civil war. Less fancifully, the English treasured the memory of an earlier Henry – Henry V*, who had modelled himself on the pattern of an ideal Christian Prince (like King Arthur himself) and had demonstrated the splendour of national unity by the glorious victory of Agincourt* in 1415. There, Henry with his inferior forces was an image of the prince whose personal destiny was identified with the destiny of his people. Whatever the truth of this image of Henry V – and it had some truth – such identification of princely and national destinies was very fact in the reign of Elizabeth.

The nation was committed to its own version of Protestantism, and so was the queen; to lose her was to lose Protestantism, and national independence as well. Elizabeth's position was vulnerable, for her mother, Anne Boleyn, had been the cause of Henry VIII's divorce of Katharine of Aragon, which had been the occasion for the separation of the Church of England from Rome. Good European Catholics were forced to regard Henry's divorce as illegal, since it had not been allowed by the Pope, and thus to consider Elizabeth an illegitimate child. Legitimacy, in that view, lay with the Catholic Mary Queen of Scots*, and she had the support of the greatest European military power, ruled by Europe's most ardently Catholic sovereign, Philip II of Spain. His attempted invasion of England in order to depose Elizabeth was defeated, against all likelihood, in 1588, and England and Elizabeth were saved. The great outpouring of Elizabethan poetry came principally in the last 15 years of her reign, after this victory over the Spanish Armada*. It was, no doubt, partly the expression of the release of national energies no longer inhibited by foreign menace, and much of it (notably Spenser's *Faerie Queene**) celebrated the glory of the queen who had become identified with national salvation. But some of this poetry, for instance the verse of Raleigh* and the plays of Shakespeare* written towards the end of the reign, had a more sombre tone, as though anticipating the darker mood of the nation in the more sombre period to come.

1.3

1603–1714

Introduction

The theme of this period, which is as coherent as a drama, is the battle for supreme power between King and Parliament, and the eventual supremacy of the latter.

How did this struggle arise? The causes were partly economic: the kings never had enough money to pay for government; consequently they went to Parliament – though they sometimes took other courses – to raise taxes. But Members of Parliament looked after their own interests; if they were to pay for government, they wished it to be conducted in accordance with those interests. And here we come to the social causes of the conflict. The centre of power in Parliament had shifted since the 15th century. No longer were the Commons* the tool of the Lords* – it was beginning to be the other way round. The House of Commons represented the merchants and the landed gentry, who were not definitely distinguished, just as the gentry were not clearly distinguishable from the class represented in the Upper House: the sons of the Lords were usually 'commoners', and could and did sit in the House of Commons when they were elected to it. The opposition to the monarchy was more geographical than social; the south and east of England were economically the most developed, and more conscious of disagreement with the policies of the king, who, when the Civil War* eventually broke out in 1642, found that his supporters lived chiefly in the more backward and conservative north and west.

Finally, there are the religious causes of the conflict. Religion, till the second half of the 17th century, still affected every department of life, and religious divisions corresponded to economic and social divisions as well. The more extreme kinds of Protestantism known as Puritanism* suited the mentality of the mercantile middle classes, and so the emotional fervour which led to the Civil War was religious fervour, even when the disagreements might in fact be practical issues of politics or economics.

After 1660, when the monarchy was restored, a major change began to affect political behaviour: religion influenced all aspects of experience less and less, and became itself a mere compartment of life. The Revolution* of 1688 was indeed made on account of the Catholicism of King James II* – yet chiefly because it was leading him into despotic practices. After 1688, men's ideas were increasingly cast in the mould of the tolerant and sceptical philosophy of John Locke*, the thinker whose ideas were to dominate the 18th century.

1.3.1. *Puritanism, the Civil War, and the Protectorate*

1.3.1.1. *The character of Puritanism*

> *One chanced, mocking, beholding the carriages of the men, to say unto them, What will ye buy? But they, looking gravely upon him, said, We buy the Truth. At that, there was an occasion taken to despise the men the more; some mocking, some taunting, some speaking reproachfully, and some calling upon others to smite them. At last things came to an hubbub, and great stir was in the Fair, insomuch that all order was confounded.*
>
> John Bunyan: *Pilgrim's Progress**

The term 'Puritan' arose early in the reign of Elizabeth I, as an expression of impatient contempt for those militant Protestants who, discontented with the attempt of the Elizabethan Settlement of 1559 to solve the religious debate, wanted to carry the purification of what they regarded as Catholic abuses of religion to limits beyond compromise. Puritanism covered a wide variety of beliefs, but its outstanding characteristics can be summarized as follows. Firstly, Puritans rejected any spiritual authority save that of the Bible – 'the pure Word of God'. Secondly, they were opposed to the appointment of official Church authorities, such as bishops, regarding the government of the Church as a matter for those whom Puritans considered to be true believers, though they disagreed among themselves about what form this government should take. Thirdly, in keeping with this objection to temporal authorities imposed from above, they believed that the Voice of God spoke in each man's individual conscience, and that no priest or other intermediary could rightfully come between. Fourthly, they insisted on extreme austerity of worship, believing that images, ornaments, altars, ritual, and embroidered surplices worn by priests were all no better than superstitions. Fifthly, in their insistence on nothing but the pure truth of religion, they tended to regard all fiction such as stage plays as deceiving vanities, tending to divert the minds of men from spiritual devotion, and they were also disapproving of costly clothing, long hair, and even innocent amusements such as dancing.

Not all these characteristics applied to all Puritans: some, for example, were much less severe on worldly amusements than others; on the other hand, something of the Puritan austerity coloured men such as the Elizabethan poet Spenser* who would not have described themselves as Puritans. Again, within the mentioned characteristics, there was plenty of room for disagreement, both in doctrine and in opinions about church organization. But the variations within Puritanism are less important to notice than the kinds of people who were attracted to it, for it was the adoption of the principles by whole classes of society that made it such a formidable political and cultural force.

Its austerity appealed to the businesslike, *ie* those who made work rather than pleasure their chief occupation; so did some of its doctrines, such as predestination, which declared that some men were irremediably damned, and that a sign of Divine Grace being on a man's side was whether he prospered in his worldly pursuits. Also, the Puritan reliance on the individual conscience tended to encourage independence of political judgement, and Puritan belief in the supremacy of religion over all other considerations accorded with a desire to control the political machine, since Puritans were seldom in doubt that true religion was identical with what they happened to believe. It was thus the hard-working, practical commercial and agricultural classes of south-eastern England that were attracted to Puritanism, and economically as well as religiously, in an age when governments were not yet predominantly commercial, they felt that they had to fight for their interests. When James I* rejected the moderate Puritan appeals to him at the Hampton Court Conference of 1604 with the terse pronouncement 'No Bishop, no King', he was speaking prophetically out of his bitter previous experience as King of Puritanical Scotland; the English Puritans felt that war had been declared upon them.

1.3.1.2 *The Stuart kings and the Great Rebellion*

KING: *Let him go, Gertrude; do not fear our person:*
There's such divinity doth hedge a king,
That treason can but peep to what it would,
Acts little of its will.

Shakespeare – *Hamlet** IV.v

That thence the Royal Actor borne
The tragic scaffold might adorn:
While round the armed bands
Did clap their bloody hands.
He nothing common did or mean
Upon that memorable scene:
But with his keener eye
The axe's edge did try:
Nor call'd the Gods with vulgar spite
To vindicate his helpless Right,
But bow'd his comely head,
Down as upon a bed.

Andrew Marvell*–*Horatian Ode* (on the execution of Charles I)

The Stuarts* had been Kings of Scotland since the 14th century. When Elizabeth died, childless, James VI of Scotland, descended from a sister of Henry VIII, was heir to the English throne; he thus became king of both countries as James VI and I*. It is impossible to know whether history would have been very different if the 17th-century Stuarts had been an exceptionally enlightened dynasty, but historians usually agree that, with the exception of Charles II* (1660–85), their personalities were unfortunate for the political circumstances with which they had to deal. James I insisted on the Divine Right of kings to rule, but the sacredness of a crowned head, which was strong in men's imaginations, was the more respected the less it was proclaimed. He also called his judges 'lions beneath the throne', whereas the English assumption had long been that the king himself was subject to the law. He combined these tactless assertions of royal status with the incompatibility of a timid personality and an ambitious foreign policy which, moreover, since it involved coming to terms with the national enemy Spain, in itself angered Parliament.

Charles I* (1625–49) had equally unfortunate qualities, but very different ones. James had lacked personal dignity, whereas his son possessed it notably, and the royal court under James was scandalously conducted, while that of Charles was cultivated and fastidious. On the other hand, Charles was bigoted and unyielding in all his opinions. He quarrelled with his Parliaments by trying to raise taxes without their consent, using imprisonment without trial, and insisting on conformity to the rites of the Anglican Church. After he had tried and failed to rule without summoning Parliament, the breach between himself and the Puritans became too great to be mended. The Parliamentary Puritans (a majority of the House of Commons and a minority of the House of Lords) tried to impose on him a puritan reformation of the Church of England. This finally divided the nation between Royalist Cavaliers (*ie* courtiers) and Puritan Roundheads (so called because they wore their hair short): between, that is to say, those who cared less for Parliamentary power than for the Anglican establishment on the one side, and those who saw in Parliament the only protector of religious truth on the other.

The 15th-century Civil Wars of the Roses* had been fought with professional soldiers, newly released from the wars in France; the Civil Wars of the 17th century were fought by a nation that lacked professional armies, since it had grown accustomed to relying upon its navies for defence. Foreseeably, victory would come to whichever side succeeded in professionalizing its army first. Thanks to the military genius of Oliver Cromwell*, this was achieved, and the war was won, by Parliament. With Cromwell's Ironsides the English military tradition was renewed; the oldest regiment of the modern British army, the Coldstream Guards, is of Cromwellian origin.

1.3.2 *Republican interlude: the Protectorate*

King Charles I was executed in 1649. From that year until 1660 England was a republic, under the rule of the House of Commons and a Council of State until 1653, and then under Cromwell as Protector, a position resembling that of the modern President of the United States.

The Protectorate, however, solved no problems; it only brought to light the reality of the English political predicament. This was not, fundamentally, a matter of religious or social differences, none of which were as final as the mismanagement by the first two Stuarts had made them seem; it was a problem of political machinery. Parliament had grown strong enough to insist that governmental policy should accord with its wishes, and the governments – whether of King or of Protector – needed Parliament's financial support. The solution might seem to be that Parliament, the legislative or law-making power, should itself become the executive or policy-making power; but, as Cromwell and the nation discovered in the years 1649–53, a body of several hundred men is altogether too clumsy to devise and execute policy. The dilemma remained, until by slow experiment over the next century and a half the Cabinet system (*1.4.1.2) was evolved.

When the great Protector, Oliver, died in 1658, after finding that he was as unable as Charles I had been to rule either with or without Parliament, he was succeeded by his negligible son Richard Cromwell. The nation recognized that if it had to live under a hereditary protectorship, it might as well recall the legitimate dynasty of kings. So came about the Restoration* of the Monarchy in 1660.

1.3.3 *The Restoration and the beginning of party politics*

Charles II was a very different man from his father. He had an intelligent, subtle mind, and in contrast to his father's bigotry he was willing to adapt himself to his circumstances to the point of unscrupulousness. He recognized that, as king, he was weaker than his predecessors had been. Parliament, on the brink of the Civil War, had destroyed the weapons forged by the 'Tudor despotism', and he knew that never again could a king raise taxes without Parliament's consent.

On the other hand, the mood of the nation was changing in ways that were helpful to the king. Puritan fanaticism was discredited, and the Anglican establishment was restored. The English were not yet a tolerant nation: in 1662 an Act of Uniformity* penalized all kinds of Puritan opinion which refused to conform to the Anglican system of belief contained in the Thirty-nine Articles*; this, however, was a political as much as a religious measure, to prevent the revival of a Cromwellian party. In other respects, the Restoration was an unexpectedly mild event; Charles and his chief minister, Clarendon*, who at one time had been a Parliamentary opponent of Charles I, knew better than to embitter public rejoicing by extensive revenge. The spirit of court and Charles II's 'Cavalier Parliament' was no longer that of the doctrinaire 'Martyr King' and his resolute archbishop, Laud*. Typical of the new age was the Royal Society*, founded for the pursuit of science. It had been started in 1645, but in 1662 it received the king's patronage: the age of philosophic reason was beginning to obliterate the age of religious passion.

But passions were still strong. T. S. Eliot* has remarked that perhaps civil wars never really end, and the differences of creed that had caused the wars of 1642–8 still impressed themselves on Parliament. Two parties resulted: the party of those who inherited the Cavalier sentiment for Church and King, and the party of those who continued the Roundhead support for Parliament and trade. Catholics and Puritans were both excluded from political representation, but those in the Cavalier tradition evoked ideas of Catholic authoritarianism and were called by their opponents 'Tories', a term of abuse for Irish Catholic rebels; in return the Tories called their opponents 'Whigs'*, a term of abuse for Scottish Puritanical rebels. So the English 'two-party system' began, and has remained till the present day; even 'Whig' and 'Tory' survived as party names until the middle of the 19th century, when they were changed to Liberal and Conservative respectively; Tory still survives as a synonym for Conservative. The interests represented by the different parties, however, have varied at different periods. In the 17th and 18th centuries, the Tories were mainly the landed gentry, the country squires who provided the majority of the Justices of the Peace, and the Whigs were an alliance of greater landowners and the middle classes of the towns.

1.3.4 *The Revolution of* 1688 *and the Act of Settlement* (1701)

The final triumph of Parliament was ensured once more by the ill-judgement of a Stuart king. Charles II* had become a Catholic, but he had been careful not to proclaim his conversion, and he died peacefully, a popular king, having cunningly frustrated Whig attempts to exclude his brother James, a much more demonstrative Catholic, from succession to the throne. James II* accordingly succeeded in 1685, but he quickly antagonized both Tories and Whigs, the former by his evident intention to supplant Anglicanism by Catholicism, and the latter by undermining Parliament's authority in order to do so. The Tories (with misgivings, because James was the legitimate king) allied with the Whigs to summon from Holland William of Orange and his wife Mary, James's Protestant daughter, to reign jointly as William III* and Mary II*. The Revolution succeeded bloodlessly, apart from some resistance from James's supporters in Catholic Ireland and the Scottish Highlands. Parliament had now achieved a decisive victory expressed in law by the Bill of Rights* (1689); it had denied the principle of the Divine Right of Kings by altering the succession, and it confirmed this victory in 1701 (the Act of Settlement) by excluding James's Catholic son from the succession, choosing instead the German Protestant House of Hanover, descended from a daughter of James I.

The Tories indeed, when they were in power just before the death of Mary II's sister, Queen Anne (1702–14), tried to withdraw this act, which was so contrary to their principles, but the Whigs obtained power just in time for George I to succeed peacefully. No longer could the kings openly challenge parliamentary sovereignty, for they themselves were the creations of Parliament. The only king later to attempt revival of monarchical power was George III (1760–1820), and he did so by trying to turn himself into a parliamentary politician.

1.3.5 *England into Great Britain: the relationship with Ireland and Scotland*

The English kings had claimed sovereignty over Ireland* since the 12th century, but they had not succeeded in making their rule effective there. In the 16th century, when England and Scotland underwent Protestant Reformations, Ireland remained Catholic, and consequently became a threat to the Protestant establishments in the other two countries. The governments of Elizabeth I and James I were in consequence aroused to subdue the country systematically, both by force of arms and by settling an Anglo-Scottish landowning class upon it. They fully succeeded in their colonizing policy only in most of the northernmost province of Ulster, which still has a Protestant majority. Later Ireland was completely subdued by the armies of Cromwell, and at the opening of the 18th century it was an unhappy, subject nation, defended only by the savage indignation of the greatest of English satirists, Jonathan Swift*.

The union with Scotland* is a very different story. James VI and I had brought about a union of the crowns, but, apart from a brief period of subjugation by Cromwell, Scotland remained an independent country with its own government until 1707. In that year, a Union of Parliaments was negotiated; Scotland lost its own Parliament in return for representation in the English Parliament, but it has kept its independent legal system and its distinct state church. The consequences for Scotland were that from being a poor and backward country, it began to share in English prosperity. In one respect only was Scotland a subjugated country: 18th-century Scottish writers (with the exception of some poets, the most notable of whom was Burns*) abandoned their traditional idiom of 'Lallans'*, and anglicized their expression completely.

1.4

1714–1815

Introduction

The 16th century was a formative period; the 17th, a period of conflict; the 18th century, upon the whole, was a period of stability. There were relatively few great social, political, or religious issues to disturb its strongly developed sense of civilization. Culturally, it was the age of classicism: of harmony, proportion, assured taste and balanced statement. It is true that the Puritan Dissenters, like the Catholics and the Jews, were excluded from participation in politics and from education at the universities, but they were not deeply resentful; they, too, had lost their fanaticism and had taken on the prevailing rationalism. It is true, too, that this serenity, like much 18th-century architecture, was often as shallow as a façade: there were disturbances of spirit within, as the Methodist religious revival showed, and it is significant that the mid-century poets (notably Collins*, Gray* and Cowper*) were characterized by frequent melancholy. Moreover, Swift*, Pope* and Johnson*, the great representatives of this Augustan* spirit which felt so assured of the values of civilization, were far from complacent about their time; they were indeed savagely critical of it for falling far below its own standards. But it was the failure of society to rise to the standards that offended them, not, on the whole, the standards themselves.

Thus, 18th-century culture was relatively stable, but it was not stagnant, and politically, in its peculiar way, it was a constructive period. Politicians went far towards solving the dilemma of how to combine the sovereignty of Parliament with efficient executive government. The process was conducted in a practical spirit, with very little attention to political theory, and it went with a moral cynicism that condoned many political abuses. However, this practical spirit nourished a critical outlook which, in the form of Utilitarianism, was the 18th century's most useful legacy to the reformism of the 19th.

The last 25 years of the period, from 1790 to 1815, show the latent disturbances of spirit coming to the surface. Politically they emerge as radicalism and culturally as Romanticism; economically, the Industrial Revolution deeply affected society. Together, these movements were as decisive for change as the Reformation and the Renaissance had been in the 16th century.

1.4.1 *The Whig oligarchy*

1.4.1.1 *Parliament in the eighteenth century*

Though Parliament was the unquestioned victor in the long struggle with the 17th-century kings, England was by no means yet a democratic country. It was not democratic electorally, for the system of the election of representatives to the House of Commons had been unreformed since the 14th century. Towns (for political purposes called 'borough constituencies') that had flourished then were in some instances no more than villages in the 18th century, but they still returned members to Parliament; these were the 'Rotten Boroughs'. Other towns that were still of some importance contained only a tiny minority of citizens with voting rights (the franchise), as in the case of the borough of Onevote in Peacock's novel *Melincourt** (1817). Furthermore, the country was still undemocratic in its state of opinion: political rights were not yet thought of as the rights of individuals, but as the rights of property owners, and the common people often thought that loyalty to the opinions of their landlords was their principal political duty. Voting, moreover, was public, and voters were in consequence open to bribery and intimidation. It is not surprising that the landed aristocrats who led the Whig party after 1714 saw no need to become electoral reformers, and the system survived the more easily because they were sensitive to commercial interests, in which they often shared; there was as yet little movement from the middle classes for reform.

This is, however, not the whole story of political corruption in the 18th century; it would be something in its defence to be able to say that business within Parliament was conducted honestly. This was not so. The political leaders had at their command a number of administrative appointments known as 'sinecures' ('sine cura' = without care or responsibility) because, though they brought the occupiers substantial salaries, they required little or no work. These posts were distributed to Members of Parliament by statesmen holding ministerial office in return for their support. In consequence, politics was apt to become a game for the profit of politicians. The game was played among the 'connexions' of the various statesmen, and genuine political disagreement, though it did not cease, was often subsidiary. Such a state of decadence was caused not merely by the degeneracy of the system, but by the absence of the Tories, whose support of the exiled Catholic Stuarts disqualified them for 50 years from playing any part in politics under the Hanoverians.

The most notoriously corrupt of the Whig statesmen in that half-century was Robert Walpole*. Yet he was in his way a great statesman, and a creative one – 'the first Prime Minister' (though he refused to admit the description) and a chief inventor of the 'Cabinet system'.

1.4.1.2 *The Prime Minister and the Cabinet system: Robert Walpole*

If the dilemma of how to combine parliamentary sovereignty with efficient executive government was solved by any one man, this man was Walpole, who controlled both the executive and Parliament from 1721 till 1742.

Circumstances assisted him. Firstly, the German kings from Hanover, George I and II, understood little of English politics or even of the English language; they needed English affairs to be 'managed' for them. Secondly, a major financial crisis, the South Sea Bubble*, burst upon the country in 1720, and Walpole had the necessary financial ability to settle it. He continued in Parliament by royal support, and by using the corrupt methods that have been described; he similarly 'managed' the elections to Parliament, which, by the Septennial Act of 1716, had to be held every 7 years.

Though Walpole's management was corrupt, in his own way he commanded majorities in Parliament, and may justifiably be called the first Prime Minister*, though in fact the title was only used against him by his hostile opponents. His importance is that he achieved by dishonourable means what other men later imitated in honourable ways.

One man, however able, cannot rule alone; whether King or Prime Minister, he has to have ministers to support him. The problem therefore remained, for Walpole, of how to keep the support of his ministers and thus preserve unity of policy. To this also he found a solution. He chose his ministers (though officially they were appointed, as they are still, by the reigning monarch) from among his friends in either House of Parliament, and consulted them in his private room or 'cabinet'. In that privacy, he used force of persuasion to secure agreement with his ideas, and if they refused to agree, he tried to secure their resignation. So, today, important policy is framed at meetings of the chief ministers ('Cabinet Ministers') at the Prime Minister's official residence, 10 Downing Street in Westminster; the meetings are never reported in the press, and all the ministers are assumed to agree with the resulting decisions unless any resign.

The crucially important institutions of Prime Minister and Cabinet government were not the work of Walpole alone. Beginnings of these ideas arose even in the reign of Charles II, and they were not fully evolved until Parliament was reformed in the 19th century. Walpole is the statesman most distinctly to be associated with them, but even so, his work might have been fruitless because of the disrepute he brought upon politics. The reputation of the political system was fortunately saved by another Prime Minister with an unusually long reign of power, at the end of the century; this was the Tory, William Pitt* the Younger.

1.4.2 *The revival of Toryism*

1.4.2.1 *The New Tories ('King's Friends')*

The political power game played by the Whigs in the first half of the century could be played by the Tories too, once they could find a way back to power. However, having committed themselves to the Catholic Stuarts, they were regarded as Jacobites* (*ie* supporters of James Stuart, the son of the deposed James II), and the nation stood by the Hanover family, not because it was popular, but because it guaranteed the security of the parliamentary system and the classes that relied upon it. The accession of George III changed the picture. George I (1714–27) and George II (1727–60) were Germans first and English kings only second; it suited both themselves and the Whigs that they should stand back from politics. George III ('Farmer George'), however, felt himself to be an Englishman, with English tastes and outlook; it was natural that such a man should despise a passive role. The Tories by this time, after the defeat of the second Jacobite Rebellion in 1746, had come to recognize that the Stuarts were a lost cause, and began to be attracted to a monarch who was not only secure on the throne but shared so many of their interests. Moreover, both the king and the Tories had an ideology provided for them in *The Idea of a Patriot King* (1749) by the veteran Tory statesman and former Jacobite, Henry St John Bolingbroke*. In this book, Bolingbroke contrasted the demoralization of politics under the Whigs with the idealistic national spirit of the reign of Elizabeth I, and drew conclusions about the capacity of the right kind of monarch to raise the country above the squalor of self-seeking politics.

In the 1760s George III succeeded in forming a party of sympathizers – the New Tories or King's Friends – in Parliament. With the help of these, he fought the Whigs and eventually secured in power for twelve years a Prime Minister congenial to him; this was the ministry of Lord North, 1770–82.

George's efforts were finally defeated by two circumstances. The first was that his government was discredited by the success of the rebellious colonists in America – the American War of Independence, 1775–83. This was a crisis which the king and his government seriously mishandled. Possibly the Whigs would not have dealt with it better, for English political assumptions were aristocratic, whereas those of the Americans were already democratic; the old nation spoke the same language as the new, but interpreted it differently, so that there was little common understanding. The second circumstance that defeated George was that, while he had been obliged to fight the Whigs with their own weapons of corruption, when he won power from them he did nothing to reform the political system which invited such conduct.

1.4.2.2 *William Pitt the Younger*

King George lost North, but he was unwilling to submit to the Whigs. This crisis was solved by the appearance of a gifted young man of 23, William Pitt, whose father had brought victory to Britain in the Seven Years' War* (1756–63). Pitt was comparatively independent of party; he kept power for 18 years (1783–1801), and was Prime Minister again for a short period from 1804 until his death in 1806.

Pitt had financial ability comparable to Walpole's, and he had integrity. He abandoned methods of government by bribery, and relied for his power on genuine votes, both in Parliament and at elections in the country; if his party had supported him, he would have carried out reforms in both. He differed from Walpole in acknowledging that he was Prime Minister, and furthermore he insisted that the office was necessary, and that it implied the collaboration of a Cabinet system as well. He thus not only purified the atmosphere in which parliamentary politics were conducted, but he transmitted to the 19th century much clearer ideas about how to conduct them. Finally, strongly influenced as he was by the ideas of Adam Smith*, he initiated the practice of Free Trade* in foreign commerce – a policy destined to have important effects both politically and economically long after his death.

1.4.3 *The French Revolution; the Industrial Revolution; the Napoleonic War*

Bliss was it in that dawn to be alive,
But to be young was very heaven . . .

Wordsworth* – *The Prelude**

A spirit of innovation is generally the result of a selfish temper, and confined views. People will not look forward to posterity, who never look back to their ancestors.

Edmund Burke* – *Reflections on the Revolution in France**

Pitt's reformism belonged to his early phase of power; in 1789 there broke out the epoch-making French Revolution*, which transformed him into a much more conservative statesman. It transformed, too, the values of English politics. For the Revolution proclaimed ideas of the rights of man which inspired the peoples of all Europe, and in England made democracy for the first time a real issue, so that political thinking was done in new terms. Enlightenment was not all on one side; those who sympathized with the Revolution – they included leading Whig aristocrats – did not always understand its significance as well as did its opponents. Two influential English books were published while the Revolution was at its height, and typify the opposition of ideas about it. In 1790, the Tory (a former Whig) Edmund Burke published his *Reflections on the Revolution in France*, one of the profoundest and most eloquent political treatises ever written; significantly, he was provoked to write it by a sermon glorifying the Revolution by a Dissenter, that is to say a member of one of the politically unempowered classes in England. Burke, who had understood the case of the American rebels and had written and spoken in their defence, also understood that the politics of revolution were more likely to be destructive than creative – he foresaw that France would have to endure despotism – and he extolled the English tradition of slow organic growth as the true way to political and social fulfilment. He may indeed have underestimated the intolerable distress that a nation may suffer by such patience. His book was thus answered by Tom Paine's* revolutionary testament, *The Rights of Man* (1791–2); 'Burke', said Paine, 'mourns the plumage and forgets the dying bird.'

History in England was to follow Burke's way rather than Paine's, but it moved with a new urgency. This urgency was provoked not only by the French Revolution and the propaganda of its sympathizers, but also by another revolution that happened more slowly, and yet, considering its nature, with astonishing rapidity. England was developing a new economy of production in factories by power-driven machinery – was, in fact, the first country in the world to experience an industrial revolution*. The process was transforming the north from an empty countryside into a region of populous cities, and the rapidly expanding middle class in them could no longer tolerate a political system run by a landed aristocracy, even though it was a commercially-minded one. The political consequences of the Industrial Revolution will be traced in the next section. The picture was complicated by the development of France into an aggressive military despotism under Napoleon* Bonaparte.

The Tories remained in power to fight this despotism. Reactionary at home, they suppressed libertarian movements like the nascent trade unions, but abroad, in the eyes of Englishmen, they seemed to stand for liberty; the English feared Napoleon as they had feared Philip II of Spain in the 16th century, and Nelson's* defeat of the Franco-Spanish navies in the Battle of Trafalgar* (1805) was a victory over another Armada. Where was the liberal-minded Englishman to direct his sympathies? The change in political opinion of Wordsworth* and Coleridge*, from enthusiastic support of the French Revolution to philosophic conservatism, was natural in the ideological confusion of the time.

1.5

1815–present day

Introduction

Burke, in his *Reflections on the Revolution in France*, argued that true political advance required political continuity with the past. He wrote with the spectacle before him of catastrophic changes in France, and the fear that they might follow in England. His fear might have been even greater if he had been able to discern all the forces making for change in his time; the changes that have come about since his death in 1797 have certainly been revolutionary. Yet they have come about according to his prescription; we have the institutions of a modern state and society, but they are the outcome of continuity, not upheaval.

1.5.1 *Political change*

1.5.1.1 *The new industrial classes*

Ill fares the land, to hastening ills a prey,
Where wealth accumulates and men decay.
Princes and lords may flourish or may fade;
A breath can make them, as a breath has made;
But a bold peasantry, their country's pride,
When once destroyed, can never be supplied.

Goldsmith* – *The Deserted Village** (1770)

A visitor to modern England realizes that he has come to one of the most densely populated countries of Europe, where the large majority of the people live in towns. When he looks at the bigger towns he will see that they are predominantly 19th- and 20th-century constructions, and that, recent replanning apart, they seem to have been rushed together in the hurry of industrial pressures rather than to be the slow growths of time. Manchester, for example, had a population of

36,000 in 1773; this population had doubled by 1801, and by 1850 it was more than three times the 1801 figure. The fact is that, until the Industrial Revolution, England was not an urban nation though it was a trading one; the only great city was London, and much of the industry (especially cloth-making) was conducted in the villages. It is the villages and small country towns that bear the marks of a long, prosperous past.

The biggest social change in English history is the transfer, between 1750 and 1850, of large masses of the population from the countryside to the towns; the basic social classes were transformed from small farmers and rural craftsmen into an urban proletariat and a lower middle class of industrial employers. The movement was hastened by two forces: (i) the agricultural revolution carried out by the landowners (Enclosures*) drove the peasants off the land, and (ii) they were drawn to the towns by the demand for labour in the factories and mills, operated by machines driven by steam-power. It affected the north of England and parts of the midlands far more than the south, and this, too, was a big transformation; hitherto it had been the south that had been advanced and relatively populous while the north had remained relatively empty, backward, and conservative, but now the north was pushing against the conservatism of the south. The evidence of the contrast is frequent in mid-19th-century novels: it is in the title of Elizabeth Gaskell's *North and South**, and for other examples, George Eliot's Silas Marner* appears in a midland village from a northern town like a man from another country, and in Dickens's *Bleak House** the rich, landed gentleman Sir Leicester Dedlock finds the northern ironmaster Rouncewell a socially incomprehensible figure although he is the son of Sir Leicester's own housekeeper.

The new industrial towns were places of great distress for the workers. The poor were indeed having the worst period of suffering since serfdom had been practically extinguished in the 14th century. The prosperous peasant farmer, the yeoman*, who had won the battles for the Plantagenet kings in the Hundred Years' War, had long been considered the solid base of English society, but by the 19th century he had largely disappeared. If he had not sunk to the level of a labourer on the land of a bigger farmer, or become a factory-worker and little better than a serf, he had turned into an industrial employer. The employers themselves often struggled very hard to get their heads above the level of wretchedness, and they commonly achieved it by a narrow range of human virtues – thrift, industriousness, sobriety – and were apt to conclude that these were the only estimable virtues, because they were the only ones that had proved useful to themselves. These were the 'philistines' who were the despair of Matthew Arnold*, and responsible for much of the ugliness of industrial England.

Two forces worked for redemption in the industrial towns. One was Methodism.

1.5.1.2 *Methodism and Nonconformity*

Methodism*, the religious movement led by the evangelist John Wesley*, was a late outburst of Puritanism*. Puritanism appealed chiefly to the middle and lower regions of society; Methodism reached the really poor. Puritanism, which in the 18th century was called Dissent and in the 19th century, Nonconformity, lost much of its fighting spirit and passion in the 18th century, but these were somewhat restored by the example of Methodism, and together they gave the industrial workers the emotional resistance that they needed to withstand the degradation and harshness of their lives. 'Cleanliness is next to Godliness', Wesley preached, meaning that the circumstances of his audiences made cleanliness the first condition of spiritual survival. The French historian Halévy has even suggested that, by giving the industrial working class something to live for, Methodism diverted them from revolution.

But Methodism and other kinds of Nonconformity did more than provide the poor with psychological resistance to spiritual degradation. The Methodist and other Nonconformist chapels were little communities that educated their members, and trained them in social organization. Nonconformity was a strong contribution to the Liberal* Party in the 19th century, and it was Nonconformity rather than Marxism* which inspired the formation of the Labour Party* at the very end of it. By that time, however, the working class had developed a more distinctly political means of education and action; this was Trade Unionism*.

1.5.1.3 *The Trade Unions*

Associations of workers for mutual relief in sickness and unemployment began as far back as the middle of the 18th century; the oldest English union claims to date from 1747. Until the 19th century, however, they were chiefly 'Friendly Societies' for such mutual insurance. In the first quarter of the 19th century, they were suppressed by the Tory governments, afraid that any 'combinations' among workers might become centres of revolution. When, after 1824, the ban was removed, Trade Unionism suffered early setback, owing to the failure of Robert Owen's* ambitious but ill-organized project, the Grand National Consolidated Trades Union. However, during the middle of the century, unionism developed quietly and respectably among skilled workers; one example was the Amalgamated Society of Engineers. When, in the 1860s, unionism was subjected to a government investigation, the verdict was wholly favourable. The result was the establishment of a federation of unions, called the Trades Union Congress (T.U.C.) in 1868. In the 1870s the Liberal and Conservative Prime Ministers competed with each other to give the Trades Union Movement full legal rights: Gladstone* secured that they could become corporations recognized by the Law, and able to own and acquire property out of the funds provided by their members; Disraeli* took the even more important step of legalizing strike action, so that in future the workers possessed an important weapon (which hitherto they had used illegally) with which to fight the employers.

In the last 20 years of the century, two important advances were made in Trade Unionism; it spread among the unskilled workers, who most needed it, especially through the victory of the Dockers' Strike in 1889, and it became the basis for more direct action through the formation of the Labour Party, of which it has remained the main financial support. By 1920, the working-class part of the nation was able to compete with the rest of the nation politically on equal terms.

1.5.1.4 *Parliamentary Reform*

By the third decade of the 19th century, both the Whigs and the Tories had come to realize that they were faced with a new social landscape, and that political institutions would have to be adapted to conform to it. The Tories were slower, but even they were aware enough to remove the political disabilities from Nonconformists and Catholics by the Emancipation Acts of 1828 and 1829. They resisted the major requirement, however, which was the reform of Parliament, and in 1830 they consequently fell from power, having held it for 50 years. The Whigs passed the First Parliamentary Reform Bill* in 1832.

The Act of 1832, however, was not broadly based enough to be democratic; voting rights, and the right to seek election, were given a systematic property basis, and only the middle classes were enfranchised. Even the Whig party was afraid of the consequences of emancipating the working classes, ignorant and even illiterate – there was as yet no universal system of education – as they extensively still were. The result of this failure to enfranchise the workers led to the working-class Chartist* movement, whose six points of reform included 'manhood suffrage' – that is, the right to vote of every adult male in the country.

But it was the middle classes who were most energetic in their own interests, and most capable of organization. Popular support for the Chartists was drawn off to support a middle-class movement which had nothing directly to do with further parliamentary reform. The new middle classes of the towns were greatly resentful that the sale of British-grown corn was 'protected' by taxes which increased the price of imported corn, since this meant that after bad harvests food was dear for the working classes, and they demanded higher wages. The industrialists, in advance of the rest of the world in the production of factory-made goods, stood to gain by a system of free competition in trade, such as had been advocated by Adam Smith* (in *The Wealth of Nations*, 1777) and already initiated by the Prime Minister Pitt. The working classes supported the movement because, more urgently than any political gain sought by the Chartists, they wanted bread. The established leaders of the Whigs and Tories, among whom the agricultural interest was strong, were reluctant to give way, but in 1846 it was a Tory Prime Minister, Robert Peel, who surrendered in the face of a famine in Ireland. He abolished taxes on imported corn by the Repeal of the Corn Laws*.

This step had two important corollaries. The first was that Britain was implicitly declaring herself basically dependent on her industrialists, and not on her food producers. This, of course, meant not that the landed class was ruined, but that it was ceasing to be the dominant class, although it remained for a generation a very prosperous one. The second important corollary was that an industrial nation could not indefinitely keep its industrial workers politically without rights, especially after the middle of the century when they were becoming progressively better informed and organized. It was not, however, until 1867 that a substantial part of the urban working classes got the vote, through the Second Parliamentary Reform Bill, passed this time by a Conservative government. It was followed in 1870 by the establishment of state education; as the politicians said, 'We have to educate our masters.'

The villages had lost much of their vitality by the movement into the towns and by the gradual loss of their crafts by competition with machine production, and their working classes received political rights even later, by the Third Parliamentary Reform Bill of 1884, and this still left some exceptions until 1918. Women everywhere in all classes had to wait longer still. The Women's Suffrage Movement conducted a fierce agitation in the early years of the 20th century, but it was the First World War of 1914–18 that did most to enfranchise them: by doing men's work while the men were fighting, women approached equality of social and economic status, and could no longer be excluded on the baseless ground that they are somehow congenitally unfitted for the conduct of affairs. Women over 30 received the right to vote and seek election in Parliament in 1918; in 1928, women were placed on equality with men over 21. It was not until 1958 that they received the right to sit in the House of Lords.

1.5.1.5 *Politics and social change*

The social and political changes so far described necessarily produced effects in the composition of Parliament itself, in its organization, and in the parties. But it is first important to notice the continuity, in its social context, of English politics.

The medieval social structure was at first fairly clearly stratified, divided into 'castes' rather than 'classes'. Families might advance in course of time, moving from serfs to yeoman farmers, becoming country gentlemen or 'franklins', receiving knighthood, and finally becoming ennobled. Or churchmen might advance the fortunes of their relatives by the road of learning, acquiring power as clerks in noble or royal households. In the later medieval centuries, there was the increasing chance of a merchant becoming a landed gentleman through his acquisition of property. Yet, at a given time, as Chaucer's Prologue to his *Canterbury Tales** shows, a man or woman had a recognizable rank and function in society, fairly easily to be distinguished from other functions and ranks. In the 16th century, the decay of feudalism, the rise of the merchants, the Tudor practice of making the fortunes of their servants rather than choosing them from among those who had inherited fortunes, all complicated the social structure and made it much more fluid. 16th-century Englishmen respected 'noble blood', and were keenly sensitive to differences in degree, yet their experience showed them that commoners could be ennobled, and could found noble families. 'Snobbery' is commonly regarded as an English vice and as marking a society of strong social divisions, and both statements are true. Yet snobbery – the feeling that 'I am better than you, because I am your social superior' – flourishes in a fluid society, that is to say, in one in which hopes may exist of improving social status, rather than in a rigidly divided society.

It might be thought that a country whose legislative assembly is divided into a House of Commons and a House of Lords is a country likely to suffer from class conflict in its politics. This has not been especially true of England. In the centuries before the Industrial Revolution, both Houses contained land-owners, many of whom had relatives and friends in the other House; similarly, since the Industrial Revolution, both Houses have contained industrialists. Moreover, since the 16th century it has been an increasingly common practice for governments to reward Commoners for political services by ennobling them, and a Labour lord today is unlikely even to want to be thought to belong to the aristocracy – he is in the Upper House to serve his party and for no other reason. Thus the members of the two Houses of Parliament have generally had too much in common to wish to quarrel; when they did, the Commons had a decisive weapon in its power: it could persuade the king to threaten the appointment of a sufficient number of Lords to ensure a majority on the Commons side of the dispute. The Lords offered stubborn resistance only once; this was in 1909, when the Liberal Government proposed a Land Tax which would severely penalize the landed proprietors. They had no power to resist the retribution that came upon them in the shape of the Parliament Act of 1911, limiting their legal powers to oppose the Commons in future.

Social continuity in English politics has also been remarkable for the persistence of a number of great family names among political leaders: the Churchills, Cavendishes, Cecils and Russells. These have depended on family tradition rather than family privilege, as is evident from their continuance even after the First Reform Bill abolished the rotten and pocket boroughs. Political tradition developed in such families a store of experience to be drawn upon and ambitions to be emulated, and at the same time a pride of independence which made for radical rather than conservative opinions, for instance among the Russells.

Nevertheless, the Reform Bills greatly broadened the social composition of the parties. True, the last great Prime Minister of the 19th century was a Cecil, of the same family as William Cecil, Elizabeth I's chief statesman; but the greatest Conservative leader of the century was Benjamin Disraeli, a man of Italian Jewish ancestry who could scarcely have achieved such a position before that time. The parties, also, developed coherent public organizations such as they had never had before, and began to represent particular classes of society in a more distinct and consistent way.

The biggest change resulted from the political rise of the working class.

The Whigs had always stood for the interests of the towns, and for the disfranchised Nonconformists who had their strength there. This meant that they represented both employers and employees. Before the Industrial Revolution, these two classes often shared interests, and even after its inception, the factory workers, though they were more generally and bitterly opposed to the Liberal manufacturing employers, were often unable to organize themselves as a distinct political force: the failure of the Chartist party is evidence of their weakness, and it was often Tories like Lord Shaftesbury and Disraeli who fought their masters on their behalf. After the workers had gained political rights, however, and had educated themselves for political action through the Trade Unions, they became actively dissatisfied with a party whose leaders were their own employers, and in 1900 the Labour Party was formed. At the same time, the employers came to feel that the Conservatives were more distinctly an upper class party than the reformist Liberals. Ultimately the result was the collapse, after World War I, of the Liberal Party, and the rise of the Labour Party to its present position of equality with the Conservatives. The Conservatives in the meantime had broadened their scope from being above all the party of the squirearchy (country gentry). Disraeli* (author of the novel *Sybil, or The Two Nations** – the nations of the rich and the poor) had been determined that the working class should see them as a party sympathetic to their plight, and about a third of the English working class votes Conservative even today. But the Conservatives remained predominantly a party of the middle and upper classes; moreover, they became the Imperial party.

1.5.2 *The British Empire*

At the end of the 19th century, Britain ruled the largest empire that the world had ever seen; today that empire has almost disappeared into the Commonwealth of Nations, and it is difficult to know whether this international body of independent nations possesses solid reality, or whether it is no more than the ghost of the empire.

Britain did not, until the African acquisitions in the last twenty years of the 19th century, acquire her Empire by deliberate policy so much as by an indirect consequence of her international trade.

There have been two British Empires – that of the 18th century, and that of the 19th. The most important part of the 18th-century empire was the American Colonies, which were lost to Britain by the American War of Independence (1775–83). When she lost these, she had just acquired Canada (which at the time seemed of little value), parts of India (ruled not directly by the Crown but by the East India Company), and some islands in the West Indies. The loss of America gave the British a distaste for colonies, but Britain was now the greatest trader and the greatest sea-power in the world, and in the interests of her commerce she inevitably acquired new territory. Later she felt the competition of other powers, and she became 'empire-conscious', a nation of 'empire builders', and invested much of her national pride in the Empire. Even then, the sentiment was stronger among Conservatives than among Liberals and Labour supporters, who tended to feel guilty about the position. Even among Conservatives, the British Empire was never comparable to the French one – never a 'Britain beyond the Seas' –

with the partial exception of such countries as Canada, Australia, New Zealand, which had been colonized principally by British settlers; it was something apart from and extra to Britain. The insularity of the British partly explains this; another explanation is the memory of George III losing America by trying to hold it too tight. His failure certainly helps to explain the transformation of Empire into Commonwealth by the invention of 'Dominion Status', *ie* the grant of self-government within the Commonwealth, beginning with Canada in 1867. It was the Liberal and Labour parties which were more ready to release these bonds of empire, and in one case the Conservatives held on grimly. This, however, was the case of Ireland – a country which, though undoubtedly a conquest, had long been accepted as a part of the very body of Britain.

1.5.3 *Relationship with Ireland*

Ireland is probably the country over which Britain has ruled most ruthlessly and unwisely. From the 12th to the 16th century, England's sovereignty was chiefly nominal and Ireland was left largely to herself, but in the 17th century, owing to the Reformation and English and Scottish fear of Ireland's Catholic majority, the Irish were pitilessly suppressed, and in the 18th century the suppression was continued, if less brutally. In the 19th century, the British fear of Catholicism lessened, and the British conscience awoke. From 1829, Irish Catholics were able to take seats in the English Parliament, and social reforms were carried out during the next fifty years on behalf of the Irish peasant. These, however, did not satisfy the Irish Members of Parliament (after 1870 called the 'Home Rule Party'); they wanted self-government. The Irish wanted this not merely because of their resentment of past oppression, but because they were divided from England in ways that the Scots and Welsh were not: they not only retained Catholicism (except the northern province of Ulster, which was extensively colonized in the 17th century by English and Scots), but they alone lacked a strong middle class able to profit from the expansion of English commerce.

Gladstone, the Liberal Prime Minister, would have given them Home Rule, but the Conservatives and many of his own party opposed him. Conservatives and anti-Home Rule Liberals allied as 'Unionists', and the embittered Irish developed increasingly intense nationalist feeling. Strong national feeling has often been fruitful for art, and the English language was enriched by the Irish literary renaissance, the most notable contribution to literature in English from outside England since the Scottish poets of the early 16th century. Politically, the consequences were the tragic Dublin Rising in 1916, and the Irish War of Independence of 1919–21. In 1921 the British Government made a treaty with the Irish, according to which the southern three provinces became the Irish Free State with complete self-government, but retaining membership of the British Commonwealth as a Dominion, on equal terms with Canada, Australia and New Zealand. This did not satisfy the more extreme nationalists, who wanted Ireland to become a republic.

In 1937, the Irish Prime Minister, De Valera, abolished the title Irish Free State, replacing it by the Erse name Eire; he also abolished the titular head of the Irish Government, the Governor General, and caused the appointment of a President. Ireland kept a shadowy connection with the British Commonwealth, however, until 1949, when, with the consent of the British Labour Government, it separated itself entirely. By the Treaty of 1921 the northernmost province of Ulster remained in the United Kingdom with special rights of self-government. The system of self-government in Northern Ireland has, however, continued the traditional hostility between Protestants and Catholics there, and this hostility, in 1969, sharpened into a new, acute crisis.

1.5.4 *Britain today: the Welfare State*

A survey of contemporary Britain suggests three observations. The first is that Britain, through her institutions, has preserved extraordinary continuity with her ancient past. The second is that this continuity has not prevented Britain from adapting herself, like other western countries, to the peculiar demands of the mid-20th century. But the third is that there is in modern Britain a widespread scepticism about the value of this inheritance, and a corresponding uncertainty about the future of Britain as a nation.

The continuity of British politics is well known. Institutions have seldom been abolished; they have been changed, and if existing institutions have at any time proved unadaptable to the demands of a new age, new institutions have grown up beside them. Out of the ancient, pre-Conquest past, medieval England inherited a king and a stratified society, composed of great landowners, small landowners, and landless men of the towns and the villages. The king ruled with the aid of a council, which from time to time he expanded into a Great Council attended by his chief landowners. In the 13th century, Edward I* found that on occasions even the Great Council was insufficient, and he added to it representatives of the Commons*, thus beginning the institution we know as Parliament*. From the 12th century the small Council served judicial as well as administrative purposes, but by the 15th century it was throwing off separate judicial and bureaucratic bodies, without losing its own identity. In the 16th century, when the Crown achieved more concentrated power, the small (Privy) Council was the main instrument of this centralization. Such centralization caused even the Church to be brought under the Crown, but the Crown preserved its main órganization in accordance with its original medieval pattern. In the 17th century, the upper classes asserted through Parliament their will to sovereignty against the Crown, but the monarchy was abolished only to be soon restored, with gradually reduced powers. In the 18th century, the superiority of Parliament endangered the efficiency of government, but this dilemma was solved by the evolution of the system of rule through a Prime Minister and Cabinet, dependent on a majority in Parliament secured by periodic general elections. In the 19th century, the Industrial Revolution* altered the structure of society by expanding the numbers and power of the middle and working classes of the towns; government through the representatives of preponderantly land-owning classes ceased to make political or economic sense. Revolution, however, was averted by the slow expansion of electoral rights, and by the growth of trade unions* to counterbalance the organizations of the richer classes. In the 20th century, new demands have been made on governments to ensure a high level of social justice, a healthy minimum standard of social welfare, and the provision of extensive services relatively cheaply. Such demands have imposed unprecedented strains on political institutions. They have been met by the expansion of central government and local government bureaucracies, and by the invention of the public utility corporations, to be explained later.

A sketch of this sort brings to mind the great, old country houses scattered about the English countryside. Outwardly their structures seem often to have remained unaltered from the past, except that one notices that each century seems to have made its own additions. Indoors, however, one sees that the ancient rooms have been adapted to modern convenience, and put to uses for which they were not originally intended. In the same way, the monarchy has become almost entirely a ceremonial institution; the House of Lords*, though it is still recruited by the awarding of noble titles to prominent men and women, is in fact scarcely more medieval or undemocratic than the second chambers of most national assemblies; the Privy Council, though it rarely meets as a body, survives as the instrument of various administrative activities, for which Parliament and the civil service are unsatisfactory.

Such continuity has had important advantages for British society. It has caused the growth of unusual respect for authority, and patient tolerance of grievances in expectation of reform. It has helped to prevent the development of fanatical theories leading to violent and futile conflict between opposing interests; it has even enabled partly conflicting interests to combine in single great parties, thus reducing the confusion characteristic of parliamentary politics in many other countries. Far from preventing change, it has tended to produce a national frame of mind which sees change as not merely acceptable but inevitable. The long history of the right-wing Conservative Party is evidence of this attitude: modern Britain shows an array of state controls and public monopolies which would have horrified Conservatives of a century ago; yet, by repeatedly adapting its political assumptions, the Conservative Party has succeeded in remaining one of the two most important parties of the state.

In its economy, Britain is partly capitalistic and partly socialistic, though basically its structure is still that of capitalist free enterprise. To combine the freedom of capitalist enterprise with the responsibility of state control, certain national industries, services, and means of communication have been organized into public utility corporations. A public corporation is managed by a suitably qualified staff, the members of which are not civil servants; that is to say, they are not members of the bureaucracy which is directly responsible to government ministers, though the government retains the right to interfere with them in certain defined circumstances, and has the duty of ensuring that the corporation fulfils the public function for which it is intended. Thus, within broad limits, the managers of public corporations are free from interference from the government and are able to take such immediate decisions as an efficiently run industry may require. Some of the corporations are required to be economically self-supporting as evidence that they are serving public needs efficiently; some (for instance the airways) have privately owned enterprises in competition with them; some are assisted by government financial grants.

A few public corporations were already established before the Second World War, but most of them were established by the Labour Government of 1945–50, or have been established since. The earliest was the British Broadcasting Corporation, incorporated by the ancient expedient of Royal Charter in 1927. It is financed by the payment of broadcasting licences. In 1954 the Conservatives set up the Independent Television Authority in rivalry to BBC television; it is financed by commercial advertising. Other corporations set up later than the BBC are as follows: the British Overseas Airways Corporation (1939); British European Airways (1946); the Bank of England* (hitherto nominally a private concern – 1945); the National Coal Board (1946); the Atomic Energy Commission (1946 and 1954); the Transport Commission (1947, subsequently divided into five separate authorities in 1962); and boards controlling the supply of electricity (1947); gas (1948); iron and steel (1952, subsequently denationalized by the Conservatives, and re-nationalized in 1966).

The Labour Government of 1945–50 also made important innovations in the public care of health and welfare. By a series of Acts passed between 1945 and 1948, the payment of weekly national insurance contributions was made compulsory for most adults, a proportion for each employee being paid by the employer. In return, the individual became entitled to grants in sickness, unemployment, and retirement, to family allowances, and to allowances to help with the expenses of maternity, and for maintenance in widowhood. In addition, national insurance payments entitle individuals to largely free medical attention, made possible by the establishment of the National Health Service in 1948.

The public corporations, national insurance, and the health service are three of the main ingredients of what we call today the Welfare State. To these we should add the system of free education established by the Education Act of 1944 (*2.1.2), the expansion of the universities, the provision (still far from sufficient) of good housing at low rents by the local authorities, and amenities which have the public assistance of the Arts Council, established (again by Royal Charter) in 1946. If, besides, we remember the low rates of unemployment since the war (relatively, that is, to the unemployment before the war) and the unprecedentedly high levels of wages, we can think of the Welfare State as being an aspect of the Affluent Society.

How then do we account for the present sense of crisis and discontent in the

British scene? The writers (such as the dramatist John Osborne* and the novelist Kingsley Amis*) who were known as the 'Angry Young Men' of the 1950s, were succeeded by the more active 'student revolutionaries' of the late 1960s and early 1970s. The explanations must be complex and numerous, and not all of them are yet discoverable. Moreover, while some of them arise from Britain's peculiar situation in the modern world, others concern the crisis shared by all the western nations.

First, Britain is a nation that has lost its former sense of greatness without discovering a new destiny to inspire and unite the people. Britain has surrendered most of her empire since 1945; she no longer has the greatest navy in the world; as an international power she finds herself, for the first time for three hundred years, in the second class. At the same time, the remnants of her empire have forced her to maintain more overseas military commitments than most second-class powers, and these commitments have been economically burdensome. They help to explain (without by any means providing the total explanation) the continuing vulnerability of Britain's position in international trade and finance. Why British trade expands more slowly than that of her competitors, and why she has so far failed to close the gap of foreign indebtedness, are questions which aroused constant anxiety in the 1960s without finding answers. One answer, perhaps, is that abiding social dissatisfactions are frustrating national energies in international competition.

Special, though not peculiar, to Britain is the legacy of strong class opposition that descends from the Industrial Revolution*. The trade unions* arose in the middle of the 19th century when the interests of employers seemed to be clearly antagonistic to those of the workers; nationalization has not altered this tradition of opposition, though it is now an opposition more of managers and employees than of proprietors and wage-slaves. The Labour Government of 1945–50 hoped to recruit trade union members among the managers of the public corporations, but on the whole they failed. Since government is part of management, this trade union insistence on preserving an opposition role in society crippled Labour governments in the decade of the 1960s.

Beyond this indigenous feature in British politics, there is the instinct of individual protest against the large organizations that have come to dominate the life of modern nations everywhere. In Parliament, party organization has become so closely controlled by party leaders that we now speak of 'party machines'. The party machine of government is thus an instrument of the executive machine, and Parliament, as a body of individuals elected to represent the interests of the people, is in the course of losing the respect of public opinion. The government, in turn, acts through its large impersonal ministries, and 'faceless' coordinating bodies such as the National Economic Development Council. Even the trade unions have become steadily fewer and larger, in danger of losing the trust of their individual members, with the consequence of numerous 'unofficial' strikes, *i.e.* strikes unsupported by the unions in the industries concerned.

Corresponding to the growth of these large, faceless organizations is the progressive decrease of respect for traditional authority. It is not new that a nation that has become predominantly agnostic should lose respect for the established Church, but it is relatively new in Britain for the political parties no longer to inspire trust as representatives of recognizable sections of opinion in society.

At the same time as the social and political organizations grow more meaningless, the media of communication (especially television) bring the facts, injustices, and conflicts of national and international life to the attention of the individual with unprecedented force, causing him to recognize the alternatives of deliberate indifference and militant action. The restlessness that this induces might culminate in revolution at last, if Britain's economic crisis should end in actual breakdown.

Work. From a painting made between 1852 and 1865 by Ford Madox Brown. The intention is to idealise labour, and to comment on various aspects of Victorian society. The working men in the centre are heroic figures; the idle rich are shown as arrogant figures in the background. On the right are the unemployed, forced to while away their idleness. Ford was accociated with, though not actually a member of, the Pre-Raphaelite Brotherhood.

2 Society and the arts

2.1

People

2.1.1 *The changing structure of English society*

2.1.1.1 *The decline of feudalism: 1350–1500*

A fair field full of folk found I there between them,
Of all manner of men, the meaner and the richer,
Working and wandering, as the world asks of them.
Some were putting out to plough, had little play-time,
In setting and sowing, sweated at their labour,
Winning wealth that the worthless wasted in their gluttony.
Some pranked themselves in pride, preciously apparelled,
Coming under colour of costly clothing.
To prayer and to penance many put themselves,
All for the love of our Lord living austerely,
In hope they might have their happiness in heaven,
Such as anchorites and hermits who hold to their cells,
And do not covet to go off gadding round the country
For bodily liking of a lecherous livelihood.
And some chose business, with better achievement,
For it seems to our sight that such are successful.

William Langland – *Piers Plowman** (modernized by Neville Coghill)

Seen from a distance in time, social class structures always get simplified. Thus the common view of English medieval society is that it comprised a greater nobility, a lesser nobility or gentry, a small but expanding middle class in the towns, and a large peasantry, many of whom in 1350 were still serfs. The outline is a true one, but it has to be elaborated greatly in order to fit the facts.

The Church occupied a very large place in medieval society, and it had a complicated social structure of its own, though it reflected that of society at large. At one extreme the bishops and the abbots of the larger monasteries* were equals of the nobility; at the other extreme is the poor parson of Chaucer's *Canterbury Tales**, brother to the ploughman. It has been estimated that out of a total population of about 3 million, there may have been as many as 40,000 men ordained as clergy. There were about 9,000 parishes in the country, so that some priests might have several assistant priests in the parish. The parish priests made up the majority of the 'secular clergy', so called because they lived and worked in the world and followed no special rule of life beyond the rules that were binding on all the fully

*Indicates mention in the reference section.

ordained clergy, such as celibacy. The 'regular clergy' lived according to the specific rules of life which were binding on their various orders. They consisted principally of the monks, who lived (or were supposed to live) cut off from the world in their monasteries, and the friars* who, like the parish priests, worked among the people. The regular clergy were fewer in number than the seculars; when Henry VIII dissolved the monasteries in the 16th century, there were about 5,000 monks, 2,000 nuns and 1,600 friars. On the other hand, the monks were disproportionately large landowners: Parliament complained that the Church owned one-third of the land of England, and most of it was in the possession of the monasteries.

The vast Church organization was of mixed advantage and disadvantage to medieval society. The disadvantages included the worldliness of many of the richer clergy; in *The Canterbury Tales*, Chaucer's monk and friar are parasites on the people they are supposed to serve. On the other hand, though his parson is represented as an ideal priest, many of the poorer clergy were ignorant and useless burdens on society: the parish priest supported himself by levies of tithes*, amounting to one-tenth of the income of his parishioners, and these were oppressive to the poor. On the other hand, the monasteries were very large employers of labour, and they served as inns, hospitals and schools in regions where such institutions did not otherwise exist. The parish priest (if, like Chaucer's parson, he was both conscientious and qualified for his position) might be the only means by which the poorer peasant could be brought to see himself as a fully rounded human being and not a mere working animal. If he was not himself almost uneducated, he might supply the beginnings of education to the brighter peasant children, who might themselves then become ordained among the clergy. The 'clerks' did not necessarily become parish priests; if, like Chaucer's Clerk of Oxford, they achieved a university education, they might obtain posts as secretaries or administrators under some great nobleman or prelate, or under the king himself. Admittedly such clerks were more likely to derive from the middle classes of the towns, and Chaucer himself is evidence that, in the 14th century, these classes were also supplying a lay bureaucracy of educated men. Nonetheless, the Church, by the recruitment of its clergy, was still the chief ladder for social advancement for those who were gifted but unprivileged by their birth. Finally, the Church was of immense social importance in another way: it provided a complete system of ethics for the conduct of social life. The immense differences in status were never allowed to become merely material differences; a man's status, high or low, dictated his social function, his responsibilities towards other members of society. The use of money itself was subject to Church law: money might not breed money in the form of the taking of interest on a loan, for the Church called this the sin of usury*, and for every article manufactured there was a 'just price', beyond which profit was sinful. It is true that by the later 14th century such an ethical system was more a matter of theory than of practice: the taking of interest, for example, was a common economic practice. Yet the theory survived, and Langland's *Piers Plowman* is evidence of it.

Class differences were stronger in medieval society than they have been at any time since, but the structure of the upper class was not clearly defined. Its chief basis was the ownership of land, but after 1350 land ownership was distributed among an increasingly wide range of the population, from the great nobleman who owned one or more of some 1,500 castles built in the Middle Ages*, down to the franklin or yeoman* who owned a farm worth 40 shillings annually. Politically, the lords could be recognized as those who were summoned individually to the Upper House of Parliament, in contrast to the smaller landowners (Knights of the Shire*) and the townsmen, who were invited to send representatives to the Lower House. Before Richard II* (1377–99), however, the term 'baron' was applied to a confusing variety of people; there was no certainty, beyond fairly narrow limits, as to who would receive a personal summons to any particular Parliament, and it was not until the 16th century that the House of Lords* became defined by the distinctive titles which the Crown conferred on its members. The foundation of such titles of nobility* is in the so-called 'feudal system' of society, but, with the exception of 'earl', they all originate in the 14th and 15th centuries, when feudalism was in decline.

The 'feudal system' is a historian's term for a condition of society prevalent in western Europe between the dissolution of the Roman Empire in the 5th century AD and the rise of the centralized nation state in the 16th century. It was never, in fact, a system, but rather the evidence of the collapse of one: an emergency arrangement for government when there was no adequate central authority. The stronger members of society agreed to protect those who were weaker, in return for support provided either economically or militarily. The nominal head of such a 'system' was the king, and the 'greater barons' swore oaths of loyalty to him, but in fact the kings were often too weak to impose their authority. English feudalism was more systematic than elsewhere, because the Norman Conquest* of 1066 was so thorough and complete. William I* (1066–87) was the effective owner of all the land in England, and he was able to exact allegiance not only from his principal military leaders, but from the lesser barons who were dependent on them. Nonetheless, English feudalism in the 12th century was not bounded by the national frontier. The barons were French noblemen as well as English ones; as a French nobleman, King Henry II* (1154–89) ruled territories in France that were larger than his English kingdom. At the same time, he was seeking to expand his effective authority by judicial and bureaucratic institutions which were not feudal at all, but the basis of the modern state.

However, by the beginning of the 13th century, the king and his greater nobility had lost their French lands, and the long wars against France in the 14th and 15th centuries consolidated the English nobles into a national aristocracy. They were not, however, poorer, for the nation itself was richer; they shared the increase of wealth, and it increased their ambitions, which they endeavoured to satisfy by struggling over the governmental machine which the English kings had by this time built up. Thus, in the second half of the 14th century – the lifetime of Chaucer

– we find that the English nobility has ceased to be the principal element of a loose feudal organization which ignored national frontiers, and has become the richest and most power-hungry section of what is already a national society of a modern type. Their distinctness as a class becomes registered by the new titles with which the king rewarded those who were friendly to him. The title of 'duke' was introduced in 1337; that of 'marquis' (between 'duke' and 'earl') in 1385; that of 'viscount' (below 'earl') in 1440. 'Baron' lost its vague significance and became a distinct title in 1387; it belongs to the lowest rank of nobility.

Chaucer's pilgrims in his *Canterbury Tales* do not include a nobleman, since such a man would not usually accompany such a mixed social group. The highest of them is a representative of the most aristocratic class in the middle ranks of society – the knight. The term 'knight' can be interpreted in three ways: as a vague social classification; in a military sense; and in relation to the aristocratic code of values conveniently denoted by 'chivalry'. Socially, a knight (like one of the 1600 knights of the shire elected at various times to the parliaments of King Edward III) was a medium landowner without a hereditary title. The nobleman took part in national politics at the king's court, whereas the knight participated in local government; in the 16th century such landowners were to be the very basis of royal authority there. Militarily, a knight was a cavalry soldier drawn from the same social group as the knights of the shire. He supplied his own horse and armour, and probably a small following of foot-soldiers as well. Until the archers of Edward III* and Henry V* revolutionized the techniques of war, the armed knight on horseback was the chief weapon of war, corresponding to the tank of modern warfare. In French, he was called a 'chevalier' – a 'horseman' – and upon him centred the code of chivalry. Knighthood in the chivalric sense, however, extended beyond the social significance of the term. Not merely the untitled gentleman, but the titled nobility belonged to the Orders of Knighthood*, for entry into which they had to prove their worth in war as squires* and as 'knights bachelor'. Thus Edward the Black Prince of Wales was knighted by his father, Edward III before the battle of Crécy (1346). Besides military courage, the knight was supposed to cultivate other disinterested virtues. Socially, as a warrior, he was supposed to protect the community. So Piers the ploughman tells the knight in Passus VI:

. . . I will sweat and see to it, and sow for us both,
And labour for your love, all my lifetime,
If you charge yourself to cherish Holy Church and myself
And chase off the wicked that lay the world to waste.
And be a hardy hunter of hares and of foxes
Of boars and of badgers that break down my hedges;
Go and fly falcons to fall upon wildfowl
That come into my croft and crop up my wheat.

(Coghill's version)

In personal relations, the knight was to be the humble but resolute protector of the weak – especially women and children. He cultivated courtesy and the art of making fine speeches, like Gawain in *Sir Gawain and the Green Knight**, and he balanced his ferocity as a soldier with his refinements as a lover. Chaucer says of the Knight's son, the Squire, that he fought well in the hope of winning his lady's favour, and that he was a poet and a fiery lover.

After the Squire has told his tale, the Franklin* praises his eloquence and fine manners, and wishes that he had a son to match him. He then tells his own tale, which expounds the generous, knightly virtues. The Franklin (the word means literally 'freeman') is himself a prosperous small landowner, but a grade lower than the knight in the scale of society. His admiration shows the way in which the civilized values are emulated by those who achieve sufficient prosperity to be able to afford the refinements of living, although they have not been educated to them. Chaucer's poetry is much concerned with such perfecting of earthly life, while Langland is concerned with how to transform the world into a gateway to Heaven for the humblest men and women – who are the most likely to get there unless their social superiors put obstacles in their way.

Langland's ploughman, like Chaucer's, is a freeman, and therefore still above the lowest level of medieval society, composed of serfs, beggars, and casual labourers. The serf's life and labour were entirely at the disposal of his lord, although serfdom contained many varieties of status, and serfs were never absolute slaves. When, moreover, the Black Death* epidemics of the middle of the 14th century swept away between a third and a half of the population, the consequent shortage of labour caused the landowners to let much of their land to small farmers (such as Chaucer's and Langland's ploughmen) and to cultivate the remainder with hired labour. But the change was accompanied by acute social conflicts, culminating in the formidable Peasants' Revolt* in 1381.

Meanwhile, the towns of England were developing their own social systems, with independent characteristics. The towns were small; London, which was the largest, had a population of about 50,000, and those nearest to it – Norwich, York, Bristol and Southampton – may have had a quarter of the number. Others, proud of their identities, would today rank as large villages. It was, however, this sense of identity which gave them importance. Towns began as small settlements, often around a castle or an abbey, and from this they developed into trading centres for the neighbourhood. The kings and the nobles, who at first controlled them as they controlled any village or hamlet of the countryside, were commonly in need of money, and in the 12th and 13th centuries they sold to the towns charters which granted limited self-government and rights of trade regulation. Such freedom encouraged the growth of merchant guilds, which were corporations for the adjustment of prices and other common interests. Later, craft guilds* grew up in each separate trade to regulate the interests of the masters, define the status of the apprentices* who were learning the crafts, and assure the rights of the journeymen* whom the masters employed. Such guilds did not restrict themselves to economic functions; they occupied themselves with the total welfare of their members, and were often partly religious organizations.

By the middle of the 14th century many forms of trade were greatly expanding, and rich merchants began to be national figures. Wars could no longer be fought with feudal levies, and the great armies required by the kings and their barons kept them in constant need of money. During the reign of Edward III* (1327–77), William de la Pole of the town of Hull became one of the first merchants to raise his family into the ranks of the nobility by helping to finance the king. One commodity, that of wool, had long been a major export to other countries of western Europe, and it was partly to defend this trade that Edward III had begun the Hundred Years' War* with France in 1338. The Merchants of the Staple, who conducted this trade, were the first great national trading company, but in the 15th century they met with increasing rivalry from the Merchant Adventurers, who exported cloth. The cloth-making* industry was deliberately encouraged by the government in the 14th century, which invited Flemish weavers to establish it in the English towns. The Staplers and the Adventurers were the first important English capitalists; they did not necessarily themselves produce the commodities they sold; the Staplers bought the wool from the sheep-farmers, and the Adventurers employed the craftsmen who made the cloth. In other kinds of trade, too, a class division began to grow. At first the craft guilds represented solidarity between the master, who was himself a workman, and his apprentices and journeymen, but in the 15th century the masters became increasingly merchants of the products which they caused to be manufactured. The guilds then became privileged associations from which the poorer craftsmen were excluded, and class conflict began to grow in the towns.

These changes were however only on the way. England during the 14th and 15th centuries was on the whole a country of small horizons commercially: the great majority of the countryside and of the towns thought only of their neighbourhoods, not of the country at large, still less of foreign countries. Relationships were defined by long-established custom, and were not rapidly or frequently changed by money. Men did not think of themselves individualistically, but corporately – as members of guilds, of knightly or religious orders, or as members of a class into which they were born – so that the classes in many ways resembled the castes of India rather than the money-based classes of the modern West. Finally, society was still largely dominated by the religious codes of the Church; even the most worldly did not deny that, whatever the delights and opportunities of life on earth, only the Church was able to declare life's true purpose.

2.1.1.2 *The alliance of land and money: 1500–1800*

English schoolchildren commonly learn that the Middle Ages ended in 1485, when the House of Tudor* ascended the throne in the person of King Henry VII*. The great feudal families had destroyed themselves in the struggle for power known as the Wars of the Roses*, and the Tudors were able to build up a new aristocracy which was civilian rather than military, and dependent on the sovereigns who had raised it and whom it served. The great social predominance of the Church was destroyed between 1530 and 1560, and the new national Church of England* not only had a far less pervasive social interest but, like the new nobility, was dependent on the Crown. There was far more opportunity for the growth of the commercial and landed middle classes, on which the Tudors themselves relied for their power and popularity. The 16th century saw great changes therefore; and yet in many outward respects English society changed slowly, not only in the 16th century but in the two centuries that followed it.

Throughout these three centuries, with the marked exception of the growth of London, England remained a country in which village life greatly predominated over urban life. There were three principal reasons for this. The first was that cloth and wool remained the most important national products; wool was produced on the farms, and cloth was manufactured in the villages rather than in the towns. A second reason for the predominance of the rural side of life was that the ownership of land retained its social prestige, and as (thanks largely to the policy of the Tudors) English society was comparatively open to change, a successful merchant could look forward to establishing himself as a landed proprietor, while on the other hand the established gentry were always glad to increase or renew their wealth through intermarriage with merchant families. The third reason was that English agriculture itself became an important commercial enterprise, and ceased to be merely a means of subsistence. In the 16th and 17th centuries, many landlords realized that sheep-farming was far more profitable than arable farming: wool was an important export, and the raw material of the principal export of cloth; it required less labour, and was less vulnerable to bad weather. The substitution of sheep for crops meant the expulsion of the arable farmers who were their tenants and, with the creation of consolidated farms, the enclosure of the common land which their tenants had shared – with consequent suffering among the peasantry and some change in the texture of rural life. But 16th- and 17th-century enclosures* affected the country very unevenly. It was not until the 18th century that agriculture was radically altered by the 'Agricultural Revolution'. This was caused by the discovery of modern methods of cultivation and cattle-breeding; it substituted large farms for small ones and obliterated the medieval system of open-field* farming. The English landscape assumed its modern aspect of hedge-bound fields, and the small peasants dwindled in number. The large landowner, however, prospered all the more. The evidence of the continued prestige of land is that Parliament was dominated by landowners; even townsmen consented, and often preferred, to be represented by landed men.

There were other reasons, besides the predominance of country over town, for the gradualness of English social change. Much agriculture and many of the rural and urban crafts remained local in their importance and preserved a close, personal relationship between employers and employed. The guild organization of town trades was a mere relic in the 18th century, and long before that it had disintegrated into a great variety of systems, but its disappearance was gradual. Even a great change like the Reformation* left society at its lower levels less changed than one might expect. The parish priest had the same relationship with his parishioners, although, after 1560, he might be a married man; he preached the same kind of sermon* after the Reformation as he had preached before it. The local landowner was often the same kind of man as the medieval knight of the shire, though he was now generally referred to as the Squire*. Most important of all, if we are considering the continuance of social values, it was not until after the middle of the 17th century that economic doctrines began to prevail over religious doctrines in men's ideas about how society should work; it was not until then, for instance, that the taking of interest on monetary loans entirely ceased to carry moral opprobrium as the sin of usury*.

A superficial observer, then, might consider that society in the age of Shakespeare had not changed decisively since the death of Chaucer in 1400. He would see greater changes by the time of Dryden's* death in 1700, and some radical differences between Dryden's England and that of Wordsworth* and Coleridge* when they published their *Lyrical Ballads** in 1798, yet even at the end of the 18th century many of the principal features of England society would not greatly have altered, at least in appearance. A less superficial observer might ask himself whether this outward continuity did not mask inward changes in the spirit of society. He might wonder, for example, what significance underlies the growth and distribution of the population. This nearly doubled from about 3 million in the 15th century to about 5½ million in 1700, and by 1800 it increased to 11 million. The increase was most striking in south-eastern England and especially in London, the population of which grew from about 50,000 in Chaucer's time to about 200,000 in Shakespeare's; by 1700 it was 674,000, and by 1800, over a million. The increase was due chiefly to London's importance as a port, and it is evidence of the growth of commercial enterprise in national life.

The natural vehicle for commercial enterprise is the capitalist system of economic life. We have seen that capitalism* had already made energetic beginnings in England by 1500, although it was much less advanced here than in some other regions of western Europe, especially Italy. Its beginnings had been in that characteristic of capitalism which divides the employer from the employee; the former owns the materials of production and the finished product, which he sells, whereas the latter commands only his skills and his labour. This had been a characteristic of some of the leading medieval industries, especially wool and cloth, and cloth-making also exhibited another characteristic of capitalism – division of labour, by which the capitalist ensures efficient production by causing the different phases of manufacture to be accomplished by different workers, each employing a special skill. But capitalism, for its full development, requires stores of accumulated wealth available for investment, and this in turn depends on a large market, offering the investor a wide choice. One of its conspicuous features is speculation: the owners of capital seek investments which offer the greatest profits, or the greatest security, and they will change their investments as the market changes. Correspondingly, traders who lack capital themselves will seek to persuade possessors of it to invest it in their enterprises.

The 16th century offered new opportunities for the growth of capitalism in various ways. One of these was that money became more available for two reasons, the first of which was national, and the second international. King Henry VIII* (1509–47) found that his government was short of gold and silver currency, and he increased the quantity of this by 'debasing' it; that is to say, he caused the gold and silver of the coinage to be mixed in the minting with cheaper metals. The increased volume of money caused a rise in prices, with the result that many small farmers could not pay their rents, and the landowners took over the arable farms and enclosed them for sheep. The international expansion of money was, however, much more important: the Spanish discovery of gold and silver in South and Central America led to an immense influx of these metals into Europe, and a great international money market grew up in the main commercial cities, one of which was London, where the Royal Exchange* was established in 1566. Prices increased still further. The Crown and the great landowners who relied on fairly constant rents were the sufferers, and so were the poor, but the smaller landed gentry and the merchants received higher prices for their crops and their merchandise (while wages remained low) and higher profits on their investments.

Investment was immensely encouraged by the most important of all the opportunities for capitalist expansion in the 16th century: it was the age of the great voyages of discovery. England was later than Spain or Portugal in joining the race to open up the little known or undiscovered lands, but after 1570 the English pursued it with great energy, and often with immense profit. Great trading companies were established. The earliest was the Muscovy (or Russia) Company (1553) which also traded with Persia; the Eastland Company (1579) traded with the Baltic; the Levant Company (1581) with the Middle East; the East India Company* (1600), first with the East Indies and later with the continent of India: there were also a number of African companies. Many were joint stock companies*; that is to say, the traders received profits according to the total sale of the merchandise, and this was to become the commonest and most tempting kind of investment.

This great expansion of mercantile enterprise conflicted with many of the traditions of rural society, the basis of the nation. The mercantile spirit was acquisitive, and easily tended to personal aggrandizement without regard for any existing order of human relations; it might also lead to unprecedented folly, resembling mania. In the reign of James I*, the comedies of Ben Jonson*, Thomas Middleton* and Philip Massinger* are full of satire against the new acquisitiveness. 'Projectors' extract money from their dupes for impossible commercial projects, as Meercraft preys upon Fitzdottrel in Jonson's *The Devil is an Ass** (1616); Mammon surrenders himself to impossible dreams of sensual indulgence in *The Alchemist** (1610); in *Volpone** (1606) the Fox finds that there are no limits to the baseness to which his dupes will descend in the hope of gain. A powerful representation of the new, ruthless, acquisitive man is Massinger's Sir Giles Overreach in *A New Way to Pay Old Debts** (1625). Overreach is not a merchant, but a landed gentleman, who impoverishes his neighbours for his own advantage, and seeks to force his daughter into marriage with a nobleman to enhance his own personal status:

Now, for these other piddling complaints
Breathed out in bitterness; as when they call me
Extortioner, tyrant, cormorant, or intruder
On my poor neighbour's right, or grand encloser
Of what was common, to my private use;
Nay, when my ears are pierced with widows' cries,
And undone orphans wash with tears my threshold,
I only think what 'tis to have my daughter
Right honourable; and 'tis a powerful charm
Makes me insensible of remorse, or pity,
Or the least sting of conscience.

He is addressing Lord Lovel whom he desires to be his son-in-law, and Lovel replies: 'I admire [*ie* 'wonder at'] the toughness of your nature.' Overreach is of course a caricature, but 'toughness of nature' had become typical of the English landed gentry and merchant classes. They had been the basis of Tudor power in the 16th century, and had gained great confidence. As magistrates*, they had been endowed with extensive power, and they used it not merely to preserve law and order and to relieve the distressed, but to enforce their own privileges, as in the preservation of game on their estates for hunting and to secure (like Overreach) the enclosure of common lands to their 'private use'. The old medieval community of interests between the knight of the shire and his tenants tended to be replaced by opposition of interests, and by the 17th century this social opposition on one side was balanced by an opposition between the gentry and the king on the other.

The Stuart kings found the rising costs of government much exceeded their traditional sources of income, many of which had fixed rates, and they sought to meet these costs by special taxation. The gentry and the rich merchants, however, did not see why their money should be used to finance governmental policies of which they often disapproved, and they resisted the king's demands. This was the economic cause of the battle for parliamentary supremacy, which began with wordy debates in the reign of James I, reached bloodshed in the Civil Wars* of 1642–51, and ended with complete Parliamentary victory in the Revolution* of 1688. The struggle was not a democratic one, in the sense of a whole people resisting the king and his hirelings, but a struggle between authority based on tradition and new economic forces. Those who sided with the king did so either on religious grounds or because they had not shared in the economic expansion.

They included a large part of all classes in the nation, especially in the north and west; the supporters of Parliament were chiefly in the south and east, and especially in London.

In some respects, the social restlessness of the middle classes in the 17th century is parallel to the restlessness of the nobility in the 14th and 15th centuries. Both were hungry for land and power. The nobility had sought them through wars in France, and when they were frustrated or defeated there they struggled for them at home. In the 17th century, the middle-class order of objectives was the reverse: at first they struggled with the king, and when Charles I tried to govern without Parliament in the 'Eleven Years' Tyranny' (1630–41), 60,000 men and women emigrated to the new colonies on the east coast of America and in the West Indies. The nobility were defeated in the 15th century because the economic and social forces were against them; the middle classes were victorious because the same forces were on their side.

When, however, we speak of the 'middle classes' as a power group, we have to remember that they were only a fraction of even the middle segment of society. It is easy to exaggerate the extent of the commercial interests, because London took the lead in the struggle. Four-fifths of the population still worked on the land, and nine-tenths of the members of the House of Commons* were landowners; of these, a large minority sided with the king in the Civil War. The world of commerce was more solidly behind Parliament, but there was a division between the great companies such as the East India Company, who sought to monopolize trade, and 'interlopers' who sought to break the monopolies. In domestic trade, the number of small traders was increasing. They had no spare wealth for investment, but they were rich enough to feel superior to the 'mechanics' whom they employed, and secure enough to feel independent of their superiors in wealth. If, like Robinson Crusoe's* father, they prospered, they often preferred to sink their money into a small landed estate rather than to speculate, though they might do both. Their sons might continue as small country gentlemen, or they might enter a profession – usually the Church or the Law, or they might re-enter commerce. Defoe* dates Crusoe's birth as 1632. The father, trying to quieten his son's wanderlust, thus expatiates on the advantages of the condition into which he was born:

> *He told me it was men of desperate fortunes, on one hand, or of superior fortunes, on the other, who went abroad upon adventures, aspiring to rise by enterprise . . . ; that these things were all either too far above me, or too far below me; that mine was the middle state, or what might be called the upper state of low life, which he had found, by long experience, was the best state in the world, the most suited to human happiness; not exposed to the miseries and hardships, the labour and sufferings, of the mechanic part of mankind, and not embarrassed with the pride, luxury, ambition, envy of the upper part of mankind; he told me, I might judge of the happiness of this state by one thing, viz. that this was the state of life which all other people*

envied; that kings have frequently lamented the miserable consequences of being born to great things, and wished they had been placed in the middle of the two extremes, between the mean and the great; that the wise man gave his testimony to this as the just standard of true felicity, when he prayed to have 'neither poverty nor riches'.

Nonetheless, the young Crusoe goes on his wanderings. The Puritan* middle class to which he belonged – Defoe's own – was torn between social and spiritual ideals of stability and the need for exploration, whether in the spirit through constant examination of the conscience, or over the sea. Yet even while they risked their lives in dangerous journeys and their sanity in the introspective caverns in which Bunyan* and his creation, Christian, nearly lost themselves, their ultimate goal was the recovery of that spiritual and material security from which Crusoe departs, and to which he returns.

This growth of a wide, moderately prosperous middle class beneath the more ambitious and wealthy one suggests a basic stability in 17th-century society, in spite of the turbulence of the political conflicts. Its existence is largely attributable to the constructive policy of the Tudor sovereigns, especially Elizabeth I*, in establishing a national system of poor relief administered by the magistrates, and culminating in the Poor Law* of 1601. Here we have a marked contrast to the previous age of social restlessness in the 14th and 15th centuries. In the earlier period, the victimized peasantry had to seek relief for their wrongs in the great popular outbreaks of the Peasants' Revolt of 1381 and Cade's Rebellion in 1450. In the 17th and 18th centuries there were no such risings, because machinery existed for relieving distress before it became desperate. When they again showed signs of occurring in the early 19th century, this was because the machinery had broken down. At the end of the 17th century, a contemporary commentator, Gregory King, computed that nearly one-fifth of the population received poor relief from time to time; they mostly belonged to the class of land workers.

The 18th century showed a greater differentiation of social classes than had been characteristic of the 16th and 17th centuries. One reason for this was a new expansion of opportunities for acquiring wealth, and new facilities for raising money. In trade, there had hitherto been no safe repositories for money apart from the domestic strong box, but in the middle of the 17th century rich men began to leave it with the goldsmiths, who thus became the first regular bankers. The Bank of England* was founded in 1694, and by the middle of the 18th century there was a nationwide banking system from which loans could be raised. The extensive wars with France enabled Britain to expand her overseas territories, and to secure her trade with them by her sea-power. Such expansion increased the availability of raw materials, especially cotton, and this, combined with newly invented machines for working cotton and wool, enabled the manufacturers to operate on an enlarged scale. Factories* came into existence, side by side with the traditional domestic system, under which the craftsmen worked up the materials in their homes. The Industrial Revolution* was thus well under way at the end of the century, but its effects on society were not yet so conspicuous as those of the Agricultural Revolution. The new methods of farming made it profitable as never before, but they required capital investment and large-scale enclosure. The peasant farmer was reduced as a class; the peasants emigrated to the colonies, sank to the level of farm labourers, or drifted to the industrial towns where there was a growing demand for labour. Even the middle class of landowners, oppressed by taxation to pay for the wars, often sold out to the great landowners, who let their estates to large tenant farmers. Thus the great landowners, after two centuries of reduced importance which had enabled the House of Commons* to exceed the House of Lords* in parliamentary power, once more became the most powerful class in the country. Such wide difference in wealth reduced social mobility from class to class, but society was still not sharply divided into castes, as it had been in the Middle Ages. Moreover, the great landed aristocracy, which now firmly controlled Parliament and the government, was fully conscious of the importance of the nation's commerce. The aristocrat might despise the merchant socially, but he did not despise the merchant's wealth. He invested his own in the great Joint Stock Companies in the management of which he often participated.

2.1.1.3 *Industrialization: 1800–present day*

Between 1801 and 1830, the population of England, Wales and Scotland increased from 11 to 16½ million; it almost doubled in the reign of George III (1760–1820). By 1875 the population of England and Wales alone was 23 million, and by 1900 it was 32½ million. This great increase occurred chiefly in England, and it was mainly urban. By 1851 over half the population lived in the towns, and today fewer than 5% work in agriculture, as compared to 80% three hundred years ago. This rapid urban growth was of course produced by the Industrial Revolution*, which converted manufacture to the factory system, thanks mainly to the introduction of steam power late in the 18th century, and to the spread of the railways in the 1830s and 1840s, greatly facilitating the transport of goods. The story of the Scottish and Irish populations is very different. That of Scotland increased from about 1 million in 1700 to just under 5 million today, but the increase was principally in the industrial parts of the south and east; the north emptied itself in repeated emigration. Ireland, which is little industrialized even today, has been one of the few countries in the world to show a large fall in population in the last hundred years. In 1830 its population of 8 million was about half that of the rest of the United Kingdom, but by 1900 over 4 million had emigrated.

The parts of England most transformed by the Industrial Revolution were the north and the northern midlands. Hitherto these regions had remained comparatively backward and barbarous, and had resisted the thrusting south. They had risen against Henry VIII's dissolution of the monasteries in the rebellion known as the Pilgrimage of Grace* (1536); it was in the north that the old medieval nobility had made its last stand in the rebellion of the northern earls (1569); the same regions had been predominantly the supporters of Charles I in the Civil War* of 1642–6. To the 19th-century southerner, like the heroine of Elizabeth Gaskell's *North and South** (1854), the north did not seem less ferocious and untamed than in the pre-industrial centuries, but its energies now expressed themselves in the throbbing factories of the dark, smoke-hung towns. Of course the north was not, and is not now, a great urbanized mass; Mrs Gaskell's *Cranford** is about a country town 15 miles from Manchester, and yet as sweet and genteel as any southern town in a novel by Jane Austen*. Emily Brontë's* Heathcliff derives his energies as much from the empty moors surrounding Wuthering Heights* as from the jungle conditions of the Liverpool slums where he spent his infancy. All the same, large areas of Yorkshire and Lancashire, centres of the wool and cotton trade, were heavily industrialized. The towns grew very rapidly, without care for dignity or for human welfare; England now suffered for her comparative lack of a strong urban tradition like that of Italy, the Netherlands, or Germany. Even if she had had one, however, it is possible that the rush into industrialization would have destroyed it. Mitchell and Leys in *A History of the English People* state that in the early 19th century only 68 of the 568 streets in the Yorkshire town of Leeds were paved, and some of these were 'floating with sewage'. In Manchester, at the same time, of every hundred children born, only 35 survived to the age of five. For a century, two of the principal social problems in England were to be the huge areas of slum dwelling in the industrial towns, and the drunkenness which was the working man's (and woman's) only easy escape from the intolerable squalor of his surroundings.

The social changes brought about by industrialization were thus most conspicuous in the changed character of the working class. The greatest indignity human beings can suffer is to be reduced to the anonymity of units in a mass. To some extent the land-worker had already been treated in this way. The medieval serf, and the small cultivator victimized by enclosures from the 16th century to the 19th, had been sacrificed to the interests and the economic advancement of the landlords. Yet their distress was partly alleviated by the Poor Laws, and the comparatively isolated living conditions of the countryman helped to sustain his individuality. The 19th-century urban worker, on the contrary, was herded into factories and overcrowded streets, and the abstract economic theories of the time reduced him to the level of a commodity, valued only according to the fluctuating demand for his labour. Women and children were at first treated no differently in this respect from the men. The Poor Law of 1601 no longer operated in either town or countryside, and the desperation of the poor expressed itself in the popular outbreaks of machine-breaking known as the Luddite* riots. England, in 1820, seemed to be drifting towards a great social uprising.

The industrial towns were no better than jungles, where the law was the survival of the fittest. The hardiest, however, had the freedom of the jungle to work themselves into the employing class, and to own and manage their own factories, though they might only be small ones. It was these newly risen men, rather than the already established merchant class, who were the ruthless employers. For them, the law of the jungle was unqualified; but they found support among the intellectual theorists of the Utilitarian* school of political economists, who were on the whole men of right feeling, but men who closed their minds to their feelings. The classic exposition of the alliance is Dickens's presentation of the Utilitarian Gradgrind and the employer Bounderby in *Hard Times** (1854):

> . . . *who* was *Mr Bounderby?*
>
> *Why, Mr Bounderby was as near being Mr Gradgrind's bosom friend, as a man perfectly devoid of sentiment can approach that spiritual relationship towards another man perfectly devoid of sentiment. So near was Mr Bounderby – or, if the reader should prefer it, so far off.*

Mr Gradgrind prides himself on his total reliance on 'facts'; Bounderby prides himself on his success in surviving the misery and deprivations of his early life. About these, as it turns out, Bounderby is lying, but his account of his career and the brutality of his ideas exemplify employers of his type:

> *I was to pull through it, I suppose, Mrs Gradgrind. Whether I was to do it or not, ma'am, I did it. I pulled through it, though nobody threw me a rope. Vagabond, errand-boy, vagabond, labourer, porter, clerk, chief manager, small partner, Josiah Bounderby of Coketown. Those are the antecedents and the culmination. Josiah Bounderby of Coketown learnt his letters from the outsides of the shops, Mrs Gradgrind, and was first able to tell the time on a dial-plate, from studying the steeple clock of St Giles's Church, London, under the direction of a drunken cripple, who was a convicted thief, and an incorrigible vagrant. Tell Josiah Bounderby of Coketown, of your district schools, and your training schools, and your whole kettle-of-fish of schools; and Josiah Bounderby of Coketown tells you plainly, all right, all correct – he hadn't such advantages – but let us have hard-headed, solid-fisted people – the education that made him won't do for everybody, he knows well – such and such his education was, however, and you shall force him to swallow boiling fat, but you shall never force him to suppress the facts of his life.*

Bounderby's implication is that he has proved his right to power by his superior strength, and that those who depend upon school education show themselves thereby to be weaklings whom he has the right to oppress. Such men were inevitably obstructive to humanitarian reform; contemptuously indifferent to the new education, they actively resented any attempt to restrict the supply of child and female labour. But other members of the increasingly powerful middle class and those of the upper class who – like the seventh Earl of Shaftesbury* – were concerned about social matters took measures to amend the worst abuses. Such of these measures as arose from Utilitarian thinking – especially the New Poor Law of 1834 – were inspired more by the desire for efficiency than by human feeling, but others, like the Factory Act of 1833, were directed against exploitation as such. It is an indication of the extent of the exploitation that this Factory Act was intended to restrict the hours of work of children, but so large was the employment of children in factories that work could not continue without them, so that its effect was to restrict the hours of work of men and women as well.

Though they were now very large and very rich, the industrial and commercial middle classes were themselves, at the beginning of the century, an underprivileged class. The system of electoral representation in Parliament was an ancient one and favoured landed society. The old towns, many of which had dwindled (even, like Old Sarum, to extinction) or had remained small were over represented. Even in these, the townsmen entitled to vote were often few, and subservient to the neighbouring landed interest. The newly grown towns, on the other hand, were represented inadequately or not at all. Furthermore, the Corn Laws*, which protected English agriculture by imposing taxes on imported corn, deprived the market of cheap food and thus weakened the industrial labour force, and the Corn Laws were only the most conspicuous example of a protective system of economic policy which frustrated the industrialists, preventing them from flooding the world with their mass-produced manufactures. They fought hard and victoriously, in the first half of the 19th century, to secure the political representation to which they were entitled, and to reform the trading laws in their favour. In this struggle, they had the working class on their side, although the parliamentary Reform Bill of 1832 enfranchised the middle class alone. The Repeal of the Corn Laws in 1846 was a turning point for British society. By inaugurating free trade* in foreign commerce, the government in effect acknowledged that Britain was no longer basically an agricultural country, but an industrial one; and by supplying the working class with its most urgent need – cheap food – it bowed to the alliance of the middle and working classes against the landed classes. The decades of the fifties and the sixties showed a lessening of social conflict, because the middle classes had achieved their aims, and national prosperity extended downwards in higher wages. After 1870 the workers tended increasingly to take their own way politically against the employers, but the growth of working class political movements was slow. The early experiments in trade unionism in the 1830s and the movement of the thirties and forties known as Chartism*, were frustrated by inexperience in organization, and by the strength of the interests which the workers shared with their employers.

Thus by 1850 the middle classes had won preponderance of political power, but this did not mean that the aristocracy were excluded or lost prestige. The aristocratic political families, often creations of the Tudors, such as the Cecils, the Russells and the Cavendishes, were still prominent in Parliament and in the bureaucracy, though they submitted to the leadership of William Gladstone*, the son of a Liverpool merchant and even of such an outsider as Benjamin Disraeli*, of Italian Jewish descent. One reason for this continuance of aristocratic prestige, which is evident in British politics even today, is the willingness of the British aristocracy to adapt themselves to change. They resisted parliamentary reform and the Repeal of the Corn Laws, but they did not seek to reverse them, and they often took the lead in reforms such as the Factory Acts. Many of the aristocracy, indeed, held to a tradition of political radicalism; they were sympathetic to the French Revolution*. Lord Byron*, the poet, defended the Luddite rioters in the House of Lords; the philosopher Bertrand Russell* continued this aristocratic radical tradition in our own time. But another reason for aristocratic survival. and a more important one, has been the continuing fluidity of English society. The aristocracy had prestige with the middle classes because it was possible for them to enter it. The sociologist, Beatrice Webb*, in her autobiography *My Apprenticeship* (1926), describes upper society as she saw it in the last thirty years of the 19th century thus:

> *There was the Court, representing national tradition and custom; there was the Cabinet and ex-Cabinet, representing political power; there was a mysterious group of millionaire financiers representing money; there was the racing set . . . representing sport. All persons who habitually entertained and who were entertained by the members of any one of these key groups could claim to belong to London Society. These four inner circles crossed and recrossed each other owing to an element of common membership; this, in the 'seventies and the 'eighties, happened to consist of striking personalities: such, for instance, as Edward, Prince of Wales, and the magnetically attractive Grand Seigneur [Lord Rosebery] who . . . won the Derby*, married a Rothschild and was destined to become Prime Minister of the British Empire [1894–5] at a time when there was a British Empire. Surrounding and solidifying these four intersecting social circles was a curiously tough substance – the British aristocracy – an aristocracy, as a foreign diplomatist once remarked to me, 'the most talented, the most energetic and the most vulgar in the world'; characteristics which he attributed to a perpetual casting out and renewal, younger sons and daughters falling out of social rank to sink or swim among their fellow-commoners, whilst the new rich of the British Empire and the United States were assimilated by marriage, or by the sale of honours to persons of great riches but with mean minds and mediocre manners, in order to replenish the electoral funds of the 'ins' and 'outs' [ie political parties 'in' or 'out' of power].*

The Victorian novelists were inclined to treat the predominance of money with angry satire which recalls the satire of Jonson and his followers on the 'projectors' and other speculators of the reign of James I (1603–25). We have the arrogant merchant such as Thackeray's Mr Osborne (*Vanity Fair**, 1848) and Dickens's Podsnap (*Our Mutual Friend**, 1865), neither of whom, in spite of their pride, was important enough for London's 'inner circle' of high society. We also have the fraudulent financier like Trollope's* Melmotte (*The Way We Live Now*, 1876) and Dickens's Merdle in *Little Dorrit**, who, for the time of their glory, were important enough.

> *Mrs Merdle reviewed the bosom which Society was accustomed to review; and having ascertained that show-window of Mr Merdle's and the London jewellers' to be in good order, replied:*
>
> *'As to marriage on the part of a man, my dear, Society requires that he should retrieve his fortunes by marriage. Society requires that he should gain by marriage. Society requires that he should found a handsome establishment by marriage. Society does not see, otherwise, what he has to do with marriage. Bird, be quiet!'*
>
> *For, the parrot on his cage above them, presiding over the conference as if he were a Judge (and indeed he looked rather like one), had wound up the exposition with a shriek.*

Against such vulgarity and ruthlessness, Thackeray set up the old-fashioned (but by no means dead) ideal of the gentleman; Dickens offered spontaneity of feeling and disinterested service; Trollope admired the respect for the obligations of rank manifested by Roger Carberry, the country squire in *The Way We Live Now*. Carberry shows the country gentleman of the old school in eclipse: those of his neighbours who, in the 18th century, would have been proud to call themselves his equals, are ruining themselves by their social ambitions in London, and Carberry finds no congenial society except among his tenants and with an old-fashioned bishop. Fascinated by the glamour of the prodigious wealth that was inflating the upper classes, people of all ranks were more inclined than ever to estimate a man by his status rather than his personal qualities. The evil aristocrat, Grandcourt, in George Eliot's *Daniel Deronda** (1876), is treated by his equals and inferiors as an institution immune to moral judgement, while he treats all who surround him with the contemptuous indifference of a man who has never found occasion to value human feeling.

Trying to estimate the spirit of the wealthy society in which she grew up, Beatrice Webb remarks: 'Some of the men and practically all the women made the pursuit of pleasure their main occupation in life.' But she goes on to say that, in her circle, 'There were very few men who were not active brain-workers in politics, administration, law, science or literature.' This highly responsible section of the influential classes counteracts the impression one often receives from the novelists, (*eg* James* and Gissing*), that English society was fast degenerating.

Moreover, the responsible middle class had beneath them a rising tide of responsible and active working-class leaders. The working classes had been oppressed by the harshness and rapidity of the earlier Industrial Revolution, but, apart from the relief afforded them by the social legislation between 1830 and 1850, they had possessed resources of their own which not only saved them from total brutalization but trained the best of them in self-help and organization. Methodism*, the 18th-century religious revival, and other Dissenting* movements in sympathy with it, were above all working-class movements. They operated through self-governing chapels in the industrial towns and the mining villages, like those to which George Eliot's Silas Marner* and the Morels in D. H. Lawrence's *Sons and Lovers** belonged; their spirit was ardent, and, despite their tendencies to narrowness and intolerance, they were important means of self-improvement and self-education. Inevitably, the relevance of Gospel teaching to the condition of the working class found an important place in their discussions, and in men like the miner and labour leader, James Keir Hardie (1856–1915) these led straight to socialism. In addition, the mining and metal working trades which were virtually created by the Industrial Revolution led to a working-class aristocracy, and provided a natural leadership in the second half of the century such as had been lacking in the first half. It was from such resources that the trade union movement grew up, and achieved national unification by the establishment of the Trades Union Congress in 1868. The Conservative and Liberal politicians saw the necessity of winning working-class support. Disraeli gave the urban workers the right to vote in elections and to sit in Parliament in 1867, and the Liberals gave it to the agricultural workers in 1884; in 1870, universal primary education was established. In the last twenty years of the 19th century the unskilled workers also achieved trade union organization, and by 1900 the working classes, with the help of such middle-class intellectuals as Beatrice Webb, were sufficiently well consolidated to form their own Labour Party*.

Between the rich middle classes and the workers, a very large lower middle class existed; its members populate the novels of Dickens and H. G. Wells* more than the members of any other class. Its bulk was the large number of small traders brought into existence by the extensive 'consumer society' which the Industrial Revolution created. At one extreme, the lower middle class met the new kind of skilled worker, the engineer and the mechanic; at the other, it met the upper middle class in the retail businesses, in the teaching and medical professions, and in banking. Social discriminations were constantly changing in the 19th century; more and more kinds of work rose in public estimation as economic organization became increasingly elaborate. The lower middle class tended therefore to be the most fluid of all the classes. It was the most unstable in its political sympathies, and consequently often the decisive section of the society in elections. Better educated than the average working-class man, its members helped to provide leadership in Labour movements, and at the same time, since it also consisted largely of small property owners, it provided a restraining influence.

Thus 20th-century society received from the 19th century a great legacy in the shape of a highly developed social conscience: the belief that widespread wretchedness is a wrong which the state ought to prevent, as it prevents crime and epidemics. The political momentum of the last century has led to the establishment of the (still imperfect) Welfare State, which can be said to have begun with the introduction of Old Age Pensions in 1909, and to have taken further shape with the establishment of universal social insurance and the health service between 1945 and 1950. But the 20th century has seen enormous events in world politics and in scientific advance which have introduced quite new social problems, so that now we seem, in common with most other countries in the world, to be living between two ages. On the one hand, we have been living with the remains of the social systems of the past, which in Britain are perhaps preserved more clearly than elsewhere; on the other hand, we are living with the beginnings of a quite new social system, which has not yet taken shape. Consequently, society is now more complex than it has ever been, although it contains fewer contrasts in the conditions of material life. The old hierarchy of the landed society survives, but in a much more meagre form than it possessed a century ago, and with much diminished prestige. Partly owing to heavy taxation, still more owing to increasing costs and the shortage of labour, the great country houses and estates have since 1914 been increasingly difficult to maintain and have gradually been abandoned; the small estate has also extensively disappeared, so that the villages have lost their squires. Village life itself began to lose its vitality in the 19th century when the village craftsman, who had contributed so much to it, was drawn away into the factories. The decline of agricultural prosperity after 1870, and the mechanization of farming (reducing the need for labour) in the 20th century further depopulated the villages. Today, English villages are often suburbs of the towns, inhabited by town workers who 'commute' by car between the two.

Below the much attenuated aristocracy, the social structure still bears the main outlines that it possessed in the 19th century, although with much less striking contrasts of wealth and poverty, and with important changes of composition. Whole sections of the middle and working class have disappeared or are disappearing. A middle-class home in the 19th century commonly had three or four servants, usually women; rich houses had many more, and of both sexes; even a prosperous working-class home might have one. Domestic servants were still fairly numerous, though much reduced in numbers, between 1920 and 1940, but since 1945 they are seldom found except in very rich houses, hotels, and public institutions such as hospitals. The cause of their disappearance has of course been the much wider range in choice of employment for women. In the middle classes, the small shopkeeper is gradually disappearing, as chain-stores spread from town to town; the small farmer often depends on the support of government subsidies; the small manufacturer flourishes in some industries, and has vanished from others.

The biggest change, however, has been in social attitudes. The obverse of the Welfare State, in which it is intended that no one shall suffer from undue distress, is the Affluent Society, in which it is assumed that all classes should share a high material standard of living. The trade unions do not fight for fair subsistence wages on behalf of their members, but for wages that will give them a standard proportionate to the prosperity of their employers. If the profits of middle-class investments do not diminish, the working class wage earner resists restraint on his own wages, even if their increase does not correspond to the increase of his productivity. This claim of a proportionate share in affluence indicates the disappearance of the old acceptance that superior classes had privileges in proportion to the superiority of their wealth. The tradition that the 'gentleman' has rights in proportion to the standards that he is expected to maintain has gone, and Britain is beginning to be, in this sense, democratic in its social standards for the first time. The explanation seems to lie in the rise of a new kind of ruling class.

Modern society is a system of large organizations, whether they are nationalized industries like the railways, or private industries like Imperial Chemical Industries. These require an immense variety of technical and managerial skills which are more specialized than those demanded by management and industry in the past. Since higher education is now, in theory at least, available to all, such skills present opportunities to any young man or woman who is sufficiently gifted to merit the rewards in money and position that they bring. But what has been called the 'meritocracy' – the rule of those who have won the race of talent – presents two almost entirely new problems of social tension. The first is that whereas the 19th-century middle- or upper-class 'gentleman' from a public school* occupied his position of power at least with a sense of obligation (imbued in him by his education and social training) to balance his privilege, the 'meritocrat' occupies it by force of his ability alone. In so far as he obeys a gentlemanly code of etiquette, this is more likely to mark his sense of belonging to an elite than to guide his moral conduct. This does not mean that 'meritocrats' are corrupt, but that there is less of a governing standard of values, inspiring trust among the governed, than once existed. The 'meritocrat' of working-class origin, or even the well-paid worker who finds himself surrounded by comparatively bourgeois circumstances, is quick to feel suspicion of the manners of the class into which he has moved, since working-class culture, especially in the north and in the midlands, has kept more of its spontaneity and integrity. This may account for the peculiar combativeness of working-class novelists in this century, from D. H. Lawrence* to Alan Sillitoe*. The other problem is that the young man who is excluded from positions of importance or wealth by the system of educational selection is more likely to feel that he has been rejected on account of his personal demerits than when he found himself excluded by lack of social privilege. The result may be a vague and frustrated hatred of 'society', leading to aimless destructiveness.

The past thus weighs heavily on the present in contemporary Britain. The social and political 'establishment'* is inherited from the 19th century and from centuries long before that. The technological, scientific requirements of modern government have altered this 'establishment' only to harden it into a crust which seems to bear little relationship to the personal needs of the 20th-century individual, seeking institutions that will relate him intelligibly to his own past. The result seems to be that the social conflicts of the past are translating themselves into a conflict between the generations more acute than the differences between old and young that have always existed – an insular manifestation of an opposition that seems to be worldwide.

2.1.2 *Education*

2.1.2.1 *Medieval education: 1350–1500*

Education in the Middle Ages* followed the division by the Greek philosopher, Aristotle*, into mechanical and liberal arts. The former trained the student in a craft, from the humblest and most practical trade, such as shoe-making, to what would now be called the fine arts of sculpture, painting and architecture. The main means of mechanical education was the guild system of the towns, by which boys began their training as apprentices*, achieved the status of journeyman* half-way through their course, and became (or might become) fully recognized master craftsmen at the end of seven years. The liberal arts were the training of the mind, and were taught at the universities, where they were divided into two stages: the Trivium consisting of Grammar, Rhetoric, and Logic, and the Quadrivium, consisting of Arithmetic, Astronomy, Music and Geometry. There were two universities* in England (Oxford* and Cambridge*) but to these we should add the Inns of Court* in London where law was (and still is) studied. A third kind of education was provided by royal and aristocratic households, where boys of noble and (like Chaucer*) some merchant families were trained as pages until later they became squires* and were finally knighted. This training did not, until later, include much formal education; the page and the squire learnt to use weapons and to hunt, to acquire courtly manners and to dance and sing. They did not necessarily learn to read and write, but by the time of King Richard II* (1377–99), when Chaucer was settled as a court poet and bureaucrat, the English nobleman was becoming too sophisticated to remain illiterate.

Liberal education was entirely in the hands of the Church, and in the middle of the 14th century, it was not widespread. The idea that 'book-learning', or even mere literacy, was in itself a desirable acquirement for every man capable of it only became generally accepted in the 16th century. The 14th- and 15th-century clergy, on the contrary, saw liberal studies as essentially a vocational training for their profession, and even as that they were required in very varying degrees – the medieval parish priest was often barely literate. However, by the end of the 14th century, literate laymen became mentioned in records; after 1415, such mentions cease, presumably because their large number now made them commonplace. Among the poor, the Church tended to discourage literacy except among those expected to become clergy; it threatened the Church's authority.

The schools, therefore, were attended principally by those intending to 'take orders', although in the 15th century young noblemen and merchants' sons were to be found in them. Small schools were sometimes attached to the monasteries; the monastic almoner, whose duty it was to relieve the poor, sometimes included education in his function, and there were also 'song schools' to provide for the monastery choirs. More numerous were the episcopal grammar schools established by the bishops in their dioceses. Among these, the most distinguished was Winchester College, founded in 1382 by the Bishop William of Wykeham for 'poor scholars' (usually of the middle classes), but intended also for noblemen's sons. This was the first of what became known as the public schools*, distinguishable from the other grammar schools both by drawing their pupils from all over the country, and by taking them from a wider social range. In the 15th century the laity, from the king downwards, also founded schools, though the teachers remained clergy: King Henry VI* founded Eton* in 1440. Many of these foundations were established by town guilds and by 'chantries', *ie* corporations of priests whose function was to sing masses for the souls of the dead. At the beginning of the 16th century, it has been estimated that there may have been 500 grammar schools in England, besides a smaller number of almonry and song schools. In noble households, education began to be conducted by private tutors, whose pupils might include a few besides members of the immediate family of the nobleman.

The principal subject of study in the grammar schools was Latin. Religious works were read, but not the Bible, which was left to interpretation by the priests. In addition, the pupils read the works of the great Roman poets, in so far as they were known, especially Virgil*. Latin was the language of learning and administration in daily life, and the pupils were forced to speak it while they were at play. By the 15th century, French was no longer the language of daily speech among the upper classes; it was sometimes taught in the grammar schools as a foreign language.

The term 'university'* derives from a medieval synonym for 'guild', and the medieval university was in effect a guild of liberal arts, analogous to the town guilds of the mechanical arts. The relationship between the tutor and the student was similar to that between the master craftsman and his apprentice. When the student had completed half of his course he might become a bachelor of arts, analogous to the status of journeyman in the craft guilds; after this he could complete his course and become a 'Master'. The two universities of Oxford and Cambridge owed their origins to 'custom'; that is to say, they were not royal or church foundations, but arose spontaneously. Oxford originated in the 12th century as a colony from Paris, and Cambridge was the offspring of Oxford early in the 13th century. The teachers were principally secular clergy, like the parish priest and reformer John Wycliffe* (1320?–84), but these had rivals among the teaching order of the friars* – the Dominicans*, from whom the modern term 'don' derives. Until the 15th century, Oxford was the more important of the two, but Wycliffe's criticism of the Church made it suspect as a centre of heresy, so that Cambridge then increased the number both of its students and of the endowments from patrons, the most important of whom was King Henry VI* (1422–61).

In the 14th century, conditions of study in the universities were bad. The students were poor, books were few, and there was constant hostility, sometimes exploding into murderous outbreaks, between students and townsmen. It was in consequence of one of these outbreaks that students, fleeing from the disorder of Oxford, established the university of Cambridge. The college system arose both as an attempt to discipline the students, and as a means of protecting them against the townsmen, but it was not until the 15th century that it extended sufficiently to be effective. Two of the greatest of the medieval colleges – New College in Oxford and King's College in Cambridge – were founded in conjunction with the great schools, Winchester and Eton respectively.

The Inns of Court* in London were begun as colleges of law in the reign of Edward I* (1272–1307). Thereafter they were attended not merely by prospective lawyers, but by numbers of gentry who sought to acquire legal knowledge in order to defend their property in the disputes over land so common in the Middle Ages. The Inns of Court were the first educational institutions to be used principally by laymen.

2.1.2.2 *The expansion of education: 1500–1800*

The Renaissance* was, among other things, the discovery by the upper classes that learning was a necessary means to personal fulfilment.

This 'discovery of learning' was made partly through the activity of the Humanist* scholars, beginning in Italy in the 14th century, and extending gradually northwards to the rest of Europe. The humanist use of disinterested scholarship awakened men to the importance and potentialities of acquiring knowledge for its own sake. The medieval aristocrat had long formed an image of nobility which far excelled the primitive one of the bloodthirsty warrior; he now began to see that the cultivation of his mind was central to his acquirement of courtly accomplishments and to the aristocratic ideal of the perfected man.

Another cause of the changed attitude to education was the invention of printing, introduced into England late in the 15th century by William Caxton.* The great obstacle to learning had so far been the lack of material; books had to be copied by hand, and most learning was conducted by discussion between teacher and student. Printing however made books plentiful, and if they were not cheap, at least they were far more accessible than they had been, to both rich and poor.

The humanist passion for education began in the universities and thence extended gradually to the rest of society, through the scholarship and writings of such men as Grocyn, Linacre, Colet, More*, and above all, the Dutch humanist Erasmus*, who resided at Cambridge from 1511 to 1514. One of the chief objects of the scholars was to clarify and enlarge Latin culture, out of which the whole civilization of western Europe had grown, but they also taught the universities to extend their studies from Latin to Greek and Hebrew texts, especially those that had constituted the original texts of the Bible*, from which the medieval Latin version, the Vulgate*, had been translated. The critical spirit of the Renaissance easily led to the reforming spirit of Protestantism, and Cambridge soon became and remained a centre of Reformation* ideas. As in literature and philosophy, so, too, in religious thought, this enlargement of understanding and activity of mind extended from the universities throughout society. The translations of the Bible into English, encouraged by Henry VIII (1509–47), and the Book of Common

Prayer*, compiled by Archbishop Cranmer* under Edward VI* (1547–53), brought English laymen close to the spiritual texts of Christianity, whereas hitherto the Bible and the liturgies had been mysteries in the control of the priests.

The Reformation, however, was not altogether helpful to the spread of education. Henry VIII dissolved the monasteries and friaries in 1536 and 1539, and since these made important contributions to the universities, Oxford and Cambridge suffered at least financially. A minor ill effect of Henry's action – minor because the numbers affected were small – was the closure of the nunnery schools, the only institutions for the education of girls. Much worse was the closing down of many grammar schools under Edward VI. Many of these, established by town guilds and by chantries, had religious affiliations, and Edward VI's Protestant politicians gladly made this the excuse for seizing the funds with which they had been endowed. Some, indeed, were refounded with the title 'King Edward VI Grammar School', with the result that for three centuries this boy king enjoyed the reputation of being a great patron of education, but in fact far more schools were lost than refounded.

These setbacks were, however, temporary. Gradually, from 1560, new schools were opened, including some (for instance, Rugby) which later became famous as public schools*. The universities also recovered from their difficulties, and it is in the reign of Elizabeth I (1558–1603) that we first find them attended by large numbers of the great men of the age, including the poets Raleigh*, Spenser*, Sidney* and Marlowe*, and the philosopher statesman, Francis Bacon*. The college system was now strongly established; it imposed effective discipline and established the relationship between tutor and student as the principal method of instruction which it is to the present day. Young men of the upper classes began to be sent to the universities as a regular practice to complete their education, unless they completed it in the London Inns of Court.

It was not until the 17th century that the great Public Schools – especially Winchester and Eton – became predominantly aristocratic. The young nobleman was more often educated, until he went to the university, by tutors in his home. Gentlemen, however, commonly went to grammar schools. At Repton, later a Public School, the first 20 names on the list of pupils in 1564 include the sons of 5 gentlemen, 13 small farmers, and 4 tradesmen. There were often entrance fees into the grammar schools, graduated according to the rank of the pupil, but some of the town schools, such as the one probably attended by Shakespeare in Stratford on Avon, were free to the sons of burgesses, *ie* established citizens.

Boys received a predominantly classical* education – chiefly in Latin literature – as they were to continue to do until late in the 19th century, though at the universities they might in addition acquire some knowledge of mathematics and the sciences and Aristotelian philosophy. The universities still followed the medieval pattern of the trivium and the quadrivium (*2.1.2.1), though thinking was much freer and more varied, and no longer subjected to theology. Teaching continued to ignore what were known as the 'mechanical arts'. It was, however, beginning to be a practical age, and in 1597 Sir Thomas Gresham founded Gresham College in London, for lectures which included physic (*ie* medicine), law, and navigation, as well as the more 'liberal' subjects. Gresham College lasted until 1768, by which time other institutions of a similar kind existed. The Inns of Court were attended especially by young men who, like the poet John Donne*, were ambitious but not wealthy, for a legal training was the most useful practical one for a public career in politics and administration as well as the law itself.

Until the later 19th century, upper-class education was commonly pursued for the general cultivation of the mind and manners; it included knowledge of the ancient cultures and the arts; increasingly, it required travel. The lower a boy (or a girl) stood in the social scale, the more practical and vocational his training had to be. It was not, however, until the reign of Queen Anne (1702–14) that much was done, apart from the increasingly expensive apprenticeship system, for the really poor. In that reign, the Church of England began the establishment of large numbers of Charity Schools* which, by the end of the reign, were giving free or nearly free elementary education to about 25,000 children throughout England. The education included religious instruction. At the end of the 18th century, children in industrial areas were employed so extensively in factories* that even charity schools were not available to them. For such children, after 1780, there were the Sunday Schools, which again were partly religious and partly concerned to inculcate the beginnings of literacy and numbers.

The Dissenting Academies were started by the large minority of the English Puritans*, who came to be called Dissenters* or Nonconformists in the 18th century, because they 'dissented from', or refused to conform with, the Thirty-nine Articles* of Anglican belief, and were thus excluded both from the universities and from most of the grammar and public schools. The Academies were often of high quality, since it was natural to the earnestness of the Dissenting mind to take education with deep seriousness. Since the Dissenters were particularly strong among the commercial classes, the tendency of their education was more scientific and technical than that of the public schools and the universities, and capable of throwing up a great scientist, such as the chemist Joseph Priestley*, who attended the Daventry Academy.

The distinction of the Dissenting Academies was the more noticeable because the universities were in a state of decadence. The historian Gibbon* describes in his autobiography the complete indifference of the Oxford authorities to whether he was present or absent as a student, although they awoke into indignation and expelled him when he underwent his temporary conversion to Catholicism. Both universities developed fine schools of mathematics in the 17th century, and Cambridge produced the most distinguished scientist of the age in Isaac Newton* (1642–1727), but the intellectual complacency which was characteristic of the weaker side of 18th-century civilization reduced them to apathy as teaching centres. The young men of fashion who attended them often learned more from the Grand Tour of Europe which they made after, or sometimes instead of, their university careers, in the company of a tutor. As for the Public Schools, the novelist Henry Fielding causes Parson Adams in *Joseph Andrews** (1742) to inveigh against them thus:

> *Public schools are the nurseries of all vice and immorality. All the wicked fellows, whom I remember at the university, were bred at them. . . . Joseph, you may thank the Lord you were not bred at a public school: you would never have preserved your virtue as you have . . . What is all the learning of the world, compared to* [*a man's*] *immortal soul? What shall a man take in exchange for his soul? But the masters of great schools trouble themselves about no such thing.*

Fielding was educated at Eton*. However, a great change was to come over the public schools in the 19th century.

2.1.2.3 *The growth of national education: 1800–present day*

In the 19th century, partly owing to the breakdown of sectarian restrictions in education, much of which was under Dissenting control, partly owing to the establishment of the non-denominational universities, the Dissenting Academies declined. However, the Industrial Revolution brought into being a new class of skilled worker: the 'mechanic' of the iron, steel and engineering industries. Such men needed brains for their skills, and their natural intelligence caused them to seek further education to advance their knowledge. This was provided by the growth of the voluntarily established Mechanics' Institutes. They began in Scotland, where education in general, since the Reformation, was more widely extended and popularly sought than in England. It was the Scottish lawyer, statesman, and man of letters, Henry Brougham*, who brought the movement to England. By 1824, the London Institute had 1,500 artisans subscribing one guinea a year for their instruction, which was conducted in the evenings. It was the beginning of the movement of education in technology which has led to the enormous expansion of technical colleges under the control of local government authorities in the 20th century, especially since 1945.

In the 19th century, however, the state was much more timid in undertaking national systems of education of any sort, and Britain was well behind the most advanced European countries, especially Prussia, in this respect. The principal reason for this slow development was the religious divisions of public opinion. The medieval assumption that education must fundamentally be the concern of the Church has faded very slowly in England. Even today, 'Religious Instruction', taught non-denominationally, is the only compulsory subject in state schools. The schools for the children of the mass of the people in the first part of the 19th century were controlled by rival Anglican and Dissenting movements: the National Society for the Education of the Poor, and the British and Foreign School Society respectively. Since the Church of England was the established Church of the state, it claimed that it should have a monopoly of religious instruction in any state system, a claim that was strongly resisted by the Dissenters. In 1833, the government for the first time acknowledged some responsibility independent of the Churches by granting a subsidy of £20,000 for school buildings, whichever society chose to build them. Since Britain was by then the richest country in the world, the sum was contemptibly small. Till 1870, the important advances towards nationwide education remained in private hands.

The most important of these advances, though it affected only a minority, was in the Public School system, which had originated in the medieval system of grammar schools. Many of these had been closed in the middle of the 16th century, but others had been established in the later 16th and the 17th centuries; in the 18th century they had again been allowed to decline. A few of them, however, had from early times achieved an importance above the rest; they had richer endowments, and drew their pupils from the nation at large and not merely from their immediate localities. These included Winchester (founded 1382), Eton (1440), Westminster (1560), Rugby* (1567), and Harrow (1571). Their discipline was bad. By the early 19th century, the pupils were predominantly upper class. They produced some great teachers and headmasters, but their educational standards varied extensively. However, in the 19th century, the character of these schools greatly changed, largely owing to the influence of one man – Thomas Arnold, headmaster of Rugby from 1828 to 1842. Arnold believed that his education should provide a boy with a training of the whole character, and not merely the mind. The guiding principle of the public schools became that of the Roman poet Juvenal, writing at a time when the Roman Empire had a corresponding greatness to the greatness of Britain after Arnold: 'mens sana in corpore sano' – 'a healthy mind in a healthy body'. A consequence of this maxim, though Arnold himself never emphasized it, was that athletics became an essential element in Public School education. Hitherto, sport had been discouraged rather than otherwise by educational institutions, as tending to disorderly conduct, but Public Schools gave it such importance that in many of them it came to exceed the prestige of scholarship. Arnold's Rugby not only introduced new standards into the Public Schools, but it had two further important results. One was that it gave real significance to boarding school education; the boys lived at the school for three-quarters of the year, not, as before, merely because conditions of travel were difficult, but because the school could thereby educate the boy during his leisure as well as in the classroom, a consideration of importance when it was a question of educating his whole character, and when sport was an essential part of this character-training. The second result was that many new Public Schools were founded, so that until 1950 a Public School education became the normal one, not only for upper-class boys but for the sons of professional men and the more prosperous business men as well. To some extent, the system was also extended to girls, but coeducational Public Schools, even today, are the exception rather than the rule.

There were special social and political reasons for this adoption of Public School education by the middle classes. One was the continuing prestige of the

English aristocracy. The middle-class business man, especially if he had raised himself from a lower rank in society, wanted his son to be a 'gentleman', and by this time he could afford the high Public School fees. We see the same ambition, without the means of achieving it so expeditiously, as far back as Chaucer's Franklin in *The Canterbury Tales**. But there was a more important reason. Britain, by 1850, was the centre of the largest overseas empire that the world had ever seen. This great empire required an unprecedented number of administrators, who had to be men of high moral quality and courage, as well as of good ability. The aristocracy could not provide them all from itself, and would have aroused social resentment had it tried; they came, therefore, from preponderantly middle-class backgrounds, and it was the Public Schools which gave them the education considered necessary to qualify them for the function.

In some respects, however, the expansion of the Public Schools had unfortunate influences on the development of English society and education. By giving the governing classes the recruits they needed, the Public Schools tended to prolong the complacent indifference of the state to its educational responsibilities. Secondly, since the Public School tradition was almost entirely an Anglican one, the Public Schools also prolonged the opposition between the Dissenters and the Anglicans over education. Thirdly, the Public Schools made more conspicuous the social gulf between the richer and poorer classes.

Universal elementary education was introduced in 1870 by the provision of State schools wherever the Church schools were inadequate. In 1902, special Local Education Authorities were created with responsibility for both these types of school, and for secondary education as well. It was, however, not until the Education Act of 1944 that the state system was improved sufficiently for the more prosperous middle classes to consent to use it instead of the private system. Even today, the prestige of the Public Schools is such that most of them continue to flourish (though their fees are now very high) side by side with the state schools.

Yet even the Act of 1944 tended to perpetuate the cleavage between the classes. Education became compulsory between the ages of 5 and 14 (15 in 1947, and soon to be raised to 16), but at the age of 11, boys and girls were (and often still are) subjected to the '11+ (eleven-plus) examination', dividing them into those who were sent to the Modern Schools (75% of the secondary-school population) and the minority who were sent to the new state Grammar Schools. The Modern School child was expected to leave school at 15, but the Grammar School child, though allowed to leave at the same age, was expected to continue to the age of 18, after which he or she could be at least partially supported by the local authority through the university, or some other institution of further education. The system was clearly intended to provide an élite comparable to that of the Public Schools, but an élite based on real merit, and not on wealth. However, it has often been criticized on the grounds that it favours children who come from materially comfortable, well-educated backgrounds, since these advantages tend to accelerate the mental development of a child. Hence, under the 1964–70 Labour Government, the 11+ selection system was extensively replaced by various forms of the 'Comprehensive School', which does not require selection when children enter the school at 11, though it may divide them according to levels of ability ('streaming') after entry.

The present (1971) school system in Britain is thus complicated though educationally rich. There is a highly developed independent sector, consisting of the Public Schools and the Preparatory Schools which prepare boys to go to them; in the state sector, the Grammar Schools and Modern Schools established by the 1944 Act are still competing against the newer Comprehensive Schools which have replaced them in many areas. The complexity is increased by the large independence allowed to each headmaster to develop his own ideas, and by the experiments which are tried by various local authorities. Education burns with controversy, but the lines of dispute are different from those of the last century.

The old religious differences of opinion have subsided, chiefly because of the spread of religious indifference, although Roman Catholics cling with determination to their own schools, and still receive state financial aid. The only serious religious disagreement is on the subject of whether religious instruction should continue to be a compulsory subject – the only one. Social differences, on the other hand, are hotly discussed, and allied to the social issues is the disagreement about the relative merits of technical and liberal education. In the 19th century most Public Schools followed the tradition of classical education in line with the tradition which predominated in the old universities of Oxford and Cambridge.

To some extent, this classical tradition was connected with Anglicanism; until 1871, Oxford and Cambridge were largely Anglican, and in the 18th century the Dissenters preferred a more scientific bias in their academies. It was thus to be expected that London University, founded in 1836 by Dissenters and non-believers, should favour 'modern' rather than 'ancient' studies, and that it should be strongly impressed by the fashionable philosophy of Utilitarianism*. Since London, numerous new universities have been founded, many of them since 1945. Nonetheless, up to the present, Oxford and Cambridge have preserved their preeminence. They broadened their syllabuses after 1870, and their religious exclusiveness was abolished by the state, so that entry to them is now free to all with the needed academic qualifications. Yet, like the Public Schools, with the oldest of which they have always had close affiliations, Oxford and Cambridge tend to be identified, even today, with the richer side of the English social division.

The serious problem which now faces British universities is whether they will be able to maintain that independence of the state for which they have hitherto been outstanding. Only one (in Northern Ireland) is a state foundation, but all are now dependent on state subsidies. The state is inclined to favour scientific education on utilitarian grounds.

2.1.3 *Women*

2.1.3.1 *The Middle Ages and the Renaissance – subjection and idealization: 1350–1600*

The social history of women is largely the story of the varying forms of their dependence on men until 1800, and of their gradual achievement of independence thereafter. On the surface it is easily told, but it has deeper implications for human relations which are of great importance in imaginative literature.

In theory, women in the Middle Ages were subjected to men in every class, as was natural in a relatively insecure society. They could own property and inherit noble titles, but their property came into the power of their husbands on marriage, and they could not dispose of it after their deaths against their husbands' wishes. Noblewomen who inherited titles were not summoned to Parliament* as noblemen were, nor were women ever elected as members of the House of Commons*. They were seldom or never allowed to enter professions such as medicine or the law, although country women were expected to understand medicinal herbs and other forms of healing. In marriage, a woman was the servant of her husband, who had the right to chastise her, just as he had the right to chastise his children; a wife who resisted her husband's will could be punished by the law, and a 'nagging wife' was punished by popular opinion. Girls, at least in the richer classes, did not usually have the power to choose their own husbands; these were selected for them by their parents on grounds of social advantage. Unfaithfulness in marriage on the part of the wife was far more seriously regarded than unfaithfulness on the part of the husband.

This subordination of women was supported by the philosophy of the Church; Chaucer's Wife of Bath* remarks that it is useless to expect a 'clerk' to speak well of women. The story of *Genesis*, according to which God fashioned the first woman out of a rib taken from the first man, seemed to affirm woman's physical inferiority to man, and her moral inferiority was affirmed by the story of the Fall, since it was Eve who surrendered to the Serpent's temptation, and Adam's sin was merely that he preferred her society to obedience to God. The medieval Church was, besides, largely a male institution; clergy in full orders, from the Pope down to a parish priest, were celibate, and it was held (with the authority of St Paul) that virginity in both sexes was superior to marriage. Women could indeed have religious vocations, but they were limited to convents, corresponding to monasteries. Some convents were large and wealthy institutions, and their prioresses and abbesses were people of importance, like women who held peerages in their own right. Nuns were, however, much fewer than monks, and they tended to be more socially exclusive; a convent was a useful place of disposal for unmarriageable daughters, and this was a problem which affected the upper classes much more than the propertiless ones.

However, the facts of female status tended to be rather better than the theory. No amount of theoretical subordination could prevent some wives from dominating their husbands, as the Wife of Bath demonstrates; nor could it prevent strong-willed and remarkable women, like Henry II's queen, Eleanor of Aquitaine, or the peasant girl, Joan of Arc*, from playing active parts in politics. The example of the Wife of Bath also illustrates the way in which widowhood could advance a woman in the working life of the community. Five times a widow, she has acquired through her husbands a cloth-making* business of renown –

Of clooth-making she hadde swich an haunt
She passed hem of Ypres and of Gaunt –

in other words, she excelled the Flemish clothiers, who were the greatest in Europe. Probably no English clothiers of either sex in fact excelled the Flemish ones in the 14th century, but there is evidence in guild records that women took part in trade, probably as widows of guild members, and their numbers increased in the 15th century. As regards marriage, the 15th-century Paston* letters, which record the life of a family of landed gentry in eastern England, provide evidence that girls sometimes obtained the husbands of their preference in spite of the prevailing materialistic evaluation of the marriage tie. Margery Brews married into the Paston family despite the inadequacy of her dowry: 'If ye love me' – she writes to John Paston in 1477 – 'as I trust verily that ye do, ye will not leave me therefore.' Another Margery, one of the Pastons, secretly engaged herself to the family bailiff and endured the violent family opposition until at last they allowed her to marry him. General acknowledgement that a girl should marry the man of her preference and not that of her family spread very gradually but it came sooner in England than in more southern European countries.

Moreover, the Middle Ages nourished some ideas about woman that were in opposition to the repressive ones of the Church and of much social theory. In pre-Christian peasant society the female was an aspect of divinity since it was identified with fruitfulness, and this passed over into Christian society in assumptions that women possess faculties of insight and knowledge denied to men; the 'wise woman' of the village had mysterious powers of healing. The belief probably did her little good, for she might easily be regarded as a witch who owed her powers to Satan; witches* were far more common than their male equivalent in medieval and Renaissance demonology. This seems to show the beliefs of the Church inverted: that Eve should have yielded to the Serpent and Adam to her is evidence both of woman's power over man and of her contact with powers to which he had less access. This element of fear and reverence for special powers in the female may have had some connection with the growth of the medieval veneration of the Virgin Mary in the Church; it is not much in evidence in early Christianity. It is difficult to know whether the reverence has any connection with the idealization of women in aristocratic society in the courtly literature* of romantic love. This literature is not only mysterious in its origins, but complicated as a phenomenon. On the one hand. it often manifested itself in tales of adulterous passion, like that of Lancelot and Guinevere in Malory's *Morte d'Arthur**, and it is therefore sometimes said to have arisen as a kind of compensation for the commercial valuation put by society upon marriage. On the other hand, it is also said to be connected with the special regard for the Virgin Mary which seems to have developed concurrently with it. Socially, at all events, it flourished in the royal and noble courts of western Europe and was connected with the reverence due to queens and noblewomen, to whom it was due not only on account of their status but by virtue of the luxury and refinement which women encouraged in such courts. Courtly manners, and the values of 'romantic love' that went with them, penetrated the middle classes later in the Middle Ages; his tales show that in Chaucer's day they were still the prerogative of aristocratic society.

The Canterbury Tales help us to sum up the complexity of the medieval image of women. In the Prologue* we find two full-length portraits of women pilgrims – the Prioress and the Wife of Bath – and a number of other women who are the heroines of the tales themselves. The Prioress is aristocratic, not devout or learned, but refined, sensitive, and courteous. To her, Alisoun, the Wife of Bath, is a strong contrast: she is arrogant, sensual, ostentatious, vulgar and practical. These two, with the support of other evidence, we may take to be extreme examples of actual types. The tales indicate rather more the idealized and the comically extravagant notions of woman in the medieval imagination. They include Emilia in *The Knight's Tale**. She has no distinct personality, but to the prisoners of the tower she is an emanation of the May season which has called her out, and embodies the inaccessible qualities of birth, freedom and joy like a Spring Goddess:

And in the gardin, at the sonne up-riste,
She walketh up and doun, and as hir liste
She gadereth floures, party whyte and rede,
To make a sotil gerland for hir hede,
And as an aungel hevenly she song.
The grete tour, that was so thikke and strong,
Which of the castel was the chief dongeoun,
(Ther-as the Knightes weren in prisoun,
Of which I tolde yow, and tellen shal)
Was evene joynant to the gardin wal,
Ther as Emelye hadde her pleyinge.

At the other extreme there is the adulterous wife of the carpenter in *The Miller's Tale**, and the young wife of the old man in *The Merchant's Tale**, both of whom express sensual joyousness in defiance of conventional principle, which had no place for it. Then there are the moral idealizations: the patient wife, Griselda, in *The Clerk's Tale*, who endures injustice and maltreatment beyond natural capacity, and the loyal wife, Dorigen, in *The Franklin's Tale**. The Man of Law and the Second Nun tell tales of holy women.

If we attempt to find a balance between theory and practice, ideal and actuality, myth and fact, we need to remember, first, that the married woman commonly had a fulfilled life of activity in the Middle Ages. The life of the peasant's wife was certainly hard: she shared her husband's labours in the fields, besides bearing children, many of whom died in infancy. The wife of the merchant was often his business partner, and the wife of the landed gentleman (as the Paston Letters show) was fully occupied in managing her large, mainly self-supporting household, over which she had full control. Secondly, we need to remember the influence on the working lives of many women of the great clothing industry. The English word still in use for an unmarried woman is 'spinster', and the word 'wife' may be related to 'weave'. Women spun and wove for their own purposes, but much cloth manufacture was also undertaken by women in their homes, and this continued until the Industrial Revolution* at the end of the 18th century. Finally we should remember the greatness of the religious vocation at its best in an age when religion, despite its frequent debasement, drew on many of the richest potentialities of human beings. Nuns of exceptional devoutness, like Juliana* of Norwich (14th–15th century), could become spiritual leaders of their time.

The 16th century did not bring marked changes in the status of women, but when Henry VIII abolished the nunneries in 1536–9 he closed up not merely a means of fulfilling a spiritual vocation, but a chief refuge for unmarried women, and the principal (though never extensive) institutions for educating girls. On the other hand, more settled society permitted women to reign in the highest places of power: England had two ruling queens in the 16th century and Scotland had one queen and a woman regent, whereas 12th-century England had broken into civil war (the 'reign' of Stephen, 1135–54) rather than endure a woman as sovereign. But women were still excluded from any lesser places of political importance. Their education varied greatly according to the households in which they were brought up, but the Tudor women – Jane Grey (the 'ten days' queen'), Mary I* and Elizabeth I* – were all very highly educated. Below the aristocratic level, women's education did not advance, nor did their status. Sir Thomas More might advocate equal education for the sexes in *Utopia** (1516), but the women in his imaginary country are still subject to men. On the other hand the immense popularity and prestige of Elizabeth I (1558–1603) combined with Platonic* idealism to reinforce the idealization of woman. Here we begin to see the beginnings of a dangerous dichotomy: the idealized women of Spenser's *Faerie Queene** are ideals merely, and not women; whereas Chaucer had juxtaposed his ideals with actuality. Many poets were like Spenser, but there were two great exceptions: Shakespeare* and Donne*. Shakespeare's heroines – especially in the last four plays – are often idealized, but the idealization is always related to flesh and blood. The poignancy of Juliet, an early heroine, is precisely that she is real, not the bloodless abstraction with whom Romeo supposes himself to be in love at the beginning of the play. The point of Sonnet 130 seems to be a satirical comment on the Platonically idealized women of most other sonneteers:

I love to hear her speak, yet well I know
That music hath a far more pleasing sound:
I grant I never saw a goddess go;
My Mistress when she walks treads on the ground.

This is no disparagement of the Mistress (the word 'reeks' elsewhere in the sonnet does not have the modern pejorative meaning) but on the contrary an extolling of a real relationship. Similarly, Donne's love poems always convey the sense of a real and present woman, not the distant goddess of such a sonneteer as Spenser or Daniel*, whose idealizations would not be incompatible with contempt for real women for falling so far short. This kind of idealization was to prove a restraint upon the freedom of women when it was joined to the unreal morality imposed on women by some kinds of Puritanism* in the 17th century.

2.1.3.2 *Women achieve social prominence: 1600–1800*
As one reads on into 17th- and 18th-century English literature, one becomes increasingly aware of women as personalities in cultured society, though not yet in politics. One might begin with the early patronesses of literature: Mary, Countess of Pembroke* (1561–1621), Sidney's sister and patroness of Daniel and Ben Jonson, and her contemporary, Lucy, Countess of Bedford, the patroness of Donne. Women became memorable letter-writers in these centuries when letter-writing* had its best period: Dorothy Osborne* (1627–95), wife of Sir William Temple, Lady Mary Wortley Montagu* (1689–1762), Mrs Delany* (1700–88), and Fanny Burney* (1752–1840). Letter-writing was their chief means of expression, but they began to take part in other forms of literature: Lucy Hutchinson (b 1620) wrote a notable biography of her husband, a Puritan officer; Aphra Behn (1640–89) was a popular dramatist and writer of romances; Anne, Countess of Winchelsea (1666–1720), and Margaret, Duchess of Newcastle (1625?–73) were minor poets of some distinction; Fanny Burney wrote enduring novels. In the middle of the 18th century, there was a fashionable circle of women intellectuals known as the Bluestockings* in London, led by Mrs Montagu; the distinguished philanthropical writer, Hannah More* (1745–1833), was associated with it. At the end of the century, Mary Wollstonecraft (1759–97), wife of the philosopher Godwin* and mother of the girl who was to marry Shelley*, made her well-known appeal for women's education – *A Vindication of the Rights of Woman* (1792). Finally, 18th-century men of letters often had a circle of close women friends with whom they corresponded; this was particularly true of some of the most eminent – Swift*, Pope*, Richardson*, and Samuel Johnson*.

Society was far more settled and orderly, and disposed to cultivate those interests and occupations which 'the weaker sex' could share. More important still, the section of society in which women had most opportunity to achieve commanding positions – the middle class – was becoming steadily more prominent. The wife of the aristocrat had to support her husband's rank; the farmer's wife had her own province in the farm economy, and it left her little leisure; but the merchant's wife in the towns not only shared directly in her husband's interests, but had leisure in which to 'improve' herself, and to influence her husband. The essays in Addison's and Steele's *Tatler** and *Spectator** in the reign of Queen Anne (1702–14) are addressed to middle-class readers, and their content often makes it clear that they have women readers in mind as well as male ones. The same is true, in the reign of George II (1727–60), of Samuel Richardson's novels. Admittedly, the writings of Addison, Pope and Swift early in the century are frequently satirical about women's minds as exhibited in their reading, amusements and behaviour, but the amount of attention they give to the subject shows that it interests them, and that they desire to improve the situation. Later in the century, the satirical note sounds less often.

The growth of the middle classes in the 17th century was naturally accompanied by the spread of their characteristic belief – Puritan Protestantism in all its forms, and this, too, probably helped women to achieve more prominence and to find some degree of independence. It is true that many of the Puritan sects, as much as the medieval Church, emphasized the subordination of women to men. On the other hand, Puritanism replaced the authority of the Church by that of the private conscience, and the collective conscience of fellow believers. In doing so, it made the family into the nucleus of the community of the faithful; this raised the status of the husband and father as the head of the household, but it also raised the status of the wife and mother, as her husband's most intimate associate and counsellor. One of the smaller but most influential Puritan sects, the Society of Friends (more commonly known as Quakers*) believed in complete sexual equality in spiritual matters: women were as fully entitled to preach the Word of God as men were, and equality in a matter of such deep importance necessarily affected all human relations. In the 18th century, the Quakers took to banking at a time when it first assumed a central role in economic life, and this necessarily extended Quaker influence to those who did not share their religious beliefs.

Women's education was probably at its best in a few enlightened households, but boarding schools for girls (like Miss Pinkerton's Academy in Thackeray's *Vanity Fair**) were being opened in increasing numbers. Mary Wollstonecraft, the great advocate of women's education, was herself educated in one and later opened one. Intelligent women began to find teaching their natural career, but it was easier to become a governess than a schoolteacher, and the pay of governesses was low. Another profession which was opening to women was the theatre. The profession of actress became possible for women after 1660; before that women's parts were acted by boys. The 18th century was the first in which acting achieved respected status as a profession, and this was thanks not only to David Garrick* but to the great tragic actress, Sarah Siddons* (1755–1831). However, it was not until the second half of the 19th century that respectable families were able with equanimity to see their daughters going on to the stage.

However, the changing position of women in society was not altogether to their advantage, and this was particularly true of attitudes to the sexual relationship, especially those of Puritanism. The medieval Church had emphasized the supreme virtue of chastity, but it accepted the reality of the sensual passions in both sexes, and the Wife of Bath leaves one in no doubt about her own. Marriage for the medieval Church, as for St Paul, was regarded as the institution into which carnality could be channelled and contained. The Puritan elevation of marriage and the family into something more sacred was incompatible with a frank acknowledgement of sensuality; in particular, the idea that it might exist in a mother, who had the morals of her children in her care, was abhorrent. The belief came into existence that a good woman does not have sexual desire. Since Puritanism was mainly a middle-class set of codes, there tended to be a cleavage between the middle and upper classes in this matter. It is evident in the difference between the upper class Fielding*, whose women are 'natural', and the idealized women in Richardson's* novels. In the 19th century, the predominance of the middle classes caused the Puritan, Richardsonian view to prevail. Thus the very century in which women were winning their social and political freedom was also the one in which they were restricted to an unnatural sexual code; men and women became divided on a deep, intimate level while they were being drawn together on the surface (public) levels of relationship.

2.1.3.3 *Women achieve independence: 1800–present day*

The period from 1800 to 1918 was the heroic age for British women. It was after 1870 that they fought their main battles for social, including marital, freedom; for the right to enter the professions of their choice; for educational equality and for political rights. The earlier years of the 19th century, however, set the stage for the conflicts which were later to come into the open, and which, in some directions, are still continuing.

By 1800, many individual women were accustomed to being treated as equals by intelligent men, but women collectively remained in subjection. In particular, there was no psychological correspondence between the facts of the feminine nature and the image of women as men required them to be. Women, at least in 'polite society', had to represent refinement of feeling, and, even while they were acknowledged to be physically desirable to men, a moral remoteness from the physical passions. It was generally acknowledged that men, in practice, were 'free' in their sexual conduct, although such freedom was not publicly approved; for a woman to practise such freedom was unacceptable. Men, particularly if they had a strong Puritan background to their ideas, were inclined to develop an attitude of very doubtful sincerity towards women. They made a distinction between 'good' women and 'fallen' women, attributing sexual appetites to the latter but not to the former, and at the same time they did not perhaps entirely believe in the distinction, although for their own needs they had to make it. No doubt it was the uneasiness of mind that resulted from such equivocation which caused sex to become a forbidden subject of discussion in polite society in the middle years of the century, while the London streets thronged with prostitutes. In earlier days, when the attitude was only beginning to prevail, Richardson seems to have dramatized his own unacknowledged doubts in his novel, *Clarissa Harlowe** (1748). Lovelace, the 'rake' who is the villain of the story, does not believe in the capacity in women for 'pure', disinterested love which is attributed to them, and in his desperate search for a 'pure' woman he acts on the assumption that women are really motivated by a combination of lust and social aspiration. He tries to prove that Clarissa is no exception to this rule, and he carries his experiment so far that he destroys both her and himself.

But Richardson's *Clarissa Harlowe* opens with a different conflict: Clarissa – like Margery Paston in the 15th century – has to resist the brutal pressures of all her family to drive her into an 'arranged' marriage with a man she does not love. An intelligent woman's happiness almost always depended on her finding a husband who suited her. Love matches were by now much more generally accepted than in the Middle Ages; the 18th century was perhaps a transitional period in this respect. But parental pressures often existed, and even if they did not, the girl was at a great disadvantage in the search. Strictly, she was not supposed to make a search at all, but from the age of about 17 (when she 'came out') she was 'on the market' at balls and other social occasions. She could not, of course, propose marriage herself, but she could use her charms to attract suitable men; her problem, of course, was partly that, as in Fanny Burney's *Evelina** (1778), they were apt to attract unsuitable men even more strongly. The worse problem, for a girl of ordinary integrity, was that the subterfuge of consciously 'attracting' men was an intolerable one, and that unless the subterfuge was a very cunning one it was apt to frighten discriminating men away. The novels of Jane Austen* (1775–1817) are often mistaken for peaceful comedies of sheltered lives; in fact they are sharp dramatizations of the very unpromising predicament in which intelligent girls usually found themselves. *Pride and Prejudice** (1813) is an example. Elizabeth Bennet refuses the offer of marriage from the rich young clergyman, Mr Collins, to the anger of her mother but to the satisfaction of her father, who does not want her to marry a fool. But, to Elizabeth's dismay, her friend Charlotte Lucas accepts him, for though he is much her inferior in intelligence and character, Charlotte sees no better prospect for herself, in the narrow country society in which they live, if she is to avoid the miseries of becoming an 'old maid'. Elizabeth herself nearly loses the man whom she really needs as a husband, in her resentment at his contempt for her family. It is typical of Jane Austen's novels that it is just Elizabeth's intelligence and distinction that nearly prevent her marrying at all; in each of them, the heroine and the hero come together only after surviving social and personal obstacles which are much more likely to prevent their union than the extravagant events of Gothic novels*. This indeed is Jane Austen's constant theme: that it is actual human nature as it is conditioned by actual society, not romantic fantasy, that can be shown to make a fine marriage a rare triumph.

Thirty years after Jane Austen's death, the novels of the Brontë sisters expressed the woman's predicament still more radically. Charlotte Brontë's best novels, *Jane Eyre** (1847) and *Villette** (1853) presented passionate love from a woman's standpoint in a way that shocked many readers, who considered that she did not show a suitable feminine reticence on the subject. It was vaguely acknowledged that women might, after all, have passions, but the public preferred them to be presented with something of the unreality of a romance; above all, the heroine should be strikingly beautiful, whereas Charlotte Brontë's heroines are moderately plain, and this made them uncomfortably real; for it brought home to the reader that *all* normal women were capable of passions, and not merely exceptional ones. Emily Brontë's *Wuthering Heights** (1847) was still more original. She contrasted different kinds of love, especially that of the normally acceptable marriage with that of instinctive passion, and thereby raised the question whether the deeper and stronger feelings of men and women could ever be acceptable to society at all. This range of deep relationship was not investigated further by an imaginative artist until the time of D. H. Lawrence* in the 20th century.

For the unmarried woman in the first half of the 19th century the possibility of finding satisfying work to take the place of marriage still hardly existed. The heroine of Jane Austen's *Emma** (1816) is fortunately placed in society, and at the age of 20 she contemplates an unmarried future complacently, but the author's irony demonstrates that it would be filled with superficial activities, skills which girls normally acquired in the course of their superficial education, and that these would be combined with damaging interference with other people's lives – damaging because there was no prospect of her achieving (outside marriage) the kind of maturity that justifies such intervention. A woman of education and middle-class standing still only had one profession open to her: that of teaching. Boarding schools (like the Belgian one in *Villette*) were still not numerous, but there were plentiful opportunities of becoming a governess in a private family. This was occasionally a happy position, but, as the experience of the Brontë sisters shows, it was more often unfortunate, even wretched. Governesses were overworked in many households, and they were seldom well paid. They were treated as a little superior to the upper servants, but as no better than servants by the servants themselves.

Even in married life, the relationships with the husband which had once given satisfaction to a wife were widely dislocated by economic changes in the 19th century. In the industrial areas, the factory system displaced the domestic system which had enabled women to work in their homes. Often the women worked in the factories, but this disrupted home life and interfered with the upbringing of young children; if, on the other hand, only the men worked in the factories, the women were left idle and dissatisfied. There were, it is true, some compensations in the factory employment of women: they began to achieve an economic independence, though at a low level, which was often denied to women of higher social rank. In the commercial middle class, business men now seldom had their offices in their homes, so that women could not, as they once did, participate in the business, and they too were left idle. In the upper class, the management of a great household which had kept 'great ladies' so busy from the 14th to the 18th centuries was now a simplified task; the industrial mass production of goods and their swift transport by rail made many household crafts redundant, and the management of servants was usually left to a competent housekeeper. It is not surprising that Beatrice Webb* should have found that late-19th-century women of the upper class occupied themselves almost entirely with seeking amusement: they had few alternatives.

Women of strong character, however, began to open up professions hitherto closed to them, or expand such as had always been open, or invent new ones. Women became writers and journalists, as the remarkable succession of women novelists in the century shows; there were at first prejudices against women writers, but these diminished. One profession that had always been open to women was nursing, but Dickens's Mrs Gamp in *Martin Chuzzlewit** (1844) shows that it was so degraded that no woman of self-respect before 1850 would have thought of entering it. This was changed by the reforming energies of Florence Nightingale (1820–1910) during and after the Crimean War of 1854–6. Doctors, on the other hand, were still exclusively men, and the struggle to enable women to take medical degrees was slow and difficult; however, in 1878 women were admitted to examinations in London University. Beatrice Webb invented for herself the profession of 'social investigator' (*ie* sociologist) and discovered that in the London trades, such as tailoring, the pay of female workers was so low that women were driven into prostitution to supplement their earnings; their status began to improve with the formation of women's trade unions in some of the worst paid (the 'sweated') industries. For educated women, teaching was itself an expanded profession after the middle of the century, and women needed university education if they were to compete with men professionally. It became steadily more widely recognized that women were entitled to the same education as men; the state Education Acts of 1870 and 1902 provided for both sexes, though as yet only at a low level.

By this time, women had found support for their claims amongst leading male writers of the day. F. D. Maurice, the Christian Socialist, was one of the pioneers of women's education, and John Stuart Mill*'s *Subjection of Women* (1869) became a gospel for emancipation. The Married Women's Property Acts of 1882 and 1892 were important legal advances, since they at last removed the husband's control over his wife's money – a matter of peculiar importance when she earned it. Yet political rights were still distant: by 1884, all men over 21 had the right to vote in parliamentary elections and to stand for election, but women were still excluded. The serious campaign for women's rights began with the election to Parliament of John Stuart Mill in 1865. Women formed political organizations, the best known of which – the Suffragettes led by Emily Pankhurst – was notorious for its use of violence in the years before 1914. World War I really decided the issue. The unprecedented mobilization of men into the fighting services made women indispensable in civilian jobs from which they had so far been excluded, and their competence in undertaking them removed the last objections to giving them political rights. Even then, the 1918 Act enfranchised only women over 30; those over 21 had to wait another 10 years.

The extraordinary reluctance of men to yield equality to women, especially in politics, must have had a deep psychological cause: it seems likely that this was connected with male reluctance to surrender the image of woman as an ideal yet dependent creature, which had been built up since the 17th century.

The challenge of women disturbed a number of profound male prejudices, some of which were more conscious than others. Men needed to feel that women were inferior, so that men could protect them and thereby satisfy their desire for self-assurance. Competition with men in the professions and politics does not, however, seem to have been of chief importance to women themselves, once the principle of their rights was recognized; women's membership of Parliament has always been lower than 10%, and they have not flooded the professions in proportion to their numbers. Their deeper, psychological need was to win equal recognition, collectively, as persons. This was countered by the fear in men that women, regarding themselves as equals, might make new demands in personal relationships to which men might find themselves unable to respond, as Skrebensky cannot respond to Ursula Brangwen's demands in D. H. Lawrence's novel, *The Rainbow** (1915). Lawrence's deep imaginative investigation into the relationship of the sexes was a great writer's response to the central human issue of his time, and partly accounts for his immense prestige. Yet though his work seemed to many readers insufferably bold and intrusive, Lawrence was not really making a break with tradition; he was carrying on the serious inspection of the hidden truths in human relationships which has been characteristic of English fiction since Richardson, and which probably has its origin in the examination of the conscience regularly practised by the Puritans.

Since 1945, the struggle for women's rights on the public level has continued: women still seldom receive equal pay for the same work as men, and there are still a few professions from which they are excluded. On the personal level, an entirely new factor is affecting relationships between the sexes: easy and cheap contraception has removed the dangers of unmarried pregnancy, which once was the perpetual threat of disgrace to those who practised 'free love'. This is sometimes said to be leading to a sexual revolution, implying that women have at last lost their most serious disadvantage as against men and are now, in the most important sense, free. Whether contraception has really granted freedom, or whether, by removing the chief danger to women of promiscuous sexual relations, it is distracting social attention from more important underlying moral and psychological problems, remains at present unknown.

2.2

Surroundings

2.2.1 *Dwellings*

Castle Hedingham, Essex (12th C). The 'keep' or central tower as it stands today. Early medieval castles consisted of single towers like this, sometimes surrounded by a curtain wall.

Stokesay Castle. In 13th C, when the land became more peaceful, many medium-sized houses ceased to be wholly fortified. The transition from the fortress to the domestic dwelling is shown here. The main building is a 13th-C great hall with an adjoining 'solar' or private room for the lord and his family.

The Great Hall of Penshurst, Kent: a 14th-C hall, showing the hearth in the centre of the room. By 15th C it became the custom to build the hearth into the wall of the room. Penshurst is the subject and title of one of Ben Jonson's most celebrated poems.

Haddon Hall: a fortified manor house. The house was restored in 20th C. The original 14th-C fortifications are already partly ornamental.

Cothay Manor, Somerset. The illustration shows the complete abandonment of fortification on many country houses in 15th C.

The 15th-C house of an important wool merchant in the main street of the village of Chipping Campden, a centre for the wool trade in the west of England.

Houses in Lavenham, a centre for the wool trade in Eastern England. They belonged to Flemish weavers who were encouraged to settle in England to stimulate cloth manufacture.

Sudeley Castle. This mansion dates partly from 15th C. The ruined tower on the right is the remains of genuine fortification, but the castellated roofline is 16th C and purely decorative. The formal garden is of the late Tudor style of design.

The Great Hall of Montacute House. The furniture and plaster relief on the end wall are of the same date as the architecture (16th C). The relief shows the 'Skimmity Ride', a traditional ordeal inflicted on one of a married couple whose life has become the subject of public scandal or mockery.

Coleshill House. Built 1650–64 entirely in the classical style of which Inigo Jones* (1573–1652) was the first great English master.

The Double Cube Room, Wilton House (1648); designed by Inigo Jones*. The portraits are by the Flemish painter, Van Dyck*, who spent much time at the Court of Charles I.

The medicinal baths at Bath. The drawing is dated 1675, but the houses were built in the early decades of the century.

The library at Kenwood House, Hampstead. Designed 1767–8 by Robert Adam.

London clubs – St James's Street, 1792.

The Quadrant from Vigo Street. The end of Regent Street, designed early in 19th C by John Nash*, and pulled down a hundred years later.

Gustave Doré's London. An example of slum houses in a big Victorian city.

Mid-Victorian suburban houses near London.

2.2.2 *Communications*

2.2.2.1 *Travel and transport*

Apart from packhorses, the main method of overland transport of goods from the Middle Ages until the 19th-C invention of railways was the stage wagon. The 'carriers' who drove the wagons were the most convenient means of transporting news and correspondence in rural districts, as well as goods.

2.2.2.1.1 *The Middle Ages: 1350–1500*

The extent of travel in any period of history depends not only on the availability of means, but on the existence of motives, and on what facilities are offered or refused by governments.

In the Middle Ages, the means of travel were bad, but pilgrimages supplied an important motive; so did trade; consequently, above the level of the very poorest class, there was more travel than one might expect when one considers the obstacles to movement. It is true that the very poor – the largest segment of the population – did not travel; the humblest of Chaucer's pilgrims, the Ploughman, is a farmer, not a paid labourer or a serf. The mass of the peasantry and many town artisans remained locked within the horizons of the small town or village, and barely emerged from them until the age of railways. They were as credulous about the outer world as many moderns are about outer space, and were natural victims to the lies told them by Chaucer's Pardoner, or by Shakespeare's ballad-seller, Autolycus, in *The Winter's Tale**. Those who could afford pilgrimages, however, often undertook at least a few short ones, for a pilgrimage was in the eyes of the Church a deed of virtue and was frequently imposed as a penance. There were professional pilgrims, called Palmers, who dedicated their lives to pilgrimage, and Crusaders*, like Chaucer's Knight, were really a military variant of the Palmer. The destinations were places of reputed holiness: Jerusalem, the Holy City; Rome, the capital of Christendom; or the shrine of some great saint, like that of St James of Compostella in northern Spain. In England, there were many places of pilgrimage, but three were outstanding: Glastonbury, the legendary starting-point of Christianity in Britain; Walsingham, which possessed a miraculous statue of the Holy Virgin; and Canterbury, the shrine of the most famous English saint, Thomas à Becket*, the 12th-century martyr. Besides pilgrimage, trade, war, and diplomacy were the most important motives. Some men were travellers in the course of business, like the Pardoner, who is a commercial traveller in sacred relics, and the pedlars or chapmen who carried their goods on their backs or on pack-horses from village to village. Chaucer, as a youth, was with Edward III's army in France; later he twice visited Italy on diplomatic missions, and went on others to France or Flanders. Although the conditions were bad, there was in some respects more freedom of movement than in modern Europe, where passports and sometimes visas are now required by almost every country with an independent government; national frontiers were not yet the barriers of prejudice that they sometimes are now. Language, too, was less of a problem for many travellers, since Latin was an international tongue for the learned, and French, until the 15th century, was spoken by the English upper class.

The conditions, however, must often have been formidable. The Romans, before their organization collapsed in Britain early in the 5th century, created a great system of paved roads; these may have survived to some extent into the Middle Ages, though they were probably sometimes pillaged for building material. Until the 18th century, hard roads were seldom constructed, apart from a few causeways which merchants sometimes arranged for over marshy places. There were not only the problems of impassability in bad weather, but also the dangers of highway robbery. A law of 1285 ordained that roads should be widened to 200 feet by the destruction of bushes and trees, so that there should be no cover for robbers lying in ambush. Travel was by foot or on horseback; heavy carriages were used by the rich, but they were very rare until the 16th century; the sick, the old, and great ladies were carried in litters supported by their servants; goods were transported in large wagons or by packhorse.

The badness of roads made water transport preferable; rivers were used whenever they were navigable. Heavy goods were transported by sea; hence the expression 'sea coal' for coal brought from Newcastle in the north of England to London.

By later standards, trade was necessarily much restricted, but many traders would risk one journey a year for the sake of gain; hence the importance of the annual fairs*. From the 14th to the 19th century, there were numerous fairs throughout England, and many survive today, although their purpose is now often entertainment rather than trade. The size of the region from which fairs drew traders varied greatly; it might consist of a few neighbouring villages, or – like the Stourbridge Fair at Cambridge – it might draw traders from the extremities of the country, and even from foreign lands.

Coal barges and 'tilt' boats (17th C). Waterways were much used for transport until roads improved in later 18th C. A 'tilt' boat was a light passenger craft.

Heavy coaches for private use began to be used in 16th C. By 18th C private carriages were varied in design, and more comfortable and elegant.

Toll gates, Hyde Park. In 18th C 'Turnpike Companies' were licensed to maintain roads as a commercial enterprise. They levied tolls on passengers to pay for road maintenance.

Lady and gentleman in a phaeton, by George Stubbs (1787). An example of one of the very light styles of carriage used for pleasure in late 18th and early 19th C.

2.2.2.1.2 *1500–1800*

The Protestant Reformation in the 16th century put an end to pilgrimage; it forbade the reverence hitherto paid to the bones of the saints, and Rome was no longer the capital of Christendom for England and Scotland. But the pilgrims were replaced by students and writers seeking enlightenment at the great sources of Renaissance culture, especially in Italy. Already in the 14th century Chaucer had learnt much from meeting French and Italian writers on his diplomatic journeys, and Wyatt* (1503?–42) was to renew this experience as a diplomatist; later Donne* (1572–1631) and Milton* (1608–74) travelled on their own account. The idea of travel as a means of education became normal among the educated classes of the 17th century, and in the 18th century it became an enthusiasm, until in 1785 40,000 Englishmen were said to be doing the 'Grand Tour'. Besides travel for education, there was the constantly increasing travel for trade. By far the most important technical advance in the 16th century was the adoption of a new structure of sail enabling ships to voyage much farther: this made possible the great voyages of discovery which, in the last 30 years of the century, enormously expanded trade.

Overland transport, however, was increasingly difficult. The increasing movement of goods about the country in huge carrier's wagons drawn by teams of six or more horses caused the bad roads to deteriorate still further. In the 16th century the care of the roads was in the charge of the country parishes under the supervision of the magistrates, but the work was neglected, since it was not the countrymen who were the chief users of the roads. In the second half of the 17th century, the 'turnpike system' was introduced, to transfer the cost of road repairs on to the road users. The turnpikes were barriers across the roads at suitable places, where travellers were compelled to pay tolls before they were allowed to proceed. The system worked with unequal success, and extended to remote regions only slowly, but in the 18th century it improved. In the second half of the 18th century roads were immensely improved by the great engineers Macadam, who invented the method of building road surfaces from broken stone, and Telford, who was also a great bridge-builder. By the end of the century, foreign observers acknowledged English roads to be the best in Europe.

The improvement naturally affected ways of travel and styles of vehicle. A system of post-horses for royal messengers already existed in the 16th century: relays of horses were established about the country to expedite their journeys. As early as 1660 stage coaches, which changed horses at fixed stages, were available; a century later the improvement of the roads made this the usual way of travelling on long journeys. The system of 'post-horses' was by then at the disposal of people who could afford to travel in privately owned or hired post-chaises; these light vehicles made it possible to accomplish in a day journeys of a hundred miles which had taken three days at the beginning of the century. By the beginning of the 19th century, various styles of vehicle existed, and John Thorpe in Jane Austen's *Northanger Abbey** (1818) boasts of the speed of his curricle in similar terms to a modern young man boasting of the 'performance' of his sports car.

For heavy transport, water was still more convenient than land, and in the 16th and 17th centuries, rivers were deepened, locks were built, and the first canals were dug. But it was again the second half of the 18th century that was the great period for the improvement of water transport. By his wealth and political influence, the Duke of Bridgewater was largely responsible for the construction of a system of canals throughout England. His enterprise was very important in advancing the Industrial Revolution*, since it not only facilitated the distribution of heavy manufactures but enabled large supplies of corn and other foodstuffs to be brought to the new population centres.

2.2.2.1.3 *1800–present day*

In 1840, England had 22,000 miles of good roads, maintained by 8,000 turnpikes; it also had a magnificent canal system for industrial use. But in 1843 it had, in addition, 2,000 miles of railway, which increased to 5,000 miles by 1848, and was to exceed 23,000 by the end of the century. The first steam-railway had been opened in 1825, a distance of 11 miles. Thus, no sooner had the 18th-century system of transport reached perfection than it was superseded by the 19th-century one. The great canal system decayed, and the road system lost most of its long-distance traffic. Railways could move passengers and goods more economically, in far greater quantities, at hitherto unimagined speeds, and perhaps not even the motor car has caused such marked changes in the economic and social life of Britain. They were the more marked, of course, because of the swiftness of the spread of railways. Steam made much slower progress at sea: in 1847, steamships represented only 116,000 tons out of a total of 3 million tons of British merchant shipping. Not until the end of the century did steamships completely supersede sailing ships on long voyages.

The Great Eastern, built in the 1850s, was ahead of its time in the ambitiousness of its scale and design. The illustration pays tribute to the immense speeding-up of communications in 19th C, with portraits of some of the scientists and industrialists who contributed to it, and depictions of Queen Victoria and the President of the United States enjoying the benefits.

The effect of railways was to bring all the regions of the country into close relation with one another, and to make extensive travel possible for all the social classes for the first time. They had, in fact, an effect on single countries comparable to that which air travel is having on the entire world in the 20th century. The formerly enclosed, regional cultures, like Hardy's Wessex*, lost their self-sufficiency, so that British civilization in the 20th century has become much more uniform than it once was. The railways were breakers of social barriers, too; they were a comparatively democratic mode of travel. Hitherto only the rich and leisured had been able to afford the money and time to travel extensively, but now the poor could manage it too; and trains mixed the social classes, despite the provision of first, second and third class coaches. Perhaps the most important effect of all was that railways greatly increased the movement of population from the countryside into the towns, although this had already begun in the 18th century. Many industrial towns in the north owed their rapid enlargement to railways, so that railways are one of the most important explanations for England becoming the first thoroughly urbanized country in the world.

Railways naturally extended the habit of foreign travel from the upper to the middle class, which visited foreign countries in the second half of the 19th century in far greater numbers than ever before.

The opening of the Liverpool and Manchester Railway, 1830.

But humbler kinds of travel also became common in the 19th century for the first time, for reasons that had nothing to do with the invention of the steam engine. Until the later 18th century, Britain was too rural for people to have much curiosity about the countryside, and travel for pleasure was chiefly limited to friendly visits and journeys to pleasure resorts such as Bath* and – when sea bathing became fashionable in the reign of George III – the seaside towns such as Brighton*. In every century from the 16th there were individuals who had the curiosity to make surveys of the entire country – Leland and Camden in the 16th century, Fynes Morrison in the 17th, Defoe* in the 18th, and Cobbett* in the early 19th – but they were interested in economic and social facts, not landscape. However, the romantic writers who were contemporary with Cobbett (Scott*, Coleridge*, Wordsworth* and Keats*) awakened a new interest in scenery as part of their new kind of attention to nature, and they walked about the countryside merely for the pleasure it gave them. Such an activity would have been incomprehensible to a medieval man, but by the middle of the Victorian period it had become an accepted one. When the pedal cycle came into popular use at the end of the century, touring the countryside for its fresh air and natural beauty extended to women as well as men.

The two greatest travel developments of the 20th century have of course been aircraft and the motor car. Since Britain is relatively small in area, aircraft have been chiefly important in foreign travel and transport, but aeroplanes have dramatically changed Britain's relationship to other countries, not only by closer communications with them, but by causing her to lose much of the defensive protection of insularity. In the war against Spain in the 16th century, the wars against France in the 18th and early 19th centuries, the war against Germany of 1914–18, England was made safe by her navies; but in World War II she depended, like every other modern country, on her air force. The change is important not only politically but psychologically; it has changed the attitude of Englishmen to their own nation, causing them to see it, for the first time, as just one among many nations, and not as a privileged exception to the depredations of history.

The first cars appeared on the roads of Britain in 1894, but it was not until after 1918 that they became widespread, and not until after 1945 that ownership of a car extended to all but those on the lowest income levels. Since then motor transport has gone far to supersede rail transport for passenger travel; not only have the roads had their revenge on the railways but road construction has not been able to keep pace with the increase of motor traffic. The mobility of the population has been intensified, and people no longer commonly die in the place in which they were born. Cars have also changed the relation of living-place to working-place, and it is now quite usual to drive every day to and from one's work over a distance which, even in the 18th century, would have been a long day's journey. Meanwhile, rural England continues to perish under the weight of urbanization which this increasingly dense traffic has produced. In trade and transport, as in some other important matters, the movement has been from the oppression of one extreme to the oppression of another: from confinement to one place in the 14th century to the confinement of belonging nowhere in particular in the 20th.

2.2.2.2 *News and opinion*

The Canadian scholar, Professor H. M. McLuhan, in *The Gutenberg Galaxy* and other books, has pointed out the immense influence on the shaping of human thought and of the responses of the mind that the media of communication exert: the changes from the spoken word to the printed word, from the printed word back to the spoken word of broadcasting, and the most recent change to the fusion of the broadcast word and the broadcast image in television, are, for McLuhan, changes in human consciousness. His opinions are controversial, but there is no doubt about the truth of his central contention: literature is communication or it is nothing, and the nature of the communication is profoundly affected by the medium through which it is made.

Thus, our response to medieval literature ought to be affected by our knowledge that it is a spoken literature. One of the few surviving pictures of Chaucer* shows him reading aloud to Richard II* and his court. However diligent the copyists, the circulation of books could only have been small before the introduction of printing, and the diffuse, limpid style of Chaucer and other medieval poets is due to their assumption that their works would be communicated to the *ears* of their public. The existence of strongly didactic poems, such as *Piers Plowman**, *The Parliament of the Three Ages**, *Pearl**, and *Winner and Waster*, shows that verse-speech had peculiar importance for didactic purposes in an oral culture; the form was so much more easily memorized than prose. This accounts, too, for the popularity of the ballad* of topical events in the 15th and the 16th centuries. But the main medium for reaching the minds of the common people was the church pulpit; the sermon* had an importance in public life which was very slow to decline.

The introduction of printing by William Caxton* in 1477 produced no dramatic change beyond the small but important circles who were influenced by Renaissance learning. The drama of the age of Shakespeare was above all a spoken art. It is true that nearly half his plays were published during his lifetime (most of them, probably, without his consent), that a collected edition came out after his death, and that he seems to have been favourite reading of, for instance, King Charles I (1625–49). But the evidence is against the view that he intended his plays to be read as much as to be heard, and we study them wrongly if we forget that they made their important impact from the stage, and not from between the covers of a book. The pulpit was as important in Shakespeare's time as it had been in the Middle Ages, and the great preachers, such as the poet–divine John Donne*, were national figures.

However, it was also in his time that printing began to make its wider mark on the public. The pamphleteers* – Nashe*, Greene*, Martin Marprelate* – who wrote on the sensational religious, moral, and social questions of the day, were the first journalists*; several of them were also the first popular fiction writers. Humble people were buying popular versions of well-known romances in the chapbooks*, sold by the chapmen, or travelling pedlars. The first English newspaper (published in Holland) appeared in 1620, and private newsletters were circulated from hand to hand. The publication of news was restricted by government censorship, but the abolition of the Court of the Star Chamber* in 1641 released a quantity of polemical pamphlets stirred up by the violent controversies of the Civil War*. When Parliament tried to reimpose censorship, Milton protested with his eloquent *Areopagitica** (1644), the first important defence of the freedom of the press. The Restoration* government established its own censorship* by the Licensing Act of 1663, but this was allowed to lapse in 1695, and since then the British press has been free, as freedom of the press has been understood by most advanced countries.

Thus the reign of Queen Anne (1702–14) was the first great age of modern journalism*, and the first age in which journalism became a distinct profession, allied to literature but distinguishable from it in that the journalist, unlike other writers, is above all concerned with the events of the passing day. Freedom of expression was still not fully accepted; Defoe* went to prison for some of his opinions, and Addison* and Steele* found it more prudent to concentrate upon social opinions and manners than upon public politics. The chief political journalists – Defoe and Swift – wrote principally under the protection of the political parties, and even then they wrote at some risk. Newspapers*, as distinct from organs of opinion like Addison's and Steele's *Tatler** and *Spectator** and Johnson's *Rambler**, were established institutions by the middle of the century, but their circulation, by modern standards, was very small. That of *The Times** in 1795 was 4,800, and this was considered large; today its circulation is a hundred times as great, and yet it is considered small in comparison with that of the more popular (though less influential) newspapers. The 18th century, however, showed the final transformation from the culture of the spoken word into a culture of the printed word. Well established newspapers were only one of the indications of the change; another was the increase in the number of printers. At the end of the 17th century, there were only 20 printers in England; 18 of these were in London, and one each in Oxford and Cambridge. A hundred years later there were about 300 of them all over the country, about half of them outside London. Still another indication is that the novel* had become the prevalent literary form; for the novel, as opposed to the drama, is essentially a product of the printing medium, intended to be read, not recited. Books were expensive, but their availability was much increased by the circulating libraries* that spread over the country after 1740.

It was in the 19th century that the great division appeared between the small but influential educated public and the great mass of half-educated, or uneducated people. Even in the first 30 years there was an evident contrast between the 'great reviews', such as the *Edinburgh Review** established in 1802, with substantial literary and political essays for reading by the leisured classes, and Cobbett's weekly *Political Register**, started in the same year, with its brief, blunt, plain articles on urgent social questions, intended to reach the poorest classes of the country. But Cobbett's language was such as the readers of the *Edinburgh* could respect, though they might hotly dispute his opinions; writers and journalists still belonged to the same world of literate standards. By the end of the century the serious writer and the popular journalist lived in different worlds; the former still belonged to the world of art, whereas the latter had moved into the world of commerce. Newspapers with massive circulations counted in millions were a commonplace by the 20th century, and Britain by 1950 had the largest newspaper-reading public in the world. The causes of this development are complex; some of them were technical. For instance the introduction of the electric telegraph in the 1840s made possible the almost instantaneous transmission of news, and this transformed the character as well as increasing the popularity of newspapers. Their readers became aware for the first time that they were reading about world events immediately after their occurrence, and not, as hitherto, when they were already several days past, so that in the meantime other events might have dramatically changed the picture.

But the growth of the mass circulations of newspapers and periodicals was especially caused by a combination of the highly developed English commercial consciousness and the universal literacy made possible by the establishment of state education in 1870. Hitherto journalists, publishers, newspaper editors and newspaper proprietors had chiefly been faced by a well educated and critical public, which required information from them, and knew the difference between information, opinion, and entertainment. The new public, however, was often hardly educated beyond the capacity to read; the majority of it felt incapable of understanding the complexities of public events, even when they were told the facts, while the same sense of restriction in their mental horizons and the tedium of their work tempted them not so much to the further arduousness of more education as to distraction and sensational excitement. The journalists sometimes took this new public as a challenge to enlightenment, but more often they regarded it as a great market for their products. This market, moreover, could be manipulated, because, unlike the old public, it was uncritical; tastes and demands could be actively stimulated, and the stimulation was directed at the baser human responses because these could be more easily aroused. Hence arose the difference so evident among 20th-century British newspapers between those which remain responsible and informative and those which appeal to the widest possible public, with far less responsibly delivered information and considered opinion, and far larger circulations. Both kinds of newspaper have to remain cheap in order to be competitive, and their low prices are made possible by reliance on advertisements for profit.

The growth of advertisement, in newspapers and elsewhere, is part of the same history of the exploitation of the human mind. Its beginnings go back to the beginnings of newspaper publication, but massive expenditure upon it by large commercial enterprises has grown with the growth of the popular press, until it has become what it is today, a highly sophisticated technique of manipulating the feelings. The accusation which many educators make against commercial publicity is the same, therefore, as the accusation they make against the popular press; that advertisers abuse language and stimulate responses with the cynical aim of profit, not the serious aim of truth, and that language thus abused becomes compromised, by its debased associations, when serious minds try to use it for the advance of human dignity.

Another important development in the transmission of the printed word is one that has changed the bookselling industry, and this has had more mixed consequences for good and bad. The Victorian novelists, of whom Dickens* is the most conspicuous example, first overcame the expensiveness of books by publishing in serial, paper-bound parts, either separately or in magazines such as Dickens's *Household Words** (started 1850). In the second half of the century, publishers found it profitable to publish cheap editions for 'railway reading', and the production of these has been enormously enlarged since 1930 by the introduction of paperbacks. One result is that the general public is more aware than it used to be of the past and of the extent of past literary culture, and self-education in many branches of knowledge has become far easier; on the other hand, the spread of cheap publications has also spread the availability of inferior writing. The average modern reader is likely to be more widely read than his forebears were; his values are also likely to be more confused.

But the truly revolutionary changes in the media of communication in the 20th century have been of course in the growth of broadcasting. Sound broadcasting became a widely used medium in Britain between 1920 and 1940; television, since 1945. The British Broadcasting Corporation, established in 1927, financed by licences and government support, is probably the most enlightened broadcasting organization in the world, but it has a monopoly of sound-broadcasting, although it competes with independent networks (financed by advertising) in television. The question whether such monopoly and privileged competition can be justifiable in what have become by far the most widespread and influential means of communication is of course very important; the obvious defence is that the B.B.C. operates with large freedom from interference either from the government or from the nearly always degrading effects of commercial finance. But beyond such a local problem, affecting Britain alone, is the great question which affects the entire world: the unforeseeable influences on the human consciousness of media which are constantly available, worldwide in their range of instantaneous communication, and above all which affect the mind in such very different ways from the printed word, or the word spoken face to face. At least in a highly developed, geographically fairly small country like Britain, it is partly the concentration of the modern media, especially the broadcasting ones, in a few hands that constitutes a danger, particularly since the broadcasting media continue the strong trend of the popular press and advertising media in the manipulation of taste and the standardization of judgement. The B.B.C. to some extent solves the threat by broadcasting programmes of two kinds on television and four on sound, one of which in each case appeals to minority tastes which could not bring profit to any commercially subsidized or promoted network. Yet even this classifying of programmes is a kind of standardization of taste, and it is by no means certain that some future authoritarian government in Britain would respect the present independence of the B.B.C. as a corporation, with rights of self-direction guaranteed to it (over a term of years) by state charter. But this hypothetical political danger is separate from the more universal danger which arises from the very nature of modern communications systems: their uninterrupted pressure on the mind, and the intensity of their effect. Artistically, television has hardly liberated itself from the techniques of the cinema, and the cinema itself has extended the art of prose fiction by little more than its greater force of illusion, but television and the cinema have much greater power to absorb attention than the printed word, as well as to reach publics measured in millions rather than thousands. Just as, in travel, we have moved since the Middle Ages from bondage in place to uprootedness from place, so, in the media of the mind, we have moved from near silence to incessant bombardment.

2.2.3 *The changing environment*

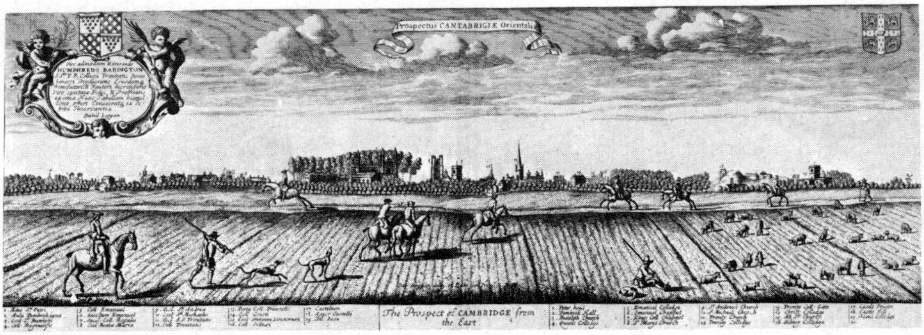

The 'open-field' system of agriculture was characteristic of the Middle Ages. From 16th to 19th C landlords by degrees united the strips of cultivated land which divided up the open fields, and made new fields enclosed with hedges. They did the same with most of the open 'common' land, used by the peasants for grazing their cattle. The upper illustration shows an 'open-field' landscape near Cambridge in late 17th C; the lower one (of Oxford at the same date) shows an 'enclosed' landscape.

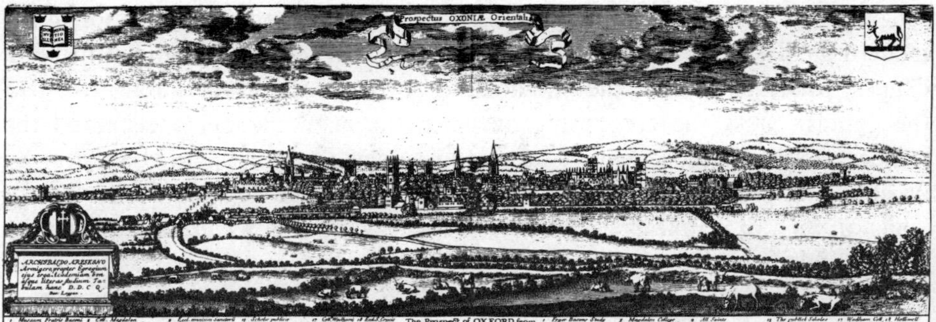

Norwich in the reign of Elizabeth I (1558–1603). An important centre for the cloth trade, and one of the largest towns in England (population 20,000).

London in the reign of Elizabeth I, showing old London Bridge — note the heads of executed criminals on stakes at the south end. London had a population of about 200,000 at the end of 16th C.

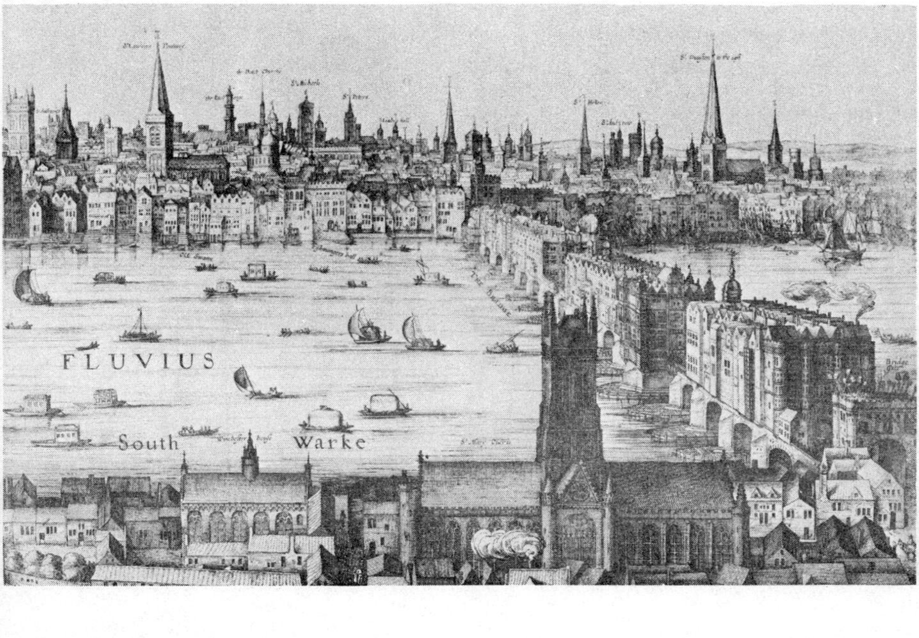

London in 1746. From a painting by the Venetian artist Canaletto. In the distance are Wren's* new St Paul's, and the towers and spires of the City churches rebuilt by Wren after the Fire of London* in 1666.

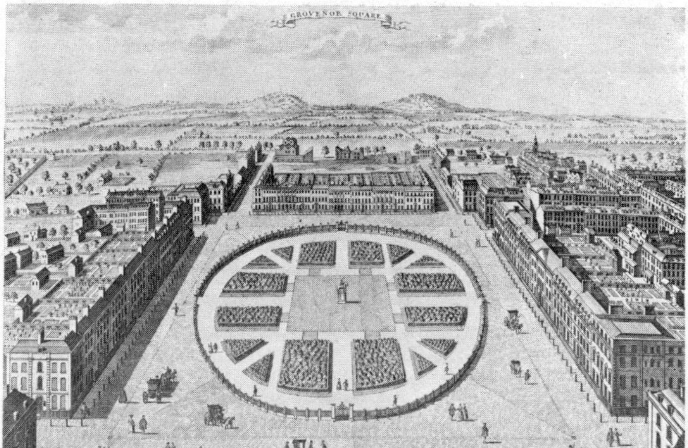

Grosvenor Square. An early example of a familiar style of English 18th-C town planning.

Gin Lane. An engraving by the 18th-C painter William Hogarth*, showing a London slum, and demonstrating the degradations produced by indulgence in strong drink.

The Mall, about 1735. A fashionable promenade alongside St James's Park in London.

Blenheim Palace. Designed for the Duke of Marlborough* by the architect-dramatist John Vanbrugh*; built 1705–27. The grand dramatic effect was considered heavy and rather vulgar by later 18th-C architects. The gardens, all originally formal, were later redesigned by the famous landscape gardener Lancelot ('Capability') Brown to suit the taste for natural-seeming scenery.

An 18th-C landscape garden: Stourhead, Wiltshire. The artificial lake, with an ornamental bridge and a Greek temple at the far end; the grotto to the left of the bridge; and the folly, or ornamental tower, at the extreme left, are typical features of the great landscaped estates.

Bradford, Yorkshire. The industrial towns which sprang up in the wake of the Industrial Revolution* were dark, dirty, crowded and confused. 'Coketown' in Dickens' *Hard Times** gives a picture of life in such a town.

A Court for King Cholera (1864), by John Leech. Leech is concerned to show the ill effects of slum housing on morals and health; cholera epidemics were frequent in mid-Victorian London.

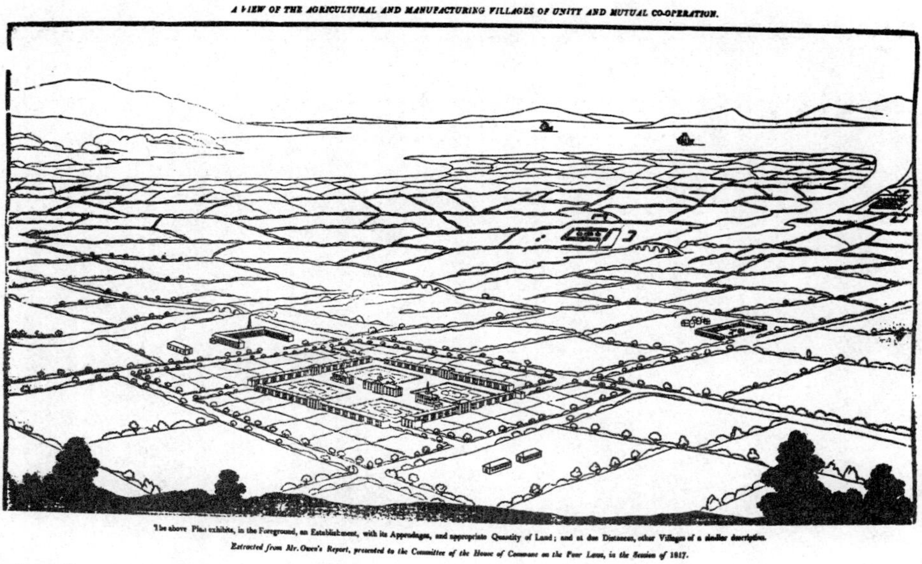

Robert Owen's plan for the agricultural and manufacturing villages of Unity and Mutual Cooperation. (1817).

Engine in the Egyptian taste. Exhibited at the Great Exhibition* of 1851. Typical of the Victorian kind of stylistic imperialism in all fields: designers felt that they had at their command any style which suited their fancies or the fancies of their clients.

2.3

The background of taste

When English medieval poetry reached its greatest period, in the half century that followed the Black Death in 1350, medieval culture already had characteristics common to many other advanced cultures: it was lavish and complex, like the castle Sir Gawain comes upon suddenly in the forest:

Into the water the wall went wondrous deep,
And then to a huge height upwards it reared
In hard hewn stone, up to the cornice,
Which was buttressed under the battlements in the best style
With protruding turrets between, equipped
With loopholes interlinked with lovely ornament.
No better barbican had ever been beheld by that knight,
And inside he could see a splendid hall
With towers and turrets on top, all tipped with crenellations,
And pretty pinnacles placed along its length,
With carved copes, cunningly worked.
Many chalk-white chimneys the chevalier saw
On the tops of the towers twinkling whitely –
And so many painted pinnacles disposed everywhere,
Congregated in clusters beyond the castle embrasures,
That it appeared like a prospect of paper patterning.

*Sir Gawain and the Green Knight** II iii, modernized by Brian Stone

The castle is functional; it is a strong place of defence in a wild and disorderly country through which Sir Gawain has been fighting his way. But the functionalism has flowered into elaborate art, just as the rich, powerful, comparatively secure nobility have – while remaining hunters and warriors – sophisticated themselves into courtly aristocrats who cultivate ceremony, brilliance and luxury. Similarly, the churchmen, dedicated to vows of poverty in emulation of their Founder, Jesus Christ, had sophisticated themselves into lovers of art, ceremony, and gorgeous colours. But churchmen and laymen did not ignore the contradiction between this earthly brilliance of a worldly Church and the austerities of the doctrine that it preached. They knew that it was like the contrast between the gorgeous cock and the poor widow who owns it in the tale told by the Nun's Priest* in Chaucer's *Canterbury Tales*; the widow lives with austere colours:

No wyn ne drank she, neither whyt ne reed;
Hir bord was served most with whyt and blak,
Milk and broun breed . . .

but the cock, whose neck she may wring when she chooses, is as resplendent as he is proud:

His comb was redder than the fyn coral,
And batailed, as it were a castel wal.
His bile was blak, and as the jeet it shoon;
Like asur were his legges and his toon;
His nayles whytter than the lilie flour,
And like the burned gold was his colour.

Chaucer's detail, comic realism, and colourfulness are analogous to qualities in 14th-century sculpture, building and painting. The pillars of the churches were crowned, just where the arches sprang upward, by carving as detailed, expressing grotesque comedy, and so were the bosses at the meeting points of the stone ribs that crossed the vaults of the roofs in elaborate patterns. English Gothic churches, like those of other west European countries, were richly painted, and their present grey austerity, together with the loss of the stained glass windows, has altered their character. In style, church architecture had begun with the massive simplicity of the round arches and plain thick pillars of the Norman* (or Romanesque) style in the 12th century. In the 13th century, this had changed into the first phase of English Gothic*, the pointed arches and fluted pillars of the far more graceful but still severe Early English style. Early in the 14th century this was elaborated into the patterning of stone tracery in windows and on roofs – the Decorated style. In Chaucer's own day, Decorated was giving way to the uniquely English Perpendicular Gothic, with huge, shallow apexed windows, unsculptured (but often painted) walls, and new elaborations of roof design. Perpendicular was as grand as but less ornate than Decorated Gothic, and it was simpler to build, partly owing to the great areas of glass. The greater simplicity of construction may have been regarded as a virtue owing to the shortage of labour which was one consequence of the Black Death*, and was perhaps accentuated by the constant civil disturbances of the 15th century. It was not, at all events, an attempt to restore the simple essentials of Christian worship.

The function of a church building was to be not merely a house of worship, but a symbol in stone and glass of the Faith that ordained such worship. It was characteristically built on the plan of the cross on which Christ died; it pointed eastwards towards Jerusalem, the Holy City; its stone spire directed the eye to Heaven; its west end had sculptured representations of the Trinity and the saints; its windows depicted the Bible stories, and even details of its interior architecture served to remind the worshipper of his religion and its meanings. To all this the elaborate ornament was often redundant and disapproved of by orthodox reformers, who wanted the building to become again a bare 'allegory in stone', the more compelling in that allegory* was intrinsic to the outlook of medieval man, who interpreted the very structure of the universe in terms of his religious beliefs.

The material allegory of the church building thus sprang from the same habit of mind which produced the great poetic allegories like *Piers Plowman** and the Morality Plays* of the 15th century. Yet the factual quality of Christian doctrine – God became an actual man, and a carpenter's son at that – made comic realism quite at home with allegory, just as ceremonial splendour was also at home with it. The Protestant reformers of the 16th century went further than medieval Catholic reformers however; they smashed the windows and the sculptures, and obliterated the paintings on the walls. Many survived, but on the whole the medieval church is a different phenomenon to us from what it was to medieval men. It appears dark and solemn, and less relevant to life as it is actually lived; yet this general effect is often contradicted by some of the detailed ornament that has survived the reformers' destruction. The difference is brought out by D. H. Lawrence in 'The Cathedral' chapter of his novel *The Rainbow** (1915). Will Brangwen has surrendered to the solemn splendour of the interior of Lincoln Cathedral but his wife Anna resists his mood because she is afraid of 'being swept forward headlong in the tide of passion that leaps on into the Infinite' . . .

> *So she caught sight of the wicked, odd little faces carved in stone, and she stood before them arrested . . .*
>
> *Apart from the lift and spring of the great impulse towards the altar, these little faces had separate wills, separate motions, separate knowledge, which rippled back in defiance of the tide, and laughed in triumph of their own very littleness.*

The writings of a 14th-century poet like Langland, in spite of his passionate appeals for a return to the life of dedicated poverty, suggest that he would not have been troubled by the comic carvings on the bosses in the midst of the allegory of stone; he had his own comic carvings. *Piers Plowman* contains many long sermons, but it also contains vivid, realistic, comic portraits like those of the Seven Deadly Sins in Passus V.

Allegory, realism, comedy were all qualities of medieval secular and religious art which the 16th century transformed rather than destroyed, though it went far to destroying their union with serious reverence. Another conspicuous quality that the Middle Ages transmitted was ceremony. Abuse of ceremony was, to the medieval mind, the abuse of order, and order was perhaps its deepest aspiration and faith. Life was centred on the great ceremony of the order of the Mass; ceremony gave order to the luxury of the royal courts, with their almost ritualistic cultivation of courtly manners, and ceremony balances realism in medieval allegory. In the 16th-century Renaissance, allegory became a deliberate device, as different from medieval allegory as spectacles are from the eyes; comedy and realism were likewise artificially cultivated by writers such as Spenser* and Sidney* who deliberately emulated the new ideals. Ceremony, however, remained the guarantee of order that itself guaranteed the meaning of life.

In building, there was no ecclesiastical architecture of importance after the completion of the final monument of Perpendicular Gothic – King's Chapel in Cambridge – but there was a great expansion of secular, especially domestic architecture. The newly rich classes of the Tudor age, the merchants and gentlemen who had been granted stretches of the spacious, confiscated monastic lands, built extensively, but in the main conservatively. The entrance was characteristically a great fortified gatehouse like that of a medieval castle, but the fortifications were reduced to the dimensions of ornamental detail, since there was no longer civil war and disorder in England. The gateway, particularly in the earlier mansions like Hampton Court*, opened on to an enclosed courtyard; in any case the central part of the building was still the great hall, in Perpendicular Gothic style, with huge windows which, though framed in heavy stonework, were evidently no longer designed for defence but to enable those outside to see the grandeur within, and those inside to survey the spaciousness of the garden and parklands. Privacy was not yet a principal object, but stateliness and ceremony still were; the hall was where the lord entertained his guests, served by members of his household, and entertained by musicians or a troupe of players which might also be in his personal service. The Tudor mansions were often heavy and sometimes vulgar, but they were confident, even exuberant structures, and asserted the grandeur of their owners. They were elaborately decorated and the ornament mingled Gothic detail with Classical detail inspired by the new Renaissance enthusiasm. As, in the first half of the century, poets like Wyatt* and Surrey* borrowed forms and devices from French and Italian literature, so the builders were infected by architectural influences from the same regions, though they assimilated them more slowly; poets and builders alike were better when they perpetuated the native traditions, although the mansions improve in classical symmetry and elegance as the century goes on.

Sculpture and painting depended much more on foreign influences. Great artists from the continent of Europe were employed at the English courts in the 16th and 17th centuries – Holbein, by Henry VIII (1509–47) and Van Dyck, by Charles I (1625–49) – but as yet no major native school grew up, despite the fine art of miniature portraits in the reign of Elizabeth I (1558–1603). Such miniatures were worn as portraits or laid on tables; but larger pictures required bare walls, and Elizabethan householders preferred to cover their walls with tapestries, which provided warmth in the chilly English winters. However, the increasing habits of foreign travel made Englishmen strongly responsive to the visual arts, which were such an important aspect of Renaissance culture. Charles I and his brother Henry were great collectors of paintings. The taste shows itself in the loving descriptions by the poets of art rivalling and excelling nature, as when Iachimo describes Imogen's room in Shakespeare's *Cymbeline** (II. iv):

The chimney
Is south the chamber; and the chimney-piece
Chaste Dian bathing; never saw I figures
So likely to report themselves: the cutter
Was as another nature, dumb; outwent her,
Motion and breath left out.

But though the extraordinary skill of the foreign artists in this kind of representation fascinated Englishmen, it roused their suspicions, perhaps rather as the suspicions of modern men are aroused by the ability of science to interfere with nature. Such interference was, indeed, already taking place in gardening; Acrasia's Bower of Bliss in Spenser's *Faerie Queene** (II. xii, 61) is a garden of artifice, and an evil, though an entirely beautiful place:

And over all, of purest gold was spread,
A trail of ivy in his native hew:
For the rich metal was so coloured,
That wight, who did not well avis'd it view,
Would surely deem it to be ivy true:
Low his lascivious arms adown did creep,
That themselves dipping in the silver dew,
Their fleecy flowers they tenderly did steep,
Which drops of crystal seem'd for wantonness to weep.

This is art used for deceitfulness, and suspicion of it was no doubt due to Puritan religious influence, which in the 16th century deeply permeated even the royal court. Puritanism saw Nature as derived from God, and Art as derived from Fallen Man.

In gardens* – a main feature of 16th- and 17th-century houses – Art normally met Nature in collaboration, as Polixenes explains to Perdita in *The Winter's Tale** (IV. iii):

You see, sweet maid, we marry
A gentle scion to the wildest stock,
And make conceive a bark of baser kind
By bud of nobler race: this is an art
Which does mend nature – change it rather; but
The art itself is nature.

Yet even this collaboration is suspect; Perdita refuses it, for she is a creature of innocence, of a pastoral Garden of Eden* where man dwelt in God-given Nature before his Fall. English pastoral literature followed classical Pastoral* in making its subject sheep and shepherds rather than arable farming, and this was not merely a matter of literary emulation; it suited the Puritan worship of Christ the Shepherd of souls, and it opposed the morally dangerous Italian influences the more effectually. Nonetheless, the English gentleman found the marriage of Art and Nature in his gardens most congenial. He was not afraid, at this date, to cultivate an architectural formality in his planning of gardens, and to emulate sculpture in the 'topiary-work' of clipped hedges and bushes. Marvell's* *The Garden* brings together classical and Biblical pastoral feeling, yet he ends it by using a typically ingenious gardening device of the time – a sun-clock of flowers – to represent the superiority of Nature over man's contrived world:

How well the skilful Gardener drew
Of flowers and herbs this Dial new;
Where from above the milder Sun
Does through a fragrant Zodiac run;
And, as it works, th'industrious Bee
Computes its time as well as we.
How could such sweet and wholesome Hours
Be reckon'd but with herbs and flowers!

Literature and gardening were two of the arts to which Englishmen took most naturally. Music was a third, and it was cultivated with an excellence which was second only to that of poetry. Since it was above all vocal, there was close collaboration between the poets and the composers, particularly in the hundred years between 1550 and 1650 (*6.1.2). But the 17th century saw the growth of a more cultivated taste in architecture, and the beginnings – though this belongs chiefly to the 18th century – of a native school of painting.

The first fully classical architect in Britain was Inigo Jones* (1573–1651). Jones designed three buildings which still stand in London: the Banqueting Hall in Whitehall, St Paul's Church (not to be confused with St Paul's Cathedral by Wren) in Covent Garden, and the Queen's House (1616) at Greenwich; the last of these was the first fully classical building in England. He replaced the often clumsy amplitude of the 16th-century mansion with the qualities of restraint, balance, proportion and elegance. These were qualities that he assimilated from the work of the Italian architect, Palladio* (1518–80) and which Palladio had learned from the study of ancient Roman remains. Jones's transformation of English building style was remarkably complete; the classicism which had merely ornamented Elizabethan houses now became the very spirit of the building. He was the first of a great line of classical architects and designers to dominate English taste: Christopher Wren* (1632–1723), John Vanbrugh* (1664–1726), Robert Adam* (1728–92), and John Nash (1752–1835) are the most famous names, though the list could be doubled at least. Literary taste shows a corresponding change, though it is not quite so rapid or so marked, and in literature the line begins with Jones's great rival in the composition of court masques*, the poet Ben Jonson* (1572–1637) whose verse is the first to be thoroughly imbued with classicism derived from the ancient Roman poets. From him, we go to his disciples, the Cavalier Poets* of the reign of Charles I, and thence to John Dryden*, Alexander Pope*, Jonathan Swift*, Henry Fielding*, Samuel Johnson* and Jane Austen* – to mention, again, only the leading examples.

Classical taste is generally thought of in opposition to Gothic taste; perhaps it is legitimate to say that classical art obeys a standard of taste, whereas Gothic does not have a standard, though it has intentions. Classicism aims at harmony and reveals itself in a discipline of the parts within the whole, whereas Gothic allows itself freedom; classicism fears redundancy whereas Gothic rejoices in abundance. This is to mark their extremes: it is possible to find many examples of Gothic art with some classical virtues, and much classical art (especially in the baroque of Wren and Vanbrugh) which has the dynamism of Gothic. If we sum up the contrast by suggesting that Classicism subjects itself to reason whereas Gothic abounds out of emotion, we have to remember that the best classical art (Wren, Pope, Swift, Johnson) shows the emotion as not less deeply felt for being disciplined.

Despite what we may call the 'classical revolution' in English taste in the 17th century, classical standards never commanded English feeling so completely as they influenced France and Italy, whose cultures had more enduring foundations in the Roman Empire; the English language is not a derivative from Latin as French and Italian are. Gothic never altogether became a synonym for outmoded barbarism; it remained a fascinating region of forbidden freedoms. This fascination found expression, first, in a new attitude to landscape and (especially in painting) to nature generally. Since the 16th century, landowners had been enclosing common lands and the farms of their tenants, not merely in the interests of more profitable farming, but to increase their own grandeur by surrounding their mansions with parkland. In the 16th and 17th centuries they had used this land for hunting over, but the 18th-century proprietors, influenced partly by painters of landscape such as the Frenchman, Claude (1600–82), and the Italian, Salvator Rosa (1615–73), saw the possibilities of 'improving' their parkland aesthetically, by modifying its features so as to form a series of ideal 'pictures', framed into a variety of perspectives. Straight paths were made to wind; groves of trees were carefully sited for the beauty of their position and grouping; lakes were created, not the regular rectangles of French classical taste as at Versailles, but irregularly shaped, like the Serpentine in London's Hyde Park, so as to seem natural; small buildings – follies – were constructed, merely to focus the view – Chinese pagodas, artificial Gothic ruins, or Greek temples. Architects such as 'Capability' Brown, Repton and Kent spent much cf their working life 'improving' estates in this way; a contemporary remarked that he hoped to die before Brown could get to Heaven and 'improve' even that. The poet, William Shenstone (1714–63), gave less time to making verse than to creating a visual poem out of his estate, Leasowes.

This movement in landscape gardening accompanied and was encouraged by a new sensibility for wild nature which agreed very well with reviving taste for Gothic art. The term 'picturesque' entered aesthetic vocabulary. The educated public of the later 18th century, under the guidance of the books of William Gilpin (1724–1804), explored the mountainous regions of Britain, such as the Lake District and the Scottish Highlands, which they had hitherto avoided, or visited, like Samuel Johnson, for the social interest of discovering the ways of life in a primitive region. Travellers and antiquarians found exciting beauty in the ruins of monasteries and medieval castles. In poetry, wild nature became a theme as early as Thomson's* *Winter* (1726) and this continued in the verse of Akenside, Collins* (*Odes*, 1747), Gray* (*Elegy*, 1750), Goldsmith* (*Deserted Village*, 1770) and Cowper* (*Yardley Oak*, 1791). Responsiveness to the ballads* of the people belongs to the same movement of sensibility, and Percy* published his famous collection of them, the *Reliques of Ancient English Poetry* in 1765. Horace Walpole*, the son of the 'first Prime Minister' and very representative of the aristocratic taste of his time, converted his house, Strawberry Hill, into 'a little Gothic castle' in the middle of the century, and wrote there the first of the Gothic novels*, *The Castle of Otranto* (1764).

The great painters of the English 18th century ranged, like the writers, from conservative classical taste, to satire in one direction, and to the poetic feeling for natural surroundings in another. Chief among the conservatives was Sir Joshua Reynolds*, a fine portrait painter and the first President of the Royal Academy*, founded in 1768. He and Thomas Gainsborough were chief among a number of portrait painters whom the rich upper classes delighted to commission to decorate the huge walls of their Palladian mansions, now long bare of the tapestries which their 16th-century predecessors had preferred. Gainsborough, however, also contributed to the sensibility for nature by his paintings in the tradition of Claude Lorraine. William Hogarth* (1697–1764) was far more realistic; his violent satire and vivid caricature had a strong influence on the novelists Richardson* and Fielding* in a style of comedy which was to reach its greatest richness in the work of Charles Dickens*. However, in Dickens the comedy is distinctly 'Gothic' in its abandonment, whereas the satire of Hogarth and the 18th-century novelists has greater affinities with a characteristically 'classical' abhorrence and ridicule of human tendencies to break out from a civilized 'norm' into extravagances of pride or degradation; it relates back to the Humours* of Ben Jonson's comedies. Another representative of the varied English 18th-century school was the landscape painter Richard Wilson (1714–82). His work was more sensitive and original than the landscape work of Gainsborough, but it is significant that as yet it lacked popularity; for that, it had to wait for the deepening of the sensibility for nature in the years in the Romantic Revival* (1790–1830).

Some of the complex later-18th-century taste for 'picturesque nature', gothic ruins, landscape gardening and folk poetry was far from superficial; the deepest element in it, perhaps, was an insight into man as a being of the wilderness, to counterbalance the strongly social conception of man, characteristic of 18th-century Augustanism*. Much of it, however, was shallow and sentimental – a false idealization of rural life by those who were too well off to understand its hardships. This aspect was bitterly attacked by Crabbe* in his poem *The Village* (1783). Crabbe, and Jane Austen in *Sense and Sensibility** (1811), are classical writers in a romantic age, but their satire on the more sentimental side of 18th-century sensibility is not really in opposition to the great early Romantic poets, Wordsworth* and Coleridge*, who had a far deeper perception of human nature, considered as the outcome of natural surroundings. Correspondingly, the novelist Walter Scott* made Gothic into something more real than Horace Walpole and his school had done, because to him it was a phase of history and not merely a fancy about the past, or about the primitive and the strange. The Romantic Age of 1790–1830 did not in all respects 'grow out of' 18th-century sensibility; it engaged as realities much that 18th-century taste had often only played with.

The young William Blake* (1757–1827), poet and engraver, received some of his art education at the Royal Academy. Joshua Reynolds was its President; he represented conservatism in 18th-century taste, and for Blake he was the great enemy of true art. 'In the midst of the highest flights of fancy and the imagination, reason ought to preside from first to last,' wrote Reynolds in his *Discourses*; and Blake wrote in the margin: 'If this is true, it is a devilish Foolish thing to be an Artist.' Painters had taken their subjects from literature and their ideas on nature from theory; they now relied much more on their own responses to what they saw, and to their own inspiration. England had its greatest landscape painters in Constable (1776–1837) and Turner (1775–1851), and there was a closer interaction between the imaginative writers and native English painters than there had ever been: the poet Keats* (1795–1821) owed much to Hazlitt*, the critic with a strong taste for painting, and to his friend, the historical painter Haydon. Yet the public and the artists, just because of the sheer individualism of the Romantics, were also less in accord than they had been; the artist was a lonelier man, and there was never to be a very coherent public for either the visual arts or imaginative writing again, in spite of the immense popularity of individual artists such as the poet Tennyson.*

Despite Romanticism, the classical rule of taste, with variations and attenuations, lasted until about the time of the death of the architect Nash in 1835. Thereafter a new 'Gothic' age swept over Britain in earnest; it was different from either the sophisticated reaction to classicism of the 18th century or the imaginative exploration of the deeper feelings of Romanticism; it was the exuberance of the upper and middle classes, intoxicated by the technological possibilities of the Industrial Revolution* which had finally reached its climax with the invention and spread of the steam railway. Machines could mould with ease materials which the hand-craftsman could only shape imperfectly, and new materials became plentiful. The rapid expansion of population demanded vast building programmes – workers' cottages and tenements, factories, railway stations, town halls and churches. The new technology made possible an extraordinary proliferation of ornament. Above all, popular excitement over the material progress which made Britain 'the workshop of the world' and the richest of the nations gave to the spirit of design a more than Elizabethan ostentation and arrogance, without the Elizabethan restraints of order, ceremony, and the requirements of spiritual decorum.

In the face of this assault by technology, the artist and the writer stood back, or, like Carlyle*, Matthew Arnold* and Ruskin*, went into opposition. The best element of Victorian taste is probably its spontaneity and vigour, and this can be felt most infectiously in the 'Gothic' energy and abundance of the novels of Dickens, but even Dickens was increasingly, bitterly critical of the inhuman aspect of his age – its tendency to put sheer accumulation of things before people. Some architects, such as the devout Catholic, Pugin (1812–52), one great art critic, Ruskin, and one artistic movement, the Pre-Raphaelites*, took Gothic with deep seriousness and tried with some success to use the energies of the age in the cause of human spiritual advancement. But although their ideas and those of the Socialist craftsman William Morris* were influential beyond their own lifetimes, they could not exercise a decisive influence on a period which was steadily abandoning respect for intellectual authority when it was unsupported by demonstrable 'scientific fact'. To relieve people of material destitution was a generally acceptable objective by the end of the century; to create an environment which would enhance human dignity met with scepticism or indifference, at least among the ruling class of financiers and industrialists. A new split came into English society: that between those whom Matthew Arnold called 'Philistines', who cared nothing for the values represented by art, and the minority who still cared for them. In Henry James's* novel, *The Spoils of Poynton* (1896), Mrs Gereth creates a work of art out of a house full of works of art, in a way that is comparable to Shenstone's creation of a work of art out of his estate in the 18th century, but Shenstone had a whole society to share his taste, whereas Mrs Gereth's Poynton is a lonely, heroic achievement. Such a theme could not have been taken by an earlier author in the history of English taste. Taste is always, above all, the outcome of caring enough about an object; the handcraftsman cared because of the labour he expended upon it, but the machine – as Ruskin points out in his chapter 'On the Nature of Gothic' in *The Stones of Venice* – removed the man from the object he made, and turned him into something like an object himself. As for the purchaser, the proliferation of standardized objects destroys interest in them, or creates an interest that has little to do with care for their intrinsic value.

One of the salient qualities of the Victorian* period was its intense interest in detail, nourished partly, no doubt, by the new technical mastery over material, partly by the sheer crowdedness of daily life, and partly perhaps by the minute scrutiny of matter characteristic of the sciences that lay behind the technology. We see this everywhere in the art of the period: in the novel (which had always been an art of the detail of daily life); in the poetry of Tennyson* and Browning*, and, in a different way, that of Hopkins*; in the paintings of every school after the death of Turner. Such concern with detail often became obsessive, especially in the painters, but in artists of great vitality, such as Dickens and Hopkins, it greatly intensified the vividness of experience. By the end of the century it was provoking a reaction in a new kind of fastidious selectiveness. This is notably true of the work of Henry James, whose latest novels (for instance *The Golden Bowl**, 1904) present characters with the least possible material and social detail in their background.

In the graphic and sculptural arts, a different kind of reaction to this love of detail showed itself in the 20th century. Victorian technology, to the disgust of Ruskin and William Morris, showed slight reverence for material, since the engineer had found that – within a wide range – he could do what he liked with it. Even the painters and architects were infected by the enthusiasm for manipulating matter so as to transform it. The 20th-century painters and sculptors, by contrast, have put their main emphases on their materials, whether considered as paint or colour, whether stone or iron. The result has been a tendency to abstraction and away from realistic representation. For example, the Victorian sculptor reproduced the human body with minute attention to accurate resemblance, but the great modern sculptor, Henry Moore, has sought to exhibit the qualities of his materials above, or even in place of, figurative representation. The great poets of the earlier 20th century, W. B. Yeats* (1865–1939) and T. S. Eliot* (1888–1965), showed a correspondingly fastidious care for language and its intrinsic properties, and so did some of the novelists, especially James Joyce* (1882–1941).

The preoccupation of the 20th-century artist with the material of his art has done much to make him still less accessible to the general public, since the influence of the great popular media of communication – the press, advertising, broadcasting – has been in the opposite direction, that of fostering realistic illusion. The predominant media for popular art have been the cinema and television; both of them are large industries with correspondingly large organizations to support them, and they have perfected techniques of illusion. The consequence for modern taste is that it is faced with a crisis which in one aspect resembles and in another is opposed to that which faced the Victorians. The technical mastery is as great as ever, and the abundance of material is even greater; the combination, as in the Victorian period, tends to produce indifference in the public. At the same time, the organizations behind this mastery of material are incomparably larger than they were in the Victorian period. Critical judgement is thus inhibited in a new way by the very force of the impressions that are imposed on the mind, and by the incessant stream of persuasions assailing it. The individual is presented with more choices than have ever previously existed in the history of taste, but he is left with less capacity to make a choice of his own.

*Foxe's Book of Martyrs** was an immensely popular work for generations because it enshrined the Protestant reformers persecuted by the Catholic Queen Mary I. This illustration from it shows two of the principal martyrs, Ridley and Latimer, being burnt at the stake.

3 Religion, philosophy and myth: 1350–*present day*

Introduction *The mental background to British culture*

The background of beliefs to a culture and the flow of ideas within it include the emotional and intellectual assumptions on the basis of which writers communicate with their publics. There are two principal difficulties in the way of understanding these beliefs and ideas. The first is that while there is continuity in the beliefs and ideas, they are at the same time always changing; we have the problem, then, of distinguishing the elements of continuity and the elements of change, of seeing in what ways Milton in the 17th century shared beliefs with Langland in the 14th, and how far the beliefs of Dickens in the 19th century had anything in common with those of either. Much of the continuity of a culture is of course social, but social continuity is the physical counterpart of ideas about human beings and their relationships; it is not a mechanical survival of forms and institutions, although the forms and institutions generally change more slowly than the ideas. The second difficulty is that beliefs affect the minds of writers variously, depending on whether they are open or secret, intellectually argued or communicated through the emotions, widely diffused through society or present only in a part of it. Moreover the relative importance of the ways in which beliefs and ideas can affect literature varies from period to period; for instance, Christian belief, in the Middle Ages, is impressed to some extent on most of the imaginative literature, whereas in the 18th century it is comparatively unimportant, and writers are being influenced by more or less sceptical philosophers whose very names are unknown to the majority of the population. We also have to take account of fictions in which belief is assumed for imaginative purposes, because such fictions correspond to emotional needs in at least a section of society. Such fictions include the use made of Greek and Roman pagan deities from Chaucer in the 14th century to Keats and Shelley in the 19th. This essay attempts to explain some of the principle ways in which beliefs of various kinds have affected English literature, how far these beliefs have kept continuity, and how far they have changed. It is necessary to distinguish the main forms of belief and thought in their categories 'religion', 'myth', and 'philosophy'.

Britain is still, officially, a Christian nation, and though less than half the population profess Christian belief, the religion has a strong influence on the habits and behaviour of the unbelieving majority. It is in fact a 'binding' belief; the derivation of the word 'religion' is from the Latin 'ligare', 'to bind'. For purposes of this essay, 'religion' will be used for beliefs that make a total demand on the emotions, whether or not they are accompanied by a reasoned philosophy. Two facts immediately become clear: the first is that Christianity was much more inclusively 'binding' up to the 17th century than after it, and the second is that in these later centuries some writers – Blake, Keats, George Eliot and D. H. Lawrence, for example – were religious although they were not Christian nor disciples of any other distinct creed. A religious attitude to experience does not, in fact, depend on a

*** Indicates mention in the reference section.**

creed of belief; it is distinguished rather by a disposition to revere what the individual feels to be 'binding' on human experience. As the official doctrines of Christianity became less 'binding' on the imaginative vision, so writers tended to shape a conception of the world that arose from their individual interpretations of the ideas current in their time, including the myths that constituted a meaningful language for them.

The word 'myth' derives from the Greek 'mythos', meaning 'a tale', or simply 'speech'. The appeal of a myth is entirely to the emotions and the imagination, but we have to distinguish myths which influence the personality without the critical interference of the intellect from those which a writer uses symbolically without any literal belief in them. It is clear, for instance, that the Judeo-Christian myth of Adam and Eve as the first man and woman had literal force for imaginative writers until the 19th century: Milton believed in the biblical mythology of his poem *Paradise Lost** whereas Chaucer in *The Parliament of Fowls**, Keats in *Hyperion** and Shelley in *Prometheus Unbound** did not believe in the Greek mythology they were using. However, the pagan mythology of Chaucer, Shelley and Keats is intended to be taken seriously – as seriously as Blake 'meant' his private mythology in the Prophetic Books – whereas Shakespeare did not expect the same kind of serious attention to be given to his ceremonial use of such mythology in Prospero's marriage masque in the last act of *The Tempest**.

There are thus three main uses of mythology in English literature: the first is part of the imaginative expression of literal religious belief, and it has the same authority as historical fact has for the modern mind; the second is the figurative expression of what is often, though not necessarily, individual belief; and the third is purely ceremonial or ornamental. In the Middle Ages, the first use was not restricted to Christian mythology, for pagan 'nature myths' still flourished in medieval England, and there is a core of pre-Christian Celtic myth in at least the earlier versions of the legends of King Arthur*. Such pagan myths survived because Christian beliefs did not totally satisfy the emotional needs of society; the second and third uses of (principally) classical mythology are also attempts to find a language to satisfy these needs, and though the writers who employed it were distinctly conscious that they were using fiction, such fiction often embodied very serious complexes of belief. We shall see that the first use of myth is scarce after the 17th century, that the second extends to the present day, and that the third, the ornamental and ceremonial use, belongs chiefly to the aristocratic segment of culture in the 16th and 17th centuries.

The influence of philosophy on literary culture varies according to its relationship to existing myth and religion, and according to whether writers agree with or resist the philosophers. Thus, in the Middle Ages, the Greek philosopher Aristotle* was quoted to sustain official doctrine, but in the 16th century the influence of Plato* operated more independently of official belief though he could be harmonized with it; the influence of the Italian political thinker Machiavelli* aroused universal hostility among late-16th-century English writers, whereas

John Locke* in the late 17th century left a kind of orthodoxy of thought for writers in the 18th century. In the 19th century, painful divisions make themselves felt: the rational, scientific thought of the time did little to satisfy the emotional needs of the individual, while at the same time it actively corroded the religious beliefs which did give this satisfaction. Thus we see the rise of 'the Victorian sage', such as Carlyle* and Ruskin*; D. H. Lawrence* was perhaps the last of this kind. In the 20th century some philosophers and scientists – notably the depth psychologists, Freud* and Jung*, and the anthropologists – have found new meaning in the ancient myths, but they remain myths, that is to say, traditional tales which, though not factual, convey important messages to the mind. Another kind of myth, however, was accepted as literally true by philosophers and scientists from the Middle Ages to the 19th century; this was 'the Great Chain of Being', used by medieval theologians to reconcile the observed world and their theology, and by 18th-century biologists as a framework to accommodate their scientific findings.

We find, then, that religion, myth and philosophy must not be studied as three distinct influences upon the human mind; each, at different times, collaborates, conflicts, or merges with the others in often unexpected ways. If we say that philosophy is totally rational, and myth irrational, we must remember, first, that total rationality is an ideal rather than an actuality, and second, that philosophy sometimes needs a conception of order which it cannot provide for itself, though mythology can. Religion has always had both its mythological and its rational aspects, though they have not at all times had the same importance. When we consider all three in relation to the imaginative writer, we realize that he is often unconscious of much in the movement of contemporary thought; at least unconsciously, however, he will respond to the important strands of it, for the imaginative writer reflects and unifies the different aspects of the mind of his time.

3.1

The Middle Ages: the Age of Faith: 1350–1500

3.1.1 *Christian doctrine and the Church*

Three events are the basis of Christian doctrine: the Fall of Adam; the Incarnation of God in Jesus Christ; and the Second Coming. Belief in these has undergone extensive modification and variation among Christian sects since 1500; in the Middle Ages*, when the Church was one, literal acceptance of them was almost universal. The Fall meant that the First Man disobeyed God, and thereby transmitted to all his descendants the curse of Original Sin, which means that the inherited propensity to sin condemns humanity to eternal punishment after death;

implied in this is the belief that man is 'imperfectible', that is to say, he cannot avoid sin by his unaided efforts. The Incarnation means that God became the man, Jesus Christ; he removed the curse on Adam's descendants by taking upon himself the punishment for man's sins, and in consequence of this, man is no longer doomed to damnation but is given the hope of salvation, if he follows Christ's Law and the guidance of the Church. The third event lies in the future: Christ, on his Second Coming, will liberate the world from all the consequences of the Fall, and will bring eternal happiness to all who are saved by God's mercy. Medieval theologians moderated the terrible opposition of Heaven and Hell by assuming the existence of a third place, Purgatory, where souls underwent purification in preparation for the Second Coming of Christ and his Last Judgement.

For the Middle Ages, the Fall was the event which began history; the Incarnation was the central fact of history; the Second Coming would bring history to its close. History was thus contained in religion. Religion also contained the life of the individual: the doctrine of the Fall dictated that he was born into sin, but the Incarnation released him from the inevitable eternal damnation consequent on this; an infant who had received baptism, like the daughter of the poet in the 14th-century poem *Pearl**, was sinless, and though the individual was certain to relapse into sin, he could as repeatedly be released through the confessional of his sins to a priest who would then give him absolution; that is to say, the priest would act as intermediary for God's pardon. On his deathbed the individual hoped to receive 'the last rites' of final absolution, and after his death he hoped to pass to Purgatory, where his sufferings could be eased and his redemption speeded by prayers said for him by the living. The central event of the religious life was the Church ritual of the Mass, in which the Eucharist – the Last Supper of Christ and his disciples – was re-enacted; by the dogma of 'Transubstantiation' it was held that the bread and the wine consumed at the Eucharist were actually transformed into the flesh and blood of Christ. Thus this Holy Sacrament constituted the vital communication between man and God, and the threat of 'excommunication', *ie* refusal of the Church to give the sacraments to the offender, was its most dreaded weapon against those who resisted it. These beliefs and practices are of course substantially unaltered in Catholic countries today, but in the Middle Ages they constituted the most central facts of existence for whole societies, which thus envisaged the goal of life in other-worldliness to an extent that is not true of any western society today. Medieval men did not entertain the notion of time as a progress to a hypothetical material happiness on earth; earthly progress they envisaged as 'the Dance of Death' processions painted on church walls, where every individual, from prince to serf, is accompanied by a skeleton. There was no hope in mortal life, and those who placed their hopes in it were subjected to the eternal revolutions of the Wheel of Fortune which brought men from poverty to prosperity and then down to despair. This was like the revolution of the seasons in every year – from the scarcity of winter through the harvest of summer back again to winter. But there was another pattern in the year which gave it a different meaning – that of the religious festivals*. The darkest season was redeemed by the celebration of the birth of Christ in midwinter; Easter, the celebration of his Resurrection, came suitably in the spring; Corpus Christi*, the festival of the Holy Sacrament, came in high summer; and there were many others dedicated to the saints and to events in the life of the Virgin Mary. Time was the enactment, through the whole of history, in every life, and in every year, of the drama of damnation and salvation, of Satan and Christ, and of death and life. The outcome of the drama was fore-ordained for good in the world, but it was in doubt for every individual person.

The conflict was thus strictly an earthly one; the battle between Good and Evil in the universe at large had been won by the heavenly powers long before man had been created. The universe was thus not dualistic – exposed to the rivalry of equal powers – but subject to God alone. Christianity, therefore, had to face the problem of reconciling this belief in an omnipotent God with the belief that God was somehow taking the side of man in his personal struggle against Evil. The problem was solved by the doctrine that God was the Holy Trinity – one God with three aspects or manifestations. In one aspect he was the Father, the all-powerful, -all righteous Judge and Creator, who ruled the universe down to the depths of Hell. In another aspect he was the Son, who had entered the earthly conflict as complete Man (the Son of Man); having achieved victory in human terms, he had left the Earth with the promise that he would return, to temper the Father's Judgement with mercy at the end of time. Till then, he left behind him God in his third aspect – the Holy Spirit, the Comforter (Strengthener), as the invisible presence of God-with-Man. Below these in the heavenly hierarchy, but also on the side of man in his earthly struggle, were Mary, the Mother of Christ, and the Saints. All these had been undoubtedly human, but they were raised to Heaven immediately on their deaths on account of their especial merit and could there intercede for men in answer to human prayers. But Heaven was principally populated by countless angels*, whose eternal vocation was the glorification of God, but who were also sent to earth as messengers (like Gabriel announcing the birth of Christ to Mary) and as special guardians, like the Good Angels of the Morality* Plays. Most important of all in its immediate influence on human life was the corporate Holy Church of Christendom. The Church, in this sense, has to be understood in its mystical meaning as the Bride of Christ. She was envisaged by the Dreamer in Langland's *Piers Plowman** (Passus I) as 'A lady of great loveliness, in a linen garment' –

> '*I am Holy Church,' said she. 'You may chance to know me,*
> *I was the first to feed you, and taught you the Faith;*
> *You brought me surety to obey my bidding*
> *And to love me loyally while your life lasted.'*
>
> (Coghill's version)

No medieval Christian in western Europe would have disputed this mystical conception of the Church, whatever quarrels might exist with the Church in its concrete political and social manifestations. It had been founded by Christ himself, when he committed authority over it to the Apostle Peter, conceived as the first Pope or Father: 'thou art Peter, and upon this rock I will build my church; and the gates of hell shall not prevail against it. And I will give unto thee the keys of the kingdom of heaven: and whatsoever thou shalt bind on earth shall be bound in heaven: and whatsoever thou shalt loose on earth shall be loosed in heaven' – *Matthew* 16: 18. It was on this text that the Church based its complete authority over morality and belief, its power to excommunicate sinners and to grant absolution from sin, and to exert the function of 'canonization' by which men and women were declared to be saints in heaven.

The antagonists of man, on the dark side of the universe, were the Fallen Angels led by Satan, whose name in Hebrew means 'antagonist'. The myth of the Fall of the Angels has very slight biblical authority, but it is nonetheless intrinsic to medieval if not to modern Christianity. Satan had been Lucifer, the Lightbringer, and the brightest of the angelic beings, but his pride had caused him to rebel against the sovereignty of God and to pervert a section of the angelic host on to his side. His penalty was to be cast out of Heaven into Hell, a region specially prepared for him, his followers, and all subsequent rebels against the Divine Will. His followers were the devils; these were, in fact, often identified with pagan gods, especially those who, like Beelzebub*, had formerly been worshipped by the enemies of Israel, as recorded in the Old Testament of the Bible.

Such were the beliefs of Christians in the 14th century. They derived principally from the Bible, but Christianity owed much to other influences as well: to ancient eastern religions which invaded the Empire of Rome when the Church was struggling for survival; to the thinking of early Christian philosophers known as the Fathers, and to ancient Greek philosophers, especially Plato* and Aristotle*. The Church had first adapted the philosophy of the former to its uses: Platonic idealism, with its belief that the true insight into reality penetrates beyond material forms into the region of spiritual forms, seemed congenial to Christian spirituality. However, in the 13th century the Italian philosopher St Thomas Aquinas* (1225?–74) substituted the philosophy of Aristotle who was more empirical – that is to say, he based his thinking more on the evidence of concrete experience. The change was in some respects an unexpected advantage, for Christianity is the most material of all supernatural religions: it preaches that, as a historical fact, God intervened in history by becoming a man, and God had originally intended the earth to be a paradise for man's pure enjoyment. However, this very earthliness of Christianity tended to induce men to attend less to the spirituality of its doctrines, so that they became increasingly occupied with opportunities of knowing, enjoying, and mastering their environment. It is possible that Aquinas, by inducing the Church to replace the idealist Plato by the empirical Aristotle as its official philosopher, hastened this change of direction.

Moreover, men were being gradually pressed in the direction of critical, if not yet sceptical, thinking. Medieval Europeans were realistic in their earthly expectations, and they realized that besides its mystical aspect, which was unquestioned, the Church had to operate through ordinary mortals with the usual mortal weaknesses, but nonetheless, in the later 14th century, there was a sense of oppressiveness and disgust under the weight of the Church's materialism. Chaucer* shows this mood at its most genial in *The Canterbury Tales**, and his friend Gower* is more explicit and expansive in *Mirour de l'Omme* and *Vox Clamantis*; Langland's *Piers Plowman** is a long discussion of the predicament of the common man who finds that his dedication to Holy Church is constantly frustrated rather than aided by the practice of the Church in the world. This worldly Church has to be understood in two ways: in its operation as by far the largest and most effectively deployed political organization in medieval Europe, and in its detailed effects on the life of society.

As a political organization, the Church was the effective heir to the Roman Empire. It was centred in Rome under the Pope, except for some 70 years in the 14th century, when the Popes lived in the French city of Avignon. Christendom was divided into provinces, corresponding in area to those of the Empire, such as the provinces of Canterbury and York in England. Each province was under the authority of an Archbishop. The provinces were further divided into districts which were also similar to those of former Roman Imperial local government; these were known as 'sees' and each was under an Episcopus or Bishop, who was served by a hierarchy of officials. The smallest division and the one that immediately affected the life of the common man was the parish; each had its parish priest, and it has been estimated that the proportion of priests to population was over ten times larger than it is in modern England. Such were the 'secular' clergy, who worked in the world. There were also the 'regular' clergy, the orders of monks and friars* who obeyed the 'regulum' or rule of their respective monasteries* and friaries. The monks were intended to live away from the world, leading lives of prayer and scholarship, but the friars lived among ordinary men and women, as did the secular clergy, teaching and preaching if they were Dominicans*, and serving the poor and sick if they were Franciscans*. Through this vast army of clergy the Church affected almost every side of social life: it controlled education through all its levels, and provided the majority of the educated members of the population; the higher clergy and the monasteries were great landowners and employers of labour; individually and collectively, the higher clergy were prominent in national politics and occupied powerful positions in the state; the Church had its own law-courts, which tried not only the offences of the clergy but many moral offences of the laity as well. More important than all this, the Church, both collectively and in the constitution of its regular orders, was thoroughly international in its organization. It is true that the kings shared some authority over it with the Pope, and often disputed, sometimes successfully, with the Pope over much authority that the latter did not agree to share; moreover, papal international power was much weaker in the later 14th century than it had been in the early 13th. Nonetheless, no national sovereignty of the modern sort could come into being so long as the clergy held so much wealth and power within the country, and could defend themselves in the use of them by appealing to superior authorities abroad. England already had a comparatively well developed national consciousness, and the internationalism of the Church was bound to provoke resentment and conflict.

However, this great political and social prominence of the Church was not incompatible with its mystical claims, and if the clergy had served their vocation conscientiously and unanimously, it is probable that such national political jealousy would not have been felt deeply, at least until later when national self-consciousness had developed still further. But churchmen set no such high example to their worldly neighbours: they were, in numerous instances, neither conscientious nor unanimous. At the top the Church was divided by political antagonisms of such a kind that, when Chaucer was writing *The Canterbury Tales* in the 1390s, there were two rival popes in Christendom, and this 'Great Schism'* was not healed until 1417. At the bottom there were bitter rivalries between the secular and the regular clergy, especially between the parish priests and the friars who competed for influence over the common people. The parish clergy were often much poorer and less educated than they should have been while the higher clergy and many of the monks and friars were extravagantly rich and scandalously self-indulgent, as instanced by the Monk and the Friar in *The Canterbury Tales*; they were often, too, unlearned men, appointed to high position by the force of strong social influences. Chaucer reminds his audience that the clergy took vows of poverty to live like their Master, Christ, but the only clergyman who does so in *The Canterbury Tales* is the poor Parson, brother of the Ploughman; Langland's Piers Plowman is, in one aspect, an emblem of Christ, and an insistent reminder of how far the wealth and worldly power of the Church deny the teaching of its Founder. It followed that the Church exercised its functions in regard to the common man not only inefficiently but often very corruptly. Chaucer's Monk does not live by prayer and learning, but by hunting and drinking; his Friar, Pardoner and Summoner – all servants of the Church, though only the first is a clergyman – are common criminals, exploiting the ignorance and superstition of the poor by deceit and terror. It is scarcely surprising, therefore, that contemporary with the poets Langland, Chaucer and Gower, was the great reformer, originally a parish priest, John Wycliffe*. He was partly an educator, and the first of the great English translators of the Bible from Latin, but he was also an outspoken critic of the power and wealth of the Church, and of its abuse of them. But critics of religious institutions have seldom been able to keep back from the invisible boundary between the institutions themselves and the doctrines that lie behind them: Wycliffe went so far as to question the truth of Transubstantiation in the Sacraments before he was silenced by his own powerful protector, John of Gaunt*, but – thanks to secular protection – he was allowed to die peacefully in his bed, safe from the wrath of the Church. His movement, the Lollards or Poor Priests, was suppressed, but he led the unsettled minds of English believers far along the road to the Reformation* though this destination was not reached for almost another century and a half.

3.1.2 *Pagan undercurrents, courtly love and learned mysteries*

The Middle Ages were the Age of Faith to the extent that few men professed to live by reason alone, but Christianity did not dominate the mind exclusively, since it did not entirely satisfy the emotional and intellectual demands of all men. In the countryside the peasants who lived off the land that they cultivated were conscious of forces of nature which they could neither explain to themselves nor control, and which they attempted to propitiate or conciliate with pagan rituals, though most of them probably did not cease to be Christian with half their minds. In courts, noblemen who were frustrated by the Christian rule of monogamous marriage and by the social rule that such marriages should afford mutual economic satisfaction rather than mutual passion, responded to the cult of courtly love (*courtly literature and romantic love), which became almost a worldly religion. In universities and other places of learning, scholars like Chaucer's Canon in *The Canterbury Tales* were fascinated by the half-superstitious sciences of alchemy* and astrology, which offered mastery over matter and insight into human destiny. We have, therefore, three avenues of non-Christian thought and feeling, affecting different classes of people, though the appeal of astrology crossed the boundary between class and class. All three have some significance for medieval literature, and the second was practically a literary cult. It is the first however that was probably the most pervasive, though it is also the most obscure, because of the illiteracy of the countryfolk and the secretiveness of the practices.

Not only were the country people isolated, ignorant, and at the mercy of their natural environment, but in about 1350 they were devastatingly reduced in numbers by the epidemics of the Black Death*, after which they engaged in fierce social conflict with their masters, the landlords, in consequence of the shortage of labour caused by the high proportion of deaths in the working community. These facts may have given impetus to underground pagan religions which had survived the general conversion to Christianity. Such religions were cults of nature, the purpose of which was to secure fertility and guard against scarcity. The chief form was belief in a god incarnated as a man or as a beast. Those who were dedicated to his service were known as 'witches'*; they were endowed with mysterious knowledge and magical powers. This god was worshipped four times a year, in winter, spring (the eve of May Day), summer and autumn, at assemblies which became known as 'witches' sabbaths', and every seven or nine years he was ritually sacrificed. In the trials of witches, common from the 14th century onwards, the god was referred to as 'the Devil', and it is to be remembered that the devils of Christian belief were often identified with the gods which Christianity had overthrown. In Britain, if the god was represented by an animal, this was usually a dog, cat or bull; if a man he was frequently 'the Green Man', so common on English inn-signs. His effigy, a ferocious face surrounded by twigs and leaves growing from the corners of his mouth, is even found in medieval churches, sometimes on bosses in the roof where the priests could not see or reach them.

The manifestation in literature of these beliefs is often disguised, indirect, or debatable. Witchcraft appears far more in Renaissance writings than in medieval works – for instance in Shakespeare's *Macbeth** (1606?) and Dekker's *The Witch of Edmonton* (1623). The immediate reason for this may have been the intense interest of King James I (1603–25) in the subject; a more general reason may be that the great medieval panoply of the Church was stripped away by Protestantism, leaving the private conscience in naked confrontation with Good and Evil, without that faith in the clarifying and cleansing power of Reason which was later to remove all supernatural matters to a distance from the mind. There is perhaps evidence for this explanation in the fact that the persecution of witches was more extensive in northern countries after the Reformation than before it, and was more intense in Scotland than under the comparatively moderate Protestantism of England. It is at all events clear that these later persecutions show a long survival of rural pagan superstition, though its importance for literature diminished as writers in general lost touch with the secrets of the countryside. Certainly in the Middle Ages poetry and drama were much closer to the life of the common people than they became later; medieval ballads* are full of a spirit of naïve magic, but they were transmitted by word of mouth, and when much later they were written down, they were also edited. It is difficult not to associate the medieval folk hero Robin Hood* – the theme of May Day Morris Dances* and the subject of many ballads – with the Green Man, but it is doubtless impossible to prove the connection. This probable association suggests a connection between the pagan cults and 14th-century social discontent, for Robin Hood was an outlaw who robbed the rich but spared the poor. There is dispute, again, as to whether the Green Knight in the great and much more sophisticated romance *Sir Gawain and the Green Knight** is also a manifestation of the Green Man, but again it is natural to make the connection, especially after Frazer's remarks in *The Golden Bough* on Jack of the Green as a vestige of the ancient pagan tree worship of the north European forests.

Sir Gawain is, at all events, related to the Arthurian cycle of legends, and in these we find the pagan cults linking, however unconsciously, with the aristocratic cult of courtly love. The legends were certainly Celtic* in their dim origins; Arthur*, and the chief knight of the earlier cycles, Gawain, probably started as pagan gods in Wales, though the Christian priests called them demons or devils – another example of Christianity blackening the deities to which it was opposed. From the 10th century to the 12th, Arthur was regarded as a Christian warrior who had defended Britain against the Anglo-Saxon invaders in the 6th century. In the 12th century, the legends passed – probably by way of the Celtic Breton minstrels – into French literature, and there they become a mixture of heroic poem and courtly love romance; Arthur's chief knight ceases to be Gawain and becomes Lancelot*. By the time of Thomas Malory's *Morte d'Arthur**, late in the

15th century, the legends have received still further overtones, this time from the monks who tried to counteract the epic chivalry and the courtly love by erecting chastity as the supreme virtue: Lancelot, the great lover, is in his turn superseded as the chief hero of the cycle by his chaste and devout son Galahad*. The history of the cycle passes from its probable origins in pagan symbolism, through a phase of epic romance and passion, to a final phase of devout Christianity. The 'quests' of Arthur's knights were originally mythical versions of the ritual ordeals undergone in pagan societies, whereby youths proved themselves as men. The object of the principal quest was the Grail*, the cup from which Christ drank at the Last Supper; only those who have led lives of perfect purity are empowered to achieve a vision of this Holy Grail.

The origins of courtly love – which the French called 'fine amour', translated by Chaucer as 'fine loving' – are very obscure, so that it is impossible to know whether they were at all related to the pre-Christian fertility cults. Since the romances treat the sexual passion as an end in itself, so that marriage and offspring are irrelevancies to it, they would seem to originate in a sterility cult rather than one concerned with fertility, and something like this view of them is expressed by the French scholar Denis de Rougemont in his book *Passion and the West*. We know, at least, that the romances first took shape in the highly sophisticated courts of southern France in the 11th and 12th centuries, and it is reasonable to see them as expressions of the refined and civilized, though amoral, relationships between the sexes cultivated in those courts. Not only do the romantic passions seldom end in marriage, but they are often adulterous, like the love of Lancelot for Arthur's wife, Guinevere*. Since medieval marriages were arranged on economic grounds, not those of mutual feeling, it seems reasonable to suppose that the courtly aristocracy of western Europe welcomed relief from the frustrations of passionate desire by purifying it into a cult of the worship of Woman, thus civilizing manners and at the same time relieving the tension. Love courtship becomes a sophisticated art, demonstrated allegorically in Chaucer's *Romaunt of the Rose*, translated from the French *Roman de la Rose** of Guillaume de Lorris. If the lover wins his mistress, he must obey a severe code of conduct in regard to her, especially in guarding her reputation, as Pandarus warns Troilus in *Troilus and Criseyde** (III, stanzas 37–47). Chaucer's earlier poem, *The Parliament of Fowls**, sets courtly love in a kind of moral and social perspective. The poet falls asleep in a mood of dissatisfaction after reading an account of the world which leaves out the fact of sexual passion, and his dream compensates him by revealing the nature of this passion. It does not belong to the sick and frantic sensuality symbolized in the dream by the Temple of Venus, but to the healthy, outdoor world of the goddess Nature. In her presence he listens to a debate among the birds, and learns that 'fine loving' is only for the noblest of them. The 'fine lover' may decide that he must idealistically live and die unwed, because his devotion to his mistress is more important to him than life although she has refused him; this at least is the faith of the eagles. The baser birds, such as the ducks and geese, corresponding to lower-class human beings, take the more practical view that sexual union is for the propagation of the species, and that if one female refuses a male, he has plenty of others to choose from. There was, of course, nothing in romantic love to contradict Christianity; it was a creed for this world, and more for the imagination than for practical living. Nevertheless, it induced preoccupation with earthly love instead of heavenly love, and in this way it was contrary to the teaching of the Church. Poets knew this, and, like Chaucer at the end of *Troilus and Criseyde*, they sometimes concluded their narratives with propitiatory prayers to the Trinity.

The half-sciences of alchemy* and astrology – the former an ancestor of chemistry, and the latter the most active part of medieval astronomy – were regarded ambiguously by the medieval Church; they were not necessary to man's salvation, but they did not necessarily conflict with Church teachings. Astrology, based on the belief that the stars and planets can influence human destiny, was cultivated in the universities and attracted keen interest in all ranks of society. It was used by physicians in the treatment of disease, and by others as well, as a psychological explanation of character. For instance, Chaucer's Wife of Bath describes her temperament in terms of the influence of the planets Mars and Venus at her birth. The fact that the planets bear the names of the ancient Roman gods also made astrology a peculiar vehicle for classical myth, which is much more vivid when it is used astrologically than when it is used on its own account. For example, Chaucer's use of Venus in *The Parliament of Fowls* is merely figurative – she had always represented sexual lust, and in this poem she is an emblem of it. In *The Knight's Tale*, however, the gods and goddesses are also astrological forces, giving the poet the opportunity for eloquent exposition of those aspects of human experience which, astrologically, were held to come under their influence. Chaucer, of course, did not believe in the pagan deities as such, though he could use them allegorically as symbols. But he probably accorded at least half belief to astrology, and he knew that he could count on as much among his readers. The result is that when the Roman deities are presented through his astrological lens, they are like emblems that suddenly take on life. Alchemy, on the other hand, was a specialist study, and like modern specialisms, it easily became a joke for the common reader; Chaucer makes it into one, in *The Canon's Yeoman's Tale*.*

3.1.3 *The philosophy of Nature*

The main energies of medieval men were dedicated not to the pursuit of knowledge but to the search for order and system. Men of later times have scorned them for their scientific apathy and for their submission to the tyranny of theology. But they considered that the Bible and the teachings of the Church contained the essential truth that man needed, whereas they felt the daily impact of the forces of disorder that threatened his survival. Disorder emanated from the Father of Lies – from Satan and his hosts; order was the visible aspect of Divine Truth. Their conception of Nature and the universe was simplified and systematized, but man, by his sinfulness, was held to have disrupted the system.

Their ideas about the shape of the physical world and the composition of matter were an imperfect inheritance from the ancient Greeks, modified chiefly by the requirements of Christian theology. The universe was a system of concentric circles with the earth at the centre. The circles corresponded to the apparent orbits of the heavenly bodies: the Moon, the Sun, Mercury, Venus, Mars, Jupiter, Saturn, the stars; the movement of these was controlled by the outermost circle, the 'Primum Mobile' or 'prime movement of Heaven'. The earth occupied the lowest place in this system as well as the central one, a position which encouraged humility in man and promoted the prestige of theology, for theology was the only science that could lead the spirit of man upwards. The Fall of Man that had begun history also influenced natural history, for by his sin of disobedience Adam had separated his world from God, and imperfection began 'under the Moon'. Matter was compounded of four elements – hot, cold, moist and dry – in accordance with Aristotle's theory, and these manifested themselves in the human body as the four humours* of blood, phlegm, melancholy and choler, which affected the health and shaped the temperament in accordance with their chance proportions in the individual. These ideas survived the Middle Ages until they were gradually eliminated by the beginnings of modern scientific investigation in the 17th century. The most embracing medieval conception, however, had a longer life, and indeed only reached its climax of prestige in the 18th century, whose 'natural philosophers' found it as convenient to use as a framework for their rational ideas of the universe as the men of the Middle Ages had found it for the harmonizing of Divine Purpose with observed nature.

This idea was the 'Great Chain of Being', the history of which is expounded by Arthur Lovejoy in his book of that name. Like other medieval conceptions of the world, it derived from ancient Greek thought; from the philosophy of Plato who expounded it in his dialogue *Timaeus*, and from Aristotle's *Metaphysics*. It attempted to answer the questions why the world exists, and how it has come to contain such an extraordinary variety of kinds and degrees. The answer to the questions implies three assumptions: the first is that the universe could not have begun unless it was created; the second is that the Creator was perfect, and because he was perfect, sought to manifest himself in creation; the third, that his infinitude of perfection necessarily expressed itself in amplitude of kinds and degrees of created beings. Aristotle originated the influential notion that there could be no interruption in the series of created things, so that every kind – spiritual, animal, vegetable or mineral – contained qualities that related it to its neighbours in the chain. The theory was extremely useful to the medieval outlook in several ways. First of all, it agreed well with the belief in a God whose central attribute is love, for love is the creative virtue. Secondly, Aristotle's opinion that there must be continuity in the chain corroborated the medieval belief in the hierarchy of angels, who filled the otherwise appalling void between man and his creator. Thirdly, it helped to explain the almost inescapable belief that some things and creatures are superior to others, each kind culminating in excellence, as minerals seem to culminate in gold, birds in the eagle, mammals in the lion, and so forth. Fourthly, the 'Chain of Being' harmonized with the social facts of the Middle Ages, when society was severely hierarchical, from the serf who spent his days in the service of his lord to the king who was God's representative in earthly matters in his realm.

The famous English literary expressions of the 'Chain of Being' are later than the Middle Ages. They include the speech by Ulysses in Shakespeare's *Troilus and Cressida** (I.iii. 85–137), Hooker* on the Law of Nature in his *Laws of the Ecclesiastical Polity* (Bk I, 1593), and Pope's lines in *The Essay on Man** (I, 207–80). The first two are concerned with the appalling consequences of the hierarchical order being broken – consequences no less than the return of chaos – and Pope invokes the 'Chain of Being' against the arrogance of men who believe that human reason can comprehend every kind of excellence. Thus all three writers express the fear that acceptance of the law of the 'Chain of Being' is no longer an assumption in the minds of everyone; it is still the only conceivable principle of order in the world, but order itself has to be defended. In fact disorder was of course much greater in the Middle Ages, but the principle of order, as operative and desirable, was more profoundly accepted. It lay behind the spacious majesty of Dante's *Divine Comedy** early in the 14th century, and, near the end of the century, behind Langland's *Piers Plowman**, a poem which, among other things, is an extended protest against the wilful and sinful refusal of men to perform the functions allotted to them in the hierarchy.

3.2

The Renaissance and the Reformation: 1500–1650

3.2.1 *The renewal of classical culture*

Renaissance* means 'rebirth'; it conveys the idea that for centuries European culture had been dead, and then, by some means, had recovered life. The Middle Ages* received their name from the men of the Renaissance because they were thought to have come between the vigorous civilizations of Greece and Rome and the reborn culture of 16th-century Europe. Yet we know that the Middle Ages had a most vigorous civilization and a most active intellectual life: European civilization had, in fact, no need of rebirth.

What actually occurred was an immense and complicated change which was *felt* as rebirth – an extension of energies and the discovery of new means of insight in almost every aspect of experience, especially in the 'rediscovery' of Greek and

Roman literature. Again, to talk of 'rediscovery' is in some respects misleading, for medieval culture had in many ways been a continuation of that of the Roman Empire: Latin had continued as a living language, the organization of the Church grew directly from the Imperial organization, and its philosophy developed from Greek and Roman premisses. However, Europe has grown not only from these classical roots but also from the very different Asiatic roots of Hebrew culture, through Christianity. It is significant that the book most sacred to the Middle Ages was the 5th-century translation into Latin of the original Greek and Hebrew texts of the Bible; it was called the *Vulgate**, for it made the Bible available to the 'vulgus' or masses, since Latin was the common language of western Europe. Thus the *Vulgate* can be regarded as a symbol of Hebraic-Christian culture conquering the pagan Latin culture of the Roman Empire, and transforming it into Christendom. The Renaissance was a counter-movement: the spirit of Greek and Roman culture reasserted itself over against the Hebraic–Christian tradition, not indeed reconquering it, but achieving independence. The essence of this independence is implicit in the movement known as humanism*.

The humanism of the Renaissance must not be confused with the modern sense of the word: it was not, as modern humanism is, the cultivation of human values without relevance to any supposed supernatural values. The Renaissance humanist was a scholar who chose to concern himself with classical literature and not with theology. He was not usually opposed to theology, though he was often opposed to the way in which much theological thinking had been conducted in the Middle Ages. Unlike the characteristic medieval thinker, the humanist was foremost a critic, studying and testing his texts for their own sake, and this meant that he practised freedom of thought even though he did not advocate it. The movement began in Italy; one of the earliest humanists was the Italian poet Petrarch* (1304–74), who collected texts of the ancient Greek and Latin writers. The practice spread, and gradually European scholars realized that not only had medieval scholarship been ignorant of many ancient authors whose works were thus being rediscovered, but that the texts of such writers as had long been known were often incomplete and corrupt. One consequence was new pride and assurance in scholarship – a feeling that it possessed larger and more reliable resources than at any time since the collapse of the Roman Empire of the West in the 5th century. The humanists developed an often unjustified disdain for medieval learning, and their confidence in supposing that they were the first to understand the classics amounted to a belief that they had rediscovered civilization itself. It was this belief that led to a new phase of European culture.

The immediate influence of the humanists was important in four ways: in literature, education, philosophy and religion.

Their constant occupation with literary tests caused them to distinguish and value 'style' in literature to an unprecedented extent. This does not, of course, mean that medieval writings had no style, but style now became distinguished from substance for its own sake. Outstanding Latin writers were emulated even more for their expression than for their thought – Cicero*, for his persuasiveness, and Seneca* for his terseness and weightiness. Such preoccupations were important not only for literary criticism; concern with literary style is likely to promote concern with other forms of style, including styles of living, and thus emphasis on literature is important in regard to education and conduct.

Medieval education had above all been directed to the production of clergy, but the secular learning of the humanists appealed to the worldliness of men, whether they were clergy or not; the 16th century was the first, in England, in which the upper classes considered education to be indispensable to a man of high rank. For 400 years they pursued an education based principally on the classics and on the classics as the Renaissance humanists began to see them – as models of style. Already in the Middle Ages the tradition of courtly love had trained the aristocracy into a richer conception of nobility than the primitive one of prowess in war and the hunting field. Humanistic style further enriched the courtly ideal by requiring that the nobleman should excel in the arts and letters, in accordance with the prescriptions of the Italian humanist Castiglione*, whose book *The Courtier* (1528) was widely read by the English upper classes. The ideal of the nobleman thus formed was the basis for the conception of the gentleman* cultivated by the 'public schools'*. Nor was this conception merely the cultivation of fine manners; classical philosophy contributed the substance of it.

The humanists were scholars rather than philosophers, but their study, criticism and editing of the Greek and Roman philosophers independently of theology led to admiration and emulation of their ideologies. The *Faerie Queene** of Spenser is a thoroughly Renaissance poem, and it shows this kind of influence; the virtues celebrated in each of the Books are Platonic ideals, but the whole poem is a summation of the 'magnanimous man' who embodies them all, and in the *Faerie Queene* – had it been completed – would have been represented by Prince Arthur, a figure borrowed from medieval romance. Distinct from Platonism and the Aristotelian 'magnanimous man', but not incompatible with it, was the Graeco-Roman philosophy of Stoicism*, known chiefly through the Roman philosopher Seneca*. Stoicism advocated the pursuit of virtue for its own sake, and the consequent disregard, not merely of material glory and prosperity, but of the influences of pleasure and pain. Stoicism harmonized easily with the Protestant emphasis on strict personal ethics, and contributed to the ideal of the gentleman in English education, but the effect of humanism in helping to bring about the Protestant Reformation arose rather through its critical spirit.

This critical spirit was naturally disinclined to spare some of the less central beliefs valued by the medieval Church. For example, the belief that the Emperor Constantine had granted to the Papacy temporal sovereignty over the West in the 4th century was exposed as baseless by the humanist Laurentius Valla in 1440. The humanists did not, however, attack those doctrines that were indispensable to the Church. On the other hand, they attacked – as medieval writers such as Langland had done – the mismanagement of the Church and the misconduct of the clergy; and the climate of the Renaissance caused such criticism to have more momentous consequences than it had had in the 14th century. The greatest of the humanists, the Dutchman Erasmus* (1466–1536) wrote a satire, *The Praise of Folly* (1509), which is directed at all aspects of society and is largely light-hearted, but becomes vehement when the subject is Church abuses. However, when a few years later the German reformer Martin Luther* began the process of leading half Europe out of the Catholic Church, Erasmus did not follow him. The humanistic spirit implied intellectual independence, because it originated in criticism and discovery, but it did not commit the humanists themselves to active reform.

The greatest of the earlier English humanists was Sir Thomas More* (1478–1535); he was a friend of Erasmus, who wrote *The Praise of Folly* in his house. More's most famous work is *Utopia** (1516), which was written in Latin. Utopia purports to be a far-away state which is organized on perfect principles. It is communistic, enjoys religious toleration, has a democratic government and elected kings who can be deposed for tyranny, and it extends education to all the population of both sexes. As a criticism of the actual state in which the author lived, *Utopia* is of course the start of a critical tradition of utopian and anti-utopian fiction, and it appears bold and very much in advance of its time. Yet it has puzzled critics, for it seems that More cannot have meant all that it seems to imply: the facts of his life, for instance, show that he was not himself a practical believer in religious toleration, and they equally show that he is not likely to have been either a communist or a liberal democrat at heart. It is more likely that the book was intended as a kind of romance, in which an unrealizable perfection was presented as an exercise of the intellect and a speculative entertainment. More himself was a realistic statesman of his age, and he died a martyr to the Catholic faith. His book, like Erasmus's, was a disinterested exertion of the mind, newly emancipated by humanistic critical thinking.

Political, economic, and intellectual emancipation went together to form the image of what we now think of as the Renaissance. Politically, the outcome was the modern state; economically, newly enriched classes shook off the remnants of the feudal 'caste' relationship. In consequence the nation was at last psychologically ready for the religious emancipation which Wycliffe had already preached, and which is known to history as the 'Reformation'.

3.2.2 *The religious reformation*

3.2.2.1. *Anglicanism*

The great religious changes which took place in the countries about the North Sea in the middle of the 16th century arose out of differences of feeling and belief that had long been growing in medieval Europe, but they also corresponded to profounder cultural differences. After the lines of disagreement had hardened, the Catholic Church was left in power chiefly in those countries which had formed part of the Roman Empire, and the Protestant ones were chiefly those that had never fallen under Roman rule. The exceptions are significant: Poland and Ireland retained Catholicism as part of their national identity, which was threatened by neighbours of a different faith; England had been part of the Empire, but it accomplished a form of Protestantism* which was nearer than any other to Catholicism – Scotland, which had never been part of it, became much more profoundly Protestant. Wherever the Roman Empire had had deep roots, the Catholic order and doctrine impressed itself more enduringly. Moreover, it was especially the material aspects of the doctrine that the Protestant movements of Reform attacked: not the doctrine of the Trinity, but those of the veneration of the Holy Virgin and the Saints, and belief in Transubstantiation. Luther's* campaign of reform in Germany was overlapped by the reign of Calvin* in Geneva, a period in which the Calvinistic Church took precedence over the political authority in the city.

The common characteristic of the Protestant movements was the determination to purify the Christian faith of excrescences which were held to conceal its truth. However, there was much disagreement about what constituted these excrescences, and how the truth should be interpreted when they were removed. Henry VIII* (1509–47) belonged to the party which chiefly restricted its hostility to the international sovereignty of the Pope, and to the international structure of the religious orders. He accordingly declared himself head of the Church in England and abolished the monasteries, but he made few other concessions to Protestant opinion beyond some encouragement of the translation of the Latin Bible (the *Vulgate*) into English. This was insufficient for the Archbishop of Canterbury, Cranmer*. In the reign of the boy king Edward VI*, he compiled an English form of Church liturgy in the Book of Common Prayer*, from which most of the ritual and doctrine without secure basis in the Bible was removed, and he altered the Communion service so that it became a commemoration of the Last Supper rather than a re-enactment of it. But the reformers went still further; the images of the saints in the churches were systematically defaced, and the holy paintings on the walls were covered over. Against this, public opinion revolted; it could tolerate changes in the church service because they were beyond the capacity of ordinary men to understand, but the destruction in the churches themselves affected centuries of custom and sentiment. Thus the nation received the Catholic reaction of Edward's sister, Mary I* (1553–8) with relief rather than resentment. However, she proved as bigoted in reaction as her brother's statesmen had been in reform, and on her death, Elizabeth I* (1558–1603) was able to restore the Protestant system. But her methods were tactfully ambiguous: Cranmer's Prayer Book was subtly modified in a Catholic direction; marriage among the clergy was tolerated but scarcely approved, and Henry VIII's title of Supreme Head was altered to the less offensive 'Supreme Governor'.

These shifts from Catholicism to extremer Protestantism, ending with a compromise, did not indicate religious indifference among the English, but diverging opinions. At least since Wycliffe, the mood had been prevalently anti-papal, and probably a majority of Englishmen desired the purification of religious practices, whether or not they favoured important changes in doctrine. The Elizabethan Settlement was opposed by two minorities: a small one of steadfast Catholics, such as the martyr Edmund Campion* (1540–81) and the poet Robert Southwell* (1561?–95) and a larger one of extreme reformers known as Puritans*. The question was whether the Anglican Church would turn out a mere compromise and collapse between these contending forces, or would develop a strong distinctive character of its own. That it did the latter is proved by the great line of Anglican preachers and poets of the 17th century. The first and doctrinally the most important of these was Richard Hooker* (1553–1600); the first five parts of his *Laws of the Ecclesiastical Polity* appeared between 1593 and 1597.

Hooker's aim was to defend the Anglican Church against the Puritan insistence on further reform. Their faith and their ideas about the relationship of the Church and society rested entirely on the Bible; to the Divine Law of God's Word all other law must give way. They believed, for instance, that the Church was the body of true believers, who were the only true saints, and that it must rest with them to appoint the government of the Church; Christ did not intend that the Church should be ruled by a single person by virtue of his office, be he king or pope, and they were still more hostile to 'episcopacy', the system, retained in the Church of England, by which this rule was delegated to royally appointed bishops. Hooker's reply to this challenge was both highly traditional and very supple in reasoning. The basis of his thought was the comprehensive philosophy of the great 13th-century Catholic thinker Aquinas*, who had in turn based his reasoning on Aristotle. Hooker agreed with the Puritans that the scriptures of the Bible were God's Law, but he asserted that the law of nature was also divinely inspired, and the same must be true of human law, which is based upon it. Moreover, human nature has been endowed with the divine gift of reason, and Hooker interpreted the use of reason as the great conservative thinkers (from himself through Burke and Coleridge to T. S. Eliot) have always interpreted it: to affirm that the long establishment of traditions is reasonable presumption of their inherent value, so that it is against reason lightly to abolish them. This is the basis of Hooker's defence of Anglican episcopacy. But Hooker was consistent in his use of reason; it might be reasonable to abolish or reform an ancient institution, but it was not reasonable to do this on the grounds that there was no scriptural authority for it. Moreover, his argument that it was man's duty to use his gift of reason he carried to the extent of challenging the Puritan assertion that what the Bible prescribed must be absolute, for it is reasonable to suppose that laws and institutions which were right for the ancient Hebrews would in many instances be wrong for 16th-century Englishmen, and were not intended to be binding upon them. This reasonableness in Hooker's thinking sets him apart from the Catholic Church with its absolute demands upon the obedience of its members. In one sense, he believed in Holy Church as much as Langland in the 14th century did, but he also believed what the Catholic Church, at least of his time, did not allow – that the earthly organization of the Church could vary in accordance with the changing conditions of time and place. Thus Hooker related the Church of England firmly to the ancient traditions of Christianity, while at the same time he asserted its independence: national churches in relation to Christendom resembled separate families in a society, not the servants of a single family.

3.2.2.2 *The Puritans*

In the middle decades of the 16th century, while England was feeling its way to the 'via media' of Anglicanism (*3.2.2.1), Scotland was swept by the doctrines of the most systematic of the protestant Reformers, the Frenchman Jean Calvin* (1509–64). Calvinism, based on Calvin's *Institutes of the Christian Religion* (1535), became known in the British Isles as Presbyterianism*, through its system of church government by means of regional, elected assemblies called presbyteries. In England, the Presbyterians were only one, and later not even the most important, of a number of extreme reform movements collectively called Puritan*. The word first appeared in print in 1567. In Scotland, Presbyterianism quickly became the national Church, which it has remained ever since, but in England Puritanism fought with Anglicanism for nearly a hundred years, and it was only in the 1660s, after the temporary triumph of Puritanism between 1642 and 1660, that the Puritans were formally excluded from the Church of England and obliged to form Dissenting* or Nonconformist churches of their own.

The essence of Puritan doctrine is its emphasis on the inherent sinfulness of man. All men are born in sin, though the sacrament of baptism creates a presumption of redemption. Furthermore, because God is eternal, he necessarily has foreknowledge of all time, and has known since the creation of man which individual men and women are to be saved for eternal joy, and which are to be eternally lost. From this arises the Puritan doctrine of predestination*: a man's fate after his death is already decided at his birth. But how is he to know that he is predestined to salvation? Chiefly by the inward certainty of his conscience, and he will achieve this inward certainty by being 'led' by the Holy Spirit into the community of the saints, which the Puritans regarded as the true believers in the world, not those who have won the special favour of God in Heaven. This community of the 'true church' will worship God under its own elected clergy which will be as shepherds ('pastors') to the 'flock 'of their righteous congregation. The members of the true church will moreover be known by the godly strictness of their earthly lives, by the avoidance of all those mortal pleasures which distract earthly pilgrims from the narrow path to salvation, and by the austerity and sincerity of their forms of worship. The last was important; the Puritans believed that Christian worship had been much corrupted by superstition, which was a mortal sin because it was a mockery of God; thus they were especially insistent that there should be no altars in churches, or holy images, for God must be worshipped in the spirit and not through concrete symbols; the clergy, likewise, must not wear costly vestments.

So far, this account of Puritanism shows it to be a strictly other-worldly religion, and it might seem that they withdrew themselves altogether from this world. In fact, they were very much concerned with it. First of all, the Puritan faiths were, on the whole, intensely communal, and the communities were strongly conscious of themselves as the right-thinking core of society. Thus they not only contended fiercely for their rights, but they believed that they had the special privilege and duty to purify society of its sinfulness and to guide it into the right paths of government. Thus they were important politically, and moreover their belief in elected authority made them very disturbing to the accepted beliefs that the only right and practicable government was through anointed sovereigns, who were God's representatives in earthly affairs however they might depart from their obligations. Secondly, the Puritans believed that the 'saint' predestined to salvation demonstrated this by the course of his life, and even that God's favour would show itself in his earthly prosperity. Thus they were encouraged to a life of industry on both spiritual and earthly grounds, and since a life of industry was best conducted in trade and commerce, it is natural that the most enthusiastic Puritans were found among the middle classes of the towns. Thus the other-worldly doctrine of predestination and the economic fact of capitalism have an intimate relationship which is not intrinsically discernible in either. Finally, the common belief that Puritanism was hostile to the arts is not entirely true. Part of the opposition of the Puritan government of the City of London to the theatre was purely prudential: the theatres easily became centres of disorder, and in times of plague they were dangerous centres of infection. The Puritan intellectuals were not indifferent to humanism; Calvin's first book had been a commentary on the Stoic philosopher Seneca, and Calvinism had much in common with the Stoic creed that pain and pleasure must be ignored for the sake of the sovereign demands of virtue. There is an element of Puritan severity in the most eminent of the 16th-century humanist poets, Edmund Spenser,* and in the 17th century John Milton* (1608–74) is the outstanding example of a writer who was profoundly imbued with the austere ethic of Puritanism and at the same time with the high learning of humanism. It is true that Milton was a pronounced individualist who by the time he came to write *Paradise Lost* had abandoned all distinct Puritan creeds for his own personal beliefs. Nonetheless, he had risked everything for the Puritan cause in its most dramatic phase, and his great epic is a meeting point of what Renaissance humanists believed to be the highest achievement of man – the sublime heroic poem – and the Puritan demand that literature must above all serve the Holy Spirit.

3.2.3 *Renaissance philosophy and its influence*

Richard Hooker was able to balance philosophy and religion by an unusual combination of conservatism and Renaissance suppleness of reason; he could appeal to a more embracing system of ideas than that relied upon by the Puritans, and at the same time he undermined their bigotry. But at least Hooker was arguing in favour of religion. Other Renaissance thinkers discovered the immense scope of the reasoning faculty when it was not serving religion, and their exertions tended in the long run to weaken the hold of religious belief on men's minds.

This disruption of the union between religion and philosophy took effect in three kinds of thinker. First there was a direct challenge from those – chiefly Italian – thinkers whom today we would loosely think of as scientists. Machiavelli* demonstrated in *The Prince* (1513) what politicians could achieve if they acted without respect for moral or human law, but solely with regard to the shortest and most effective means of gaining their own ends. Galileo* early in the 17th century, showed what the solar system looked like through his telescope, without respect for theological doctrines about what it ought to look like. Neither of these, nor Copernicus*, the astronomer whose theory anticipated Galileo's experiments, was concerned to overthrow traditional theology; they were specialist thinkers who happened to show that the part of the universe and of human experience with which each was concerned did not correspond to the image of the whole which the theological philosophers had hitherto preached. Thinkers of a second kind did concern themselves with the 'whole' of the universe. These were the Platonists,* such as the Italian Ficino (1433–99), who based their philosophy not only on Plato but on Plato's still more mystical successors, such as Plotinus (3rd century AD). They also did not intend to supplant Christian theology, but they tended to supplement it with their own mysticism and thus introduced into it an extraneous element which had its independent appeal. Thus, imaginative works influenced by Platonism, such as Sidney's *Arcadia** and Spenser's *Faerie Queene**, are in many ways more Platonic than they are Christian, though both Sidney and Spenser were devout Protestants. The third kind of philosopher was more important in his effect on mental attitudes than either of the other two, and the most illustrious example this time is an Englishman, Francis Bacon* (1561–1626). His influence was directed to changing men's ideas about the field in which the human reason could operate to the best purpose. Men had long acknowledged that there are several kinds of cause in nature: there is the 'First Cause' of all reality; there are the 'Second Causes' operating in the daily observed process of change; and there are the 'Final Causes', or purposes for which things exist. Medieval thought had given much attention to the First Cause of all things, namely God, and also to Final Causes, but it had neglected Second Causes – the immediate explanations of phenomena – either because they were irrelevant to their concern with the universal whole, or because they were somehow explained as logical consequences of their total philosophy. But Bacon believed that Second Causes particularly required investigation, because they are accessible to reason, whereas the First Cause is accessible only to faith. Moreover the discovery of Second Causes gave knowledge, and knowledge is the secret of power. Bacon thus openly made that division between religion and philosophy, forcing the mind to separate them as fields for quite different kinds of thinking and feeling, which has lasted till the present day.

Of all the thinkers in these schools of thought, Machiavelli made the most distinct, personal impression on literature. The reason is obvious: he presented a new and shocking conception of the human being. It is true that politicians have always behaved as though the end justifies the means, and never more so than in the 16th century, but Machiavelli seemed frankly to preach immoral conduct as right conduct. In supposing that he did this the Elizabethan English were unjust to him in only one respect: they ignored the fact that he was a great patriot who strongly desired the unification of his country and who knew that the hope of this was a futile one in the face of the unscrupulousness of those giant intruders, France and Spain, unless every means for realizing it was judged, not according to its morality, but according to its expediency. Extracted from the practically hopeless predicament which his country was facing, Machiavelli appeared in a unique sense to be an emancipated man – one who feared neither God nor the Devil, but was equally ready to serve either, or both at once if it suited his personal aims. But the way in which he, or characters modelled on him, is presented in Elizabethan dramas shows that his ideas were not merely feared and hated but were also regarded with fascination. The Renaissance mind was in love with action, and the Machiavellian, totally liberated from moral restraint, was logically the most effective man of action of them all. Moreover the Renaissance – or at least the Renaissance Englishmen under Elizabeth – admired men who committed themselves against destiny, as Marlowe's Tamburlaine* commits himself to mortal ambition and his Faustus* to earthly knowledge, and as Shakespeare's Antony* commits himself to love and his Coriolanus* commits himself to fame. The Machiavellian, like Marlowe's Barabbas in *The Jew of Malta** and Shakespeare's Richard III*, commits himself to getting the better of his fellows by any means. In so far as he is evil his downfall is dramatically desirable, but in so far as his total commitment means that he has more vitality than his fellows, who, like most men, compromise between good and evil, this downfall has its tragic side. His candid rejection of all morality made him a more popular character than his counterpart, the Puritan, who declared that morality was everything but that only he and his fellows could lay claim to it; the Puritans figured in the dramas only as objects of satire.

In contrast to both the devilry of the Machiavellian and the bigotry of the Puritan was the deliberately cultivated nobility of the self-conscious nobleman. Such Platonic idealism took three main forms: the emblems of virtue represented by the knight-heroes of Spenser's *Faerie Queene*, with their ancestry in Arthurian legend; the passionate lover who idealizes his mistress as the embodiment of all beauty like Sidney's Astrophel*, the Renaissance representative of the medieval courtly lover; and the mage, like Shakespeare's Prospero in *The Tempest**, who has achieved supernatural powers by years of contemplation which enable him to combine ideal virtue with ideal wisdom. Such perfection of moral beauty was however restricted to the noble class, for the traditions of the Great Chain of Being operated morally and spiritually as well as physically and socially. Socially, indeed, only the aristocrat who was free from the necessity to earn his bread had the opportunity to cultivate – as a Sidney* or a Raleigh* did – the many-sided excellence which the courtly and the Platonic ideal demanded. There was also the belief that nobility of nature was inherited with noble blood. Caliban, in *The Tempest*, is bestial because he has base origins, but the 'Salvage Man' of the woods in *The Faerie Queene* has noble instincts because he is of noble birth, though he has grown up like an animal. Perdita in *The Winter's Tale** grows up with the virtues of a princess because she is one, though she believes she is a shepherd's daughter; Prospero's daughter, Miranda, has had, apparently from infancy, an innate sweetness of spirit which wild nature can strengthen but cannot spoil.

There were, in fact, two attitudes to wild nature in the Renaissance; one was inherited from the Middle Ages, and the other educed from classical literature. In medieval times, nature was held to be originally from God, and as a procreative principle could be personified as a goddess, as in Chaucer's *Parliament of Fowls*; on the other hand, wild nature was also fallen nature since Adam's expulsion from Paradise, and this was degraded and degrading. Against such nature, man had to struggle for his salvation, and this was why the Church preached that celibacy was a higher vocation than matrimony. The Greeks and the Romans, on the contrary, had, in their pastoral* poetry, held an elevated view of life in natural surroundings because it encouraged virtues which the city corrupted, and the Renaissance poets found such pastoralism a congenial medium for exemplifying the pure virtues of Platonic idealism. It is true that they could only do this by envisaging such a world of shepherds and shepherdesses in classical terms, and with a free ornamental use of classical myth. Actual English pastoral life belonged still to the medieval fallen world, and was best brought into the picture for ironic contrast, as Shakespeare brings it into *As You Like It** and *The Winter's Tale.** Thus two pastoral myths were brought into association during the Renaissance: the literary myth of the Golden Age from the classics, and the myth of Adam in Paradise from the Bible.

In its attitude to nature, the Renaissance mind was thus in a dilemma: nature in myth attracted the imagination, but nature in reality repelled it. This dilemma, however, only covered a still deeper one: the Renaissance mind was divided between action and self-doubt. Human energies had been liberated in many ways – in commerce, politics, art and science. The most representative activity of the age was perhaps exploration, typified by the great voyages of Da Gama, Magellan, Columbus, Drake, Frobisher, Gilbert and the rest. The deepest impulse behind such exploration was desire for mastery of the outer world, but while this outer world magnetized men, the great spiritual tradition of Christianity held them back, for it taught that the Final Cause or purpose of man was to relate himself in humility to the First Cause. It was the Devil that showed Christ in the wilderness 'all the kingdoms of the world in a moment of time' and tempted him with the words 'If thou therefore wilt worship me, all shall be thine' (*Luke* 4). It is the temptation of Marlowe's Faustus. The solution to the dilemma was offered by Francis Bacon, with immense consequences for the future of British culture. Nature, he reasoned, need be neither worshipped nor abhorred; it need only be understood.

'Men fear death as children fear to go in the dark; and as that natural fear is increased with tales, so is the other.' This opening sentence of Bacon's essay on Death is typical of his dry, cool, confident wisdom. The *Essays*, the first collection of which appeared in 1597 and the last in 1625, are essentially practical comments on life and its conduct, and it is the temper of mind that they reveal so clearly and so tersely which has made them memorable, rather than the substance of their thought. This is true also of Bacon's philosophical works: *The Advancement of Learning* (1605), *Novum Organum* (1620), and *De Augmentis Scientiarum* (1623). He was the first great propagandist for scientific thought, yet he ignored the great scientists of his own day, such as Galileo; he did not fully understand the principles of scientific method, and he offered no new and comprehensive scheme of ideas. On the contrary, he dealt with the traditional religious system of thought by evading it. It has often been the practice in English politics to get rid of a powerful but unwanted politician in the House of Commons by giving him a title and 'promoting' him to the House of Lords, which has prestige but little power; Bacon did something like this to religion. The great mysteries, he declares in Book IX of *De Augmentis*, he leaves to Faith; his own concern is with 'the small vessel of human reason', and how best to use it in the world around us. Thus he awakened no conflict, for he refused to engage in one; he merely argued that men could use their minds much more effectively than they were doing. In *Novum Organum* he describes the chief obstacles to the proper use of the mind as 'idols': there are Idols of the Tribe which are common to all human beings and include wishful thinking and prejudice; the Idols of the Cave, which arise from individual bias and predilection; the Idols of the Market-place which are caused by mistaken uses of language; and Idols of the Theatre which are fallacious systems of thought. Against these idols he advocates empiricism – the formation of generalizations about nature on the basis of experience and experiment. This is the 'inductive' method of acquiring knowledge of what were known as Second or Immediate Causes of Phenomena. In the Preface to *De Augmentis* he admits that such thinking may at first seem to lead towards atheism, but he promises that deeper experience of it will show the thinker that 'the upper link of Nature's chain is fastened to Jupiter's throne'. By thus invoking the Great Chain of Being, the traditional conception of the design of the universe, Bacon shows that he assumes an ultimate goal to the advancement of learning. It is, however, a very distant one, and by making it so distant Bacon also distances the religious emotions that it awakens. Thus his important influence became not so much philosophical as psychological; he not merely separated philosophy from religion, but the reason from the feelings.

In *The Seventeenth Century Background*, Chapter III, Basil Willey remarks: 'Bacon was pleading for science in an age dominated by "religion"; Browne is already – at least in the *Religio Medici* – pleading for religion in an age that was beginning to be dominated by science.' Sir Thomas Browne's* 'The Religion of a Physician' was published in 1642, and it shows a mind which is intensely interested in natural phenomena and at the same time deeply excited imaginatively by the religious mysteries of the universe. However, the deliberate art of his richly eloquent style already shows his religious emotion to be to some extent a self-consciously 'poetic' one. Browne is not a Metaphysical* in the same sense as was Bacon's immediate contemporary, the poet and preacher John Donne*, whose emotions and intellect are more closely related to each other, both in his verse and in his sermons. By the middle of the century, men's minds were more widely perplexed by the scriptures as evidence of Divine Truth than they had been hitherto. Some thinkers evaded the problem by great concessions to rationalism. Earliest among these was Lord Herbert* of Cherbury (1583–1648), brother of the great Anglican Metaphysical poet George Herbert. In his book *De Veritate* ('Concerning the Truth', 1624) he maintained the existence of a 'natural religion' discoverable by reason from a study of the religions of the world. He has been called the Father of Deism*, a belief widespread among intellectuals of the 18th century, which sought to establish supernatural religion on a rational basis. Even Milton, the devoted Puritan and believer in a divinely inspired Bible, declares in his posthumously published *Treatise Concerning the Christian Religion* that the truth of the Bible is not to be taken literally; God has 'accommodated' himself to our understanding, and shown in his Book in figurative language how man should conceive him morally and spiritually. This 'moral and spiritual' truth is what is presented in *Paradise Lost*; it explains why Milton, who had known and admired Galileo, still uses the pre-Copernican, Ptolemaic* pattern of the universe in his poem. The literal, scientific fact is not his concern; he is occupied with the spiritual truth,

> *That, to the height of this great argument,*
> *I may assert Eternal Providence,*
> *And justify the ways of God to men.*

The great fact of Divine Revelation which is central to Christianity was being increasingly interpreted as an inward experience in the believer. Even Lord Herbert found it in an inner certainty not unlike the faith of the Puritans.

3·3
The Age of Reason: 1650–1790

3.3.1 *The philosophers*

Bacon started the process in which reason became separated from the feelings. The century and a half between the execution of Charles I of England in 1649 and that of Louis XVI of France in 1793 was dominated by philosophers who at first explored the empire of reason, and later defined the limitations of this empire. The Age of Reason was not, however, one of inertia of feeling. The prose of the great British philosophers of the period – Thomas Hobbes* (1588–1679), John Locke* (1632–1704), George Berkeley* (1685–1753), and David Hume* (1711–76) – has a life and ease which arises from the release of feeling and is incompatible with the suppression of it. The thinkers of the Age of Reason despised the sort of learned man – typified in their opinion by the 'scholastics' of the Middle Ages – who never relates his ideas to his experience, and thus produces mountainous but worthless systems such as Bacon stigmatized as 'the Idols of the Theatre'; philosophy, they maintained, was for the world, and thus it must talk to a man's feelings as well as to his brain. If they separated reason from the feelings and judgement from the imagination, this was because they believed that the feelings should be cultivated like plants in a garden, which, left to itself, becomes a jungle in which the baser vegetation destroys the nobler. This is why the word 'enthusiasm', especially the 'enthusiasm' of the Puritans* and Methodists*, was always used disparagingly in the 18th century; it meant an outpouring of feeling unrestrained by reason. Reason was the great instrument of cultivation; its separation from the feelings did not mean disconnection from them, but control.

That the reason should rule the passions was indeed maintained by the medieval philosophers also: when the dramatists of the age of Shakespeare compared the mind to the state, with reason as its lawful sovereign, they were speaking in traditional terms, not anticipating the Enlightenment. But just as in a medieval monarchy the king was conceived to be the head of merely a section of a much larger hierarchy extending to God himself – otherwise he would not be truly a king – so the reason of the individual was unavailing to him if it did not subscribe to faith, and faith – through revelation – appealed beyond reason to the emotions and the imagination. But in the Age of Reason, according at least to John Locke, the most influential of the philosophers, this order was reversed, and faith itself had to subscribe to reason. Such immense reliance on reason came from its now evident victories in science from Copernicus* (1473–1543) to Isaac Newton* (1642–1727); these victories were given official recognition by the establishment under the king's patronage of the Royal Society* for Promoting Natural Knowledge in 1662. Addison*, himself a mediocre thinker, was an admirable popularizer of leading ideas, and he expresses the feeling of the intellectuals of his time in his essay on 'Imagination and Science' (*Spectator* 420, 1712):

> *The Understanding, indeed, opens an infinite Space on every side of us, but the Imagination, after a few faint Efforts, is immediately at a stand, and finds herself swallowed up in the Immensity of the Void that surrounds it: Our Reason can pursue a Particle of Matter through an infinite variety of Divisions, but the Fancy soon loses sight of it, and feels in itself a Kind of Chasm, that wants to be filled with Matter of a more sensible Bulk.*

The Age of Reason was thus felt to be not merely the liberation of the mind, but the liberation of the whole personality, and consequently the perfectly civilized society was felt to be for the first time within reach.

However, it is convenient here to distinguish between two conceptions of the function of reason. According to the first, it is the faculty which directly apprehends the truth, and its effect is to unify the individual's opinions into single-minded belief. According to the second it is the instrument for the destruction of error, and it operates analytically. Each function, of course, implies the other, and in many writers the two functions cannot be clearly distinguished. Yet even if the difference is chiefly one between attitudes to the purpose of reason rather than between the ways in which it actually operates, it is important because it separates British thinkers into opposing schools from the 17th century to the 20th. Very generally, we may say that the religious thinkers and the imaginative writers have tended to adopt the first attitude to reason, seeing it as primarily an integrative function, and the philosophers and the scientists have adopted the second attitude, seeing reason as an analytic instrument. During the so-called Age of Reason it was the second attitude which prevailed, not merely among the philosophers but among the majority of thinking men.

The first great exponent of the analytic use of reason was the French philosopher Descartes*, whose *Discours de la Méthode* appeared in 1637. Descartes set himself to discover an unassailable starting-point for philosophical inquiry – a truth that it was impossible to doubt – and he found it in the formula: 'Cogito, ergo sum' (I think; therefore I exist). Having proved at least his own existence to himself, he set himself to prove the existence of the external world. He discovered that the evidence of the senses is illusory, and that though external nature can indeed be known, it can only be apprehended as a certainty through the intellect. Descartes then authenticated intellectual knowledge by an independent proof of the existence of God. This last proof, however, is neither original nor compellingly convincing, and so Descartes leaves us with the mind and external nature in very insecure relationship. This gap between the mind and nature remained in the thought of British philosophers; the analytic reason, by itself, was unable to fill it. The tendency was to affirm one side rather than the other: either that all is matter or that all is mind, but the choice seems to have been dictated less by the force of abstract reasoning than by the circumstances surrounding the philosopher's life.

Thus Thomas Hobbes was a materialist because the events of his lifetime caused him to believe that men have no control over their sensual appetites, however they may disguise them; he deduced from this that the 'state of nature' is one of brutal anarchy, and that peace and civilization are artificially produced. He was born in 1588, the year of the attempted invasion by the Spanish Armada*, and he declared that the crisis was responsible for the timidity of his temperament; he grew to middle age under progressively weakening governments which had eventually foundered in the Civil Wars* of 1642–51. In 1651 he published his treatise *Leviathan**, in which he argued that strong government is necessary to human happiness. Life without government would be 'nasty, brutish and short', and he reasoned that human beings had been sensible enough to invent government by making a 'contract' with one another to surrender a quantity of liberty in order to safeguard their lives and property. Hobbes did not believe that men were capable of sustained will-power for good or evil; they were solely material, and the puppets of their material desires. Consequently, even a tyranny was better than a weak government, for it released the passions of a single man, whereas weak governments let loose the passions of many. He was not, it is true, bold enough to admit himself an atheist – still an unthinkable admission to be made publicly – but he asserts that it is for the public good that men should accept the faith of the ruler of the country.

Just as Hobbes was influenced in the formation of this cynically defensive philosophy by the historical events of his lifetime, so John Locke was influenced in an opposite way by the events of 1688. This was the year of the 'Glorious Revolution', when King James II was expelled from the throne without bloodshed (at least in England) and Parliament, then representing the secure, propertied classes of the country, took to itself the essential powers of government which it has retained to the present day. Almost all his important work was written within six or seven years of that peaceful yet crucial event, which, to Locke, brought up as he had been on the Parliamentarian and Puritan side of the Civil War, was the start of a new age of hope. The Revolution of 1688*, indeed, settled the facts of British society and politics for a century, and for just so long the philosophy of Locke dominated the majority of educated English minds.

Like Hobbes, Locke was a realistic thinker, but whereas history taught the former that freedom and tolerance are impossible, it gave the latter faith in them. His two *Treatises of Government* (1690) are a defence of the form of government which the Revolution had established. He follows Hobbes in postulating a 'social contract' as the original basis of all governments, but he differs from Hobbes in regarding the ruler as a trustee of power for the people, who have the right to remove him if they consider that he has broken the trust committed to him. His *Letters concerning Toleration* (1689–92) argue that nothing is gained and great dangers are risked by religious intolerance. The reasonableness of his views on the two questions that had most tormented the British Isles in the 17th century is consistent with the dispassionate argument of his basic work, the *Essay concerningHuman Understanding** (1690). This is almost as radical a theory as Descartes' *Discours*, but it is constructed in a different way. Like Descartes, Locke regards awareness of the self as the basis of knowledge, but he assumes that the mind is originally like a blank sheet of paper, and he goes on to investigate how it builds up its knowledge of the outside world. Awareness of the world reaches us through the senses, but true knowledge is built up by comparing and relating to one another these 'ideas' that we experience at first in a simple form. He further maintains that the qualities of objects are of two kinds: those about which there can be general agreement, such as weight and size, and those which are subject to difference of judgement, such as colour and beauty. The former are the 'primary' qualities of things, and the latter are the 'secondary' qualities.

Though Berkeley was later to point out that this distinction between 'primary' (objective and more real) and 'secondary' (subjective and less real) qualities is fallacious, the theory is consistent with ordinary experience, and it had considerable influence on 18th-century imaginative writers. Defoe*, for example, conveys his realistic fiction largely through detailed descriptions of 'primary qualities' and thus gives an impression of being severely factual, and Swift*, in the same way, gives an illusion of plausibility to the fantastic countries visited by Gulliver. But – though the geniality of Locke's style prevents one from feeling it – the suggestion that the primary qualities of objects are the real truth about them implies a world of facts without values. Locke, indeed, never pushes his theories to extremes, so that he never actually says that art and poetry are irrelevant to human experience, but he does say that the reason or judgment is the ultimate measure of truth, so that even divine revelation – the reality of which he accepts – must be intelligible to the reason, for if it is not, how are we to know that it is divine? His conception of morality is similarly practical: initially the human will is motivated by the desire for happiness, but he does not identify this desire with the brutal satisfaction of the appetites, as Hobbes does. For Locke, whether or not men are purely material, they have will-power capable of restraining their appetites for the sake of a higher good, and it is by means of this that God draws men upwards to himself. Yet God, though Locke required him as logically indispensable to the fact of the existence of the world, is not an immanent reality in this system; even revelation has a function chiefly for unreasoning, uneducated humanity. In spirit, Locke's philosophy is content with this world, and offers contentment in it in specifically practical ways.

George Berkeley observed that Locke's ideas did nothing to mend the duality of mind and matter which had originated with Descartes. He demonstrated that things and people are real to us to the extent that they are known to us in our minds; from this he argues that it is mind-stuff, the world of the spirit, that is the true reality. His aim was to counteract the atheism which he considered implicit in the philosophies of Descartes and Locke, but his reasoning is philosophically persuasive without appealing, as Locke's does, to practical common sense; Johnson considered that he refuted Berkeley's ideas when he remarked to an exponent of them: 'Pray, Sir, don't leave us; for we may perhaps forget to think of you, and then you will cease to exist.' David Hume was more disconcerting. He carried the reliance on reason so far that he exposed its limits. Even the apparently logical relationships of cause and effect are the consequence of habitual association in our minds, not demonstrable realities, and in the essay *Of Miracles* he maintains that Christianity, far from being 'reasonable', actually defies reason in the claim it makes upon belief, so that religious faith can only exist in the mind by a continuing miracle. Men are therefore thrown back upon their feelings, and in the later 18th century it is the culture of the feelings rather than that of the reason which preoccupies them.

3.3.2 *Reason and Nature in religion and society*

Under the influence of Locke, the first half of the 18th century seemed to achieve a newly unified conception of man. Religion was in danger of collapsing into an optimistic worldly wisdom, according to which the conduct of life had to be guided by reason, and reason had to be based on judgement of what contributes to human happiness. God, in this view, becomes an intellectual hypothesis, chiefly useful for understanding how the universe 'hangs together' in that orderly design which, inherited from the past in the form of the 'Great Chain of Being', seemed to be increasingly demonstrated as fact by the scientists ('natural philosophers' as they were called) such as Isaac Newton. However, his serene confidence was not as secure as it seemed. All through the century it was countered by other currents of thought, and in the end nature, conceived as the best of all possible worlds, proved treacherous to the optimistic rationalists. Nature, we may say, resumed its authority by removing itself from the domain of reason, and since the reliance on reason had made man the measure of value, this change mediated a new kind of spirituality of thinking.

However, early in the second half of the 17th century, before Locke wrote, reason seemed to one group of thinkers to be the means by which true spirituality could be restored to religious thinking. These were the theologians known as the Cambridge Platonists*: John Smith (1618–52), Nathaniel Culverwell (d 1651 ?), Benjamin Whichcote (1609–83), Henry More (1614–87), and Ralph Cudworth (1617–88). They sought to oppose two distinct tendencies of their time: Puritan bigotry, based on literal interpretation of the Bible, and the materialism of Hobbes and Descartes which tended to atheism. They were Anglican clergymen who favoured the Puritan side in their ideals of sobriety and sincerity in religious worship and behaviour, but they were opposed to the Puritan emphasis on the sinfulness of man; against this they asserted a natural disposition to virtue in human beings. At the same time they countered the Puritans' literal use of biblical texts as the sole authority for religious doctrine by interpreting them as lucid philosophical statements appealing to the reason rather than the emotions; thereby, in the tradition of Hooker, they hoped to remove doctrine from the bitterness of heated controversy and restore to it the function of spiritual enlightenment. This reasonableness with which they countered Puritanism necessarily bore a different aspect in their opposition to the philosophers, who themselves relied upon reason. Whereas Descartes and Hobbes had used reason analytically for the destruction of fallacies, the Cambridge Platonists used it as Plato had – as the faculty for the direct apprehension of spiritual truth. Like Berkeley later, they preached that the heart of reality is God, but whereas Berkeley did this analytically, by exposing the fallacies in Locke, they relied on the religious tradition according to which God could be known only through direct experience; for this experience the reason was merely an instrument and was secondary to the Christian revelation and divine grace as they are felt by the individual. Such experience is clearly mystical, and vulnerable to misinterpretation by a writer who is without mysticism but who finds the ideas behind the mysticism congenial. Such a writer was Anthony Ashley Cooper, the third earl of Shaftesbury* and grandson of the first earl, whom Dryden had satirized in *Absalom and Achitophel**.

Shaftesbury's ideas were much admired in his own time in both England and France, though he has been little read since. In his writings, the mysticism of the Platonists is diluted by the rationalism of Locke, and converted into the abstract religion of deism.* He follows the optimistic view of human nature with which the Platonists had countered the Puritans, and he adopts the optimistic view of nature itself implicit in Locke. Nature he sees as essentially good and sublime, and since man has a natural propensity to virtue, he concludes that it is by following nature that he can best become virtuous. He opposed the reasoned pessimism of Hobbes by pointing out that the latter had arbitrarily chosen to judge humanity by its baser impulses. Not only do men possess natural affections, but these affections have developed in the course of history with the growth of civilization, so that they have extended from the sexes to the family, from the family to the clan, and from the clan to the nation. Religion is thus natural – as, a century before, Lord Herbert had said it was – and revelation, indispensable to the Cambridge Platonists, becomes for Shaftesbury almost redundant.

Shaftesbury's enthusiasm for his 'natural religion' and the enthusiasm of many of his contemporaries for his ideas can only be understood today if we appreciate what nature and the idea of the 'Great Chain of Being' meant to them. From earlier sections of this essay we have seen that western Europe adopted this idea from Plato, and that it was central to the thought of the Middle Ages and the Renaissance. Then it was useful in giving a sense of order amid the otherwise bewildering proliferation of natural phenomena, and in adding a moral significance to the differences among human beings brought about by the social structure. However, in the hundred years between 1650 and 1750 it was not only found useful in new ways, but it was found inspiring. The scientists were finding it useful as a means of classifying and arranging their discoveries, and for other men this meant that it offered an infinite field for exploration by the human mind. Man, in fact, could now participate in the Chain of Being through his reason, whereas hitherto he had been restricted to his limited section of it. It was accepted, indeed, that he could never know the whole scheme, but this itself became a basis for optimism, for it seemed to some minds to solve the problem of evil in the universe; evil merely *seems* to exist, because man is not in a position to understand the significance of what looks like imperfection in the whole plan. Man, therefore, as Pope says in his *Essay on Man*, must stop complaining:

Cease then, nor order imperfection name:
Our proper bliss depends on what we blame.
Know thy own point: this kind, this due degree
Of blindness, weakness, Heaven bestows on thee.

Submit, in this, or any other sphere,
Secure to be as blest as thou canst bear:
Safe in the hand of one Dispensing Power,
Or in the natal, or the mortal hour.
All Nature is but art, unknown to thee;
All chance, direction, which thou canst not see;
All discord, harmony not understood;
All partial evil, universal good:
And, spite of pride, in erring reason's spite,
One truth is clear, Whatever is, is right.

However, there were many 18th-century thinkers who resisted this optimism which made morality so 'natural' that it was merely a part of rational behaviour, and accepted evil so readily that it became 'good'. Bishop Joseph Butler (1692–1752), in his *Analogy of Religion* (1736) sought to re-establish the central importance of divine revelation in religious belief by demonstrating that faith in the great order of nature was basically no more rational; faith in the latter was facile, by his argument, and not worth having, and so was the morality (Shaftesbury's kind of morality) based upon it. John Wesley* (1703–91), the great reformer, demonstrated by the extent of his Methodist* religious revival amongst the poor that the 'natural religion' which made much of reason and little of suffering was meaningless to the majority of the nation, who were too ignorant to philosophize and too wretched to be serene about wretchedness.

Besides these, three writers stand out above all others in the 18th century as challengers to its self-satisfaction. These are Jonathan Swift* (1667–1745), Samuel Johnson* (1709–84) and Edmund Burke* (1729–97).

Swift was an Anglican clergyman, but his famous writings are all satirical, and not ostensibly religious. There are clearly reasons for this. His public were too assured in their half religious, half materialistic philosophy to respond vividly to direct religious appeals; either they would translate such appeals effortlessly into their own abstract idiom, or they would despise them as they despised the 'enthusiasm' of the Puritans, against whom the age was in such strong reaction. For that matter, Swift himself belonged to this reaction, and clearly had no desire to discourage it. His parable of the 'Three Coats' in *The Tale of a Tub** (1704) is about the Reformation; the three brothers in it – Jack, Martin, and Peter – stand for Calvinism, Anglicanism and Catholicism respectively. Only Martin comes out at all well from the parable, but Swift's invective against Jack, the Puritan, is markedly more vehement than that against Peter, the Catholic. However, the chief objects of Swift's attack are the deists and natural philosophers who believe that they have achieved 'enlightenment', and the men of fashion who believe that they are themselves the perfection of civilization. Both groups thought themselves the late, fine flower of human history, but Swift thought them arrogant, heartless, and often extremely stupid. They believed in analytic reason, but Swift shows in the

'Digression on Madness' in *The Tale of a Tub* that they did not carry their belief to its logical conclusion; if they did, they would be horrified at their self-discovery. At the end of *Gulliver's Travels**, he makes his fine gentleman grovel to kiss a horse's hoof, in token of the humiliation of the whole human race. Swift, like Hume later in the century, though with the weapons of the satirist and not those of the philosopher, used reason against the cult of reason, and they both leave the reader with the feeling that his resources have been emptied away.

Johnson was a devout Anglican, more devout than Swift, but like Swift he was also a product of the Age of Reason. So much was he a product of it, indeed, that for the last twenty years of his life he was generally revered as almost an embodiment of the culture of his generation. He was this, but it was a culture with more body to it than the aspect of it exhibited by the deists. Of Pope's summing up of the deistic faith in The *Essay on Man*, he remarks: 'Never was penury of knowledge and vulgarity of sentiment so happily disguised'. It is however important to remember that Pope's deism in the *Essay on Man* was unconscious and largely attributable to his friend Bolingbroke. Johnson is much more outspokenly indignant in his famous review of Soame Jenyns's deistic book, *A Free Enquiry into the Nature and Origin of Evil* (1757). Jenyns relies on the theory of the Great Chain of Being for his argument that what we call evil is really those parts of the 'plan' of the universe which we do not understand and which disturb our comfort. Johnson exposes fallacies in the theory more lucidly than they had ever been exposed before, but he is especially scornful of Jenyns's argument that our sufferings may (somehow justifiably) be for the good of beings higher in the scale of the Chain: 'Many of the books that now crowd the world may be justly suspected to be written for some invisible order of beings, for surely they are of no use to any of the corporeal inhabitants of the world. The only end of writing is to enable the readers better to enjoy life, or better to endure it: and how will either of those be put more in our power by him who tells us, that we are puppets, of which some creature not much wiser than ourselves manages the wires?'

Burke wrote his greatest work, *Reflections on the Revolution in France** (1790) just after the outbreak of the French Revolution*. The intellectual inspiration for this event was largely the extreme rationalism of the Age of Reason. Ever since Locke first made his strong impression on French intellectuals such as Voltaire early in the century, they had been concluding that a tyrannous government could legitimately be overthrown by the people whom it oppressed, and could be remodelled by 'the light of reason'. But Burke, in deep anxiety about the extent of British sympathy with the Revolution, argues that the revolutionary view is based on a fallacious idea of society; it presupposes that society is a kind of machine which can be destroyed and reconstructed according to a new and improved design. Society for Burke, on the contrary, is organic – that is to say, a natural growth, more like a tree than a machine. It can be reformed, and the conditions for reform should exist within its structure, since 'A state without the means of some change is without the means of its conservation.' But a society has deep roots in ancient soil, and to ignore them is to reduce life to the brutality which Hobbes had described as being indeed the state of nature. Addressing the French, Burke writes:

> *If, as I suspect, modern letters owe more than they are always willing to own to ancient manners, so do other interests which we value full as much as they are worth. Even commerce, and trade, and manufacture, the gods of our economical politicians, are themselves but creatures; are themselves but effects, which, as first causes, we choose to worship. They certainly grew under the same shade in which learning flourished. They too may decay with their natural protecting principles. . . . Where trade and manufactures are wanting to a people, and the spirit of nobility and religion remains, sentiment supplies, and not always ill supplies, their place; and if commerce and the arts should be lost in an experiment to try how well a state may stand without these old fundamental principles, what sort of a thing must be a nation of gross, stupid, ferocious, and, at the same time, poor and sordid barbarians, destitute of religion, honour, or manly pride, possessing nothing at present, and hoping for nothing hereafter?*

Thus politics, culture, commerce and religion constituted an interdependent whole for Burke, and change must have respect for this whole. It is vain to suppose that politics can be taken apart for the improvement of national prosperity without regard for traditional beliefs and ways of life; if that is done, civilization and the welfare of all must be destroyed. Burke asserts, in fact, in his book, that analytic reason is helpless to improve the human condition without reason considered as sympathetic understanding: the intellect must join with the imagination. No doubt, as Tom Paine* was to point out in his *Rights of Man* (1792), Burke himself misconceived the situation in France, but his view that a society has to be sympathetically understood before it can be radically reformed is nonetheless as wise as it is nobly expressed. Thus the 19th century opened with a new duality: that of Reason and Imagination.

3·4

The Age of Change: 1790–1914

3·4·1 *The Romantic Imagination*

There is No Natural Religion (1788)

The Argument

Man has no notion of moral fitness but from education. Naturally he is only a natural organ subject to sense.

I

Man cannot naturally perceive but through his natural or bodily organs.

II

Man by his reasoning power can only compare and judge of what he has already perceived.

III

From a perception of only 3 senses or 3 elements none could deduce a fourth or fifth.

IV

None could have other than natural or organic thoughts if he had none but organic perceptions.

V

Man's desires are limited by his perceptions: none can desire what he has not perceived.

VI

The desires and perceptions of man, untaught by any thing but organs of sense, must be limited to objects of sense.

Conclusion

If it were not for the Poetic or Prophetic Character, the Philosophical and Experimental would soon be at the ratio of all things, and stand still, unable to do other than repeat the same dull round over again.

William Blake* (1757–1827)

Blake was the earliest and the most uncompromising of the six poets – the others being Wordsworth*, Coleridge*, Byron*, Shelley*, and Keats* – whom we nowadays call the great Romantics. He was not in any usual sense a philosopher, but, as the Conclusion to these six propositions shows, a professed visionary. The propositions are a synopsis of the ideas of Locke, but the title shows that Blake intends to use Locke's own ideas in order to refute them. Locke, and his disciple, the psychologist David Hartley* (1705–57), assumed that though our knowledge derives initially from our physical senses, nonetheless we can build up a system of moral and spiritual ideas on the basis of these perceptions. The function of education, as they thought, is to guide the mind towards spiritual truths by instructing it in the appropriate association of ideas. Blake shows that this assumption, on their theory of the human faculties, is illogical. The theory, on the contrary, if it proves anything, proves that reality is all material. If reality is not – and Blake assumes that it is not – then Locke's account of the mind is incomplete.

At the time of the French Revolution, Blake had among his friends some of the chief rationalists of the day, such as the chemist, Joseph Priestley* and the political philosophers, William Godwin* and Tom Paine*. Like them, he was at first a strong supporter of the Revolution, for they all believed that the régime that was being overthrown in France was a gigantic and deceitful system of repression, but whereas his rationalist friends believed that society would henceforth flourish by the single light of reason, Blake saw, or soon came to see, that human nature itself lives from contradictions, and that to impose the rule of reason upon it – even when you have destroyed the rapacious elements and institutions in society – was only to impose upon it a new system of enslavement. In *The Marriage of Heaven and Hell** (1790), he writes: 'Without contraries is no progression. Attraction and Repulsion, Reason and Energy, Love and Hate, are necessary to Human existence.' Human life is thus an endless warfare of contrary forces within the mind, and he dramatized these in the mythology of his 'Prophetic Books'. It was a private mythology, for two reasons. The first is that the 18th century had destroyed the habit of mythological expression, except as a literary ornament; for the Age of Reason respected only those truths that could be expressed as plain statement. The other reason is that Blake felt himself to be exploring the drama of the mind in entirely new terms, for even Christianity had been falsified and 'institutionalized' by the clergy and the Church. He was himself a man of strong religious feeling, and came from a Nonconformist background; it has always been part of the Puritan-Nonconformist tradition in England to despise ecclesiastical institutions and priestly authority, and to see the individual mind and heart as the only true battlefield of spiritual forces. However, whether there is a battle, and what form it takes, are questions which necessarily depend on individual temperaments, and when the 18th century had moderated the Puritan passions of the 17th century by a large degree of practical tolerance, many Nonconformists decided that their 'inner light' was the light of reason; consequently they became conspicuous rationalists, as did Blake's friend Joseph Priestley. What was left of Nonconformity – apart from the new Methodists – was narrow and dogmatic, demanding too little of either the reason or the passions of men. Blake's mind was too strong to subscribe to such creeds, and his passions were too strong for the limitations of rationalism. Moreover he was of humble social origin, and received no regular education except in engraving; he was therefore both unimpeded and unguided by the values and learning of the middle and upper classes. This was a mixed blessing, for while it left him free to discover his own rich but perplexing religious philosophy, it left him almost without an audience and deprived him of his power to exert an influence upon his contemporaries. Nevertheless, none of the Romantics arouses stronger interest among readers in the 20th century.

Romanticism is a vague term, but, before it was invented, the word 'romantic' had long signified whatever is wild, irregular, and mysterious. The Romantics, as opposed to the men of the Age of Reason, were explorers even more than critics, imaginative as much as rational, and integrative rather than analytical. They sought, that is to say, for 'wholeness' of experience and were dissatisfied with the kind of knowledge on which the 18th century had prided itself. 'He who sees the Infinite in all things,' wrote Blake in another set of Propositions, 'sees God. He who sees the Ratio only, sees himself only.' The 'ratio' or proportion, is of course 'rational' and therefore discerned by reason. The great achievement of the 18th century was really its shaping of experience to the elegant proportions of its conception of civilization, but the price it paid was the exclusion of all that might break the design. The Romantics needed convincing emotionally, independently of their reason. 'I can never understand how anything can be *known for truth* by a process of abstract reasoning,' remarks Keats in one of his letters. For Wordsworth, the truth about nature was not what could be stated about it, but what could grow out of relationship with it. For the 18th century, the reason provided an illusion of stability, but for the Romantics, the interplay between thought and feeling made preoccupation with growth, change and decay inescapable. This made it difficult for them to work in coherent forms, so that they are at their best in forms which are fluid and variable like the ode. The most eminent thinker among them, the writer who was most learned in philosophy, was Samuel Taylor Coleridge, and he was never able to order his abundant perceptions and reasonings into a system.

Coleridge in his early days was a follower of Locke and Hartley, and like Blake and Wordsworth, an enthusiastic supporter of the French Revolution. Also like them, he became disillusioned with it when he saw that the rationalism of men like Robespierre* was leading the movement into a system that was as tyrannical as the one it had overthrown. He found a new way forward through the influence of the German idealists, especially Immanuel Kant* (1724–1804). With the help of these he rejected Hartley's assumption that the mind is initially blank so that its acquisition of experience is a process in which it is, in the first instance, passive. He came to think of the mind as endowed with certain faculties which are active from the start and enable it to perceive moral and spiritual truths which are not available to the senses. He did not, however, abandon the whole method of 18th-century reasoning; he enlarged it by introducing distinctions into some of its concepts. Wordsworth taught him that nature is living and active, and he had already come to feel that the 18th century idea of it was dead and passive. This did not mean that this idea was false, but that there were two ways of 'knowing' nature: as a living relationship, and as an inert field for analytic reasoning. Coleridge therefore made a distinction between two sorts of reason: the intuitive and integrative sort which he *called* Reason ('namely that intuition of things when we possess ourselves as one with the whole'), and the 18th-century form of analytic reasoning which he called 'Understanding'. This distinction is paralleled by another, that between 'Imagination' and 'Fancy'. Hitherto, they had been synonymous terms, but Coleridge, in Chapter XIII of *Biographia Literaria**, defines the imagination as the vital faculty which creates new wholes out of disparate elements, whereas the fancy merely associates unlike elements together, wittily or ornamentally, without creating new wholes. The 'understanding' (in science) and the 'fancy' (in literature) are both faculties of 'the head disjoined from the heart', but the reason and the imagination are activities of the whole man, for 'deep thinking is attainable only by a man of deep feeling, and . . . all truth is a species of revelation'.

Coleridge's Reason and Imagination are like Blake's 'prophetic power'; they operate as unifying (Coleridge coined the words 'coadunating' and 'esemplastic') faculties in a world of opposing forces. Reason, however, can only fulfil its function through Faith, which, in *Aids to Reflection*, he defines as the synthesizing of Reason and Will joining themselves to God. He does not attempt to 'prove' the existence of God analytically, for he considers the analytic Understanding to be useless for the purpose, since it operates without the feelings through which God has to be experienced. On the other hand, only by the fact of God's existence can the unifying faculties of the Reason and the Imagination fulfil themselves, since without him they are cut off from the world by being isolated in the individual. Between the individual and God there must, as always, be the Church, but again Coleridge makes a distinction between two kinds of Church. There is the 'Holy Church' of all believers which Langland believed in, but Coleridge also wanted a 'National Church', to which the Church of England only corresponded in part. In *The Constitution of Church and State* (1829) he described society as rightly composed of 'three estates', the first two of which were the landowners and the mercantile community. The National Church should be the third. He did not consider it as purely what is normally considered a religious body; it should be composed of the teachers, writers and scholars who comprise what we nowadays call the 'intelligentsia' and Coleridge called the 'clerisy'. Its function would be the cultivation of 'the harmonious development of those qualities and faculties that characterize our humanity' for 'we must be men in order to be citizens'.

The force of Coleridge's influence was felt only near the end of his life and after his death. One reason for this was the scattering of his ideas among his few short books, his many essays published in *The Friend* and elsewhere, his lectures, his letters, and the reports of his conversation. Yet the collective impression of his thought, when at last it was assimilated, was great, for his many-sided mind brought together and showed the interrelation of the dispersed activities of society: its politics, religion, education, literature and philosophy. He brought back to life regions of experience which the 18th century had left dormant, offered a comprehensive idea of civilization greater than any since Hooker, and elaborated a constructively conservative philosophy which expanded the outline of the one offered by Burke in his *Reflections on the Revolution in France*. Thus his influence extended far down the 19th century: he was one of the inspirations of the revival of the Church of England in what became known as the Oxford Movement* after 1830; his conception of a responsible, collaborating 'clerisy' anticipates Arnold's* ideas of a vitally living culture in *Culture and Anarchy* and *The Function of Criticism*; his philosophical distinction between the Reason and the Understanding gave 19th-century thinkers a more fertile and generous conception of the operation of the mind than 18th-century thinkers had possessed. Yet Coleridge did not have the dominating influence over the 19th century that Locke had exerted over the 18th. Apart from the dispersion of his ideas among so many fragments of talk and writing, there were two important reasons for this.

The first of these was the serious weakening of the hold of the Christian tradition on men's minds. The reaction against 18th-century abstraction did not necessarily imply a return to strongly held Christian beliefs. After all, the Church had been a conservative part of the 18th-century social system, and Romanticism was a reaction against this system as much as against modes of thinking. We have seen that Blake, in participating in both reactions, had found that he was driven to wrestling with the problems of the individual spirit, and that this led to his evolution of a private mythology. This, though it ended in an essentially Christian interpretation of human destiny, was far from being one which was comprehensible to the common mind. Except for their reverence for the person of Jesus Christ, Keats and Shelley ignored Christianity; like Blake, they turned to mythology as the language of their intellectual and emotional insight. They were not like Blake, however, in his choice of an invented, private system of myths. Keats's *Hyperion** (1819) and Shelley's *Prometheus Unbound** (1820) contain the gods and goddesses of the ancient Greeks and Romans, though these receive a more personal interpretation than they had ever received before in English literature. Another expedient was that used by Coleridge in his greatest poem, *The Ancient Mariner** – a return to the world of romantic legend and the employment of it in new symbolic terms. A weakness in the revival of both classical myth and romantic legend is that they are too obviously fiction; the power of myth upon the mind has always depended on a degree of faith. This had been destroyed by the Age of Reason, and it had to await the rise of the science of deep psychology for its revival.

Another reason for the limitation of Coleridge's influence was that the 18th-century rationalist tradition which he had tried to counteract was both adaptable enough and strong enough to survive Romantic criticism. This tradition had two sides to it: it had been not only a force for repression of the imagination, but a critical force against 18th-century society; this critical force had been one of the main inspirations of the French Revolution, and the Revolution, in turn, was one of the inspirations of Romanticism. So it came about that the atheistic rationalist William Godwin, a disciple of Hartley and Locke, could inspire the most romantic of the poets, Percy Bysshe Shelley, who believed that the Golden Age might be restored by a combination of Godwin's faith in reason and his own Platonic idealism. Furthermore, the rationalist tradition was still working with the tide of history, whereas Coleridge's thought was in several ways working against it. The Industrial Revolution* of the late 18th and early 19th centuries brought with it many horrors, but it also immensely increased material production, and enlisted the help of the scientists, technologists and inventors who found analytic reason their most useful intellectual instrument. The industrialists and traders who profited by this immense expansion were inevitably 'pragmatists': they valued ideas to the extent that ideas assisted material progress, and disregarded those that did not. Society was still organized – as Coleridge himself recognized – too much in the landed interest, and the social and political institutions that suited the landed proprietors worked obstructively for the rest of the nation. The men of commerce and industry were vehement for their reform, and the rationalist critics in the 18th-century tradition were their useful allies. These were the thinkers who were known at first as the Philosophical Radicals or Benthamites, and later as the Utilitarians.

3.4.2 *The Utilitarians and Reason*

Jeremy Bentham* (1748–1832) began his career as a legal reformer whose ideas were strongly influenced by those of Locke. Philosophically, he identified what is good with what makes for happiness, and he believed, like Hobbes, that human beings necessarily pursue their own self-interest. Hobbes, in *Leviathan*, had pointed out the logical conclusion to this assumption: that human beings would destroy one another unless they had the sense to surrender some of their liberty to a strong, even tyrannical, government. Bentham was a benevolent man who grew up in milder times than Hobbes, and his solution was less drastic. He saw the duty of the state to be the protection of the weaker against the rapacity of those who were stronger, and he examined institutions critically to judge their effectiveness in this function. Initially, since he had a legal training, he concentrated on the English penal system, which, in the 18th century, punished a great many offences by death. He pointed out that since the aim of a penal system was to prevent crime, the English one was ineffective, for juries acquitted many undoubted criminals rather than see them condemned for small crimes. He advocated the abolition of capital punishment for all but the most serious offences, and this reform was made before the end of his life.

Bentham's attitude to capital punishment illustrates his essentially practical approach to all problems, social, political, and ethical. His test of a law was always its necessity and its effectiveness; of an institution, its necessity and its efficiency; of an idea, its truthfulness to evident facts. The British constitution was heavily laden with antiquated laws and institutions which had outlived their original purpose; obviously, their reform was delayed only because they brought incidental profit and advantage to small but powerful political and social interests. By temperament he was a conservative in politics; he saw no meaning in revolutionary ideologies such as Paine's *Rights of Man*. On the other hand, he was quite without feeling for the past, without reverence for institutions merely because they had been long established. He condemned the Church of England, for example, because it was responsible for practices that were quite baseless in reason; for instance, teaching children the Apostles' Creed before they were capable of understanding it. His attitude to religion is simply to inquire whether it increases human happiness on earth; in *The Analysis of the Influence of Natural Religion on the Temporal Happiness of Mankind* (1822), he concludes that religion diminishes happiness. Thus the tendency of Bentham's thinking was distinctly revolutionary although his disposition was not, for, by his tests, no institution was safe from the threat of abolition if it did not quite evidently serve human happiness interpreted in the simplest way.

Bentham's chief follower was James Mill (1773–1836), who transformed Benthamism into a political and social programme of reform and tried to supply it with a coherent philosophical basis. He accepted Hartley's doctrine that the mind is built up on the principle of the association of ideas, based on Locke's assumption that it is initially a blank page, and he accepted the strong emphasis made by the French 'philosophe' Helvetius on the consequent importance of education. He rejected religion on Bentham's principle that its doctrines are baseless in reason and its practices obstructive to the furtherance of human happiness. The direction of his ideas was towards the transformation of all forms of study into exact sciences, and the most important of these sciences was to be that of Political Economy, with politics and society as its field. Thus a group of thinkers gathered round himself and Bentham, employing themselves in strict scientific inquiry into social facts and their consequences. In 1803 one of these, Thomas Malthus*, published the final form of his *Essay on the Principle of Population*, in which he argued the influential idea that population will always tend to increase beyond the means of subsistence, with the chilling implication that the poorer classes must be persuaded to breed less. In 1817 David Ricardo published his *Principles of Political Economy and Taxation*; its theory that all economic value inheres in the labour involved in manufacture had important influence on the growth of socialist ideas, since it implied a severe criticism of the profits made as a result of capitalist investment. It was indeed in these years that socialism first made its appearance in the ideas and practice of the industrialist Robert Owen*, another friend of Bentham; in 1827 the word 'socialist' was invented to describe Owen's school of thought. However, although socialism derived partly from their ideas, James Mill and the other Philosophical Radicals were opposed to it, and its advance was postponed until later in the century when it acquired a new philosophy from Marx.

By the time Bentham and James Mill died, Philosophical Radicalism had already exerted a strong influence on governmental policies, but the greatest thinker in the school was still a young man. This was Mill's son, John Stuart Mill* (1806–73). The younger Mill's importance is that while he seeks to retain all the practical power for good in Benthamite thinking, he nonetheless came early to see its appalling narrowness, and its consequent inadequacy as a social philosophy. At the end of his life he was to describe in Chapter V of his *Autobiography* how, in his early manhood, he underwent the crisis of discovering that he could not live his own life merely in terms of Benthamite principles. Not long after this crisis he discovered that what was deficient in his father's and Bentham's thought was supplied by Coleridge, and in an essay upon each (1838 and 1840) he explained his belief that the ideas of the two men were not truly contrary but complementary. Bentham had been content to ask of 'any ancient or received opinion' the question 'Is it true?' but Coleridge asked the question 'What is the meaning of it?' Coleridge's question is the deeper one, because it brings to light hidden truths and needs of human nature, whereas Bentham's question leaves such truths unobserved. Mill considered that Coleridge's conservatism was quite different from the materialistic conservatism of the politicians, and that, indeed, it was not likely to appeal to them, for its criticism of contemporary institutions was as radical in its own way as that of the Philosophical Radicals themselves. A striking example of the difference between Bentham and Coleridge was in their attitudes to the Church: Bentham, considering merely whether it promoted human happiness, saw no use in it; Coleridge, considering the human needs to which it corresponded, thought that it was indispensable but must be made to have real meaning. The Benthamite philosophy, for all its apparent logicality, contained a major logical weakness: it held that men always act from self-interest and that it is the function of the state to prevent self-interest from becoming socially destructive, but it never explained what could induce the self-interested politicians to make the state fulfil this function. Mill's explanation for this gap in the argument is that Bentham never includes among his human 'springs of action' – fundamental motivations – such concepts as 'conscience', 'sympathy', 'self-respect', 'honour', 'beauty', or 'affection'. It was this whole range of moral and spiritual feelings that Coleridge felt to be the field of action for the Church, and Mill – atheist though he was – recognized that no account of human beings or society could leave them out.

It was John Stuart Mill who first used the term Utilitarian* for the Benthamite school of thought, and though he was the first great critic of Utilitarianism, he remained basically loyal to it. This was because he rejected Coleridge's central thesis: that human beings are endowed from birth with a faculty – his version of Reason as opposed to his version of Understanding – which directly apprehends truth. For Mill, no such faculty exists: truth can only be built up in the mind by experience; there is no other way of apprehending it. Thus Mill was faced with the task of reconciling his strictly rationalistic conception of the working of the mind with his firm belief in the values in which Coleridge believed. He tries to reconcile the two in his essay *Utilitarianism* (1863) by insisting that – contrary to Bentham's belief – 'Some kinds of pleasure are more desirable than others', so that people ought to cultivate those that are evidently more valuable, and to be educated to do so. It is open to question whether his argument is truly logical in this essay, or whether he so enlarges the Utilitarian concept of happiness as virtually to destroy it.

Mill's two works of largest scope are his *System of Logic* (1843) and *The Principles of Political Economy* (1849). The first attempts to establish the reality of 'moral science', that is to say, a study which is truly one of moral values, and at the same time pursuable by recognizably scientific methods. The second makes an important distinction between economic progress (in the sense of a steady accumulation of capital, expansion of trade, and increase of population) and social improvement, seen as an advance in the quality of civilization, an advance which may only begin when progress has been brought to a halt in the 'Static State' (vol. II, bk iv, chap. 6). Neither of these two ambitious books, however, is now read so much as Mill's classic statement of liberal philosophy in his essay *On Liberty** (1859). From the German thinker von Humboldt he takes as an axiom that the aim of civilization must be 'human development in its richest variety'. His theme is that the condition of this development is liberty of thought and discussion, and he sees such liberty as threatened by two dangers: the tyranny of the majority, and public apathy. To counteract these, he advocates constant debate and discussion of opinions even when no genuine opposition to them exists, for otherwise they may survive only as dead matter in the thought of the time, and their activating influence will be lost. *On Liberty* is a rich and humane development of Bentham's principle that every proposition, no matter how fully accepted, must be tested and debated; the dangers which Mill saw of the standardization of thought by the majority have intensified in the 20th century.

Mill was influenced by the French Positivist philosopher, Auguste Comte* (1798–1857). Comte maintained that there were three stages in the history of human thought: the religious, the metaphysical (or philosophical), and the positive (or scientific). In one central principle, however, Mill opposed Comte: while Comte used society as his field of values, Mill laid emphasis on the individual. Society, after all, is composed of individuals, and unless the individual can develop his potentialities, society cannot develop its own 'in richest variety'.

3.4.3 *Religious revivals: 1830–50*

The Church of England* was established precariously in the 16th century with political compromise, and for long periods it has seemed to rely on a basis in the political establishment. However, it developed its own intellectual and spiritual life between 1590 and 1640, and its sense of identity as a true Church and no mere political institution has never been lost, even during the period of its greatest inertia in the 18th century. During that century, its intellectual and spiritual traditions were maintained by a few notable figures: Bishop Butler (1692–1752) defended it against the deists with his *Analogy of Religion* (1736); Bishop Berkeley* (1685–1753) defended it against the materialist tendencies of the philosophers; William Law (1686–1761), by his *Serious Call to a Devout and Holy Life* (1729), awakened the great reformer John Wesley* (1703–91) to the neglected moral realities of the Christian life. Wesley's Methodist Movement was the principal religious event of the 18th century, but the opposition of the Church forced the Methodists to form a separate organization among the Nonconformists. Nonetheless, Wesley found supporters within the Church of England (which he himself never left); these became known as the Evangelicals*. In the first half of the 19th century, they were active and important in the life of the nation, and individuals among them, such as William Wilberforce* (1759–1833) and the seventh Earl of Shaftesbury* (1801–85) were great leaders in the reform of social abuses.

The Church was thus revitalized by the opening of the 19th century; it had at least escaped the worldly complacency which in the 18th century had been threatening its spiritual life. However, if the Anglican Church has always been in danger in consequence of its political origins, it has also been in danger of disintegration in consequence of its spiritual origins. In the reign of Elizabeth I, it was 'a middle way' between Catholicism and the more extreme forms of Protestantism.

It appealed to a broad range of opinion on the assumption that Hooker clarified – that it is unreasonable to divide and destroy religious life on issues that are not essential to the Christian faith. In times of apathy, when people care little about what they believe, large disagreements within Anglicanism have not seriously disturbed its peace, but in times of revival such disagreements often become important. Some Anglicans have emphasized their closeness to the parent Catholic tradition, and others have insisted upon their Protestant differences from that tradition. Partly owing to the very fact of the Evangelical Revival, the decades between 1830 and 1850 were a time when such antagonisms were unusually keen. However, the crisis rose chiefly out of a question incited by the political aspect of the Church's life: the question how far a state Church can and ought to resist the claims of the state to govern it. The resulting divisions in the Church of England did not destroy its organization, but they led to the curious terminology by which these divisions are known even today. What is called the Low Church originated in the Evangelical Movement, and it emphasizes the strictly Protestant view of Anglicanism. On the other hand, the High Church, which originated in the Oxford Movement* of the 1830s, affirms the continuity of Anglicanism with Catholicism. In addition the term Broad Church, especially associated with Thomas Arnold* (1795–1842) and like thinkers, implies that High and Low Church differences are of small importance compared to the use of religious energies to permeate society.

Politically and socially, the most important of these three movements in the 19th century was probably the Low Church, but the other two were more important in English literary and artistic life. The Evangelicals were content to operate within Parliament to achieve the reforms of those abuses which affronted their conscience; it was of slight account to them that Parliament could pass laws at will to change Anglican institutions. However, other Anglicans regarded some of the reforming tendencies of the age with great alarm. Some of the reformers were instigated by Benthamite Utilitarianism, and were indifferent to the spiritual independence and authority of the Church. Furthermore, in 1828 and 1829, the two Test Acts were repealed by Parliament. These had excluded both Nonconformists and Catholics from the right to vote in elections and to seek election as Members of Parliament. Now that they were able to do both, the Church might be at the mercy of politicians who not only did not profess to be Anglicans but were openly opponents of Anglicanism. Anglicans who were alarmed at this prospect also saw with concern that the ceremonies and order of religious worship were widely neglected by the clergy, and that the spirit of Anglican religion was in danger of losing its spiritual tradition altogether, for the sake of strong ethical convictions which, after all, were shared by Nonconformists, Catholics, and non-believers in Christianity.

In 1833, a counter-attack on these secularizing tendencies was begun in Oxford with a sermon preached by John Keble; since the movement that developed from this was centred on a group of Oxford scholars, it has become known as the Oxford Movement*. Its most eminent member at the time was Edward Pusey, from whose name it was also known as 'Puseyite'; still another name for it was Tractarian, from its practice of conducting propaganda through a long series of tracts*. Many of these tracts were written by a young scholar called John Henry Newman*, who is by far the best-known member of the group, and even at the time was its principal inspiration. The purpose of the Oxford Movement was to reassert the spirituality of the Church of England, its dignity, and its right to independence from political interference with its affairs. The writers of the tracts appealed to the spirit of the great early Anglicans such as Hooker*, Andrewes* and Jeremy Taylor*, and like Hooker they maintained that the tradition of Anglicanism was that of medieval Christendom. They declared that the Church of England had not seceded from the Catholic Church, but on the contrary that the Catholic Church had seceded by wrongfully excommunicating Queen Elizabeth in 1571. At the same time, to restore the dignity of Anglicanism, they revived much of the neglected ritual and ceremony.

For the first time for well over a century, Anglicanism began to make a strong appeal to the aesthetic feelings and the imagination of its followers. It became a focus for the expression of the growing interest in the Gothic* forms of medieval art. A taste for Gothic, which in the early 18th century had represented cultural barbarism, had been growing since the later 18th century, and had been given new substance by the great Romantics, especially Coleridge* and Walter Scott.* Newman's own prose was extraordinarily eloquent and his personality as a preacher was strongly inspiring, but his mind was disciplined and his intellect keen; to a large section of educated opinion, much that in Romanticism had seemed merely wild and disturbing was now receiving its true form and meaning in the intensity and sincerity of his personality and his writings.

However, other sections of opinion had been equally stirred by Evangelicalism, with its rooted prejudices against Catholicism or anything that resembled it. Thus the Oxford Movement aroused as much bitter hostility as enthusiastic support. When Newman published his *Tract XC*, in which he argued that the Thirty-Nine Articles – the official basis of Anglican beliefs – was not really directed against Catholic doctrine or incompatible with it, the Bishop of Oxford requested that he should cease writing the tracts. Newman was then forced to reconsider the true basis of his own faith, and the consequence was his withdrawal from the Church of England and entry into the Catholic Church in 1845. When he was lost to it, the Oxford Movement lost the main force of its spirit, although the High Church is still an important element in the religious life of the country. In the meantime, Anglicanism was showing its vitality through another and different but equally commanding personality – that of Thomas Arnold.

Arnold was strongly influenced by Coleridge's conception of the role of the Church as expressed in *The Constitution of Church and State*. He was opposed to the Evangelicals because they ignored the spiritual relevance of the Church as a body to the State as a body; he was also opposed to the Oxford Movement because he considered that its members ignored the true function of the Church for the sake of subtleties of doctrine and worship. He saw this true function as the creation of a whole Christian society, beginning with the education of its leaders – Coleridge's 'clerisy'. It is this that gave him such importance as the headmaster of Rugby* School, for in that capacity he gave the English Public School* system a new inspiration which raised it, at its best, to the level of one of the greatest educational systems of the world. In spite of his opposition to both the Evangelicals and the Oxford Movement, Arnold shared some of the convictions of each: with the former he emphasized the ethical imperatives of Christianity; with the latter he believed that the spirit of religion required a basis which was much broader and more intellectual than any allowed by the Evangelicals, who revived the Puritan insistence on the Bible as the sole repository of doctrine. His assertion of the relevance of Christianity to every aspect of society made him the initiator of the central, humane school of Anglican thinking, which included such men as F. D. Maurice (1805–72), the founder of Christian Socialism. However, unintentionally, by his refusal to allow doctrinal disputes to interfere with religious practice, he also became the initiator of another body of thought to which some of the best mid-19th-century minds belonged: those which emphasized the humane values of Christianity rather than its doctrine, in which they might even disbelieve. Of these, his son Matthew Arnold* was one of the most distinguished representatives.

3.4.4 *Science and the humane sceptics: 1830–80*

Science is a long-established word in the English language. Its original meaning is 'knowledge' or 'the pursuit of knowledge', and until the 19th century it was not differentiated as a special kind of thinking. In the 18th century, men of science were called 'natural philosophers'; they were merely philosophers who concerned themselves with the nature of the physical world, and they might easily combine this study with other kinds of thinking; for instance, Isaac Newton was also a religious thinker. There were no barriers in the world of the mind.

The word 'scientist', on the other hand, is a mid-19th-century invention. It marks an important change in intellectual history, for not merely a new word but a new kind of man was entering into existence. By 1850 it was becoming recognized that the pursuit of knowledge was not the same as the study of wisdom – as philosophy. Science was acquiring special techniques which were different from those of philosophy and theology, and the pursuit of knowledge could no longer afford the restraints that traditional notions and systems of belief had imposed upon it. The natural philosophers had worked within such systems: they not merely found the 'Great Chain of Being' to be a valuable framework within which they could classify their discoveries, but they considered the existence of God to be an indispensable hypothesis. The 19th-century scientist, on the other hand, found that the expansion of knowledge was such that no framework could contain it and that the 'God hypothesis', far from being indispensable, had less and less obvious relevance to their investigation into natural structures and forces. A great dilemma began to face the human mind: if science is really the pursuit of knowledge, and if the pursuit of knowledge has now to be conducted without reference to what has always been regarded as the spiritual life of man, what becomes of those religious beliefs which have embodied the light of meaning for human life and which, themselves, have claimed to be forms of knowledge? Moreover the character of scientific discovery was seriously disturbing to 19th-century minds. Instead of providing evidence that the universe is both stable and transparent to the intellect, it showed the universe to be incessantly changing and probably governed by the laws of chance. For the first time, at least to a greater extent than ever before, the implications of science seriously disturbed the ordinary man, so that he had either to ignore them or somehow to confront them. A large number of intellectuals after 1830 were forced into religious disbelief, or into some form of personal religion which, though it might contain elements of Christianity, was essentially untheological.

The sciences that caused this disturbance of belief were, at first, geology, and later, biology. In *The Principles of Geology* (1830–3), Charles Lyell* demonstrated that the age of the world was far greater than had been supposed, or than religious beliefs had led men to suppose, and he also propounded the theory that the earth had taken its present form by a constant but very gradual succession of changes. In his books *On the Origin of Species* (1859) and *The Descent of Man* (1871), Charles Darwin revealed that living creatures (in their existing forms) are in fact not 'creatures' at all, in the sense of having been created, but have taken their forms through a similarly slow process of change and adaptation in an endless 'struggle for survival'. Man himself is not a 'created spirit' but has apparently evolved like any other animal from primitive beginnings as an apelike mammal. Both the geological and the biological discoveries were incompatible with literal acceptance of the accounts of the creation of the world and of man in the Bible, and the belief that such a literal acceptance was indispensable to religious faith was still widespread. This, however, was not the most discomforting effect of the scientists. Enlightened believers, having already abandoned literal interpretations of the scriptures, were prepared in advance for the scientific attack. Coleridge, for instance, in his posthumously published *Confessions of an Enquiring Spirit*, had expanded the already existing view that the Bible must be interpreted as a spiritual guide, not as a handbook to every kind of knowledge. The scientists themselves were not all outright disbelievers. The biologist Thomas Huxley* (1825–95), who invented the term 'agnostic' for his own position of suspension between belief and disbelief, declared that atheism was philosophically untenable. Amongst the leading Christian thinkers, Newman* in his *Apologia* (1864) pointed out that the scientific discoveries presented no outright challenge to theology because they were constantly evolving and implying changing conclusions.

The more serious challenges presented by scientific thought were indirect, and implied two questions: whether Christian doctrine, once subjected to any radical criticism of its texts, could still be shown to be true in any but a nebulous sense;

and whether, true or not, it was indispensable to the well-being of mankind and the meaningfulness of human destiny. The first of these challenges was most distinct in the new 'scientific' criticism of the Bible, especially in Germany. The purpose of this criticism was to discover whether the Bible is true in the sense that any other ancient record can be established as true. Once the belief that the Bible was literally inspired by God was abandoned, it was implicitly admitted that the authors, being merely human, were liable to make mistakes. If that was so, then the miraculous elements of the Bible – including the Resurrection of Christ, belief in which is central to Christian doctrine – might not be historical facts but merely the interpretation of facts by primitive minds for whom myth was not distinguishable from history, and for whom the use of the imagination was not differentiated from the use of reason. In England, an example of this kind of biblical criticism was Charles Hennell's *Concerning the Origins of Christianity* (1838). He concluded that Jesus Christ was never resurrected except in the imagination of his disciples; Christ's importance was that he possessed outstanding qualities of courage and spiritual insight, and that the belief of his disciples in his divine origin led to a new and far nobler moral vision of the goal of history than had existed before.

Hennell's decisive influence on the great novelist George Eliot* (Mary Ann Evans, 1819–80) is typical of the history of some of the best mid-19th-century minds. Her father was a conservative Anglican; he was devout, but he did not feel the deep Evangelical disturbance of spirit that his daughter knew as a girl. When she read Hennell's book, the same earnestness of spirit which had caused her to respond to Evangelicalism led her to admit the cogency of his arguments. She went on to translate from the German Strauss's *Life of Jesus* (1846) and Feuerbach's *Essence of Christianity* (1854), both of them books with the same critical approach as Hennell's and written with stronger scholarship. They left her convinced of the truth of the emotional and moral values of Christianity, but doubting its historical doctrines. She no longer accepted that a merciful Providence had created and was guiding the human race, and had proved his love by taking on the human flesh of the man, Jesus Christ, but she believed all the more strongly in the duty of understanding and responding to human needs. To intellectuals of her kind, the reverence that had once been due to God was now due to humanity, and her novels are the subtle and rich testimony of such reverence. These minds found the most articulate and systematic exposition of their outlook in the writings of the French philosopher Auguste Comte* (1798–1857), who declared that the development of science made possible a new 'religion of society', as ordered and authoritative as the Catholicism of the Middle Ages. For others, like the novelist and poet Thomas Hardy* (1840–1928), the spiritual outlook was more sombre. For Hardy, if there was no longer a merciful Power sustaining the human race, there were still powers, but they were indifferent to its destiny.

However, one receives a false impression of an age if one concentrates merely on the exceptional minds. The majority of mid-19th-century Britons were absorbed in the extraordinary technological advances that were giving the nation unprecedented wealth and prestige. The Darwinian theory of the evolution of the species did less to disturb their acquiescence in traditional Christian doctrines than it did to excite their minds with new hopes. Evolution seems to imply an automatic principle of progress in nature, according to which improvement was inevitable so long as natural energies were allowed their freedom. Such optimism was especially typical of the urban commercial middle class. Hardy was a countryman, who lived among a declining rural peasantry; it was not surprising that he should see Darwinian evolution as remorseless and ambivalent – as destructive of life and happiness as it was creative. The now huge urban middle class, on the other hand, found itself with great and expanding advantages, and its assumption that this was in the order of nature seemed to receive support not only from the biologists, who appeared to justify them as successful competitors in the struggle for survival, but from the most popular and eloquent of the historians, Thomas Babington Macaulay* (1800–59), whose *History of England* expounded a general law of historical progress which, he found every reason to think, would extend indefinitely into the future.

Still other Victorian intellectuals detested this ingenuous, materialistic optimism, and were determined to fight it. Finding that the widespread agnosticism deprived them of the weapon of traditional Christianity, they cultivated a spirituality of outlook which was intense but undoctrinal, and they commonly gave it substance by enlisting activities of the mind which had not hitherto had any specific association with religious thinking. The most influential of them, Thomas Carlyle* (1795–1881), brought history in evidence. Benjamin Disraeli* (1804–81) sought to propagate a new faith in politics. John Ruskin* (1819–1900) taught the spiritual value of the graphic arts, and Matthew Arnold* (1822–88), that poetry and culture would provide civilization with the inspiration and standards of value which religion was ceasing to supply. These were the Victorian Sages – men who were not philosophers, because they spoke as much to the imagination as to the reason, and not artists because they were, above all, preachers.

Carlyle's 'religion of hero worship' was a cult of great men. He was a Scotsman, whose father was a socially humble Presbyterian* Calvinist. Carlyle greatly revered the energy and distinction of mind which Scottish Presbyterianism gave to men of his father's kind, but he himself suffered the loss of his religious faith – a loss which, in his case, was due more to the legacy of 18th-century scepticism than to the advance of science. However, the influence of Romanticism greatly strengthened his imagination, and he refused to give way to the emotional poverty which he saw as characteristic of the commercially-minded, pragmatic, English middle classes. His fictional autobiography, *Sartor Resartus** describes his energetic rebellion against spiritual despair and his conversion to the worship of a principle of divinity in nature and the great historical leaders. In his essay on Chartism* (1839), he showed how the meanness of contemporary social ideas justified the working-class revolutionary movement that went under that name, and in *Past* *and Present* (1843) he used the history of an episode in English medieval monastic life to expose, by force of contrast, the mediocrity of contemporary ideals. This use of history was an important innovation, which Carlyle owed partly to the conservative thinking of Coleridge and partly to the historical novels of Walter Scott. Coleridge had shown that the past could illuminate the present if its ideas and institutions were studied sympathetically for the purpose of understanding their meaning and intention. Scott had sought to make the past actual for the readers of his own time by showing what it was like to live among the facts of medieval England or 17th-century Scotland, and not merely – like the 18th-century Gothic fantasists – to entertain some untruthful notion about life in those times. Thus Scott raised up the past in a new way for the judgement of the present; Carlyle showed that to do this was to compel the present to judge itself in the light of the experience. Thus in his studies of great men of the past – Frederick the Great, Cromwell, Shakespeare, Dante – Carlyle showed his public how small were the values which they thought fit for their own society, and how mean was their denial of the merest human dignity to the under-privileged working class.

Carlyle was not a clear or original thinker, but he was a man of enormous energy and fearless individuality, and it is difficult to exaggerate the impression he made on his time. He largely inspired, for instance, the stream of 'social problem' novels between 1830 and 1860, notably some of the best by Elizabeth Gaskell*, Disraeli*, and Dickens*. Even to Matthew Arnold and John Stuart Mill, who later despised and distrusted his vague and idiosyncratic rhetoric, he was at first an inspiration and liberation, and Ruskin was the chief among his more devoted disciples.

Perhaps Ruskin's principal service to the culture of Britain was his passionate belief that no society could flourish and at the same time ignore its material environment. At no previous period would such a gospel have been necessary: squalor and impoverished conditions had surrounded the very poor, and they had always constituted a large fraction of the population, but the total population had been small, so that this sort of environment had never been extensive – even 18th-century slums had been within reach of green fields. In mid-Victorian Britain, the total population was very much larger, and it chiefly swelled the towns; the Industrial Revolution* not only did much more to multiply the squalor than to alleviate it, but it debased and vulgarized the taste of the richer classes. Such degradation has afflicted all modern industrial nations more or less, but Britain, being historically the first of them, was swept into it without any opportunity of foreseeing its onset. Ruskin's importance was that he was not merely a great art critic with an aesthetic message, but a moralist who understood that if men are indifferent to the objects they use they will themselves become such objects, merely to be used. Like Carlyle he used history, but the history of art, to convey his message; with unequalled vividness he demonstrated the human enrichment to be found in the great art forms of the past, especially in the spontaneity and variety of the Gothic Middle Ages. When, in the four essays published under the title of *Unto This Last* (1862), he turned his attention to Political Economy, this was an extension of the theme of his art criticism rather than a departure from it. His argument is that the science then called Political Economy had no title to the name, for it was really only 'commercial economy'. The science had been originated by the Utilitarians and like-minded thinkers; John Stuart Mill, the most clear-headed of these, had already seen its limitations, but its apparent basis in reason and its usefulness to commerce had made it something like a new religion for the middle class. Ruskin demonstrated that its basis in reason was much more apparent than real, and that quite a different conception of the relationship between employers and employees must succeed the one that it offered if society was ever to become healthy. Despite the furious opposition of the business men, his revised theory of Political Economy passed into common acceptance, with the result that *Unto This Last* is now read less than it ought to be.

Matthew Arnold, on the other hand, raised questions about society and culture which are today as important and as difficult to answer as they were in his own time. The subject is dealt with in Essay 7, on Critical Thought, in this volume. What is important to notice here is his conception of the incompleteness of even the most just arrangements for social welfare if these do not include adequate means for the enlargement of the human mind in terms of values intrinsic to 'the best that is known and felt in the world' (see *The Function of Criticism*). Arnold brings to a point many of the conflicts of ideas and feelings of the mid-19th century: the parts played by reason and by the emotions in the fulfilled human being; the problem of what can replace the 'binding force' of religion as a means of human integration; the question whether religion can survive the abandonment of a supernatural faith; above all, how to get beyond the pressing materialism which is implicit in either a capitalist or a socialist economy. The last was the most important, because it was, and still is, the most concrete and immediate. It became still more urgent after Arnold's death, for the end of the 19th century saw the energies of many reformist thinkers channelled into the new, ruthless, analytically logical forces of Marxist socialism.

3.4.5 *The growth of socialism and of modern journalism: 1880–1914*

British socialism was not, in its original forms, Marxist, nor has it ever been inspired entirely by Marx*. It began with the industrial experiments of Robert Owen* after 1815, but these failed, largely because his assistants and deputies could never carry out his ideas, which became increasingly vague and unpractical. In the second half of the 19th century, a new socialist inspiration arose indirectly from the writings of Ruskin, who saw the mass-production of the new capitalism as degrading to man, whether he worked in factories or bought their standardized products. From Ruskin, the Pre-Raphaelite* and the later aesthetic* movements grew up; they made a cult of beauty and its power to redeem the mind from industrial vulgarity, and though this did not necessarily give them sympathies with socialism, their opposition to the commercial world easily became opposition to capitalism. The chief figure in these movements was William Morris* (1834–96), who was a distinguished writer but a still more notable designer and craftsman. He tried to counter industrialism by his practice and encouragement of manual crafts, and in 1884 he founded the Socialist League. But Morris, as Marx's associate Engels remarked, was more a utopian than a socialist; that is to say, he worked for a world in which human beings would be liberated from the capitalist profit motive, but he gave small attention to the actual working of economics and politics.

The effective beginnings of British socialism were necessarily more practical. The great Utilitarian, John Stuart Mill, declares in his *Autobiography* (1873) that he and his friends had become socialist in their sympathies through their strong sense of the injustices of contemporary society, but they repudiated the tyranny of society over the individual which most socialist societies have inflicted. 'The social problem of the future we considered to be how to unite the greatest individual liberty of action with a common ownership in the raw material of the globe and an equal participation of all in the benefits of combined labour.' He saw the process as a gradual one, partly because of the lack of universal education, and partly because he saw the change from a competitive to a co-operative way of life as requiring 'an equivalent change of character . . . both in the uncultivated herd who now compose the labouring masses and in the immense majority of their employers'. So far as the 'herd' was concerned, the beginnings of the change he required occurred with the establishment of universal education in 1870; however, its principal early effects were not all as he would have wished, for it made available to commercially-minded journalists and their newspaper proprietors an unprecedentedly large public which had been taught to read but not to think. Meanwhile, in the intelligent middle class, a left-wing élite began to form, and in 1884 – the same year as Morris established his Socialist League – they founded the socialistic Fabian Society*. And in the last year of the century, the Fabians united with the now strong and flourishing Trade Union movement to form the Labour Party.

There had been a steadily growing ferment of discussion about social injustice ever since 1830. One of the founders of the Fabian Society, Beatrice Webb*, wrote in her autobiography *My Apprenticeship* (1926) that 'the origin of the ferment is to be discovered in a new sense of sin among men of intellect and property'. She gives a list of names of men who had contributed to this 'sense of sin' which thus found its expression in the socialist movement. They include Utilitarians*, such as J. S. Mill*; the Evangelical* conservative, Shaftesbury*; the Broad Church Christian Socialist, F. D. Maurice; 'Karl Marx* and his English interpreters'; General Booth, the founder of the Salvation Army*; the Catholic Cardinal Manning; and writers and artists such as Carlyle*, Dickens*, Ruskin* and William Morris*. Among such men, Marx had been less important in the shaping of the social conscience than Evangelicals and Nonconformists, for whom the phrase 'consciousness of sin' had an ancient and central significance. Thus late-19th-century British socialism was produced by the convergence of widely different streams of thought and feeling, but the most effective of them all was Utilitarianism: Beatrice Webb and her associates built up a body of knowledge based on the investigation of social facts, and developed critical methods for the scrutiny of institutions, which they derived ultimately from Bentham.

The period between 1880 and 1914 was one of vigorous public discussion in which social issues were central; literature was marked by strong polemical tendencies. Even the aesthete Oscar Wilde* showed his socialist sympathies in his essay *The Soul of Man under Socialism* (1895); even Rudyard Kipling* owed his popularity as much to his feeling for the common man as to his celebration of British imperialism. The polemics were conducted in a new journalistic style designed to capture the large public which universal state education was now making accessible. Socialism and rationalism were opposed by the Catholic writers G. K. Chesterton* and Hilaire Belloc*, who used witty and ebullient styles to demonstrate that Catholicism could be as reasonable and socially relevant as socialism, and far more emotionally appealing. Their chief antagonists were the novelist H. G. Wells* (1866–1946) and the dramatist George Bernard Shaw* (1856–1950). These were by far the most popular writers of their time.

Wells and Shaw were socialists and members of the Fabian Society. Wells's writing is a product of 19th-century scientific culture working on a man who had raised himself from low social origins, and who despised the conservative, predominantly literary culture of the upper classes. He saw Darwin's theory of biological evolution as an example for the advance – through socialism – of the human race, with science and technology as its indispensable instruments. The liveliness and comedy of his novels were remarkable, but these qualities could not compensate for the narrowness and shallowness of Wells's ideas on what constitutes humanity. Shaw, who accepted Marx's analysis of history as a record of class conflict, tried to give his writings additional depth and excitement by borrowing the idea of the 'superman' from the German philosopher, Nietzsche*, and that of the 'creative life force' – a kind of spiritualizing of Darwin's evolution theory – from the French philosopher, Bergson, but these are not the aspects of his work which still make him seem a commanding dramatist. Both Wells and Shaw brought the optimistic and materialistic aspects of Victorian thinking to their logical conclusion. The First World War destroyed such optimism for ever.

3·5

The dispersal of shared beliefs and the growth of new sciences: 1914–present day

Modern intellectual history has seen a greater disturbance of accepted beliefs and values than any period since before the Middle Ages. This has been partly due to the shocks of political events. The 18th-century Age of Reason and the 19th-century Age of Progress together accustomed men to the belief that civilization had advanced beyond the possibility of extensive horrors. Yet the 20th century has seen the appalling slaughter of World War I, a Revolution in Russia which far exceeded the French in its ferocity and thoroughness, the Nazi concentration camps, and World War II with its revelation that science is as likely to be used for immediate total destruction as for rapid material advance. Wells registered his new pessimism in *Mind at the end of its Tether* in 1945. However, the faith in automatic progress had never dominated the profounder minds of the 19th and early 20th centuries, and though they could not have anticipated these 20th-century horrors, they anticipated other developments which often seem to be the most present dangers to reflecting modern minds. Carlyle, Arnold, Mill, Newman and Ruskin all in their different ways foresaw that the instrument might become stronger than the agent: that the human being might so subject himself to his man-made environment as to end in a slavery perhaps greater and less escapable than the enslavement of primitive man to his natural surroundings.

Many 18th-century minds believed that they had found the true use of Reason, and that this discovery was the key to all the doors that lock human nature out of contentment; hence the early hopes in the French Revolution. Many 19th-century minds believed that these hopes might still be realized if reason could be cultivated together with the sympathetic imagination – if reason could be joined to the love of fellow-men; hence the late-19th-century hopes in socialism. But in the 20th century, words like 'reason', 'truth', 'love', 'freedom', 'morality' have lost much of their power to sway the mind. We grant them substance only in a context – scientific, social, psychological, religious – and the contexts often lack relationship with one another. One indication of this modern tendency for fields of thought to lose contact with a relating centre is the absence of any consent about the word we should use to express the essence of a human being. 'Soul' and 'spirit' have a clear sense only in religious doctrine; 'mind' – preferred by scientists and many philosophers – signifies for most other people only the conscious and thinking part of the human being; 'person' and 'personality' are suspect psychologically, for the words derive from the Latin one for the mask worn by Roman actors, and consequently imply only the public and exhibited side of the self. Thus it has become difficult to *think* any longer of a human being as an identity, although we still *feel* that he is one. When we 'think' of a human being, we find rather that he has a number of identities – social, psychological, physical, and so forth – and though we may accept only one of these identities as the real one, we cannot deny the existence of other opinions about him, so that we then face the difficulty of conversing intelligibly about human beings with anyone who disagrees with us.

One great problem of the century has been that the advances in technology and in social and political justice have been accompanied by a withdrawal – often in the name of democracy – from the centres of spiritual and moral guidance such as

Coleridge had meant his 'National Church' to provide, and such as Matthew Arnold had wanted from 'the State'. The intellectual achievements have been outstandingly scientific, and it is scientific thinking, because of its spectacular successes in technology, which alone receives universal respect. This has meant that philosophy, which for centuries had been the more or less uneasy ally of religion, or its direct rival, has moved into partnership with science.

The dominant school of British philosophy since 1914 has been that of Logical Analysis, which has abandoned speculation into universal values and concepts in favour of the clarification of statements. A typical approach is that by Gilbert Ryle in the opening of his Introduction to *The Concept of Mind* (1949):

> *This book offers what may with reservations be described as a theory of the mind. But it does not give new information about minds. We possess already a wealth of information about minds, information which is neither derived from, nor upset by, the arguments of philosophers. The philosophical arguments which constitute this book are intended not to increase what we know about minds, but to rectify the logical geography of the knowledge which we already possess.*

This school began with G. E. Moore* (*Principia Ethica*, 1903). Since Moore, its principal representatives have been Bertrand Russell*, Wittgenstein, A. J. Ayer, and Ryle himself. Hitherto, philosophers had created, or at least groped towards, systems of thought which endeavoured to give a coherent intellectual image of the world, both as it could be 'known' intellectually and as it could be 'felt' morally. The Logical Analysts, on the contrary, have maintained that all such 'systems' were illusory, and would never again be possible. Bertrand Russell puts the case at the close of his *History of Western Philosophy* (1946):

> *Intellectually, the effect of mistaken moral considerations upon philosophy has been to impede progress to an extraordinary extent. I do not myself believe that philosophy can either prove or disprove the truth of religious dogmas, but ever since Plato most philosophers have considered it part of their business to produce 'proofs' of immortality and the existence of God. . . . All this is rejected by the philosophers who make logical analysis the main business of philosophy. They confess frankly that the human intellect is unable to find conclusive answers to many questions of profound importance to mankind, but they refuse to believe there is some 'higher' way of knowing, by which we can discover truths hidden from science and intellect.*

The philosophy of Logical Analysis thus implies religious scepticism, but it does not necessarily contradict religious faith, which has always proceeded from the total experience – the feelings as well as the mind – of the believer. It is certainly true that there is more outspoken religious disbelief in Britain now than there ever has been before, and yet the intellectual doubters of the mid-19th century would probably be surprised at the number of believing intellectuals in

Britain a century after Darwin's *Origin of Species* (1859). Religious thought does not cease to be intellectually respectable merely because the philosophers cease to take cognizance of religious experience. However, we have to distinguish between the language that expresses that experience and the language that formulates the doctrines behind it. The language of ordinary doctrinal theology remains caught in a dilemma: without sacrificing the concreteness of Christian belief, it cannot depart from its traditional terminology, and yet this terminology is an affront to the modern mind, which cannot distinguish it from the language of ancient mythology and superstition. The language of religious experience, on the other hand, is intelligibly symbolic (for instance in Eliot's *Ash Wednesday* and *Four Quartets**) since it concerns the individual's engagement with what by definition goes beyond his capacity to define by concepts; much of the work of the great 20th-century writers has been symbolist in this sense, not only among Christians (notably T. S. Eliot*) but among non-Christians, such as D. H. Lawrence* and W. B. Yeats*. Moreover, it has been reanimated by the arrival of analytical psychology, which is possibly the most momentous development of 20th-century thought.

Since the first impact of Freud's* psycho-analytical theories on Britain just before 1914, psychological thought has multiplied into many schools, and there is still dispute about the claims even of Freudian psychology to be considered a science. But its importance as a language for the description of human experience is scarcely affected by such disputes. Its importance is not merely that it has provided new, more intelligible ways of describing the personality, but that it restored to the mind an 'unseen world' just when the physical sciences had seemed to deprive the mind of the traditional unseen world of Christian metaphysics. This is the 'inner space' of unconscious mind, accessible only through dreams and the discovery by analysis of forgotten experiences, the buried memories of which still influence conduct. Psychological analysis of the mind – despite its varying and sometimes contradictory conclusions – has permanently altered our conception of human nature in both life and literature. It has taught us that human beings cannot be judged, for good or ill, merely by their behaviour, and that details of experience may be as significant as conspicuous features of it. It has in some respects increased our self-doubt and scepticism, since it has made more difficult the acceptance of public formulations of belief and feeling – the acceptance, indeed, of any sort of expression at its face value. On the other hand, analytical psychology offers some promise of recovering a unified conception of human identity – though probably not on Freud's terms – and of arriving at a true account of human relationship.

Charles Dickens from an engraving made at his death. His great popularity as a novelist was based especially on his immense range of characters drawn from all sections of society.

4 Narrative literature from romance to the novel: 1350–*present day*

4.1

Myth, romance, and allegory: 1350–1600

Introduction: the dramatic vision

Man has always needed to feel mastery over his surroundings, or at least relationship with them. Nowadays, he has this through science and technology, products of experiment and the analytic reason. In his pre-scientific stages, he responded to environment emotionally, though ritual and myth.

Ritual is the dramatic expression of changes in nature, such as the turn of the year from cold and darkness back towards warmth and long days; it enacts these changes, gives form to the desire that they may come about, and may be felt actually to assist their occurrence. What is dramatized in a ritual may be narrated in a myth. Thus the *Mummers' Play* – about St George and the Turkish Knight, their duel, death, and resurrection by the Doctor – is an ancient ritual enacting the death and revival of the year, as performed until recent times by English country-folk; the Greek myth of Demeter* and Persephone is also about death and life and the cycle of the year.

Christian beliefs about the death and resurrection of God and man harmonize with pagan beliefs about the death and resurrection of every year; the Christian Church patterned the year with festivals corresponding in date and meaning to the pre-Christian pagan ones. But, because they accorded so well, the Christian beliefs and rituals did not obliterate the pre-Christian practices. Pagan myths continued to flourish, although they were no longer officially acceptable, because they still expressed the fears and longings of Christian countrymen – however they acquired the myth; for the coming together of races and cultures in the Middle Ages resulted in the meeting of myths from various sources. Thus, besides the Christian tradition of a religious poem like *Piers Plowman**, there were Arthurian* legends with characters deriving from Celtic gods, the folk-legends of Robin Hood* who may have derived from the Norse god Odin*, and a poem such as *Sir Orfeo*, which is an anglicized version of the ancient Greek myth of Orpheus* and Eurydice.

The pagan myths dramatizing natural changes on which life depended, and the Christian beliefs about the origins of the world and the destiny of man, were intelligible images of mysteries impenetrable to the human mind; they alike operated through the medium of 'allegory'*, a word derived from ancient Greek and meaning 'speaking in other terms'. We still use allegory when we wish to express

*Indicates mention in the reference section.

concretely what we think abstractly, but medieval allegory was not merely a device of expression but a way of thinking and feeling about the universe. Far from reducing complex experience to simplified appearance, allegory enabled medieval men to live out the conflicts inherent in their world – conflicts of dearth and plenty (*Winner and Waster**), of soul and body (*Everyman**), of sexual passion (*The Romaunt of the Rose**), of wild nature and courtly civilization (*Sir Gawain and the Green Knight**).

This incessant awareness of life as conflict accounts for the dramatic vision of the age. This is not to say either that the drama was the dominant form of expression, though it was more central than other forms, or that all the notable work in the period was dramatic in feeling. It means that it was natural to the medieval mind to express itself through dramatic interchange, and especially by the disputes or flytings* between opposing parties. Whole poems are cast in this form, from *The Owl and the Nightingale* (13th century), and flytings boil up in poems that are cast in other forms, as in some of the gayest passages of *The Canterbury Tales**. The drama is the subject of another essay, but to realize how spontaneous was dramatic feeling in the narrative art of the Middle Ages is to understand the apparently sudden flowering of the theatre, especially in the work of Shakespeare*, at the very end of the period.

4.1.1 *Kinds of medieval narrative*

Men of the Middle Ages, like those of any other period, were intensely interested in the world of their daily life. They were different from men of later periods in our literature, however, in their having distinct conceptions of other worlds to which the 'real' world of every day could be related. One of these other worlds was that of supernatural faith, taught by the priests – the spiritual world of religious allegory. There was also the world of magic, which belonged to a region of feeling that the priests did not reach, and was older than that of Christian faith. This was the world in which men struggled with natural forces, and were still more aware of 'gods' than of God. Finally, there was the world of idealized feeling, which the priests regarded with official disapproval although (since they were often also worldly men) they might indulge in it themselves. This was the world of the illusion that the most absorbing of earthly passions, sexual love, could – because for spells of time it actually did – make a heaven out of earthly experience. Later generations of writers, of course, have written of other worlds born of faith and fancy; medieval writers were different chiefly in the seriousness with which they used their other worlds as different ways of presenting human experience and of interpreting it. They did not keep this world and the other worlds in separate compartments; the life of the senses penetrated the worlds in which daily fact was in one way or another transfigured. It was this transfiguration which revealed the meaning of daily life; the way into the transfiguration, in many narratives, was for the poet to describe how he fell asleep and had a dream, that is to say, a 'vision'.

4.1.2 *Fabliau, fable, allegory, and romance*

It was, perhaps, the beginning of a substantial middle class in the 14th century that encouraged the growth of the comic tale restricted to the material of real life, and often to the lives of middle-class men. This was the fabliau*. The best examples of it are told by the Miller*, the Reeve* and the Merchant* in Chaucer's *Canterbury Tales*. The Wife of Bath's Prologue**, also in the Tales, belongs to this kind of narrative. It is not formally a tale, but a fictional autobiography, interspersed with the kind of lively dispute, or flyting*, which was a common device in medieval narrative, especially when the tone was comic; another notable example is Dunbar's *The Two Married Women and the Widow*. That the daily life of human beings should above all be treated as comic is intelligible when life was hard, and robust humour, drawing life from the passions most familiar to human nature and finding expression in the flytings, was the most natural resource for outfacing its trials.

The French word 'fabliau' is cognate with 'fable'*. Fables have come chiefly to signify light-hearted tales of birds and beasts, told so as to illustrate the moral experience of human beings. The first great writer of fables was the ancient Greek poet Aesop*, whose popularity from the 14th century was immense, though the fables offered under his name, for instance those by the Scottish poet Henryson*, were often not really translations but original works written in emulation. Once again, the finest example in English is by Chaucer, *The Nun's Priest's Tale** in *The Canterbury Tales*. Chaucer's tale is of the farmyard, and preserves the comic liveliness of a fabliau; though fables inculcated moral lessons, the animal characters and the human types they represent still kept them in touch with common life.

A fable is an allegory, and essentially fanciful. But allegory* was characteristically much more than a fanciful device in the Middle Ages: it was a method of interpreting the universe and human destiny; a method which seemed more meaningful than any other, and was therefore as natural to a medieval writer as intellectual analysis is to a writer of the 20th century. The greatest English medieval allegory is *The Vision of Piers Plowman** by the 14th-century poet William Langland. In this poem, the society of England is tested against the religious faith that it professes, and is found to fail both in its secular institutions and in the institutions of the Church. The poem works through the embodiment of these institutions, and the doctrines and social traits that go with them, in characters that are pungently human (and often comic) in their turns of speech, and complex in the many-sidedness of their relationships. Other poets, like the anonymous authors of the 14th-century *Parliament of the Three Ages** and *Winner and Waster**, show the same assurance of imparting a wisdom which is both visionary and practical. In these poems, it is a wisdom inherited from the long history of human conflict with nature rather than derived from Christian teaching, though these did not necessarily conflict. One of the greatest 14th-century narrative poems, the anonymous *Sir Gawain and the Green Knight**, is a tale which appears to have its roots in pagan myth, yet its author may be the same as that of the deeply Christian allegory, *Pearl**.

Sir Gawain and the Green Knight is a romance*, and therefore belongs to the most conspicuous of all the medieval narrative forms – the courtly literature* of romantic love. The word 'romance' originates from the term for 'Roman' (*ie* Latin) languages, spoken round the western Mediterranean. It was here, but especially in southern France, that the typical romance tale evolved. Its characteristics were at first heroic adventures full of magical and supernatural incidents drawn from legend, but by degrees its main theme came to be that of sexual passion, not treated comically as in the fabliaux, but with a seriousness otherwise used only for religious themes. Its authors were professional minstrels who recited the romances in the castles and courts of the aristocracy, such as the court of Eleanor of Aquitaine, wife of Henry II of England (1154–89). The French romance, like the narrative forms of all periods when they have an assured public, tended as time went on to be written to a formula, and to become relatively lifeless. At the time of Eleanor, English was a neglected 'provincial' language, not spoken by the upper classes in England itself, but when English adopted the romance from France in the 13th century, this provinciality showed itself to be in some ways an advantage, for English poets were in touch with a wider, more vigorous, more popular taste than the French court minstrels were. At first the English romance (like the 13th-century *Havelock the Dane*) was chiefly heroic rather than amorous, but already *King Horn* (which may be earlier than *Havelock*) is showing the predominance of amorous interest. In the 14th century the author of the much maturer *Sir Gawain* uses the older alliterative verse (as does Langland) and he uses it with such mastery that it seems likely that the alliterative tradition was never really lost. But it was once more Chaucer, returning to rhymed and metrical verse, who brought perfection, in *The Knight's Tale** (*Canterbury Tales*) and above all in his masterpiece *Troilus and Criseyde**. In Chaucer, the provincialism of the earlier English romance has gone, but the vigour of a wide human appeal which comes from contact with the whole of a society has been maintained. By the middle of the 15th century – on the whole a barren period for distinguished English narrative verse, though much verse was written – Malory was retelling the Arthurian romances in prose. Though his prose often rises to great eloquence, his *Morte d'Arthur* (1469) already betrays the weakening often consequent on a form becoming divorced from the invigorating influences of popular taste.

4.1.3 *The ballad*

The ballad* form requires a separate note, partly because it had a longer history than the other medieval narrative forms, and partly because it has distinctive features that separate it from them. Many English and Scottish ballads are difficult to date, because they belonged mainly to the common people and were transmitted by word of mouth long before they were written down and collected in the 18th century by men like Thomas Percy*. The earliest versions can seldom be traced back farther than the 15th century, although they may deal with events that occurred earlier. The printed broadside* ballads, on the other hand, began in the 16th century, continued until the 19th century, and have their equivalents in the popular literature of today. Some old ballads, like *Thomas the Rymer*, may have been composed by professional minstrels performing in aristrocratic houses; others, like the Robin Hood* ballads, were of peasant origin. The ballad subject-matter varies widely; it includes magic (*The False Knight upon the Road*), romantic tragedy (*Sir Patrick Spens**), history (*Otterbourne** and *Chevy Chase**), and the tragedy and comedy of topical events, which was the main subject of the broadsides. In style, the ballad was the most dramatic of all the medieval narrative forms: most of these lent themselves to amplification, whereas a ballad tells its story with economical brevity omitting comment and relying for emphasis on a few rhetorical devices such as repetition. Its strong, singing rhythms and the common use of refrains show that ballads were always intended to be sung, and that their origins were close to those of the carol*; both were at first dance songs.

4.1.4 *Kinds of narrative in the sixteenth century*

Our need to reduce the confusions of history into some order leads to the use of such terms as 'Middle Ages'*, for English history up to the 16th century, and 'Renaissance'* for that century itself. They may lead us to assume a change of mentality, as though a man of 1550 was fundamentally different in outlook and feeling from his grandfather of 1450. But ways of thinking and feeling do not change so decisively in a century, or, if they do, this is true of ourselves rather than of our forebears. It is true that institutions changed: the Church became a national institution instead of an international one, and the nation became 'the state' of modern political experience. Moreover thought and opinion changed among the educated, who rediscovered Plato* and were affected by Luther*. But humble men felt these changes less or not at all; they heard the same kinds of sermon from the village priests, and looked upon their surroundings with eyes that, for the most part, saw few changes to bewilder them. Developments which did affect them – the Reformation* and the upthrusting, profiteering middle classes – caused them to see the world yet more as one of conflicting forces, but still on a basis of accepted normality. Drama had been central to English life in the Middle Ages; in the 16th century, educated men gave thought to drama as never before, and their ideas met popular feeling in the minds of Shakespeare and his contemporaries, so that the theatre – with strongly conservative assumptions behind it – became a truly national art form.

But the Renaissance was also the time when education finally burst the bonds of the Church, which had so far confined it, though less and less closely; and a 'literature for the educated' emerged, in which popular taste, though it exerted influence, did not extensively share. Edmund Spenser* (1552?–99), the first poet to match Chaucer of two centuries before, was a product of this change. His great work *The Faerie Queene** is a 'romantic epic', that is to say, a narrative poem with much in common with the long romances of the Middle Ages, but pervaded by the Renaissance educated taste for 'ideas'. Ideas for Spenser, however, were not abstractions but ideal qualities to be presented beautifully and recommended persuasively. In his letter to Sir Walter Raleigh*, used as a preface, he wrote: 'The generall end therefore of all the booke is to fashion a gentleman or noble person in vertuous and gentle discipline', and he goes on to say that he has chosen a 'historicall fiction' to 'delight' his readers, 'rather for variety of manner, then [than] for profite of the ensample [example]'. Spenser's *Faerie Queene* is a noble and beautiful poem, but, though it contains combats and adventures, it is not by much dramatic interest that it appeals to modern readers. It is a poem that had greater influence on the post-dramatic, reflective spirit of the later 17th century.

Spenser uses allegory throughout *The Faerie Queene*, but it is used as we use it – as a literary figure, not in the medieval way of transforming indistinct but powerful emotions into actualities. In the popular imagination, the older use of allegory survived another century, as John Bunyan* was to show, but it is no longer characteristic of most 16th-century narrative writing, emanating as this did from London, or at least from court circles.

The romance of courtly love and the comic tradition of the fabliau survived, but in the new forms of the prose 'Elizabethan novels'* which were very popular in the last quarter of the century. None of them is great literature, though some still live as literature; they include Sidney's *Arcadia**, Nashe's *Unfortunate Traveller**, and Deloney's* *Thomas of Reading*. These three illustrate their variety. Sidney was a courtier who, like Spenser, was affected by Platonic idealism, and to our taste cared too much for verbal beauty unrelated to matter. Nashe also cared greatly for words in themselves, but in a more vivid way as a parodist of contemporary styles; and he resembled a modern journalist in his subject-matter – the lives of rogues and the 'underworld' of the day. Deloney stands on his own as a realistic narrator of middle-class daily life; at his best, he is a vivid one, and anticipates the quality of Daniel Defoe.

4.2

Reason, prose, and satire: 1600–1720

Introduction: growth of the descriptive vision

In the 17th century, old traditions reached conclusion, and new ones originated. In narrative, two works of the first order appeared, both in long-established forms

– Milton's epic, *Paradise Lost**, and Bunyan's allegory, *Pilgrim's Progress**; both, moreover, came late in the century. The new kinds of author wrote predominantly in prose: the biographers, John Aubrey* and Izaak Walton*; the diarists, Evelyn* and Pepys*; the historians, especially Clarendon*; the (Theophrastian) character* writers, especially John Earle; the travel writers; and the essayists, Bacon*, Cowley,* and above all Addison* and Steele* early in the 18th century.

Such 'new' writers seem to have little to do with imaginative fiction; they are, at least ostensibly, concerned with fact. But they are imaginative in the sense that they are describing scenes and people (including, often, themselves) as they wish them to be known or as they seem to be significant; they present them with a stylistic 'tone' that colours the responses of the reader. When we look at these 17th-century writers in this way, we find in them a fresh kind of reaction to surroundings, which we can call 'curiosity'.

Curiosity was of course not a new emotion in the 17th century, but it became in the course of it a 'key' emotion; it was, after all, the century of the founding of the Royal Society* for Promoting Natural Knowledge (1662) and of Isaac Newton*. To understand the force of curiosity for imaginative writing, we have to remember that it accompanies a passion for enlightenment; it goes with a desire to act in the light of reason, and it refuses to dispense with reason for the sake of emotion, especially religious emotion. The 'curious' man is an inquirer; for personal and social conduct, he needs to know himself, and then to inform himself about other men and their manners. The century opened with John Florio's translation of that great self-inquirer, the French essayist Montaigne*, and early in the 18th century (1711), Addison was prescribing for himself the role of Spectator – the detached observer qualified to describe the human nature of his day: 'Thus I live in the World, rather as Spectator of Mankind, than as one of the Species; by which means I have made myself a Speculative Statesman, Soldier, Merchant and Artisan, without ever medling with any Practical Part in Life.' Addison worked through fictional representatives (the most memorable of whom is Sir Roger de Coverley*) so that he can be read as an embryonic novelist. In doing so, he was using with more particularity the method of the character writers of a hundred years before, such as Earle in *Microcosmographie* (1628); they had written generalized descriptions of human and social types.

The 17th century began still in the age of conflict, of 'dramatic vision', of the spiritual struggles of such men as the poet and preacher John Donne* (1572–1631). The great Civil Wars* of the 1640s were the culmination of this conflict, in its religious and political terms. Yet, before this, Bacon had already propounded his philosophy of scientific method (*Novum Organum**, 1620), and Thomas Browne* had written his self-revelatory testament of tolerant religious faith – *Religio Medici**. The year 1662, that of the founding of the Royal Society, brings the signs that civilized men were choosing the way of Bacon, and following the tolerance, though not the mysticism, of Browne.

When we look more closely at Milton's epic (1667) and Bunyan's allegory

(1678), we can see that the spirit of the age has, after all, accounted for them too.

4.2.1 *Epic: Milton*

'Epic'* derives from a Greek word meaning 'story', but in western European literature it has always meant 'heroic story' – a form of narrative that takes a great subject and treats it in the grandest way. This identification of epic with grandeur is due to Homer's *Iliad** and *Odyssey**, the earliest great poems known to us and built on the grand scale. Grand narrative poems have, of course, arisen in other cultures, and they existed in northern Europe before the poets of Iceland, Scandinavia, Germany and England were aware of the Homeric models. By the Renaissance, however, it was the Homeric epics which had become the ideal. In the 1st century BC the Roman poet Virgil* emulated them magnificently in his *Aeneid*,* the epic that celebrated the mythical origins of Rome and linked it with Homeric Greece. Virgil himself was, for the Middle Ages, a link between pagan Rome and European Christendom. The 13th-century *Divina Commedia** by the Italian poet Dante* is not an epic in the Homeric or Virgilian sense, but it has epic grandeur of scale, and Dante introduced Virgil into it in the character of his guide. The Virgilian epic left a legacy to the British Middle Ages in the legend (for which Virgil was not responsible) that Britain had been founded by Brutus, a great-grandson of Aeneas*, Virgil's mythical progenitor of Rome; this legend survived into the 17th century.

Milton (1608–74) was a poet of the Renaissance, and as such he revered Homer and Virgil. However, he was also an ardent Puritan*, and revered the Bible and the Christian myth of the Fall of the Angels that supplemented the biblical stories. In *Paradise Lost* he sought to combine the two traditions: he wrote a Virgilian epic whose content was Judeo-Christian myth. But to understand what Milton was undertaking, we have first to distinguish between the Homeric epic vision and that of Virgil whom Milton was specifically emulating; secondly, we have to take into account the circumstances in which Milton wrote his poem.

Scholars (*eg* C. S. Lewis in *Preface to Paradise Lost*) have distinguished between 'primary' and 'secondary' epics. Primary epics are exemplified by those of Homer; they narrate heroic events to a public for whom such stories would have contemporary significance, *ie* a society with the same values and structure as those of the epic heroes. Secondary epics, like Virgil's *Aeneid*, are written for a different sort of society, for whom the interest of the epic is that it is an imaginative account of the society's own beginnings. Thus the secondary epic is an attempt to carry into the present a sense of the greatness of the past, whereas a primary epic celebrates the greatness of its own time. Milton was writing a secondary epic, but not only that – he was imitating another secondary epic, though his had very different content and was written in very different circumstances.

Virgil wrote his epic to celebrate the greatness of Rome when he was high in the favour of the first Roman Emperor, Augustus: Milton wrote his when his party, the Puritan Republicans, had been defeated, and he had for a time gone in fear of losing his life at the hands of the anti-Puritan royalist government. He was writing a Christian poem in a Christian country, but the Church of England was against him and he was against the prevailing spirit of Restoration* Society. Thus he felt himself in opposition – against the current of his time:

> *though fallen on evil days*
> *On evil days though fallen, and evil tongues,*
> *In darkness, and with dangers compass'd round,*
> *And solitude . . .*
>
> (From the opening of Book VII)

Thus *Paradise Lost*, unlike epics in general, is a 'resistance' poem. To this is due, perhaps, the well-known paradox – at least an apparent paradox – about Satan, the great antagonist to the sovereignty of God and to the human race, who nonetheless compels admiration:

> *A mind not to be changed by place or time.*

Whether Milton unconsciously identified himself with Satan, the Fallen Angel, contrary to his intentions for his poem, or whether Satan dominates much of the poem merely because it is easier for the reader to feel sympathy with rebellion than with authority, is critically controversial, but most readers feel that there is some identification.

But *Paradise Lost* is a 'resistance' poem in another sense also. Its Latinate grandeur has long seemed foreign to English idiom and tradition. The English language 'sunk under him' commented Addison early in the 18th century, and Johnson later added: 'He was desirous to use English words with a foreign idiom'; Keats, early in the 19th century, protested that 'English ought to be kept up', as he tried to free his own work from Miltonic influence, and 20th-century critics and poets have made still severer strictures of the same kind on Milton's language. The immediate cause of this Latinacy is of course that Milton was using a Latin poet for his model, but this in itself had a deeper cause. Milton shared with his enemies a deeply classical culture, and he was using this culture to display Puritan values and Hebraic mythology with which they were out of sympathy. It is as though he were saying: '*This* is what ought to be inspiring your devotion and disciplining your classical culture, and look how sublime it is when I use *my* classical culture to expound it!' Prevailing tastes of his time did not of course reject the doctrine of Milton's subject, but he considered that they were turning away from the spirit of that doctrine. He was right, and he was also successful, for the public of the day greatly admired the poem.

In so far as Milton may have unconsciously identified himself with Satan's great 'resistance movement', his poem contains dramatic conflict, but this, in any case, is true only of the first two books. The rest of *Paradise Lost* is a great display of Bible story and Christian myth presented in the manner most likely to impress his contemporaries – an outcome of the 'descriptive vision', not the 'dramatic vision'.

4.2.2 *Satirical epic: Butler, Dryden, Pope*

Satire is hostile to its subject, and therefore the opposite to epic, which sustains and elevates the dignity of its subject. An effective kind of satire, therefore, is to pretend to use epic, and then to show the subject to be unworthy of it, thus exposing the distance between the actual subject under satire and one that deserves epic treatment. This may be done in various ways, and the period 1660–1760 – the great age for English satire – contains diverse examples of 'satirical epic'. Butler's *Hudibras** (1663–78) is a satire against the Puritans; Butler adapts the method of the Spanish writer, Cervantes, author of the early-17th-century comic romance, *Don Quixote**. Two men – a Presbyterian and an Independent – who pretend to elevated ideals, are shown to be rascally in practice; they have adventures which, instead of exhibiting them heroically and tragically, are laughable and end contemptibly. Dryden's *Absalom and Achitophel** (1681) had a political purpose – to discredit the Whig opposition to James Duke of York (later James II*), the brother and heir of King Charles II*. Dryden's method is to describe the political events in terms of King David and his son Absalom, and to identify the Whig leaders with those shown in the Bible story to have been against the divinely appointed king. Since it is part of Dryden's purpose to show not merely that the Whigs are wrong, but that they are dangerous, he does not on the whole diminish them by contempt, but makes them formidable by expounding their selfish and destructive ferocity:

In friendship false, implacable in hate,
Resolv'd to ruin or to rule the state . . .

Such portraits, though hostile, are balanced and living creations of men driven by real psychic forces.

Alexander Pope* (1688–1744) wrote two great satirical epics, each different in method from the other. His *Rape of the Lock** (1714) seeks to expose the triviality of the cause of a bitter quarrel between two families. He does this by reducing the 'epic machinery' to miniature, using diminutive fairies to intervene in human affairs, instead of gods and goddesses as in Homer and Virgil, or bright and dark angels as in Milton, and the affairs which concern them are trivialities such as a lady dressing herself and the protection of her coiffure. His purpose was ostensibly to reconcile the quarrelling families by making them laugh at themselves, but he goes beyond this, to depict a whole society occupied with trifling daily vanities and gratifications, and treating small things on equal terms with great ones. So at the royal court –

Hither the heroes and the nymphs resort
To taste awhile the pleasures of a court;
In various talk th'instructive hours they pass'd;
Who gave the ball, or paid the visit last;
One speaks the glory of the British Queen,
And one describes a charming Indian screen;
A third interprets motions, looks and eyes;
At every word a reputation dies.
Snuff, or the fan, supply each pause of chat,
With singing, laughing, ogling, and all that.

Pope's *Dunciad** (1742) is an altogether more massive work. Its theme is the destruction of a civilization by the forces making for inertia in a variety of unexpected ways. The epic machinery is used with all the spaciousness natural to it, but its constituents are just those with which serious epics do not concern themselves; the presiding deity of the poem is the goddess Dulness. Yet they are powerful forces: they bring the possibility of epics to an end, which is more than the greatest natural or political catastrophe can do, and so they have, paradoxically, an epic grandeur of their own –

For public flame, nor private, dares to shine,
Nor human spark is left, nor glimpse divine!
Lo! thy dread empire, Chaos! is restored;
Light dies before thy uncreating word;
Thy hand, great Anarch! lets the curtain fall
And universal darkness buries all.

These satirical epics of Butler, Dryden and Pope were not negative, destructive works. Their positiveness is rich; in particular, they build up in the reader a many-sided sense of proportion by disclosing to him the ways in which 'what ought to be' differs from 'what is', thereby impressing the mind strongly with 'fact' in relation to 'value'. Milton's epic, on the other hand, draws the mind away from the concreteness of fact into the finally inapprehensible regions of pure good and pure evil.

4.2.3 *Allegory in transformation: Bunyan*

The work that most interestingly marks a bridge between old and new is Bunyan's *Pilgrim's Progress.**

John Bunyan* (1628–88) was a Puritan evangelist who suffered 12 years of imprisonment for his faith during the reign of Charles II. He had a humble social origin. During his childhood, he heard village clergymen preaching sermons in the allegorical idiom natural to the Middle Ages, for the Reformation scarcely affected the traditional form of the village sermon. He also grew up with the popular chapbook* versions of medieval English romances, about the adventures of knights in fairylands of giants and monsters. Unaffected by the new 'scientific' curiosity of educated men, his natural idiom was the concrete proverbial expression of the countryman and the language of the Bible stories by which the Puritans lived.

This background makes *Pilgrim's Progress*, in its main features, a highly traditional work: an allegory in which life is seen as a dangerous journey between 'the City of Destruction' which is this world, and the 'Holy City' of the Christian Heaven. Its hero, Christian, does much of the journey as a knight-at-arms, fights the devil in the form of a monster like a figure from a fairy tale, Apollyon, and is imprisoned in the Castle of Giant Despair. The landscape through which he passes is that of Bunyan's native countryside, and yet continuously figures the difficulties and dilemmas of the spiritual life.

Yet Bunyan was much more than a teller of medieval fairy tales and allegories in the spirit of Puritan Bible-religion. His spiritual autobiography, *Grace Abounding*, in which he relates his personal spiritual and psychological crisis, is only the most distinguished of a number of 17th-century Puritan books of the same kind; *Pilgrim's Progress* is partly a translation into allegory of his own experience. The allegory, however, is especially remarkable for the ways in which it shows understanding of the variety of human experience; Christian meets pilgrims, as devoted as himself, whose differences of temperament cause them to have quite other trials. Thus, Christian's inward-turning temperament causes him nightmare experience in the Valleys of Humiliation and the Shadow of Death, but Faithful's outward-turning one brings him only the simple temptations of fleshly lust and social pride from such as Wanton and Shame. But the outward-turning man tends to be the most conspicuous in action, and so it is Faithful whom the judges condemn to death in the Town of Vanity Fair*.

Bunyan's discernment of the differences of the human psychology and their consequences gives his allegory a quite new kind of interest. Though the characters have names that seem to designate them by identifying them with particular characteristics, such as Christian, Faithful, Hopeful, Little Faith, Talkative, Ignorance etc., such a name does not sum up the whole of a character but merely denotes a dominant quality implying susceptibility to a particular kind of trial and the likelihood of the owner's failure or success in undergoing it. So Little Faith is a coward, but he has just enough faith to get him through life successfully; Hopeful has the courage of optimism but is susceptible to the perils of an optimist, while the pessimistic Christian might have perished under Giant Despair were it not that Hopeful accompanied him; and Talkative has all the right ideas for the good life but does not understand the difference between talking about them and living by them. This kind of psychological wisdom looks forward to the art of the novel, and reminds us that the 18th-century novel had strong elements of Puritan tradition behind it. Bunyan, after all, was a contemporary of the philosopher John Locke* (1632–1704), the author of *Letters concerning Toleration*; though they belonged to different segments of society and mental background, they had in common the belief that understanding and true description were productive, where bigotry and fanaticism were destructive.

4.2.4 *Growth of interest in character*

When we look at the extraordinary variety of narratives in this period, have they anything in common? They have attention to human character. There are the generalized types of John Earle, the representative individuals of Addison, the Whig politicians of Dryden, the political portraits in Clarendon's History, the men of fashion and learning in Pope, the gallery of Fallen Angels by Milton, the seekers and the betrayers of truth in Bunyan – not to forget the biographical portraits of Aubrey* and Walton* and the self-portraits of the diarists. Everywhere there is the instinct for portraiture, and the instinct grows rapidly after 1660. What is new is not representation of character as such, since this had always been the subject of narrative literature and was conspicuous in Shakespeare's dramas, but the interest taken in what the individual has of his own, as distinct from what he shares with all human beings, or at least other members of his class. Much of this new interest is contributed from the drama, and in the 17th century it is in many ways misleading to consider narrative and drama separately, though in this book drama has to be the subject of another essay. In both drama and narrative, the growth of attention to human character for its own sake was part of the whole movement of society, and of the withdrawal, after 1660, of religion from its position of supremacy over all the actions and thoughts of men into the position of near-equality with other departments of thought and action.

4·3

First period of the novel: 1720–1820

Introduction: the judicial vision

The form of narrative we call the novel arose in Britain during the period which is often called the 'Age of Reason', when nature and man seemed transparent to the human mind, and men valued, above all, the qualities of harmony, proportion, balance. Yet not till the work of Jane Austen* early in the 19th century do we find these values explicit in the novel: the tales of Defoe* and Smollett* are shapeless; those of Richardson* are diffuse; Fielding* is extravagant, and no novelist has been more eccentric than Sterne* except, perhaps, Joyce. The novel, of course, is a form that has always resisted definition; by its nature it lends itself to untidiness and experiment. So we have the apparent contradiction that the very age that valued order and regularity itself produced the form of literature which is most wayward in such qualities.

The explanation is partly that the ideals of the age did not altogether accord with the social facts of it. An art form is a social product; if the society is tidily coherent, its art is likely to be so, but if the society is mixed and confusing, the art will be, at least in some of its manifestations, adaptable and elusive. English society in the 18th century had a rich landed aristocracy, a vigorous commercial class, and a very strong class of middle landowners – the squires*. But the boundaries between these classes were not distinct: they were crossed by intermarriage, they were confused by changes of fortune, and the classes were brought together by many of the same interests; for instance, all classes valued land, and acquired it when they could, and at the same time all classes were permeated by a business-like, often commercial, energy. In religion, fanaticism (except among the socially humble Methodists*) had gone, and religious faith was a conservative force, whether for property and status as among the squirearchy, or as a guarantee of orderly social conduct among the Dissenters*, the former Puritans. The professions and background of the writers are themselves an indication of the cultural conditions: Defoe began as a Dissenting business man and became one of the first modern journalists; Swift*, of a ruined Cavalier* family, combined journalism and the Church; Richardson was a printer, and Fielding was the grandson of an earl; Smollett was a doctor; Sterne, a clergyman, and Jane Austen, the daughter of one. The list shows a predominance of the middle classes, but an even more varied middle class than the professions suggest, and their books were more various still.

Yet all these writers belonged to the Age of Reason in a real sense. The 'Reason', however, of aristocrats like Lord Chesterfield, or of a fashionable poet such as Pope, became something different in the minds of middle-class adventurers like Defoe and Smollett, to whom it presented itself as a strong sense of fact; for Jane Austen it was discrimination between the subtleties and incongruities of human behaviour, and for Richardson – the self-conscious moralist – it was a duty to create ideal models of conduct. Moreover, the very clarity and objectivity that Reason implies invite their opposite, the desirability of cultivating the feelings; and the philosophers not only distinguished the faculties of emotion and reason, but tended to rest morality on 'the tenderness of the affections'. Furthermore, their respect for reason and order itself made 18th-century writers sensitive to the disorderliness of actual human life. In painting, the elegance and sweetness of Gainsborough (1727–88) were counterbalanced by the grotesque realism of Hogarth* (1697–1764), and Hogarth made a strong impression on the novelists.

The novelists belonged to the Age of Reason especially in the assurance of their judgement. Faith in the possibility of arriving at true judgements was a deep assumption in the age which was inaugurated by the physics of Isaac Newton* (1642–1727), and included the philosopher David Hartley* (1705–57) who aspired to be the Newton of human psychology. However, this faith in the faculty of reasoned judgement was paradoxically connected with a new kind of scepticism originating in the thought of the French philosopher Descartes* (1596–1650), who asked the question 'What do I know?' and concluded that initially he could know only the fact that he existed. Descartes thus undermined the long tradition, paramount in the Middle Ages, that knowledge was imposed on the mind by authority – the authority of accepted tradition and the Church. Descartes' postulate grew into the assumption that it was for the individual to discover the truth for himself, through the use of his own faculties working through his social experience. Exactly this was to become the material of the novelist: the individual discovering his own nature through his society. His religious faith, even his ethical ideals, became secondary to social fact as it impinged on him. In the second half of the 17th century the English philosopher John Locke* reinforced Descartes' insistence on reliance on individual judgement, but he also provided a hypothesis which was helpful to the novelist in another way. If our judgements are essentially individual, how, when we describe them, do we convince others of the truth of the facts we observe? Locke, in his *Essay concerning Human Understanding** (1690) distinguished what he called the 'primary qualities' of objects (their weight, shape, measurement, etc.) about which all observers can agree, from their 'secondary qualities' (smell, colour, beauty, etc.) about which individual judgements may disagree widely. By the 19th century, more complex ideas of imaginative truth were to make Locke's primary qualities seem very inadequate for the scope of the novel, but for the 18th-century novelist his theory offered a useful technique for presenting the imaginary – even impossible – worlds convincingly to the mind's eye of the reader.

4.3.1 *The beginnings of the novel: Defoe and Swift*

Defoe's first work of fiction, *Robinson Crusoe**, appeared in 1719. It became famous especially for its first part, which contains the account of Crusoe's long solitude on the desert island. Defoe had never been on one, though he had talked to Alexander Selkirk who had; and he had never travelled, though he had read travellers' tales. Yet the story is built up with such careful attention to factual detail, and Crusoe's practical anxieties and pride in achievement are so convincing, that the book reads like a personal memoir. Before he became a novelist, Defoe was one of the first of the modern newspaper journalists; the craft of journalism and the art of the novel have always been related, for the material of both is the facts of daily living.

This prominence of factual detail originated in the life of the class of people to whom Defoe belonged. He was the son of a London butcher, and he had the tradesman's preoccupation with the detail of life. He was also of Puritan background, and he shared the Puritan's religious devotion to productive work, for this and the success it brought were considered to be signs that God's Grace was on a man's side. Yet it is significant that Crusoe gives little of his time to thinking about God, except when reminded of him in illness and times of danger. It is also significant that when Crusoe refers to God, he often does so under the name of Providence –

ie 'the Power that Provides'. When Crusoe settles the island with other colonists, he has to be reminded by a French Catholic priest that he has forgotten to arrange for their religious life. The Puritans, by now known as Dissenters, were losing their insistent concern with God, and were relying more upon their personal endeavours – as Crusoe does – than upon prayer. It was still, however, an unthinkable notion – though Crusoe at times comes near to thinking it – that there might, after all, be no Providence to sustain human endeavours.

Robinson Crusoe is in many ways a strangely limited book. In construction it is 'episodic', that is to say, it consists of a succession of episodes each of which is fairly complete in itself, and it lacks, or appears to lack, unity of theme. Its absence of plot matters little; what matters is that the man Crusoe is not built up into a complete, many-sided human being. His relationship with women is almost ignored; his happiest friendship is with his servant Friday, whom he values in that capacity; the happiness of his relationships with other men depends on whether they are good 'business partners'; God himself is presented as the Senior Partner of all commercial partnerships. Crusoe has no sense of beauty; we infer that his island is beautiful, but Crusoe describes it only as productive.

Yet the book has been significant and deeply satisfying to many readers. Human beings have always had to struggle with the hard facts of the surroundings in which they live; moreover they have usually had to continue the struggle from generation to generation, so that no one in a single lifetime could claim the satisfaction of victory, but only of continuance and survival. In the Middle Ages, and in earlier, mythologizing times, men transfigured the repetitive tedium of the struggle by dramatizing the sequence of reviving and subsiding life in the revolutions of the seasons. A change came about when colonizing began, such as that of the Puritan settlers during the 17th century on the eastern American seaboard, for the colonists were able to see the transformation of wilderness into cultivated land in the space of a lifetime; labour then took on the shape of heroic enterprise. Defoe, by showing how Crusoe constructed for himself a habitable and even prosperous settlement by his unaided effort and ingenuity, achieved a kind of prose epic of the humdrum, and his book became a permanent inspiration to sober, patient and practical men such as his fellow Dissenters of the 18th century.

Swift's *Gulliver's Travels** (1726) was written partly in emulation of the success of *Robinson Crusoe*, but with an intention very different from Defoe's. Swift's book is a unique, unclassifiable work, of much greater complexity than *Robinson Crusoe*, and not a novel at all in the usual sense of the word. Moreover, the success of *Robinson Crusoe* is partly that Defoe never goes beyond the limits of the possible, whereas Swift works in terms of what is impossible: a land of people six inches tall, another where they measure 60 feet, a third inhabited by people of excessively developed intellect, a fourth where they are immortal, a fifth where the horses are civilized and the humans are brutes – these are the vehicles of his allegorical satire of the illusions and false pretensions of the human race. It is a book that needs to be interpreted on many levels. Yet on one of these levels Swift's method is similar to

Defoe's, though his style is much more powerful. Gulliver, like Crusoe, is a plain 'man of sense' who records these marvels with careful detail, in the language of the traveller who expects to be believed. Also, Swift is careful to restrict the impossible elements to only one aspect of Gulliver's surroundings at a time, and to present them with the same care for sober particularity as the normal elements. In consequence, the reader is not led away into fantasy, but taught to see how much his habitual outlook and valuations rest upon unexamined assumptions, for instance, about the normality of the spatial dimensions in his habitual environment. Gulliver, like other 'men of sense', assumes that human beings have an inborn kingliness that sets them apart from other animals, but when he finds himself with the dimensions of a small animal in a world of giants – terrified of falling off a table – he takes on much of the mentality of a small animal; his sense of superiority has really depended on apparently insignificant material factors to which he would have supposed himself spiritually superior. In the last tale, Gulliver is enabled to see the human race quite objectively, since the intelligent beings in the land of the Houyhnhnms* are non-human: he painfully learns that the 'normal' human qualities on which he has prided himself are strange peculiarities, and most repulsive ones. All this is 'novelistic', for it gives a heightened sense of ordinary experience and of habitual ways of feeling.

The novel, like any other fictional form, is not merely a device for telling a tale, but a way of envisaging human experience. Like any other envisagement, it became habitual only gradually, and was shaped by many influences and other kinds of narrative. Defoe, no doubt, was the first writer to be recognizably a novelist, but Swift – and also Bunyan – were both of them profounder writers than Defoe, and contributed even more than he did to the development of the novel-form as the most prevalent medium for the recording of modern experience in depth.

4.3.2 *Inward versus outward: Richardson and Fielding*

Two important contributions to the shaping of the novel were the 18th-century practice of letter-writing,* and the theatre of the Comedy of Manners*.

Letter-writing was having its best period. The more prosperous classes had the requisite leisure and cultivation of mind; communications were good enough to make postal delivery reliable, and not so good as to facilitate frequent personal meetings. A letter was a work of literature, to be composed with care and at length; proficiency at it was an art, respected even by the Dissenting middle classes who regarded other forms of art as at best irrelevant to the serious business of living. They did not consider irrelevant one of the main purposes of a letter-writer of the time – to produce 'a faithful and chaste copy of real life and manners'.

This was Samuel Richardson's* tribute to the famous French letter-writer, Madame de Sévigné. He was himself a member of the serious-minded middle classes, and well known for his gifts in the 'epistolary art'. Some booksellers (the publishers of the day) asked him to compile a guide to letter-writing for literate but inexperienced country girls, and the resulting book also gave guidance on 'how to think and act justly and prudently in the common Concerns of Human Life'. *Familiar Letters for Important Occasions* was Richardson's inspiration for his first novel, written entirely in letters between imaginary characters – *Pamela**, *or Virtue Rewarded* (1741). This too was intended as a guide to prudent conduct, by showing how a girl who is at great social disadvantage nonetheless succeeds in making a great social position for herself without losing her virtue, but it was also a work of art, which, to Richardson's alarm and disgust, attracted criticism in regard to its truth to real experience and the genuineness of its moral values.

The most formidable of his critics was Henry Fielding*, a man of aristocratic background, with the rich classical education of such men of the time, and much wider social experience than Richardson had. He had been a dramatist in the Comedy of Manners tradition, satirizing the society and politics of the age; to him, *Pamela* was hypocritical and narrow. He replied to it with *Joseph Andrews** (1742), written as a straight narrative, part parody and part social satire. Fielding had all the freedom of outlook of the dramatists of the Comedy of Manners; he was quite without Richardson's false delicacy in sexual matters, and he excelled in the sharp, vivid dialogue characteristic of that school of the theatre. But his book has an older form than Richardson's: it is in the picaresque convention of events linked together not so much by the logic of a plot as by the chances of a journey. It was the method of the Spanish and Italian romances of the 16th and 17th centuries, such as *Don Quixote**, and of the older Arthurian romances which had their effect, through popular versions or imitations, on Bunyan's *Pilgrim's Progress*.

A duel had opened between Richardson and Fielding, and this first encounter was to Fielding's advantage. But Richardson was in some ways a superior artist to his rival, in spite of the latter's superiority in education, experience, and breadth of sympathy. Richardson's next novel, *Clarissa Harlowe** (1747–8), was a masterpiece which showed the great virtues of his epistolary method. The first of these virtues shows itself in the treatment of time: letters give the reader the illusion, as perhaps no other narrative form does, of living in the time-scale of the characters. There is no author whose voice is narrating the events from a point in the future, and so the reader feels that he is enduring the sequence of events at the same rate of time as the character is. Thus, as Defoe and Swift caused the reader to feel the incessant pressure of space, so Richardson now added time pressure. A second virtue of the method is one that helped to overcome his personal limitations as a novelist. Inhibited as he was by his moral principles against frivolity and vice, and ignorant of the influence of the sexual instincts on his own nature, he was all the more determined to expose the nature of vice and frivolity, and to do so he had to include characters of whom he disapproved. But the epistolary method demands that a character should write his own letters, and he is therefore enabled to state his own case; the consequence is that *Clarissa* is a novel of dramatically varied outlooks, and the narrowness of *Pamela*, in which too many of the letters are written by the heroine, is avoided. A third virtue also helped Richardson the artist to overcome Richardson the man. The 18th-century style of ample letter gave the writer much opportunity for self-analysis; not only did this cause *Clarissa* to become known as the first great 'psychological' novel, but the over-idealized heroine comes more to life than one might expect, with the result of making her more human and less above the reach of common human sympathy.

Fielding himself admired *Clarissa*, yet his own next novel, *Tom Jones**, is a kind of answer to Richardson's masterpiece. Fielding again uses straight narrative, but he is more evidently conscious of attempting something new than Richardson is. In *Joseph Andrews*, he tells the reader that he is writing a 'comic epic', thereby claiming that he is innovating on a tradition that goes back to the dim figure of Homer. The expression 'comic epic' implies a structure, and *Tom Jones* has more coherence than any previous prose fiction in English; the range of character is also again wider, more humane, and in some ways more convincing than Richardson's. This time, however, the psychological penetration into character is shallower, and the emotional texture is loose and uneven by comparison with Richardson's minuteness. Fielding's vision is all on surfaces; Richardson's, all inward.

But Fielding also contributed a feature which derived from the essay tradition of Addison* and Steele*: he intersperses his narrative with essays that present quite nakedly his authorial point of view. It is not a device much favoured by 20th-century novelists, and even in the 19th century 'authorial intrusion' (in George Eliot* for example) is interspersed within the narrative. But Fielding's method has merits. In a realistic art like that of the novel, the relationship of the author to his subject must always be controversial. He may pretend to invisibility (like Jane Austen*) but the reader has to connive at the convention; or he may identify himself with the central character (like Defoe) but this limits his scope of treatment. Fielding's self-exposure has the advantage of winning the reader's confidence. On the other hand, it was another merit of the epistolary method that Richardson could achieve invisibility quite effortlessly.

4.3.3 *The novel reaches maturity: Sterne to Jane Austen*

The epistolary method was used by novelists after Richardson, notably Tobias Smollett (*Humphry Clinker**, 1771) and Fanny Burney* (*Evelina**, 1778); they had much less insight than Richardson into its possibilities, and the vivid life of these two books could equally well have been conveyed by straight narrative. After them, the method ceased to be used by important novelists. Its disappearance probably has social causes – the special cultivation of the letter as a form of personal communication began slowly to decline, so that the medium became fictionally less convincing. More significant, undoubtedly, were its artistic limitations; it restricted the author in his treatment of narrative, especially by slowing up the story if it was used realistically.

How to write a novel began to occupy the minds of novelists increasingly, as they became more aware of the newness of the form. The most original of the experimenters was Laurence Sterne*, whose *Tristram Shandy** appeared in successive volumes between 1760 and 1767. His approach was to make the business of writing itself into comedy, by exposing all his problems to the reader. At what point should the writer begin his narrative? In what sense, if at all, is the writer digressing when he is elaborating the characters that surround his central character? What are the limitations, if any, to the devices by which the writer may use the medium of print to affect the reader? Sterne succeeds in writing one of the most entertaining novels in English literature while pretending that he can never really begin. And since his nominal theme is *The Life and Opinions* of Tristram Shandy, his critical difficulties are as relevant to the parallel art of biography as to the art of the novel.

These arts are never far apart. As the novel moved towards maturity, English biography achieved its principal masterpiece in James Boswell's *The Life of Samuel Johnson** (1791). The obvious restrictions on the biographer, when compared with the novelist, are that he can neither achieve the inward knowledge of his subjects that the novelist is able to assume for his own creations, nor, except at moments, can he give them the same immediacy. Boswell however is unique in going far to break down these barriers, especially the second one; he did this by spending many hours with his subject, and recording much of his conversation. Thereby he not only achieved a great and vivid work of art, but he showed ways in which the biographer can give lessons to the novelist. The chief of these is the discipline of the historian of human life. The novelist, it is true, writes fiction, not fact, but novelistic fiction has the peculiarity that it must (generally) give the reader an illusion of fact. It is not the novelist's function to idealize his characters, as Richardson had done, and it *is* his function to give a convincing image of the human mind, changing yet consistent in vicissitude, as Defoe and Fielding had not done. The biographer is forced by the nature of his material to remember these requirements, but the novelist is tempted to forsake them for effects which are better achieved in other forms of literature.

The first novelist in English literature to understand what the novel should not attempt, and what it can do supremely well, was Jane Austen*. Her restricted subject-matter – the small section of society that she treats, the scarcity of startling episode, the narrow range of her settings – has been attributed to the restricted experience of life of this unmarried clergyman's daughter. The real explanation is artistic. She knew that significant experience did not always or necessarily arise from extraordinary conditions, that conversations about what is commonplace may reveal character even more effectively than conversations about what is exceptional, and that the depth of a reader's impression of a story is proportionate to the extent to which he has found it convincing. She came at the end of a century in which the art of irony had been practised with unprecedented skill. With this instrument she exposes the inwardness of her characters while they never cease to conform to the obligations imposed by the outward social circumstances, and thus she unifies the inner and outer imaginative approaches of Richardson and Fielding. Hers are the first novels in English to show full and true artistic discipline, yet without sacrifice of human depth. Later novelists, writing under different social conditions, enriched the art by breaking the limits she imposed on herself, but it would be a mistake to assume from this that her art was excessively conventional. It was Jane Austen who first brought to light what was to be one of the principal themes of the later-19th-century novel: the predicament of the individual, particularly of the woman, who requires personal fulfilment in society, and finds that society imposes far more obstacles than opportunities for realizing the desire.

4.3.4 *The narrative poem: 1790–1825*

Jane Austen wrote her balanced, restrained, 'classical' novels well aware that she was living in an age that was deeply disturbed. Prose, since the beginning of the Age of Reason in the 17th century, had steadily usurped from verse its centrality in imaginative expression. But the French Revolution* had battered the assumptions of the Age of Reason, although it was itself partly caused by them. Accordingly, it was accompanied and followed by a period of emotional release and spiritual conflict, both of which found their natural medium in verse.

The range of narrative verse during these 45 years is remarkably large: we have the 'prophetic poems' of Blake*, new kinds of epic with a personal psychological symbolism; imitations of the medieval ballad and romance by Scott*, Coleridge* and Keats*; the attempt to revive classical epic by Keats and others; a new use for classical myth by Shelley*, to dramatize contemporary ideological conflict; Byron's* exotic tales, and his partly autobiographical, partly satirical social surveys in *Childe Harold** and *Don Juan**; Wordsworth's* deep but quiet tales of man in nature, and Crabbe's* epigrammatic, realistic tales of man in society.

This extensive body of work can be approximately divided into a large group of poems, some of which are profound in their subject, some superficial, but all remote in time or place from Britain and its society, and a smaller group of comparatively 'realistic' narratives. The larger group contains a few masterpieces, especially three by Coleridge, but the successes are comparatively rare, perhaps because the poets lacked the shared tradition of myth that gave medieval romances like *Sir Gawain and the Green Knight* their significance.

It is from the smaller group that more works of living interest survive. This group includes from Wordsworth at least the first two books of *The Prelude**, *Michael**, and *Margaret or The Ruined Cottage*, and from Crabbe, his tales in the 1812 volume. Byron is extravagant or realistic at his pleasure, but it is possible to see the last four books of *Don Juan* as moving towards a novel in verse. Perhaps it is natural, since the mood of the age was still mainly 'novelistic' in spite of the verse revival, that the larger proportion of the most living verse narratives should be those which come nearest to novelistic subject matter. At all events, these poems were in an important respect actually in advance of the novels of the time: the poets, especially Wordsworth and Crabbe, show sensitive and deep awareness of the relationship between characters and their physical environment.

4·4

Individual and environment: 1815–80

Introduction: the comprehensive vision

Literary forms commonly develop their greatest amplitude when the nations that produce them are living through a period of heightened vitality. The vitality of England in the reign of Elizabeth I culminated in the drama of Shakespeare and his contemporaries; the dynamic of the Industrial Revolution* made the reign of Queen Victoria* (1837–1901) the great period of the novel in Britain.

Britain was for a time the richest country in the world, but at the price of being the first to encounter the immense social problems that arise from the rapid development of urban industry. As humanitarian individuals, the novelists could see no solutions beyond the enlightening and sensitizing of the social conscience. As artists, they were awakened to the factor of environment, in the sense both of the social structure as it affected the individual, and of the physical surroundings conditioned by the social structure. Writers of previous centuries had, of course, also been aware of environments, but they had felt them either as permanent and static backgrounds to people (*eg* the 18th-century novelists) or as fields of natural forces. The Victorian novelist saw environment either as change, especially social change, or as a force for social stability. The life of the great towns and of nationwide high society was the life of change, bewilderment and distress, but it also made for energy and the optimism that energy brings; the life of the small towns and the villages was orderly, permanent, traditional and comparatively safe, but it depended on a balance of society and social values that was growing precarious, and it also made for narrowness of outlook and frustration of energy.

The new consciousness of society and environment as active forces to be characterized equally with individuals was stimulated from other sources besides the Industrial Revolution. The political French Revolution of 1789 aroused questions about the nature of societies, their histories, and the histories of particular national societies; and the French Revolution itself was the product of the critical and inquiring spirit of the century behind it. The 18th century built up an antiquarian interest in the reconstruction of the past, one outcome of which was historical works, of which Gibbon's *Decline and Fall of the Roman Empire** (1776–88) was the most splendid. Historical writing led to the historical novel, which Sir Walter Scott* practically invented. To reconstruct in a novel a society of the past is to look at that society as a whole and from the outside, in a way that is strictly impossible in regard to the society of one's own time. Moreover, Scott wrote his first and best novels about Scotland, a small country which became politically united to England in 1707, and had undergone marked changes of development in the 17th and 18th centuries. Looking back upon his country in those centuries, Scott could see the formative influence of events on the Scotland of his own day. The past worlds of *Old Mortality** (1816) and *The Heart of Midlothian** (1818) were meaningful to him as the worlds of medieval and 16th-century England of his later and inferior novels were not. He was the first novelist writing in English to achieve a comprehensive vision of man in his social environment.

4.4.1 *Man in the great town: Dickens (1812–70)*

Dickens* was principally an urban writer, and the setting of all his novels (except *Hard Times**, about a northern industrial town) is at least partly London. People create towns, and the towns then shape the inhabitants. Consequently, a Dickens character is vivid often to the extent that he can be 'placed' in characteristic surroundings; the surroundings partake of his life and contribute to him a vitality that has become their own. In the later novels, the inanimate surroundings are often intensified impressively and menacingly, seeming both to emanate from social evil and to symbolize social evil that has escaped the possibility of human control; such are the fog that opens *Bleak House** and the River Thames in *Our Mutual Friend**. Part of Dickens's peculiar power as a novelist is thus his 'sensational' force, his capacity to make the reader feel an environment acting upon him.

His sense of the life that emanates from the inanimate gives added substance to his characters as social beings, for, to an even greater extent than rural surroundings, urban ones are impressed with social differences. Thus the social peculiarities of a Dickens character commonly impress themselves with an intensity proportionate to that of his surroundings. But this strong feeling for social varieties and gradations goes with a feeling for human character that goes back through Fielding and Ben Jonson to Chaucer; often called caricature in Dickens, it is really a delight in primitive vitality and belongs to the comic genius, though in Dickens it sometimes softens to tearful sentimentality and sometimes hardens into grim and violent drama. It fights against the arbitrariness of social classification, and, especially after 1850, the resultant clash between the individual and society intensifies into increasingly sombre drama.

London elated Dickens by its energies and appalled him by its indifference, and London and society were associated in his mind. However, the Victorians were great cultivators of family life, and in Dickens as in some other novelists the happy family was like a subculture where the distressed could ultimately hope for refuge from the ruthlessness of society at large. Such refuges were often associated with an almost pastoral nostalgia for the freshness and sweetness of the countryside and the traditional values of human life. Dickens took, if anything, an even grimmer view of society in the past; and saw more hope in new ironmasters than in old landed aristocracy; on the other hand the squirearchy or middle landed gentry, like Mr Wardle of Dingley Dell in *Pickwick Papers**, sustained humane values from age to age – 'the religion of Christmas'.

4.4.2 *Humanity in the countryside: George Eliot, Hardy, Emily Brontë*

The period 1830–80 changed England from a predominantly rural country into a predominantly urban one; the first thirty years of it were the last in which the farmer's way of life seemed the basic norm of existence, and during the whole period the contrast between town and country was more pronounced than ever before. The contrast led certain novelists without an urban background to be more conscious than hitherto of the rural surroundings of the regions where they had spent their youth; it also caused them to be aware of the changes in those regions, so that they commonly wrote about them as they had been a generation before the time of writing.

Emily Brontë's* only novel, *Wuthering Heights** (1847) has always been regarded as one of the most singular and isolated of English novels, and it is often seen as one of the remotest from familiar social conditions. But there are plenty of signs in it that the author knew where she was in relation to her time. Until the Industrial Revolution, the north of England had commonly been perhaps a hundred years behind the south; now its industrial districts were in advance of the rest of the country, but its moors and hills still contained regions that followed ways of life forgotten elsewhere, and to ensure the relative primitiveness of the setting of her novel, Emily Brontë dated the events in it back to the end of the 18th century. Wuthering Heights, in the moorland, is a household which is still almost medieval in its outlook in comparison with the up-to-date Thrushcross Grange down in the valley, where Jane Austen might have been on visiting terms. But there is an element more primitive in the book than the moorland farm; this is the waif, Heathcliff, who is never assimilated even by that household, though he is introduced into it as a child. The principal heroine, Catherine Earnshaw of Wuthering Heights, is torn between her devotion to Heathcliff with the freedom of instinctual life that he gives her, and her desire to advance herself by marriage to Edgar Linton of the Grange. The book, like *Pilgrim's Progress*, stands on a frontier, looking back into the past and anticipating the future: Emily Brontë anticipates the restlessness of women in the 20th century, refusing a code of civilization that repressed their energies, but she also raises the question whether a 'tamed' society can ever properly assimilate the wildness of instinctual impulse in all human beings. Such questions were not to be raised again by a novelist until D. H. Lawrence*.

Her exceptional insight proceeded from her exceptional surroundings; a more familiar English rural background is that of the Wessex novels of Thomas Hardy*, whom we have to consider here though his career as a novelist (1870–96) extends beyond the period we are at present discussing. Hardy was born in south-western England, whose ancient name of Wessex* he revived. Of all the major English novelists, he was nearest, by social origin, to the peasantry which, until the later 19th century, formed the great majority of the English population. In his early life he shared their folk-culture of ballad and song; by the time he became a novelist he was aware how this regional culture, the basis of all he most loved, was decaying and being destroyed. This, and his loss of religious faith which was part of the same tradition, instilled into him a tragic and fatalistic vision; his books contrast the ancient continuity of rural society – which he by no means sentimentalizes – with the rootless and dispersed, though more adaptable, energies of the newer kind of man. *The Mayor of Casterbridge**, for example, contrasts the Wessex man, Michael Henchard, a country man of the old style whose monolithic personality gives the whole of itself into every activity, with the wandering Scotsman, Donald Farfrae, who lives by cool-headed ingenuity. Both are admirable men, but Henchard fails in his rivalry with Farfrae because of the latter's far greater adaptability to changing circumstances. It is Henchard who makes the greater impression on the reader, not just because his tragedy is the theme of the book, but because he is unified by the force of his native surroundings into a simpler, more impulsive, but much larger being than Farfrae, whose personality is divided into compartments, each of which is brought to life at the appropriate time of need. Hardy did not reject the social developments which were changing people with their circumstances, but he saw the loss as well as the gain. And the loss was not to be estimated merely in the perishing of old customs, but in the passing away of a kind of humanity which would never be replaced.

Midway in time between *Wuthering Heights* and Hardy's earliest Wessex novel come the earlier novels of midland rural life by Mary Ann Evans, who wrote under the pen-name of George Eliot*. Her father managed a great estate in Warwickshire, Shakespeare's county, and her early experience gave her an extraordinary knowledge of the range of country society, from the aristocracy to the humblest villager. Like Hardy, she lost her religious faith, and this intellectual scepticism gave her, as it gave him, all the greater emotional attachment to the qualities of stability and wholeness to be found in the long-established traditions of village life. They emerge most clearly in *Adam Bede** (1859) and *Silas Marner** (1861). Yet George Eliot was no more inclined than Hardy to sentimentalize the village and the country town; the first of these two novels contains a tragedy which shows the precariousness of the balance of village relationships, and the second exposes the dreary nullity of the household of the widowed Squire Cass, once it has lost the refining and humanizing influence of a dedicated woman. Village life was rigid, and the Victorian village was growing stagnant; once it lost any of its important components, it tended to become empty. The role of womanhood in it was crucial, and yet sharply defined, allowing no scope for the free development of the original spirit; this is Maggie Tulliver's tragedy in *The Mill on the Floss** (1860).

4.4.3 *Women and the human environment: Elizabeth Gaskell to Henry James*

Probably no other culture has produced a succession of women artists to equal that of the English women novelists of the 19th century, and it seems that their existence must be connected with the struggle of women towards personal independence during the period. It was not a self-consciously conducted campaign, as it was to become in the 20th century, but it showed itself in an increasing awareness among both sexes that women were developing a will to self-determination which the established social tradition had no space for. Women characters thus acquired a kind of importance in imaginative literature, such as they had never had before. Defoe's heroines in the 18th century were, through misfortune, outcasts from society, struggling to reach positions of safe material respectability; Richardson's are patterns of feminine virtue of the conventional kind, forced into unnatural isolation by the viciousness of men. The women in Victorian novels, on the contrary, are more likely to have strongly characterized identities within the social framework, and these identities are of various kinds, though the novelists use them for two principal functions.

In many novels, women tend to become value-indicators in the turmoil of a still predominantly masculine world; a conspicuous example is Little Dorrit* in Dickens's novel of that name. But in this function they are not necessarily benign influences: Thackeray's *Vanity Fair** (1848) is a panorama of wealthy, hypocritical society which the little adventuress Becky Sharp exploits to her best advantage; Trollope's* *Barchester Towers* (1857) is about a cathedral town whose old and dignified church customs are challenged by an ambitious, vulgar, but practical and reforming bishop's wife, Mrs Proudie. They are antagonists to the humane values, which in both books are presented conservatively, but it is significant that these women have on the whole superior vitality, as creations, among the characters. In novels of social conflict, such as Elizabeth Gaskell's* *Mary Barton** (1848) and *North and South** (1855), women play the reconciling roles that are natural to them; more original is her use of the feminine society of *Cranford** (1853) as an index of the values of the active, male world outside it.

The other function to which novelists put their leading women characters is to make the vulnerability of women in social and domestic contexts the theme of a novel. Examples of this are Lucy Snowe in Charlotte Brontë's* *Villette** (1853), Molly Gibson in Mrs Gaskell's *Wives and Daughters** (1865), and Clara Middleton in Meredith's *The Egoist** (1879). In the second of these, the heroine's life and relationships are complicated by her father's second marriage; in the third, the heroine sets herself against the arrogance of the man proposed to her for marriage, and finds herself in conflict with a whole tradition of masculine assumptions of superiority. The first is the most radical of the three; Charlotte Brontë's heroine has to seek her living by adventuring alone into a foreign country, and her subsequent experience not only reveals a clash between feminine and masculine values, but between these of Anglo-Saxon Protestant individualism, and Latin Catholic authoritarianism. The two richest examples of this kind of novel are George Eliot's *Daniel Deronda** (1876) and Henry James's *The Portrait of a Lady** (1881). The first receives its title from the hero, but it is the heroine, Gwendolen Harleth, who matters. Her personality is rich in proportion as the social demands upon her are narrow; her tragedy is that it is her attempt to break through these limits by meeting them at their largest promise – 'a great marriage' – that dooms her to her most deathly frustration; George Eliot makes the marriage a test of the values of 'great society' and reveals these values as illusive and static. Henry James's theme is a similar one, but he alters the perspective by making his heroine, Isabel Archer, an American (that is to say, already comparatively an 'emancipated' woman) and rich, yet Isabel's 'free' choice proves to be as deadly to her as Gwendolen's 'compelled' one.

These novels of the feminine predicament have the deep theme of the need for the individual to fulfil herself in relationship with a society which hardly provides the conditions for fulfilment. The predicament was particularly distinct for women, but it existed also for men. George Eliot's next-to-last novel, *Middlemarch** (1872), is peculiarly central because it uses both functions of the woman character: the personal predicament of 'woman in society' becomes indicative of the whole web that entangles the individual and society together. *Middlemarch* is the most comprehensive of the Victorian novels, coming nearest to a portrayal of a 'whole society'.

4.4.4 *The dramatic monologue*

Verse narrative, having undergone revival in the first quarter of the 19th century, continued to be written extensively throughout its remaining years, but it is chiefly read now in one of the forms that it took – an invention of the Victorian period.

The 'dramatic monologue'* has resemblances to the 'confessions' of some of Chaucer's characters, for example the Prologues of the Wife of Bath and the Pardoner in his *Canterbury Tales.* The true origins of the form, however, are in the early-19th-century 'conversation poems' (especially those by Coleridge) in which the poet meditates freely and at length, as though addressing a friend or one of his family. In Tennyson's early work, this meditation becomes a speech in the mouth of an imagined character, such as the Greek hero Ulysses, or the seer, Tiresias. The value of this device is that the poet can express through his character emotions and attitudes for which he would have had difficulty in finding a form, had he sought to express them in his own person. But the dramatic monologue is especially associated with Robert Browning*, who used it rather differently: where Tennyson used it to release emotions otherwise difficult to formulate, Browning tried to penetrate the experience of men in other periods, and styles of mind different from his own. Browning's use of dramatic monologue, for instance in *The*

Bishop Orders his Tomb, begins to approach novelistic presentation of character. In *The Ring and the Book* (1868–9) he comes near to making a new kind of verse novel in this medium, and Arthur Hugh Clough's *Amours de Voyage* (1849) – done in verse letters – comes nearer still, at a less ambitious level. In the end, however, the dramatic monologue moved away from narrative into a new form of reflective and analytic verse. It found itself most convincingly in *Prufrock* by T. S. Eliot*, and *Hugh Selwyn Mauberley* by Ezra Pound*.

4·5

Art and reality: 1880–1930

Introduction: the analytic vision

The exceptional vigour and variety of the mid-19th-century novel (1830–80) was due to its responsiveness to popular taste and the rapidly changing and widely varied ways of life in the society which was its subject. The novel during this period resembles in these respects the drama between 1590 and 1620. Sometimes novels were formless; the best of them had, with a few exceptions, a looseness and amplitude of form which was partly caused by publication in serial parts. Each of these parts had to be filled out to a required number of words, and to be given a degree of self-sufficiency for the sake of the current readers. Serious critics tended to ignore the novel: 'the minds and hearts of the greatest depth and elevation', wrote J. S. Mill*, 'are commonly those which take the greatest delight in poetry; the shallowest and emptiest . . . are . . . not the least addicted to novel-reading.' (*Poetry and its Varieties*, 1859)

A change began in the last 20 years of the century. Two major novelists, Henry James and Joseph Conrad, brought to their writing a taste educated by the more fastidious French and Franco-Russian traditions in the form. They admired the strong moral concern in the English novel, but they considered that it ought to be matched with an equal concern for artistic integrity. Since human life is infinitely mysterious and complex, they considered that it requires for its portrayal a strenuous concentration on language, form, and clarity of intention, and that the reader must share in this spirit of serious responsibility on the part of the writer. In James's essays, serious criticism of the art of the novel had its beginning.

But the loose and adaptable English tradition did not succumb; other writers found it indispensable to their purposes. The period 1880–1914 was lively with movements towards social and political reform. The socialist novelist H. G. Wells* opposed the artistic fastidiousness of James and Conrad by insisting – like his contemporary G. B. Shaw* in relation to drama – that the novel had work to do:

as popular entertainment, it could enlighten and arouse a wide public, as essays on political economy could not, for they would not be extensively read.

Thus, by 1914, the novelists were more conscious and critical of their medium than they had ever been. They analysed it, they used it to analyse society, and they analysed their public. World War I shook long-established prejudices about morality and class, and thus increased the ardour for analysis and experiment; new directions of thought and feeling had to be related to the older patterns, the foundations of which, though not destroyed, had been gravely loosened. Moreover, the influence of the new science of deep psychology, initiated by Sigmund Freud* and spread by his disciples and rivals, was penetrating the art of the novel, to which it was particularly relevant. The decade 1920–30 was particularly rich in experiment and achievement, especially in the work of writers who had grown up before the war – D. H. Lawrence*, James Joyce*, and E. M. Forster*. Ways of writing novels were more diversified than ever before; uses for the novel were better understood; ambitions for it were at their height. Intense analysis and strong creative momentum, for a few years, coincided.

4.5.1 *The novel as art: Henry James and Joseph Conrad*

Both these novelists were foreigners: James*, an American, settled in London as a writer in 1876, after a year in Paris, where he met the Russian novelist Turgeniev and the French novelist Flaubert*. Conrad*, a Pole, joined the English merchant service in 1878, and turned to writing only in 1886. Both of them came to the English novel enthusiastically, but from the outside; their interest in French and Russian novelists was as great as in the English ones. The development of the novel in England had been insular; it had not excluded foreign influences, particularly in the 18th century, but its chief impetus had come from the eventfulness of English social change. Other novelists in Britain at the end of the 19th century were affected by foreign influences, for instance George Gissing*. James and Conrad, however, were men of finer genius than any of their British contemporaries. They enriched the English novel, at a time when its native impetus was slackening, with the freshness of their vision of the English scene, the extensiveness of their international experience, and the new intensity with which they upheld the vocation of novelist.

It is their cosmopolitanism which strikes an English reader first. Like any other narrative form, the novel thrives on human contrasts and peculiarities; these, hitherto, in the English novel, had been chiefly social, since English society had been notable for the variety and vigour of its social structure. In James, however, the social contrast was replaced in many of his novels by the continental contrasts of America and Europe, for instance in *The Portrait of a Lady** (1881) and *The Ambassadors** (1903). Superficial comparisons of national type are of course shallow in interest and often misleading, but James knew the cultures deeply, and he was especially impressed with the opposition between the austerity combined with social freedom of his native New England background, and the cultural exuberance combined with social rigidity of Europe. The contrast became a moral one, between innocence with openness of mind, and experience with sophistication that amounted to corruption. The opposition of innocence and corruption were transferred to his novels of English life, *eg What Maisie Knew** (1897) and *The Awkward Age** (1899), in which childhood and youth are set against the adult world. Conrad's cosmopolitanism was even wider, and was less imbued with cultural traditions than with psychological dispositions characteristic of various European nations. His career as a sailor, also, gave him both a sense of the antagonism between man and nature, especially the sea, and a feeling of the difference between the small, coherent society of a ship's crew, united by co-operation in common need (*The Nigger of the Narcissus*, 1898) and the loose, uncomprehending relationships of men on land (*eg* in *Nostromo**, 1904, and *The Secret Agent**, 1907). In *Under Western Eyes** (1911), he wrote of the contrast between the authoritarianism of Czarist Russia, with its appalling menace to the individual conscience, and the safe, rather complacent liberalism of western Europe, in which political decisions were no longer issues of heroic moral choice. In all his books there is the tragic vision of the loneliness of men, whether faced with the indifference of nature or the self-interest of fellow-men, but in all of them, too, there is reverence for the dignity of the human spirit.

The impressiveness of these two writers, however, arises not from their cosmopolitanism and the moral values they drew from it, but from the new poetic intensity in their way of writing. Their best novels have a concentration hitherto unmatched in English novels, even by Jane Austen and Emily Brontë, though in those writers also it is true that no sentence can be missed if the whole is to be understood. They combined this new concentration with other qualities unshared by previous novelists. In James there is awareness of the elusiveness of human personality, and also of the true significance of human interchange; this, especially in his later novels, caused James to present characters indirectly through dialogue, and to make dialogue operate through implication. In Conrad there is a new freedom in the handling of the time sequence of events, especially by breaking up temporal succession by sudden shifts of the point of view to the future, rather as spatial effect in films is changed by sudden movements of the camera. In both, there is a new treatment of narrative, whereby the total effect of the book depends less on the mounting climax of the story than on effects in each episode, and on contrast and association with other episodes, each, by itself, almost sufficient to itself as a story. These peculiarities of method caused James and Conrad, in their own day, to be writers for comparatively limited publics. Their reputations, however, have survived those of their contemporaries whose popularity was greater in their lifetimes.

4.5.2 *Novelists of social materialism: H. G. Wells, Arnold Bennett, John Galsworthy*

These are the novelists whom most ordinary novel readers, between 1910 and 1930, would have singled out as the outstanding writers of the time; they probably continue to be more widely read than Conrad and James. Serious students of literature, on the other hand, give them much less attention. We have here a divergence of taste between those readers who require novelists to engage their interests without arduously engaging their minds and those who require the novel to make a total demand on the attention such as James and Conrad considered it should make.

We have seen that 19th-century critics, such as J. S. Mill, thought novels to be almost negligible literature. Yet modern critics, with seriousness comparable to Mill's, give the same degree of attention to his contemporaries George Eliot and Charles Dickens as they do to James and Conrad, or as he gave to poetry. Mill, presumably, was aware of the inferiority of most of the large number of novels that were being published every year of his life; the modern critic knows only the best of them, and realizes that the best novelists were struggling in interesting ways to relate the inwardness of human experience to the vast but ephemeral surfaces of life. James and Conrad confronted this inwardness more uncompromisingly, but not necessarily more revealingly, than previous novelists had done. The ordinary reader would probably maintain that Wells* Bennett* and Galsworthy* are the obvious pursuers of the Victorian tradition. What, then, are the shortcomings which have caused serious readers to neglect these novelists?

One of their younger contemporaries, D. H. Lawrence*, was to write of Galsworthy:

> *Why do we feel so instinctively that the Forsytes are inferiors? It is because they seem to us to have lost caste as human beings, and to have sunk to the level of the social being . . . the fatal change today is the collapse from the psychology of the free human individual into the psychology of the social being, just as the fatal change in the past was a collapse from the freeman's psyche to the psyche of the slave.*
>
> ('John Galsworthy' in *Phoenix*)

Here we have the view that while the Victorian novelists (Lawrence cites Dickens and Meredith) were acutely aware of the human being existing for himself in spite of society, Galsworthy has given up the distinction and decided for the lesser reality – the human being wholly shaped by the social environment. Referring to all three novelists, another contemporary, Virginia Woolf*, wrote, 'If we fasten, then, one label on all these books, on which is one word "materialists", we mean by it that they write of unimportant things; that they spend immense skill and immense industry making the trivial and the transitory appear the true and the enduring' ('Modern Fiction' in *The Common Reader*). This opinion, which is consistent with Lawrence's, may be paraphrased as saying that if the individual in society is to some extent like the kernel of a nut in its shell, then we have here three novelists who gave most of their attention to the shell, ignoring the kernel.

They nonetheless differed greatly from one another. Wells was the best writer of science fiction yet to appear in English, and his realistic novels – *eg Kipps* (1905), *Tono-Bungay* (1909), *Mr Polly* (1910) – are graphic comedies in the Dickens tradition and acute social commentaries as well. He preferred the title of 'journalist' to that of 'artist', and he is one of the best of the journalist–novelists. Bennett, on the other hand, was a serious artist, who was deeply affected by the materialist philosophy of Herbert Spencer*, and by the French novelist Zola*, himself influenced materialistically by 19th-century biological science. Bennett wrote chiefly of the industrial midlands, and his best novels (*eg Clayhanger**) are clear-sighted accounts of the preponderant importance of material environment in the now long-industrialized parts of England. Galsworthy's sequence *The Forsyte Saga* began with *The Man of Property* (1906). He is the most neglected of the three by modern critics; yet in 1967 the *Saga* was a popular television serial. This suggests that his achievement was not negligible: it was the creation of a panoramic, if not very profound, social spectacle.

4.5.3 *Novelists of human culture: E. M. Forster, D. H. Lawrence*

Virginia Woolf censured Wells, Bennett and Galsworthy for the excessive importance they attached to the material aspect of society; James and Conrad, on the other hand, in their later work, did not always sufficiently substantiate the environment of their characters. The escape from materialism may lead to an atmosphere too thin for human flesh and blood.

In the first decade of this century, E. M. Forster's* position lay between the two sides: his first four novels (1905–10) insist discomfortingly on the materialism of British civilization; at the same time, by ironic comedy not found in the English novel since Jane Austen, he analyses the qualities of mind that delude people into accepting this materialism, and discloses the qualities of intelligence that make for release from it. His enlightenment thus gives him the importance of centrality within this period, although his achievement as a novelist (with the possible exception of his last novel, *A Passage to India**, 1924) is not of the first rank. The freshness of his novels arises from his keen and subtle comedy – his critical force. His limitations are in his 'poetic' power: he has not been able to create a substantial image of what it means to be fully human. D. H. Lawrence's* very high reputation is due precisely to his possession of this 'poetic' power. Lawrence is also central in a much more important way than Forster is: he has a wider range of social experience, an equal capacity to face and understand the materialism of 20th-century civilization, and a larger, more radical intelligence, able to see more of the issues, and more deeply into them.

Lawrence's best work is generally considered to comprise three of his novels –

*Sons and Lovers** (1913), *The Rainbow** (1915), and *Women in Love** (1921) – besides a number of shorter tales, such as *St Mawr** (1925). His starting points were that a society is inseparable from the human beings that compose it, that its quality (or 'civilization') therefore depends on the quality of the individuals characteristic of it, and that the quality of these individuals arises from the relationships with other human beings that they are able to achieve. *Sons and Lovers*, an autobiographical novel about Lawrence's own childhood and youth, is remarkable for its unprecedented insight into relationships within the family – the nucleus and beginning of all other relationships. *The Rainbow* concerns the changes in the character of relationships between the sexes and within the family, over the three generations that preceded the war of 1914–18. *Women in Love* is the most ambitious of the three; it penetrates the quality of human relationship, and hence of humanity itself, in the kind of society that existed at the outbreak of that war. Lawrence's conception of the novelist's vocation was as high as that of James and Conrad, and he had the genius commensurate with the conception: he understood how to condense very large subjects into the immediacy of personal themes. He also inherited the strong conviction, recurring in English fiction since Bunyan, of the regenerative power of art, and in particular of the novel, which alone he considered capable of presenting man as a whole; see 'Why the Novel Matters' in *Phoenix*. He included elements of the human experience which had never been included before, and which shocked the reading public. His conception of experience entailed also the expression of levels out of reach of normal articulacy; this he achieved through a remarkable use of symbolism, drawn from natural surroundings and animal life. His technique in this respect was revolutionary, although on the surface it was closer to Victorian technique than that of many of his contemporaries.

In Lawrence, therefore, we find something like a resolution of the dilemmas that faced other novelists between 1880 and 1930; he is also a climactic figure in the history of the English novel, at least as it had been developing since 1830.

4.5.4 *The search for viewpoint: 1920–30*

The decade that followed *Women in Love* looks now as if it may have been a crisis period for the English novel. Lawrence himself took to wandering about the world. In the next ten years that ended with his death, he produced disturbing work, much of which (the notorious example is *Lady Chatterley's Lover**, 1928) is very controversial, both in its merit and in its implied doctrines. Other novelists, his close contemporaries, now reached their height: E. M. Forster with *A Passage to India* (1924), James Joyce* with *Ulysses** (1922), Virginia Woolf* with *To the Lighthouse** (1927), T. F. Powys* with *Mr Weston's Good Wine* (1927), Wyndham Lewis* with *The Childermass* (1928), Aldous Huxley* with *Point Counter Point* (1928). Others again, who were to make their reputation during the following ten or twenty years, achieved their first fully original writing: Henry Green* with *Living* (1929), Ivy Compton-Burnett* with *Pastors and Masters* (1925), L. H. Myers* with *The Near and the Far* (1929).

Such a list is necessarily open to discussion and incomplete; disagreement is still very strong about most of the books mentioned in it, and many readers would consider that names omitted from it (Somerset Maugham, Arnold Bennett, John Galsworthy) ought certainly to be included. Its special interest, and the reason for making it, is that it is the record of almost as many distinct approaches to the writing of novels as there are names.

It was a period like that which succeeded the French Revolution of 1789: the spirit of the time was calling all traditions – social, moral, religious, philosophical, psychological – in question, and thinking men were no longer sure of what it means to call oneself a human being. Even less were they certain of human values, or how to evaluate human experience. If novels were still to be what they had always been, images of life as it is lived from day to day, then some novelists considered that such images should take new forms, and these forms varied according to their personal conceptions of how experiences are received, or how they ought to be received, or how they can be made significant. These are the 'experimental' novelists, whose methods are strictly personal and inimitable though each necessarily depends on influences from the past, whether English, French, or (an important one at this time) Russian. Ivy Compton-Burnett, for example, develops Jane Austen's method of narrating through dialogue almost without the supporting descriptions, and James Joyce carries to one extreme – though he was to carry them still further – the realistic criteria of the French novelists from Flaubert.

The older tradition of an explicitly evaluative function for fiction was however still vigorous; it is clearest in the work of Forster and Myers, and also in Lawrence. Even here, the reader finds new ways of going to work. Forster, for instance, in *A Passage to India*, elaborates a symbolic method which he had already developed in his earlier books; the symbolic pattern unfolds a fable within the realistic story, and the fable discloses the moral significance which it is Forster's main purpose to impart. Myers found it necessary to abandon contemporary Europe with all its distractions of material detail, and to set his novels in remote places and times in order to elucidate his spiritual meanings. Powys reduced his novels to outright fables, using a childlike bareness of diction for his pagan treatment of the basic experiences of life – sexual love and death.

This great variety of highly distinctive work shows, if nothing else, remarkable vitality within a single decade. The variety provokes questions, however: whether a single direction could emerge from such dissimilarities; whether works so personally conceived had enough breadth and depth of interest long to outlast their time; and even whether the novel, as an art, was exploding under the intensity of the creative pressures which the divergences of the time and the tempting flexibility of the form inspired.

4.6

The novel since 1930

Distinctiveness of vision does not, of course, necessarily accompany spaciousness of imagination; it may very well be a symptom of narrow imaginative convictions in a writer who nevertheless has the artistic intelligence to find the defining form for them. The writers who showed their first promise in the 1920s – Henry Green, Ivy Compton-Burnett, L. H. Myers – produced their best work in the 1930s, but they did not carry their kinds of vision much further. Indeed, of the notable writers of the 1920s, only James Joyce did this, by following his extraordinary achievement of *Ulysses** (1922) with the still more extraordinary one of *Finnegans Wake** (1939). This is the most ambitious attempt of modern times to realize a comprehensive vision of human experience. But, significantly, it is a lonely achievement by an isolated man writing of the whole of humanity and yet always of his birthplace, Dublin, in language so abstrusely contrived that general readers will never penetrate it.

The English writers who have achieved eminence since 1930 have partaken of at least three characteristics. One of these is topicality, especially considered as a return to questions of what society does to the individual. The last four decades have been a time of crisis and change in society: the great economic depression of the 1930s, the upheaval of World War II, the prosperity of full employment and the efforts towards a socially just society since that war. Never before have national and world events been brought so close to the ordinary man, making him aware of other societies as well as his own, and never before has he felt so surely that the materially good life is his right and within his reach. The novelist, himself affected by all this in his personal life, has necessarily felt these social changes as drama which he cannot ignore.

Yet the second characteristic that novelists tend to share has been conservatism – not necessarily in opinion, but in expression. The explanation is partly that the changes have proved compatible with continuity of social structure and of leading national institutions. Such continuity has encouraged a style of novel which is nearer to the 19th-century tradition than that of the 1920s; how to express has again come to seem less important than *what* to express. Some novelists have been eclectic, *eg* Joyce Cary* and Angus Wilson*, borrowing styles from the past as it has suited them; others, *eg* John Wain* in *Hurry on Down* (1954), have gone back to the 18th-century style of the picaresque novel, in the manner of Defoe and Fielding.

It is the third characteristic that most differentiates mid-20th-century fiction from that of previous periods: the recurrent concern with man as he is alone. It arises, seemingly, from a feeling peculiar to our time, that the social circumstances that press so closely on the individual turn out, in the end, to be irrelevant to the meaning of experience: society no longer carries within it the resources for justifying individual existence even against itself. It is a feeling already prominent in D. H. Lawrence (*Women in Love*, 1921), and his influence has been strong.

The social content takes different forms: comedy of upper class society in Evelyn Waugh* (*Brideshead Revisited*, 1945), in Anthony Powell's* sequence *The Music of Time* (*eg Casanova's Chinese Restaurant*, 1960), and in Angus Wilson (*Anglo-Saxon Attitudes*, 1956); intense evocation of environment in Graham Greene* (*eg Brighton Rock*, 1938); preoccupation with the qualities which make for material success, and with their effect on personal relations, for instance in C. P. Snow's sequence *Strangers and Brothers* (*eg The Masters*, 1951); the theme of the newly prosperous working-class man, such as Sillitoe's* *Saturday Night and Sunday Morning* (1958) and Storey's* *This Sporting Life* (1960). The working class field of experience again looks back to Lawrence (*Sons and Lovers*, 1913), and it is one of the most distinctively 20th-century aspects of the novel.

Yet the theme of the loneliness of the character within the social context pervades most of these novels, as well as others which do not concern themselves so prominently with environment. Its most surprising aspect is perhaps the revival of religious themes, such as would not have been anticipated in the agnostic atmosphere of the mid-Victorian novel. This is plain in the Catholic novels of Graham Greene (*The Heart of the Matter*, 1948), and in the Protestant tradition of Joyce Cary (*A Prisoner of Grace*, 1952). Another manifestation of the theme of loneliness is the preoccupation with psychology and particularly with the psychology of childhood, *eg* in L. P. Hartley's* *The Go-Between* (1953).

The theme of loneliness is perhaps evidence for widespread doubt, even desperation, arising from a society without deep commonly held convictions, and without even a materialistic sense of direction. It is a state of uncertainly perceived conflict that has helped the revival of drama in the last two decades. The yearning for 'meaning' that it implies, has stimulated in some novelists a new emphasis on the fable aspect of the novel, already so prominent within the novels of E. M. Forster. This helps to account for the prodigious success of the novels of William Golding*, a novelist of pronounced religious vision of a kind that recalls the sternness of the old Puritans. His novels, unlike the fable-novels of T. F. Powys, preserve a realistic surface, but the fable is so pronounced (*eg The Lord of the Flies*, 1954) that it tends to distort the realistic surface to its own purpose. Fables have close kinship with allegories; the novel began to break its shell in the allegory of *Pilgrim's Progress* by John Bunyan. Since then the English novel has travelled a long way, but its spirit has seldom been very far from its point of entry.

The Triumph of Isabella. The illustration is not from a medieval English source, but based on a 17th-C Flemish picture. Nevertheless, it is a practical assistance to forming a mental picture of the medieval English pageants which circulated in English towns on certain feast days.

5 Drama in Britain

5.I

Age of dramatic vision: 1350–1642

Introduction: religious and social drama

Drama is made from conflict. Primitive society has to struggle for its survival with natural forces. But these natural forces are like wayward gods: they are not consistently hostile, nor are they always friendly in due season; they have to be conciliated as well as fought, and they fight amongst themselves when the weather fluctuates and season reluctantly gives way to season. It is probably with this that we have to start our story of English drama: with the common people of medieval England, thinly spread over the countryside in villages, depending for life on their harvests, their crops periodically ravaged by pests and bad weather, the cattle perishing and the men and women decimated by disease.

What we know about medieval folk culture shows us that it was a way of life which took naturally to dramatic expression. But medieval society was stratified into divisions which resembled castes rather than the modern money-divided classes, in which size of income makes the social standard. The landlords depended on their peasantry and shared much of their outlook. However, they also had the outlook of their own rank: that of warriors, hunters, and men of some wealth who cultivated the refinements of civilization in manners and conduct as well as in material goods. The peasantry in their festivals enacted the drama of their lives as it operated through the seasonal changes. The lords in their halls listened to tales sung and recited by minstrels; these too were full of dramatic feeling, and evoked the struggle with the natural environment, but they also appealed to the contemplative faculties of an audience which could afford to look beyond the immediate struggle for existence.

Of course England of the 14th century contained towns. The townsman, even if he was a Londoner, still lived very close to the countryside, but he had his distinct way of life, differently organized, more subject to daily variety, more self-conscious, better informed. The town craftsmen and merchants organized themselves into guilds, and these were fraternities which concerned themselves with the lives of their members in matters which went much beyond matters of trade.

The all-embracing organization of medieval life, affecting townsman, peasant, and lord alike, was the Church. The Church had its seasonal festivals* which corresponded in date with those of the countryside, some of which antedated Christianity. In the towns, Church, town, and country met during Church

*Indicates mention in the reference section.

festivals to witness the Mystery Plays*, which were created from the record of the Christian revelation as men interpreted it from the Bible and Church teaching, and which were performed by the town guilds. Many of these plays, in 15th-century versions, have come down to us, and they constitute the written record of the beginnings of English drama. Though their principal inspiration and purpose is Christian, the experience of medieval men was too integrated to exclude strong secular elements; the seasonal struggle for survival and the tragicomedy of daily life are in the plays too.

The Mystery Plays originated in the heart of the Church; they evolved from the Mass itself. By the 15th century they seem to have disengaged themselves from the Church and to have got into secular hands. However, another form of medieval drama arose from the clergy* or Churchmen, who were still the majority of the educated class in England; this new form is called the Morality Play*. This was a kind of dramatized sermon, with human life presented as continuous moral conflict; in the Middle Ages, the sermon itself was dramatic, concerned as it was with individual salvation and damnation. Dramatically the Morality was an advance on the Mystery, in that the action no longer depended mainly on biblical text, but was concerned with human beings as they actually live their lives. On the other hand, Church doctrines of what constitute the chief trials of human beings severely limited the scope of the writers; only one of the Moralities, *Everyman**, has survived as major dramatic literature.

But in the 16th century the restrictions of a single embracing Church began to break down, and eventually fell away. Men still saw their lives collectively: the same perils threatened them all, and the same salvation rewarded their survival of these perils. But life was lived less in a frame of surrounding Christendom, and more in a frame of the surrounding nation; the Church became the spiritual and moral manifestation of the nation. The society of this nation was now more diversified, social divisions were no longer so firm, and movement from one class to another was easier. Finally, the forces that worked upon the individual were more varied; education was no longer Church-dominated, there were many opinions about religion, and wealth and fame could be won by more various means. As society broke up into new formations, so drama also began to break up and diversify; the Moralities continued, their purpose was still ethical, but their themes were as likely to be educational or political as religious. Some plays abandoned ethical purpose and aimed candidly at entertainment; many of these belong to the category of the Interludes*, but the Interlude is often indistinguishable from the Morality in its now more broadly conceived form. Yet traditional Moralities and Mysteries continued to be performed until the end of the century: the break with the Middle Ages was at no time sharp.

Thus the great age that opened in the last 20 years of the 16th century had behind it a period of several centuries in which men had thought and felt dramatically, and the forms of this traditional expression were still in existence when Shakespeare began writing. However, it seems to be true that only in the 16th century did the drama become a natural means of expression for those who were highly educated, or who belonged to the richer classes. In so far as this meant that such people were taking a more lively interest than ever before in the sophisticated dramatists of ancient Greece, and particularly in those of ancient Rome, the result might have been that the age would have produced a number of more or less skilful imitations, but very little of intrinsic interest. But the age was producing a new kind of ideal of human being: the man of complete culture, whose culture found its meaning in a life of noble action – men, in short, like the Earl of Surrey*, Sir Philip Sidney* and Sir Walter Raleigh*. Important among the means of education of such men, and important also as a form of action in which they prided themselves, was the art of rhetoric or persuasion, for which the stage was a natural vehicle. Moreover the spiritual and intellectual diversity of the century presented to such men new conflicts; not the conflicts of struggle with environment, nor the conflicts inherent in the attempt to lead the good life according to the Church's prescription, but the conflicts arising from how to become a great man of action without making wrong choices, or even choosing evil. This was the material which made possible the flowering of tragedy at the very end of the century. To this flowering, not merely the scholarship of the humanists* but the older and richer experience of the common people contributed importantly.

5.1.1 *Drama in the Middle Ages: 1350–1500*

5.1.1.1 *Folk drama*

The so-called Mummers'* Play is still performed in a few English villages at Christmas time, though it is now an artificial survival. The actors wear furry costumes, and the main characters are St George, the Turkish Knight, and a Doctor. St George and the Turkish Knight fight together and St George is killed. The doctor then comes forward, and after a recital of the diseases that he can cure, he revives St George with a club. The fight continues, and in the end the Turkish Knight is slain. There are commonly other characters, including Father Christmas. Almost within living memory, this crude drama was performed in villages all over England, and there is a description of it in Hardy's novel, *The Return of the Native** (1878).

St George's Day is the 23rd of April; it occurs, therefore, in the spring, and in a number of countries in Europe peasants have long associated it with rejoicing at the return of life to the land. Christmas is also a turning point in the year, because it comes just after the shortest day; the people can look forward with hope to gradually increasing light and warmth. If St George, then, is associated with life and life-giving properties, the Turkish Knight would seem to be the opposite. In the Middle Ages, the Turks were thought of as powers of evil because they were the chief force of Islam, the only religion to menace Christianity, and because they controlled the Holy City of Jerusalem; thus, for the common man there was very close association between a Turk, an Infidel (or unbeliever), and the powers of darkness. As for the Doctor and his club, there are widespread pagan traditions of a sacred tree with reviving properties; the ancient Celts in Britain treated the mistletoe plant as sacred when it grew on the oak tree – in many countries a sacred tree – and it is an indispensable element in British Christmas decorations to this day. Thus, scholars are inclined to think, the Mummers' Play, though not in its surviving form pre-Christian, is nonetheless the survival of a pre-Christian dramatic ritual celebrating and assisting the return of fertility and life to the winter land of death.

In the Middle Ages the principal English rural festivals were four: Plough Monday just after Christmas, May Day* or the 1st of May, Midsummer, and Harvest Home in the late summer or early autumn. There is evidence that Plough Monday was once celebrated with a play similar to the Mummers' Play, and the Lord of Misrule who reigned on the Twelfth Night after Christmas seems to belong to a tradition of New Year feasting that goes back to the ancient Roman Saturnalia. But the principal revels were on May Day, very close to the Church feast of St George. The May Day Revels included the mysterious half dramatic Morris Dances*; these were mimes based on the folk-legend of the outlaw Robin Hood* and the characters associated with him, such as Friar Tuck, and Maid Marian who was sometimes also identified with the Queen of the May. The dancers blackened their faces, from which some scholars have concluded that 'Morris' derives from 'Moorish'; others, however, surmise that the blackening originated in the ashes of a sacrificial fire, and that Robin Hood is the same as Jack of the Green or the Green Man of folk myth: the Spirit of Vegetation. In some of the villages, Jack of the Green himself was a character in the dances.

Such games, dances, and primitive dramas have left nothing behind that can be called a literature; the dramatic literature of the Middle Ages was almost all of it religious. But for this very reason it is important to remind ourselves of their existence. Moreover the non-Christian rural festivals occurred at nearly the same time as those of the Church: Plough Monday was near Christmas, May Day not far from Easter, and Midsummer was near the Feast of Corpus Christi* when the great cycles of the Mystery Plays were performed. It would not be surprising if in the contriving of these plays, the deep reverence of the people for the Christian stories became mingled with their emotions about the natural world.

5.1.1.2 *Mystery plays*

The first great drama of Europe, that of ancient Greece, grew out of Greek religious ceremony reflecting natural sequences. And the Mystery Plays grew out of the Catholic ritual of the Mass, by the interpolation of 'tropes'. The Mass itself is a dramatic ceremony, commemorating the Incarnation of God as Jesus Christ, and the redemption of mankind through his sacrifice; thus, in the Church year, Good Friday and Easter, commemorating and re-enacting the Crucifixion and the Resurrection of Christ, has always had the quality of a dramatic climax in Church ritual. A 'trope' was a short interpolation into the Mass at Easter; it constituted a short passage of dramatic dialogue, and its function was further to dramatize the climax of the Resurrection. These dialogues seem to have grown into short plays, and the plays grew in length and popularity until they were acted outside the Church walls. By the mid-14th century the Mystery Plays were out of the hands of the priests and under the control of the craft guilds* of the towns. Performed at the feast of Corpus Christi*, which was only fully established in 1264, they were indeed not only a great religious occasion, but the climax of the town year, when all the guilds collaborated in a great dramatic festival.

The Corpus Christi plays were performed in cycles; a typical cycle dramatized the Christian story from the Creation to the Last Judgement. The longest of them took several days to perform, and it is likely that some of the longest were never performed in full; appropriate plays in the series were performed at other festivals in the year, such as Christmas and Easter. They were performed on wheeled stages ('pageants') which moved from point to point round the town, so that by waiting at one point a spectator could see the whole series, or he could follow his favourite play round the town and see it several times. The separate plays were the responsibility of particular guilds, and were often related to the craft concerned; for example, at York, the shipwrights presented Noah and his Ark, and at Chester the Last Supper was presented by the bakers. Four cycles have come down to us; those by the names of York, Chester, Wakefield and Coventry. There are, however, doubts about whether the Coventry and Wakefield plays are correctly ascribed, and the latter are often called 'the Towneley Mysteries' from the name of the family into whose possession the manuscript came. Of these, the finest are those of York and Wakefield; each is marked by the distinctive styles of a poet of unusual talent in some (not all) of the plays. These poets are commonly referred to as 'the York Realist' and the 'Wakefield Master' respectively. Both are probably 15th-century writers.

The York Realist can be exemplified by his Play of the Crucifixion, in which four Roman soldiers are carrying out the task of nailing Christ to the cross, and then fixing the cross into the ground. Like any other soldiers who have been allotted an unpleasant, awkward, tedious task, they carry it out callously with grim humour; every stage of the horrible process is presented convincingly, and the actors were from the Guild of Pinners and Painters, whose craft qualified them for the work. Christ makes only two speeches, calling on God the Father to forgive his tormentors; to the second of them the first soldier cries out, 'Wee! hark! he jangels like a jay.' The impressiveness of the short play is in its economy and its stark contrast between compassion and callousness: this is God, and this is the world that God is saving. No cynic could be more ruthless, and yet the play is the opposite of cynical; the writer maintains a balance between savage comedy and tragic dignity in a way that is characteristic of the Middle Ages, and with an art whose tradition survives among the great Elizabethans, such as Shakespeare in *King Lear**.

The Wakefield Master wrote perhaps nine of the Wakefield plays; notable among these are the comedies of the two Shepherds' Plays, in which the shepherds are summoned to worship at Christ's birthplace in the Bethlehem stable. Each is distinctive, though far from unique, for the secular episode that precedes the scriptural story. In the First Shepherds' Play, the episode is a kind of comic fantasy about dearth and plenty; in real dearth, the shepherds have a fantastic illusion of being surrounded by large flocks and rich pasture. They are brought back to the reality of actual scarcity, but then a boy enters and announces to them that plenty has indeed been miraculously restored to them. The fable fits the Christian message of God's salvation of an undeserving world, but it also reads like a record of natural magic (the fact that the Shepherds behave as though plenty has been restored to them actually helps to bring the restoration about); we may, in fact, have here something not far removed from the Mummers' Play. The Second Shepherds' Play, which opens with the comedy of Mak the Sheep Stealer hiding his stolen sheep in a cradle and pretending that it is a baby, reads so far like a parody of the birth of Christ, the subject of the second half. But it may be a parallel rather than a parody; the birth of God as man is paralleled by the rebirth of an older, pagan horned god (like the Greek Pan*) whose return (like the return of the Greek Dionysus*) is the return of fertility and wealth.

Some of the Mystery Play comedy proceeds from perennial themes of daily life: Noah is presented as a hen-pecked husband. But a notable feature of comedy in these plays is the comic presentation of evil characters such as Herod, who is commonly a bombastic, ranting tyrant, who, in one play, is made to leap from the stage and carry his raging into the street. This may be an example of the preacher's art of attacking vice most effectively through ridicule, but dramatically it is effective in releasing the baser human passions in all of us by reducing their terror while acknowledging their vitality: we remember Shakespeare's Richard III and his Iago. Another version of the comedy of evil was the 'clown-devil' Tutivillus, or Titivil; he also had a future, in the comic Vice of the Morality Plays, and the comic villainous servant of the Elizabethans, like Ithamore in Marlowe's *Jew of Malta** or Mosca in Jonson's *Volpone**.

The Mystery Plays were timeless dramas; in them past and future (the Last Judgement) united with the present, and characters from the English countryside mingled with Roman soldiers and Pontius Pilate. The stage was used for simultaneous representation of varieties of place, showing the gates of Hell and Heaven, and the three worlds made by God. Similarly, the emotions were mingled: reverence and ribaldry, tenderness and cruelty, laughter and fear. It is important to recognize these fusions of time, space and feeling, for they are the basis of the dramatic presentation and vision in the age of Shakespeare.

5.1.1.3. *Morality plays*

I stonde lyk a clerk in my pulpet,
And when the lewed[1] *peple is doun y-set*[2],
I preche, as ye han herd bifore,
And telle an hundred false japes[3] *more.*
Then peyne I me to strecche forth the nekke,
And est and west upon the peple I bekke[4]
As doth a dove sitting on a berne[5].
Myn hondes and my tonge goon so yerne[6],
That it is joye to see my bisinesse.

[1]ignorant [2]seated [3]jokes [4]beckon [5]barn
[6]eagerly

The preaching of Chaucer's Pardoner* was really a kind of acting; the medieval pulpit was one of the early sources of theatre. The preacher exhorted the people through dramatic images and allegorical symbols; he might act the qualities of vice and virtue with gesture and facial expression. Chaucer's *Pardoner's Tale* is really a form of medieval sermon. He begins by preaching against the vices of swearing, drunkenness and gambling, and follows this up with an 'exemplum' ('example') in the story of the three rioters who set out to slay death. The story is like a Morality Play* in narrative form; it was at about this time (the late 14th century) that Morality Plays came into existence. Few of those that have survived till our day are intrinsically vital as literature, but the form had dramatic potentiality. The Mysteries, that is to say, did not lead beyond themselves, whereas the Moralities were capable of indefinite development, because they concerned themselves with life as it is actually lived.

The late-15th-century anonymous play *Everyman** perhaps of Dutch origin, shows the Morality at its best. At the beginning of the play, Everyman, a rich man in the prime of life, is visited by a vision of Death. Life for him, henceforward, is a long pilgrimage away from the world. In grief and panic, he summons to his support all his past friends – Cousin, Fellowship, Kindred and Goods – only to discover that they are entirely bound up with this world and will not go with him. He then turns to Good-Deeds, the personification of the good actions he has done in his life; Good-Deeds is willing, but by himself he is too weak and helpless. Everyman is now near the extreme of desperation, but at this moment Knowledge appears to him – the only friend who comes without being summoned – and she shows him the way. She causes him to submit to Confession, and then introduces him to his human qualities: Strength, Discretion, Five-Wits, and Beauty. Everyman is now happy, but he has not reached the end of his pilgrimage. As his death approaches, his human qualities – all that make him valuable as a man in the flesh – depart from him in due order: Beauty, Strength, Discretion, and Five-Wits. Even Knowledge will not enter the grave with him; only Good-Deeds will do that. Although when it is summarized the play may seem to be peopled by bodiless abstractions, in performance or in reading it presents a true account of the human condition; moreover it is an account which does not depend on Christian doctrine, although it is that which it is seeking to expound. Everyman is first shown as a man who lives only from moment to moment; because he ignores his mortality, his life is unreal. It is only when he takes his eventual death into account that he is led to discover the unreality of his values; the only reality in them is constituted by his good deeds – the ways in which he has impressed himself creatively on the world. Knowledge – who is also Christian faith – comes to him by God's Grace when he has fully understood the extent of his vanity. She teaches him how to live; the lesson begins with admission of his own shortcomings (Confession) and then he learns the true value of his human qualities, which so far he has merely taken for granted. Yet his death is still a lonely event: Everyman enters the grave with only his good deeds to comfort his isolation. In the Christian meaning, he goes to salvation, but death is a terrible transition for Christians as for any others, and the dramatist makes it appear so.

In *Everyman* we find a dignity and spaciousness of feeling unmatched in English drama hitherto. But although the other Moralities have less merit, some of them show possibilities for development that *Everyman* lacks. One is the verbal dispute (flyting*) of which medieval writers were so fond, for example when the virtues and the vices debate for the soul of man in *Pride of Life* (1410?). Also, the Morality, even more than the Mysteries, offered possibilities for the comedy and satire of daily life, especially through the personification of the Vice as a clown, *eg* in *Mankind* (1475?). Both Moralities and Mysteries of the traditional sort survived into Shakespeare's lifetime and are alluded to in his plays, for instance when Hamlet says of a certain kind of acting that 'it out-herods Herod', and Feste compares himself to 'the old Vice' at the end of *Twelfth Night** IV.ii. The Moralities and the Mysteries lead us into an understanding of Shakespeare by a way that will take us further than any other road.

5.1.2 *Prelude to the Great Age: 1500–90*

5.1.2.1 *Political and social influences*

The kind of development undergone by English medieval drama in the Middle Ages was not very different from, for instance, that of French drama. Yet for most of the 16th century, English drama seemed to most Englishmen to lag far behind the drama of France and Italy. But the century ended with the beginnings of an age of drama unexcelled in the history of the world's literature. This cannot be explained by such a formula as 'the miracle of genius'; Shakespeare, and the best of his contemporaries, were not miracles, but men who took to writing drama because the conditions of their society were exceptionally favourable to it.

English society developed in some respects differently from that of the rest of Europe in the 16th century. It shared with other countries a growth in the power of the monarchy and a corresponding decline in the power of the old nobility, an increasingly rich middle class, and a secularization of outlook in consequence of Humanist* criticism of traditional doctrines and ideas. But in England, the monarchy did not centralize the power of government through the maintenance of a strong army and the gradual dismantling of feudal privilege. Feudalism largely destroyed itself by the civil Wars of the Roses* in the 15th century; the Tudor* kings and queens of England raised to power new men who were dependent on the royal favour and served them in the government, and the authority of this government was exercised in the provinces by magistrates chosen from the local gentry, whose own interests were best served by their service of the Crown. What was true of the nobility and gentry was true also of the merchants in the towns. In consequence, England was less subdivided than ever before into rigid divisions of court, aristocracy, and people; there was much movement between the classes, and less tendency to form stratified levels of culture. A. P. Rossiter (in *English Drama from Early Times to the Elizabethans*) offers what he calls 'a suggestive Elizabethan lineage': the great humanist Sir Thomas More*, Henry VIII's Chancellor, had a sister who married John Rastell, a lawyer, playwright and printer from the provinces; Rastell's niece married another playwright, John Heywood, who gained favour from Princess (later Queen) Mary as a musician; Heywood's daughter married a London ironmonger, and their child was John Donne*, the courtier, adventurer, and poet who ended as Dean of St Paul's Cathedral in London, that is to say in one of the most eminent offices of the Church of England. The lineage is illuminating because it shows how relatives could belong, at one extreme, to the highest circle in the land, and at the other extreme, to the London middle class, and because it shows how the world of art penetrated both. Shakespeare's own ancestry is indicative: his grandfather was tenant-farmer to the great aristocratic family of Arden; his father, a Stratford-on-Avon merchant, married Mary Arden, who probably belonged to a junior branch of the great family.

As well as having, in terms of class, a comparatively open society, England had an expanding one, increasing in wealth, in self-confidence, in national consciousness, and in pride. Such a society usually expresses itself forcefully through whatever artistic forms its traditions have nourished; that form, in England at the end of the 16th century, was literature, and above all the drama.

5.1.2.2 *Growth of the professional theatre*

The dramatic medium required not only writers of plays, but actors who could do them justice, and theatres, suited to the plays, to act them in. As to the public, we have seen that there had long been a great popular audience for the medieval drama; what was needed, in England even more than in other western countries, was a more educated public of high intelligence who could respond to the best dramatists at the highest reach of their genius. All these came into existence in the first three-quarters of the 16th century.

In the Middle Ages the Mystery Plays were performed by amateurs, though they were amateurs who, by their regular performances and the popularity of the work they performed, probably achieved something like professional standards. How the professional actors emerged from these amateurs is not clear, but it seems that first of all the Morality Plays were performed by associations of actors from one town or another, and they were paid for their services; such associations began to resemble modern amateur dramatic societies who achieve approximately professional status. By the end of the 15th century we already hear of companies of actors (or 'players' as they were then called) attached to important households including the king's; they probably grew up from the class of professional minstrels who had long worked in such households, reciting and performing songs, ballads and romances for their patrons. By the second half of the 16th century, such companies, though they still bore the titles and badges of particular households and went under such names as 'Lord Leicester's Players', were only nominally attached to the patrons, and were in fact independent of them. Individual 'strolling' players were classed as 'vagabonds' – *ie* potential criminals – for society was permanently suspicious of the criminal potentialities of its poorer members unless they were respectably classified; a man who called himself an actor or a pedlar might be a robber seeking his opportunity, like Autolycus in Shakespeare's *The Winter's Tale**. The serious actor, therefore, required membership of one of the companies with a recognized patronage, and such membership increased his sense of professionalism, of belonging to an established 'craft'.

But for a long time they had no theatres. The lords, the lawyers in the Inns of Court*, the Colleges at Oxford* and Cambridge*, all had great halls, and at the

The New Inn, Gloucester. This is a 15th-C inn yard, of the kind in which plays were performed both before and after the building of the first London theatres. The plan of these yards became the pattern for the design of the Elizabethan theatres. The actors would erect a temporary stage and would probably incorporate the staircase and the arcaded gallery. The mass of the audience would watch from ground level; those of superior status would occupy the gallery on the left.

same time provided the most educated audiences. When the actors performed for the general public, they erected temporary stages in the yards of the bigger inns. But as the companies became better organized, they needed permanent homes of their own. Thus in 1576 James Burbage*, the first of the great business men of the theatre world, erected the first theatre in England since the Roman occupation. This was called simply 'The Theatre', and stood in Shoreditch, just outside the City of London. It was the first of a number of theatres or 'playhouses' to be built in Shakespeare's lifetime, and it is important to understand the general characteristics of their structure if we are to interpret the acting conventions of his plays correctly.

Most historians consider that these early English theatres were in design a kind of compromise between the inn yards where plays continued to be performed, and the bull- and bear-baiting pits, where the London public enjoyed the spectacle of animals being worried to death by dogs. The inn yard commonly consisted of a large open courtyard, surrounded by the buildings of the inn and overhung by balconies. The actors performed on a temporary stage at one end of the yard, with a balcony above them where musicians might play and which might also serve as an upper stage if a character was required to appear for instance on the wall of a castle, as the king does in Shakespeare's *Richard II**. One sketch that has survived from the time, and a number of written indications, suggests that the theatres

The Swan Theatre, 1596. From the sketch by a Dutch visitor, Johannes de Witt. From what we can learn from the builder's specifications for the Fortune Theatre (1600) it seems that this sketch may not be entirely accurate, or at least not altogether typical of other theatres. In particular, the exit and entrance doors were probably farther apart, and flanked a recess screened by a curtain and constituting a rear stage. The gallery above could either be used for spectators or as an upper stage.

followed this pattern, resembling also the bear-pits in that their shape was usually hexagonal or round (like Burbage's Globe Theatre*). The main stage ('apron stage') projected among the audience, who stood or sat on benches on the unroofed floor of the theatre. Roofed galleries surrounded this space. Behind the apron stage, there might be a rear stage for such scenes as Prospero's cell in *The Tempest**, though the surviving sketch does not show one. The rear stage was flanked by doors for exits and entrances, and above it were one or two galleries; if there were two; the first would serve as an upper stage, and the second as a musician's gallery. The apron stage was half covered by a roof or canopy, and had beneath it an underground space known as the 'cellars', as 'hell', or as 'hades' – terms which give point to Hamlet's cries to the Ghost in Act I, scene v.

From these basic features we can draw some conclusions about the presentation of plays in Shakespeare's day, and so about the ways in which such presentation influenced their composition. We notice, first, that the stage was the opposite of the modern 'picture-frame' stage, which gives the audience the feeling of being separated from the action, as though they are looking at a pictorial illusion of life; for the Elizabethan audience the action was happening in their midst. They were not able to forget themselves by entering into the action, as into a dream-world, mentally identifying themselves with the characters of their preference, as the modern audience is inclined to do. For example, the modern audience is inclined to accept Hamlet* as a complete illusion of a man, living in a completely illusory world; however, just because these illusions are complete, the modern audience is inclined to regard the dramatist as though he were a conjurer, who will enable them for two hours to forget the real world outside the theatre and lose themselves in his world in its place. The Elizabethans, on the contrary, were not in the position to forget the world outside the theatre so easily: Hamlet would not be for them the illusion of a real man, but a role performed by an actor; they would be much less inclined to identify themselves with the character, and they would be more disposed to keep a critically detached interest in the role that the character was performing.

Related to this conclusion is another: that the Elizabethan theatre was not well adapted, as the modern theatre is, to scenic illusion. In the public theatres, *Macbeth** would have been acted in the broad daylight of a London afternoon, although most of the action is supposed to take place in darkness. There was no painted scenery, although objects ('props') such as a tree, a throne, or a 'grassy bank', were introduced on to the stage to indicate scenes. This did not only mean that the Elizabethans dispensed with the realism of a modern theatre; it meant also that they were less inclined to give complete illusion of place. The stage always looked the same, apart from the changing props, whether the scene represented London, Paris, or a battlefield, as happens in *Henry V**. It was therefore much more natural for Elizabethan dramatists to ignore 'unity of place' than it was for the neo-classicists of the later 17th century, who were already accustomed to the 'picture frame' stage.

A third conclusion that we can draw from the character of the Elizabethan stage is that it was consistent with the staging of the medieval Moralities and Mysteries. The details of staging were different, but in neither age could perfect illusion have been the aim. In both, the bareness of scene encouraged rapid action and emphatic, colourful speech. In both, the audiences were encouraged to witness the performances more as symbolic extensions of their lives than as substitutes for their private experience. This state of mind responded more readily to fantasy in the theatre than does our own: when we watch a play about passionate love with all its irrationalities, we still demand psychologically plausible circumstances, so that we can enter into the dramatic illusion with conviction; the Elizabethan was content to accept the frank make-believe of the Court of Illyria in Shakespeare's *Twelfth Night**, for he did not himself need to forget reality in order to enjoy the spectacle of fantastic extensions of real experience.

Three final facts need to be pointed out about Elizabethan play production. The first is that though the Elizabethans did not employ scenery, they attached importance to costume. The costume was not realistic in the sense of being historically or geographically accurate (though minor concessions were made when ancient Rome was the scene), but it was ostentatiously gorgeous or eccentric, and expressive of character. The second fact is that women, until after 1660, very seldom acted in plays; female roles were taken by boys. The third fact is that, as far as we can judge, acting was more formal, both in speech and gesture, than modern acting is; it was also closely related to a much esteemed branch of contemporary education – that of rhetoric. Elizabethan schoolboys and university students were taught rhetoric as a form of creative composition as well as persuasive argument, and appropriate gestures as well as speech were part of the subject. This suggests that the audiences must have been better qualified than modern audiences are to appreciate and criticize styles of acting; it also shows that spoken language had then a force and importance that it is scarcely regarded as possessing today.

Yet, when we have acknowledged all this, we need to acknowledge that the Elizabethans were in the process of changing their fundamental ideas about the theatre. We have to remember the Masque*, a court spectacle in which language, music, and scenery were of equal importance. Hamlet (III.ii) warns the players against exaggerated rhetoric, and if we find so many of Shakespeare's characters fully realistic, this may be because he was breaking through to realism. It is certainly true that when the Puritans* closed the theatres in 1642, plays of a very different kind from those of fifty years before were being shown, and they were being presented in a different way.

5.1.2.3 *Later Moralities and Interludes: dramatic evolution, 1500–90*

In the 16th century, the traditional, religious drama of England mingles with new kinds which arise from political and cultural changes.

As an advance, the change is most noticeable in comedy. The fine tragic feeling in the Mystery plays of the Crucifixion depended on a kind of religious intensity that was passing away, but the comedy of the Mysteries and the Moralities expanded naturally in the new more secular drama. The play sometimes credited as being the first 'true' English comedy, *Ralph Roister Doister** (written 1551?), is still lively reading, whereas the play so much admired in its own day as the first 'true' English tragedy, *Gorboduc** (1561), is for us an intrinsically dead work, of historical interest only. 'True' here is to be understood as measuring up to the standards of dramatic construction and consistency of tone to be found in the drama of Greece and Rome; both plays followed Roman examples: those of Terence* and Plautus* in comedy, and of Seneca* in tragedy. However, whereas *Ralph Roister* has the life of a native tradition of comedy as well, *Gorboduc* is a painstaking imitation, its native inspiration chiefly a responsible concern for the national future. Besides *Ralph Roister*, a number of other plays survive from the middle of the century with lasting comic vitality. The kind of play in which comedy most freely displays itself is known as the Interlude*.

Unlike Mysteries and Moralities, Interludes are difficult to classify as a clearly defined form. Some Interludes are indistinguishable from Moralities, and they varied in length and seriousness of intention. There is even disagreement about the meaning of the term 'Interlude'. One of the modern uses of the word is to signify a pause between the acts of a play; in accordance with this, 16th century Interludes are thought to have been intended as short dramatic performances in the intervals of business, such as meetings of a town council, or in the course of some other entertainment, such as a feast in a great house. On the other hand, the Latin words 'inter' and 'ludo' together mean 'play between'; in this sense an Interlude may merely have implied a short dramatic performance with a number of characters opposed to one another. In either case, the word suggests something unambitious and probably rather short. Many Interludes consist of debates between conflicting viewpoints; these made up the witty plays of John Heywood*, such as the *Play of the Weather* (1533), in which representatives of either sex and of various classes, trades and ages make incompatible demands on the gods for their own preferred kinds of weather. Heywood's plays are little more than dramatic anecdotes, but they show an excellent sense of the theatre, and an ability to involve the audience as participants in the joke. When a Heywood character speaks a soliloquy, he is addressing the audience as a man addresses bystanders in the street; he is not thinking aloud before invisible witnesses in the way that we nowadays – probably wrongly – think of Hamlet and Iago as doing.

Meanwhile, the traditional kind of Morality continued to be performed, but the newer Moralities proceeded from the altered fields of men's thought. The growth of the state, the reduced claims of the Church on men's lives, caused men like John Skelton* (1460?–1529) to write political Moralities such as his *Magnificence* (in which a ruler with right feelings is first ruined by bad advisers, and then restored by good ones with such names as Good Hope and Perseverance). The finest play in this style is a Scottish one, Sir David Lindsay's* *Satire of Three*

Estates (1540), in which Rex Humanitas ('King Humanity') is flanked by Diligence and Wantonness, as a man in the older form of Morality might be flanked by his good and bad angels; the play develops at some length, with other allegorical characters both virtuous and vicious, and Pauper (the Poor Man) as the victim of the episodes. John Bale (1495–1563) used the political morality in a historical setting in his *King John* (1547?), in which the events of the reign of the English King John (1199–1216) are used as a commentary on the struggle between Henry VIII (1509–47) and the Roman Catholic Church. Thus Bale began the union between the political Morality and the history play which reaches its climax in Shakespeare's series of plays on the reigns of Richard II*, Henry IV* and Henry V* between 1595 and 1599; in Shakespeare, the sources in the Morality tradition of the history plays are by no means invisible.

One other great secularizing influence on the religious Morality was Humanism*. Humanism was primarily a great educational movement, awakening men's interest in the sources of European culture in ancient Greek and Latin literature. More important still was its effect in rousing men to a desire for secular education as a means to full human development in this world, as well as a guide to right living that would lead them to the destination they desired in the next. The centre of Humanism in early-16th-century England was the household of Sir Thomas More*, who himself took a great interest in drama. From this circle came plays like Medwall's *Nature*, in which Reason, not religious piety, is the crowning virtue, and the setting is the London of the day and not far removed from Falstaff's surroundings in Shakespeare's *Henry IV*. Redford's *Wit and Science* and John Rastell's *Four Elements* concentrate more strictly on the spiritual rewards of right education.

The Humanists not only helped to give a different turn to the Morality tradition; they developed the beginnings of a drama for the intelligentsia by studying the Latin dramatists, Terence, Plautus, and Seneca, and by adapting plays from France, Italy and Spain, which were themselves more or less based on those classical models. These classical dramatists were studied, translated, and imitated in the grammar and public schools, in the universities of Oxford and Cambridge, and in those important centres of the English intelligentsia, the corporations of lawyers in the London Inns of Court. One consequence of this study was the gain of experience in dramatic structure, to supplement the vivid sense of theatre which the best writers of Interludes and Moralities were already masters of. Another effect was the introduction into English plays of classical situations and characters, some of which fused with similar features of the native English tradition. For instance, Ralph in *Ralph Roister Doister* is the boastful but cowardly soldier of Plautus's *Miles Gloriosus*. The 16th-century comic Vice, or buffoon, is a combination of the comic devil of the Moralities and the mischievous servant in the Latin dramatists. Such a character is Matthew Merygreek in *Ralph Roister Doister*, and Diccon the Bedlam in *Gammer Gurton's Needle** (1566), a play in which classical comedy is completely transported into the environment of English village life.

They anticipate a variety of intriguers in plays of the great age: Mosca, in Jonson's *Volpone** (1606) is a clear example, but Shakespeare's Iago in *Othello** is a relative of the family.

The 1560s and 1570s were the climax of this slow process of the maturing of Renaissance drama. Plautan intrigue comes out most clearly, and most independently of the native English tradition, in Gascoigne's* *Supposes* (1566), an adaptation of the Italian Ariosto's* *I Suppositi* (1509). It is based on a cunning exploitation of confusions and disguises, and anticipates Shakespeare's comedies (*Two Gentlemen of Verona**, *The Merchant of Venice**, *Much Ado About Nothing**) also set in Italy, which to Elizabethan Englishmen was the land where civilization had reached its height, corruption its depth, and cunning intrigue was the distinguishing feature of behaviour. This was also the period of attempts at solemn tragedy, though it was nearly always mixed with comedy. The educated audiences of the Inns of Court wanted a 'high style' fit for their serious minds, but they were better accustomed to comedy of intrigue and savage debate; the result was a number of tragicomedies* by a group of dramatists forgotten except by scholars: *Cambises* (1561?) by Preston, *Damon and Pythias* (1565?) by Edwardes, *Apius and Virginia* (1565?) by R.B., and *Promos and Cassandra* (1578), the basis of Shakespeare's *Measure for Measure** (1603?). Such dramatists wished to escape what they considered to be the barbarity of the English tradition, but they had not felt their way either into true tragic experience or into the use of comedy as a subtle and refined commentary on human behaviour. To their audiences they were probably exciting as the progenitors of serious drama; to us they are important as the basis for the more creatively gifted University Wits of the 1580s.

This interest in tragedy caused the sixties to be the decade in which attention focused on Seneca. Seneca* was a philosopher as well as a dramatist; as neither does he count among those of the first rank in the history of European culture. Yet to Englishmen of this period both his stoical philosophy and his drama of revenge seemed of particular relevance to their society. His plays were translated into English between 1559 and 1581; they inspired the form and feeling of *Gorboduc*, and later helped to inspire the much more vital tradition of Revenge Tragedy* from Kyd's *Spanish Tragedy** (1589?) to Middleton's *The Changeling** (1623).

5.1.2.4 *University Wits*

The group of young men who were writing plays when Shakespeare began his career are called the 'University Wits' because they had studied at the universities of Oxford or Cambridge and then set up as professional writers, selling their learning and their 'wits' to the London public of playgoers, and to the reading public as well, for they were none of them merely playwrights and two of the group wrote little for the stage. Greene*, Nashe* and Marlowe* came from Cambridge; the first was a journalist as much as a writer of plays, and the second almost wholly a journalist; Marlowe wrote (but did not finish) one of the finest narrative poems of the age, *Hero and Leander*. Lyly*, Peele*, and Lodge* were at Oxford: Lyly wrote the most popular prose tales of the age (*Euphues**); Peele designed pageants for the City of London, and Lodge is chiefly remembered for his romance *Rosalynde*, the source of Shakespeare's play *As You Like It**. With these six, Thomas Kyd* is always associated; he was not strictly a University Wit since he seems not to have attended a university, but he was of the same calibre, and, after Marlowe, he was the most influential playwright of them all.

Attendance at a university was of course nothing unusual for a playwright. Hitherto, however, playwrights with a university background had either been scholars who were permanently resident there, or, like Thomas Sackville, part-author of *Gorboduc*, they had been gentlemen who had passed through university into the world of the court and the aristocracy, practising literature as only one of the activities that engaged the gentlemen of the time. The 'Wits' were different from these. They were not primarily scholars, though they had all, including Kyd, been influenced by humanistic scholarship. Except Lyly, they started their careers outside court circles: Nashe was the son of a parish clergyman, Greene and Marlowe were the sons of tradesmen; Peele and Lodge, the sons of richer merchants. Lyly was more a man of the older generation; he began his career under the patronage of the Earl of Oxford, and used literature as a means to advance himself at court. The others were among the earliest professional writers of the modern sort, selling their talents for whatever the public would pay. Shakespeare himself was a writer of the same sort, and so was his chief rival in the theatre, Ben Jonson.

Probably any dramatist would aspire to the court, but these were not courtiers, and they competed for audiences in the new public theatres as well. The audiences in these were socially and educationally mixed, but they shared a taste for language at a time when English was passing through what was possibly its most vivid phase – not yet segmented by social distinction into rigid class dialects, nor emasculated by insistence on a limited clarity. The learned were not ashamed to use the concrete, sensuous language of the common people, while at the same time they struggled to increase their articulacy by borrowing from the classical and the other modern languages, and by inventing new terms. Prose writers and readers allowed words to carry the multiple suggestiveness that has always been allowed them by poets, and the writing, reading, singing, and reciting of verse was very widely practised at a time that was as rich in its eminent musical composers as it was in its lyric poets. Education reached pretty far down urban society; good schooling and sometimes university teaching were available to the sons of city tradesmen, as the examples of Greene and Marlowe show. The less educated, if they could read, had the jest books, like those associated with the comic actor Tarlton,* consisting of anecdotes like those which make the starting-point of Nashe's romance, *The Unfortunate Traveller** and the lighter episodes of Marlowe's *Doctor Faustus**; whether they could read or not, they had the broadside ballads* on topical events, read and sold in the street by such men as the pedlar Autolycus in Shakespeare's *The Winter's Tale**, and they listened to the great popular preachers, some of whom were national figures, like Henry Smith, 'the prime preacher of the nation'. For both the learned and the unlearned members of society, language was more than we take it to be: whereas we use it as a means of exchange for information and ideas, for the Elizabethans it had a transfiguring power. The learned had a boundless faith in the persuasive force of rhetoric, in the capacity of words to express the whole of knowledge and wisdom, and in their power to embody a reality that would remedy the imperfections of nature. Those who lacked learning still had a belief in words as a form of magic – in the deadly power of the curse, and the beneficent and maleficent effects of spells.

A man trying to sell his literary talents to such a public could use wide resources, unless, like Lyly, he made his appeal to only a section of it. Lyly, who stands apart from the rest of the Wits, was a court dramatist. He wrote his plays for boy actors, in prose that appealed candidly to a taste for artificial wit and ornament, though even his dialogue is not quite divorced from the character of common speech. He cultivated his artificial graces, not as a writer does when he has lost contact with language that is more humanly vivid, but as one who is deliberately removing himself from it. His prose is the foundation of Shakespeare's language when he is representing courtly manners in their most self-conscious form, as in *Love's Labour's Lost*, or when he is burlesquing such manners as Falstaff does in *1 Henry IV* II.iv. Peele and Greene were more typically ready to appeal either to the courtly or to the popular taste, or to both together. Peele helps to illustrate the variety of styles of play in the later years of Elizabeth. His *The Arraignment of Paris* (1584) was a courtly pastoral in the style of Lyly, but his *Battle of Alcazar*, whose hero, Thomas Stukely, is an illegitimate son of Henry VIII, belongs to the world of the broadside ballad; his history play *Edward I* was actually based on a ballad. *David and Bethsabe*, on the other hand, is a solemn tragedy based on the Bible, and his most lively play, *The Old Wives' Tale* (1593?) is in the tradition of the country folk-tale. Greene is most remembered as a dramatist for two plays – *Friar Bacon and Friar Bungay** (1589?) and *James IV*; in these he mingled elements of folklore with elements of courtly romance, and his use of the romantic heroine anticipated Shakespeare's famous women, such as Rosalind in *As You Like It* and Viola in *Twelfth Night*. Kyd's *Spanish Tragedy** (1589?) is more important than any play by Peele or Greene. He was not their superior as a poet, but excelled them in dramatic construction and in theatrical appeal; he also started the fashion for the tragedy of revenge which culminated in Shakespeare's first great tragedy, *Hamlet*, itself probably based on a lost play of the same name by Kyd. But the greatest of all the Wits was Marlowe. He and Shakespeare were born in the same year (1564), and when he died in 1593 it is questionable whether his achievement was inferior to Shakespeare's at the same date. He belongs to the Great Age, and is discussed in the next section of this essay.

5.1.3 *The Great Age: 1590–1620*

5.1.3.1 *Elizabethan drama: 1590–1600*

Probably no country has ever produced drama of such richness and variety as England did during the 30 years, 1590 to 1620. Such variety, however, points to the limits of this achievement. On the one hand it was the sign of a confluence of many kinds of imaginative power in an excited and vigorous society; on the other hand, it was also the sign of deep emotional uncertainty and insecurity of values. The price paid for the variety was the absence of a clear conception of the frontier and scope of dramatic art: part of the interest in studying the period is that one never knows what a dramatist will attempt next, or how he will attempt it, and the disappointment of such a study is the unevenness of the dramatic execution. Shakespeare wrote perhaps a dozen great plays without serious weaknesses, and Jonson* wrote three; of the other leading dramatists – Marlowe*, Chapman*, Webster*, Tourneur*, Middleton* – it is hardly possible to say that they produced a single play in which great achievement is not matched by serious weaknesses. The drama is a form of art in which distinctness of idea is so important as to be almost indispensable; it took the very great genius of Shakespeare to achieve clarity of vision amidst the paradoxes of thought and feeling so characteristic of his time. But exceptional energy of spirit was also characteristic of the time, and this energy enabled some other dramatists to achieve it, altogether in a few plays by Jonson and one by Middleton, and intermittently in many plays by these dramatists and by others. When this energy declined, as it began to do even in the second decade of the reign of James I* (1603–25), the drama could no longer express the deepest feelings of the age, and it began to decline too.

The great period of the University Wits was little more than five years, from 1588 to 1593, when Marlowe died. He left behind the two-part play *Tamburlaine the Great**, *The Jew of Malta**, *Doctor Faustus**, and *Edward II* – probably written in that order – besides lesser work. His great achievements were two: he developed the medium of blank verse* from its original inflexible stateliness into a supple instrument for a range of tones from pathos to grandeur; and he replaced the stilted heroes of former Renaissance* drama by men of vitality and passion – in short he created the Renaissance hero for the English drama. The men of the Renaissance valued knowledge, learning, reason, and the arts of persuasion, but all these were instruments for fulfilment in action; action, in turn, was valued for its prizes of fame and power. They worshipped beauty because it was the outward sign of this fame, and part of beauty was ceremony, pageantry, and the other emblems of order and rank. They were exhilarated by their new confidence in the reach of the mind, but for them the mind reached towards a finite end: sovereignty over either the world or the self. The lines spoken by Tamburlaine (*1 Tamburlaine* II.vi) are often quoted because they embody one side of this humanistic passion:

Nature, that fram'd us of four elements
Warring within our breasts for regiment,

Doth teach us all to have aspiring minds:
Our souls, whose faculties can comprehend
The wondrous architecture of the world,
And measure every wandering planet's course,
Still climbing after knowledge infinite,
And always moving as the restless spheres,
Will us to wear ourselves, and never rest,
Until we reach the ripest fruit of all,
That perfect bliss and sole felicity,
The sweet fruition of an earthly crown.

To a modern mind, the last line is not so much a climax as an anticlimax. This shows the difference between our mind and the Renaissance mind; it also marks the difference between the Renaissance and the Middle Ages. The men of the Middle Ages would perhaps have considered a crown in heaven preferable to an earthly crown, though no doubt they sometimes only pretended to have this preference; and Tamburlaine is of course an Asian pagan, not a European Christian. But he is also, in Marlowe's conception, a Renaissance man, who is fascinated by the vision of heaven on earth.

But Marlowe knew the immense cost of such a vision. First, Tamburlaine, who goes from the conquest of one earthly crown to that of many, is unable to conquer death, the inevitable frustration of all who forsake everything for personal glory. Second, Tamburlaine is ruthlessly cruel even beyond gaining his ends; cruelty and treachery are requirements for the attainment of his 'sole felicity', and this becomes a theme of tragedy culminating in Shakespeare's *Macbeth**. Marlowe's grim farce, *The Jew of Malta**, deals expressly with this aspect of the man grasping for power; whereas Tamburlaine is portrayed as a terrible force of nature, pitiless but amoral rather than evil, Barabbas is presented as a monster of evil, into whom an element of grotesque comedy enters, recalling the Herods of the medieval Mysteries and anticipating Jonson's Comedy of Humours*.

A third and deeper cost of the lust for power is connected with a profound conflict in the Renaissance mind. Renaissance men were not so different from medieval men in wanting heaven on earth as in dissociating heaven from earth to a greater extent than the Middle Ages did. English churches in town and village are mostly medieval, at least in design, and they often bear spires which point heavenward; the churches were the focus of communal life, and by their very design they were bonds between the here and the hereafter. But Renaissance men wanted both, and were keenly aware that they endangered their chances of heaven – so real, but so remote – if they concentrated on earth, so immediate, and so desirable. Marlowe himself was accused of atheism, but it was not the modern kind of disbelief; it was an arrogant display of what the mind could do for itself, *if* it chose to reject divine teaching. His greatest play is consequently *Doctor Faustus*, in which he grafts on to the medieval Morality tradition a Renaissance man who at the end, in one of the greatest passages of dramatic poetry in any literature, faces the truth that his soul is lost.

When Marlowe was killed in 1593, Shakespeare* may have written four history plays (*1*, *2*, *3 Henry VI** and *Richard III**), a violent tragedy of revenge (*Titus Andronicus**), a deft comedy adapted from Plautus* (*The Comedy of Errors**), and a slight but charming romantic comedy (*The Two Gentlemen of Verona**). Of all these, only *Richard III* equals and in some ways excels Marlowe's work in power; yet if Shakespeare had died in the same year, it is possible that we would still think that he had the greater promise of the two. We would notice his superior powers of dramatic construction, and the variety and appeal of his women characters – few and relatively dull in Marlowe. We would above all notice his greater variety of form and tone; we would have the sense of a young man experimenting in the wide variety of forms now available to a dramatist. It was not for nothing that the envious Greene*, while he was dying in 1592, seems to have meant Shakespeare when he described 'an upstart crow beautified with our feathers' – though some think that he meant Shakespeare's acting. Shakespeare was certainly learning his art from the variety offered by the Wits, but most of all he was learning how to develop Marlowe's blank verse line. He continued to experiment for at least another three years, producing a courtly comedy that excelled Lyly in *Love's Labour's Lost**; a domestic comedy of rough, homely humour – the antithesis of romantic comedy – in *The Taming of the Shrew**; a romantic comedy in which classical myth combined with English folklore in *A Midsummer Night's Dream**, a romantic tragedy in *Romeo and Juliet**, and another history play, *King John**. 'Experiment', of course, is a misleading term if it suggests imperfection, for several of these are masterpieces. By now he has shown clearly not only that he can equal the Wits, but that he can excel them.

Shakespeare's pre-eminence is of course due to his extraordinary originality; but to begin to understand his originality, we have to interpret the word correctly. It does not mean that he invented a kind of drama that was quite different from that to which his age was accustomed, or that he invented new ideas for his dramatic subjects. It means that as part of his poetic talent and his imaginative intensity he possessed an unusual critical power. This, too, must be properly defined. He left no assessments of his own or of anybody else's work, but a great imaginative writer must use criticism to test the vitality of the literary forms of his age. He tests them, rather than invents new ones, because entirely new forms would be neither intelligible to his audience nor continuous with the imaginative expression that has nourished him. Thus in *Love's Labour* he takes the theme of 'courtly love' and treats it in comedy: the courtiers are forced to unwind their delicate web of ideality, and face reality. In *Romeo and Juliet*, Romeo, the courtly lover, has to forget his abstract ideal of a lady, and come to terms with brutal reality, and a girl of flesh and blood. In *King John*, the Bastard, an outsider to all the political pageantry because of his illegitimate birth, uses against it his vigorous but humane and increasingly responsible satire. In *The Merchant of Venice**, the singular figure of Shylock the Jew, another outsider, has the distinctness of reality in contrast to the other much less distinctive characters and the conventional fable, as though Shakespeare were deliberately contrasting an accepted world of fantasy (though it points to real values) with an outlook that rejected the convention wholly. In *Henry V** we are shown the man who, in national opinion, represented the ideal Christian king, and we see how difficult, or strictly impossible, it is for the man and his role to be united. In *As You Like It**, the most pastoral* of all Shakespeare's plays, pastoralism, romantic love, and court manners are all satirized. In all these plays, Shakespeare is not rejecting the accepted forms of theatrical tradition; he is revitalizing them by bringing them into relationship with the actualities of real experience.

In other plays of the period, such as *Richard II** (1595?), *1 & 2 Henry IV** (1597–8?), *Julius Caesar** (1599?) and *Twelfth Night** (1599–1600?), we see a different use of the critical faculty; the themes are again traditional enough, but they are refreshed by a new density of characterization. The process is most easily illustrated by the Henry IV plays. They have sometimes puzzled readers because they seem to split into two layers: one layer consists of a heroic political conflict presented through aristocratic characters speaking eloquent poetry, and the other layer consists of broad comedy of low life, centring on Falstaff, and presented chiefly in prose. Both layers contain vivid characterization, but apart from the importance of Prince Hal in each, they seem to have little in common. In fact, beneath their vivid surface life, the plays are firmly based in the Morality tradition. Falstaff is, in Christian terms, the old Adam who lives by the desires of the flesh, and Hotspur, who seeks worldly honour much as Tamburlaine does, resembles the sin of Pride. Prince Hal, the heir to the throne, stands between these different destructive forces, and the drama consists in his triumph over them in the name of England. Both plays are about rebellion, but in Renaissance thinking there was a correspondence between the individual man considered as a moral society of the appetites, passions, will and reason, and the political state; thus Falstaff, the rebellious flesh in us all and the spirit of 'riot' in the state, is a more difficult enemy to defeat than is Hotspur, the open enemy of society. In Part 2, the Prince is still faced by Falstaff, though Hotspur is dead; on his other side, like a good angel confronting a bad one in a Morality, he has the Lord Chief Justice, who is Justice in essence and not merely by his profession as a judge. The Prince identifies himself with the latter by force of will under guidance of reason, and when he discards Falstaff after his coronation –

I know thee not, old man: fall to thy prayers

– we are witnessing, not the rejection of an old friend by an ungrateful young one, but the rejection by a Christian Prince of the self-indulgent temptations to which he, like all of us, is privately subject, and which constitute a public, political source of disorder as well. This is the Morality basis of the play, but because of its vivid realization in characters and language the older political Moralities and history plays – even including Marlowe's *Edward II* – look insubstantial beside it.

5.1.3.2 *The Jacobeans: rediscovery of tragedy: 1600–25*
Most periods of literary taste consider that they understand the term 'Tragic Drama'. This often means that readers conceive an idea of it based on the form it took in the last age in which it actually flourished. In no country has it flourished in every period of dramatic writing; in its greater manifestations it is always rediscovered in a new form. Thus in the Middle Ages, although as we have seen the Mysteries and at least *Everyman** among the Moralities contained genuine tragic feeling, there was no real tragic drama. The conventional view of tragedy was that of Chaucer's Monk*, and was associated with the operation of the Wheel of Fortune: the way in which a man may rise to greatness of prosperity, and then, by the inexorable course of events, sink again into insignificance or misery.

The 16th century inherited this general conception, but in its closing years, two more interesting ideas were growing up. Kyd* took from Seneca* the conception of the tragedy of revenge, a form which has special meaning for a society like the Elizabethan one, where ideals of law and order were much in advance of the means to enforce them. In a highly civilized society a man who desires justice for murder or injury to a friend or a relation can appeal with some reliance to the courts of justice; but in a society in which there are practically no police and 'great men' can frustrate the working of the law, such a man may feel that it is his duty to exact justice by private revenge, which Bacon called 'a kind of Wild Justice'. Thus Seneca's 'tragedies of revenge' appealed to the Elizabethans, not merely by their intrinsic literary excitement, but by their relevance to the conditions and practice of their own society. Revenge Tragedy* took root in the Elizabethan imagination, and from Kyd's *Spanish Tragedy** (1589?) through Shakespeare's *Hamlet** (1601?), Tourneur's(?) *Revenger's Tragedy** (1607), Webster's *Duchess of Malfi** (1613?) and Middleton's *Changeling** (1623?), it was the source of a remarkable series of dramas.

The other tragic idea that developed in the last 15 years of the century was more fruitful still. It was a variant of the medieval conception of the Wheel of Fortune, and may be said to start with Marlowe's Tamburlaine plays. Death is a tragedy for Tamburlaine not in the sense that it is for Everyman, who, as every man, must meet it alone, but because of the ironical paradox that such a man, who feels infinite potentialities within himself, *can* die. Marlowe's *Faustus* is richer, because Faustus is caught between two conceptions of eternity: the illusory eternity of physical ecstasy that he enjoys with Helen, and the ultimate eternity of damnation or salvation. Thus, Marlowe's tragic idea implies the common human desire to have heaven on earth, but Marlowe hardly developed the idea beyond the elementary barrier to its fulfilment – that man is mortal. It was left to Shakespeare to develop the much more important obstacle – that man is spiritually unworthy.

So far, then, we have seen the tragedy of the Great Age as arising from the work of two pioneers: the social Tragedy of Revenge begun by Kyd, and what we may call the personal tragedy of the Renaissance Hero, begun by Marlowe. These two lines of development were, however, related by their interpretation of the world in terms of correspondence, such as that between individual man considered as a moral society in himself, ruled by reason, and the state ruled by the sovereign. This kind of correspondence between public and private was supported – not always consistently – by the various kinds of thinking of the time. Spiritually it had its foundation in the Christian religion, divided though this now was. Philosophically, it found support in Aristotle* and Plato* among the Greeks, and in Seneca's philosophy of Stoicism* among the Romans, all of whom taught the advantage of ordering the passions to the benefit of the well-ordered state. Physically, the sciences of physiology, psychology and medicine were related by the doctrine of the correspondence between the four elements* in nature and the four humours* in man, and by the importance of a due balance among them being maintained in both. Astronomy and astrology taught that man's personal order was deeply influenced by the order that governed the outer sphere of his universe. But though the Elizabethans believed that they could attain perfect understanding of a perfectly ordered universe, society, and private life, all in harmony, they could not agree about how best to achieve it, nor were they under any illusion about the difficulty of achieving it. They were very conscious of evil as an active force, and of the cunning and deceitfulness of its working: a man, seeking good, might act evilly; or, possessing good, might destroy it, mistaking it for evil.

The great period of tragic drama, beginning with *Hamlet* in about 1601 and ending with Middleton's *The Changeling* in 1623, is concerned with these two aspects of evil: the deceitfulness of its working, and the destructiveness of the human passions.

The deceitfulness of evil was often represented through the kind of character known to the Elizabethans as the 'Machiavel' or 'Politician', because they deeply abhorred the ideas of the Italian philosopher Machiavelli* (author of *The Prince*, 1513) who maintained that if political objectives were desirable, they should be pursued without the restraint of any moral principles. Such a 'Machiavel' was Shakespeare's Richard III and another was Marlowe's Barabbas; Iago in Shakespeare's *Othello** is clearly related to the type. Characteristic of Machiavels is that they glory in their evil, making no disguise of it except before those whom they hope to deceive. *Hamlet* is more deeply interesting than any English tragedy that preceded it because it deals with the problem of how to recognize evil when it does not declare itself, and how to act effectively when it is recognized. Claudius, the villain, is not actually *seen* to be evil. Hamlet – and the audience – have to depend on the evidence of the Ghost that Claudius has gained the throne and the Queen by murder. On the other hand, it is important that Hamlet's awareness of evil begins before the Ghost declares it; evil is implicit in the unnaturally hasty marriage of his uncle and his mother after his father's death – a marriage that was incestuous according to 16th-century law. Claudius, in his first speech, addressed to the court, shows his embarrassed knowledge of this indecency by his grotesque imagery, and he reminds the court that they have connived at the ugly situation. 'Something is rotten in the state of Denmark' says one of Hamlet's honest friends. Not the crime merely, but the 'rottenness' that includes it is the evil. It extends, in Hamlet's consciousness, beyond Claudius the murderer to all those who abetted him in taking the crown and marrying Hamlet's mother, even though they were ignorant of the murder: it extends to the Queen herself, to the sycophantic courtiers, perhaps even to Ophelia. Revenge Tragedy in *Hamlet* is no longer a 'detection' problem of first finding the murderer and then finding a means to kill him; it has become the problem of whether revenge can be carried out at all. A scarcely less fine play on the deceitfulness of evil is Middleton's *The Changeling*, in which the heroine, Beatrice Joanna, convinces herself that she can keep free of the loathsomeness of murder by getting a man whom she loathes to commit it, only to find that she is as intimately bound up with him as she is with the loathsome aspect of her own nature.

The clearest examples of tragedies of destructive passion are Shakespeare's *Antony and Cleopatra** and *Coriolanus**. These are 'Roman' plays; that is to say, they are set in a period and a society about which the unhistorically-minded Jacobeans had a clear, if limited, historical consciousness. Rome, for them, was the summit of human civilization, but it was pagan. Its paganism implied an important difference from the Christian world, in which the highest type of humanity was the saint; but saints could not exist under paganism, whose highest type was therefore the hero. At the same time, this difference had special significance for men of the Renaissance, since they themselves were inclined to seek the ideal of the hero rather than that of the saint. The hero's most obvious field of action was the battlefield, but all the nobler passions would work in him more strongly than in common men. Thus Antony is greater than his rival Octavius, not merely because he is greater in war, but because he is greater in love; his tragedy is that war and love, by pulling in opposite directions, destroy him. So much is clear to any reader on first reading, but closer examination shows us further destructiveness in the theme. The war is an extension of politics, and politics without spiritual authority is a kind of cannibalism, as men, in their striving for power, conspire to destroy one another. Moreover, love, as sexuality, is also a kind of war, with men and women striving for mastery over one another; Cleopatra, the devourer of men, is, however magnificent, another kind of cannibal. She loves Antony because he is a hero and therefore a man of war, yet it is war that draws him from her, so that, in order to possess him, she has to destroy him as a warrior and therefore as a man. Coriolanus is also a Roman warrior, a hero who seeks honour and fame as they are estimated by his caste. But his caste, the Roman patricians, compromise with the common people whom they despise; Coriolanus refuses to compromise and to conceal his contempt. In the name of compromise he is cast out of Rome; in the name of honour, he returns with Rome's enemies to destroy the city, only to find that he is defeated by his mother from whom he has derived all his values, and who yet forces him to renounce them since he loves her still more. It is important, in these plays, to observe that the hero does not fail through weakness but is brought down by those very virtues that have made him the great man he is: he lives to the full in the light of the values which other more politic men acknowledge as their own but which in practice they accept only with reservations.

The destructive passions are the principal theme of the leading tragic writers amongst Shakespeare's contemporaries – Jonson*, in *Sejanus**; Chapman* in *Bussy d'Ambois*; Tourneur*(?) in *The Revenger's Tragedy**; Webster* in *The White Devil** and *The Duchess of Malfi**. Jonson's play (1603) is probably the finest of these, but its theme of an ancient Roman politician intoxicated by ambition to the extent that he eventually causes his own collapse and death leads in the direction of Jonson's powerful and highly personal comedy, and it will be discussed in the next section of this essay. The others are all set in princely courts of the time, and all abroad: Chapman's play in France, and Tourneur's and Webster's plays in Italy. Any serious writer, even if he is writing 'historical' drama or narrative, is primarily interested in his own age and its principal social centres of interest: there were reasons why these writers should write about princely courts, and why they should not write about English ones. The courts were the centres of Renaissance societies – the focus of their politics, culture, manners and morals. It was however against the law for dramatists to write about the contemporary English court, and moreover it was the French and above all the Italian courts which exhibited the extremes of civilization in their luxury, refinement, licence and corruption. The dramatists and their audiences were fascinated by the vividness of court life and they were appalled by its moral anarchy, especially when this was masked, and made more sinister, by princely ceremony, the mockery of an order which was supposed to have its basis in nature. In such courts, as the dramatists conceived them, the sensual appetite for heaven on earth created hells; morality and humanity were overthrown. *Bussy d'Ambois* (1604?) shows one answer to this challenge: Bussy is a man of unquenchably independent spirit whose valour for a time successfully defies the subtleties of courtiers' intrigues, though eventually his own refusal to subdue his fiery spirit causes his death. *The Revenger's Tragedy* (1607?) offers a second answer: without virtue himself but filled with a hatred of the court viciousness that has led to the death of his betrothed, Vindice, the 'Revenger', sets about the wholesale destruction of the court, and succeeds, at the cost of his own life when a saner régime is restored. The violence of this play is grotesque, but the poetry is vital and not merely sensational; it is near the spirit of Marlowe's tragic farce, *The Jew of Malta*. A third answer, dramatically much less successful, is provided by Chapman's *The Revenge of Bussy d'Ambois* and Tourneur's *The Atheist's Tragedy*, both written about 1607. In these, the heroes – Clermont d'Ambois and Charlemont respectively – have such finely tempered spirits that they can rise above their passions and above those of their enemies; they are consecrated to virtue, contemptuous of suffering, resigned to the sacrifice of happiness. This is the answer of Roman stoicism, an answer much favoured by the Jacobeans, but dramatically they were much more interested in the extremes of emotion that are commonly the outcome of violence. In the plays of Shakespeare, and in those so far mentioned by other dramatists, the violence is shaped into coherence by a high order of spiritual vision. It was essentially the medieval vision enriched rather than contradicted by the Renaissance sense of the potentialities of man, and already in the second decade of the reign of James I it was being transformed and weakened. Violence began to be allowed its inherent theatrical appeal without the unifying inspiration of the traditional beliefs, and Webster's two plays, *The White Devil* (1611?) and *The Duchess of Malfi* (1613?), have marvellous intensity in particular scenes and passages, rather than dramatic excellence in the whole play. For the destructive passion to be truly dramatic, rather than being sensationally theatrical, some positive and active embodiment of greatness and goodness must be present at least in implication, as they are perhaps even in the apparently negative *Revenger's Tragedy* by Tourneur. The passion of Shakespeare's masterpieces is consonant with the heroes' greatness, and even with the source of their greatness.

In what are commonly considered to be his finest achievements in tragedy – *Othello* (1604–5?), *Macbeth** (1605–6?), and *King Lear** (1605–6?) – the themes of the destructive passion and the deceitfulness of evil combine. Othello and Desdemona achieve heaven on earth by their single-hearted love for each other, but Iago does not believe that mortal men and women deserve such bliss, and his envy of it induces him to set about its destruction; by playing on Othello's trust in him as a fellow soldier – who, ideally, was considered to be the opposite of the subtle politician – he demonstrates that Othello does not deserve the wholeness of Desdemona's heart by winning him to the belief that she must be disloyal. King Lear brings about his own destruction by the conviction, natural to him as a father and as a king, that his daughters will still give him their first loyalties when he has relinquished power without relinquishing status; it is the deceitfulness of his older daughters, Goneril and Regan, that facilitates this fatal change. He finds, when he has made it, that the nature that he considered bound to support him in the rights of his role and of his affections, is really a jungle in which selfish passions make the law – though his third daughter proves to him that nature is still a creative order when all its obligations are observed. Macbeth, the warrior whose impetuosity saves his country, is carried by his passions to murder, usurpation, and then to further murder and massacre, but it is the Witches who, by siding with his passions, deceive him into believing that he is merely fulfilling his destiny. In all these plays there is violence as much perhaps as in Webster's plays, but in none of them is violence the principal dramatic intention; all of them are imaginative affirmations that even the good in man must be related to a greater good.

The excellence of imaginative art can never be evoked in summary. Elizabethan and Jacobean drama is wholly made out of language; even the scenery and the time of day had to be evoked in words on stages which had no artificial lighting, and no painted sets. In any age or country, if drama is to be at its best, the language has to be highly developed for literary purposes: rich in its vocabulary, supple in its syntax; capable of rhythms which are an eloquent component of meaning, and possessing a range of diction that is intimate with the emotions and with the subtleties of the intellect. Before Shakespeare's lifetime, English had emotional immediacy but it lacked intellectual refinement; after it, the language began to lose in emotional concreteness while it gained in its capacity for intellectual abstraction. During his lifetime, and for a short period afterwards, the qualities of immediacy and sublety were evenly compounded. In comedy as well as in tragedy, the old ways of feeling and thinking were meeting our own.

5.1.3.3 *Jacobean comedy and tragicomedy: 1600–20*

In all countries, until the 19th century, the characters of tragedy were drawn from the class of princes and nobility, though England, in Shakespeare's time, had some 'bourgeois' tragedy too, such as the anonymous *Arden of Feversham* (1592) and *A Yorkshire Tragedy* (1605?) and Thomas Heywood's* *A Woman Killed with Kindness* (1603). The emphasis on aristocracy in tragedy is natural when we remember that contemporary social ideas credited the class with superior capacity for the more refined and more heroic virtues, as well as for the more dangerous vices. Moreover, the consequences for others of a man's virtues and vices tend to increase in proportion as his status is higher and his power, therefore, greater.

Comedy, on the other hand, has always invited a mixing of the classes. For instance, the middle class may wish to exalt itself by proving its equal worth with the upper class, symbolized by a romantic marriage between members of each; Dekker's *The Shoemakers' Holiday** (1599) appeals to this kind of sentiment. Or the dramatist may wish to burlesque the middle-class desire to escape from the daily practicalities of its habit of life into naive romance; this is the theme of Beaumont's *The Knight of the Burning Pestle** (1609). These two plays survive by their vitality, but they lack the dramatic force of the best middle-class comedy of the period: this took as its theme the vices characteristic of the middle class, though by no means exclusive to them.

Ben Jonson*, Shakespeare's most formidable rival, was the greatest writer of comedy in the period. In his own day he was equally famous for his masques*; these displays, in which music, poetry, and scenic design shared equal importance, were essentially court entertainments, and though they were one of the starting-points of the art of opera, they were too restricted in literary scope and too much directed towards meeting the requirements of particular court occasions to have left an outstanding impression as literature. Jonson also wrote two tragedies. One of these, *Sejanus*, is one of the finest dramas of its time, but it is better understood in the light of Jonson's comedy than in that of Jacobean tragedy; it belongs to the tradition of the violent farce of Marlowe's *The Jew of Malta*, even though it is also close to Marlowe's 'primitive' tragedy, *Tamburlaine*. Sejanus, like Marlowe's heroes, seeks fullness of earthly power, and pursues it through domination of the Roman Emperor, Tiberius, a monster of self-indulgence. His confidence swells till it becomes blinding presumption, and this conceals from him the fact that Tiberius, who is as cunning and keen-sighted as he is corrupt and lethargic, has no intention of submitting to an all-powerful favourite. The Emperor sets up a conspiracy against him through another favourite, Macro, and Sejanus is torn to pieces by the Roman mob; Macro replaces him, but Rome will fare no better – for Macro is another Sejanus, as ambitious, pitiless, and unscrupulous.

Sejanus is a *satiric* tragedy, founded on the conception that men who seek to live to the full tend to satisfy their appetites to the full, whatever the cost to themselves or to other people. They destroy others, but they are their own self-destroyers. This is the essence of Jonson's Comedy of Humours*. A humour, according to the physiology and the psychology of the time, was one of the liquid constituents of the body, each of which had its peculiar emotional propensity: the 'sanguine' humour of the blood led to excessive optimism; 'melancholy', one kind of bile, tended to despair, and so forth. Jonson, however, interpreted the humours more liberally. In his early comedy, *Every Man in hisHumour* (III.i), a character describes a humour as 'a monster bred in a man by self-love and affectation, and fed by folly'. All human beings tend to be self-lovers, and they all consequently tend to breed in themselves these 'monsters'. Much more of a scholar than Shakespeare, Jonson, on the basis of his classical learning, believed in comedy as an artistic end in itself and as a moral means to the correction of human folly. He cultivated comedy as a distinct medium. Shakespeare saw comedy as a medium which was in its essence artificial; when its artificiality was penetrated by the vitality of real life, it led towards tragedy, and tragedy in turn led to a realization of the re-creative potencies of life. Shakespeare's comedy thus ended in the tragicomedies* of his last four plays. Jonson's comedy is self-sufficient and leads nowhere beyond itself; his tragedy, on the contrary, implies his comedy.

Jonson's acknowledged masterpieces are *Volpone** (1606) and *The Alchemist** (1610). In these the humours are identified with appetites and absurdities in the society of Jonson's day, but they also have clear and close relationships to the personified sins of the old Moralities and of Marlowe's *Doctor Faustus*. Each principal humour is a passion amounting to monomania absorbing the whole character, and the central characters are intriguers who deceitfully profit from the maniacal vice and folly of their neighbours, thus 'over-reaching' them; but since they are themselves victims of their own greed and lust, they end, with the exception of Face in *The Alchemist*, in destroying themselves, just as Sejanus destroyed himself. The Ben Jonson world seems at first one of vigorous caricatures, but the energy of his language takes his characters beyond the mere satirical distortion that the word 'caricature' conveys. A caricature reduces a character by force of ridicule, but a Jonson humour is larger than life; his vitality matches him with a Renaissance hero such as Tamburlaine, or even Antony. But whereas the tragic hero takes the accepted values of his world beyond the limits of his world's capacity to accept them, the Jonsonian humour distorts such values by his appetites beyond the limits within which he is acceptably human; whereas the hero is an enlarged human being, the humour is a monstrous one. Thus Jonson gave comedy an intensity that paralleled the intensity given to tragedy by Shakespeare, and in this sense he may be said to have rediscovered the serious art of comedy, as Shakespeare rediscovered tragedy. His Comedy of Humours established a tradition in his own generation. The most notable representatives of it were two writers of Citizen Comedies*: Thomas Middleton* (*A Trick to Catch the Old-One*, 1608; *A Chaste Maid in Cheapside**, 1611) and Philip Massinger*, in *A New Way to Pay Old Debts** (1625) and *The City Madam** (1632).

Jonson's comedy was a scholarly art, inasmuch as it was a 'studied' form with a distinct definition, function, and mode of operation. Most dramatists of the 'Great Age', however, though they drew upon the classical scholarship of the time, were more concerned with how to appeal to the now highly developed theatrical taste among the public. This taste was not predominantly formed by a scholarly conception of drama, but grew out of the mixed serious and comic appeal that had long characterized the English tradition. It seems that between 1590 and 1610, the vitality of public interest in the theatre was at its height, and audiences responded to the drama as the imaginative expression of their strongest and deepest emotions; after that, a slow lessening of vitality of interest began, and the drama was seen more as a vehicle for strong but transitory impressions. Tragicomedies, rather than the serious tragedies of Shakespeare and the weighty comedies of Jonson, came into fashion. This decline in taste helps to explain the immense popularity of the work of John Fletcher*, who usually collaborated with another dramatist. Beaumont and Fletcher's *Philaster** (1610?) is one of the earliest examples of these new tragicomedies, which still strongly appealed to literary taste in the second half of the 17th century. They are plays that often show a very skilful command of theatrical effect, yet they are not shaped by a strong, unifying imagination, but rather appeal incidentally to fashionable tastes for pathos, grace, verbal wit, and exalted sentiments unsupported by deep conviction. Fletcher's work, from 1609 to the year of his death in 1625, marks the beginning of the downward movement of the 'Great Age'.

However, not all tragicomedy was decadent art. At about the time that Fletcher was beginning his career, Shakespeare was also writing the four tragicomedies that concluded his. These plays – *Pericles* (1608–9), *Cymbeline* (1609–10), *The Winter's Tale* (1610–11), *The Tempest* (1611–12) – do not indicate a decline in his power, though the first two are very imperfect. He abandons the comparatively realistic style of his great tragedies (1603–8), and freely uses imaginative licence in the symbolic plotting of his narrative, and in the introduction of magic (especially in *The Tempest*). Nevertheless, not only is each play a coherent imaginative unity, but all four are united by a common imaginative vision. In each, there is tragic loss and miraculous recovery; in the first three, the loss is symbolized by the supposed death of a daughter, and in all four, a daughter, like Persephone* in the Greek myth, is the instrument of the recovery of the lost happiness. Time, in Shakespeare's sonnets and in a number of his earlier plays, *eg Troilus and*

Cressida (1601–2), is a destructive force; in these last plays – the 'Romances' and the 'Reconciliation Plays'* as they have been variously called – Time is re-creative, the healing and restoring power.

The reconciliation plays are a natural extension of Shakespeare's tragedies, because while the tragedies express the destructive force of nature, especially human nature, the reconciliation plays express the forces of renewal. But their fanciful form, the opportunities they give for masque-like display, and the sophistication of their symbolism, all suggest that Shakespeare was writing for the same audience as Fletcher. It was a much less 'mixed' audience than formerly, for it was on the way to becoming what it was to be after the Restoration* in 1660 – a public of fashionable playgoers rather than the representatives of a whole society that shared a dramatic vision of life itself.

5.1.4 *The beginnings of decline: 1625–42*

Charles I* (1625–49) was a more cultivated though a less learned man than his father and predecessor, James I. His court was a refined one, whereas that of his father had been gross, and it was the centre of civilized ideals. Yet it was less the meeting-point of strong national currents of feeling; no English royal court was ever again to be that. It provided the centre of enlightened taste for the theatre, but it was now a socially limited, no longer a humanly limitless, taste.

The principal dramatists of the period were Philip Massinger* (1583–1640), John Ford* (1586–1640?), and James Shirley* (1596–1666). They still used the blank verse* medium introduced into the drama by Sackville and Norton, given life by Marlowe, and enormously enriched by Shakespeare. They used it, however, with a fluency that made it almost as pliant as prose; the tension and the wide range of expressiveness in Shakespearian blank verse was now gone. The same slackening of intensity and dilution of feeling is to be felt in the tragedies of the period. The most notable of these are Ford's: *'Tis Pity She's a Whore*, *The Broken Heart*, *Love's Sacrifice*, between 1628 and 1633, and *Perkin Warbeck* in about 1634. They are plays of melancholy refinement, combined (especially in *'Tis Pity*) with a morbid violence which seems to be intended to excite tastes which are no longer naturally stimulated to tragic feeling.

Comedy survived better in this decline. Massinger, as we have seen, wrote *The City Madam* in the fine tradition of Jonson's Comedy of Humours. Shirley's comedies – *Love in a Maze* (1631), *Hyde Park* (1632), *The Lady of Pleasure* (1635) – are nearer the later Comedy of Manners; that is to say they are beginning to be more concerned with absurdities of social behaviour judged by polite standards than with aberrations of human appetites judged by moral ones. The standards of criticism are still broader than they were to be later, but the theatre is no longer what it was – the testing-ground for the deepest insights into human passion.

In 1642, the Puritans*, who from the first had been hostile to the drama and were now in triumphant revolt against the King and his court, seized power in

London and closed the theatres, which did not reopen until the Restoration in 1660.

5.2

The theatre of entertainment: 1660–1890

5.2.1 *Changes in society and in the theatre*

Theatres have always been places of entertainment; Shakespeare himself would have achieved nothing if he had not been an excellent entertainer. But the English word 'entertain' has more than one meaning. In its common contemporary sense it signifies 'to give pleasure', usually in a light-hearted way and at a superficial level. In an older sense, which survives in the expression 'to entertain an opinion', it is closer to 'sustain' or 'give support or nourishment to'. When the theatre 'entertains' its audiences in the older and more serious meaning, it reaches the heart of human concerns. The 230 years from the reopening of the theatres in 1660 to the revival of serious dramatic art in the 1890s is the history of how the modern, commonly accepted use of 'entertain' came to predominate over the older, more serious meaning.

The influences making for decline were partly social. We have seen that when the Puritans closed the theatres in 1642, the dramatists were already writing for a more limited kind of audience drawn from the upper class, with tastes representative of that class rather than of a national civilization. The serious damage done to dramatic art by the closure was not so much that it stopped these dramatists writing, as that it accentuated this social narrowness in the audiences. Disapproval of the theatre by many of the large middle class was combined with hostility to court society, so that it was a small class round the court in the west end of London that constituted the theatrical public when the monarchy was restored in 1660. Only two theatres were needed to satisfy this public in the second half of the 17th century, whereas in Shakespeare's lifetime there had been many more. And theatrical taste was almost as limited as the theatre buildings were few; ever since the 17th century, the term 'the West End Theatre' had denoted an entertainment industry directed at the tastes of the more prosperous section of the London public.

The middle classes, however, did not stay away from the theatres for ever. By the end of the 17th century, Puritanism was moderating, and the middle classes were anxious to extend and refine their cultural appetites. They did not, unfortunately, moderate all their moral prejudices, and their sharp disapproval of the moral licentiousness of the fashionable theatre is expressed in Jeremy Collier's* influential pamphlet *A Short View of the Immorality and Profaneness of the English Stage* (1698). The middle classes were, in fact, making a bid to displace the fashionable audiences, and were demanding a new kind of play to suit middle-class taste. Well within the first quarter of the 18th century, this revolution was successful, but it was not an enriching change. The fashionable public may have had few moral principles, but at least they had taste, and there is at least strong character in the comedy, if not the tragedy, of the Restoration period, which, for the drama, may be said to have lasted from 1660 till 1710. The middle classes had no well-developed taste, and more moral prejudice than principle. The English theatre contributed nothing memorable to English literature, apart from the work of Goldsmith* and Sheridan* – candle flames in a great darkness – until Shaw began making his massive appeal to the English intelligentsia in the 1890s.

Yet English society was not undergoing cultural deterioration, but cultural change of direction, and this, even more than the social causes, contributed to the decline of the drama. The 16th century had found the drama to be its natural imaginative vehicle because even London society felt close to the rural environment which was itself dramatic in the seasonal processes on which it depended, and because men felt their conflicts – both those within the individual and those within society – to be such that they could be dramatized but could not be reasoned away. Eighteenth-century society was more conscious of its basis in trade, and it believed that reason could resolve its most important conflicts. This was the century of the reflective essay, of didactic poetry, and of the discursive novel. The novel was

The Dorset Theatre, 1673; a scene for Elkanah Settle's *The Empress of Morocco*, engraved by William Dolle. The illustration shows the recession of the stage behind a proscenium arch, and elaborate scenic design. The theatre was under the management of Sir William Davenant.

particularly important as a rival to the theatre, since part of its appeal was dramatic, as the 19th-century novelist Dickens well knew when he hastened his own death by the strain of reading his novels aloud to enthusiastic audiences. A society seldom sustains two major literary forms together, and in the 18th century the attraction of the novel form progressively obliterated fascination with the theatre.

Finally, the decline of the theatre was hastened by changes in the theatre itself. These were of two kinds: the changes in stage design and in the methods and conditions of acting, and the change in the law relating to theatres.

The changes in stage design and in the acting profession are relevant to the kind of drama that was produced in the theatre. After 1660 the original Elizabethan style of 'public theatre', with a stage surrounded by the audience and open to the sky, soon disappeared, and was replaced by a style which developed steadily in the direction of theatre design as we know it today. It was roofed, had painted sets, and in the 18th century it began to develop more sophisticated methods of stage lighting. Still more important, the stage was now recessed beyond the 'proscenium arch', which began to approximate to the modern 'picture frame'. The projecting 'apron-stage' was not, it is true, abandoned at once; a half-stage, at first, extended in front

Drury Lane Theatre, 1808, after its rebuilding by Sheridan in 1794. The Licensing Act of 1737 restricted the London theatres to a handful of very big ones. Drury Lane was one of the largest; it was said to impose a great strain on actors' voices, and to have coarsened acting techniques. Note the painted backcloth: scenery grew increasingly elaborate throughout 19th C.

of the arch, so that the actor, on suitable occasions, still stepped amongst the audience. Nonetheless, the theatre of illusion was beginning, and it was assisted by the engagement of women actors, replacing the boys who had taken the women's roles of Shakespeare's day. In the 19th century, acting costumes were made to suit the period and place of the play, and the setting for a complete theatre of illusion was achieved. Such a theatre was of course not necessarily inferior artistically as a medium to the Shakespearian stage, but it encouraged a different relationship between the actors and their audiences; just because the theatre was superior as a means to illusion, it was more divorced from the realities of daily life outside the building.

The theatre of illusion gave more opportunity, and therefore more responsibility to the actor. A few outstanding actors, such as Tarlton*, the younger Burbage*, and Edward Alleyn*, achieved great popularity and even high social status in Shakespeare's lifetime. It was, however, David Garrick* (1717–79) who really established the profession of acting among the fine arts; in the 18th and 19th centuries, the great names in the English theatre are those of actors far more than those of dramatists. This was both a service and a disservice to literature. It was a service, inasmuch as Garrick was a man of culture as well as of acting genius; the English repertoire of fine plays was now extensive, and Garrick, as well as other actors and actresses, increased public acquaintance with them, especially with the work of Shakespeare. But this was a disservice inasmuch as the very existence of such a repertoire obstructed the productions of new dramatists; moreover, a fine actor can transform even an inferior play. The modern bad practice of visiting the theatre (or the cinema) more for the sake of the actor than for the sake of the work in which he is performing probably began in the 18th century.

Government policy was also unpropitious for the literary drama. Ever since the reign of Elizabeth, governments had looked on the stage with suspicion, as a possible platform for discontent. In the 18th century, Henry Fielding's* dramatic satires on the political leadership of the time caused the government to impose the Licensing Act (1737) which restricted the theatres in London to two – Drury Lane* and the Haymarket* opera house. The Licensing Act was not repealed until 1843, and the limitation it imposed on dramatic production is obvious; talented writers who might have taken to drama chose more promising opportunities, and Fielding himself became a novelist.

Popular drama of a sort did not die, however. Even under Puritan rule, between 1642 and 1660, musical performances escaped Puritan prohibition of the drama, and in the 18th century the government permitted musical drama – *ie* melodrama* in its earliest form – and pantomime* to be performed in unlicensed theatres. Both were crude forms of art, but they flourished, and pantomime has remained popular until the present time. Again, most of the impact of the performances came from the actors. Pantomime and melodrama derived their techniques from the French and Italian 'Commedia dell'Arte', in which the action was chiefly improvised by the actors. The theatre and the serious writer, in short, drifted apart in the 18th century, and remained apart through most of the 19th. The only promising change was that the London monopoly of the drama was broken, and theatres were for the first time built in the provinces.

5.2.2 *The last phase of tragedy and the rise of the Comedy of Manners: 1660–1714*

English drama in the Great Age (1590–1620) had been essentially indigenous; that is to say, although the dramatists learnt much from France, Italy and ancient Rome, their best plays were in a style that had evolved in England and defied the rules and movements of other countries and times. The period now before us is, in this respect, very different. The king, many of his court, and some leading men of letters such as William Davenant*, spent most of the decade before 1660 in France, and France was passing through the greatest phase of her drama. This began with *Le Cid* by the tragedian Corneille* in 1636; it reached its highest peak in the art of tragedy with the career of Racine* (from *Andromaque*, 1667, to *Athalie*, 1690) and in comedy with that of Molière* (from *Les Précieuses Ridicules*, 1659, to *Le Malade Imaginaire*, 1673). France was having the first of her two heroic ages in every aspect of her national life, and it was an age in which the monarchy and the aristocracy were exalted; the French court was a concentration of the national spirit as the English court never was after Elizabeth I* (1558–1603).

In some respects, English minds were close to the French ones in feeling and outlook; the forces that made the French language a powerful instrument of logical thinking and rhetorical persuasiveness were working also in the English language. Unfortunately these forces did not, in England, work towards great dramatic tragedy. In France the logic and rhetoric of the language were impelled by passions arising from social convictions; in England there was no longer a centre on which such passions could focus. It was not a heroic age in England, nor an aristocratic age with a devotion to aristocratic codes of conduct, but an age of scepticism, satire, and reassessment of accepted ideas. Consequently the imitators of French tragedy, the most notable of whom was John Dryden* (*eg Aureng-Zebe*, 1675), were following the form of French tragedy without being able to emulate its spirit. The best tragedies arose from a revival of the Elizabethan dramatic spirit, for which Dryden, as critic, was largely responsible. The most notable of such works were Dryden's own *All for Love** (1677) based on Shakespeare's *Antony and Cleopatra*, and Otway's* *The Orphan* (1680) and *Venice Preserved* (1682). These plays do not possess the dense verbal life to be found in the work of Shakespeare and his best contemporaries, but they revive some of the freedom and variety of Elizabethan emotion, and combine it with the new classical concern with surface elegance and shapeliness; in them the Elizabethan vitality exhibits its last pulsations.

The changed spirit of the language, however, offered new resources to comedy. The qualities of speech among the educated classes were such as we identify in certain kinds of good modern prose: lucidity in reasoning, easy and graceful movement, a capacity for clear and pungent epigram. The best Restoration comedy, unlike the tragedy, was in such prose. The old, weighty Comedy of Humours of the Jonson tradition – the presentation of characters as the embodiments of obsessions – survived in the work of Thomas Shadwell, *eg The Sullen Lovers* (1668), but it is the lighter, more superficially pleasing Comedy of Manners* satirizing behaviour as it is distorted by social pretensions, that we associate with the Restoration. The leading examples of it are Etherege's* *The Man of Mode** (1676), Wycherley's* *The Country Wife** (1672–3) and *The Plain-Dealer* (1674), Congreve's* *Love for Love** (1695) and *The Way of the World* (1700), Vanbrugh's* *The Relapse* (1696) and Farquhar's* *The Beaux' Stratagem* (1707). All these plays depend principally on the self-conscious grace and wit of their dialogue; they owe much to Molière, and are in line with similar qualities already emerging in Fletcher and Shirley between 1610 and 1640. Structure is seldom a strong point in these Comedies of Manners, and they all exhibit some degree of moral licentiousness and cynicism, but their surviving popularity is due to the high though limited value that the dramatists attached to the language, which excels in qualities that are expertly contrived – qualities of elegance, timing, wit, balance and diction, within a narrow range characterized by sophisticated assurance.

After the first decade of the 18th century, little of intrinsic literary value was produced in the English theatre for 180 years, except for the brief but charming revival of the Comedy of Manners by Goldsmith and Sheridan in the 1770s. Their three memorable plays are Goldsmith's *She Stoops to Conquer** (1773), and Sheridan's *The Rivals** (1775) and *The School for Scandal** (1777). The setting is more middle-class and has a more provincial frame of reference; there is more sentiment and no coarseness; the dialogue is fresh and vivacious, but the comedy depends more on ludicrous situation and on variety of social type. The serenity of these three comedies derives from a typically 18th-century assurance about the pattern of society and manners. Soon after, the French Revolution* and the Industrial Revolution* dispersed this assurance. Wilde's social comedies of the 1890s are much more idiosyncratic in their appeal.

But perhaps the most significant fact in the history of drama in this period is Milton's *Samson Agonistes** (1671). It is significant less for its intrinsic merit – about which opinions differ considerably – than for the spirit in which it is written. Milton chose a form – that of ancient Greek tragedy – which he knew to be unsuitable to the contemporary stage which he despised and rejected. The divorce between the poet and the working theatre was to last for nearly three centuries and it has various causes, but Milton's play was its earliest manifestation. In the 19th century almost every poet of importance and many unimportant ones attempted poetic drama. This was partly because the criticism by such writers as Coleridge* (1772–1834), Lamb* (1775–1834), Hazlitt* (1778–1830) and De Quincey* (1785–1859) caused Shakespeare to be more admired than ever before and led to the rediscovery of his contemporaries. Not one of the 19th-century poets, however, really understood the theatre; their plays are seldom if ever amongst their best poetic work, and they survive for readers, not for audiences.

However, the succession of serious and famous actors continued; the theatre had glamour, and in its more vulgar manifestations of melodrama, pantomime and music-hall it had popularity. Music-hall was especially lively; its songs had the topical character of the broadside ballads sung in the London streets since the 16th century, and they developed into a kind of urban folk literature.

5·3

Experiments in renewal: 1890–1965

5·3·1 *Drama of wit and discussion: Bernard Shaw (1856–1950); Oscar Wilde (1856–1900)*

For reasons that remain mysterious, the notable dramatists in the English theatre in the 18th, 19th, and early 20th centuries were all Irish, although Ireland, until the 20th century, had no indigenous theatre of significance. Part of the reason may be that Ireland was entirely an agricultural country, so that the English spoken there, even by the educated classes, was less overlaid by the analytic spirit of the increasingly technological and commercial society of England, and retained more ebullient vitality. The plays of Oscar Wilde* (*Lady Windermere's Fan*, 1892; *A Woman of No Importance*, 1893; *An Ideal Husband*, 1895, and – above all – *The Importance of Being Earnest*, 1895) certainly show a brilliance of verbal wit that much excels any previous comedy since those of Sheridan and Goldsmith. However, their distinctiveness no doubt owes more to the histrionic qualities of the aesthetic* movement – with its doctrine that life itself should have the aesthetic qualities of art – than to Wilde's Irish origins.

Bernard Shaw* is a much more important figure. His extraordinary achievement arises partly from the talent for witty rhetoric with which the English have always credited the Irish, but it also proceeded from the combination of three other factors. First, he was an excellent music critic before he took to the theatre, and he learnt much about the effective arrangement of rhetorical speeches from opera, and particularly from the employment of the aria by Mozart. Second, a dramatic revival was at work elsewhere in Europe in the second half of the 19th century; Shaw was the disciple of the greatest of these new dramatists – the Norwegian Henrik Ibsen* (1828–1906); especially, Shaw admired that phase of Ibsen's career in which he presented social criticism through drama, for example *A Doll's House* (1879) and *Ghosts* (1881). Third, Shaw, through his drama of social criticism, was able to revive an intelligent audience for the theatre, and it was precisely the absence of such an audience that had been one of the principal causes of the theatre's long decadence. The end of the 19th century was a period in which ideas of social reform flourished and multiplied: socialists, feminists, and others were excited by ideas, analysed them, and used them as weapons against the established traditions, and Shaw became the new dramatist of ideas. Whereas, with other dramatists, characters provoke ideas in consequence of the predicaments into which they are cast, in Shaw's comedies the predicaments are themselves produced by the conflicts of ideas, and the characters are the mouthpieces of the ideas. But Shaw's delight in ideological conflict was such as to make his dramas of ideas as light and witty as any comedy of manners; even though most of his propaganda is out of date, his art still holds his plays on the stage.

Shaw's career, from *Widower's Houses* in 1892 to *In Good King Charles's Golden Days* in 1939, was long. Many would say that his masterpiece was *St Joan* (1924), but his greatest impact on the theatre and on public opinion was between 1900 and 1914. During this period he inspired others in the drama of social problems. His most noteworthy contemporary in this field was Galsworthy* (*eg Strife*, 1909) whose plays at least dignified the stage by their serious concern.

5.3.2 *The revival of poetic drama: 1900–50*

Shaw restored an intelligent audience to the theatre. He would not have denied that he was as much a journalist of the stage as an artist. This is not to his discredit, but it means that he was more concerned with valuable teaching than with the establishment of values, which has always been the artist's principal and inestimable function.

At the end of the 1890s, W. B. Yeats* began seeking another national audience. He formed the Irish National Theatre Movement, through which he hoped to establish the values of the Irish nation, which was struggling for independence. He was a verse dramatist, and the first since the 17th century to understand the need to shape his art to the medium of the stage. His plays, from *The Countess Cathleen* (1892) to *Purgatory* (1939), are none of them among the best of his poetic achievements, but they show a deep understanding of the theatre, and a new shaping of poetic language to its needs, in an age which had come to assume that plays should be written in prose. Yeats was also an able theatre manager, the creator of the first and best of the literary theatres of this century in the British Isles. So far as his ambitions for Ireland were concerned, he failed, and resigned his management of the Abbey Theatre* in Dublin in 1909. However, his experiment was not futile. Besides producing his own distinguished verse plays, he discovered the talent of J. M. Synge* (1871–1909), who is one of the most interesting of modern dramatists. Synge contributed six plays to the Abbey Theatre, and one of them – *The Playboy of the Western World** (1907) – is a masterpiece. He wrote in prose, but it was prose of the vivid, figurative speech of the Irish peasantry, and he used it with poetic effect. His own origins were Irish middle class, and by education he was a cosmopolitan intellectual, but he had the unusual gift of being able to use his broad culture to expand the significance of his peasant themes, without losing the authenticity of his peasant characters and their speech; in consequence, no dramatic dialogue since the great Shakespearian age is so imaginatively rich.

Yet the Irish Movement was, after all, a minor one. Yeats's dramas are short and intimate in the scope of their appeal, not suited to the holding of big audiences in big theatres. Synge was unique in being able to use peasant dialect with such rich effect, and perhaps he wrote at the latest point in history at which it could be done. Their Irish contemporaries did not match them in power, nor did their successors, for though the plays of Sean O'Casey* (*eg Juno and the Paycock*, 1924) have power, they show a less profound and original talent. Perhaps Yeats's most important achievement in the theatre is that he closed the fatal gap between the poet and the theatre, and showed English poets a way to the future. It was partly his example, partly the work of the great German dramatist Bertolt Brecht, that inspired the lively dramatic experiments of W. H. Auden* and Christopher Isherwood (*The Dog Beneath the Skin*, 1935; *The Ascent of F6*, 1937; *On the Frontier*, 1938), but they lacked the originality and depth of Yeats and Synge, and the theatrical genius of Brecht.

Mermaid Theatre, Blackfriars (opened 1959). An avant-garde London theatre. By the middle of the present century a complete reaction to 19th-C ornateness reduced the stage to something like the bareness of the Elizabethan stage. The theatre itself is converted from a former warehouse. The scene is for a production of Bertoldt Brecht's *Life of Galileo*.

Much more interesting experiments were made by the poet T. S. Eliot (1888–1965). He had already brought into his poetry the spoken idiom of his time; several of his best early poems are Dramatic Monologues*, with more dramatic tension in them than the 19th-century Dramatic Monologues by Tennyson and Browning. He was a profound critic of the Elizabethan and Jacobean drama from 1590 to 1640, and he understood better than any of his contemporaries the difficulties and potentialities of poetic speech in the theatre. His first completed verse play, *Murder in the Cathedral* (1935), was designed for a small audience on a religious occasion, but after it he composed a succession of verse plays for the big West End theatres of London. Yeats had proved that a poet could once again be a dramatist, but he had failed to capture the ordinary theatre-going audience; Eliot made this capture his aim, and in a sense he succeeded too well. He understood that the mistakes of the 19th-century dramatic poets had been not only their failure to learn effective dramatic construction, but their persistence in continuing the much worn blank verse* rhythm of Shakespeare and his contemporaries. They needed instead a new rhythm, more closely related to the spoken rhythms attuned to the ears of their contemporaries, who were so much accustomed to the rhythms of prose. Eliot invented such a rhythm. It is so inconspicuous in its beat that, like the blank verse of Massinger and Shirley, it is indistinguishable from prose to the listening ear, and yet it enables the dialogue to gain concentration by its patterning, and it is used to heighten or relax tension as the progress of the play requires. Eliot thus attempted to restore poetry to the drama by stealth; even the titles of his dramas – *Murder in the Cathedral*, *The Cocktail Party* – disguise under labels that suggest the crime story and the drawing-room comedy what are in fact plays of wholly religious import. It is possible that Eliot was too timid, or compromised too far; at all events, the successive plays each drew closer to the theatrical style of the dull West End, in spite of the seriousness of their religious intention. *Murder in the Cathedral* and *Family Reunion* (1939) are imperfect but original and moving, and *The Cocktail Party* (1950) still justifies its verse medium. *The Confidential Clerk* (1954) and *The Elder Statesman* (1958) lose the virtues of this medium, without gaining quality by other means. The West End won the duel, and captured Eliot. Yet he taught the audiences that after all poetry has its advantages. Christopher Fry's exuberant though poetically commonplace verse dramas, from *A Phoenix Too Frequent* (1946) to *Curtmantle* (1961), attracted delighted audiences.

5.3.3 *The recovery of prose idiom: 1955–65*

Yeats and Eliot may yet prove to be the precursors of a great revival of poetic drama, but at present the effect of their influence seems to have been a different one. The superiority of their best work is due not so much to the depth of their themes, or the originality of their ideas about the drama, as to their demonstration that dramatic speech requires unusual qualities: it requires to be as natural as talk, and yet as carefully directed to the artist's intended effect as is the language of lyrical poetry. Yeats and Eliot believed that these almost incompatible requirements were best achieved through the strict discipline and the varied effects of verse, but the special problems of suiting verse to a public that was so little accustomed to it partly defeated them. The present generation of dramatists, concerned above all to express the common mind of their age at a level of expression that it cannot ordinarily sustain, have seen that they may succeed better through artistic handling of prose dialogue – of 'talk'.

It has been easy to forget that a genuine idiom of 'talk' has not been heard in the theatre since the time of Goldsmith and Sheridan. Shaw's characters do not even pretend to talk; they make speeches, and the characters of the ordinary run of 'entertaining' plays use the lifeless idioms of various theatrical conventions. The first play by John Osborne*, *Look Back in Anger* (1956), is not a masterpiece, but it won attention by the intensity with which he poured into it the idiom of the actual speech of young men and women of the 1950s.

The years since World War II have released energies in the working class of Britain in a way that is comparable to the release of the energies of the middle class a hundred years ago, and the new drama is related to this social change. Though the 19th-century popular art of music hall songs is dead, some of the modern dramatists have tried to use its forms of expression; for instance, Osborne in *The Entertainer* (1957). Harold Pinter*, perhaps the most original of the younger dramatists, has cultivated an idiom drawn from the speech of the least articulate sections of society (*eg The Caretaker*, 1960) and has thereby isolated in dramatic dialogue a pathos and dignity in human beings who would otherwise seem to be below the attainment of either. Arnold Wesker, in his trilogy *Chicken Soup with Barley*, *Roots*, and *I'm Talking about Jerusalem* (1960) has tried to replace the middle-class standpoint in usual dramatic interpretations of society by centring his plays on working-class outlooks. The most intelligent of all the movement seems to be John Arden*, whose plays have remarkable variety of setting and theme; he explores ideas with the thoroughness of Bernard Shaw, without Shaw's sometimes facile solutions to ideological conflicts, and with some of the force of the German dramatist Bertolt Brecht, for instance in *Sergeant Musgrave's Dance* (1959). All these plays are of serious interest, but the only dramatist to achieve a perfectly articulated drama in the new style of carefully cultivated 'talk' belongs to a rather older generation; this is the Irishman, Samuel Beckett*, whose masterpiece, *Waiting for Godot* (1952), belongs in the first place to French rather than English literature, since it was originally written in French, and translated into English in 1954.

It is of course impossible to say whether these and other contemporary dramatists will ensure that the art of the theatre will have a future, or whether the drama will pass, as sometimes seems likely, to the media of broadcasting and television. It is perhaps indicative that Beckett is also the author of a few outstanding broadcast plays, the most notable of which is *All That Fall* (1957). So long as television and sound broadcasting offer only a few plays such as this one by Beckett in a dramatic idiom that is truly distinct from that of the theatre or the cinema, the traditional stage play is no doubt secure against extinction. Television, however, is beginning to offer possibilities of a new kind of function for drama. The facts of current problems (for instance, bad housing) may be presented in the kind of programme called 'a documentary'; the documentary producer selects, cuts, and organizes his material into what is sometimes a strikingly dramatic form. A television dramatist may go a stage further: he may organize documentary material into an actual play, combining fictional character with environmental fact, and enforcing both with the subtle techniques that television makes available to him. This was done by Jeremy Sandford in his enormously influential television play about the housing problem, *Cathy Come Home* (1966). John Hopkins, in his series of four plays, *Quartette* (1968) used the technique memorably in order to dramatize familiar problems of 20th-century family life. The potentialities of a new, serious dramatic art for the mass public of television are thus real and important.

We can at least say of English drama today that it is alive, and that it possesses more life than at any other time in the last 250 years.

Chaucer reading his poems to a company of Courtiers. A frontispiece (1400?) to his poem *Troilus and Criseyde.* The illustration is a useful reminder that Chaucer wrote for the ear of the listener, rather than the eye of the reader like much poetry after the invention of printing.

6 Poetic form since 1350

Introduction: *rhythm and metre; the relationship of poetry and speech*

All language is rhythmical. The most ordinary English sentence has a rhythm which arises from the accenting of certain syllables, and the unconscious spacing of these accents so that they strike the ear with some regularity. Here is an example:

'Will you bríng up the bóx which I léft downstáirs?'

The syllables marked with an accent (í) are spoken with slightly more emphasis, a slight change in the pitch of the voice, and a little more slowly; those that are unaccented are spoken more lightly and quickly, and often with a slight alteration in the quality of the vowel to make it shorter and less distinct. If the sentence is slightly altered, the accent may shift from one syllable to another so as to keep rhythmic pattern:

'Bríng up the bóx which I léft in the dównstairs róom.'

The accent on 'downstairs' has moved from the second syllable to the first, so as to introduce a space between the last two accents.

It is important to notice that the length of time an English sentence takes to say depends more on the number of accented syllables in it than on the total number of syllables. Thus, 'Will you bríng up the bóx which I léft downstáirs?' has a total of 11 syllables, but it has only 4 accented syllables, so that it takes very little longer to say than 'Bríng the bóx I léft downstáirs', which contains only 7 syllables but still has 4 accented ones.

Rhythm is a music of speech which contributes to ease of speaking, but it also contributes to meaning. If I say 'I knéw him lóng yéars agó', I mean something different from 'I knéw him mány yéars agó'; 'lóng yéars' – with its successive accents – gives prominence to the length of time *since* I knew him, whereas the second sentence gives prominence to the fact that I *did* know him. The difference of meaning issues in the difference of rhythm, as well as in the different choice of words.

Speech has other forms of music which heighten meaning. In the sentence 'His death was a bitter blow to me', the expression 'bitter blow' is emphasized by the repetition – *ie* alliteration* – of the sound represented by the letter 'b'. Alliteration often occurs in familiar idiomatic phrases, such as 'good as gold', 'with might and main'. Rhyme also occurs in such phrases, *eg* 'hither and thither', 'out and about'. Rhyme, however, is less common than alliteration, or than repetition in such a phrase as 'again and again'. Other forms of music in speech are intonation, the use of pauses, and the use of 'assonance', *ie* the rhyming of vowels without the rhyming of consonants, in such a phrase as 'hard and fast'.

Poetry emphasizes the musical properties of ordinary speech. It is unable to insist on distinct patterns of intonation, since it is impossible to indicate the rise and fall of the voice clearly in writing except when the poem is set to music,

*Indicates mention in the reference section.

and music has different principles from spoken intonation. On the other hand, rhyme is used much more extensively in poetry than in ordinary speech because the obviousness of its musicality is more obtrusive than is tolerable in the spoken language; even poets have dispensed with it when – as in most drama – they wish their poetry to sound as close to speech as possible.

The musical characteristics of poetry vary with the language in which it is written. This is especially true of rhythm. Ancient Greek and Latin were languages in which syllables were more or less distinctly long or short. This fact encouraged a quantitative rhythm (metre*) in their poetry. The line was divided into feet, each foot composed of varying combinations of long and short syllables. Thus an iambic* foot was composed of a short syllable followed by a long; a trochee, of a long syllable followed by a short; a dactyl*, of a long syllable followed by two short ones; an anapaest*, of two short syllables followed by a long one, and so forth. English syllables vary greatly but very unevenly in length, and lines of verse cannot be measured (or scanned) easily in quantitative units. When such terms as 'iambic' are applied to English poetry, they are applied to combinations of accented and unaccented syllables; for example, an English iambus is a combination of syllables such as that in the word *agáin*.

We have seen that the length of time that an English sentence takes to say depends more on the number of accented syllables in it than on the total number of syllables. In keeping with this quality, old English poetry followed rhythms which depended for their rhythmic conformity on the consistency from line to line of the number of accented syllables in each; the total number of syllables was allowed to vary. After the Norman Conquest, however, French influence encouraged a more flowing rhythm which required uniformity in the number of syllables in every line. The accentual poetry seems to have continued alongside metrical poetry until the age of Chaucer. Accentual rhythms combined naturally with alliteration, so that this older poetry is commonly referred to as 'alliterative' poetry, but metrical rhythms encouraged the use of rhyme. Thus, with the important exception of blank verse* which was introduced in the 16th century, English poetry became not only increasingly metrical but increasingly rhymed after 1200.

This essay is a brief account of the leading forms in English poetry. Poetic forms are not accidental, or mechanically devised patterns. For small poets, forms are often merely moulds into which language is poured to achieve an effect of coherence, but the forms do not often originate with small poets. In great poetry the form is a living organism which grows from the civilization surrounding the poet as well as from his individual mind. 'Form' includes a medium of expression such as blank verse, and a pattern of expression such as the sonnet*; both undergo changes as the spirit of the age changes. A study of poetic form is thus one of the main subjects of literary study.

6.1

The Middle Ages and Early Renaissance: 1350–1580

6.1.1 *Fourteenth-century alliterative poetry; Chaucer's metrical poetry*

In a somer seson – when soft was the sonne,
I shope me in shroudes – as I a shep were,
In habite as an heremite – unholy of werkes
Went wyde in this worlde – wondres to here.
Ac on a May mornynge – on Malvern hulles
Me byfel a ferly – of fairy, me thoughte;
I was wery forwandred – and went me to reste
Under a brode banke – by a bornes side,
And as I lay and lened – and loked in the wateres
I slombred in a slepyng – it sweyved so merye.

William Langland: Prologue to *Piers Plowman* lines 1–10

In a summer season, when soft was the sunlight,
I shook on some shreds of shepherd clothing
And habited like a hermit, but not a holy one,
Went wide in this world, watching for wonders.
But on a May morning, on a Malvern hilltop,
A marvel befell me, as might a fairy-tale.
I was weary and far-wandered and went to rest myself
On a broadish bank by a running brook,
And as I lay leaning and looking in the water
I slipped into a slumber, it slid away so merrily.

(Modernized version by Nevill Coghill.)

*Piers Plowman** was completed in its final version in about 1393, when Chaucer was writing *The Canterbury Tales**. The main features of alliterative verse are evident in these lines. Each line contains four strongly accented syllables, and is marked by a strong pause in the middle; the modern translator has abandoned the consistent use of the pause. Two of the strong accents precede the pause, and two follow it; the first three are alliterated (*ie* begun by the same letter), but the fourth need not be. The four accents are occasionally increased to five, and the number of unaccented syllables is allowed to vary freely. The accented syllables need not be spaced with precise regularity, except that there must be at least two in each half line, and an accent nearly always falls on the final word in the half line.

Any rhythm depends on two elements: 'flow' and 'rigidity'. A sound that is all flow, like water from a tap, has no rhythm because it has no rigid parts to break it up; sounds without flow, like monosyllables spoken irregularly, are irregular because there is no principle of continuity leading the ear from one sound to the next. Any rhythm must therefore contain both elements, but one may be stressed rather than the other. Alliterative rhythm is comparatively rigid. Because it emphasizes the beginnings of syllables (not, as rhyme does, the ends of them) it draws attention to individual words rather than to the line as a whole, and since the final word of the line is accented, it emphasizes the line rather than the paragraph. We shall see that rhyme also tends to emphasize the line unit of rhythm, but the running rhythm that normally accompanies rhyme sometimes passes over the line ending, so as to make rhythmical continuity with the next line, perhaps through a whole paragraph.

The following lines are the opening of the Prologue to Chaucer's *Canterbury Tales*:

Whan that Aprill with his shoures sote
The droghte of March hath perced to the rote,
And bathed every veyne in swich licour
Of which vertu engendred is the flour;
Whan Zephirus eek with his swete breeth
Inspired hath in every holt and heeth
The tendre croppes, and the yonge sonne
Hath in the Ram his halfe cours y-ronne,
And smale fowles maken melodye,
That slepen all the night with open ye,
(*So priketh hem nature in hir corages*):
Than longen folk to goon on pilgrimages
(*And palmers for to seken straunge strondes*)
To ferne halwes, couthe in sondry londes;
And specially, from every shires ende
Of Engelond, to Caunterbury they wende,
The holy blisful martyr for to seke,
That hem hath holpen, whan that they were seke.

(Paraphrase: 'When April with his sweet showers has pierced the dryness of March to the root, and bathed every vein with that moisture the virtue of which is to engender the flower, when Zephirus (*ie* soft breezes) also with his sweet breath has inspired life in the new shoots in woodland and heath, and the young sun has run half his course into the constellation of the Ram, and the small birds are singing, sleeping all night open-eyed, because nature so excites them in their breasts, then do people long to go on pilgrimages (and palmers to seek foreign shores) to distant holy places, famous in various countries; and in England especially, from the end of every shire, they journey to Canterbury to seek out the holy sainted martyr who helped them when they were ill.)

The rhythmic principle of these lines is that every line has 10 syllables, and every second syllable is accented. (To make the lines consistent, the final 'e' of words ending with that letter is pronounced when the next word begins with a consonant.) Alliteration has not vanished, but it is used only occasionally ('maken melodye', 'seken straunge strondes') and not as a unifying pattern. The lines rhyme* in pairs (couplets*); the regularity of the metre (*ie* measured rhythm) causes the ear to expect the fall of the rhyme in its due place, but it also allows the sentence to flow smoothly on through the 18 lines.

The alliterative rhythm used by Langland and the running rhythm of Chaucer make for different kinds of communication. The rigid alliterative rhythm, emphasizing individual words and phrases, is direct and forceful, conveying fact in simple syntax. This is not to say that the great alliterative poems (*Piers Plowman*, *Sir Gawain and the Green Knight**, and *Pearl** are possibly the best) are primitive poems, embodying crude or elementary feelings; they are highly developed works of art, rich in thought, profound in meaning. However, a large part of their strength arises from the direct vividness of their statements, the solidity of the images, the achievement of subtlety through the accumulation and juxtaposition of varied detail and incident, each presented in simple terms. It is not however a style which lends itself to the concentration and blending of varied experiences in a few lines. It is part of Chaucer's merit that he does not lose the simplicity of alliterative poetry, but his running rhythm has more suppleness: statement merges naturally with statement, idea with idea. Thus Langland's opening lines are statement laid beside statement, whereas those of Chaucer lead from the renewal of natural life to the renewal of spiritual life; moreover the natural life is not presented as merely physical but as psychologically painful (by the use of 'perced', 'priketh'), and pilgrimages are not merely religious, but physically exciting experiences.

Chaucer's use of the 10-syllable line was to be of the very greatest importance to English poetry, and his choice of the rhythm showed sensitive perception of the character of the language. The 8-syllable line – already in use before his day – is light and lacks dignity; the 12-syllable line (the alexandrine*) which is so natural to French is too ponderous for common use in English. The 10-syllable line is light enough for grace, ease, and humour, but it has weight sufficient for solemnity and tragedy. He himself used it with unexcelled versatility, but often with a slight irregularity natural to poetry which – since he wrote before the age of print – was commonly read aloud.

Chaucer's other important formal innovation was the 7-line stanza later known as the rhyme-royal*; perhaps it was so called because King James I of Scotland* used it for his poem *The King's Quair** early in the 15th century. Chaucer wrote his greatest single poem, the romance of *Troilus and Criseyde**, in it. The following two stanzas show Troilus riding down the street after battle, watched by Criseyde, who suddenly – against all her resolution – falls in love with him:

His helm to-hewen was in twenty places,
That by a tissew heng, his bak bihinde,
His shelde to-dasshed was with swerdes and maces,
In which men mighte many an arwe finde
That thirled[1] hadde horn and nerf and rinde;
And ay the peple cryde, 'here cometh our joye,
And, next his brother, holdere up of Troye!'

For which he wex[2] a litel reed for shame,
Whan he the peple upon him herde cryen,
That to biholde it was a noble game,
How sobreliche he caste doun his yën.
Criseÿda gan all his chere aspyen,
And leet so softe it in her herte sinke,
That to hir-self she seyde, 'who yaf[3] me drinke?'

The first three lines have interlacing rhymes, and the last four are rhyming couplets; each stanza, therefore, seems first to delay, and then to advance forward. The stanza is formal enough for the ornament and ceremonious description appropriate to a romance, and yet fluent enough for the realistic and humorous narrative of this particular romance, which is ironic as well as serious. Rhyme-royal was the first important narrative stanza of greater complexity than the quatrain in English; like the 10-syllable couplet, it had a future, though a less extensive and important one. Spenser* used it in his *Four Hymns* and adapted it for his elegy *Daphnaida*; some scholars have wondered whether it is not the basis of the Spenserian stanza*. Other examples of its use are Shakespeare's narrative poem *The Rape of Lucrece* (1594) and Wordsworth's *The Leech-Gatherer** (1802).

6.1.2 *The short poem: the Middle Ages and Wyatt*

The short poem is usually called the lyric, but the identification may cause confusion. The word 'lyric'* originated in ancient Greece for a poem intended to be sung, whereas many so-called lyrics in European literature were written without reference to music.

Yet short poems begin in song and dance in most cultures, and English medieval examples may rightly be called lyrics. Some of them are preserved as carols*, now almost entirely associated with Christmas, and the word 'carol' originally meant a

[1]pierced [2]grew [3]gave

dance in a ring. The poet often added refrains (or 'burdens') for the dancers or audience to sing in chorus at the end of each stanza sung by one voice. The refrain was sometimes in Norman French, and often it was a Latin phrase that had passed into common speech from Church liturgy:

As I me walked in one morning
I heard a bird both weep and sing.
This was the tenor of her talking:
  Timor mortis conturbat me.

Not all medieval lyrics are religious, though it happens that a majority of those that have come down to us from the 14th and 15th centuries are religious or at least moral. Some are light-hearted, secular poems, and some have hints of pagan belief and feeling, such as the famous quatrain

Western wind when will thou blow
  The small rain down can rain?
Christ, if my love were in my arms
  And I in my bed again!

F. W. Bateson (in *A Guide to English Literature*) suggests about this, that the speaker is a girl associated with the soil to be softened by April showers, so that she stands for natural fertility, like the Greek nature goddess, Persephone*.

Many of these lyrics certainly originated among the common people, though no doubt, in the form that we know them, they were edited by the clerks who wrote them down; some were written by minstrels, or adapted by them from French lyrics. The line from folk poetry to professional poetry with its aristocratic audience was continuous; courtly poets developed sophisticated forms out of popular ones, for instance the French ballade* which Chaucer imitated in English. In the 16th century, the popular and the courtly traditions were still close. It is true that courtier-poets like Sir Thomas Wyatt* and Henry Howard, Earl of Surrey*, travelled in France and Italy and cultivated foreign forms (such as the sonnet) which were and remained alien to the popular taste, but Wyatt's more distinguished poems are in the tradition of the medieval lyric. As a courtier, he wrote for a circle of courtiers and he used the courtly convention of the love lyric designed to be sung to the accompaniment of the lute, but his language is not conventional. It is the language of a man who feels deeply and seriously, and reveres the shape and weight of simple words used by deep and serious men, most of them anonymous, for over two centuries of lyrical poetry. Like other sophisticated poets, he kept the refrain of popular poetry and put it to his own purposes. In the following poem, the refrain of 'Forget not yet' has a mounting affect of reproach and bitterness as he pleads with the lady – is it also the king in whose service he has laboured? – not to take his devotion entirely for granted:

Forget not yet the tried intent
Of such a truth as I have meant;
My great travail so gladly spent
Forget not yet.

Forget not yet when first began
The weary life ye know since whan
The suit, the service none tell can
Forget not yet.

Forget not yet the great assays,
The cruel wrong, the scornful ways,
The painful patience in denays,[1]
Forget not yet.

Forget not yet, forget not this,
How long ago hath been and is
The mind that never meant amiss,
Forget not yet.

Forget not then thine own approved,
The which so long hath thee so loved,
Whose steadfast faith yet never moved,[2]
Forget not this.

[1]denials [2]changed

Wyatt's rhythms do not always run smoothly, and it has been suggested (*eg* by D. W. Harding in *The Pelican Guide: The Age of Chaucer*) that Wyatt preferred the rhythm of natural emphasis in the spoken language to a consistently 'running' rhythm, and that he was capable of using the strong pause familiar in alliterative poetry when it suited him. Certainly his original word order, despite its awkwardness to an ear attuned to running metre, is usually more expressive than the amended version published in Tottel's *Miscellany** of 1559. But Tottel's alterations show the change of taste of the second half of the century. The Renaissance*, which only fully arrived in England during the reign of Elizabeth I* (1558–1603), believed that highly worked form was the enhancement of nature. The world of nature, wrote Sir Philip Sidney* in his *Apology for Poetry** in about 1580, 'is brazen, the Poets only [*ie* not other writers] deliver a golden', and he criticized the English poets of his day for failing to deliver it. It was Spenser – even more than Sidney himself – who provided the civilizing influence that Sidney and other critics desired.

6.2

The High Renaissance: 1580–1660

6.2.1 *The influence of Spenser*

She fell away in her first age's spring,
Whilst yet her leaf was green and fresh her rind,
And whilst her branch fair blossoms forth did bring,
She fell away against all course of kind.
For age to die is right, but youth is wrong;
She fell away like fruit blown down with wind.
Weep, Shepherd! weep, to make my undersong.

Spenser – from *Daphnaida*, 1591

The stanza is from an elegy inspired by the death of a young girl. It resembles the stanza of Chaucer's rhyme-royal, but instead of the last four lines forming two couplets, all the rhymes are interlaced: *a b a b c b c*. This rhyme arrangement increases the melodiousness of the stanza, and makes it more self-contained by removing the suggestion of forward movement in rhyme-royal – *a b a b b c c*. The lingering effect of this pattern is suited to the theme, for though the poem contains narrative, it is essentially a meditation on early death.

The melodiousness and close workmanship of the stanza make it characteristic of Spenser. The phrase 'fell away' has a short first syllable and a long diphthong; the music of this cadence conveys the suddenness of the girl's death and the inconsolable mournfulness of her lover, and this music is sustained by the assonance of 'age's'. 'Spring' gives a slight lift from this mournfulness and leads on to the fresh beauty of the girl's youth, emphasized by assonance in the second line ('leaf' – 'green') and by alliteration in the third ('branch' – 'blossoms' – 'bring'). The fourth line repeats the cadence 'fell away', and the syllables 'all course' have the sombre colouring characteristic of rounded vowels pronounced at the back of the mouth. The fifth line is a plain statement of the peculiar sadness and injustice of early death, but it is made in terse, elliptical syntax – '[for] youth [to die] is wrong' – which concentrates the force of the statement and is further emphasized by the alliterated 'right' – 'wrong'. The sixth line has the key cadence 'fell away' once again, and the three heavy syllables 'fruit blown down' are an epitome of the heaviness of the lover's grief and of its cause. The last line recurs in a later stanza as a refrain; it contrasts with the easy flow of the other lines by its two strong pauses, enforcing the injunction for sympathetic response. The rhythm cannot be 'scanned' into a mechanical pattern of iambic feet, as for instance 'she féll / awáy / like frúit / blown dówn / with wínd', since it is natural in speaking the words to give almost as strong an accent to 'blown' as to 'fruit' and 'down'. Yet 'blown' does not carry quite so strong an accent; the metrical pattern is firm, but not so rigid that it frustrates the natural emphasis of the voice. The singing 'n' and 'ng' in the end-rhyme of each line unifies the feeling of the stanza: the feeling that sorrow is transcended, without being denied, by being transmuted into poetry.

The chief aim of Spenser's career was to make poetry an instrument of high ceremony; in him poetic language is consecrated to the heightening and the formalizing of feeling. He found English in a barbarous state for his purpose. Chaucer – whom he greatly admired – had possessed an unselfconscious command over the resources of medieval English as well as an easy and discriminating openness to what foreign literatures could teach him; Wyatt did not exceed the limits of the short poem. But in their Renaissance admiration for wide learning and for the sophistication of French and Italian writers, many English writers had lost assurance or had grown overbold: they had borrowed undiscriminatingly, and had learnt to despise in their native tongue qualities which were not contemptible. 'So now', Spenser wrote to his humanist friend Gabriel Harvey*, 'they have made our English tongue a gallimaufry or hodgepodge of all other speeches.'

Spenser wrote these words in a prefatory letter for his first important poetic experiment, *The Shepherd's Calendar** (1579). This series of poems, one for each month of the year, is in the tradition of the classical pastoral* of Theocritus* and Virgil*, and he learnt also from the recent French and Italian pastoralists, Marot and Sannazaro. The poems vary in theme; they include love laments, moral fable and satire, and eulogy of Queen Elizabeth; their style varies from the Chaucerian couplets, containing revivals of archaic Chaucerian language to emphasize the virtues of native English (*February*), to elaborate and sophisticated song stanzas (*April* and *November*). The *Calendar* has, moreover, various intentions and is based on an equal range of convictions. Spenser is, first of all, relating English poetry to ancient starting-points and to modern renewals – to the high tradition of European culture. Secondly, he uses pastoral because it is a simplified world in which ideals can be expressed in their simplicity, uncomplicated by the dilemmas and complications of the real world of contemporary society. Thirdly, Spenser was a strong patriot, and part of this patriotism was acceptance in a fairly extreme form of the English Protestant* establishment, the discipline and moral austerity of which he wanted to contrast with what he considered to be Catholic luxury and indulgence. Finally and above all, he wanted to demonstrate the varied potentialities of English as a poetic medium.

In his Reformation* or Protestant aspect Spenser was severe and even censorious, but in his Renaissance* and Platonic* aspect he was an idealist with a high conception of order and ceremony as outward signs of the beauty of holiness. His ceremonious poetry had among its main purposes the display of his idealism through an art both elaborate and disciplined, splendid and unworldly, aesthetic and spiritual; these adjectives were not inconsistent to him, but on the contrary each implied the other, and made natural his chosen means of intricate but stately stanzas. He used various forms, but he is famous for the 'Spenserian stanza'* consisting of 9 lines and ending in a 12-syllable line of alexandrine*. He devised it for the long, uncompleted romantic epic, *The Faerie Queene**.

And is there care in heaven? and is there love
In heavenly spirits to these creatures base,
That may compassion of their evils move?
There is: else much more wretched were the case
Of men, than beasts. But, O! th'exceeding grace
Of highest God, that loves his creatures so,
And all his works with mercy doth embrace,
That blessed angels he sends to and fro,
To serve to wicked man, to serve his wicked foe.

The design makes for stateliness rather than narrative movement; Spenser was a master of description rather than narrative. The best parts of *The Faerie Queene* are pageantlike spectacles with an atmosphere like that of dream, but the poem had a practical intention: 'The general end', Spenser wrote to Raleigh*, 'is to furnish a gentleman or noble person in vertuous and gentle discipline' – in other words, to shape a conception of a truly civilized man. Just as the nobleman, who should be the exemplar for base-born men, had to subdue his sinful nature if he was to be truly noble, so the poet had to subdue the language if it was to render the beauty which was the shape of that nobility. This was the aim of Spenser's civilizing mission as a poet.

6.2.2 *The development of blank verse*

Before Spenser, Thomas Wyatt* and Henry Howard, Earl of Surrey* had both sought the refinement and civilization of English poetry by the standards of French and Italian Renaissance* verse. Surrey, the lesser of the two poets but the more famous in his day, emulated the Italian humanists by translating part of the *Aeneid**, the epic by the greatest of the Roman poets, Virgil. The attempt was not new in English; Chaucer had translated fragments in the 14th century; Caxton* published a prose version in the 15th, and the Scottish poet, Gavin Douglas*, produced a distinguished version in Chaucerian rhyming couplets (1512–13). Surrey however was characteristically in the humanist tradition by seeking a closer resemblance to the original Latin by dispensing with rhyme. To do this he abolished the rhymes of the Chaucerian couplet, and achieved the first experiment in blank verse*:

They whisted all, with fixèd face intent,
When prince Aeneas from the royal seat

Thus 'gan to speak. O Queen, it is thy will
I should renew a woe cannot be told,
How that the Greeks did spoil and overthrow
The Phrygian wealth and wailful realm of Troy,
Those ruthful things that I myself beheld,
And whereof no small part fell to my share:
Which to express, who could refrain from tears?

Surrey's experiment is chiefly of historical interest, for his blank verse metre was used by Sackville* and Norton in their attempt to write the first English tragedy on the model of the austere classical tradition:

Your wonted true regard of faithful hearts
Makes me, O King, the bolder to resume,
To speak what I conceive within my breast:
Although the same do not agree at all
With that which other here my lords have said,
Nor which yourself have seemèd best to like.

Gorboduc, 1561

This also is not memorable, but the dignity and orderliness of *Gorboduc** impressed Sidney when he wrote his *Apology for Poetry** in about 1581, and Sidney, when we consider the poetic and dramatic confusion prevailing at that time, was right to be impressed.

Better dramatists than Sackville and Norton adopted blank verse, and in the blossoming years about 1590, the gifted group known as the University Wits* – Greene*, Peele*, and Marlowe* – brought the medium to poetic life. Marlowe was the greatest. His double drama *Tamburlaine** (1590) is about the Asian shepherd whose gigantic and pitiless energy raised him from the level of a petty chieftain to that of conqueror of kings. The same passion that drives him to the height of power also drives him to the height of ecstasy in love:

What is beauty, saith my sufferings, then?
If all the pens that ever poets held
Had fed the feelings of their masters' thoughts,
And every sweetness that inspir'd their hearts,
Their minds, and muses on admirèd themes;
If all the heavenly quintessence they 'still[1]
From their immortal flowers of poesy,
Wherein, as in a mirror, we perceive
The highest reaches of a human wit –
If these had made one poem's period

[1] distil

And all combin'd in beauty's worthiness,
Yet should there hover in their restless heads
One thought, one grace, one wonder, at the least,
Which into words no virtue can digest.

The energy of Tamburlaine is Marlowe's own poetic energy. His typical figure of speech is hyperbole – not exactly in its dictionary meaning of 'exaggeration' but rather the charging of language with feeling until it achieves an intensity which exceeds the literal meanings of the words. He does this largely through rhythm, by causing sentence structure to collaborate with rhythmic pattern so that the lines are fused into the whole speech. The first line asks the question which the remainder of the passage answers; the line has two pauses, which suspends it for the ear as the question is suspended in the mind. The succeeding 13 lines are all one sentence. Each line is self-contained by its rhythm, often reinforced by alliteration, while the rhetorical syntax carries the ear on to the climax and conclusion which is enforced by the pauses – 'One thought, one grace, one wonder . . .'. The words themselves are not especially 'poetical' or ornate; they are even rather plain, and get their strength from the rhythm and from their purposefulness – the sense that they give to the reader of being 'meant'.

Shakespeare's dramatic blank verse shows plainly the influence of Marlowe at the beginning of his career, for instance in *Richard III** (1592–3), and his first decade shows him broadening the scope of the medium, giving it variety and modulations beyond Marlowe's reach. In the next decade he achieved full mastery. In the following passage (1605–6?), Macbeth* is contemplating the murder of his sovereign, relative and guest, King Duncan (I.vii):

If it were done – when 'tis done – then 'twere well
It were done quickly: if th'assassination
Could trammel up the consequence, and catch,
With his surcease, success; that but this blow
Might be the be-all and the end-all here,
But here, upon this bank and shoal of time,
We'd jump the life to come. But in these cases
We still have judgement here; that we but teach
Bloody instructions, which, being taught, return
To plague th'inventor; this even-handed justice
Commends th'ingredients of our poison'd chalice
To our own lips.

So far in the speech, we see Shakespeare following Marlowe's use of sentence structure to enforce rhythm, and rhythm to enforce syntax, but he carries the principle further. Tamburlaine's speech reads rather like a set-speech, obedient to rhetoric rather than responsive to the turbulence of a mind; Macbeth's disturbance is felt rhythmically by the succession of mid-line pauses (lines 1, 2, 4) and onrushes over the end of the line (1–2, 2–3, 4–5). Shakespeare has sufficient command of blank verse rhythm to vary its pattern without weakening the force of its movement; thus, at the beginning of line 9 the accent falls on the first syllable of 'Bloody' instead of in its normal place, on the second syllable of the line, so that line 9 follows without break from line 8. However, this variation had long been in use. A more notable one is the joining of lines by the addition of light, eleventh syllables at the ends of lines, as in 7, 10 and 11. But the most important rhythmic feature of the passage is the combination of these run-on lines with strong pauses within the lines, so that the rhythm is extended throughout the paragraph. Apart from rhythm, the speech shows intensification of the enforcement of meaning by the character of the words. The word 'done' in lines 1 and 2 falls heavily like a blow, and this monosyllabic dullness of sound is combined with the alliterated s's of the polysyllables ('assassination', 'consequence', 'surcease', 'success') the hissing of which conveys the agitation of Macbeth's mind. The contrasting of Latin polysyllables with Germanic monosyllables – 'assassination', 'blow' – is an often remarked feature of Shakespeare's language. The monosyllable is commonly the familiar and spontaneous word, and the polysyllabic word is more likely to arise from reflection, so that the effect of their combination – as here – is to show the whole mind of the speaker engaged in the speech, from the sensational level to the intellectual one.

The speech ends –

Besides, this Duncan
Hath borne his faculties so meek, hath been
So clear in his great office, that his virtues
Will plead like angels, trumpet-tongued, against
The deep damnation of his taking-off;
And pity, like a naked new-born babe,
Striding the blast, or heaven's cherubim, hors'd
Upon the sightless couriers of the air,
Shall blow the horrid deed in every eye,
That tears shall drown the wind. – I have no spur
To prick the sides of my intent, but only
Vaulting ambition, which o'erleaps itself,
And falls on the other.

If Marlowe's distinguishing image is hyperbole*, Shakespeare's is metaphor*. Macbeth envisages the effect on the public of his crime. It will be the virtues of his victim that will make the peculiar shock of his murder, and Shakespeare does not merely describe this state of horror, but enacts it, with the alliterated and assonantal 'trumpet-tongued' and the alliterated 'deep damnation'. The tender childlike emotion of pity will be like a force of nature, striking like the wind on every individual; then pity is heightened to the angels of God riding the winds ('sightless' = invisible) as messengers of divine vengeance. Strong wind makes the eyes smart and water; so the pity will be so great that it will overwhelm the horror. Shakespeare thus uses the image of wind three times, but by twice using synonyms – 'blast', 'couriers of the air' – he obliterates the repetition and conveys the storm of horror, compassion and indignation which Macbeth's horrified imagination calls up to his mind. Macbeth now sums up his own position by comparing it with both a horseman and a horse: a horse needs a spur to urge him on, and so does he, but his spur is only that of excessive ambition that will bring ruin on himself – *ie* horror at the murder will annul the value of the fruits of the crime – just as an over-eager horseman will leap over a horse's back instead of on to it. This last image is confused, but it is confused with dramatic intention: so far in the play, Macbeth has moved as though hypnotized by the bloody urgency of his desire for power, but at this moment his reason is trying to recover control – he is both the horse *and* the rider.

Concentration of poetic force could not be carried further than in the blank verse of *Macbeth* and in that of the other great tragedies by Shakespeare written between 1603 and 1609, but the medium of blank verse could be made still more flexible. In *The Tempest** (1612?) Antonio is urging on his friend Sebastian the expediency of a cold-blooded double murder of sleeping men, and Sebastian asks him about his conscience:

ANTONIO: *Ay, sir; where lies that? If 'twere a kibe*[1]
'Twould put me to my slipper: but I feel not
This deity in my bosom: twenty consciences,
That stand 'twixt me and Milan, candied be they
And melt, ere they molest! Here lies your brother,
No better than the earth he lies upon,
If he were that which now he's like, that's dead;
Whom I, with this obedient steel, three inches of it,
Can lay to bed for ever; whiles you, doing thus,
To the perpetual wink for aye might put
This ancient morsel, this Sir Prudence, who
Should not upbraid our course. For all the rest,
They'll take suggestion as a cat laps milk;
They'll tell the clock to any business that
We say befits the hour.

[1] corn

The imagery still has its force: ordinary public opinion usually conforms to the wishes of those in power and commonly conforms involuntarily, as a cat involuntarily takes to its favourite food. The blank verse is still metrical; but the lines flow so naturally into one another that the syntax now dominates the metre.

Four of the $14\frac{1}{2}$ lines end in light additional syllables, and line 8 has 13 syllables. Four of the other lines (2, 10, 11, 14) end in weak words on which the voice cannot pause because the syntax drives it on to the suitable syntactic pause. Six of the lines have strong pauses in the middle without pauses of corresponding strength at the end. This loosening of the rhythm does not indicate that Shakespeare's art is weakening, but it does raise the question of what will happen to blank verse when its flexibility is increased still further.

The following extract comes from Massinger's* *A New Way to Pay Old Debts**, published about 20 years after *The Tempest* was written. Sir Giles Overreach has been asked whether his conscience is affected by his unscrupulous financial transactions:

Yes, as rocks are,
When foamy billows split themselves against
Their flinty ribs; or as the moon is moved
When wolves, with hunger pined, howl at her brightness.
I am of a solid temper, and, like these,
Steer on, a constant course: with mine own sword,
If called into the field, I can make that right,
Which fearful enemies murmured at as wrong.

This is nearer prose than Antonio's speech in *The Tempest.* Massinger is less careful than Shakespeare to relate his rhythms to the syntax of his speeches. 'Yes, as rocks are, when foamy billows split themselves against their flinty ribs' is as forceful when it is written as a prose sentence as it is in verse lengths, whereas Shakespeare has not forgotten the advantages of the verse medium. For instance, in the third line of Antonio's speech, a specially strong accent is thrown on '*twen*ty', by the pause that separates this accented syllable (*ie* '*twen*'-) from the unaccented one that usually precedes it immediately; in the fourth line the same device throws emphasis on '*can*died', and then the inversion of the verb and subject ('be they') followed by the expected stress on 'melt' – with a pause after it – in the fifth line, disposes the emphasis exactly as Shakespeare wanted it. It could not so distinctly nor so strongly be distributed in a prose version.

When blank verse had loosened as far as Massinger loosened it, the way was open to a prose drama. But blank verse was still to have a long history in other poetic fields.

6.2.3 *The sonnet*

The sonnet* is merely one kind of short poem, but it has a distinctly defined character. However, it requires a separate account, less because of the individuality of its form than because of its strong appeal to English poets, who, at the end of the 16th century, put it to uses different from those of other short poems.

The origins of the sonnet are obscure, but it had been evolved by the 13th century and in the Middle Ages some of the best poets used it, notably two of the great Italians, Dante* and Petrarch*. It consisted of 14 lines divided into two parts: one, called the octave, had 8 lines and a rhyme scheme *a b b a a b b a*; the other, called the sestet, had 6 lines and a varying rhyme scheme. The special prestige of the sonnet arose no doubt partly because the strictness of its form was a challenge to poetic craftsmanship, but partly it must have been because this strictness was such as to offer peculiar scope. The division of octave and sestet invited contrasting treatment of the subject, offering an opportunity for complexity in harmony with grace. Thus a fine sonnet was an epitome of the qualities which a poet who was also a refined artist sought to achieve. This epitome was at the opposite of the alternative ideal – that of the amplitude and drama of the various forms of long poem, especially the epic – but the disadvantages of the restriction of the form were evaded by the practice of writing sonnets in sequence, like those of Petrarch to Laura. A single sonnet could express a mood and allow scope for the contradictions of feeling that so often make up a mood; a sequence could build a number of moods into a whole attitude of mind. Personal relationships are natural subjects for such treatment, and sonnet sequences were preponderantly about love.

English poetic genius was at first reluctant to receive the sonnet. Chaucer did not use it, though he emulated other short forms current in France, nor did any other poet before Wyatt and Surrey in the 16th century. One reason commonly given is the paucity of rhymes in the English language by comparison with French and Italian. A better explanation is that the spirit of English poetry from the 14th to the mid-16th century did not favour elaborate and precise forms; the best poetry, including Chaucer's and Wyatt's, had the kind of freshness that goes with informality, though not with formlessness. Even the sonnets of Wyatt are not amongst his best work, and though their publication, together with those by Surrey, in Tottel's *Miscellany** (1557) initiated a fashion, the form did not immediately take root. The sonnets of Wyatt and Surrey, however, began the establishment of the English pattern by ending with a couplet, unlike French and Italian sonnets.

It was Philip Sidney's* sequence *Astrophil and Stella** which really established the sonnet form; he composed it in or soon after 1580, but it was not published until 1591, after his death in 1586. The publication was the start of a decade of prolific sonnet writing, as though English poets suddenly discovered what the sonnet could do. But although Sidney was the first English poet to understand the form thoroughly, its popularity can best be understood by recalling the kind of influence which had been disseminated by Spenser. Spenser's own sonnets (*Amoretti*, 1595) are inferior to Sidney's, but their form resembles an expansion of his own 9-line Spenserian stanza. The sonnet was, in fact, a natural medium for the qualities of ceremony, refinement, stateliness and ideality which Spenser, in all his work, held up as the criterion of civilization. Spenser, we may say, did most to create the climate for the sonnet, and Sidney revealed its proper handling; the most influential foreign model was the Petrarchan, and the theme of the sequences – *Astrophil and Stella* is typical – was a lover's worship of his disdainful, imperious, and ideally perfect mistress. The situation was conventional; the woman concerned might be fictitious, or if she was real, the poet was perhaps not seriously in love with her; her essential function was to serve as a symbol for what was unattainable but infinitely desirable. The only sure weapon the lover possessed was the reminder of mortality, as in this example from Daniel's* *Sonnets to Delia* (1592):

Time, cruel time, come and subdue that brow
Which conquers all but thee; and thee too stays,
As if she were exempt from scythe or bow,
From love or years, unsubject to decays.
Or art thou grown in league with those fair eyes,
That they may help thee to consume our days?
Or dost thou spare her for her cruelties,
Being merciless like thee, that no man weighs?
And yet thou see'st thy power she disobeys;
Cares not for thee, but lets thee waste in vain;
And prodigal of hours and years betrays
Beauty and Youth to Opinion and Disdain.
Yet spare her, Time, let her exempted be;
She may become more kind to thee or me.

This is the Elizabethan sonnet as it finally evolved; it does not consist of an octave and sestet like French and Italian sonnets, but of three quatrains and a couplet. The lover first calls on Time as an ally against his mistress (first quatrain); then, since Time and her beauty are equally destructive, he fears that Time may already have become her ally (second quatrain); he next warns Time that her contempt for lovers is also a contempt of Time, since she is behaving as though her youth and beauty are indestructible (third quatrain); finally, in the couplet, he prays that her beauty may yet be spared – a reversal of his opening lines – in the hope that she may yet realize her approaching danger, and surrender her beauty to him before it has passed away. Under the disguise of addressing Time, the poet is really addressing the lady, and he makes his appeal by way of a fusion of reproach, threat, and high compliment. The matter is so united to the form, that the form seems designed for what the poet has to say; we do not have the feeling that the poet is merely 'filling out' a pattern.

But Time in Daniel's sonnet is a mere figure of speech, though a graceful one, and his attitude to the lady is basically conventional. Still better poets – Sidney among them – used the convention, but at the same time passed beyond it. Thus in the following sonnet (64 in his sequence) Shakespeare uses the convention for a very serious meditation on Time – the paradox that the very winning of the beloved is itself the beginning of tragedy, since mortality has already doomed the lover to loss of the beloved:

When I have seen by Time's fell hand defaced
The rich proud cost of outworn buried age,
When sometime lofty towers I see down razed
And brass eternal slave to mortal rage;
When I have seen the hungry ocean gain
Advantage on the kingdom of the shore,
And the firm soil win of the watery main,
Increasing store with loss, and loss with store;
When I have seen such interchange of state,
Or state itself confounded to decay,
Ruin hath taught me thus to ruminate,
That Time will come and take my love away.
This thought is as a death, which cannot choose
But weep to have that which it fears to lose.

A good sonnet characteristically presents a delicately achieved balance of contrasted states of feeling. The English substitution of quatrains and a couplet instead of the octave and sestet made possible more dramatic progression in the presentation of the feelings, and invited an epigrammatic summing up in conclusion. The deeper the feeling, the more the dramatic element was emphasized, as we can see in this sonnet by Shakespeare; as in his blank verse, the regular pattern of accents is modified by the force of the dramatic stress – 'And the fírm sóil wín of the wátery máin'. But the distinctive quality of the sonnet form is its completeness, the sense it communicates of nothing more to be said; and this requires that the dramatic element must be contained within the sonnet. After 1600, the enthusiasm for the form suddenly abated, and though it continued to be used in the 17th century and was revived in the 19th, it never recovered the quality that distinguished it from other short poems. This quality depended on the ability of the poet to feel contradictions of emotion within a larger state of finality, beyond which there was no need to speculate. The experience of living with immediate contradictions of feeling within ascertainably final values belonged especially to the last 20 years of the 16th century – the period of the influence of Spenser – of the high Renaissance in English poetry. In the 17th century, in the hands of Donne*, Herbert* and Milton*, the sonnet became a vehicle of religious feeling, and a way of dramatizing the poet's relationship with God. Their sonnets are amongst their best poems, but in different ways they altered the character of the form, and it no longer insists on separate treatment in this essay.

6.2.4 *The short poem*

The end of the 16th century and the beginning of the 17th was one of the greatest periods of English music. In the same period, the drama flowered from a union between the dramatic life of popular festivals, both seasonal and religious, and a learned cultivation of classical literature and contemporary rhetoric. Similarly, folk music of village May* games and London street ballads united with philosophical ideas about music as the harmony of the universe and music as an indispensable courtly attainment; and the union produced the flowering of English lyric poetry. We shall see that the drama too had an important effect on the growth of this poetry.

The traditions of European music at this time were predominantly vocal, and, until the Reformation* in the first half of the century, the most elaborate vocal music was, in England, church music. The Reformation was damaging to musical tradition – especially in England – because it dispersed the monastic choirs and abolished the Catholic Mass; the new Anglican* liturgy did not offer the same opportunities for musical settings. In the second half of the century, however, secular music greatly expanded, partly through the cultivation of the Italian song-form known in England as the madrigal*, for which different singers sang different melodies, and sometimes different words, simultaneously. Side by side with the madrigal was the air, or song for the single voice. Books of madrigals and airs were numerous and famous, for example *England's Helicon* (1600), which included poems by many of the most famous poets of the time.

Because music was mainly vocal, the collaboration between musicians and poets was close. Composers such as Byrd (1543–1623) and Morley (1557–1603) did not attempt to make their settings predominate over the language, but used the words to suggest musical ideas. The poets, at the same time, learnt from the musicians' treatment of language. Musical rhythms and harmony led the poet to new opportunities of accent and emphasis, and they also taught him greater attention to the choice and placing of words, so that the musician could elicit their significance and feeling naturally and appropriately. This collaboration partly accounts for the quality, often noticed in the Elizabethan lyric, of impersonality, as though the poet were listening for the composer's contribution of emotional expression. It also partly explains one of the critical controversies of the time.

Gabriel Harvey* and other humanists thought that English poetry should return to classical quantitative rhythms, abandoning rhyme, and his opinion was shared unexpectedly by one of the best masters of rhyming verse in the period – the poet Thomas Campion* (1567–1620), who was also a composer. Campion's point in *Art of English Poesy* (1602) seems to have been that 'the fatness of rhyme' distracted the ear from the true rhythms of poetry, and that rhyme was therefore not merely redundant but a hindrance. In practice, he knew that the variety of English syllabic lengths was too great for strictly classical quantitative verse, and Harvey himself was unconsciously advocating accentual verse like that of the old alliterative poets rather than classical quantity. Harvey's and Campion's arguments were fruitful in drawing attention to rhythmical art and emphasizing the danger of the mere tunefulness of rhyme. Thus scholarly interest in classical rhythms unites with concern for musical properties in the art of a lyric like the following, from Ben Jonson's* play, *Cynthia's Revels* (1600):

Slow, slow, fresh fount, keep time with my salt tears;
Yet slower, yet, O faintly, gentle springs:
List to the heavy part the music bears,
Woe weeps out her division,[1] *when she sings.*
Droop herbs, and flowers;
Fall grief in showers;
Our beauties are not ours:
O, I could still
(Like melting snow upon some craggy hill)
Drop, drop, drop, drop,
Since nature's pride is, now, a wither'd daffodil.

[1] musical modulation

This, considered as a poem, has its own verbal music, but it is not the music of Spenser. Spenser's music depends on metrical pattern, with only slight variations, whereas the Jonson lyric, except for the last line, is not obviously metrical (in the sense of being manifestly divisible into the metrical units of verse feet) although it is rhythmical in a way that enables the music to bring out the emotional stresses with due rhythmic variety in each line.

Jonson was as careful and conscious an artist as Spenser; he was also one of the most scholarly poets of his day. His scholarship was not an end in itself, but a means to balance personal feeling with the feeling of past writers, so that what is individual is related to what is shared, and brought into proportion with it. Thus Jonson achieved his civilized wit: personal emotion is critically disciplined by reason, and seen in the perspective of general truth. An example is the following poem, based on the Latin style of epigram, on the death of his daughter. It was published in *Epigrams* (1616) but was perhaps written in 1598:

Here lies to each her parents' ruth,[1]
Mary, the daughter of their youth:
Yet, all heaven's gifts, being heaven's due,
It makes the father less to rue.
At six months' end, she parted hence
With safety of her innocence;
Whose soul Heaven's Queen (whose name she bears)
In comfort of her mother's tears,
Hath placed amongst her Virgin-train:
Where, while that sever'd doth remain,
This grave partakes the fleshly birth,
Which cover lightly, gentle earth.

[1] compassion

Music and scholarship made for discipline of form; the drama encouraged release, and the writer of short poems who most clearly shows the force of dramatic idiom, though he did not use blank verse, was John Donne*. Most of his best love poems, according to Ben Jonson, were written in the 1590s.

My face in thine eye, thine in mine appears,
And true plain hearts do in the faces rest,
Where can we find two better hemispheres
Without sharp North, without declining West?
Whatever dies, was not mixt equally;
If our two loves be one, or, thou and I
Love so alike, that none do slacken, none can die.

This is the third and last stanza of Donne's *The Good-morrow*. In the first stanza, the lover tells his mistress that his life began with their love, and in the second he says that together they make up a complete world that needs no other. In this one he completes the comparison: as one hemisphere is the image of the other, so they bear each other's images in the pupils of their eyes. While, in this, they resemble the physical world, they are also superior to it, for their compass lacks either the bitterness of northern cold or the promise of decline associated with the west because the sun sets there. He concludes by inferring, from the science of the day, that their love must be immortal because it is equal, whereas death is caused by the inferiority of one element to another. The poem is characteristic of Donne in three ways: the first is the direct idiom of the spoken language, like that of the contemporary verse drama; it is the opposite of the Spenserian charm of consecrated language. The second characteristic is that a personal interchange is communicated – again as in the drama, but in contrast to the Petrarchan love poem, in which the mistress is not present, or at least is unresponsive. The third and most important characteristic is the way in which the image of the world is worked out as a full analogy to the personal relationship, with extensive logical consequences. It is this working out of the image (or conceit*) that caused Samuel Johnson* in the 18th century to designate Donne and his successors as the Metaphysical* School of poets, because they wrote like philosophers even when they were not writing philosophical poetry. The name has lasted, although it is misleading if it suggests that they wrote exclusively about what lies beyond physical experience – about the supernatural. It is true that Donne became a deeply religious poet, and that his successors in his style were predominantly religious, but they were less metaphysical in this sense than was Milton*, who, except in some of his early work, does not show their influence. It is more important to observe how Donne's 'metaphysical conceit' works rather in the same way as Shakespeare's dramatic images (*eg* those of blood, darkness and sleep in *Macbeth*) by embodying the situation which is the subject, and not merely illustrating it.

Spenser, and the younger men, Jonson and Donne, were all working in the decade 1590–1600, and each had extensive influence over later poetry. Spenser first diffused wide influence over younger poets, and later on Milton; through Milton and also more directly, he impressed himself on some poets of the 18th century, and more strongly still on those of the 19th, when he became known as 'the poet's poet'. His was the poetry of what I have called 'consecrated language'. Jonson's immediate followers were the Cavalier Poets* of the 1630s, whose cultivation of balance and shapeliness made them the natural predecessors of the Augustan* poets, who began with Dryden* and dominated the 18th century. Jonson's was the poetry of civilized reasonableness, ordering the feelings even more than expressing them. Donne's dramatic imagination led to the 17th-century Metaphysical school (Herbert*, Vaughan*, Crashaw*, Marvell* and Cowley*), some of whom (Marvell, notably) shared his influence with that of Jonson. Donne's boldness and irregularity were displeasing to the Augustans, and antipathetic in a different way to the poets of the 19th-century Romantic Revival*, drawn as they were to the opposed Spenserian influence. In the 20th century Donne has become at last understood and appreciated; as his reputation has risen, so has that of Spenser fallen.

6.3

Classicism to High Romanticism: 1660–1830

6.3.1 *Epic and satire: the renewal of blank verse and the predominance of the heroic couplet*

The Renaissance* was a period of exploration rather like the archaeological uncovering of ancient cities, but the humanists* did not feel that they were uncovering a dead past; the classical world of Greece and Rome was their own living past, out of which they felt they could build a worthy present. In England, the period of the Renaissance in literature was above all the 16th century; the 17th and 18th centuries stemmed directly from the 16th-century findings. The 17th century, until its last quarter, was influenced by that religious extension of the Renaissance which we know as the Reformation*. The Reformation did not run entirely counter to the Renaissance, whose inspiration was pagan Greece and Rome, but instead gave many humanist scholars a deep sense of mission: they believed that the classical civilizations represented the greatest glory available to this world, and they considered it to be the privilege of Christians to emulate this splendour for the glory of God. So the men who were most morally impressed by the Reformation were often those who responded most vividly to classical culture; this is true of Edmund Spenser* (1552?–99), and it is also true of John Milton* (1608–74). On the other hand, the Renaissance was also a secularizing movement which sought learning for its own sake; the humanists believed that their learning contained all that was necessary for the building of a perfect civilization, and some rather turned away from religion, not because they were atheists, but because God was beyond understanding, whereas society could be understood. Religious passions wore themselves away in the wars of the 17th century, and then the secular aspect of the Renaissance came uppermost. On the one hand, Milton at the opening of *Paradise Lost** (1667) prayed that he might 'assert Eternal Providence, And justify the ways of God to men'; but on the other hand, Pope opened the second Epistle of his *Essay on Man** with the injunction:

Know then thyself; presume not God to scan;
The proper study of mankind is man.

In composing his epic *Paradise Lost*, Milton was building a great monument, intended to rival that epic monument of Rome, Virgil's *Aeneid**. Because he intended both to emulate Virgil and to excel him, Milton considered that his epic should be comparable: it should have a similar structure, and the verse should have a parallel texture. It seemed to him, as it had to Surrey, that the English 10-syllable blank verse line was the nearest medium he could get to the unrhymed Latin hexameter. Blank verse, when Milton took it up, had passed through a whole cycle of life in the drama towards the laxity of speech rhythms in the decadent verse of poets such as Massinger. For Milton this pliability had the advantage that it could be used expansively over long paragraphs, but he needed to replace the fluidity of the speech rhythm by renewing the tension of the line so as to make it capable of the sustained grandeur of the epic style. To achieve this, Milton stiffened his sentences with suspended periods, according to a syntax which was more natural to Latin than to English; he also heightened his diction with sonorous words, often of Latin derivation, such as diffuse the attention rather than concentrate it. Critics came to talk of Milton's 'sublime organ music': it is poetry that goes straight to the emotions through the ear, not through all the senses to the mind as well as to the emotions, as Shakespeare's does. This is how Milton described the fall of Satan:

The infernal Serpent; he it was whose guile,
Stirred up with envy and revenge, deceived
The mother of mankind, what time his pride
Had cast him out from Heaven, with all his host
Of rebel Angels, by whose aid, aspiring
To set himself in glory above his peers,
He trusted to have equalled the Most High,
If he opposed, and, with ambitious aim
Against the throne and monarchy of God,

Raised impious war in Heaven and battle proud,
With vain attempt. Him the Almighty Power
Hurled headlong flaming from the ethereal sky,
With hideous ruin and combustion, down
To bottomless perdition, there to dwell
In adamantine chains and penal fire,
Who durst defy the Omnipotent to arms.

Paradise Lost I.34

In the first sentence, down to 'vain attempt', Milton is communicating facts: Satan revenged himself against God by tempting Eve, because his rebellion had failed and he and his fellows had been cast out of Heaven. The facts can be stated simply, but the phrasing ('Raised impious war in Heaven and battle proud') draws out the statement, so that the reader can feel the elevating march of the rhythm, for this is no ordinary rebellion and no ordinary revenge. In the second sentence, the facts are communicated through the movement, at least if we read according to the rhythm which the words themselves dictated, and not according to an abstract metrical pattern. In 'Húrled heádlong fláming fróm the ethéreal sky' the first two accents come together, and 'heádlong fláming fróm the' reverses the usual order of accented and unaccented syllables, so that we feel the fact and do not merely listen to the words. The adjectives 'flaming', 'ethereal', 'hideous', 'bottomless', 'adamantine' convey sensations rather than distinct meaning; similarly the resonant polysyllable 'Omnipotent' (for 'God') seems to ride in serene grandeur over the headlong fall – an example of Milton's use of a Latin word for an impressiveness of sense through sound.

This is art of strong character, and it left a long-lasting impression on English poets. But Milton was writing in later life, and the younger poets, though they listened to him with admiration, were moving in a different direction. The most notable of these was John Dryden* (1631–1700), whose working life lay chiefly between 1660 and 1700. This was an age of reconstruction after civil conflict excited by just such religious passion as inspires *Paradise Lost*. The attention of men like Dryden was occupied by society and its politics. They sought clear ideas and orderly standards, and considered that poetry – for the first time – should emulate the virtues of lucid prose, aiming at clarity of focus and critical persuasiveness. The best instrument for these was not the nebulous sublimity of Miltonic blank verse, but the rhymed couplet, for the rhymes invited the mind to bring conflicting ideas into balance, and to clarify them with epigrammatic point. Henceforward it was to be known as the 'heroic couplet', both because – since Chaucer and in spite of Milton – it was the measure in which serious narrative verse had chiefly been written, and because it was the English equivalent to the French couplet of 12-syllable lines (alexandrines) which was the medium of the French grand style. In English, however, the most memorable works that have been written in it since 1660 have been satirical, sometimes the satire of mock epic* or mock-heroic*, in which the grandeur of epic poetry was parodied for the purpose of ridicule. Dryden was the first master of the satirical and epigrammatic heroic couplet, notably in his mock epic *Absalom and Achitophel** (1681), but he had a still greater successor in Alexander Pope* (1688–1744). A good example of Pope's satirical use of the couplet is the portrait of the statesman Philip Wharton from Epistle I of the *Moral Essays* –

Wharton, the scorn and wonder of our days,
Whose ruling passion was the lust of praise.

The description continues to display the paradox that Wharton represents – the paradox of a man with immense gifts, but with a temperament which drives him to seek admiration not only among those whose high opinion is worth having, but among those who are beneath contempt. It ends:

Thus with each gift of nature and of art,
And wanting nothing but an honest heart;
Grown all to all; from no one vice exempt;
And most contemptible to shun contempt;
His passion still, to covet general praise;
His life, to forfeit it a thousand ways;
A constant bounty, which no friend has made;
An angel tongue, which no man can persuade;
A fool, with more of wit than half mankind;
Too rash for thought, for action too refined;
A tyrant to the wife his heart approves;
A rebel to the very king he loves;
He dies, sad outcast of each church and state,
And, harder still! flagitious,[1] *yet not great.*
Ask you why Wharton broke through every rule?
'Twas all for fear the knaves should call him fool.

[1] deeply criminal

Occasionally Pope's compression, or the exaction of rhyme, makes superficial confusion in his syntax; thus 'which' in lines 7 and 8 is the subject of the verb in each line, not the object as the word order suggests, but this is an accepted variation of the usual English syntax to which his mature poetry nearly always adheres. He writes as the well-bred members of society whom he is addressing talk, and he seldom wastes words. One of his aims is precision – to write 'what oft was thought but ne'er so well expressed' – and every word, including the unusual 'flagitious', is chosen for its exactitude. Another of his aims is the achievement of balance in fine proportion, the outstanding quality of the Augustan age* of English culture, of which he is one of the two or three chief exponents. Thus he not only balances line against line, but contrasts opposites within single lines, so subjugating his disorderly subject to the discipline of the conspicuous order of his art. Yet Pope was not a constricted poet. He could use his couplets to render images that were bold enough for Donne, showing that his discipline was no mere constraint, but united to intense feeling. An example is the following epitomization of spiritual mediocrity from his *Elegy to the Memory of an Unfortunate Lady*:

Most souls, 'tis true, but peep out once an age,
Dull sullen prisoners in the body's cage:
Dim lights of life, that burn a length of years
Useless, unseen, as lamps in sepulchres:
Like eastern kings a lazy state they keep;
And, close confined to their own palace, sleep.

Pope here is using words with the same precision, but his satire has led him to a style that is metaphysical not only in the narrower sense of the tradition of Donne, but in the broader sense of displaying the spiritual in bondage to the material. The image expands and changes as those of Donne do: 'peep' and 'dull sullen prisoners' express the fear of ordinary people to go beyond the safe limits of conventional life at all, and their resentments at any such demands upon them. The light in the sepulchre is their living death, and the sleeping kings the potential grandeur that they waste. For Pope, satire was no mere vehicle of envy and hate, but the voice of the conscience of civilized society.

No other poet used the couplet with such dexterity and versatility, but the medium found very different voices. The most notable of these, still strongly in the Augustan tradition, was the massive satire of Samuel Johnson* (*Vanity of Human Wishes*, 1749). Goldsmith* used a mellifluous tone to idealize the life of the villages, which he saw as menaced by the enclosure* policy of the landlords:

Sweet Auburn! loveliest village of the plain,
Where health and plenty cheered the labouring swain,
Where smiling spring its earliest visit paid,
And parting summer's lingering blooms delayed . . .

*The Deserted Village**, 1770

His idealism was motivated by a characteristically Augustan social indignation, but he was countered by the equally Augustan social common sense of Crabbe*, who knew the village better, and resented Goldsmith's sentimentalizing the life of the peasant:

No; cast by Fortune on a frowning coast,
Which neither groves nor happy valleys boast;
Where other cares than those the Muse relates,

And other shepherds dwell with other mates;
By such examples taught, I paint the Cot,
As Truth will paint it, and as the Bards will not . . .

The Village, 1783

Crabbe was the last master of the heroic couplet. With him and Goldsmith, we enter the relationship of man and natural environment, a great theme of the Romantics, and one that found its best medium, not in the heroic couplet, but in yet another mutation of blank verse.

6.3.2 *Blank verse and the poetry of contemplation*

Milton was not an Augustan, yet his grand style appealed strongly to one side of the Augustan temperament. It was a tendency of feeling inherited from the Renaissance and particularly from Spenser, through whom it went back to medieval Christianity tempered – but also, in some respects, intensified – by 16th-century Protestantism. According to this conception, the universe was vast, orderly, and sublime, and demanded from man all his powers of reverent contemplation. But Milton himself was the last poet who could unselfconsciously unite the biblical, the philosophical, and the epic–heroic aspects of this emotion. The strongly rational direction of thought after 1660 was too sceptical for the younger poets to write as he did; they might contemplate the Universe and feel much as Milton did, but they could not make Satan wander about it like Robinson Crusoe, or make God speak like a divine schoolmaster, as Pope remarked of Milton's God. 'The proper study of mankind is man'; however, the natural philosophers* of Pope's day occupied themselves with nature as well as with man, and this growth of natural science gave the poets a field of contemplation which satisfied their inclination to reverence without offending their pronounced respect for fact. Thomson's *Seasons** (1726–30) were the first important poems of this new kind; he used his subject for a mixture of solemn description and moral reflection, and presented it in the heightened Miltonic style:

Where now, ye lying vanities of life!

but it is his strong sensibility for the natural scene, evident in spite of rather than by means of his 'high style', that makes his poems – in parts – memorable:

The keener tempests rise: and fuming dun
From all the livid east, or piercing north,
Thick clouds ascend; in whose capacious womb
A vapoury deluge lies, to snow congeal'd.
Heavy they roll their fleecy world along;
And the sky saddens with the gathered storm.

Through the hushed air the whitening shower descends,
At first thin wavering; till at last the flakes
Fall broad and wide and fast, dimming the day
With a continual flow. The cherished fields
Put on their winter-robe of purest white.

Winter

This is still Augustan in its way; Thomson is almost using poetry as a public act of worship. But Augustanism was very much an urban phase of culture, and this very fact alienated some minds from it. The appeal of natural environment led to the contemplation of wide, lonely landscapes, in which the man who for some reason fears and hates urban society may find himself more at home than in the city. William Cowper* (1731–1800) was such a man; he suffered fits of pathological depression, and fled from London to the country where he took refuge with some friends to whom he addressed his long, reflective poem *The Task* (1785):

God made the country, and man made the town.
What wonder then that health and virtue, gifts
That can alone make sweet the bitter draught
That life holds out to all, should most abound
And least be threaten'd in the fields and groves?
Possess ye, therefore, ye, who, borne about
In chariots and sedans, know no fatigue
But that of idleness, and taste no scenes
But such as art contrives, possess ye still
Your element; there only can ye shine,
There only minds like yours can do no harm.
Our groves were planted to console at noon
The pensive wand'rer in their shades. At eve
The moonbeam, sliding softly in between
The sleeping leaves, is all the light they wish,
Birds warbling all their music.

Book I, 749–764

The often quoted first line is not a new sentiment: the idea that country life enhances health and virtue whereas the city corrupts both, goes back to classical pastoral*, and in English, to Spenser at least. What is new here is the relaxed quality of the verse. Cowper is not aspiring to Miltonic grandeur; his moral reflections are expressed in language of dignity, but he does not attempt sublimity. Even the rhetorical address to the town-dwellers ('Possess ye, therefore . . .') is ironical, not an attempt to elevate the tone. The difference between Cowper and Thomson is evident if we compare the lines 'The moonbeam, sliding softly in between' and 'Through the hush'd air the whitening shower descends'. Both are good lines, but in the Thomson, 'whitening shower' is an elevated phrase for 'snow', and 'descends' is elevated for 'falls'; Cowper's line is an attempt to convey as exactly as possible the effect of moonlight penetrating foliage, without any attempt to heighten this effect. Thomson is contemplating the sublimity of nature, and he is conscious of the distance of ordinary experience from appreciation of this sublimity; Cowper sees nature as the world of truth, and he is trying to find his own truth within it.

The French Revolution* and the English Industrial Revolution* together did much to fragment the social ideas of the Augustans. The young poets Wordsworth* (1770–1850) and Coleridge* (1772–1834) felt alone, not so much because personal sufferings alienated them from society – as happened to Cowper – but because they no longer had a coherent society to relate themselves to. They sought to discover themselves in their solitude and in their friendships. Their poems explored their own natures in relation to surrounding nature, and they addressed their poems to each other, or to others – such as Wordsworth's sister Dorothy – who knew them best. Wordsworth's childhood in the Lakeland mountains gave him a peculiarly intimate sense of the interpenetration of his surroundings and his own mind. He was the first English writer to express man's continuity with nature; he saw nature not only as the source of human life but also as the principle of human growth and enlargement. His joint publication, with Coleridge in 1798, of the *Lyrical Ballads** includes his *Lines composed a few miles above Tintern Abbey.* In the following passage, he tries to express the essence of this union of nature and man:

These beauteous forms,
Through a long absence, have not been to me
As is a landscape to a blind man's eye:
But oft, in lonely rooms, and 'mid the din
Of towns and cities, I have owed to them,
In hours of weariness, sensations sweet,
Felt in the blood, and felt along the heart;
And passing even into my purer mind,
With tranquil restoration: – feelings too
Of unremembered pleasure: such, perhaps,
As have no slight or trivial influence
On that best portion of a good man's life,
His little, nameless, unremembered, acts
Of kindness and of love. Nor less, I trust,
To them I may have owed another gift,
Of aspect more sublime; that blessed mood,
In which the burthen of the mystery,
In which the heavy and the weary weight
Of all this unintelligible world,

Is lightened: – that serene and blessed mood,
In which the affections gently lead us on, –
Until, the breath of this corporeal frame
And even the motion of our human blood
Almost suspended, we are laid asleep
In body, and become a living soul:
While with an eye made quiet by the power
Of harmony, and the deep power of joy,
We see into the life of things.

These lines are even simpler in their expression than Cowper's. There is a clue to this determined simplicity half-way through the passage in the use of the word 'sublime'. For Milton and for Thomson, the 'sublime' was the object of contemplation *beyond* the mind, but for Wordsworth it has penetrated within. Because this experience is 'within' (though it comes from outside) he cannot objectify it, as Milton could 'objectify' Heaven, or Thomson a winter landscape. And because it is more elemental, more like sensation, than any intellectual concept, he cannot use abstractions to express it. At the same time, Wordsworth is still Augustan enough to have a strong sense of fact, and he avoids the kind of symbolism (such as Coleridge uses in similar poems) that might take the reader beyond the co-ordination of the intellect and the senses. The experience he is expressing is the purest part of the very act of living – 'Felt in the blood, and felt along the heart'. It is life felt as pure meaning, in which resistance to the mind from surroundings vanishes away – 'We see into the life of things'. Language itself is a means to overcome the resistance of surroundings to the mind, and fully to accomplish his purpose here, Wordsworth would have to cause language to refine itself away. Since this is impossible, he uses a diction which is as directly apprehensible as possible, and a rhythm so discreet that it affects the ear with the gentlest possible movement.

Minds can interpenetrate with minds, as well as minds with nature; although Wordsworth and Coleridge intended their blank verse poems for the public, they commonly addressed them to individuals, for their intimate appeal can be public only if it is personal first. We are thus now far away from the epic of Milton or the verse epistles of Pope, for though the latter were addressed to individuals too, the person addressed was only a pretext for the writing of a public poem. *Tintern Abbey** is the new form which Coleridge called the Conversation Poem, and it is a form that guided all Wordsworth's other writing in blank verse, including narratives such as *Michael**, and the long autobiographical *Prelude**.

6.3.3 *Revival of popular verse forms*

The Restoration* of the English Monarchy in 1660 and the French Revolution* in 1789 were events of great influence upon the writing of poetry. The Restoration was a victory of reason over fanaticism, and it encouraged the discipline of the imagination by a rational, intellectual order which made for poems of some length. The Revolution, on the other hand, was a victory of passion over conservative system, and it encouraged the release of the imagination in bursts of insight, which made for a revival of the short poem, although it provided new pretexts for the long poem as well. Poets searched for the springs of spontaneity, and the search brought them back to folk poetry, in particular the ballad*, which the Augustan poets had neglected, although Augustan antiquarians had shown a keen interest in it. This meant a new cultivation of the quatrain*, that is to say, the simplest kind of rhymed stanza of 4 lines.

The quatrain has of course always been in use for rhymed verse, much of it of a very sophisticated kind such as Gray's famous *Elegy in a Country Churchyard** (1750), but it was particularly associated with traditional ballads like *Sir Patrick Spens**:

The king sits in Dunfermline town,
Drinking the blude-red wine.
'O where will I get a skeely[1] *skipper*
To sail this new ship o' mine?'

[1] skilful

Sir Patrick Spens is not strictly metrical, but this stanza shows the pattern of the quatrain in what is called common metre*: the lines alternate with 4 and 3 accents, and they sometimes have alternating rhymes, and sometimes – as here – only two lines rhyming. Common metre was also used in church hymns*, for instance those by Isaac Watts (1674–1748):

Time like an ever-rolling stream
Bears all its sons away;
They fly forgotten as a dream
Dies at the opening day.

It was the first generation of the Romantics, writing between 1789 and 1810, which particularly cultivated the idiom of popular poetry in the quatrain. Blake's* *Songs of Innocence** (1789) and *Songs of Experience* (1794) are short, symbolic poems, mostly in quatrains, but in very varied rhythms and line lengths. Some resemble hymns in the Watts tradition, like this stanza from *The Divine Image* in *Songs of Innocence*:

To Mercy, Pity, Peace and Love
All pray in their distress;
And to these virtues of delight
Return their thankfulness.

The resemblance to Watts is deceptive, however, for the poet is not offering the accepted Christian teachings as he seems at first to be; Blake goes on to point out that we know these virtues only because we find them in human beings, and when we worship God we really worship the divine in human beings. In another poem, *London* in the *Songs of Experience*, Blake seems to be writing in the tradition of the broadside ballads* of the London streets. These were often protest poems against social injustice, but Blake, in four quatrains, expresses the essence of injustice in the retribution it brings on the social institutions which are supposed to require respect:

How the Chimney-sweeper's cry
Every black'ning Church appals;
And the hapless Soldier's sigh
Runs in blood down Palace walls.

His idiom is popular, but his imagination is comprehensive and deep. Often it is also mysterious, as in the famous *The Tiger* or in *The Sick Rose* (*Songs of Experience*):

O rose, thou art sick!
The invisible worm
That flies in the night,
In the howling storm,

Has found out thy bed
Of crimson joy
And his dark secret love
Does thy life destroy.

If this symbolism is in a popular tradition, it is surely the very ancient non-Christian one suggested by such a medieval stanza as 'Western wind when will thou blow' (*6.1.2). The medieval poem uses human longing to imagine the aridity of the soil waiting for rain; Blake uses natural imagery in a similarly terse, enigmatic way to express the aridity of possessive passion.

Blake was a very unusual poet; he was also an unusual man, eccentric and solitary. Paradoxically, his unusualness was partly due to his ordinariness. He used the popular stanzas with originality and truthfulness because he belonged to popular culture; he was more a man of the people than were the other leading poets of his time, and his contemporaries knew little about him. Wordsworth, independently of Blake, wrote in the tradition of the broadside ballad, which not only drew him by its inherent simplicity but satisfied his respect for ordinary fact, as the more romantic and traditional ballads did not. But he had not grown up with the sound of the street ballads in his ears as Blake had, and he sometimes failed to see that his admiration for their simplicity degenerated into mere tolerance for their occasional flatness. To do him justice, his critics themselves often disagree about when his own simplicity is mere flatness, though they agree that the tendency is his principal weakness. Wordsworth's peculiar accomplishment was to convey through the communication of simple, literal facts a vision that transmutes them; the experience that one of his very simple poems leaves in the mind is different from the experience received in the act of reading it.

A slumber did my spirit seal;
I had no human fears:
She seemed a thing that could not feel
The touch of earthly years.

No motion has she now, no force;
She neither hears nor sees;
Rolled round in earth's diurnal course,
With rocks, and stones, and trees.

(1800)

A young girl belongs so much to life that it is impossible to connect the idea of death with her, or even that of ageing; but she dies, and is part of the earth. These are the facts, and the poet seems to state no more, apart from the implication that he loved her. The first line tells us only that he did not think of the possibility of the actual event; it is only on reflection that the reader notices that the poet 'slumbered' while the girl lived, and awoke when she was beyond slumbering, in death. The second stanza does not merely say 'she died'; it says that the girl has lost her individuality – has no motion of her own, but is impelled by the motion of the turning earth. It is of this that he now thinks, and his tragic loss has thus become a human enlargement, for while she lived his imagination had not extended to the globe that sustains life just as it contains death. Thus the poem is not merely a statement about a girl who has been loved and has died, but about our attitudes to life and death.

Both Blake and Wordsworth used the popular stanza for their own purposes; their admiration for simplicity arises from meditation on the significance of simplicity, so that they are commonly least simple in their meanings when they are simplest in their expression. Neither was really 'a poet of the people' in the sense that many anonymous medieval poets were. The close connection between popular and sophisticated culture in England had broken soon after the 16th century. Scotland preserved the relationship between the two levels to a greater extent, and the lyrics of Robert Burns* (1759–96) used popular idiom as Wordsworth, and even Blake, scarcely attempted to use it – to make a genuine popular poetry which was also sophisticated. Walter Scott* (1771–1832) was further from the common people than his compatriot Burns was, but he had intense antiquarian interests, and he not only collected and edited traditional ballads, but composed ballads in the authentic idiom, such as *Proud Maisie*. But it was the English poet, Coleridge, who used the form of the traditional ballad for poetry on the grand scale, by directing the style with his fully equipped, intellectual imagination.

Where the broadside ballad, used by Wordsworth, had been topical and realistic, the traditional ballad, followed by Coleridge, was legendary and sometimes magical. Both forms were usually distinct and concrete in detail, gaining their effects by concentrating on bare statement of dramatic high points. Coleridge's *The Ancient Mariner** (1798) is a mystical poem about the infection of the mind by desolation and its recovery of the sources of spontaneous life. The theme is mysterious and obscure, but the traditional style of ballad released it for Coleridge so that he could express it in distinct imagery that appeals directly to the imagination even when it is obscure to the reason. The remarkable strength of the poem is the quality of intense sensation associated with states of mind:

Down dropt the breeze, the sails dropt down,
'Twas sad as sad could be;
And we did speak only to break
The silence of the sea!

All in a hot and copper sky,
The bloody Sun, at noon,
Right up above the mast did stand,
No bigger than the Moon.

Day after day, day after day,
We stuck, nor breath nor motion;
As idle as a painted ship
Upon a painted ocean.

The quatrain and similar popular stanzas were the media of much of the very best poetry of the Romantic Period, but most of it appeared between 1789 and 1805. The style required great clarity in the imagination and singleness of conviction. The complexities of the age destroyed these, and the later phase of the period drove poets to complex forms.

6.3.4 *Revival of the elaborate stanza*

The cultivation of simplicity – of the direct response of the child and of the humble man and woman – was the earliest phase of romanticism; its other and on the whole later manifestation was the outpouring of emotion by the force of strong psychic pressures, and this resulted in very varied and liquid verse forms. When the emotion issued from brief but intense illumination or from strong indignation, the Miltonic sonnet was a natural medium. Milton had transformed the sonnet into a short poem with close unity of feeling throughout. Wordsworth revived the sonnet in this form; in his later years he often used it mechanically, but his earlier sonnets are some of his best short poems, for instance, *Upon Westminster Bridge*. Shelley* (*eg Ozymandias**) and Keats* (*eg When I have fears that I may* *cease to be*) are the other great sonnet writers; they varied the rhyme pattern, but they nearly always used the form as Wordsworth and Milton did. For long poems – they were often narratives – the Romantics tried or revived almost all the recognized possibilities, from the long lines and free rhythms of Blake's* prophetic books to the exacting pattern of the Spenserian stanza*, used by Byron* in *Childe Harold**, by Shelley in *Adonais**, and by Keats in *The Eve of St Agnes**. Sometimes a form is used carelessly, as Byron used the 10-syllable couplet in some of his narratives and as Keats used it in *Endymion**, chiefly because it was familiar and seemed easy; sometimes it was a careful emulation of style, like Keats's use of Miltonic blank verse in his *Hyperion**; sometimes it was an invention for special needs, like the almost free verse of Blake. It is a main weakness of the Romantic poets after 1805 that their form is too often mechanical (in the later Wordsworth) or excessively fluid – like the early Keats and much of Shelley. The later and best work of Byron (*The Vision of Judgement**, 1822, and *Don Juan**, 1819–24) shows how he solved the problem: he found in the 8-line stanza (ottava rima*) a supple form in which he could write relaxed and skilful anti-poetry, which he used to mock the insincerity of manners confused with morals, and of styles adopted without conviction. At the same time, if he chose, he could stiffen the medium into real eloquence when his own convictions overcame him. Yet it is not true that the other poets found no style of their own after the quatrain and the conversation poem in blank verse had outlived their usefulness; they evolved the Romantic Ode, and this was a development which by its very nature shows their dilemma in regard to form.

The English ode* has a history that goes back to the Elizabethan poets. It had two forms, each of which derives from classical literature: the Pindaric Ode, originated by the Greek poet Pindar*, and the Horatian Ode derived from the work of the Roman poet Horace*. The latter was really a solemn style of lyric; it was emulated very nobly in very different ways by various poets, notably Andrew Marvell* (*Cromwell's Return from Ireland*, 1650) and William Collins* (*eg Ode to Evening*, 1747). The Pindaric Ode was originally an elaborate hymn, designed to be sung by a choir divided into two parts, and to be accompanied by dance. Its verse form was strictly functional in relation to the music, but without the music the form seems to be highly irregular, with stanzas and lines of uneven lengths. English imitators from Ben Jonson* (1572–1637) to Thomas Gray* (1716–71) varied greatly in their understanding of the true nature of the Pindaric Ode, but they all used it for the kind of inspiration that proceeded from a noble theme demanding the fullest scope of the poet's orchestration of language. Before 1800, the finest examples were undoubtedly the marriage hymns (*Epithalamion*, 1595, and *Prothalamion*, 1596) by Edmund Spenser, but these were analogies rather than imitations.

The Romantic Ode differed from those of previous periods chiefly in its strongly personal rather than public expressiveness. Wordsworth's *Ode to Duty* is in this respect not typical, either in its mood or in the strictness of its stanza form; the poem is called an ode for the traditional reason that it has a very solemn theme. His *Ode: Intimations of Immortality** (1802–6) has the irregularity of the Pindaric movement, and it is a personal record of the nature of the visionary imagination in early childhood, its slow passing in later life, and his desperate clinging to its vestiges. The poem is 207 lines long, and has 11 stanzas which vary in length from 9 to 38 lines; each stanza has its independent rhyme scheme, and varying line lengths. Coleridge's *Dejection: an Ode** (1802) has a comparable theme – both are poems about creative power – and it has a similar though less extreme irregularity of form. Here is the fourth stanza.

O Lady! we receive but what we give
And in our life alone does Nature live:
Ours is her wedding garment, ours her shroud!
  And would we aught behold, of higher worth
Than that inanimate cold world allowed
To the poor loveless ever-anxious crowd,
  Ah! from the soul itself must issue forth
A light, a glory, a fair luminous cloud
  Enveloping the Earth –
And from the soul itself must there be sent
  A sweet and potent voice, of its own birth,
Of all sweet sounds the life and element!

In both Odes, though the stanza pattern is fluid, the basic rhythm is that of the familiar 10-syllable line. It is the rhythm that influences the reader's response most intimately, so that he is made to feel that he starts with a recognizable formal principle, and he is then swept to the edge of formlessness by the stanza variation; this range from recognizable form to something near the dissolution of form corresponds to the range from assurance to dissolution of assurance in the poetic emotions expressed. The predominant effect is that of movement, like the pressure of a strong wind, and in the 7th stanza of *Dejection* Coleridge uses the wind as an image of creative passion. Shelley uses the same image in his *Ode to the West Wind* (1819). This poem has an unusual but much more regular stanza pattern, with no resemblance to the traditional Pindaric shape, but the same effect of strong movement. The stanzas are 'terza rima'* (*ie* of 3 lines, rhyming *a b a b c b c d c* etc.) and grouped into 5 paragraphs of 4 triplets and a rhymed couplet each. The sentences drive through the stanzas with impetuous rhythms, so that the force of the wind is conveyed by the language, and it is this movement, rather than the stanza divisions, that the reader – still more the listener – notices. If we use these three poems as a basis for describing the Romantic Ode as a poetic form, we can say that the word 'Ode' is no longer being used to indicate a particular verse structure (as 'sonnet' still is) but to indicate a poem of medium length and high intensity which is sustained throughout; the characteristic theme is, in general, the force that makes for intensity of living, and in particular it is the act of poetic creation.

These are again the themes of the greatest odes of the period, those by John Keats: *Indolence*, *A Grecian Urn*, *Melancholy*, *Psyche*, *A Nightingale*, and *Autumn*, all written from March to September in 1819. Of these, the *Ode to Psyche* is nearest to the Pindaric shape which Wordsworth and Coleridge recognizably imitated; the others have consistent length and rhyme scheme in their stanzas. The first stanza of the last and greatest, the *Ode to Autumn*, is as follows:

Season of mists and mellow fruitfulness,
   Close bosom-friend of the maturing sun;
Conspiring with him how to load and bless
   With fruit the vines that round the thatch-eves run;
To bend with apples the moss'd cottage-trees,
   And fill all fruit with ripeness to the core;
      To swell the gourd, and plump the hazel shells
   With a sweet kernel; to set budding more,
And still more, later flowers for the bees,
Until they think warm days will never cease,
   For summer has o'er-brimmed their clammy cells.

It is a poem of fulfilment, almost of excess, but the third and last stanza hints the approach of winter and of death. Keats reconciles within the poem the opposing principles in life which had tormented him in his other odes – the principles of fulfilment and of denial. Each of the writers of odes whom we have been considering was concerned with the same or similar themes, but only Keats found a resolution of the split without some loss of integrity caused by wishfulness taking the place of authentic vision. The strong pressure of movement in the odes by the other poets is partly the pressure of desire to force the poem through to a solution of the unease which inspired it, but the urgency in Keats is marked by density rather than movement; the difference is partly suggested by the consistency of form in his odes, though they still have the amplitude characteristic of the Pindaric tradition.

The lyric in the ballad tradition, the conversation poem, and the ode, together make up the most characteristic and the most impressive achievements of the High Romantic period, but of the three, perhaps only the conversation poem made an important contribution to poetic form later in the century.

6.4

Late Romanticism to Post-Romanticism: 1830–1940

6.4.1 *Dramatic monologue and derivative forms*

The year 1830 marks a halt in the history of English poetry. This is partly owing to biographical accident. Four of the six great Romantics were dead, and Crabbe, the fine belated Augustan, died in 1832; Coleridge died in 1834, and he had long ceased to produce important work. Only Wordsworth lived on until 1850, but his great period also was over. The outstanding new poet was Alfred Tennyson*; he published his first significant volume in 1830, but it was not until 1833 that he began to show his real power, and in that year also his chief rival, Robert Browning*, started publication. The phase of what we may call late Romanticism began with these two, but the auspices were unhappier for the new period than they had been for that of high Romanticism. When, in 1824, the grief-stricken boy Alfred Tennyson went on to the moors and wrote on a rock 'Byron is dead', he showed more foresight than he knew; the last period in which poetry dominated imaginative literature had ended. It was first shaken in the second half of the 17th century, when poets for the first time felt the need to emulate the virtues of prose, but the confusion of the French Revolution caused emotional disturbance of a kind that poetry was better fitted than prose to resolve. However, 1830 or thereabout is the beginning of an age dominated by a practical logic which not only diminished the public demand for poetry, but inhibited poetic creation. The Industrial Revolution* and the steam railway concentrated the minds of the middle classes on the gaining of wealth, and those of the working classes on finding practical remedies for their hardships. In philosophy, the hard reason of the political economists sought efficient means for the accomplishment of concrete ends, and the physical sciences, beginning with Lyell's* *Principles of Geology* (1830–3), were already changing the vision of the human past from the material of myth into material for statistical measurement. The human imagination still demanded satisfaction, but found it in the novel, which could place social statistics in a human context. The poet still had a public function: he was expected to transfigure the hard facts by a golden aura, or sweeten the present by a nostalgia for the past that was, or seemed, free of them. But the poet was also a man of his age; how could he satisfy men's longings for the ideal when he was himself afflicted by doubt?

Tennyson found a partial solution by evolving the 'dramatic monologue'*, a form in which a figure, from legend or history or the poet's invention, was used as a voice for the emotions the poet chooses to express. The device was essentially new, though it had a history: Chaucer had made his Wife of Bath and Pardoner render full confessions of their lives; Shakespeare and dramatists contemporary with him caused characters such as Hamlet to address their thoughts aloud, from time to time, in 'dramatic soliloquy' to the audience; Wordsworth and Coleridge had talked to each other and to their friends in 'conversation poems'. The Victorian dramatic monologue probably found readers predisposed in its favour through recalling the blank verse of dramatic soliloquy, but it was with the conversation poem that it had closest connections. The difference between the two forms is that the Victorian poet felt the need to evade identification with the emotions that he was expressing, either because they might offend the optimistic rationalist prejudices of his age, or because they were too complex for the poet himself to understand. Tennyson's characters (Oenone, the Lotus-Eaters, Ulysses, Tithonus, Teiresias, the unnamed character in *Maud*) spoke Tennyson's emotions, but the disguise both concealed and released them. We can see the way in which this happens if we examine a passage from *Ulysses* (1842). The theme is not from Homer but from Dante's *Inferno*; the hero wanderer, having reached his homeland, is contemplating one last voyage.

This is my son, mine own Telemachus,
To whom I leave the sceptre and the isle, –
Well-loved of me, discerning to fulfil
This labour, by slow prudence to make mild
A rugged people, and through soft degrees
Subdue them to the useful and the good.

. . . .

Death closes all; but something ere the end,
Some work of noble note, may yet be done,
Not unbecoming men that strove with gods.
The lights begin to twinkle from the rocks;
The long day wanes; the slow moon climbs; the deep
Moans round with many voices. Come, my friends,
'Tis not too late to seek a newer world.
Push off, and sitting well in order smite
The sounding furrows; for my purpose holds
To sail beyond the sunset, and the baths
Of all the western stars, until I die.

There are three voices in these two extracts, though the whole poem is the speech by a single man. When Ulysses speaks of Telemachus, he uses the voice of the public conscience in Tennyson, expressing approval of social advancement of a practical kind. When he addresses the sailors directly ('Come, my friends . . .') he uses the voice of public enterprise, and the diction recalls clichés from Elizabethan blank verse ('Some work of noble note') to remind the reader of the adventuring merchants of Elizabethan days. The third voice is the true one, and brings the verse to life with Tennyson's remarkable command of vowel music and rhythmic pauses – 'The long day wanes; the slow moon climbs' – and it is used when the speaker contemplates the actual voyage or its outset. The poet is contemplating an experience, the richness, beauty and drama of which has nothing to do with social engineering or public enterprise.

In his greatest poem, *In Memoriam** (1833–50), the dramatic monologue becomes a meditation in Tennyson's own voice, because here he has a pretext for the expression of his grief and doubt – a reason that he can publicly acknowledge: the death of his friend Arthur Hallam. In *The Princess* (1847) and the *Idylls of the King** (1859–85) he turned from monologue to romantic narrative, a much less original form in which he wrote less interesting poetry because he was giving the public what they liked, not what he felt. Other poets – Matthew Arnold* in *Empedocles on Etna* (1852) and Arthur Hugh Clough* in *Dipsychus* (1869) – expressed their doubts in poems which have a mixture of monologue and dialogue. Arnold also criticized his age in meditative poems like *Dover Beach* which resemble the early Romantic conversation poem more closely than the dramatic monologue does, and in Keatsian odes like *The Scholar Gipsy** and *Thyrsis*. Arnold and Clough did not yield to a compromise with the spirit of the age as Tennyson did, except that they used the 'consecrated language' of the Spenserian tradition which gives their verse – especially Arnold's – the effect of poetry of withdrawal. Only Robert Browning really attempted the voice of actuality.

Browning is the poet with whom the dramatic monologue form is most closely associated. Through his monologues he displayed attitudes to a wide range of subjects, but his poems show him as less interested in the subjects than in his characters – in the textures of their states of mind. His imagination thus bore closer resemblance to that of a novelist than Tennyson's did, and his most ambitious poem, *The Ring and the Book* (1868–9), is a bold experiment at a verse novel, constructed by juxtaposing monologues each of which presents an independent view of the same event. His monologues also bring to mind the 'confessional' speeches of Chaucer's characters in *The Canterbury Tales*. However, this comparison shows an important difference: a Chaucer character, virtuous or otherwise, is the shape of one kind of human life seen in relation to a whole philosophy of human life, whereas a Browning character is merely an attitude to one aspect of life, and this attitude is unrelated to a coherent philosophy, for Browning did not possess one. Yet his speakers use the diction and cadence of men and women really struggling with living problems, and poetry badly needed that kind of invigoration at the time Browning wrote. The following extract is from *Andrea del Sarto* (1855). Del Sarto was a Renaissance artist so perfect in technique that he was called 'the faultless painter', but his facility exceeded his strength of feeling. Browning shows him recognizing the difference between himself and men of lesser talent but more inspiration; the artist is talking to his mistress:

At any rate 'tis easy, all of it,
No sketches first, no studies, that's long past –
I do what many dream of all their lives
– Dream? strive to do, and agonize to do,
And fail in doing. I could count twenty such
On twice your fingers, and not leave this town,
Who strive – you don't know how the others strive
To paint a little thing like that you smeared
Carelessly passing with your robes afloat –
Yet do so much less, so much less, Someone says,
(I know his name, no matter) so much less!
Well, less is more, Lucrezia! I am judged.

The strength of Browning's portraits is in the detail: the flavour of actual converse, and the catching of transient particulars like 'Carelessly passing with your robes afloat'. He brings our imaginations close to the subject, often with the loss of what surrounds it; his insistence on the expression of the speaker's voice is often at the expense of all that underlies the voice – the psychological, inexpressible depths. His poetry betrays the weakness of Victorian* materialist bias, which felt human minds as objects, and objects as final and irreducible. But the 20th-century consciousness does not feel like this: objects dissolve under analysis into fields of force, and the mind is a field in which conflicting forces strive to find balance and coherence. The difference means that we have a much less distinct sense of well-defined human identity.

The chief 20th-century master of the dramatic monologue is T. S. Eliot*; he brought to bear upon it his training as a sceptical philosopher, a strong admiration for French 19th-century symbolism*, and a radical rethinking of the problem of poetic rhythm based partly on revaluation of the Jacobean* dramatists of Shakespeare's time and just after. His early longer poems are monologues in a new style: *Prufrock* and *Portrait of a Lady* (1917), and *Gerontion* (1920). *The Waste Land** is a disguised dramatic poem to which many voices contribute, a 20th-century mutation of the 19th-century literary drama such as Arnold's *Empedocles* or Clough's *Dipsychus*. From *Ash Wednesday** (1930) to his greatest poems, *Four Quartets** (1935–42), Eliot moved from the monologue to the meditation in verse.

In *Reflections on Vers Libre* (1917) he wrote: 'But the most interesting verse in our language has been done either by taking a very simple verse form, like the Iambic pentameter, and constantly withdrawing from it, or taking no form at all, and constantly approximating to a very simple one.' Eliot used changing rhythms and verse patterns for different ranges of feeling in the same poem, and related them by images held together by association, not narrative or logical sequence as in most previous poems. This makes some of his poems peculiarly difficult, especially *Prufrock* and *The Waste Land*. *Prufrock* is a man arguing with himself, as Browning's characters argue, but the argument is not conducted as though he is speaking to a listener, but as his conflicting feelings arise and sink. *The Waste Land* assembles round images which in turn assemble round a central image, the title of the poem, and the images are communicated through different voices each of which communicates through its characteristic rhythm. This is how the poem opens:

April is the cruellest month, breeding
Lilacs out of the dead land, mixing
Memory and desire, stirring
Dull roots with spring rain.
Winter kept us warm, covering
Earth in forgetful snow, feeding
A little life with dried tubers.
Summer surprised us, coming over the Starnbergersee
With a shower of rain; we stopped in the colonnade,
And went on in sunlight, into the Hofgarten,
And drank coffee, and talked for an hour.
Bin gar keine Russin, stamm' aus Litauen, echt deutsch.
And when we were children, staying at the arch-duke's,
My cousin's, he took me out on a sled,
And I was frightened. He said, Marie,
Marie, hold on tight. And down we went.
In the mountains, there you feel free.
I read, much of the night, and go south in the winter.

What are the roots that clutch, what branches grow
Out of this stony rubbish? Son of man,
You cannot say, or guess, for you know only
A heap of broken images, where the sun beats,
And the dead tree gives no shelter, the cricket no relief,
And the dry stone no sound of water.

The opening 7 lines are perhaps an example of 'taking no form at all, and . . . approximating to a very simple one'. The lines evoke the opening of Chaucer's *Prologue*; like Chaucer's lines, they evoke impersonally the effect of the seasons on the mind, and they approximate to a simple stanza pattern. But the images merge into a different rhythm and a different voice for lines 8–18. The basis is the iambic pentameter (10-syllable line), but the traditional rhythm is relaxed so as to express the trivial cadence of 'smart' conversation – the idiom of rich cosmopolitans, for whom the seasons mean nothing but a change of amusement and place of residence. At line 19 ('What are the roots . . .') the voice and the rhythm change again: the 10-syllable line is still the base, but the loose chattering rhythm has been replaced by the grave cadences of the English Bible. The land of no seasons is a desert – a 'waste land' – for it is a land which takes no account of birth, death, growth, and renewal. The rich can escape bad climates by travel, but the spiritual desert travels with them.

The long poem and poems of medium length between 1830 and 1914 showed the poet withdrawing into 'consecrated language'; the clearest example is probably Algernon Swinburne*, whose working life lasted from 1860 to 1908. The 'poetic' quality of the later Tennyson, of D. G. Rossetti*, William Morris* and Swinburne is above all a surface quality, and in this respect Browning is not an exception: he offers a different kind of surface to the mind. The importance of Eliot was his renewal of poetic language by restoring to it the dimension of depth. This does not mean that he used more philosophical or spiritual diction, but that he used language so that the mind can move within it, and feel its own depths. He achieved this by showing that some of the rules that govern prose are not necessarily relevant to poetry, by directing imagery and symbolism to a level of the mind beneath that at which it operates logically (as it does in prose), and by a more studied use of a wider range of rhythms than most poets of the 19th century attempted.

6.4.2 *The short poem*

It seems to many modern readers and critics that most poetry from 1830 to 1914 lacked certain kinds of strength to make it permanently very impressive. At least two poets are important exceptions to this generalization. These are the Jesuit, Gerard Manley Hopkins* (1844–89); and the poet and novelist Thomas Hardy* (1840–1928), whose most interesting work was written after he abandoned novel-writing near the end of the 19th century. Both were masters of the short poem, and to them we must add a poet who was greater than either: W. B. Yeats* (1865–1939), whose best period is contemporary with Eliot's, but who began his career in the Victorian period.

In his early poetry, Hopkins closely followed the style of John Keats. He seems to have renounced poetry in 1868 when he entered the Jesuit Order, but in 1875 he returned to it by writing *The Wreck of the Deutschland**, and from that poem onwards he wrote in a startlingly innovating style. Almost none of his poetry was published until 1918, and he accomplished only a small body of work. It is work of exceptional excellence, however, and its quality not only demonstrates the weakness of so much of the verse of his contemporaries, but anticipates qualities that 20th-century poets have aspired to. Part of his unusual strength was contributed by the coherence of Catholic philosophy; more important still was his distinguished critical power, enabling him to rethink problems of expression in a way that is comparable to Eliot's later reassessments. His rethinking led him to conclusions about rhythm, syntax, and diction. He saw that rhythm in contemporary poetry had become needlessly subservient to metrical patterns, and that medieval alliterative* verse and traditional popular verse such as the ballads* and nursery rhymes* followed the natural emphasis of accented syllables rather than the measured syllabic regularity of metre. This led him to syntax: he realized that the syntax of ordinary speech does not merely reflect the speaker's movement of thought, but operates on the mind of the listener and shapes it, as much as the choice of words does. In regard to diction, he remained a follower of Keats in the use of words to express the life of the senses, but while other Victorian poets – who also followed Keats in this respect – made their words mere reflections of sensuous life, Hopkins appreciated that Keats had given sensuous body to his words so that they constituted and aroused quite fresh sensations. He went beyond Keats by forming new words by combining existing ones, a practice common in Shakespeare and his contemporaries, and natural to the spirit of the English language in such formations as 'daredevil'. These principles give his poetry unusual concentration, which makes them difficult for general readers. One of the simplest is *Spring and Fall*, addressed to a child who is mourning the loss of leaves in Autumn; the accent marks (′) are Hopkins's own:

Márgarét, are you gríeving
Over Goldengrove unleaving?
Leáves, líke the things of man, you
With your fresh thoughts care for, can you?
Áh! as the heart grows older
It will come to such sights colder
By and by, nor spare a sigh
Though worlds of wanwood leafmeal lie;
And yet you wíll weep and know why.
Now no matter, child, the name:
Sórrow's spríngs áre the same.
No mouth had, no nor mind, expressed
What heart heard of, ghost guessed:
It ís the blight man was born for,
It is Margaret you mourn for.

The grace, brevity, and poise of this resembles Jonson's poem on his dead daughter (*6.2.4 – p. 291), but whereas Jonson sought a point of detachment, Hopkins makes his poem a personal address by balancing speech against metre in his emphases. The rhythm has four accents but an uneven number of syllables in each line; thus the parenthesis 'no nor mind' in the twelfth line is an example of the way in which Hopkins makes the syntax penetrate the reader's understanding, whereas the surface naturalness of Browning's speech rhythm commonly stops at the ear. In the eighth line 'wanwood leafmeal' are examples of Hopkins's word combinations: 'wan' + 'wood' gives to the falling of the foliage as the sap withdraws an immediate expression of failing life and 'leafmeal' is analogous to 'piecemeal' (*ie* 'in small pieces') as well as conveying the impression of the leaves as countless on the ground, like the 'meal' that is the edible grain separated from the wheat.

Hopkins is so fresh and original partly because he knew himself so isolated; he had no reading public save a few fellow-poets, who could at least be brought to understand his intentions even if they did not appreciate the result. Paradoxically, Hardy, who was a much more conservative poet, owes his originality precisely to his conservatism, but this conservatism, like Hopkins's innovations, derives from special circumstances. Unlike most of his contemporaries, he was socially of humble origin, and had grown up amidst the folksong and ballad of the west of England countryside. His conservatism was not of the passive sort, but derived from an active love of a traditional way of life. He wrote ballads in the traditional style, but his personality was distinctive. His atheism was, in its seriousness, closer to Hopkins's Catholicism than the conventional religion of most Victorians; at root it was the fatalism common to countrymen, and he infused into it strong compassion for the unhappiness of the human condition, and peculiar honesty. He had no use for theoretical innovation in poetry, and loved the tunefulness of the traditional lyric, but he could fill it with his personal diction, cadence, and exact observation, for instance in *At Day-Close in November* (1914):

The ten hours' light is abating
And a late bird wings across,
Where the pines like waltzers waiting,
Give their black heads a toss.

Beech leaves, that yellow the noon-time,
Float past like specks in the eye;
I set every tree in my June time,
And now they obscure the sky.

And the children who ramble through here
Conceive that there never has been
A time when no tall trees grew here,
That none will in time be seen.

The tunefulness of these lines comes near to jingle, especially with the double rhymes – 'through here,' 'grew here' – but the sense always imposes itself over the tune: in the first line the accent falls naturally on 'through', but in the fourth the sense shifts it to 'here', so that the tiresome jingle is lost. The symbols and the diction are never merely mechanical: the comparison of the pines with waiting dancers, as though the tempest makes them seem eager to spring from their roots, is unexpected, and so is 'yellow' used as a verb, and incidentally evoking the sunlight of noon.

Hardy wrote a great quantity of poetry, and much of it is slight; moreover it shows very little progression during his working life from the 1860s till his death in 1928. W. B. Yeats was in some respects as innovatory as Hopkins; in others, as conservative as Hardy; and his development, from his first volume in 1889 to his last poems in 1939, is very remarkable. He began in the aestheticism which was the legacy of Tennyson, though in him it was modified and strengthened by his strong feeling for his Irish homeland, at a time when Ireland* was undergoing historic invigoration. In the 1900s he showed himself to be the first poet of genuine dramatic talent since the 17th century, and it was partly the discipline of dramatic writing that caused him to achieve between 1910 and 1930 a mature style that greatly excelled the style of his early work. Yeats learnt from a wide variety of poets: from the objectivity of Chaucer, the strenuousness of Donne and the classical toughness of Jonson, the visionary symbolism of Blake and Shelley, the verbal melodiousness of the Pre-Raphaelites* (D. G. Rossetti and William Morris) who hung over his youth, and, to a less extent than Eliot, from the French 19th-century symbolists*. So wide a range of assimilation took time, and partly explains why Yeats's poetic personality matured only in advanced middle age, when he was over 50. By this time the Irish movement had exploded into civil war, and Yeats's style is not only armoured against the disrupting forces of national events and those of western Europe as a whole, but also tempered like fine steel to express his piercing insight into the confusion. On the one hand, he created his own world of changing symbols for the movements of the mind through history, and he enacted many different roles; on the other hand, he set against this multiplicity and experimentation with the consciousness a strict cultivation of traditional stanzaic forms and a full-bodied and yet austere diction – what he called 'a powerful and passionate syntax, and a complete coincidence between period and stanza' ('A General Introduction to my Work' in *Essays and Introductions*). This fusion of passion and exact form is exemplified in his *An Irish Airman Foresees his Death* (1919).

Yeats renewed, culminated, and counteracted the Romantic tendencies of the 19th century. He culminated them by the intensity of his cultivation of rhymed and metrical forms; he renewed them in the strength of his assurance in noble and heroic idealism, which the early Romantics recovered from the Renaissance, but which their successors could only associate with the past and with legend. He counteracted them by the vehemence of prophetic feeling with which he confronted what he felt to be the catastrophic quality of his own time. Yeats was probably the last poet who is a recognizable descendant from the Renaissance.

6.5

Modern English poetry: 1940–present day

Yeats and Eliot are great names in English poetry. Yeats died in 1939, and Eliot accomplished his best work with the completion of the *Four Quartets** in 1942.

Their influence, particularly that of Eliot, will be permanent, but its very strength has sent modern British poets looking elsewhere for inspiration. It has been, in Britain, an age of the short poem, for in every field of intellectual and imaginative life the spirit of the time is one of questioning; we are not in a climate of thought that nourishes ample forms sustained with intensity, as the long poem demands. Even the long poems of the 19th century sustained themselves by admitting passages that are as relaxed as prose – an expedient which the criticism and poetry of T. S. Eliot has made no longer tolerable to us. Behind the modern short poem can be seen the operation of at least three pressures: one is the desire for release from an over-organized society; a second, distrust of abandonment to emotion; and the third is the need to explore the limits of human experience.

Dylan Thomas* (1914–53) was a striking and controversial personality who achieved extraordinary prestige by what seems wild and random poetry, strongly rhythmical and extravagant in imagery. It resembles, rhythmically and in diction, the poetry of G. M. Hopkins, but Hopkins's poetry is only apparently extravagant, and is imbued with a tightly controlling discipline, whereas Thomas's work is often libertine. His popularity is partly due to reaction against the fastidious restraint of Eliot and the aristocratic passion of Yeats. Thomas was generously vulgar, in the sense of being a man of the crowd; he often read his poems publicly and his hypnotic, exuberant rhythms expressed for his audiences the joyful abandonment of pressing but often meaningless controls. Words in his poetry are released for unprecedented uses, as 'dumb' is in the following stanza from one of his lyrics:

The force that through the green fuse drives the flower
Drives my green age; that blasts the roots of trees
Is my destroyer.
And I am dumb to tell the crooked rose
My youth is bent by the same wintry fever.

Thomas wrote often uncritically, and his really good poems are few. In other poets he aroused distrust. One of the most characteristic figures of post-war English literature has been the young academic poet, who distrusts emotional abandonment because it is associated with the monstrosities of Nazism in the recent past, and with the hysteria of world-wide antagonisms in the present. Thus, in the 1950s the so-called Movement arose; it consisted of a group of poets who were concerned chiefly with the achievement of complete honesty of feeling and meticulously careful language. Among recent poets, the influence on this school has been neither Eliot nor Yeats, but – if anybody – Thomas Hardy. The reason for this is partly the feeling that neither Eliot, the American immigrant, nor Yeats, the Irish patriot, really understood the direction that English poetry was taking (for instance, in Hardy's work) when they stepped in and changed it. An example of the quiet, intelligent, sceptical poetry of the Movement is *On the Death of a Child* by D. J. Enright (born 1920):

The greatest griefs shall find themselves inside the smallest cage.
It is only then that we can hope to tame their rage,

The monsters we must live with. For it will not do
To hiss humanity because one human threw
Us out of heart and home. Or part

At odds with life because one baby failed to live.
Indeed, as little as the subject is the wreath we give–

The big words fail to fit. Like giant boxes
Round small bodies. Taking up improper room,
Where so much withering is, and so much bloom.

The words are simple, the rhythm almost unnoticeable and yet carefully judged; even the rhyme is inconspicuous, almost as though it might be accidental. But the thought is not simple, and the imagery bears the mark of a poet—one of a generation – who has concentrated attention on the considered 'conceits' of the Metaphysicals, especially George Herbert (1593–1633). We are far away from the Romantics.

Behind the third pressure upon modern poetry – the need to explore the limits of human experience – stands the remarkable genius of D. H. Lawrence* (1888–1930). Lawrence was a minor poet, though he was a great novelist, but his prose and his poetry are closely related in a way that is rare among writers who use both media. In both he explored the physical nature of man, where he believed the true life sources to be, and this led him to write with liveliness, sensitiveness, and originality about animals. Just because he discerned the continuity of the animal nature with man, he was careful not to confuse the two: animals in his prose and poetry possess their own life, and are brought within our reach by the delicate perceptions of the writer. The poetry of Ted Hughes (born 1930) has the same theme. The following example by Hughes, *The Thought-Fox*, expresses the sensation of original, imaginative thought arising in the mind. Because it is original, it is new and strange to the thinker, like a wild animal:

I imagine this midnight moment's forest:
Something else is alive
Beside the clock's loneliness
And this blank page where my fingers move.

Through the window I see no star:
Something more near
Though deeper within darkness
Is entering the loneliness:

Cold, delicately as the dark snow,
A fox's nose touches twig, leaf;
Two eyes serve a movement, that now
And again now, and now, and now

Sets neat prints into the snow
Between trees, and warily a lame
Shadow lags by stump and in hollow
Of a body that is bold to come

Across clearings, an eye,
A widening deepening greenness,
Brilliantly, concentratedly,
Coming about its own business

Till, with a sudden sharp hot stink of fox
It enters the dark hole of the head.
The window is starless still; the clock ticks,
The page is printed.

The poem is both the exploration of an animal, and an expression of the physical affinity of the human mind; behind it lies a long chain of influences. The fox is a metaphysical conceit for the awakening of thought; the pre-conscious experience of the process of awakening is like Wordsworth's; the light, careful rhythm and the familiar but carefully chosen words sensitively placed are modern.

The three pressures behind contemporary English poetry are not really so unrelated as they may seem. Thomas's transporting rhythms and violent experiment in imagery and diction are related to Hughes's attempt to reach into life-experience beyond the human consciousness, just as what Hughes is doing is also to release the imagination from its lifeless controls. The sceptical, measured, self-critical poetry of the poets of the Movement – who now write independently of one another – is a justified control of feeling through the educated judgement. Hughes's kind of poetry is perhaps the most interesting that is being written today, because it is pointing in the direction in which we may expect English poetry to move – the direction of the question 'What is human?' It is a question that will gain importance as the traditions of European civilization receive ever less unquestioned acceptance.

A Literary Party at Sir Joshua Reynolds's. This shows Dr Johnson, the great critic, in the company of some members of his circle, including David Garrick and Reynolds himself. He held an unusually central position in English intellectual society, drawing his friends and admirers from almost every branch of it.

7 The history of English critical thought

Introduction

At no time is literary criticism, as a body of writing, equivalent to the total body of meaningful literary ideas. Critical writing in English was, in fact, inconsiderable before the reign of Queen Elizabeth I* (1558–1603), and it was only after 1660 that criticism became a recognized profession – that is to say, a pursuit to which men of ability and even genius gave the best part of their energies and their time. But this does not mean that Chaucer* in the 14th century wrote with no critical theory behind him, or that the reason Shakespeare* seems to have ignored the leading critical teachings of his age was that he was uncritically indifferent to them. Literary criticism is the application of thought to the business of writing, and it is therefore an inevitable part of imaginative writing, although the imaginative writer is only recognized as a critic if he expresses his ideas on literature to the public. It follows that imaginative writing of a high order can exist without the accompaniment of any explicit literary criticism at all, but it cannot exist without ideas about literature. We need therefore to consider three questions: first, where did these ideas come from, in periods when there was no discoverable literary criticism? Second, if the professional critic is unnecessary for the production of fine literature, why did he ever come into existence? Third, what is the value of literary criticism, apart from the guidance that it offers to the imaginative writer?

Part of the answer to the first question has already been given: the imaginative writer has always been his own critic. But ideas do not operate in isolation, and imaginative creation is a social activity. The poet, before the age of printed books, must have learned his art by listening to poems already in existence, and by sharing the response of the rest of the audience; in other words, when he began writing he found himself in a tradition of writing. He might, in his own thinking, depart from this tradition, but he could not start afresh as though no literature had ever existed, for his own mind was influenced by the way of life which had shaped the literature of his age. This way of life, in turn, was shaped by material forces – such as the methods of food production and distribution – and by ideas about the proper social regulation of these forces. Thus the poet would also write in the light of the general ideas, the philosophy, that prevailed over himself and his audience. Literary thought proceeded, and still extensively proceeds, from three sources, apart from literary criticism: from the writer's own mind in the act of creating, from the tradition that has shaped his mind, and from the philosophy and religion which has shaped the tradition.

The critic came into existence owing to an increase in the size of the public for literature. Before the introduction of printed books and the extension of interest in education caused by the Renaissance*, the well-informed public for literature was small. By 1580 printing had been in use in England for a century. The Renaissance had prevailed, and 1580 was the approximate date of the writing of the first important critical essay in English – Sir Philip Sidney's *Apology for Poetry**.

***Indicates mention in the reference section.**

But Sidney was a nobleman, for whom literature was not a profession but one of the activities regarded as fit for an aristocrat of the time. Printing and the enlarged audience for books, however, produced the professional man of letters who pursued literature as a whole-time activity. As books became more and more widely available, the professional writer sometimes sought public support for his ideas, so as to encourage a climate of taste favourable to him; we have the debate of 1602 between the poets Campion* and Daniel* about the value of rhyme.

This desire to influence a large public gives us an important part of the answer to our third question, about the purposes of literary criticism. It has seldom been directed principally at imaginative writers, but rather at their publics, and critics have often been imaginative writers who desire, in Wordsworth's* phrase, to create the taste by which they are to be appreciated. Yet criticism has always been more than a kind of literary publicity. When it has been directed at contemporary work, it has been one of the chief instruments for the assessment of the character and quality of contemporary civilization, since the literature of any period is a principal manifestation of its civilization. When it has been directed at literature of the past, it has been one of the chief instruments for understanding the contribution that the past makes, or could make, to the civilization of the present. The critic only fully entered into these larger functions in the 18th century, and in doing so the great critics – Samuel Johnson* (1709–84) and Matthew Arnold* (1822–88) became themselves memorable exponents of the phase of civilization that they represented.

But literary criticism has elaborated since the 16th century, and it early becomes difficult to describe the critical function simply. We can make a broad distinction between applied criticism, concerned with the assessment of particular works or writers, and theoretical criticism, concerning the relationship of imaginative literature to the rest of human experience, but even this separation of functions becomes unreal when it is used for a critic of any spaciousness of mind. Moreover we need, once again, to remind ourselves that literary ideas are not the monopoly of the critic, so that we cannot afford to ignore some imaginative and didactic writers who have written little or no specifically literary criticism although they indirectly exemplify thinking about literature.

7.1

From the Middle Ages to the High Renaissance (1350–1660): the beginnings of English criticism

Touching thy lettre, thou art wys y-nough,
I woot[1] *thou nilt it digneliche*[2] *endyte;*
As make it with these argumentes tough:
Ne scrivenish[3] *or craftilie*[4] *it wryte;*
Beblotte it with thy teres eek a lyte;
And if thou wryte a goodly word al softe,
Though it be good, reherce it not to ofte

[1] know [2] scornfully [3] like a professional letter-writer
[4] in a studied manner

Chaucer – *Troilus and Criseyde** II.147

Nature never set forth the earth in so rich tapestry as divers Poets have done, neither with pleasant rivers, fruitful trees, sweet smelling flowers, nor whatsoever else may make the too much loved earth more lovely. Her world is brazen, the poets only deliver a golden.

Sidney – *Apology for Poetry**

These quotations illustrate approaches to literature in the Middle Ages* and the Renaissance*. The extract from Chaucer* is part of Pandarus's advice to Troilus on the composing of a love-letter; Pandarus is giving a lesson in persuasive writing – that is to say, what the Middle Ages and the Renaissance called the Art of Rhetoric. The extract from Sidney* concerns the justification for imaginative writing. Sidney and his contemporaries were as interested in rhetoric as the medieval writers were, and the latter, too, attended to the problem of whether the imaginative writer – we will call him the poet, since most imaginative writing hitherto had been in verse – served a useful purpose in society. Sidney, however, discusses this problem in terms that revive the ancient discussion of it by the Greek philosophers, Plato* and Aristotle*, in the 5th–4th centuries BC. By doing so, he made himself one of the earliest (though not the first) writers of what we now recognize as literary criticism.

Medieval men scarcely had a use for what we call literary criticism, although they valued rhetoric. They inherited the Roman system of education, according to which studies were divided into the Quadrivium*, (arithmetic, geometry, music, astronomy), and the Trivium (grammar, rhetoric, logic). Medieval rhetoric classified various kinds of oratory – persuasive speech – and elaborated principles of order and technique in effective persuasion. Such principles influenced the poets – for instance Chaucer – by giving them a rhetorical structure for the argumentative poems that are so common in medieval literature. But imaginative writing is really distinct from rhetoric; the purpose of the latter is chiefly to induce action, whereas the poet seeks above all to awaken the imagination and give pleasure to the mind. Medieval thinkers were aware of this difference, but their framework of ideas supplied no terms by which the activity of imaginative literature could be independently justified as an important one. They saw that poetry could serve rhetoric and grammar as exemplification of their principles; they saw that it could serve theology, as Dante's *Divine Comedy** and Langland's *Piers Plowman** can be said to do, by giving true guidance; they tolerated secular poetry, if it did not conduce to vice, as harmless recreation. Otherwise, the Church, which governed the medieval intellect, distrusted imaginative literature. In the Church's beginnings under the Roman Empire, classical literary culture had been one of its chief opponents. The rise of allegory* and fable* in the Middle Ages was partly due to the medieval vision of the surrounding world, but it also arose from the need to justify the study of pre-Christian classical literature by making out that its fictions were capable of moral interpretation; commentators developed habits of interpreting texts according to four classes of meaning – the literal, the moral, the allegorical, and the spiritual. Literature that resisted this kind of handling was potentially dangerous, and the drama was distrusted most of all. The Middle Ages were intensely dramatic in feeling, and the Mass – the official ritual of religious worship – was itself a drama, but the Church could find no justification for a secular drama. Even the Mystery* plays, which had Bible subjects and originated in the Mass, and the Moralities*, which instructed the public in right living through allegorical fictions, were suspect because of the secular elements that intruded into them. It is understandable, then, that Chaucer, in his Prologue to *The Canterbury Tales** (725–742), should seek to prevent disapproval by warning his readers that he means to write of men as they are, as a narrator should –

> *Or elles he moot telle a tale untrewe*
> *Or feyne a thing, or finde wordes newe*

– that is, tell lies or use an unnatural diction. Christ himself, he reminds them, used 'broad' language in the Holy Scriptures, and Plato had said that, for discriminating readers, 'The wordes moot be cosin to the dede' – that is to say, human language had to be consistent with human behaviour.

Chaucer's use of Christ and Plato as evidence in favour of his own practice illustrates the background against which medieval men thought about literature. Plato was the pagan philosopher whom the early Christian Church found most congenial, and in the tenth book of his *Republic** he argues that poets should be banished from the ideal state. He agrees that poets are 'inspired', and that for this reason they deserve the greatest respect, but he declares that since they create images of earthly objects and happenings, they only make imitations of imitations, for it was the essence of his philosophy that earthly objects are only imperfect reflections of heavenly forms. This philosophy harmonized conveniently with Christian thinking about the relationship of the earthly and the Divine: theology, medieval thinkers said, was the 'poetry of God', and the best that earthly poetry could do was to act as an assistant to that sacred poetry. The Roman rhetoricians Cicero* and Quintilian based literature strongly in ethics and thus gave further support to the medieval conception of literature under the discipline of a theologically controlled philosophy. The ancient writer who might have countered this whole line of thought was Aristotle. In the 13th century he superseded Plato as the leading influence upon medieval philosophy, but his *Poetics** was not rediscovered until 1498, in Italy. The date is significant: the Italian Renaissance was in full tide, and in consequence both classical verse and contemporary poetry were more highly esteemed by scholars and philosophers – by the Renaissance 'humanists'* – than it had been for many centuries.

The Renaissance arose from the rediscovery, chiefly by Italians, of many more texts of Greek and Latin literature than the Middle Ages had previously known. This rediscovery acted like a slowly mounting flood of illumination upon western Europe. It led to improved scholarship in the editing and publishing of texts, and to a much heightened esteem for education. This was no longer seen as predominantly a means for supplying the Church with the 'clerks' that it needed; it became an independent means of intellectual fulfilment. The humanists did not seek to antagonize the Church, but their absorption in classical literature and the ardour for education that they propagated necessarily had a secularizing influence, and this was encouraged by the rise of the modern state, in which sovereigns like Henry VIII* (1509–47) were inclined to subject the Church, within their frontiers, to themselves. This new political society found that it had in common with ancient Greece and Rome an interest in 'great men'. Rhetoricians like Roger Ascham* (1515–68) still emphasized the need for moral instructiveness in literature, and the poets commonly agreed, but they now exercised this function through stories of the lives of 'great men', as in the *Mirror for Magistrates** (1559). Moreover, this moral instructiveness of the lives and fortunes of great men now justified the existence of serious secular drama such as Sackville and Norton's *Gorboduc** (1561).

The study of Aristotle's *Poetics* by Italian humanists greatly contributed to this new prestige of drama, since drama is Aristotle's main subject, but his book did more: it provided a philosophical justification for poetry that was independent of theology, and it also provided a new terminology for literary criticism. Aristotle seems to have been writing in reply to Plato's philosophical condemnation of poetry; he shows that both Plato's conception of the nature of poetic imitation, and his idea that poetic art morally damages the public, are mistaken. Aristotle agrees with Plato in supposing that poetry 'imitates' nature, but he disagrees with him in his refusal to accept Plato's narrow interpretation of imitation as mimicry. Poetry is imitation of nature *in a given medium*, that is to say in language, and specifically in one or another literary form – epic, tragedy, comedy, or the lyric. To imitate nature in a medium is to re-create it in that medium, in such a way that not only can it not confuse the public in their perception of spiritual realities, but in its finest achievements it will have a most healthful influence on this perception.

In the first half of the 16th century, Italian critics such as Julius Caesar Scaliger (1484–1558), not only welcomed Aristotle's theories but expanded them, and in the second half, English critics, under Italian influence, began to do the same. Possibly the first of them was George Puttenham*, whose *Art of English Poesy* was published in 1589 although he may have written it in the 1560s. Puttenham describes poetry as the most ancient of arts and poets as the originators of learning, 'the first philosophers, the first astronomers and historiographers and orators and musicians in the world'. From this early eminence Puttenham regards the status of poet as having fallen into contempt, 'for commonly who so is studious in the art or shows himself excellent in it, they call him in disdain a *fantastical*; and a light headed or fantastical man (by conversion) they call a poet'. 'Fantasy' and 'imagination' are distinguished in modern English, the former having the sense of 'extravagant and falsifying imagination', but in the 16th century they were often synonymous. Consequently, Puttenham goes on to distinguish, consistently with Aristotle, between the bad delusive use of the imagination and the good, creative use of it, 'and of this sort of fantasy are all good Poets, notable Captains . . . all cunning artificers and engineers, all Legislators, Politicians, and Councillors of State, in whose exercises the inventive part is most employed, and is to the sound and true judgment of man most needful'.

That the imagination is the crucial faculty for all, whether scientists or artists, who employ original thought ('the inventive part') needs no argument today, but in the 16th century, partly because it was a highly imaginative period, the imagination was regarded as a treacherous, deceitful and dangerous faculty, in need of constant discipline by the reason. This indeed was why Puttenham had to defend it, and a still more persuasive defence was made by Sir Philip Sidney* in his *Apology* (*ie* Defence) *for Poetry*, which was written soon after 1580 and published in 1595. It remains the single famous classic of English 16th-century criticism, and it may have been provoked by the attack on the poetry of the day by Stephen Gosson in his *School of Abuse* (1579). Gosson had been a poet who was converted to extreme Protestantism (*ie* Puritanism*), which carried on, with much less tolerance, the medieval tradition of distrust of imaginative art. He consequently took the Platonic side against poetry. Sidney's Anglican Protestantism was much broader in its cultural vision; he answered Gosson in Aristotelian terms, yet also in the spirit of Platonic and Christian idealism. He saw the function of poetry in relation to the traditional medieval conceptions of nature; on the one hand, nature is the work of God, and man is the summit of this work; on the other hand, nature is itself creative and man is the most creative and therefore Godlike of natural beings:

> *Neither let it be deemed too saucy a comparison to balance the highest point of man's wit with the efficacy of Nature: but rather give right honour to the heavenly Maker of that maker, who, having made man to his own likeness, set him beyond and over all the works of that second nature which in nothing he showeth so much as in Poetry, when with the force of a divine breath he bringeth things forth far surpassing her doings, with no small argument to the incredulous of that first accursed fall of Adam: sith* [since] *our erected wit maketh us know what perfection is, and yet our infected will keepeth us from reaching unto it.*

Sidney is saying that although man's corrupted will is incapable of restoring a perfect world, his mind ('wit') is capable of conceiving one imaginatively: the vision of art can and should *improve on* the actuality of nature, by imitating a perfect nature. Such is the potentiality of poetry; what actual poetry at a given period achieves is another matter. Sidney and Puttenham thought the poetry of their day (Sidney laid special emphasis on poetic drama) badly needed guidance.

Renaissance critics valued Aristotle's *Poetics* not only because it justified poetry against Plato's condemnation of it, but because it seemed to contain principles and methods by which poetry could be evaluated. He was, of course, writing only about the epics and tragedies known to him, and there is no reason why his principles should apply to work of other times and countries, such as Spenser's romantic epic *The Faerie Queene** or the plays of Shakespeare*. However, Renaissance reverence for classical literature and philosophy caused the belief that Aristotle deduced his theories from nature, so that they had the validity of general truths. Besides accepting his plain statements, critics developed what they believed to be hints in his work, and evolved the 'Rules of Unity'. The Unity of Action, plainly stated by Aristotle, affirmed that every part of a work should be relevant to the whole; Unity of Time, barely implied by Aristotle, required that a tragedy should be restricted to the fictional limit of about 24 hours; that of Place, which Aristotle scarcely mentioned, required that the action should have a single setting. These and other 'rules' have often been condemned as irrelevant tyrannies on the poet, but to appreciate their value we have to remember the serious confusion in, or absence of, artistic principle in much 16th-century imaginative writing. Critics like Sidney were conducting a campaign for 'decorum' – for the order, dignity and clarity which they found in classical writing from Homer down; such decorum they believed necessary for the poetry of their own time if it was ever to rival the great poetry of the Greeks and ancient Romans. It was, in fact, the classical Latin literature of the Romans that Europe of the Renaissance found linguistically most akin and spiritually most congenial, and there too they found a teacher, in Aristotle's disciple Horace*, whose *Ars Poetica* (Poetic Art) was a leading critical text from the 16th century to the 19th. It was Horace who encouraged Puttenham and

Sidney to make such high claims for the poetic function, for the eminence due to poets, and for the moral excellence of the true poetic character. In some ways, moreover, Horace's short critical essay in verse was a more explicit and more lucid guide to critical method than Aristotle was, and he had more effect on actual artistic practice.

'Ut pictura poesis' – 'a poem is like a picture' – is a much-quoted phrase from Horace's *Ars Poetica*, and it is of course a version of Aristotle's theory of art as imitation. But this preoccupation with the imitativeness of art drove out the allegorical method of interpreting literature. Allegorical interpretation implied that the story existed for the guidance it gave to behaviour; the imitation theory taught that the story was an end in itself. This does not mean that allegory and allegorical interpretation abruptly ceased in the 16th century; on the contrary, they were so deeply rooted that the habit and the form persisted, though less coherently because the dispersal of ideas in the Renaissance obstructed the desire to see the different aspects of experience as reciprocally explanatory; yet even at the end of the century Spenser conceived his *Faerie Queene* on the principle of multiple meaning. But Spenser* (1552?–99) was consciously conservative, concerned to expound the chivalric values of the Middle Ages in terms of Renaissance idealism. Poetically, he was the last and greatest shaping influence of the English Renaissance.

Ben Jonson* (1572–1637) was one of the leading examples of its products. One of Spenser's main endeavours had been to demonstrate that English, uncontaminated by foreign borrowings, was as 'poetic' a language as any other, and his diction, as Jonson remarked in his conversations with Drummond, is often archaic owing to his reaction against the fashionable experiments of his contemporaries in 'improving' the language by verbal innovation. Jonson wrote with more confidence; he took the state of the language for granted, and used a contemporary idiom naturally, without feeling that he needed to show any special reverence either for the diction of foreign scholarship or for that of the English of the past. He did not, however, take the art of writing for granted. He believed, on the contrary, that it had to be cultivated with a care which was equal to his conception of its nobility. He agreed with Horace that poetry is like painting, but he considered it nobler, in that it reached more of the personality:

> *Poetry and picture are arts of a like nature, and both are busy about imitation. It was excellently said of Plutarch*, poetry was a speaking picture, and picture a mute poesy. For they both invent, feign, and devise many things, and accommodate all they invent to the use and service of Nature. Yet of the two the pen is more noble than the pencil; for that can speak to the understanding, the other but to the sense. They both behold pleasure and profit as their common object; but should abstain from all base pleasures, lest they should err from their end, and, while they seek to better men's minds, destroy their manners. They both are born artificers, not made. Nature is more powerful in them than study.*
>
> *Timber; or Discoveries* (published 1640)

This passage is typical of much Renaissance thinking about literature. The arts are 'busy about imitation' says Jonson; yet he also says that they 'invent, feign and devise'. For the modern mind, invention is incompatible with imitation, but this is because we have divorced 'invent' from its Latin origin in *invenio*, 'find, discover'. For the Renaissance mind, invention was not so much making something new as discovering it, and imitation was not so much imitating something that already existed as reproducing in art the action of what exists already in nature. Thus 'invention' implied an element of receptivity in its meaning whereas we now think of it as wholly active, and 'imitation' implied a strong element of creativity whereas we now understand it as mainly passive. Both words were understood in association with one of the important Renaissance uses of the word 'Nature'. In this sense, nature was the world as it had been created by God; it was a moral reality as well as a physical one, and it required moral interpretation and obedience rather than – as we now think – physical interpretation and understanding. 'In being able to counsel others,' Jonson writes elsewhere in *Discoveries*, 'a man must be furnished with a universal store in himself, to the knowledge of all nature – that is the matter and seed-plot: there are the seats of all argument and invention'. Thus if art, particularly poetry, neglects to improve the 'manners' of man – that is to say, his morals – it is being false to nature and 'unreal' in a sense that we do not know, because we think of artistic realism in merely physical and psychological terms.

When Jonson goes on to say that artists are 'born . . . not made', he is again echoing Horace, but neither he nor Horace thought that for that reason study was needless for the true poet. On the contrary, Jonson insists in another place in the *Discoveries* on the importance of poets studying the ancient writers, and his own poetry is conspicuous evidence of such study. Dryden* was to say of him later in the century: 'He was not only a professed imitator of Horace, but a learned plagiary of all the others: you track him everywhere in their snow.' For Jonson, study and emulation of the ancients was a form of imitation only less important than the imitation of nature, and again we have to understand his point of view in the light of general Renaissance ideas. For moderns, ideals of civilization are for the future: if we have any hopes of actualizing them, we allow ourselves to trust in 'progress'. For the Renaissance, excellence existed in the past: religion taught them that man had fallen from a state of created perfection, and it was natural to believe that his condition had on the whole grown progressively worse. The civilizations of ancient Greece and Rome were nearer in historical time to man's paradisal state, and they were undeniably the foundation of all that Renaissance men revered in their own civilization, apart from the Jewish sources of Christianity. Men like Jonson therefore believed that the road to advancement in civilization did not lie in the future, but on the contrary depended on thorough understanding of the ancient past, and the cultivation of its finest values. But this did not mean servility to the past and refusal to face the realities of his own time; ancient example and modern actualities had to be kept in balance, 'For to all the observations of the ancients we have our own experience: which if we will use and apply, we have better means to pronounce. It is true they opened the gates and made the way, that went before us; but as guides, not commanders.'

Puttenham, Sidney, Spenser and Jonson themselves opened the way to the main lines of critical thinking in Britain during the 17th and 18th centuries. Some of their ideas – notably Sidney's conception of poetry as a means to the envisagement of Platonic ideals and a perfected world – were greatly modified; others were greatly simplified and modified in the later 17th century. On the whole, the principles and terminology of the Renaissance were developed rather than forgotten or refuted in these centuries; 'imitation', 'invention', 'nature' continued to be staple terms. The Renaissance classification of the main kinds of poetry, based on classical categories, received further definition; Sidney in his *Apology* had listed them as 'Heroic, Lyric, Tragic, Comic, Satiric, Iambic, Elegiac, Pastoral and certain others', and such a classification caused poets to write with a more distinct purpose than they had in the Middle Ages, when the definition of kinds had been vaguer. Tragedy was restored to the theatre whence the Middle Ages had excluded it owing to their disapproval of secular drama; for the Middle Ages, tragedy had meant little more than a tale of misfortune, and the 16th-century practice had mixed tragedy and comedy on the stage, but Sidney carefully defined what was due to each. Critics cannot legislate for poets, and in the outcome Shakespeare's practice demonstrated that Sidney's definition was far too limited, but at least his disentanglement of tragedy and comedy facilitated clear discussion. Jonson, the only great dramatist of the period who was also a distinguished critical theorist, evolved his own conception of comedy as a deeply serious form of art through his Comedy of Humours*, his ideas about which are interspersed in his two early plays, *Every Man in his Humour** (1598) and *Every Man out of his Humour* (1599). Sidney's other classifications refer to non-dramatic verse; they endured, except for 'Iambic' poetry, since this designated a particular rhythm, not a form of vision or of subject-matter.

Moral disapproval of imaginative writing continued to be vigorous so long as the Puritans were important as a distinct force in English cultural life – that is to say, until the end of the 17th century – but it was chiefly restricted to attacks on the theatre. The real enemy to poetry was not moral in the 17th century, but intellectual; it was elusive, to some extent unconscious, manifested itself indirectly, and arose from the reverence for and dependence on the faculty of the reason. The first faint indication of this movement of mind occurs in Bacon's *Advancement of Learning** (1605). Bacon discusses poetry in similar terms to Sidney's in the *Apology*, but he uses a significantly different tone. He calls poetry 'feigned history', which heightens the image of experience in its fictions because 'the events of true history have not that magnitude which satisfieth the mind of man'. There is a noticeable coolness in Bacon's language; poetry, he says, had always been considered partly divine 'because it doth raise and erect the mind, by submitting the shows of things to the desires of the mind' – poetry, he seems to imply, encourages our wishful fantasies – 'whereas reason doth buckle and bow the mind unto the nature of things'. He leaves the subject after a brief discussion of it with a gesture of disdain: 'But it is not good to stay too long in the theatre.' Bacon's essentially practical thinking was of course one of the starting-points of modern science, but there is no inevitable antagonism between science and poetry. What is more important is his concentration on the merely rational propensities of the mind; when the 19th-century Industrial Revolution* caused this kind of mental bias to dominate our culture, poetry came to seem not so much morally dangerous as wastefully extravagant. The movement towards this attitude of mind lay through the Age of Reason, between 1660 and 1800.

7.2

The Age of Reason (1660–1789): the critic in authority

> *Mr Lock[e] has an admirable Reflection upon the Difference of Wit and Judgement, whereby he endeavours to show the Reason why they are not always the Talents of the same Person. His Words are as follows: 'And hence, perhaps, may be given some Reason of that common Observation, That Men who have a great deal of Wit and prompt Memories, have not always the clearest Judgement, or deepest Reason. For Wit lying most in the Assemblage of Ideas, and putting those together with Quickness and Variety, wherein can be found any Resemblance or Congruity, thereby to make up pleasant Pictures and agreeable Visions in the Fancy; Judgement, on the contrary, lies quite on the other side, in separating carefully, one from another, Ideas wherein can be found the least Difference, thereby to avoid being misled by Similitude, and by Affinity to take one thing for another. This is a Way of proceeding quite contrary to Metaphor and Allusion; wherein, for the most Part, lies that Entertainment and Pleasantry of Wit which strikes so lively on the Fancy, and is therefore so acceptable to all People.'*
>
> Addison* quoting Locke* in *The Spectator**, 1711

The quotation is from Locke's *Essay concerning Human Understanding** (1690), a philosophical work which dominated educated minds for a century. In the quoted passage, Locke does not mention poetry, but it is clear that his opposition between 'wit'* and 'judgement' is parallel to the opposition between 'poetry' and 'reason' in Bacon's *Advancement of Learning* (1605). The later 17th and earlier 18th centuries are an age in which poets themselves used wit to cultivate judgement, for they felt the cultivation of judgement, or 'right reason', to be the cultivation of civilization. But reason operates more naturally through prose than through verse; we find, therefore, that English prose, after 1660, is subjected to a campaign of conscious improvement. Earlier English prose had a vivid sensuous life that it shared with poetry. Bacon may have written his philosophical works after the *Advancement* in Latin partly because only in that language could he escape the poetic suggestiveness that was liable to confuse the rational course of his argument. The disciplining of English prose into what Bishop Sprat in 1667 called 'a close, naked, natural way of speaking' was one of the aims of the Royal Society* for Promoting Natural Knowledge, which was given, in 1662, a central place which it has never lost in British intellectual life. It was a society of scientists – 'natural philosophers'* as they were then called – but poets also belonged to it, and among these was the great poet–critic, 'father of English criticism', John Dryden* (1631–1700). Dryden's own prose set a standard in the qualities that Sprat required, and it was Dryden more than any other single writer who endowed poetry with the virtues that the new prose achieved. Thus in Dryden and his disciples – notably Pope* – the relation between the diction of prose and poetic diction was reversed: before 1660 (though of course the date must not be taken as a precise dividing line) prose had had the virtues of poetry; after 1660, for over a century, poetry tended to emulate the virtues of prose.

However, Dryden was not the only dominating figure in English poetry: there was also John Milton*, whose epic *Paradise Lost** was published in 1667. His vast poem impressed the age in three ways: it was an ambitious emulation of the most admired works of the ancients, the epics by Homer* and by Virgil*; it gave a grand, heroic scale to the origins and destiny of mankind; it sought to reconcile the two sources of the European tradition which Europeans have always found it difficult to harmonize: the secular stream emanating from the Greeks, and the religious one from the Jews. The men of the Age of Reason inherited from the Renaissance the conception that poetry must 'elevate' the mind of man; they admired and tried to imitate the neo-classic, heroic tragedies by Corneille* and Racine* in contemporary France. The limitations of the Age of Reason lay in the narrowness of its conception of art rather than in any lack of lofty ideas; the influence of French critics such as Boileau* (1636–1711) systematized and developed the disciplines implied by Aristotle's *Poetics* and Horace's *Ars Poetica* and so heightened their already great authority, but to these was now added a third classical authority: the *Treatise on the Sublime* ascribed to the Greek critic Longinus* (3rd century AD). Longinus was translated by Boileau in 1674, and he was subsequently translated several times into English. His influence was great, and encouraged 18th-century critics to apply the word 'sublime' to works such as Milton's *Paradise Lost*, which they admired. But Longinus was as rational and as conscious of art in writing as were Aristotle and Horace. He did not encourage work that arose from idiosyncratic passions, without basis in generally accepted truths, nor eccentric and merely ingenious figures of expression. Such work was likely to be disdained by 18th-century critics as Gothic*, because they associated it with the Middle Ages, before the Renaissance recovered the ancient classical ideas of order. Thus Addison, later in the essay quoted at the beginning of this section, remarks: 'Were I not supported by so great an Authority as that of Mr Dryden, I should not venture to observe, that the taste of most of our English poets, as well as Readers, is extremely Gothick.'

It is helpful to consider the literary thought of the later 17th century and the early 18th through the uses of such words employed in it, and also through the words employed about it. The age itself is called 'Augustan'*, from an essay (1759) by Oliver Goldsmith* in his periodical *The Bee*, though Goldsmith meant specifically the early 18th century in Britain. This label refers back to the reign of Augustus Caesar (Emperor 27 BC–AD 14) when Latin literature reached its height of excellence. By that age, and also by the standards of contemporary neo-classical France, the British Augustans judged themselves, and tried to form their taste. But the greater critics of the age were not as narrow as this suggests; Dryden, Pope, Addison and Johnson* all pointed out that sublime poetry could not be seriously weakened by what they and their lesser contemporaries considered to be defects in 'correctness', so long as these were minor ones. Addison distinguishes (*Spectator* 160) between geniuses who produce great works in spite of their deficiency in art and learning – he mentions Shakespeare – and those who have 'formed themselves by rules, and submitted the Greatness of their natural talents to the Corrections and Restraints of Art', amongst whom he includes Milton and Bacon, but he does not give preference to the second class. Critics found it useful, as they do today, to distinguish the greatest artists, who could afford to neglect or observe the rules as they pleased, as 'geniuses'; the creative faculty in lesser writers was called 'wit', and as this word is seldom used in such a sense today, it requires special study.

In its oldest sense, wit meant simply 'mind', or one of the faculties of the mind. In the 16th century it came also to be used in the sense of the mind at its highest – the intellect; and in the 17th century it was also used to mean 'imagination'. But 17th- and 18th-century writers were restless about the word; they repeatedly redefined it, and the definitions do not agree. At one extreme we have Cowley*, in his ode *Of Wit* (1647), expressing the idea that wit brings into harmony what are dissimilar in nature, thus creating a new unity in the poem:

In a true piece of Wit all things must be,
Yet all things there agree,
As in the Ark, join'd without force or strife,
All creatures dwelt, all creatures that had life.

His opinion had prestige, but though the definition by Locke at the beginning of this section resembles Cowley's, it also modifies the idea: 'the Assemblage of Ideas . . . wherein can be found any resemblance or congruity'. Dryden produced two definitions, the earlier of which is also a modified version of Cowley's: 'the faculty of imagination . . . which, like a nimble spaniel, beats over and ranges through the field of memory' (Preface to *Annus Mirabilis**, 1667). His second definition (in *The Author's Apology*, 1677) is so broad as to be almost useless: he calls it the 'propriety of thoughts and words'. This is almost saying that wit is the quality of exact prose, but it is also appropriate to the qualities that Dryden is by this time trying to cultivate in his poetry. He is really ascribing to wit something of the quality that Locke ascribes to judgement: Locke evidently believes that the exercise of judgement enlightens the reader, whereas wit merely delights the reader by startling him; but Dryden, by the time he arrives at his second definition, believes that wit should be enlightening too. What, then, becomes of Locke's distinction between wit and judgement? Pope, in his *Essay on Criticism** (1711), says that 'true wit' is disciplined by art; that is to say, it is subjected to the judgement; the gymnastic wit of a poet such as Cowley only leads to ostentatious 'conceits'*, which glitter with their own brilliance but accumulate in mere incoherence:

Some to Conceit alone their taste confine
And glittering thoughts struck out at every line;
Pleas'd with a work where nothing's just or fit;
One glaring chaos and wild heap of wit.
Poets, like painters, thus, unskill'd to trace
The naked Nature and the living grace,
With gold and jewels cover every part,
And hide with ornaments their want of art.
True wit is Nature to advantage dress'd;
What oft was thought, but ne'er so well express'd;
Something, whose truth convinced at sight we find,
That gives us back the image of our mind.

Essay on Criticism, lines 289–300

It is evident that the concept 'wit' mattered to the Augustan writers, for otherwise they would not have discussed it so often; it is also evident that their discussions led to some confusion, especially when we remember that the year of Addison's essay, in which he approves of Locke's earlier definition, is also the year of Pope's *Essay on Criticism*. What accounts for this sustained interest in the word, and why did it lead to such disagreement? The explanation is that the same word 'wit' is being used to express the poetic faculty of two distinct poetic schools of thought. Cowley was the last of the group of poets which Johnson, in his *Life of Cowley* (1779), was the first to call the Metaphysicals*. They flourished in the first half of the 17th century and included Donne* (1572–1631), Herbert* (1593–1633), Marvell* (1621–78) – who outlived Cowley, but wrote most of his poetry as a young man – as well as many lesser names. Modern critics distinguish sharply between the earlier poets in the group, who use wit with boldness and sincerity in their search for equivalences between the experiences of the heart and those of the head, and its decadence, represented by Cowley (1618–67), who used wit with the kind of barren ostentation that Pope condemns in the lines that have been quoted.

Dryden, Pope, and the other Augustans differed from modern critics in seeing Cowley as representative of *all* the Metaphysicals. They were blinded to the deep emotional and spiritual conflicts of poets such as Donne and Herbert by their own faith in the power of intellectual understanding to penetrate mysteries, but they admired, in Donne and Cowley alike, the Metaphysical ingenuity of intellect, which they regarded as indispensable to the kind of poetry which they – the Augustans – themselves wanted to write. They therefore accepted the term 'wit' as the name for the poetic faculty used by themselves and by their predecessors, but they considered that they could improve the Metaphysical employment of wit by their own employment of art; Johnson, in his *Life of Cowley*, recalls that 'Dryden confesses of himself and his contemporaries, that they fall below Donne in wit, but maintains that they surpass him in poetry'.

It is, in fact, Johnson in his Cowley essay (1779) who puts the history of the word 'wit' into clear perspective up to his own time. But Johnson was himself an Augustan, and he gives the clearest definition of the Augustans' appropriation of the word, in contrast to their use of it when they had the Metaphysicals in mind – a use which Locke and Addison failed to distinguish:

> *If . . . that be considered as Wit, which is at once natural and new, that which, though not obvious, is, upon its first production, acknowledged to be just; if it be that, which he that never found it, wonders how he missed; to wit of this kind the metaphysical poets have seldom risen.*

Distinctively Metaphysical wit he goes on to distinguish as:

> *a combination of dissimilar images, or discovery of occult resemblances in things apparently unlike. Of wit, thus defined, they have more than enough. The most heterogeneous ideas are yoked by violence together; nature and art are ransacked for illustrations, comparisons, and allusions; their learning instructs, and their subtilty surprises; but the reader commonly thinks his improvement dearly bought, and, though he sometimes admires, is seldom pleased.*

Thus the Augustans, from Dryden to Johnson, wrestled with the Metaphysicals over the term 'wit', and eventually, by the great authority of Johnson, gained a superior meaning of it – superior, that is, according to their lights – for themselves. Their victory led to the commonest meaning attached to the word today. Wit in the Augustan sense lent itself to the epigram, in the practice of which Pope excelled, and to the aphorism, of which Johnson was a master; so we, today, understand wit as the practice of intellectual humour, in which the weight of thought is often as impressive as the comedy. The victory was, however, expensive to the reputation of the Augustans as 19th-century critics viewed them, and it was also in some ways a paradoxical conclusion to their literary thought. It was costly to their reputation, since later critics saw the Augustan age as the Age of Wit as well as the Age of

Reason, and they saw these labels as indicating not so much the cultural excellence of the period as its limitations. Thus we find Matthew Arnold* writing in his essay on Gray* (1888):

> *The difference between genuine poetry and the poetry of Dryden, Pope, and all their school is briefly this: their poetry is conceived and composed in their wits; genuine poetry is conceived and composed in the soul.*

Such a comment points to the paradox of the Augustan appropriation of wit, for, after all, they began by priding themselves, not on their wit but on their use of art and judgement; 'wit' they were prepared – until Johnson – to allow to be the peculiar excellence of their predecessors in the first half of the 17th century.

If, then, we think of the Augustan men of letters as they would probably have preferred to be remembered, we think of them less as the men who perfected 'wit' than as the men who perfected 'art'. Yet even this view, if we are to do them justice, requires proper understanding of their use of the word 'art'. The meanings we attach to the word are influenced by 19th-century conceptions of it, and those were often large, but vague and confusing; in general the 19th century tended to discuss 'Art' either in opposition to, or at least in relation to, 'Life'. This is a more ambitious employment of the word than the one which the 18th century inherited from the Middle Ages by way of the Renaissance; an artist was not fundamentally different from an 'artisan', and 'art' was associated with 'craft', 'workmanship' and what today is comprised in technology. 'Poetry' – from ancient times – had never been quite identical with the 'art' of poetry; the former was thought to proceed from a 'divine rapture' for which the poet was not himself entirely responsible, but his art was his responsibility to his readers. When Ben Jonson told Drummond that Donne 'deserved hanging' for not 'keeping accent', he meant that Donne's genius, with which he was endowed, did not excuse him for his disregard of his responsibility, as an artist, for the perfection of his rhythms; and Jonson, of all his great generation, was closest in spirit to the Augustans.

The Augustan view of art, so described, may seem narrow and mechanical, but to understand its full dignity and scale we have to observe how they repeatedly measured their conception of Art against their conception of Nature. Thus Pope writes in his *Essay on Criticism* (lines 68–73):

> *First follow Nature, and your judgement frame*
> *By her just standard, which is still*[1] *the same:*
> *Unerring Nature, still*[1] *divinely bright;*
> *One clear, unchanged, and universal light,*
> *Life, force, and beauty, must to all impart,*
> *At once the source, and end, and test of Art.*
> [1] always

The best Augustans, however much they respected the 'Rules' of Art, never forgot that these rules were valid only in so far as they were felt to be, in the philosophical sense, 'natural'. So Pope again (lines 88–91):

Those rules of old discover'd, not devised,
Are Nature still, but Nature methodized:
Nature, like liberty, is but restrain'd
By the same laws which first herself ordain'd.

He means by the last couplet that God, who created Nature, also created the laws which regulate her. Pope and his contemporaries saw these laws as unchanging, and as constituting philosophical evidence of the existence of the Creator. The laws of Nature implied the laws of Art, for Art implied an ordered view of Nature.

Nature, from the Middle Ages to the 19th century, was always related to God, its Creator, on one side, and to Man, its principal production, on the other. Emphasis could fall variously: until the 17th century it fell on the relationship of God with Nature, and in the 19th century it fell on the relationship of Man with Nature. In the Augustan period, emphasis fell in between. Newton* (1642–1727), the great mathematical physicist, and Locke (1632–1704), the great philosophical rationalist, gave confidence in the study of the laws of nature, interest in which was promoted by the Royal Society. Such interest gave a more detached view of nature, art and man than had ever existed before, or has existed since. Nature was truth, man was part of this knowable truth, and art must conform to it. Man was notoriously paradoxical and inconsistent, but he too must have a prevailing law which would explain his complexity. Pope thought he had found one in his idea of 'the ruling passion' (*Essay on Man**, 1732), and the philosopher Hartley* (1705–57) believed that he had found another of a different sort in his principle of the association of ideas. No one, of course, believed that all was known about nature and about man: there was merely the belief that all was knowable.

Since nature was not wholly understood, it was not enough to condemn an artist outright merely because he did not conform to the 'rules'; it may be that a poet is conforming to the truth of nature in an unfamiliar way. 'There is always an appeal open from criticism to nature', wrote Dr Johnson in his Preface to Shakespeare (1765), in defending the apparent 'irregularities' of Shakespeare's art. Thus, while their confidence that their principles of judgement were derived from the truth of nature gave the Augustans unusual assurance in their judgements, their conception of the largeness of nature also gave the best of them great modesty and warm generosity in their appreciation. The limits to their appreciation were not due to their arrogance in believing that they had arrived at the ultimate 'rules of art', but to their seriousness in believing that it was the function of art to make clear the relevance of poetry to nature considered as general truth. The generosity is most evident in Dryden; the insistence on relevance is clearest in Johnson.

Johnson called Dryden 'the father of English criticism' because he was 'the writer who first taught us to determine upon principles the merit of composition', and he goes on to name Dryden's *Essay on Dramatic Poesy** (1668) as 'the first regular and valuable treatise on the art of writing'. It is a dialogue among four characters who discuss the relative merits of ancient and modern, and of French and English drama, but its interest for us derives less from these general comparisons than from the particular appreciations of Shakespeare and of Ben Jonson's *Epicoene*, or The Silent Woman* (1609), which constitute the first valuable assessments of individual writers and works in English criticism. Again, in his *Preface to the Fables* (1670), Dryden displays warm and discriminating admiration for the poetry of Chaucer, although his own limitations in scholarship and stylistic preferences prevented him from fully understanding Chaucer's outlook and technique. Dryden does not abandon his neo-classical principles in such appreciations, but he shows how to apply them largely – how to acknowledge the vitality of forms and diction which proceed from quite different outlooks. He uses his critical reason to illuminate his honest feelings, instead of allowing it to obscure them. The gracious persuasiveness of his writing makes his various essays and prefaces agreeable to read even when his opinions have lost their force. This careful cultivation of pleasing style which establishes a friendly personal relationship with the reader is characteristic of the Augustans. Literary taste was not the speciality of scholars and courtiers, as it had been during the Renaissance, but a part of social relationship and of the quality of civilized life as educated men lived it daily in their houses and gardens and in the cultivation of their leisure. Social life was seen as an art to which all the arts contributed, and aesthetic judgements always had their moral aspect; it is most richly expressed in the poetry of Pope, all of which is permeated by the operation of his critical faculty. The Augustans accepted that high standards were difficult to sustain, but they assumed that if they were sustained at all, it was by the general body of educated men and women: 'I rejoice to concur with the common reader' wrote Dr Johnson in his *Life of Gray*.

Samuel Johnson was great as a poet, critic, biographer, essayist, and conversationalist, but in all these activities he was consistently a moralist. 'The only end of writing', he declares in a review of a book by Soame Jenyns (1704–87), 'is to enable the readers better to enjoy life, or better to endure it.' He had, himself, a great capacity for enjoyment, but he was a stern realist, subject to despondency, and familiar for many years with severe poverty. He tested literature by its capacity to appeal to the deepest moral needs, and his sense of the community of human beings gave him special conviction in one of the strongest Augustan doctrines – that imaginative writing must appeal to what is general in human experience, not to what is particular:

> *Nothing can please many, and please long, but just representations of general nature. Particular manners can be known to few, and therefore few only can judge how nearly they are copied. The irregular combinations of fanciful invention may delight awhile, by that novelty of which the common satiety of life sends us all in quest; but the pleasures of sudden wonder are soon exhausted, and the mind can only repose on the stability of truth.*

There is much in this often-quoted paragraph from the Preface to his edition of Shakespeare that is strongly neo-classical and Augustan: an implicit acceptance of the Aristotelian doctrine that art is imitation, the Augustan dislike of eccentricity in art, and the faith in 'the stability of truth' – the discoverable facts and laws of nature. Johnson never used neo-classical principles from mere habit; he was a critic of strongly independent judgement. The idea that art must be general, not particular, in its references is as much based on his own firm opinion that art must be evidently relevant as it is derived from Aristotle and Horace. The same sense of relevance is the cause of his strictness in criticizing diction. He says, for instance, in the *Lives of the Poets**: 'There was . . . before the time of Dryden no poetical diction, no system of words at once refined from the grossness of domestic use, and free from the harshness of terms appropriated to particular arts'; he means that, since words necessarily carry associations, the poet must be sure that his words carry the right associations. However, he was no propagandist for an artificial 'poetic' diction; he says of Gray – in a censure from which he excludes Gray's *Elegy** – 'He has a kind of strutting dignity, and is tall by walking on tiptoe'. For Johnson, where there is superfluous ornament there is no genuineness of feeling; he is thus ruthless about Milton's elegy *Lycidas**, because it is cast in a pastoral framework – 'Where there is leisure for fiction there is little grief'. Most readers consider that Johnson misunderstood Milton's intention, just as he misunderstood the intention of Shakespeare's 'plays on words' when he dismissed them as 'quibbles', and that of Donne's 'metaphysical' conceits where, in the *Life of Cowley*, he cites them as ludicrous. The very strength of Johnson's Augustan principles, in fact, causes him to exhibit startling limitations in judgement, but they are always limitations of literary training, never limitations of human feeling; he is indeed the most profoundly humane of all the Augustan writers. Even when he makes mistakes, they are always made in the cause of the dignity of literature as he saw it, resting, as he believed it should, on community of right taste.

The Augustan community of right taste depended, in turn, on the idea of a tradition of culture which the Augustans believed to have been initiated by the Greeks and perfected by the Romans. But like any other age, the 18th century exhibited divergency of opinion. Its careful balance tended to inertia, self-satisfaction and complacency; in its religious aspect, the Anglican compromise of the 16th century had hardened into a strong establishment, chiefly menaced by the Dissenting* sects, successors of the 17th-century Puritans; in its philosophical aspect, the natural philosophers were producing new scientific speculations which were sometimes important, sometimes extravagant, but always unsettling. The writers whom we think of as the 'great' Augustans – especially Pope, Swift, and Johnson – were certainly not complacent, but they tended to be conservative. While they were scornful of the smart society which skated on the surface of civilization without ever penetrating to the substance, they hated the Dissenters for their unbalanced emotionalism, and they distrusted the natural philosophers for their unbalanced intellectualism. Their conservatism led them to rely upon the classical heritage, and this fact gives some importance to a controversy that started in France in the late 17th century and affected England – the battle between 'the Ancients and the Moderns'. Regarded as a mere argument about the relative merits of individual classical writers and individual modern ones, this controversy has often been despised as a mere pastime for scholarly gentlemen. Dryden participates in it interestingly in his *Essay on Dramatic Poesy*. However, Swift's* *Battle of the Books* (1704), despite its playfulness, has more importance. It includes his fable of the Spider and the Bee. The Spider, who is the Modern, spins his art from out of himself, 'that is to say' (says the Bee) 'you possess a good plentiful store of dirt and poison in your breast', whereas the Bee is the writer who cultivates the Ancients, and 'by an universal range, with long search, much study, true judgement, and distinction of things, brings home honey and wax'. The ancient writers in the story adopt the Bee as their emblem, believing that they provide 'mankind with the two noblest of things, which are sweetness and light'.

'Sweetness and light' were to be used as a symbol by Matthew Arnold* in the mid-19th century in his campaign against the 'Philistine'* middle classes, who, as he believed, thought they could dispense with a communal culture based on a disinterested care for the values of human society. Swift* (1667–1745), who wrote very little distinctively literary criticism, gave much attention to criticism of the social values of Britain during his lifetime. At the same time as his *Battle of the Books* he published *A Tale of a Tub**, in which, with brilliantly complex satire, he attacks the Dissenters and all whom he considered to be propagators of 'false learning', including the natural philosophers. Pope, too, in his greatest poem *The Dunciad**, Part IV (1742), attacks those pedants, amateur scientists and superficial men of fashion who, as he considered, were threatening to level culture down to their own mediocrity. The issue was an important one, for it was ultimately the question whether a civilized society can survive without a high tradition of imaginative art; it was to be taken up again and again from age to age. In the 19th and 20th centuries it was to become more explicit, and the first to revive it, in the new conditions of the still early phase of the Industrial Revolution, was William Wordsworth.

7·3

The Romantic Age (1790–1830): the critic as explorer

A multitude of causes, unknown to former times, are now acting with a combined force to blunt the discriminating powers of the mind, and unfitting it for all voluntary exertion, to reduce it to a state of almost savage torpor. The most effective of these causes are the great national events which are daily taking place, and the increased accumulation of men in cities, where the uniformity of their occupations produces a craving for extraordinary incident, which the rapid communication of intelligence hourly gratifies. To this tendency of life and manners the literature and theatrical exhibitions of the country have conformed themselves . . . When I think upon this degrading thirst after outrageous stimulation, I am almost ashamed to have spoken of the feeble endeavour made in these volumes to counteract it; and, reflecting upon the magnitude of the general evil, I should be oppressed with no dishonourable melancholy, had I not a deep impression of certain inherent and indestructible qualities of the human mind, and likewise of certain powers in the great and permanent objects that act upon it, which are equally inherent and indestructible; and were there not added to this impression a belief, that the time is approaching when the evil will be systematically opposed, by men of greater powers, and with far more distinguished success.

Wordsworth*: Preface to the second edition of the *Lyrical Ballads** (1800).

Writing only 15 years after Johnson's death, Wordsworth (1770–1850) was aware that he and his readers were living in a world that was already startlingly different from Johnson's. Indeed, in some features it was already our world: the world of big industrial cities, of rapid historical change, of quick transmission of news ('intelligence'), of the exploitation by an amusement industry of a public taste that was intellectually apathetic and nervously restless. Wordsworth and his friend Coleridge* (1772–1834) believed that poetry could purify society from the malignant effects of the forces that were afflicting it, but that in order to do so poets must become more aware of elemental forces both in human beings and in their surroundings than they had hitherto been. These forces were the deep impulses of life in man and in nature, and it is to them that he is referring when he writes of 'certain inherent and indestructible qualities of the human mind, and likewise of certain powers in the great and permanent objects that act upon it'.

His awareness of the social need and of the healing power which the poet could educe from his inner life meant a new kind of poetry, but it also meant a new kind of criticism. The Augustan critics had taught educated men the duty of sustaining and refining the civilization they had inherited; the task of the critic, as of the philosopher, was to maintain clear vision in the light of well-defined axioms, and that of the imaginative writer was to renew the emotional freshness that underlies vision by his 'wit' and 'invention'. Wordsworth, however, teaches in his Preface that the educated vision is not enough; indeed, the simplest men are more likely to be aware of their deep resources of life, for the complex social life of the educated man will commonly overlay the more fundamental, but also more elementary human insights. For this reason Wordsworth directs his readers to 'humble and rustic life', because, amongst other things, simple countrymen 'hourly communicate with the best objects from which the best part of language is originally derived'.

Wordsworth might seem to be bringing the poet farther into the community of human beings than critics had ever brought him before: he was to be the voice of common humanity in all men. In reality, however, his major purpose was much more difficult and unusual than this; he was seeking to enlarge the educated consciousness from within, by showing that just the kind of basic experience which the educated man despised as primitive and to be outgrown was in reality the truest and the most important to sustain. In attempting this, Wordsworth really separated himself from his readers, as a poet-critic, in a way that Dryden, Pope and Johnson never did. They had addressed audiences that were open to their ideas, but Wordsworth was addressing an audience that needed to be converted to his. He had to reconsider and define terms that had long been assumed and unexamined. He had to define what he meant by a poet and by poetry, what he considered to be good poetic diction, and the function of metre and rhythm. Embracing all these, though it was the subject of his poetry rather than of his prose criticism, was his new vision of nature, and of man's relationship to it.

However the Preface not only contains startingly new opinions; it also contains strikingly conservative ones, and this is most evident when Wordsworth sets about his task of redefinition, though the conservatism includes implications of new ideas:

> *Aristotle . . . has said, that Poetry is the most philosophic of all writing: it is so: its object is truth, not individual and local, but general and operative; not standing upon external testimony, but carried alive into the heart by passion; truth which is its own testimony, which gives competence and confidence to the tribunal to which it appeals, and receives them from the same tribunal. Poetry is the image of man and nature.*

Here we find that Wordsworth is still holding to Aristotle's doctrine that poetry is imitation, and he agrees with Johnson that its object is general – not individual and local – truth, but we also find a difference. Johnson might have agreed that poetry 'gives confidence and competence to the tribunal to which it appeals', for did he not define 'wit', in its operation on the reader, by saying 'he that never found it, wonders how he missed'? Yet, though many of Wordsworth's ideas are congruous with Johnson's, we commonly have to translate them into Johnson's terms to see the agreement and, as in all translation, something is lost. The eloquent phrase 'carried alive into the heart by passion' is not Johnsonian; Johnson's description of the operation of wit and invention always suggests the response of 'recognition' by the reader, whereas Wordsworth's language expresses *union* – something felt rather than recognized. Wordsworth describes a poet as follows:

> *He is a man speaking to men: a man, it is true, endowed with more lively sensibility, more enthusiasm, and tenderness, who has a greater knowledge of human nature, and a more comprehensive soul, than are supposed to be common to mankind; a man pleased with his own passions and volitions, and who rejoices more than other men in*

the spirit of life that is in him; delighting to contemplate similar volitions and passions in the goings-on of the Universe, and habitually impelled to create them where he does not find them.

Johnson would again acknowledge the thoroughly Aristotelian operation of Wordsworth's conception of the poet's mind, but he would notice that 'enthusiasm' has changed its meaning from the pejorative sense of undisciplined outpouring of feeling to the favourable sense of a spontaneous outpouring; no doubt also, Johnson, who said 'men are evidently and confessedly so corrupt, that all the laws of heaven and earth are insufficient to restrain them from crimes', would have questioned the right of any man to be 'pleased with his own volitions and passions'.

A discussion between Johnson and Wordsworth would thus have been fruitless, for they would have proceeded from different premises. Even the critical vocabulary was changing. For instance, the term 'wit' to express the poetic faculty, so much in use in the 17th and 18th centuries, does not recur in this sense in criticism, nor, very much, does 'invention'. Both words, however defined, suggest the activity of the conscious mind, but Wordsworth's conception of the part played by the mind in poetic creation is more passive:

I have said that poetry is the spontaneous overflow of powerful feelings: it takes its origin from emotion recollected in tranquillity: the emotion is contemplated till, by a species of reaction, the tranquillity gradually disappears, and an emotion, kindred to that which was before the subject of contemplation, is gradually produced, and does itself actually exist in the mind.

Thus, for Wordsworth, the poet's mind 'recollects' and 'contemplates' what he describes as something like a chemical process of the emotions; the mind is the spectator, and it is the emotions that are active. Johnson would perhaps not so much have disagreed with this as considered it a useless speculation; asked about the nature of poetry, he replied: 'Why Sir, it is much easier to say what it is not. We all *know* what light is; but it is not easy to *tell* what it is.' Johnson and the other Augustans were interested in poems as achieved products of the mind, and in the poetic faculty – 'wit' – as it operated on the reader's mind. Wordsworth, on the other hand, because he is trying to awaken the reader to a new conception of poetry, had to convey to the reader some idea of the way the poet's mind operates. Later, his friend Coleridge was to amend Wordsworth's account by giving a much more positive role to the mind in poetic creation, but instead of using the term 'wit' to denote it, he used 'imagination' – a word which did not so distinctly imply participation by the reason. Coleridge, in fact, is further removed from Johnson than is Wordsworth, and to understand Coleridge's development it is necessary to see how he came to depart from the accepted ideas of psychology in England at the time.

Wordsworth took his ideas of the mind from the rationalistic psychology of

David Hartley's *Observations on Man* (1749). Hartley maintained that the mind is built up from physical sensations; with these, ideas of pleasure and pain become associated in a structure, which – with proper education – may be trained into a moral structure, enabling the individual to recognize disinterestedly the differences between good and bad, and the degrees of either. It was a simple and reasonable theory, and it facilitated Wordsworth's task, for it enabled him to account for the powerful effects of very early experiences. Thus he describes the influence of wild nature on him in his own childhood:

By day or star-light thus from my first dawn
Of childhood didst thou intertwine for me
The passions that build up our human soul;
Not with the mean and vulgar works of man,
But with high objects, with enduring things –
With life and nature – purifying thus
The elements of feeling and of thought,
And sanctifying, by such discipline,
Both pain and fear, until we recognize
A grandeur in the beatings of the heart.

(*Prelude* I.405–14)

Here Wordsworth expresses his own experience of being invaded by nature, and Hartley's theory fits well with it. Coleridge, too, at first accepted the theory; a characteristic image in his poetry for the mind of the poet is the 'aeolian harp', strung across a window and played upon, not by hands, but by the breezes as they rise and fall. Yet Coleridge came to reject Hartley. He recognized that his own characteristic weakness was precisely excessive passiveness to experience, and he came to see it as a source of evil, and inadequate as an explanation of the creative process. Thus, in 1802, we find him writing in *Dejection: an Ode**:

O Lady! We receive but what we give
And in our life alone does Nature live:

and accordingly he found it necessary to evolve a new psychology as a basis for critical theory.

It is with Coleridge, more than with Wordsworth, that English literary thought becomes distinctly 'Romantic'. In general, nonetheless, the word has to be used with some caution; the English writers did not recognize themselves as Romantics; for instance in 1820 we find Byron writing disapprovingly of the Romantic–Classical controversies in Germany and Italy, and hoping that they would never spread to Britain. The word 'romantic' had long been used in regard to whatever was wild and disturbing to the imagination; it had been associated with 'Gothic', and with the tales in Romance languages during the Middle Ages. But 'Romantic' and 'Classic' had never been opposed to each other, or regarded as incompatible.

'Romantic', in fact, was applied in the mid-19th century as a label to English literature between 1790 and 1830 only because of its habitual use in continental European literature during the same period. The importance of Coleridge in the evolution of what came to be considered as English Romanticism is particularly that he was the principal channel of contemporary German* thought – Fichte, Schelling, Kant* – as well as of the earlier mystic, Jacob Boehme*. He pays his debt of acknowledgement to these and other writers in Chapter IX of his *Biographia Literaria** (1817), in the course of which he remarks that students of philosophy during 'the two or three last centuries' must have recognized a conspiracy among thinkers 'not to pass beyond a certain limit in speculative science'. The Germans, for Coleridge, had broken through these limits. Whereas the French and English philosophers and literary critics during the 17th and 18th centuries had in effect restricted discussion to man as he existed in the society that was present to them, the Germans had dared to ask questions about the very basis of being in man and in nature. Largely owing to Coleridge, German thought became influential in Britain between 1800 and 1850. It was never to predominate as the French influence had done a hundred years before, but it helped to end the predominance of reason over imagination in literary thinking, and thereby broke the frontier between life and art: art was no longer thought of so much as a highly skilled profession, but more as a way of life. The critic became an interpreter rather than an evaluator, and the imaginative writer became the man living out human problems in imaginative terms, rather than the poet holding a mirror up to nature for the judgement of reason. 'Reason', Shelley was to write in *A Defence of Poetry* (1821), 'is to the imagination as the instrument to the agent, as the body to the spirit, as the shadow to the substance'.

In his *Biographia Literaria* Coleridge attempted a philosophical basis for and a critical exemplification of this new outlook in literary thought. The first 13 chapters compound philosophy and autobiography, for it was characteristic of his approach that nothing could be taken for granted: the poet had to elucidate himself while he elucidated his philosophy, for this could no longer rely for its persuasiveness on an impersonal 'light of reason'. This section ends with his famous definitions of the Primary and the Secondary Imagination and of Fancy. The second and last section consists of literary criticism, and six of its nine chapters are devoted to the poetry and opinions of Wordsworth. Their close friendship and collaboration over the *Lyrical Ballads* had been decisive in Coleridge's development, though they had drawn apart since. His admiration for Wordsworth's poetry survived the breach, but he had also become critical of some of it and of the ideas in Wordsworth's Preface. He used the disagreement positively, to clarify his own ideas: for instance, he showed that Wordsworth's theory of poetic diction was based on the radical social philosophy that he held at the time, rather than on sound literary practice, and that his ideas on metre were more influenced by his desire to remove the prejudices of readers against poetry than on true understanding of the effects of rhythm on the human mind.

The outstanding value of Coleridge's literary thought is its psychological depth: he was the first critic to show that no theory of artistic creation was valid unless it showed how the artist was totally involved in the process of creation as a man; and this, of course, demands a total response by the reader: 'The poet brings the whole soul of man into activity' (Chap. 14). This is where his rejection of Hartley's psychology, and his own definition of imagination, become important. In Chapter 12 he reasons out his own theory by starting with the 18th-century assumption, basic to Hartley, that, in any theory of knowledge, there must be subject and object, knower and known, man and nature. He goes on to argue that behind this duality there must be a unity – neither a subject nor an object, but a principle of being which 'manifests itself in the SUM or I AM'. This is God – the infinite, creative, unifying power for which he invents the adjective 'esemplastic' (shaping into one). At the end of Chapter 13 he declares that this infinite creative power, which he terms 'the primary imagination', manifests itself as 'the secondary imagination' in acts of creation. It differs from fancy, which hitherto had loosely been regarded as synonymous with imagination, because fancy is merely a mode of memory with no capacity to re-create, but only to combine images in surprising associations, whereas the imagination 'dissolves, diffuses, dissipates, in order to re-create'. Thus, in Coleridge's terms, it becomes difficult any longer to think of the poet as making Aristotelian imitations of nature, for this implies judgement of the poem in the light of nature regarded as an object. For Coleridge, poetic truth is not that of the object, but a union between the subject and the object, of a union of the poet and nature; poetry is 'esemplastic', and creates new wholes out of

> *opposite or discordant qualities: of sameness, with difference; of the general, with the concrete; the idea, with the image; the individual, with the representative; the sense of novelty and freshness, with old and familiar objects; a more than usual state of emotion, with more than usual order; judgement ever awake and steady self-possession, with enthusiasm and feeling profound or vehement; and while it blends and harmonizes the natural and artificial, still subordinates art to nature; the manner to the matter; and our admiration of the poet to our sympathy with the poetry.*

In short, 'The poet, described in ideal perfection, brings the whole soul of man into activity.'

What has been the importance of Coleridge's literary philosophy? The *Biographia* has had more influence on 20th-century critics than on 19th-century ones, though Coleridge made a strong impression on his century through his miscellaneous writings and his talk. The book, regarded as a document of its time, is perhaps especially interesting as the most articulate expression of a spirit which had been slowly taking shape even within the Augustan, neo-classic 18th century. The very rationality of that age caused it to see limits in the range and power of reason. Words like 'sentiment' (feeling), 'sentimental', and 'sensibility' – both for the power and the sensitivity of the feelings, and for the capacity to appreciate beauty – became prominent in literary currency. Jane Austen's novel *Sense and Sensibility* (1811) contrasts the two aspects of the late Augustan period: admiration for sound reason ('Sense'), and cultivation of taste for the imaginative pleasures. The words 'sentimental' and 'sentimentality' received their modern derogatory meaning of 'merely playing with the emotions' early in the 19th century, and no doubt this derived from the intensely serious attitude to the faculty of the imagination, so bound up with the feelings, which Coleridge and Shelley exemplify. If it is through the feelings and the imagination that men must struggle to fulfilment, then the feelings must not be 'played with'. True literary thinking was now seen as involved with the spiritual conflicts of poets as men; consequently some of the best literary thought of the period is to be found in its poetry – Wordsworth's *Prelude* and Coleridge's *Kubla Khan** and *Dejection* – and in letters, especially those of John Keats* (1795–1821).

All three men were profoundly concerned with the principles of growth and the rich exfoliation of the human being, and Wordsworth and Coleridge lived long enough to be concerned, too, with the cessation of growth, and the principle of desiccation. One of Wordsworth's most valuable insights was that the child enters the world with a sense of the wholeness of experience through its bond with the mother, and moreover it actively participates in this wholeness –

Even as an agent of the one great Mind
Creates, creator and receiver both,
Working but in alliance with the works
Which it beholds.

Prelude, II.257–60 (1805)

In *Tintern Abbey** (1798) he describes the difficult transition from this homogeneity of experience into adult detachment, and in his *Intimations of Immortality** (1802–6) he writes of the more difficult transition into middle life when the original vision fades, and of his determination to live from its vestiges. Similarly, Coleridge's *Kubla Khan* is a marvellous symbolic expression of creative life, but in *Dejection* (1802), Coleridge writes of the breaking of his powers under the strain of his sufferings, and the gradual smothering of his 'shaping spirit of Imagination' by the speculative intellectual faculty which he developed to compensate for his suffering:

And haply by abstruse research to steal
From my own nature all the natural man –
This was my sole resource, my only plan:
Till that which suits a part infects the whole,
And now is almost grown the habit of my soul.

Wordsworth and Coleridge were 28 and 26 respectively when they published their first important poems in their joint work *Lyrical Ballads*; their view of the growth of the imaginative life is restrospective, as they look back on their earlier careers. At 26 Keats was dead, having achieved his best work at 24; his view was concurrent, like a running narrative on the relationship of art to life. His development as a poet was also his spiritual development, and the justification for the truth that he offered in his poetry was that it arose out of his struggle to experience truth: 'Axioms in philosophy', that is to say, had to be 'proved upon our pulses' (letter 64), and he invented the famous phrase 'Negative Capability' (32) (Forman's edition) to express the quality that forms 'a Man of Achievement' – 'that is, when a man is capable of being in uncertainties, mysteries, doubts, without any irritable reaching after fact and reason'. He cites Shakespeare as a man who possessed this quality, and Coleridge as one who lacked it. He described the world as 'The vale of Soul-making' (123): 'There may be intelligences or sparks of the divinity in millions – but they are not Souls till they acquire identities, till each one is personally itself'. This struggle to form oneself, to create an identity 'is the very thing in which consists poetry; and if so it is not so fine a thing as philosophy – For the same reason that an eagle is not so fine a thing as a truth' (123). Philosophy and poetry, or perhaps rather the labour of thought and the life of the senses, competed in Keats for predominance, but one sees how in both his verse and his letters the latter became a means to realizing the former. Their union, for Keats, constituted Beauty, which for him was a more distinct concept than it has been for most writers. Hitherto, when writers had speculated about Beauty as an absolute quality (Spenser's *Four Hymns*, 1596) they had conceived it as some kind of Platonic ideal of form. For Keats it was the active quality in which suffering was surpassed by the human spirit. He writes of 'the pleasure of trying the resources of his spirit', about a man under misfortune (31), and in the same letter: 'I am certain of nothing but of the holiness of the Heart's affections and the truth of the Imagination – What the imagination seizes as Beauty must be truth.' The process of reconciling suffering and delight in Beauty is the theme of his great Odes*, but it is in his unrevised and unfinished late poem, *The Fall of Hyperion* (**Hyperion*), that he is most distinct about the subject, though he uses symbolic language to express it. The poet finds himself first in a luxuriant garden – the life of the senses – from which he passes into a vast temple where a veiled figure is enthroned at the top of a flight of steps. The poet finds that he must mount the steps or die on the temple floor, but to take the first step proves an almost intolerable ordeal. The reason seems to be that the act symbolizes achievement of disinterested sympathy, for

> '*None can usurp this height*,' *return'd that shade*,
> '*But those to whom the miseries of the world*
> *Are misery*, *and will not let them rest*.'

When the veiled figure unveils, she exhibits a terrible pallor which the poet finds intolerable to contemplate, were it not for the 'benignant light' radiating in blank splendour from her eyes. The vision recalls Keats's sonnet of 1818 on reading *King Lear*, where he writes of 'burning through' 'the fierce dispute Betwixt damnation and impassioned clay', that is to say, the encounter of vulnerable but vital humanity with excess of pain.

Keats, until tuberculosis wrecked him, sought to bring the life of the senses progressively into accordance with moral experience, and to enlarge his moral experience until it could extend to universal sympathy. Wordsworth and Coleridge, in their separate ways, saw poetry as an enlargement of the poet's and the reader's personalities through the extension of their sympathies. This concern with growth from within the personality was what distinguished the Romantic period of 1790–1830 from the 18th-century Augustan period, and it constituted a change of direction from attention to the outer world of social civilization to the inner world of the human spirit. Yet it was not a deliberate turning away from society: Wordsworth declared that he spent many hours deliberating about social problems compared to the few that he devoted to literary ones. The change was largely due to a change in the conception of society. The Augustans had felt deeply critical of their society, but they believed that it contained all the elements necessary to the fulfilment of man in a high civilization. The Romantics – partly owing to the deep disturbance of social ideas resulting from the French Revolution* but still more owing to the new methods of production in the Industrial Revolution* – felt that society denied essential human needs, which could only begin to be satisfied by new influences from imaginative literature acting on the inner lives of individuals. Thus Shelley*, in *A Defence of Poetry* (1820) wrote:

> *The cultivation of poetry is never more to be desired than at periods when, from an excess of the selfish and calculating principle, the accumulation of the materials of external life exceed the quantity of the power of assimilating them to the internal laws of human nature.*

Shelley's essay was written in answer to one by his friend Peacock*, *The Four Ages of Poetry* (1820). Peacock had argued – in line with 18th-century rationalism – that poetry and the poetic imagination belonged to the primitive ages of civilization and were to be outgrown. It was not a very seriously presented thesis, but Shelley's reply is passionate and eloquent. It is not very closely argued, however, though it contains illuminating phrases and a few passages that are directed to the problem of contemporary culture, like the one just quoted. Nor did Charles Lamb* (1775–1834) and Thomas de Quincey* (1785–1859), two of the leading Romantic critics, contribute much to the discussion, though they helped to widen the literary interests of their generation, especially by drawing attention to neglected 16th- and 17th-century writers, and thus extended the material for debate. The most notable of the Romantic critics, apart from Wordsworth, Coleridge and Keats, was probably William Hazlitt* (1778–1830), whose book *The Spirit of the Age* (1825) is a sequence of terse commentaries on contemporary writers and thinkers. His contribution is a better 'defence of poetry' than Shelley's, for he shows how the abstract social philosophers, such as Bentham*, ignored the concrete particulars which were the very subject for the poets.

Hazlitt's book reminds us how easy it is to distort the character of a literary period by concentrating on those writers whose reputations have best survived from it. We forget that Keats and Shelley were comparatively neglected writers, and that Wordsworth and Coleridge only reached the height of prestige after 1830. Looking at the 'Romantic Period' more closely, we see that it was dominated by the 'Great Reviews' (*Reviews and Periodicals), notably the *Edinburgh** (founded 1802), the *Quarterly** (founded 1809), and *Blackwood's Magazine** (founded 1817), and that these were conservative – even Augustan – in the bias of their taste. They nonetheless gave extensive attention even to Romantic poetry, and it was not always unfavourable attention, nor always unjust even when bitterly hostile. Hostile attention, moreover, is better than neglect; after 1830 the reviews gave less space – though it remained considerable – to imaginative writing, and more space to politics. It was in this period, succeeding that of the great Romantics, that the battle for literary culture became for the first time acute.

7·4

The Victorian Age (1830–1914): the critic against society

I felt that the flaw in my life, must be a flaw in life itself; that the question was, whether, if the reformers of society and government could succeed in their objects, and every person in the community were free and in a state of physical comfort, the pleasures of life, being no longer kept up by struggle and privation, would cease to be pleasures. And I felt that unless I could see my way to some better hope than this for human happiness in general, my dejection must continue; but that if I could see such an outlet, I should then look on the world with pleasure; content as far as I was myself concerned, with any fair share of the general lot.

This state of my thoughts and feelings made the fact of my reading Wordsworth for the first time (in the autumn of 1828) an important event in my life. . . . What made Wordsworth's poems a medicine for my state of mind, was that they expressed, not mere outward beauty, but states of feeling, and of thought coloured by feeling, under the excitement of beauty. They seemed to be the very culture of the feelings, which I was in quest of. In them I seemed to draw from a source of inward joy, of sympathetic and imaginative pleasure, which could be shared in by all human beings; which had no connexion with struggle or imperfection, but would be made richer by every improvement in the physical or social condition of mankind.

John Stuart Mill* – *Autobiography* (1873) Chap. 5

J. S. Mill (1806–73) was educated in that 18th-century stream of thought which had the most powerful influence on 19th-century thinking. His father, James Mill, was a follower of Jeremy Bentham* (1748–1832) who assessed society according to his own severely rationalistic philosophy: since the goal of human life was happiness, that society was happy in which the most pleasure was available to the greatest number, together with the least possible subjection to avoidable pain. Bentham and James Mill tested institutions and ideas according to their practical effectiveness in promoting human happiness thus primitively calculated; they despised imagination and relied entirely on reason in their social accountancy. 'All poetry is misrepresentation', the younger Mill quotes Bentham as declaring. James Mill trained his son from a very early age in every mode of study that cultivated the reason, but poetry was ignored except as a kind of rhetoric, 'useful' because 'people in general attached more value to verse than it deserved'. Christianity was left out of this education altogether. John Stuart was thus brought up to be a practical political reformer, and he was already a leader of the young intellectuals in the Benthamite school of thought when, at the age of 22, he suffered the spiritual crisis referred to in the extract quoted above. He discovered that he was devoting all his energies to the means of reform, without any satisfying conception of human nature as the end which the reforms were to serve.

Mill recovered from his crisis when, like Hazlitt in *The Spirit of the Age*, he saw the truth that the Benthamite philosophers ignored: that abstract propositions about society have meaning only in relation to individuals, the concrete particulars that make it up. The quality of a society must therefore depend on the quality of individual experience, and this in turn must depend on the faculties through which the individual acquires his experience – his feelings and his imagination. He saw that contemporary social thinkers were divided along the line that separated Bentham from Coleridge – the thinker who relied entirely on reason and based the deductions of reason on practical evidence, and the thinker who associated reason with imagination as the faculty which gives direct insight into reality. Mill himself remained on the Bentham side philosophically, but he realized that Benthamism could only account for the truth outwardly, and that Coleridgean thinking asked the right questions about the inward nature of the truth. His essays on Bentham (1838) and on Coleridge (1840) are an attempt to relate the two sides: to bring 18th-century rationalism into alliance with, instead of antagonism to, 19th-century Romantic intuition.

Mill wrote on Coleridge as a philosopher, not as a poet or a critic; he was himself a philosopher, who wrote a few intelligent literary critical essays. He is nonetheless an important and characteristic figure in the literary thought of his time, so much of which is more interesting when it raises questions about the relationship of imaginative writing to the life of society than when it discusses literary art directly. There are two reasons for this bias of interest: the first is that many leading Victorian* thinkers were deeply troubled, beyond those of any previous society, by the rapidity of social change and by its lack of direction. The second is that critics were unable, until the last twenty years of the century, to see that the most lively imaginative production was now flowing along channels which were unrecognized by traditional literary culture. From Homer downwards, imaginative writing had meant poetry, and poetry had nearly always meant verse. There had, of course, always been imaginative writing in prose, and in the 18th century the growth of prose fiction first threatened the preponderance of verse, but until 1830 the majority of the finest imaginative writers still cultivated the verse forms. After 1830, verse ceased to be the preponderant medium, and the prose novel became the most vigorous imaginative form. It was also, of course, the most popular, and a great proportion of the very large output was worthless. It is understandable, therefore, that the critics, who were anxious to find writings that would raise popular taste, and had themselves been educated in the great poetic masterpieces of the past, regarded all current novels with suspicion and disdain; particular novels received extensive critiques in the reviews and literary journals, but the novel considered as an artistic form was largely ignored as an inferior product of the poetic art.

On the other hand, the serious critics were also dissatisfied with the quality both of contemporary verse and of the high Romantic verse that had preceded it, which seemed to them lacking in intellectual force; an exception was commonly made for Wordsworth, but he was sometimes accused of lacking emotional spontaneity. Thus Mill, who was one of the earliest admirers of Tennyson*, complained of the lack of the capacity to think apparent in his early volumes of 1830 and 1833; in his essay *Poetry and its Varieties* (1859) Mill similarly criticized Shelley for his lack of 'logical and scientific culture'. John Ruskin*, writing about the Pathetic Fallacy (in *Modern Painters* III, 1856), defined this term as a pleasant but usually weakening tendency in poets to represent nature as though it behaved in accordance with human emotions; the poets whom he quotes as exemplifying it are all of the 18th and 19th centuries. He does not wholly condemn the tendency, 'For . . . it is in general a sign of higher capacity and stand in the ranks of being, that the emotions should be strong enough to vanquish, partly, the intellect, and make it believe what they choose.' However, the greatest poets are only exceptionally subject to it, for 'it is still a grander condition when the intellect also rises, till it is strong enough to assert its rule against, or together with, the utmost efforts of the passions'. He cites Dante and Homer as exemplars of this finer order of poet, but he quotes an example from Wordsworth too. In general, desiring as they did that poetry should amply counteract the pettiness which they considered commercialism to be imposing on human nature, the Victorians demanded heroic proportions from their poets, and they found such men of genius (apart from the German poet Goethe*) only in the distant past. The strongest and most eloquent expression of the potentiality of poetry is that made by Matthew Arnold* (1822–88) in his essay *The Study of Poetry* (*Essays in Criticism** II, 1888):

The future of poetry is immense, because in poetry, where it is worthy of its high destinies, our race, as time goes on, will find an ever surer and surer stay. There is not a creed which is not shaken, not an accredited dogma which is not shown to be questionable, not a received tradition which does not threaten to dissolve. Our religion has materialized itself in the fact, and now the fact is failing it. But for poetry the idea is everything; the rest is a world of illusion, of divine illusion. Poetry attaches its emotion to the idea; the idea is *the fact. The strongest part of our religion today is its unconscious poetry.*

Arnold's claim for the greatness of the role of poetry in civilization is in keeping with the great claims made for it by Wordsworth and Coleridge, but it is more comprehensive and far-reaching. The extensiveness of Arnold's claim recalls rather Shelley's *Defence of Poetry* (1821), and this in turn recalls Sidney's *Apology** (1595). Neither Sidney nor even Shelley, however, was so specifically concerned with poetry as a remedy for the ills of contemporary society. For Sidney the world was by its nature (though not in its origin) a fallen one for any society, and Shelley was appealing for poetry as a function, though a supreme one, among competing functions of the mind. Arnold, on the other hand, is concerned with the action of poetry on his own society, and in a sense his mind is more engaged with his society than with poetry. So, on the whole, were the minds of Ruskin, Carlyle* and Mill when they wrote about poetry, but Arnold, by far the most memorable of the mid-19th-century critics, made the most specific diagnosis of the evils of his age. In his essay *The Function of Criticism at the Present Time* (*Essays in Criticism* I, 1865), he made a plea, not for poetry, but for criticism to counterbalance the headlong material advances which overlay much human misery and obscured any vision of finer social ideals. Arnold says, in effect, that the men and women of his time, rich or poor, simply could not see by what high standards they should judge the quality of human life, for lack of an enlightened critical function. The essence of this function he describes as 'the idea of a disinterested endeavour to learn and propagate the best that is known and felt in the world, and thus to establish a current of fresh and true ideas'. He considered that English life had lost this spirit of culture – the spirit that had been so central and vital in the age of Shakespeare. Even the first 30 years of the century, remarkable as it had been poetically, had suffered from its lack: 'the English poetry of the first quarter of this century, with plenty of energy, plenty of creative force, did not know enough. This makes Byron so empty of matter, Shelley so incoherent, Wordsworth even, profound as he is, yet so wanting in completeness and variety.' In his book *Culture and Anarchy* (1869), Arnold divided English society into three classes; these were the Barbarians, or upper classes, the Philistines, or middle classes, and the Populace, or uneducated working classes. The Barbarians were civilized, but their civilization was external only, a matter of fine manners and gracious living. But Arnold was mainly concerned with the Philistines, for it was the middle classes that gave English civilization its distinctive quality. He goes on to describe this quality as 'Hebraism' – following the tradition of the Biblical Hebrews in the pursuit of right conduct in accordance with obedience to a narrow ethical law. His criticism of Hebraism is not that it is wrong, but precisely that it is narrow, and he proposes to correct this narrowness by what he calls 'Hellenism' (from 'Hellene' = 'ancient Greek') by which he understands the breadth and richness of a generous, life-giving culture, the diffusion of the Bee's 'sweetness and light' in Swift's *Battle of the Books*. He summarizes the difference thus: 'The governing idea of Hellenism is *spontaneity of consciousness*; that of Hebraism, *strictness of conscience*.'

Arnold believed that no social or political reform could lead to a truly enlightened society, or even to a proper understanding of contemporary abuses, unless it was guided by a 'hellenic' consciousness, and this led him in the direction of authoritarianism. He was impressed by the high level of culture in contemporary France, with its governing Academy (*Literary Influence of Academies*, in *Essays in Criticism* II) and by the success of von Humboldt in the organizing of Prussian education. These examples of enlightened authority brought him in his Conclusion to *Culture and Anarchy* to declare that the State must be made the 'expression of our best Self', but he did not show how this could be done without surrendering to an 'élite' – presumably elected by an 'élite' minority of the nation. This difficult attempt to give political reality to the concept of 'Culture' sets Arnold apart from Mill, who, in his essay *On Liberty** (1859) confines himself to arguments for the defence of minority opinion against the tyranny of majorities, in order to safeguard the many-sided requirements of human development. Mill, on the other hand, gives no account of the kind of culture he so clearly desires as the objective of social improvement, though in his essay *Civilization* he is much more lucid than Arnold about the political means of securing one. Ruskin's four essays *Unto This Last** (1862) do something to fill the gap between Mill and Arnold: he examines the assumptions behind the political and economic terminology in current use, and he shows how the very fact of their prevalence made it impossible to think clearly about the culture of society.

Such works have little to do with literary criticism in a strict sense, but they have much to do with the sort of society in which a high literary culture can flourish, and especially with the consequences for any society of doing without one. These consequences were seen by Arnold and Ruskin – and also by Mill, though he is much less explicit about it – to be a kind of spiritual meanness; the sort of meanness to which the richer classes of Victorian Britain condemned the working classes, and in which these richer classes often themselves lived, without the excuse of lack of better opportunities. Ruskin, though he was primarily a critic of the plastic arts, preached enlargement and release through the study of great poetry in his lectures to working-class audiences, *Sesame and Lilies* (1865); Arnold did likewise in his *Essays in Criticism* (1865 and 1888), especially in the famous essay, *The Study of Poetry*. Central to Arnold's view is his statement (in the essay on Wordsworth in the same volume) that 'poetry is at bottom a criticism of life . . . the greatness of a poet lies in his powerful and beautiful application of ideas to life – to the question: How to live.' In *The Study of Poetry* he expands this:

> *But for supreme poetical success more is required than the powerful application of ideas to life; it must be an application under the conditions fixed by the laws of poetic truth and poetic beauty. Those laws fix as an essential condition, in the poet's treatment of such matters as are here in question, high seriousness; the high seriousness which comes from absolute sincerity.*

For Arnold, nothing less than the very best will do to demonstrate the very great potentialities he sees in poetry, and to measure the very best he recommends 'touchstones' from the most exalted poets of European literature – from Homer, Dante, Shakespeare and Milton. Arnold is a sensitive critic, and when he rejects less exalted poets – Chaucer, Dryden, Pope and Burns – who, for him, do not exhibit the necessary quality of 'high seriousness' – he manages to do so without belittling them. Yet his 'high seriousness' – and a similar charge might be made against Ruskin – is a narrowing criterion for taste: the desire of these critics to 'raise' taste leads them to poetry that is 'elevated', but these critics forget that the 'vitalization' of taste is important before 'raising' it can be. Moreover 'high seriousness' may mislead a reader into admiring poetry that is serious by intention though it fails in achievement, and if he tries to check his judgement by reference to 'absolute sincerity' he may find this an elusive term. Critics in the 20th century have found less to admire in Milton than Arnold did, and much to admire in Donne – whom Arnold does not mention – just because Donne directly faces the problem of sincerity in his poetry in a way that Milton does not. Arnold's great claims for poetry need to be substantiated by a wider range of detailed assessments than he has left us. Thus Arnold remains for 20th-century readers a tantalizing figure: a great critic who wrote relatively little specific criticism, but, as T. S. Eliot* has said, (*Arnold and Pater*, 1930) achieved fine propaganda for criticism.

Memorable literary criticism of the specific kind that one misses in Arnold occurs chiefly in the last 30 years of the 19th century. The remarkably original poet G. M. Hopkins* (1844–89) shows in his letters and his notebooks the kind of insight that his age badly needed into poetry and the state of the language. For him, poetic language is 'current language heightened, to any degree heightened and unlike itself, but not an obsolete one'. He understood better than any writer of his lifetime that poetry should draw its rhythms from the spoken language, thus carrying a weight of meaning immediately into the reader's sensibility, activating the sensibility rather than reducing it to the trancelike, passive receptivity characteristic of too much poetry of the period. Arnold, Ruskin, and other critics seem to have desired that poetry should operate like this, but they were too much affected by the Spenserian and Miltonic influence so prevalent over the previous two centuries to see how it could be achieved, and contemporary prejudice from the same influence was too strong to allow the publication of Hopkins's own poetry. Hopkins's practice of criticism – none of which was published in the 19th century – was strict but constructive. So was that of Leslie Stephen* (1832–1904).

Stephen's reputation is the most curious of those of the great Victorian critics; his approach is commonly acknowledged to be the nearest to that of mid-20th-century criticism, and yet his name is more honoured than his works are read. He avoided the extremes of 19th-century criticism – the narrow reverence for what is spiritually exalted on the one hand, and the lazy tolerance of any literature that is entertaining on the other – and he sought to give his assessments the kind of validity that is found in conscientious and responsible scientific and philosophic thinking.

Much of the literary criticism of the later 19th century is decadent, both in the sense that it lacked Leslie Stephen's rigour, and in the sense that it lacked the concern for the relevance of literature to humanity which has characterized so much of the best criticism in English. One form of this decadence arose from excess of the historical approach, in itself a healthy belief that literature must be judged in the setting of its historical period. An example is the distinguished writer George Saintsbury* (1845–1933), who was a great literary scholar rather than a great critic. The historical and scholarly approach is, of course, useful and necessary, and yet, in so far as it encourages a merely descriptive treatment of writers, it can be sterile, since it ignores the most important responsibility of any criticism: the revaluation of a writer's work in the light of its relevance to *present* history. Another form of decadence arose from aestheticism. It stemmed from Walter Pater* (1839–94), who, at his most humane, was a disciple of Arnold, but without Arnold's passionate preoccupation with society. The most useful service performed by the aesthetic movement was that it helped to release the English critical tradition from the wrong sort of insistence on the moral purpose of art. Art, although the aesthetes thought otherwise, cannot exist for its own sake, but a work of art is obedient to its own laws, and cannot be obedient to any particular moral theory. Art, at its best, at least when it takes the form of imaginative writing, is concerned with moral exploration, and this the aesthetic critics, with their preoccupation with form, failed to understand. One critic, however, was keenly aware both of the importance of artistic form and of the relevance to art of moral exploration; this was the Anglo-American novelist-critic, Henry James* (1843–1916).

James's criticism is important in at least four ways. First, he was the first systematic critic of the novel form in English; there had been many long reviews of novels in the 19th century, but no writer had hitherto attempted to form a conception of the scope of the novelistic vision, of ways in which the novel could be organized, of its characteristic limitations and its evident advantages. Secondly, James opened a window on to the artistically much more self-conscious French novel, and thereby raised questions of form for the English novel. Thirdly, James, like Wordsworth at the beginning of the century, was creating the taste by which he was to be appreciated, and thus reveals the principles of his own very distinctive art. Fourthly, his basically pessimistic mind was intensely occupied with the idea of civilization as the order men build out of chaos, and with the tragic paradox that the quality of innocence – what is spontaneously good in human nature – undergoes almost inevitable corruption or destruction when it is subjected to the civilization of the western world. This cultural aspect of James's criticism is much more the theme of his fiction than it is of his specifically literary criticism, but it emerges here and there when he touches on the paramount importance of finding the right treatment of a theme, the form that is essential to it. So he writes in the Preface (1906–7) to his novel *The Spoils o Poynton* (1897): 'Life being all inclusion and confusion, and art being all discrimination and selection, the latter, in search of the hard latent *value* with which alone it is concerned, sniffs round the mass as instinctively and unerringly as a dog round a buried bone.' He himself probably thought that the 18 Prefaces to the Collected Edition of his novels were the important part of his critical writing, but the essays that will most endure are the early *The Art of Fiction* (1884) and his studies of French novelists, notably those on Flaubert*, de Maupassant, Balzac and Zola*. In the early essay he distinguishes the essential requisites of the serious novel – the close interrelationship of all its parts and aspects, the importance of allowing to the novelist complete freedom in choice of theme and treatment of it, the requirement that the novelist should be as consistent and responsible to the truth of his fiction as the historian is to the truth of his facts, and above all the insistence that the value of a novel is directly proportionate to the intelligence of the novelist. Some of his points now seem obvious enough, but James was the first critic, in English, to make them, and in making them he was demanding very belated recognition of the principle that the writing of novels should be one of the most serious occupations of the human mind. That it is also one of the most difficult, he demonstrates in his accounts of French novelists, especially Flaubert, and yet, in them, he finds limitations of imaginative intelligence which in the end caused him to revert to the English tradition. He considered that it was the business of art, especially of the novel, to explore the values of human living; the exploration of 'reality' in any other sense was not enough. He was first drawn to the French because he found them so much freer than the English in their treatment of actualities of character and environment, but he withdrew from the French tradition when, as he put it, he found the moral soil too thin to sustain him. Nonetheless, he learnt from the French the true exigency of the novelistic art, not only for the novelist but for the reader, and some of his best criticism is contained in tales of the writing life, such as *The Figure in the Carpet* and *The Lesson of the Master* in which he shows the lonely struggle of the artist to maintain his dedication to art despite the inferiority of the public taste on which he has to rely.

In his critical essays James dealt only with literature; his criticism of society he kept for his fiction, yet each kind of criticism implies the other. When we look back over the 19th-century thinkers who gave attention to literature, we find this theme recurring although in very various forms: the place of imaginative literature in society, and the importance and difficulty of sustaining it there. It was the fastidious seriousness of James's taste which caused him to be the first to give the art of the novel its proper eminence, but his taste was perhaps too fastidious to see the full scope and richness of its potentiality. In the 20th century a novelist-critic of richer vision than James gave a more fertile account of its reach. This was D. H. Lawrence.

7·5

The twentieth century (1914–present day): the responsibility of the critical function

A critic must be able to feel the impact of a work of art in all its complexity and force. To do so, he must be a man of force and complexity himself, which few critics are. A man with a paltry, impudent nature will never write anything but paltry, impudent criticism. And a man who is emotionally *educated is rare as a phoenix. The more scholastically educated a man is generally, the more he is an emotional boor.*

D. H. Lawrence* – *John Galsworthy* (1928)

And the most important qualification which I have been able to find . . . is that a critic must have a very highly developed sense of fact. This is by no means a trifling or frequent gift. And it is not one which wins popular commendations. The sense of fact is something very slow to develop, and its complete development means perhaps the very pinnacle of civilization.

T. S. Eliot* – *The Function of Criticism* (1923)

To those who take a serious interest in literature it must often seem as if their interest were curiously irrelevant to the modern world; curiously, because a serious interest in literature starts from the present and assumes that literature matters, in the first place at any rate, as the consciousness of the age. . . . The world, it will be retorted, has something else to be interested in; those who see the desperate need for action, political and other, can have no concern to spare for the state of poetry and literary criticism. The need for political action few will deny. But it seems pertinent to inquire the worth of political action or theory that is not directed towards realizing some idea of satisfactory living. I do not assert that traditional culture and literary tradition are identical, but their relation is such that those who are aware of it will not expect one to survive without the other; and it seems romantic to expect that an adequate idea will issue out of amnesia – out of a divorce from the relevant experience of the race.

F. R. Leavis* – *What's Wrong with Criticism?* (1932)

The third of these quotations shows continuity with the greatest 19th-century critic, Matthew Arnold: it continues his point of view that, in order to think about literature, the critic has to interest himself in all that relates to it, so that he ends by becoming the critic of the whole culture of his society. This is true of all three of these critics. But the first two quotations show a more distinctively 20th-century quality which is even more characteristic of all three: intentness on the writer and the work that is to be judged, and concern with the qualities required of the critic who is assuming judgement. These two attitudes to the scope and task of criticism are of course related: a culture, and a cultural tradition, are expounded in art, and especially in literature; but the exposition varies very greatly in merit, interest, and kind, so that if a society is to learn from its literature it will depend heavily on the quality of the critics who interpret the literature to it.

This superior balance between substantial comment on literature and comment on the environment of literature has made the 20th century, since 1914, the richest period yet in English literary thought. However, the superiority of criticism in our age is by no means a ground for self-satisfaction: the best critics have often been those who have written in response to what they see to be a desperate need. In the 18th century, Samuel Johnson (in his *Life of Gray*) could declare: 'I rejoice to concur with the Common Reader', but no important critic since has had his confidence. Wordsworth in his *Preface*, Coleridge in Chapter 10 of his *Biographia*, Arnold in *The Function of Criticism*, and James in his essay on Balzac, have all in different ways pointed to the dispersion of common educated taste, or to influences degrading it. Moreover they pointed out that this increasing confusion and degradation has not merely meant a communal decline in expertness of readership, but an increasing inability in society to agree on any values at all, unless they are commercial ones: civilization has declined qualitatively as it has increased quantitatively.

It is possible of course to question the qualifications of literary thinkers to be judges of their civilization, but it is difficult to ignore the insistence of their warnings, and it is necessary to allow due importance to the grounds on which they assume their authority, and to respect their serious attitude to the critical function. James (in *The Art of Fiction*) said that the quality of a novel will always be proportionate to the quality of mind in the novelist, with the implication that novel writing is futile unless it exerts all the novelist's intelligence and unless that intelligence be a good one. Lawrence, in the quotation above, makes a similar statement about the personal qualities required of the critic, and he is implying that the judge of writing must be qualified to be a judge of living. Eliot, in the second quotation, is more specific and more cryptic: by a 'sense of fact' he means direct consciousness of reality, a consciousness not filtered through other people's consciousness nor through unconscious and therefore unexamined assumptions about reality. Like Lawrence, he requires for the critic what he requires for the imaginative writer. Thus, writing about William Blake (1920), he makes the point more clearly:

> *It is important that the artist should be highly educated in his own art; but his education is one that is hindered rather than helped by the ordinary processes of society which constitute education for the ordinary man. For these processes consist largely in the acquisition of impersonal ideas which obscure what we really are and feel, what we really want, and what really excites our interest. It is of course not the actual information acquired, but the conformity which the accumulation of knowledge is apt to impose, that is harmful . . . Blake . . . knew what interested him, and he therefore presents the essential, only, in fact, what can be presented, and need not be explained. And because he was not distracted, or frightened, or occupied in anything but exact statements, he understood. He was naked, and saw man naked, and from the centre of his own crystal . . . He approached everything with a mind unclouded by current opinions. There was nothing of the superior person about him. This makes him terrifying.*

The importance of the critic being fully open to the work of art (Eliot), and engaged with it not only intellectually but morally (Lawrence) is relevant to the point made by Leavis in the third quotation: that the literature of a period is 'the consciousness of the age', and that the significant literature of the past is 'the relevant experience of the race'. Eliot, also, put this point in *Tradition and the Individual Talent* (1917):

> *Someone said: 'The dead writers are remote from us because we* know *so much more than they did.' Precisely, and they are that which we know.*

As often with Eliot, the statement is too cryptic: we need to understand what he means by 'know'. In the context of the whole important essay, Eliot seems to mean assimilation of what Leavis was later to call 'the relevant experience of the race', with emphasis on 'relevant'. The literature of the past is not important as an undiscriminated mass, and 'know' does not mean 'examination knowledge' of arbitrarily chosen texts, but assimilation of the texts in such a way that – to adapt a phrase Eliot used about Donne – they 'modify the consciousness' of the modern mind. Eliot was the first critic to formulate clearly this vital relationship of the past to the present in English literature, though of course it had pre-existed his formulation, and from Sidney in the 16th century to Arnold in the 19th century it had extended to the ancient literature of Rome. Indeed, Eliot was forced to undertake his formulation owing to the breakdown in the 19th century of a living continuity with the ancient classics, for this breakdown necessitated new understanding of how the past of a culture relates vitally to the present, and of the true meaning of 'tradition'.

In his essay *Tradition and the Individual Talent*, Eliot redefines 'tradition' in a way parallel to that in which Wordsworth, in his poetry, redefined 'nature' at the opening of the 19th century. In the 18th century 'nature' had tended to mean the inert substance of reality which the mind could 'know' objectively, as information, but Wordsworth re-expressed nature as that in the human environment which humanity could assimilate emotionally, so that he 'knows' it by active relationship and the enlargement of his personality. Similarly, Eliot teaches that 'tradition' is not, as it is still commonly understood to be, the 'dead hand of the past' forcing the present into conformity with it, but all that is alive from the past, capable of assimilation by the present, and of being altered by it. It follows that a contemporary who is a truly 'traditional' writer is also a truly modern one, for he continues the tradition by adding to it and changing its shape, whereas the writer who is commonly called 'traditional' no more truly belongs to the tradition than a forgery belongs to a gallery of great pictures:

> *The existing monuments form an ideal order among themselves, which is modified by the new (the really new) work of art among them. The existing order is complete before the new work arrives; for order to persist after the supervention of novelty, the* whole *existing order must be, if ever so slightly, altered; and so the relations, proportions, values of each work of art toward the whole must be readjusted; and this is conformity between the old and new.*

Eliot is here speaking of the imaginative writer's relationship to tradition. Leavis expresses the idea for the critic a generation later in *The Responsible Critic* (1953):

> *The serious critic's concern with the literature of the past is with its life in the present; it will be informed by the kind of perception that can distinguish intelligently and sensitively the significant new life in contemporary literature.*

These convictions led Eliot and Leavis to take the lead in what is probably the most important critical achievement of this century: a revaluation of English literature to an extent and thoroughness such as had never been equalled before.

Eliot's revaluation is substantially contained in his *Selected Essays 1917–32*. Its extent is perhaps partly due to his having, like James, American origins. These enabled him to see English poetry as a whole more readily than an English-born critic might; it also enabled him the better to see it, as James saw the English novel, in relation to the European tradition. Thus he was able, for example, to see that French later-19th-century poetry could contribute influences to 20th-century English poetry of a more interesting kind than those offered by English poetry contemporary with it, and he was able to show the relevance of Dante to the whole European tradition, including the English part of it. In English literature itself, he was able to demonstrate that Milton's gigantic reputation was in some ways disproportionate and harmful, because it had helped to obscure, for two and a half centuries, the quite different vitality of language among the Metaphysical School of poets, especially, in the first half of the 17th century. For Eliot, the importance of the Metaphysicals is that in their work the intellect and the emotions are fused by the imagination into single operation, whereas after the middle of the 17th century the mind and the emotions separated, and the separation resulted in poetic impoverishment: 'Tennyson and Browning are poets, and they think; but they do not feel their thought as immediately as the odour of a rose. A thought to Donne is an experience; it modified his sensibility.' After the middle of the 17th century, 'something happened to the mind of England', and Eliot describes this something as a 'dissociation of sensibility'*:

> *In the seventeenth century a dissociation of sensibility set in, from which we have never recovered; and this dissociation, as is natural, was aggravated by the influence of the two most powerful poets of the century, Milton and Dryden. Each of these men performed certain poetic functions so magnificently well that the magnitude of the effect concealed the absence of others. The language went on and in some respects improved . . . But while the language became more refined, the feeling became more crude. The feeling, the sensibility, expressed in the* Country Churchyard *(to say nothing of Tennyson and Browning) is cruder than that in the* Coy Mistress.
>
> *The Metaphysical Poets*, 1921

Eliot's diagnosis has several times been challenged, particularly in regard to his injustice to later poets. But the phrase 'dissociation of sensibility' has passed into critical currency, partly because it suggests, better than any other, certain aspects of what were undoubtedly changes in 'the mind of England' at about the time of the Restoration of the Monarchy in 1660, and partly because it helps to explain the very general revival of interest in Donne and the Metaphysical poets in this century.

Whether or not the 17th century is the age of the 'dissociation of sensibility', it certainly contained the greatest Civil War* in British history. It was a war that divided the people in complex ways, but the most evident division was the religious one (with cultural implications) between the Anglican* Church, with its 'half-way' conservative tradition between Catholicism and Protestantism, and the thorough Protestants or Puritans*, who later came to be known as 'Dissenters' or 'Nonconformists'. Eliot has remarked that the differences that break into Civil War never really heal while a culture persists, and it is curious that the most vehement disagreements in 20th-century English criticism have lain between Eliot, the convert to Anglicanism and the increasingly conservative critic of literature and society, on the one side, and Lawrence and Leavis, with their Nonconformist background, on the other. The differences were apparent from the first between Lawrence and Eliot, but it is only from Eliot's book *After Strange Gods* (1934) that they become important between Eliot and Leavis. That book shows Eliot narrowing his ideas on tradition to orthodoxy, and discussing Lawrence as a man of profound intuition but no intellectual training, no background in social tradition, with a strong reliance on his 'Inner Light' and a comparable disposition to see himself as a Messiah. Lawrence is, in fact, for Eliot 'an almost perfect example of the heretic', and Eliot's book is subtitled 'A Primer of Modern Heresy'. The issue, which goes far beyond those of strictly literary criticism, is between the advocacy of free intelligence by Lawrence, and intelligence responsibly guided by authority, advocated by Eliot. However, it is not true that Lawrence lacked intellectual training any more than Shakespeare did, nor that his Nonconformist background provided no social tradition; it is true, however, that he came from the other side of the 'Civil War' to Eliot, who was thus disqualified from even seeing Lawrence's kind of self-discipline and restraint. This was a discipline derived from the Puritan–Nonconformist sense of ethical responsibility: the belief that the enlightenment of the mind was never valid unless it was allied to the enlightenment of the conscience.

Unless the word 'Puritan' is properly understood here, it is of course seriously confusing to apply it to Lawrence, since it is with 'anti-puritanism' that he identified himself. 'Puritanism', in the loose, broad sense of what he opposed, has come to be identified with the vices with which its 17th-century enemies associated it: prudishness in sexuality, hypocrisy, philistinism and bigotry. Of these, Lawrence was undoubtedly the foremost opponent of the age. On the other hand, the Puritan virtues tended to be the obverse of these vices: responsibility in human relationship, highly developed conscience, a sense of the relevance of art to the conduct of life, and loyalty to deeply felt convictions. These qualities Lawrence possessed, but he possessed, too, the Puritan's suspicion of imposed authority. Morality for him, in consequence, could not be a system; it was an aptitude for living which had to be educated, as he explains in the last paragraph of his posthumously published essay *Why the Novel Matters*:

> *In life, there is right and wrong, good and bad, all the time. But what is right in one case is wrong in another. And in the novel you see one man becoming a corpse, because of his so-called goodness, another going dead because of his so-called wickedness. Right and wrong is an instinct: but an instinct of the whole consciousness in a man, bodily, mental, spiritual at once. And only in the novel are* all *things given full play, or at least they may be given full play, when we realize that life itself, and not inert safety, is the reason for living. For out of the full play of all things emerges the only thing that is anything, the wholeness of a man, the wholeness of a woman, man alive, and live woman.*

In the essay *Art and Morality* (1925), Lawrence associates the morality of true art with something very like the 'sense of fact' that Eliot requires for the critic: 'The true artist doesn't substitute immorality for morality. On the contrary, he *always* substitutes a finer morality for a grosser. And as soon as you see a finer morality, the grosser becomes relatively immoral.' True morality, in other words, is always the outcome of the fullest possible awareness of reality, and it is such awareness that true art promotes. The novel seemed to Lawrence the fullest medium for the cultivation of this awareness. Potentially, it was 'the one bright book of life' (*Why the Novel Matters*), but it could be this only on condition that the novelist was allowed complete freedom to realize his vision, and on condition that he was conscientiously true to it. In the essay *Morality and the Novel* (1925) he argues that the novel is the finest medium for conveying the truth – that is to say, the kind of truth that is relevant to the conduct of life – because, unlike philosophy, religion and science, which 'are all of them busy nailing things down, to get a stable equilibrium', the novel allows reality to find its own equilibrium. But there is such a thing as immorality in the novel; this is when the novelist, influenced by personal fear or wishfulness, 'puts his thumb in the pan' and destroys the equilibrium that arises from the honest and free use of his imagination.

Apart from his general essays on literature and art, several of which have been cited, Lawrence wrote criticism on recent and contemporary writers such as Thomas Mann, Verga, the American novelists, and Galsworthy and Hardy. The interest of these essays is not so much the value of the individual assessments as the vivid insights into the art of fiction which relate them to the general essays. For instance, the essay on Galsworthy attacks the merely social reality of his characters:

> *The human individual is a queer animal, always changing. But the fatal change today is the collapse from the psychology of the free human individual into the psychology of the social being, just as the fatal change in the past was a collapse from the freeman's psyche to the psyche of the slave.*

His main criticism of contemporary and recent novelists was that they did not take enough into account, in their estimates of human nature, but he blames the novelists for this less than he blames the belittling effects of contemporary civilization. It is characteristic of Lawrence's writing – and in keeping with his constant concern with human 'wholeness' – that in order to understand his conception of the scope of fiction one has to pass from his literary critical essays to the essays that express his philosophy of human nature, such as *Apropos of Lady Chatterley's Lover*, written just after the banning of that book, in 1929. There he defends the central position he gives to the sexual relation in his novels. True emotional relationships, he considered, had been replaced in western civilization by counterfeit emotions – mental 'ideas' of emotion – for 'All the emotions [truly] belong to the body, and are only recognized by the mind.' The sexual relationship he saw as the only one that cannot lie; or rather, when it is false or trivial, the lie in it is immediately apparent. He had no use for sex as a game, for the promiscuity of the permissive society; indeed, no Puritan ever disapproved of it more uncompromisingly. Lawrence, just as much as Eliot, was aware of a fatal 'dissociation' in the modern consciousness, but whereas Eliot came to see the solution as a recovery of religious orthodoxy (*After Strange Gods*), Lawrence saw hope in art, whose task it should be to reconstitute the psyche. He went out to awaken humanity, whereas Eliot withdrew watchfully into a fortress.

Leavis, the third of the leading English literary critics of this century, was not, like Lawrence and Eliot, an artist using criticism to serve the ends of his art, but a teacher using it for the ends of education. Like many other 20th-century English and American critics, he worked in and through a university, but unlike others he also worked against the university system, in that he fought the tendency inherited from the 18th and 19th centuries for universities to turn inwards, away from society, or to serve it only as a supply of scientific experts. His aim – expressed in *The Idea of a University* – was to make universities into centres of thought and trained sensibility, permeating society with positive criticism. The aim aligns him with Arnold in his *Function of Criticism* – to 'propagate the best that is known and felt in the world, and thus to establish a current of fresh and new ideas' – but Leavis's campaign for criticism was more desperate: Arnold wrote as though such a nucleus of informed and mature judgement was possible, but Leavis has written as though it is *barely* possible. *Scrutiny**, the great review that he edited from 1932 to 1953, was an attempt to secure such a nucleus, and its influence has been extensive in education at all levels. It also contributed to a new kind of literature of critical-sociological inquiry, though this perhaps owes more to the initiative of the book *Fiction and the Reading Public* (1932) by Mrs Leavis. This development is represented by such books as Richard Hoggart's *The Uses of Literacy* (1957), an enquiry into the state of working-class culture, and Raymond Williams's *Culture and Society, 1780–1950* (1958), a study of the bearings of the concept 'culture' on working-class history. Leavis's own writing led into a somewhat different critical investigation of the relationship of society and criticism. The influence of Arnold upon him was tempered by that of Mill, as is evident from his edition of *Mill on Bentham and Coleridge* (1950). That book shows him concerned to combine the study of imaginative literature with the study of social and philosophical literature as complementary expressions of the cultured mind.

> *Without the sensitizing familiarity with the subtleties of language, and the insight into the relations between abstract or generalizing thought and the concrete of human experience, that the trained frequentation of literature alone can bring, the thinking that attends social and political studies will not have the edge and force it should.*
>
> 'Literature and Society' in *Scrutiny*, 1943

In other words, abstract thought on society and politics must draw life from the stuff of individual experience, which is the material of the best imaginative writing.

This concern with 'the sensitizing familiarity' led Leavis to an extensive revaluation of the English literary tradition – an enterprise that became a co-operative one in *Scrutiny*. His revaluations, many of which are published in *Revaluation* (1936) and *The Common Pursuit* (1952), were more thorough and more extensive than those of Eliot, who attended almost entirely to poetry, whereas Leavis gave equal attention to poetry and prose; he treated imaginative writing as a single tradition. His achievement, however, was most notable in the field of the novel; *The Great Tradition* (1948) and *D. H. Lawrence: Novelist* (1955) established for the first time the criterion of a great artistic development in English prose fiction. He distinguishes sharply, in a way that recalls Leslie Stephen in the 19th century and

Johnson in the 18th, between the writing that he finds fully significant for human life from that which is merely entertaining or possesses 'charm'. This has caused him to be sometimes regarded as a negative and discouraging influence on creativity. It is true that there is in his criticism a strongly censorious tone that recalls the old Puritan conviction that what is not positive in its influence is probably harmful – at least, in Leavis's terms, when it is allowed to obscure, with ephemerality, the profound relevance of the greater work. The criterion for the latter is the depth and vitality of the 'felt life' in the work. For the critic to respond to such depth of life in a writer, he must, as Lawrence points out in the passage quoted at the head of this section, be capable of comparable qualities in himself. Thus criticism becomes a kind of spiritual ordeal for the critic, and the feeling that they had suffered a kind of moral condemnation as men caused many critics and critical journals to ostracize Leavis through much of his career: the reason was probably fear rather than actual hostility. In fact, however, it is Leavis's generously affirmative judgements which stand out, when his work is surveyed. In modern writing, his *New Bearings in English Poetry* (1932) remains the most enlightening book on poetry in the 20th century, and the high reputations of Eliot and Lawrence owe more to his appreciations than to any other single critic. His treatment of individual writers shows him nearer to Lawrence than to Eliot, and it is Lawrence's side that he takes in the antagonism between them. His method is certainly far less intuitive, far more rigorous than that of Lawrence, but his mind moves with the same determined freedom, without respect for any dogma, literary or other. The criterion is Lawrence's 'fullness of life', disciplined by the same strongly developed but adventurous ethical consciousness. He is, however, much more securely based than Lawrence: there was some point in Eliot's attack on Lawrence's 'messianism' and reliance on his own 'Inner Light'. Leavis's control is the continuity of the English tradition, assessed corporately in *Scrutiny*: we live from the past, but not from abstract *concepts* of the past.

None of the critics so far mentioned has been chiefly important as a critical theorist – a function which, indeed, has seldom greatly appealed to the pragmatic English mind. Coleridge, indeed, was the only important theorist of the principles underlying criticism before the 20th century; after him it is necessary to come to I. A. Richards* (b 1893). In his books *Principles of Literary Criticism* (1924), *Science and Poetry* (1926), and *Coleridge and the Imagination* (1935), he tried to outline the process of the imagination and the effects of poetry on the reader, in accordance with his conviction, taken from Arnold, that the civilized consciousness will depend on poetry as it once depended on religion. His approach, however, is scientific, through psychology, and philosophical in accordance with the linguistic philosophy of Bertrand Russell* and Wittgenstein. He considered, perhaps, that to make great claims for the potential effect of poetry is of little use while poetry counts for so little in most educated minds. In an age when the common man is convinced by little unless it is presented to him by what purports to be scientific method, Richards attempted to use one in describing the authority that poetry can exercise over the human mind. The essence of the theory is that the personality can be described as a tangle of disordered impulses, among which poetry can produce a degree of order and balance; the value of the poetry depends on the degree of order and buoyancy that a poem causes. It is not, now, a theory with strong influence; it has been regarded as a somewhat misguided attempt to make concessions to the Benthamite, utilitarian grounds for disregarding poetry as a fully serious activity – an attitude which was much more widespread when Richards wrote his *Principles* than it had been when J. S. Mill discovered its unsatisfactoriness a hundred years before. On the other hand, Richards has had great influence through his books *Practical Criticism* (1929) and *Speculative Instruments* (1955) in which he shows that it is poetry that raises in the richest and most interesting ways the complexity of language and the elusive relationship between language and meaning. Much of his writing – in books not mentioned here – has been devoted to semantics, the science of meaning, and the semantic approach to poetry which he originated has given new instruments to the critic, and a fresh kind of assurance, responsible for what is still known as the 'New Criticism' in the United States. In England, it contributed to Leavis's advocacy of close textual criticism as an educational method. It also assisted the decline of 'historical criticism' in the Saintsbury tradition, by emphasizing that the value of an imaginative work must always be intrinsic, and that the extraneous interest which historical criticism commonly affords is often more distracting than useful.

The characteristically 20th-century concentration of criticism upon texts, upon language as the whole material of the literary work of art has been fertile in the criticism of the last 40 years. It has led, for instance, to new attitudes in the assessment of Shakespeare. During the 19th century, criticism of Shakespeare tended to be in terms of his characters, culminating in the still-admired *Shakespearian Tragedy* (1904) by A. C. Bradley*. According to the new school of thought, character criticism inclines to fallacy and to incompleteness, since it easily leads to an account of fictional character as though it is identifiable with the historical character of actually existing persons, and at the same time tends to ignore important elements such as the imagery in a Shakespeare drama. The most eminent exponent of this new approach has been Wilson Knight (*The Wheel of Fire*, 1930; *The Imperial Theme*, 1931; *The Crown of Life*, 1947) who treats the plays as poems metaphorically dynamized into 'expanded metaphors'. Knight describes his books as 'interpretations' rather than as critical assessments, and 'interpretation', even in these earlier and more influential books, can be given a licence as extravagant as any used by the 'character critics' of the 19th century. Yet the fresh conception afforded of Shakespeare's work by Knight and others who, at least partly, share his ideas (of whom L. C. Knights and Leavis are the most notable) amounts to the most thorough and complete exposition of Shakespearian art yet achieved.

The most remarkable criticism since 1930 is undoubtedly that by William Empson* (b 1906), originally a pupil of Richards. His most notable books are *Seven Types of Ambiguity* (1930), *Some Versions of Pastoral* (1935), and *The Struc-*

ture of Complex Words (1951). As the titles suggest, they carry Richards's conception of the art of poetry as the richest of the arts of communication to extreme length. Empson's exploration of the possible varieties of meaning conveyed from the conscious and the unconscious levels of the poetic imagination has extended critical expectations in the interpretation and evaluation of poems. The stimulus from Richards and Leavis for this kind of criticism is important, but it owes much to the earlier rediscovery, by Eliot and other critics, of the importance of the early-17th-century 'Metaphysical' poets, to the discovery of the poetry of Hopkins (first published in 1918, but not widely appreciated until the second edition of 1930), and to the richness of verbal texture in the leading 20th-century poets, especially that of Eliot himself, and that of Yeats. 'Complexity' and 'ambiguity', in this later criticism, have become subjects of exploration by critics, and themselves have become words of positive evaluation, not only in poetry but in prose fiction. A danger of this development is a new, false academicism: the elucidation of a work of literature may become an end in itself, and its relevance to the whole of human experience, so strongly emphasized by Eliot, Lawrence, and Leavis, may be forgotten. From this danger it is perhaps the sociological critics, such as Raymond Williams, who may be our rescuers.

The reference section

A

Aaron /ˈeərən/

In the Bible, the founder of the Jewish priesthood; he assisted Moses* in leading the Jews out of Egypt to the frontiers of Canaan, the 'Promised Land'. His rod was a sacred emblem which Moses and he held up above the battle when the Jews were fighting the Amalekites (*Exodus* 17); it is the 'rod of God' committed to Moses by God in *Exodus* 4 – a miracle-working implement and symbol of the mystery of life. The novel *Aaron's Rod* (1922) by D. H. Lawrence*, is about a coal-miner who transforms his life with the aid of his flute.

Abbey, Abbot

* *Monasteries.*

Abbey Theatre, Dublin

The home of the Irish National Theatre Society from 1904 until a fire destroyed the building in 1951. The Society, usually known by the name of its theatre, grew from a fusion of the Irish National Dramatic Company, led by the actor W. G. Fay, and the Irish Literary Theatre founded by the poet W. B. Yeats*, his friend Lady Gregory, and others. The time was propitious: there was an intense national feeling in Ireland, and an accompanying literary revival; Europe was undergoing the awakening influences of Ibsen and Strindberg; Yeats was a major poet with strong interest in the drama. Consequently the Abbey Theatre was a focus for creative energies which made it a unique institution in the history of the English-speaking theatre. However, the movement was neither the mere mouthpiece of Irish patriotism, nor just a vehicle for European fashions. Though Ibsen was a stimulus and dominated at least one of the Irish dramatists (Edward Martyn), its most outstanding contributor, J. M. Synge*, was in reaction against Ibsen, as was Yeats himself. Neither of them tolerated the prejudices of the cruder nationalists. Synge's masterpiece, *The Playboy of the Western World**, caused a riot in the theatre when it was produced there in 1907. Synge used poetic idiom in peasant diction, Yeats used verse of increasing vigour and austerity in a renewal of poetic drama that ranked the Abbey with the most interesting experimental theatres of the time in Europe – the Théâtre Libre in Paris and the Freie Bühne in Berlin. The heroic period of the Abbey Theatre ended with Synge's death and Yeats's retirement from its management in 1909; but under Lennox Robinson the Abbey remained a theatre of distinction. Its most notable playwright after that time was Sean O'Casey*.

* 5.3.2.

Abbotsford

The home of the novelist Sir Walter Scott*, purchased by him in 1812, and greatly expanded in a romantic style of architecture corresponding to his antiquarian interests.

Abel /ˈeibl/

In the Bible, the second son of the first man and woman, Adam and Eve. His elder brother, Cain, killed him, because Abel's offering of animals in sacrifice was accepted by God whereas his own offering of 'the fruits of the ground' was rejected. Abel is thus the victim of the first murder. See *Genesis* 4.

Abelard, Peter (1079–1142)

A philosopher of great influence in the University of Paris early in 12th C. At the height of his fame, he fell in love with a young orphan girl, Heloise (Eloise), and became her tutor. She bore him a child, and to appease the anger of her uncle, Abelard proposed that they should be secretly married; open marriage was out of the question as it would obstruct Abelard's career in the Church. The marriage took place against Heloise's wishes, for she did not want her lover to risk his future prospects for her sake, and she refused to admit to it when challenged to do so. She took refuge in a convent, and her uncle revenged himself on Abelard by causing him to be mutilated. Thereafter a famous correspondence took place between them. Abelard continued his career as a teacher, but, at the instigation of Bernard of Clairvaux, he was eventually condemned for heresy (1141). The trial broke his health, and he died; his remains were secretly conveyed to Heloise, who died in 1164 and was buried in the same grave. Their love affair became legendary, and the subject of imaginative literature. Pope's *Eloisa to Abelard** (1717) is a poem on the subject. George Moore's* novel, *Héloïse and Abélard*, appeared in 1921.

Abigail /ˈabigeil/

In the Bible (*1 Samuel* 25), the wife of King David.* In addressing him, she calls herself 'thine handmaid'. Beaumont and Fletcher gave the name Abigail to a 'waiting-gentlewoman' in their play *The Scornful Lady*. From this, the name came to be used generically in English, for superior women servants.

Abraham (Abram)

In the Bible (*Genesis* 12–25), the legendary founder of the Jewish nation, and first of the Patriarchs (racial ancestors). He is represented as a nomadic chieftain or 'sheikh' who is directed by God (Yahweh, Jehovah) into the land of Canaan, with promises that in return for his obedience to God's will he is to become the father of a great nation. His only legitimate son is Isaac*, by his wife Sarah; however, he has other sons by his concubines, the most notable of whom is Hagar, the mother of Ishmael. These illegitimate sons became the forebears of the hostile tribes which surrounded Israel in the Old Testament. An important episode is that in which Abraham obeys God's command to sacrifice Isaac, for whom a young ram is substituted at the last moment. The incident seems to signify the end of human sacrifice among the Jews.

The phrase 'Abraham's bosom', used by Christ in the parable of the rich man and Lazarus (*Luke* 16), is a synonym for heaven. In the words of the Hostess in Shakespeare's *Henry V* (II.iii) the phrase becomes 'Arthur's bosom', by a confusion between the ancient British and the ancient Jewish hero.

Abraham Man

In 16th-C England, a beggar who shammed sickness or madness. Real lunatics, not dangerous enough to be shut up, were entitled to beg, but inadequate poor relief after the closing of the monasteries* (1536–9) tempted many destitute people to simulate their condition.

Absalom and Achitophel

A political satire* in heroic couplets* by John Dryden*, published in 1681, and continued (Part II) mainly by Nahum Tate, published in 1682. Dryden used the biblical story of King David* and his rebellious son Absalom (*2 Samuel* 13–19) to portray allegorically a current crisis about who should be the next king after the death of Charles II*. Charles had no legitimate son, so that his heir was his brother James, Duke of York, a professed Catholic. His succession was feared as a menace to the Church of England and the liberty of Parliament; in consequence, the opposition (Whig*) party tried to pass a law excluding James from the throne and substituting Charles's illegitimate son, the Duke of Monmouth*. Dryden's poem was intended to influence the public against the Whigs and their leader, Anthony Ashley Cooper, Earl of Shaftesbury*. His use of the biblical story simultaneously blackened the opposition and sanctified the King, who supported his brother, and their party. The biblical David stands for Charles; Absalom for Monmouth; Achitophel (Absalom's evil tempter) for Shaftesbury. Other correspondences are: Zimri = Duke of Buckingham; Corah = Titus Oates*; Shimei = Sheriff of London. The satire is Dryden's most famous work.

*** 4.2.2.**

Acephalous

From the Greek = lacking a head or beginning. In the study of poetic metre*, the term is used for a line that lacks an initial syllable to complete the metrical pattern.

Achilles /ə'kiliːz/

The principal Greek hero in *The Iliad**, Homer's* epic* of the siege of Troy*. His mother had plunged him in his infancy into the River Styx in the underworld. This made him invulnerable except for his heel, by which she had held him. Hence a person's 'Achilles' heel' is his weak point, where he is most vulnerable.

Acrostic

A literary game in which the initial letters of the lines of a poem spell a word when read downwards in order.

Kind sister! aye, this third name says you are;
Enchanted has it been the Lord knows where.
And may it taste to you like good old wine,
Take you to real happiness and give
Sons, daughters and a home like honied hive.

The initial letters spell 'Keats'; and it is the third verse of an acrostic poem to Georgiana Augusta Keats, by her brother-in-law John Keats*. A double acrostic can also be read downwards with the last letters of each line.

Act

In politics: a law, when it has been passed through both Houses of Parliament*, and accepted by the monarch. Until this process is completed, it is called a Bill; many famous Acts of Parliament are commonly referred to as Bills, *eg* the Bill of Rights* of 1689, and the Parliamentary Reform Bill of 1832.

In drama: a division of a play; acts are sometimes subdivided into scenes. The ancient Greeks did not use divisions into acts; the practice was started by the Romans, and the poet-critic Horace* (1st C BC) in his *Ars Poetica* laid down the principle that the number of acts should be 5. Since the Renaissance of classical learning in the 16th C, most dramatists have used act divisions, and many have obeyed Horace's precept. All Shakespeare's plays are divided into acts and scenes in modern editions, but it is certain that he did not write them in labelled scenes, and uncertain whether he thought in terms of acts; some of the first printed versions of his plays show act divisions, and some do not. The fact that editorial division of all his plays into acts seldom or never disagrees with Shakespeare's development of the dramatic plot suggests that he thought in terms of 5-act divisions, even if he did not write them in.

Acting, The Profession of

Acting began to achieve recognition as a profession in the reign of Elizabeth I*. The important date is the building of the Theatre – the first theatre in England – by James Burbage* in 1576. It was followed by many others in London, and theatres soon became big business. Previously, actors had performed where they could, especially in inn yards and the halls of palaces, mansions, and colleges. They continued to do so, but the existence of theatres gave them a base and (though they still required an official licence) independence such as they badly needed in order to win social recognition.

Until mid-16th C acting was practised by many kinds of people: ordinary townsmen at festivals, wandering entertainers, boys and men from the choirs of the great churches, and members of the staffs of royal or aristocratic households. It was from these last that the professional actors emerged. They still wore the liveries – uniforms and badges – of the great households, but the connection was now loose (good performers could transfer from one household to another) and was chiefly a means of procuring a licence to perform. This licence was essential because the City of London, around which dramatic activity concentrated, feared the theatre as providing centres of infection for the recurrent plague* epidemics (which from time to time sent the companies away on tour) and disliked acting as a morally harmful and anomalous way of life. Moreover, the royal court, which favoured the stage, was nonetheless on guard against it as a potential source of sedition. Censorship and licensing, however, had the advantage of helping to distinguish the serious performers from the vulgar entertainers.

By the time of Elizabeth's death two great companies were dominant: the Lord Chamberlain's* Men, for whom Shakespeare wrote, and the Lord Admiral's* Men, headed by the leading actor of the day, Edward Alleyn*. Women did not perform; their parts were taken by boys who enlisted as apprentices. Companies of boy actors from the choirs of St Paul's* and the Chapels Royal also had prestige (see *Hamlet* II.ii), especially in the 1570s. The establishment of the profession owed most to the dramatists, but much to the energy of actor-managers and theatre proprietors such as Philip Henslowe*, Edward Alleyn, James Burbage, and his son Richard.

Actresses were introduced after the Restoration* of the monarchy (1660). The status of the profession continued to rise, aided by the theatre's ceasing to be the possession of all classes and becoming a fashionable pleasure of the London West End. In 18th C the genius and culture of David Garrick* greatly enhanced the prestige of the profession. From his time on, there is a long roll of great acting names; the drama, however, declined until the end of 19th C, partly because the intrinsic value of plays came to be considered secondary to the merit of their performance.

* *Puritanism; Theatres.*

Adam

The name in the Bible of the first man; see *Genesis*. His eating of the forbidden fruit of the Tree of Knowledge led to his expulsion from Paradise (the Garden of Eden*).

* 3.1.1.

Adam, Robert (1728–92)

Architect. His work is representative of the middle period of Augustan* taste, as the earlier period of it is expressed in the buildings of Wren* and Vanbrugh*. The earlier period is bold and dramatic in its display of shapes and ornaments; the Adams period is graceful and delicate. He was a particularly fine interior designer, and is famous for the designs of his ceilings and mantelpieces. His taste was much influenced by ancient Roman architecture in Italy, for instance the ruins of the town of Pompeii, and the palace of the Emperor Diocletian (AD 245–313) at Spalato (Split). The last he used as the pattern for a fine urban development (see *Georgian* Illustration) overlooking the Thames in London; he carried it out with the help of his brother James, and thus called it the Adelphi from the Greek for 'brothers'. His work in London, like most good 18th-C architecture there, has been

ruined or destroyed, but Edinburgh has preserved some of his best street architecture, and a number of country houses survive, either designed throughout by him or ornamented in part. These include Harewood House (Yorkshire), Mersham-le-Hatch (Kent), Syon House (near London), and Ken Wood (Hampstead, London).

* 2.3; *Georgian.*

Adam Bede (1859)

A novel by George Eliot*. The setting is a village in the English Midlands, and the events take place at the beginning of 19th C. Adam Bede is the village carpenter, a young man of stern morals and great strength of character; he is in love with Hetty Sorrel, the vain and frivolous niece of a farmer, Martin Poyser*. She is seduced by the village squire*. Another principal character is the young and beautiful Dinah Morris, a Methodist preacher whom Adam marries after Hetty has been transported for the murder of her child. The novel belongs to the early phase of George Eliot's art when her principal subject was the rural civilization which had been the background of her youth; the fine parts of the novel are those scenes, such as the Poyser household, which are directly concerned with this way of life.

Addison, Joseph (1672–1719)

Poet, politician, and essayist, Addison is now read for his essays in two periodicals: the *Tatler* (1709–11), and the *Spectator* (1711–12 and 1714). These were almost entirely written by himself and Richard Steele*. The *Tatler* appeared thrice weekly, and the *Spectator*, daily. The essays are reflective comments on manners, morals, literature and philosophy, aimed at a wide audience. The circulation of some issues of the *Spectator* may have reached 30,000, and Addison reckoned that each copy was read by at least twenty people. Particularly famous is the account of the daily life and opinions of a country gentleman, Sir Roger de Coverley*, in a series of sketches – mainly by Addison – which anticipate the way of looking at experience soon to be exploited by 18th-C novelists. Addison had a mission: he wanted to bridge the distance between the small circle of London elegance and wit – the public for the comedies of Congreve* – and the large, serious but unsophisticated middle classes who were the public for the journalism of Defoe*; and he wanted to do this without sacrificing the virtues of either. More than anyone else, he stands behind the idea of the 'gentleman', regarded as a moral as distinct from a social phenomenon. His style, in its combination of grace, poise, and familiarity, is the expression of his gospel, and communicates itself today. In volume form, the *Spectator* remained popular throughout 18th C.

Son of a parson, Addison was steeped in the classical education which the age regarded as the basis of culture. He made his name with a poem – *The Campaign*, 1705, celebrating the victory of Blenheim (1704); his classical tragedy, *Cato*, nowadays ignored, was then enthusiastically admired. He had a respectable career as a Member of Parliament on the Whig* side, and for a short time, though not very successfully, was a Secretary of State.

* *Augustan Age; Reviews and Periodicals;* 7.2.

Bib: Samuel Johnson's Life of Addison, in *Lives of the Poets;* Smithers. P., *Life*; Beljame, A., *Men of Letters and the English Public in the 18th Century;* Dobree, B., *Essays in Biography*; Lewis, C. S., in *Essays Presented to David Nichol Smith:* Leavis, Q. D., *Fiction and the Reading Public.*

Admiral's Men, The Lord

A company of Elizabethan actors under the protection of Lord Howard of Effingham, who became Lord Admiral in 1585. They are first heard of in 1574, and were at their height in the 1590s, when they were led by one of the two chief actors of the time, Edward Alleyn*, and when their only rivals were the Lord Chamberlain's* Men who were led by the other, Richard Burbage*. As Burbage was Shakespeare's leading actor, so Alleyn and the Admiral's Men are associated with Christopher Marlowe*. The chief financial management of the company was under Alleyn himself and his father-in-law, Philip Henslowe*, a financier. In the reign of James I (1603–25) the company came under the patronage of his eldest son, Prince Henry; and on his death under that of James's son-in-law, the Elector of the Palatinate. The company came to an end in 1628.

Adonais (1821) /adə'neiis/

A poem in 55 Spenserian stanzas* by P. B. Shelley*, mourning the death of the poet John Keats* in Rome. Shelley based his poem on the *Lament for Adonis* by the Sicilian-Greek poet, Bion (1st C BC). Adonis* was a beautiful youth slain by a wild boar. Keats died of tuberculosis, but Shelley (like Byron*) considered that his death had been hastened by a long and violent attack in the *Quarterly Review** on Keats's poem *Endymion** (1818). In his preface, Shelley surmises that the review may have been written in a kind of brutal ignorance of its possible effect; the reviewer, in other words, had behaved like the savage animal that had killed the mythical Adonis – hence the title that Shelley chose for the poem. Shelley felt himself the more involved because of the political motivations that lay behind the attack on Keats's poem. Keats himself was non-political in his poetry, but he was a close friend of Leigh Hunt*, the leader of the London radicals, and this undoubtedly accounted for much of the ferocity of the attack on him by the *Quarterly*, which was the mouthpiece of the most right-wing political opinion in Britain. Shelley himself was a pronounced radical, a bitter opponent of the *Quarterly* and all it stood for. The poem mourns the death of Keats, attacks his critics, and celebrates his immortality.

Adonis /ə'dəunis/

A supremely beautiful youth in Greek myth. Beloved by Aphrodite*, he was cured of a mortal wound by Persephone on condition that he spent half the year with the latter in the underworld and half with the former on the earth. The myth thus symbolized the change from winter to summer; images of Adonis were surrounded by gardens of flowers; hence the Garden of Adonis in, *eg*, Spenser's *Faerie Queene**, Bk. III.

An 'Adonis' became a name for a strikingly handsome young man; also, in 18th C, of a kind of wig.

Advancement of Learning, The

A philosophical treatise by Francis Bacon*, published in 1605 in English; Bacon later expanded it in his Latin work, *De Augmentis Scientiarum* (1623).

The book is addressed to King James I, one of the most learned men ever to occupy the English throne. Its purpose is to suggest ways in which the prestige of the pursuit of knowledge can be enhanced and its methods improved. It is divided into two parts: Book I treats first those characteristics of scholars and of scholarship which have led to the discredit of both, and then the characteristics that contribute to the dignity of the life of learning; Book II is a survey of the branches of learning, and of the mental faculties.

The importance of *The Advancement* is of two kinds: as a work of philosophy and as a work of literature. As philosophy, the *De Augmentis* is more important as a fuller development of Bacon's thought, but *The Advancement* is distinctive for the modernity of its approach to the pursuit of knowledge and to the obstacles to it arising from mistaken uses of the mind. As a work of literature, it is distinguished for the terseness and lucidity of Bacon's prose, and, critically, for the beginnings of a discrimination between the rational and the imaginative faculties that was to become a basic belief in the 'Age of Reason' that opened in 1660. In the section on Poetry in Book II, Bacon says that poetry submits 'the shows of things to the desires of the mind; whereas reason doth buckle and bow the mind unto the nature of things'. This implies two different uses of language: the imaginative and the rational, corresponding to the poetic and the prosaic. The distinction was not securely made by most of Bacon's contemporaries, so that the poetry of Shakespeare, Donne* and Herbert* is enriched by a strong intellectual interest in ideas, and at the same time the prose of Donne and even of Bacon himself is enriched by a pronounced figurative use of language which we think of as 'poetic'. An example of this poetic expression is Bacon's use of 'buckle and bow' in the sentence quoted.

* *Dissociation of Sensibility.*

Advocate

A professional pleader in Scottish courts of justice, corresponding to the English barrister. Advocate is sometimes used synonymously for barrister. The Lord Advocate is the principal law officer in Scotland.

Aeneas /iː'niːas/

Hero of the Latin epic, *Aeneid** by Virgil*. Traditions about him had existed long before Virgil's poem. He was the son of Anchises and the goddess Aphrodite*, and the son-in-law of Priam*, king of Troy*. In Homer's *Iliad** (v) he is represented as the chief of the Trojans and one of the most formidable defenders of Troy against the Greeks. Other records stated that after the fall of Troy, he set out to seek a new kingdom with some of the surviving Trojans, and eventually settled in central Italy. By Virgil's time, the Romans were already worshipping Aeneas as the father of their race.

Aeneid /'iːniid/

An epic* poem by the Roman poet Virgil* (70–19 BC). The poem tells the story of Aeneas*, son-in-law of Priam* of Troy*, from his flight from Troy during the confusion of its destruction by the Greeks to his establishment as king of the Latins in central Italy and his death in battle with the Etruscans. The poem thus begins at a point near where Homer left off in the *Iliad**, and its description of the wanderings of Aeneas is parallel to the description of the wanderings of Odysseus in Homer's *Odyssey**. It is divided into 12 books, of which the second, fourth and sixth are the most famous: the second describes the destruction of Troy; the fourth gives the tragedy of Queen Dido* of Carthage, who dies for love of Aeneas; the sixth shows his descent to the underworld and the prophetic visions of those who are to build the greatness of Rome. It was these books that Virgil selected to be read to the Emperor Augustus and his family.

Virgil's purpose was much more than merely to emulate Homer, the greatest epic poet of Greece. He wrote at a climax of Roman history, when Roman power was nearing its height, and Rome itself had become a settled and luxurious civilization. Luxury implied dangers of degeneration into complacent mediocrity; Virgil wished to relate the Rome he knew to her heroic past, and to inspire her with a sense of her great destiny in world history. The *Aeneid* is thus a central document for Roman culture, and inasmuch as Roman culture is the basis of the culture of Western Europe, it has remained a central document for European culture too; from 16th to 19th C, knowledge of at least the important parts of the poem constituted an indispensable element in the equipment of the educated man.

The most notable English translations of the *Aeneid* are those by the Scottish poet Gavin Douglas* (1553) and by John Dryden* (1697). Henry Howard, Earl of Surrey*, translated Books II and III into the earliest example of English blank verse*.

Aeolian /iː'əuljən/

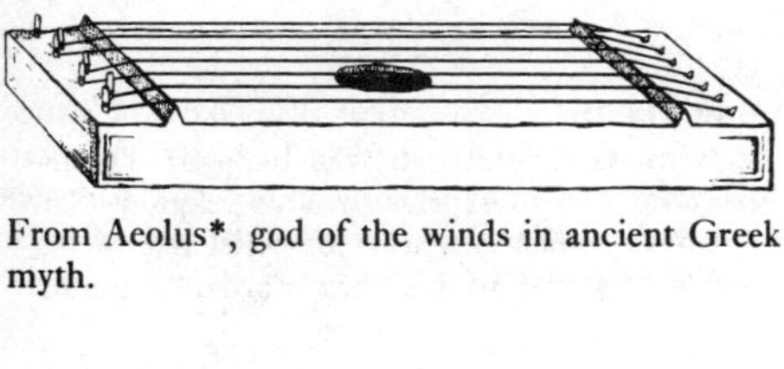

From Aeolus*, god of the winds in ancient Greek myth.

An Aeolian harp is a stringed instrument, placed across a window or outside a house, so that the wind causes the strings to vibrate and make music. The poet Coleridge* possessed one; hence his poem *The Eolian Harp* (1795), and references to the instrument in *Dejection* (1802). For him, it symbolized his conception of the poet 'played upon' by Nature.

Aeolists /'iːəlists/

In Swift's satire *A Tale of a Tub** (1704), a fictional sect of believers in direct inspiration: 'The learned Aeolists maintain the original cause of all things to be wind . . .'. Swift's satire is an attack on all pretensions to truth not in accord with right reason or properly constituted authority, and the Aeolists, in Section VIII, are a kind of climax to the work. He associates them particularly with the Dissenters*, who based their religious faith on belief in direct intimations from the Holy Spirit to the individual soul; Jack, who represents Presbyterianism* in the *Tale*, is a leader of the sect.

Aeolus /'iːələs/

In Greek myth, the guardian of the winds, which he kept on the Aeolian Islands, and could subdue or enrage at will. He was the son of Poseidon*, the sea-god, and in Roman myth was himself promoted to the status of god.

Aeschylus (525–456 BC) /'iːskiləs/

With Sophocles* and Euripides*, one of the three great tragic poets of ancient Greece. Only seven of his seventy plays survive; of these the best known are *Agamemnon*, *Choephori*, *Eumenides*, making up the *Oresteia* trilogy. Aeschylus is the great starting-point of all European tragedy, but it was the derivative tragedy of the Latin poet Seneca* which influenced the great period of English tragedy between 1590 and 1630. Reacting against this, Milton* deliberately based his tragedy *Samson Agonistes** (1671) on the Greek pattern. Shelley's* masterpiece *Prometheus Unbound** (1820) was written as a sequel to Aeschylus's *Prometheus Bound*, but without pretensions to Greek form. T. S. Eliot* used the Oresteia myth for his verse drama *The Family Reunion* (1939). The works of Aeschylus have been frequently translated into English.

* *Orestes; Tragedy.*

Aesculapius /iːskju'leipiəs/

The Roman god of medicine and healing (Greek Asclepius). On recovery from an illness it was usual to sacrifice a cock to him.

Aesop /'iːsop/

A Greek composer of animal fables* of 6th C BC. He probably did not write them down, but fables purporting to be his were collected by later classical writers, and they and imitations of them have had a wide popularity in European literature. The most notable Aesopian fable in English literature is Chaucer's *Nun's Priest's Tale** of the Cock and the Fox in the *Canterbury Tales*.

Aestheticism /iːsˈθetisizm/

A movement of late 19th C. As a movement, it was not well defined; it was one of the reactions against the materialism and commercialism of the Victorian* industrial era. Previously, Arnold* had attacked Victorian cultural narrowness; Carlyle* had attacked Victorian spiritual mediocrity; Ruskin* had tried to educate Victorians in the moral inspiration of beauty. There had also been two well-defined movements: the Oxford Movement*, reverting to Catholic ritual in the Church of England*, and the artistic Pre-Raphaelite* movement preaching the virtues of medieval culture. All these made up the background to aestheticism, but its immediate inspiration was the writings of the Oxford don, Walter Pater*. His two most influential books were *Studies in the History of the Renaissance* (1873) and *Marius the Epicurean* (1885). These show him as a ritualistic moralist, laying emphasis on the value of ecstatic experience. Apart from Pater and his predecessors, the aesthetes owed much to the current French doctrine of 'L'Art pour l'Art' (Art for Art's sake) but they retained, if sometimes not obviously, a typically English concern with moral values and issues. The outstanding aesthete was Oscar Wilde* (1856–1900), and a characteristic aesthetic product was his novel *The Picture of Dorian Gray* (1891). As the movement lacked a programme, writers of very different character were influenced by it: the naturalistic novelist, George Moore*; the poet Lionel Johnson who was a Catholic convert; Swinburne*, a main channel for the art for art's sake doctrine; W. B. Yeats*, the Celtic revivalist. A characteristic aestheticist periodical was *The Yellow Book** (1894–7), so called because French novels, conventionally considered 'daring', were printed on yellow paper. Its main illustrator was Aubrey Beardsley*, whose line drawings were notorious for their sensuality. Yet some of its contributors, such as H. G. Wells*, had nothing to do with aestheticism; this was typical of the movement's vagueness of tendency.

Bib: Aldington, R. (ed.), *The Religion of Beauty: Selections from the Aesthetes.*

Agamemnon /agəˈmemnən/

In Greek myth, the king of Argos and commander of the Greek forces which besieged Troy*. He was the brother of Menelaus*, the abduction of whose wife, Helen*, was a cause of the siege.

Age, Coming of

'To come of age', 'to reach one's majority', means to become a fully responsible adult in the eyes of the law. The individual is then able to hold property, marry without the consent of parents or guardians, be responsible for his debts, vote in political elections, etc. In English law the age is now 18.

Ages, Golden, Silver, etc.

The Greek poet Hesiod (8th C BC) in *Works and Days* writes of an ideal golden age in the past, comparable to the Garden of Eden* in Christian and Jewish story; from this period, he considered that there had been a progressive decline through the silver, bronze, and heroic ages until his own time. His classification has been adapted by other writers to describe cycles of history. The terms have also been applied more or less loosely: so one speaks, for example, of the Elizabethan period* as being the golden age of English drama. Thomas Love Peacock's* essay *The Four Ages of Poetry*, which provoked Shelley's* well-known *Defence of Poetry* (1821), is an example of a conscious adaptation of Hesiod's terms. The term 'heroic age' is often used without reference to any supposed decline from a golden age, in order to describe a period of major and inspiring conflict, *eg* 'The French Revolution was the heroic age of democracy.'

Other uses of 'age' in connection with a descriptive word are to express supposed dominant qualities in a period, as when the Middle Ages* are described as the Age of Faith owing to the unanimity of religious belief in the period, or the Age of Chivalry, from the institution of knighthood and its courtly code.

Finally there are the classifications of literary history; for these see: Periods of English Literature.

Agincourt (1415) /ˈadʒinkoː/

A battle in the Hundred Years' War*, in which the English king, Henry V*, defeated a much larger French army. The victory was the more inspiring because it was especially a victory for English yeoman* archers – humble foot-soldiers – over the aristocratic French cavalry. It helped to give Henry his reputation as the leader of a whole people, not merely of an aristocracy as other medieval kings were; it also symbolized the nation acting in unity, especially by contrast to the disturbances during the previous reign of Henry IV (1399–1413), and the extensive civil wars during the next one, that of Henry VI (1422–61). This explains its importance in Shakespeare's play, *Henry V**, written at a time when the English had become more conscious of themselves as a united nation than ever before, and yet feared that civil war (either through the death of Elizabeth I* without heirs, or arising from religious disagreements) might soon revive. Another famous representation of the battle is Michael Drayton's* *Ballad of Agincourt* (1606–19).

* *Archery.*

Agnes, St

A Christian martyr in the reign of the Roman Emperor Diocletian (AD 284–313). She became the patron saint of virgins; her day of celebration is 21 January. It was a popular belief that ceremonies performed on the night before this day would cause a girl to dream of the man she was destined to marry. This is the idea behind Keats's *Eve of St Agnes**.

Agnosticism

The term was invented by the biologist Thomas Huxley in 1869 to express towards religious faith the attitude which is neither of belief nor of disbelief (atheism*). In his own words, 'I neither affirm nor deny the immortality of man. I see no reason for believing it, but on the other hand I have no means of disproving it.' Agnosticism was widespread among writers between 1850 and 1914; it arose from the scientific thought of the time, especially that of Huxley himself, and that of another biologist, Charles Darwin*.

Ainsworth, William Harrison (1805–82)
Novelist. His best novels are historical: *Jack Shepherd* (1839), *The Tower of London* (1840), *Guy Fawkes* (1841), *Old St Paul's* (1841), *Windsor Castle* (1843). He tended to idealise the heroic criminal, *eg* Dick Turpin* in *Rookwood* (1834) and Jack Shepherd; this was a literary fashion in the 1830's and 40's and censured by Thackeray* in his early reviews under the designation 'The Newgate School of novelists'. He edited *Bentley's Magazine* 1840–42, *Ainsworth's Magazine* 1842–53, and *New Monthly Magazine* from 1853.
Bib. Ellis, S. M., *W. H. Ainsworth and his Friends.*

Ajax /'eidʒaks/
In Greek legend, the son of Telamon, king of Cyprus, and one of the principal heroes of the Trojan War. In Homer's *Iliad**, he is described as a man of enormous stature and strength, second only to Achilles* in heroic courage. He rescued the body of Achilles from the hands of the Trojans, but he lost the competition with Odysseus* for Achilles' armour, and, according to Homer, his rage at this disappointment caused his death. In another legend, his rage caused him to attack a flock of sheep in mistake for the enemy, and he took his own life after returning to his senses, from shame at this humiliation. Virgil* describes him as meeting his death in consequence of arousing the wrath of the gods by his boastfulness. In Shakespeare's *Troilus and Cressida**, Ajax is shown as boastful, brutal, and stupid.

Albert of Saxe-Coburg-Gotha (1819–61)
Husband (with the title of Prince Consort) of Queen Victoria*. They were cousins. The Queen was devoted to him, and the marriage was of considerable political importance; Albert did much to shape the Queen's ideas of her political duties as a constitutional monarch who could not interfere directly in politics but could nonetheless exert great personal influence. Albert was a man of tact, intelligence, high principles, and considerable (though one-sided) culture. In his youth he had given much attention to the study of natural science and political economy, and he exercised considerable influence in the application of science to contemporary technology. The Great Exhibition of 1851 was organized on his suggestion. Unfortunately, his foreign origin caused his influence to be regarded with considerable suspicion in the country. His death was a cause of immense grief to the Queen; it led to her retirement from public appearances between 1861 and the Jubilee of her reign in 1887, and as these appearances were now popularly regarded as the most important part of the royal function, her popularity declined during this period.

Albion
The most ancient name for Britain, used in Greek by Ptolemy* and in Latin by Pliny*. The word possibly derived from Celtic, but it was associated by the Romans with the Latin *albus* = white, referring to the white cliffs of Dover. From the Middle Ages on it has often been used poetically to stand for Britain.

Alcestis /al'sestis/
In Greek myth, the wife of Admetus, king of Pherae. The god Apollo* granted Admetus that he should be saved from death if another person would take his place. Alcestis gave herself. She descended among the dead in the underworld, whence she was brought back by Heracles*.

Alchemist, The
A comedy by Ben Jonson*, first acted in 1610. The scene is a house in London during a visitation of the plague; its master, Lovewit, has taken refuge in the country, leaving his servant, Face, in charge. Face introduces two rogues: Subtle, a charlatan alchemist, and Dol Common, a whore. Together they collaborate in turning the house into a centre for the practice of alchemy* in the expectation that they can attract credulous clients who will believe that alchemical magic can bring them their heart's desire. Their expectations are realized, and their dupes are representative social types. Sir Epicure Mammon dreams of limitless luxury and the satisfaction of his lust; the Puritans, Ananias and Tribulation Wholesome, hope to enrich their sect; Drugger, a tobacco merchant, wants prosperity for his business; Dapper, a lawyer's clerk, seeks a spirit to guarantee him success in gambling; Kastril, a young country squire, desires a rich husband for his sister (Dame Pliant) and knowledge of the secret of fashionable quarrelling. Only Pertinax Surly, a friend of Mammon, sees the fraudulence of the enterprise, but Face and his colleagues manage to turn the clients against him and he is routed. Each of the clients has to be deceived by a separate technique, depending on his peculiar brand of social credulity, and this requires swift changes of role by the cheats, especially Subtle. They are equal to all emergencies until Lovewit suddenly returns – a crisis which only Face survives. He expels Subtle and Common, and then wins over his master who admires his ingenuity and is satisfied with the plunder, which includes Dame Pliant. The play is one of Jonson's best; it has energetic wit and extraordinary theatrical ingenuity. Moreover the characterization has behind it the force of Jonson's conviction that human folly is limitless and can only be cured by exposure and castigation.

Alchemy
A pseudo-science started by the Alexandrian Greeks in the early Christian centuries and widely pursued in Europe until 17th C. Essentially a primitive form of chemistry, it was popularly identified with experiments to transmute base

metals into gold through the discovery of what was called 'the philosopher's stone'. As such it was a field for dupes and charlatans, and is ridiculed in Chaucer's *Canterbury Tales** (*The Canon's Yeoman's Tale*) and satirized by Ben Jonson in *The Alchemist**.

* *Elements, The Four.*

Ale and Beer

Since the Middle Ages*, the most usual alcoholic drinks in England. They are now identical, but formerly ale was distinguished from beer by being brewed without an infusion of hops, a crop introduced into England in 16th C. Ale is thus the older, and in compounds denoted a feast: Whitsun-ale (Pentecost), lamb-ale (at shearing time), bride-ale (from which comes 'bridal'), etc. Ale and beer were widely drunk by all classes, and by both men and women, until the latter took to tea and coffee in 18th C. 'Small beer' was a weak brew especially for children and servants. Hence Prince Hal says in Shakespeare's *2 Henry IV**: 'Belike, then, my appetite was not princely got; for, by my troth, I do now remember the poor creature, small beer.' To be 'small beer' is to be unimportant; 'to think no small beer of oneself' is to have a high opinion of oneself, etc.

Alexander the Great (356–323 BC)

He succeeded to the throne of Macedon in 336 BC after the assassination of his father Philip II. Macedon was on the northern frontier of ancient Greece and had absorbed Greek culture, *ie* had become 'hellenized'. The great 5th C achievements in Greek culture were by now being assimilated into a self-conscious Hellenic identity, not only for the politically still disunited Greek states but for their hellenized neighbour, over against alien civilisations of which the most important was Persia. Philip had used this hellenic consciousness to assert military leadership over the Greek states, and Alexander began by consolidating his father's hegemony. Then he embarked on an amazingly rapid career of conquest which took his armies as far as the valley of the Indus in north-west India.

Alexander became a prominent figure in European medieval literature, especially in that of France; a long 12th-C French poem entitled *Li Romans d'Alexandre* was written in lines of 12 syllables, hence originating the term 'alexandrine'* for a line of that length. The ultimate sources for medieval narratives about Alexander were three: the Greek narrative by the 'Pseudo-Callisthenes' (c 200 BC); the Roman narrative by Quintus Augustus, dating from the reign of Augustus, and a hostile account by the Christian Orosius (5th C AD) in his *Historia versus Paganos*. These diverse accounts, much overlaid by legend, resulted in medieval versions of comparable diversity, depending on whether the writer was secular in his inspiration, using Alexander as a type of chivalric greatness, or morally inspired, seeing him (in contrast to Diogenes*) as a man governed by his will and appetites, or theologically influenced by Orosius as a diabolic type bedevilled by satanic pride. Another line of interest derived from the fact that he had had Aristotle* as a tutor and was supposed to have corresponded with philosophers, so that he could be seen as a type of Platonic 'philosopher-King'. This diversity was further embroidered by the legend that Alexander was not in fact the son of Philip but of the magician Nectanebus, the last independent king of Egypt, who visited Alexander's mother Olympias, in the shape of a dragon.

An Anglo-Norman poem in French by Thomas of Kent dates from about 1250, and this is the basis of a 14th-C rhymed poem in English, the *Lyfe of Alisaunder*. In addition two fragments of English alliterative romances survive, edited by Skeat, and a 15th-C poem in Northumbrian dialect entitled by Skeat *The Wars of Alexander*. In Scots dialect, we have *The Scots Buik of the most noble and vailzeand Alexander the Great* (15th C) based on translations from French sources. Chaucer's Monk (*Canterbury Tales**), uses the 'storie of Alisaundre' as one of his tragedies; this exemplifies Alexander as a tragic chivalric hero. Gower* in *Confessio Amantis* (Bk III) uses him to preach the lesson of self-control, and Lydgate* in the *Fall of Princes* presents him as an exemplar of excess of pride. In the 17th C a minor Restoration* dramatist, Nathaniel Lee, wrote a tragedy called *The Rival Queens* on the theme of Alexander's fatal love for two women, Statira and Roxana. In the Renaissance, Alexander always figures among 'the Nine Worthies'*.

Alexandrine

A twelve-syllable line of verse, possibly owing its name to French medieval poems about Alexander the Great. It is common in French poetry but unusual in English, where the commonest line length is of ten syllables. Michael Drayton* used it in his long poem *Poly-Olbion* (1613–22), but its most famous use is in the last line of the Spenserian stanza*, invented by Edmund Spenser for his *Faerie Queene**.

Alfred, King (871–901)

The greatest of the Anglo-Saxon* kings, though he ruled over only the south-western part of England (Wessex*). He was famous for his successful resistance to the Danish invaders, and still more for his vigorous encouragement of Anglo-Saxon culture. He raised the standard of learning and religion, spread education among the nobility, laid the foundations of English prose, and initiated the *Anglo-Saxon Chronicle**, the first historical record in the English language.

Alice's Adventures in Wonderland; Through the Looking-Glass

* *Carroll, Lewis.*

All Fools' Day

1 April, also called 'April Fools' Day'. It was once a festival, probably of pagan origin, to celebrate the Spring equinox. It is now merely a day of licence, chiefly observed by children, for 'making fools' of people, *ie* playing practical jokes on them.

All for Love, or The World Well Lost
A tragedy by John Dryden*, published in 1678; it is based on Shakespeare's *Antony and Cleopatra**. The difference between the two plays is a measure of the change that had come over English literary taste between Shakespeare and Dryden. In dramatic structure and in verse movement, Dryden has sought economy, shapeliness, elegance and fluency; these qualities replace Shakespeare's range of thought, abundance of imagery, and depth of dramatic vision. Dryden's artistic achievement is a very much smaller one than Shakespeare's, but *All for Love* is still a masterpiece in its own kind, and Dryden's best play.

All the Year Round
A periodical published by Charles Dickens* from 1859, in succession to *Household Words**, until his death in 1870. Novels which appeared in it in instalments included Dickens's own *A Tale of Two Cities** and *Great Expectations**.

All's Well that Ends Well
A play by Shakespeare in which the heroine, Helena* de Narbon, pursues Bertram, Count of Rousillon, whom she loves but who seeks to elude her. He is misled by a dishonourable young courtier, Parolles; she eventually ensnares him by a trick. The plot is taken from Painter's *Palace of Pleasure** (1566–7) but the play is difficult to date precisely owing to its mixture of styles. Sir Edmund Chambers* dates it 1602–3. This agrees with the kind of difficulty with which it faces critics: uncertainty about Shakespeare's intention; the play seems to be a romantic comedy, but the treatment of the subject is often unromantic and the comedy is often harsh. Thus *All's Well* resembles other problem plays* of Shakespeare written between 1600 and 1604: *Hamlet**, *Measure for Measure**, *Troilus and Cressida**.

Allegory
From Greek 'speaking in other terms'. A way of representing thought and experience through images, by means of which (1) complex ideas may be simplified, or (2) abstract, spiritual, or mysterious ideas and experiences may be made immediate (but not necessarily simpler) by dramatization in fiction.

In both uses, allegory was most usual and natural as a medium of expression in the Middle Ages*. Catholic doctrine prevailed as deeply as it did widely; even the physical structures of the universe and of man seemed to be living images of spiritual truth. The morality plays, notably *Everyman** (15th C), were practical applications of this doctrine to ordinary experience. But the tendency to see experience in allegorical terms extended to secular literature, *eg* the romances of sexual love, such as *The Romance of the Rose* (14th C) in part translated from the French by Chaucer*. When Chaucer wrote a romance in which there was no overt allegory, *eg Troilus and Criseyde**, the allegorical spirit was still implicit within it (see C. S. Lewis, *Allegory of Love*). Such implicit allegory extended into much Renaissance* drama, *eg* Shakespeare's *1 & 2 Henry IV*.

In the Renaissance, however, explicit allegory, though still pervasive, was greatly complicated by the break-up of the dominant Catholic framework; various Christian doctrines competed with one another and with non-Christian ones such as neo-Platonism*, and also with political theories. Thus in a work like Spenser's *Faerie Queene** religious, political and Platonic allegories are all employed, but intermittently and not with artistic coherence.

Since 17th C deliberate and consistent allegory has continued to decline; yet the greatest of all English allegories, *The Pilgrim's Progress** by John Bunyan, is a 17th-C work. The paradox is explained by Bunyan's contact with the literature of the village sermon, which apparently continued to be conducted by a simple allegorical method with very little influence from the Reformation* (see Owst, *Literature and Pulpit in Medieval England*). Moreover allegory has continued into modern times, partly as an indispensable habit of explanation, partly in a suppressed form (*eg* the names of characters in Dickens's novels), and partly as a resource in the expression of mysterious psychological experience incommunicable in direct terms; here allegory merges with symbolism*, from which, however, it needs to be distinguished.

* 4.1.2; *Fable*.

Allegro, L' (1632)
A poem by John Milton*. The title is Italian, and means 'the cheerful man'. It was written as a companion piece to *Il Penseroso** (= 'the reflective man') and celebrates the active life of the countryside and the city.

Alleyn, Edward (1566–1626) /'alin/
Son of an innkeeper, Alleyn rose to become one of the two foremost tragic actors of the great age of English drama. In 1586 he was performing for Lord Worcester's Men; in 1592 he married the step-daughter of the financier Philip Henslowe*, and together they built up the prosperity of the Lord Admiral's Men*. In this company he was celebrated for his performances of Christopher Marlowe's* heroes: Tamburlaine, Faustus, Barabas. He became the main owner of the Rose* and the Fortune theatres, and a wealthy man by his speculation in land. He founded Dulwich College, to this day a leading public school. After the death of his first wife, he married the daughter of John Donne, the poet and Dean of St Paul's. His acting was highly praised by contemporary dramatists and other writers – Nashe*, Heywood*, and Ben Jonson* among them – and was likened to that of the Roman actor, Roscius*.

**Acting*; *Theatres*.

Bib: Bradbrook, M. C., *The Rise of the Common Player*; Hosking, G. L., *Life and Times of Alleyn*.

Alliteration
* *Figures of Speech*.

Amaryllis /amə'rilis/
A name used for a shepherdess in Greek and Latin pastoral poetry, *eg* by Theocritus*, Virgil*, and Ovid*, and borrowed by English pastoralists such as Spenser.
* *Pastoral.*

Amazons
A race of female warriors occurring in ancient Greek legend, and said by the historian Herodotus to live in Scythia, north of the Black Sea. The word is often used to describe aggressive women, women hostile to men, or women in power instead of men.

Ambassadors, The **(1903)**
A novel by Henry James*. It belongs to his last period, during which he saw America more with European eyes than as a native American.

Lambert Strether, a conscientious, middle-aged American, is engaged to the rich American widow, Mrs Newsome. She sends him over to Paris to bring back her son Chad to run the family business. He arrives to find Chad immersed in Parisian culture, and absorbed in a love affair with the Comtesse de Vionnet. Strether, instead of persuading Chad to return, finds his sensibilities released by the freedom and richness of Parisian life, and delays his own return. Chad's sister, Mrs Pocock, and her husband, Jim, are now sent over by Mrs Newsome; Strether decides to go back, abandoning his friendship with the intelligent and sympathetic Maria Gostrey, an American expatriate. Chad, however, remains.

Mrs Newsome is an authoritarian American matron, full of rectitude and prejudice. Strether has the highly developed New England conscience (it is his conscience that forces him to return) and a hitherto starved imagination. The Pococks stand for American philistinism, without imagination or sensibility. Together with *The Golden Bowl** (1904) and *The Wings of the Dove** (1902), the novel shows James's art at its most highly-wrought and difficult stage; the writing is condensed and full of innuendo.

Ambrosia
* *Nectar.*

Amerigo Vespucci (1451–1512)
A Florentine merchant who claimed to be the first European to set foot on the continent of America, in 1497. His claim was for some time believed, and hence the American continents were named after him; it is, however, now discredited.

Amis, Kingsley (b 1922) /'eimis/
Novelist, poet and essayist. Novels: *Lucky Jim* (1954, filmed 1957); *That Uncertain Feeling* (1955, filmed as *Only Two Can Play*, 1962); *I Like It Here* (1958); *Take a Girl Like You* (1960); *One Fat Englishman* (1963); *The Egyptologists* (1965); *The Anti-Death League* (1966); *I Want It Now* (1968); *Girl, 20* (1971); *The Riverside Villas Murder* (1973); *Ending Up* (1974).

Verse: *A Frame of Mind* (1953); *A Case of Samples* (1956).

Essays: *New Maps of Hell* (on science fiction*, 1960); *The James Bond Dossier* (1965); *What Became of Jane Austen?* (1975).

Amos Barton, The Sad Fortunes of the Rev
The first of the three tales composing *Scenes of Clerical Life* (1858) by George Eliot*.

Amphibology, Amphiboly
A sentence having two possible meanings owing to the ambiguity of its construction. Example, a line from Elizabeth I's* *The Daughter of Debate:*

Our rusty sword with rest shall first his edge employ

meaning, not 'employ his edge with rest', but 'rusty with rest'.

Amphibrach
A verse foot composed of a long syllable between two short ones, or an accented foot between two unaccented ones. It is rarely used in English verse.

Ana, -ana
A collection of memorable quotations from a writer, or sayings by a famous person, or anecdotes about him, *eg* Shakespeariana, Johnsoniana. Usually a suffix at the end of a name, as in these examples.

Anacoluthon /anəkə'lu:θon/
* *Figures of Speech.*

Anacreontics /ənakri'ontiks/
Any kind of melodious verse, lyrical, and concerned with love and wine. From the Greek poet Anacreon (6th–5th C BC). Byron* called his friend Thomas Moore* 'Anacreon Moore,' because he translated the Odes of Anacreon into English.

Anacrusis /anə'kru:sis/
The use at the beginning of a line of verse of a syllable additional to the number required by the given metrical pattern.

Anadyomene
* *Aphrodite.*

Anagram
A literary game in which a word is disguised by changing the order of its letters so as to make a different word, *eg*

How well her name an Army *doth present,*
In whom the Lord of hosts did pitch his tent!
(George Herbert*)

'Army' is here an anagram for Mary, *ie* the Mother of Christ.

Anapaest /'anəpi:st/
A metrical foot having two short or unaccented syllables followed by a long or accented one. It is usually mixed with iambics, as in the following lines:

She is com/ing my own,/my sweet

Were it ev/er so air/y a tread

From *Maud* by Tennyson*

where the first two feet in the first line are anapaests, and the last is an iambic foot. The second line consists of three anapaests.

Anatomy of Melancholy, The

A treatise by Robert Burton* (1577–1640) on a psychological disorder which had increasingly interested Elizabethan* and Jacobean* writers. In modern times, the book has received praise from scientists, but its literary influence has been far greater. This has been because Burton's curiosity and extensive learning led him so deeply into his subject as to make it something like a study of Man in the whole of his nature, and because his wide range of literary allusions and witty and colourful expression provides much entertainment. This explains his extensive influence, *eg* on Sterne*, who borrowed his anecdotes, and Lamb*, who followed his style.

Ancien Régime

A French phrase, commonly used in English, to signify the political and social order in France before the Revolution of 1789.

* *French Revolution.*

Ancient Mariner, The Rime of the

A ballad by S. T. Coleridge* (1772–1834), and his most famous poem. The theme is sin and expiation, and the form is the traditional English ballad style, naïve but economical and powerful in its effect, exploited with subtle but disguised sophistication by the poet, who had a profound and philosophically trained intellect. It was first published in *Lyrical Ballads** (1798), a collection of poems composed by Wordsworth and himself.

Ancients and Moderns

A literary dispute carried on in France and England towards the end of 17th C, and in the beginning of 18th. The dispute arose naturally in an age so dominated by admiration for ancient Greek and Latin literature; this raised the question whether and how far the writers of the time could compete with their classical predecessors. More important, the standards of ancient culture were used as a weapon of criticism against modern culture and particularly against the vulgar scientific optimism of the 'natural philosophers' of the school of Locke*. The most notable contributor in England was Jonathan Swift*, whose *Battle of the Books* (1697, pub. 1704) was a witty satire on the whole dispute, rather on the side of the ancients. His attack on the arrogance of the scientific natural philosophers was fierce in *Gulliver's Travels* (1726), where he satirizes them in 'A Voyage to Laputa'. Pope*, in his *Essay on Man** (1732–4), indirectly contributed to this side of the discussion by expressing the smallness of man in the scale of nature, and his vulnerability in his search for self-sufficiency. This political and scientific aspect of the dispute was more characteristic of England than of France.

* *Natural Philosophy.*

Andersen, Hans Christian (1805–75)

Danish author, known in Britain almost entirely for his children's fairy tales, which began to appear in Denmark in 1835 and were translated into English first in 1846. Their poetic quality has been much imitated by English writers, *eg* Oscar Wilde*.

* *Children's Books.*

Andrewes, Lancelot (1555–1626)

A bishop and leader of the Church of England* during the most formative century (1550–1650) of its thought. His sermons* were famous in an age when preaching was a high art; their prose was vivid and condensed, and an important contribution to the development of English prose at a time when it still shared with the greatest period of English poetry a rich imagery and imaginative suggestiveness. For these qualities, Andrewes is compared to John Donne*, poet and Dean of St Paul's, whose prose comes near his own poetry. As an intellectual defender of the Anglican* religious position, Andrewes was the successor of Richard Hooker*; but whereas Hooker was mainly concerned to defend Anglicanism against the Puritans*, Andrewes defended it against the Catholics. Both he and Hooker are great representatives of Anglicanism as the *via media* between the two.

Bib: Eliot, T. S., 'Lancelot Andrewes' in *Selected Essays*; Higham, F., *Lancelot Andrewes*; Welsby, P.A. *Lancelot Andrewes.*

Androcles and the Lion

A comedy (1912) by Bernard Shaw* based on a tale by a 2nd-C Latin writer, Aulus Gellius. The lion has a wounded paw which Androcles, a runaway slave, heals; subsequently the lion meets Androcles in an arena combat, and spares his life.

Andromeda /an'dromidə/

In Greek myth, daughter of king Cepheus of Ethiopia; she was sacrificed to the wrath of Poseidon* because Cassiopeia*, wife of Cepheus, had boasted of being more beautiful than the sea-nymphs. Andromeda was chained to a rock to await death from a sea-monster sent by Poseidon, but she was rescued by the hero Perseus*, who slew the monster and married the princess.

Angel

From the Greek 'messenger' (of God). The best known example of this function of messenger is the annunciation by the Angel Gabriel* to the Virgin Mary of the birth of Christ. Biblical information on angels comes especially from *Revelation*, but there is further detail in the Book of Enoch (not included in the Bible or Apocrypha).

In general, angels are conceived as a range of beings extending between man and God. The medieval view was that they have a hierarchy in this descending order: seraphim, cherubim, thrones; dominions, virtues, powers; principalities, archangels, angels – the nine orders being grouped into three choirs, of three orders each. A more widespread notion was that angels have as leaders seven Archangels: Uriel, Raphael, Raguel, Michael, Sariel, Gabriel, Jerahmeel. These names derive from the Book of Enoch, but only three of them are well known: Michael the Warrior, Gabriel of the Annunciation, and Raphael, who is sent to warn Adam in Eden in Book V of Milton's *Paradise Lost**.

As in the last three centuries Christian belief has become increasingly rationalized, so angels have been increasingly sentimentalized. Thus cherubs and seraphs are represented in 18th- and 19th-C art as the winged heads of children, and 'cherub' is a common designation for a pretty child; so also we speak of 'a seraphic smile' – often a baby's.

The name 'angel' was also given to a coin; see Noble.

* *Angels, Fallen; Angels, Guardian*

Angels, Fallen

The myth of the Fall of the Angels is expressed in the Book of Enoch and is therefore not scriptural; it is based, however, on *Genesis* 6:2: '. . . the sons of God saw the daughters of men that they were fair; and they took them wives of all which they chose'. Thus this doctrine would make the angelic fall subsequent to the fall of man in *Genesis* 3. Another version derives from *Isaiah* 14:12: 'How art thou fallen from Heaven, O Lucifer, son of the morning!' – where Lucifer* was the morning star (planet Venus) but became identified with Satan* in his unfallen condition. Corroboration, not for the angelic fall but for the existence of evil angels, comes from *Daniel*, where the guardian angels* of the heathen nations oppose Michael, the guardian angel of Judah. These heathen guardians were presumably their gods. Milton in *Paradise Lost** uses the Lucifer myth and also gives to the angels that fell with him the names of pagan gods.

Angels, Guardian

The idea that individuals each have guardians allotted to them is alluded to in the New Testament; see especially *Matthew* 18:10. It agrees with the classical pagan idea of a guardian genius, alluded to by Shakespeare:

. . . and, under him,
My Genius is rebuk'd; as, it is said,
Mark Antony's was by Caesar.

(*Macbeth* III.i)

Angles

The name of one of the three Germanic tribes which invaded the Roman province of Britannia in 5th C AD. They formed the kingdoms of Northumbria in the north-east, Mercia in the centre (Midlands), and East Anglia in the east. Their dialect was the first to be put into writing, and 'English' (derived from Angle) came to be used for the language and people of the large part of the island overrun by the Angles, Saxons*, and Jutes* (*ie* excluding Wales and Scotland).

* *Anglo-Saxon; English Language.*

Anglican

From medieval Latin, *anglicanus* = English. The Catholic Church of medieval Christendom divided Europe into provinces for administrative purposes; England was the 'Anglican' province. Since the separation of the Church of England* from Rome in 16th C, 'Anglican' has been used adjectivally for the Churches in Britain, the U.S.A., and the Commonwealth which are in communion with the Church of England, as well as for that Church itself. Anglicanism = doctrine and practices of the Church of England and kindred Churches.

* 3.2.2.1; *Church of England; Episcopalian; Reformation.*

Anglo-Saxon

The name is practically identical with Old English in denoting the language, literature and culture of the English before the Norman-French conquest of 1066, and also after it until it becomes fused (Middle English) in 13th C with the insular Norman-French; it was later occasionally used, *eg* in Disraeli's* *Coningsby** and *Sybil**, to differentiate the common people from the aristocracy of (supposedly) Norman-French descent.

* *Angle; English Language; Saxon.*

Anglo-Saxon Chronicle

A history compiled by monks at different centres and at different periods, begun in the reign of Alfred* (871–901), and covering the period from the invasion of Julius Caesar in 54 BC to 1154, when it was completed. Its famous passages are those which describe Alfred's struggle with Danish invaders and the miseries of the people during the civil wars under King Stephen (1135–1154). It was written in English.

Anglo-Saxon Literature

The four centuries preceding the Norman Conquest of 1066 was a period during which the Teutonic tribes who invaded Britain in the 5th C after the fall of Roman dominion achieved a settled and individual civilization capable of first resisting and then assimilating the 8th-C invaders from Scandinavia. The conversion to Christianity of the Angles in the north and east of England, the Saxons in the south and the Jutes in Kent, partly by Irish and partly by continental missionaries, led to the establishment of monasteries which became centres of a literate culture and new creation. Anglo-Saxon writings can be classified as follows:

[1] The Latin writings of the monastic clerks. Works have survived by the Venerable Bede and by Alcuin in the northern kingdom of Northumbria, and by Aldhelm in the southern kingdom of Wessex. The historian Bede* (672–735) was the most enduringly influential of this group. Alcuin (735?–804) was the most generally famous in his time as a result of his importance in the court of

the Emperor Charlemagne as an educational reformer and pioneer from about 790. He compiled manuals of knowledge in the form of dialogues. Aldhelm (640?–709) wrote treatises in prose and in verse in praise of virginity, showing a mastery of Latin unusual in his time and combining it with a vigorous imagery characteristic of vernacular writing of the Anglo-Saxon period.

[2] Vernacular narratives of the pre-Christian era. The most famous of these is the epic *Beowulf**. *Widsith* and *Deor* are shorter poems about the life of the 'scop' or minstrel among the princes and tribes and their deities on the Teutonic mainland.

[3] Elegiac poems in the vernacular, mainly pre-Christian in feeling. The most famous of them is the 100-line *Seafarer*, partly because it has received a masterly rendering in modern English by the American poet Ezra Pound*. It has vivid poignancy in its counterbalancing of the wretchedness of the seafaring life with its irresistible attraction. *The Wanderer* extends the grief of a young man on the death of his lord to general reflections on the transitoriness of earthly existence.

[4] Songs of war. *Brunanburh*, a fragment, describes the victory of an English army in 937 over invading Scots and Norsemen from Norse colonies in Ireland. *Battle of Maldon* is a fragment about the defeat of an East Saxon army by invading Norsemen near the Thames estuary. Its spirit has been compared to that of the French epic, *The Song of Roland*.

[5] Riddles. These do not resemble the petty style of joke which we term a riddle. Some of them are vernacular renderings of questions put by the Latinist Aldhelm who used them for didactic purposes. The vernacular riddles are not so much didactic as lyrical, evoking natural phenomena by metonymy and metaphor (see Figures of Speech).

[6] Vernacular Christian poetry. These are Biblical and devotional poems rendering Christian myths and traditions into native idiom. An important half-legendary figure in this field is the poet Caedmon, whose story is given by Bede in his 'Ecclesiastical History of the English People'. Religious poems attributed to Caedmon survive, but are now held to be paraphrases or derivatives. *Judith*, paraphrased from a book in the Apocrypha*, and the epic fragment, *Fall of the Angels*, on the theme later used by Milton in *Paradise Lost**, are anonymous poems in this genre. The 8th-C Northumbrian poet Cynewulf is considered to be the author of a poem known as 'Christ' about the Ascension, and others on the lives of the Saints.

The influence of French literature and language after the Conquest made Anglo-Saxon (Old English) into a foreign language for the literate classes. The substitution of French rhyme and running metre predominated over the freer Anglo-Saxon rhythms and alliterative music, although the emergence of great alliterative poems in the 14th C* argues some continuity culminating in an important alliterative revival. Nonetheless from the 16th to the 19th C English literature was assumed to have been fathered by Chaucer* who wrote in English but used rhyme and running rhythm. In the 19th C, patriotism and a new interest in German culture caused scholars to make claims for Anglo-Saxon as the real beginning of our literature. In the 20th C it is more usual to regard Anglo-Saxon as a separate study, in some ways related to our later literature but in important respects distinct from it.

Anjou, House of

* *Plantagenets*.

Annus Mirabilis (Wonderful Year)

A poem by John Dryden* written in 1667 dealing with the twelve months between the summer of 1665 and that of 1666, especially the fierce sea battles against the Dutch and the Great Fire* of London. It is written in quatrains, and is Dryden's first noteworthy poem, displaying some of the influence of the metaphysical* school whose style he was later to abandon.

Anthology

A collection of short works in verse or prose, or selected passages from longer works, by various authors. Some anthologies have claims to authority as representing the best written in a given period, *eg* the Oxford Books (of Sixteenth Century Verse, etc.) and others are standard examples of taste at the time of compiling, *eg* Palgrave's *The Golden Treasury of the Best Songs and Lyrical Poems in the English Language*, 1861. Others have had an important influence on taste, or on later literary development: *Percy's Reliques**; *Tottel's Miscellany**; *The Mirror for Magistrates**; *The Greek Anthology**.

Anthology, The Greek

A collection of poems begun by Meleager of Gadara (about 60 BC) and later expanded, especially by Constantius Cephalas (10th C AD), till it included selections from over 300 writers. Many of the pieces, which number over 4,500, are epigrams. The *Anthology* has been, from 16th C onwards, an important source of information on Greek culture.

Anthropophagi

In Greek legend, a race of cannibals who lived north of the Black Sea.

Antichrist /'antikraist/

The word occurs in the New Testament, *1 John* 2 and *2 John* 7, and is explained as the being who denied Christ; there was an older Jewish tradition of a mighty ruler at the end of time, the great antagonist of God. In later centuries, Antichrist was identified with various contemporary rulers; some reformers, *eg* Wycliffe*, applied it to the Pope.

Anti-climax

* *Figures of Speech*.

Antigone /an'tigəni/

In Greek myth, the daughter of Oedipus*, condemned by her uncle Creon, ruler of Thebes, to be buried alive for insisting on carrying out burial rites for her dead brother although he had been a rebel. She is the subject of a tragedy by Sophocles*.

Antiquary, The (1816)

A novel by Walter Scott*. It is the third of his 'Waverley Novels' coming after *Waverley** (1814) and *Guy Mannering* (1815), and, like the previous two, the scene is set in Scotland in 18th C. The main story is an ordinary romance. A young officer, Major Neville, falls in love with Isabella Wardour, whose father rejects him on account of his supposed illegitimacy. Neville follows the father and daughter to Scotland, where the three have sundry adventures; Neville saves their lives, and rescues Sir Arthur Wardour from impending ruin. He also turns out to be the son and heir of a Scottish nobleman. Thus the objections to the union between Neville and Isabella are removed. The real distinction of the novel arises from the subsidiary characters: Jonathan Oldbuck, a learned antiquarian scholar (like Scott himself), and Edie Ochiltree, a wandering beggar who epitomizes the feelings and traditions of the Lowland Scottish peasantry. The most vivid passages are the speeches of this peasantry. Scott states in his preface that he agrees with Wordsworth's opinion (expressed in the Preface to the Lyrical Ballads*) that the peasantry have an eloquence in expressing the basic and most universal passions which is lost to the educated classes.

Antithesis

* *Figures of Speech.*

Antony and Cleopatra

A tragedy by Shakespeare, probably written in 1606–7, and first printed in the First Folio edition of his collected plays in 1623. The source is North's* translation (1587 edition) of Plutarch's* *Lives.*

Mark Antony, with Octavius Caesar and Lepidus, is one of the 'triumvirate' (43–31 BC) which rules Rome and its empire, and he is Rome's most famous living soldier. At the opening of the play, he is the lover of Cleopatra, Queen of Egypt, and, to the disgust of his officers, is neglecting Rome and his political and military duties. All the same, he cannot ignore Rome, and from time to time he reacts strongly against Cleopatra when he remembers his public position and his reputation. His strained relations with Octavius Caesar are temporarily mended when he marries Caesar's sister, Octavia, but he soon abandons her and returns to Cleopatra. Caesar is enraged, and is in any case anxious to secure sole power over the empire for himself. Open war breaks out between them, and Antony is defeated at the sea battle of Actium, largely owing to Cleopatra's attempt to participate personally in the campaign. After Antony's final defeat on land, he attempts to kill himself, and eventually dies of his wounds in the arms of Cleopatra, who has taken refuge in her 'monument'. This is a mausoleum which she had built so that she and Antony could lie together in death; it serves as a kind of miniature fortress. After Antony's death, she makes a bid for survival by pitting her wits against Caesar's. When she sees that she has failed, she takes her own life. The two death scenes, her own and Antony's, are amongst the most famous scenes in Shakespeare's work.

One of the ironies of the tragedy is that Cleopatra loves Antony just because he is a great Roman hero, and yet, in order to get full possession of him, she has to destroy this part of him. At a deeper level, Rome and Egypt are set in dramatic contrast: Rome stands for the political world, with its ruthless and calculating manoeuvring for power; Egypt stands for the heat and colour of passion, tending always to dissolution and corruption. The play belongs to Shakespeare's maturest period. As in his other 'Roman' plays, *Julius Caesar** and *Coriolanus**, Shakespeare shows awareness of writing about the pre-Christian era, in which the hero represents the highest human type, instead of the saint.

Dryden's *All for Love** is also a tragedy about Antony and Cleopatra; a comparison of the two plays is instructive in showing the changes that had come about in English verse in the intervening period. Shaw's play *Caesar and Cleopatra** (1901) is about Cleopatra's earlier relationship with Julius Caesar.

* *North; Plutarch; Shakespeare.*

Aphorism, apophthegm

A terse sentence, weighted with sense; with more weight of wisdom than an epigram need have, but less elegance, *eg* 'The shepherd in Virgil grew at last acquainted with Love, and found him a native of the rocks' (Samuel Johnson*: Letter to Lord Chesterfield, 1754); 'Crafty men contemn studies, simple men admire them, and wise men use them . . .' (Francis Bacon*: *Of Studies*, 1625)

Aphrodite

In Greek myth, goddess of physical beauty and sexual love. Her cult was widespread; in Rome she was known as Venus; in Syria, and the Middle East as Astarte, Ashtaroth, Ishtar. Because she originally sprang from the sea she was also called Anadyomene ('sprung from the foam'); because this occurred near the island of Cythera, she was Cytherean. Zeus* married her to Hephaestus*, but owing to his ugliness she was unfaithful to him with Ares*. She was the mother of Eros (Lat. Cupidos) the boy-god of desire. She was the rival of Persephone* for the love of Adonis* and thus features in a vegetation myth. She competed with Hera* and Athene* for the prize of a golden apple for the greatest beauty, to be awarded by Paris*, and won the contest.

Apocalypse

From Greek 'disclosure'. A kind of visionary literature, especially *Revelation* in the Bible. The essence of such literature is that it expresses in symbolic terms truths and events which surpass the ordinary reach of the human mind.

Apocrypha /ə'pokrifə/

[1] Books of the Old Testament* not counted as the genuine Word of God by the Jews, nor as sacred by Protestants: *1 and 2 Esdras*; *Tobit*; *Judith*; the *Rest of Esther*; *Wisdom*; *Ecclesiasticus* (not to be confused with *Ecclesiastes*); *Baruch*; the *Song of the three Holy Children*; *Susanna*; *Bel and the Dragon*; *Manasses*; *1 and 2 Maccabees*. They remain in the Catholic Bible, and continued in the English one until the British and Foreign Bible Society excluded them in their 19th-C editions. There have also been books apocryphal to the New Testament*, not included in any Bible.

[2] Also sometimes used for works alleged on uncertain grounds to be by a given author. Shakespeare apocrypha: plays said to be wholly or in part by Shakespeare, but not generally acknowledged as such, *eg Edward III*.

Apollo (Phoebus: Phoebus Apollo)

In Greek and Latin mythology, the son of Zeus*. Apollo was a god identifiable with the sun; he was god of music and poetry, and thus associated with the lyre; he had command of prophecy, and was famous for his oracles*, especially that of Delphi*; he was associated with the founding of states and colonies; he was regarded as the ideal of young manhood and male beauty.

Apollyon

In the Bible, *Revelation* 9:11: 'And they had a king over them, which is the angel of the bottomless pit, whose name in the Hebrew tongue is Abaddon, but in the Greek tongue hath his name Apollyon.' He is chiefly famous in English literature for his appearance in Bunyan's *Pilgrim's Progress**, where he is identifiable with Satan. Apollyon means 'destroying'; in Bunyan's allegory, Christian is escaping from the City of Destruction (*ie* this world) when he meets and has to do battle with Apollyon in the Valley of Humiliation.

Apologia, Apology

In ordinary speech, *apology* has the sense of an expression of regret for offensive conduct, but as a literary term it commonly has the older meaning still conveyed by *apologia*: defence, *eg* Philip Sidney's *Apology for Poetry**, or explanation, vindication, *eg* Cardinal Newman's* *Apologia pro Vita sua*.

Apologue

A little story, very often a fable*, with a moral.

Apology for Poetry, The

A critical essay by Sir Philip Sidney*, written in about 1580 and published in 1595 after his death. Its aim is partly to defend the art of poetry against accusations of moral harmfulness made by the Puritans*; in 1579, Stephen Gosson had dedicated to Sidney an essay making such accusations, entitled *School of Abuse*, and this may have incited Sidney to give a more balanced account. He does not deny that poetry (by which he understands all that we would call imaginative literature) may be morally harmful, but he insists that the main purpose of the art is to elevate humanity: '[Nature's] world is brazen, the Poets only deliver a golden.' Sidney follows Aristotle's* view (which he learnt from Italian critics such as Scaliger) that poetry is the art of imitation, but he also takes the Platonic view that an ideal reality lies beyond visible phenomena, and that it is this ideal that should be imitated. However, no art can achieve this high purpose of ennobling the imagination unless it is allowed its due dignity by society. Sidney insists that poetry in England lacks proper respect, and that the practice of the art in his time (about 1580) is unskilled and backward. He gives an account of the reverence with which it was regarded in the past, classifies the different kinds of poetry, and censures the faults that he finds in English verse and drama. He recommends reforms on the neo-Aristotelian Italian principles of shapeliness, consistency, and order. His ideas were soundly based if we consider the actual state of English poetic literature at the time, even though the actual development of this literature after 1590 seems to go against some of his theories. Sidney was not an original critic, but the *Apology* is nonetheless one of the first important critical essays in English, and the only one in the period to be widely known. It is written with vivacity and charm, and the argument is developed methodically and persuasively.

* Poetics (*Aristotle's*); *Unities*; 7.1.

Apophthegm

* *Aphorism*.

Apostrophe

* *Figures of Speech*.

Apple Cart, The (1929)

A 'discussion' comedy by Bernard Shaw*, presenting an imaginary constitutional crisis in England set in modern times. '*The Apple Cart* exposes the unreality of both democracy and royalty as our idealists conceive them' (Shaw in his Preface, 1930). The title is from the English idiom 'to upset the apple-cart', *ie* to cause confusion in the settled order of things. The play is about a fictional English king, King Robert, who refuses to conform to the traditional constitutional role, according to which the King does not interfere with his ministers in their conduct of the government. He thus causes a political crisis, which he cleverly turns to his own advantage. Shaw's satire is directed at the idea of responsible democratic government: this, according to the play, does not really exist in 20th-C Britain, because the ministers have to subject themselves to their bureaucracy, which is much more experienced in the problems with which the government has to deal. The King, on the other hand, is much better qualified to govern, since, like the bureaucracy, his office is a permanent one and is not affected by periodic parliamentary elections which change the ministers. The play is a good example of Shaw's genius for transforming political ideas into witty comedy.

Apple of Discord
* *Paris.*

Apprenticeship
A system of training undergone by youths entering on a trade or craft. The apprentice was indentured to a master in the craft, *ie* entered into a contract with him, to serve him in return for maintenance and instruction for seven years, usually between the ages of 16 and 23. The apprentice was a member of the master's household, and the master was responsible for his behaviour before the law. Thus apprenticeship provided social control, as well as a form of education, and tended to maintain standards in manufacture and professional conduct. It also had the social advantage of mixing the classes and ensuring that the landed classes retained interest in trade, for the smaller landed gentry commonly indentured their younger sons, who had no land to inherit, to master craftsmen, especially in London. Until 18th C (when the gentry, grown richer, tended to despise trade) this admixture of classes, as well as large numbers, made the London apprentices a formidable body of public opinion both politically and, for instance, in the Elizabethan theatre. Apprenticeship was systematized by law under the Statute of Artificers, 1563, and was steadily reduced to insignificance by the growth of capitalism in 17th and 18th C, and by the Industrial Revolution* in 19th. It had its beginnings in the Middle Ages*. Until 17th C, apprenticeship was the only way to enter most trades and professions.
* *Craft Guilds; Journeyman; Master Craftsman.*

Aquinas, St Thomas (c 1225–74)
/ə'kwainəs/

An Italian thinker, author of an extensive system of philosophy and theology, *Summa Totius Theologiae*, on the principles of Aristotle*. This work came to be considered the most authoritative product of scholastic thinking, and, more than any other, was responsible for Aristotle's superseding in the Middle Ages* the philosophy of Plato*, who, however, recovered influence in the Renaissance* of 16th C. Aristotle's philosophy was less easy to harmonize with Christian ideas than was Plato's, and as the former's prestige was very great, Aquinas's reconciliation of Aristotle and Christianity was an important strengthening of Christian thought.

Arabian Nights Entertainments
Also known as *The Thousand and One Nights*, this collection of stories supposed to be told by Scheherazade was probably put together by an Egyptian story-teller about 15th C. The stories became well known and popular in Europe early in 18th C. English translations have been made by Edward Lane in 1840 and, with greater literary merit, by Sir Richard Burton in 1885–88.

Arcadia
A mountainous district in Greece, with a pastoral economy, and in ancient times the centre of the worship of Pan*, the god of shepherds and huntsmen. The country was idealized by Virgil* in his *Eclogues*, and again in the Renaissance* in pastoral* works, notably *Arcadia* by Sannazzaro (1504), and Sir Philip Sidney's* *Arcadia*. By this time Arcadia was thought of purely as an ideal country of the imagination, uncorrupted by the sophistications of civilization; 'Arcadian simplicity' is the expression for such ideality.
* Arcadia *by Sidney.*

Arcadia, The
Begun by Sir Philip Sidney* in 1580 during a period of retirement from court, and published in 1590, *The Arcadia* is a long prose romance with a loose plot which accommodates a number of subsidiary tales. The stories are heroic, amorous, or pastoral, with some comic relief; the characters are simplified types of nobility, wickedness or comedy. The intention was to cultivate high aristocratic morality, as well as to entertain; and part of the entertainment lay in the elaborate musical style which now makes the book unfashionable. Its contemporary influence was great, however, in encouraging pastoralism and romanticism in the poets between 1590 and 1640. The prose is interspersed with poetry of delicate musicality, also important for its influence, though not so distinguished as the best of Sidney's *Astrophil and Stella** sonnets.

Archer, William (1856–1924)
Dramatic critic and translator. He is chiefly remembered as the translator of the Norwegian dramatist, Ibsen*. Ibsen has had other translators, but it is chiefly through Archer's version that he is known to the British public.

Archery

The art of shooting with the bow and arrow. Archery played an important part in English history in the Middle Ages.* Three kinds of bow were used: the short-bow; the crossbow, which fired a metal bolt released by a trigger; the longbow. The first of these was a comparatively primitive weapon, but it was much in use until 13th C. During the same period, the crossbow became the principal firearm of west European armies, except English ones; it had a longer range than either of the others, although it could not be fired so quickly, nor was it as accurate as the longbow. The virtues of the longbow were proved to the English by the Welsh, who first developed the weapon. It enabled the English to defeat the Scottish commander, Sir William Wallace*, at the battle of Falkirk (1298), after which it became for two centuries the principal weapon of the English foot-soldiers, bringing them victory again and again in their wars against the French and the Scots. The secret of this success was partly the constant encouragement, and even enforcement, of the practice of archery as a sport by the medieval kings; Edward III*, for instance, in 1363, forbade all sport except archery on Sundays and other holidays. But the English skill with the longbow also resulted from their distinctive way of using it; in 16th C, Bishop Latimer* described how in his youth he was taught 'not to draw with the strength of the arms as . . . other nations do, but with the strength of the body'.

The importance of archery in medieval England is exemplified by the commonness of the surname Fletcher, which means a 'maker of bows and arrows'. The bows were made from wood of the yew-tree, and this timber was imported in quantity. To ensure cheap supplies, the government of Richard III* (1483–5) ordained that merchants had to include yew staves with every ton of other goods imported. This care for a plentiful supply of bows and for widespread training in their use was due to the dependence of the medieval kings on the peasantry for the defence of the realm. They had no large standing armies of professional soldiers, and needed to be able to call on the 'militia' of ordinary yeomen* in every shire.

The invention of gunpowder and the spread of muskets and pistols in 16th C gradually made the longbow obsolete, although 16th-C governments continued to enforce or at least to encourage the practice of archery. The military importance of the longbow, however, was past by 1500; its most dazzling victories had been those of the Hundred Years' War* against France; in particular, the battles of Crécy* (1346), Poitiers (1356), and Agincourt* (1415).

Archimedes (3rd C BC)

Greek mathematician and inventor. He lived in the Greek colonial city of Syracuse in Sicily. He wrote a number of mathematical treatises which survive, and is particularly associated with the Archimedes Principle in the science of hydrostatics. The anecdote about his discovery of this is famous: Archimedes was puzzling how to discover whether the king's crown was pure gold or contained an alloy of silver; stepping into his bath, and noticing the displacement of the water level by his body, he realized that his problem could be solved by placing the crown and an equal weight of gold in two waterfilled vessels, and then observing whether the crown shifted the water-level further, owing to the extra bulk of the alloy. In his delight at his discovery, he leapt out of his bath and ran naked through the streets crying 'Eureka!' (I have found it.) His ingenious machines of war protracted the Roman siege of Syracuse to three years. When the Romans sacked the city, he was killed by a Roman soldier as he sat solving a mathematical problem. A saying attributed to Archimedes is: 'Give me a place to stand, and I will move the earth.'

Arden, Forest of

Formerly an extensive forest in the neighbourhood of Stratford. It gave its name to the important landed family of Arden; Shakespeare's mother, Mary Arden, may have belonged to a junior branch. The Forest of Arden in Shakespeare's *As You Like It** is the Flemish forest of the Ardennes, but Shakespeare may have had the English forest in mind as well, when he used the name.

Arden, John (b 1930)

Dramatist. First play: *All Fall Down* (1955). In 1956 he won a B.B.C. drama prize with *The Life of Man*. This brought him to London's best-known theatre for serious modern drama, the Royal Court Theatre, where his next three plays were produced: *The Waters of Babylon* (1957); *Live Like Pigs* (1958), and *Sergeant Musgrave's Dance* (1959). The last attracted much attention among critics, though it was not a popular success. It is a play about an army sergeant who deserts with three soldiers from his unit which is stationed in a colonial territory; they come to a mining town in the north of England with the mission to inspire the people with a hatred of war; they seek alliance with the miners who are in conflict with the mine-owners. The multiple conflict that arises from this situation is used to propound complex ideas about the nature of conflict and its resolution; but the play ends in tragedy without a solution to the problems. No dramatist in England since Bernard Shaw* had used the theatre for such thorough exploration of political and social ideas, but whereas Shaw made the ideas central to his dramas and the characters merely instrumental to them, Arden makes his characters central, presenting them through a dialogue which sometimes achieves poetic intensity without sacrificing truth to the northern idiom. This play is one of the most substantial achievements of the dramatic revival which most distinguishes English literature in recent years. The most important shaping influence on this and others of Arden's plays seems to be that of the German dramatist Bertolt Brecht, most noticeably in the simple energy of the dialogue and the dramatic use of lyrics. Later plays: *Soldier Soldier* (1960); *The Happy Haven* (1960); *The Business of Good Government* (1960); *Wet Fish* (1962); *The Workhouse Donkey* (1963); *Ironhand* (1963); *Ars Longa Vita Brevis* (with Margaretta D'Arcy, 1964); *Armstrong's Last Goodnight* (1964); *Left-handed Liberty* (1965); *Friday's Hiding* (1966); *The Royal Pardon* (1966); *The Hero Rises Up* (1968); *Island of the Mighty* (1972); *The Ballygombeen Bequest* (1972). His later plays show him trying to meet the problem of combining an appeal to substantial popular audiences with richness and subtlety of dramatic ideas.

* 5.3.3; *Beckett, Samuel; Osborne, John; Pinter, Harold.*

Areopagitica /ariopə'dʒitikə/

A pamphlet* published in 1644 giving the text of a speech by John Milton* (1608–74) in defence of freedom of the press. The Civil War* was in progress, and Parliament, at war with King Charles I, had ordained that no book should be published without parliamentary licence so that opinion hostile to it could be restrained. Milton, who was on the parliamentary side during the war, argued that restraint of the press was wrong according to Parliament's own principles, that it was useless, and that it was bad for a vital, growing nation. One of Milton's important prose works, *Areopagitica* is famous for its eloquence. The title derives from Areopagus, the hill in ancient Athens where the supreme judicial tribunal met.

Ares

In Greek myth, the god of war, identifiable with the Roman Mars. He was the son of Zeus* and Hera*, the king and queen of the gods. He symbolized the rage of war, or blood-thirstiness, and was attended by the minor deities Deinos (Fear), Phobos (Fright), Eris (Strife), Enyo (Destroyer of cities), and the Keres, who drank the blood of the dying. He was constantly opposed to Athene*, associated with wisdom and intelligent courage, and was the weaker of the two. He conducted a love-affair with Aphrodite*, who was lawfully wedded to Hephaestus*, the physically grotesque craftsman of the gods. Hephaestus made a public exhibition of the lovers by binding them down in their bed when they were asleep together, with an invisible net.

Aretino, Pietro (1492–1556)

One of the 16th-C Italian writers much read in England, especially between 1580 and 1640; he was much enjoyed for his licentiousness, especially by Thomas Nashe*, and proportionately deplored on the Puritan* side, for instance by John Milton in *Areopagitica**, 1644.

Argonauts

In Greek legend, travellers on the ship *Argo* conveying the hero Jason in search of the golden fleece of a certain sacred ram. The legend is very old, and was known to Homer. The story is told in English in a narrative poem by William Morris*: *Life and Death of Jason* (1867).

Ariadne /ari'adni/

Daughter of King Minos* of Crete and Pasiphae, daughter of the sun-god. She fell in love with Theseus* and helped him to guide himself through the labyrinth, where the Minotaur* was kept, with a clue of thread. Later, abandoned by Theseus, she was found and married by Dionysus*, god of wine.

Ariel /'eəriəl/

In Shakespeare's *The Tempest**, a spirit of the air through whom the magician Prospero performs his magic; Ariel is contrasted with the other servant of Prospero, Caliban*, a creature of the mud.

The name is also applied to a fallen angel in Milton's *Paradise Lost**, Bk. VI, and to a sylph in Pope's *Rape of the Lock**.

Ariosto, Ludovico (1474–1533)

Italian poet; author of the romantic epic *Orlando Furioso**, one of the most famous and influential poems of its kind. The poem is 'epic' by virtue of its heroic exploits, and 'romantic' by virtue of its extravagance of fictions and the loose interlacing of them through the poem. His most distinguished follower in England is Spenser in the *Faerie Queene**. *Orlando* is full of humour and irony; Spenser's intention was to surpass it by his high seriousness.

Aristides the Just (6th–5th C BC) /aris'taidi:z/

In Greek history, a statesman and general of Athens, who took a leading part in resisting the Persian invasion of Greece. He was politically and militarily conservative, desiring that Athens should depend on her army, and not build a great navy, according to the policy of his rival Themistocles. He nonetheless loyally supported Themistocles in the naval campaign of Salamis which saved Greece. He seems to have earned his epithet 'just' by his just apportionment of the financial contributions from the allies of Athens in the Delian League. When the Athenians were voting between himself and Themistocles, an illiterate shepherd who did not know him asked him to write the name Aristides for rejection. Aristides asked him whether he had ever injured the shepherd, who replied: 'I do not even know Aristides, but it irritates me that one can't hear his name spoken without "the Just" '.

Aristophanes (c 444–c 380 BC) /aris'tofəni:z/

A great Athenian comic dramatist who satirized the manners, politics, statesmen and literary men of his age, but always with serious intentions. His nearest English equivalent is Ben Jonson* in such plays as *The Alchemist** and *The Devil is an Ass*. Aristophanes did not, however, have important influence on English comedy at any period.

Aristotle (384–322 BC) /'aristotl/

A great Greek philosopher, born at Stageira, and so sometimes called the Stagirite. He was first a pupil of Plato*, later developing his thought on principles opposed to those of his master. He was tutor to the young Alexander (the Great). His thought covered varied fields of knowledge, in most of which he has been influential. His best known works are his *Ethics*, *Politics*, and *Poetics*; it is the last that most concerns English literature, but the pervasive influence of his thought as a whole must first be touched on.

The difference between Aristotle and Plato has been described as follows: Plato makes us think in the first place of an ideal and supernatural world by turning our minds to ideal forms which are the truth in terms of which imperfect earthly things can be known and judged; Aristotle turns us towards the natural world where things are what they are, perfect or imperfect, so that knowledge comes through study and classification of them in the actual world. It can thus be seen that whilst Plato leads in the direction of mysticism, Aristotle leads towards science. Until 13th C, Christian thought tended to be dominated by Plato, but thereafter medieval Christian thought, owing to the work of Thomas Aquinas*, found Aristotelianism more convenient, since it could show how the human reason supplemented divine revelation more aptly than the mysticism of Platonism could. So it arose that while Aristotelian thinking dominated the medieval period, Plato offered an alternative base for the Renaissance* intellectuals in their attempts to emancipate themselves from official thinking. For instance, Aristotelian ideas on morality prevailed in the Middle Ages*, but in the Renaissance they competed with Platonic ideas; an example is Spenser's *Faerie Queene**, considered as an allegory of the virtues; the basic plan is Aristotelian, but the inspiration is Platonic.

The *Poetics** is based on the study of imaginative literature in Greek. On this basis of an essentially informatory study, Italian critics such as Scaliger and Castelvetro, of 16th C, and French dramatists and critics of 17th C such as Corneille, Racine* and Boileau* constructed a system of rules which acted partly as a discipline, but partly as a tyranny over imaginative writers. Sidney* knew Aristotle chiefly through the Italians, who had derived from Aristotle some rules not to be found in him – notably the unities* of time and place. The great critics of 17th and 18th C, Dryden* and Samuel Johnson*, were respectful of and deeply influenced by French neo-Aristotelianism, but they refused to be bound by it, unlike some second-rank critics such as Thomas Rymer*, famous for his condemnation of Shakespeare's *Othello**. The 19th C reacted strongly against the attitude, but in this century the elimination of the neo-Aristotelian superimpositions of the Renaissance has revived interest in the discernment displayed in the *Poetics*.

Armada, The (Spanish), 1588 /aːˈmaːdə/

The fleet dispatched by Philip II of Spain to transport a Spanish army from Flanders to land in and conquer England. The attempt was defeated by the English fleet under Lord Howard of Effingham and his sea-captains, some of whom were already famous for other exploits, such as Drake*, Hawkins, Frobisher. The event was of great importance for these among other reasons: (1) England had a rapidly growing sense of national identity and this was centred on the person of Queen Elizabeth I*, against whom the invasion attempt was specifically aimed; the victory was thus not merely a personal triumph for the Queen but an inspiration to the whole people, finding expression in adulation of Elizabeth in idealized roles during the immense poetic outburst of the last 15 years of her reign (1588–1603). (2) England was the most important country to have renounced papal authority; her defeat might have been disastrous to the Protestant side in its struggle against the Catholic powers, of which Spain was then the chief. Instead, the English victory meant a decisive check to the formidable (Counter-Reformation*) attempt of Catholicism to recover the northern countries of Europe. (3) The English victory was a milestone in the shift of power from the Mediterranean region to the Atlantic powers of England, France and Holland, which henceforth increasingly led the European expansion over the globe.

Armageddon /aːməˈgedn/

In the Bible (*Revelation* 16:16), the last great battle that will end the world; the name may derive from Megiddo, a place associated with frequent battles in Israelite history.

Arminianism

* *Predestination.*

Arms and the Man

An early play by Bernard Shaw* with the theme that the glamour of war and of military heroism is essentially a civilian fiction. The hero, Bluntschli, is a Swiss mercenary soldier and unheroic 'anti-hero' such as was to become common in 20th-C literature, but, with his ironic intelligence, was a type special to Shaw.

Arnold, Matthew (1822–88)

Poet, critic, and educationist, son of Thomas Arnold, the famous broad churchman, headmaster of Rugby and creator of the modern type of public school*.

As a poet, Arnold had distinction but was representative of his time rather than outstandingly an original voice within it. Most of his verse was published from 1849 to 1867: *The Strayed Reveller*, 1849; *Poems*, 1853; *Poems, Second Series*, 1855; *Merope, a Tragedy*, 1858; *New Poems*, 1867. From these volumes, the best known poems today are: *Sohrab and Rustum* (1853), a narrative in epic style; the reflective and elegiac *Scholar Gipsy* (1853) and *Thyrsis* (1867), and a short lyric, *Dover Beach* (1867 – perhaps written much earlier). His poetry is fastidious, elevated, meditative, and melancholy; deeply felt, it now seems rather remote, 'But the poet's vision gave the prose writer his goal' (Trilling).

As a critic, Arnold remains strongly influential on 20th-C critical thought. This influence does not come from his studies of individual writers but from his studies of contemporary culture and of the relationship, actual and potential, of literature to industrial civilization. His best known critical works are *Essays in Criticism**, First and Second Series, 1865 and 1888; *On Translating Homer*, 1861; and *Culture and Anarchy*, 1869. In such essays as 'The Function of Criticism at the Present Time' in *Essays in Criticism I** his easy, ironic, but subtle and persuasive thought has been felt to be deeply relevant to 20th-C problems by such critics as I. A. Richards, T. S. Eliot, F. R. Leavis and Lionel Trilling.

Arnold's work as an inspector of schools and educationist was related to his most serious critical preoccupations, and the two worlds meet in such a work as *Culture and Anarchy*.

*** 6.4.1; 7.4.**

Bib: Trilling, L., *Matthew Arnold*; Jump, J. D., *Matthew Arnold*; Brown, E.K., *Arnold: a Study in Conflict*; Tinker, C. B. and Lowry, H. F., *The Poetry of Arnold*

Arnold, Thomas (1795–1842)

The famous headmaster of Rugby School and father of Matthew Arnold*.

* 2.1.2.3; 3.4.3; *Public Schools*.

Ars Poetica (Art of Poetry)

* *Horace*.

Artemis

In Greek myth, the moon-goddess; identifiable with the Roman Diana. She became gradually less associated with the moon, which was given a distinct goddess, Selene*. She remained, however, associated, like Apollo*, with light, and they are connected by their alternative names – Phoebe and Phoebus respectively. Both were armed with bow and arrows; both inflicted sudden death – Artemis usually on women. However, she had her benevolent aspects, and presided over childbirth. She was a huntress, and as a virgin she was identified with chastity. The Greeks regarded her as Apollo's twin sister. Other versions of her character, however, differed considerably. Her cult in the Asian city of Ephesus (where her temple was one of the Seven Wonders of the World*) represented her as a fertility goddess with almost opposite qualities to those of the Greek Artemis.

Arthur, King

King Arthur may have been a Celtic chieftain who resisted Anglo-Saxon* invaders in about 5th or 6th C AD, after the Roman garrisons had abandoned Britain. Some Welsh legends of uncertain date show him as a god for laymen and a demon for the Christian priests. The earliest known mention of him is by the chronicler Nennius (who lived on the borders of Wales) in his Latin *History of the Britons* (900?). Nennius describes him as 'war-leader of the kings of Britain' against the Saxons. Early in 12th C Geoffrey* of Monmouth in his Latin *History of the Kings of Britain* expands Nennius's account, and it is his narrative which is the main basis of the King Arthur of medieval romance. Arthurian romances were written in England, France and Germany, but the principal ones are French. It has puzzled scholars to explain how Welsh legends should have been taken up by French court poets. The connecting link was probably Brittany, the Celtic-speaking north-west province of France which no doubt shared the Celtic legends of Wales. Although Geoffrey of Monmouth, like Nennius, lived on the borders of Wales, he is thought to have had Breton origins.

The medieval Arthurian romances grew up in three main stages. In the first stage, Arthur is a heroic warrior, and his chief knight is Gawain*. To this stage belongs the 12th-C English alliterative poem *Brut** by Layamon, who drew his material from Geoffrey by way of a French poem by Wace. The second stage starts late in 12th C with the French poet, Chrétien* de Troyes. The interest moves from Arthur himself to his knights, the chief of whom is Lancelot* (Launcelot). By this time 'courtly love' or 'fine amour' has become a main theme of French literature, and Lancelot is a great lover. The third stage is differentiated from the second by the emphasis on chastity above 'fine amour'. Lancelot tends to be superseded in turn by his son, Galahad*, the chaste knight, and the knights' adventures centre on the search for the mysterious Holy Grail*. English medieval Arthurian literature relates to all three stages. There are two 14th-C poems, one alliterative and one in metrical stanzas, entitled *Morte Arthur* ('Death of Arthur') which belong to the first stage, and the stanzaic one was used by Malory* in his prose *Morte d'Arthur** (15th C) though he relied chiefly on French material belonging to stage three. The greatest of the English Arthurian romances, the anonymous 14th-C *Sir Gawain and the Green Knight**, relates to all three stages.

Arthur remained a national hero and a historical figure for Englishmen until the end of 16th C. Spenser's *Faerie Queene** (1596), with its wandering knights each emblematic of a virtue, and Prince Arthur as the embodiment of the sum of virtues, is a romance of the Arthurian tradition with Renaissance platonic idealism added. As late as 19th C, Tennyson* tried to ennoble industrial England with an idealized retelling of the Arthurian tales in *The Idylls of the King** (1842–85).

Aryan

A linguistic term referring to the Indo-European family of languages. Sometimes used racially for the speakers of these languages, or their ancient forefathers.

As You Like It

A comedy by Shakespeare. Produced about 1599, and first printed in the Folio* of 1623. Its source is Thomas Lodge's* romance, *Rosalynde*.

The story is romantic and pastoral. A Duke, the father of the heroine, Rosalind, has been turned off his throne by his ruthless brother, the father of Rosalind's devoted friend, Celia. He has taken refuge with a few loyal courtiers in the neighbouring Forest of Arden. An orphan son, Orlando, is tyrannized over by his wicked elder brother, Oliver. Orlando and Rosalind fall in love. Rosalind is banished from court, and goes to the forest in male disguise, calling herself Ganymede; Celia goes with her as Rosalind-Ganymede's sister, Aliena, and they are also accompanied by the court jester, Touchstone. Orlando follows them. He does not penetrate Rosalind's disguise, however, when, as Ganymede, she makes him 'play-act' courtship with her, episodes which are used by Shakespeare as light satires on the conventions of romantic love. Another pair of lovers in the forest are the shepherd and shepherdess, Silvius and Phebe, a couple who are drawn from the most artificial pastoral* mode. Phebe (true to her convention) disdains Silvius, but falls embarrassingly in love with Rosalind (in her disguise) at first sight, and in spite of Rosalind's rudeness to her. Touchstone engages the affections of an unromantic and realistic village girl, Audrey, and thus frustrates her unromantic village lover, William. There is also Jaques, a fashionable and affected young man in the Elizabethan style, attached to the court of the exiled Duke. Rosalind, who is extremely plain-spoken except when she remembers that she is in love, exposes his affectations. In the end the couples are sorted out appropriately, and Rosalind's father regains his dukedom.

Shakespeare thus plays off real life against literary convention. The play is gay, satirical and romantic, all in one. Together with *Twelfth Night** it is his best work in the style of romantic comedy.

* *Courtly Literature.*

Ascham, Roger (1515–68) /ˈaskəm/

An enlightened and influential humanist, tutor to Elizabeth I* as princess and Queen, and Latin secretary to Mary I*. Puritan* in moral sympathies, he hated the licentiousness of the influence of Italian manners, while at the same time he admired the Italian humanist view (especially in Castiglione's *The Courtier* – 1528) that education should aim to produce the harmonious man, on the Platonic pattern. He taught the importance of physical education in *Toxophilus* (The Archer) published in 1545. In the *Schoolmaster* (1570) he taught that education should be persuasive in its method rather than intimidatory. His style is eloquent but plain, and important in the development of English prose.

* *Humanism.*

Ash Wednesday

[1] The first day of the religious season of Lent*; a day of penitence when, in the Catholic Church, the penitents had their foreheads marked with ash.

[2] *Ash-Wednesday* is the title of a sequence of poems, 1930, by T. S. Eliot* (1888–1965), marking poetically the conversion of the poet to Christianity: he became a member of the Church of England in 1927.

Ashtaroth

* *Aphrodite.*

Assonance

* *Figures of Speech.*

Astarte

* *Aphrodite.*

Astraea

In Greek myth, 'the star maiden', usually considered to be the daughter of Zeus* and Themis. During the Golden Age* she lived on earth as the benefactress of humanity. When, in the bronze and iron ages, humanity degenerated until they no longer deserved her blessings, she took her place among the stars as the constellation Virgo.

Astraea Redux ('Astraea Returning', 1660) is a poem by John Dryden about the restoration* of King Charles II*.

* *Ages, Golden, etc.*

Astrophil and Stella

A sequence of sonnets* by Sir Philip Sidney* (1554–86) supposed to be addressed by the Star-lover (Astrophil) to the Star (Stella). They were written about 1580, but not published until 1591. The poets Wyatt* and Surrey* had already tried the sonnet form, introducing it from Italy, but it had not become established. Sidney's sequence, which contains some of the finest sonnets in English poetry, was the start of a vigorous tradition, although the immediate fashion only lasted about a decade. Stella is based on Penelope Devereux, daughter of the Earl of Essex. Her marriage with Sidney was proposed in 1576, but instead she married Lord Rich. Sidney makes sardonic play with his name in sonnets 24, 36 and 37.

Atalanta

In Greek legend, a beautiful girl, famed for her speed. Suitors, to win her, had to beat her in a race, and be killed by her dart if they lost. She was eventually beaten by Milanion, who distracted her from the race by throwing down three golden apples. She is also associated with another legend, of the killing of the Calydonian Boar. *Atalanta's Race* is a poem by William Morris* in *The Earthly Paradise* (1868–70); *Atalanta in Calydon* (1865) is a poetic drama in Greek style by Algernon Swinburne*.

Atheism

Disbelief in God. In the Middle Ages and 16th and 17th C, atheism was abhorrent, it was equivalent to a denial of conscience – an attitude shown in the play *The Atheist's Tragedy* (1611) by Cyril Tourneur*. On the other hand, sheer adventurousness of mind induced some Renaissance* men to play with atheism, and Christopher Marlowe* was charged with it in 1593. However, this kind of intellectual risk-taking was different from the systematic belief that man's reason suffices for his welfare. This belief grew in 18th C and emerged in the French Revolution*, influencing such English intellectuals was William Godwin* and through him P. B. Shelley*, whose atheism caused him to be expelled from Oxford, and for whom Platonism sufficed. Different, but still 18th C in its sources, was the atheism of Utilitarians* such as James Mill (1773–1836) and John Stuart Mill*, who were less naïve about Reason than Godwin but, as practical men, saw religion as unnecessary in their scheme for human betterment. The scientific ideas of the Victorian* period, especially those of Charles Darwin* and Thomas Huxley*, were more productive of agnosticism* than of atheism. Modern atheism is exemplified by the Rationalist Press, but it remains a minority attitude among writers, in contrast to agnosticism, which is rather commoner than professed faith.

Athenaeum, The

A London men's Club*, founded in 1824. Members are elected from those who have gained distinction in literature, science, art and scholarship.

Athene

Also known as Pallas, Pallas Athene (Lat. Minerva). In Greek myth, the goddess of wisdom, and in general of the intellectual and active sides of life, *eg* industry and politics. She sprang fully armed from the head of her father Zeus*, who had swallowed her mother (Metis = 'counsel') fearing that their progeny would usurp his power. Owing to her gift to man of the olive, the city of Athens was called after her.

Athens

Chief city of ancient Greece, and the source for Europe of the greater part of the enormous influence which Greek culture has exercised. Her greatest period was 5th C BC but she continued to be the cultural metropolis of the ancient world, after her military decline, well into 4th C. To the earlier part of these two centuries belong Greek tragedy*: Aeschylus*; Sophocles*; and Euripides*; and comedy: Aristophanes*. To the later part belong the outstanding philosophers: Plato* and Aristotle*.

* *Greek Literature.*

Atlantis

A legendary island in mid-Atlantic, described by the Greek philosopher Plato* in his dialogue *Timaeus.* It is said to have had immense power and prosperity until it was submerged by the sea. Its existence was believed in during the Middle Ages* partly owing to legends about other mysterious western lands, such as Avalon* in the Isle of the Blessed, and Lyonesse*, both in Arthurian legend. Such places were imagined as earthly paradises, and in the Renaissance* the myths were used to demonstrate ideal governments and countries, in the Platonic style. Hence *The New Atlantis** (1626) by Francis Bacon*, an uncompleted account of a fictitious country governed through the wisdom of natural philosophers.

Atlas

In Greek myth, a Titan* who was turned to stone (Mount Atlas) and was supposed to bear the heavens upon his shoulders. The name came to be used for a volume of maps; frontispieces of Atlas bearing the heavens appeared in early atlases.

Attila (d AD 453)

King of the Huns*. His kingdom centred on Hungary; from it he made devastating attacks on the Eastern Roman Empire and on the Germanic kingdoms which had replaced the Empire in Western Europe. He was eventually defeated (451) by an alliance between Aetius, a Roman general, and Theodoric, king of the Visigoths. The terror that he inspired caused him to be known as 'the scourge of God', and he has remained a symbol of destruction.

Aubrey, John (1626–97)

Antiquarian and biographer, chiefly remembered for his *Brief Lives* chiefly of contemporaries. He compiled these for Anthony à Wood's history of Oxford University (1674). He is thus one of the early English biographers. The lives contain many inaccuracies but are entertainingly written in a personal and anecdotal style.

* *Biography.*

Bib: Powell A., *Aubrey and his Friends.*

Auden, Wystan Hugh (b 1907) /ˈoːdn/

Poet. Son of a doctor and a devoutly Anglo-Catholic mother; educated at Gresham's School, a public school* with liberal ideas about education, and at Oxford University. He spent much of his early life in the industrial midlands of England. He thought first of becoming an engineer; in some respects his attitude to poetry has been to treat it as a branch of technology – he takes great pleasure in technical virtuosity. His middle-class intellectual background produced in him an extreme example of openness to ideas characteristic of that class in England, together with a sense of responsibility towards problems equally typical of it. These two qualities have made for a strong didactic* tendency in his poetry; he has been a teacher both in an English school and in English and American universities. He emigrated to the United States in 1939, and became an American citizen, a move apparently provoked by the desire to live where the crises of modern civilization were felt at their most intense, and not obscured or disguised by the strong traditionalism of the English way of life. His emigration was also perhaps inspired by a sense of uprootedness: the English way of life no longer even seemed self-sufficient, as it did in 19th C. Western civilization itself was exposed to destructive forces from within itself. Yet in certain respects he has always remained very English; his moral purposiveness and his landscapes of open hillside are in sympathy with the poetic tradition from Wordsworth*.

His first book, *Poems* (1930), was published during the great economic crisis which originated in the United States in 1929. In the decade of the thirties this book was followed by *The Orators* (1932), the 'charade' *The Dance of Death* (1933), the drama *The Dog Beneath the Skin* (with Christopher Isherwood, 1935), *Look, Stranger!* (1936), the drama *The Ascent of F.6* (with Isherwood, 1936),

Letters from Iceland (with Louis MacNeice 1937), the drama *On the Frontier* (with Isherwood, 1938), *Journey to a War* (with Isherwood, 1939), and *Another Time* (1940). His verse was full of topical reference to the social and international crises of the time; it gave direct expression to the anxieties of the contemporary intelligentsia as no other writing did, and Auden was recognized as the leader of a group of writers, chiefly poets, that included Spender*, Day Lewis, MacNeice and Isherwood, all with similar preoccupations. His verse showed a wide interest in verse technique, and a range of influences extending from the alliterative* styles of Old and Middle English to T. S. Eliot* and the late work of Yeats*. Psychologically and socially he adopted critical standpoints from Freud* and Marx*, but more centrally he evolved an ideology of love and responsibility of choice which, with the help of the 19th-C Danish philosopher Kierkegaard and the 20th-C German-American theologian Niebuhr, brought him after 1940 to Anglo-Catholic Christianity.

Since his emigration to America, Auden has published long poems: *New Year Letter* (1941), *For the Time Being* (1945), *The Age of Anxiety* (1948), and then more shorter poems: *Nones* (1952), *The Shield of Achilles* (1955), *Homage to Clio* (1960). He has also written criticism: *The Enchafèd Flood* (1951), *The Dyer's Hand* (1963), and libretti for operas, and he has edited a number of anthologies. He is now an isolated figure, whereas during the first decade of his writing he seemed to be the voice of a generation – perhaps, in reality, only of the generation of the younger middle class.

Bib: Hoggart, R., *Introductory Essay*; Muir, E., and Daiches, D., *The Present Age*; Drew, E., *Directions in Modern Poetry*; Beach, J. W., *The Making of the Auden Canon*; Spears, M. K., *The Poetry of W. H. Auden*; Everett, B., *Auden* in the Writers and Critics Series.

Augustan age

A period in the history of a literature when it reaches its highest standards in certain easily identified qualities: refinement, clarity, elegance, balance of judgement. This coincided in Roman literature with the reign of the Emperor Augustus (27 BC–AD 14). Oliver Goldsmith* seems to have been the first to use the term in regard to English literature ('Augustan Age in England' in *The Bee*, 1759) and he applies it to the reigns of Queen Anne, *ie* the age of Addison* and Swift*, and William III. Other writers have extended the English Augustan age back to Dryden* and forward to include the work of Pope* and Samuel Johnson*; in fact, to include all those English writers who shared the literary ideals of the reign of Anne. This period of English culture was indeed one in which there was an especially high admiration for the classical Augustan age, the age of Virgil*, Horace*, and Ovid*, and for the standards of criticism prescribed by Horace in his Art of Poetry (*Ars Poetica*).

It is reasonable, on the whole, to identify the English Augustan age with 18th C. The whole century assumed the sovereignty of reason, but from about 1750 we see an increasing value attached to the feelings, especially the social ones such as the sense of justice, delicacy of taste, sympathy. The change occurred partly through the influence of the philosopher David Hume* who carried the analytical use of reason so far as to undermine the basis of the faculty itself. But Hume did not destroy faith in reason; he merely proved that it is unreasonable to assume that reason is the origin and justification of our moral values, which must be based on our feelings. He thus kept for reason its sovereignty as the critical and analytical faculty of the mind, while proving its limitations in the conduct of life. The earlier Augustans, such as Pope, Swift, Addison, are distinguishable for the value they attach to reason permeating society; the later Augustans, such as Johnson, Gray*, Goldsmith, are distinguishable for their attention to the sensibilities; both assume that man fulfils himself socially and not in solitude, and both rely on reason as the guide to fitness of taste and conduct.

* *Eighteenth Century Literature*

Auld Lang Syne /ˈoːldlaŋˈsain/

A song by Robert Burns* (1759–96), with the refrain:

For auld lang syne, my dear,
For auld lang syne,
We'll tak a cup o' kindness yet
For auld lang syne.

The second and fourth lines mean 'for the sake of times gone by'. The song is often sung on anniversaries when old colleagues meet, or at the end of similar gatherings. The quoted refrain is in fact not by Burns but perhaps by Sir Robert Aytoun (1570–1638); Burns inserted it in his song.

Austen, Jane (1775–1817) /ˈostin/

Novelist. Her novels in order of publication are as follows: *Sense and Sensibility** (1811), *Pride and Prejudice** (1813), *Mansfield Park** (1814), *Emma** (1816), *Northanger Abbey** and *Persuasion** (1818). The last two, published posthumously, are her first and last work respectively in order of composition. Fragments and early drafts include: *Lady Susan* (pub 1871), *The Watsons* (1871), and *Sanditon*, on which she was working when she died, published in 1925.

She restricted her material to a narrow range of society and events: a quiet, prosperous, middle-class circle in provincial surroundings. However she treated this material with such subtlety of observation and depth of moral penetration that she is ranked among the best of English novelists. A French critic, Louis Cazamian, writes of her method that it is 'so classical, so delicately shaded . . . that we are strongly reminded of the great French analysts'. Her classicism arises from respect for the sane, clear-sighted judgement of the Augustan* age that had preceded her, but its vitality is enhanced by the romanticism* of her own period, so that her heroines acquire wisdom by a counterbalancing of the two. She brought the English novel, as an art form, to its maturity, and the wide range which that form covered later in 19th C owed much to the imaginative assurance which she had given it.

Her father was rector of the village of Steventon in Hampshire, where she was born. Her life as a clergyman's daughter was outwardly uneventful, but it is probably not true that this accounts for the absence of sensationalism in her novels; her circle of relatives and friends was such as could have given her a wide experience of contemporary society. The restriction of the subject matter of her fiction seems to have been dictated by artistic considerations.

* 4.3.3.

Bib: Austen-Leigh, J. E., *A Memoir of Jane Austen*; Lascelles, M., *Jane Austen and her Art*; Mudrick, M., *Jane Austen: Irony as Defence and Discovery*: Trilling, L., 'Mansfield Park' in *The Opposing Self*; Leavis, Q. D. *A Critical Theory of Jane Austen's Writings* (*Scrutiny x, xiii*); Southam, B. C., (ed) *Jane Austen: The Critical Heritage*.

Authorized Version of the Bible

* *Bible in England.*

Autobiography

The word came into English at the very end of 18th C. In 19th and 20th C the writing of the story of one's own life has become a common literary activity. However, the practice already had an ancient history, and English autobiography may be divided into three overlapping historical segments: [1] the spiritual confession; [2] the memoir; [3] the autobiographical novel.

[1] The spiritual confession has as its basic type the Confessions of St Augustine of Hippo (345–430) who described his conversion to Christianity. Such records of the inner life existed in the English Middle Ages, *eg* the *Book of Margery Kempe* (15th C), but the great age for them was 17th C, when the Puritans, depending on the Word of God in the Bible and the inner light of their own consciences, made a practice of intensive self-examination. By far the best known of these records is Bunyan's* *Grace Abounding to the Chief of Sinners** (1666). It is characteristic of such works that they contain detailed accounts of the emotional life, but little factual description of events.

[2] The memoir, on the other hand, of French derivation, originates largely in 17th C and owes much to the practice of extensive letter-writing which then developed, *eg* the letters of Madame de Sévigné (1626–96). An unusual early example of this class is the recently discovered autobiography of the musician Thomas Whythorne (1528–96), published in 1964 and entitled *A Book of Songs and Sonetts*. An example from 18th-C England is the fragmentary *Memoirs* (pub 1796) by the historian Edward Gibbon*. But the objective memoir and the subjective confessions come together in the *Confessions* of the French-Swiss Jean-Jacques Rousseau*, and this is the most prevalent form of the outstanding English autobiographies of 19th C. The varieties of this form are extensive: they may be a record of emotional struggles and experiences, *eg The Confessions of an English Opium Eater**, by Thomas de Quincey*; *Sartor Resartus** by Thomas Carlyle*. They may be essentially a history of the growth of ideas, convictions, and the strengthening of vocation, in the life of the writer, *eg Autobiography* (1873) by John Stuart Mill*, *My Apprenticeship* (1926) by Beatrice Webb*; *Apologia pro Vita Sua* (1864) by Cardinal Newman.* In any case, an autobiographical element becomes prominent in works which are not strictly autobiographies from the early 19th C on; *eg* Wordsworth's* *Prelude, or Growth of a Poet's Mind** (first version 1805); the periodical essays of Charles Lamb* in *Essays of Elia** (1820–3) and Coleridge's* mixture of autobiography with philosophy and literary criticism in *Biographia Literaria** (1817). It may be said that from 1800 on it becomes the instinct of writers of many kinds to use autobiographical material, or to adopt from time to time an autobiographical standpoint.

[3] Thus we come to the autobiographical novel; this begins with the novels of Charlotte Brontë* (*Jane Eyre**, 1847, and *Villette**, 1853), and Charles Dickens's *David Copperfield** (1849–50). This method of writing a novel really came into its own, however, with Samuel Butler's* *Way of all Flesh** (1903), which led to many successors in 20th C, notably James Joyce's *Portrait of the Artist as a Young Man** (1916), and D. H. Lawrence's* *Sons and Lovers** (1913).

Avalon /'avəlon/

In Celtic myth, a place in a mythical land to which King Arthur* was taken after his last battle. It was somewhere in the west across the ocean, and has similarity with other mysterious western lands, such as Plato's Atlantis*.

Avon

The river of Shakespeare's birthplace, Stratford-on-Avon, from which he is called the 'Swan of Avon' by Ben Jonson* in his poem *To the Memory of Shakespeare*. The word derives from Celtic *afon* = 'river'; three other rivers with the same name exist in England.

Awkward Age, The (1899)

A novel by Henry James*. Nanda Brookenham is a young girl brought up in a smart but corrupt section of London society; her mother and her mother's circle are willing to carry on immoral intrigues so long as respectable appearances are scrupulously protected. Nanda is in love with Vanderbank, who, as she learns later, is her mother's lover, and she has affection for Mitchett, a young man of less charm than Vanderbank, but with an attractive simplicity of heart. Unlike the other members of her mother's circle, she is free and candid in her feelings and open in her conduct; this alarms Vanderbank and inhibits him from declaring his love for her. Her elderly friend, Mr Longdon, an admirer of her dead grandmother, gives Nanda a dowry to attract Vanderbank, but this only increases the latter's fastidious reluctance to declare himself. Meanwhile, the Duchess, Mrs Brookenham's friend and rival, conspires to capture Mitchett for her own daughter, Aggie, whose appearance of immaculate innocence immediately breaks down when it has served its purpose of qualifying her for the marriage market. Vanderbank's mixture of scrupulousness and timidity remains a permanent barrier between himself and Nanda. Mr Longdon adopts her, and they remain together in their love of truthful feeling, isolated from the sophisticated but essentially trivial society which has hitherto constituted Nanda's environment.

The novel is an example of James's interest in the survival of integrity in a materialistic society blinded by its own carefully cultivated artificiality.

Ayre

* *Madrigal*

B

Baal /ˈbeiəl/

Baal = 'chief god', applied to the pagan gods of the tribes surrounding the Old Testament Jehovah-worshipping Hebrews; Baalim is plural. Bel, alternative form used in Babylon. 'The worship of Baal' is false worship.

Babes in the Wood

* *Children in the Wood.*

Babylon

A city which was the centre of one of the most important ancient civilizations. Its remains border the River Euphrates, about 70 miles south of Baghdad, capital of modern Iraq. In its last and most spectacular period under Nebuchadnezzar II* its empire extended over Judah, and Nebuchadnezzar carried the inhabitants to Babylon. The 'Babylonian Captivity'* lasted from c 603 till 536 BC, when the Jews were released by Cyrus, King of Persia, who had captured Babylon in 539 BC. The subjects of the conquest, exile, and return of the Hebrews are the material of some of the most dramatic and eloquent passages of the Old Testament, *eg* the fall of Judah – *2 Kings* 24, 25; the exile – *Daniel*; the return and the reconstruction of Jerusalem – *Nehemiah*.

The part played by Babylon in Jewish history later caused it to typify the powers opposed to true religious practice in the world. Hence *Revelation* 17, concerning 'Babylon the Great, Mother of Harlots and Abominations of the Earth'. In the Middle Ages* the disciples of St Francis stigmatized the Church as the Great Babylon on account of its materialism, and 17th-C English Puritans* described the Catholic Church as 'the Whore of Babylon'.

Babylonian Captivity

[1] The period of exile (603–536 BC) when the Jews were carried from Judah to Babylon* by King Nebuchadnezzar*. In the Bible, *Psalm* 137 is the famous lament for this exile.

[2] The term was also used to describe the period when the Popes were in exile in Avignon (1309–78), much to the disgust of the English, who resented the consequent domination of the Papacy by French interests. This and the subsequent Schism* (1378–1417) underlay the English reformist movement of Wycliffe* and his successors, the Lollards, anticipating the Reformation* of 16th C.

Bacchanalia /bakəˈneiljə/

Roman revelry in honour of the god Bacchus (Dionysus*). Bacchanals were devotees of Bacchus, and the word is also used for his rites and ceremonies. Bacchantes were priestesses of Bacchus.

Bacchus /ˈbakəs/

The Greek and Roman god of wine.

* *Dionysus*

Bacon, Francis (1561–1626)

Statesman, philosopher, and essayist: as a thinker, one of the most formative minds in European thought during the last 400 years; as a prose writer, an important influence on the development of English rational (as distinct from poetic and imaginative) expression; as a statesman, he reached the highest political and judicial office (the Lord Chancellorship) from which, however, he was dismissed for accepting bribes in 1621. The combination of greatness of thought with mediocrity of conduct provoked the poet Pope's* description of him, a century later, as 'the wisest, brightest, meanest of mankind'.

His strictly philosophical work comprised notably three books: *Advancement of Learning** (1605); an expansion of the Advancement, *De Augmentis Scientiarum* (1623); *Novum Organum** (1620). His *Instauratio Magna** (Great Renewal of the Sciences) was left unfinished. It included the *De Augmentis* and *Novum Organum* as its first two Parts, fragments of Parts III–V, and nothing of the projected Part VI, which was to have been a scientific synthesis of conclusions. Apart from the *Advancement*, Bacon wrote his philosophy in Latin under the belief that it would remain indefinitely the language of international learning. His concern was the whole field of knowledge; his importance for the development of thought was his ability to distinguish strictly scientific aims and methods, and to define illuminatingly the obstacles to them. Such obstacles he called 'Idols', and they include mistaken or ill-distinguished personal or popular prejudices, misuse of language, and wrongly based traditions of thought. In his positive recommendations he advocated inductive, experimental methods. He made a lucid analysis of the shortcomings, scientifically speaking, of the traditions of study at a time when English universities* still pursued medieval scholastic systems. He also prescribed new methods of study, and defined the scope of various sciences. In this way he cleared the field for later natural philosophers. Yet Bacon was not fully alive to the importance of the scientific advances of his own time.

The movement away from the poetic and imaginative towards the scientific and rational received, in English, a notable advance through the explicitness, directness, and terseness of Bacon's prose. Apart from the *Advancement of Learning*, his famous works in English are his *History of Henry VII* (1622); *New Atlantis** (1626), an uncompleted study of an imaginary culture dominated by natural philosophers: and, above all, the *Essays**. To the general reader the last are by far the best known of his writings. The first 'essays' in English, they did not resemble the extended, flexible, searching investigations of the originator of the form, Montaigne*, but owed more to the terse observations of the Latin writer Seneca*, and originally (1597) resembled a collection of aphorisms. They were expanded and increased in number until the final collection of 1625, but continued to exhibit an aphoristic style, which causes sentences from them to be quoted in the style of proverbs, *eg* 'Men fear death as children fear to go in the dark.'

* 3.2.3.

Bib: Anderson, F. H., *The Philosophy of Francis Bacon*; Willey, B., *The Seventeenth Century Background*; Knights, L. C., *Bacon and the seventeenth century dissociation of sensibility* in *Explorations*; Anderson, F. H., *The philosophy of Bacon.*

Bacon, Roger (1214?–94)

Franciscan* scholar, student at Paris and Oxford, and author of treatises on sciences such as grammar, logic, physics, and mathematics. He was an acute and independent thinker, and one of the leading philosophers of the Middle Ages*. His originality in devoting himself to experimental methods caused him to be known in Paris as Doctor mirabilis = Wonderful Doctor, but his opposition to the theoretical, inadequately based scholarship of his time resulted in his imprisonment for heresy. In popular tradition he came to be regarded as a magician, and the inventor of a brazen head that could speak. It is in such a role that he is represented in *Friar Bacon and Friar Bungay** (1594), a romantic comedy by Robert Greene*.

Baconian Theory, The

The first and best known of the theories that someone else was the real author of Shakespeare's plays, in this case, Francis Bacon*. The theory has survived partly because little is known about Shakespeare's life, and partly because Shakespeare is commonly supposed to have had comparatively little education, though about that also almost nothing is known. Neither the Baconian theory nor any of the rival theories which allege that Shakespeare did not write the plays ascribed to him has any respectable scholarly support today. Scholarship is, in fact, not needed to dispose of the Baconian theory; nobody doubts that Bacon wrote his own essays, and it is impossible to believe that the same personality was responsible for these and for works so different as the plays of Shakespeare. Nor is there anything unusual about our lack of information about Shakespeare's life: the same is true of many other famous Elizabethans.

Badman, The Life and Death of Mr (1680)

A moral allegory* by John Bunyan*, author of *The Pilgrim's Progress*, and, apart from the more famous work, the only one of Bunyan's fictions to remain widely known. It is the biography of a wicked man told by Mr Wiseman, and contains vivid and dramatic detail. Its realism of detail and its psychology make it one of the forerunners of the novel.

Baedeker, Karl (1801–59) /ˈbeidikə/

The author of famous guide-books, which were carried on by his son and eventually covered most of the civilized world. Their frequent mention in English 19th- and 20th-C fiction shows how indispensable they were to English middle- and upper-class tourists of the last hundred years, especially in visits to countries in which monuments and works of art are plentiful, such as Italy. He wrote in German, but English editions were produced after his death, from 1861 onwards.

Bagehot, Walter (1826–77) /ˈbadʒət/

A writer on political and economic affairs; best known for his book *The English Constitution* (1867) which, despite historical change, is still a classic study of the spirit of English politics, and notably of the function of monarchy in providing the imaginative appeal of the state, and ensuring the dignity of government without hindering desirable conflict of opinion.

Bagehot was also the author of a number of critical essays, the best known of which is *Wordsworth, Tennyson, and Browning or Pure, Ornate, and Grotesque Art in English Poetry* (1864). It is republished in *English Critical Essays* ed. by E. D. Jones (World's Classics).

Bib: Stephen, Leslie in *Studies of a Biographer*; Buchan, A., *The Spare Chancellor.*

Bailey, The Old

The building that houses the Central Criminal Court in London. A 'bailey' is an outer fortified wall, such as once existed on the site as a medieval defence for the City of London.

Balaam and his Ass /ˈbeilam/

In the Bible, *Numbers* 22-4. Balaam was sent by Balak, the King of Moab, to curse the Israelites who, with the blessing of God, were invading his territory. His ass, as he rides towards the Israelites, is stopped by an angel, invisible to Balaam. When Balaam beats the ass to make it advance, the animal is suddenly given the power of speech, whereupon Balaam sees the angel and knows that he is not to proceed. In the end, instead of cursing the Israelites, he prophesies their happiness. The story is important because it is an early example of a heathen acknowledging the God of the Jews. Proverbially, Balaam's ass is a fable of the humble and ignorant being endowed with power to warn the wise.

Ball, John
A priest and a leader of the popular rising known as the Peasants' Revolt* (1381). He was a disciple of the reformer, John Wycliffe*, who, through his critical attitude to the wealth and worldliness of the Church, was himself partly sympathetic to the rebels. To Ball has been attributed the slogan of the rebellion:

> When Adam delved and Eve span,
> Who was then the gentleman?

Though formidable, the Revolt failed, and Ball was executed in the same year.

Ballad
The word derives from Old French, *baller* = to dance; compare modern English, ball = a dance to which guests are invited. The derivation suggests the probable origin of the traditional form, showing that it was, at least in the Middle Ages*, a dance song. Thus, many old ballads have repeated lines, *ie* 'refrains', as the second and fourth of the four-line stanzas, these refrains often having no relation to the rest of the matter, as though they were intended for singing by a dancing group while a single voice sang the alternate lines. Other features of the ballad in its traditional form are these: the matter is often a highly dramatic narrative; the narrative is a bold outline, with graphic detail but only the most essential connecting links; frequently, stock epithets are used – 'golden', 'silver', 'milk-white', etc. – but epithets of other kinds are used sparingly; there is often a conventional patterning of numbers, with a preference for 3, 7, 9. The stories are often versions of similar themes used in ballads throughout Europe, showing that the ballad often drew from a widespread store of folklore.

This traditional popular ballad was an oral, not a written form; ballads began to be published (apart from exceptions) in 18th C in such collections as Allan Ramsay's *Evergreen* and *Percy's Reliques**. Such publications had two important effects: the ballads became to some extent civilized and sophisticated in their published form; and they awakened the interest of the sophisticated poet, both in the ballad form itself, and in the poetic virtues of the simple, uneducated people. Thus Wordsworth and Coleridge's collection of their own verse, *Lyrical Ballads** (1798), for the most part contains poems not in ballad form but concerned with people in common life; on the other hand, it also includes one of the masterpieces of the form, Coleridge's* *Ancient Mariner**, using the simplicity and vividness of the traditional style for subtle and sophisticated purposes. Walter Scott*, notable for his keen and energetic interest in the past, made his best poetry out of adaptations and imitations of traditional Scots ballads, *eg Proud Maisie*, and published a collection of Scots ballads, *The Minstrelsy of the Scottish Border*.

The traditional ballads often showed popular feelings about actual events, but were rarely immediate comments on events. Another class, the broadside* ballad, printed for a popular audience (see Shakespeare's *Winter's Tale** IV.iii), was common in Elizabethan days, but unlike the traditional folk ballad produced few masterpieces. (This kind of topical ballad has been revived in England today.) Among famous English and Scottish folk ballads are: *Chevy Chase**; *Edward, Edward*; *Sir Patrick Spens**; *A Lyke-Wake Dirge*.
*4.1.3.

Bib: Speirs, J., *The Scots Literary Tradition*; Hodgart, M. J. C., *The Ballad*.

Ballade /ba'la:d/
A sophisticated lyrical form, having nothing in common with 'ballad'. It was introduced into English in 14th C by Geoffrey Chaucer*. Its form varied, but it commonly had these features: [1] it had three stanzas, or was divided into sets of three; [2] the stanzas varied in length, but usually had 7 or 8 lines; [3] each stanza had an identical concluding line or refrain; [4] the whole poem was restricted to three or four rhymes, repeated in each stanza in the same order; [5] the poem ended with a short stanza called an envoi – but this was often omitted in English ballades. Chaucer and Lydgate* (15th C) used the ballade; after the Middle Ages* it was not used till in later 19th C it was revived by poets like Swinburne* and Rossetti* as part of the cult of the Middle Ages.
* 6.1.2.

Ballet
* *Madrigal*.

Balthazar
By tradition one of the three magi* or wise men who brought gifts to the Christ child at Bethlehem (*Matthew* 2). The name means 'Possessor of treasure' and he was held to be King of Chaldea.

Banbury
A market town in Oxfordshire famous early in 17th C for its Puritans*; hence satirical allusions to Banbury men by Jacobean* dramatists, the Puritans being foes to the theatre. 'Banbury cakes' were famous then and are still. Banbury Cross was a large stone crucifix such as existed in the centres of many English country towns; it is the subject of a well-known nursery rhyme – 'Ride a cock-horse to Banbury Cross'. The Puritans destroyed the cross in 1610.

Bank of England, The
The Bank of England was founded in 1694 on the basis of suggestions of William Patterson. It first existed as a corporation with a special charter to raise loans for the government of William III* to pay for the wars against France. By degrees, in 18th and 19th C it became the keeper of the government's funds, as well as of the funds of other banks. Thus it grew into the first 'Central Bank' in the world. Although nominally a private corporation until 1946, when it was nationalized, it had for long worked so closely with the Treasury (*ie* British finance ministry) that its independence of the government had been only nominal.

Bankside
The south bank of the Thames in London. It was famous in Shakespeare's day for its theatres. The City of London refused to allow public theatres within its bounds; hence the famous theatres such as the Globe*, the Rose* and the Fortune all had to be built in Southwark* on Bankside.
* *Theatres.*

Bannockburn (1314)
A battle in central Scotland, in which a Scottish army under Robert the Bruce* defeated a large invading English force under Edward II*. The battle decided Scottish independence until the two countries became united under a Scottish king (James VI and I, 1603–25). As a heroic episode, it has had a force of inspiration for the Scots similar to the victory of Agincourt* for the English.

Banshee
In Celtic myth, a spirit, said to foretell deaths by lamenting in the neighbourhood of a dwelling. Usually, the household was aristocratic, and great families had their special banshees. The banshee is particularly associated with Ireland, and the word derives from the Celtic, *bean sidhe.*

Baptism
The ritual by which a child is admitted to the Christian Church by a symbolic purification, either by sprinkling with water or by total immersion.

Baptists
An important sect of Nonconformist Protestants; originally one of the three principal branches of English Puritanism*, the other two being the Independents (Congregationalists*), and the Presbyterians* (Calvinists). Their especial doctrine is to maintain that the rite of baptism* must be administered to adults, and not to infants. They began as an offshoot of the Independents in the first decade of 17th C, and made rapid progress between 1640 and 1660 – the period of the Civil War* and the Interregnum*, when the Puritans usurped the position of the Church of England*. One of the foremost exponents of the Baptist Church in the second half of 17th C was John Bunyan* (1628–88). In New England the Baptists opened their first congregation in 1639, and they flourished there to the extent that they are now the largest Protestant community in the U.S.A.

Barabbas /bəˈrabəs/
In the Bible, the robber whom the Roman governor, Pilate* released at the demand of the Jews, instead of Jesus, whom Pilot offered as an alternative. (See *Matthew* 27.)

Barbara Allan
Heroine of two famous Scottish ballads*; her refusal of her lover caused his death from grief.

Barbary Corsairs
Barbary refers to the north-west coast of Africa, from Berber, the principal inhabitants. After the expulsion of the Moors from Granada in Spain, 1492, Moorish pirates (corsairs) revenged themselves by attacking the merchant shipping of Christian nations, first only in the Mediterranean, but from 17th C more distantly. The piracy was assisted by Christian nations allying with the corsairs against one another, and by intermittent reinforcement from Christian renegades. The main purpose of the piracy was the slave trade; it was not finally suppressed until the French conquest of Algiers in 1830.

Barbour, John (1316?–95) /ˈbaːbə/
Scottish poet; author of a long narrative in 8-syllable couplets about the Scottish War of Independence – *The Bruce* (about 1375). It tells the story of the defeat of the English attempt to conquer Scotland (1296–1328) and extols the principal hero of the War – Robert the Bruce*, who ended his career as king of Scotland. Barbour wrote other poems, but it is for this that he is sometimes called the 'father of Scottish poetry'.
* *Scottish Literature.*
Bib: Neilson, G., *Barbour; Poet and Translator.*

Bard
A privileged caste of poets among the ancient Celtic peoples. After the Roman conquest of Britain in 1st C AD, the strongholds of the bards in Britain became Wales and Ireland. The term became known to later English writers from references by Latin ones, *eg* Lucan* (1st C AD), and in 17th and 18th C poets such as Shakespeare, Milton and Pope use the word for any kind of serious poet. In the romantic period the cultivation of druidism, with which the ancient bards had been involved, led to 'bard' being used for a mysteriously or sacredly inspired poet. Merlin*, in the Arthurian* cycle of legends of Celtic origin, was a type of bard. Gray's* ode, *The Bard* (1757), is an example of an early romantic conception of such a poet.
* *Druids; Eisteddfod.*

Barleycorn, John
Malt liquor personified; a barleycorn = a grain of barley, from which malt, the basis of ale*, etc., is made.

Barnaby Rudge (1841)
A novel by Charles Dickens*, published as part of *Master Humphrey's Clock*. The only other novel that he published in this proposed series was *The Old Curiosity Shop**; Dickens then abandoned it.

It is set in 18th C, and its central episodes are descriptions of the fierce anti-Catholic disorders called 'the Gordon Riots'*, which terrorized London for several days in 1780. These scenes, and the characters directly concerned in the riots (such as the half-wit Barnaby Rudge, the locksmith Gabriel Varden, and his apprentice Simon Tappertit), constitute the part of the book which is most memorable and most representative of Dickens's genius. The main story is a romantic one about the love affair of Emma Haredale, whose father has been mysteriously murdered, and

Edward Chester, the son of Sir John Chester, a suave villain who helps to instigate the Riots. Sir John and Emma's uncle, Geoffrey Haredale, a Catholic, are enemies, but they unite in opposition to the marriage of Edward and Emma. During the riots, Geoffrey Haredale's house is burnt down, but Edward saves the lives of both Emma and her uncle, and thus wins his approval of the match. The murderer of Emma's father turns out to be the father of Barnaby.

Barnaby Rudge is one of Dickens's two historical novels, the other being *A Tale of Two Cities**. Its combination of a romantic, upper-class love affair and vigorously delineated lower-class characters and crowd scenes recalls the work of the historical novelist, Walter Scott*.

Barnard's Inn

* *Inns of Court*

Barnes, William (1801–86)

A west of England clergyman and poet. He wrote in the Dorset dialect, *Poems of Rural Life*, and is one of the few successful dialect poets in England (as distinct from the rest of Britain) after the Middle Ages*.

Bib: Baxter, L., *The Life of Barnes by his Daughter.*

Barnum, Phineas Taylor (1810–91)

A famous American showman who first made a success through the exhibition of 'George Washington's nurse', alleged to be 161 years old; he later made the American Museum, a collection of curiosities, one of the most popular shows in America. He started a circus in 1871, which, as Barnum and Bailey's in 1881, became the type and pattern of all later circuses in England and America, since he toured in both countries. The name of his famous elephant 'Jumbo' is synonymous with 'elephant' to this day.

Barrie, Sir James Matthew (1860–1937)

A Scots dramatist, nowadays chiefly famous for his creation of *Peter Pan** (1904). Early in this century he was extremely popular for the theatrical skill and the humour and sentimentality of his plays, which sometimes carried penetrating satire, *eg The Admirable Crichton* (1902).

Bib: Darton, F. J. Harvey, *Barrie*; Hammerton, J. A., *Barrie, the story of a genius*; Mackail, Denis, *The Story of J.M.B.*

Barsetshire

An imaginary English county invented by Anthony Trollope* for a series of novels some of which centre on an imaginary town in it, the cathedral city of Barchester. It is a characteristic southern English setting. The novels are the best known of his works. Titles: *The Warden**, *Barchester Towers*, *Doctor Thorne*, *Framley Parsonage*, *The Small House at Allington*, *The Last Chronicle of Barset*.

Bartholomew Fair (1614)

A vigorous prose comedy of London Life by Ben Jonson*. The scene is that of a famous fair held annually in Smithfield, London, from 12th C till 1855. The cast includes traders, showmen, dupes, criminals, a gambler, and a hypocritical Puritan* – the best-known character, called Zeal-of-the-land Busy. It has very lively surface entertainment, and some of Jonson's characteristic force of satire by which the vicious pursue their vices with eloquence but such extravagance that they overreach themselves, and not only produce their own doom but bring ridicule on their own heads by self-caricature.

* *Comedy of Humours*

Bas bleu

* *Bluestocking.*

Basilisk

Also called a cockatrice. In Greek myth, a reptile whose breath and gaze were deadly. Hence a 'basilisk stare', meaning a very fierce one.

Bastard

A bastard is born out of wedlock, *ie* has no legal parents; in law, he is *filius nullius* = the son of no one. When land, and with it, status, derived from the legal father, the bastard could inherit nothing by his own right. In early medieval times an exception was sometimes made for bastards in ruling families; thus William I* of England (1066–87) took the appellation William the Bastard. But in general a bastard was by law something of a social outcast. Hence Edmund* in Shakespeare's *King Lear** (I.ii) 'Why brand they us / With base? with baseness? bastardy? base, base?' However, a bastard was not debarred from making for himself a position in society, acquiring land, marrying legally, and bequeathing his property – all depended on his natural worth, abilities and energies: 'Thou, nature, art my goddess;' says Edmund (I.ii.1) 'to thy law / My services are bound.' In Edmund, as in the bastard Philip of Shakespeare's *King John**, there is the idea that the bastard is compensated for his lack of rights by unusual natural energies; the same is implicit in Fielding's *Tom Jones**. Bastards could inherit by the testament, *ie* legally admitted last wishes of the father. When, by 18th C, property owning became more varied and flexible, the bastard's social dilemma was relieved.

Bath

A city in the west of England with hot springs with certain mineral properties which afford relief to those with rheumatic diseases. In 18th C, largely owing to the energies of Richard ('Beau'*) Nash, the city became a brilliant social centre; nearly everyone of eminence in politics, literature or the arts at some time visited or lived there. Hence its prominence in the literature of the time. Nash, who virtually ruled Bath, was a civilizing influence on fashionable society: by his discipline he improved the manners of the rich but ill-bred country gentry, and by refusing to allow the wearing of swords in

Bath : Royal Crescent

public assemblies he helped to reduce the practice of duelling.

Bathos * *Figures of Speech.*

Baudelaire, Charles (1821–67)

French poet. His work is mainly contained in a single book – *Les Fleurs du Mal* (1857). This book marks a turning point in French 19th-C poetry, between the age of the Romantics such as Lamartine and that of the Symbolists* such as Mallarmé. Baudelaire seems to cultivate the morbid side of Romantic subjectivism, but he is in fact concerned with the human condition at a religious level. His poetry has the discipline and precision of the great French classical poets; at the same time his sense of the suggestiveness of objects and sensations, relating unlike experiences so as to transfigure them into experience of greater depth than seems to belong to them, was fertile for the cultivation of symbolism in later French and English poets.

Among the English poets, his first admirer was Swinburne*, who reviewed *Les Fleurs du Mal* in the *Spectator* in 1862. Swinburne responded to the sensualism of Baudelaire – 'the weariness of pain and the bitterness of pleasure – the perverse happiness and wayward sorrows of exceptional people.' This was the kind of Baudelairean influence which Swinburne passed on to the 'decadent' poets of the 1890s, such as Ernest Dowson, and it was for this that Robert Buchanan stigmatized Swinburne in his notorious essay 'The Fleshly School of Poetry' (1871): 'All that is worst in Mr Swinburne belongs to Baudelaire'. T. S. Eliot's judgement – see *Baudelaire* (1930) in *Selected Essays* – stands in contrast to Swinburne's. He praises Baudelaire for his 'sense of his age', his use of 'imagery of the sordid life of the great metropolis', and his 'elevation of such imagery to the first intensity'. For Eliot, Baudelaire is above all a religious poet, for whom 'the recognition of Sin is a New Life . . . It is apparently Sin in the Swinburnian sense, but really Sin in the permanent Christian sense, that occupies the mind of Baudelaire.' Baudelaire was in fact a 'modern' writer in that he was the first to carry exploration of the human condition with conscious risk of despair as far as his spiritual consciousness could take him, thus looking forward to the work of such a writer as Samuel Beckett*.

Beaconsfield, Lord

* *Disraeli.*

Bear and Ragged Staff

A crest borne by the Earls of Warwick, one of whom was particularly famous for the decisive part he played in the Wars of the Roses* in 15th C. The crest shows a bear climbing a tree-trunk. Another, but legendary, Guy of Warwick was the subject of a 14th-C poem.

Bear-baiting, Bull-baiting

In the Middle Ages and 16th C a popular pastime, in which a bull or bear was tied to a stake and then attacked by bulldogs or mastiffs. Bull-baiting continued longer, and these 'sports' were only made illegal in 1835. In Elizabethan times, bear-baiting was an alternative amusement to drama; 'bear gardens' (notably the Paris Garden) were situated in the same region as the theatres – Southwark, on the south bank of the Thames. The theatres themselves were used for the purpose. Earlier in the century, Erasmus* speaks of herds of bears being kept in the country to supply the bear-gardens. The Puritans* disliked the meetings as scenes likely to lead to disorder, but humane disapproval does not come before the middle of 17th C, when the famous diarist, Evelyn*, speaks of being 'heartily weary of the rude and dirty pastime'; Steele* attacked the cruelty of the sport in *The Tatler**. In country places, badgers were often used as cheap alternatives to bulls and bears – see the poem by John Clare* (1793–1864): *Badger.*

Beardsley, Aubrey (1872–98)

An artist famous in the 1890s for his black and white illustrations to writers such as Oscar Wilde* and Ernest Dowson. He contributed to the periodicals, *The Yellow Book** (the first four covers of which he designed) and *The Savoy* (including his tale, *Under the Hill*), which were regarded as organs of the aesthetic movement. The flowing lines and sumptuous compositions of his illustrations expressed what was considered most bold and most daring in the movement.

* *Aestheticism.*

Beatrice and Benedick

Two characters in Shakespeare's comedy *Much Ado About Nothing**. They hate each other and engage in witty exchanges of repartee. The hatred is only apparent, however, and they are brought together in love by a trick. Quarrelsome lovers are often compared to them.

Beau (Brummel, Nash)

'Beau' is a French word which came into use in 18th C for an elegant young man, especially as suitor to a lady. The word also prefixed the names of certain famous men of fashion and elegance, notably Beau Nash (1674–1762) the famous Master of Ceremonies at Bath*; and Beau Brummel (1778–1840), friend of George IV in his Regency* days (1810–20), and leader of London fashion.

Beaumont, Francis (1584–1616) /ˈbəumənt/

Dramatic poet and collaborator with John Fletcher*. They wrote comedies (*eg The Knight of the Burning Pestle**, perhaps by Beaumont alone); tragedies (*eg The Maid's Tragedy**); romantic dramas (*eg A King and No King* and *Philaster**). Fletcher also collaborated with other writers – Shakespeare, Massinger – and wrote plays on his own. The general superiority of those he wrote with Beaumont has suggested to modern critics that Beaumont may have been the more talented partner. Their plays were immensely popular in 17th C, but they are now regarded as the beginning of the decadence of the great period of English drama. The plays have fluent charm and are theatrically dexterous, but they lack the force of profound relevance to lived experience that is characteristic of the great work of the time.

Bib: Macaulay, G. C., *Beaumont: a critical study*; Appleton, W. W., *Beaumont and Fletcher: a critical study*.

Beauty and the Beast

A fairy story, best known in the French version of Madame de Villeneuve (1744). The theme is that of a young girl who learns to love a monster who holds her in his power; her freely given love transforms him into a young prince.

Becket, St Thomas à (1118?–70)

A priest who served Henry II* (1154–89) in various offices culminating in the highest – that of Lord Chancellor. The period was one of constant disputes between the Church and the Crown over spheres of power, especially in the courts of justice. Becket's efficiency and devotion in offices that did not conflict with the Church led Henry to suppose that his services would also heal disputes in which the Church and State were directly concerned. Accordingly, he secured that Becket became Archbishop of Canterbury (1162). Becket, however, now that he was head of the Church in England, resisted the King so vehemently that Henry first drove him into exile, and later, on Becket's return, expressed his rage in terms that were interpreted by his followers as instructions for the Archbishop's assassination. Becket was killed in Canterbury Cathedral (1170). The King did penance, however, so that the event was a great victory for the Church. Becket was canonized in 1173, and his shrine in the cathedral became one of the great centres of European pilgrimage.

Becket's martyrdom has been the subject of several dramas, by far the most noteworthy of which is T. S. Eliot's* *Murder in the Cathedral* (1935).

Beckett, Samuel (b 1906)

Dramatist and novelist. Born in Dublin of Jewish parents, he was educated at Trinity College there. He became a lecturer in English at the Ecole Normale Supérieure in Paris (1928–30) and was then a lecturer in French at Trinity College. Since 1932 he has lived chiefly in France, and has written in both French and English. In Paris he became the friend and associate of the expatriate Irish novelist, James Joyce* (1882–1941), whose 'stream of consciousness' subjective method of narrative has strongly influenced Beckett's own novels; another important influence upon him has been the French novelist Marcel Proust (1871–1922).

Poems: *Whoroscope* (1930); *Echo's Bones* (1935).

Novels and stories: *More Pricks than Kicks* (1934); *Murphy* (1938); *Watt* (1944); *Molloy* (French-1951, English-1956); *Malone Meurt* (1952, trans. *Malone Dies* 1956); *L'Innommable* (1953, English 1960); *Comment C'est* (1961, English 1964); *Imagination Dead Imagine* (1966, from French); *Nouvelles et Textes Pour Rien* (1955); *Le Depeupleur* (1971, trans. 'The Lost Ones', 1972); *First Love* (1973); *Mercier et Camier* (1974).

Plays: *En Attendant Godot* (1952, trans. *Waiting for Godot* 1954); *Fin de Partie* (1957, trans. *End Game*); *Krapp's Last Tape* (1959); *La Dernière Bande* (1961); *Play* (1963). Plays for radio: *All that*

Fall (1957); *Embers* (1959); *Cascando* (1964); *Breath and Other Short Plays* (1972); *Not I* (1973).

Beckett is the most singular and original writer to appear in English, or possibly in French, since 1945. Like Joyce an Irish expatriate, he seems to belong to Ireland and to Europe; his characters are commonly Irish, and his cultural background the desolation of European culture. In both narrative and drama, (it is in the second that his achievement is perhaps the more remarkable) his method has been to create art out of increasingly simplified material, reducing his images of humanity to the sparest elements. In so far as he is related to the English literary tradition, it is to the generation between the wars of 1914–18 and 1939–45 when, most notably in the work of James Joyce, communication with an audience was often secondary to experiments in the medium of language. His novels have accordingly had no influence on English fiction. His plays, on the other hand, especially *Waiting for Godot* and the plays for radio, have shown new possibilities in the handling of dialogue, by which speech is used less for communication than for the expression of minds that feel themselves in isolation, or on the point of sinking into it. Such use of dialogue perhaps had its beginnings in the late 19th-C dramatists, the Russian Chekhov* and the Belgian Maeterlinck, and has superficial parallels with the work of the contemporary English dramatist, Harold Pinter*. Since speech from isolation tends towards silence, however, Beckett's more recent *Imagination Dead Imagine* suggests a drawing together of drama and narrative in a kind of drama without dialogue, peculiarly effective in radio.

* 5.3.3.

Bib: Kenner, H., *Samuel Beckett, a Critical Study*; Jacobsen, J., and Mueller, W. R., *The Testament of Beckett*; Esslin, M. in *Theatre of the Absurd*.

Beddoes, Thomas Lovell (1803–49)

Poet. He was nephew of the novelist Maria Edgeworth*, and son of a physician, Thomas Beddoes, who was famous for his radical politics and for his public-spirited dissemination of medical education through his writings. The poet was also a doctor and shared his father's political convictions; no doubt these convictions helped to make the work of Shelley* especially congenial to him. He spent most of his adult life in Germany and Switzerland, repeatedly in trouble for his revolutionary ideas. Like Shelley and others among the Romantics, he was deeply interested in the Jacobean* dramatists, and sought to revive drama in their spirit. He knew, however, that mere imitation of the Jacobeans was inadequate. He wrote, 'I am convinced the man who is to awaken the drama must be a bold, trampling fellow – no creeper into wormholes – no reviser even, however good. These reanimations are vampire cold.' (Letter to Kelsall Beddoes.) He later suppressed his first work, written while he was at Oxford, *The Improvisatore* (1821); it was followed by *The Bride's Tragedy* (1822) which shows his Jacobean inspiration. He then embarked on *Death's Jest Book or The Fool's Tragedy*, which he continued to revise all his life and was published posthumously in 1850. Despite occasional grandeur, these plays have been adjudged failures due to his inability to master dramatic structure. His reputation rests chiefly on his lyric verse in the tradition of Shelley, such as *Dream Pedlary*. Beddoes died by suicide.

Bib: Donner, H. W., *Beddoes: the Making of a Poet*.

Bede, The Venerable (673–735) /bi:d/

Scholar, and author of the first important English history, which he wrote in Latin: *Historia Ecclesiastica Gentis Anglorum* = Ecclesiastical History of the English Race, completed 731. For this he has been called 'the Father of English history'. The work is considered a masterpiece. He was also author of theological and scientific works. Bede was a native of the Angle kingdom of Northumbria, and spent his life in the monasteries of Wearmouth and Jarrow.

Bedivere, Sir /ˈbedivɪə/

In Malory's *Morte d'Arthur** (15th C) and Tennyson's poem of the same name (1842), the knight who with King Arthur survives the last battle. By Arthur's orders, he hurls the king's sword into the lake and bids him farewell as he is borne away to Avalon*.

Bedlam /ˈbedləm/

A famous lunatic asylum. Originally it was a priory, founded 1247, for members of the religious order of the Star of Bethlehem. Lunatics were admitted to it in 14th C, and in 1547, after the dissolution of the monasteries, it was handed over to the City of London as a hospital for lunatics. The name became shortened to Bedlam, and a Bedlamite, Tom o'Bedlam, Bess o'Bedlam, became synonyms for lunatics; Bedlam, itself, for lunatic asylum. In modern English, 'bedlam' is a scene of uproar and confusion.

Beefeater

Popular name for the Yeomen* of the Guard instituted in 1485 by Henry VII as wardens of the Tower of London*. The name is thought to originate in a comment made on them by the Grand Duke of Tuscany when he visited England in 1669: 'They are great eaters of beef, of which a very large ration is given them daily at the court, and they might be called "Beefeaters".'

Beelzebub /biˈelzibʌb/

Baal-zebub, 'Lord of the Flies'. In the Old Testament (*2 Kings* 1:2) he is a heathen god; in the New Testament, *eg Matthew* 12:24 'prince of the devils'. Hence in Milton's *Paradise Lost** (Bk. I) he is second only to Satan.

* *Baal*.

Beer

* *Ale and Beer*.

Beerbohm, Max (1872–1956)

Essayist, cartoonist, writer of fiction. When he be-

gan his career he belonged to the so-called 'decadent' generation of the aesthetic school in the 1890s; this included Yeats* in his Celtic Twilight* phase, Oscar Wilde*, Aubrey Beardsley*, and the poets Lionel Johnson and Ernest Dowson. He showed his affiliation to this school by the playful fastidiousness of his wit, especially in his cartoons and in his parodies. *A Christmas Garland* (1912) contains parodies of contemporary writers including Wells*, Bennett*, and Conrad*. But it is in his cartoons that his satirical wit is displayed with most pungency and originality, *eg Caricature of Twenty-five Gentlemen* (1896), *The Poet's Corner* (1904), *Rossetti and his Circle* (1922). As a writer he was above all an essayist; he entitled his first slim volume with humorous impertinence *The Works of Max Beerbaum* (1896), to which he added *More* (1899), *Yet Again* (1909), *And Even Now* (1920). He also wrote stories (*Seven Men* 1919), and he is probably now most read for his burlesque romance *Zuleika Dobson* (1911), about the visit of a dazzling beauty to the University of Oxford where she is responsible for a mass suicide among the students.

Beerbohm was educated at Charterhouse and Merton College Oxford. He contributed to the *Yellow Book**, and in 1898 succeeded Bernard Shaw* as dramatic critic on the *Saturday Review*. From 1910 he lived in Italy. His personal and literary fastidiousness caused him to be known as 'the Incomparable Max', and as such Ezra Pound* commemorates him as 'Brennbaum the Impeccable' in section 8 of *Hugh Selwin Mauberley*, though Beerbohm was not a Jew.

Bib: Riewald, J. G., *Beerbohm*: a critical analysis with a brief life and a bibliography.

Beeton, Mrs (1836–65)

The author of a book on cooking and household management, published serially in *The Englishwoman's Domestic Magazine* (1859–61). The book met the needs of the rapidly broadening Victorian middle class, which was strongly attached to the domestic virtues and satisfactions. It was soon regarded as an indispensable handbook.

Beggar's Opera, The (1728)

By the poet John Gay*, a play with numerous songs to the music of folk tunes. It is the earliest and by far the most famous of the 'ballad operas',

which were light entertainment as opposed to the serious Italian operas fashionable in England, and dealt with life in low society. In part it was a political attack on the Prime Minister, Robert Walpole. The daughter of a receiver of stolen goods falls in love with Macheath, a highwayman who is imprisoned in Newgate*, where the warder's daughter also falls for him and procures his escape. As a class of literature, *The Beggar's Opera* belongs to the mock heroic, another example from the time being Fielding's novel *Jonathan Wild the Great**, (1743), which is about a master criminal. The effect of such works was to make their appeal through the lawless zest for life of the characters, coupled with an ironic exposure of their baseness. *The Beggar's Opera* is a classic of the English stage, and its music has been reset by later composers – Arthur Bliss and, more recently, Benjamin Britten. It was adapted by the German dramatist, Bertolt Brecht in *Die Dreigroschenoper* ('The Threepenny Opera'). *The Beggar's Opera* had an overture by the German musician Pepusch, also arranged from folk tunes.

* *Opera in England.*

Beggars, Sturdy

An expression used in 16th C for the able-bodied poor who were unemployed and lived by begging. Unemployment was a serious social problem throughout 16th C for a succession of causes. Henry VII* (1485–1509) disbanded the private armies of the nobles; Henry VIII* (1509–47) dissolved the monasteries, and threw into unemployment the numerous servants and craftsmen who had served them; the nobles enclosed extensive tracts of arable land for sheep-farming, which required less labour, or simply to surround their great houses with ornamental parks; prices rose, and periods of inflation sometimes made it impossible for poor men to support themselves without begging. The beggars were regarded as a serious social threat, since they often moved about in bands and took to robbery with violence. In the reign of Elizabeth I* (1558–1603), the government made serious and fairly successful attempts to deal with the problem: they instituted a succession of Poor Laws*, culminating in the Great Poor Law of 1601, in accordance with which the aged, sick and crippled were given financial relief by the parishes, but the 'sturdy beggars' were forcibly set to work. Not all the 'sturdy beggars' were from the poorer classes; in an age of enthusiastic financial speculation, richer men were sometimes suddenly ruined, and forced to take to the roads. It has been suggested that this social mixture may explain the third line of the old English nursery rhyme:

Hark, hark, the dogs do bark,
The beggars are coming to town,
Some in rags, some in jags, some in a velvet gown.

Behemoth /bi'hi:moθ/

Perhaps from ancient Egyptian (= hippopotamus), the word occurs in the Bible (*Job* 40:15), and is used in later literature to mean 'enormous monster'.

Behmnen, Jacob

* *Boehme.*

Bel and the Dragon

In the biblical apocrypha*, formerly part of the Book of Daniel. It concerns idolatrous worship in Babylon (Bel = Baal*) and its exposure by the prophet.

Belcher

An article of clothing to go round the neck (*ie* neckerchief) of distinctive design, named after a famous boxer, Jim Belcher (1781–1811), and fashionable in his time.

Belial /'bi:ljəl/

In ancient Hebrew means 'worthlessness', but given as a proper name in the Bible (*Deuteronomy* 13:13), it was used by 17th-C Puritans* to describe fashionable and dissipated people – 'sons of Belial'. Milton makes Belial a fallen angel:

and, when night
Darkens the streets, then wander forth the sons
Of Belial, flown with insolence and wine.
(*Paradise Lost**, Bk. I.)

Bell Savage Inn

A famous inn which formerly stood not far from St Paul's Cathedral in London, and was used in Elizabethan times for bull-baiting and for dramatic performances.

Bellerophon /bə'lerəfən/

In Greek myth, a hero of the city of Corinth. When he was guest of Proetus, king of Tiryns, his host's wife fell in love with him, but Bellerophon scorned her. In revenge, she told her husband that he had tried to seduce her, and Proetus sought ways to put him to death. He was unwilling to kill a man who was his guest, so he sent him to his father-in-law, Iobates, with secret instructions that Iobates should find a way of destroying him. Iobates sent Bellerophon on a number of impossibly dangerous tasks, the most famous of which was the slaying of the monster, Chimaera*. Bellerophon slew Chimaera with the aid of the winged horse, Pegasus*, given to him by the goddess Athene*. His repeated successes won Iobates' respect, and Bellerophon married his daughter. Bellerophon ended in tragedy and disgrace, however. His children, Laodamia and Isander, were slain by the god Ares and the goddess Artemis, and he himself was disgraced by attempting to fly up to Olympus* on Pegasus; he was cast down from the mountain of the gods by Zeus, their king, and ended his days a cripple and an outcast.

Belles Lettres

French for 'fine literature'; the term was borrowed by Jonathan Swift* in 1710 and was for long used to denote refined forms of imaginative literature. It has nowadays fallen into disrepute, and is commonly used to describe elegant but not really serious forms of writing.

Belloc, Hilaire (1870–1953) /'belok/

A versatile writer (novelist, poet, essayist, biographer, historian) now especially remembered for his association with G. K. Chesteron* in Roman Catholic propaganda. The most important phase of his career was before 1914, when he was one of a generation of popular, vivid, witty propagandists; Shaw*, Wells*, and Chesterton were his equals, and the first two (as agnostic socialists) his opponents. With Chesterton, he maintained the doctrine of Distributism – an alternative scheme to socialism for equalizing property ownership. Among his best works is his earliest: *The Path to Rome* (1902), a discursive account of a journey through France, Switzerland and Northern Italy. He is now chiefly read for his light verse, *eg Cautionary Tales*, *A Bad Child's Book of Beasts.*

Bib: Hamilton, R., *Belloc: an introduction to his spirit and work*; Speaight, R., *The Life of Belloc.*

Belphoebe

A character in Spenser's *Faerie Queene** (1596), and one of the symbolic representations of Queen Elizabeth* in the poem. As a model, Spenser also has in mind the Greek moon-goddess, Phoebe (also called Artemis*, and in Latin, Diana); thus Belphoebe is represented as chaste and a huntress.

Belshazzar (6th C BC) /bel'ʃazə/

In the Bible (*Daniel* 5) the son of Nebuchadnezzar* and King of Babylon. He gave a great feast where he and his nobles 'praised the gods of gold, and of silver . . .', when mysterious words suddenly appeared on the wall. Only the Hebrew prophet-in-exile Daniel could interpret that they foretold Belshazzar's overthrow, at the hands of Cyrus, King of Persia. The feast has been the subject of poems and dramas in English, including a poem by Byron*.

Belvoir Hunt /'bi:və/

A famous example of one of the fashionable fox-hunting associations which flourish especially in 'the Shires', *ie* the east midlands of England. It was founded in 18th C.

Ben, Big

The biggest bell in the clock tower of the Houses of Parliament; often used as the name of the tower itself. The name commemorates the official under whose authority the bell was cast – Sir Benjamin Hall, Commissioner of Works, 1855–8. The loudness and melodiousness of the chime are well known to all English people, and, from the position of the clock high above the Houses of Parliament so as to be a landmark, both the chime and the tower itself have become symbols of corporate national life.

Benedictines

The first and most important of European monastic orders, founded by St Benedict in 529 in Italy. St Augustine of Rome (d 601), first Archbishop of Canterbury and the founder of Catholic (as distinct from Celtic) Christianity among the Anglo-Saxons, was a Benedictine; so also were Lanfranc* and Anselm, the first two Archbishops under the Norman* kings. The fact that all three men were Italians shows not only how the Church transcended national frontiers in the early Middle Ages, but also the degree to which the Benedictine Order was instrumental in helping it to do so. Moreover the Benedictines were notable for learning and teaching, so that they were then the most important channel for the flow of intellectual culture from the more to the less civilized regions. For instance, the first great English scholar, the Venerable Bede* (673–735), was a Benedictine monk. The Benedictine monasteries were in fact by far the most important centres of learning in England until the universities of Oxford and Cambridge became important in 13th–14th C. At the dissolution of the monasteries under Henry VIII*, in 1536 and 1539, there were 300 Benedictine houses in England, including most of the principal monasteries of the country.

* *Monasteries.*

Bennett, Arnold (1867–1931)

A leading English novelist of the first 30 years of this century. His principal novels: *The Old Wives' Tale** (1908); the Clayhanger trilogy – *Clayhanger** (1910), *Hilda Lessways* (1911), and *These Twain* (1916) – all three reprinted as *The Clayhanger Family* (1925); *Riceyman Steps* (1923); *The Grand Babylon Hotel* (1902). His distinctive characteristics as a novelist are his regionalism and his naturalism*. His books mainly concern life in the industrial Five Towns* of the north-west Midlands (the Potteries), the particular characteristics of which differentiate his fiction considered as an image of English society. Secondly, he was strongly influenced by the naturalism of French fiction-writers such as Zola* and Maupassant. This led him to emphasize the influence of environment on character, and to build his artistic wholes by means of a pattern of mundane details. This importance that he attached to environment caused a reaction against his artistic methods not only on the part of subjective novelists like Virginia Woolf* (see her essay 'Modern Fiction' in *The Common Reader, First Series*, 1925) but on the part of D. H. Lawrence*, who found Bennett too rigid in his notions of form and too passive in the face of environmental influence. Nonetheless, Bennett lacked the ruthlessness of the French naturalists, and softened his determinism with a sentimentality that recalls Dickens.

* 4.5.2.

Bib: Allen, W., *Life*; Muir, E., in *Scrutinies*, ed. Rickword, E; Wain, J., *The Quality of Bennett* in *Preliminary Essays.*

Bentham, Jeremy (1748–1832) /bentəm/

An extremely influential thinker, founder of the school of thought called Utilitarianism*. The basis of his thought was: [1] that human motives are governed by the pursuit of pleasure and avoidance of pain; [2] that the guiding rule for society should be the greatest happiness of the greatest number; [3] that the test of value for human laws and institutions should be no other than that of usefulness. These views he expounded in *Fragment on Government* (1776) and *Introduction to Principles of Morals and Legislation* (1780). His principal associates were James Mill (1773–1836) and John Stuart Mill* (1806–73); collectively they were known as the Philosophical Radicals, and together they established a practical philosophy of reform of great consequence in 19th-C Britain. But their excessive rationalism frustrated sympathy and imagination in education and the relief of poverty – see Dickens's novel, *Hard Times** (1854). Bentham's thought derived from the sceptical 18th-C French 'philosophes' such as Helvétius and 18th-C English rationalists* such as David Hartley* and Joseph Priestley*. It was, in fact, the outstanding line of continuity between 18th-C and 19th-C thinking.

* 3.4.2.

Bib: Stephen, L., *The English Utilitarians*; Pringle-Patterson, A. S., *The Philosophical Radicals and other essays*; Atkinson, C. M., *Life.*

Bentley, Richard (1662–1742)

Distinguished as a classical scholar and noted for his despotic personality as Master of Trinity College, Cambridge. He is satirized by Jonathan Swift* in *The Battle of the Books* and by Alexander Pope in the *Dunciad** (Bk. IV, 201–75).

Beowulf /'beiəwulf/

The earliest known English epic, written in Anglo-Saxon* (Old English). The written version is 10th C, but the poem may go back to the 7th; Christian and heroic-pagan elements mingle. Though the myth was introduced by the Angles*, the events and characters are Scandinavian. Hrothgar, king of the Danes, had built a great hall, Heorot, but it is constantly ravaged by the monster Grendel. The Swedish prince Beowulf, nephew of the king of the Geats, slays the monster by wrestling with it and wrenching out its arm. Grendel's mother then seeks vengeance by carrying off one of the Danish nobles, but Beowulf enters the mere beneath which she lives and kills her too. Beowulf returns home and in due course becomes king of the Geats. When he has reigned fifty years, his kingdom is invaded by a fiery dragon which he manages to kill with the aid of a young nobleman, Wiglaf, when all the rest of his followers have fled. However, he receives his own death wound in the fight, and as he dies, he pronounces Wiglaf his successor. His body is burnt on a great funeral pyre, and the dragon's treasure is buried with his ashes; twelve of his followers ride round the funeral mound celebrating his greatness. This bare skeleton is amplified by many episodes and additional characters. Although the material of the narrative is Norse rather than Anglo-Saxon, its spirit resembles that of contemporary Anglo-Saxon poems rather than the Norse Sagas, and its epic form has caused scholars to attribute Virgilian* influence. Whatever its sources, the written form which we have received is probably the work of a Northumbrian monk.

Berkeley, George (1685–1753) /'ba:kli/

Irish philosopher in the tradition of Descartes* (1596–1650) of France, and Locke* (1632–1704), but the opponent of the latter. Locke had affirmed the independence of matter and mind; Berkeley held that the reality of anything depended on its being perceived by a conscious mind; thus mind (and spirit) had primacy over matter. Nature is the experience of consciousness, and the evidence of Universal Mind, or God. He considered that Locke's insistence on external matter and physical causes led to atheism; but his own lucid and precise prose is as much the vehicle of reason as Locke's. While Locke led towards scientific scepticism, Berkeley's faith, combined with reason, maintained the religious vision in an essentially rational century. His philosophy is expressed in *A New Theory of Vision*, 1709, and in *Principles of Human Knowledge*, 1710. His *Dialogues of Alciphron* (1732) are distinguished for their grace of style.

* 3.3.1.

Bib: Wild, J., *Berkeley: a study of his life and philosophy*; Luce, A. A., *The Life of Berkeley*; Warnock, G. J., *Berkeley* (Penguin).

Bess

One of the many short forms of the name of Elizabeth. Hence, 'Good Queen Bess' = Queen Elizabeth*, in the form of an endearment. It tends to be a tradition in English to use familiar forms of endearment for great and revered men and women in this way, *eg* 'Winnie' for Winston Churchill.

Bestiaries

Tales in which animals personify human qualities, as when the lion = courage, the fox = cunning, the wolf = greed, the owl = wisdom. Such tales were especially popular in the Middle Ages. The most popular character of all was Reynard the Fox.

* *Aesop; Fable; Reynard.*

Betjeman, John (b. 1906)

Poet and critic of architecture. His poetry is highly nostalgic but written in a style which has given it wide popularity: *Mount Zion* (1931); *Continual Dew* (1937); *Old Lights in New Chancels* (1940); *New Bats in Old Belfries* (1945); *A Few Late Chrysanthemums* (1954); *Summoned By Bells* (autobiography in verse, 1960). The verse is witty as well as nostalgic, and sometimes very poignant; some of it is pastiche and much of it is influenced by late Tennyson. As an architectural critic, Betjeman has done much to encourage a taste for Victorian architecture.

Bib: Brook, J., British Council Pamphlet, *Writers and their Work* 153.

Beulah, The Land of /'bju:lə/

In the Bible, *Isaiah* 62:4. A Hebrew word = 'married'. In Bunyan's *Pilgrim's Progress** it lies in sight of the Heavenly City and beyond the reach of Giant Despair. It has also been a common name for a nonconformist chapel. It signifies the state in which the soul is 'married' to God, in a state of perfect assurance.

Bevis of Hampton /'bi:vis/

A popular metrical romance of 13th-14th C. Bevis's father has been murdered by his mother's lover, Sir Murdour. Bevis is sold as a slave and has many adventures – with his horse Arundel and his sword Morglay – before the happy ending with Bevis married to Josiane. The story was circulated in the chapbooks* of 16th C and is retold in Drayton's* *Poly-Olbion.*

Bible in England

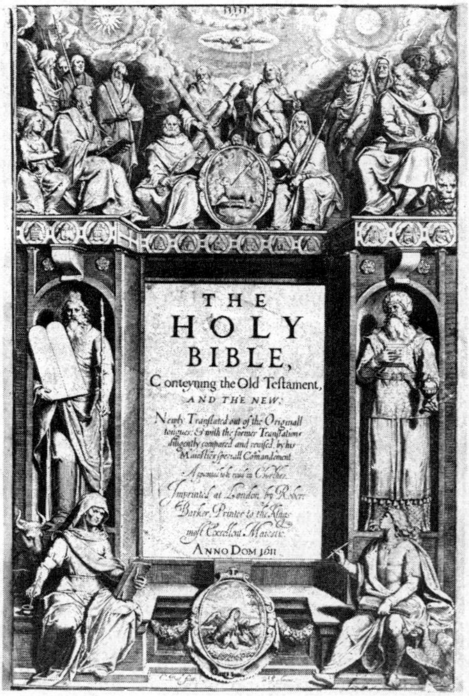

In the Middle Ages the only version of the Bible authorized by the Church was the Vulgate*, *ie* the translation into Latin by St Jerome, completed in 405. Partial translations were made into Old English before 11th C. Thereafter the objective of translating the Bible was associated with opposition to or suspicion of the Church, which seemed to reformers to keep the Bible out of English so that plain men without Latin should not have the means of seeking guidance for themselves, but should depend on Church authority. The Church indeed maintained that study of the Bible was in itself insufficient for such guidance, and that the commentaries of the Holy Fathers, and the decisions of the Church Councils were needed for amplification, definition, and explanation. The Reformers, however – from 16th C known as Protestants – considered that as the Bible was divinely inspired, no other source was needed by good men studying it conscientiously. (There were, however, intermediate positions, such as that of the Anglican Church.)

Thus, from 14th C, all the earlier translations were by reformers. The main translators were these: Wycliffe* (14th C); Tyndale*, and Coverdale (16th C). The last-named was the producer of the *Great Bible* (also called Cranmer's* Bible after the Archbishop of the time), but Henry VIII*, concerned for his intermediate position between Catholics and Protestants, ended by restricting its use. Under the Catholic Mary I* (1553–8) English reformers produced the *Geneva Bible* abroad, with annotations suited to Puritan Calvinist* opinion; and in 1568 the so-called *Bishops' Bible* was issued by the restored Anglicans to counteract Puritan influence. Finally, in 1611 the Authorized Version was produced with the approval of James I* (1603–25). For three centuries it was to be the only one in general use, and it is still the prevailing version. In 19th C it was revised (Revised Version) and very recently a new translation has been authorized and produced (New Testament 1961; Old Testament and Apocrypha 1970) under the direction of representatives of all the major Protestant Churches in England, Scotland, Wales and Ireland. A Catholic translation (the Douai Bible) was issued at about the same time as the Authorized Version.

In spite of various other translations, Catholic and Protestant, in 19th and 20th C, the Authorized Version is by far the most important for its literary and social influence. It was based on previous translations, especially that of Tyndale, so that the cast of its prose is characteristically more 16th than early 17th C in style. Nonetheless much of it is of supreme eloquence, *eg* the Book of *Job*, and the last 15 chapters of *Isaiah*. It was for many people in 17th and 18th C the only book that was constantly read, and it was familiar to all from its use in church and education. Consequently, Hebrew mythology became better known to the ordinary Englishman than any national mythology; ancient Hebrew ethics of the Old Testament mingled with the Christian ethics of the New and were used for social as well as personal instruction (*eg* the English attitude to the keeping of Sunday); differing textual interpretations caused important religious disagreements leading to the proliferation of sects; and Biblical idiom entered extensively into popular English. Finally, the musical cadence of Authorized Version prose can often be heard in the prose of English writers, whether or not professing Christians. It is conspicuous in John Bunyan's

*Pilgrim's Progress**, but it can also be heard in the prose of 20th-C novelist T. F. Powys*, *eg Mr Weston's Good Wine* (1927).

* *New Testament ; Old Testament.*

Bib: Daiches, D., *The King James' Version of the Bible.*

Bill of Rights (1689)

An Act passed by Parliament, according to which the powers of the king were restricted. In particular, he could no longer suspend laws without the consent of Parliament; nor could he dispense with laws in individual cases. The importance of the Act was less the specific ways in which royal power was limited than Parliament's implicit decision to take over the sovereignty of the government from the Crown. This Bill and the events that led up to it, the flight of James II (1685–8) and his replacement by William III* and Mary II (the Glorious Revolution), were the real starting-points of 'constitutional monarchy' in England, *ie* a monarchy under which it is accepted by both Crown and people that the representatives of the people are the real sovereigns of the country.

Billingsgate

The London fish market, situated by one of the gates of the City by the riverside. In 17th C the market was famous for the abusive language used in it; hence 'billingsgate' has become synonymous with violent and abusive language. Similarly, 'to scold like a fishwife'.

Biographia Literaria (1817)

A work of mingled autobiography, philosophy, and literary criticism, by S. T. Coleridge*. The autobiography relates to his struggles as a young writer and editor, and to his beginnings as a poet and co-author of *Lyrical Ballads**. The philosophy is directed to establishing a philosophical and psychological basis for literary criticism; and the criticism is especially devoted to the poetry of William Wordsworth*, and to expressing his disagreement with Wordsworth's ideas on the nature and function of poetry as shown in Wordsworth's Preface to the second edition of *Lyrical Ballads*. The book is disorderly in construction, but, though it received little attention on publication, it has been very influential since. With its psychological approach pursued by acute if abstruse thinking, it is perhaps the starting point of modern criticism. Coleridge shows how the whole personality of the poet, and not merely particular faculties, engages in the act of creation. He makes the first profound statements about the nature and operation of metre. His distinctions between understanding and reason, between two sorts of imagination, and between imagination and fancy, though they are sometimes found to be over-refined or unsatisfactory, stimulated deeper and clearer thinking about works of art and their making.

* 7.3.

Biography

The chief source of inspiration for English biographers was the Greek, Plutarch* (1st C AD), whose *Parallel Lives* of Greek and Roman great men was translated into English by Sir Thomas North* in 1579 and was widely read. Biography had been practised before in England; there had been the lives of the saints in the Middle Ages, and in 16th C Cavendish's life of the statesman Cardinal Wolsey* had appeared. The regular practice of biography, however, starts with 17th C, not merely owing to the influence of North's translation of Plutarch, but as part of the outward-turning, increasingly scientific interest in many kinds of people (not merely saints and rulers) which in 18th C was to give rise to the novel. Biography is a branch of history, and the art of historical writing advanced with biography: Edward Hyde, Earl of Clarendon*, included fine biographical portraits in his history of the Great Rebellion, written between 1646 and 1670. Izaak Walton's* lives of John Donne (1640), Sir Henry Wotton (1651), Richard Hooker (1665), George Herbert (1670) and Bishop Sanderson (1678) are closer to our modern idea of biography, and they are landmarks, if not originals, in the form inasmuch as the subjects, though eminent men, were humble enough to lead ordinary lives in touch with usual experience. In 18th C the writing of biographies became habitual; and also biography, or autobiography, became a way of disguising pure fiction, *eg* in the novels of Defoe*. Samuel Johnson* was a master of biography in his *Lives of the Poets** (1779–81), most notable among which is his *Life of Mr Richard Savage*, previously published in 1744. The outstanding biography of the century, however, and unquestionably the greatest in English, is the life of Johnson himself by James Boswell*, 1791. As an intimate and vivid account of a great man, it was never equalled in 19th C when so many biographies were written and some classic ones, amongst them and perhaps pre-eminent, Elizabeth Gaskell's* life of her friend, Charlotte Brontë* (1857). 19th C was, however, more outstanding for its achievements in the largely new form, autobiography*. 20th C saw a new approach to the art in the work of Lytton Strachey* (1880–1932). His *Eminent Victorians* (1918) sought for the truth in the lives of its subjects in unexpected details, and instead of expounding their greatness exposed the weakness of their mere humanity. His masterpiece was perhaps his *Queen Victoria* (1921). He established the psychological, analytical, reductive approach to the art of biography which has been characteristic of much of it since.

Black Death

An epidemic which struck England in 1348–9 and reduced the population by between one-third and one-half. The economic consequences were far-reaching, especially the shortage of labour. Landowners tended to change from arable to sheep-farming, which required less labour; peasants had better bargaining power and were in a position to commute their serfdom into paid labour; a fierce class struggle resulted from attempts by the landed classes to keep down wages, culminating in the Peasants' Revolt* of 1381.

Black Douglas

* *Douglas.*

Black Friars (Blackfriars)

Dominican Friars, called 'Black' in England owing to the colour of their robes. Their convent in London was dissolved by Henry VIII* (1509–47), but the district has continued to bear their name. Part of the old convent was adapted as a theatre by James Burbage*. The Blackfriars theatre was at first in the hands of boy actors – the Children of the Chapel – and only came to the Lord Chamberlain's Company* in 1608. It was a 'private' theatre with a less mixed, more refined kind of audience than frequented the public theatres such as the Globe*. The change of audience encouraged a change in mode of drama, and helps to explain the less popular, romantic style of Shakespeare's last phase. The theatre was gradually becoming an upper class entertainment, instead of one for all classes.

* *Theatres.*

Black Hole of Calcutta

Suraj-ud-Daula, ruler of Bengal, decided in 1756 to expel the East India Company from its base in Calcutta. He surprised the city, and imprisoned 146 Europeans in a small punishment cell in the barracks; only 23 survived till next morning. The incident was followed by the campaign of Robert Clive, the Battle of Plassey of 1757, and the conquest of Bengal.

Black Prince, The (1330–76)

Edward, Prince of Wales, eldest son of Edward III*. He was famous for his military exploits, especially his defeat of a French army at Poitiers, 1356; in consequence he became a national hero comparable to Henry V*. His designation 'Black' seems to originate with 16th-C chroniclers; it probably refers to his terrible reputation as a warrior. His son was Richard II*.

Blackwood's (Edinburgh) Magazine

Founded in 1817, it was particularly interesting and influential in the first fifteen years of its existence. It was one of 'the Great Reviews' that dominated the literary scene. The first and most eminent of these was the *Edinburgh Review*, founded 1802, and 'Whig' in political outlook, *ie* without being radically reformist it was moderately 'left' in politics. Against it the *Quarterly Review* was founded in London, 1809, on the 'Tory' or right wing. *Blackwood's* was also in opposition to the *Edinburgh Review*, but called itself a 'magazine' to indicate a rather wider range of reading matter, some of it lighter in content than the other reviews provided. It took its stand against the brilliant younger poets – Byron*, Shelley*, Keats* – on political grounds, and, like the *Quarterly*, it was particularly hostile to Keats, although he did not engage in politics. This was because he was a friend and associate of Leigh Hunt*, the radical journalist; Hunt, Keats and their circle were stigmatized as the 'Cockney School', partly because they worked in London, and partly for snobbish reasons. *Blackwood's* began with a brilliant group of contributors, especially Walter Scott*, Lockhart (known because of fierce criticism as 'the Scorpion'), the poet Hogg*, and John Wilson* who wrote under the pen-name of Christopher North. Between 1822 and 1835 the magazine ran a series of brilliant dialogues called the *Noctes Ambrosianae* – Nights at Ambrose's, a well-known inn. In 1857 it published George Eliot's *Scenes from Clerical Life**. It is still published.

* *Reviews.*

Blake, William (1757–1827)

Engraver, poet, and mystic; the self-educated son of a London hosier. He engraved, instead of printing, his poems, and combined each with pictorial engraving that displayed the poetic theme in visual terms. Thus, as other poets had written poems intended to be completed by music, Blake invented a new form by which the poem was completed visually. Most famous, partly because most intelligible and partly because in them Blake is secure in his form, are the *Songs of Innocence** (1789), and *Songs of Experience* (1794). These are lyrics, naive but strong in diction and mysterious in content. *Tiriel* (1788–9) is an early example of Blake's prophetic books, in which he evolved a new type of allegory with characters named by his own invention and representing psychological or spiritual forces. The prophetic books are thus not fully objectified artistically, and are not only often obscure but formally vague. Yet they contain passages of highly original illumination, and, though they were little known in Blake's own time, they have fascinated students and even general readers ever since. Blake wrestles with contrasts: innocence and experience, energy and control, cruelty and meekness. Partly because of his high integrity, partly because of his lack of public, he does not mediate these oppositions through traditional mythologies, *eg* the Prometheus and Zeus of Shelley's *Prometheus Unbound** (1820), but allows them to take the embodiments that arise in his own imagination. Sometimes, however, there is a clue, *eg* the tyrannical figure of Urizen, who, like others, recurs, seems by his name to be bound up with Reason and Horizon – *ie* the inhibiting powers of control and restriction. Politically, Blake was radical, and a supporter of the French Revolution when public opinion was most fiercely against it in London.

His prophetic books include: *The French Revolution*, 1791; *America*, 1793; *Visions of the Daughters of Albion*, 1793; *The Book of Urizen*, 1794; *The Book of Ahania*, *The Book of Los*, 1795; *Europe*, 1794; *The Song of Los*, 1795; *Vala*, 1797, subsequently rewritten as *The Four Zoas; Milton* and *Jerusalem*, 1804. In 1790, a work of different character, *The Marriage of Heaven and Hell**, expresses his disdain of conventional (18th-C) notions of order and contentment, and contains his epigrammatic and penetrating 'Proverbs of Hell'. His later work includes some extremely fine lyrics. Blake's peculiarities of thought and imaginative vision have in many ways proved far more congenial to 20th C than they were to 19th.

* 3.4.1; 6.3.3.

Bib: *Selected Poems*, ed. Saurat, D.; Gilchrist, A. *Life*; Sloss, D. J., and Wallis, J. P. R., *The Prophetic Writings of William Blake*; Blackstone, B., *English Blake*; Bronowski, J., *The Man without a Mask*; Keynes, G., *Blake Studies*; Wickstead, J., *Blake's Innocence and Experience*.

Blank Verse

Verse which is unrhymed, and composed of lines which normally contain 10 syllables and have the stress on every second syllable, as in the classical iambic* pentameter.

The first user of the iambic pentameter in English was Chaucer* and he used it in rhyming couplets, *eg* The Prologue to *The Canterbury Tales**. The first user of blank verse was Henry Howard, Earl of Surrey* (1517–47), who adopted it for a translation of the second and third books of Virgil's *Aeneid* in order to get closer to the effect of the metrically regular but unrhymed Latin hexameters. The effect in Surrey is that Chaucer's measure is being used but without rhyme:

> *They whisted all, with fixèd face attent,*
> *When prince Aeneas from the royal seat*
> *Thus gan to speak.*

The measure is used in the same rather rigid way by Sackville and Norton in their tragedy, *Gorboduc** (1561). The dramatist Christopher Marlowe* (1564–93) first gave blank verse its great distinction. In his plays, he combined the rhythm of the verse with the normal rhythm and syntax of the sentence, so that the effect begins to be like natural speech expressed with unusual music and eloquence:

> *Hell hath no limits, nor is circumscrib'd*
> *In one self place; for where we are is hell,*
> *And where hell is, there must we ever be . . .*
>
> (*Dr Faustus*)

Blank verse as used by Marlowe was carried on by Shakespeare, who employed it with steadily increasing flexibility and power. His contemporaries did the same, but in his immediate successors' work the flexibility exceeded the power, and the result is something which the ear sometimes finds difficult to distinguish from prose; great freedoms are taken with the metre, and the rhythm of the sentence begins to dominate over that of the line, so that the effect (*eg* in Massinger's *A New Way to Pay Old Debts**) is of rhythmic paragraphs of speech.

Massinger's paragraphs conclude the really valuable part of the dramatic history of blank verse; the next phase is the epic use of blank verse by Milton in *Paradise Lost** (1667). Milton gave the weight of Latin syntax to the long sentences, which, in Massinger, have the fluency of ordinary speech. His achievement was thus a massiveness quite dissimilar to the dramatic blank verse. The

Miltonic music was accordingly away from speech rhythms, whereas the movement from Marlowe to Massinger had all been towards them. Wordsworth* and Coleridge* at the beginning of 19th C lightened the Miltonic effect back towards colloquialism. 20th-C-poets such as Eliot and Pound derived from the Jacobean* dramatists new free measures which cannot strictly be described as blank verse at all.

6.2.2.

* *Free verse; Metre.*

Bleak House (1852–3)

A novel by Charles Dickens*. It was published, like most of his novels, in monthly parts. It opens with an attack on the part of the legal system called the High Court of Chancery. The rest of the novel expands this opening into a dramatization, through a wide range of characters, of the various forms of parasitism that society lends itself to, and of the ways in which institutions (especially legal ones) falsify relationships and degrade human beings. Most of the story takes place in London. The telling of the story is shared by two contrasted narrators: the savagely sardonic but impersonal author, and the ingenuous, unresentful girl, Esther Summerson*, who is ignorant of her parentage, though she knows that she is illegitimate. She is adopted by a philanthropist, John Jarndyce, who also adopts two young orphan relatives, Richard Carstone and Ada Clare, who are 'wards in Chancery' (*ie* legally under the care of the Lord Chancellor) while the distribution of an estate to which they have claims is endlessly disputed in the Court of Chancery (the case of 'Jarndyce and Jarndyce'). Through Richard, Ada, and Mr Jarndyce, Esther becomes acquainted with a large number of characters, some of whom are also despairing participants in Chancery Suits, and others (such as Skimpole*, the parasitic man of letters, Mrs Jellyby*, a well-meaning but incompetent philanthropist, and Turveydrop*, the self-styled model of fashionable deportment) who live off society without giving anything substantial in return. Another focus in the novel is Sir Leicester Dedlock, a simple-minded but self-important landowner, whose one redeeming feature is his devotion to his wife, the beautiful and silent Lady Dedlock. Lady Dedlock is in fact the mother of Esther Summerson, a fact known to the family lawyer, Tulkinghorn, who blackmails her. Her former lover, Captain Hawdon, is still alive, but lives in destitution and misery. His only friend is the crossing-sweeper, Jo, who resembles Sir Leicester in that they are equally simple-minded and equally capable of one great love for another person. In social respects they are so differentiated, by the lack of any advantages in the one case and by excess of privilege in the other, that it is hard to think of them as belonging to the same species. A large number of other characters contribute to Dickens's panorama of society as mainly constituted by parasites and the victims of parasites. The theme is conveyed partly through the atmosphere of contrasted houses: Bleak House, which is in fact the cordial and life-giving home of Mr Jarndyce; Chesney Wold, the vast but empty mansion of Sir Leicester; Tom-all-alone's, the slum dwelling where Jo finds his sole refuge; the clean and orderly household of the retired soldier, Bagnet; the squalid one of the money-lender, Smallweed, and so forth. For the main characters, the story ends with the corruption of Richard Carstone, the death in despair of Lady Dedlock, the murder of Tulkinghorn, and Esther's marriage to the young doctor, Woodcourt. The case of 'Jarndyce and Jarndyce' was based on an actual case centring on a Birmingham millionaire, William Jennings. The character of Skimpole is partly based on Leigh Hunt*, and another character, Boythorn, on Landor.

Blenheim (1704) /'blenim/

An important battle in the War of the Spanish Succession* in which the forces of John Churchill, Duke of Marlborough*, and Prince Eugene of Savoy defeated the French forces of Louis XIV under Marshal Tallard, near the village of Blindheim (anglicized, Blenheim) in Bavaria.

Blood, Tragedy of

* *Revenge Tragedy.*

Bloody Assizes

Judicial trials of unusual ferocity held after the failure of Monmouth's* Rebellion against James II. Judge Jeffreys condemned large numbers of the small rebel army to death, and sentenced many more to transportation to penal colonies.

Bloomers

Women's trousers worn under a skirt; they were invented in U.S.A. about 1850, favoured by the American movement for women's rights, and publicized by the editor of the American women's magazine *Lily*, Mrs Amelia Bloomer.

Bloomsbury Group, The

An exclusive intellectual circle that centred on the house of the publisher, Leonard Woolf, and his wife, the novelist, Virginia Woolf*, in the district of London round the British Museum, known as Bloomsbury. It flourished notably in the 1920s, and included, besides the Woolfs, the economist Lord Keynes, the biographer Lytton Strachey*, the art critics Roger Fry and Clive Bell, and the painters Vanessa Bell and Duncan Grant, as well as others. The group owed much to the Cambridge philosopher G. E. Moore* and the importance he attached to the value of friendship. Their close relationships which resulted from this, in addition to their fastidiousness which arose from their critical attitude to the prevailing culture of English society, gave them an apparent exclusiveness which made them many enemies. Moore's influence also contributed to their scepticism about religious tradition and social and political conventions; they tended to be moderately left wing and agnostic. Positively, they were innovators in art and represented an important section of the English avant-garde. Their more constructive opponents attacked them for excessive self-centredness and an aestheticism which was too individualistic and self-regarding to be really creative in social terms. Such an enclosed intellectual élite is unusual in English cultural life, which has not easily lent itself to coteries. They had some affinities with the circle that had surrounded George Meredith*, the novelist.

Blue-coat School

A term used for a number of schools formerly dependent on public subscription; the boys in them wore blue uniforms. Much the best-known example is Christ's Hospital, now a famous public school*; it was founded under Edward VI* (1547–53).

Blues, The

[1] The Regiment of Royal Horse Guards, so called from the colour of its uniform.

[2] As dance music, the blues were a jazz setting to melancholy 3-line verse, of American Negro origin (to feel blue = to feel gloomy).

[3] An Oxford or Cambridge blue is an athletic distinction, owing its name to the colours (dark and light blue respectively) representative of these universities.

Bluestocking

A woman of very serious intellectual, especially literary, taste. In mid-18th C Mrs Elizabeth Montagu started parties in her house for serious discussions instead of card-playing. It became the habit to wear blue woollen instead of black silk stockings at such meetings, as a token of seriousness. The idea came from a similar circle in 17th-C Paris. The men wore the stockings, but the word now refers only to women, often rather derisively.

Blunden, Edmund (b 1896)

Poet and critic, and author of one of the most famous books of World War I, *Undertones of War* (1928). His lyrical poetry produced during and just after that war is drawn especially from the English countryside, and its sincerity and dignity redeemed what was becoming a hackneyed convention of 'nature poetry'. His literary studies have been important especially for the 'romantic' period, *eg Life of Shelley*, *Charles Lamb and his Contemporaries*; and he played a great part in editing and raising the reputation of the poet John Clare*.

Bib: Hart-Davis, R., *Edmund Blunden* (Brit. Coun).

Boadicea (d AD 61)

A Celtic queen (also Bonduca, Boudicca) who is a national heroine because of her rising against the Roman occupying forces. Her people were the Iceni of what is now the country of Norfolk; she was defeated by Suetonius Paulinus and killed herself. Poetically she has been celebrated by William Cowper*, Alfred Tennyson*, and in the tragedy *Bonduca* by John Fletcher*.

Boar's Head Inn

Particularly famous in literature because it is the setting of some of the scenes in which Falstaff* figures in Shakespeare's *King Henry IV, Parts I and II**. An actual inn existed in Eastcheap, London, in Shakespeare's day; it was pulled down in 1831.

* *Inns.*

Bobby

A nickname for a policeman. Bobby is an endearment form of Robert; it was Sir Robert Peel who first established the London Metropolitan police – the first of its kind in the world – in 1828.

Boccaccio, Giovanni (1313?–75)

/bo'ka:tʃiəu/

Italian poet, writer of prose tales, and one of the first of the 'humanists' – *ie* revivers of Greek and Latin studies. He is particularly known in England as the author of the cycle of prose tales called the *Decameron**, from which English writers have borrowed extensively. Indeed, no other foreign writer in medieval or modern literature has been so much a source of borrowings by Englishmen. A brief list is as follows: Chaucer* adapted his poem *Filostrato*, making it into his greatest long poem, *Troilus and Criseyde**, and his *Teseide*, making it into *The Knight's Tale**; tales from the *Decameron* were included in William Painter's anthology *The Palace of Pleasure**, which was then used as a plot-source by Elizabethan dramatists, for instance in Shakespeare's *All's Well That Ends Well**; Dryden adapted two tales making them into *Sigismonda and Guiscardo* and *Cymon and Iphigenia*; Keats* derived his *Isabella, or the Pot of Basil* from the Decameron; the 15th-C poet John Lydgate* based his *Falls of Princes* on Boccaccio's *De Casibus Virorum Illustrium*. Thus in most periods of English literature major writers have been indebted to Boccaccio. Borrowings are, however, not the same as influences; if one means by 'influences' effects on attitudes to experience, style, and feeling, Boccaccio has been less important in English literature than his compatriots Petrarch* and Dante*.

* *Humanism.*

Boehme, Jacob (Behmen) (1575–1624)

A German Protestant mystic and source of the doctrine called after him Behmenism. Spiritual knowledge comes from within – God within rather than God above; it comes to light by an act of will; good and evil, body and spirit, are antitheses, but they are not from separate sources; evil, from the wrath of God, serves God's purposes in bringing about a synthesis according to the Divine Will. Boehme influenced an important English religious thinker, William Law (1688–1761), author of *Serious Call to a Devout and Holy Life* (1729), which in turn influenced John Wesley* and therefore the Methodist religious movement.

* *Methodism.*

Bohemian

Applied to artists and those who live a life supposedly dedicated to the spirit of the imaginative arts, it means living freely, refusing to observe social conventions, especially when they depend on mere habit, snobbery, or fear of 'seeming different'. Literally, Bohemian of course means native to Bohemia, now the western part of Czechoslovakia. In 15th C gipsies* were supposed to have come from there; in 19th C, French students were supposed to live like gipsies and hence to be 'bohemian'. The word was then introduced into English with this meaning by the novelist William Makepeace Thackeray*. His novel *The Newcomes** is one of the first studies in English of Bohemianism.

Boileau, Nicolas (1636–1711) /ˈbwa:ləu/

French critic and poet. Through his *Art Poétique* (The Poetic Art) (1674), based on Horace's* *Ars Poetica* and his translation of the Greek critic Longinus'* treatise *On the Sublime*, he disciplined French literature by the strictness of classical form, setting the example by the quality of his own style. His influence was potentially a hindrance to freedom and invention; but he lived at the time of the great French dramatists Molière* and Racine*, whose energies were only enhanced by his principles. In England, his influence was also important, and enhancing to the kind of poetry written by Dryden*, who revised a translation of Boileau's *Art Poétique*, and Pope, whose verse *Essay on Criticism** was partly based on it.

Bolingbroke, Henry (1367–1413) /ˈboliŋbruk/

In Shakespeare's *Richard II** he deposes his cousin, King Richard, to make himself King Henry IV*.

Bolingbroke, Henry St John (1678–1751) /ˈboliŋbruk/

Brilliant political leader, and writer chiefly on political matters. On the death of the last Stuart* monarch, Queen Anne (1702–1714), he led the Tory party; after the victory of their opponents, the Whigs, and the establishment of the new royal house of Hanover, he fled abroad, but was later pardoned. In 1749 he published his *The Idea of a Patriot King*; with its notion of a king in the role of a national leader, taking politics out of the hands of corrupt politicians, this had much influence on political alignments and the behaviour of the monarchy in the coming thirty years. Bolingbroke was a friend of the great English poet of the time, Alexander Pope*; he was also a deist, *ie* his belief in God was purely rational and did not depend on revelation; the influence of Bolingbroke's deism appears in Pope's *Essay on Man**, although Pope himself was a Catholic.

* *Deism; Whig and Tory.*

Bond Street

In London; famous for its fashionable shops and its art galleries. Divided into 'New' and 'Old' Bond Street, it runs from Oxford Street* to Piccadilly*, through the smart quarter known as Mayfair*.

Boreas

In Greek myth, the personification of the North Wind, and brother of Zephyrus*, the west wind, and Notus, the south wind.

Borough

One of the synonyms of 'town', used specifically for a town which has been incorporated and given privileges of limited self-government; also used until 20th C for a town with the right to elect a Member of Parliament. 'The Borough' is a term for Southwark*, south of the Thames, to distinguish it from 'the City' (of London) to the north.

Boswell, James (1740–95)

Author of the *Life of Samuel Johnson*, published 1791, the greatest English biography. Boswell met Johnson* in 1763, and saw him frequently thereafter. He projected the biography long before Johnson's death, and one of the excellences of the book is his transcription of Johnson's talk in direct form; this is of peculiar value since Johnson excelled in talking. More important still, Boswell had a talent for presenting personalities; his subject's personality was impressive, and, as a great man of letters, Johnson encountered many of the most important people of his day, from the king (George III) downwards. Thus Boswell's *Life* is also a record of unique value for the age. It is no accident that the greatest English biography was written in the century of the first important novelists, since the outlook of a novelist has much in common with that of a biographer.

Boswell was a Scotsman by nationality, and a lawyer by profession. His *Journals* are vast, and have recently been published; but it is as a biographer rather than as a diarist that he shows genius.

Bib: Bronson, B. H., *Boswell's Boswell:* Stauffer, D. A., *The Art of Biography in Eighteenth-Century England*; Pottle, F. A. *James Boswell: The Earlier Years 1740–1769.*

Botany Bay

In New South Wales, Australia, near Sydney. Captain Cook landed there in 1770 and took possession of it for the British Crown. From 1787 Australia was used for convict settlements, *ie* convicted criminals sentenced to transportation were sent there. They were not in fact sent to Botany Bay, but the name was used in common speech to cover convict settlements in Australia generally. The bay received its name from Joseph Banks, a botanist accompanying Cook, because of its rich plant life.

* *Penal System.*

Bottom, Nick

A comic character in Shakespeare's *Midsummer Night's Dream**. He is a weaver, and the most prominent of the 'Athenian artisans'.

Bow Bells /bəu/

The church of St Mary-le-Bow in Cheapside*, London, has always been famous for its peal of bells. The church is in the middle of the City of London, so that to be born within hearing of the Bow bells has been the test of being a true Cockney*, *ie* Londoner.

Bow Street /bəu/

In London, immediately next to Covent Garden Opera House. The chief Magistrates'* Court in London has been situated there since 1735, when it opened in the house of the first Bow Street Magistrate. His successor, the novelist Henry Fielding*, was given a house in Bow Street separate from the court-house. Fielding was exceptionally successful as a Magistrate in ridding London of its crime. He and his brother established the Bow Street Runners, the predecessors of the London police.

Bowdler, Thomas (1754–1825) /'baudlə/

Famous for *The Family Shakespeare*, 1818; an edition in which 'those words and expressions are omitted which cannot with propriety be read aloud in a family'. He later published an edition of Gibbon's *Decline and Fall of the Roman Empire** similarly expurgated. From these we get the word 'bowdlerize' = to expurgate.

Bradley, A. C. (1851–1935)

Literary critic; famous for his 'character-study' method of Shakespearian study. His approach to Shakespeare had dangers in so far as it might lead to treating the fictional characters out of context of the immediate dramatic setting to which the dramatist had limited them; it might even lead to discussion of the kind appropriate only to historical figures. Bradley was on the whole aware of these dangers, but he was not perhaps aware of the third danger: that of treating characters as though they appeared in a 19th-C novel, whereas dramatic characters before the age of the novel were based on different assumptions about the nature of fictional reality. For these reasons, Bradley's criticism has fallen into some disrepute, and more recent critics (*eg* Professor Wilson Knight) have preferred methods which concentrate more on the language of the plays, in particular on study of the use of symbolism. Bradley's most famous work was *Shakespearian Tragedy* (1904).

* *Shakespeare – Criticism.*

Bradley, F. H. (1846–1924)

Brother of A. C. Bradley, the literary critic. He was himself an eminent philosopher, author of *Ethical Studies* (1876); *Principles of Logic* (1883); *Appearance and Reality* (1893), and *Essay on Truth and Reality* (1914). His position philosophically was an idealist one, and in this he has been opposed by most British philosophers ever since, beginning with G. E. Moore. Bradley, however, had a strong influence on T. S. Eliot*, the poet and former philosophy student, whose early thesis on him has recently been published. Bradley's philosophy certainly illuminates some of the difficulties of Eliot's poetry.

* *Idealism ; Realism.*

Bib: Kenner, H., *The Invisible Poet* (for Bradley's influence on Eliot); Eliot, T. S., *Knowledge and Experience in the philosophy of F. H. Bradley*; Woltheim, R., *F. H. Bradley.*

Braine, John (b 1922)

Novelist. His most famous novels are *Room at the Top* (1957, filmed in 1958) and *Life at the Top* (1962, filmed 1965). Both of these deal with the new kinds of social mobility and anxiety, characteristic of Britain since the Second World War. Later Novels: *The Jealous God* (1964); *The Crying Game* (1968); *Stay with me till Morning* (1970); *The Queen of a Distant Country* (1972); *The Pious Agent* (1975).

Bridewell

A royal palace until 1555, then a penitentiary, *ie* a place where the socially undesirable such as wandering beggars and prostitutes were taken for discipline. It was largely destroyed in the Fire* of London in 1666. New Bridewell, used for the same purpose, was built in 1829 and pulled down in 1864. The idea of a penitentiary lies behind the more modern idea of the reformatory, *ie* the place to which offenders are sent when they are considered too young to be sent to prison, and in 19th C 'Bridewell' was used as a synonym for such institutions. (Reformatories are now known as Approved Schools, and Bridewell is no longer a term applied to them.)

Bridges, Robert Seymour (1844–1930)

Poet (Poet Laureate*, 1913–30). His first volume of verse was published in 1873, after which he wrote prolifically: his collected *Poetical Works* (1936), excluding eight dramas, are in six volumes. He was a fine classical scholar, and an innovator in minor ways, *eg* experiment with classical rhythms. His most ambitious poem was the long, philosophical one *The Testament of Beauty*, which appeared in five parts from 1927 to 1929. He is now remembered more as the chief correspondent and literary executor of the poet G. M. Hopkins* than for his own work, though some critics, notably Yvor Winter in his book *The Pursuit of Criticism*, have argued that this is very unjust. A selection of his work, *Poetry and Prose*, has been edited by John Sparrow.

Bib: Smith, N. C., *Notes on The Testament of Beauty*; Guerard, A. J., *Bridges: a study of traditionalism*; Thompson, E., *Robert Bridges.*

Brighton

An English seaside resort on the south coast, one of the first to become fashionable when in 18th C sea-bathing was first held to be good for health and George III (elsewhere) entered the water to the music of 'God Save the King'. Early in the next century the Prince Regent (*Regency) made Brighton his favourite resort and ordered the erection of the oriental-style Pavilion there. Since then, Brighton has remained one of the largest of a line of seaside resorts extending almost the whole length of the south coast.

Britain, British, Briton

Britain (Latin: Britannia) was the name given by the Romans to the island that includes modern England, Wales and Scotland, though the Roman *province* of Britain (AD 43–410) only reached the south of Scotland. Speaking of pre-Roman times, we call the island Ancient Britain and we call its mixed people Ancient Britons.

The term was revived when King James VI of Scotland became also James I* of England (including Wales) in 1603 and called himself King of Great Britain. It was officially adopted by Parliament when England and Scotland were united in 1707. In 1801 the United Kingdom of Great Britain and Ireland was formed, but most of Ireland became separate again in 1922. Terms now in use are:

British Isles: Great Britain and all Ireland, geographically.
United Kingdom: Great Britain and Northern Ireland.
Great Britain, or *Britain*: England, Scotland and Wales, geographically.
British, referring loosely to the U.K. or to Britain.
Briton: a native of the U.K., but the term is rarely used. A native calls himself an Englishman, Scotsman, Welshman or Ulsterman (N. Ireland).
Britisher: American name for a Briton.
England and *English*: These are often loosely and wrongly used for Britain and British, simply because England is the largest partner and English is the common language.

Britannia

The Latin name for Britain. It became a poetic name for Britain in personification. Since 1672 Britannia has been represented with helmet, shield, and trident on certain coins. The poem *Rule Britannia* by James Thomson (1700–48) has been sung to music by Arne as an unofficial national anthem.

Broadside Ballads

Popular ballads* sold by pedlars and ballad-singers in the streets and at fairs, especially in 16th C. 'Broadside' meant that only one side of the paper was printed. Proclamations, items of news, political propaganda and manifestos of all sorts were also often published by this quick and cheap method of printing. An example of a broadside ballad pedlar is Autolycus in Shakespeare's *The Winter's Tale**. The subject of such ballads was commonly sensational news of the moment, such as accounts of notorious crimes; another theme was popular social protest.

The term 'broadside' was transferred to naval war, and designated the simultaneous firing of the guns on one side of a ship.

Brontë, Anne (1820–49) /'bronti/

Novelist and poet. The younger sister of Charlotte and Emily Brontë. She wrote under the name of Acton Bell, contributing to the volume of poems by all three sisters. Her two novels are *Agnes Grey* (1847) and *The Tenant of Wildfell Hall* (1848). They are books of some distinction, but are not on the same level of importance as the work of her two sisters.

* *Brontë, C.; Brontë, E.*

Brontë, Charlotte (1816–55) /'bronti/

Novelist; the third among five daughters of Patrick Brontë, a Yorkshire clergyman of Irish origin. All the daughters seem to have been more or less gifted; two – Charlotte and Emily – outstandingly so. All the daughters, and their single brother, died before their father; their mother died in 1821.

In 1846 Charlotte, with Emily and Anne Brontë published a volume of poetry under the pen-names of Currer, Ellis, and Acton Bell; only Emily's verse is particularly noteworthy. Charlotte's first novel, *The Professor**, was not published until after her death; her second, *Jane Eyre** (1847), was immediately successful. Her third novel, *Shirley**, came out in 1849; *Villette**, based on her period of teaching in Brussels, in 1853. *Villette* is her maturest. The impressiveness of her writing comes from the struggle – experienced by herself, related through her heroines in *Jane Eyre* and *Villette* – to preserve her independence of spirit in circumstances which are overwhelmingly adverse. Her novels are the first truly autobiographical ones; that is, the reader experiences events through the personality of the writer in the guise of her narrating heroine, who yet is objectified as independently as the other characters. *Jane Eyre* is spoiled by wish-fulfilling fantasy, but *Villette* is almost if not entirely free from such defects. *The Professor* is really *Villette* in an earlier and more imperfect form; and *Shirley*, the only one not to have autobiographical form, is less admired.

Bib: Gaskell, E., *Life*; Cecil, D., *Early Victorian Novelists*; Ratchford, F., *The Brontës' Web of Childhood*; Hanson, L. and E. M., *The Four Brontës*

Brontë, Emily (1818–48) /'bronti/

Novelist and poet. She has been described as the greatest woman poet in English literature. It is, however, for her only novel, *Wuthering Heights** (1847), that she is chiefly famous. The novel is unique in its structure and its vision; the former is so devised that the story comes through independent narrators in no way identified with the author, whose personality is therefore completely absent from the book. Her vision is such that she brings human passions (through her characters Heathcliff and Catherine Earnshaw) against society (represented by the households of Wuthering Heights and Thrushcross Grange) with extraordinary violence, while at the same time retaining a cool artistic control. This enables the reader to experience a highly intelligent criticism of society's implicit claim to absorb all the energies of the individual, who potentially is larger in spirit than society ever can be.

* 4.4.2.

Bib: Kavanagh, C., *The Symbolism of Wuthering Heights*; Sanger, C. P., *The Structure of Wuthering Heights*.

Brooke, Rupert (1887–1915) /bruk/

A young poet of exceptional promise who died in World War I. Several of his romantic poems were much quoted, especially *The Great Lover* and *The Old Vicarage, Grantchester*.

Brooks's

A fashionable London club founded in 1764; towards 1800 the centre of aristocratic Whig politics. The playwright Sheridan* was an important member of it.

* *Clubs; Whig and Tory*.

Brougham, Henry Peter, Lord (1778–1868) /bruːm/

One of the founders (1802) of the *Edinburgh Review**, and possibly author of the satirical essay in it which provoked Byron's* first important poem – *English Bards and Scotch Reviewers* (1809). Brougham was a brilliant lawyer, who defended Queen Caroline against George IV and his ministers when they tried to exclude her from the title on his accession in 1820; the defence was successful and celebrated for its boldness. Brougham was Lord Chancellor in Lord Grey's ministry which passed the first Reform Bill* in 1832. As a politician he took a leading part in the Reform Movement of that time; it was then that he was raised to the peerage. He took a lead also in the founding of London University (1828), an event of great importance since it was the first in England to be free of religious restrictions (**Universities*). His versatility and the influence of his imposing personality are illustrated by three minor points: he gave his name to a well-known horse-carriage of his own design – the brougham; he made the reputation of Cannes, in the south of France, as a health resort; and by the age of 25 his reputation as a rising scientist was such as to secure his election as a Fellow of the Royal Society*, though this reputation never matured.

Browne, Sir Thomas (1605–82)

One of the most eminent of 17th-C prose writers; by profession, a physician. His works: *Religio Medici**; *Pseudodoxia Epidemica* (*Vulgar Errors*) (1646); *Urn Burial** and *Garden of Cyrus** (1658), *Christian Morals* (pub 1716). Browne's reflective, fanciful mind drew on his wide range of learning – archaeological, classical, scientific, pseudo-scientific. His prose style has a controlled, musical amplitude and shows a mastery of cadence. His thought lacks the forthrightness of Bacon* and the urgency of Donne*; but he is one of the first English prose writers to reveal self-consciously his own personality in his writing, and to try to 'make a friend' of the reader. His books, especially the *Religio Medici*, reflect the growing tolerance and scepticism of 17th C, and its gradual abandonment of the appeal to an overriding authority.

Bib: Stephen, L., *Hours in a Library* (*Second Series*); Gosse, E., *Sir Thomas Browne*; Willey, B., *The Seventeenth-Century Background*.

Browning, Elizabeth Barrett (1806–61)

Poet. Born Elizabeth Barrett, she was rescued from ill-health and life under an oppressive father by the poet Robert Browning*, who married her in 1846. Her first publication was *Battle of Marathon* (1820). Then came *Essay on Mind: with other poems* in 1826, and her last poems were published in 1862 after her death. Her verse novel *Aurora Leigh* (1857) was popular with the Victorian public, but she is now chiefly remembered for her love poems, *Sonnets from the Portuguese* (1850). She translated *Prometheus Bound* from the Greek of Aeschylus*. Her romance with Robert Browning has been used as a subject for both fiction and drama, notably the play *The Barretts of Wimpole Street* (1930) by Rudolf Besier, and *Flush, a Biography* (1933), in which Virginia Woolf* reconstructs the events from the point of view of Elizabeth Barrett's dog.

Bib: Royds, K. E., *Elizabeth Barrett Browning and her Poetry*; Hayter, A., *Elizabeth Barrett Browning* (British Council: *Writers and their Work*); Miller, B., *Robert Browning: a Portrait*.

Browning, Robert (1812–89)

Poet. The son of a clerk in the Bank of England, he married the poet Elizabeth Barrett in 1846 under dramatic circumstances, and lived with her until her death in 1861 in Italy. He spent the rest of his life in London.

From the first his poetry was exuberant, and he began as an ardent follower of Shelley*: *Pauline* (1833); *Paracelsus** (1835); *Strafford* (a verse tragedy, 1837); *Sordello* (1840). Between 1841 and 1846 he published 7 more plays, the dramatic poem *Pippa Passes*, the collection *Dramatic Lyrics* (including *The Pied Piper**), and *Dramatic Romances* – all published together under the title *Bells and Pomegranates*. During his married life he produced *Christmas-Eve and Easter-Day* (1850) and, his best-known work, *Men and Women** (1855). Nonetheless, public recognition only came with *Dramatis Personae** (1864) and *The Ring and the Book* (1868–9). The latter was his most ambitious work and consists of 10 verse narratives, all dealing with the same crime, each from a distinct viewpoint. It was based on an actual trial, the record of which he discovered in Florence. The period 1850–70 was his best; the later work has endured less well: *Prince Hohenstiel-Schwangau* (1871); *Fifine at the Fair* (1872); *The Inn Album* (1875); *Pacchiarotto* (1876); *La Saisiaz* (1878); *Dramatic Idylls* (1879–80); *Ferishtah's Fancies* (1884); *Asolando* (1889).

Browning was keenly aware that he was writing poetry in an age of science, of vigorous technology, and of prose, particularly of prose fiction. He made poetry compete with prose in these conditions, and the curiosity and delight in detail that were part of his temperament fitted him to do so. Where other poets, notably Tennyson*, wrote in a style that moved apart from and above the preoccupations of daily living, Browning delighted in the idiom of ordinary speech and in the peculiarities of minds and objects. He was not the only practitioner of the dramatic monologue, but he is especially associated with it; he chose characters out of history or invented them in special predicaments, and made them think aloud so as to display their distinctive mentalities. He was not afraid of obscurity, and both his earlier and his later poems suffer from it (*Sordello* and *Fifine*); even in his best work the difficulty of some of the language is not always justified by the actual value of the thought. His contemporary, G. M. Hopkins*, who excelled him in the employment of speech rhythms in verse, despised his intellect. This relative shallowness of mind has caused him to be comparatively neglected in 20th C, and has obscured the importance of the influence of his diction on Ezra Pound*, and of the monologue form on T. S. Eliot* (*eg Prufrock*).

4.4.4; 6.4.1.

Bib: Griffin, H. W. and Minchin, H. C., *Life;* Miller, B., *Life*; Cohen, J. M., *Robert Browning*; Devane, W. C., *A Browning Handbook*; Duckworth, F. G. R., *Browning: Background and Conflict*; Duffin, H. C., *Amphibian: a Reconsideration of Browning*; Herford, C. H., *Robert Browning*; James, H., in *Notes on Novelists*; Johnson, E. D. H., *The Alien Vision in Victorian Poetry*; Raymond, W. O., *The Infinite Moment*; Litzinger, B., Smalley, D., (eds), *Browning: the Critical Heritage.*

Brownists

A Puritan* religious sect founded by Robert Browne (1550?–1633?); from about 1640 they were known as Independents, and since 18th C they have been Congregationalists. Their best-known doctrine is that on the evidence of the New Testament each religious congregation should be self-governing, so that there should be no overriding Church, *eg* no government through bishops under a central figure such as the Pope, or, in the Anglican system, the Crown.

* *Congregationalism.*

Bruce, Robert the

King of Scotland (1306–29) and hero of the Scottish War of Independence (1296–1328), during which he successfully resisted the efforts of Edward I* and Edward II* to conquer the country. Bruce's decisive victory was the Battle of Bannockburn* (1314).

In about 1375 a Scottish poet John Barbour* wrote an epic poem describing the war, called *The Bruce.*

Brummagem /ˈbrʌmədʒəm/

A colloquial term for the midland industrial town of Birmingham, or for an article made there; based probably on an old spelling of the town's name – Bromwicham.

Brut (Brutus)

According to some early chroniclers (esp. Geoffrey of Monmouth*) the founder of Britain, which was fancifully derived from his name. He was said to be grandson of Aeneas*, legendary founder of Rome and son-in-law of Priam, King of Troy. Brut was exiled from Italy, made his way to Britain, and founded New Troy (London). The myth was the subject of 12th-C poems by Wace and Layamon and others.

Buckingham Palace

The principal residence of the British royal family in London. The original house belonged to the Dukes of Buckingham, from whom it was bought by George III in 1762. It was rebuilt by the architect John Nash in 1825, who designed Marble Arch as a gateway to it, but the Arch was removed to its present position near the entrance to Hyde Park* in 1851. It was Queen Victoria* (1837–1901) who first made the palace her principal residence.

Bull, John

* *John Bull.*

Bunyan, John (1628–88) /ˈbʌnjən/

Author of the greatest English allegory, *The Pilgrim's Progress**. The allegory is related to his own spiritual experiences described in his spiritual autobiography, *Grace Abounding to the Chief of Sinners** (1666). He also wrote other works, but only two have survived in literary reputation; both are again allegories: *The Life and Death of Mr Badman** (1680), and *The Holy War** (1682).

Bunyan was of humble origin, the son of a tinsmith in the village of Elstow, near Bedford, where he was born. His life covered the period of greatest crisis in the Puritan* struggle for the survival of their various versions of extreme Protestant faith, and he himself was of Baptist* sympathies. He took part in the Civil War*, but next to nothing is known of his soldiering career. After the Restoration* of Charles II, the Puritans underwent severe persecution and he himself was imprisoned twice for his preaching, once for twelve years. It was during his second and shorter term that he wrote Part I of his masterpiece; the milder tone of Part II may be partly a reflection of the spirit of greater tolerance of religious differences prevailing in England later in his life.

The great reputation of *Pilgrim's Progress* arises from the depth of Bunyan's experience, the spaciousness of his imagination, and the courage, honesty, and nobility of his personality, all of which raise the book far above its narrow, sectarian basis. Moreover, though nominally an uneducated man, Bunyan was fed by a rich, but in some ways primitive, culture. The main source of this was the English Bible which, like other Puritans, he knew with extraordinary thoroughness; there is also an element of popular secular culture from his youth represented by such widely known romances as *Bevis of Hampton**; finally there is the allegorizing tradition of the village sermon which persisted into his youth from the Middle Ages, very little affected by the Reformation*. One should add the strenuous training in self-examination, argument, persuasion, and preaching, characteristic of 17th-C Puritans.

* 4.2.3.

Bib: Talon, H., *John Bunyan, The Man and his Works*; Sharrock, R., *John Bunyan*.

Burbage, James (d 1597) /ˈbə:bidʒ/

Actor and theatre manager. In 1576 he built the first English theatre, called simply The Theatre, on the north side of London. In 1596 he opened the Blackfriars Theatre, where the Children of the Chapel performed. He was the first manager of the Lord Chamberlain's Company*, to which Shakespeare belonged as actor and playwright.

* *Black Friars; Theatres.*

Burbage, Richard (1567?–1619) /ˈbə:bidʒ/

Son of James Burbage. On his father's death, he dismantled The Theatre and rebuilt it as the Globe* on the south bank of the Thames. As actor-manager of the Lord Chamberlain's Company* he took the leading part in plays by Shakespeare*, Jonson*, Fletcher* and others, using the Globe* and (after 1608) the Blackfriars Theatre. He and Alleyn* were the best actors of the time.

Burgundy, Duchy of

A province in the south-east of France, with which it was united in 1477. In the phase of the Hundred Years' War associated with Henry V* of England (1413–22) Burgundy was for the time an important ally of England against France.

Burgundy is famous for its wines.

* *Wine.*

Burke, Edmund (1729–97) /bə:k/

Statesman and thinker; one of the most distinguished 18th-C prose writers. He was of Irish origin, but Protestant, and he pursued his political career in England. He was a Member of Parliament for much of his life, but never held very high office, partly because of his independence of mind, and partly owing to his lack of high social status in a century when power was largely in the hands of the landed aristocracy. His intellectual influence, however, through his parliamentary speeches and even more through his writings, was very great; it was chiefly in politics, but not in the narrow sense of political propaganda.

One of his first works was *A Philosophical Inquiry into the Origin of our Ideas of the Sublime and the Beautiful* (1756), an essay in aesthetics with Longinus* as its starting-point, but with associations of mystery and sublimity which owed more to Milton*. The essay is an example of how the leading thinkers in a century dominated by the rationalism* of Locke* came to feel that reason needed to be aided by imagination and a true understanding of non-intellectual, instinctive response. This way of thinking is related to his attitude to the French Revolution, expressed in perhaps his greatest work, *Reflections on the Revolution in France** (1790). In this he argues for the organic, evolutionary development of society as opposed to the brutal surgery and mechanical reconstruction by revolution. Society is a live organism, and reform must respect its organic nature.

Such an attitude may go with reactionary politics, and Burke sometimes inclined to this, but on the whole his political life and writing stood for sanity, liberality, and justice in the causes of the time, *eg* his defence of Parliament and free elections in *Thoughts on the cause of the Present Discontents* (1770); his defence of the rebellious Americans in *On Conciliation with the Colonies* (1775), and his upholding of the rights of the Catholic Irish in *Letters to Sir Hercules Langrishe* (1792). His prose has vividness and passion, and in the history of political arguments it is outstanding as a vehicle for moral conviction; it is outstanding also at a time when the more characteristic qualities of prose inclined to precision and elegance, even to the point of narrowness of expression.

* 3.3.2.

Bib: Cobban, A., *Edmund Burke and the Revolt against the Eighteenth Century*; Willey, B., *Eighteenth Century Background*; Magnus, P., *Edmund Burke*; Morley, J., *Burke*; MacCunn, J., *The Political Philosophy of Burke*; Copeland, T. W., *Edmund Burke. Six Essays.*

Burlesque

A form of satirical comedy (not necessarily dramatic) which arouses laughter through mockery of a form usually dedicated to high seriousness. Thus, Chaucer's *Sir Thopas** in the *Canterbury Tales** is a burlesque of medieval romance, and the *Beggar's Opera** is a burlesque of early 18th-C Italian opera. The word is from the Italian *burla* = 'ridicule'. Burlesque is similar to parody*, but parody depends on subtler and closer imitation of a particular work.

* *Satire.*

Burney, Frances (Fanny), Madame D'Arblay (1752–1840)

Novelist, diarist, letter-writer. She was the daughter of the musical historian Dr Burney who belonged to the circle of men distinguished in art, letters and politics surrounding Dr Johnson*. In 1786 she received a Court appointment for attendance on Queen Charlotte, wife of George III, and in 1793 she married a French exile, General D'Arblay. From 1802 to 1812, she lived in Paris under Napoleon. After the Napoleonic Wars she spent the rest of her life in England.

Her novels are *Evelina** (1778), *Cecilia* (1782), *Camilla* (1796), *The Wanderer* (1814). Her reputation as a novelist rests almost entirely on the first, which had a great success on publication, and was read with enthusiasm by the most distinguished men of her father's circle, including Johnson and Burke*. Fanny Burney was an admirer of Samuel Richardson* and wrote in the epistolary form, *ie* presenting the narrative through letters between the characters. Her social observation was keen, fresh and lively, and it constitutes the book's permanent charm and interest. Her later novels lose this freshness without notable compensations in the gain of other qualities; nonetheless, *Cecilia* and *Camilla* both exerted some influence on Jane Austen*.

Apart from *Evelina*, Fanny Burney is well known for her diaries and letters, which are a vivid record of contemporary society, including Dr Johnson's circle, Court Society under George III, and Brussels during the battle of Waterloo*.

* *Diaries.*

Bib: Macaulay, T., in his *Critical and Historical Essays*; Scholes, P., *The Great Dr. Burney*; Hemlow, J., *The History of Fanny Burney.*

Burns, Robert (1759–96)

Scots poet, and the best known of a line of poets who used Lowland Scots as a poetic language from the Middle Ages on, and had their golden age at the beginning of 16th C. His immediate predecessors in this school were two other 18th-C poets, Allan Ramsay and Robert Fergusson. He was born in poverty, the son of a peasant or 'cottar', but he became well-read in some parts of English literature, and in the Bible; he knew Shakespeare and the 18th-C English writers, and he read French including Racine*. He had in common with other writers of his century that his art is eminently social: people in their relationships are his subject, not, as with the Romantics (**Romance*) of whom he is often said to be a forerunner, man in his solitude with nature. On the other hand, thanks to the robust character of his Scots idiom, he drew on older traditions in which it was natural to write concretely of ordinary experience, as Chaucer did. His best work was written between 1785 and 1790, and most of it in 1785; these poems were published at Kilmarnock in *Poems Chiefly in the Scots Dialect* (1786), and they brought him fame. He has always been more popular, however, for his extremely musical sentimental pieces such as his songs – *Auld lang syne**, *Ae Fond Kiss*, *Highland Mary*, etc. which, in the view of those who know his work are minor works compared to his satires: *To a Louse*, *Holy Willie's Prayer*, *The Twa Dogs*, *Tam o' Shanter**, *The Jolly Beggars.*

Burns has become something of a national symbol for Scotsmen all over the world, who celebrate 'Burns Night' in January and can usually quote a great deal of his poetry. It is not possible to give a single reason for this. Burns was convivial, a boon companion who revelled in 'wine, woman and song'; he was a rebel against conventional morality and repressive Presbyterianism*; he had a strong sense of humour; he had a profound sympathy for the down-trodden, whether man or mouse; his emotions, of fire or of pathos, were deeply sincere; his vivid portrayal of country life was based on experience, not (as in the Wordsworth* school) on mere observation; he was in all things an unashamed patriot.

* *Lallans; Scottish Literature.*

Bib: Lindsay, M., *Life*; Daiches, D., *Robert Burns*; Speirs, J., *The Scots Literary Tradition.*

Burton, Sir Richard Francis (1821–90)

Explorer and travel writer. *Scinde, or the Unhappy Valley* (1851); *First Footsteps in East Africa* (1856); *The Lake Region of Central Africa* (1860); *The Pilgrimage to Al-Medinah and Meccah* (1855). He also translated the 'Arabian Nights' (*The Thousand Nights and a Night* – 1885-8) and *The Lusiads of Camoens* (1880). See Travel Literature.

Bib: Lady Burton, *Life;* Schonfield, A. L., *Richard Burton Explorer;* Wilson, A. T., *Richard Burton.*

Burton, Robert (1577–1640)

Oxford scholar, author of *The Anatomy of Melancholy**. He was the son of a country gentleman, and was educated at grammar schools until he went to Oxford University in 1593. He remained there for the rest of his life, first at Brasenose College and later at Christ Church. The writing of the *Anatomy* was practically a life work. The first edition (under the pen-name 'Democritus Junior') appeared in 1621; altered and expanded editions appeared in 1628, 1632, 1638 during his lifetime; the fifth and sixth editions, published in 1651 and 1652 after his death, contain further alterations. His original pseudonym 'Democritus Junior' was chosen because Burton was emulating the Greek philosopher Democritus (5th C BC) who, according to tradition, had spent his closing years studying the causes and the cure of the same disease.

Bib: Wood, A., in *Athenae Oxonienses*; Whibley, C., in *Literary Portraits*; Mueller, W. R., *The Anatomy of Burton's England.*

Buskin

A long thick-soled boot worn by ancient Athenian actors in Greek tragedy; hence associated with acting or writing in the spirit of tragic drama. Its purpose was to increase the stature of the actor, in keeping with the grandeur of his tragic role.

* *Tragedy.*

Butler, Samuel (1612–80)

Chiefly known for his satirical poem *Hudibras**. It

is a mock epic written in eight-syllable rhymed couplets ridiculing the two principal Puritan* sects of the time – the Presbyterians* and the Independents (*Congregationalism). The hero is a Puritan hypocrite and mock knight-errant in the style of Don Quixote. He is taken from a Hudibras in Spenser's *Faerie Queene** who is 'not so good of deedes, as great of name'. The poem has wit and pungency, and is the high point of a tradition of burlesques*. The motive was political – the Puritans seeming at the time to be a menace to the royal establishment and the Anglican* Church – but it was intended also to have the moral purpose of exposing hypocrisy. He also wrote *Characters* on the classical model of Theophrastus*; and another satire, *The Elephant in the Moon*, against a contemporary scientist.

4.2.2.

Bib: Jack, I., *Augustan Satire: Intention and Idiom in English Poetry 1660–1750.*

Butler, Samuel (1835–1902)

Satirist, scientific writer, author of an autobiographical novel, *The Way of All Flesh** (pub 1903) in a form which became a model for a number of 20th-C writers. His satires *Erewhon** (*Nowhere* reversed) and *Erewhon Revisited* (1872 and 1901) are anti-utopias, *ie* instead of exhibiting an imaginary country with ideal customs and institutions in the manner of Sir Thomas More's *Utopia** (1516), Butler describes a country where the faults of his own country are caricatured, in the tradition of Swift's Lilliput*. He attacks ecclesiastical and family institutions; in Erewhon, machines have to be abolished because their evolution threatens the human race – a blow at Darwinism.

His scientific work concerned Darwin's* theory of evolution, to which he was opposed because he considered that it left no room for mind in the universe; he favoured the theory of Lamarck (1744–1829) with its doctrine of the inheritability of acquired characteristics. His disagreements and his own theories are expounded in *Life and Habit* (1877), *Evolution Old and New* (1879), *Unconscious Memory* (1880) and *Luck or Cunning?* (1886).

The Way of All Flesh attacks the parental tyranny which Butler saw as the constant feature of Victorian family life (despite much evidence to the contrary); so close did he keep to his own experience that he could not bring himself to publish the book in his own lifetime.

Shaw* admitted a great debt to Butler's evolutionary theories, and to Butler's stand against mental muddle, self-deception, and false compromise in society. Writers as different from Butler and from each other as D. H. Lawrence* and James Joyce* wrote autobiographical novels after him in which the facts were often as close to their own experience.

Bib: Cole, G. D. H., *Butler and The Way of All Flesh*; Henderson, P., *The Incarnate Bachelor*; Joad, C. E. M , *Samuel Butler*; Muggeridge, M., *Earnest Atheist*; Pritchett, V. S., 'A Victorian Son' in *The Living Novel.*

Byron, George Gordon, Lord (1788–1824) /ˈbaiərən/

Poet; his work, and even more his dramatic personality became immensely influential throughout Europe. In his own day, it was the 'romantic' aspect of his poetry which was most popular, such as the first two Cantos of *Childe Harold** (1812) and his verse tales, *The Giaour**, *The Bride of Abydos*, *The Corsair*, *Lara*, *The Siege of Corinth* – these and others all appearing 1812–16. His dramas came out between 1820 and 1824 – *Cain**, *Marino Falieri*, *Sardanapalus**, *The Two Foscari*, *Werner*, *Heaven and Earth* – and they, too, were admired, and contributed, by their sombre passions and the mysteriousness of some of them, to public fascination with the Byronic legend. Modern eyes see a rather different aspect of Byron: critics remember more his admiration for the classicism of Pope, and stress his satirical work, and its contempt for false feeling and the kind of hypocrisy which goes with oppression. Thus it is the 'daylight', Augustan Byron of *Childe Harold III* and *IV* (1816–18), *The Vision of Judgement** (1822), and above all, *Don Juan* (1819–24) which are now admired.

The fascination of Byron's personality starts with his personal good looks and charm; it is also bound up with the mysterious scandals surrounding his broken marriage and exile (1816), his alleged love for his half-sister, his later love affairs, and his close association with the liberation movements of Italy and then of Greece, where he died in 1824. Above all, it arises from his pride, independence of spirit, courage, and vigorous wit. He became a symbol of the successful defiance of all that less gifted (and less privileged) mortals have longed to defy in 19th–20th-C social oppressiveness.

Byron's poetic style is loose, fluent, and vivid; since his day it has been stigmatized for its carelessness and for its bad influence on second-rate talents. In his own work it has its justification in the often well-sustained vigour of his imagination.

Bib: Briscoe, W. A., *Byron the Poet*; Calvert, W. J., *Byron: Romantic Paradox*; Chew, S. C., *Byron in England: His Fame and After Fame*; Knight, G. W., *Lord Byron: Christian Virtues*; Leavis, F. R., 'Byron's Satire' in *Revaluations*; Lovell, E. J., *Byron: the Record of a Quest*; Read, H., *Byron*; Rutherford, A., (ed) *Byron: the Critical Heritage.*

C

Cacodemon /kakə'di:mən/

In Greek myth, an evil spirit. In astrology, a region of the heavens supposed to have an evil influence.

Cade, Jack /keid/

A leader of a popular rebellion in the counties immediately south of London in 1450, during a time of misrule under the weak king Henry VI* (1422–61). The rebellion had temporary success, but later grew disorganized, and Cade was killed.

Cadmean Victory

One gained at too great a cost.

* *Cadmus; Pyrrhus*

Cadmus

In Greek myth, the son of Agenor, king of Phoenicia, and brother of Europa*, who was carried off by Zeus, disguised as a bull. He went in search of her until warned to desist by the oracle of Delphi*; instead, he was to follow a certain cow until she reached a place where she would lie down. On this spot he was to found the city of Thebes. When he reached the place, his companions encountered a dragon which killed them, and which was in turn killed by Cadmus. The goddess Athene instructed him to sow the dragon's teeth in the ground. From the buried teeth a race of armed men sprang up and threatened him; but by throwing a stone amongst them he caused them to fight among themselves until only five were left. These became the ancestors of the great families of Thebes, but for killing the dragon Cadmus was forced to do a penance of eight years. From this legend arises the phrase 'Cadmean victory'.

Caduceus /kə'dju:siəs/

In ancient Greek and Roman times, a staff signifying the function of herald or messenger, entitling him to safe and respectful treatment. Most famous is the caduceus of the Messenger of the Gods – Hermes*. In its most familiar form it consisted of a rod with two serpents intertwined on it, and a pair of wings at the top. Hermes was associated with peace, sleep, and healing; hence the caduceus of Hermes is also associated with the art of healing.

Caedmon (7th C) /'kadmən/

The first Anglo-Saxon Christian poet; he is said to have received the gift of poetry miraculously. Various poetic versions of the Biblical scriptures have been ascribed to him, but the only work known to be his is his first Hymn, said to be composed by Caedmon in a dream, and preserved in the Venerable Bede's* *Historia Ecclesiastica*. Other so-called 'Caedmon poems' are later.

* *Anglo-Saxon literature*

Caesar /'s:izə/

The name of an aristocratic ('patrician') family in ancient Rome; the family claimed descent from the legendary Aeneas*, supposed founder of Rome. The name was made famous by the general and statesman Gaius Julius Caesar*, whose adopted son, Octavianus, also called himself Caesar. Octavianus became Augustus Caesar*, the first Roman Emperor, and thereafter Caesar became the adopted name of all the Roman Emperors, until the fall of Constantinople* in 1453. The German Holy Roman Emperors, claiming to be the heirs of the Roman Emperors of the West, adopted the title Caesar as 'Kaiser'; similarly the Russian Emperors, claiming to be heirs of the Roman Empire of the East, adopted it as 'Czar'. Thus from the first century the family name of Caesar virtually became a title, 'Emperor'. As Julius Caesar became dictator of Rome, 'Caesarism' has come to mean belief in autocracy.

Caesar, Augustus (Gaius Julius Caesar Octavianus) (63 BC–AD 14)

Nephew of Julius Caesar, and his adopted son. He adopted the surname Caesar, and was awarded the title of Augustus by the Roman Senate. He overcame the political enemies and assassins of his uncle, Julius, and after defeating his other rivals (notably Mark Antony), he achieved complete power and became first Emperor of Rome. His reign was contemporary with the best period of Latin literature; in consequence, 'an Augustan age'* has become a term to describe a high peak of literary achievement in any culture, whenever such achievement shows similar qualities of elegance, restraint, and eloquence. In these qualities, France in 17th C and England in 18th C consciously emulated the Augustan age of Rome.

Octavius Caesar, in Shakespeare's *Antony and Cleopatra**, is a portrait (based on Plutarch) of Augustus during his struggle with Antony.

Caesar, Gaius Julius (102?–44 BC)

Roman general, statesman, and writer. He conquered Gaul (*ie* modern France) and in 55 and 54 BC undertook two expeditions to Britain. He described these wars in *De Bello Gallico*, a work long and widely used in English education for instruction in Latin. His victories led to civil war against his chief political rival, Gneius Pompeius, generally known in English as Pompey*, whom he defeated. He then became dictator in Rome, but he was assassinated by other patricians, led by Marcus Brutus, for overthrowing Roman republican institutions. For the Middle Ages, Julius Caesar represented all that was great in Rome. His life was described by the Greek biographer Plutarch* and this with Plutarch's other biographies, was translated into English by Sir Thomas North*. Shakespeare used it as the basis of his play *Julius Caesar**.

Caesar and Cleopatra (1901)

A play by Bernard Shaw*, concerning the relationship of Julius Caesar* and the young Cleopatra*,

Calais

Queen of Egypt. It is an example of Shaw's demonstration of the Life Force manifesting itself in the great man – the spearhead of progress.

Caesura /si'zjuərə/

In Greek and Latin verse, a pause occurring in the middle of a verse foot, caused by the ending of a word. In English verse, a main pause about the middle of a line usually at the end of a verse foot and related to a pause in the syntax; *eg* the pauses marked / in the following lines would be called caesuras:

Now Heaven in all her glory shone, / and rolled
Her motions, / as the great First Mover's hand
First wheeled their course; / Earth, in her rich attire
Consummate, lovely smiled; / Air, Water, Earth,
By fowl, fish, beast, / was flown, was swum, was walked,
Frequent; / and of the sixth Day yet remained.

(Milton – *Paradise Lost**, Bk. VII, 499–504).

Cain

In the Bible (*Genesis* 4:1) the eldest child of the first man and woman, Adam and Eve. Cain's sacrifice to God of the fruits of the earth was rejected, while the beast-offerings by his shepherd brother Abel* were accepted. In a rage Cain killed Abel, so becoming the first murderer. He was driven out of the settled community. By tradition, Cain and Judas Iscariot, the betrayer of Christ, both had red hair; hence *Cain-coloured*, to describe such hair or beard, in Elizabethan plays.

In *Cain: A Mystery* (1821), a verse drama by Lord Byron*, the episode was dramatized with Cain in the role of tragic hero, questioning the justice of the Almighty. Cain, as the first of outcasts from human society, would naturally appeal to the imagination of Byron.

Calais /'kalei/

A port on the north coast of France captured by the English under Edward III* in 1347. It was the last of the extensive conquests by the English kings to be regained by the French, in 1558. In the intervening two centuries, Calais was of great commercial importance as the 'wool staple town,' *ie* the channel through which wool exports passed into Europe.

Caledonia

Roman name for what is now known as Scotland; used poetically for that country, as Albion* is for Britain.

Caliban /'kaliban/

A character in Shakespeare's play *The Tempest** (1611). The word is almost an anagram for 'Cannibal', and Caliban represents in part man at his most primitive as reported by travellers of the day. He is also an unnatural monster, child of the witch Sycorax, and as much animal as human. Shakespeare also seems to have intended him to symbolize the mere body, unredeemed by any spark of spirit. Unlike his counterpart, Ariel*, who is composed purely of the element of air, Caliban is mere earth. Both of them are slaves of the magician Prospero, who dominates the play.

Caligula, Gaius Caesar (reigned AD 37–41) /kə'ligjulə/

Roman Emperor, famous for his cruelties. He was probably mad, and considered himself a god. He was eventually murdered.

Callisto

In Greek myth, a nymph, and companion of the hunting goddess Artemis*. Zeus* loved her, and his jealous queen, Hera, transformed her into a bear, in which shape she was killed by Artemis.

According to another version, she was nearly killed by Arcas, her son by Zeus, but Zeus saved them by turning them into constellations – Callisto into the Great Bear.

Calvary

From the Latin, *calvaria* = 'skull'. The name of the hill on which Jesus Christ was crucified. Also called Golgotha. A Calvary is a life-size image of the Crucifixion before which prayers may be said.

Calvin, Johannes (1509–64) /'kalvin/

French religious reformer, and author of the *Institutes of the Christian Religion* (1535). He settled in the Swiss city of Geneva*, of which he became the ruler. He was the starting-point of the best organized, most disciplined, and most militant of the branches of Protestantism*. The Presbyterian* Church of Scotland, the Scottish national church, is based on his doctrines, and his teaching was widely influential in England in 17th C, as well as in France and Switzerland. His doctrine was austere, and laid great emphasis on the inborn sinfulness of man. His theory of Church government was that it should be elective. Taken with his belief that the Church should be independent of the state, and at the same time that the state had obligations towards the Church, this had great political importance in leading to the Civil War* of 1642–46. Calvin's influence was especially strong among the merchant classes of the towns.

Calypso /kə'lipsəu/

[1] In Greek myth, a nymph, who entertained the hero Odysseus* on his way home from Troy, and kept him on her island of Ogygia for seven years. He refused to renounce his intention of returning home, even for the promise of immortality, and eventually she had to release him on the orders of the gods.

[2] A West Indian ballad-like song.

Cambridge Platonists

* *Platonists.*

Cambridge University

One of the two oldest English universities. Its origins are obscure, but it was in existence early in 13th C, and was probably founded by students emigrating from Oxford. Like Oxford, it is famous for the organization of its students and scholars into colleges, these being independent self-governing bodies whose governing members usually, though not necessarily, hold office in the university as well. It achieved importance equal to Oxford only in 15th C. From then onwards the two universities have been rivals as leaders of English intellectual life, a position they retain in spite of the founding of many other universities in 19th and 20th C. In literature, it has been noted for the number of outstanding English poets educated there, *eg* Spenser, Donne, Milton, Dryden, Wordsworth, Coleridge, Byron, Tennyson.

* *Universities*

Camelot /'kamilot/

In Arthurian legend, the place where King Arthur* held his court. Its whereabouts are unknown, though the principal English writer of Arthurian romance, Sir Thomas Malory*, identified it with Winchester.

Campbell, The Clan /'kambl/

A Scottish clan, headed by the Duke of Argyll, which in 17th and 18th C was one of the most powerful clans in the Highlands*. The heads of the clan became dukes in 18th C; their ancient Gaelic title is Macallum Mhor – the great Campbell. It was steadfast under its chiefs in its support of the Presbyterian* Church and the Protestant Succession*, and in this it was opposed to other leading Highland clans who tended to support the Catholic House of Stuart.

Campbell, Roy (1902–57) /'kambl/

A South African poet, mainly resident in England, and well-known in the 1930s for his resolute opposition to the dominant left-wing school of poets led by Auden*, Spender*, and Day Lewis* whom he satirized under the composite name of Macspaunday. Much of his best verse was satirical in heroic couplets, a form otherwise very rare in 20th-C English verse. He also wrote eloquent, clear-cut lyrics. He was notably vigorous in all he wrote, but not distinctively original. Among his best known works are: *The Flaming Terrapin* (1924), exalting the instinctive, vital impulses in man; *The Wayzgoose* (1928), a satire on South African writers; *Adamastor* and *Georgiad*. He was a Catholic and fought for Franco in the Spanish Civil War. Amongst his finest works is his translation of the poems of San Juan de la Cruz, *St John of the Cross* (1951). *Collected Poems* in 3 volumes, 1960.

Campion, Edmund (1540–81)

English Catholic, member of the Society of Jesus, martyred for his preaching of the Catholic faith. He won the admiration even of his opponents for his heroism and his dignity under trial.

* *Jesuits.*

Campion, Thomas (1567–1620)

English lyric poet and musician. He wrote and composed when the art of English song was at its height; the words do not exist merely as a pretext for the music, but are so composed that the music brings out their expressiveness. This led naturally to metrical experiment, and the resulting increase of rhythmic flexibility no doubt influenced the playwrights in the great range of expression which they achieved in blank verse. Campion wrote ayres, madrigals* and masques*. Despite his fine command of the rhymed lyric, he wrote an essay against the use of rhyme, *Observations in the Art of English Poesy* (1602). This provoked a reply in one of the more important Elizabethan critical essays, Daniel's* *Defence of Ryme*.

* 6.2.4.

Bib: Colles, H. C., *Voice and Verse*;
Kastendieck, M. M., *Thomas Campion, England's Musical Poet*;

Mellers, W., *Music and Poetry*;
Pattison, B., *Music and Poetry of the English Renaissance*;
Warlock, P., *The English Ayre*;
Smith, H., *Elizabethan Poetry*.
Fellows, E. H., *English School of Lutenist Song Writers*.

Canary Wine

* *Wine*.

Candida /ˈkandidə/

One of the *Plays Pleasant and Unpleasant** by Bernard Shaw, published in 1898. Its theme is the conflict between two views of life: the lofty, vague one of the poet Marchbanks, and the narrow but practical one of the Christian Socialist clergyman Morell. Both men are rivals for the love of Morell's wife, Candida.

Candlemas

A Church festival, on 2 February: the feast of the Purification of the Virgin Mary. It also commemorates the presentation of Jesus Christ in the Temple. It used to be celebrated by processions with burning candles.

* *Festivals*.

Canterbury Tales, The [begun about 1387]

A cycle of verse and prose tales by Geoffrey Chaucer*; one of the greatest works of its kind. A miscellaneous body of pilgrims meet at the Tabard Inn*, Southwark, in order to set out on a pilgrimage to Canterbury (a distance of about 70 miles – 112 km) to offer their devotions at the shrine of the martyr St Thomas à Becket*.

The pilgrims are widely representative of the society of the time (excluding the extremes of riches and poverty) and are described in the Prologue*. They number 31 and are joined during the journey by two more, a Canon and his Yeoman or servant. They are described in this order:

[1 & 2] The Knight* and his son the Squire*, who represent the gentry and the spirit of chivalry; they are accompanied by

[3] a Yeoman *or servant. Next is a group of clergy, headed by

[4] an aristocratic Prioress*, who has in attendance

[5–8] a Nun and three Priests;

[9] a Monk*;

[10] a Friar*.

[11] A Merchant*.

[12] The Clerk of Oxford is a scholar, but in 14th C this means that he belongs to the clergy, and he is in fact awaiting a Church appointment.

[13] A Lawyer.

[14] The Franklin* is a prosperous middle-class landowner. Next,

[15–19], is a group of middle-class townsmen: a Haberdasher, or dealer in small articles of dress; a Carpenter; a Weaver, a Dyer; and a Tapicer, or maker of tapestry.

[20] A Cook.

[21] A Shipman, or sailor.

[22] A Physician.

[23] The Wife of Bath is an example of 'the new woman', in that she owns a prosperous cloth-making business.

[24] The Parson or village priest is socially the humblest of all the clergy, though the only one – of those described at length – who is entirely worthy of his sacred vocation.

[25] The Ploughman is the parson's brother and is a peasant farmer.

[26] A Miller.*

[27] The Manciple* is a steward whose work is to find provisions for one of the London inns of court*.

[28] The Reeve* would now be called a land agent, having the duty of supervising a landowner's estate.

[29] The Summoner* is an officer of a Church court, and

[30] the Pardoner* sells indulgences, *ie* remission of punishment for sins – an important and much criticized source of Church income. The summoner and the pardoner are the most disreputable of all the pilgrims.

Finally there is

[31] the poet himself.

After supper the Host of the inn proposes to accompany the pilgrims and to beguile the time on the journey by acting as judge in a contest of tale-telling; each pilgrim is to tell two tales on the way to Canterbury, and two more on the return journey. Thus the Prologue ends. The remainder of the *Canterbury Tales* consists of tales and link passages preserving the setting. The cycle, however, is not completed: there are only 23 tales, two of which (the Cook's and the Squire's) are unfinished. Moreover, seven link passages are missing.

Most of the tales are, like the Prologue, in rhymed ('heroic') couplets*, but two are in prose (Chaucer's own *Tale of Melibeus** and the Parson's); four (the Lawyer's, the Prioress's, the Clerk's, the Second Nun's) are in a 7-line stanza known as rhyme-royal*; and the Monk's tale is in an 8-line stanza. They can be classified in four groups:

[1] the romances, or tales of love, magic, and knightly adventure: the Knight's, the Wife of Bath's, the Squire's, the Franklin's;

[2] those of piety and moral edification, told by the Lawyer, the Clerk, the Second Nun, the Pardoner, the Prioress, Chaucer in his *Melibeus*, the Physician, and the Parson;

[3] the comedies or 'fabliaux'* told by the Miller, the Reeve, the Cook, the Friar, the Summoner, the Merchant, the Canon's Yeoman, the Shipman;

[4] the animal fables, told by the Nun's Priest and the Manciple. The Monk's series of 'tragedies' about the downfall of great men and Chaucer's burlesque romance *Sir Thopas**, both of which are interrupted by disgusted listeners, do not fall into any of these categories.

There are marked contrasts between some of the tales in any one class, *eg* the harshly ironical *Pardoner's Tale* and the sweetly pious *Prioress's Tale*; the two animal fables are different in kind and object; and some tales, such as the Franklin's, partake of two classes, in his case of the first and second. Yet the classification is perhaps useful as indication of the range of subject matter and treatment in the *Canterbury Tales*. Finally, the link passages are by no means secondary. They preserve a framework of actuality for the tales and have a distinct raciness of their own, and two of them – the prologues by the Wife of Bath and the Pardoner – are long and amount to additional tales of great merit.

Of the tales proper, many are traditional or derived and adapted from other writers; the *Knight's Tale**, for example, is an adaptation of Boccaccio's* *Teseide*; the *Clerk's Tale** comes from Petrarch and ultimately from Boccaccio, and so forth. Others, especially among the comedies, seem to be Chaucer's inventions. The collection naturally varies considerably in merit, and the following are perhaps the most famous:

The *Knight's Tale*, about the tragic love of Palamon and Arcite for Emilia, sister-in-law of Theseus of Athens;

the *Pardoner's Tale**, a parable about the coming of death;

the *Nun's Priest's Tale**, about the cunning of the fox and the vanity of the cock – a masterpiece from the way in which Chaucer has fused a hackneyed fable with realistic comedy;

the *Merchant's Tale**, about the outwitting of an old man by his young wife;

the *Franklin's Tale**, about Dorigen's devotion to her husband Arveragus, the attempt of her lover Aurelius to gain her favours by witchcraft, and his surrender before the honourable generosity of the husband and wife;

and the scurrilous, highly comic tales of the Miller* and the Reeve*, the Friar* and the Summoner*, in which each pair tells tales which are reciprocally insulting. There are, however, merits in all the tales; the tastes of readers in choosing the masterpieces vary considerably.

Canto /'kantəu/

Used in Italian literature as a division of a long poem, such as might be sung or chanted at one time (canto = song). The term has been borrowed for some long poems in English, *eg* Spenser divided the books of his *Faerie Queene** into cantos.

Canute (Cnut) (1016–35)

A Danish king of England. He is especially remembered for the story recorded by 16th-C chronicler Holinshed* about his rebuke to his flatterers. When they declared him all-powerful, he sat down by the seashore and forbade the incoming tide to wet his royal feet. When nonetheless the waves came on, he demonstrated to his courtiers that a king had no more power over nature than an ordinary man.

Capitalism

The system by which the means of production is owned privately, production is for private profit, and productive enterprise is made possible by large-scale loans of money rewarded by the payment of interest.

Before about 1350, in England as in much of the rest of Europe, there was little opportunity for capitalism. On the land, the economic unit was the manor (corresponding approximately to a village) which consumed its own produce and had little left over for sale; the economic relations were feudal, *ie* the landlords provided protection to the peasants in return for economic services, and the peasants were mostly serfs, *ie* they were bound to the land they worked on, and were unable to sell their labour freely. The towns were small, and manufacture was by master craftsmen*, who worked with their own hands, and employed apprentices* and journeymen* only in small numbers. The masters combined in craft guilds* which regulated trade and limited profits to a communally arranged 'just price'. Moreover, commerce, except for the export of wool, was mainly limited to the districts round the towns. Finally, it was difficult to borrow money for capital investment, partly because the Church disapproved of the taking of interest on money loans, since it regarded this as the sin of usury. The economic bond was not, in fact, a money relationship but a personal one, bound up with an elaborate system of rights and duties; these divided society into something more like castes than the modern social classes, which are differentiated chiefly by wealth.

But already by the lifetime of the poet Chaucer* capitalism was making beginnings. Towns were growing, and they now contained a substantial middle class, as the *Prologue* to *The Canterbury Tales** illustrates. Master craftsmen were gradually becoming employers of labour rather than workers themselves; this was particularly true in the manufacture of cloth, which required a variety of processes impossible for one man, or even one guild, to undertake alone. The Craft Guilds were becoming supplemented by the Merchant Companies, such as the Merchants of the Staple, who had a monopoly of the export of wool to the cloth manufacturers of Flanders, and later (15th and 16th C), the Merchant Adventurers, whose export of cloth became even more important than the older commerce of the export of wool. The economic cause of the Hundred Years' War* was Edward III's* determination to protect the English wool staple towns – *ie* those through which the export of wool was channelled into Flanders – from the threat of France. To sustain the war,

Edward III and Henry V* had to borrow extensively from foreign bankers, who were finding methods of escaping the Church's prohibition of usury. Meanwhile, on the land the serfs were becoming independent wage-earners, able to sell their labour freely and where they pleased; this was thanks to the shortage of labour that resulted from the Black Death* epidemics (about 1350). Lack of labour caused many landowners to turn their arable land into pasture and to enclose open land with hedges. This process continued in Tudor times for economic reasons, despite a labour surplus. It weakened the landowners' ties with the peasantry and encouraged the 'drift to the towns' which drained the countryside in 18th–19th C.

The rapid growth of capitalism in 17th and 18th C was aided by the Reformation*, since certain of the Puritan* sects – notably the Calvinist Presbyterians – found that religious individualism gave support to and was supported by economic individualism. The dramatists of the great period of English drama (1580–1640) found the Puritans to be against them, and they (*eg* Ben Jonson*, Middleton*, Massinger*) tended to stand for the traditional values, and to satirize the money-loving, socially ambitious middle classes, among whom the Puritans had their main strength. By the end of 17th C, however, Puritanism was losing its ferocity; the traditional non-economic bonds of community were by then gravely weakened, and the novels of Defoe* depict the loneliness of men guided predominantly by economically individualistic motives.

The full triumph of capitalism came only with the fulfilment of the Industrial Revolution* in 19th C. Workers were, for the first time on a large scale, employed in the mass, in factories. The employers (backed by a number of gifted theorists, such as Adam Smith*, Bentham*, Malthus*, Ricardo) developed a ruthless philosophy, according to which their relationship with their workers should be governed entirely by the economic laws of supply and demand, with which the state interfered, in their opinion, only at the cost of wrecking national prosperity, even if the interference were dictated by the need to save the workers from intolerable misery. This stream of opinion among the industrialist employers was however progressively opposed by Evangelical Christians among the politicians (*eg* Lord Shaftesbury*), by socialists of the school of Robert Owen*, and by the very popular novelists between 1830 and 1860, such as Elizabeth Gaskell*, Benjamin Disraeli* and Charles Dickens*. Gradually industrial capitalism became less inhumane, and in the last twenty years of the century, socialist opinion grew, aided by the leadership of intellectuals such as Bernard Shaw* and Beatrice Webb*. England has not yet become a socialist state, but more and more economic activity has been taken over by the state in order to bring about a society in which nobody shall suffer social injustice. Today, the railways, broadcasting, the banks, electricity, gas, coal production, medicine and steel production are all controlled indirectly by the state, and the list is not complete. The principal issue now dividing the main political parties is how much economic activity should be left in private hands, and how much freedom this 'free enterprise' should be allowed: the Conservatives support a greater amount of capitalist enterprise, and the Labour Party* emphasizes the value of state control. This compromise between capitalism and socialism since the Second World War has produced the Welfare State*, where nobody can starve, and nobody is supposed to suffer social injustice, though many still do. The Welfare State has combined with full employment and better education since the war to produce a more prosperous and more articulate working class than has ever been seen in England before; one result of this has been a much larger production of novels, plays and films with working-class themes, *eg* the plays of Arnold Wesker and the novels of Alan Sillitoe*.

*** 2.1**

Capitol, The

In ancient Rome, the hill on which stood the temple to Jupiter, chief of the gods. Here the chief officers of the Roman Republic, the Consuls, took their vows, and the sacred Sibylline (*Sibyl) books were kept.

In the U.S.A., the Capitol is the building where the National Congress meets in Washington.

Captain Singleton, Adventures of (1720)

A novel by Daniel Defoe*. Like the heroes and heroines of Defoe's other novels, the hero has at first no morality and takes to a life of wandering adventure; some of this takes place in Africa (which Defoe knew only from reading and hearsay). Later he becomes a pirate in the Indian Ocean and further east; finally he settles down in England, a respectable married man, converted to a religious life. The story is told in the first person.

Capuchins /ˈkapuʃinz/

An order of Friars*, founded in Italy about 1520. It was an offspring of the older Franciscan* Order, and the name derives from the pointed hoods that were worn.

Capulet /ˈkapjulet/

In Shakespeare's *Romeo and Juliet**, the name of the family to which Juliet belongs. The inveterate hostility between the Capulets and the Montagues, the family to which Romeo belongs, causes the tragedy.

Caractacus (Caradoc) (1st C AD) /kəˈraktəkəs/

An ancient British chieftain who resisted the Roman conquest of Britain under the Emperor Claudius*. His courage and dignity before the Emperor, after he had been captured, caused him to be pardoned and released.

Carew, Thomas (1595–1640) /ˈkeəri/

A poet, whose work combines two of the main streams of poetic tendency in the first half of 17th

C: the classical discipline of form from Ben Jonson*, and the 'metaphysical'* ingenuity of imagery of John Donne*. One of his best poems is his *Elegy* upon the death of Donne. His works show the qualities of wit, seriousness, and bold imagination characteristic of the best poetry of the time. He belonged to the sophisticated court circle of Charles I*, and was one of the so-called 'Tribe of Ben', as the disciples of Jonson were called.
Bib: Williamson, G., *The Donne Tradition*; Selig, E., *Carew – a Critical Study*.

Carker, James

A character in Dickens's novel *Dombey and Son**. He is a vicious character and one of Dickens's most successful depictions of villainy.

Carlton Club

A fashionable political club, and centre of the Conservative Party, in London. It was founded in 1831 by the Duke of Wellington.
* *Clubs*.

Carlton House

A London mansion near Buckingham Palace, which became famous as the residence of George IV before he came to the throne.

Carlyle, Thomas (1795–1881) /ka:'lail/

Scottish essayist, historian, philosopher. The term 'philosopher' is inappropriate to him if it implies the use of the reason for the logical investigation of truth; his friend John Stuart Mill*, who was a philosopher in this sense, called Carlyle a poet, meaning that he reached his conclusions by imaginative intuition. In his old age he became known as 'the sage of Chelsea'; a sage is a 'profoundly wise man', and this is certainly the kind of admiration that he received in England between 1840 and his death. He hated spiritual mediocrity, mere contentment with material prosperity, moral lassitude, and the surrender to scientific scepticism and analytic reasoning. All these he regarded as characteristic of British civilization in mid-19th C. Part of their cause was the overwhelming technical advances resulting from the Industrial Revolution*; he also considered that the immense popularity of the poet Byron* had helped to disintegrate spiritual wholeness because of the cynicism and pessimism of his poetry, and he distrusted equally the influence on the English mind of the coldly logical French philosophers. To counter Byron, he pointed to the spiritual health which he found in Goethe*, and to counter the French he advocated the more emotional and intuitive 18th and 19th C German thinkers like Richter and Goethe.

Carlyle's influence derives even more, however, from his own character and the environment from which he sprang. His father had been a Scottish peasant, with the moral energy and intellectual interests which are so characteristic of the Scottish peasantry, and come partly from the influence of Scottish Calvinism (Presbyterianism*). This religious tradition in Scotland had much in common with 17th C Puritanism* which had left such a strong mark on the English character; the resemblance between the two traditions helps to account for the hold which Carlyle established on the English imagination. His own personality was strong and individualistic; this, combined with his intention of counteracting the abstract intellectual thought of writers like Bentham*, caused him to write in an eccentric prose style, distorting natural word order and using archaic language. His *Sartor Resartus** ('Tailor Repatched', 1833–4) is a disguised spiritual autobiography in which he faces the tendencies to intellectual scepticism and spiritual denial in himself, and dedicates himself to a life of spiritual affirmation. He is unable to base this affirmative spirit on the traditional religious beliefs that had supported his father, so that he has to base it on his own will, his imaginative response to nature, and the inspiration provided by the lives of great men.

History was for Carlyle the storehouse of example of these great men, his 'Heroes' – and it is in this spirit that we have to approach his historical works: *French Revolution* (1837), *On Heroes and Hero Worship* (1841), *Oliver Cromwell's Letters and Speeches* (1845) and *Frederick II of Prussia* (1858–65). In *Past and Present* (1843) he reconstructed the life of a medieval abbot to contrast his vigour with the mediocrity of 19th-C middle-class values, and in *Latter-Day Pamphlets* (1850) he attacked the quasi-scientific treatment of social questions by the rationalist political economists. In 1867 *Shooting Niagara – and After?*, written at the time of the Second Parliamentary Reform Bill, reflects his total disbelief in the efficacy of of mere political reform.

As a historian, Carlyle wanted history to be related to the life of the ordinary human being, and his inspiration here was his compatriot, the historical novelist Sir Walter Scott*. As a social thinker, his advocacy of the imaginative approach to man in society relates him to the thought of Coleridge*, whom he knew through his friend John Sterling (*Life of John Sterling*, 1851), and also to his own disciple, John Ruskin*.
* 3.4.4; *Utilitarianism*.
Bib: Trevelyan, G. M., *Carlyle Anthology*; Froude, J. A., *Life*; Neff, E., *Carlyle and Mill*; Harrold, C. F., *Carlyle and German Thought, 1819–34*; Symons, J., *Carlyle: the Life and Idea of a Prophet*.

Carmelites

An order of friars* and nuns. The friars were called 'White Friars' in England, from the white cloak worn over a brown under-garment.

Carol

A hymn of praise, especially associated with Christmas. The origin of the carol may have been pagan, and connected with New Year and spring festivals. Dancing and singing in early medieval churches was common, for instance round the Christmas 'crib', or model of the Christchild's birthplace in the stable at Bethlehem. English Christmas carols, like those of other nations, are freer of the restricted sentiment of church piety than other hymns. Examples dating from 15th C are 'Joseph was an old man' and 'I saw three ships come sailing in'. The earliest collection in English is by Wynkyn de Worde in 1521.

Caroline Period, The /'karəlain/

From Carolus (Lat.) = Charles; applied to the reign of Charles I* especially to denote the literature of the reign. Caroline poets include so-called 'Cavalier poets'* such as Carew*, Lovelace* and Suckling*; Caroline dramatists were the last to write in the Elizabethan tradition, *eg* John Ford* and James Shirley*. The Caroline writers exhibited the graceful qualities associated with Charles I's court; they had more refinement and elegance than the poets and dramatists of the previous (Jacobean*) reign of James I, such as John Donne* and Webster*, but less vigorous feeling and thinking. The Caroline divines followed the leadership of Charles I's Archbishop of Canterbury, William Laud*, in taking up the extreme Anglican position in the matter of church ritual, so that the Puritans* regarded them as essentially Catholic and therefore 'superstitious'.

* *Periods of English Literature.*

Carroll, Lewis (Charles Lutwidge Dodgson) (1832–98) /'karəl/

Writer for children; author of *Alice's Adventures in Wonderland* (1865) and *Through the Looking-Glass* (1872). By profession, a mathematics lecturer at Oxford University. The 'Alice' books describe the adventures of a child in dreams, and owe their distinctiveness to the combination of childlike naivety with an authentic dream atmosphere, so that events succeed and language is used with dream logic instead of daylight logic. Thus these two books mark an epoch in the history of dream literature; the dream state is not merely a pretext for fantasy, but is shown to follow its own laws. Consequently Carroll's two masterpieces have had as much appeal for adults as for children. Dodgson was also a master of 'nonsense' verse which shows the same characteristics; his most famous poem is *The Hunting of the Snark* (1876). His other book for children, *Sylvie and Bruno* (1889), is less memorable.

Bib: Gardner, M., *The Annotated Alice*
Collingwood, S. D., *The Life and Letters of Lewis Carroll*; Empson, W., 'Alice in Wonderland' in his *Some Versions of Pastoral*; Green, R. L., *The Story of Lewis Carroll*; Sewell, E., in *The Field of Nonsense*; Hudson, D., *Lewis Carroll.*

Cartesianism /ka:'ti:zjənizm/

The philosophy of Descartes*.

Carthage /'ka:θidʒ/

A great city on the North African coast in the Gulf of Tunis; it was practically destroyed by the Arabs in AD 698. In 3rd C BC Carthaginian troops invaded Italy under the great general Hannibal, and came near to destroying Rome. Rome succeeded in destroying Carthage (Third Punic War) in 2nd C BC, but the city was rebuilt by the Emperor Augustus (27 BC–AD 14), and remained an important port of the Roman Empire.

Carthusians /ka:θjuz:jənz/

An order of monks founded in France in 11th C. The name derives from Chatrousse (Chartreuse), the village where its first monastery was built. Their monasteries were called Charterhouses in England; the most famous of them, the London Charterhouse, was taken from the monks in 1535 during the Reformation*, and in 1611 was turned into a school (now a famous public school* and moved to Godalming).

Cary, Arthur Joyce Lunel (1888–1957)

Novelist. He was born in Northern Ireland, where Protestantism* is strong; he was brought up against a background of devout Anglicanism*, lost his faith, and later constructed an unorthodox but strongly ethical faith of his own in the Protestant tradition. He came late to the writing of novels. He studied as an art student in Edinburgh and Paris before going to Oxford University. In 1912–13 he fought, and served in the Red Cross, in the Balkan War. In 1913 he joined the Nigerian political service, fought against the Germans in West Africa in the First World War, and returned to the political service after it. His first novel, *Aissa Saved*, appeared in 1932. His subsequent works were: *An American Visitor* (1933); *The African Witch* (1936); *Castle Corner* (1938); *Mister Johnson* (1939); *Charley is my Darling* (1940); *A House of Children* (1941); the trilogy *Herself Surprised* (1941), *To Be a Pilgrim* (1942) and *The Horse's Mouth* (1944); *The Moonlight* (1946); *A Fearful Joy* (1949); another trilogy, *Prisoner of Grace* (1952), *Except the Lord* (1953), and *Not Honour More* (1955); *The Captive and the Free* (1959). He also produced two volumes of verse, *Marching Soldier* (1945) and *The Drunken Sailor* (1947), and a number of political tracts – *Power in Men* (1939), *The Case for African Freedom* (1941, revised 1944), *Process of Real Freedom* (1943), and *Britain and West Africa* (1946).

In the first 30 years of 20th C novelists tended to be open to foreign influences and experimental in expression; Cary was among the first distinguished novelists of the last 30 years to return to English traditions and direct narrative, although he here and there uses the stream-of-consciousness technique of narration evolved by novelists of the 1920s, notably Joyce*. He is one of the most eclectic of modern novelists, both in method and in subject. In his comedy and his loose, vigorous narrative he has been compared to 18th-C novelists – Smollett* and Defoe*; in his characterization, to Dickens*; in his attitude to human nature, to D. H. Lawrence*; in his concern with heroic morality, to Conrad*; in his endeavour to present experience with immediacy, to Virginia Woolf* and Joyce; in his interlocking of human destiny and social patterns he might be compared with George Eliot*. His first three novels and *Mister Johnson* are products of his African experience; *Charley is my Darling* and *A House of Children* are novels of childhood, and his two trilogies – thought by some to be his major work – are attempts, in his words, to see 'English history, through English eyes, for the last 60 years'. His characters are similarly varied, but have in common strong idiosyncrasies; his work as a whole is unified by what Walter Allen has called 'very English Existentialism . . . the working of the Protestant, Nonconformist spirit.' (From *Joyce Cary*, Writers and their Work, British Council.)

Bib: Wright, A., *Joyce Cary: a Preface to his Novels*; Mahood, M. M., *Joyce Cary's Africa*; Bloom, R., *The Indeterminate World.*

Casanova De Seingalt, Giacomo (1725–98) /kazə'nəuvə/

An Italian adventurer, author of scandalous Memoirs. His name has become synonymous in English with 'licentious lover'.

Cassandra /kə'sandrə/

In Greek legend, a daughter of Priam*, King of Troy. The god Apollo gave her the gift of prophecy, so that she foresaw the fall of the city. At the end of the war she was made captive by Agamemnon*, leader of the Greek forces, and was later murdered by Agamemnon's queen, Clytemnestra*. In English, a 'Cassandra' is a prophet of disaster; sometimes, merely, a fearless prophet or critic of the times.

Cassibellaun (Cassibellan: Cassivellaunus)

Ancient British chieftain who commanded the Catuvellauni against the Romans during Julius Caesar's* second invasion of Britain in 54 BC. Caesar eventually succeeded in forcing tribute and hostages from him. In medieval legend he was the brother of the mythical King Lud*, said to have built walls round London.

Cassibelan is mentioned in Shakespeare's *Cymbeline** as one who fought against the Romans.

Cassiopeia /kasiəu'piːə/

In Greek myth, wife of Cepheus, king of Ethiopia. She boasted that she excelled even the nereids, or nymphs of the sea, in beauty; she thus incurred the wrath of the sea god, Poseidon*, who transformed her into a constellation. She was the mother of Andromeda*.

Castalia, Castalian Spring /kas'teiljə/

A fountain which rises in Mount Parnassus*, near Delphi, Greece. In ancient times, it was sacred to Apollo*, god of poetry, and in both classical and later literature it is referred to as the source of poetic inspiration.

Castiglione, Baldassare (1478–1529)

Italian humanist, and author of *Il Cortegiano* (1528) translated into English (1561) as *The Courtier* by Sir Thomas Hoby. It is a dialogue at the court of the Duke of Urbino, and concerns the many-sided virtues, intellectual, moral, physical, of the ideal courtier, the ideal of Renaissance* man. The book was immensely influential in 16th-C England; it was extolled by Roger Ascham* who otherwise regarded Italy as morally pernicious, and was the pattern for the life of such courtier-poets as Wyatt*, Surrey*, Raleigh* and Sidney*, and for Spenser's *Faerie Queene**, which, like *The Courtier*, 'purported to fashion a gentleman or noble person in vertuous or noble discipline'. *The Courtier* is neo-Platonic in inspiration, *ie* had as ideal a conception of perfect wholeness in man, attainable by those of noble origin.

Castle of Indolence, The (1748)

A poem in Spenserian stanzas* by James Thomson* (1700–48). It combines Spenserian music, sensuousness, and reflectiveness with Augustan* concern with the virtues of civilized society. The first canto deals with the delights of the enchanted castle; the second with its overthrow by the knight of Industry.

Castle of Otranto, The (1764)

One of the first so-called gothic novels*, by Horace Walpole* (1717–97). The fantastic events are set in the Middle Ages, and the story is full of supernatural sensationalism. The story concerns an evil usurper, a fateful prophecy about his downfall, a mysterious prince disguised as a peasant, and his eventual marriage to the beautiful heroine whom the usurper had intended as his own bride. It reflects the 18th-C view of the medieval (gothic) period as barbarous but excitingly mysterious. The novel set a powerful fashion which extended into 19th C.

Castlereagh, Viscount (1769–1822) /'kaːslrei/

Statesman, and Secretary of State for Foreign Affairs during and after the downfall of Napoleon, from 1812 to 1822. This period coincided with a phase of political reaction in Britain, and to the radicals of the time he represented the oppressiveness of the government. Hence the attack on him by Shelley in the *Mask of Anarchy**.

Castor and Pollux (the Dioscuri)

In Greek myth, twin sons of Zeus* and Leda, and companions in the voyage of the Argonauts*. They were made into the constellation of Gemini (the Twins). In their divine capacity, they came to be considered as the friends of sailors, with power to calm a storm.

Catalectic /katə'lektik/

A term used in metrical analysis, when the last foot of a line of verse is cut short, or omitted altogether, *eg* the lines:

Best and brightest, come away!
Fairer far than this fair day,
Which, like thee to those in sorrow,
Comes to bid a sweet good-morrow

(Shelley – *The Invitation*)

are written in 'falling', trochaic feet – an accented syllable followed by an unaccented one – and have lines 3 and 4 complete, but lines 1 and 2 are catalectic, lacking the final unaccented syllable of the last trochee.

Cathay /ka'θei/

The name by which China was known to medieval Europe, still used as a poetic term for the country.

Catholic Emancipation, The Act of (1829)

A law by which Roman Catholics in England were awarded full political rights, *eg* to be elected as Members of Parliament. They had been deprived of these rights by legislation of various kinds since the time of the Reformation*.

Catholic Majesty, His Most

A title awarded to the kings of Spain early in 16th C by Pope Alexander VI.

Catholicism (Roman) in English Literature

Until the Act of Supremacy* (1534) by which King Henry VIII* separated the English Church from Roman authority, and the more violent revolution in Scotland a little later, both countries had belonged to the European community of Catholic Christendom. This community was a genuine culture, allowing great unity of belief and feeling together with great variety of attitude. In 14th and 15th C both Scottish and English poetry shows highly distinctive regional character, together with a stronger understanding of the literature of other countries (notably of France and Italy) than was to be typical of the post-Reformation (**Reformation*) centuries. In 16th C this community of cultures broke up, owing not only to the Protestant* rebellions but also to the increase of national self-consciousness, the influence of non-Christian currents (especially Platonism), and the gradual release of various fields of activity – political, commercial, philosophical – from religious doctrine. The Counter-Reformation* after the Catholic Council of Trent (1545–63), even more than the Reformation, tended to define Roman Catholicism in contrast to Protestantism. Thus, although the dramatists and lyric poets in England from 1560 to 1640 show a plentiful survival of medieval assumptions about the nature of man and his place in the universe, in conflict with newer tendencies of thought and feeling, the Roman Catholic writer in the same period begins to show himself as something distinct from his non-Catholic colleagues. The clearest example in 17th C is the poet Richard Crashaw*. Milton's epic of the creation of the world, *Paradise Lost**, is in many ways highly traditional – for instance it uses the Ptolemaic conception of the universe (**Ptolemy*), accepted in the Middle Ages, instead of the modern one substituted by Copernicus and Galileo in 16th and early 17th C – but the feeling that inspires it is entirely post-Reformation. By 18th C, however, religion of all kinds was becoming a mere department of life, no longer dictating ideas and emotions in all fields, even when sincerely believed; it is thus seldom easy or important to remember that the poet Alexander Pope* was a Roman Catholic. By 19th C, writers of strong religious conviction were increasingly feeling themselves in a minority in an indifferent and even sceptical world. They therefore tended to impress their work once more with their faith, and this was especially true of the few Catholic writers, since Catholic faith was dogmatically so strongly defined, *eg* the poet Gerard Manley Hopkins*. The century also saw a revival of Anglo-Catholicism. To understand Anglo-Catholicism, it is important to remember that the English Reformation was the most moderate of all, and that from its beginnings under Henry VIII there was a school of opinion which sought to remain as close to Roman Catholicism as Anglican* independence allowed. This wing of the Church was important under Charles I*, but in consequence became identified with monarchical and anti-parliamentarian politics, and lost prestige until it was revived by the Oxford Movement*. Since then it has remained important in the strength of its imprint on literature. Thus in 20th C the Anglo-Catholicism of the poet T. S. Eliot* is as conspicuous as and more profound than the Roman Catholicism of the novelists Evelyn Waugh* and Graham Greene*.

Catiline (1611) /'katilain/

A tragedy by Ben Jonson*, about the attempt by Lucius Sergius Catilina to overthrow the government of the Republic of Rome in 1st C BC. It is an example of Jonson's great classical scholarship, but this scholarship impedes the dramatic impact of the tragedy instead of enhancing it as in the case of his other Roman tragedy, *Sejanus**.

Cato, Marcus Porcius (95–46 BC) /'keitəu/

'Cato the younger', great-grandson of Cato the Censor*. He tried to maintain the Republic against the ambitions and popularity of Julius Caesar*. He was noted for his disinterested devotion to duty and disregard for his own personal interests. The later Roman stoics* looked back to him as the pattern of stoic man. He was eventually defeated by Caesar at Utica (46 BC).

Cato the Censor (234–149 BC) /ˈkeitəu/

Marcus Porcius Cato, an austere statesman of ancient Rome, famous for his hostility to unnecessary luxury imported from Greece, and for his endeavours to maintain traditional Roman simplicity. He was the first important Latin prose writer, and the first of the great Roman historians. His most important work was *Origines* ('Origins') in which he described the history of Rome and the rise of other Italian states. Later in the Roman Empire, Cato's emphasis on discipline and austerity in private and public life was admired as an ideal from which the sophisticated Romans of the Empire had fallen away.

** Cato, Marcus Porcius ('the younger'); Latin Literature.*

Catullus, Gaius Valerius (84?–54 BC) /kəˈtʌləs/

A great Roman lyrical poet, famous especially for his Lesbia cycle of love poems. He was one of the Latin poets who had an extensive influence over English lyric poets in 16th and 17th C. For instance, John Skelton's* *Book of Philip Sparrow* (1503–7) echoes Catullus on Lesbia and the sparrow; Ben Jonson's* *Song to Celia* is modelled on Catullus, and so is Marvell's* *To his Coy Mistress*. Jonson, with his sensitive and profound Latin scholarship, was the most important English follower of Catullus, and he transmitted the strength and delicacy of the Latin poet to the 'Cavalier'* lyrists and to Marvell. The most important period for Catullus' influence on English poetry was therefore 1600–50.

Cavalier

A word, meaning 'horseman', which was used for the supporters of Charles I*, in the Civil War*. It was first used as a term of reproach against them by their opponents, the supporters of Parliament (Roundheads*); in this sense it meant an arrogant and frivolous man of the court. Soon, however, it was accepted with pride by the Royalists themselves. It is a mistake, however, to think of the Cavaliers as merely members of the court and of the aristocracy; many of the aristocracy supported Parliament, and many of the Cavaliers were fairly modest country gentlemen who never came near the court. The Cavalier Parliament sat from 1661 to 1678 after the restoration of Charles II* and was so called because the king's supporters won most of the seats.

Cavalier Poets

A name given to a large group of poets owing to their association with the court of Charles I*, and the reflection in their verse of a number of its characteristic qualities. The three most famous names are Thomas Carew*, Sir John Suckling*, and Richard Lovelace*. The main influences acting upon them were those of Ben Jonson* and, less important, of John Donne*. Jonson transmitted to them the firmness, grace, and detachment which he in turn had derived from the ancient Latin poets such as Catullus* and Horace*; Donne was the source of their ingenious and witty imagery which is especially noticeable in Carew. Native to them, and a product of the court, is the easy liveliness of their diction, characteristic of aristocratic poets up to the time of Byron.* The Cavalier poets to some extent resemble the Restoration* poets who appeared after the restoration of the monarchy (Charles II*), but differ from those by their greater refinement of taste, the absence in their work of the Restoration tendency to confuse wit with licence. On the other hand, they differ from the older generation of poets such as Donne and Herbert*, by their inferiority in depth and force. Some of the best poets of Charles I's reign, notably Herrick* and Marvell*, share some of the qualities of the Cavalier poets without normally being included in their number.

** Metaphysical Poets.*

Caxton, William (1422?–91)

The first English printer. He established his press in Westminster in 1476, and in the years 1477–91 he issued nearly 80 books, many of them translations from the French, and many of these made by himself. Of English works that he printed, some of the most important are Chaucer's *Canterbury Tales**, *House of Fame**, and *Troilus and Criseyde**, and Sir Thomas Malory's *Morte D'Arthur**. Caxton was also a good translator, and has his place in the development of English prose. No great writer had set a standard for prose as Chaucer had for poetry. The language was in a fluid state, with no accepted standards of spelling, grammar or style. Caxton had to fix these for himself, not only as a printer but as a publisher aiming to be intelligible to the widest possible public. With few English prose works available for printing he had to fall back on producing his own, by translation.

Bib. Bennett, H. S., *English Books and Readers, 1475–1557*; Awner, N. S., *Caxton: A Study of the Literature of the First English Press.*

Cecilia, St

Patron saint of music and the blind; martyred for her faith, in Rome, AD 230, or possibly in Sicily rather earlier. Her association with music depends on a passing reference in the medieval account of her life. Her legend is told by Chaucer in the *Canterbury Tales* (*Second Nun's Tale**) and she is further commemorated by Dryden* in one of his most famous poems, *Song for St Cecilia's Day*, and by Pope* in his *Ode for Music on Saint Cecilia's Day*. Handel set both these poems to music.

Celestial City

The name by which Heaven is denoted in John Bunyan's *Pilgrim's Progress**. It is contrasted with the City of Destruction, a typical earthly town standing for worldliness, from which Christian flees on hearing that it is doomed.

Celestial Empire

One of the literary names for the Empire of China. It is a translation of a native Chinese title.

Celt /kelt/

So far as the British Isles are concerned, the Celts are taken to be the inhabitants of the western regions where a Celtic language survives, or survived until the comparatively recent past. They are: Wales, Ireland, North-west Scotland, the Isle of Man, and Cornwall. Such regions have, to varying degrees, Celtic traditions of culture surviving in spite of the encroachment of Anglo-Saxon* culture from 12th C onwards. With these regions, the north-western province of France, Brittany, is commonly associated.

Celtic Literature

* *Irish Literature; Wales.*

Celtic Twilight, The

Originally *The Celtic Twilight* was a book of short stories by the poet W. B. Yeats*, published in 1893. The book concerned the widespread beliefs in magic and the supernatural which were current among Irish peasants. Since then, the term Celtic Twilight has been widely used to describe the idea that the Celts, especially in Ireland, preserve a mystical, imaginative, poetic vision which the practical and materialistic Anglo-Saxons (both in England and in southern Scotland) have lost. At the end of 19th and beginning of 20th C Yeats and other Irish poets used this conception of the Celtic character as a weapon in the cause of Irish nationalism, and they cultivated ancient Irish legends about heroes such as Cuchulain* and heroines such as Queen Deirdre* so as to build up a distinctively Irish literary consciousness to replace the dominant English culture. The belief in the inherent poeticality of Celts* receives some support from two sources: the vividness of English dialect as spoken by Irish peasants and used by the dramatist J. M. Synge*, and others; and the survival of literature in the Welsh language, with an audience not merely among the intelligentsia but among the common people of Wales.

Cenci, The (1819) /ˈtʃentʃi/

A poetic drama by P. B. Shelley*, concerning the hatred of the evil Roman nobleman, Count Francesco Cenci, for his children, and the incestuous passion infecting him for his daughter Beatrice. Beatrice, her brother Bernard, and her stepmother Lucretia succeed in killing the Count who has thus darkened their days, and are executed for the murder. Poetically the play, as with all English verse dramas of early 19th C, owed much to the blank verse drama of the Jacobean* period, especially that of John Webster*, whose work Shelley imitates without assimilating it into a style of his own. The play is however one of the most successful of the romantic school of drama, though this is not to claim very much for it. It is also interesting as representing Shelley's emotions about the oppressiveness of the older generation. In this he was influenced both by his relationship with his own father and more, symbolically, by the restoration of the forces of reaction and oppression in Europe after the downfall of Napoleon.

Censorship and English Literature

Systematic censorship has never been an important restriction on English writing except in times of war; but English writers have certainly not always been entirely free.

Until 1640 the kings exercised undefined powers by the Royal Prerogative. Early in her reign, Elizabeth I* ordered dramatists not to meddle with politics, though this did not prevent *Gorboduc** with its warnings on national disorder; but Ben Jonson*, Chapman* and Marston* found themselves in prison for *Eastward Hoe* (1605) because it offended the Scots friends of James I*. In the reign of Charles I* the term Crop-ears was used for opponents of the king who lost their ears as a penalty for criticizing the political or religious authorities. Moreover printing was monopolized by the Stationer's Company, whose charter might be withdrawn by the Crown, so that the monopoly would cease.

In the Civil War, Parliament was in control of London, and issued an edict that the publication of any book had to be licensed. The edict provoked John Milton's *Areopagitica**, a noble appeal for freedom of expression. Its influence was not immediate; after the Restoration* of the Monarchy, Parliament issued a similar edict in the Licensing Act of 1663. The Act was only for a period, however, and in 1696 it was not renewed. The lapsing of the Licensing Act was the starting point of British freedom of the press except for emergency edicts in times of war in 20th C, although in early 19th C the government attempted a form of indirect censorship by imposing a tax on periodicals which restricted their sale amongst the poor. Nonetheless there are still laws extant which restrict freedom of political expression beyond certain limits: it is, broadly speaking, an offence to threaten, in print, Queen or Parliament with direct violence. The limit is so remote, however, as not seriously to embarrass anybody.

More serious are the English laws of libel and of obscene libel. The first exists to punish attacks on private reputation, and the second concerns the defence of sexual morals. These restrictions are serious restraints on opinion because they are vaguely defined, so that it is difficult for a publisher or writer to know when he is infringing them. Moreover, prohibition under obscene libel is frequently reversed, *eg* D. H. Lawrence's *The Rainbow** was suppressed for obscenity, but in 1965 it was a prescribed text for a public examination taken in schools.

Censorship in the theatre has been a special case since 18th C. Henry Fielding's* comedies attacking the Prime Minister, Robert Walpole*, led in 1737 to the restriction of London theatres to two 'patented' ones – Covent Garden and Drury Lane – and the Court official, the Lord Chamberlain, had to license plays. In 1843 the Theatres Act removed the restriction on the theatres and defined the Lord Chamberlain's powers to the restraint of indecency. The Lord Chamberlain's censorship came to an end in 1968.

* **2.2.4.2.**

Centaurs /'sentɔ:z/
In Greek myth, a race of beings who were part horse and part man. They are mainly known for their war with a neighbouring race of men, the Lapithae, to whose women they had offered violence, and for one of their number, Cheiron, famous for his knowledge of medicine, music, and archery. Heracles, in his war with the Centaurs, wounded Cheiron incurably in the knee, and Zeus translated him into the constellation of Sagittarius (the Archer).

Cephissus
The river that flows near Athens.

Cerberus
In Greek myth, a dog who guarded the entrance to the underworld to prevent the escape of the dead or the entry of those who were still alive. He is variously described as having two, three, or fifty heads. Visitors to the underworld, *eg* Aeneas*, threw him a cake which he stooped to devour, and thus let the visitor pass. Hence the idiom, 'a sop to Cerberus'. Orpheus*, on the other hand, charmed him to sleep with his lyre.

Cervantes Saavedra, Miguel de (1547–1616)
A Spanish writer whose worldwide fame derives from his mock-romance *Don Quixote*.

Chaldea /kal'di:ə/
Used in the Old Testament of the Bible as synonymous with Babylonia, *ie* the ancient civilization between the rivers Tigris and Euphrates, which the Chaldeans ruled from c 626 BC; the Chaldeans were, however, a distinct race from the Babylonians. They were famous for their wisdom in astronomy, astrology, magic and prophecy. Hence 'Chaldean' is often used as synonymous with soothsayer or prophet.

Chamberlain's Company, The Lord
The more important of the two leading companies of actors in the reigns of Elizabeth I* and James I*, and the one to which Shakespeare belonged as both an actor and playwright. All companies of actors had to have licences in order to perform, and this meant that they had to have the patronage of some leading nobleman, or to be attached to the royal household. The Lord Chamberlain's Company seems to have been formed in 1594 by a regrouping of various companies depleted by a plague epidemic. Its patron was Lord Hunsdon who held the office of Lord Chamberlain at the royal court. After the accession of James I, the King himself became its patron, and the company was known as 'the King's Men'. It was first managed by James Burbage*, builder of the first English theatre (1577), and from 1597 to 1619 by his son, Richard Burbage*, who was one of the leading tragic actors of the day. It played at court, and at a number of theatres in London under the control of the Burbages; its most lasting homes were at the Globe* on the south bank of the Thames, and at the Blackfriars* on the north bank. No doubt it was the popularity of Shakespeare's plays, both at court and among the general public, which gave the Company its commanding position, though the quality of Burbage's acting must also have counted. Its chief rival was Edward Alleyn's* Lord Admiral's Company. The King's Men retained their supremacy among the acting companies until the closing of the theatres by Parliament in 1642.
 * *Acting.*

Chambers, Sir Edmund (1866–1954)
Scholar. The exceptional breadth and exactness of his work on English literature make his books indispensable reference works for students of English literature in the medieval and Elizabethan periods. His best-known works are: *The Medieval Stage* (1903); *The Elizabethan Stage* (1923); *William Shakespeare* (1930).

Champagne
A province in Eastern France, which produces one of the most famous of all wines. Its best-known form is a sparkling white wine, which has long been considered indispensable on occasions of special festivity, such as wedding parties. It is mentioned frequently in literature as far back as the second half of 17th C.
 * *Wine.*

Chancellor, The Lord
The office of Lord Chancellor existed before the Norman Conquest (1066), and has always been one of the most important in the state, although its outstanding political importance diminished after the resignation of Sir Thomas More* in 1532, owing to his disagreement with Henry VIII's religious policy. In the Middle Ages the Chancellor was the king's secretary, and keeper of the seal which authorized public enactments. This closeness to the centre of power often meant that he was second only to the king himself. In 14th C he took upon himself the task of hearing appeals from subjects who were unable to get justice through the Common Law Courts. He thus became the head of a new Court of Law, the Court of Chancery operating a new department of law, called the Law of Equity. The Lord Chancellor also presided over meetings of the Great Council of the Barons in medieval times, and he still presides over its historical descendant, the House of Lords, *ie* the Upper House of Parliament. As the House of Lords contains judges who meet as the highest court of judicial appeal in the country, the Lord Chancellor presides over this too, and in this capacity he is the head of the English judicial system. Finally, the Lord Chancellor is *ex officio* a member of every Cabinet, and the nearest equivalent in England to a Minister of Justice.
 * *Court of Chancery; Courts of Law.*

Changeling, The (1623)
A poetic tragedy by Thomas Middleton* and William Rowley. Rowley seems in fact to have been responsible for the comic subplot, the value of which is contested; the play is sometimes produced

or broadcast without it, since the connection between the two plots is loose. The main plot, by Middleton, concerns the murder by Beatrice-Joanna of her prospective husband, Alonso de Piracquo, so that she can marry another man. To execute the murder she employs one of her admirers, De Flores, a man who physically revolts her, as though by employing such a man she could herself remain free of the guilt and horror of the crime. Instead, De Flores insists that they are now partners and equals in the sin of bloodshed, and blackmails her into becoming his mistress. The play is one of the greatest in English after Shakespeare; it is written in sober, forceful blank verse* which is one of the finest late Jacobean* examples of this medium. The main plot is taken from *God's Revenge against Murther* by John Reynolds.

* 5.1.3.2.

Chanticleer /tʃanti'kliə/

The name for a cock in medieval bestiaries*, or animal fables, in imitation of Aesop. His best known appearance in English Literature is the Nun's Priest's Tale* of *The Cock and the Fox* in Chaucer's *Canterbury Tales.* As the fox (Reynard) represents unscrupulous cunning, so the cock represents male vanity.

Chapbooks

The name for a kind of cheap literature which flourished from 16th to 18th C, after which they were replaced by other forms. They were so called because they were sold by 'chapmen' or travelling dealers. Their contents consisted commonly of traditional romances retold, often from the French, in crude form: *Bevis of Hampton**, *Guy of Warwick*, *Till Eulenspiegel*, *Dr Faustus*, are examples. Some of them, such as *Dick Whittington*, about the poor boy who ended up as Lord Mayor of London, have survived as children's stories to the present day, and are the theme of the Christmas theatrical entertainment known as pantomime.

Chapman, George (1559?–1634?)

Poet and dramatist. As a poet he is particularly famous for making one of the best-known translations of Homer's *Odyssey** and *Iliad**. It is, however, a very free translation, expressing more of Chapman himself, as an Elizabethan intellectual with strong philosophical interests characteristic of his time, than of the spirit of the ancient Greek poet. He saw the epics as heroic exemplifications of moral greatness, in accordance with Stoic* ethical categories much later than Homer. In his conception, the great man had strong passions, but also strong pride which raised him above the corrupting influences of society; on the other hand, this passion and pride must be tempered by philosophical fortitude and discipline if they are not to be self-destructive. The dramatic conflicts implied in this view of Homer dominate Chapman's tragedies (1603–31): *The Tragedy of Bussy d'Ambois*; *The Conspiracy and Tragedy of Charles Duke of Byron*; *The Revenge of Bussy d'Ambois*; and *Caesar and Pompey*. Of these the first is acknowledged to be the finest; all of them contain fine passages, and none is without fairly serious imperfections. Bussy is a magnificent portrayal of the heroic man who dominates his morally mean environment but cannot control his passions; Clermont, his brother, in *The Revenge*, is a less successful example of the man of tempered passion and stoical calm. Chapman also wrote eight comedies of less fame, and completed the narrative poem *Hero and Leander*, left unfinished by Christopher Marlowe*.

* 5.1.3.2.

Bib: Ellis-Fermor, U.M., in *Jacobean Drama*; Ure, P., in *Pelican Guide to English Literature*, Vol. II; Jacquot, J., *Chapman: Sa Vie, Sa Poésie, Son Théâtre, Sa Pensée.*

Characters, Theophrastian

In early 17th C a form of essay devoted to the description of human and social types grew up, and collections of such essays were known as 'Characters'. The origin of the fashion is in the brief sketches by one character of another in the comedies of the time – *eg* those of Dekker* and Jonson* – and in the verse satires of such poets as Donne* and Hall*. The tone was always light and often satirical; as a literary form, Characters displaced the satirical pamphlet popular in the last decade of 16th C written by such men as Greene* and Nashe*. The basic pattern of the form was the *Characters* of the ancient Greek writer, Theophrastus (3rd C BC); hence the designation 'Theophrastian'.

The two most famous collections were that of Sir Thomas Overbury – partly by other hands – published in 1614, and *Microcosmographie* by John Earle*, published in 1628. The fashion continued, though it became less popular, throughout 17th C and into 18th. It was eventually superseded by the more elaborate and individualized studies by Addison* and Steele* in the *Spectator*, especially the De Coverley papers, and by the growth of the 18th-C novel.

Charge of the Light Brigade, The

A famous poem by Alfred, Lord Tennyson* about the episode in the battle of Balaclava (1854) in the Crimean War, between the English and the French on one side and the Russians on the other. The charge was of great heroism but an act of folly based on a misunderstood order. Tennyson celebrates the heroism in vivid terms. Curiously enough his poem called *The Charge of the Heavy Brigade*, which occurred in the same battle and was successful, is much less well-known, although it has equal merit.

Charity Schools

* *Schools in England.*

Charles I

King of Great Britain and Ireland (1625–49). He had limited intellectual abilities, and the causes of religious and economic conflict were so strong during his reign that it ended in civil war, his defeat, and his execution. On the other hand, he was morally upright in personal (if not political) relations, devoted in his affections and in religion, and he created around him a court of taste, refinement and distinction. His connoisseurship led to a fine collection of pictures later dispersed by Oliver Cromwell*, who sold them to obtain international currency. His patronage of the Flemish artist Van Dyck resulted in some highly flattering portraits which have done the king much good with posterity. His fine personal qualities, his tragic end and his nobility in its endurance, were the basis of a strong sentimental, sometimes even a religious, devotion to his memory. For example, there are churches dedicated to Charles the Martyr in a few places (*eg* Tunbridge Wells) in Britain.

* *Civil War.*

Charles II

King of Great Britain and Ireland (1660–85). The Restoration* of the Monarchy brought him back from exile after the Interregnum* since the execution of his father, Charles I, in 1649. Politically unscrupulous and of low personal morals, he was nonetheless one of the most intelligent kings in English history, and his court was a centre of culture and wit as well as of moral licentiousness. His lack of scruple enabled him to raise the monarchy to a new pitch of popularity, in spite of the growing strength of Parliament and its increasing independence of royal authority. His was the last royal court in England to be a centre of cultural vitality.

* *Cavalier Poets.*

Charon /ˈkeərən/

In Greek legend, the ferryman who took the souls of the dead across the River Styx* to Hades. Charon's toll was a small coin placed in the mouth or hand when ancient Greeks were buried; it was to pay for the crossing of the Styx.

Charter Companies

These were joint stock companies* authorized by the Crown to make treaties, to set up trading colonies, and to employ armed forces for their protection. The British Empire in India, the Far East and Africa was developed almost entirely by them. The British government only took over their responsibilities when forced to do so by political pressure, *eg* in India (1858), in Nigeria (1900), in Rhodesia (1923). Some, like the Hudson's Bay Company and the Muscovy Company, still operate although no longer chartered.

* *Companies, Joint Stock; East India Company.*

Charterhouse

* *Carthusians.*

Chartist Movement

A working-class political movement which flourished between 1837 and 1848. It arose because the Reform Bill* of 1832 had reformed Parliament in favour of middle-class political rights, but had left the working-class without them. The Chartists wanted Parliament to be closely responsible to the nation as a whole, and to reform an electoral system according to which the poor were excluded from membership of Parliament and denied the right to vote others into membership by their lack of the necessary property qualification. Some regions were more heavily represented in Parliament than others, and all voting was subject to bribery or intimidation because votes had to be declared publicly. Consequently they put forward their Charter containing Six Points: [1] votes for all males; [2] annually elected Parliaments (instead of general elections every seven years); [3] payment of Members of Parliament (so that poor men could have political careers); [4] secret voting (voting 'by ballot'); [5] abolition of the property qualification for candidates seeking election; [6] electoral districts equal in population. The movement seemed to be a complete failure, but all these points became law between 1860 and 1914 except the demand for annually elected parliaments. The Chartists attracted an ardent following, but they were badly led. Allusions are made to them in those novels between 1840 and 1860 which were concerned with 'the Condition-of-the-People Question', *eg Sybil** by Benjamin Disraeli. This serious discussion of the social crisis of the second quarter of 19th C was greatly stimulated by Carlyle's* essay *Chartism* (1839), one of his fiercest and most influential writings.

* 1.5.1.4.

Charybdis

* *Scylla and Charybdis.*

Chaste Maid in Cheapside, A (1611)

A comedy by Thomas Middleton*. It is one of the 'citizen comedies'* of the Jacobean* period, with a characteristic theme of a merchant (Yellowhammer) scheming against Sir Walter Whorehound, a dissolute landed gentleman, so as to secure marriage with his daughter and entry into the landowning class, while Whorehound in turn tries to marry off his mistress to Yellowhammer's son and thereby gain Yellowhammer's money. These intrigues of the gentry and the citizenry against each other were a common theme of the comedies of the time. The play makes mock of both classes, and has a characteristic robustness in the way in which it uses the social satire at a deeper level than the merely topical relationships, so as to bring out basic types of human greed, vanity, and lust, in the tradition of Ben Jonson's* 'comedy of humours'.

* *Humours, Comedy of.*

Chatterton, Thomas (1752–70)

Poet; he is chiefly famous for forging medieval poems purporting to be by Thomas Rowley, a non-existent 15th-C monk. These he claimed to have found among old documents in the church of St Mary Redcliffe, Bristol, where his uncle was sexton. Chatterton was too young and inexperienced to be a really competent forger, but the poems showed undoubted talent and charm, and for a time they deceived a number of people including,

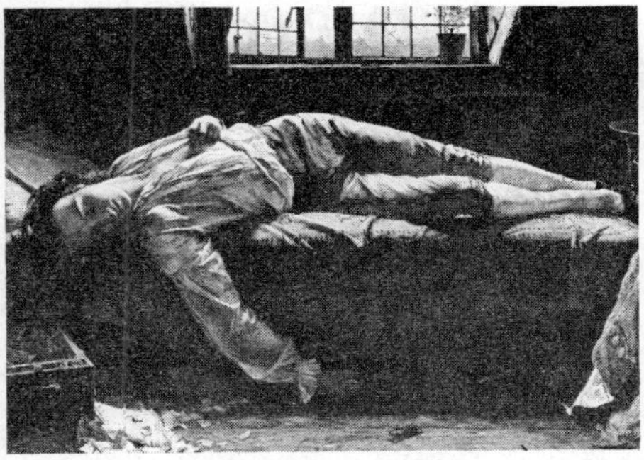

briefly, the leader of the fashion for medieval revival, Horace Walpole*, author of *The Castle of Otranto*. Chatterton, despite his gifts, could get no adequate reward for his literary productions, and while he was not yet 18 he committed suicide, although the forgeries were not actually exposed until 1777. There was then a reaction in his favour; his early and tragic death gave a romantic lustre to his truly talented work, and the English romantic poets idealized him as a martyr for the cause of poetry, particularly of the new, anti-Augustan style. Wordsworth refers to Chatterton's end in his poem *The Leech-Gatherer**; Coleridge* composed *A Monody on the Death of Chatterton*; Keats dedicated his *Endymion** to Chatterton, and Shelley commemorates him as well as Keats in *Adonais**. One reason for Chatterton's influence was that, although his forgeries purported to be medieval, he made much of Elizabethan poetry, especially Spenser – an important element in Romanticism. The modern view inclines to the feeling that whereas his contemporaries unjustly neglected his merits, the next generation over-estimated them.
Bib: Meyerstein, E. H. W., *Life of Chatterton*.

Chauncer, Geoffrey (1340?–1400) /ˈtʃɔːsə/

Poet. His work has often been regarded as the effective starting point of English literature. This view has been unfortunate in so far as it has led to the comparative neglect of the other great 14th-C poets – William Langland*, and the anonymous author or authors of *Sir Gawain and the Green Knight** and *Pearl**. It is also misleading in so far as it assumes that a great poet can spring from nothing. But it is true that Chaucer established the East Midland dialect of Middle English as the medium of all later major English literature, with the exception of some Scottish poets, that later poets emulated his employment of rhymed and regular metre, and not the alliterative* forms of the other great 14th-C poets, and that the next poet in time comparable in stature to Chaucer – Edmund Spenser* – freely acknowledged his indebtedness to Chaucer.

His greatness is due to his capacity to assimilate the techniques of French and Italian poets, using them to enrich and enhance his native idiom. One of his earliest works was the translation of the French poem *Roman de la Rose** ('The Romance of the Rose') by Guillaume de Lorris and Jean de Meung; some of this translation may be by another poet, but the first 1,700 lines have been generally accepted as Chaucer's. In 1369 he wrote *The Book of the Duchess*, showing the influence of the French poets Machault and Froissart. These poems are in 8-syllable rhymed couplets; so is *The House of Fame**, which perhaps shows the influence of the *Divine Comedy* by the Italian poet, Dante*. *The Parliament of Fowls** (1380?) is in the 7-line stanza, called 'rhyme-royal'*. These are all allegorical poems in a general European tradition, and all in different ways have the theme of romantic or courtly love, a theme that originated in France. *The Legend of Good Women** (1385?) is the first of the poems in the 10-syllable rhymed couplets which Chaucer used with such assurance that the 10-syllable line became the principal rhythm for later poets. All the poems so far mentioned are still fresh and living literature, but his first great masterpiece was *Troilus and Criseyde* (1386?) – in rhyme-royal. This was based on the Italian poem *Il Filostrato* by Boccaccio*, and at first glance it is a characteristic treatment of romantic love; but Chaucer greatly expanded and altered Boccaccio's poem, and he presented the theme with qualities of real life experience such that some critics have described *Troilus and Criseyde* as the first of the great novels. It was followed by the best known of his works, *The Canterbury Tales**, which may have occupied the last decade of Chaucer's life. It is unfinished, but unique among the medieval and renaissance* collections of tales in being not merely a collection but an artistic whole.

Through most of his life Chaucer was in the royal service; he was a court poet at a time when court society had not yet turned in upon itself, away from the wider interests of society. He thus drew his imaginative life from a wide range of sources, so that his poetry shows inclusiveness and variety both in its subject matter and in its approach to the subject matter; he knew the idiom and the passions of men and women from contrasting backgrounds, was at ease with them all, and wrote at a time when all shared in a closer community of values than later times knew. His knowledge of French and Italian literature was assisted by his travels in France and Italy on diplomatic missions for Richard II*, under whom he also occupied a number of administrative posts.
Bib: Lloyd, L. J., *A Chaucer Selection*; French, R. D., *Chaucer Handbook*; Speirs, J., *Chaucer the Maker*; Curry, W. C., *Chaucer and the Medieval Sciences*; Lewis, C. S., in *The Allegory of Love*.

Cheapside

A street in the City of London. In the Middle Ages it was the site of a busy market, and owed its name to the Old English word *céap*, 'to buy and sell'.

Chekhov, Anton Pavlovich (1860–1904) /tʃekof/

Russian dramatist and short story writer. In his last four plays (*Seagull*, *Uncle Vanya*, *Three Sisters*, *Cherry Orchard*) he evolved a dramatic form and idiom of dialogue which were highly original and had a great influence on 20th-C drama. His originality lay in his combination of faithfulness to the surface of life with poetic evocation of underlying experience. This he achieved partly by exploiting the character of human conversation when it seems to be engaged in communication, but is actually concerned with the incommunicable. This leads on to the non-communicating dialogue in the work of playwrights such as Beckett in France and Pinter in England, when the characters on the stage alternately baffle and enlighten the audience by the undercurrents implicit in their words. The realism of Chekhov's stories is similarly subtle and original; they have similar faithfulness to surface combined with delicate artistic pattern, giving significance to seeming irrelevance and slightness of incident. An outstanding exponent of the method in English is the New Zealand writer Katherine Mansfield*.

Bib: Magarshack, D., *The Plays of Anton Chekhov.*

Chelsea

A district in the West End of London, bordering the north side of the Thames, and well known for its literary and artistic associations. Sir Thomas More*, author of *Utopia*, lived there, and so did Thomas Carlyle*, the 'Sage of Chelsea'. In 19th C it became, and has remained, a centre for painters. Its most famous architectural monument is the Chelsea Hospital, designed by Christopher Wren* and founded as a home for disabled soldiers by Charles II*.

Cherub

In the Old Testament of the Bible (pl. cherubim(s)), angelic beings who in *Genesis* 3:24 guard Paradise; in *Ezekiel* 1 attend the divine chariot; in *1 Kings* 6 and 8 are pictured in Solomon's Temple. They are depicted with the wings of birds and with human or animal faces. In medieval Christian tradition they were held to be the second of the nine orders of angels. When classical influence widely affected Christian art in 16th and 17th C cherubs came to be represented as winged (bodiless heads of) children. They lost all grandeur of mystical and religious symbolism and were chiefly used as decorative motifs. They even become closely associated with the classical image of the child god of love, Cupid* used in a similar way as a decorative motif on furniture, walls, etc. In modern English usage a 'cherub' is commonly a way of referring to a pretty child.

Cheshire Cat

A grinning cat, best known as a character in Lewis Carroll's* *Alice's Adventures in Wonderland* (1865). The idiom 'to grin like a Cheshire cat' is an old one, however, though its origin cannot be satisfactorily explained.

Cheshire Cheese, The

A tavern off Fleet Street* in London, and a favourite resort of Ben Jonson*, and, after it was rebuilt, of Samuel Johnson. It still exists.

Chester Plays

* *Mystery Plays.*

Chesterfield, Philip Dormer, Lord (1694–1773)

Statesman, diplomatist, letter-writer. He is chiefly remembered as the last. His letters to his son were published in 1774 after the latter's death. They were intended to educate the son, Philip Stanhope, in good breeding and worldly wisdom, and their elegance, wit and fine descriptions have made them famous as a portrait of the age. They are outstanding examples of the golden age of English letter-writing. A similar body of letters to Chesterfield's godson (also a Philip Stanhope) were published in 1890. He was a man of high culture, a friend of the greatest poet of the age, Alexander Pope*, but antagonized the other literary giant, Samuel Johnson*, by his failure to act generously as a patron when Johnson was struggling to complete his Dictionary. Johnson's letter to him (quoted in Boswell's* *Life of Johnson*) is a classic of ironical comment on the system of literary patronage on which writers extensively relied until 19th C. Politically, Chesterfield is chiefly remembered for his brilliant administration of Ireland, 1745–6.

* *Letter Writing.*

Bib: Shellabarger, S., *Life*; Coxon, R., *Chesterfield and his Critics.*

Chesterton, Gilbert Keith (1874–1936)

An extremely versatile writer of essays, stories, novels, poems; G. K. Chesterton is best described as a polemicist, since polemics entered into everything he wrote, whether it was detective stories (the Father Brown series, 1911, 1914, 1926, 1927) or comic verse, or religious studies such as *St Francis of Assisi* (1923) or *Aquinas* (1933). He wrote against life-denial, whether manifested in the denial of humanity in Victorian political economy, or the sceptical withdrawal into aestheticism* of the 1890s. His basis of attack was a conviction that life is to be enjoyed with all the faculties; he also had the belief that such fullness of life required a religion large enough to comprehend all the spiritual and moral potentialities in man, and he found this religion in Roman Catholicism. He was not received into the Catholic Church until 1922, but from *The Napoleon of Notting Hill* (1904) – a fantasy about a war between London boroughs – he shows the romantic medievalism which for him was a large part of the appeal of Catholicism. The period of his greatest influence was probably between 1900 and 1914, when he belonged to a group of vigorous witty polemicists, including Shaw*, Wells*, Belloc*. He was from the first an ally of the Catholic Belloc against the agnostic socialists, Wells and Shaw. He had in common with both his antagonists a genius for vivid particularity strongly reminiscent of the Victorian novelist, Charles Dickens*; with Shaw he shared a delight in witty and disturbing paradox, which he used as Shaw did, to startle his readers out of the acceptance of platitudes into genuine thinking. In spite of his homely, zestful humanity, one notices nowadays a journalistic superficiality about Chesterton's work, as though he felt that his audience demanded entertainment as the indispensable reward for receiving enlightenment, and this may account for the neglect of his work since his death.

Politically, with Belloc, he preached an alternative to socialism in Distributism, a vision of a society of small proprietors. His critical work perhaps survives better than his other work; it included studies of Browning* (1903) Dickens (1906), Thackeray* (1909), Chaucer* (1932), and *The Victorian Age in Literature* (1913). He is otherwise perhaps best read in selection, for instance in the *Stories, Essays and Poems* (Everyman Series), or *An Anthology of Chesterton* (World's Classics).

Bib: Belloc, H., *The Place of Chesterton in English Letters*; Hollis, C., *G. K. Chesterton*; Ward, M., *Gilbert Keith Chesterton*; Evans, M., *G. K. Chesterton*.

Chevalier of St George /ʃevəˈliə/

'Chevalier' means literally horseman, and in medieval France was equivalent to knight. After the Revolution of 1688* and the Act of Settlement of 1701 excluding the Catholic members of the House of Stuart* from the English throne, James Stuart, the son of James II*, was known as the Chevalier of St George as a courtesy title; he was otherwise known as the Old Pretender* (*ie* claimant to the throne) in distinction from his son, Charles Stuart, known both as the Young Pretender and the Young Chevalier.

Chevy Chase, The Ballad of

A famous English ballad*, probably dating from 15th C. It issues from the border wars which were intermittent between England and Scotland from 14th to 16th C. Lord Douglas, head of the principal Scottish border family, attacks Percy*, Earl of Northumberland, who has defied him by coming for a three days' hunt on the Scottish side of the border. Both Percy and Douglas are killed in the ensuing battle. The ballad has been well-known since Bishop Percy published it in his *Reliques* in 1765, but, earlier, Addison* praised the poem in the *Spectator* (70), and so did Sidney* in his *Apologie*.

* *Otterbourne, the Battle of; Percy's Reliques.*

Child Labour

The use of children in agricultural labour was widespread, and not necessarily pernicious, up till 19th C, but their use in factories and mines after 1800 and during the Industrial Revolution* aroused widespread indignation and led to reform. The Factory Act of 1833 (**Factories*) limited their working hours in factories, and in 1847 their hours were restricted to ten. In 1842 the Mines Act forbade the employment of women and of children under 10 underground; this evil was very old, but had become much severer with the expansion of the coal industry in 18th C after the invention of steam-powered machinery. An old abuse, too, was the employment of little boys to clean chimneys; the boys were made to climb inside the chimneys. Public indignation against the practice was aroused by Charles Kingsley's *Water Babies** (1863), but it was only effectively prohibited in 1875. It was above all in the reign of Queen Victoria* that understanding of the nature and needs of children most rapidly developed

(**Children's Books*); the age saw the abolition of all the worst abuses of children, as well as the establishment of the first universal system of education in England. Since 1939 it has been illegal to employ children under 15.

Childe /tʃaild/

Before a name, *eg* Childe Harold, the word is the relic of a medieval title used for young men awaiting the order of knighthood*.

Childe Harold's Pilgrimage

A poem by Lord Byron*, written in Spenserian stanzas* and divided into four Cantos or parts. Cantos I and II were published in 1812, Canto III in 1816, and Canto IV in 1818. From the start, the poem is manifestly autobiographical, and in the fourth canto Byron abandons the fiction and writes in the first person. The subject is the wanderings through Europe of a young man seeking escape from his disgust and disillusionment with a life of pleasure at home. The first two cantos describe his wanderings round the Mediterranean, and end with a lament for Greece enslaved by the Turks. The third and fourth cantos are more concerned with events and people: in the third, Byron describes Brussels on the eve of Waterloo* – the description of the interrupted ball (stanzas XXI–XXV) is one of the most famous passages – and includes accounts of travels along the Rhine and in the Alps and Jura mountains; in the fourth he describes the great Italian cities of Venice, Rome and Florence, and great Italians such as Boccaccio*, Petrarch* and Tasso*. The first two, more 'romantic', cantos made Byron famous in his own time, and present, through Childe Harold, the image of the famous Byronic personality – self-regarding, proud, independent. In the last two the more balanced, critical Byron is present, still vivid and emotional, but more analytical and objective, as in the assessment of Napoleon* (III, XXXV-XLV) and of Rousseau* and Voltaire*.

* *Childe.*

Childe Roland to the Dark Tower Came

One of the most famous poems by Robert Browning*. He called it a 'Dramatic Romance' and it was published in *Men and Women**, 1855. It describes a journey or 'quest' (in the tradition of medieval knightly romances) which has lasted so long that Roland is almost in despair. In the poem, he reaches his destination, the tower, which stands in the middle of a great wasteland full of the signs of death. The poem ends with his sounding his horn to signal his arrival. In spite of its sombreness, the poem has a vigour of style, characteristic of Browning, which communicates itself as the most important part of its otherwise cloudy meaning. Browning, too often associated with facile optimism, is the poet here of courage and energy in the face of desperate circumstances.

The title is a quotation from Shakespeare's *King Lear**, where it may be an echo of a still older ballad.

Children in the Wood (*Babes in the Wood*)

A ballad (1595) well-known for its story which is often retold in books of children's fairy tales. It concerns the plot of a wicked uncle to murder his little nephew and niece, whose property he means to seize. The hired murderers abandon the children in the forest, where they perish and the birds cover them over with leaves. The wicked uncle is then punished by God, with the loss of his son, his wealth, and eventually his life.

Children's Books

Until 19th C, the child was not regarded as a being with its own kind of experience and values, different from those of adults, but as an imperfect adult. In so far as educated adults acknowledged that a child has his own world, this was confused with the world of the uneducated adult. The literature available to the child was thus that which circulated among the common people: popular versions of old romances such as *Bevis of Hampton**, magical folk-tales such as *Jack the Giant-Killer**, circulating in the chapbooks*. Such tales were read especially by children of the lower classes like the young John Bunyan, whose *Pilgrim's Progress** was not intended for children but appeals to them because it shows a childlike (as well as an extremely intelligent) imagination. In 18th C educated men developed that kind of interest in the past and in the primitive elements of society which is known as 'antiquarianism', and they collected ballads and folk-tales. French fairy stories, collected by Perrault*, were translated in 1729, and became popular as *Mother Goose's Fairy Tales*. The famous collection of German folk-tales, collected by the brothers Grimm*, was made later, and appeared in England as *German Popular Stories* in 1824.

Blake in his *Songs of Innocence** and Wordsworth* in the poems of his great decade (1788–1807) were the first English writers to recognize that childhood experience is a world of its own, the starting-point of the adult's world, yet in many ways superior to it, and by no means merely an imperfect version of it. They did not write for children, but at about the same time a fairly large literature for the child public began to grow up. Most of it, however, was written still with the idea that the child needed to be 'improved'. Some writers (*eg* Mrs Sherwood, author of *The Fairchild Family*, 1818) wanted to banish fairy-tales (such as Perrault's) as morally frivolous. Much of this 'improving literature' is nowadays regarded as comically ridiculous examples of ignorance of the child's mind; for instance, the cautionary tales in verse (1804 and after) by Anne and Jane Taylor are still remembered because they were brilliantly parodied by Hilaire Belloc* (in *The Bad Child's Book of Beasts*, etc.) a century later. Other writers, however, such as Thomas Day (*Sandford and Merton*, 1783–9) and Maria Edgeworth* (*Moral Tales*, 1801) combined the inculcation of moral principles with a real attempt to understand the child's nature. This more intelligent literature for children owed much to the novel *Émile*, on the subject of education, by the French thinker, Rousseau*.

It was not till the Victorian period* that writers began extensively to try to please children, without also attempting to improve them. Two of these wrote books that are nowadays admired still more by adults than they are by children: Edward Lear's* *Book of Nonsense* (1846) consists of verse fantasies of remarkable originality and humour; Lewis Carroll's* two prose fantasies, the *Alice* books (1865 and 1872), explore dream worlds with a verbal wit and inventiveness which has fascinated 20th-C imaginative writers, such as James Joyce*, who share the modern scientific interest in the workings of the unconscious mind. Romance and magic had a strong appeal to the Victorians, and fairy tales from all over the world were presented in versions for children, the most notable being the collections by Andrew Lang. The most remarkable fairy tales, however, were the original compositions by the Dane, Hans Andersen*, English translations of whose work were published in 1846. His strongly symbolic and poetic tales have had many British emulators, and his nearest equivalent in Britain is perhaps the Scottish writer George Macdonald (1824–1905). Another field of fiction for children appealed to the active and realistic tastes of boys. This drew especially on the tradition of travel-literature* (strong since Hakluyt* in 16th C), the literature of sea-life, and of desert islands – *Robinson Crusoe** was widely read by boys. Frederick Marryat's* *Masterman Ready* (1841) is a sea-story which became a minor classic; Robert Louis Stevenson's *Treasure Island** (1883), in the desert island tradition, is even better known. Charles Kingsley's *Water Babies** (1863) combines free fantasy comparable to Lear's and Carroll's with the robust style of story-telling that is closer to Marryat and Stevenson; at the same time, it preaches Christian morals and a social conscience and is thus in line with the 'improving' literature earlier in the century. Mrs Ewing (1841–85) and Mrs Molesworth (1839–1921) wrote delicately vivid, somewhat sentimental stories which are still read (*eg Lob-lie-by-the-fire* by the former and *The Tapestry Room* by the latter) in which the fantasy element is usually superior to the over-softened child characters; another woman writer, E. Nesbit (1858–1924) is still immensely popular owing to her realistically delineated children and her ingeniously interwoven realism and fantasy, *eg The Amulet*.

The Victorian period showed a dangerous tendency to become nostalgic about childhood, and to use children's literature as a release for fantasies which were really symptomatic of arrested development in the adult writer; of these, early in 20th C, James Barrie's stories about Peter Pan*, the boy who would never grow up, are the notorious example. Of this danger 20th-C children's writers have become increasingly aware; on the other hand, modern psychology tends to inhibit writers of children's stories from entering the child's world with the naive freedom and adult sensibility which gave the Victorians their rich distinctiveness. Some of the best books are by writers who show an ability to treat children as equals, in a way that was difficult for Victorians, while they continue to use a Victorian kind of fantasy, *eg* Phillipa Pearce in *Tom's Midnight Garden* (1958) and Mary Norton's *The Borrowers*. Another Victorian tradition survives in magical fantasy in the tradition of George Macdonald, for instance C. S. Lewis's *Tales of Narnia* and J. R. Tolkien's *The Hobbit*. The poet and story writer de la Mare*, in whom the childlike sensibility pervades equally his children's and his adult books, had a unique quality as a children's writer, especially of poems, *eg Peacock Pie* (1913).

Chiltern Hundreds

A region in the Chiltern Hills north of London belonging to the Crown. It is a rule that Members of Parliament may not resign between elections, and another rule precludes their holding offices of profit under the Crown. If a Member wishes to resign between elections, he applies for the Stewardship of the Chiltern Hundreds (to which no duties are now attached) and on receiving it, he becomes automatically disqualified from sitting in Parliament. The income from the office is now merely nominal.

Chimaera /kaiˈmiərə/

In Greek myth, a fire-breathing monster with the head of a lion, the body of a goat and the tail of a dragon. Considered to be the personification of a storm cloud.

* *Bellerophon*

Chippendale, Thomas (1718–79)

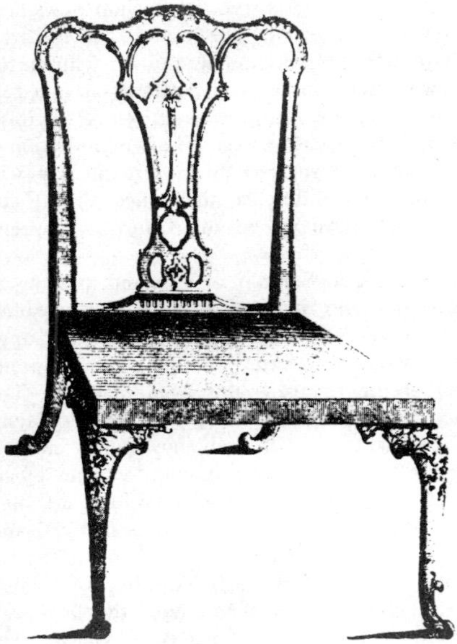

A famous furniture designer, noted for the combination of elegance and solidity in his designs. His work was very much imitated so that 'Chippendale style' is the most familiar pattern of 18th-C furniture in England.

* *Furnishings and Furniture.*

Chloe /ˈkləui/

In ancient Greek pastoral*, a name for a shepherdess, *eg Daphnis and Chloe* (2nd C AD). In 17th and 18th C mock-pastoral, the name was sometimes given to disguise actual ladies when they were referred to in poetry or prose, *eg* Pope uses the name for Lady Suffolk in *Moral Essays** ii.

Cholera

A deadly disease flourishing in dirty living conditions and bad sanitation. The rapid and insanitary growth of industrial towns in England in the first half of 19th C (the Industrial Revolution*) led to its first occurrence here in 1832; it came again in 1848. The threat of it accelerated the improvement of sanitation in English towns, but slums were not eliminated in the 19th C, and it continued to be feared. However the last visitation in 1892–5 caused so few deaths that by then it was clear that the danger had been mastered.

Chrétien de Troyes (12th C)

A French compiler of Arthurian legends, and a main source for the versions of them in Middle English, *eg* his *Perceval* is partly the basis for *Sir Gawain and the Green Knight**. *Perceval* is part of his *Conte du Graal*, which is a source for the grail* quest stories, as told, for instance, by Sir Thomas Malory in *Morte d'Arthur**. His *Le Chevalier de la Charrette* concerns the adventures of Lancelot*, and his *Chevalier au Lion* those of Yvain (Gawain).

* *Arthur*

Christabel

An unfinished narrative poem by S. T. Coleridge*. He wrote the first part in 1797 and the second in 1800; it was published in 1816. The story has the characteristics familiar from the popular folk-ballad tradition: Christabel, daughter of Sir Leoline, finds a distressed lady in the woods and takes her back to the castle. The lady, Geraldine, is really an evil enchantress. Christabel discovers her evil nature, but is forced by a spell to keep silent. *Christabel* is written in lines with four stresses and varying numbers of syllables, the length altering like the rhythmic beat with the variations of mood in the poem. This variation is suggested and licensed by the ballad-like matter of the poem; but, as with the *Ancient Mariner**, the supernatural element has the power of a highly sophisticated intellect behind it. *Christabel*, by comparison with Coleridge's other masterpiece, suffers from being uncompleted, but it, too, vividly actualizes a visionary, supernatural theme.

Christian King, Most (His Most Christian Majesty)

A title assumed by the kings of France from not later than 15th C. (Compare: 'Most Catholic King' for the kings of Spain, 'Defender of the Faith' for kings of England.)

Christmas

The Christian festival of the birth of Jesus Christ.

The Festival is close to the date of the winter solstice (shortest day of the year), when there were pagan festivals in many countries in pre-Christian times. The pagan customs survived into Christian times, and many still survive in a more or less Christianized form. Thus the modern habit of decorating the home with green vegetation, especially holly and mistletoe, goes back to the ancient Romans decorating their temples with greenery for the Saturnalia*, the ancient Britons picking the sacred plant mistletoe with its white berries, and the Anglo-Saxons using holly with its red ones. In northern countries, huge fires were burned to strengthen the failing sun-god; this survived in England in the burning of the yule log – abandoned in these days of small grates, electric fires, and central heating. Christmas trees are said to date from the conversion of Germany by the English missionary, St Boniface (680–755), who in honour of Christ substituted the fir tree for the sacred oak dedicated to Odin. The Christmas tree was introduced into England only in 19th C, when the German Prince Albert* became the husband of Queen Victoria*. These pagan elements in Christmas made it an occasion for secular merry-making as well as religious rejoicing. In the Middle Ages the festival lasted for twelve days (until Epiphany on 6 January, commemorating the coming of the Magi*). Lords of Misrule were appointed, as symbols of the reign of licensed abandon; special food was prepared, of which the Christmas pudding and the roast turkey are modern survivals. The 17th-C Puritans*, with their insistence on the strict austerity of religious observance, strongly disapproved of such merry-making, and when they achieved power they suppressed it by law (Act of 1644). The old customs were restored however with the Restoration* of the monarchy in 1660; and the strong, secular element in Christmas has if anything become more and more marked. For example, the first Christmas cards (in the 1840s) illustrated Christmas puddings rather than the birth of Christ. Father Christmas, the old man with a white beard and a red cloak, who drives his reindeer over the rooftops on the night before Christmas day, descends chimneys and fills children's stockings with toys, is thought of as a purely fairy tale figure, though his other name, Santa Claus (contraction from St Nicholas*, the patron saint of children), shows a derivation with religious associations. The modern conception of 'the Christmas spirit' owes much to the celebration of it in novels and stories by the young Charles Dickens*, in the 1830s and 40s.

* *Festivals.*

Christmas Carol, A (1843)

A story by Charles Dickens*, about a miser, Scrooge, who is converted by a series of visions from a condition of mercantile avarice and misanthropy into an embodiment of the Christmas spirit, with its generosity and good will to men in general. By no means one of the best of Dickens's works, it nonetheless represents entertainingly his celebration of the virtues associated with Christmas (especially characteristic of his early work). He represented these virtues as the cure for the puritan narrowness of feeling and inhumanity of outlook which were the dark side of Victorian commerce. Compare the Christmas scenes in his *Pickwick Papers** (1837).

Christmas Carols

* *Carol.*

Christy Minstrels

Any company of entertainers disguised as negroes, usually singing comic songs. The original band was founded by George Christy of New York (19th C).

Chronicle Plays

* *History Plays.*

Church of England

The Middle Ages. In this period, the Church in England was a division of the Catholic Church of Western Europe. Ultimate authority over it, as over the rest of the Catholic Church, was vested in the Pope in Rome, though in practice the English king shared authority with the Pope, inasmuch as the clergy were his subjects except in spiritual matters. These clergy consisted of an order of priests who, at the humblest level, had in their charge the village churches and the parishes (each more or less coincident with a village) that surrounded them. The parishes were grouped into regions known as 'sees', each of which was governed by a bishop, and the sees (bishoprics) were grouped into two provinces under two archbishops, those of Canterbury and York, the Archbishop of Canterbury being the senior. The bishops and the archbishops attended Parliament, and the Church had its own assemblies or convocations, attended by the senior clergy and representatives of the lower clergy, *ie* the parish priests. This organization of the Church has survived to the present day, with the important difference that since 16th C the Pope has ceased to be the Church's supreme authority.

16th C. The Church of England became an independent organization in 1534, when Henry VIII* caused Parliament to pass the Act of Supremacy* which declared him to be the 'Supreme Head of the English Church and Clergy'. This action was political rather than religious; Henry was conservative in his religious beliefs, and reaffirmed the traditional Catholic doctrines by his Act of the Six Articles (1539). However, a Protestant* party, influenced by the German reformer Martin Luther*, had long been growing in England and was favoured by the Archbishop of Canterbury, Thomas Cranmer*. Under the boy King Edward VI*, the Protestants seized power, and Catholic doctrine was modified by Cranmer's two Books of Common Prayer*. These changes were accompanied by the destruction of images and the covering up of holy wall-paintings in village churches; such actions, combined with the rapacity of the nobles who seized church money, were unpopular, and partly reconciled the nation to a return to the Catholic Church under Mary I*. She too, however, became unpopular owing to her persecution of Protestants, and her successor, Elizabeth I*, attempted a compromise Settlement, by means of which she hoped to keep in the Church of England both the Catholics and the extremer Protestants. She succeeded, in so far as her Settlement prevented religious conflict breaking into civil war during her reign. On the other hand, she failed in that the Pope forbade English Roman Catholics to worship in the Church of England, and the extreme Protestants – now for the first time called Puritans* – continued to agitate for further reforms, although they did not yet establish independent churches. Her Settlement was, however, popular with the majority of her subjects.

17th C. The Roman Catholics were and remained a small minority, but the Puritans grew in numbers and determination, especially in the south and east of England, with particular strength in London. Their political convictions, their dislike of religious direction by bishops, and their desire for simple forms of worship without ceremonial, were all in accord, and in the Civil War* they were able to overthrow the king, Charles I*. Under the Protectorship of the Puritan Oliver Cromwell*, all forms of Protestant belief and worship were tolerated, but the Church of England ceased to exist as a state religious organization. In 1660 the monarchy and the Church of England were restored, and the Act of Uniformity* and other laws during the reign of Charles II* excluded the Puritans from the Church of England, from political rights (*ie* the parliamentary vote, election to Parliament, and the holding of public office) and from attendance at the Universities of Oxford and Cambridge. The test imposed on them was acceptance of the Thirty-Nine Articles* of religious belief laid down under Elizabeth I. Puritans now became increasingly known as Dissenters* or Nonconformists; they proceeded to set up their independent Churches such as exist at the present day. Within the Church, religious differences remained, and were the basis of the political parties that now first arose: the Whigs were more in sympathy with the Puritans, and the Tories were nearer to the Roman Catholics, from whom they nevertheless sharply distinguished themselves.

18th C. For about a century, the Church was dominated by the political outlook of the state, and was a passive, conservative force in society and politics. In the middle of 18th C this passivity, and a growing coolness among the Nonconformists, caused a religious revival, chiefly active among the poorer classes and led by John Wesley*. Wesley did not originally intend to separate his followers from the Church of England, but his choice of clergy proved unacceptable to the Church. The Wesleyan Methodists thus formed the last and largest of the Nonconformist Churches. However, Wesley's example inspired some Anglicans* to revive religious fervour within the Church of England. This revival became known as the Evangelical Movement*, which by 19th C was making an impact on the state by its advocacy of various kinds of social reform.

19th and 20th C. In the 1830s, some Anglicans, led by a group at Oxford University of whom the most active was John Henry Newman*, grew alarmed at the power of the state over Church affairs. The resulting Oxford (or Tractarian) Movement* affirmed the spiritual independence of the Church, and their resistance to the state led them to insist on the continuity of the Church of England with the medieval Catholic Church, in spite of the break made by the 16th-C Reformation*. They were able to do this the more easily because Henry VIII had preserved the essentials of Catholic belief, because his daughter Elizabeth I had been deliberately vague in some of her prescriptions for belief and worship, and because the great leaders of the Church in the reigns of James I and Charles II had been eloquent exponents of this continuity with Catholicism. Newman eventually became a Roman Catholic, and the Oxford Movement lost in him its main inspiration. He left behind him, however, divisions of opinion within the Church that exist today: the High Church is composed of Anglicans who are essentially Catholic in belief, though they reject the authority of the Pope; they can be said to be descendants from Henry VIII's Reformation. The Low Church feels itself to be Protestant, and can be said to favour the Reformation of Edward VI. A third group, prominent in mid-19th C but not to be distinguished now, was the Broad Church; it developed from the Evangelical Movement and was especially active in social and political reform. These have all existed under the common organization of the Church.

Today, the Church of England is the state Church, under the Crown, only in England; in Scotland, Wales, the Commonwealth, and the U.S.A., members of churches originally derived from the Church of England are known as Episcopalians*.

The history of the Church of England is closely bound up with the political and social history of England: not only have the divisions within it given rise to the political parties (Whigs and Tories becoming Liberals and Conservatives respectively) but social divisions have tended to follow a parallel development, the upper classes being more sympathetic to the High Church, and the lower classes more likely to follow the Low Church, or Nonconformists.

Cibber, Colley (1671–1757) /ˈsibə/

Comic actor and dramatist, very popular in his own day; now chiefly of historical importance as one of the innovators of a comedy of sentiment, in reaction against the cynical comedy of the Restoration* wits. For instance, in his *Love's Last Shift* (1696) his dissolute hero is brought to virtue by the devotion of his wife, thus satisfying an emotional wish in his increasingly middle-class audience. Cibber was a skilled craftsman but no artist: his sentiment no longer carries conviction. His success in spite of his limitations, together with his disparagement of some other writers, may have been the cause of the hostility he aroused among now more famous men: Pope, who made him hero of the second version of his satire *The Dunciad**, Swift*, Fielding* and Johnson*. It is chiefly through the attacks made on him by these writers that he is now known to the general reader. However, the sentimental comedy had its importance as being one of the forerunners of the novel of sentiment (*eg* Richardson's *Pamela**). His memoirs (*An Apology for the Life of Colley Cibber*, 1740) contain valuable insights into the theatre of his time.

Cicero, Marcus Tullius (106–43 BC) /ˈsisərəu/

Roman statesman, and writer on rhetoric, politics and philosophy. Politically he is famous for his vigorous resistance to the conspiracy of Catiline against the government of the Republic. This is the theme of Ben Jonson's tragedy *Catiline**, of which Cicero is the hero. Cicero's mastery of eloquence in his various writings, and his prestige in ancient Rome, caused him to be much admired in the Middle Ages and afterwards. Cicero's *Somnium Scipionis* (*Dream of Scipio*) influenced Chaucer's *Parliament of Fowls**, and in 16th C the growing body of English prose writers, such as Roger Ascham*, tended to take as a model either the rolling, musical sentences of Cicero or, by contrast, the terse pointed sentences of Seneca*. Cicero's work, especially his letters, was always a central subject of study (chiefly for stylistic reasons) so long as the Latin classics remained dominant in English education, *ie* until well into 19th C.

CID /ˈsi:aiˈdi:/

Criminal Investigation Department of police force, especially that of the London Metropolitan Police in Scotland Yard, whose experts are always available to help other forces.

Cimmerian /siˈmiəriən/

A race known to ancient Greek writers (*eg* Homer* and Herodotus*) and supposed to live in constant darkness (hence such phrases as 'Cimmerian gloom').

Cinderella

A widespread fairy tale, known in English from its version by the French collector of fairy tales, Charles Perrault*, whose work was translated into English in about 1729. Cinderella means the 'little cinder girl', because in the story she is made to do all the hard work of the house by her cruel elder step-sisters, and is dirty with the ashes of the fire. Aided by her fairy godmother, she wins a prince in marriage. Cinderella is widely thought of as the symbolic representative of people who are unjustly neglected and persecuted contrary to their real merits.

Circe /ˈsə:si/

In Greek myth, a sorceress who lived in the island of Aeaea. In Homer's *Odyssey**, she changed the companions of Odysseus into swine. Odysseus himself, protected against her by the magic herb moly*, forced her to restore them, but nonetheless he lived with her for a year, forgetting his wife and family.

Circulating Libraries

A library from which books may be borrowed. Such libraries were in private hands in 18th C and subsisted on subscriptions from clients. The first circulating library started in 1740, and as the institution spread so the reading public greatly increased. It was the more important since, apart from chapbooks*, books were very expensive in 18th C. Q. D. Leavis gives a valuable account of their influence in her *Fiction and the Reading Public*.

Citizen Comedies

Comedies, especially between 1600 and 1640, using contemporary London and its middle class as their setting, *eg* Ben Jonson's *Bartholomew Fair** (1614), Middleton's *A Chaste Maid in Cheapside** (1611), and Massinger's *The City Madam** (1632).

City, The

The customary way of referring to the oldest and most central part of London*, occupied now chiefly by commercial offices, and with only a small resident population. The term is also used to designate collectively the chief financial institutions of the country, situated there, such as the Bank of England* and the Stock Exchange*. Despite its smallness, the Lord Mayor of the City of London has outstanding importance as a ceremonial representative in the nation for business and commercial interests.

City Madam, The (1632)

A comedy by Philip Massinger*. It is about a London merchant whose wife and daughters grow outrageously extravagant in their tastes. To teach them a lesson, the father, Sir John Frugal, temporarily retires from the world and leaves his affairs in the hands of his hypocritically humble brother, Luke. Once he has power in his hands, Luke throws off his pretence, becomes arrogant and harsh, and humiliates his nieces and sister-in-law. Like so many comedies of the age, *The City Madam* ridicules the extravagance and pretentiousness of the new urban bourgeoisie.

City of Destruction, The

In Bunyan's *Pilgrim's Progress** the town from which the pilgrim, Christian, flees to the Celestial City, *ie* Heaven. The City of Destruction stands for the world divorced from spiritual values, doomed to the destruction that is to overcome all the merely material creation.

City of Dreaming Spires

Oxford, from a description in Matthew Arnold's* poem, *Thyrsis*.

City of Seven Hills

Rome, said to be built on seven hills, *ie* the Palatine, Aventine, Capitoline, Caelian, Esquiline, Viminal, and Quirinal.

Civil Wars, English and American

England has had two periods of Civil War:

[1] The more important, in 17th C, also called the Great Rebellion. It was fought between the king (Charles I*) and Parliament, and divided into the First Civil War (1642–6) ending with the parliamentary victory at Naseby (1645) and the capitulation of Oxford (1646), the royalist capital. The Second Civil War (1648–51) also ended with parliamentary victory, this time over the Scots, who had been the allies of Parliament in the First Civil War, but took the king's side in the Second. The issues were complicated; simplified, the economic interests of the urban middle classes coincided with their religious (Puritan*) ideology, and conflicted with the traditional economic interests of the Crown, correspondingly allied with Anglican* religious belief. *See also* 1.3.1.2.

[2] The other period of civil war occurred in 15th C and is usually known as the Wars of the Roses*.

The American Civil War, or War of Secession (1861–5) was fought on the issue of whether the southern states of the United States had the right to secede from the Union and establish their independence. Their wish to do so arose from the northern opposition to the slave holding on which the southern landed economy was based.

Clare, John (1793–1864)

Poet. The son of a farm labourer in the midlands. He had a limited success with his earlier work, but his publisher tried to impose on him a literary sophistication which did not accord with Clare's own freshness and originality. In 1837 he became insane and spent the remainder of his life in lunatic asylums, where he continued to write. Earlier work: *Poems Descriptive of Rural Life* (1820); *The Village Minstrel* (1821); *The Shepherd's Calendar** (1827); *The Rural Muse* (1835). In 20th C Clare's reputation has grown extensively, and hitherto unpublished work has appeared: *Poems of Madness*, ed. G. Grigson (1949); E. Robinson and G. Summerfield's *The Later Poems* (1964); in addition to the *Poems* ed. J. W. Tibble (1935). The poetry is mostly of natural scenery and rural life, and at its best has remarkably close observation, freshness of diction, and poignancy of feeling. No other poetry of the period (including Wordsworth's*) shows such sensitive and intimate experience of the English countryside.

Bib: Tibble, J. W. and A., *Life*; the same authors have made a Selection with an introduction. Other selections with introductions by G. Grigson and J. Reeves.

Clare, Order of St

A Clare is a member of an order of nuns founded by St Clare in about 1212 in imitation of the Franciscan* Order. Often called 'the poor Clares.'

Clarendon, Edward Hyde, Earl of (1609–74)

Statesman and historian; author of *The True Historical Narrative of the Rebellion and Civil Wars in England*, about the Civil War*, during which he had supported King Charles I*. The published history combines two separate manuscripts: a history written 1646–8 while the events were fresh in his mind, and an autobiography written between 1668 and 1670 in exile and without the aid of documents. In consequence, Books I–VII are superior in accuracy to Books VIII–XV, with the exception of Book IX, containing material written in 1646. Besides its unevenness in accuracy, the history suffers from Clarendon's inability to understand the real issues of the war, and the point of view of his opponents. Nonetheless, Clarendon's History is a literary classic because of its series of portraits of the participants in the war. His book is a notable contribution to the rise of the arts of biography and autobiography in England in 17th C, and contributed to the attitude to reality which in 18th C produced the first English novels.

As a statesman, Hyde was at first a leading opponent of Charles I, but his strongly Anglican* faith led him to take the Royalist side shortly before the war. He became one of the king's chief advisers. He followed the royal court into exile, and was Lord Chancellor and Charles II's* chief minister at the Restoration* (1660). The king's brother, the future James II*, married his daughter, so that he became grandfather of Queen Mary II and Queen Anne. He was made the scapegoat for the unpopularity of Charles II's government in its early years, however, and was driven into exile in 1667. He lived the remainder of his life in France.

* *Histories and Chronicles*

Bib: Huehns, G., *Selections from the History of the Rebellion and the Life*; Wormald, B. H. G., *Clarendon, Politics, History and Rebellion*; Firth, C., *Essays, Historical and Literary*

Claret

* *Wine.*

Clarissa (1747–48) /klə'risə/

A novel by Samuel Richardson*, and his masterpiece. It is slow-moving, of great length, and composed in the form of letters passing especially between Clarissa Harlowe and her friend Miss Howe*, and between the villain Robert Lovelace* and his friend John Belford. Clarissa's mercenary family want her to marry a repulsive man of their choice for their financial convenience; she resists with the aid of Lovelace, who, however, is a complete cynic about feminine virtue, and has made a vocation of seduction. Her virtue is exemplary and she resists him steadfastly even when he succeeds in carrying her off and keeping her captive and completely deceived about the nature of her surroundings and all her circumstances. Eventually he succeeds in raping her when she is drugged. She dies of shame and Lovelace is killed in a duel. Lovelace's viciousness is partly a protest against the profound sexual hypocrisy of the age, and Clarissa's chastity is partly a matter of self-deception; thus his unnatural villainy and her rigorous virtue are made to a great extent convincing, though the main characters lack the complexity of later novelists' work. The other characters and the clashing viewpoints of both the major and minor ones are graphically presented through the various epistolary styles.

* 4.3.2.

Classic, Classics, Classical

These words are apt to cause confusion. A classic is a work of outstanding merit and permanent value in its class or kind, *eg David Copperfield** is a classic. 'Classics' is the study of ancient Greek and Latin literature. 'Classic' is used as an adjective as well as a noun, *eg* Dickens wrote many classic novels. 'Classical' is mainly used as the adjective for 'classics', *eg* classical scholarship.

Classical Education and English Literature

Classical education is based on the study of the 'classics', *ie* the literature of ancient Greece and Rome, principally from Homer* to the great Latin poets and prose writers (*eg* Virgil*, Ovid*, Cicero*) of 1st C BC – 1st C AD. Latin is more closely bound up with western history and culture, and is the easier language for English speakers to study; consequently it has been more widely used in schools than Greek, and it has been studied at earlier stages of education. Roman literary culture was, however, based on that of the Greeks.

Medieval Europe (Christendom) grew out of the ruins of the western Roman Empire; the Church, like the Empire, was still ruled from Rome; its philosophy was deeply influenced by the Greek philosophers, and its language continued to be Latin. The Church controlled the universities, and the classics were the basis of medieval university education, especially that part of it known as the 'Trivium' – grammar, rhetoric and logic. Nonetheless, many of the Greek and Roman writers were known principally through inferior versions of their texts, and they were valued chiefly in so far as the Church could use them for its own purposes.

The movement known as the Renaissance* started in Italy in 14th C; it was, first of all, the enthusiastic rediscovery and collection by scholars of ancient classical texts, and the development of new and more accurate methods of studying them. It did not long remain merely a scholarly movement; the scholars influenced the writers and artists, and these in turn, in 15th and 16th C, aroused enthusiasm in the upper classes of all western Europe. The Renaissance practice of studying the classics for their own sake, and not under the direction of the Church, was like the recovery of Europe's youth, and the discovery of a new principle of growth in literature and the other arts. To be civilized meant to have classical learning, and to become instructed in the classical styles of architecture and sculpture; for gentlemen, such education became indispensable.

The Renaissance first seriously affected England early in 16th C. Scholarship was influenced first; imaginative literature was strongly influenced only in the second half of the century, and the other arts were affected more gradually still. The pattern for classical education in the national public schools and the more local grammar schools was formed by such men as John Colet (1467?–1519), High Master of St Paul's School. Sir Thomas More*, author of *Utopia* and Chancellor to Henry VIII*, gave prestige to humanist* values in the royal court. Erasmus* visited England from Holland and made friends among these and other English humanists; his liberal, reasonable, witty and critical mind typified Renaissance enlightenment – free and yet disciplined, serious without superstition, scholarly and at the same time courtly.

But ancient Greece, and Rome in its greatest days, were pagan; their values were social rather than religious. Thus there was the possibility of divided loyalty between the Rome that was the starting-point of so much European art, thought and politics, and the later Rome that was the centre of the originally Hebrew and very unclassical religion of Christianity. The Roman Catholic Church in 15th and early 16th C at first responded to the humanists favourably, even when they were critical of its traditions and practices. The thought and outlook of pagan Greece and Rome nevertheless did not agree well with the ancient Hebrew roots of Christianity as shown in the Old and New Testaments of the Bible. The 16th-C Protestant Reformation* was partly the outcome of humanist criticism of the Church, but it was also a return to the Word of God as the Bible displayed it. Thus, from 1560 to 1660, much English imaginative writing has two aspects: the poets Spenser* and Milton*, for example, have a Protestant aspect, which is biblical and Hebraic; and a classical aspect, strongly inspired by the classical Renaissance. The poet Ben Jonson* is much more classical than Protestant, while George Herbert* is strongly religious in the moderately Protestant, Anglican* tradition, and despises the kind of subject matter (*eg* 'classical pastoral') which Ben Jonson accepted. Both, however, had an equally classical education.

Another division arose from the difference between native literary traditions, which continued in their non-classical character, and the classical qualities and standards which many writers felt should permeate and regulate the native tradition. This division did not correspond to religious differences: the most Latin of all English poets is the Puritan*, John Milton. Shakespeare is well-known for his indifference to the classical 'rules' which critics like Sir Philip Sidney* thought necessary to good drama, while his contemporary, Ben Jonson, favoured them, though not slavishly.

Classical and native traditions of literature rivalled and nourished each other until the middle of 17th C, and so did Protestant biblical and secular classical philosophies of life. But after the Restoration* in 1660, religious passions declined and sceptical rationalism began to take their place. Scientific rationalism – the discipline of prose appealing to reason as opposed to the discipline of poetry appealing to the imagination – was congenial to classical scholarship and the rationalism of Greek and Latin philosophy. Thus began the most classical period of English art and literature, the so-called Augustan* age of 18th C. Yet within their neo-classical horizon, the best English writers even of this period retained strong elements of native idiom; this is true of the poets, Dryden* and Pope*, and of the prose writers Swift* and Samuel Johnson*.

The French Revolution* of 1789 was the outcome of 18th C reason, criticism, and scepticism, but it challenged the 18th-C classical qualities of order, intellectual proportion and balance, and the view of man as fulfilled only in a civilized structure of society. The English Romantic* Movement was partly an outcome of the French Revolution; it challenged many of the classical values, attaching more importance to the cultivation of the feelings of the individual than to the cultivation of the reason of man in society; it rediscovered the Middle Ages, which for three centuries had been despised as 'gothic', *ie* barbarous. At the same time, that part of English society which had always been more biblical than classical in its culture – the commercial middle classes – was now stronger (thanks to the Industrial Revolution*) than it had ever been before. So we find the critic Matthew Arnold*, in his *Culture and Anarchy* (1869) distinguishing between two categories of mind in contemporary society: the majority were the 'Hebraizers', who devoted themselves to the virtues of private conduct and practical achievement; the 'Hellenizers', like himself, valued contemplation, reason, and critical discrimination. England, he considered, was becoming barbarous owing to the preponderance of the former over the latter.

Since Arnold, classical education has lost its long-held place in the centre of education. One cause of this displacement is the strong need in our time for scientific and technical training; another, the increased attention to modern languages in consequence of closer communications with other lands; a third cause is the increased understanding of our own culture and its history. Thus we have educational disciplines that are the equals and rivals of the old classical disciplines. But a deeper cause still is the democratization of education; this has led to the importance of 'vocational' training for particular trades and professions, and also to the decline of the ideal of the 'gentleman'*. When education (beyond elementary stages) was the privilege of the upper classes, *ie* until the later 19th C, its purpose was to shape the completely cultured man, and for this purpose the classics were in many ways admirably suited. Nowadays, not only do the upper classes have to compete with the poorer ones for positions in the professions and industry, but the complexity of our civilization is such that 'the completely cultured man' has become an impossible ideal.

Classical Mythology

Ancient Greek mythology can be divided between the 'Divine Myths' and the 'Heroic Myths'.

The divine myths are known in differing versions from the works of various Greek poets, of whom the most notable are Homer and Hesiod. Hesiod explained the origin of the world in terms of a marriage between Earth (Ge or Gaea) and Sky (Uranus). Their children were the 12 Titans: Oceanus, Crius, Iapetus, Theia, Rhea, Mnemosyne, Phoebe, Tethys, Themis, Coeus, Hyperion, and Cronos. Cronos overthrew his father, and he and Rhea became the parents of the 'Olympian gods', so called from their association with the sacred mountain Olympus*. The Olympians, in their turn, overthrew Cronos and the other Titans.

The chief Olympians were Zeus and his queen Hera. The other gods and goddesses were the offspring of either, but as Zeus was usually at war with Hera, they were not the joint parents. They seem to have been seen as male and female aspects of the sky; their quarrels were the causes of bad weather and cosmic disturbances. The principal offspring of Zeus were Apollo, Artemis, Athene, Aphrodite (sometimes represented as a daughter of Uranus out of the sea), Dionysus, Demeter, Hermes, and Ares. Zeus also had two brothers: Poseidon who ruled the sea, and Hades who ruled the underworld. In 3rd C BC the Olympian gods were adopted by the Romans, who used the Latin names more commonly used by later European writers. Uranus, Apollo, and some others remained the same. Gaea became Tellus; Cronos = Saturn; Zeus = Jupiter (or Jove); Hera = Juno; Athene = Minerva; Artemis = Diana; Hermes = Mercury; Ares = Mars; Hephaestus = Vulcan; Aphrodite = Venus (and her son Eros = Cupid); Demeter = Ceres; Poseidon = Neptune. There were numerous minor deities such as nymphs and satyrs in both Greek and Roman pantheons.

The Olympian deities mingled with men, and rivalled one another in deciding human destinies. They concerned themselves particularly with the destinies of the heroes, *ie* those men, sometimes partly divine by parentage, who were remarkable for the kinds of excellence which are especially valued in primitive societies, such as strength (Heracles), or cunning (Odysseus). Each region of Greece had its native heroes, though the greatest heroes were famous in legend all over Greece. The most famous of all was Heracles (in Latin, Hercules) who originated in Thebes. Other leading examples of hero are: Theseus (Athens); Sisyphus and Bellerophon (Corinth); Perseus (Argolis); the Dioscuri, *ie* Castor and Pollux (Laconia); Oedipus (Thebes); Achilles (Thessaly); Jason (Thessaly); Orpheus (Thrace). Like the Greek gods and goddesses, the Greek heroes were adopted by Roman legend, sometimes with a change of name – for instance Odysseus became Ulysses (or, in the correct form, Ulixes). The minor hero of Greek legend, Aeneas, was raised to be the great ancestral hero of the Romans, and they had other heroes of their own, such as Romulus, the founder of Rome, and his brother Remus.

The classical deities and heroes lived on in European literature through the Middle Ages to the present day. After the downfall of the Roman Empire of the West, they no longer had the vitality of universal racial or popular folk myths, although the science of astrology, until it fell into disrepute in 17th C, gave them a kind of popular reality through the planets and zodiacal signs which are named after them, and which, according to astrologers, influence human fates. Thus in Chaucer's

*The Knight's Tale**, Mars, Venus, Diana and Saturn occur, and owe their force in the poem as much to medieval astrology as to classical legend. Otherwise their survival has depended chiefly on their importance in the works of the classical poets, such as Homer, Hesiod, Virgil* and Ovid*, who have meant so much to European culture. In Britain, important poets translated and thus helped to 'naturalize' the great Greek and Latin poems; *eg* Gavin Douglas* in 16th C and Dryden* in 17th C translated Virgil's *Aeneid**; Chapman* in 16th C and Pope* in 18th C translated Homer's epics. In 16th and 17th C, poets used major and minor classical deities to adorn and elevate poems intended chiefly as gracious entertainment, and occasionally they added deities of their own invention.

While European culture was understood as a more or less distinct system of values, the poets used classical deities and heroes deliberately and objectively. In 19th C, however, the deep disturbance of European beliefs and values caused European writers to use classical myth more subjectively, as symbols through which they tried to express their personal doubts, struggles, and beliefs. Thus John Keats in his unfinished epic *Hyperion** tried to emulate Milton's great Christian epic, *Paradise Lost**, but instead of Christian myth he used the war of the Olympian gods and the Titans to embody his sense of the tragedy of human experience. Tennyson* wrote dramatic monologues in which personifications of Greek heroes (*eg* Ulysses, Tithonus, Tiresias in poems named after them) recounted the experiences associated with them in classical (or, in the case of Ulysses, medieval) legend, in such a way as to express the emotional conflicts of a man like Tennyson himself. In 20th C, writers have used figures from the classical myths differently again; they are introduced to establish the continuity of the emotions and attitudes characteristic of modern men with emotions and attitudes of men in the past. It is thus that T. S. Eliot* uses Tiresias in his poem *The Waste Land**, and James Joyce uses the Odysseus myth in his novel *Ulysses**. In a comparable way, modern psychologists have used the Greek myths as symbolic expressions of basic psychological conflicts in human beings in all periods. Freud's theory of the Oedipus complex is the most famous of these reinterpretations.

* Classical deities and heroes under their Greek names.

Claudius /'klo:djəs/

[1] The Roman Emperor (AD 41–54) who began the systematic conquest of Britain. Subject of the novels by Robert Graves*, *I, Claudius* and *Claudius the God*.

[2] King of Denmark in Shakespeare's *Hamlet**. He mounts the throne after secretly murdering his brother, young Hamlet's father, and he marries Hamlet's mother. At the opening of the play, young Hamlet does not know that his father's sudden death was due to murder, but he is disgusted by the situation on three counts: Claudius's marriage with his sister-in-law is technically incestuous according to the law of the time, besides indicating lack of due grief on the part of his mother, and Hamlet himself should naturally have succeeded to the throne, although the law of succession was elective in Denmark. It is not until scene v of Act I that Hamlet learns, from his father's ghost, that his uncle is a murderer.

Claudius differs from most evil men portrayed by Shakespeare and by his contemporaries. In contrast to Iago in *Othello**, Macbeth, and Richard III, he is scarcely shown to be evil by direct enactment. We hear of the murder at second hand, from the Ghost; Claudius's own confession of wickedness in the chapel (III.iii) excites the audience's compassion rather than their indignation, since his remorse is so evident; his conspiracies against his nephew are in self-defence, since he knows that Hamlet is plotting revenge. The fact that Claudius is not self-evidently a cruel tyrant is one of the features that differentiates *Hamlet* from other Revenge Tragedies* of the period; dramatically, it helps to make intelligible Hamlet's doubt and hesitancy in carrying out his revenge.

Clayhanger (1910)

One of the best novels by Arnold Bennett*. It is the first of a series, later published as *The Clayhanger Family* (1925), consisting of *Clayhanger*, *Hilda Lessways*, and *These Twain*. Its setting is Bennett's characteristic one: that part of the industrial west Midlands known as the Five Towns or the Potteries, where the ceramics industry has its centre. The period of the story is the later 19th C.

Until Bennett wrote, there had been remarkably little fiction centred in industrial, urban England outside London. Elizabeth Gaskell in *Mary Barton** and *North and South** Dickens in *Hard Times**, George Eliot in *Felix Holt**, had all written about the social problems of industrialization in northern towns, but neither they nor any other considerable novelist had attempted to convey the texture of daily life in large industrial towns as Bennett did. He thus inaugurated a new setting for the English novel, one which was also used by D. H. Lawrence* (in *The Lost Girl*) and by a number of novelists since 1945, *eg* John Wain*, Allen Sillitoe*, David Storey*. *Clayhanger* dramatizes the contrast between the generation of 'self-made men' who by enormous efforts rise from poverty to wealth, and their successors who are in a position to form ambitions quite beyond the imagination of their parents. At the time about which Bennett was writing, this younger generation was frustrated, not only by the lack of sympathy of the older generation, but because it was not yet practicable for the young to free themselves from the provincial restrictiveness of their environment by escaping to the larger possibilities offered by London.

Cleopatra of Egypt (51–30 BC)

The last of the dynasty of the Ptolemies. The chief authority for the facts of her life is the Greek historian Plutarch* (1st C AD) in his life of Antony. She was joint sovereign of Egypt with her younger brother Ptolemy Dionysus. Driven out of Egypt, she withdrew to Syria, where she met the Roman general Julius Caesar* while she was preparing to counterattack. Caesar took her side, re-established her on the throne, and made her his mistress. When Caesar was assassinated, she became the mistress of Caesar's ally Mark Antony, until they were jointly defeated by Caesar's nephew and adopted son, Octavianus. She then committed suicide. Her love affair with Caesar is the subject of Bernard Shaw's play *Caesar and Cleopatra**; and that between herself and Antony is the subject of Shakespeare's *Antony and Cleopatra** and Dryden's *All for Love**. Samuel Daniel's* verse tragedy, *Cleopatra* (1594), has as subject her dealings with Octavian after Antony's death.

Clergy

Collectively the body of men in holy orders in a Church. In the Middle Ages, 'clergy' was the collective noun of 'clerk' = a man in holy orders; as, in earlier times, only the clergy were learned, 'clerk' was also used for student, intellectual, or scholar. All men not in holy orders are collectively the laity.

The different kinds of clergy in the Church of England of today are commonly the same as in pre-Reformation England, but they do not always correspond to their equivalents in other countries, and the existence of other Protestant churches and of the Roman Catholic Church side by side with the Church of England may lead to confusion in the minds of readers. Consequently, a brief alphabetical list of ranks and designations may be found useful.

Archbishop. The head of one of the main regional divisions of the Anglican church. England is divided into two archdioceses or provinces; of the north, centred on York, and of the south, centred on Canterbury. The Archbishop of Canterbury has always been the senior. There are also archbishops of Anglican provinces outside England, and Roman Catholic archbishops.

Archdeacon. An official who assists a bishop in the care of a diocese; he is especially responsible for the discipline and good order of the clergy and churches in the bishop's care.

Bishop. The head of a diocese, or subdivision of an Archbishop's province.

Canon. A member of a chapter, or body of clergy attached to a cathedral, with the duty of preaching in the cathedral and other churches in the diocese.

Churchwarden. A layman given responsibility for the care, upkeep and good order of a particular church.

Clerk. In the Middle Ages, a man in holy orders as explained at the beginning of this entry. After the Reformation, the clerk was a layman with special duties in church services (reading the lesson, leading the singing, etc.) and in connection with the keeping of records of baptisms, marriages, etc. Its church use is now rare, but 'clerical' is still used as the adjective for both clergyman and office clerk.

Curate. Assistant to a parish clergyman, or vicar.

Deacon. In the Church of England, one who is not yet fully ordained (*ie* in holy orders) but able to undertake some duties in church services etc. In other protestant churches, a layman with practical responsibilities in running the church, *eg* for its finances.

Dean. The head of a cathedral chapter, responsible for the cathedral building and the services in it, and for the work of the canons.

Minister. Though generally synonymous with clergyman, it is particularly used for a clergyman of the Church of Scotland or of one of the various churches independent of the Church of England.

Parson. A rector or vicar. Now commonly used of any clergyman.

Pastor. From Lat. = shepherd. Clergymen of all denominations are figuratively shepherds of the laity, but the word, like 'minister', is especially used in nonconformist denominations.

Priest. A clergyman in the Roman Catholic or Anglican Church. The other Protestant denominations have largely abandoned the designation, however, and it is now chiefly used for the Roman Catholic clergy.

Rector. A parish clergyman in the church of England who was entitled to the tithes* of his parish.

Vicar. A parish clergyman who was not entitled to tithes and who was paid a stipend instead. Since the abolition of tithes, the difference between vicar and rector has ceased to matter.

Clerihew /'klerihju:/

A lightweight epigram, usually in four lines of varying length, so called after its inventor E. Clerihew Bentley. For example:

Alfred de Musset
Called his cat 'pusset'.
His accent was affected –
That was to be expected.

Cliché /'kli:ʃei/

A word borrowed from the French, used to denote a phrase or idiom employed by habit instead of meaningfully, *eg* 'her skin was *as white as snow*'. It is a stock phrase, employed without thought and heard (or read) without visualization.

Clifford's Inn

* *Inns of Court.*

Climax

* *Figures of Speech.*

Clio

* *Muses.*

Cloth Manufacture

The export of wool was the foundation of English commercial prosperity, but in 14th C cloth-making began to overtake it in importance. It was carried on in villages and small towns in East Anglia, in the Cotswold hills and other regions of the west, and in the hill country in the north. Since it required the combination of several crafts – carding, spinning, weaving, fulling, dyeing and finishing – it gave rise to the first great capitalist industrialists, the clothiers, who gave out the work to the various craftsmen often in scattered villages, and then marketed the finished product. Cloth-making was in fact the first important trade to break out of the non-capitalistic, guild-organized craft industry of the Middle Ages. The growth of the industry was encouraged by the government in 14th C, and it led to the settlement in England of Flemish craftsmen – often bitterly unpopular – in order to establish the finer skills. Chaucer's Wife of Bath in the *Canterbury Tales** is an example of a 14th-C member of the class. The clothiers' pride and wealth made them into a commercial aristocracy, around whose leading members legends, like those collected by Thomas Deloney*, were built up.

* *Capitalism; Craft Guilds.*

Clough, Arthur Hugh (1819–61) /klʌf/

Poet. He was the son of a Liverpool cotton merchant, and was educated at Rugby School under the great headmaster, Thomas Arnold*, and at Balliol College, Oxford. At Oxford he came for a time under the influence of Newman, afterwards a Roman Catholic but at the time one of the leaders of the Anglican religious revival known as the Oxford Movement*; later, when Clough was a senior member (Fellow) of Oriel College, he became a sceptic in religious belief. It was necessary (until 1871) to accept the doctrines of the Church of England in order to be a senior member of an Oxford College; thus Clough's religious doubts caused him to resign. He travelled in Europe, was for a short time Principal of a students' hostel in London University (where no religious restrictions operated) and lectured in America. Finally (1853) he accepted a post under the government in the Education Office. He was the close friend and correspondent of the poet and critic, Matthew Arnold*, who commemorated his death with the elegy *Thyrsis* (pub 1867). Almost all of Clough's letters to Arnold have disappeared, but Arnold's letters to him (see *Letters to Clough*, ed. H. F. Lowry) are interesting for what they reveal of the minds of the two men. Both were religious doubters, and both were dismayed by the course of 19th-C civilization. Arnold was desolated by the loss of his friend, and attributes his death to premature despair ('Too quick despairer, wherefore wilt thou go?') Clough's best known poem, the lyric 'Say not the struggle nought availeth', has a desperate tone, though it ends in hope.

Clough's long poems, however, have a lighter, though scarcely a serener, spirit. The best-known ones are the two verse novels, *Tober-na-Vuolich* (1848) and *Amours de Voyage* (1849, pub 1858), and the uncompleted dramatic dialogue, *Dipsychus* (1850, pub 1869). The first two are written in a metre unusual in English, the Latin hexameter*. *Dipsychus* employs a wide variety of metres. The subject of the first poem is a young man of advanced intellectual opinions but emotionally immature, and his love affair with a Scottish Highland peasant girl who has the emotional maturity that he lacks. *Amours* is about a self-doubting man who loses the girl he loves through his inability to arrive at conclusions as to the truth of his own feelings. *Dipsychus*, 'the man in two minds', is a colloquy between a self-doubter and the spirit who haunts him, who admits to the name 'Mephistophilis' and yet is not certainly evil. The other leading poets of the age (Arnold, Tennyson* and Browning*) were as much afflicted by the torments of doubt as Clough was, but Clough differed from them in relating doubt to the conduct of ordinary daily life, and in his use of a kind of irony which is much more characteristic of 20th-C poets (*eg* T. S. Eliot* in *Prufrock*) than it is of 19th C ones. He has recently attracted much more critical interest than he has received in the past.

* **6.4.1.**

Bib: Chorley, K., *Clough: the uncommitted mind*; Houghton, W. E., *The Poetry of Clough*; Goode, J., Hardy, B., essays in *The Major Victorian Poets* (ed. Isobel Armstrong).

Clubs

Private associations, organized for a common recreational purpose; sometimes recruited from men of common beliefs or opinions, *eg* the political clubs; sometimes from a particular profession such as the authors' and actors' clubs; sometimes from the casual gatherings of friends. They have been important in English life since mid-17th C, when they first appear by name in association with particular coffee houses – as important in English social life then as the café in France later. But the principle may be said to go back to the later years of 16th C, when (according at least to tradition) poets met in taverns, *eg* the Mermaid in London, attended by Shakespeare, Jonson*, Raleigh*, Donne* and others. (See Beaumont's* lines *Master Francis Beaumont to Ben Jonson*, describing meetings at this tavern.) In the early years of 18th C there is frequent mention of clubs in the periodical essays of Addison* and Steele*; Swift *was a leader of the Brothers' Club and founded the Scriblerus*. Dr Johnson* founded the Literary Club in 1764; the painter Reynolds*, the statesmen Burke* and Fox*, the writer Goldsmith*, and Garrick* the actor were all members of it; it met at the Turk's Head Tavern. In the later 18th and early 19th C clubs began to leave the taverns and use their own buildings, and the most famous of all literary and artistic clubs, The Athenaeum*, was founded in 1824 and moved to its present building in 1831. The Carlton Club* (Conservative, 1831) and the Reform (Liberal, 1834) are the outstanding political clubs of 19th C, but Brooks's and White's* had been the corresponding bodies in 18th C, and both still exist. In 19th C it was usual for men of the middle and upper classes to belong to clubs of some description, and clubs have always varied very much in prestige. Working class clubs were usually for education, politics, or some other practical objectives. They are still common, especially in the north, but have become more recreational. Women were never admitted to membership of men's clubs, and did not start their own until late in 19th C.

* *Coffee and Coffee-Houses.*

Clytemnestra /klaitimˈnestrə/

In Greek myth, wife of Agamemnon*, king of Argos. While her husband was absent, commanding the Greeks in their war against Troy, Clytemnestra took as lover Aegisthus, Agamemnon's cousin, in whose charge the kingdom had been left. When Agamemnon returned, he was murdered by his wife and her paramour; in retribution she herself was later murdered by her son Orestes*. The story is the subject of several of the greatest ancient Greek tragedies: *Agamemnon*, *Choephori*, and *Eumenides* by Aeschylus*; *Electra* by Sophocles*; *Electra* and *Orestes* by Euripides*.

Coal

* *Fuel.*

Cobbett, William (1762–1835) /'kobit/

Journalist and political leader of the working class, especially of the rural labourer. The son of a small farmer and self-educated, he remained identified with country pursuits and interests; he was always a peasant, but a fully articulate one. The work by which he is especially known is *Rural Rides**, an account of tours through England on horseback, written for the enlightenment of a working-class public, and published between 1820 and 1830 in his periodical *Political Register**, which he edited from 1802 until his death. The *Rides* are famous for their racy, vigorous description of the countryside. His language is always clear, plain and lively; in an autobiographical fragment he declares that his first inspiration in the writing of prose was the work of Jonathan Swift*, though he is completely without Swift's ironical suavity. His next most famous work is his *Advice to Young Men* (1829); his *Grammar of the English Language* (1818) is an outstanding guide to the writing of vigorous English.

Apart from the still appreciated vividness of his writings, Cobbett has remained a hero of forthright, independent political journalism. When he was in America (1792–1800) his *Porcupine's Gazette* and various pamphlets were in defence of Britain against the prejudices of the newly independent Americans; once back in England, he refused offers of government patronage, and though he started his *Register* in support of the Tories, then in power, in a few years he moved over to radical opposition, and spent two years in prison. In 1832 he was elected Member of Parliament in spite of his refusal to use the corrupt methods for influencing electors common at the time; in Parliament he went into opposition to the Whig government as an extreme left radical. He was excessively quarrelsome and prejudiced, but also exceedingly brave and eloquent in support of the cause of justice as, at any given time, he saw it.

* *Whig and Tory.*

Bib: Cole, G. D. H., *Life; Opinions of William Cobbett*; Lobban, J. H., (ed.) *Rural Rides*; Hughes, A. M. D., *Selections*; Hazlitt, W., in *Spirit of the Age*; Carlyle, E. I., *Cobbett.*

Cockney

A native of the old city of London, noted for the 'cockney accent' of his dialect. Country people use the word contemptuously for the typical city-dweller. The word derives from 'cock's egg'; the medieval countryside belief was that small or ill-shaped eggs were laid by cocks.

Cockpit

A small arena where the sport of cockfighting (making one cock fight another) took place. The sport was widely popular in England from the Middle Ages until 19th C. The term was extended to describe any region where war often takes place (*eg* Belgium, the 'cockpit of Europe') or a small usually sunken space, *eg* the cockpit of an aircraft.

Coffee and Coffee-Houses

Coffee was introduced into England from the east in mid-17th C, and from the Restoration* until mid-18th C coffee-houses were fashionable public resorts in London. Certain coffee houses became acknowledged meeting-places for supporters of particular political parties, or for the members of particular professions. Will's Coffee-House* became the centre for men of letters; the Cocoa Tree Chocolate-House became the home of Tory politicians, while the Whigs went to St James's Coffee-House; Lloyd's* became popular with merchants, and so forth. In the later 18th C more tea was imported, and as such luxuries were now distributed more widely, ordinary people took to drinking it in their homes. So the flourishing century of the coffee-house was replaced by the domestic tea-party as the typically English social occasion. Some of the coffee-houses survived in other forms; thus Lloyd's became the central office in London for marine insurance, and White's became one of London's most fashionable clubs*.

* *Whig and Tory.*

Cole, King

Old King Cole: a familiar English nursery rhyme*; Coel is a legendary ancient British king mentioned by Geoffrey of Monmouth* and said to be the founder of Colchester.

Coleridge, Samuel Taylor (1772–1834) /'kəulridʒ/

Poet and critic. He is well known to general readers for four poems (*The Ancient Mariner**, *Christabel** *Kubla Khan**, *Dejection**) and one volume of criticism, *Biographia Literaria**. His poetic production, though small, was of course larger than this, and his criticism was very much larger. In both poetry and criticism his work is outstanding, but it is typical of him that his critical work is very scattered and disorganized, that two of his best-known poems (*Christabel* and *Kubla Khan*) are unfinished, and that he was most famous among his contemporaries for his talk. He introduced to England the 18th-C German philosophy of Kant and others; he was also an original thinker, and he attempted to give to his literary criticism a profound philosophical basis. Coleridge had a most versatile mind and comprehensive vision; his tragic failure was his inability to organize his ideas into completed and published work.

His poetry begins to be important at the time of his first association with the poet William Wordsworth* in the 1790s. Together they published *Lyrical Ballads** (1798), the book which is the effective starting-point of the English Romantic movement, the great period of which extended until 1830. The principle of the collaboration was that while Wordsworth was to reveal the poetic significance in the commonplaces of life, Coleridge was to dramatize human emotions aroused by extraordinary events. Coleridge wrote all his best poetry between 1797 and 1802. This includes the supernatural poems (*Ancient Mariner*, *Christabel*, *Kubla Khan*), the 'conversation' poems* (*Frost at Midnight*, *The Nightingale*, *This Lime-tree Bower*) and *Dejection: An Ode*. This last (1802) reads like a farewell to poetry, and though he continued to write it occasionally until near his death, his two most productive years were 1797 and 1798. Coleridge's poetry shares with Wordsworth's a quite new simplicity of diction and fluency of movement; he was bolder than Wordsworth (partly because more scholarly) in rhythmical experiment, and he showed, as Wordsworth seldom did, intense and delicate visuality of detail. The 'romanticism' of both poets comes out in their reverence for the spontaneity and inherent dignity of the feelings, and their cultivation of truthful and profound expression of them.

Coleridge's most important criticism is in his *Biographia Literaria* though much of interest is scattered among his letters, notes for lectures, and jottings. Besides his insight into numerous individual authors – Coleridge was one of the first critics to give close critical attention to language – his most important contribution to critical thinking was his conception of the profoundly organic nature of poetic (and all artistic) creation, involving the whole personality of the poet. Philosophically and critically, under the influence of German philosophers, he opposed the limitedly rationalistic trends of 18th-C thought. Politically he began, like Wordsworth, as an enthusiastic supporter of the French Revolution, but by 1800 he was reacting against it into a philosophical conservatism which, however, was radically different from the politically sterile conservatism of the Tories in power. Coleridge's conservatism was deeply thought in the tradition of Burke*, whereas the Tories were merely negative and superficial. Coleridge suffered from bad health for much of his life, and after 1800 became an opium addict, a fact which is often adduced to explain the relative smallness of his literary production.

* **6.3.2-4**; **7.3**; Romantic Revival.

Bib: Raysor, T. M., *Shakespearian Criticism; Miscellaneous Criticism*; Margoliouth, H. M., *Wordsworth and Coleridge*; House, H., *Coleridge*; Lowes, J. L., *The Road to Xanadu*; Richards, I. A., *Coleridge on Imagination*; Muirhead, J. H., *Coleridge as Philosopher*; Wellek, R., *History of Modern Criticism* (Vol. 2); Mill, J. S., (ed F. R., Leavis) *Bentham and Coleridge*; Chambers, E. K., *Coleridge: A Biographical Study*; Beer, J. B. *Coleridge the Visionary*; Jackson, J. R. de J., (ed) *Coleridge: the Critical Heritage*.

Colin Clout

[1] The name adopted by Spenser* in his pastoral sequence, *Shepherd's Calendar** and again in his pastoral allegory *Colin Clout's Come Home Again*, written to describe his visit to London and the court, 1589–91. The second poem is partly a tribute to the glory of Elizabeth (Cynthia in the poem) and the splendour of her court, and partly a satire on court vices and intrigue. It is dedicated to Sir Walter Raleigh*, who in the poem is represented as the Shepherd of the Sea.

[2] *Colin Clout* (or *Colyn Clout*) is the title of a satire by Skelton* on the vices of the clergy, written about 1519.

College of Arms

* *Heralds' College*.

Collier, Jeremy (1650–1726)

A clergyman, chiefly known for his attack on the contemporary theatre, *Short View of the Immorality and Profaneness of the English Stage*, 1698. He contrasted the indecency of the English stage of the time, citing Dryden*, Congreve*, Vanbrugh*, and others, with the comparative decency of the ancient Latin and Greek drama. This angered some of the dramatists, notably Congreve, and started a controversy that lasted some 10 years, but the pamphlet did not have direct substantial influence, though it was later thought to have had. The witty cynical comedy of the late 17th C was soon to disappear from other causes – a change in public taste which led to the rise of sentimental comedy, such as Colley Cibber's*.

Collins, Mr

A character in Jane Austen's *Pride and Prejudice**. His combination of pomposity in relation with his social equals, superciliousness to inferiors, and servility to his social superiors is comically caricatured, and satirizes the excessive wordliness of the less deserving English clergy of 18th and early 19th C. A 'Mr Collins' came to be a designation for a merely conventional letter of thanks for hospitality, after such a letter written by the fictional Collins.

Collins, Wilkie (1824–89)

Novelist; the first detective* novelist in English. His two famous novels are *The Woman in White* (1860), first published in *Household Words**, a magazine edited by Charles Dickens, and *The Moonstone** (1868). His mastery was especially over plot-construction, in which he influenced Dickens; his characterization is less distinguished, but in *The Woman in White* he excels in this, too, and in the creation of disturbing atmosphere. Collins, like other novelists of detection, is to be read essentially for his plots; unlike Dickens, whose plots are merely a framework for the more important effects of a poetic order. He collaborated with Dickens in a few stories in *Household Words* and in *All the Year Round**: *The Wreck of the Golden Mary*, *A Message from the Sea*, *No Thoroughfare*. Collins's other novels include *No Name* (1862) and *Armadale* (1866) which has been praised for its melodrama.

Bib: Robinson, K., *Life*; Phillips, W. C., *Dickens, Reade and Collins: Sensation Novelists*;

Eliot, T. S., Preface to *The Moonstone*, World's Classics edition.

Collins, William (1721–59)

Poet; especially famous for his Odes (*To Simplicity*, *The Passions*, *On the Popular Superstitions in the Highlands*, *To Evening*, etc.), his *Dirge in Cymbeline*, and the lyric *How Sleep the Brave*. He was one of the most inward-turning of the 18th-C poets, and one of those less concerned with the theme that dominated the century – the relationship of man and society. His interest in nature was not unusual for the time, and he shared with contemporaries (Gray* and Thomson* for example) the influence of Milton* in cadence and diction to evoke the awesomeness of nature's influence on the mind. But in addition he had a highly original sensibility capable of expressing natural influences subjectively better perhaps than any other poet in English before Wordsworth* and Coleridge*. Yet he was a truly 18th-C poet in the formality that he derived from the study of classical poetry, especially Horace*.

* *Augustan Age.*

Bib: Johnson, Samuel, *Lives of the Poets*; Ainsworth, E. G., *Life*; Garrod, H. W., *Collins.*

Colonel Jack (1722)

The History and Remarkable Life of Colonel Jacque, a novel by Daniel Defoe*. Jack is abandoned by his parents, becomes a thief, a soldier, a slave on an American plantation, a planter, and eventually a rich and repentant man back in England. The sequence through crime, suffering and repentance, and from poverty to prosperity, is typical of Defoe's novels.

Colossus of Rhodes

In ancient Greece, a huge statue that stood by the entrance of the Harbour of the Island of Rhodes; according to later tradition, it stood astride the harbour entrance, forming an arch under which ships could pass. It represented the sun god, and was reckoned one of the Seven Wonders of the World*.

Columba, St (AD 521–597)

Son of an Irish chieftain, he became a Christian evangelist to Scotland, where he founded the monastery of Hy on the Island of Iona.

Columbine

* *Commedia dell'Arte.*

Comedy

* *Humours, Comedy of; Manners, Comedy of.*

Comedy of Errors (?1592)

An early comedy by Shakespeare who adapted it from *Menaechmi* by Plautus*. The spirit of the play is similar to the Latin original, and depends on deft handling of situation for the comedy, not on poetry and character as in the characteristically Shakespearian comedy. Shakespeare, indeed, seems to have been attempting to beat Plautus at his own game: he adds to Plautus' original pair of indistinguishable twin brothers an equally indistinguishable pair of twin slaves to the brothers. The twins are separated in infancy by shipwreck and live in different cities, each unaware of the other's survival. One of them marries, in Ephesus, and the other arrives there. Highly confused and improbable situations result in very deftly managed farce, but the play is chiefly to be regarded as Shakespearian apprentice work.

Commedia dell'Arte

A kind of Italian comedy, developed in 16th C, in which the plot was written, but the dialogue was improvised by the actors. Certain characters regularly recurred in these plays, and in 18th C they were adopted in England (by way of France) and became part of the English puppet shows (*eg* Punch and Judy*) and of the pantomime* tradition. Such characters, anglicized, include Harlequin, his mistress Columbine, Pantaloon*, Punch.

Common Land

Land held in common by the peasantry of a village, and used for the pasturage of their cattle. By 19th C farms were grouped into fairly large holdings all over the country, and such commons as had not been enclosed were used chiefly for recreation, *eg* cricket and various field sports.

* *Enclosures.*

Common Law

A system of law in use in Great Britain (excluding Scotland), some parts of the Commonwealth, and the United States, which retained the system after renouncing English political authority. The term arose in the Middle Ages and meant the law common to the whole people as distinct from law governing only sections of it, such as the Law Merchant or local customary law. It is also distinguished from Statute Law, made by Act of Parliament, and from Equity, a system supplementary to Common Law beginning in 15th C. Common Law is 'case-made', *ie* based on precedent judgements, and originally derived from acknowledged custom. The Common Law system differs from the law in most other European countries (including Scotland) in that the English legal system did not undergo the influence of the study of Roman Law in 16th C. The difference is important politically, since Roman law emphasizes the power of the state, and by its avoidance the English lawyers of 17th C were better able to defend the liberties of the subject against the claims of the Stuart* kings.

* *Courts of Law.*

Common Metre

A 4-line stanza with alternating four and three stresses and alternating rhymes, *eg*

Bíd me to líve, and Í will líve
Thy Prótestánt to bé;

Or bid me love, and I will give

A loving heart to thee.

(Robert Herrick*)

It is especially common in hymns*, carols* and ballads*.

* 6.3.3.

Common Prayer, The Book of

The prayers and order of church services for use in the Church of England. It was prepared under the supervision of Archbishop Cranmer on the basis of the 'Primers', containing prayers and aids to religious devotion for the laity, written in English and in use since the Middle Ages. The religious reformation of Henry VIII* was above all the establishment of a national Church, independent of papal domination from Rome, and such a conception required that services and prayers should be in the native language, and not, as hitherto, in Latin. The first *Book of Common Prayer* was issued in 1549, revised in 1552. It is of great importance as a work of literature, for, though English prose was still in an early stage, Cranmer succeeded in combining the plainness and directness of the language with the dignity and sonority so outstanding in the Latin, thereby proving the resourcefulness of English for expression. Church attendance was compulsory in 16th C and normal for a majority of all ranks of society until 19th C, so that the Prayer Book language became a familiar and formative influence in speech and writing second only in importance to the Bible itself.

Doctrine is sometimes ambiguously phrased, allowing for more than one interpretation so as to accommodate variations in religious belief; such phrasing owes most to the revision under Queen Elizabeth I* in 1559 which made clear the centrality and inclusiveness of Anglicanism among the various bodies of Christian opinion. The Prayer Book authorized in 1662 after the Restoration* was substantially the 1559 revision and is the only legally approved version today. As the head of the Church of England is the Crown, revision can only be carried out by royal consent; and as the powers of the Crown are in practice exercised by Parliament, the consent of Parliament is indispensable. Thus a fairly extensive revision was blocked by Parliament in 1928, though its use is tolerated. More recently Parliamentary approval has been gained, service by service, for alternative forms for experimental use.

Commons

As a political term, the 'commons' of England are all those who do not hold a title of nobility, or the office of Bishop in the Church of England. Commoners elect their representatives to the House of Commons whereas the lords or peers and the bishops are entitled to sit in the House of Lords. This does not mean that the House of Commons does not include members of the aristocracy: the sons of peers may hold courtesy titles (*eg* the eldest son of a duke is called a marquis but is accorded this title only 'by courtesy') but politically they are considered to be commoners, and are entitled to vote for representation in the House of Commons, or to 'stand' for election themselves.

* *Parliament.*

Communism

Communism may be interpreted in two ways. [1] the older, imprecise sense covering various philosophies of the common ownership of property; [2] the relatively precise interpretation understood by the Marx–Leninist Communist Parties throughout the world.

[1] The older philosophies derive especially from the Greek philosopher Plato*. His *Republic* proposes that society should be divided into classes according to differences of ability instead of differences of wealth and birth; the state is to provide for the needs of all, and thus to abolish rivalries and inequalities between rich and poor; children are to be educated by the state, and women are to have equal rights, opportunities, and training with men. In England, one of the most famous disciples of Plato is Sir Thomas More* in his *Utopia** (1516). More's prescriptions are similar to Plato's in many respects, but though he also requires equal opportunity and training for men, he goes against Plato in keeping the monogamous family intact, whereas Plato wanted a community of wives and children to be brought up by the state. Both Plato and More require for their schemes an all-powerful state in the charge of an intellectual aristocracy; what we should call enlightened totalitarianism. With the growth of the power of the state in 20th C, however, all forms of totalitarianism were regarded with abhorrence by liberal intellectuals, and so arose the 'anti-utopian' class of literature, for example Aldous Huxley's **Brave New World* (1932) and George Orwell's *Animal Farm* (1945) and *Nineteen Eighty Four* (1948), vehemently satirizing totalitarian communism.

In practical experiment, the vows of poverty taken by members of orders of monks and friars and the communal ownership of property in such communities may have kept alight for men in general the ideal of the freedom of the spirit attainable by the renunciation of selfish material ambitions and competition. Protestant sectarian beliefs emphasizing the equality of souls led to such an abortive communistic enterprise as that of the Levellers in the Interregnum*. In America, a number of experiments were undertaken by immigrant sects such as the Amana community, and under the influence of the English socialist Robert Owen* and the French socialists Fourier and Cabet, but few of them lasted long.

[2] Modern so-called scientific communism, based mainly on Marx*and Lenin, differs from the various forms of modern socialism by affirming the necessity for revolutionary as distinct from evolutionary method, to be followed by a period of dictatorship. This form of communism is supported in Britain by a small but fairly influential political party which is active in the trade unions but has no place in Parliament or in local government. For the influence of Marxist ideas on English artists and intellectuals in 19th and 20th C, see *Marx*.

Companies, Joint Stock

Companies whose profits are distributed among the shareholders. They began in 16th C and largely superseded the older 'regulated company' whose members traded each on his own account, and combined only for common protection. The greatest of the regulated companies was the Merchant Adventurers, founded in 15th C; the greatest of the joint stock companies was the East India Company* founded in 1600.

* *Charter Companies.*

Complaints

In medieval times and in 16th C – less commonly thereafter – a 'Complaint' in poetry was not a mere expression of grievance though that might be included, but was equivalent to 'Lament' or even (*eg* the 18th-C poem subtitled *Night Thoughts** by Edward Young) might indicate a serious, reflective poem with a sombre subject.

The Compleat Angler

A discourse on the sport of fishing (in full, *The Compleat Angler, or the Contemplative Man's Recreation*) by Isaak Walton*, first published in 1653; its 5th edition has a continuation by Charles Cotton (1630–87) and came out in 1676. The book has been described (Legouis and Cazamian: *History of English Literature*, p. 555) as perhaps the only handbook of art and craft to rank as literature. This is because Walton combines his practical instruction with digressions about his personal tastes and opinions, and sets it in direct, fresh description of the English countryside which may be contrasted with the artificial pastoralism which had hitherto been characteristic of natural description. The book has the form of a dialogue mainly between Piscator (Fisherman) and Venator (Hunter), which takes place along the banks of the river Lea near London. Cotton's continuation is transferred to the banks of the river Dove between Derbyshire and Staffordshire.

Compton-Burnett, Ivy (1892–1969)

/ˈkʌmtn bɔːˈnet/

Novelist. Her first novel, *Dolores* (1911) is distinguished from all her others by an approach to the method of novel-writing similar to that of 19th C, in particular that of George Eliot*, and a disposition to accept usual conceptions of moral retribution. From *Pastors and Masters* (1925) both the method and the moral vision change radically. The novels are narrated almost wholly through dialogue, in a manner that derives from Jane Austen*, but with even less attempt to present visualized environments. The period is always 1890–1914; the setting, a prosperous household of the period; the characters include some who are arrogant to the point of evil, and are able, without retribution, to dominate those who are selfless or weak; the plots are melodramatic but never break up the surface of respectability. The dialogue is epigrammatic and pungent, with the consequence that the novels are each exceptionally concentrated structures. The effect is commonly of sardonic comedy with tragic conclusion, which is, however, dominated by the comedy that accompanies it.

After 1925 the novels are as follows: *Brothers and Sisters* (1929); *Men and Wives* (1931); *More Women than Men* (1933); *A House and its Head* (1935); *Daughters and Sons* (1937); *A Family and a Fortune* (1939); *Parents and Children* (1941); *Elders and Betters* (1944); *Manservant and Maidservants* (1947); *Two Worlds and Their Ways* (1949); *Darkness and Day* (1951); *The Present and the Past* (1953); *A Father and his Fate* (1957); *The Mighty and their Fall* (1961); *A God and his Gifts* (1963). Few distinguished novelists have shown such uniformity of treatment and lack of development throughout their career. Probably *A House and its Head* and *A Family and a Fortune* are her two outstanding achievements.

Bib: Hansford Johnson, P., *Ivy Compton-Burnett* (British Council); Liddell, R., *The Novels of Ivy Compton-Burnett*.

Comte, Auguste (1798–1857)

French philosopher. He sought to expound a scientifically based philosophy for human progress, deducing laws of development from the facts of history and excluding metaphysics and religion – Positivism. His chief works were translated into English. In them he sought to establish a system that would be the scientific equivalent of the Catholic system of philosophy. In this he failed, but his work led to the modern science of sociology. In England, his chief disciple was Frederic Harrison, but he also deeply interested the philosopher John Stuart Mill* and the novelist George Eliot*. The character of his beliefs suited radically reformist and religiously sceptical English intellectuals such as these; on the other hand, his systematization of ideas was alien to English habits of mind, and was criticized by the philosopher Herbert Spencer*.

* 3.4.2.

Comus

/ˈkəuməs/

As described in the original title, *A Masque, presented at Ludlow Castle, 1634, before the Earl of Bridgewater, Lord President of Wales* by John Milton*. A typical masque* provided as much opportunity for spectacle and music as for poetry; the words were often of subsidiary importance. In this sense *Comus* is not a true masque; nor is its composition sufficiently dramatic for it to be a true poetic drama. It is a poetic act of praise of the Puritan* virtues of temperance and chastity, combining renaissance splendour with moral austerity in the tradition of Spenser's *Faerie Queene**, though with a verbal energy in some speeches recalling the fieriness of the best Elizabethan* dramatists. Its mode is that of classical pastoral*: a girl is lost in a wood and separated from her two brothers; she falls into the hands of Comus, son of Bacchus*, and of Circe*, the evil enchantress of Greek legend. Comus tries to subdue her, but she clings to her virginal purity and resists him. Eventually she is rescued by her brothers with the aid of a shepherd called Thyrsis, and of Sabrina*, spirit of the River Severn that flows by Ludlow. As usual with masques, the principal characters were not, on the occasion for which *Comus* was written, acted by professional actors but by ladies and gentlemen – in this case the lady was performed by the 15-year-old daughter of Lord Bridgewater, and the brothers by her own younger brothers. The music was composed by Henry Lawes, who had requested Milton to write the words. *Comus* is a masterpiece of Milton's early style, before he had evolved his Latinate epic periods (*eg* in *Paradise Lost**) and while he was still in touch with the nimbler and more varied Elizabethan idiom. The name Comus is from the Greek for 'revel', and in later Greek myth he was the god of revelry.

Conceit

Now used chiefly to mean undue satisfaction with oneself, 'conceit' originally meant the faculty of imagination or fancy; hence in 16th C a conceit was an ingeniously witty and imaginative expression or similitude. The term is especially employed for the metaphysical* poets of the first half of 17th C – Donne*, Herbert*, Vaughan*, Crashaw*, Cowley*, etc. An example from Donne:

Our two soules therefore, which are one,
Though I must goe, endure not yet
A breach, but an expansion,
Like gold to ayery thinnesse beate.

Confessio Amantis (1386–90)

A collection of tales of courtly love, in verse, by John Gower*. The verse is strongly influenced by Chaucer*, Gower's contemporary and friend. The poet makes confession to Genius, priest of Venus, goddess of love, and Genius tells him exemplary stories of the Seven Deadly Sins* and their remedy. In the end the poet is dismissed from the court of Venus as being too old for love. The tales were thus set in a framework like Chaucer's *Canterbury Tales**, though there had been French and Italian antecedents, especially Boccaccio's *Decameron**. The stories are mainly taken from the Latin poet Ovid*, though some may have come from Chaucer. The language is Chaucerian and fluent but without Chaucer's genius. The combination of courtly love with ethical moralizing anticipates a characteristic combination in 15th C.

* *Courtly Literature and Romantic Love.*

Confessions of an English Opium-Eater (1822: enlarged ed. 1856)

An autobiography, and the most famous work of Thomas De Quincey*. Like Coleridge*, De Quincey began taking opium to ease physical suffering, and eventually increased the dose until he became an addict. The book contains eloquent, prose-poetic accounts of his opium dreams and also graphic descriptions of his life of poverty in London. In the former aspect the prose evokes the high musical rhetoric of the 17th-C masters – Thomas Browne*, John Milton*, Jeremy Taylor*; in the latter, it is typical of the 19th-C mode of transmitting intimate, minute personal experience, resembling the increasingly close-textured psychology of the novel. In his tenderness for and understanding of childish suffering, De Quincey represents a development that was new in the history of literature, and came to fruition in the Victorian novelists, notably Dickens.

Congregationalism

The doctrine of an extreme Protestant sect which maintains that local churches should be independent of wider authority in the conduct of their affairs and worship. In Elizabeth I's* time, followers of this belief were called Brownists*, after their founder, Robert Browne; by mid-17th C they were called Independents. It was at this period that the movement had special importance; it became widely influential amongst the Parliamentary opponents of Charles I* and numbered among its supporters Oliver Cromwell*. The Independents constituted the core of his fine army and enabled him to defeat the Presbyterian* Scots when, in the Second Civil War of 1648–51, they sided with the king.

* *Civil War.*

Congreve, William (1670–1729) /'koŋgri:v/

The most famous writer of comedies in the Restoration* period of English drama, which lasted approximately from 1660 to 1710. His two outstanding plays were *Love for Love** (1695) and *The Way of the World** (1700). Other comedies: *The Old Bachelor* (1693); *The Double Dealer* (1694). His one tragedy was *The Mourning Bride* (1697); he also wrote a slight but entertaining novel, *Incognita* (1691). He wrote at a time when English prose had matured into unprecedented refinement, grace and suppleness; his public was an aristocratic society which was cynical and easy-going, but valued wit, subtlety and intelligence. His dialogue in consequence has an exceptional pointedness and terseness. The plays, as is common with Restoration dramatists, are not notable for excellence of construction nor for depth of feeling; this was the period of the 'Comedy of Manners' when the nimble wit which fashionable society esteemed found its natural scope on the surface of human behaviour. Thus he lacks the depth and feeling to be found in the French comic dramatist, Molière*, who was the acknowledged master of English Restoration comedy, but none of Congreve's contemporaries so nearly merit comparison with Molière.

* 5.2.2; *Manners, Comedy of.*

Bib: Hodges, J. C., *Life*; Dobree, B., *Restoration Comedy*; Palmer, J., *The Comedy of Manners*; Johnson, S., in *Lives of the Poets.*

Coningsby, or The New Generation (1844) /'kʌniŋzbi/

A political novel by Benjamin Disraeli*. By means of it, the rising politician, Disraeli, expresses his contempt for the lack of principle behind the contemporary Tory (right wing) party, whose side he nonetheless took against the expediency and materialism of the Whigs* and Utilitarians*. Against them he advocates a revived, platonically idealized aristocracy with the interests of the people at heart and respected by them as their natural leaders. Such a new aristocrat is the hero of the novel, Coningsby, and he and his friends form a group comparable to the Young England group which Disraeli himself led in Parliament. Coningsby is the grandson of Lord Monmouth, type of the old, unprincipled, predatory aristocracy, whose inveterate enemy is the industrialist Millbank, representing the new and vital middle class. Coningsby falls in love with Millbank's daughter, is disinherited by his grandfather, and eventually is elected to Parliament with Millbank's support. The novel is essentially one of propaganda of ideas, but written with great feeling, liveliness, and intelligence. Lord Monmouth was based on the actual Lord Hertford, also used as the basis of Lord Steyne in Thackeray's *Vanity Fair**. Another excellently drawn character is the detestable Rigby, based on John Wilson Croker, politician and journalist, and author of the notoriously abusive review of Keats's *Endymion**.

Conquest, The (Norman)

The conquest of England following the defeat of Harold by the Norman* invading force led by William I* at the Battle of Hastings in 1066.

Conrad, Joseph (1857–1924) /'konrad/

Novelist. His name in full was Teodor Josef Konrad Korzeniowski. He knew hardly any English when he was 20; yet before he was 40 he had completed his first English novel, *Almayer's Folly* (1895), and ten years later he had published one of the masterpieces of the novel in English: *Nostromo** (1904). The background to Conrad as a novelist is complicated and important for understanding the richness of his art. [1] Early life. His father was a Polish patriot and man of letters, exiled from the Polish Ukraine by the Russian government, which then ruled it, for his political activity. [2] Life at sea. From the tales of sea life (in translation) by the English writer Captain Marryat*, the American Fenimore Cooper, and the Frenchman Victor Hugo, he became fascinated by the sea and joined the crew of a French ship in 1874, and of an English one in 1878. By 1884 he was a British subject and had qualified as a master (ship's captain). In his voyages Conrad had visited the Mediterranean, South America, the Far East, and Central Africa. [3] Writing life. Ill-health stopped Conrad's seamanship. He began writing in about 1886 with at least as good an acquaintance with French language and literature as English. He brought to the English novel an admiration for the French realists*, Flaubert* and Maupassant. He also had a knowledge of many peoples, and a profound feeling of the contrast between the tightly enclosed communities of ships' crews and the loose egocentric individualism characterizing land societies. In addition, he knew, from his childhood experience in Russian Poland and Russia itself, the tragic impingement of political pressures on personal life, in a way that was unusual in the West until after the outbreak of the First World War in 1914. In his preoccupation with the exploration of moral issues he was in the English tradition. Though the sea enters more or less into most of his books, two of the best concern a contrast of political attitudes between East and West and have entirely land settings: *The Secret Agent** (1907) and *Under Western Eyes** (1911). *Nostromo* is about the creation of an imaginary state on the coast of South America. Other novels were: *An Outcast of the Islands* (1896); *Lord Jim* (1900); *Chance* (1914) – the first to bring him a big public; *Victory* (1915); *The Arrow of Gold* (1919); *The Rescue* (1920); *The Rover* (1923). He was writing *Suspense* when he died. Some of his best work is in nouvelles or long tales: *The Nigger of the Narcissus* (1898); *Youth, Heart of Darkness, Typhoon* (1902); *The Shadow Line* (1917), and others. *The Mirror of the Sea* (1906) is essays, and *Some Reminiscences* (1912) is autobiographical. His prose is among the richest and most sensuously beautiful among the writings of English novelists.
* 4.5.1.

Bib: Baines, J., *Life*; Bradbrook, M. C., *England's Polish Genius*; Gordan, J. D., *Joseph Conrad: the Making of a Novelist*; Hewitt, D., *Conrad: a Reassessment*; Leavis, F. R., in *The Great Tradition*; Guerard, A. J., *Conrad the Novelist*.

Constantinople

The name given to Byzantium by the Roman Emperor Constantine when he rebuilt it as his capital in AD 330. It is now a part of Istanbul.

Conversation Poem

A reflective poem, usually in blank verse*, in which the poet meditates aloud, ostensibly talking to a friend. The form is especially associated with Coleridge* who first used the term; *eg The Eolian Harp* (1795), *This Lime-Tree Bower* (1797), *The Nightingale* (1798), and *Frost at Midnight* (1798). Wordsworth's* *Tintern Abbey* (1798), written under the influence of Coleridge, is another example.

The conversation poem resembles the verse epistle, which originated with the Roman poet Horace*. Alexander Pope had brilliantly revived the Horatian epistle in his *Moral Essays** and *Imitations of Horace**. But the Horatian style is studied, epigrammatic, and outward-looking, whereas the conversation poem is spontaneous, relaxed, and introspective. The verse epistle, as used by Horace and Pope, is suited to a public, society-minded poetic expression characteristic of 18th-C Augustanism*, and the conversation poem is suited to poetic expression of the mind in solitude, a characteristic of the Romantics*. Cowper* was transitional between Pope and Coleridge in his long, reflective, blank verse poem *The Task* (1784), the style of which resembles that of Coleridge. A further development was the evolution of the dramatic monologue* out of the conversation poem, after 1830.
* 6.3.2.

Copernicus (1473–1543)

This was the Latinized form of surname of Nicolas Koppernik, a Polish astronomer. In *De revolutioni-*

bus orbium coelestium (*Concerning the revolutions of the heavenly spheres*) (1543) he expounded for the first time since classical times the belief that the earth and other planets move round the sun. This was contrary to the hitherto accepted theory of the Egyptian astronomer Ptolemy* according to which the earth was the centre of the solar system. The Ptolemaic system suited the traditional Christian conception of the universe and the place of man within it – it is still assumed, for instance, in Milton's epic of the Creation, *Paradise Lost** – but the Copernican theory caused little scandal since at the time it was regarded merely as an ingenious hypothesis. Only when Galileo* claimed its validity, on demonstrable grounds, after the invention of his new telescope, did the Church condemn the theory outright, in 1616.

Cophetua, King /kə'fetjuə/

A legendary king of North Africa who was indifferent to women until he loved and happily wedded a beggarmaid. The legend occurs in an old English ballad published in *Percy's Reliques** and there are several allusions to it in Elizabethan plays and elsewhere. The maid's name is Penelophon in the ballad, but given as Zenelophon in Shakespeare's *Love's Labour's Lost**.

Coppard, A. E. (1878–1957)

Writer of short stories. He was largely self-educated, and began serving in a shop at the age of 9. Later he began writing while working as an accountant, and his literary interests were nourished when he obtained a post at Oxford where he met and made friends with the intelligentsia. The best of his stories are chiefly in the earlier volumes, *Adam and Eve and Pinch Me* (1921), *Clorinda Walks in Heaven* (1922), *Fishmonger's Fiddle* (1925) and *The Field of Mustard* (1926). Later volumes include: *Pink Furniture* (1930), *Easter Day* (1931), *Rummy* (1932), *Tapster's Tapestry* (1938), *You Never Know Do You?* (1939), and *The Dark-Eyed Lady* (1947). He also wrote poems: *Collected Poems* (1928) and *Cherry Ripe* (1935), and an autobiography, *It's Me, O Lord* (1957).

Coppard had a remarkably acute ear for the spoken word, and his best tales have the freshness and simplicity of aural folk-tales. Although his subject matter was often more sophisticated than this suggests, many of his finest stories are about the life of the countryside. He was influenced by Thomas Hardy's* short stories, and he often shows a stoically resigned attitude to human destiny which is similar to Hardy's outlook, but he combined this with a remarkable talent for sharp comedy, again reminiscent of peasant folk tales.

Copyright, The Law of

The right of writers, artists, and musicians to refuse reproduction of their works. The right is now established law in every civilized country. The first copyright law in England was passed under Queen Anne in 1709. Before this, it was possible for publishers to publish books without the author's permission, and without allowing him any profits from sale, a practice very common during the lifetime of Shakespeare. Until 1909, the laws of the United States did not adequately safeguard British authors against having their works 'pirated' there, *ie* published without their permission and without giving them suitable financial return. Dickens was a main sufferer from this state of affairs, and it greatly angered him.

* *Shakespeare, Plays of; Stationers.*

Coriolanus (1608?) koriə'leinəs/

A tragedy by Shakespeare about a legendary Roman hero (5th C BC). Shakespeare took the story from the *Lives* by Plutarch* translated into English by Sir Thomas North*. A war is being waged between Rome and the neighbouring city of Corioli, capital city of the Volscians. The hero of the play, Caius Marcius, wins the title Coriolanus for his heroism against the enemy. But Rome is morally at war within herself: the arrogant patricians (aristocrats) despise the plebs, or common people, who in turn are factious and disorderly. Coriolanus differs from his fellow patricians only in being still prouder than they are, in that he cannot stoop to flatter the plebs for their votes. They succeed in expelling him from the city, whereupon he allies himself with the Volscians and returns to destroy it. His mother Volumnia, who embodies the qualities of the arrogant patricians and has herself bred her son to value his pride above all, succeeds in deterring him; he is then assassinated by the Volscians as a traitor. The tragedy has peculiar interest for its study of social influence on the individual. It is less popular than some other tragedies by Shakespeare, but it is certainly among the finest of his plays.

Corn Laws, Repeal of the, 1846

The Corn Laws existed to protect English home-grown corn from competition from imported foreign corn. Their existence made for higher food prices, and assumed the superior importance of agricultural interest over urban industrial interests. In the first half of 19th C the Tory party derived its main support from landowners, whereas the Whigs owed much of their support to the new industrialists of the rapidly growing industrial towns. The Whig Anti-Corn Law League consequently represented not merely opposition to a particular measure but rivalry between main segments of society; moreover the workers, anxious above all for cheap food, supported the urban middle class and the Whigs. It was nonetheless a Tory Prime Minister, Robert Peel, who repealed the Corn Laws under pressure of a severe famine in Ireland. The abolition of the Corn Laws was of historic importance in several ways: [1] it divided the Tory party, sending its most brilliant younger leader, Benjamin Disraeli*, into opposition, with his supporters, against Peel; [2] it began the era of free trade (*ie* trade unrestricted by import or export taxes); [3] it acknowledged implicitly that industrial interests were henceforth to be regarded as more important than agricultural interests; [4] it relieved the almost revolutionary restlessness of the working class, so that England was one of the few countries in Europe not to undergo upheaval or serious threat of upheaval in the Year of Revolutions, 1848.

Corneille, Pierre (1606–84) /ko:'nei/

One of the three great poetic dramatists in France whom exiled Englishmen encountered during the English interregnum and whose influence thereafter pervaded the English stage, in both tragedy and comedy, for the rest of the century. The French Court under Louis XIV (1643–1715) was one of the richest, most aristocratic and most cultured that Europe has ever seen, and its splendour was the symbol of France in one of its greatest political periods. Corneille gave expression to this spacious, aristocratic culture with a drama of lofty rhetoric in *Le Cid* (1636–7) and *Horace*, *Polyeucte*, *Cinna*, between 1640 and 1643. His tragedies, unlike the Elizabethan ones in England, take place at a highly conscious level of choice between passion and honour, and became increasingly disciplined by the neo-classic conception of the unities. His critical essays (the *Examens* and *Discours*) were pioneers in serious dramatic criticism. However, the English genius, the Court of Charles II, and the English literary tradition were all alien to the French influence: the genius operated more at the instinctual level than at the rational; England was a second rank power more conscious of its internal disagreements than its external greatness, and the court, though cultivated, was comparatively impoverished and did not directly nourish drama in the way that the French court did. Consequently the drama in England in the later 17th C did not match French attainments, despite English efforts at emulation.

Cornhill Magazine, The

A monthly periodical, at the height of its fame soon after its foundation by Thackeray*, the novelist, in 1860. Contributors included Ruskin*, Matthew Arnold*, Mrs Gaskell*, Trollope*, and Leslie Stephen*, besides Thackeray himself. It is still published.

Corpus Christi, The Feast of

A festival of the Roman Catholic Church in honour of the Holy Sacrament. It was ordained in 1264 by Pope Urban IV. By 15th C it was the principal Church feast in the year, and was particularly celebrated by the performance of mystery plays* dramatizing the redemption of Man by the Incarnation of Christ of which the Sacrament was the perpetual miraculous evidence. The Protestant* movements of the Reformation* on the whole rejected the doctrine of the Real Presence of Christ in the bread and wine of the Sacrament, so that in Protestant countries the feast ceased to be observed.

Corsair, The (1814)

A narrative poem in heroic couplets by Lord Byron* about a pirate chief, Conrad, his conflict with Seyd, a Turkish pasha, and the love for him

of two women, Medora and the rescued slave Gulnare. Medora dies of grief, and Conrad mysteriously disappears. It was once one of the most popular of Byron's poems, and illustrates the romantic* aspect of his work: exoticism, passionate love, the tragic hero.

Cortegiano, Il (The Courtier)

* *Castiglione.*

Corybantes

* *Cybele.*

Costume

The purpose of this entry is first to give readers an outline of the development of English costume, and secondly to explain by illustration some costume terms.

14th Century

The illustrations are from memorial brasses in English churches. The lady is wearing a cap or *coif* of pleated linen. The main garment is the *cotehardie*, tight-waisted and covering the gown to the feet. Over this, buttoned down the middle, is the *surcote*, perhaps trimmed with fur; it is open-sided, revealing the cotehardie beneath. Men wore versions of both garments: the cotehardie extended to the hips, and the surcote was long and loose, without open sides.

The male surcoat was worn over the main garment or *tunic*; here the surcoat is divided in front, showing the tunic beneath. The ornamented sword-belt, from which a pendant hangs, is worn like a *baldric*, *ie* from the shoulder to the hip. The shoes are sharply pointed, in mid 14th-C fashion.

14th Century (cont)

The woman's head-dress covering the head and neck is a *wimple*, surrounded by a veil, which falls to the shoulders. The main garment is a long, loose surcote, worn under a mantle fastened across the bosom.

The man's surcote covers the arms to just above the elbows, showing the tunic sleeves fastened by buttons which might be jewelled. Over the surcote he wears a *shoulder cape* with a hood attached.

15th Century

(Monumental brasses) The lady on the left wears a horned head-dress under a veil, a mid 15th-C fashion. The dress is still the tight-waisted cotehardie, worn under a mantle with ornamental fastenings. The tall head-dress (*above, centre*) is called a *hennin*; it has a butterfly veil over it, wired to keep its shape. Necklaces and pendants are now worn, as well as ornamental girdles round the hips. The other figure wears a plainer style of dress, with a fur or velvet hood similar to those worn later, in the Tudor period. The men all wear the voluminous outer garment, fashionable in 15th C for both men and women, known as a *houppelande*. The full sleeves were known as *pokys*. The tight sleeves of the cotehardie can be seen at the wrists. The short hairstyle of the figure on the right, with the head shaved up to the hairline, is typical of the reign of Henry VI (1422–61).

16th Century

(Brasses and portraits) The Elizabethan lady (*left*) has a cap or coif resembling a French hood, and the large Elizabethan *ruff* framing her head and the décolleté neck-line. The bodice of her gown is pointed in the *peasecod belly* style, and the skirt opens in front to show the richly-embroidered under-gown. She wears a *wheel farthingale* made of whalebone to make the dress stand out. The *gable hood* head-dress (*centre*) belongs to the first half of the century, while the *French hood* (*right*) is slightly later. The high shoulders and full skirt of the figure on the right foreshadow the exaggerations of the Elizabethan period.

A Gentleman in Red (portrait, about 1548). He wears a red velvet *doublet* under a gown with puff sleeves that gives the square silhouette typical of the period. The *breeches* or *trunk-hose* swell above the tight-fitting hose, and the *codpiece* at the crutch is conspicuous.

Portrait of the Earl of Leicester, in the reign of Elizabeth. His face is framed by a *ruff*; he wears a *jerkin* (a kind of doublet) with the characteristic 'peasecod belly', and trunk hose.

17th Century

Etching (*left*) of a woman representing Spring. An example of more ornate mid 17th-C costume, though not necessarily Cavalier. Her *bodice* is separate from her gown, laced across, ending in a silk bow. Note the numerous lace ruffles about the neck and cuffs. Autumn (*centre*) shows a plainer style of the same date. The collar or *falling-band* and the cuffs are plainer; the head is covered by a hood. The apron is not necessarily a mark of Puritan or lower-class dress. The high head-dress (*right*), from the end of the century, is called a *fontange* or *tower*.

Van Dyke's portrait of the Earl of Peterborough (*left*, about 1635). The *jacket*, or loose coat, has a lace falling-band and cuffs, and lace is also worn at the knee. Note the long, curled hair. The centre figure wears the sober dress and shorter hair of the Roundhead (Puritan supporters of Parliament against the King). The figure on the right shows the ordinary dress of the middle-class citizen – the doublet and cloak are plain without austerity.

18th Century

Fashion plate, 1794. The head-dress is composed of a *turban* and the high ostrich plumes which a little later were worn only as court dress. The waistline is now very high, and hoops were abandoned, muslin was the chief material and gowns were mostly white or spotted, no longer heavily embroidered.

Engraving, 1744. The hat is straw. The gown (probably silk) extends sideways over *hoops* and has the loose, ample lines of the kind known as a *sack*; it is open at the front to reveal the undergown. She carries the indispensable fan.

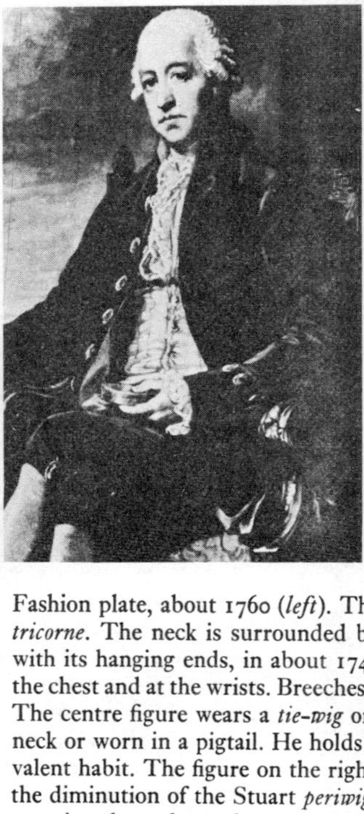

Fashion plate, about 1760 (*left*). The three-cornered hat was known as a *tricorne*. The neck is surrounded by a *stock* which replaced the *cravat*, with its hanging ends, in about 1740. The white linen shirt is frilled on the chest and at the wrists. Breeches continued to be worn until the 1790s. The centre figure wears a *tie-wig* or *Ramillie wig*, tied at the back of the neck or worn in a pigtail. He holds a snuff-box – snuff-taking was a prevalent habit. The figure on the right wears an earlier, fuller wig, showing the diminution of the Stuart *periwig*, long and curled. Powder was worn on wigs throughout the century.

19th Century – Regency and George IV (1800–30)

Fashion plate, 1809. A walking dress, showing the cultivation of the classical simplicity of the *Empire style* (named after the French Empire). The child wears a tunic over a white muslin or cotton gown. (*Right*) Fashion plate, 1816. A ball dress. It is a little fuller than the earlier Regency style, and shorter. The lace wings at the shoulder recall the Elizabethan period, so fashionable in the literature of the time. Note the flowers in the hair and the embroidered flowers at the hem.

Fashion plate, 1820. A carriage dress; a straw hat with plumes. The black silk upper garment is a *spencer*, a waist-length coat for outdoor wear. The lace collar and the puffed and slashed sleeves are again Elizabethan reminiscences.

Left: fashion plate, 1806. Walking dress. Wigs were abandoned around the end of the century. The loosely knotted stock or cravat is a symptom of the new 'romantic' simplicity and carelessness. Waistcoats are much shorter and commonly striped; the coat is a cut-away *tail coat*. *Trousers* replaced breeches entirely over the period 1790–1830. The *beaver hat* is made of the fur of that animal. The two figures above show one style of heavy top coat, the *redingote*, and the *frock coat*, cut square at the waist, worn as evening dress.

Victorian (1840–1900)

Fashion plate, 1854. Unlike the Regency period, mid 19th-C fashions sought to conceal the feminine figure rather than reveal it. Skirts filled out after 1830 until they arrived at the bell-shaped *crinolines* of the '50s and '60s. Bonnets, on the contrary, kept close to to the head, thus completing the triangular shape typical of the time. Materials were frequently heavy, and sombre in colour.

Fashion plate, about 1870. In the mid-sixties the crinoline flattened at the front and sides leaving only the *bustle* protruding at the back. Gowns often had heavy frills called *flounces*. Outdoors, heavy silk shawls were worn.

Fashion plate, 1878. Evening dress. Gradually the bustle became smaller and disappeared, though skirts remained very long until the last years of the century. Dresses once more conformed to the shape of the body; long *trains* were worn for evening dress.

Fashion plate, 1843 (*left*). Male evening dress assumed the style and blackness which it has retained ever since. The *bow tie* appears.

Fashion plate, 1871 (*centre*). The *top hat* was now always of silk. Ties are now worn; trousers (looser than at the beginning of 19th C) are often striped or checked. The cutaway tail coat has returned for everyday wear.

Fashion plate, 1890. Sports wear. The loose knee-breeches are *knickerbockers*; the *Norfolk jacket*, cap and knickerbockers are all of tweed cloth.

Cotter's Saturday Night, The
A poem by Robert Burns*. Written in Scots diction and Spenserian stanzas*, it celebrates the simplicities of Scots peasant life.

Counter-Reformation
A movement in the Catholic Church to counter the Protestant* Reformation*. It arose from the Council of Trent (1545–63) composed of the ecclesiastical leaders of the Catholic Church; they dealt with questions of doctrine and discipline raised by the Protestant revolt. The only important English writer to be influenced by the Counter-Reformation is the poet Richard Crashaw*.

Countess Cathleen, The (1892)
A verse play by W. B. Yeats*. Its theme is a woman who sells her soul to the devil in order to save the poor from starvation. It marks the beginning of Yeats's career as a poetic dramatist, and was one of the plays used by the Irish Literary Theatre as a starting-point.
 * *Abbey Theatre.*

Country Wife, The (1672–3)
A comedy by William Wycherley*. The naive jealousy of Mr Pinchwife, instead of keeping his country wife (whom he brings to London) in virtue, only puts into her head ideas which the libertine, Horner, encourages. On the other hand the naive confidence of Sparkish in Alithea, whom he is to marry, leads to her being carried off by someone else. It has been cited as an example of the dramatic deftness of wit and situation characteristic of Restoration* comedy, together with the moral cynicism and confusion also typical of it.

Couplet
A pair of rhymed lines of verse of equal length. The commonest form is the so-called heroic couplet of 10 syllables and five stresses in each line. It was first used in Chaucer's *Legend of Good Women**.

A thóusand tímës háve I hérd men télle
That thér is jóye in héven, and péyne in hélle . . .

The heroic couplet (*6.3.1) had its great period between 1660 and 1790 when most major poets from Dryden to Crabbe used it; its great master was Pope*:

Most sóuls, 'tis trúe, but péep out ónce an áge,
Dull sullén pris'ners ín the bódy's cáge
(Elegy to an Unfortunate Lady.)

Blank verse* (the medium of Elizabethan* and Jacobean* drama, including Shakespeare's, and of Milton's *Paradise Lost** and Wordsworth's *Prelude**) was a derivative of the couplet.

The 8-syllable (octosyllabic) couplet gives a lighter, less dignified rhythm. It was also used by Chaucer (*The Romaunt of the Rose*, *The Book of the Duchess*, *The House of Fame*) in his earlier work. It is less common after 1600 than before, but a notable later user of it is Jonathan Swift* (*eg On the Death of Dr Swift*). Keats* used it for *The Eve of St Mark* (1819), and W. H. Auden* for his *New Year Letter* (1941).

The poet John Skelton* sometimes used a very short, rapid, irregular couplet of two or three stresses commonly known as the 'Skeltonic couplet'.
 * 6.1.1.

Coursing
Hunting game (usually hares or rabbits) with hounds by sight and not by scent. A 'course' is set; the previously captured hare is released, and fast hounds (greyhounds) are sent in chase. The sport thus becomes a race to see which hound shall first catch the hare, and a prime interest is betting upon the hounds. The sport was widely popular from the Middle Ages onwards, and is even more so today, when it has been mechanized (with electric hares) and become simply 'dog-racing'. The sport was taken up by the aristocracy in 16th C, and regular coursing clubs were set up in the later 18th C.
 * *Field sports; Hunting.*

Court of Chancery
A Court of law under the Lord Chancellor*, head of the English judicial system. The Court grew up in 15th C to deal with cases which for any reason could not be dealt with efficiently by the established law courts administering Common Law*. The practice developed a system of law supplementary to Common Law, known as Equity. Equity dealt with special fields of jurisdiction, *eg* trusts, the rights of women, orphans, and lunatics. By 19th C its procedure became excessively complex, its relationship with other courts of law was ill-defined, and judgements were often delayed for years – hence the satire to which Dickens subjected the Court in his novel, *Bleak House**. The system was reformed by the Judicature Act, 1873. (The idiom 'in chancery' means 'remaining undecided indefinitely'; a 'ward in Chancery' is an orphan whose interests are in the care of Chancery.)
 * *Courts of Law.*

Courts of Law
The following is an alphabetically arranged list of some law courts commonly mentioned in English literature. It is not, of course, a complete account of the English judicial system; moreover it must be remembered that the Scottish one is different.
Assize Courts. Judges of the High Court of Justice go on circuit to try both criminal and civil cases outside London three times a year. These judicial sessions in the provinces are called Assizes.
Central Criminal Court. A stationary court – part of the High Court – for trying the more serious criminal offences in the London area. It meets in the building known as the Old Bailey.
Chancery. A court for trying civil cases under the branch of English law called Equity. It is presided over by the Lord Chancellor, and since 1873 it has been a branch of the High Court.
County Courts. Stationary courts in the provinces (*ie* in centres outside London) for trying minor civil cases. They meet under special County Court Judges.

High Court of Justice. This concerns itself with only the most important civil cases and criminal offences. It is now divided into three branches: Chancery under the Lord Chancellor; the Queen's Bench under the Lord Chief Justice; and a department under the name of Admiralty, Probate and Divorce which combines various ancient special forms of law, under a President. The Lord Chancellor is senior judge of the High Court.
House of Lords. As well as being politically the Upper House of Parliament, the House of Lords has kept its ancient function of being the senior Court of Law in the country. For this purpose certain judges are appointed as life-peers (*ie* their title is not inheritable) and are known as the Law Lords or Lords of Appeal. Only these judges and the Lord Chancellor, president of the House of Lords in both its political and its judicial capacity, meet when the Lords is in judicial session. It is now the senior Court of Appeal for civil and (not for Scotland) criminal offences. Until this century, peers had the right to be tried in the first instance by the House of Lords when charged with a criminal offence.
Magistrates' Courts. These courts try only the smallest criminal charges without a jury. The Magistrates*, or Justices of the Peace, are usually ordinary citizens without legal training appointed by the Lord Chancellor, nowadays on the recommendation of the local authorities. They now have very little civil jurisdiction, but until 19th C they had a great deal.
Petty Sessions. A name sometimes given to meetings of Magistrates' Courts.
Police Courts. Magistrates' Courts, as they are generally known to the public. The term is inaccurate, since the police have no more authority in these courts than in any others; but see the separate entry, *Magistrates.*
Queen's Bench. The division of the High Court concerned with the more important civil and criminal cases under Common Law. It provides judges for the Assizes, and its senior judge is the Lord Chief Justice.
Quarter Sessions. Criminal courts for trying intermediate offences, *ie* more serious than those in the jurisdiction of the Magistrates' Courts but less serious than those dealt with by the High Court. It meets either under a judge known as a Recorder, or under a group of magistrates whose chairman has had legal training.

* *Chancellor, Lord; Court of Chancery; Common Law; Jury System; Penal System.*

Courtly Literature and Romantic Love

We use the term 'Courtly Literature' for a type of literature which was nourished by the royal and aristocratic courts of western Europe from 12th to 16th C. Its outstanding theme was 'courtly' or 'romantic' love, in the medieval French courts known as 'fine amour', translated by Chaucer* as 'fine loving'. 'Fine loving' required elaborate codes of conduct and an elaboration of symbolism which only the leisured aristocracy could cultivate in the Middle Ages. This is indicated by the idioms 'to go courting' and 'to court a girl', frequent in common speech today, when all classes can hope for leisure.

For the medieval courtier or knight, 'fine loving' or 'courtly love' implied the tempering of warrior courage with gentleness to and reverence for women; for the lady, it implied fidelity, delicacy of feeling, and candour of heart at least towards the lover. The masculine ideal survived to educate the middle classes of 18th and 19th C in the virtues of 'the gentleman'; the feminine ideal combined with Puritan* abhorrence of sensuality in 17th C to produce the unnatural belief that 'good' women were immune from sexual passion. Nonetheless, the medieval courtly love romances were a literature of strong, though refined, sensuality, and although their whole tendency was to idealize the sexual relationship, their themes were often those of adultery and seduction; at least they comparatively seldom celebrated the institution of Christian marriage. This did not necessarily mean, however, that courtly love was contrary to the Christian ethic; Dante* was writing in the tradition when he made the Florentine girl Beatrice into a symbol of Theology in his *Divine Comedy.*

Among the royal courts which were particularly important for the cultivation of the literature of courtly love was that of Henry II* of England and his wife, Eleanor of Aquitaine. Their court was French-speaking, and became a centre for the southern French troubadour* poets, with whom the concept of courtly love seems to have originated. By the end of 14th C the language of the English royal court had become English. Richard II* had one of the most splendid courts in Europe. Its preeminent poet was Chaucer*. Chaucer's *Romaunt of the Rose* – a translation from the French – is an allegory of courtly love, and epitomizes its leading characteristics: love at first sight, love as a kind of parody of religion, the campaign of the lover as a parallel to a siege of a castle, the tendency of the lady's courtesy to betray her chastity, and so forth. The *Romaunt* is in fact a kind of textbook of courtly love, but Chaucer wrote other and still better poems on the theme, including *The Knight's Tale** and his masterpiece, *Troilus and Criseyde**. However, although the latter poem is one of the most moving and eloquent of all the medieval romances, it is written in a critical spirit; the fine madness of the lovers' passion is counterbalanced by a spirit of irony and moral sanity. Chaucer used an ancient legend as the basis of this poem, as was the usual practice of the medieval romancers. The most famous of these legends were the Arthurian cycle, which made an even more important contribution to French literature than to English; the best known version of them in English is Malory's *Morte d'Arthur**, which is itself based on French sources.

The 16th C brought the Renaissance* to England; the royal courts were patrons of the arts more than ever before. Platonic philosophy revived, and contributed Platonic idealism to the courtly tradition. It was the age of Castiglione's* *The Courtier* which expressed the ideals in accordance with which young noblemen formed their conduct. The pattern had much in common with that of medieval knighthood, but it was larger, in keeping with the more varied and more complex cultural interests of the age. The court of Elizabeth I*, partly because of her exceptional culture and partly because she was identified with the national destiny, had unusual importance as a centre of literary patronage. Spenser idealized her as Queen Gloriana, the counterpart of Arthur, in his courtly poem *The Faerie Queene**, but it is significant that there is a deliberate archaism about this poem of knightly adventures on the Arthurian model. From now on, one is less inclined to speak of 'courtly love' and more of 'romantic love', which is less defined by a code of conduct and not so restricted to a courtly, aristocratic class. Shakespeare's plays of romantic love (*eg Romeo and Juliet*, *As You Like It*, and *Twelfth Night*) have an astringent element which counteracts the traditional idealistic sentiment. There was a strong fashion for courtly love sonnets in the tradition of those by the Italian poet Petrarch*, but even Sidney in his sonnet sequence *Astrophel and Stella** used sonnets for psychological exploration as well as for idealization of his mistress, and this tendency becames much more marked in the sonnets of Shakespeare. The love lyrics of John Donne* are not in the least courtly. The last truly courtly poets were those at the court of Charles I*, the Cavalier Poets*, such as Carew*, Suckling* and Lovelace*.

Romantic love, the heir to the courtly tradition, had a history extending to this century. It deeply permeated 18th- and 19th-C novel, and acquired new interest and importance as women gradually moved to social equality with men. It also became trivialized in popular literature and the film. When Rupert Birkin, in D. H. Lawrence's *Women in Love**, tries to refuse the word 'love' to express his feelings for Ursula Brangwen, it is partly because of his distaste for the decadence of the tradition.

* 3.1.2.

Covenant and Covenanters

[1] When Charles I* tried to impose an Anglican religious settlement on Presbyterian* Scots, supporters of the Presbyterian system met from all over Scotland and signed the Covenant (1638), by which they solemnly undertook ('covenanted') to defend their common religious belief. Supporters of the Covenant were called Covenanters.

[2] The Solemn League and Covenant (1643) was the treaty between the Scottish supporters of the Presbyterian church and the Puritan* Parliamentarian rebels in England to preserve the Scottish Church, reform the Anglican* one in England, and resist the advances of Catholicism.

* *Civil Wars.*

Covent Garden

Originally Convent Garden. It was until recently the site in London of the chief vegetable market, and is still the site of London's opera house which goes by the same name. The present opera house dates from 1858. Before that the site had two successive theatres: the first opened in 1732 and burned down in 1808; the second was burned down in 1856. Conspicuous on one side of the square where the vegetable market was held is the severely classical portico of St Paul's Church (not to be confused with St Paul's Cathedral) designed by Inigo Jones*; the opening act of Bernard Shaw's *Pygmalion** is set there. In 18th C Covent Garden was a well-known London pleasure resort. In 18th C and up to 1843, Covent Garden was one of the only two theatres in London licensed by the government, the other being Drury Lane*.

* *Theatres; Jones, Inigo* (illustration).

Coventry Plays

* *Mystery Plays.*

Coverdale, Miles (1488–1568)

* *Bible in England.*

Coverley, Sir Roger de /ˈkʌvəli/

A fictional character invented by the essayist Sir Richard Steele* for the pages of the *Spectator**, and developed by his colleague Joseph Addison*. The name was taken from a north country dance, Roger of Coverley. Sir Roger was at first a member of an imaginary club, the Spectator Club, where Steele in his journalistic guise of the 'Spectator' purported to be studying human nature. In the hands of Addison, Sir Roger came to take up much more space than the other members; the papers devoted to describing his life (20 by Addison, 8 by Steele, and 2 by Budgell) are much the best known parts of the *Spectator*. In his conservatism, his devotion to the Church of England, and his kindly but despotic control of his tenants, he is a typical squire* of the time, but in his civilized manners he is deliberately made superior to the general run of country squires (compare Squire Western in Fielding's *Tom Jones**). In his simplicity and idiosyncrasies he was individual, with a literary relationship to Don Quixote. Though the 'Coverley Papers' are not a novel, the envisioning of the character is distinctly novelistic, so that they rank among the precursors of the English novel. Addison's especial aim, beyond entertainment, was to civilize the country squire; a secondary aim was the political one of making fun of the Tory English gentry.

Cowley, Abraham (1618–67) /'kauli/

Poet and essayist. His great prestige in his own time has never revived, but his verse is still living poetry, and should be read by anyone who wishes to understand the great change which English literature underwent between the beginning and the end of 17th C. His poetry is transitional between that of the Metaphysicals* (among whom he is usually included), with their balancing of feeling against reason and their conception of wit as a synthesis of imagination and intellect, and that of Dryden* and the Augustans* with their assertion of reason over feeling, and their use of wit to establish order and proportion. His language is often as ingenious as that of Donne*, but his conceits* are criticized for seeking ingenuity for its own sake, while at the same time he pays tribute to neo-classical ideals of decorum (see his ode, *Of Wit*). It was characteristic of him that he introduced into English the classical Pindaric* ode form, which allows considerable freedom within certain distinct limits; that he began the first epic on classical models in English, *Davideis* (1656), and that he was one of the founders of the scientific Royal Society*. His prose Essays (pub 1668) combine the moral analysis of Francis Bacon's* *Essays* with the personal element which, in the English essay, steadily increased through the work of Addison* and Steele* to that of Lamb.

Bib: Johnson, S., in *Lives of the Poets*; Loiseau, J., *Life*; Nethercot, A. H., *Life*; Williamson, G., *The Donne Tradition.*

Cowper, William (1731–1800) /'ku:pə/

Poet; he comes between the master of Augustanism, Alexander Pope* and the master of Romanticism, William Wordsworth*. He resembles the former in his sense of balance and proportion and in his sententiousness, and the latter in his compassion and his sensibility to natural surroundings. In direct comparison, he seems at first to lack the greatness of either his predecessor or his successor. It is a mistake, however, to read Cowper as a modified Pope or an immature Wordsworth. Though he lacked their power and originality in vision and control of medium, his personal humility led him to assess his limitations correctly and to write out of the attractive simplicity of his humane nature, without the pretentiousness of much of the poetry of the time. His nature was capable of great humour; *John Gilpin* (1785) is one of the most famous comic poems in the language. However, he was also deeply religious, influenced by the intense but narrow religious revivalism of the later 18th C to the point sometimes of insanity. His *Olney Hymns** (1779) include some of the best-known hymns sung in English church services; but one of his finest lyrics is inspired by religious despair – *The Castaway* (1799). His eight satires, 1782, written in Pope's* measure of the heroic couplet, are uneven; his major enterprise, the long reflective poem in blank verse, *The Task* (1785), is diffuse, but contains passages of sensitive description and sincere comment on life in town and in the country. This is the work most representative of his talent. In accordance with the modesty and integrity of this talent, Cowper's letters are among the most famous in English literature. He translated Homer's epics, the *Iliad* and the *Odyssey* (1791), but not memorably.

* 6.3.2.

Bib: Cecil, D., *The Stricken Deer*; Hartley, L. C., *William Cowper*; Nicholson, N., *William Cowper*; Thomas, G., *William Cowper and the Eighteenth Century*; Ryscamp, C., *Life*; Sainte-Beuve, C.-A., in *Causeries du Lundi*; Hartley, L., *Cowper, the Continuing Revaluation.*

Crabbe, George (1754–1832) /krab/

Poet. Born in the late Augustan* literary epoch, during which he wrote in heroic couplets *The Library* (1781) and *The Village* (1783), he produced most of his major work in the Romantic period, still using the same Augustan measure: *The Parish Register*, 1807; *The Borough*, 1810; *Tales in Verse*, 1812; *Tales of the Hall*, 1819. This makes him seem at first merely a belated Augustan unable to adapt himself to the changed idiom and vision to which Wordsworth and Coleridge had begun to convert the English public since their *Lyrical Ballads** of 1798. In fact Crabbe is a markedly original poet. He preserved some important qualities of the Augustan age: its moral assurance, its concern with man-in-society, its values of balance and proportion, its vigorous rationalism. But he added to these the grasp of significant detail, an intelligent understanding of the simple human being, and an ability to portray realistic circumstance typical of and even excelling some of the romantics in their best work. His verse tales (especially those of 1812) are a new form – short stories in which Crabbe uses the heroic couplet to enhance precision of description and incisiveness of comment. His art is to a great extent that of the novelist, and in forceful economy he is superior to any novelist of his time or before it except Jane Austen*, who admired him. As early as *The Village* he was countering the usual 18th-C descriptions of nature – usually to some extent influenced by literary pastoralism* – with bitter, vigorous realism, showing nature as it was known to the poor. His *Tales* are unique in English literature.

Bib: Crabbe, G. (junior), *Life*; Huchon, R., *Crabbe*; Haddekin, L., *The Poetry of Crabbe.*

Craft Guilds

Medieval societies for the protection and regulation of trade. They grew up in 13th C out of the already existing merchant guilds, the difference being that the merchant guilds were associations of all the traders in a town, whereas the craft guilds were each limited to a particular craft or line of business.

By degrees the craft guilds eliminated the merchant guilds by making them redundant. Each town had its own guilds, and part of their function was to protect the trade of that town against competition from 'foreigners'. They gave much-needed security to the exercise of trade in disorderly times, provided some social security to their members in times of need, and settled standards of work and conditions of sale. The members were master craftsmen*. Guilds declined fairly rapidly in 16th C as the capitalist, free-enterprise employers became more numerous; the guild system was too restrictive of trade to be compatible with capitalism*. For the study of literature, one of the main interests of the craft guilds was their performance of mystery plays* at festivals, especially Corpus Christi*.

2.1.1.1.

Cranford **(1853)**

A novel by Elizabeth Gaskell* (1810–65), first published in *Household Words** (ed. Charles Dickens) 1851–3. It is the best known of her novels. The town of Cranford is actually based on Knutsford, some 17 miles from Manchester. The book describes the life of the predominantly feminine genteel society of the place. Though apparently very slight, it contains graphic description, subtle, ironic humour resembling Jane Austen's*, and acute discernment in discriminating between the vulgar arrogance of the merely rich and the sensitive, humane pride of true gentility. Its most famous characters are the blatant and ostentatious Honourable Mrs Jamieson and, in contrast, the timid, retiring, yet distinguished Miss Matty.

Cranmer, Thomas (1489–1556) /ˈkranmə/

Archbishop of Canterbury, and responsible for the Book of Common Prayer (1549 and 1552) containing the liturgy of the Church of England. He was made Archbishop of Canterbury by Henry VIII* during the king's conflict with the Papacy, and supported his rejection of the Pope's authority (Act of Supremacy*, 1534), the starting-point of the Church of England. Under Henry's Roman Catholic daughter, Queen Mary I*, Cranmer renounced his opinions, but repudiated his renunciation when he was burnt at the stake in 1556. For English literature, he is especially important for the high literary value of his Prayer Book.

* *Common Prayer, Book of.*

Crashaw, Richard (1612?–49) /ˈkraʃoː/

Poet. He belongs to the Metaphysical* school of English poets, but in a special sense. In 1645 he became a Roman Catholic, despairing of the survival of the Church of England at that stage of the Civil War*. He earlier came under the influence of the work of the Italian baroque poet, Giovanni Battista Marino (1569–1625) whose extravagance of imagery to some extent resembled the drawing together of unlike ideas into a single image that typified the English metaphysicals. Although Crashaw was perhaps the most sensuous of the English poets of this tendency, his Catholicism and the influence of Marino give to Crashaw's ecstasy an impersonal quality quite different from the direct, very personal devotional poetry of Donne* and Herbert* – the latter of whom had been Crashaw's first master. Crashaw's masterpiece is his *Hymn to Saint Theresa*; the one that shows his extravagances most obtrusively is *The Weeper*. His poems were published in 1646 in one volume under the titles *Steps to the Temple* and *The Delights of the Muses*.

Bib: Warren, A., *Richard Crashaw*; White, H. C., *The Metaphysical Poets*; Williamson, G., *The Donne Tradition*.

Crécy, Battle of (1346) /ˈkresi/

The first major victory of the English in the Hundred Years' War*. In military history and patriotic sentiment it was important as being brought about by the English yeomen* as archers, using the longbow. For military history, this meant the beginning of the end of the domination of war by the horsed knight in armour, and the beginning of the importance of infantry. Nationally, the English victory was not merely a victory of the English feudal aristocracy over that of the French, but one in which the common people shared. The English forces were commanded by Edward III*, and the French by King Philip VI.

* *Archery.*

Creoles
British, French, and Spanish settlers in South and Central America, Louisiana, and the West Indies, and their descendants of any colour. In English literature it applies especially to British sugar planters in the West Indies, who were very prosperous in 18th C.

Cresseid, The Testament of
* *Testament of Cresseid, The.*

Cressida /ˈkresidə/
Heroine of a medieval legend of Latin origin, telling the story of the tragic love of Troilus and Cressida during the Trojan war. The legend is used by Chaucer in his long narrative poem, *Troilus and Criseyde**, by Henryson in his *Testament of Cresseid**, and by Shakespeare in his drama *Troilus and Cressida**.
* *Troilus and Cressida : the Legend.*

Cricket
The English national game. It is of obscure origins, but was played in some form by the common people in the Middle Ages. According to the *Encyclopedia Britannica*, it began to become popular with the upper classes during the Interregnum*, when the absence of a royal court and fashionable life in London caused the gentry to spend more time in their country houses. By 18th C the game was rapidly becoming popular among all classes especially in the south-east of England. Village played against village, and county against county; the gentry played alongside the common people. It was usually played, as it is today, on the village green. In 19th C, cricket spread overseas, but with curious irregularity. Thus the game has become popular in South Africa, Australia, New Zealand, India, Pakistan, and the West Indies, but not in most other parts of the Commonwealth, nor even in Scotland and Ireland. It is still the game, as distinct from sport, which most unites the various social classes in common enthusiasm.

Cricket on the Hearth, The (1846)
A Christmas book by Charles Dickens*, one of a series started by *A Christmas Carol*, 1843. It is a tale in which the evil schemes of old Tackleton to injure the married love of Peerybingle and his young wife, Dot, and to marry May Fielding are frustrated by the magic of the Cricket and by a mysterious stranger.

Cromwell, Oliver (1599–1658)
Chief commander of the Parliamentarian forces in the Civil War* against Charles I* and Lord Protector of the Realm (1653–8) in place of a king. He belonged to the landowning class in the east of England, and supported the Independents among the Puritans*. It was his generalship that defeated the forces of Charles I, and the Scottish supporters of Charles II* after the execution of Charles I. His brief period of rule increased Britain's international prestige. After his death, his son, Richard Cromwell, succeeded as Lord Protector for some months, after which Charles II was restored by the action of one of Oliver's generals,

General Monk, in 1660. After 1660 he suffered the censure of his political opponents, and it was not until Carlyle* published *Oliver Cromwell's Letters and Speeches* (1845) that his greatness was generally appreciated.

Cromwell, Thomas (1485–1540)
Chief minister of Henry VIII*; organized the dissolution of the English monasteries in 1536 and 1539. His sister married Morgan Williams; their son adopted the name of Cromwell, and was the direct ancestor of Oliver Cromwell.

Cronos /ˈkrəunəs/
In Greek myth, the son of Uranus* and the father of Zeus*. He usurped his father's position as ruler of the universe and was in turn overcome by Zeus.

Crotchet Castle (1831)
A novel by Thomas Love Peacock*. The plot is unimportant, and the novel consists mainly of witty talk, burlesquing and satirizing contemporary attitudes and ideas. A crotchet is an eccentric and frivolous notion or prejudice. Some of the characters are representatives of intellectual tendencies, *eg* MacQuedy, a Scots economist whose name suggests 'Q.E.D.' (Quod erat demonstrandum), stands for the excessive rationalism of the political economists and utilitarians of the age. On the other hand, Mr Skionar stands for the poet, critic and philosopher, S. T. Coleridge*, and burlesques his transcendental mysticism. Mr Chainmail stands for the sentimental cult of the 'gothic', *ie* the romance and sensationalism of the cult of the Middle Ages, familiar from the historical novels of Walter Scott* and from the gothic novels* of the previous generation. Sanity is represented by Dr Folliott, a

clergyman, a character of robust and cheerful common sense.

Crown of Thorns
The crown put in mockery on the head of Christ before the Crucifixion. *Matthew* 27:29.

Cruikshank, George (1792–1878) /ˈkrukʃaŋk/

Illustrator, with a strong satirical and moralistic bent; famous especially for his illustrations to Charles Dickens's novel *Oliver Twist**.

Crusades, The
Military expeditions to recover the Holy Land, and in particular the Holy City of Jerusalem, from the Muslims. There were eight principal crusades, from the first, proclaimed by Pope Urban II in 1095, which made Godfrey de Bouillon the King of Jerusalem in 1099, to the last on which St Louis (Louis IX of France) died in 1270.

Crystal Palace
* *Exhibition, The Great.*

Cuchulain /kuˈhu:lin/
In Irish myth the hero of a cycle of prose legends called the Cuchulain or Ulster cycle (9th–13th C AD). In English, he is chiefly known by the poems and plays about him by W. B. Yeats*. Yeats's work issued from his support of Irish nationalism, which revived interest in the Irish myths, and led to the publication of English versions of them – see E. Hull, *The Cuchullin Saga.*

Culloden (1746) /kəˈlodn/
A battle in the north of Scotland in the 1745 Jacobite* Rebellion on behalf of the House of Stuart* in the attempt to recover the British throne from the House of Hanover, which had been installed by Parliament in 1714. The Jacobites, consisting mainly of Scottish Highland clans commanded by Prince Charles Edward Stuart ('Bonnie Prince Charlie'), were decisively defeated by the Duke of Cumberland – Butcher Cumberland to his enemies. Not only did Culloden end the rebellion, but it practically put an end to the Highland clan system, which remains chiefly in name by force of romantic nostalgia.

Cunobelin
In legend, Cymbeline*. An ancient British king, father of Caractacus* who resisted the Roman conquest of Britain in 1st C AD.

Cupid
The Roman boy god of love, identical with the Greek Eros. He was son of Venus (the Greek Aphrodite) the goddess of sexual beauty. He seems to have been represented as a boy by the Greeks and Romans because love is mischievous. He is always represented with wings, and with arrows and a bow, with which he shot into the heart of his victims. He is made use of countless times in English love poetry, especially at the end of 16th C.
* *Psyche.*

Cybele /saiˈbi:li/
In Greek myth, identical with Rhea. A goddess originating in Asia Minor, known to the Romans as The Great Mother of the Gods, she stood for the productive forces of nature. Her priests were the Corybantes, who celebrated her festivals with delirious dances and the clashing of cymbals which were supposed to drown the cries of the infant Zeus*, king of the gods, thereby preventing his father, Cronos*, from discovering and destroying him.

Cyclops /ˈsaiklops/
In Greek myth a race of one-eyed giants in Sicily. In Homer's *Odyssey**, Polyphemus* was their chief.

Cymbeline (1609–10) /ˈsimbili:n/
A late tragi-comedy by Shakespeare; sometimes called a romance because of its avoidance of realism. Much of the play is set in the court of the ancient British king Cymbeline (1st C AD) and the climax is the defeat of a Roman invasion; on the other hand the love triangle of Posthumus, the British princess Imogen, and the Italian Iachimo* is thoroughly Renaissance*; Shakespeare has in fact combined a story of ancient British history from the chronicler Holinshed with a love-story from Boccaccio's *Decameron**. Thus a victory of British patriotism over Roman imperialism is fused with a more up-to-date victory of English single-minded devotion over Italian duplicity. *Cymbeline* has also been called a reconciliation play*, because, like *Pericles** before it and *The Winter's Tale** and *The Tempest** after it, it steadily darkens with murderous conspiracy from the outset to the middle, and then lightens towards a general clarification in candour and love at the end. Also like the other

three plays, *Cymbeline* has as a central theme the loss to the world (and, except in *The Tempest*, to the father) of a young girl, whose recovery expresses the recovery of the qualities of youth, purity, beauty, trust, and potentiality.

Cymri /ˈkimri/

A Celtic word meaning Welsh.

Cynewulf (8th C) /ˈkiniwulf/

Anglo-Saxon poet. Author of four poems: *The Ascension*, *The Legend of St Juliana*, *Elene* – about the discovery of the true cross on which Christ was crucified – and the *Fates of the Apostles*. The work shows Cynewulf to have been a scholar, familiar with Latin, and technically a skilful poet. *Elene* and the *Ascension* are most praised.
 * *Anglo-Saxon Literature*.

Cynics, The

A school of ancient Greek philosophers founded by Antisthenes in 4th C BC. Their belief, that the only realizable aim in life was the fulfilment of the individual by the strict application of reason to practical issues, led them to an extreme individualism, according to which social considerations were irrelevant, ambition was a distraction, pleasure a corruption, and poverty and disrepute were of active assistance in promoting self-reliance. The word 'cynic' seems to derive from the Greek word for 'dog', and they agreed in taking this animal as their emblem. The word has degenerated to imply an attitude of disbelief in the goodness of human motives and even in the reality of human values.
 * *Diogenes*.

Cynthia

A name given to Artemis*.

Cypress

A coniferous tree planted in cemeteries in southern Europe as symbolic of death and mourning, presumably from its sombre foliage. In English literature there are references to it in this sense, as to its northern equivalent, the yew tree. Coffins were sometimes made of cypress wood. 'Cypress lawn', on the other hand (in Shakespeare's *Twelfth Night** III.i and Milton's *Il Penseroso**), refers to a dark cloth from Cyprus.

Cythera

 * *Aphrodite*.

D

Dactyl /ˈdaktil/

A verse foot consisting of an accented syllable followed by two unaccented ones. It thus gives a light falling rhythm, and is commonly used with trochees in lines which end in an accented syllable or an iambus:

> *Mérrily, / mérrily, / sháll I / live nów*
> *Únder the / blóssom that / hángs on / the bóugh.*
> (Ariel's song in Shakespeare's *Tempest*)

These lines could be scanned as each consisting of two dactyls followed by a trochee and ending with an iambus.
 * *Metre*.

Daedalus /ˈdi:dələs/

In Greek myth, an artist of wonderful powers. He made wings for himself and his son Icarus*, and flew from Crete to Sicily to escape the wrath of King Minos*, for whom he had built the labyrinth. The fact that he was the type of the artist explains the use of a form of the name by James Joyce – Dedalus* – in *Portrait of the Artist as a Young Man*.

Dagon /ˈdeigon/

In the Bible, a god of the Philistines*. He seems to have been a corn god, although by a mistaken derivation he is traditionally described as half man, half fish.

Daily Mail

 * *Newspapers*.

Daisy Miller (1879)

A novel by Henry James*. It concerns the visit of an American girl to Europe, and is one of the stories in which James contrasts American freshness of impulse, moral integrity, and candour of heart with the complexity and deviousness of the European mentality. It is not now usually regarded as one of his best works, but it brought James some fame on publication.

Dame Schools

Schools for poor children in 18th and 19th C, especially in country towns and villages. Unlike the charity schools, they were run by private initiative, especially by single women supplementing their income by teaching reading and writing.
 * *Schools in England*.

Damocles /ˈdaməkli:z/

In Greek legend, a flatterer who declared Dionysius, ruler of Syracuse, the happiest of men. To demonstrate to Damocles the perilous life of princes, Dionysius invited Damocles to a feast where he was made to sit beneath a sword suspended from the roof by a single hair. Hence to live 'under the sword of Damocles' is to live in the constant threat of danger.

Damon /ˈdeimən/

A shepherd poet in Virgil's* eighth eclogue.

Hence the name is sometimes used in English pastoral* poetry for a shepherd, and sometimes as a pseudonym for a real person.

Damon and Pythias

In Greek legend, symbols of loyal friendship. Pythias was condemned to death by Dionysius of Syracuse, and asked for temporary release from prison to arrange his affairs. Damon gave himself as pledge for Pythias's return to prison in time for his execution, and Pythias duly returned so that his friend should not be killed in his place. In admiration, Dionysius forgave him. The legend is told in an alternative form according to which it is Damon who has been condemned, and Pythias stands pledge. In the original legend Pythias was called Phintias. The story is the subject of an early Elizabethan play, *Damon and Pythias* (1564) by Richard Edwards.

Danae /'daneii:/

In Greek myth, daughter of Acrisius, king of Argos. He shut her up in a bronze tower owing to a prophecy that her son would kill him. However Zeus* fell in love with her and visited her there in the form of a shower of gold; she gave birth to Perseus*.

Dance of Death (Danse Macabre)

A theme widespread in medieval painting and poetry, representing a procession of all ranks of society being led to their graves by a skeleton emblematic of death. The theme seems to have been inspired by the epidemics of the black death* in 14th C; they are said to have reduced the population of England alone by almost a half. There are no famous direct representations of the theme in medieval English literature, but the constant imminence of death is in the state of mind implied by much of it, *eg* the *Pardoner's Tale** in Chaucer's *Canterbury Tales*. A grimly ironical humour reminiscent of the dance of death is also characteristic of the Renaissance*, *eg* the grave-digger scene in Shakespeare's *Hamlet**.

Danegeld /'deingeld/

A tax raised by Anglo-Saxon kings as tribute to the Danes to prevent their invasions of southern England.

Daniel

In the Bible, a book devoted to a prophet (Daniel) who upheld the Jewish faith during the Babylonian captivity*. The book is much referred to in English literature owing to the dramatic character of some of its episodes such as the story of Belshazzar's* feast, and of Daniel in the lions' den. In the latter story, Daniel was found praying contrary to the edict of the Persian King Darius*, who had conquered Babylon. Darius ordered him to be thrown into a den of lions; next morning, however, he was found unharmed, because the angel of God had 'shut the lions' mouths'. Darius then acknowledged the God of Daniel as 'the living God'. The phrase 'a Daniel come to judgement', used by Shylock in Shakespeare's *Merchant of Venice** is a reference to the passage in *Daniel* 6, where Darius is said to have appointed Daniel as one of the three 'presidents' of his empire.

Daniel, Samuel (1562–1619)

Poet. He is best known for his sonnet sequence, *Delia* (1592). These love poems show his distinctive qualities: they are serious, serene, beautifully cadenced, limpid in diction, without conflict or mystery or emotional complexity. The absence of the last three qualities sets him apart from Sidney* and Shakespeare* as a sonnet writer, and in opposition to the violent Donne*. He most resembles Spenser*. The qualities that give him true though limited distinction as a sonnet writer also make for success in his *Complaint of Rosamond* (1592) – a lament in which the mistress of Henry II* confesses her sinful love – and in his masques, *eg Tethys Festival* (1610) and *Hymen's Triumph* (1615). On the other hand, the same qualities frustrate success in his longest work, *Civil War* (1595–1609), in which he describes the struggles for power between the House of York and the House of Lancaster in 15th C in narrative form, as Shakespeare had already done (*1, 2, 3 Henry VI** and *Richard III**) in dramatic form. The account is no doubt more accurate than Shakespeare's but the style is too uniformly sober for the dramatic fluctuations and violence of the events. The same limitations restrict his dramas, *Cleopatra* (1594) and *Philotas* (1605). His *Poetical Epistles* (1604) and his philosophical didactic poem *Musophilus* do not in their nature suffer from his limitations, and are admired in parts by some critics, though now little known. His contemporaries, such as Spenser (who admired his talent) and Jonson (who said he was no poet), thought he lacked energy of poetic spirit, but the romantic poets such as Wordsworth*, Southey*, and Coleridge*, searching in early 19th C for a restrained and truthful poetic diction, admired him for his sobriety of expression.

His prose *Defence of Rhyme* (1602) in answer to Thomas Campion's* *Art of English Poesy*, is a sane and practical treatment of poetic techniques, unusual in its time for the precise use of words, refusal to be dazzled by generalities, and concern with the condition of the English language and poetry of the age without excessive reverence for classical (Greek and Latin) precedent.

Bib: Rees, J., *Daniel*; Lewis, C. S. in *History of English Literature in the Sixteenth Century*; Ure, P., in Pelican Guide Vol II *The Age of Shakespeare*.

Daniel Deronda (1876)

A novel by George Eliot* (Mary Ann Evans). It contains a double story: that of the hero, Daniel Deronda, and that of the heroine Gwendolen Harleth. Daniel is the adopted son of an aristocratic Englishman, and a young man of gracious personality and positive values; he discovers that he is of Jewish parentage, and ends by devoting himself to the cause of establishing a Jewish homeland, and to marrying a Jewish girl, Mirah. Gwendolen belongs to an impoverished upper class family, and marries (under pressure from her clergyman uncle) a rich, and entirely self-centred aristocrat, Henleigh Grandcourt, to redeem their fortunes. Her story is the discovery of the truth of her own nature, just as Deronda's story is the discovery of his origin and vocation. Their stories are linked by the almost casual but entirely beneficent influence of Deronda over Gwendolen, whom he saves from despair after the death of her husband in circumstances that compromise her conscience. Critics have observed that the story of Gwendolen is one of the masterpieces of English fiction, but that that of Daniel is comparatively flat and unconvincing; fortunately, readers find it practicable to read the former with very little attention to the latter.

Dante Alighieri (1265–1321) /'danti/

Italian poet, and one of the greatest figures in European literature. He was a native of the north Italian city of Florence, which became involved in the quarrel between the Pope and the ruler of the Holy Roman Empire* that was dividing Europe; Florence itself was divided, and Dante spent the later part of his life in exile. By far his most important work was the *Divine Comedy* (or *Divina Commedia*), in which the poet imagines himself guided through Hell (*Inferno**) and Purgatory (*Purgatorio**) by the Latin poet Virgil*, and then through Heaven (*Paradiso**) by Beatrice, who was at once an earthly girl whom Dante had adored from a distance, and a spiritual embodiment of theology. Lesser works include his *Vita Nuova* (New Life) describing his encounter with and love for Beatrice, and his *Convivio* (Banquet), a maturer, philosophical poem.

Dante's importance is in summary as follows:

[1] He did for Tuscan Italian what Chaucer did for the East Midland dialect in English, *ie* established it as the literary vehicle of Italian culture.

[2] His *Divine Comedy*, based above all on the philosophy of Thomas Aquinas*, is by far the noblest and profoundest expression of the medieval cosmos – its theology, its conception of human destiny, and its vision of the nature of man. This makes him the most central of all European writers in the culture of Christendom.

[3] His combination of mysticism, lucidity, concreteness, and control of poetic medium, assisted by intimacy with the Latin poet, Virgil, was the basis, guide and inspiration for much of the greatest medieval and Renaissance* poetry both within Italy and in other countries of Europe.

Just because Dante's influence was so pervasive, it is difficult to pinpoint his impact on English literature; it is far easier to trace the specific effect of lesser Italians, such as Boccaccio* and Petrarch*, who themselves owed Dante so much. For example, Chaucer*, the dominating figure for the course of English poetry, read and was influenced by Dante both in detailed idiom and in spiritual vision, but he was a very different kind of genius. English poets who attempted profound and inclusive imaginative expressions of the spirit of man – Spenser*, Milton*, Blake*, Keats* (in the second *Hyperion**), T. S. Eliot* – are all conscious in some degree of Dante's example, but often indirectly. Perhaps one should say that the running rhythms and verbal harmonies of most English poets from Chaucer onwards owed much to Dante's use of them, and that his spiritual vision can never be ignored. Apart from the totality of that vision, his spiritualization of romance by the transfiguration of Beatrice is the fusion of two contradictory strains in European imaginative writing.

* *Terza Rima*.

Bib: Eliot, T. S., in *Selected Essays*; Wickstead, P. H., *Dante & Aquinas*; Toynbee, P., *Life and Works*.

Daphne /'dafni/

In Greek myth, the daughter of a river god and beloved by the god Apollo*. When he pursued her, she was changed by her mother, the earth-goddess, Ge, into a laurel tree. Hence the laurel (or bay tree) became the favourite tree of Apollo, god of the arts, and triumphant poets were crowned with it on his feast-days.

D'Arblay, Madame

* *Burney*.

Darius the Great (521–485 BC) /də'raiəs/

King of Persia; he greatly extended the Persian Empire but was defeated by the Athenians at the battle of Marathon (490 BC). In the Bible he is said to have declared the greatness of the God of the Hebrews after Daniel had survived the lions' den (*Daniel** 6:26).

Dark Ages, The

As late as early 19th C 'Dark Ages' was synonymous with Middle Ages*, *ie* the period between the downfall of the Roman Empire in Western Europe (about AD 500) and the beginning of the Renaissance*. However, historical studies in 19th C caused a revision of the idea that the medieval period had as a whole been one of ignorance and intellectual stagnation, and the term is now usually applied to the earlier part of it only, from about AD 500 to about 800. The expression is used also to describe any period of comparative ignorance or backwardness in a particular field of knowledge or affairs.

Darling, Grace

A girl who achieved legendary fame for her heroism in putting out into a stormy sea in a small boat with her father, and rescuing passengers from a wrecked ship. The incident occurred in 1838.

Darwin, Charles Robert (1809–82)

Biologist. His book *On the Origin of Species by means of Natural Selection* (1859) not only expounded the theory of the evolution of natural organisms (which in itself was not new, for it had been held by, among others, Darwin's grandfather, the poet Erasmus Darwin) but presented persuasive evidence for the theory. In brief, this was that species naturally tend to produce variations, and that some of these variations have better capacity for survival than others, which in consequence tend to become extinct. Darwin's conviction partly began with his study of Malthus* on population, and it thus belongs to the rationalistic* tradition which 19th C inherited from 18th. The book greatly disturbed many religious people, since it apparently contradicted the account of the creation of the world of *Genesis* in the Bible; it also raised serious doubts about the existence of the soul and its survival after the death of the body. However, it is possible to exaggerate the importance of the Darwinian theory as a cause of religious disbelief: on the one hand, Lyell's* *Principles of Geology* (1830–3) had already done much to upset traditional beliefs (those, for instance, of the poet Tennyson*) and so had scientific scholarship on biblical texts by men like Charles Hennell (as in the case of the novelist George Eliot*); on the other hand, intelligent believers such as Coleridge* had long ceased to accept the Bible as a sacred record of fact in all its books. The effect of Darwin's ideas was probably rather to extend religious doubt from the intelligentsia (who were already deeply permeated by it) to wider circles. Another kind of effect was to produce in the popular mind a naïve optimism that man was subject to a general law of progress; it thus encouraged an uncritical view of history and society.

Darwin wrote a number of other scientific works, including *The Descent of Man* (1871). His *Journal of Researches into the Geology and Natural History of the various countries visited by H.M.S. "Beagle"*, a report of his first important scientific expedition (1831–6), is a fascinating travel book. He also wrote a brief but interesting *Autobiography* (edited with additions by Nora Barlow, 1958).

* 3.4.4. *Agnosticism.*

Bib: Huxley, L., *Charles Darwin*; Stevenson, L., *Darwin among the Poets*; West, G., *Darwin: the Fragmentary Man*; Darwin, F., *Life and Letters.*

Davenant (D'Avenant), Sir William (1606–68) /ˈdavnənt/

A minor poet and dramatist, of historical interest because he was a link between the age of Charles I*, with its qualities of elegance and increasing simplicity of poetic expression – still touched, however, by something of the emotional vigour of the Elizabethans – and the Restoration* era after 1660, with its emphasis on classicism, reason and economy of form. He belonged to the court, and was a channel for the French classical influence on drama and poetry. His comedy *The Wits* (1636) was one of those that anticipated Restoration Comedy; his *Siege of Rhodes* (1656) was the first English opera, helped to keep continuity in the drama during the Interregnum*, and began a new conception of the theatre as spectacle. After 1660 he became a theatre manager, and adapted Elizabethan plays, including Shakespeare's, to suit the new taste. In 1651 he published a long romantic epic of a kind more familiar in 16th C; its romantic diction excited the criticism of a more important transitional poet, Abraham Cowley*.

* *Opera in England.*

Bib: Harbage, A., *Sir William Davenant*; Nethercot, A. H., *D'Avenant, Poet Laureate and Playwright.*

David, King

In the Bible, the Jewish hero and the second King of Judah; historians believe his reign to have been approximately 1010–970 BC. His story is mainly told in *1 Samuel* from chap. 16, *2 Samuel*, and *1 Kings* 1–2. Salient features of it are: his slaying, while still a shepherd-boy, of the Philistine giant Goliath with a stone from his sling; his adoption as court favourite by King Saul, and Saul's subsequent jealous hatred of him; the devoted friendship between David and Saul's son, Jonathan; his period of outlawry ending in the overthrow of Saul and David's accession to the throne; his capture of Jerusalem, never hitherto in Jewish hands; the rebellion by and defeat of his son Absalom. David seems to have been a poet and musician, and tradition ascribed to him authorship of the *Psalms*, but modern scholarship dissents. It was declared that the Messiah, or Deliverer of the Jewish nation, would be born of the House of David – hence Joseph, earthly father of Jesus Christ, is said in *Luke* 1 to be of this descent.

* *Pastoral*

David, Saint (6th C)

A Welsh prince who became bishop, and is the patron saint of Wales.

David Copperfield (1849–50)

A novel in autobiographical form by Charles Dickens*. 'Of all my books I like this the best; like many fond parents I have a favourite child and his name is David Copperfield.' Some commentators have thought that the hero is representative of Dickens himself, and point to the resemblance of initials: C.D. and D.C. It is true that in outline Copperfield's experiences – his sense of early rejection, child labour in a warehouse, experience as a journalist and final success as a novelist – are similar to Dickens's own. But it seems just to conclude that the parallels are distant: Dickens's purpose was to present an imaginative picture of growth from childhood to manhood in his own period of history, using his own experience as some of its material but without intending a biographical record. The social landscape of this novel is broader than an autobiography would be likely to achieve. It includes the moralistic and sadistic oppressiveness of Copperfield's mercantile stepfather, Murdstone, and the intimate study of selfish hedonism in Copperfield's aristocratic friend, Steerforth; the spontaneous cordiality of the humble Yarmouth boatman, Peggotty and his sister, and the cunning deviousness of Uriah Heap, whose servile humility is disguise for his total ruthlessness in making his way from bleak beginnings to a position of power. The novel is strong in dramatic contrasts, and particularly interesting in the counterbalancing of the women characters. Copperfield is fatherless, and his gentle, guileless mother (who becomes victim in matrimony to Murdstone) is like an elder sister to the child; both are children to the motherly, protective servant,

Clara Peggotty. She is replaced by the harsh and loveless Miss Murdstone who plays the role of cruel stepmother. Copperfield runs away, and takes refuge with his idiosyncratic aunt, Betsey Trotwood, who has shaped for herself an eccentric independence of men, retaining for a harmless lunatic (Mr Dick) a compassionate tenderness which she now extends to her nephew, in spite of having rejected him at birth because he was a boy. Copperfield's first wife, Dora Spenlow, is a simulacrum of his mother – a child wife, on whom Ibsen* seems to have based Nora in *A Doll's House*. Two other representatives of Victorian womanhood are Agnes Wickfield (whom he eventually marries), the type of defenceless womanly sanctity and nearly a victim of Heap's rapacity, and Little Em'ly who is first under the protection of Peggotty and then becomes 'the fallen woman' when she is seduced by Steerforth. Another very striking portrait is Rosa Dartle, companion to Steerforth's mother and poisoned by vindictive hatred of him because of his cool assumption of social and masculine privilege. Though not the richest and deepest of Dickens's novels, it is perhaps psychologically the most revealing, both of Dickens himself and of the society of his time.

Davy Jones

In the mythology of English sailors, the sailors' devil. 'Davy Jones's locker' is the grave of those drowned at sea.

Day Lewis, Cecil

* *Lewis.*

De la Mare, Walter (1873–1956) /dəlɘ'meə/

Poet, novelist, writer of short stories. He was born in Kent, and educated at St Paul's Cathedral Choir School. From 1890 to 1908 he was a clerk in the offices of the Anglo-American Oil Company; he was then given a government ('Civil List') pension to enable him to devote himself to writing. Many of his poems and his stories were addressed to children. Books of verse of this sort were: *Songs of Childhood* (1902); *A Child's Day* (1912); *Peacock Pie* (1913). Children's stories: *The Three Mulla-mulgars* (1910); *The Riddle* (1923); *The Magic Jacket* (1943); *The Dutch Cheese* (1946). He had conspicuous talent for retelling traditional fairy tales: *Told Again* (1927); and compiled two unusual anthologies: *Come Hither* (for children, 1923) and *Love* (for adults, 1943). His most remarkable prose fiction for adults is probably *On the Edge* (stories, 1926) and *Memoirs of a Midget* (novel, 1921). His books of verse for adults include: *The Listeners* (1912), *The Veil* (1921), *Memory and other poems* (1938), *The Burning-glass and other poems* (1945); *The Traveller* (1946); *Inward Companion* (1950); *Winged Chariot* (1951) and *O Lovely England and other poems* (1953).

His poems are conservative in technique, with the melody and delicacy of diction characteristic of the best poetry of the late 19th and early 20th C, but are unusual in the quiet intensity with which they express evanescent, elusive, and mysterious experience. His stories have a singular quietness of tone and are written in an unassuming style, but they convey with great sensitivity material which is on the borderline of conscious experience. *The Three Mulla-mulgars*, also published under the title of *The Three Royal Monkeys*, is one of the most original stories for children in English literature. De la Mare's unusual combination of intensity and innocence makes the border line between his work for children and for adults an almost imperceptible one.

Bib: Mégroz, R. L., *De la Mare: a biographical and critical study*; Reid, Forrest, *De la Mare: a critical study.*

De Quincey, Thomas (1785–1859) /də'kwinsi/

Essayist and critic. Most famous for his autobiography, *Confessions of an English Opium-Eater**. His work was mostly for periodicals and is voluminous, but only a few pieces are now much read. His strong points as a writer were his exceptionally sensitive, inward-turning imagination, and his breadth of understanding. The first produced not only his autobiography, but a fragment of exceptional literary criticism, *Knocking at the Gate in Macbeth*, *The English Mail Coach* (1849), and *Murder Considered as One of the Fine Arts* (1827), show the quality of an exceptional psychological novelist. His second gift produced studies of German philosophy (Kant, Lessing, Richter) and able translations of German tales, besides some original historical criticism. He was very much a representative of the first generation of English romanticism, and as the poets of that generation found new ranges of expression for their medium, so De Quincey expanded the poetic range of prose, partly by recapturing some of the quality of the early-17th-C prose writers.

* 7.3.

Bib: Eaton, H. A., *Life*; Abrams, M. H., *The Milk of Paradise*; Clapton, G. T., *Baudelaire et De Quincey*; Jordan, J. E., *Thomas De Quincey, Literary Critic*; Saintsbury, G., in *Essays in English Literature*; Sackville-West, E., *A Flame in Sunlight.*

Debrett /də'bret/

An annually issued register of the peerage of Great Britain, first published in 1802.

Decameron, The (1348–58) /di'kamərən/

A collection of tales by the Italian writer Boccaccio*. They came from many sources and have in turn been drawn upon by English writers including Chaucer (for the *Canterbury Tales**), Shakespeare (*All's Well that Ends Well** and *Cymbeline**) and Keats* (*Isabella and the Pot of Basil*).

Declaration of Independence (1776)

The assertion of independence by the American colonists, starting-point of the United States. It was signed by 13 states.

Decline and Fall of the Roman Empire, The (1776–88)

The most eloquent and imposing historical work in the English language. By Edward Gibbon*.

It begins at the height of the Roman Empire in 1st and 2nd C AD – an age with which Gibbon's own era, so deeply imbued with Latin scholarship, felt strong kinship. He then proceeds to record the successive stages of Roman decline, the rise of Christianity, the struggle with the Eastern Roman Empire (the Byzantine) centred on Constantinople* (Byzantium), and that empire's eventual extinction by the capture of Constantinople in 1453. As an account, it has of course been to some extent outdated in consequence of later research, but as an imaginative epic (still regarded as substantially true) and an expression of the background to modern Europe as understood in 18th C, it remains a much read and very important work. Its structure is as spacious as the subject, and is sustained by the energy of Gibbon's style. The attitude is one of 18th-C truth-seeking, and of urbane irony towards the Christian religion, whose growth he sees as one of the agents of destruction of classical civilization. Gibbon's sceptical mind is at the same time constantly critical of human pretensions to self-sufficiency, the attainment of wisdom, and integrity of motive; in such respects he is in the tradition of the great satirists of his century – Alexander Pope* and Jonathan Swift*.

Dedalus, Stephen /ˈdiːdələs/

Principal character in Joyce's novel *Portrait of the Artist as a Young Man**; he is also a main character in Joyce's *Ulysses**. The surname derives from the mythical artist of ancient Greece, Daedalus*.

Defender of the Faith (Fidei Defensor)

A title awarded to King Henry VIII* by Pope Leo X in 1521, in recognition of Henry's *Defence of the Seven Sacraments* written against Luther. English monarchs have used the title ever since.

Defoe, Daniel (1660?–1731) /diˈfəu/

Novelist and journalist. He is now chiefly remembered as the first of the English novelists, and in particular as the author of *Robinson Crusoe**. He made his living largely by political journalism.

He was born into the middle-class, Puritan section of society, the son of a London butcher. He engaged in a number of commercial enterprises which failed, but his *Essay on Projects* (1698) shows that in regard to social economy and institutions he was in advance of his time. He was already employed by the government of William III* to write in defence of its policies, when they were under attack from the Tory right wing, which was uneasy about the deposition of James II* and jealous of William's prestige among the Protestant powers in Europe. He tended in his writings to encourage the Puritans* (known then as Dissenters) to compromise with their consciences in coming to terms with the Church of England's religious and political establishment. This policy antagonized them, and he was friendless on both the right and the left when he was discovered to be the author of *The Shortest Way with the Dissenters* (1702), an ironical criticism of the government's religious policy which caused him to be imprisoned. On his release in 1704, he wrote for and edited periodicals, and served the government under the moderate Tory leader Robert Harley, until its downfall in 1714.

Defoe's novels appeared when his career as a political journalist was substantially over. *Robinson Crusoe*, 1719; *Captain Singleton**, 1720; *Moll Flanders**, *A Journal of the Plague Year**, *Colonel Jack**, 1722; *Roxana**, 1724 – these are the most famous of a number of fictitious or semi-fictitious works, told with such careful realism that there was doubt at the time whether some of them were not authentic records. Defoe wrote in a factual style without elaborate, romantic description even when the incidents seemed to demand it. This was true to the spirit of his time – the age of the philosophy of Locke*, who emphasized that reality could be truthfully described only by its primary, *ie* measurable, qualities. Characteristic also are his individualistic heroes and heroines, often criminals who, although they reform in the end, feel themselves in a world where self-reliance is indispensable, and God, often referred to as Providence, seems remote, if indispensable in the end.

In 1724 appeared Defoe's guide, *A Tour through the Whole Island of Great Britain.*

4.3.1.

Bib: Sutherland, J. R., *Life*; Dottin, P., *Daniel de Foe et ses Romans*; Watt, I., in *The Rise of the Novel*; Moore, J. R. *Defoe, Citizen of the Modern World.*

Deirdre /ˈdiədri/

In Irish myth, a harper's daughter who was to be the bride of king Conchobar of Ulster, but who fell in love with and was carried off by Naoise to Scotland. Conchobar beguiled them back and treacherously slew Naoise and his brothers. Dramas were made on her story by W. B. Yeats* in 1907, and by J. M. Synge* (pub 1910). They are two of the finest products of the Irish dramatic movement.

Deism

A form of religious belief which developed in 17th C; it was an outcome of the Reformation* in 16th C. The Reformation involved two conclusions: first, in the belief of many sects, that the truth of Christian doctrine could be discovered only by individuals for themselves; and second that toleration of differences in religious opinion was indispensable. Edward Herbert* evolved the idea that, while religion revealed in the Gospels was true, it was preceded by 'natural' religion, according to which by his own inner light a man could perceive all the essentials of religious truth: the existence of God, the duty of worshipping him, the duty of repentance for sins, the reality of life after death, and the consequences of reward and punishment. Herbert's deism was further expounded in 18th C by a number of minor thinkers (often in such a way as to suggest that the Christian revelation as presented in the Gospels was redundant), and it suited the 18th-C cool and rational habit of mind which tended to see God as abstract and remote. Bishop Butler among the theologians and Hume* and Kant among the philosophers exposed the unsoundness of deistic arguments in 18th C, and in 19th C the growth of the genetic sciences demolished the basic assumptions of deism, *ie* that human nature and human reason have always been constant, in a constant environment.

* 3.3.2.

Dejection: an Ode (1802)

A poem by S. T. Coleridge*. Its first version was a verse-letter (4 April) to Sara Hutchinson, Wordsworth's* future sister-in-law, with whom Coleridge, already married to another woman, was in love. A letter of 19 July, to his friend Sotheby, includes long selections from the poem, but the person addressed in it is now named as Wordsworth (see *Letters*, ed E. L. Griggs). The public version appeared in the *Morning Post** on 4 October, Wordsworth's wedding day and the seventh anniversary of Coleridge's own unhappy marriage. The letter-versions are very personal: they are appeals for sympathy for his unhappy domestic life, and for his distress that his poetic gift seemed to be leaving him. The public version is still addressed to Sara Hutchinson, but she is apostrophized as 'Lady' so that her identity is concealed. The poem still concerns Coleridge's personal predicament as a poet who feels his creative powers to be failing him, but the tone is much less personal; its subject is less Coleridge himself than the 'shaping spirit of Imagination', considered both as that which shapes the requirement for creative art, harmony in the poet's soul, and that which shapes the poem itself.

The poem is intimately bound up with Wordsworth, who had already written the first four stanzas of his *Intimations of Immortality**, also a poem about failing poetic powers, when Coleridge wrote his first version. *Dejection* chimes with these stanzas, and it is itself answered by Wordsworth's *The Leech-Gatherer** (May–July 1802), a poem about the revival of moral courage, and by stanzas v–xi of *Intimations*, in which Wordsworth proves to himself that he can sustain his creative powers. Thus, the three poems resemble a dialogue between the two poets.

Dekker, Thomas (1570?–1632)

Dramatist and pamphleteer. His best-known play is *The Shoemaker's Holiday**, based on Thomas Deloney's* *The Gentle Craft* – a narrative about the London crafts. The play celebrates the proud traditions of the citizens, and the romantic zest of its plot and dialogue has kept it alive. His next most known play is *The Honest Whore*, Pt. I (1604). He was essentially a dramatist of middle life. He collaborated with Rowley in *The Witch of Edmonton* (1623); with Middleton* in *The Roaring Girl* (1611), and with Massinger* in *Virgin Martyr* (1622).

His pamphlets are perhaps more notable than his plays, especially *The Wonderful Year* (1603), a vivid account of an epidemic of plague in London, and *The Gull's Hornbook*, a satire on the manners of a fashionable young man. He was a master of the racy, vigorous, colloquial prose of his time. Dekker is an example of a minor talent who has survived by sharing in the unusual vitality of an outstanding literary period.

Bib: Jones-Davies, M. T., *Dekker* (written in French); Gregg, K. L., *Dekker, a Study in Economic and Social Backgrounds*; Judges, A. V., *Elizabethan Underworld*; Knights, L. C., *Drama and Society in the Age of Jonson.*

Delany, Mrs Mary (1700–88) /dəˈleini/

One of the famous letter writers of 18th C. She had a wide circle of friends among the famous men of her day.

* *Letter-writing.*

Delia

One of the names of the Greek goddess Artemis* who was said to have been born on the Greek island of Delos.

Delia is also the name of a sonnet sequence by Samuel Daniel*.

Delilah /diˈlailə/

In the Bible (*Judges* 16) a woman beloved by the Jewish hero Samson. She betrayed him to the Philistines by cutting off his hair in which lay his divinely given supernatural strength. In Milton's *Samson Agonistes** she appears under the name of Dalila, and she is Samson's wife.

Deloney, Thomas (1543?–1600?) /dəˈləuni/

Pamphleteer and ballad writer. He was a silk-weaver, and his best writings are legendary narratives about the crafts and cloth-merchants: *Thomas of Reading* (1600), *Jack of Newbury* (1597), and *The Gentle Craft* (1598), about clothiers, weavers, and shoemakers respectively. His style was plain and direct, and the description of the murder of Thomas of Reading is an early masterpiece of realistic* narrative, anticipating Defoe*, but in its pathos superior.

* *Elizabethan Novels.*

Bib: Chevalley, A., *Life.*

Delphi

In ancient Greece, the seat of a temple to Apollo* on the slopes of Mount Parnassus*, and of the most famous oracle* of the ancient world. The oracles were spoken by a priestess of Apollo, called the Pythia*.

Demeter (Lat. Ceres) /diˈmi:tə/

In Greek myth, the corn goddess, daughter of Cronos* and sister of Zeus.* Her daughter Persephone* (Lat. Proserpina) was carried off to the underworld by its god Hades (Lat. Pluto). Zeus, however, released Persephone to the upper world for half the year, in compassion for Demeter's grief. The myth symbolizes the planting of the corn, and its shooting above the surface in spring.

Demiurge /ˈdi:miə:dʒ/

Plato* used the word for the maker of the world. The early Christian heretics, the Gnostics (2nd C AD), held demiurges to be spiritual powers, partly or wholly evil, between the Supreme Being and Man.

Demogorgon /ˈdi:məˈgo:gən/

In early Christian mythology, a terrible deity of the underworld; according to Boccaccio*, a primeval pagan god. In Shelley's *Prometheus Unbound** a spiritual principle superseding false gods

Demosthenes (4th C) /di'mosθəni:z/

In ancient Greece, a great Athenian orator; he is often referred to in English literature as the pattern and ideal of all orators. He is especially famous for his speeches warning the Athenians of the danger from the growing empire of Philip of Macedon, father of Alexander the Great. Hence the word 'philippic' for an aggressive political speech.

Derby, The /'da:bi/

The most famous English horse-race, run annually since its foundation in 1780 by the Earl of Derby. It takes place at Epsom, near London; the day of the race is called Derby Day.

Descartes, René (1596–1650) /dei'ka:t/

French philosopher, mathematician. In ethics and religious doctrine he was traditional, but in method of thought he was the starting point of the total reliance on reason – rationalism* – that was pre-eminent in the later 17th C and 18th C. In his *Discours de la Méthode* (1637) he reduced knowledge to the basic principle of *Cogito, ergo sum* (I think, therefore I am), from which intuition he deduced the existence of God and thence the reality of the external world. He also distinguished mind and matter, finding their source of combination again in God. It was the influence of Descartes' writings that drew the English philosopher, John Locke*, the dominant figure in English rationalism, to the study of philosophy.

* 3.3.1.

Deserted Village, The (1770)

A poem by Oliver Goldsmith*, and his finest. It was written in protest against the 18th-C practice of enclosures*. Goldsmith paints an idyllic picture of Auburn before enclosure, and contrasts this with its desolation after. On the other hand, as George Crabbe* pointed out in his poem *The Village* (1783), Goldsmith exaggerated the prosperity and contentment of the traditional English village. Goldsmith's poem belongs partly to the artificial mode of 18th-C pastoral, and partly to the period's more vigorous strain of invective.

* *Village, The English.*

Detective Fiction

This branch of literature is usually easy to distinguish from the much wider literature of crime and retribution in drama and in the novel. Unlike the latter, detective fiction seldom relies on the presentation of deep emotions or on subtle and profound character-creation. Character, emotion, psychological analysis of states of mind, social reflections, will all be present as flavouring, and may even be conspicuous, but the indispensable elements are always a mysterious – but not necessarily horrible – crime, and a detective, who is commonly not a professional policeman, but who has highly developed powers of scientific deduction. It is essential that the surface details should be convincing, and that the author should keep no clues from the reader, who may thus have the satisfaction of competing with the detective at his game. Thus a good detective story is always a highly developed work of craftsmanship but it is very seldom a work of art, and is usually better when it has no pretensions to being one. The vogue derives from Arthur Conan Doyle* more than anyone else, and it is significant that he based his detective, Sherlock Holmes, on a distinguished surgeon with outstanding diagnostic powers. Detective fiction is really a manifestation of our scientific culture. Earlier than Doyle, the novelist Wilkie Collins* wrote distinguished detective stories (*The Woman in White*, 1859–60, and *The Moonstone**, 1868); he was a serious writer who used detection as a means to his purposes as an artist.

Perhaps it is because most detective novels do not pretend to be literature but only a relaxing recreation that the consumption of such reading matter has become so great in 20th C. Any attempt to list the successful writers of detective fiction would certainly result in the omission of particular favourites. Readers of other literature may meet reference to fictional detectives such as Hercule Poirot (the Belgian detective of books and plays by Agatha Christie), Father Brown (G. K. Chesterton*) and Lord Peter Wimsey (Dorothy Sayers).

Deuteronomy /dju:tə'ronəmi/

In the Bible, the fifth book of the Old Testament, containing the laws of the ancient Jews, with commentaries.

Devil

[1] The Greek version of the Hebrew Satan*, and identifiable with him.

[2] In Christian myth, an inhabitant of the underworld with Satan as its king; one of the fallen angels* cast out of Heaven for their rebellious pride; traditionally depicted with horns, tails, and goats' legs and hooves, derived from the ancient Greek woodland gods (satyrs*) whose chief was Pan*; identifiable with pagan gods dethroned by the true God of Christianity, *eg* in *Paradise Lost** by John Milton. In this version, devils have links with secret pagan survivals in Christian countries, and the attempts of the Church to identify the old gods with the powers of evil.

[3] In the legal profession, 'to devil' for someone is to assist as a junior barrister in preparing work for a senior one.

[4] A printer's devil is a printer's assistant, usually a boy.

Devil is an Ass, The (1616)

A satirical comedy by Ben Jonson*, attacking the speculators, financial tricksters, and their dupes, in contemporary London. The young dupe, Fitzdottrel, is cheated out of his land by the 'projector' Meercraft with elaborate projects of land reclamation; Pug, an inferior devil trying his hand at deceiving and betraying humanity, finds that he is not the equal in this to human beings themselves. It has been described by a leading historian as 'by far the best introduction to the economic history of the period'.

Diana

* *Artemis.*

Diaries

As a form of literature in English, diaries begin to be significant in 17th C. The spirit of criticism from the Renaissance* and the stress on the individual conscience from the Reformation* combined with the political and social turbulence of 17th C to awaken people to a new awareness of personal experience and its possible interest for general readers. Thus the art of the diary arose with the art of biography* and autobiography*. Diaries of course are commonly written for the eyes of the authors alone, but when the authors do not destroy them they presumably expect that others will read them, or that they may even be published. Thus diaries may first be divided into the two classes of those clearly meant to be strictly private, and those written more or less with an eye to eventual publication. A further division may be made between those which are interesting chiefly as a record of the time in which the writer lived, and those which are mainly a record of his personality.

The best of the English diaries is that of Samuel Pepys* (1633–1703) because it was both purely private (written in code) and entirely unself-conscious, as well as an excellent record of the time. His contemporary, John Evelyn* (1620–1706), is less famous partly because his diary is a more studied, self-conscious work. Jonathan Swift's* *Journal to Stella* (covering the years 1710–13) is a personal revelation but unusual in that it was addressed to the woman Swift loved. The diary of the Quaker, George Fox* (1624–91), is a record of his spiritual experience for the education of his followers. In 18th and early 19th C the most famous is that of the novelist Fanny Burney* (Madam D'Arblay, 1752–1840) considered as a record of the time ingenuously imbued with her own personality. The diary of the great religious reformer, John Wesley* (1703–91), is comparable to that of Fox as a spiritual record, with a wider outlook on his time. In 19th C the diaries of Thomas Creevey (1768–1838) and Charles Greville (1794–1865) are famous as records of public affairs, and that of Henry Crabb Robinson* (1775–1867) for impressions of the leading writers who were his friends. In 20th C the *Journal* of Katherine Mansfield* is an intimate and vivid record of personal experience, and that of Virginia Woolf* is an extremely interesting record of a writer's experience of artistic creation.

Dick, Mr

A character in Dickens's novel *David Copperfield**. A harmless lunatic, he has an obsession with King Charles's head (*ie* Charles I*, decapitated in 1649) – hence this is commonly used as synonymous with obsession, like the idiom 'a bee in one's bonnet'.

Dickens, Charles (1812–70)

The most popular and internationally known of English novelists. His father was a government clerk who liked to live prosperously, and his sudden impoverishment and imprisonment for debt in the Marshalsea* was a drastic shock to the boy Dickens; prisons recur literally and symbolically in many of his novels, which are also filled with attacks on the injustice of social institutions and the inequalities between the rich and the poor. He began his writing career as a journalist, and all his novels were published serially in periodicals, especially in two edited by himself – *Household Words** started in 1850, and *All the Year Round** started in 1859, both of them weeklies.

His first book, *Sketches by Boz** (1836), was a collection of stories and descriptive pieces written for various papers in the tradition of the essayists – Lamb*, Hazlitt*, Hunt* – of the previous generation, with the especial difference that Dickens wrote about the hitherto neglected lower middle class. *Pickwick Papers** (1836–37), at first loosely connected but gathering unity as it proceeded, was immensely successful. There followed: *Oliver Twist** (1837–38), *Nicholas Nickleby** (1838–39), *The Old Curiosity Shop** and *Barnaby Rudge** (1840–41). This concludes the first, comparatively light-hearted phase of Dickens's writing, in which he developed his characteristic comedy and melodrama. *Martin Chuzzlewit** (1843–44) begins a more impressive style of writing in which the comedy and melodrama deepen into new intensity, though critics observe that the beginning of the novel is still in the earlier manner. In 1843 begins his series of Christmas Books, including *A Christmas Carol** and *The Cricket on the Hearth**. Thereafter come his mature masterpieces: *Dombey and Son** (1846–48); *David Copperfield** (1849–50); *Bleak House** (1852–53); *Hard Tines** (1854); *Little Dorrit** (1855–57); *A Tale of Two Cities** (1859); *Great Expectations** (1860–61); *Our Mutual Friend** (1864–65). Dickens was writing *Edwin Drood** when he died.

* 4.4.1.

Bib: Forster, J., *Life*; Johnson, E., *Life*; Wilson, E., in *The Wound and the Bow*; Chesterton, G. K., *Charles Dickens*; Gissing, G., *Charles Dickens: A Critical Study*; House, H., *The Dickens World*; Leavis, F. R., in *The Great Tradition*; Collins, P., *Dickens and Crime*; *Dickens and Education*; Gross J., *Dickens and the Twentieth Century*; Leavis, F. R. and Q. D., *Dickens the Novelist.*

Dictionary of the English Language, A

Usually known as *Johnson's Dictionary*, it was compiled by Samuel Johnson*, was published in 1755, and was accepted as authoritative for about a hundred years. The excellence of the work is not so much its scholarship as its literary intelligence. It is weak in etymology, for this was still an undeveloped science, but it is strong in understanding of language, and in particular the English language. In the Preface, Johnson writes a short grammar, but he points out that English simplicity of forms and freedom from inflexions make an elaborate one (as grammar was then understood) unnecessary. He makes clear that the spirit of the English language had been unduly influenced by the spirit of French, and he rejects the idea that correctness should be fixed by the authority of an Academy, since the inherent mutability of language will always cause it to follow its own laws. Johnson thus began the Englishman's habit of relying upon current English dictionaries and manuals of usage when he wishes to discover the best existent expression: Fowler's *Modern English Usage* and the Oxford *New English Dictionary* are 20th-C equivalents of Johnson's Dictionary.

Didactic Literature

Literature designed to teach, or to propound in direct terms a doctrine or system of ideas. In practice, it is not always easy to identify; so much literature is didactic in intention but not in form; sometimes writers renounce didactic intentions but in practice use didactic forms. Thus Spenser declared that *The Faerie Queene** was meant to 'fashion a gentleman . . . in vertuous and gentle discipline', but the poem may be enjoyed for its imaginative vision without much regard to its didacticism, and the same is true of Bunyan's *Pilgrim's Progress**. In 18th C much poetry had at least didactic leanings, such as Pope's *Essay on Criticism**, his *Essay on Man**; minor work by other poets is much more unmistakably didactic. The prevalence of didactic poetry in 18th C arose from the especially high regard this century had for ancient Greek and Latin literature: Hesiod's *Works and Days* (Greek, 8th C BC) and Lucretius' *De Rerum Natura* (Latin, 1st C BC) being the great examples of didactic verse. The Romantic poets of the early 19th C (Wordsworth*, Coleridge*, Shelley*, Keats*) reacted against the 18th-C Augustans*, and since then there has been a persistent prejudice against explicit didacticism. In fact much of Wordsworth (*eg The Excursion**, 1814) and of Shelley (*eg Queen Mab**, 1813) was highly didactic, though the undisguised passion to some extent conceals the fact. The 19th-C novelists, especially Dickens* and George Eliot*, used didactic digressions, but in the former such passages are especially of passionate social invective, and in the latter they are usually more integrated into the imaginative art than is apparent. In the 1930s there was a revival of verse didacticism, especially in the work of W. H. Auden*, *eg New Year Letter* (1941). In general, the view now is that poets and even novelists may be didactic if they choose, so long as they remain artists. True didacticism, however, requires a body of assumptions commonly held by author and reader, as was true of the age of Pope, but is not so today.

Dido (Elissa) /ˈdaidəu/

In Roman legend, the daughter of a king of Tyre, and the reputed founder of the city of Carthage*. Virgil* brings her into his epic of the founding of Rome, the *Aeneid**; she falls in love with Aeneas when he is shipwrecked on the North African coast, and when he forsakes her to fulfil his destiny, she kills herself. The Romans identified her with the guardian goddess of Carthage.

She is the subject of a tragedy, *Dido* (1594) by Christopher Marlowe* and Thomas Nashe*, and of the opera* *Dido and Aeneas* by Nahum Tate to music by Henry Purcell*, produced in 1689–90.

Diogenes the Cynic /daiˈodʒiniːz/

A Greek philosopher who sought to achieve spiritual independence by renouncing property (even a drinking bowl) and lived in a tub. When the great conqueror, Alexander of Macedon, offered to fulfil his wishes, Diogenes asked him to stand out of the way of the sunshine. Whereupon Alexander declared 'If I were not Alexander I would choose to be Diogenes'.

* *Cynics.*

Diomedes /daiəˈmiːdiːz/

A Greek hero in the Trojan war, and king of Argos. In Chaucer's *Troilus and Criseyde** and Shakespeare's *Troilus and Cressida**, he seduces Cressida (Criseyde) from her devotion to the Trojan prince, Troilus.

Another Diomedes owned the man-eating mares that Heracles* had to capture as one of the twelve Labours of Hercules.

Dionysus /daiəˈnaisəs/

In Greek myth, a vegetation god especially associated with wine. He was the son of Zeus* and Semele*. His festivals were celebrated by incantations or choruses, which eventually gave rise to Greek tragedy. He is said, like other vegetation gods, to have died and risen again, and the ceremonies by which he was worshipped were orgiastic. He was also known, in both Greek and Latin, as Bacchus. Dionysus is sometimes contrasted with Apollo: 'Dionysiac' writing is passionate and explosive; 'Apolline' writing is contemplative and serene.

Dismal science, The

Political economy; so called by Thomas Carlyle* because the social thought of such writers as Adam Smith*, Jeremy Bentham*, Thomas Malthus* and David Ricardo tended to be pessimistic about the alleviation of poverty and inhumanly indifferent to the consequences of economic laws as they saw them.

Disraeli, Benjamin [Lord Beaconsfield] (1804–81) /disˈreili/

Statesman and novelist. He was of Spanish-Jewish descent; his grandfather settled in England in 1748. His political career was brilliant; he entered Parliament in 1837; in the 1840s he was the leader in the House of Commons of a small number of Tory (**Whig and Tory*) politicians who, as the 'Young England' group, wanted a revival of the party and of the national spirit in an alliance between a spiritually reborn aristocracy and the common people; by 1848 he was leading the Conservatives in the House of Commons; in 1868 and in 1874–80 he had his two periods as one of the most brilliant of English Prime Ministers. Both politically (he secured the vote for the urban working class) and socially (*eg* his trade union legislation) he at least partly succeeded in securing support for his party from the working class. He was made Earl of Beaconsfield in 1876.

The novels which now chiefly hold attention are his 'Young England Trilogy': *Coningsby** (1844); *Sybil** (1845) and *Tancred* (1847). All were written to promulgate his doctrine of Tory Democracy, and they all have imperfections, partly because for Disraeli literature was second to politics. On the other hand they have great liveliness of characterization, and show keen insight into the structure of society with its cleavage between rich and poor, which Disraeli called 'the two nations'. His other novels are: *Vivian Grey* (1826); *The Young Duke* (1831); *Alroy*, and *Ixion in Heaven* (1833); *The Infernal Marriage*, and *The Rise of Iskander* (1834); *Henrietta Temple*, and *Venetia* (1837); *Lothair* (1870) and *Endymion* (1880).

Bib: Blake, R., *Life*; Monypenny, W. F. and Buckle, G. E., *Life*; Jerman, B. R., *The Young Disraeli*; Holloway, J., in *Victorian Sage*; Dahl, C., in *Victorian Fiction* (ed. L. Stevenson); Pritchett, V. S., in *The Living Novel*.

Dissenters

A term used for those Puritans* who, owing to their 'dissent' from the established Church of England, were refused certain political, educational, and (at first) religious rights from the second half of 17th C. That is to say, they could not enter Parliament, they could not enter a university, and, until 1688, they could not join together in worship. Puritans were not thus formally restricted before 1660. They were released from their political restraints in 1828. In 19th C it became more usual to call them Nonconformists or Free Churchmen. The term does not apply to Scotland, where the established Church is Presbyterian, not the episcopalian Church of England.

* 3.2.2.2.

Dissociation of Sensibility

A critical expression invented by T. S. Eliot*, and used in his essays *The Metaphysical Poets* (1921, included in his *Selected Essays*). He states: 'In the seventeenth century a dissociation of sensibility set in, from which we have never recovered; and this dissociation . . . was aggravated by the influence of the two most powerful poets of the century, Milton* and Dryden*.' Eliot's argument is that before 1660 poets, in particular the Metaphysical Poets*, were 'engaged in the task of trying to find the verbal equivalent for states of mind and feeling', and that after that date 'while the language became more refined, the feeling became more crude'. Poetry, henceforward, is put to more specialized purposes: 'Tennyson* and Browning* are poets, and they think; but they do not feel their thought as immediately as the odour of a rose. A thought to Donne* was an experience; it modified his sensibility.' The implication behind the argument is that poets (with exceptions) ceased to bring all their faculties to bear upon their art: 'Racine* or Donne looked into a good deal more than the heart. One must look into the cerebral cortex, the nervous system, and the digestive tracts.'

The theory has had great influence. Those who uphold it support it with the evidence provided by the rise of modern prose after 1660, and the gradual displacement of poetry from its centrality in literature thereafter; poetry either subjected itself to the rational discipline of prose (*eg* Pope*), or, in 19th C, it tended to cultivate areas of feeling to which this rational discipline was not relevant (*eg* Swinburne*). However, the theory has been attacked for various reasons. Eliot himself felt that he had used the expression in too simplified a way (*Milton*, 1947, in *Poets and Poetry*), and that the causes of the process were more complicated than his earlier essay had implied. Other writers have suggested that such a dissociation did not happen; or that it happened in different ways at different periods; or that, if it did happen, no deterioration in imaginative writing can be attributed to it. See Frank Kermode, *The Romantic Image* and F. W. Bateson in *Essays in Criticism*, vol. 1.

* 7.5; *Seventeenth-century Literature.*

Dithyramb /'diθiram/

A Greek choric hymn in honour of the god Dionysus* (Bacchus), and irregular and vehement in rhythm. 'Dithyrambic' is used to describe verse with similar rhythm, such as Dryden's* *Alexander's Feast.*

Dives and Lazarus /'daivi:z/

A parable in the Bible (*Luke* 16) about the relationship between a rich man (*dives* in the Vulgate) and a poor man (Lazarus) in this world and after death. From this, Dives is generally used as synonymous with 'rich man'.

Divina Commedia (Divine Comedy)

The greatest poem by the Italian poet *Dante**. For an account, see under its sections: *Inferno**, *Paradiso**, *Purgatorio**.

Divorce

Until 1857, divorce was possible only through Church courts which had kept their authority over matrimonial relations since before the Reformation*, while losing it in nearly all other private affairs of laymen. Even after a marriage had been dissolved by a Church court, a special ('private') act of Parliament was necessary before the divorce was legalized. In consequence, divorces were rare and only occurred among the rich and influential. Adultery and cruelty were the accepted grounds, and the wife was commonly in an unfavourable position, so that no divorce was granted on account of a husband's adultery until 1801. The law of 1857 added desertion as a ground for divorce, and proceedings were taken out of the hands of the Church courts and put under the courts of the realm. Since 1938, unsoundness of mind may also be pleaded as a cause of divorce, and it has been further facilitated in other ways.

* *Women, Status of.*

Doctor Faustus, The Tragical History of

A tragedy in blank verse*, with comic episodes in prose, by Christopher Marlowe*, and his greatest work. The play resembles a medieval morality play* in that its theme is Faustus's sacrifice of his soul to the devil (represented by Mephistophilis) for the sake of unlimited power, glory and enjoyment in this world. On the other hand, it is also thoroughly Renaissance* in its treatment: the conflict of choice is made convincing as it would not have been in a medieval play, and the psychology not only of Faustus but of Mephistophilis is presented with moving insight. The medieval and the Renaissance outlooks fuse in *Doctor Faustus*, showing the very important continuity, as well as the contrast, between the two outlooks.

There are two uncertainties about the play. One is about its date. Marlowe uses the material of the German Faustbook, which is about an early 16th-C scholar who had claimed powers of black magic, and fuses this historical figure with medieval legends about a man selling his soul to the devil. The earliest surviving English version is dated 1592, and the maturity of the poetry also suggests a date for the play late in Marlowe's life. On the other hand, other critics have found good reason to date *Faustus* at least as early as 1588. The other uncertainty concerns the extent of Marlowe's authorship. Did he have a collaborator for the comic parts? And were some of these added after his death? The edition of 1616 has considerably extended comedy, as compared with the first edition of 1604. The main reason for suspecting a collaborator is that much of the comedy is superfluous as well as trivial. It is, however, a mistake to suppose that the mere presence of comedy is injurious to the highest tragedy; the combination is frequent in Elizabethan serious drama – tragedies and history plays – including Shakespeare's, and it is one of the inheritances from medieval mystery* and morality plays, with which English Renaissance drama kept close relationship. Some of the comedy in *Faustus* enriches the tragedy by extending its relevance to common life, *eg* in the parody in which Faustus's servant, Wagner, also tries his hand at summoning the devil.

* *Faust Myth* and *Goethe's Faust*.

Doctor's Dilemma, The (1906)

A comedy by Bernard Shaw*. It is simultaneously a satire on the practice of medicine, and a criticism and exploration of the conventional moral code. The immoral artist causes less actual harm by his naked selfishness than do the highly moral doctors in the perfectly lawful discharge of their profession.

Dogberry and Verges

Comic constables in Shakespeare's play *Much Ado about Nothing**. Dogberry is famous for his misuse of words – compare Mrs Malaprop* in Sheridan's *The Rivals*.

Doggerel

Any carelessly made, irregular verse, often of a frivolous nature. The term is used by the host in Chaucer's *Canterbury Tales** in regard to the tale of *Sir Thopas**, told by Chaucer himself as one of the pilgrims: '"This may wel be rym doggerel," quod he.' John Skelton* is the only eminent poet to have used doggerel as a deliberate style, except in burlesque.

Dollar

The dollar in 16th C was the English name for the large silver German coin called a 'thaler' (pron. tarler). It was also the English name for the Spanish peso, sometimes called a 'piece of eight' because it was worth eight of a smaller coin called a 'real'. In 1785 the dollar was adopted as the coinage of the U.S.A.

Dombey and Son (1847–48)

One of the earliest of the mature novels by Charles Dickens*. Dombey is a proud and heartless London merchant whose sole interest in life is the perpetuation of his name in connection with his firm. For this reason he neglects his deeply affectionate daughter Florence for the sake of his little son, Paul, whom, however, he values not for himself but as the future embodiment of his firm. The boy is motherless, deprived of affection, and physically delicate – he dies in childhood. To prevent Florence from marrying a mere clerk in his firm, Dombey sends her lover – Walter Gay – on business to an unhealthy colony in the West Indies. Dombey's pride makes him susceptible to flattery; he is preyed upon by Carker, his manager, one of Dickens's most notable villains, and by Major Joe Bagstock. He is led into marriage with a cold, disillusioned girl, Edith Granger, who runs away from him with Carker. Both his pride and his wealth are eventually taken from him, and he finds himself in the end dependent on the forgiving Florence and Walter Gay. A particular interest of the book is that railways play an important part in it just at the time when they were transforming English life. The sombreness of Dombey's mansion is opposed to the warm-hearted if unbusinesslike environment of the shop of Solomon Gills, Gay's uncle.

Domesday Book /ˈduːmzdei/

(Dome = doom, *ie* judgement, implying a complete and final record as on the Day of Judgement at the end of the world.) The record of a survey carried out by the order of William I* and completed in 1086. It contains a description of the greater part of the landed property of England, and was compiled to assist taxation and other government purposes.

Dominicans

An order of preaching and teaching friars* founded by St Dominic (1170–1221). They established themselves in England in 1221, and were known here as the Black Friars* from their dress. Their influence was very great, but by 14th C they were under criticism for their accumulation of wealth despite their professions of poverty. The English order was dissolved, like the other orders of friars and monks, in 16th C.

Don Juan /donˈdʒuːən/

The hero under different names of legends in various European countries, but in formal literature first the subject of the Spanish play *El Burlador de Sevilla* by Tirso de Molina (1571–

1641), who gave him his distinctive character of sensual adventurer. Plays and stories were woven round him in French and Italian, and he has the title-role in Mozart's opera. In English literature by far the most important work about him is the satirical epic *Don Juan** by Lord Byron; he was also the subject of a forgotten play *The Libertine* (1676) by Thomas Shadwell, and, in a modernized form, of Shaw's* *Man and Superman*. John Clare also wrote a long poem, *Don Juan*, identifying himself with Byron.

Don Juan (1819–24)

Byron's unfinished satirical epic in 16 cantos, based very freely on the legendary figure of Don Juan*. It is written in ottava rima*. After a love affair in Spain (Canto I), Juan is sent abroad by his mother; he is shipwrecked and washed up on a Greek island where he is cared for by a Greek maiden Haidee (II); III and IV describe their love and the breaking of their relationship by Haidee's pirate father, Lambro; in V he has been sold as a slave to a Turkish princess who loves him; in VI, VII and VIII he has escaped and is serving the Russian army against the Turks in the siege of Ismail; in IX he has attracted the attention of the Russian Empress, Catherine the Great, who sends him on a mission to England. The remaining cantos concern England, Juan's experiences in English society, his affair with a duchess, and a rather deeper emotion for an English Catholic girl. Juan not only has fewer mistresses than in earlier versions of the legend, he is also more often seduced by women than the seducer (Shaw's* view of the character is consonant with this). Moreover the poem has numerous satirical digressions which are the best part of it; the reader is aware more of Byron himself than of his hero. *Don Juan* is quite the most readable poem of great length in the English literature of the last 200 years, and Byron's masterpiece.

Don Quixote de la Mancha (1605 and 1615) /don'kwiksət/

A satirical romance by the Spanish writer Miguel de Cervantes (1547–1616). It begins as a satire on the medieval and Renaissance* style of romance about wandering knights and their adventures in the pursuit of the rectification of injustices – see the Arthurian cycle. It deepens into an image of idealism perpetually at odds with the pettiness, vulgarity and meanness of the real world. Don Quixote is an impecunious gentleman whose mind has been turned by reading too many romances. He sets out on his wanderings accompanied by his servant, Sancho Panza*, the embodiment of commonplace credulity and a shrewd sense of personal advantage. He takes as his patroness a peasant girl, Dulcinea del Toboso, whom he transfigures in his imagination and who is quite unaware of his devotion. The book was translated into English in 1612–20, and again a hundred years later in a more famous version by Peter Motteux. Its influence on our literature has been extensive. In 17th C the burlesque element is emulated by Beaumont in his play *The Knight of the Burning Pestle** and by Samuel Butler in his mock epic *Hudibras**. In 18th C the theme of idealists misunderstanding and misunderstood is followed in Fielding's *Joseph Andrews** and Goldsmith's *Vicar of Wakefield**. The influence can likewise be traced in Sterne* and Smollett*, and, in 19th C, in Dickens (especially in *Pickwick Papers**).

Donne, John (1572–1631) /dʌn/

Poet and writer of sermons and devotions. His earlier years were those of an Elizabethan courtier and adventurer; he took part in the naval expeditions of the Earl of Essex against Spain, and was secretary to a minister of the Queen, Sir Thomas Egerton, until he lost his favour by secretly marrying his niece. However, in 1615 he took orders in the Church of England (though originally a Roman Catholic) and became Dean of St Paul's. The two halves of his career caused him to contrast Jack Donne, the lover of ladies and the theatre, with Dr John Donne, the great preacher, so as to indicate the dramatic nature of the transformation; his writing career covers both halves, however, and has continuity.

As a poet, Donne is the originator of the Metaphysical* school, having among his notable followers George Herbert*, Andrew Marvell*, Henry Vaughan*, Richard Crashaw*, and Abraham Cowley*. His satires and elegies were mainly written before the death of Queen Elizabeth (1603) as were many of his love lyrics – *Songs and Sonets**. This work showed a notable contrast to the other Elizabethan lyric poets whose work was pure, serene, tuneful, smooth-running; Donne's poems had the vigorous rhythms of the contemporary dramatic poets, with the vitality of speech, realism in imagery, and intellectual ingenuity characteristic of Shakespearian metaphor. His religious poetry began in 1609, and shows the same vigour and toughness as the earlier phase. In both phases his lyrics are dramatic in that they arise out of dialogue and incident; in the earlier phase it is dialogue with his mistress or his wife (not merely adoration as with the more usual Elizabethan lyric in the tradition of Petrarch*); in the later it is dialogue with God about his spiritual sufferings. His religious poems are notably: *The Litany* (1609); the two *Anniversaries* (1611 and 12) and the *Holy Sonnets*, mostly after 1621.

Donne's sermons, often preached before the king, and his *Devotions*, are in rich, imaginative prose which exhibits the same kind of physical vigour and intellectual complexity as his poetry. His prose is often used to exemplify the strength of the 'unified sensibility' of English writing before rational prose objectives had become separated from imaginative poetic ones – a process that is especially dated from the Restoration* but had already begun in Donne's lifetime in the prose of Bacon*.

The rational 'civilizing' of verse under the dominion of prose values caused Donne to be neglected in 18th C, and though he had more appreciation from such critics as Coleridge* and Lamb* at the beginning of 19th, it was the more musical, rapturous influences of Spenser* and Milton* which really counted then. In 20th C Donne's reputation has strongly recovered, together with those of some of his Metaphysical successors; 20th-C poets, as different as W. B. Yeats* and T. S. Eliot*, have emulated the unification of intellectual strenuousness, spoken vitality, and alert sensibility which Donne's poems present.

* 6.2.4. *Nocturnal upon St Lucy's Day.*

Bib: Bald, R. C., *Life*; Leishman, J. B., *The Monarch of Wit*; Louthan, D., *The Poetry of Donne*; Spencer, T., *A Garland for John Donne*; Eliot, T. S., 'The Metaphysical Poets' in *Selected Essays*; Leavis, F. R., in *Revaluations*; Smith, J., 'Metaphysical Poetry' in *Determinations* (ed. Leavis).

Dorset, Lord

* *Sackville, Thomas.*

Doubting Castle

In Part I of Bunyan's *Pilgrim's Progress**, the castle belonging to the Giant Despair, where Christian and Hopeful lie prisoners. In Part II the Castle is destroyed by the champion Greatheart.

Douglas, Black

The Douglases were a family of the Scottish medieval border nobility, constantly at war with the English Percy* family on the south side of the border. Two famous Douglases bore the epithet 'Black': James Douglas (1286?–1330), supporter of Robert the Bruce* in the Scottish War of Independence, and eventually killed fighting the Moors in Spain; Archibald Douglas (also called 'the Grim'), another famous warrior, who lived later in 14th C.

* *Chevy Chase, The Ballad of; Otterbourne, The Battle of.*

Douglas, Gavin (1475–1522)

Scottish poet. He is especially famous for his translation of Virgil's *Aeneid**, printed in 1553; it is the first translation of a great classical author in English, and is sometimes said to be the greatest English version of this poem. It belongs to the history of Renaissance* humanism*, but his two other major works are medieval in spirit: an allegory of man's life and death, *King Hart* (perhaps by another author), and a dream allegory in the tradition of the *Roman de la Rose** called *The Palace of Honour.*

* *Scottish Literature.*

Bib: Speirs, J., *The Scots Literary Tradition*; Lewis, C. S., in *The Allegory of Love*, and in *Oxford History of Sixteenth-century Literature.*

Downing Street

A short street in London near the Houses of Parliament, containing the official residences of the Prime Minister (no. 10) and of the Chancellor of the Exchequer (no. 11). The street is named after a leading supporter of Oliver Cromwell, Sir George Downing, whose grandson left money for the foundation of Downing College, Cambridge.

Doyle, Sir Arthur Conan (1859–1930)

Novelist; chiefly noted for his series of stories and novels about the amateur detective, Sherlock Holmes, a genius in minute deduction and acute observation. His friend, Dr Watson, is represented as the ordinary, ingenuous man, who needs to have everything pointed out to him and explained, and this offsets the ingenuity of the detective. The combination of acute detective and obtuse colleague has been imitated in many detective stories ever since. The stories include: *A Study in Scarlet* (1887); *The Adventures of Sherlock Holmes* (1891); *The Memoirs of Sherlock Holmes* (1893); *The Hound of the Baskervilles* (1902); *The Return of Sherlock Holmes* (1905). Conan Doyle also wrote historical novels of merit; *eg Micah Clarke* (1888), *The White Company* (1891), and *Rodney Stone* (1896).

* *Detective Fiction.*

Bib: Lamond, J., *Conan Doyle: a Memoir*; Conan Doyle, A., *The True Conan Doyle*; Carr, J. D., *The Life of Conan Doyle*; Roberts, S. C., *Holmes and Watson.*

Drake, Sir Francis (1540?–96)

National hero for his seafaring exploits. He engaged in numerous voyages in which he successfully raided Spain and her American colonies, and circumnavigated the world in his ship the *Golden Hind*, 1577–81. He was one of the commanders of the English fleet against the Armada* during the attempted Spanish invasion of 1588. A legend declares that Drake's drum (in a museum in his native county of Devonshire) will sound again when the nation is in danger.

Dramatic Monologue

A poetic form in which the poet invents a character, or, more commonly, uses one from history or legend, and reflects on life from the character's standpoint. The dramatic monologue is a development from the conversation poem* of Coleridge* and Wordsworth*, in which the poet reflects on life in his own person.

Tennyson* was the first to use the form, *eg The Lotus-Eaters** (1833), *Ulysses* (1842), and *Tithonus* (pub 1860). In these poems, he takes the standpoint of characters in Greek myth and causes them to express emotions relevant to their predicaments. The emotions, however, are really Tennyson's own; the disguise enables him to express himself without inhibition, and particularly without involving himself in the responsibility of having to defend the attitudes that he is expressing. His most ambitious poem in this form is the monodrama *Maud** (1855).

However it was Browning* who used the form most profusely, and with whom it is most associated, *eg My Last Duchess* (1845); *Fra Lippo Lippi, Andrea del Sarto, The Bishop Orders His Tomb, Bishop Blougram's Apology*, all in *Men and Women** (1855); *Mr Sludge the Medium* in *Dramatis Personae** (1864), and *The Ring and the Book* (1869). Browning used it differently from Tennyson: his characters are more detached from his own personality; the poems are attempts to explore a wide variety of attitudes to art and life. His monologues have little to do with drama, though superficially they resemble soliloquies in plays of the age of Shakespeare. They have an even closer resemblance, though still a rather superficial one, to the medieval convention of public confession by characters such as the Wife of Bath and the Pardoner in Chaucer's *Canterbury Tales**. Most of all, however, they emulate the exploration of character and society in the novel of Browning's own day, and his *The Ring and the Book* is really an experiment in the novel; the tale unfolds through monologues by the various participators in and spectators of the events. Still another use for the dramatic monologue is that to which Clough* puts it in his poem *Dipsychus* (*Divided Mind*, 1850). This poem is in the form of a dialogue, but it is a dialogue between the two parts of a man's mind: that which tries to sustain moral principle, and that which is sceptical of principle, seeking only pleasure and material well-being.

Both Browning and Clough used irony, but Browning's irony is to modern taste superficial. The more searching irony used by Clough was untypical of his age. But this searching irony was natural to 20th C, and its use by T. S. Eliot* brought the dramatic monologue to its most sophisticated form in *The Love Song of J. Alfred Prufrock* (1915) and *Gerontion* (1920). The monologues of Eliot are profound judgements on the culture of the time.

4.4.4; 6.4.1.

Dramatis Personae (1864)

/'dra:mətis pɔ:'səunai/

A collection of poems by Robert Browning*, including a number of his more famous ones: *Abt Vogler*, *Rabbi Ben Ezra*, *A Death in the Desert*, *Caliban upon Setebos*, *Mr Sludge the Medium*.

Drapier's Letters (1724)

A pamphlet by Jonathan Swift* against a monopoly to issue copper coins in Ireland, granted by the English Government to the Duchess of Kendal (George I's mistress) and sold by her to William Wood – 'Wood's halfpence'. The Irish considered that the monopoly would be economically harmful to them. Swift wrote in their support in the semblance of a Dublin 'drapier' (=draper), *ie* an ordinary shopman. The pamphlet is an example of his apparently moderate, plain style carrying an immense force of irony; it was so effective that the Government had to withdraw the monopoly.

Drayton, Michael (1563–1631)

Poet. Born a year before Shakespeare, he came from the same county of Warwickshire, and from the same middle class of society. As a poet he was versatile, and though he was not a great original genius, his work is commonly fresh, individual and forceful. One of his best known poems is *Nymphidia** (1627), a delicate fairy fantasy; his *Endimion and Phoebe* (1595) exhibits characteristic Elizabethan strength in its combination of highly conscious art with spiritual dignity; his love sonnets to *Idea* (1594) similarly combine formality with eloquent emotion. He wrote narrative love-letters in the tradition of Ovid*, and historical poems of which his most famous is the *Ballad of Agincourt*. His most ambitious work was a survey in verse of England – *Poly-Olbion* (1613–22). He wrote pas-

torals (*The Shepherd's Garland* 1593) in which he matched Spenser*, and satires, in which he was not so successful.

Bib: Newdigate, B. H., *Drayton and His Circle*; Smith, H., in *Elizabethan Poetry*; Elton, O., *Michael Drayton, A Critical Study*.

Dreadnought

The name of a class of large battleship first built for the British navy in 1905. The name was taken from two ships of historical fame – one in the reign of Elizabeth I, and one that engaged in the Battle of Trafalgar in 1805.

Dreams, Gates of

According to Greek myth, dreams came from the underworld, through a gate of horn if they were true, and a gate of ivory if they were false. See Homer's *Odyssey** xix.562; Virgil's *Aeneid** vi. 894.

Dresden China

In 18th C a factory was established at Meissen, near Dresden, capital of Saxony in Germany, to produce china figures in the Chinese and Japanese tradition. The delicacy and charm of these figures made them internationally famous.

Drinks

Ale* was a universal drink in the Middle Ages, until in 16th C beer (like ale, brewed from malt) became more popular; a thin brew called 'small beer' was used for children and servants and by the poor. The reason for this general use was the frequent pollution of water. A 16th-C traveller was surprised to be offered, in some parts of the country, milk instead of beer. Wine* was drunk freely by the richer classes from the early Middle Ages; most of it was imported from France, Germany, or the Mediterranean countries, but the grape vine was cultivated to some extent until 18th C. In the countryside, wines were made out of local plants and fruits (elderberry, cowslip, dandelion) extensively until 19th C; cider and perry, from fermented apples and pears respectively, were rivals to ale and beer in some parts. Another very common country drink was the ancient mead, from fermented honey, now seldom found. In 17th C tea and coffee were introduced, and for a hundred years (approximately 1650–1750) London enjoyed a flourishing 'café' life with its coffee-houses. Chocolate, as a drink, was also fashionable by mid-18th C. Tea had become a national drink by 19th C; the English habit of spoiling it with milk was not until then usual. It replaced beer as a normal drink for women, especially in the middle classes. For a short time in 18th C the working classes, especially in London, took to gin in preference to beer, with great injury to their health. Even after the imposition of taxes on this spirit (distilled from malt) in 1751, drunkenness, from excessive drinking of comparatively cheap spirits in so-called 'gin palaces', remained a national problem until 20th C. This accounts for the extent of teetotalism, *ie* temperance movements, appealing for total abstinence from alcoholic drinks, in working-class religious and political circles in 19th C.

Druids

The wise and holy men of the ancient Celts* in Gaul, ancient Britain, and Ireland. Knowledge of them comes to us from Roman writers, *eg* Julius Caesar in *De Bello Gallico*, and from Welsh and Irish myth. They held the oak and the mistletoe as sacred, worshipped in oak groves, and believed in the survival of the soul and its transmigration after death into other bodies. There seems to be some doubt whether they ever flourished in southern Britain, where in any case they were eliminated by the Roman conquest in 1st C AD, but they were important in Ireland and in Scotland, and the early Welsh bards* or sacred poets called themselves druids. Caesar does not mention bards but ascribes to the druids a bardic, or sacred poetic, function. In 18th and 19th C an unscientific cult of the druids grew up in England, attributing to them mysterious knowledge and wisdom where modern science finds only superstition.

Drury Lane

A famous theatre in London, named after the street in which it stands. Originally a cockpit*, it was made into a theatre under James I*. In 18th C it was one of the few London theatres allowed to survive by the Licensing Act of 1737 (with Covent Garden* and the Haymarket*). The present building dates from 1812.

* *Theatres.*

Dryads and Hamadryads

In Greek and Latin myth, nymphs* of the woods and trees, which it was their duty to guard.

Dryden, John (1631–1700) /'draidn/

Poet, critic, dramatist; he is now chiefly valued in the first two capacities.

By family background and personal sympathies he was on the Puritan*, anti-monarchical side during the Interregnum*, and his first considerable work was *Heroic Stanzas* (1659) in honour of Oliver Cromwell*, who died in 1658. However, he welcomed the Restoration* with *Astrea Redux* (1660) and *Panegyric* (1661). No doubt this was not altogether insincere: others who had supported Cromwell felt that the return of the monarchy was the only political solution after his death. He dominated English letters in the reign of Charles II*, and became Poet Laureate* in 1668. On the accession of the Roman Catholic James II* in 1685, Dryden himself became a Catholic, and kept his new faith when James was deposed in 1688 and the Protestant William III* succeeded. This lost him the Laureateship and other royal appointments, but he was respected as the chief poet of the age until his death.

As a poet, Dryden's outstanding achievement was his verse satires: *Absalom and Achitophel** (1681–2), *The Medal** (1682), and *Mac Flecknoe** (1682); of these, Part I of the first is much the most famous. In them Dryden so handled the heroic couplet* as to reveal its incomparable virtues for satire, intellectual conciseness, and terse and vivid delineation, with the result that it became the most favoured medium for the next century. By the time of the satires, he had written some of his best prose, and his satirical verse exhibits the virtues of his prose expression – its lucidity, economy, suppleness and persuasive power. He had grown up, however, in the decadence of the great Metaphysical* school; his earliest work (*Elegy on the Death of Lord Hastings*, 1649) shows the tasteless ingenuity of that sort of verse when it had lost its motive power in imaginative contemplation of the paradoxes of experience. The mature Dryden converts the Metaphysical paradox into the symmetrical antithesis. The poem on Cromwell, those on the Restoration, and above all *Annus Mirabilis** (1667) are transitional, with some of the reach of the Metaphysical conceit* and the concise generalizing power of his satirical work. It was in accordance with the classical basis of his literary culture that he wrote the two long didactic poems, *Religio Laici* (1682) and *The Hind and the Panther** (1687), on the religious question which at the time divided his sympathy. They contain fine passages, but the didactic mode is one that moderns find hard to appreciate. Similarly the contrived (as opposed to inspired) rhetoric of his Pindaric Odes (*eg Alexander's Feast*, 1697) tends to be regarded now as 'artificial', a word which he would not have thought a disparaging adjective. Dryden's poetry is in fact mostly 'public' and impersonal in accord with the social culture of his age; and yet this mode is compatible with moving elegies of personal tribute as in the elegy to Oldham.

Dryden has been called 'the Father of English criticism' and deserves the description in so far as he is the first to make extended, systematic surveys of individual writers and works, relying on classical authority but qualifying it with his independent judgement. His criticism is extensive; the most notable pieces are the *Essay on Dramatic Poesy** (1668), and the *Preface to the Fables* (1700). He did not bring to his criticism the weight of personal feeling that makes the work of Samuel Johnson* of permanent value, but he was a master of the new, persuasive prose, and this, combined with his independence of judgement despite his respect for the neo-classicism* of the French school of Boileau* and Rapin, gives Dryden's criticism abiding life.

It was to drama that Dryden gave the greater part of his energy in the prime of life; between 1663 and 1681 he wrote almost a play a year. This, however, is the part of his work that has worn the least well. He adapted Shakespeare, and his *All for Love** (1677), an entirely new version of *Antony and Cleopatra**, is now his only play regarded as having classic status. He was the chief writer of heroic dramas on the grand model of the French dramatist Corneille*, but without the power of Corneille's passion and intellect; *The Indian Empress* (1667), *The Conquest of Granada* (1669–70), and *Aureng-zebe* (1675) have been called the best. He also wrote comedies and operas.

*** 4.2.2; 5.2.2; 6.3.1; 7.2**

Bib: Johnson, S., in *Lives of the Poets*; Ward, C. E., *Life*; Eliot, T. S., in *Selected Essays*; Leavis, F. R., in *Revaluation*; Van Doren, M., *The Poetry of Dryden*; Schilling, B., *Dryden and the Conservative Myth*; Young, K., *John Dryden*; Nichol Smith, D., *John Dryden*; Kinsley, J. and H., *Dryden: the Critical Heritage*.

Dubliners (1914)

A volume of short stories by James Joyce*. Joyce later wrote: 'My intention was to write a chapter of the moral history of my country and I chose Dublin for the scene because that city seemed to me the centre of paralysis. I have tried to present it . . . under four of its aspects: childhood, adolescence, maturity and public life. The stories are arranged in this order.' He adds that he has used in them 'a style of scrupulous meanness', by which he is evidently referring to the bare realism of the stories, and the moral and spiritual poverty which they present. This poverty of spirit is no doubt what Joyce means by speaking of the 'paralysis' of Dublin, the capital city of Ireland. The stories are based on Joyce's theory of the 'epiphanies', by which he meant that deep insights might be gained through incidents and circumstances which seem outwardly insignificant. Their effect is thus often through delicate implication, like the stories of Chekhov*. Some of them have sharp humour, however, notably 'Grace', and more have very sensitive poignance, especially the last and longest, 'The Dead', which is often regarded as a masterpiece.

Duchess of Malfi, The (1613?)

With *The White Devil**, one of the two famous verse tragedies by John Webster*. The plot is taken from a tale by the Italian writer, Matteo Bandello, in an English version included in William Painter's *Palace of Pleasure**. Set in Italy, the drama concerns the vengeance taken upon the young Duchess for marrying her steward, Antonio, against the commands of her brothers, the Cardinal, and Ferdinand Duke of Calabria, who is her twin. Ferdinand employs an impoverished malcontent* soldier, Bosola, as his instrument for the mental torturing of the Duchess, but Bosola has a character of his own, and is filled with remorse. The Duchess is finally strangled, but Ferdinand goes mad with horror at his own deed, and ends by killing Bosola, who has already killed the Cardinal.

Two main problems arise in assessing the drama. The first is whether the Duchess is purely a guiltless victim. She is a young widow who marries a man of lower degree for love: commentators argue that contemporary opinion was against the remarrying of widows, that the Duchess offends against the principle of degree by marrying beneath her, and that her deception of her brothers offends against the principle that a just life must be led in openness. None of these arguments is likely to have force with modern audiences, and those contemporary with the play must have been chiefly impressed by the proud dignity with which the Duchess sustains her cumulative afflictions. The more important problem is that of the brothers' motives. That of the Cardinal is intelligible: he is a cold Machiavellian* who resents his sister's humiliation of the family, and no doubt the fact that by her second marriage she now has heirs to her estate. But Ferdinand's prolonged sadism, and his madness after her death, seem in excess of their ostensible causes. The natural explanation is that he is incestuously in love with his sister, and insanely jealous at her marriage; this is doubted by some critics who point out that incestuous passion is nowhere explicit in the play which was written at a time when such motives were rarely left to the audience's inference. Webster may have preferred to leave the question open, since the bond between a twin sister and brother might itself sufficiently explain Ferdinand's extravagance. Another explanation, since the play is remarkable for its strikingly effective individual scenes, might be that Webster was more interested in opportunities for dramatizing situations than in the exposition of a dominant theme. Even this reductive judgement cannot obscure the grandeur with which Webster dramatizes extreme passion and the horror of its degradation, and in contrast the dignity with which an individual can outface suffering.

Duelling

Two kinds have existed: the judicial combat, and the duel of honour.

Judicial combat was practised from 12th C until 16th C in England, though never so freely as in France. By this practice, a dispute which would now be settled by court of law was decided by combat before a judge or the king, on the assump-

tion that God would defend the right. Shakespeare, in his play *Richard II**, introduces a duel of this kind, between Mowbray and Bolingbroke.

The more familiar 'duel of honour', by which an alleged injury by one gentleman to another was settled by combat privately arranged between them, was never legal and did not become common until 17th C. Before this, such an injury would more probably be settled by the hiring of assassins. The social code regulated the duel of honour strictly, and so long as the regulations were kept, the survivor was likely to escape legal penalty. These duels were fought with either pistols or swords; by degrees, especially when towards the end of 18th C the wearing of swords by gentlemen went out of fashion, pistols became the more usual weapon. The frequency of occurrence can be judged by the frequency with which duels are introduced into 17th and 18th-C plays and novels. In the early 19th C the law was used much more severely against duellists, and the religious ('evangelical') revival of the time condemned duels as immoral. After 1840 they ceased to occur.

Duessa

A character in Spenser's *Faerie Queene**. She is the daughter of Deceit and Shame; in Book I she represents the Roman Catholic Church, and in Book V, Mary Queen of Scots* who with international Catholic support had been a claimant to the English throne.

Duke

The highest rank in the English peerage. The title was introduced into England by Edward III* in 1337, and into Scotland by Robert III in 1398. Dukes are addressed by the title 'Your Grace'.

* *Titles of Nobility.*

Du Maurier, George (1834–96)

Graphic artist and novelist; born in Paris. His grandparents had been refugees in England from the French revolution; his father was a naturalized British subject; his mother was English. In 1865 he joined the staff of *Punch**, and became one of the best known British humorous artists, satirizing the upper classes rather in the style of Thackeray*. He wrote three novels: *Peter Ibbetson* (1891), *Trilby* (1894) and *The Martian* (posthumous, 1896). The first two were extremely popular, but their sentimentality has put them out of fashion.

Dunbar, William (1460?–1520?) /dʌnˈbaː/

One of the finest of the Scottish medieval poets. He wrote in contrasted styles: his allegories (*eg The Golden Targe*, and *The Thrissel and the Rois*) are in ornate diction and rhymed stanzas,—court poetry; his satires, invective, and comic verse are in robust, homely, caustic and more distinctively Scottish diction. One of the best of the latter kind, *Tua Mariit Wemen and the Wedo* (Two Married Women and the Widow) is in an unrhymed, alliterative style like such English medieval poems as *Sir Gawain and the Green Knight** and Langland's *Piers Plowman**. Other famous poems are *Lament for the Makaris* (= poets) with its typical medieval use of a Latin refrain; *The Flyting* of Dunbar and Kennedy*, an example of a dialogue game in which two individuals see which can abuse the other most successfully, and the eulogy *To the City of London*, which is not certainly by Dunbar. English critics have called Dunbar one of the Scottish Chaucerians, but he does not resemble Chaucer very closely, though both use themes and modes of writing drawn from a common store of medieval culture.

* *Scottish Literature.*

Bib: Baxter, J. W., *Life*; Speirs, J., in *The Scots Literary Tradition.*

Dunciad, The (1728–42) /ˈdʌnsiad/

A verse satire by Alexander Pope*. It is written in heroic couplets*, and divided into four Books. The form is mock-epic, *ie* mean, contemptible, or merely small objects are presented as though they were majestic, heroic, to be revered, yet they still keep their own nature. Thus Dullness is represented as a goddess; suitably bad writers are elevated for her honour in terms of ironic eloquence, and bad books are expounded – without disguising their badness – in a tone appropriate to great ones. The effect is of gigantic caricature, but it is not repulsive reading thanks to the agility of Pope's wit and the liveliness of his similes. He used the poem to revenge himself upon his literary enemies, rather as Dante* put his enemies into hell, but *The Dunciad's* visionary quality arises from Pope's conception of the desolation of culture by the triumph of low standards, corrupt ambitions, and general deterioration of mind. Each Book has its own theme: Book I – the poet Bayes (Pope's enemy, Colley Cibber*) is chosen by Dullness as her Laureate; II – sports, on the analogy of the ancient Greek Olympic Games, are organized for the writers who are said to honour Dullness by their practice; III – Bayes, asleep on the lap of Dullness, has visions of her future empire; IV – these visions are realized. Book IV is usually considered to be

THE
DUNCIAD,
VARIORVM.
WITH THE
PROLEGOMENA of *SCRIBLERUS*.
DEFEROR IN VICVM
VENDENTEM THVS ET ODORES
LONDON.
Printed for A. DOB . 1729.

the most successful. It was published under the title *The New Dunciad* in 1742. The four books were published together in 1743.

* 4.2.2.

Duns Scotus, John (1265?–1308?) /ˈdʌnzˈskəutəs/

One of the most influential medieval philosophers. He was born at the village of Duns in Scotland, studied at Oxford, and taught at Paris and Cologne. He was the chief opponent of Thomas Aquinas* in the late medieval Church. He opposed Aquinas's belief in the harmony of reason and religious faith by declaring that some doctrines were incapable of proof (*eg* the immortality of the soul); he declared, in opposition to Aquinas, that the will was not necessarily subordinate to the reason; he insisted that individual objects contain a principle of reality distinct from that of the class to which each belongs. The last doctrine was of importance to the Catholic poet G. M. Hopkins* in his formation of the terms 'inscape' and 'instress'. His philosophy underwent much criticism in 16th C by both the humanist* scholars influenced by Plato, and the Protestant* reformers. His followers, the Scotists, were regarded as the enemies of the New Learning*, and in consequence a 'Dunsman' or 'Dunce' became eventually, in common speech, synonymous with a stupid person, impervious to education.

Durrell, Lawrence (b 1912) /ˈdʌrl/

Novelist and poet. He began writing before the war, and published an experimental novel, *The Black Book* (1938) in France. His autobiographical narrative *Bitter Lemons* (1957) received a literary prize, but his present high international reputation is based on the sequence *Alexandria Quartet* comprising *Justine* (1957); *Balthazar* (1958); *Mount Olive* (1958) and *Clea* (1960). Later Novels: *Tunc* (1968); *Nunquam* (1970); *Monsieur, or the Prince of Darkness* (1974); *The Best of Antrobus* (1975).

His *Collected Poems* were published in 1961 (Second edition, 1968).

The Alexandria Quartet has achieved fame partly by its lavishly exotic appeal, and partly by Durrell's experimental technique: in the successive volumes the same events are seen, and interpreted quite differently, by the different characters participating in them. This experiment was partly anticipated by Robert Browning's* verse narrative, *The Ring and the Book*.

E

Earl

English title of nobility, equivalent to French 'comte'; an earl's wife is a 'countess'. The word is Old English. The title was the highest among the English nobility until the rank of 'duke' was introduced in 14th C.

* *Titles of Nobility*.

Earle, John

* *Characters, Theophrastian*.

East India Company

The greatest of the Charter Companies*, given a monopoly of Eastern trade by Queen Elizabeth* in 1600. Competition with the Dutch in the East Indian islands turned its attention to the Indian mainland, where in 18th C its extensive commercial influence developed into political power. To protect its Chinese trade, it gained control of the Burmese and Malayan coasts down to Singapore, which it founded in 1819. After the Indian Mutiny of 1857 it was taken over by the British government, which had shared its rule in India since the younger Pitt's* Indian Act of 1784. It was familiarly known as John Company, and its ships as East Indiamen.

* *Companies, Joint Stock*.

Easter Day

The Christian festival of the Resurrection of Jesus Christ, in the Spring. The festival occurs near the Spring equinox, when in pre-Christian England the festival of the Saxon goddess of the dawn and of the spring, Eostre, was celebrated.

* *Festivals*.

Eatanswill

The town where the election of a Member of Parliament takes place in Dickens's *Pickwick Papers*. The description is a famous burlesque of parliamentary elections before secret voting (introduced 1872) put an end to intimidation and bribery. Dickens, who began his career as a parliamentary reporter, is noted for his contempt for the conduct of politics.

Ecclesiastes /iˈkliːziˈastiːz/

In the Bible, one of the books of the Old Testament. Traditionally it was held to be by King Solomon, but it is now dated much later, about 200 BC. It consists of a collection of discourses, sombre in general character, made by a sage called Koheleth. The essence of its teaching is that life, as we know it, is mere vanity. Chapter 12 is one of the most poetic passages in the English Authorized version of the Bible.

Eclecticism /ekˈlektisizm/

In ancient Greece, a term for the kind of philosophy that did not follow any one school of thought (*eg* Platonism*) but selected its doctrines from a number of schools. The term is now applied to thinkers, artists and writers who follow this principle in the formation of their thought or artistic methods.

Eclogue /ˈeklog/

A short pastoral dialogue, usually in verse. The most famous example is the *Bucolics* of the Latin poet, Virgil*. The word is often used as equivalent for idyll, or pastoral* poem without dialogue. The most famous example of eclogues in English is Spenser's *Shepherd's Calendar**.

Eden, Garden of

In the Bible, and therefore in Hebrew and Christian myth, the dwelling place of the first man and woman, Adam and Eve. Eden is thought of as a place of perfect bliss where there was no conflict, sickness or suffering, and human needs were satisfied by the fruit of the garden. But it also contained the trees of life and of knowledge; eating the fruit of the latter would give Man the knowledge of good and evil, and so God forbade it to him. Eve succumbed, however, to temptation by the serpent, and Adam followed her example. In consequence, God drove them from the garden. Their disobedience is the symbol of the myth of 'the Fall of Man': had Adam also eaten the fruit of the tree of life he would have been equal to God by being endowed with immortality; by eating only from the tree of knowledge, he succumbed to sin (*ie* separation from God), suffering and death. Other consequences were the identification of the serpent with the Devil, and the subjection of woman to man because she had first yielded to the temptation. The story is contained in *Genesis* 2 & 3. Christian paraphrases of the story commonly say little of the tree of life. The most famous paraphrase is Milton's *Paradise Lost** which also includes an account of the fall of the angels*.

Eden is also the name of a squalid and unhealthy settlement in the United States in Dickens's novel *Martin Chuzzlewit**; Dickens uses the settlement as part of his satire on American ingenuousness and false idealism.

Edgeworth, Maria (1768–1849)

Novelist. Her tales are commonly set in Ireland. Her work is minor, but still read for its vivacity, good sense, and realism. *Castle Rackrent* (1800) and *The Absentee* (1812) are two of her works still in print. She was also an excellent writer for children (see *Tales* ed. by Austin Dobson). She collaborated with her father, a noted educationist, in *Practical Education* (1798), influenced by the French-Swiss thinker, Rousseau*.

Bib: Clarke, I. C., *Life*; Newby, P. H., *Maria Edgeworth*.

Edinburgh

Since the middle of 15th C the capital of Scotland. The union of the crowns in 1603, when James VI of Scotland became also James I* of England, left Edinburgh still with its same political status, since the governments of the two countries remained separate. In 1707, however, the union of the parliaments removed the political capital to London, and for half a century greatly reduced Edinburgh's prestige: it was now only the centre of the Scottish legal and Church systems. In the second half of the century, however, Edinburgh had a notable revival. Brilliant intellectuals such as the philosopher Hume*, the historian Robertson, the economist Adam Smith*, challenged the intellectual domination of London; in the early 19th C the poet-novelist Walter Scott* and the very influential *Edinburgh Review** made it possible to say that, culturally, Britain contained two metropolises. However this was at the expense of an independent Scottish culture, since the Scottish writers mentioned all tended to adopt English styles and standards.

* *Scotland.*

Edinburgh Review

A quarterly review founded in 1802 by some of the most brilliant writers of the time: Francis Jeffrey*, Henry Brougham*, Sydney Smith. It was the first of the 'great reviews' which extensively influenced British intellectual life in, especially, the first half of 19th C. Reviews had existed before, but the *Edinburgh* had more independence and authority than its predecessors. It exercised its influence on the Whig* side in politics, and gave much space to the criticism of literature. This criticism was conservative in regard to the new generation of English poets – Wordsworth* and Coleridge*, Shelley*, Keats*, and Byron* – but it was often just, and sometimes admiring. Scott*, though a political opponent, wrote for it, and so did Hazlitt*; later contributors included Carlyle*, Macaulay* and Gladstone*. The *Edinburgh Review* came to an end in 1929, but by then it had long lost its importance.

* *Reviews and Periodicals.*

Education and the State

The main stages in the growth of state provision of education in Britain are as follows:

[1] 1833. The government began the practice of making an annual grant of £20,000 for the erection of school buildings. The grant was available to the National Society and the British and Foreign School Society only. The former was controlled by the Church of England and the latter by the Nonconformist (or Dissenting) religious denominations.

[2] Forster's Act of 1870. This provided state education for all at the primary level, to the age of 11. In 1876 primary education became compulsory for all children.

[3] Balfour's Act of 1902. This provided compulsory education up to the age of 14, and placed the secondary schools under the authority of the local government County Councils.

[4] The Act of 1944. This paved the way for the raising of the school leaving age to 15 in 1947. Secondary schools were divided into three groups: grammar schools, attendance at which could extend to the age of 18, after which children might continue their education with state financial aid at universities or technical colleges; modern schools, which pupils normally left at 15, though further education might take place at technical colleges; a small number of technical schools, with emphasis on industrial or business training. Children were obliged to enter primary schools at the age of 5, and submitted to a test at the age of 11 to decide the secondary school best suited to their abilities.

This so-called '11+' examination soon came under heavy criticism, and the local authorities often invented other expedients for arranging the secondary education of children. Much the most important of these has been the spread of comprehensive schools, which are entered by children of all levels of ability without a preliminary test. The modern educational scene in Britain consequently exhibits much variety: grammar schools, modern schools, and the 11+ test remain usual, but comprehensive schools increased widely in the 1960s, with the encouragement of the Labour governments.

* 2.1.2.3; *Schools in England.*

Edward the Confessor (reigned 1042–66)

The last but one of the Anglo-Saxon* kings. He was not politically efficient, but he was very pious, and the legend grew up that his had been a very just reign. He is presented in this way, as the royal saint able to work miraculous cures, in Shakespeare's *Macbeth* (IV.iii).

Edward I (1272–1307)

King of England. He is famous for the importance of his laws, the conquest of Wales, and the attempted conquest of Scotland.

Edward II (1307–27)

King of England. His reign is chiefly noted for his decisive defeat by the Scots in the Scottish War of Independence (battle of Bannockburn*, 1314) and for his conflicts with the barons over his excessive indulgence of favourites, especially Piers Gaveston.

Marlowe's* play *Edward II* presents him as a decadent sensual prince in Renaissance* style, but pitiable in his horrible death by assassination. The date of the play is uncertain, but it may be the last that Marlowe wrote – in 1593. This puts it later than Shakespeare's three plays on Henry VI*, but it is still one of the best early attempts at historical drama. The difference from Shakespeare comes out partly in *Edward II*'s inferiority of structure, and partly in that Shakespeare's dramatic interest is always political as well as psychological, whereas Marlowe's study depends on psychological pathos and horror without the broader social and political implications.

Edward III (1327–77)

The king of England under whom the Hundred Years' War* with France began. Up to 1360 he was notably successful, and the English armies won the battles of Crécy* (1346) and Poitiers (1356). He was succeeded on the throne by his grandson, Richard II*, his eldest son, the Black Prince* having died in 1376.

The play *Edward III* has sometimes been ascribed to Shakespeare, at least in part. It was published in 1596.

Edward IV (1461–83)

First of the kings of England belonging to the House of York; he was victorious in the civil war called the Wars of the Roses* over the last king of the House of Lancaster, Henry VI*.

Edward IV plays a prominent part in Shakespeare's *Henry VI, Part 3**, where he first appears as the Earl of March, and in *Richard III*, in which he dies and his throne is seized from the rightful heir, his son, by Edward IV's brother, Richard, Duke of Gloucester.

Edward V (1483)

The boy-king, son of Edward IV*. He was deposed in the year of his accession to the throne by his uncle, Richard, Duke of Gloucester, who became Richard III*. Edward and his younger brother were imprisoned by their uncle in the Tower of London, and were never heard of again. Legend (and the 16th-C chroniclers) always insisted that he had them murdered there.

Shakespeare introduces Edward into his play *Richard III** as a dramatic contrast to his uncle, of childish innocence facing sophisticated villainy.

Edward VI (1547–53)

The boy-king who succeeded Henry VIII*. Under the regency of the Protectors (the Duke of Somerset and, later, the Duke of Northumberland) Henry's essentially political Reformation* became more Protestant* in doctrine, though the new Book of Common Prayer* was a wise compromise. Persecution of Roman Catholics in Edward's reign led to a reaction against Protestantism when his sister Mary* succeeded him.

Edwardian /ed'wo:djən/

A term descriptive of the political, social and cultural characteristics of the early years of 20th C, roughly corresponding to the reign of King Edward VII (1901–1910). The period is often remembered nostalgically for its luxury and brilliance, soon to be darkened by the horror of World War I (1914–18) and obliterated by the relative austerity of the post-war years. This life of luxury, easy foreign travel, low taxation, etc. is also thought of as being relatively free from the close moral restraint commonly associated with the preceding Victorian* period. It is sometimes remembered, however, that such brilliance was restricted to the upper class and the wealthier members of the middle class, and that life for four-fifths of the population was at best dull and at worst squalid and impoverished. This darker aspect of the time was responsible for the rise of the socialist Labour party* and the prominence of polemical writers, whether socialists like Bernard Shaw* and H. G. Wells*, or Catholics like G. K. Chesterton* and Hilaire Belloc*. Such writers attacked the social injustice and selfishness of the upper classes in an idiom designed to reach wide audiences. A subtler and perhaps profounder critic of the dominant materialism was the novelist E. M. Forster*. Arnold Bennett* was a more representative novelist: his novels were not polemical and convey a materialistic vigour and excitement which were important elements in the harsh but inspiriting environments of the more prosperous provincial towns. Thus some aspect of materialism is generally associated with Edwardianism, whether it is being enjoyed, suffered or criticized. Politically, the period was one of disturbance and rapid development: trade unionism was militant, women fought for political rights, and the social conscience inspired legislation which was later to mature into the Welfare State* of the 1940s.

Edwin Drood, The Mystery of (1870)

A novel by Charles Dickens, unfinished at his death. The novel begins in a cathedral town (based on Rochester); the plot turns on the engagement of Edwin and Rosa Bud, who do not really love each other, and the rivalry for Rosa's love of Edwin's sinister uncle, John Jasper, and an exotic newcomer to the town Neville Landless. Edwin disappears and Neville is arrested for his murder; Rosa flees to London to escape Jasper; on her behalf the forces for good are rallying in the shape of Rosa's guardian, Mr Grewgious, a clergyman called Crisparkle, and a mysterious stranger, Mr Datchery, when the story breaks off. The fragment is quite sufficient to show that Dickens was not losing his powers. The sombreness and the grotesque comedy are equal to the best in his previous works.

Egdon Heath

A gloomy tract of country which is the Dorsetshire setting for Hardy's novel *The Return of the Native**. As often in Hardy's novels, the place is not merely a background to the events, but exercises an active influence upon them.

Egoist, The (1879)

One of the most admired novels by George Meredith*. The 'egoist' is the rich and fashionable Sir Willoughby Patterne*, who is intolerably self-centred and conceited. The story concerns his courting of Clara Middleton, and her fight for independence from his assertiveness. Willoughby is opposed by Vernon Whitford, who is austere, honest and discerning, the tutor of Willoughby's poor relation, Crossjay, a boy whose vigorous animal spirits are accompanied by deep and spontaneous feeling. Partly owing to Crossjay, Clara is eventually enabled to evade Willoughby's advances, which have been backed by her father whose luxurious tastes Willoughby has indulged. She marries Whitford, a conclusion which is a victory for integrity over deceitful subtlety. The story is told with the brilliance of Meredith's rather mannered wit, and is interspersed with exuberant passages of natural description symbolically related to the theme. Though Meredith's mannerism has lost the book some of its former prestige, his analysis of self-deceit and his understanding of the physical components of strong feeling make *The Egoist* an anticipation of kinds of fiction more characteristic of 20th C.

Eighteenth-century Literature

The 18th C in English literature is an age of great prose, of a smaller quantity of distinguished verse, and of the last flickers of the comedy of manners which had flourished in the second half of 17th C.

To take only the most salient names, the prose includes the work of Addison*, Swift*, Defoe*, Fielding*, Richardson*, Sterne*, Johnson*, Goldsmith*, Gibbon*, and Burke*. The list of names evokes a rich variety of styles and matter, and could be greatly enlarged to include other writers (for instance the philosophers Berkeley* and Hume*) who remain lively influences on civilization. They also represent a quality of civilization which goes under such names as the 'Age of Reason', and 'the Augustan* age', both of which terms suggest a feeling for right proportions, inevitably accompanied by a keen sense of the ridiculous; a reliance on reason, and a distrust of intuition; an interest in fact, with an ironical awareness of the extent to which appearances mislead; above all a high esteem for all the values that contribute to a refined, elegant, intelligent social life. Of the stronger emotions, indignation (*eg* in Swift, Fielding, Johnson and Burke) is the one most finely expressed, and wit (often in the form of irony) is the most common instrument of expression. Of the various literary forms, the novel (Defoe, Richardson, Fielding, Sterne and others) is the most conspicuous because it is new. Johnson is one of the greatest English critics, Swift the greatest satirist, Gibbon perhaps the greatest historian, Burke the most eloquent political polemicist, and Berkeley and Hume unexcelled as philosophers.

On the other hand the century is often seen as one of the poorest in the production of distinguished poetry. The poverty can easily be exaggerated. Its most characteristic poet was Alexander Pope*, and he was great. When the poetry is outstanding (Pope, Swift, Johnson), it is so in many of the qualities characteristic of the prose: it is rational, weighty, lucid and witty. This is the influence from Dryden*. Milton* was also an extensive influence, but more prominent (though he is important in Pope) among the poets later in the century who cultivated the sensibilities as distinct from the reason – Thomson*, Gray*, Cowper*. The first group tended to use the heroic couplet*; the second, blank verse* or stanza forms. This is not to imply two distinct schools of poetry, however; the Dryden-Pope tradition was predominant, and it is not merely coincidental that in the 'age of reason' the poets of sensibility and private feeling in several instances went insane or suffered from psychological disorders: Collins*, Gray, Cowper, and Smart*.

In drama 18th C was undistinguished except by comparison with 19th C. Goldsmith and Sheridan both produced comedies of charm, wit and elegance.

In the histories of cultures, of course, centuries do not begin and end with the century years. In many respects it is natural to begin the 18th from the Revolution of 1688*, which established in superior power over the monarchy the aristocratically dominated Parliament. Culturally, the end of the century is perhaps the French Revolution* of 1789, which upset the basic assumptions behind aristocratic privilege. Yet the poet George Crabbe* and the novelist Jane Austen* were deeply imbued with 18th-C taste, though both of them wrote their best work in 19th C.

* *Manners, Comedy of.*

Eisteddfod /ais'teðvod/

An annual congress in Wales, held to encourage literature in the Welsh language, music, and other aspects of Welsh national culture. Its origins are ancient; the word is Welsh, and means 'a session'.

* *Wales.*

El Dorado

(Span. = the Gilded One) According to Spanish legends circulating in the first half of 16th C, the priest or king of an Indian tribe in the interior of South America covered himself with gold dust at a yearly festival. Then the expression was attached first to a legendary city (Manoa) and afterwards to a country in which treasure was abundant. The legend seized the imagination of Sir Walter Raleigh*, who went in search of it in 1595. Finally, any territory where gold or jewels were thought to be plentiful was labelled an 'El Dorado'.

Electra

In Greek myth, the daughter of Agamemnon*, king of Argos, who was murdered by his wife, Clytemnestra*. Electra supported her brother Orestes in avenging their father by killing their mother. She is the main character of plays bearing her name by Sophocles* and Euripides*.

Elegy

An elegy is usually taken to be a poetic lament for one who has died, or at least a grave and reflective poem. In ancient Greek and Latin literature, however, an elegy was a poem written in a particular metre (lines of six dactylic feet alternating with lines of five feet) and it had no necessary connection with death or gravity; the Latin poet Ovid* used it for love poetry. Following his example, the English poet John Donne* wrote a series of elegies with amorous or satirical themes. Most of the famous elegies in English, however, follow the narrower and more widely accepted definition: Milton's *Lycidas** is inspired by the death of his friend Edward King; Shelley's *Adonais** laments that of the poet Keats*; Arnold's* *Thyrsis*, that of his friend Clough*. All three of these are in the pastoral* convention, in imitation of a 3rd-C BC Greek elegy called the *Lament of Moschus for Bion*. The best known of English elegies is Gray's *Elegy in a Country Churchyard**. None of these attempt to follow the original classical elegiac metres.

Elegy in a Country Churchyard (1750)

The best known poem by Thomas Gray*, and one of the most quoted in English. It is written in four-line stanzas, each line having 10 syllables, in rising rhythm. The poet reflects in a village cemetry on the graves of the humble and poor that surround him. It is a typically 18th-C poem in its generalizing treatment of traditional themes and in the representative images evoking the country scene. The verse is beautifully adapted to this generalizing manner which consequently does not attract the charge of insincerity sometimes made against 18th-C poems of the kind. The perfect fitting of the language to the generalities has caused some of the lines and phrases to have an almost proverbial familiarity, *eg*

Full many a flower is born to blush unseen,
And waste its sweetness on the desert air.

Elements, The (Four)

The 'four elements' are the ancient Greek and medieval conception of the basic components of matter; they are air, fire, earth and water. It was a division made by Empedocles* of Sicily and adopted by Aristotle*. Aristotle was writing before the beginnings of chemical analysis, and considered matter in regard to the 'properties' or qualities that he believed all things to possess; these he found to be 'hotness', 'coldness', 'wetness', and 'dryness'. His four elements contained these properties in different combinations: air = hot and wet; fire = hot and dry; earth = cold and dry; water = cold and wet. These, therefore, were the basic constituents of nature. Aristotle's great prestige in the Middle Ages caused his theory to dominate the thought of the time. The medieval alchemists, forbears of the modern analytical chemist, noticed that the properties of various kinds of matter change, *eg* iron becomes rust, and they deduced from Aristotle's theory that materials could be changed, provided that they retained the same basic properties, *eg* lead could be changed into gold. The theory dominated European thought until 17th C, when the English 'natural philosopher' and chemist, Robert Boyle (1627–91) taught that an element is to be regarded as a substance in itself, and not as a substance with certain basic properties. Since Boyle, chemists have discovered that elements are very much more numerous than the original four, and that air, fire, earth, and water are not in fact elements at all. Nonetheless, the pervasiveness of these so-called 'four elements' in our environment has caused them to keep their hold on the modern imagination, when it is not engaged in scientific thinking, so that they are still employed as symbols for the basic constituents of our experiences of the world in some imaginative literature, for instance in T. S. Eliot's poems *Four Quartets**.

The theory of the 'four elements' was connected in classical and medieval times with the medical and psychological theory of the 'humours', or four basic liquid constituents of the body. The blood humour ('hot and wet') is linked to air; choler ('hot and dry') is associated with fire; phlegm ('cold and wet') corresponds to water, and melancholy ('cold and dry') to earth. The preponderance of one or other of these humours in the make-up of a person's character was supposed to determine the temperament.

* *Humour.*

Elf

In old English myth, a tiny supernatural being, neither good nor bad in itself, but commonly responsible for mischief. It is of Teutonic origin, but it became increasingly associated with the fairy – of Latin origin – a less malicious kind of creature. Spenser, in the *Faerie Queene** uses the word in places for the Queen's knights. The more mischievous kind of fairy comes to be called a goblin, *eg* Puck in Shakespeare's *Midsummer Night's Dream**.

* *Fairies.*

Elgin Marbles

Greek statues and friezes, once belonging to the temple of the Parthenon in Athens, by the sculptor Pheidias (5th C BC). They are now in the British Museum, and were brought to England by Thomas Bruce, Earl of Elgin. He was British ambassador in Constantinople from 1799 to 1802, and it was then that he conceived the purpose of removing them. He was accused of vandalism, and defended himself in the pamphlet *Memorandum on the Earl of Elgin's Pursuits in Greece* (1810). The collection was purchased by the nation for £36,000 and placed in the museum in 1816. Lord Elgin had spent over £50,000 on removing them. They are amongst the finest sculptures in Europe, and made a deep impression on contemporary artists and poets, especially John Keats* and his friend Haydon. Byron* expresses his indignation at Elgin's action in *Childe Harold* (II, st.xi–xv).

Elia

* *Essays of Elia.*

Elijah /iˈlaidʒə/

In the Bible, a Hebrew prophet whose career is described in *1 and 2 Kings*. He was militant against foreign gods such as Baal* on behalf of the one God of the Jews. The stories about him are vivid and dramatic: his triumph over the prophets of Baal; the ravens feeding him in the wilderness; God speaking to him in a 'still, small voice' after the violence of the whirlwind; the chariot of fire, witnessed by his successor Elisha, carrying him up to heaven – these are some of the most remembered. He was fearless in condemning the wickedness and failings of the kings of Israel; in consequence he is often referred to as the basic type of the relentless critic of society.

Eliot, George (1819–80) /ˈeljət/

Pen-name of the novelist, Mary Ann Evans (at different times of her life she also spelt the name Mary Anne, Marian and Marianne). She was the daughter of a land-agent in the rural midlands (Warwickshire); her father's work (the management of estates) gave her wide experience of country society, and this was greatly to enrich her insight and the scope of her novels. Brought up in a narrow religious tradition, in her early twenties she adopted agnostic opinions about Christian doctrine, but she remained steadfast in the ethical teachings associated with it. She began her literary career with translations from the German of two works of religious speculation (**German Influence*); in 1851 she became assistant editor of the *Westminster Review*, a journal of great intellectual prestige in London. Her friendship with George Lewes*, led to a union between them which they both regarded as amounting to marriage; this was a bold decision in view of the rigid opposition in the English society of the time to open unions not legalized by the marriage ceremony.

Her first fiction consisted of tales later collected together as *Scenes of Clerical Life**. Then came her series of full-length novels: *Adam Bede** (1859), *The Mill on the Floss** (1860), *Silas Marner** (1861), *Romola** (1862–63), *Felix Holt** (1866), *Middlemarch** (1871–72), and *Daniel Deronda** (1876). Up till *Romola* the novels and tales deal with life in the countryside in which she was brought up; the society is depicted as a strong and stable one, and the novelist combines in an unusual degree sharp, humorous observation and intelligent imaginative sympathy. *Romola* marks a dividing point; it is a historical novel about the society of the Italian city of Florence in 15th C. As a work of imaginative literature it is usually regarded as scholarly but dead; however, it seems to have opened the way to the more comprehensive treatment of English society in her last three novels. Each of them (*Middlemarch* less than the others) has serious faults, but they also have strongly successful themes in which the relationship of the individual to society is interpreted with an intelligence outstanding in the history of the English novel, and often compared with the genius of the Russian novelist, Leo Tolstoy*. George Eliot's depth and scope of fictional art has caused the greatest critic of the English novel, F. R. Leavis*, to give her a central position in *The Great Tradition* that extends from Jane Austen* to D. H. Lawrence*.

George Eliot's poetry (*The Spanish Gipsy*, 1868, and *The Legend of Jubal*, 1870) is now little regarded, but her essays for the *Westminster Review* include work of distinction, and she published a collection, *The Impressions of Theophrastus Such*, in 1879.

In 1880, George Lewes having died, she married John Walter Cross, but she died in the same year.

* 3.4.4; 4.4.2.

Bib: Haight, G. S., *Life*; Leavis, F. R., in *The Great Tradition*; Bennett, J., *George Eliot: Her Mind and her Art*; Harvey, W. J., *The Art of George Eliot*; Pond, E. J., *Les Idées Morales et Religieuses de George Eliot*; Hardy, B., *The Art of George Eliot*.

Eliot, Thomas Stearns (1888–1965)

/ˈeljət/

Poet, critic, and dramatist. Born in St Louis, Missouri, he later settled in England, where his first important long poem—*The Love Song of J. Alfred Prufrock* – appeared in the magazine *Poetry* in 1915; his first book, *Prufrock and Other Observations*, appeared in 1917. From 1917 to 1919 he was Assistant Editor of *The Egoist*, a magazine advocating an advanced theory of poetry called Imagism*. His most famous poem, *The Waste Land**, came out in 1922, in which year he established the *Criterion*, one of the two most influential literary reviews of this century. In 1927 he became a naturalized British subject, and in the same year he demonstrated his conversion to Christianity by becoming a member of the Church of England. His remaining important volumes of poetry were *Ash Wednesday** (1930) and *Four Quartets** (1935–42). The total body of his verse is not large, but it is one of the most important collections of the century. His poetic influences were preponderantly the French 19th-C symbolists (Baudelaire, Mallarmé, Laforgue, de la Corbière), and the early-17th-C dramatists (Middleton*, Webster*, Tourneur*, the later Shakespeare) and their contemporaries the Metaphysical* poets. The great sermon writers of the same period – Donne*, Jeremy Taylor*, Bishop Andrewes* – exercised a double influence on his style and his thought, and so did the great Italian medieval poet Dante*. The contemporary who influenced him most and, in particular, greatly contributed to his early poetic development, was his fellow American Ezra Pound*. Finally, the idealist philosophy of F. H. Bradley*, whom Eliot studied as a student at Harvard and Oxford, was an important formative influence on Eliot's mind; his early academic thesis on Bradley was published in 1963.

Eliot's importance as a critic is linked with his importance as a poet, inasmuch as his really influential criticism was concerned with a reassessment of the past in such a way as to lead up to his own poetic production. Thus *The Sacred Wood* (1920) came between his first two volumes of verse. The most important of these early essays were republished in *Selected Essays* (1932). His later criticism, *eg The Uses of Poetry* (1933) and *On Poetry and Poets* (1957), lacked the motive power of the earlier fusion of poetic and critical production; consequently its shaping influence on general thinking has been much less. His work as a critic of society and civilization, *After Strange Gods* (1933) and *Notes Towards a Definition of Culture* (1948), has been such as to produce less fruitful, more sectarian discussion than his best literary criticism.

Eliot's experiments in the revival of verse drama had behind them a deeper, intenser study of the great age of English dramatic verse than any critic had brought to bear on it hitherto. Consequently his plays have abiding importance, although they are seldom rated amongst his best work. On the whole, the originality and substance are considered to diminish with the sequence of production: *Murder in the Cathedral* (1935) is admired more than *The Family Reunion* (1939); *The Cocktail Party* (1950) aroused controversy; *The Confidential Clerk* (1954) and *The Elder Statesman* (1958) aroused relatively little interest.

Eliot's non-dramatic poetry and his early

criticism have had the effect in this century of reordering and renewing literary taste both in this country and in America. He was not alone, but he was outstanding, in reviving admiration for the Metaphysical poets, and reducing the relative status of the Spenserian and Miltonic strains in the English tradition. His poetry permanently enlarged the range and form of poetic expression as a medium of the modern consciousness.

* 6.4.1-2; 7.5.

Bib: Hayward, J., *Selected Prose*; Matthiessen, F. O., *The Achievement of T. S. Eliot*; Kenner, H., *Invisible Poet*; Williamson, G., *A Reader's Guide*; Smith, G., *Eliot's Poetry and Plays*; Drew, E., *T. S. Eliot: The Design of his Poetry*; Gardner, H. L., *The Art of T. S. Eliot*.

Elision /iˈlɪʒn/

The suppression of sounds in words with the effect of drawing words together, *eg* 'the poor cat i' th' adage' (Shakespeare: *Macbeth* I.vii).

Elizabeth I (1558–1603)

Queen of England. Her reign was an extremely critical one, in which the personal fate of the Queen was unusually bound up with that of the nation and the national Church. As a Protestant*, she broke Mary's* ties with Rome and restored her father's independent Church of England*, but tolerance and compromise won her the loyalty of Catholics and Puritans* alike. For 30 years she successfully played off against each other the two great Catholic powers, France and Spain. While she remained single, there was always a chance that her Catholic cousin Mary, Queen of Scotland and widow of a French king, might succeed her. Even when Mary, deposed by the Scots, took refuge in England and connived at plots to murder her, Elizabeth avoided reprisals for nearly 20 years. Mary's eventual execution was followed in 1588 by Philip of Spain's attempted invasion of England, which resulted in the defeat of his powerful fleet, the great Armada*, by English seamanship and English weather. This was a great triumph for Elizabeth personally, and in her person the English nation saw its own triumph.

The reign saw an efflorescence of national spirit in other ways. It was the period of the first great achievements in English seamanship. Elizabeth's court was the focus of the real flowering of the English Renaissance*, expressing itself through music and literature; especially, the great age of English poetic drama began. Commerce expanded through the joint stock merchant companies, and with it a wealthy upper class, partly landed and partly mercantile, who left their mark in the immense country mansions which they built all over the land. The Queen herself, though cautious in statesmanship, was spirited and highly cultivated, able to rise to the heroic demands which the historical accidents of national destiny had thrust upon her.

* *Companies, Joint Stock; Drake; Elizabethan Period of English Literature; Raleigh; Sidney; Sixteenth-century Literature.*

Elizabethan Novels

The events in a 'novel' or 'novella' are not drawn directly from traditional or legendary sources but are invented by the writer, so that they are new (or 'novel') to the reader. The 'novels' of the Elizabethan period are distinguishable from the long prose romances, such as Sidney's *Arcadia**, by their comparative brevity, but *Arcadia* is sometimes included among them.

The Italian novella began its history in 13th C, and one of its best practitioners, Giovanni Boccaccio*, was already well known in England, especially from Chaucer's* adaptation of his work. In the first twenty years of Elizabeth's reign, various Italian 'novelle', especially those of Bandello (1480?–1562), were translated into English, notably by William Painter in his collection *The Palace of Pleasure**. These translations created a taste for the form, and led to the production of native English 'novels'. John Lyly's *Euphues** (1578) was the first of these. Best known among those that followed are: Lyly's *Euphues and his England* (1580), Barnabe Rich's collection *Farewell to the Military Profession* (1581), Robert Greene's* *Pandosto** (1588) and *Menaphon* (1589), Thomas Lodge's* *Rosalynde* (1590), Thomas Nashe's *Unfortunate Traveller** (1594), and Thomas Deloney's* *Thomas of Reading*, *Jack of Newbury*, and *The Gentle Craft* (all between 1596 and 1600). The style of these works varies greatly. Rich, Greene and Lodge wrote mannered and courtly tales in imitation of Lyly; Nashe's rambling narrative is sometimes strongly realistic, and his style parodies a wide range of contemporary prose styles; Deloney addressed a middle-class public and at his best (in *Thomas of Reading*) anticipates the sober vividness of Daniel Defoe*. The taste for the form lapsed in early 17th C. There is no continuous development between the Elizabethan novel and the novel form as we know it today: the latter has its beginnings in the work of Defoe in early 18th C, though it had late-17th-C fore-runners.

Both the Italian and the English novels were used as sources for plots by contemporary English dramatists. Shakespeare's *Twelfth Night** is drawn from *Apolonius and Silla* in Rich's collection, adapted from an Italian original; his *As You Like It** is based on Lodge's *Rosalynde*; his *Winter's Tale** draws on Greene's *Pandosto**.

* 4.1.4.

Elizabethan Period of English Literature

The term 'Elizabethan' is used confusingly in regard to literature.

[1] It is generally applied accurately to the lyric poetry and prose (*eg* Elizabethan Novels*) which flowered during the reign of Elizabeth 1* and especially during the last half of it.

[2] On the other hand the term 'Elizabethan drama' is sometimes made to cover not only the beginnings of the great poetic drama (roughly 1588–1600) but also the greater period that succeeded this in the reign of James 1* and even to include the period of its final decline under Charles 1*, *ie* until the closing of the theatres in

1642. But critics usually distinguish the mature phase as Jacobean* and the decline as Caroline*. By this more accurate designation, an Elizabethan dramatist would be such as Marlowe*, the early Shakespeare*, Greene*, Lyly*, or Peele*; the Jacobean drama would include mature and late Shakespeare, Jonson*, Tourneur*, Webster*, Middleton*; and the Caroline drama, the later work of Massinger*, John Ford* and Shirley*.

[3] In literary terminology, 'Elizabethan' has further to be distinguished from Tudor. The Queen was herself the last of the House of Tudor*, but Tudor drama, the Tudor lyric, Tudor prose, etc. commonly refer to work during the previous reigns, *ie* between the accession of Henry VII* in 1485 and her own accession in 1558.

* Periods of English Literature.

Ellis, Henry Havelock (1859–1939)

Psychologist and essayist. Part of his work was scientific: *Man and Woman* (1894); *Studies in the Psychology of Sex* (1897–1910). Part of it was literary and expressed in reflective essays: *Little Essays in Love and Virtue* (1922); *Impressions and Comments* (1914–23); *The Dance of Life* (1923). In the latter work he exemplified the revival of the essay* as a reflective form early in this century.

Bib: Calder Marshall, A., *Life*; Collis, J. S., *An Artist of Life*.

Eloisa to Abelard (1717)

A poem by Alexander Pope*, based on the famous love of the great medieval philosopher Abelard* (1079–1142) for Heloise (Eloisa) – an affair which ended tragically. In the poem Eloisa expresses the tragedy in the classical manner of the Latin poet Ovid*. The lovers had fled together, but rather than ruin Abelard's career in the church by obeying her relatives' demand that they should marry, Eloisa has entered a convent. The poem purports to be a letter from her in the convent.

Elsinore

A seaport in Denmark (Danish = Helsingør); the castle there is the scene of Shakespeare's tragedy *Hamlet**.

Elyot, Sir Thomas (1499?–1546) /'eljət/

Chiefly famous as the author of *The Governor* (1531) in which he argued in favour of a class of land-owning magistrates, qualified for their office by the classical culture (*ie* education in the ancient Greek and Latin authors) which was being promulgated by his humanist* contemporaries, Erasmus* and Sir Thomas More*. The book had an important influence in 16th-C England, helping to bind the educated classes to the service of the more modern and centralized kind of state which the Tudor sovereigns had been in the course of consolidating.

Elysium /i'liziəm/

In ancient Greek myth, an imaginary island where the souls of the virtuous enjoyed perfect happiness after death. The Latin poets transferred it to Hades*, or the Underworld. In English literature it is sometimes used synonymously with Heaven.

Ember Days

Days appointed by the Church in ancient times as beginning a period of a week's fasting and prayer; they were also prescribed for the ordination of the clergy. There are three such days for each season of the year: the Wednesday, Friday and Saturday following the first Sunday in Lent (Spring); Whit-Sunday (Summer); Holy Cross Day, 14 September (Autumn) and St Lucy's Day, 13 December (Winter).

Emblem-books

Books, very popular in England in 16th C containing pictures of ordinary objects (compasses, bottles, flowers, etc.) together with short poems showing how the object could be used to teach a truth applicable to life or conduct. The fashion influenced the imagery of the 17th-C Metaphysical* poets who commonly used simple objects as more or less complex illustrations of human experience, as when the poet Donne* in *Valediction Forbidding Mourning* compares the relationship of himself and his wife when he goes on a journey to a pair of geometrical compasses whose points can divide but which yet remain united. Poets such as Quarles*, Wither, and Herbert* wrote verses sometimes shaped like such objects – a bottle, wings, etc.

Emerald Isle, The

A poetic name for Ireland, suggested by the intense greenness of its landscape.

Emma (1816)

A novel by Jane Austen*. The heroine, Emma Woodhouse, has wealth, social prestige, good looks, and intelligence. But her good fortune and the admiration she elicits are in reality her greatest disadvantage: they blind her to the need for self-knowledge and self-criticism. In what she imagines to be pure generosity of heart, she sets about trying to control the fate of her orphan friend of illegitimate birth and insignificant character, Harriet Smith, imagining her to be the daughter of an aristocrat and deserving a marriage socially worthy of her paternity. Later she also becomes involved with a young man, Frank Churchill, who unknown to her is secretly engaged to a girl, Jane Fairfax, who is superior to Emma in talent but much inferior in worldly fortune. Jane Austen is in fact expanding the theme of the way in which romantic fantasy can blind a character to the realities of experience, more overtly used in earlier novels, *Northanger Abbey**, and *Sense and Sensibility**. Emma, who has imagination and ability but nothing on which to employ them, is first trying to make a real-life novel with Harriet Smith as heroine, and then participating in a mysterious drama, which she misconceives as her own fantasy wants it to be, with Jane Fairfax as main protagonist. But Harriet decides that she is to marry the man, George Knightley, with whom Emma herself has long been unconsciously in love; Emma also discovers that Churchill, with whom she has been conducting a flirtation, has merely been using her as a tool to mask his secret engagement. She realizes, in fact, that she has caused herself to be a victim of the first of her romances, and has been made to play an ignominious and unworthy role in the second. Only good fortune and the good sense of Knightley save her from heartbreak and shame. The novel is perhaps Jane Austen's finest, displaying her irony at its most subtle.

Empedocles (5th C BC) /em'pedəkli:z/

A philosopher and statesman of the Greek colony of Agrigentum in Sicily. He is said to have led the people against the tyrannous government of a powerful class, and then to have refused to become their king. According to a legend he met his death in the volcano of Etna, though in reality he seems to have died in Greece. There are various allusions to his legendary end in English literature, and it is usually ascribed to dangerous curiosity. The most famous account of it is the poem *Empedocles on Etna* (1852) by Matthew Arnold*; in this his death is represented as deliberate suicide by a disillusioned and banished political leader. Arnold uses the poem to express his own scepticism about the hopefulness of human destiny.

Empson, William (b 1906) /'empsn/

Critic and poet. At Cambridge University he studied mathematics, and then English literature under I. A. Richards*. He spent a number of years before and after World War II teaching first in Japan and then in China; in 1953 he became Professor of English Literature in the University of Sheffield. His main critical works are: *Seven Types of Ambiguity* (1930), *Some Versions of Pastoral* (1935), *The Structure of Complex Words* (1951), and *Milton's God* (1961). Poetry: *Poems* (1935), and *The Gathering Storm* (1940).

As a critic, he has been very influential, especially through his analysis of the nature of language when it is used in imaginative writing, particularly poetry. His approach has been influenced by the attitudes to language of 20th-C linguistic philosophers, especially Bertrand Russell* and Wittgenstein, who concentrated on the tendency of language, by the ambiguities inherent in it, to confuse clear thought. Empson's teacher, Richards, in his *Principles of Literary Criticism* (1924), discussed the kinds of truth that are to be found in poetic statements, and how these truths differ from, without being less valuable than, the truths of philosophical and scientific statement. Empson's first book (*Seven Types*) discusses the ways in which various kinds of semantic ambiguity can be used by poets, and shows the relevance of this study to the proper assessment of poems. His later books develop the psychological (particularly Freudian) and philosophical aspects of this approach, but *Seven Types of Ambiguity* is still Empson's most influential book.

The criticism of poetry through the study of ambiguities of language is particularly appropriate to the 17th-C Metaphysical* poets, and Empson's own poems are a conscious revival of the Metaphysical style; his work especially recalls that of Andrew Marvell*. At their best, they are among the finest short poems of the century, but their merit does not always equal their difficulty. Their intellectual ingenuity seems to be less a method of controlling emotion, as in Metaphysical poetry, than a defence against emotion. In this respect, Empson has influenced poets writing since 1945; reacting against the surrender of mind to emotion, exemplified by German Nazism, they have also tended to guard themselves by keeping their feelings cool.

* 7.5.

Enclosures

The enclosure of land into large units of cultivation or ownership was a feature of English agriculture from 16th C to 19th. It was nearly always motivated by the personal advantage of the landowner. In 16th and 17th C the motive was especially to profit from the market for wool, in preference to the fairly small rents obtainable from the arable farms of smallholding tenants. Less excusably, the landowner sometimes wished to use the land for no productive purpose but merely to surround his mansion with a large ornamental park. In 18th C, the aim of the landowner was to replace the small farms cultivated on the 'open-field' system by larger, economically more efficient farms with hedge-divided fields. Goldsmith's *Deserted Village** (1770) is a protest against the practice. Agricultural enclosures caused emigration to the colonies, and also into the rapidly rising industrial towns. Enclosures did not merely affect arable land, but also the common land*. It was the second sort that persisted into 19th C.

Encyclopaedists

The collaborators in the production of the great French encyclopaedia (*L'Encyclopédie*) of 18th C. The enterprise began with a translation of the English *Cyclopaedia* by Ephraim Chambers, but the French version was intellectually altogether more impressive. Its editors were two leaders of the 'philosophes' – D'Alembert and Diderot – and its contributors were the leading minds of France, such men as Voltaire* and Rousseau*. The inspiration was faith in reason and the desire to destroy superstition and beliefs thought to arise from it. The movement contributed to the influences which later led to the French Revolution*, and it reinforced rationalism* throughout Europe. In England the movement influenced Jeremy Bentham*, and through him the Utilitarians* of 19th C.

End-rhyme

Rhyme occurring in the usual position, *ie* at the end of a line; internal rhymes occur in the middle of a line, and head-rhymes are the correspondence of the beginnings of words, *ie* alliteration.

End-stopped lines

Lines of verse, especially blank verse, which end at the end of a sentence or at strongly marked pauses within the sentence:

These arms of mine shall be thy winding-sheet;
My heart, sweet boy, shall be thy sepulchre,
For from my heart thine image ne'er shall go;
My sighing breast shall be thy funeral bell;
And so obsequious will thy father be,
E'en for the loss of thee, having no more,
As Priam was for all his valiant sons.

(Shakespeare – *3 Henry VI* II.v)

The opposite effect is produced by run-on lines, when the syntax makes the voice go on to the next line without pause:

You cram these words into mine ears, against
The stomach of my sense. Would I had never
Married my daughter there! for, coming thence,
My son is lost; and, in my rate, she too,
Who is so far from Italy removed,
I ne'er again shall see her.

(Shakespeare – *Tempest* II.i)

In this passage it is unnatural to pause at the ends of the first two lines; in lines 3 and 4 the pause at the end is weaker than the pause in the middle of the line. The difference between the two quotations is representative of the difference between earlier and later plays of Shakespeare, *ie* the proportion of end-stopped lines tends to diminish.

* *Enjambment.*

Endymion (1818) /en'dimiən/

A long poem by John Keats*. It is based on an ancient Greek myth about a shepherd with whom the moon goddess fell in love. The poem has passages of great freshness and beauty, but, as Keats soon came to realize, it has many defects of immaturity. Its classicism is no longer a firm guide and basis as classicism had been in 18th C but a resource for the free embroidering of fanciful stories; the theme, the indulgence of the senses, is such as Keats quickly outgrew.

Endymion is also the title of a play (1591) by John Lyly* and of a novel (1880) by Disraeli*.

England's Helicon (1600)

An Elizabethan verse anthology* including many of the principal examples of the pastoral* poetry from the best poets of the reign. It is important evidence of Elizabethan literary taste.

English Language

Historically the language is divided into three periods: Old English extending to 12th C; Middle English, from 12th C to 16th; and Modern English.

Old English is compounded of Anglo-Saxon* and Jutish (*Jutes) dialects, and is called English because the language of the Angles* is the earliest discoverable in writing. Old English was strongly modified by Scandinavian elements in consequence of the Danish invasions, and Middle English by an extensive infusion of French vocabulary.

Middle English was divided into a variety of dialects; Langland*, for instance, the author of *Piers Plowman**, wrote in the West Midland dialect; the author or authors of *Sir Gawain and the Green Knight** and of *Pearl** wrote in a dialect farther north, and Chaucer* in the East Midland dialect. Because London was the chief city of England and the seat of the royal court, and because Caxton* established his printing press there in 15th C, East Midland became the forebear of Modern English. Since 15th C English has not undergone important structural changes; social differences of speech as between the classes have been of greater importance, at least for literary purposes, than regional ones.

Exceptions to this statement have to be made, however, for the form of English spoken and written in southern Scotland, and for those regions of the British Isles where until comparatively recent times Celtic languages were predominant: north-west Scotland, Wales, and above all Ireland. In Ireland especially, the spoken language tends to follow the structure of Erse (Irish Gaelic) and this peasant idiom is exploited by Irish writers such as the dramatist J. M. Synge* and the poet W. B. Yeats*. Normally Irish or Welsh writers of course use standard English if they do not adhere to the surviving Celtic languages. Southern Scots is more important: it is a variant of English rather than an English dialect, and has been the native language of southern Scotland for as long a period as southern English has in England. The literature in Scots (known in the Middle Ages as Inglis and today sometimes as Lallans*, *ie* Lowlands) is considerable and advanced, whether one thinks of the late medieval poets such as Dunbar*, Douglas*, or

Henryson*, an 18th-C poet such as Burns*, or a 20th-C one like Hugh MacDiarmid*. However from 17th C eminent Scottish writers took to writing in southern English, and this became universal amongst prose writers of 18th C (Hume*, Robertson, Adam Smith*).

'The Queen's English' is the term used for the language spoken by the educated classes in England; linguists, however, prefer the term 'Standard English'. Pronunciation most in use among educated people is known as 'Received Pronunciation'.

English vocabulary is basically Germanic, but it also contains a very large number of Latin words. French, of course, developed from Latin, and many of these Latin words entered English in their French form after the Norman* Conquest in 11th C. For about two and a half centuries the upper classes were French-speaking. Vestiges of this social difference survive in such distinctions as the word 'sheep' used for the live animal, and 'mutton', for the same animal when it is eaten at table; the English shepherds who cared for the sheep ate very little meat, whereas their Norman-French masters were chiefly concerned with the animal when it had been transformed into food. Even after the aristocracy became English-speaking in 14th C, the adoption of French words continued to be frequent owing to the strong influence of French culture and ways of life on the English educated classes. Latin words, however, have also entered English independently of their French forms; the 'clerks', *ie* the literate class of the earlier Middle Ages, used Latin as a living language in their writings; they were churchmen, and Latin was the language of the Church all over western Europe. In 16th C, there was a new and different kind of influx from Latin owing to the fresh interest taken by scholars in ancient Latin culture.

The Latin contribution to the basically Germanic English vocabulary has resulted in a large number of Latin and Germanic synonyms, with important consequences for subtleties of English expression. The associations of Latin with the medieval Church and with ancient Roman literature cause the words of Latin origin to have suggestions of grandeur which the words of Germanic origin do not possess; thus we use 'serpent' in connection with religious and mythological ideas, *eg* the story of the Garden of Eden*, but 'snake' will do in reference to the ordinary reptile. On the other hand, the Latinate word is emotionally less intimate than its Germanic synonym; when we wish to lessen the painfulness of death, we say that a man is 'deceased', instead of saying that he has 'died'. This kind of differentiation is, however, often despised, as indicating insincerity or artificiality of feeling. Thus, socially, it is often considered vulgar to use the synonym of French or Latin construction, as suggesting a disposition to speak stylishly rather than truly; many people consider it vulgar to use the French 'serviette' instead of the older 'napkin'; the latter is also of French origin, but it is more fully anglicized.

Some English writers, *eg* Milton* and Samuel Johnson*, and some periods of literature, especially 18th C, are often singled out for their preference for the Latin part of the vocabulary, and in 19th C the preference was sometimes regarded as a fault. Correspondingly, some literature is admired for its reliance on mainly Germanic vocabulary, *eg* the ballads*, and the poems of John Clare* and Christina Rossetti*, but in this kind of judgement Latin and French words adopted long ago and grown fully familiar are allowed to have the same merit as words of Germanic descent. Language which shows sensitiveness to the value of contrasting Latinate and Germanic vocabulary is always allowed peculiar merit; such is the case with Shakespeare.

English has borrowed words from many other languages; the chief of these is ancient Greek, which contributed extensively during 16th C Renaissance*, and coloured the language similarly to the Latin contribution at the same time. Borrowings from other languages are more miscellaneous and less distinctive; the most distinctive are the modern borrowings from colloquial American diction.

English has not only borrowed more freely than most other languages; it has also spread itself abroad more freely than any language. It is not only the first language of the larger parts of North America and Australasia, but it is spoken widely, often as a first language, in Africa and Asia (especially India), where it is a 'lingua franca' in countries which have a variety of indigenous languages. This has complicated the study of literature in English; as the various territories of the former British Empire have acquired independence, so they have developed their own literatures, which, although in the English language, have distinctive styles and directions. Only a few 20th-C American writers, for instance, can be included in the truly English tradition; it is now necessary to talk of 'American literature'. It is similarly difficult to think of the Austraiian Patrick White or the West Indian V. S. Naipaul as English writers, in the sense of belonging to the English literary tradition.

Enjambment /in'dʒammənt/

A term describing the continuing of the sense from line to line in a poem, to the extent that it is unnatural in speaking the verse to make a pause at the line ending. The effect is that of 'run-on' lines.

I caught this morning morning's minion, king-
dom of daylight's dauphin, dapple-dawn-drawn Falcon, in his riding
Of the rolling level underneath him steady air and striding
High there, how he rung upon the rein of a wimpling wing
In his ecstasy!

(G. M. Hopkins* – *The Windhover*)

This is an extreme example; it is unusual in enjambment to go so far as to divide a word, as Hopkins does at the end of line 1.

* *End-stopped lines.*

Ephesians /i'fi:ʒjənz/

Inhabitants of the ancient city of Ephesus in Asia Minor, where there was an early Christian community. St Paul addressed to these one of his letters of doctrinal exposition: *Epistle to the Ephesians* in the New Testament. The presiding goddess was Artemis* (Diana), to whom there was a famous temple. Shakespeare (in *2 Henry IV* II.ii and *Merry Wives of Windsor* IV.v) uses 'Ephesians' to mean close comrades in pleasure.

Epic

[1] A narrative of heroic actions, often with a principal hero, usually mythical in its content, offering inspiration and ennoblement within a particular cultural or national tradition. [2] The word denotes qualities of heroism and grandeur, appropriate to epic but present in other literary or even non-literary forms.

Epics occur in almost all national cultures, and commonly give an account of national origins, or enshrine ancient, heroic myths central to the culture. For European culture at large, much the most influential epics are the *Iliad** and the *Odyssey** of Homer and the *Aeneid** by Virgil. C. S. Lewis in *Preface to Paradise Lost* makes a helpful distinction between primary and secondary epics: primary ones, such as Homer's, are written for a society which is still fairly close to the conditions of society described in the narrative; secondary epics are based on the pattern of primary epics but written for a materially developed society more or less remote from the conditions described, *eg* Virgil's *Aeneid*. In English literature the Old English *Beowulf** may be counted as a primary epic. A number of attempts at secondary epic have been made since 16th C, but John Milton's *Paradise Lost** is unique in its acknowledged greatness and its closeness to the Virgilian structure. Spenser's *Faerie Queene** has many epic characteristics, but, in spite of the important classical influences upon it, the poem's structure is derived from the 'romantic epic' of the 16th-C Italian poets, Ariosto* and Tasso*; moreover, though allegory often plays a part in epics, the allegorical elements in *The Faerie Queene* are so pervasive as to present a different kind of imaginative vision from that normally found in them.

Many other works in English literature have epic qualities without being definable as epics. For example, Shakespeare's two historical tetralogies (*1, 2 & 3 Henry VI*, *Richard III*; *Richard II*, *1 & 2 Henry IV*, *Henry V*) may be called 'dramatic epics' about the English monarchy, though this is only one way of seeing them. Fielding described *Tom Jones** as a comic epic, and it is this as much as it is a novel: a series of adventures of which Tom is the hero, but of which the consequences are loss of dignity rather than enhancement of dignity. Melville's prose romance *Moby Dick* (1851), has true epic scale, seriousness of treatment, and relevance to the human condition. James Joyce's *Ulysses** uses the *Odyssey* as the ground plan for a narrative about a day in the life of a Dublin citizen, and though the intention of this and of Joyce's succeeding work *Finnegans Wake** is in part comic, there is also in both books deep seriousness, such as derives from the authentic epic tradition. In fact, this tradition, in the last three hundred years, has mingled with other literary forms, such as the romance, the comic romance (*eg Don Quixote**), and the novel, and it is in this mixed rather than in its original pure form that it has proved most productive.

* **4.2.1**; **6.3.1**.

Epic, Mock

A form of satire practised with most success in English by Alexander Pope*. The method is to employ the dignified expression associated with epic about subjects in themselves either trivial or base. Thus *The Rape of the Lock** describes a family quarrel provoked by a young man robbing a girl of a lock of her hair; it uses a dignity of style appropriate to the Rape of Helen which gave rise to Homer's *Iliad**, and applies it to the minute detail and obviously trivial scale of emotion appropriate to the slightness of the episode. In Pope's *Dunciad** the method is rather different, because here Pope is describing what is base rather than what is petty; the contrast is not, as with *The Rape*, an ironic one between grandeur of treatment and pettiness of subject, but between the nobility of the style and the depth of meanness in the subject.

Another form of mock epic is the mock heroic* poem, in which a bad man committing base deeds is described in epic style, without disguising the badness. Such are Dryden's *Absalom and Achitophel** and Butler's *Hudibras**; Fielding's novel *Jonathan Wild* is also in the tradition.

The mock epic is especially the product of the century 1660–1760, when admiration for Greek and Latin satire and epic was particularly high.

* **4.2.2**; **6.3.1**; *Epic*; *Mock Heroic*.

Epic Simile

Prolonged similes, commonly used in epic or heroic poetry, giving the subject described a spaciousness suited to its grandeur. Thus in *Paradise Lost** Bk. I, Milton wants to say that the fallen Satan is as big as a whale; this would be to use an ordinary simile. He expands it to an epic simile thus:

As huge as . . .
. . . that Sea-beast
Leviathan, which God of all his works
Created hugest that swim th'Ocean stream:
Him haply slumbring on the Norway foam
The Pilot of some small night-founder'd Skiff,
Deeming some Island, oft, as Sea-men tell,
With fixéd Anchor in his skaly rind
Moors by his side under the Lee, while Night
Invests the Sea, and wishéd Morn delayes:
So stretcht out huge in length the Arch-fiend lay . . .

* *Epic*.

Epicoene, or The Silent Woman (1609) /'episi:n/

A comedy by Ben Jonson*. Epicoene means having

the characteristics of either sex. The main character Morose, who has an extreme hatred of noise, wants to disinherit his nephew and marry a silent woman if she can be found. A completely silent one is found, but after marriage she finds the use of her tongue and is anything but silent. Morose promises to reinstate his nephew as his heir, with an additional reward, if he can free his uncle of the wife who is now the opposite of what he hoped. The nephew then discloses that the wife is a boy disguised. Though not one of the greatest of Jonson's comedies, it has always been one of his most popular, owing to a large cast of lively comic characters. The play is given a close analysis in Dryden's *Essay on Dramatic Poesy**.

Epicurean

* *Epicurus.*

Epicurus (342–270 BC) /epiˈkjuərəs/

Greek philosopher and founder of the Epicurean school of philosophers. He is best known for his principle that pleasure is the beginning and end of the blessed life. This has commonly been misunderstood to mean that the purpose of life is pleasure seeking; in fact Epicurus meant by pleasure the acquisition of a mind at peace, and this implied, for him, the pursuit of virtue, and hence a life of asceticism rather than excess. His best-known disciple is the Latin poet Lucretius*, who expounded the philosophy in his poem *De Rerum Natura* (Concerning the Nature of Things). The Epicureans were rivals of the Stoics*, who taught that the end of life was fortitude and liberation from the passions.

Epigram

For the ancient Greeks the word meant 'inscription'. From this, the meaning extended to include very short poems notable for the terseness and elegance of their expression and the weight and wit of their meaning. The richest of the ancient Greek collections is the Greek *Anthology**; the greatest Latin masters were Catullus* and Martial. Ben Jonson's *Underwoods** contains epigrams in their tradition. After him, epigrams became shorter and most commonly had satirical content; Pope* was the greatest master of this style, and his poems include many epigrams, *eg*

Now Europe balanced, neither side prevails;
For nothing's left in either of the scales.

* *Aphorism.*

Epiphany

A Church festival celebrating the showing ('epiphany' means manifestation) of the Christ child to the Magi*, otherwise known as the three Wise Men or the Three Kings (*Matthew* 2). The festival is twelve days after 25 December, or Christmas Day, so that it is also called Twelfth Night, or the Twelfth Night of Christmas; it concluded the season of Christmas festivities.

The novelist James Joyce* began his career by writing what he called 'epiphanies', *ie* sketches in which the incident, though often in itself slight, manifests or reveals the inner truth of a character. This is the method he pursues in *Dubliners**.

Episcopalian

From the Latin 'episcopus' = 'bishop'. 'Episcopacy' is the system of government of Christian Churches by bishops; an 'episcopalian' is a member of such a Church, or the supporter of such a system. The belief on which the system is based is that Jesus Christ consecrated his apostles in authority over the first disciples, and that this consecrated authority has been transmitted down the centuries to all succeeding bishops. Thus the Roman Catholic Church is governed by bishops under the supreme authority of the Pope who, as Bishop of Rome, is said to be the successor of St Peter, chief of the apostles and first Bishop of Rome.

During the Reformation*, episcopacy was opposed by various sects of reformers, and alternatives were set up, such as Presbyterianism* (government by elected elders) and Congregationalism* (self-government by each community of worshippers). The Church of England*, however, retained the episcopalian system. One of the chief causes of dispute between the Roman Catholic Church and the Church of England is over the question whether the English episcopacy is valid; the issue has special importance since bishops in turn consecrate all junior members of the priesthood. Thus, if the Anglican bishops are not entitled to their authority, all the orders of the Anglican priesthood are invalid.

Epitaph

An inscription on a tomb, or a short verse or prose inscription that might serve such a purpose. As literary compositions, epitaphs became popular in the age of Shakespeare, and as the requirement of brevity gives epitaphs a resemblance to epigrams*, 18th C, the great age of the epigram, was also that in which the epitaph was most cultivated. Some epitaphs are famous poems, *eg* several of Ben Jonson's*, and Milton's* sixteen-line epitaph on Shakespeare. This, however, is longer than epitaphs of 18th C. The following is characteristic of Pope's* epigrammatic style, on the physicist, Sir Isaac Newton*:

Nature and Nature's laws lay hid in night;
God said; 'Let Newton be', and all was light.

Epithalamion

* *Ode; Spenser.*

Erasmus, Desiderius (1466–1536)

Dutch humanist and man of letters. He had immense international influence; in the fields of classical and theological scholarship he is the leading figure of the Renaissance*. Humanism* was basically the rediscovery and direct study of ancient Greek and Latin literature, the effect of which was a fresh inspiration to the culture of Christendom, and a new critical attitude to the authority of medieval (scholastic*) interpretation of the Bible and of the Greek and Latin authors. Erasmus, for example, retranslated the New

Testament from the Greek into Latin, showing that the existing Bible (the Vulgate*), in use all over Europe, contained mistranslations. Erasmus was also a witty and reasonable critic of social and ecclesiastical abuses; his most popular work, *Encomium Moriae* ('The Praise of Folly', written at the instigation of Sir Thomas More*) ridiculed the princes of the Church and those of the state alike, as all subject to folly. Like his other works, it was written in elegant Latin. Erasmus was a contemporary of the great German religious reformer, Martin Luther*; characteristically, he refused to take sides for or against Luther, since it was contrary to the spirit of humanism as he expounded it to adopt a narrow outlook, either in the form of intolerance or of sectarianism.

Erasmus's contacts with England were important, both for himself and for the development of English culture. He was a friend of the English humanists, Colet, Linacre, Grocyn and More. He seems to have owed to Colet his interest in theological criticism. He helped to give impetus to classical studies as the education of a gentleman, and he owed much to the liberality of English patrons.

Erato

* *Muses.*

Erebus /ˈeribəs/

In ancient Greek myth, a god of the underworld, son of Chaos. The word is often used to signify the underworld or hell itself.

Erewhon (1872) and *Erewhon Revisited* (1901) /ˈeriwon/

Satirical anti-utopias by Samuel Butler*. Sir Thomas More's *Utopia** is a description of an ideal country as different as possible from England. Erewhon ('Nowhere' written backwards) represents a country many of whose characteristics are analogous to English ones, caricatured and satirized. Thus Butler satirizes ecclesiastical institutions through the Musical Banks, and parental tyranny through the Birth Formulae; machinery has to be abolished before it takes over from human beings. In *Erewhon Revisited*, Higgs, the English discoverer of Erewhon, finds that his previous departure by balloon has been used by Professors Hanky and Panky ('hanky-panky' is deceitful practice) to impose a new religion, according to which Higgs is worshipped as a child of the sun. Butler's method in these satires resembles Jonathan Swift's satirical technique in the Lilliput of *Gulliver's Travels**.

Eros

* *Cupid.*

Erse /ɜːs/

The native Celtic language of Ireland.

* *Irish Literature.*

Esau /ˈiːsoː/

In the Bible, the brother of Jacob*.

Escorial (Escurial), The

The great palace of the Kings of Spain, including a convent and a mausoleum, built by Philip II (1556–98).

Esmond (1852)

A historical novel by William Makepeace Thackeray*. It is a very careful reconstruction of early-18th-C English aristocratic and literary society. The hero's father has been killed fighting for James II*, *ie* he was a Jacobite*. The politics of the book are involved with Jacobite plotting by the Roman Catholic branch of the House of Stuart* to recover the throne of Britain from the Protestant branch. There are portraits of some of the distinguished personalities of the time – the Duke and Duchess of Marlborough*, and the writers Steele*, Addison*, and Swift*. The style emulates that of Addison himself. The theme is the devotion of the young Henry Esmond to his relatives, Lady Castlewood, eight years older than himself, and her proud and ambitious daughter, Beatrix. These relationships are complicated by political intrigues, and by family mysteries – Esmond is in reality himself the heir to the title and properties inherited by Lady Castlewood's husband. In the end, Esmond marries the widowed Lady Castlewood, and emigrates to Virginia; his story continues in *The Virginians* (1857–9).

* *Historical Fiction.*

Essay, The

'Essay' derives from the French *essai*, meaning 'experiment', 'attempt'. As a literary term it is used to cover an enormous range of composition, from schoolboy exercises to thorough scientific and philosophical works, the only quality in common being the implied desire of the writer to reserve to himself some freedom of treatment. But the essay is also a recognized literary form in a more defined sense: it is understood to be a fairly short prose composition, in style often familiarly conversational and in subject either self-revelatory or illustrative (more or less humorously) of social manners and types. The originator of the form was the great French writer Montaigne*.

Montaigne's essays were published in completed form in 1595, and translated by John Florio* into English (1603). His starting-point is 'Que sais-je?' ('What do I know?') and it leads him into a serious inquiry into his own nature as he feels it, and into investigations of facts, ideas, and experiences as he responds to them. In 1597 the first great English essayist, Francis Bacon*, published his first collection of essays, of a very different kind: they are impersonal and aphoristic, weightily sententious. The character writers, Sir Thomas Overbury* and John Earle (1601?–65) use the classical model of the Greek writer Theophrastus*, reminding one that with so indefinite a form it is impossible to be too precise about the dating of starting-points. Abraham Cowley* published the first essays in English closely corresponding to what is now understood by the form, and perhaps shows the first sign of its degeneracy: easiness of tone, which in Montaigne is a graciousness of manner introducing a serious and interesting personality, but which in less interesting writers may be an agreeable cover for saying nothing in particular.

In the early years of 18th C Addison* and Steele* firmly established what is now known as the 'periodical essay' – a kind of higher journalism, intended often to please rather than instruct, but in their case to instruct through pleasure. In creations such as Sir Roger de Coverley*, they developed the Theophrastian character into a personal, idiosyncratic portrait anticipating the characterization of the novelists a little later in the century. Their graciousness and lightness of tone take point and interest from their serious and conscious social purpose. Dr Johnson* in *The Rambler* and in his essays as 'The Idler'* used the weighty, impressive style soon to be regarded as unsuitable for the medium. Oliver Goldsmith* in *The Citizen of the World* (1762) perfected the graceful, witty manner which came to be considered ideal for it.

If 18th C was what may be called the golden age of the English essay, the early 19th, in the work of Charles Lamb*, William Hazlitt*, Leigh Hunt* and De Quincey*, was perhaps its silver age. In these writers, social comment combines with a confessional, autobiographical element which had never been so prominent in the English essay before. This was true to the autobiographical spirit of so much 19th-C literature. These essayists were links between the early Romantic poets – especially Wordsworth* – and the mid-Victorian novelists; they shared the close interest in material surroundings characteristic of those poets, and their essays often contained character delineations related to such environmental settings. The earliest work of Dickens, *Sketches by Boz**, is in the essayists' tradition.

After 1830, the periodical essay in the tradition of Addison, Goldsmith, Hazlitt and Lamb dissolved into the morass of constantly increasing journalism; though they had emulators in 20th C, the form was increasingly despised by serious writers, and the famous essayists of the later 19th C were the more specialized sort, such as Matthew Arnold* and John Stuart Mill.* Yet it is not true to say that the informal essay of serious literary interest has disappeared. In the later 19th and 20th C, essays of natural description of remarkable intensity were produced by Richard Jefferies* and Edward Thomas*. More important still is the use of the essay for unspecialized but deeply serious social and cultural comment by – to take leading examples – D. H. Lawrence*, George Orwell*, and Aldous Huxley*.

* *Characters, Theophrastian.*

Essay concerning Human Understanding (1690)

A philosophical treatise by John Locke*. Locke emphasizes the reason as the dominant faculty of man. All knowledge is acquired through experience based on sense impressions; there are no 'innate ideas', *ie* no knowledge arises in the mind independently of impressions received from the outside world. These impressions divide into primary qualities, *ie* the measurable ones such as size, number, form, etc., and secondary ones, such as colour, sound, scent, which are not demonstrably part of the object, but dependent on the observer. Knowledge begins with perception of agreement or disagreement in the qualities observed in the objects or, as Locke calls them, 'ideas'. He distinguishes between rational judgement, which identifies and analyses ideas, and 'wit', which relates them by their resemblances; the distinction is practically one between reason and imagination and gives advantage to reason. Faith, *eg* in religious doctrine, is not distinct from reason, but the assent of the mind to a belief that accords with reason. Thus Locke appeals to clear definition in language and expression; he depreciates the intuitive and imaginative faculties of the mind and elevates the rational ones. His thesis accords with the reaction at the end of 17th C against the intolerance and fanaticism of the religious conflicts which had prevailed during the first half of it. The influence of his philosophy is impressed on the imaginative prose literature of the first thirty years of 18th C, for instance in the realism of Defoe*. Later in the century, the novelist Laurence Sterne* makes ingenious use of Locke's theory of the association of ideas in *Tristram Shandy**.

Essay on Criticism (1711)

An essay in verse, in heroic couplets*, by Alexander Pope. The ideas are not original, nor intended to be; they derive from Greece (Aristotle* and Longinus*), Rome (Horace* and Quintilian), and 17th-C France (Boileau*). This is to say that the critical code which Pope is expounding is that of classical civilizations based on conceptions of just taste, reasoned judgement, shapely execution, and a rational analysis and representation of nature. Pope's art, in practice as well as theory, accords with these standards but, like most English critics sympathetic to classicism, he refuses to regard any set of rules as unquestionable; they may be broken when the artist knows what he is doing, and the right sort of critic is 'Blest with a taste exact, yet unconfin'd'. Pope was only 21 when he wrote the poem, so that it is an early example of his art, but he justifies the use of verse for his prosaic theme by the witty conciseness that his handling of the heroic couplet gives to the expression and by the breadth and suggestiveness which the poetic medium adds to the ideas. However, the theories belong to Pope's youth, and do not necessarily reflect his later practice.

Essay on Dramatic Poesy (1668)

A critical essay in dialogue form by John Dryden*. The four speakers (given classical names) represent Dryden himself ('Neander') and three of his friends. They compare the classical drama with that of England and France; French drama with English, and English drama of the Elizabethan period* with that of Dryden's own day. It is the first systematic discourse on dramatic principles in English to compare with Corneille's* *Examens* and *Discours* (1650–56), and Dryden's criticism, like Corneille's, has the special interest of being the explorations of a prominent working dramatist. The essay is representative of the time in its respect for the classical principles and attention to form, but these rules are treated with breadth of mind, so as to be compatible with enthusiastic eulogy of Shakespeare, who had not acknowledged them. The essay includes the first example in English of close criticism of a single work – *Epicoene** by Ben Jonson, a dramatist who, with Beaumont* and Fletcher*, was esteemed in Dryden's day as highly as Shakespeare, their contemporary, himself. The essay is a fine example of the lucid, supple, graceful Restoration* prose, of which Dryden was outstandingly a master.

* 7.2.

Essay on Man (1733–34)

A philosophical poem in heroic couplets* by Alexander Pope*. It consists of four epistles, or verse letters, addressed to his friend Lord Bolingbroke*, to whose deism*, though Pope himself was a Catholic, the thought of the poem owes much, as it does to the optimism of another contemporary philosopher, Lord Shaftesbury*. But the poem exhibits conviction, not versified second-hand ideas, and it is deeply representative of the thought and feeling of the time. The traditional concept, characteristic of the Middle Ages and the Renaissance*, of a 'chain of being' according to which man is midway between God and inert matter, is combined with Newtonian science of Pope's own day, concentrating on man as he is knowable – in himself and as a social being. Epistle I is concerned with man in the scale of nature; II with man in himself; III with man in society, and IV with man and his aim of happiness. Together they make a central document for understanding the Augustan* age.

Essays, Bacon's

Francis Bacon* published ten essays in 1597, increased them to thirty-eight by 1612, and in his third edition of 1625, to fifty-eight. They contain maxims on men and affairs, on conduct, on pleasures and their uses, and on great themes affecting human destiny such as *Truth* and *Death.* The expression is terse, impersonal, practical, but it is also epigrammatic and vivid with imagery, so that some sentences have almost a proverbial force and familiarity, such as 'Men fear death as children fear to go into the dark.' The quality of poetic force in the imagery is characteristic of a time when prose had much of the imaginative force of poetry; the directness of communication and the practical wisdom of Bacon's counsel is akin to his work as one of the great European initiators of the scientific approach to human affairs.

Essays in Criticism

The two volumes (First Series 1865; Second Series 1888) that contain much of the most important of Matthew Arnold's* literary critical work. The first volume opens with 'The Function of Criticism at the Present Time', a discussion of the relevance of criticism both to creative literature and to society and civilization; it is an example of what T. S. Eliot* was later to call Arnold's 'propaganda for criticism', and it has been influential among 20th-C critics. The second essay, 'The Literary Influence of Academies', makes a case for authoritative standards in culture, and constitutes an implicit criticism of the habits of English culture, again in a way that is still relevant. The remainder of the first volume comprises essays on foreign writers and literature. The Second Series opens with a striking essay on 'The Study of Poetry', in which Arnold puts his view that poetry will supply to the modern world the kind of inspiration that was afforded by great religions in the past – a view which has also been put forward in 20th C, notably by I. A. Richards* in *The Principles of Literary Criticism*, though he expresses the view in other terms. The remainder of the Second Series consists principally of studies of English poets of 18th and 19th C. On the whole, Arnold's fame rests more on the broad themes of the relationships of literature and society than on his particular studies, though some of these, *eg* on the German poet Heine in the First Series, are of great interest.

Essays of Elia (1823; 1833)

A series of essays by Charles Lamb*, published in *The London Magazine** and then in a collected edition. They emulate the essays of Addison* and Steele* in the *Spectator* and *Tatler* of a century before, but depend less on their content than on Lamb's attempt to win the affection and interest of the reader for himself as a person. The style is whimsical and self-conscious, owing something to the musical and humorously eccentric appeal of Burton's *Anatomy of Melancholy** which to some extent it emulates. However, there are passages of witty observation, and acute character sketches.

Establishment

A term which has come into use since World War II to describe the institutions which by long tradition have prestige and authority in England. It probably originates in the official description of the Church of England* as 'the Established Church' – *ie* the official state church, having the Queen at its head. The Monarchy itself, and Parliament, are obviously part of the Establishment, and so is the government bureaucracy loosely known as 'Whitehall'*. Beyond this nucleus, the constituents of the Establishment vary according to the point of view of any particular user of the term, but it nearly always includes the following items: the fashionable men's clubs* in London, especially those with long-established intellectual or political prestige, such as the Athenaeum and the Carlton; the older members and leaders of the older political parties – the Conservatives and Liberals, and sometimes also of the Labour party; the 'ancient Universities' of Oxford and Cambridge, and within them, certain colleges of special prestige, such as All Souls and Christ Church at Oxford and King's and Trinity at Cambridge; the Public Schools*,

Eton College

especially the older and more fashionable ones, such as Winchester, Eton, Harrow, Westminster, and Rugby; *The Times** newspaper, with its special prestige, and the officer corps of the fighting services, especially the Navy. Apart from these, the term may be made to include almost anyone or anything that has prestige from tradition or happens to occupy or constitute a position of authority.

The term 'Establishment' is generally used by those who are at least fairly young, and by such as are opposed to, or at least critical of, the traditions of existing authority. The war left Britain with reduced importance in the world, but without urgent crises to absorb social energies. The result was a feeling of restless discontent among the young, who felt – and to some extent still feel – the nation to have become static and dissatisfying. This mood produced a number of lively, if usually superficial, cults such as 'the Angries' or 'Angry Young Men' of the 1950s who dissented from the traditions of the nation as represented by the 'Establishment'. The names of the playwright John Osborne* and the novelists Kingsley Amis* and John Braine* were prominent among these writers.

Etherege, Sir George (1634?–1691?) /'eθəridʒ/

Dramatist; one of those who set the style of Restoration* Comedy after the return to the throne of Charles II* in 1660. He wrote three plays: *The Comical Revenge, or Love in a Tub* (1664); *She Would If She Could* (1668); *The Man of Mode** (1676). The last of these is best known. The plots are unimportant, the comedy depending on deft handling of witty and often cynical dialogue among characters in smart society. Etherege provided several comic types exploited by other dramatists of the school, such as Wycherley*, Congreve* and Vanbrugh*, and his fluent, easy dialogue set a standard for them in style and quality.

* 5.2.2; *Manners, Comedy of.*

Bib: Dobrée, B., *Essays in Biography; Restoration Comedy*; Palmer, J., *Comedy of Manners*; Underwood, D., *Etherege – A Critical Study.*

Eton College

Probably the best known of the great Public Schools*. It was founded by King Henry VI* in 1440 and was associated with Henry's other foundation of King's College, Cambridge, to which the Eton boys could pass, usually between the ages of 14 and 18. 24 scholarships are still reserved at King's for Eton boys capable of passing the requisite examination, though the earliest age of entry has for some time been 18. Scholarships to Eton are open to all boys who are British subjects and between the ages of 12 and 15. The fall of Henry VI, and the Wars of the Roses* that brought his fall about, caused Eton College to take fee-paying boys to make up for loss of income by royal patronage; hence the majority of Eton boys were soon not the 'poor scholars' for whom it was founded but sons of nobility and other wealthy families. In this way Eton early became associated with the aristocracy, and it retains this reputation to the present day. It also retains, however, a very high academic reputation, as does the sister foundation of King's at Cambridge. The average number of boys exceeds 1,100.

Ettrick Shepherd, The

* *Hogg, James.*

Euclid (Eucleides) (4th C BC) /'ju:klid/

Greek mathematician who lived at Alexandria in Egypt. Elementary geometry based on his work has long been a main study in schools.

Euphemism /'ju:fimizm/

* *Figures of Speech.*

Euphues /ju:fju:i:z/

A prose romance by John Lyly*, in two parts; the first, *Euphues: the Anatomy of Wit* was published in 1578; the second, *Euphues and his England*, in 1580. The tales have very little story; they have been described as 'pattern books' for courtly behaviour, especially in love. Their most striking quality is their elaborate style: long sentences balance clause against clause and image against image, so as to produce an effect of ornament taking priority a long way over sense. Falstaff in *1 Henry IV* II.iv parodies Euphues when he is burlesquing the king, *eg* 'for though the camomile, the more it is trodden on, the faster it grows, yet youth, the more it is wasted, the sooner it wears'. Though often parodied as the language of fops, the style was much imitated especially by Elizabethan romance writers such as Robert Greene* in *Menaphon* (1589), and Thomas Lodge* in *Rosalynde* (1590). The name 'Euphues' is from Greek, and means, generally, 'well-endowed by nature'. Roger Ascham in *The Schoolmaster* had already used it to designate a man well endowed for learning and able to put it to good use. Ascham was an admirer of Castiglione's* *The Courtier*, and Lyly's cult of the courtly virtues is in the same tradition. Basic to it is the conception that nature is not to be imitated but to be improved upon.

Euphuism

* *Figures of Speech.*

Euripides (480–406 BC) /ju'ripidi:z/

The last of the three great Athenian writers of tragedy, the other two being Aeschylus* and Sophocles*. Like them, he had no direct influence upon the great Elizabethan period of English drama, though Gascoigne's* *Jocasta* (1575) is a translation of an Italian adaptation of Euripides' *Phoenissae*. Like Aeschylus and Sophocles, however, Euripides was admired by Milton*, who emulated the Greeks in *Samson Agonistes**. Among Euripides' surviving plays are *Alcestis*, *Medea*, *Hippolytus*, *Andromache*, *Hecuba*, *Bacchae*, *Electra*, *The Trojan Women*, *Orestes*, *Heracles*, *Iphigenia at Aulis*, *Iphigenia among the Tauri*, *Ion*.

Europa /ju'rəupə/

In Greek myth, daughter of Agenor, king of Phoenicia, and bride of Zeus, who disguised himself as a bull and carried her off to the island of Crete. There she became mother to Minos*, Sarpedon, and Rhadamanthus*.

Eurydice

* *Orpheus.*

Euxine /'ju:ksain/

In ancient Greek, the Black Sea. The word means 'hospitable', but this is euphemism, an example of the Greek use of a good name for an evil thing to ward off ill luck.

Evangelical Movement

A movement for Protestant* revival in the Church of England in late 18th and early 19th C. It was stimulated partly by John Wesley's* Methodist revival and the activities of other sects (especially among the lower classes) outside the Church of England; it was also a reaction against the rationalism* and scepticism of 18th-C aristocracy, and against the atheism of the French Revolution*. Politically, the movement tended to be conservative, and was therefore strong among the Tories, whereas the Whigs* (especially their aristocratic leaders such as Charles James Fox*) retained more of the 18th-C worldliness and scepticism. In doctrine the Evangelicals were inclined to be austere, to attach importance to strength of faith and biblical guidance, and to oppose ceremony and ritual. Socially they developed a strong sense of responsibility to their fellow human beings, so that one of their leaders, William Wilberforce*, devoted his life to the cause of abolishing slavery and the slave trade in British dominions, and later Lord Shaftesbury (1801–85) made it his life-work to alleviate the social and working conditions of the working classes. The leaders of the movement were laymen rather than clergy, and upper class rather than lower class, among whom the Nonconformist sects were more actively influential. As the Nonconformists were to contribute to English socialism later in the century a religious rather than a Marxist inspiration, so the Evangelicals led later to generations of highly responsible, independent-minded intellectuals such as the historians Macaulay* and Trevelyan, and the novelist E. M. Forster*.

* 3.4.3.

Eve

In the Bible, the first woman, made by God from a rib of the first man, Adam*, and accorded to him as his wife (*Genesis* 2). Her comparative weakness exposes her to temptation by the Serpent, for which she is punished through her descendants by subjection to the husband and pains of childbirth (*Genesis* 3). After the expulsion of Adam and Eve from the Garden of Eden*, she gives birth to their sons Cain* and Abel* (*Genesis* 4). Cain murdered Abel, and Eve gave birth to a third son, Seth, to replace her dead one.

According to later Jewish tradition, Adam had a wife before Eve: she was Lilith, who flew away from him and became a demon, with evil power over children.

Eve of St Agnes (1819)

A narrative poem by John Keats*, based on the legend that on the night before the day dedicated to this saint, girls may have visions of their lovers. Madeline's lover Porphyro is an enemy to her family; nonetheless he steals into their castle and her chamber so that she wakes to see him as no mere vision but in the flesh. Keats uses the encounter in Madeline's chamber as a pretext for celebrating the life of the senses in their variety by intense verbal luxuriance, while the beginning and end of the poem are equally intense with evocations of cold, age, menace, darkness and death. The poem is one of his best apart from the Odes*, and is characteristic of his confrontation of vivid life with tragic deprivation.

Evelina (1778) /'evi'li:nə/

A novel in letters by Fanny Burney*. Evelina has been abandoned by her aristocratic father, and her socially much humbler mother is dead. She has been brought up by her guardian, a solitary clergyman. As a beautiful, well-bred, and intelligent young girl, she pays a visit to a friend in London, where she falls in love with a handsome aristocrat, Lord Orville, is pursued by an unscrupulous rake, Sir Clement Willoughby, and is much embarrassed by vulgar relatives, especially her grandmother Madame Duval. The convincing and delightful part of the novel consists in its acute and lively social observation, in many ways superior to anything of the sort yet accomplished in the 18th-C novel, and anticipating the maturer art of Jane Austen* in early 19th C.

Evelyn, John (1620–1706) /ˈiːvlin/

Chiefly remembered as a diarist. His diary, published in 1818, covers the years 1641–97, and includes impressions of distinguished contemporaries, customs and manners, and accounts of his travels. He was a man of taste and culture, and published in his lifetime translations from the Greek, Latin, and French, as well as essays on the practical arts (gardening, the cultivation of trees, engraving, architecture). He also wrote an interesting biography of a court lady (*The Life of Mrs Godolphin*, unpublished until 1847).

* *Diaries.*

Bib: *Diary*, ed. E. S. de Beer; Ponsonby, A., *Life*; Hiscock, W. G., *John Evelyn and his Family Circle*; Marburg, C., *Mr Pepys and Mr Evelyn.*

***Every Man in his Humour* (1598)**

The first important play by Ben Jonson*. By 'humour' is to be understood a passion generated by irrational egotism, and amounting sometimes to a mania. The play – which is better known in its revised form with English characters than in the first version of 1598 with Italian characters – is a comedy of misunderstandings bred largely through the deceitfulness of Brainworm, a mischievous servant, acting on the absurd humours of the other characters: the jealousy of the merchant Kitely, the credulity of his young wife, the susceptibility of her sister, the bullying boastfulness of the cowardly soldier Bobadill, etc.

* Humours, Comedy of.

***Every Man out of his Humour* (1599)**

The second of Ben Jonson's* comedies of humours*, with a range of satirical portraits: Fastidious Brisk, the foppish courtier with the sharp tongue; Sordido, the landowner who delights in dearth because it increases the price of his grain; Deliro, the infatuated husband; Puntarvolo, the knight who takes out an insurance on his pets; Fungoso, the would-be courtier who is always behind the fashion, etc. The method of satire is partly through character sketches in the tradition of Theophrastus* and partly through the method which Jonson developed from Marlowe* (in *The Jew of Malta**) of making a character carry his extravagance to the point of self-caricature. This play is, however, too narrow in the range and depth of its satire to rank among Jonson's great ones. The opening scene includes a speech (by Asper, lines 93–120) which contains an explicit account of what Jonson meant by a 'Humour'.

* *Characters, Theophrastian.*

Everyman

A famous morality play*, possibly originating in Holland, where it was published in Dutch in 1495. Whether or not the English version is the original or a translation, it remains one of the major classics of medieval literature. Everyman, prosperous and in the prime of life, is visited by Death who warns him to prepare himself. In great fear he turns to his wordly friends – Fellowship, Kindred, Goods – but all abandon him. He then remembers Good Deeds, who is willing to help him but weak from neglect. Everyman's awareness of his unfitness to meet death is now the cue for his rescue by Knowledge, who comes to him uncalled, since she is, in modern terms, faith accorded by Divine Grace. Everyman repents of his sins, and his life, represented by his faculties reordered by Knowledge, is renewed. The time comes for his entrance to the grave, and his faculties one by one desert him; Knowledge accompanies him to the edge of the grave, but only Good Deeds may enter it with him. The play has moving solemnity and much greater economy of form than is usual with morality plays. Its literary importance is exceeded only by the work of the greater Elizabethans, and it has proved itself in modern theatres.

Evil, The

* *King's Evil, The.*

Examiner, The

A weekly periodical founded by John and Leigh Hunt* in 1808, famous for its radical politics. It had no political allegiance, but criticized public affairs, in the words of Leigh Hunt's friend John Keats*, 'from a principle of taste'. In 1813 the Hunts were sent to prison for two years for exposing the gross flattery in another paper of the Prince

The Great Exhibition

Regent (future George IV). *The Examiner* helped to establish the prestige of weekly political journalism, and had a large circulation. It lasted till 1880.
* *Reviews and Periodicals.*

Excalibur /eks'kalibə/

Originally 'Caliburn'; according to Geoffrey of Monmouth*, the sword of King Arthur*. Malory* and Tennyson* describe, in *Morte d'Arthur* and *The Coming of Arthur* respectively, how Arthur alone was able to draw the sword from a stone where its blade was embedded, thus fulfilling a prophecy about the succession to the British throne. At the end of Malory's *Morte d'Arthur* and in Tennyson's *Passing of Arthur* the legend is told of how, as Arthur lay dying, his sword was thrown out over a lake, where an arm rose above the water, caught it, and withdrew. In the oldest legends, Excalibur is the property of Sir Gawain, Arthur's nephew.

Excursion, The (1814)

A didactic* poem, in blank verse* and in nine books, by William Wordsworth*. It was intended to be the middle part of a three-part philosophical poem, to be called *The Recluse*, but the other two parts were never written. Book I comprises a poem written some years before: 'Margaret, or the Ruined Cottage'; it is often regarded as Wordsworth's masterpiece. This book introduces the Poet and the Wanderer, who tells the story of Margaret. The Wanderer is a philosophical pedlar, and he introduces the poet in Book II to his friend, the Solitary, who lacks faith in man and God. Book III is an account of his despondency; Book IV shows how the Wanderer seeks to correct it; Book V introduces the Pastor, who in Books VI and VII tells stories of some of his former parishioners buried in the churchyard. After Book I, these are perhaps the finest of the books. Books VIII and IX take up problems of rural economy especially under the influence of the new industrial penetration of the countryside, and the advantages to be expected from education under a just government. In spite of the great first book and fine passages elsewhere, the poem is generally considered to betray Wordsworth's decline as a poet; it was a disappointment even to Wordsworth's friend Coleridge*, who had instigated the writing of it. The general grounds of complaint are that Wordsworth lacked capacity as a systematic philosopher, and that large stretches of the poem lack sufficient poetic intensity to compensate for this.
* *Jeffrey, Francis.*

Exhibition, The Great

Held in 1851, in Hyde Park in London, it was the first great international exhibition of the products of industry, and celebrated the peak of the British industrial revolution*. It was regarded as a triumph for British prosperity and enlightenment, though by some critics, *eg* the philanthropist Lord Shaftesbury*, as concealing the scandal of immense urban slums. Its principal building, the Crystal Palace, was a pioneer construction in the materials of glass and cast-iron. The architect was Joseph Paxton.
* *Albert of Saxe-Coburg-Gotha.*

Existentialism /egzis'tenʃəlizm/

A modern school of philosophy which has had great influence on European imaginative literature since the last war. Its basic concern is the freedom of the individual in his dependence on his own choice within a given environmental context. Investigation of this freedom involves investigation of the nature of being, and this has caused Existentialism to form two main streams, the first atheistic, which interprets the free individual existence as self-created, and the second religious, which interprets individual existence as dependent on transcendent Being. The best-known leaders of Existentialism have been Heidegger and Jaspers in Germany and Sartre and Marcel in France. Marcel represents the religious stream whose ultimate progenitor was the 19th-C Danish thinker Kierkegaard. Other progenitors have been Marx, with his emphasis on the industrial environment alienating the individual, and Nietzsche with his doctrine of self-creation. Existentialism has had little influence on British philosophy, although the novelist and philosopher Iris Murdoch* has termed modern British empiricists Existentialist in her essay *The Sovereignty of Good.* Correspondingly, although Existentialism has lent itself to exposition in fiction and drama in France (Sartre and Camus), it is difficult to point to its specific influence on post-war British literature. One explanation may be that in France Existentialism was an imaginative force under the German occupation when individuals were faced with challenges of an Existentialist character. It is also true that literature in Britain has rarely tolerated the pressures of predetermining philosophies, and this second explanation may imply a third: in so far as Existentialism is itself a reaction against still more predetermining philosophies, the British, with what seems to be an inherently empirical cast of mind, have felt less need of its releasing influence.

Extravaganza /ekstravə'ganzə/

Any composition which relies on its fantastic content for its effect. It is usually comic and irregular in its construction. Unlike farce*, however, it is not a defined literary mode; consequently it more often describes a critical reaction to a work than the author's intention in the work. *Pickwick Papers** might be described as an extravaganza, but the word is usually applied to more ephemeral works.

F

Fabian Society /'feibjən/

A large society of socialistic intellectuals, closely bound up with the British Labour Party*. It was founded in 1884, and named after the Roman general Fabius Cunctator – 'Fabius the Delayer' – who in the 3rd C BC saved Rome from the Carthaginian army under Hannibal (*Carthage), by using a policy of attrition instead of open battle, *ie* he destroyed the army by small attacks on isolated sections of it, instead of risking total defeat by confronting Hannibal with the entire Roman army. The Fabian Society similarly advocates socialism by piecemeal action through parliamentary reform instead of risking disaster by total revolution; this policy has been summarized in the phrase 'the inevitability of gradualness'. The Fabians were among the principal influences leading to the foundation of the Labour Party in 1900. The years between 1884 and 1900 were those of its greatest distinction; they were led by Bernard Shaw* and Sidney and Beatrice Webb*, and made their impact through the Fabian Essays on social and economic problems. They always advocated substantial thinking on solid evidence, in contrast to the more idealistic and 'utopian' socialism of such writers as William Morris*.

3.4.5.

Fable

In its narrower, conventional definition, a fable is a short story, often but not necessarily about animals, illustrating a piece of popular wisdom, or explaining unscientifically a fact of nature. Animals are commonly used as characters because they are readily identified with simplified human qualities, as the fox with cunning, the lamb with meekness, the wolf with greed, the ass with stupidity. In primitive folklore, fables are worldwide. The tales in Rudyard Kipling's* *Just So Stories* (1902) for children resemble the kind of primitive fable which seeks to explain facts of nature (such as how the leopard got its spots) without the aid of science. Sophisticated literatures favour the moral fable, the leading European tradition for which was established by the Greek fabulist Aesop*. To this tradition belongs the medieval Latin and German beast satire of Reynard the Fox, from which is derived the best strict fable in English – Chaucer's *Nun's Priest's Tale** of the Cock and the Fox in the *Canterbury Tales*. Almost equally good are Robert Henryson's* *Thirteen Morall Fabillis*. However, though fables are plentiful in English as in every literature, used illustratively and ornamentally amongst other matter, English literature is comparatively poor in strict fabulists. John Gay's* *Fables* are usually regarded as pleasant minor work; Dryden's* *Fables Ancient and Modern* (1699) are mostly not fables. Rudyard Kipling's *Jungle Books* (1894, 5), like his *Just So Stories*, are minor children's classics. T. F. Powys's* *Fables* (1929) are original and beautiful, and George Orwell's* *Animal Farm* (1945) is very well known.

A broader interpretation of the term 'fable' allows a wider range of depiction: a tale which is a comment in metaphor on human nature, less directly figurative than allegory, and less roundabout in reaching its point than parable. In this broader meaning, English literature perhaps produced the greatest of all fables, Swift's *Gulliver's Travels**. But this broader interpretation admits an aspect of fable into almost any serious fiction; thus critics sometimes speak of a novelist's 'fable' in trying to express the underlying intention implicit in a novel. A modern view of this broader interpretation of the Fable is expressed by William Golding* in his essay 'fable' in *The Hot Gates*, and its practice is exemplified in his own novels.

* 4.1.2; *Allegory; Bestiaries; Parable.*

Fabliau

Derived from 'fable', the term applies to a class of humorous tales in medieval French, often coarse and realistically illustrative of low life. The English equivalent is best exemplified by the comic-realist stories in Chaucer's *Canterbury Tales**, notably those told by the Miller*, the Reeve*, the Summoner* and the Friar*.

* 4.1.2.

Factories

In the sense of industrial buildings in which large numbers of men were at work under one roof, as opposed to domestic industry with the workers in their own homes, factories existed to some extent in 16th C. It was in 18th C, however, with the invention of labour-saving machines and then of steam power to drive them, that the factory system became general. Pockets of domestic industry continued well into 19th C, but it became increasingly the exception. Large industrial towns grew up haphazardly to accommodate the new factories; there is a vivid description of an extreme example in Benjamin Disraeli's novel *Sybil**. The employment of masses of labour tended to dehumanize relations between employer and employees, and instigated a new kind of class war; Elizabeth Gaskell's novels *North and South** (1854-5) and *Mary Barton**, and Dickens's *Hard Times** illustrate this. The first Factory Act to have an important effect in the improving of conditions was that of 1833; by then the public conscience was truly aroused, and the Ten Hours Act of 1847 restricted hours of labour. The main intention of the early Factory Acts was to prevent the employment of young children and to limit the hours of employment of women; they were made effective by the use of Factory Inspectors. Later Factory Acts have sought to prevent the use of dangerous machinery, and to ensure that factories were healthy places to work in. Employers came to see that it was in their own interests to make factory conditions as healthy and pleasant as possible; Andrew Undershaft in Shaw's* play *Major Barbara* is an example of an enlightened factory owner of the 20th-C sort.

Another use of the word 'factory' is to denote a centre for 'factors', *ie* men of commerce who transact trade on behalf of their employers. In the 18th C the East India Company established such factories in India, *eg* at Madras.

* *Industrial Revolution.*

Faerie Queene, The (Books I-III 1589; IV-VI 1596)

An unfinished allegorical romance by Edmund Spenser*, originally designed in twelve books. The Faerie Queene, Gloriana (representing Glory in general and Queen Elizabeth I* in particular), has despatched twelve of her knights, one on each of her twelve days of festival, on separate adventures. So much is explained in the introductory letter addressed to Sir Walter Raleigh*; the poem itself begins with the Red Cross Knight*, who stands for true religion and the Anglican* Church. The five remaining completed Books have themes as follows: II Guyon (Temperance); III the maiden-knight Britomart (Chastity); IV Friendship, with the four characters of Cambel, Triamond, Scudamour and Amoret; V Artegall (Justice); VI Calidore (Courtesy). The basis of Spenser's choice of virtues is Aristotle's* philosophy adapted to Renaissance* and Protestant* requirements; and just as Aristotle subsumed all the virtues under the comprehensive one of 'magnanimity' so Spenser introduced Prince Arthur (of the medieval Arthurian legend) as 'magnificence', himself in quest of the Faerie Queene, to help out the various knights when their particular virtues were unequal to the ordeals they had to face. Though the framework owes so much

to Aristotle, the idealizing spirit of the poem owes much more to the idealism of Plato*. Spenser's aim was explicitly to excel the Italian Ariosto's romantic epic *Orlando Furioso** although, again, he is closer in spirit to Tasso's* more recent *Jerusalem Delivered* – like Spenser's, a far more solemn work than Ariosto's poem. The allegory* of *The Faerie Queene* is much more complicated than typical medieval allegory had been, taking sometimes political and sometimes religious forms, as well as a prevailing Platonic one. For purposes of the poem, Spenser invented the Spenserian stanza*, later adopted by other poets.

The Faerie Queene was Spenser's masterpiece; both its rhythmical music and its selective diction haunted the imagination of English poets through the next three centuries, merging with the style of Milton* (whom Spenser influenced) to create assumptions about poetic style in general which prevailed widely though not universally until this century. 20th C, however, has seen a reaction against *The Faerie Queene*, the influence of which is now felt to have been a narrowing one, causing poets to limit their subject matter and their treatment of it to what was thought to be 'poetic', *ie* idealized and removed from the immediacy and variety of habitual human experience. Consequently, though few deny that the poem is a major achievement, it is now chiefly read and admired for its finest episodes, such as the Seven Deadly Sins (I.iv); the Cave of Mammon (II.vii); the House of Busirane (III.xi,xii); the Gardens of Adonis (III.vi); the dance of the Graces (VI.x).

The poem ends with the so-called Mutability Cantos, no doubt a fragment of the projected Book VII, considered by some critics to be the allegorical centre of the entire projected work. They are undoubtedly one of the finest parts of the extant poem. Their quality, like that of the other passages mentioned, is of noble symbolism conveyed musically and intensely, in the manner of highly imaginative pageants*. In this kind of writing, Spenser is unexcelled; he is much weaker in straight narrative, which is one of the strongest features of Ariosto.

* **6.2.1**; *Arthur, King.*

Fagging

A system in English Public Schools*, especially the older ones, by which junior boys work as part-time servants for senior boys. The system existed at Eton at least as early as 16th C, and the great 19th-C reformer of the public school system, Arnold* of Rugby, regarded it as being educationally valuable. It was supposed to teach humility to the 'fag' and a sense of responsibility to the 'fagmaster' who was answerable for his fag's well-being. The system continues in some public schools, but it has never been universal among them, and is not used in state schools.

Fairs

The early fairs were large markets held at particular times of the year in or near country towns; they attracted buyers and sellers from a distance. Until this century, every country town held its weekly market day on which the farmers of the district brought their cattle and vegetable produce for sale; a fair was a grand market, attracting trade from a wider region, and lasting for a week or more. They became established institutions after the Norman* Conquest, and the largest, such as the Stourbridge Fair at Cambridge, were of national and even international importance. Towns found them profitable, not merely because they profited local craftsmen, but because the town corporations were able to collect special payments or 'dues' from the visiting merchants. Apart from commerce, fairs afforded entertainment of many sorts; today their commercial importance is slight, and a fair is thought of as merely a travelling collection of roundabouts, swings, peepshows etc. attractive mainly to children. These would formerly have been regarded as mere 'sideshows'; however they always had prominence, and particularly popular were the exhibitions of 'monsters' such as 'the fattest woman in the world', animals with two heads, and other abnormalities.

Fairies

Supernatural beings such as provide material for folk-tales all over the world. In Britain, as in many other countries, fairies have been regarded as neither good nor evil, but sometimes mischievous and sometimes beneficent, as human behaviour has given opportunity and invitation (see for instance Mercutio's speech on Queen Mab in Shakespeare's *Romeo and Juliet*, I.iv). Belief in them has been thought to be a vestige of pre-Christian beliefs in nature-spirits. Stories about them sometimes include elements of medieval romance and classical myth; thus in Shakespeare's *Midsummer Night's Dream**, Oberon* derives from a 13th-C French romance, *Huon de Bordeaux*, Titania* is used as a version of Diana the huntress in Ovid's *Metamorphoses**, and Puck*, also called Robin Goodfellow, is from English folklore. Spenser's Faerie Queen Gloriana gives Queen Elizabeth I the allure of romance at the same time as identifying her with the Platonic ideal of Glory. Although witches* play a part in fairy stories, witchcraft, as exemplified by 16th and 17th C belief and manifested in Shakespeare's *Macbeth** is altogether more serious and sinister, and requires separate treatment.

Belief in fairies – or half-belief – may have been widespread among all classes in England until 17th C, but since then it has steadily shrunk even among country folk. It has persisted longest in Wales, north-west Scotland, south-west England, and especially in Ireland; hence the comparatively serious use to which fairies are put in the verse of the Irish poet W. B. Yeats*, *eg The Man Who Saw the Fairies.*

Among popular beliefs about fairies have been these: that they are small, hence sometimes called 'the little people'; they are used to explain natural phenomena such as 'fairy rings' on grass, said to be the traces of their midnight dances; they foretell the fortunes of children (fairy godmothers); they are supposed to steal human babies and leave fairy children ('changelings') in their stead. Many subdivisions of fairy exist, such as elves (*Elf), pixies, gnomes*, brownies, goblins.

Falstaff, Sir John /ˈfɔ:lsta:f/

A character in Shakespeare's history plays, *1 & 2 Henry IV**, and in the comedy *Merry Wives of Windsor**. His death is described in *Henry V** II.ii. In the history plays he is a very active comic character, embodying fleshly indulgence, and considered to be the chief injurious influence on Prince Hal (Henry), the heir to the throne. Though a fully realized character in his own right, he clearly carries also some force from medieval allegory*, representing the temptations of physical indulgence or 'riot'. Accordingly Hal, once anointed as King Henry V, casts him off at the end of *2 Henry IV*. In *The Merry Wives* he is much less substantial, and plays the role of a comparatively commonplace buffoon.

Far from the Madding Crowd (1874)

A novel by Thomas Hardy*. The title is a quotation from *Elegy in a Country Churchyard** by Thomas Gray. It is one of Hardy's Wessex* novels, and the first of real substance, following the comparatively slight *Under the Greenwood Tree**. The central character is Bathsheba Everdene, who is loved by three men: Farmer Boldwood, a solid but passionate squire*; Gabriel Oak, a shepherd, who loves her with quiet constancy and wins her in the end, and the glamorous soldier, Sergeant Troy, whom she marries first. Troy combines fascinating gallantry with ruthless egoism; he allows his wife-to-be, Fanny Robin, to die in a workhouse, and is capricious and cruel to Bathsheba; he is eventually murdered by Boldwood. A crude outline such as this brings out the ballad-like quality of the story, characteristic of all Hardy's novels but more subtly rendered in later ones. Its distinction of substance is in Hardy's intimate understanding and presentation of the rural surroundings of the characters, and in the contrast between the urbane attractions of Troy and the rough but environmentally vigorous qualities of Boldwood and Oak. Bathsheba herself is a capricious and colourful heroine, not presented with psychological depth but with confident assertiveness which makes her convincing.

Farce

A term used for comedy in which realism is sacrificed for the sake of extravagant humour. Its derivation is from stuffing used in cookery, and as a literary term it was applied to light and frivolous material introduced by actors into the medieval mystery plays*. Normally it is now applied to lightweight comedies only, but T. S. Eliot* gave the term special critical force by applying it to Marlowe's *Jew of Malta** – 'the farce of the old English humour, the terribly serious, even savage, comic humour . . . which spent its last breath in the decadent genius of Dickens' ('Christopher Marlowe' in *Selected Essays*, 1932). Eliot's view of Dickens as 'decadent' is typical of his disdain for popular culture in modern times; Dickensian farce has much in common, not only with a high tradition of comedy in English literature, but with the humour of 19th-C music-halls.

Farquhar, George (1678–1707) /'fa:kwə/

One of the last Restoration* dramatists to write a comedy of manners* of distinction. His plays were: *Love and a Bottle* (1699); *The Constant Couple* (1700); *Sir Harry Wildair* (1701); *The Inconstant* and *The Twin Rivals* (1702); *The Stage Coach* (1704) in collaboration with Motteux; *The Recruiting Officer* (1706); *The Beaux' Stratagem* (1707). The last two are his best; they are more spontaneous, less artificial and sophisticated, and more substantial than the characteristic plays of the school, though also less refined and subtle in their wit than the best of Congreve*. His plays show a transitional tendency to a more moralistic and sentimental mode of drama. Like most of the good dramatists of 18th and 19th C, Farquhar was Irish.

* 5.2.2.

Bib: Connely, W. C., *Life*; Boas, F. S., *An Introduction to Eighteenth-century Drama*; Dobree, B., *Restoration Comedy*; Palmer, J., *The Comedy of Manners*; Perry, H. T. E., *The Comic Spirit in Restoration Drama*; Hazlitt, W., *The English Comic Writers*.

Fascist

The fasces, a bundle of rods bound round an axe, were the symbol of the civil power of ancient Rome. The symbol was adopted by Mussolini's Fascist party which ruled Italy from 1922 to 1945. It was right-wing and anti-communist. The National Socialist Party in Germany (1933–45) and the Falangist Party that helped to bring Franco to power in Spain in 1938 were akin to the Italian Fascist party, and to some extent modelled on it. This is also true of the smaller Fascist parties in other countries, though Oswald Mosley's British Union of Fascists was never politically significant. All such parties favoured strong nationalism, political dictatorship, the suppression of communism and socialism; under German influence, they were usually marked by racialist prejudice.

English writers, especially between 1930 and 1945, were preponderantly left-wing in sympathy, and used the term 'Fascist' in the sense of right-wing, despotic, reactionary, brutal, etc. and applied it to any person or body of people whose politics they disliked. This abusive use of 'Fascist', though tiresome and misleading, is not due merely to political prejudice: few political ideas of historical importance have been so closely associated with brutality as Fascism, and few have contributed so little of significance to political thinking. Nonetheless, Fascists emphasis on leadership and (implicitly) on aristocracy of the sort that requires a trained élite and not hereditary privilege, appealed in varying degree to some leading British and American writers of the period 1920–40, such as W. B. Yeats* and Ezra Pound*. T. S. Eliot*, Wyndham Lewis*, and D. H. Lawrence* have also been accused of Fascist leanings. All these writers had right-wing tendencies because they reacted strongly against the simplifications of social theory resulting from the traditions of 19th C liberalism and from Marxist Socialism; only Pound became deeply identified with Fascism.

Fathers of the Church

Early Christian writers, important in the formation of Christian doctrine. They included Cyprian (3rd C), Athanasius (4th C), Gregory of Nazianzus (4th C), Augustine of Hippo (4th–5th C), Pope Gregory I, the Great (end of 6th C). Those Fathers who were nearly contemporary with the original Apostles of Christ are often called the Apostolic Fathers; they include Clement of Rome, Polycarp of Smyrna, Ignatius of Antioch – all of 1st C or 1st and early 2nd C.

Fauns

In ancient Roman myth, Faunus was a nature-god. Under Greek influence, he became identified with the Greek nature god Pan*, and is depicted with horns and goat legs. Like Pan, he was credited with a following of merry and mischievous little fauns.

Faust /faust/

The Faust myth is much older than those legends which crystallize round the historical figure of Faust and form a part of it. The myth of men seeking great earthly power from demons at the cost of their immortal souls goes back to the ancient Jews at about the time of Christ, and centres round several figures of medieval European Christendom. In 16th C the myth received new vitality through the influence upon it of various bodies of ideas: Renaissance* humanism, in its sceptical and critical spirit; neo-Platonic mysticism, in its conception of the potentially immense reach of the human mind; and the Protestant Reformation*, in its adherence to the pure Word of God as opposed to humanist* claims for reason and Catholic claims for authority alike. The real Faust was an early-16th-C German philosopher who was ridiculed by other intellectuals for his extravagant pretensions to magical powers. Nonetheless, pamphlets and plays built up a widespread, partly comic and partly serious image of him as the pattern of human arrogance eternally damned for his preference of human learning over the Holy Word. Mephistopheles*, the devil with whom Faust made his bargain, was himself condemned to eternal suffering and regarded himself in this light. Christopher Marlowe's *Doctor Faustus** is much the most interesting product of the tradition. Marlowe's poetry creates a genuine drama out of Faustus's predicament by making his dilemma real: the earthly ecstasies which are his temptation are made concrete (embodied notably in the vision of Helen of Troy) while his prospective heavenly ones are hypothetical, and his damnation has tragic force through being shown to be the consequence of his despair.

Wolfgang Goethe's* masterpiece *Faust* (Pt. I 1808; II 1832) gives an entirely new turn to the myth. Mephistopheles is no longer the evil spirit in eternal torment, but 'the spirit that denies', *ie* that refuses to acknowledge the intrinsic reality of any human or spiritual value. Goethe's Faust does not believe (as Marlowe's does) that the compact is binding upon him, though he goes through the formality of signing it. He will be damned, he says, only when one of the devil's temptations satisfies him, when he calls on the passing moment to remain. When he does in fact do this, it is because he is rejoicing at the engagement of his powers in the service of man, *ie* virtuous activity. Consequently the powers of Hell fail to capture him. Thus Goethe's version of the myth became itself one of the great myths of modern man. The struggle is no longer between earthly power and spiritual holiness; it is between the cynicism of those who deny that there is goodness in the search for goodness, and the dedication of those who make the search.

Felix Holt the Radical (1866)

A novel by George Eliot*. The hero is a talented young working man who makes it his vocation to educate the political intelligence of his fellow-workers. His rival for the love of Esther Lyon, the daughter of a nonconformist minister, is the local landowner, Harold Transome, also a radical politician though pursuing a more conventional political career. George Eliot makes Holt utter high-minded speeches which weaken the reality he is supposed to possess. On the other hand, a subsidiary theme which concerns Harold Transome's mother, the secret of Harold's illegitimacy, and his hostility to the lawyer, Jermyn, who is really his father, is treated so well that it is among the best examples of George Eliot's art.

Fen

* *Fenland.*

Fencibles, The

The part-time soldiers or 'militia' raised for the defence of the country against the French in the wars at the end of 18th C. The word means 'capable of making defence', *ie* fit for military service.

Fenians /ˈfiːnjənz/

An Irish patriotic and revolutionary society founded by Irish immigrants to the United States in 1858; its aim was to unite Irishmen all over the world to secure the independence of Ireland from British rule. The original Fenians were a semi-legendary band of warriors under the leadership of Finn Mac Coul, said to have lived in 3rd C AD.

* *Finn.*

Fenland

A stretch of country in eastern England, extending from Lincoln south to Cambridge. It is below sea-level, and until 18th C large parts of it were under water for much of the year. The reclamation of the fens in 17th and 18th C, carried out with the assistance of Dutch engineers, was one of the earliest examples in England of large-scale capitalist enterprise. It is now one of the richest regions for arable farming in Britain.

Ferdinand

The most conspicuous characters bearing this name in English literature are

[1] the King of Navarre in Shakespeare's *Love's Labour's Lost**

[2] the son of King Alonso of Naples and lover of Prospero's daughter Miranda in Shakespeare's *The Tempest**

[3] the Duke of Calabria, villain of John Webster's play *The Duchess of Malfi**.

Ferrar, Nicholas

* *Little Gidding.*

Ferrier, Susan (1782–1854)

Novelist. She was born in Edinburgh, and was a friend of Sir Walter Scott*. Her novels (*Marriage*, 1818; *The Inheritance*, 1824, *Destiny*, 1831) were considered at the time to be a kind of Scottish equivalent to those of Jane Austen, but she lacks the latter's subtle irony and represents a distinctively Scottish tradition in the robust humour of her social observation.

Bib: Grant, A., *Life*; Parker, W. M., *Susan Ferrier and John Galt* (British Council).

Festivals

Festival days are those regularly set apart every year, either by religious authority for sacred observance, or for the celebration of a change of season by popular tradition. Thus the commonest festival is the weekly Sunday, consecrated by the

Church to religious worship, and prescribed as a day of rest for all.

The medieval year contained numerous festivals (feast-days) commemorating the saints, but these were abolished at the Reformation*, and only the main Christian festivals were retained. Side by side with the Christian festivals were folk festivals, which often showed signs of pagan antecedents. These too have passed away in the last two centuries, as Britain has changed from a largely agricultural country into a largely industrial one. The efforts of the Church to assimilate the pagan instincts of the common people have much to do with the fact that the two kinds of festival often come near to each other in date, so that the celebrations of the folk could be given a Christian direction. The two kinds, however, never became fully identified.

The main Christian feasts of importance in the past have been the following:

*Epiphany** (Twelfth Night). 6 January. Celebrating the visit of the Magi* to the Child Jesus.

Candlemas. 2 February. Celebrating the presentation of Jesus at the Temple.

Lady Day. 25 March. Celebrating Our Lady, the Virgin Mary.

*Easter**. A movable feast, occurring late in March or April. Celebrating the Resurrection of Jesus Christ.

Ascension Day. 40 days after Easter. Celebrating the ascension of Christ into Heaven.

Whitsun. 50 days after Easter. Also called Pentecost. Celebrating the descent of the Holy Spirit to the disciples of Christ.

*Corpus Christi**. Celebrating the Holy Sacrament.

Lammas (Loaf-Mass). 1 August. Celebrating the Harvest.

Michaelmas. 29 September. The feast of St Michael and all Angels.

All Saints' Day. 1 November. (All Hallows Eve; Hallow E'en 31 October.) Celebrating particularly those Saints otherwise omitted from the Church Calendar.

Martinmas. 11 November. The feast of St Martin.

*Christmas**. 25 December. Celebrating the birth of Jesus Christ. It corresponded to the pre-Christian feast of Yule*.

Of these, only Christmas and Easter are universally remembered, especially because they coincide with public holidays. Christmas, Easter, and All Saints' Day coincide with pre-Christian pagan festivals of the seasons, corresponding to the Winter, Spring and Autumn seasons respectively. All Hallows, in particular, is associated with the belief that the night before it is one on which ghosts and witches walk abroad.

The main non-religious festivals were as follows:

New Year's Day. 1 January.

Plough Monday. The first Monday after Epiphany. Celebrating the start of ploughing. Folk plays similar to the Mummers'* play performed at Christmas and the New Year were performed on it.

*May Day**. 1 May. A Spring festival, on which Morris Dances* and other revels were performed.

Midsummer. 24 June.

Harvest Home. Coinciding with Lammas (1 August).

Of these, New Year's Day and May Day still have a general importance, the latter chiefly for left-wing political parties. New Year's Day is a public holiday in Scotland.

* *Quarter days*

Feuilleton

In French, a leaflet. Also used in French for that part of a newspaper devoted to literature, non-political news, and gossip. In English the term was once used for the instalment of a serial story.

Fidessa

A character in Spenser's *Faerie Queene** I.ii. The name implies 'faithful', and as such she is taken under the protection of the Red Cross Knight*. She is really the treacherous Duessa* in disguise, however, and her intention is to lead the knight (standing for the true faith of the Church of England*) into captivity.

Field, Nathaniel (1587–1633)

Actor; he was one of the most famous in the lifetime of Shakespeare. He is mentioned in the first folio* edition of Shakespeare's works as having played parts in them, and he also took leading roles in plays by Ben Jonson*, and the chief one in Chapman's* most famous play *Bussy d'Ambois*. He wrote two 'citizen comedies' in the style of Jonson: *A Woman is a Weathercock* and *Amends for Ladies*.

Field of Cloth of Gold

The name given to the meeting-place of the English Henry VIII* and the French Francis I, in France. The object of the meeting near Guisnes in 1520 was to arrange an alliance, but the encounter is less memorable politically than it is for characteristically Renaissance* splendour.

Field sports

Sport taking place in the open countryside, consisting of some sort of hunting or racing. The main kinds have been:

*Coursing**. The pursuit of animals (usually hares) with hounds using sight and not scent; a combination of hunting and racing.

Falconry. *See* Hawking.

*Fowling**. The hunting of birds, by hawking, trapping, shooting.

*Hawking**. The hunting of birds with hawks specially trained for the purpose. Shooting drove this sport out of fashion in the later 17th C.

Horse-racing. This originally took place across country. It became extremely fashionable in the reign of Charles II* and has remained so ever since.

*Hunting**. Usually implies hunting on horseback with hounds.

Shooting. Usually at birds. Until 17th C the usual weapon was the long bow or the crossbow, but guns called fowling-pieces or bird-pieces came in during 16th C and in the second half of 17th C became general.

Fielding, Henry (1707–54)

Playwright, novelist, magistrate. He was of aristocratic birth; his family was supposed to be related to the Austrian House of Habsburg, whose greatness, said the contemporary historian Gibbon*, would be long outlasted by that of Fielding's masterpiece, *Tom Jones**.

He began his career as a playwright, theatre manager and producer, but his comedies are not among his great work. One of them, however, the *Historical Register for the Year 1736*, was a satire on the government sharp enough to provoke the Licensing Act of 1737, restricting the liberty of the theatre (**Theatres*). Fielding soon after gave up drama.

In 1740 Samuel Richardson published his extremely successful novel *Pamela, or Virtue Rewarded**. Fielding, who thought that the reward in Richardson's book was really to smugness and hypocrisy, was probably the author of the parody *Shamela*, and in any case produced another parody – his first major work – *Joseph Andrews** (1742) in which the hero was supposed to be Pamela's brother and counterpart in 'virtue'. The book contains excellent satire directed much more widely than merely against the theme of *Pamela*, and the main character becomes not Joseph, but his friend Parson Adams, an English Don Quixote*. In 1743 he published his satire on criminal life, *Jonathan Wild the Great**, and a less well-known satire, *A Journey from this World to the Next*. In 1749 his finest novel, *Tom Jones*, showed his genius at its most expanded and vigorous; *Amelia* (1751) is low-spirited by comparison and much concerned with social abuses and the misery of poverty.

He edited four periodicals: *The Champion* (1739–41) and (using the pen-name Sir Alexander Drawcansir) *The Covent Garden Journal* (1752); *True Patriot* (1745–46) and *Jacobite's Journal* (1747–48).

In 1748 Fielding was made Justice of the Peace (magistrate*) for Westminster; his record is distinguished in the suppression of London crime, and he was the author of a number of pamphlets on the subject, notably *Enquiry into the Causes of the late Increase of Robbers* (1752). It is this kind of preoccupation which dominates his novel *Amelia*.

In 1754, his health in serious decline, Fielding went to Portugal and died there in the same year, but left his *Journal of a Voyage to Lisbon*, published 1755, to show that his qualities of animation and humane feeling lasted to the end.

Fielding is above all important for his contribution to the development of the novel; his outstanding works are *Joseph Andrews* and *Tom Jones*. He saw these novels as 'comic epics', and his method is a panoramic narrative of manners and behaviour seen externally, rather than that of the inward psychological exploration of his rival Richardson. The two novelists represent complementary aspects of the art: as *Joseph Andrews* challenges *Pamela*, so, though less directly, *Tom Jones* counterbalances Richardson's masterpiece *Clarissa**.

* 4.3.2; * *Bow Street*.

Bib: Cross, W. L., *Life*; Butt, J., *Fielding*; Wright, A., *Fielding*; Sacks, S., *Fiction and the Shape of Belief*; Paulson, R., (ed.) *Fielding: A Collection of Critical Essays*; Digeon, A., *Les Romans de Fielding*; Murry, J. M., in *Unprofessional Essays*; Paulson, R., Lockwood, T., (eds) *Fielding: The Critical Heritage*.

Fifteen, The

The rebellion or rising of 1715, *ie* the first of the two main Jacobite* attempts in 18th C to regain the throne of Great Britain for the Catholic son of James II, James 'the Old Pretender'.

Fifteenth-century Literature

The 15th C in English literature, by comparison with Scottish writing in the same period, and with 14th C, is, or at least seems at first sight, comparatively barren. The writers of contemporary fame, such as John Lydgate* and Thomas Hoccleve (1370?–1426?) are as prolix as Gower*, Chaucer's contemporary, but without his accomplishment and without the force of Chaucer or the 14th-C alliterative* poets. One possible explanation is that sophisticated literature had lost touch with popular idiom without having had time to gain confidence on its own level; another, commonly given, is that the language was changing in such a way that poets could not use Chaucer's verse technique effectively, nor could they ignore it.

On the other hand, 15th C, and the beginning of 16th, was the finest age of Scottish poetry. Since the Scottish War of Independence (1296–1328), Scotland had gained confidence as a nation without yet being overshadowed by the greatly superior wealth and size of England. The northern English dialect had flowered into an independent though closely related language (Lowland Scots or Lallans*) capable of its own kind of imaginative expression. In 14th C, John Barbour* was a pioneer with his epic about the war against England, *The Bruce*. The first notable work was *The King's Quair**, probably by King James I of Scotland*, a love poem. After James came three outstanding poets: Robert Henryson*, William Dunbar*, and Gavin Douglas*. They are often called 'the Scottish Chaucerians', but although it is true that they learnt much from Chaucer, they were so far from being mere imitators as to have a strong national character of their own, apart from the force of their individual personalities.

When we consider anonymous writing, 15th C in England begins to seem less empty. It is from this period that the oldest surviving ballads can be dated, Scots as well as English, such as *Chevy Chase**, *Sir Patrick Spens**, and *The Nut-Brown Maid**. Fine anonymous lyric poems have survived (*eg* *Quia Amore Langueo*) sometimes in more sophisticated forms than those of 14th C. Above all, in the drama, it was the century in which the Mystery (Miracle) Play* reached its culmination; the finest collections are the York and the Towneley (Wakefield) cycles, though there are moving individual plays from other cycles as well. The earliest texts of the Morality Plays* also date from 15th C, and this mode of drama continued into 16th C; few of them have enduring interest as works of art, but one of them, *Everyman**, which is possibly of Dutch origin, is one of the noblest fruits of the medieval imagination.

In prose, as in poetry, there were few notable writers whose names are still known. By far the most famous is Sir Thomas Malory*, whose *Morte d'Arthur** is an episodic work of uneven merit, but at its best it is written in prose which has unprecedented fluency and poignant music. It was printed by William Caxton*, whose introduction of printing into England in 1477 opened a new era for literature.

Fifth Monarchy Men

A sect of Puritans* who believed, on the basis of a prophecy in the Bible (*Daniel* 2), that Oliver Cromwell's* rise to power was a preparation for the Second Coming of Christ, and the establishment of the great fifth and last monarchy; the previous four had been the Assyrian, the Persian, the Greek and the Roman. In disillusionment, they began to turn against Cromwell, and after the Restoration* of the monarchy in 1660 they tried to raise a rebellion in London. It was easily suppressed and the leaders were executed.

Figures of Speech

Alliteration The beginning of accented syllables near to each other with the same consonantal sound, as in many idiomatic phrases: 'safe and sound'; 'thick and thin'; 'right as rain'. Alliteration is thus the opposite of rhyme, by which the similar sounds occur at the ends of the syllables: 'near and dear', 'health and wealth'. Alliteration dominated the pattern of Anglo-Saxon poetry; after the Conquest, French influence caused rhyme to predominate. However, in the 14th C there seems to have been an 'alliterative revival', producing such important poems as *Piers Plowman** and *Gawayne and the Green Knight**. Alliterative verse was accentual, *ie* did not depend on the regular distribution of accented syllables in a line, but on the number of accented syllables in the line:

In a sómer séson　　whan sóft was the sónne
I shópe me in shróudes　　as I a shépe wére
In hábite as as héremite　　unhóly óf wérkes
Went wýde in this wórlde　　wóndres to hére.

(Langland: *Piers Plowman*)

This can be contrasted with the following rhymed lines by Chaucer, in which the accents are regularly distributed:

Whan thát Aprílle wíth his shóures sóte
The dróghte of Márche hath pérced tó the róte,
And báthed évery véyne in swích licóur
Of whích vertú engéndred ís the flóur;

(Prologue to *The Canterbury Tales*)

The example from Langland shows the usual pattern for alliterative verse: each line contains a strong pause (caesura) and four accented syllables; the first three accented syllables are alliterated, while the fourth is free; the pause comes after the first two.

After the 14th C, rhyme and the regular count of syllables became the normal pattern for English verse. Alliteration, however, continued to be used unsystematically by every poet. Sometimes it is a means of causing the sound to echo the sense, as in these lines from Tennyson's *The Princess*:

The moan *of doves in imm*emorial *elms,*
And murmuring *of innumerable bees.*

Often it is used for emphasis, as in the following opening line of a sonnet by G. M. Hopkins:

I wake and feel *the* fell *of* dark, *not* day.

Anacoluthon From the Greek: 'not following on'. Strictly speaking, this is not a figure of speech, but a grammatical term for a sentence which does not continue the syntactical pattern with which it starts. However, it may be used deliberately with the virtue of intensifying the force of a sentence *eg* by the sudden change from indirect to direct speech:

And he charged him to tell no man: but go, and shew thyself to the priest, and offer for thy cleansing . . .

(Luke 5:14 Authorized Version)

Anti-climax
* *See Bathos below.*

Antithesis A method of emphasis by the placing of opposed ideas or characteristics in direct contrast with each other:

To err is human, to forgive, divine.

(Pope: *Essay on Criticism*)

Apostrophe A form of direct address often used by a narrator in the middle of his narrative as a means of emphasizing a moral lesson.

The peple out-sterte, and caste the cart to-grounde
And in the middel of the dong they founde
The dede man, that mordred was al newe.
O blisful god, that art so just and trewe!
Lo, how that thou biwreyest mordre alway!
Mordre wol out, that see we day by day.

(Chaucer: *The Nun's Priest's Tale*)

Assonance The rhyming of vowel sounds without the rhyming of consonants.

Nothing is so beautiful as spring –
When weeds, in wheels, shoot long and lovely and lush

(G. M. Hopkins: *Spring*)

Bathos From the Greek: 'death'. The descent from the sublime to the ridiculous. This may be the result of incompetence in the writer, but Alexander Pope used it skilfully as a method of ridicule:

Here thou, great ANNA! whom three realms obey
Dost sometimes counsel take – and sometimes tea.

(*The Rape of the Lock*)

Pope wrote an essay *Bathos, the Art of Sinking in Poetry*, as a travesty of the essay by Longinus, *On the Sublime* (1st C AD). Longinus had great prestige as a critic in Pope's time.

Climax From the Greek: 'a ladder'. The climb from lower matters to higher, with the consequent satisfying of raised expectations, as in these lines from Part 2 of Marlowe's *Tamburlaine the Great*:

What is beauty, saith my sufferings, then?
If all the pens that ever poet held
Had fed the feeling of their masters' thoughts,
And every sweetness that inspir'd their hearts,
Their minds, and muses on admired themes;
If all the heavenly quintessence they still
From their immortal flowers of poesy,
Wherein, as in a mirror, we perceive
The highest reaches of a human wit;
If these had made one poem's period,
And all combin'd in beauty's worthiness,
Yet should there hover in their restless heads
One thought, one grace, one wonder, at the least,
Which into words no virtue can digest.

Euphemism A mild or vague expression used to conceal a painful or disagreeable truth, *eg* 'he passed on' for 'he died'. It is sometimes used ironically, *eg* 'Mr Wopsle's great-aunt conquered a confirmed habit of living into which she had fallen . . .'

(Dickens: *Great Expectations*, Ch. 16)

Euphuism A highly artificial quality of style resembling that of John Lyly's *Euphues**.

Hyperbole Expression in extreme language so as to achieve intensity. It is a conspicuous figure in the poetry of Christopher Marlowe*, *eg* Tamburlaine's speech of grief for his dying wife, Zenocrate:

Black is the beauty of the brightest day;
The golden ball of heaven's eternal fire,
That danc'd with glory on the silver waves,
Now wants the fuel that inflam'd his beams;
And all for faintness, and for foul disgrace,
He binds his temples with a frowning cloud,
Ready to darken earth with endless night.

Innuendo A way of expressing dislike or criticism indirectly, or by a hint; an insinuation:

A petty sneaking knave I knew –
O! Mr Cromek, how do ye do?

(William Blake)

Irony From the Greek: 'dissimulation'. A form of expression by which the writer intends his meaning to be understood differently and less favourably, in contrast to his overt statement:

It is a truth universally acknowledged, that a single man in possession of a good fortune must be in want of a wife.

This opening sentence of Jane Austen's *Pride and Prejudice* is to be understood as meaning that the appearance of such a young man in a neighbourhood inspires very strong wishes in the hearts of mothers of unmarried daughters, and that these wishes cause the mothers to behave as though the statement were indeed a fact.

Dramatic Irony occurs when a character in a play makes a statement in innocent assurance of its truth, while the audience is well aware that he is deceived. A well-known instance occurs in Shakespeare's *Macbeth*. King Duncan has just been informed of the execution of the traitorous Thane of Cawdor, when Macbeth enters:

Duncan: *There's no art*
To find the mind's construction in the face:
He was a gentleman on whom I built
An absolute trust.

(Enter Macbeth)

Macbeth: *O worthiest cousin!*

The audience is aware that Macbeth has been meditating the murder of Duncan, and the irony is the stronger for the fact that Macbeth has just inherited Cawdor's title.

Litotes Emphatic expression through an ironical negative, *eg* 'She's no beauty', meaning that the woman is ugly.

Malapropism A comic misuse of language, usually by a person who is both pretentious and ignorant. The term derives from the character Mrs Malaprop in Sheridan's play *The Rivals** (1775):

Sir Anthony: *Why, Mrs Malaprop, in moderation now, what would you have a woman know?*

Mrs Malaprop: *Observe me, Sir Anthony. I would by no means wish a daughter of mine to be a progeny of learning; I don't think so much learning becomes a young woman; for instance, I would never let her meddle with Greek, or Hebrew, or algebra, or simony, or fluxions, or paradoxes, or such inflammatory branches of learning. . . . But, Sir Anthony, I would send her, at nine years old, to a boarding-school, in order to learn a little ingenuity and artifice . . .*

This comic device had in fact been used by earlier writers, such as Shakespeare in the portrayal of Dogberry in *Much Ado About Nothing**.

Meiosis Understatement, used as a deliberate method of emphasis by irony, *eg* 'Would you like to be rich?' – 'I should rather think so!'

Metaphor A figure of speech by which unlike objects are identified with each other for the purpose of emphasizing one or more aspects of resemblance between them. A simple example: 'the camel is the ship of the desert'. Great writers, notably Shakespeare, use metaphor as the means to express a unified vision of disparate elements of experience:

Macbeth: Life's but a walking shadow; a poor player
That struts and frets his hour upon the stage,
And then is heard no more . . .

This has several meanings:

[1] Life is an illusion, as an actor's role is an illusion.

[2] Life only yields us the shadow of what our desires and hopes lead us to expect, just as an actor seems impressive but is only the shadow of the great man he is supposed to represent.

[3] People are self-important but unreal and ephemeral, just as an actor seems impressive, but is nobody when he has ceased performing.

[4] People go through the motions of living without achieving the reality of life.

[5] We think we are watching an illusion at a play, but perhaps our own lives are the true illusion.

Mixed Metaphor is a confused image in which the successive parts are inconsistent, so that (usually) absurdity results: 'I smell a rat, I see it floating in the air, but I will nip it in the bud', *ie* 'I suspect an evil, and I can already see the beginnings of it, but I will take action to suppress it.' However mixed metaphor is sometimes used deliberately to express a state of confusion, *eg* Hamlet's 'Or to take arms against a sea of troubles' in his 'To be or not to be' soliloquy (*Hamlet** III.i). The point of this image is that life's problems are too manifold for any single-minded resistance or simple solution – as though a man should try to fight the waves.

Dead Metaphor is one in which the image has become so familiar that it is no longer thought of as figurative, *eg* the phrase 'to take steps', meaning 'to take action'. However a Dead Metaphor can be brought back to life, *eg* Samuel Johnson's* comment on the Metaphysical Poets* – 'if their conceits were far-fetched, they were often worth the carriage' (Essay on Cowley in *Lives of the Poets*). Here the resuscitated metaphor is 'far-fetched'.

Metaphysical Conceit
Metaphysical Poets*.

Metonymy The naming of a person, institution or human characteristic by some object or quality which is clearly associated, as when a King or Queen may be referred to as 'the Crown'.

Sceptre and Crown
Must tumble down,
And in the dust be equal made
With the poor crooked scythe and spade.
(James Shirley*: *The Levelling Dust*)

Here 'Sceptre and Crown' refer to Kings, and perhaps more broadly to the classes which control government, while 'scythe and spade' stand for the humble peasantry.

Oxymoron A figure of speech formed by the conjunction of contrasting terms; it derives from two Greek words meaning 'sharp and dull'. An example from Shakespeare's *Romeo and Juliet**, where Romeo speaks of love:

Why, then, O brawling love! O loving hate!
O any thing, of nothing first create!
O heavy lightness! serious vanity!
Mis-shapen chaos of well-seeming forms!
Feather of lead, bright smoke, cold fire, sick health!
Still-waking sleep, that is not what it is! –
This love feel I, that feel no love in this.
(I.i)

The oxymorons of lines 1, 3, 4, 5, 6 image the contradictory emotions Romeo is feeling. The emotions associated with love stimulate their opposites, *eg* 'sick health' – a condition in which love animates the whole being, and yet seems to destroy the personality it animates.

Palindrome A word or sentence that reads the same backwards or forwards, *eg*

Lewd did I live; evil I did dwel
(Phillips, 1706)

Paradox A statement that challenges the mind by appearing to be self-contradictory:
The child is father of the man.
(Wordsworth*: *My heart leaps up*)

Pathetic Fallacy A term invented by the critic John Ruskin* (*Modern Painters*, Vol. III, Pt iv, Ch. 12) to denote the tendency common especially among poets to ascribe human emotions or qualities to inanimate objects, *eg* 'an angry sea'. Ruskin describes it by dividing writers into four classes: those who do not use it merely because they are insensitive; superior writers in whom it is a mark of sensitivity; writers who are better still and do not need it because they 'feel strongly, think strongly, and see truly'; and writers of the best sort who use it because in some instances they 'see in a sort untruly, because what they see is inconceivably above them'. In general, he considers that the pathetic fallacy is justified when the feeling it expresses is a true one.

Personification A kind of metaphor, by which an abstraction or inanimate object is endowed with personality:

and wither'd murder
Alarum'd by his sentinel, the wolf,
Whose howl's his watch, thus with his stealthy pace,
With Tarquin's ravishing strides, toward his design
Moves like a ghost.
(*Macbeth*, II.i)

Play on Words A use of a word with more than one meaning or of two words which sound the same in such a way that both meanings are called to mind. In its simplest form, as the modern pun, this is merely a joke:

And in her wondrous eyes
Love lies – and lies and lies.

In 16th and 17th C poets frequently played upon words seriously; this is especially true of Shakespeare and dramatists contemporary with him, and of the Metaphysical poets*, such as Donne* and Herbert*. Thus Lady Macbeth says to her husband after the murder of Duncan:

Give me the daggers. . . .
. . . If he do bleed,
I'll gild the faces of the grooms withal;
For it must seem their guilt.

(II.ii)

Here, 'guilt' is being punned with 'gild', and when later Macbeth refers to Duncan's 'golden blood' (II.iii) the pun is deepened in meaning and in irony, but it has no humour. Again, in John Donne's *Hymn to God the Father* beginning 'Wilt thou forgive . . .', his refrain relies on a pun upon his name:

When Thou hast done, Thou hast not done;
(*ie* Donne) For I have more.

This very serious use of puns or plays upon words went out by 18th C, when the great Samuel Johnson censured Shakespeare's fondness for puns (or, as Johnson called them, 'quibbles'). The reason for this disappearance of the serious 'play upon words' was the admiration of educated men for what Bishop Sprat in his *History of the Royal Society* (1667) called 'mathematical plainness of meaning', a criterion emulated by poets as well as by prose writers. In 19th C, the play on words was revived by humorous writers and writers for children, such as Thomas Hood*, Edward Lear* and Lewis Carroll*. Although their use of the pun was ostensibly comic, its effect in their writings is often unexpectedly poignant or even profound, especially in Carroll's 'Alice' books. Puns continued to be despised by the adult world of reason, but they could freely and revealingly be used in what was regarded as the childish world of nonsense and fantasy.

Modern poets and critics have recovered the older, serious use of the play on words. Ambiguity of meaning which in 18th C was considered a vice of expression, is now seen as a quality of rich texture of expression, though of course 'good' and 'bad' types of ambiguity have to be distinguished. James Joyce* used the technique with unprecedented elaboration in *Finnegans Wake**; William Empson* revived the serious punning of Donne and Marvell* in his poems, and investigated the whole problem in *Seven Types of Ambiguity* (1930). Just as admiration for mathematics and the physical sciences caused the decline of the play on words, so the revival of it has been partly due to the rise of another science, that of psycho-analysis, especially the school of Freud*, with its emphasis on the interplay of conscious and unconscious meanings in the use of language.

Pun
See Play on Words above.*

Rhyme A verbal music made through identity of sound in the final syllables of words. Several varieties of rhyme exist:

End-rhyme When the final syllables of lines of verse are rhymed:

Most souls, 'tis true, but peep out once an age,
Dull sullen pris'ners in the body's cage.

(Pope)

Internal Rhyme When one at least of the rhyming words is in mid-line; as in 'fair' and 'air' in the following couplet by Swinburne:

We have seen thee, O Love, thou art fair; thou art goodly, O Love;
Thy wings make light in the air as wings of a dove.

Masculine Rhymes are single stressed syllables as in the examples already given.

Feminine Rhymes are on two syllables, the second of which is unaccented, as in the following from Marlowe's *Passionate Shepherd*:

And I will make thee beds of roses
And a thousand fragrant posies;
A cap of flowers, and a kirtle
Embroder'd all with leaves of myrtle.

Half-rhymes (pararhymes) are the rhyming of consonants but not of vowels (contrast *Assonance*). They are sometimes used as an equivalent for full rhymes, since consonants are more noticeable in rhyme music than vowels. However some poets, notably Wilfred Owen*, used half-rhymes for a deliberate effect of discord:

And by his smile, I knew that sullen hall,
By his dead smile I knew we stood in Hell.

(Owen: *Strange Meeting*)

Change in pronunciation sometimes has the effect of changing what was intended as full rhyme into half-rhyme, as in the following example from Pope:

Tis not enough, taste, judgement, learning, join;
In all you speak, let truth and candour shine:

In 18th C, 'join' was pronounced as 'jine'.

Simile Similar to metaphor, but in similes the comparison is made explicit by the use of a word such as 'like' or 'as':

O my Luve is like a red, red rose

(Robert Burns*)

Syllepsis A figure of speech by which a word is used in a literal and a metaphorical sense at the same time, *eg* 'You have broken my heart and my best china vase'.

Synecdoche A figure of speech by which a part is used to express a whole, or a whole is used to express a part, *eg* 'fifty sail' is used for fifty ships, or the 'smiling year' is used for the spring. In practice, synecdoche is often indistinguishable from metonymy.

Transferred Epithet The transference of an adjective from the noun to which it applies grammatically to some other word in the sentence, usually in

such a way as to express the quality of an action or of behaviour, *eg* 'My host handed me a hospitable glass of wine', instead of 'My hospitable host handed me. . . '.

Zeugma A figure similar to syllepsis; one word used with two others, to only one of which it is grammatically or logically applicable, as in Pope's line:

See Pan with flocks, with fruits Pomona crowned

where a visualization of Pan 'crowned' with flocks is entertainingly ridiculous.

Filostrato

* *Troilus and Criseyde.*

Finn (Find, Fionn, Fingal)

In Irish myth, a hero of the so-called Ossianic or Fenian cycle of legends; he is supposed to have lived in 3rd C AD and to have been leader of a band of warriors called the Fenians*. He was the father of Ossian (or Oisin*), the subject of a famous 18th-C poetic forgery.

Finnegans Wake (1939)

A novel by James Joyce*. It is the most original experiment ever undertaken in the novel form, and the most difficult to read. It purports to be one night in the life of a Dublin public-house keeper, H. C. Earwicker, and as he is asleep from the beginning to the end of the book, his experiences are all those of dream. The advantage of dream experience is that it is unrestricted by self-conscious logic, and operates by free association unrestrained by inhibitions. The basis of the 'story' is his relationships with his wife, Maggie, his daughter, Isobel, and his twin sons Kevin and Jerry; it reaches out, however, into Irish and European myths as these are suggested to his sleeping consciousness by objects in his mean little house and neighbourhood. Joyce intends in fact to make Earwicker a type of 'Everyman'. The language is made by fusing together words so as to cause them – as in dreams – to suggest several levels of significance simultaneously; this is a device which had already been used playfully by Lewis Carroll* in his poem *Jabberwocky* in the dream story for children *Through the Looking-Glass* (1872). Joyce, however, in his desire to universalize Earwicker, freely combines words from foreign languages with English ones, so that Earwicker's mind becomes representatively European while remaining his own. The movement of the narrative is based on the ideas of the 18th-C Italian philosopher Vico, who believed that ages succeed each other – gods, heroes, men – and then recommence; this is followed out in Earwicker's successive identifications, until at the end of the book the final sentence is completed by the first sentence at its beginning. Another important influence on Joyce was the psychological ideas of Sigmund Freud* on the mechanism of repression and the characteristics of dream association. Study necessitates the assistance of such a work as *A Skeleton Key to Finnegans Wake* by Campbell and Johnson.

Finsbury

A district in London on the north boundary of the City. It is said to owe its name to the draining of a marsh or 'fen' in 16th C. Part of this fen was known as Moorfields, and was laid out for public recreation, much used as a resort in 17th C *eg* by the diarist Pepys*. Bunhill Fields, a celebrated burial place for nonconformist religious sects in 17th and 18th C, contains the graves of Bunyan*, Defoe*, and George Fox*.

Firbank, Ronald (1886–1926)

Writer of witty fantasies whose extravagant humour derives from the subtly calculated and highly wrought style. His best known tales are probably *Vainglory* (1915); *Valmouth* (1919); *The Flower Beneath the Foot* (1923); *The Artificial Princess* (1934). He can perhaps best be described as a late outcome of 1890's aestheticism, combined with the fascination for stylistic experiment characteristic of the 1920s.

Bib: Fletcher, I. K., *Memoir*; Forster, E. M., in *Abinger Harvest*; Brooke, J., *Ronald Firbank*.

Fire of London, The Great

A celebrated disaster in 1666; over 13,000 houses, 87 churches, and the old St Paul's Cathedral* were destroyed. Celebrated accounts of it occur in the contemporary diaries of John Evelyn* and Samuel Pepys*. Owing to disagreements among the citizens, the great architect Christopher Wren* was not allowed to carry out his great plan for rebuilding the City, whose streets accordingly still follow the twisting lines of the old City; but he rebuilt St Paul's and many other churches. A beneficial consequence of the fire was that it ended the terrible epidemic of plague which had devastated London in 1665.

* *Plague of London, The Great.*

First Gentleman of Europe

George IV – so described by his flatterers, because of his pursuit of elegant luxury and gaiety. His tutor had predicted of him, at the age of 15, that he would be 'either the most polished gentleman or the most accomplished blackguard in Europe – possibly both'.

Fitz-Boodle, George Savage /fits'bu:dl/

The pen-name assumed by the novelist Thackeray* for the 'Fitz-Boodle Papers' contributed to *Fraser's Magazine*, 1842–43.

FitzGerald, Edward (1809–93) /fits'dʒerəld/

Poet; chiefly known for his extremely popular translation of the Persian poem *The Rubaiyat of Omar Khayyam** (1859). He also published *Euphranor* (1851), a Platonic dialogue; translations of *Six Dramas of Calderon* (1853), and, in 1865, a translation of Aeschylus'* *Agamemnon**. His delicate praise of a life of pleasure and enjoyment of beauty evident in his *Rubaiyat* countered the moral earnestness of the age and influenced the 'anti-Victorian' Pre-Raphaelite* and aesthetic* movements later in the century.

Bib: Benson, A. C., *FitzGerald*; Terhune, A. M., *Life*; Campbell, A. Y., in *Great Victorians*, ed. Massingham, A. J. and H.

Five Towns, The

A group of industrial towns in the English midlands (Staffordshire) where ceramics are manufactured: Tunstall, Burslem, Hanley, Stoke-upon-Trent, Longton. The novelist Arnold Bennett* used them as the setting for his novels, calling them Turnhill, Bursley, Hanbridge, Knype, Longshaw. The towns are now one 'conurbation' of Stoke-on-Trent.

Flanders Mare

Henry VIII* so described Anne of Cleves. He married and divorced her in the year 1540; the marriage had been arranged by his Secretary of State, Thomas Cromwell*, for the political purpose of building up a grand anti-Catholic alliance with the German states.

Flaubert, Gustave (1821–80)

A French novelist whose scrupulous and strenuous attention to his art established a new criterion of method. His most famous novel is *Madame Bovary* (1857). He also wrote *Salammbô* (1862), a historical novel about Carthage; *L'Education Sentimentale* (1869); *La Tentation de Saint-Antoine* (1874) and the unfinished *Bouvard et Pécuchet* (1881). His realism* was close, exact and consistent in a carefully wrought design; he achieved a new conception of artistic integrity in the relationship of the artist to his material, as opposed to the hitherto vaguer and looser relationship between the author considered as a person and his experience. After Flaubert, both English and French novelists show a more austere and rigorous attention to technique than was usual among writers before him.

Flecknoe, Richard (17th C) /'fleknəu/

A poet who was the victim of a satire by Andrew Marvell*: *Fleckno, an English Priest at Rome* (1645). Dryden*, when he was writing his satire against his rival Shadwell, chose the title *Mac Flecknoe**, *ie* son of Flecknoe.

Fleet Prison, The

A royal prison in London from 12th C (Falstaff* is sent there at the end of Shakespeare's *2 Henry IV**), used for debtors after 1641, and demolished in 1848. It is described in Dickens's *Pickwick Papers**. Clergymen imprisoned in the Fleet sometimes conducted secret marriages, *ie* without the formalities of licence or 'banns'. Such marriages were legal though the clergyman was liable to a fine – a penalty which was no deterrent to one already bankrupt.

Fleet Street

A street in London, the headquarters of most of the national newspapers. 'Fleet Street' is often used as a synonym for 'journalism'.

Fletcher, Giles (the Elder) (1549?–1611)

Author of a book on Russia (1591), suppressed by the government at the request of the English joint stock Russia Company as likely to offend the Russian government and hinder trade. He also wrote a sonnet sequence, *Licia, or Poems of Love* (1593) in emulation of Sidney's *Astrophil and Stella**.

* *Companies, Joint Stock.*

Fletcher, Giles (the Younger) (1585–1623)

Poet; author of allegorical religious poems, especially his epic* in Spenserian stanzas* *Christ's Victorie and Triumph* (1610). He was the younger son of Giles Fletcher the Elder*.

Fletcher, John (1579–1625)

Dramatist; nephew of Giles Fletcher the Elder*. The 1679 edition of his work contains 57 plays – the largest of all the Elizabethan collections – but most of them were collaborations.

Among the works probably by himself alone are: *The Faithful Shepherdess* (1610), a pastoral*; the tragedies *Bonduca* (Boadicea*) and *Valentinian* (1614); the tragi-comedies, *The Loyal Subject* (1618), *The Humorous Lieutenant* (1619); the comedies, *The Wild Goose Chase*, *Monsieur Thomas*, *The Pilgrim* (1621).

It was in collaboration with Beaumont* that Fletcher produced his most famous work; their best plays are commonly held to be the tragicomedy *Philaster**, and the tragedy *The Maid's Tragedy**. Another tragedy, *A King and No King* (1611) was greatly admired by Dryden; the domestic comedy *The Scornful Lady* (1610) has also been highly praised.

Fletcher seems to have ceased collaborating with Beaumont in 1613, and to have joined briefly with Shakespeare. *Henry VIII**, formerly attributed to Shakespeare entirely, is now thought to be partly Fletcher's work, and Shakespeare is also thought to have written part of *The Two Noble Kinsmen**.

Fletcher's name has also been linked with several other dramatists, including Jonson*, but especially with Massinger* between 1619 and 1622. Among these Massinger collaborations are *Thierry and Theodoret* and *The False One*.

Fletcher's reputation stood highest at the Restoration*, when he was ranked with Shakespeare and Jonson. The opinion of most 20th-C criticism is that he was an extremely skilful theatrical craftsman, a master of striking but superficial dramatic effects; his verse, similarly, is admitted to be fluent and musical, but is felt to lack authentic depth and strength of feeling. He is thus felt to be representative of decadence in the great Shakespearian period, and even to be the principal decadent influence.

5.1.3.3.

Bib: Waith, E. M., *The Pattern of Tragicomedy in Beaumont and Fletcher*; Bradbrook, M. C., *Elizabethan Tragedy*; Danby, J., *Poets on Fortune's Hill*; Maxwell, B., *Studies in Beaumont, Fletcher and Massinger*; Oliphant, E. H. C., *The Plays of Beaumont and Fletcher*; Thorndyke, A. H., *The Influence of Beaumont and Fletcher on Shakespeare*; Appleton, W. W., *Beaumont and Fletcher*; Leech, C., *The John Fletcher Plays*.

Fletcher, Phineas (1582–1650)

Elder son of Giles Fletcher the Elder*; allegorical poet in the tradition of Spenser. Principal work: *The Purple Island, or the Isle of Man* (1633), an allegorical representation of the human mind and body.

Flodden, Battle of (1513)

The invading Scottish forces under king James IV, fighting in alliance with France which had been invaded by Henry VIII* of England, were heavily defeated by the English general the Earl of Surrey. James himself was killed, as well as large numbers of his nobility. The battle was commemorated by a famous dirge *The Flowers of the Forest*, the best-known version of which is by Jane Elliot (1727–1805). *Marmion, A Tale of Flodden Field** is the most celebrated of the narrative poems by Sir Walter Scott.

Flora

In Roman myth, goddess of springtime and flowers, later identified with her Greek equivalent, Chloris. She is used in English pastoral* poetry.

Florimell

A character in Spenser's *Faerie Queene**, Books III and IV. She is one of Spenser's representations of chaste love.

Florio, John (1553?–1625) /'flo:riəu/

Translator of the *Essays* by the French writer Montaigne; the translation was published in 1603. He also published an Italian-English dictionary, *A World of Words* (1598). He was the son of an Italian Protestant refugee.

Bib: Yates, F. A., *John Florio*.

Fluellen

A character in Shakespeare's history play *Henry V**. He is a Welsh officer in the army of Henry, fighting in France. He is presented as a brave and fine soldier, but also as a comic character, with the weaknesses of emotional and irritable pride associated with the Welsh in the English mind of Shakespeare's time. The name is a corruption of Llewellyn.

Flyting

A verbal combat, in which the combatants compete against each other in satirical abuse. It may have had its origins in pagan ritual in contests which symbolized the change of the seasons, etc., and is said to have connections with the boasts and abuse hurled at each other by rival heroes and other characters in epics* and tragedies. Episodes which could be called 'flytings' occur in Shakespeare's tragedies and history plays, *eg Julius Caesar** V.i, and the ferocious dialogue between Timon and Apemantus, in *Timon of Athens** IV.iii. The device was particularly common in medieval literature, *eg* Dunbar's* *The Flyting of Dunbar and Kennedy*, and Chaucer's *The Parliament of Fowls**.

Folio

As applied to books, a folio is one for which the paper has been folded once, and therefore of the largest size. The expression 'the first folio' commonly refers to the first collected edition of Shakespeare's plays (1623); there were three other folio editions of Shakespeare's plays in 17th C.

The 1623 volume is edited by two fellow actors of the Lord Chamberlain's Company* of Players – Heming and Condell – and contains a preface by them and prefatory poems, notably one by a great rival Ben Jonson*. Following the poems there is a list of the 'principal actors in all these plays'; the list includes Shakespeare himself, Richard Burbage*, Nathaniel Field*, and of course the editors. The edition opens with the print of a rather inferior engraved portrait of the poet by Martin Droeshout. Thirty-seven plays are included; one of these, *Henry VIII**, is now thought by most critics to be partly by John Fletcher*; *Pericles**, included by modern editors, is omitted. Eighteen of the plays had already been published in small quarto* editions (some of them close to the folio version and some differing substantially), and the remainder were being published for the first time. The plays are undated, and grouped into Comedies, Histories, and Tragedies; some have divisions into acts and scenes, and some are without them.

Food

1350–1500: Chaucer's poor widow in the *Nun's Priest's Tale** (*Canterbury Tales*) lived off 'white and black', *ie* milk and coarse rye bread. Also in 14th C, another peasant, Langland's Piers Plowman*, declares that he can only afford green cheese (from thin milk), curds and cream, oatcake, and bean-loaves. Porridges made out of beans and peas (pease pudding) were also common. Poor peasants probably saw little meat up to the end of 18th C, though they might have eggs and bacon. By contrast, other 14th-C poems (*eg Winner and Waster*, *Sir Gawain and the Green Knight**) describe the tables of the nobility as overflowing with meat dishes. Mutton, beef and veal were the common diet of richer peasants, and, as deer abounded, so was venison. Chicken was the most frequent bird-dish, but wildfowl, such as pheasants and partridges, and also small birds such as larks and linnets, never eaten now, were luxuries for the rich. Great houses and monasteries kept fishponds, and fish was substituted for meat on Fridays and in the Lent fast. Sea-fish was not fresh by the time it reached inland consumers; it had often been dried in the sun without salt and was called 'stockfish'. Meat and fish were often in a tasteless or unpalatable condition, and required a plentiful use of sauces, compounded of vinegar, pepper, salt and garlic. As there were no root crops to feed cattle during the winter, surplus animals were killed off, salted, and eaten with sauces in that season. Herbs and spices were much used for savouring, and honey for sweetening; a foreign observer in the reign of Elizabeth I* mentions bad teeth in the middle and upper classes as a consequence of English addiction to sweet food. Skin infections also seem to have been prevalent, owing to deficiency of vegetables in proportion to meat.

From 1500. Salads ('sallets') began to come into general use among the middle and upper classes in 17th C. The potato, introduced by Sir Walter Raleigh in the 1580s, spread slowly, and it was not until 19th C that it became really common, and a staple food among the poor. Sugar was another important innovation; cane sugar was cultivated in the West Indies in 17th C and took the place of honey and other sweeteners that had gone by the name of sugar in earlier times. By 18th C vegetables were extensively cultivated by all classes, and were eaten with meat as plentifully as they are today. Overeating of meat continued to be a chief cause of bad health among the richer classes, hence the frequent apoplexies in 18th-C novels and plays. Lavish orchards were a feature of great houses at least as early as 16th C, and fruits such as dates, figs and oranges were imported. Diet greatly expanded in 18th and 19th C with the increase in variety of imports, and it was revolutionized by the invention of canning in 19th C: canned meat was on show at the Great Exhibition* of 1851, but did not become general until this century. Fruits, such as the banana and pineapple, originally imported cheaply from the Empire as a fashionable novelty, have remained popular to the present time.

Fools, Professional (Court Fools and Jesters)

The profession of licensed jester is ancient and widespread. In England it existed before the Conquest* of 1066; Charles I* was the last monarch to have one. Fools wore distinctive costume; characteristically, the coat was motley, *ie* made of patches of various colours; leggings were tight, each leg a different colour; a hood was worn over the head, perhaps with ass's ears projecting; the fool carried a bauble, *ie* a stick ending with a grotesque head and a balloonlike bladder for striking people with. Fools were licensed to speak with unusual freedom to their employers, though they ran risks in doing so. This made them useful to the dramatist, as is evident in the example of Shakespeare's three famous fools: Feste in *Twelfth Night**, Touchstone in *As You Like It**, and King Lear's* Fool; the first is used to set off the genuine folly of the other characters (as distinct from the professional's assumed folly), the second is a vehicle of satirical comment on society and behaviour, and the third is like an ironic choral accompaniment to his master's deepening tragedy.

The Elizabethan professional fool was different from the clown; the latter was unintentionally funny in the manner of an ignorant, credulous rustic, whereas the former was alert, acute and sophisticated. When Court Fools went out of fashion their role was eventually taken over by the Circus Clown, who like the clown of the Renaissance stage provided comedy inadvertently, but no longer bore relationship to the ignorant rustic.

Football

The game is ancient, but the first distinct mention of it in England is in 12th C. For centuries it was played without rules, and was extremely violent and dangerous; for this reason it was condemned by a number of writers including King James I*, and was especially disapproved of by 17th C Puritans*. It continued to be widely popular, however, though essentially a game for the masses and for students – Oxford forbade it but Cambridge allowed it – until it became a 'gentleman's game' in 19th C, when it was taken up by the public schools*. At least three versions then evolved in England: [1] Rugby Union, the origin of American football, was evolved by Rugby School*, and continued the old, more violent version of the game in a systematic form; [2] Rugby League is played in the north of England, and resembles Rugby Union; [3] Association football ('soccer') is played all over the world, and so called from the forming of the Football Association in 1863 to control it. Professionalism entered soccer in 1885, and Rugby League in 1895; Rugby Union remains amateur.

Ford, Ford Madox (1873–1939) (Ford Hermann Hueffer)

Novelist, critic, poet. His father was of German origin, and became music critic for *The Times**; his mother was daughter of the Pre-Raphaelite* painter, Ford Madox Brown. Ford was first known as an aesthetic writer of fairy stories, but he became deeply interested in contemporary French writing and culture, and became a propagandist for the rigorous discipline of French art, exercising a strong personal influence on Joseph Conrad* and Ezra Pound*. He was a prolific writer, but is now chiefly remembered for the four novels known in England as *The Tietjens Tetralogy* (after the name of its hero), and in America as *Parade's End*: *Some Do Not* (1924), *No More Parades* (1925), *A Man Could Stand Up* (1926), and *Last Post* (1928). This is regarded by some critics as the most memorable fiction about the war of 1914–18 (in which Ford served, although he was 40 on enlistment), and as the most remarkable account of the upheaval in English social values in the decade 1910–20.

Ford has an undoubted importance in literary history because of his personal influence. In 1908–9 he was editor of the brilliant but short-lived *English Review*, to which Thomas Hardy*, Henry James*, H. G. Wells*, Joseph Conrad and the Russian novelist Leo Tolstoy* all contributed. He was an early encourager of D. H. Lawrence*. Brought up in the relatively narrow Pre-Raphaelite and aesthetic* movements, in the 1900s he was a central figure among the writers who were thinking radically about problems of artistic form, especially in novel-writing. He regarded the 19th-C English novel as too much a product of the accident of genius, and, aligning himself with James and Conrad, was in opposition to H. G. Wells who preferred the title of journalist to that of artist. But it might be said that, though he thought radically about artistic form, he did not think as radically as they or D. H. Lawrence did about the nature of feeling.

Since 1918, Ford's influence has declined and his imaginative writing has been neglected, apart from a limited revival of interest after 1945. Of present day novelists, he has perhaps had most effect on Graham Greene*. Apart from *The Tietjens Tetralogy*, novels selected for praise include the historical trilogy about Tudor England (*The Fifth Queen*, 1905; *Privy Seal*, 1907; *The Fifth Queen Crowned*, 1908) and *The Good Soldier* (1915).

Bib: Critical studies of the novels by Cassell, R. A., Meixner, J. A., and Ohmann, C.; British Council Pamphlet by Kenneth Young; Life (*The Last Pre-Raphaelite*) by Douglas Goldring.

Ford, Henry (1863–1947)

American manufacturer, famous for the mass-production of the Ford car, and often regarded by writers between 1920 and 1940 (*eg* Aldous Huxley* in *Brave New World*, 1932) as typifying a new civilization of soulless mechanism. Confronted by a great picture, he is said to have remarked: 'What's the use of it? There's only one.'

Ford, John (1586–?1640)

The best of the Caroline* dramatists. He is best known for two tragedies, *'Tis Pity She's a Whore* and *The Broken Heart* (1633), and a tragic history play, *Perkin Warbeck* (1634). Less well-known are *Lover's Melancholy* (1629) and *Love's Sacrifice* (1633). He collaborated with other dramatists, notably with Dekker* and Rowley in *The Witch of Edmonton* (1623). In spite of sensational themes and incidents (*eg 'Tis Pity* is about incestuous love) Ford's characteristic tone is the melancholy of private, frustrated passion; pathos rather than tragedy.

* 5.1.4; *Warbeck, Perkin.*

Bib: Eliot, T. S. in *Selected Essays*;
Sargeaunt, M. J., *John Ford*; Sensabaugh, G. F., *The Tragic Muse of John Ford*;
Leech, C., *Ford and the Drama of his Time.*

Forster, E. M. (1879–1970)

Novelist. He was himself a religious sceptic, but his 19th-C forebears belonged to the prosperous evangelical* middle class and had been familiar with leading figures in it, such as William Wilberforce*, the leader of the movement for abolishing slavery. This section of society led public opinion in the Victorian* period, and Forster's writings are much concerned with its cultural and political legacy to 20th C. He was educated at Tonbridge School (a public school* whose ethos is characterized by Sawston in the first two novels) and then at King's College, Cambridge, of which he was later made an honorary fellow. He travelled in Europe, lived in Italy and Egypt, and spent some years in India, where he was for a time secretary to a rajah after World War I.

Forster's novels are: *Where Angels Fear to Tread* (1905); *The Longest Journey* (1907); *A Room with a View* (1908); *Howard's End** (1910); *A Passage to India** (1924); and *Maurice* (1971), published posthumously. He published two collections of short stories: *The Celestial Omnibus* (1914) and *The Eternal Moment* (1928). These are mainly early work; they were published in a collected edition in 1947. His high reputation rests mainly on his fiction, but he has also written biographies and essays which are important for understanding his outlook as an imaginative writer. The biography of his friend Goldsworthy Lowes Dickinson (1934) is about a Cambridge scholar who was an important leader of liberal political opinion; that of his great-aunt, Marianne Thornton (1956), is enlightening about Forster's background. *The Hill of Devi* (1953) is an account of his experiences in India. The essays in *Abinger Harvest* (1936) and *Two Cheers for Democracy* (1951) include expressions of his opinions about politics, literature and society. *Aspects of the Novel* (1927) is one of the best-known critical works on the novel form. Forster also wrote a history of and guide to Alexandria (1922).

Forster's dominant theme is the habitual conformity of people to unexamined social standards and conventions, and the ways in which this conformity blinds the individual to recognition of what is true in what is unexpected, to the proper uses of the intelligence, and to his own resources of spontaneous life. Spontaneous life and free intelligence also draw on traditions, and Forster shows how English traditions have on the one hand nourished complacency, hypocrisy, and insular philistinism, and on the other hand, humility, honesty, and sceptical curiosity. In each of the novels (except *The Longest Journey*, in which the contrast is between urban and rural traditions of life) and especially in *Passage to India*, British culture is contrasted with a foreign tradition with virtues that the British way of life is without. His style is consistently light, witty and subtle, with a use of irony which recalls Jane Austen* and a use of comedy of situation which recalls Meredith*. But Forster's most original contribution to the art of fiction is probably his very subtle and pervasive use of symbolism, especially evident in *Passage to India*. His mind and art belong to the central tradition of British liberal culture.

* 4.5.3.

Bib: Trilling, L., *E. M. Forster*; Macaulay, R., *The Writings of Forster*; McConkey, J., *The Novels of Forster*; Gransden, K. W., *E. M. Forster*.

Forsyte Saga, The

A sequence of novels constituting a study of Victorian* and Edwardian* society by John Galsworthy*. They comprise: *The Man of Property* (1906); *The Indian Summer of a Forsyte* (1918); *In Chancery* (1920); *Awakening* (1920); *To Let* (1921).

Forties, The Hungry

The decade 1840–50, so called because bad harvests caused serious food shortages, leading to mass agitation for abolition of the tax on imported corn (Anti-Corn Law League) and for a more democratic political system (the Chartist Movement*).

* *Corn Laws; Free Trade*

Forties, The Roaring

An exceptionally stormy region of the ocean, latitude 40–50 degrees south.

Fortunate Isles

In Greek and Roman myth, islands in the Atlantic where the souls of the virtuous dead spend eternity.

Fortnightly Review, The

* *Reviews and Periodicals.*

Forty-five, The

The rebellion or rising of 1745, *ie* the second of the two main Jacobite* attempts in 18th C to regain the throne of Great Britain for the Catholic branch of the House of Stuart*. It was led by Charles Stuart ('Bonnie Prince Charlie' to his Scottish supporters, the 'Young Pretender' to his enemies), elder son of the claimant James Stuart (the 'Old Pretender'). Charles succeeded in rousing the Highlands* and occupying Edinburgh*. He then advanced into England and reached Derby. He had by then attracted very few English supporters, and retreated to Scotland. He was defeated by the Duke of Cumberland in 1746 at the Battle of Culloden* in northern Scotland, but escaped abroad.

Forty Shilling Freeholders

The class, outside the towns, who from 13th C until the Reform Bill* of 1832 possessed the minimum property qualification to vote for a representative in Parliament, or to be elected as one. 'Freeholder' implies owning land, not renting it from another landowner; 'forty shillings' is the annual value of the land.

* *Franchise; Yeoman.*

Fosse Way /'fos 'wei/

The old English name for a road originally built by the Romans. It ran from Lincoln in the east to Bath in the south-west. A modern road system follows largely the same route.

Foundling

Used of a child abandoned by its parents, usually because it was illegitimate or the parents were too poor to provide for it. Such children were sometimes left at night on the doorsteps of the rich, and so were 'found' at daylight. In 1745 a Foundling Hospital was established in London for such children; baskets were hung on the outer wall for their reception, and taken in every morning.

Four P's, The (1568)

One of the amusing Interludes* written by John Heywood*. It begins with a competition between a palmer, a pardoner and an apothecary, judged by a pedlar, to find the best liar.

Four Quartets

Four poems written between 1935 and 1942 by T. S. Eliot*, eventually published as a single work. They are contemplative, religious poems, each concerned with a distinct aspect of spiritual experience. Each has as its symbolic centre a place; each uses symbolically one of the four 'elements'* of medieval physics; each has a structure analogous to the movements and the instruments of a musical quartet; the theme that unites the four is that of the human consciousness in relation to time and the concept of eternity. *Burnt Norton* (the element of air) centres on the rose garden of a ruined country house (Burnt Norton) in Gloucestershire and plays on the differences and relationships between the actual present, the past in memory, and speculation on what might have been. *East Coker* (earth) is based on a village in Somerset, whence the poet's ancestors derived, and it includes quotations from *The Governor* (1531) by Sir Thomas Elyot*; the poem is concerned with man as part of the process of nature. *Dry Salvages* (water) is named after rocks off the coast of Massachusetts; the poem is concerned with racial time and memory, larger than the time of history and of the seasons, and embracing the more unconscious regions of the mind. *Little Gidding** (fire) derives its title from the religious community in the reign of Charles 1*, who is supposed to have visited it when broken by defeat at the battle of Naseby. Fire in this poem is used as destruction (with reference to the raids on London during World War II), purification, illumination, and as an emblem of Divine Love. (*See* Elizabeth Drew – *T. S. Eliot: The Design of his Poetry*.)

Four Quartets was Eliot's last major work in non-dramatic poetry; the remainder of his career was devoted to poetic drama.

* 6.4.1.

Fourteenth-century Literature

In the middle years of 14th C, English gained predominance over French as the spoken language of the upper classes. The fact is important, because English literature was no longer subordinate to French in part of society, but could become the expression of the whole of society. Thus, although in important respects there is continuity between old (pre-Conquest*) English literature and modern English literature, 14th C is one of energetic renewal; after it, there are no serious gaps in the development of the English tradition.

The lyrics that have survived (*eg The Hawthorn Tree*, *The Maiden of the Moor*) show a vigorous link with the past; they are songs, perhaps for festivals such as May Day*, and have the spontaneity and simplicity we associate with early carols*, but are by no means naïve or crude. The 14th-C lyric shows a strength that abides in English literature: it drew its life from the life of the people, all the more, no doubt, because English had been the language of the less privileged.

But it is the long poem that is the special glory of 14th C. The 2,000-line poem *The Owl and the Nightingale* shows that in mid-13th C the Old English rhymeless, unmetrical forms had been superseded by the rhyme and metre of medieval French and Latin verse, in which romances such as *King Horn* and *Havelok the Dane* were written. Yet in 14th C, the alliterative form revives in full splendour in the west and north-west. Langland's long didactic poem, *Piers Plowman**, and the anonymous poems, perhaps by a single author, *Sir Gawaine and the Green Knight** and *Pearl**, are amongst the greatest long poems in English, and there are a number of distinguished works of secondary value, such as *Patience** and *Purity** (probably by the same author), *The Parliament of the Three Ages**, and *Wynnere and Wastoure*. But Geoffrey Chaucer*, one of the two or three greatest English poets of any age, used metrical and rhymed verse so consummately well that he established it as the form that became both most natural and most richly potential for the English poets after him. Chaucer was a Court poet in the positive sense of being metropolitan and not provincial, and he was both strongly national in his character and intelligently international in his culture. His friend and contemporary John Gower*, who wrote in French and Latin as well as English, was also a sophisticated poet, though he lacked the strength of individuality which in Chaucer impressed for ever the quality of national character upon English literature.

English prose writing in 14th C is often underrated, in the view of some scholars, because its range and development was far less than that of the poetry. As far back as the first half of 13th C, *Ancrene Riwle* (Rule of the Anchoresses) was the earliest in a distinguished tradition in religious devotional and mystical writings, and this was continued in 14th C in the works of Richard Rolle of Hampole, James Hilton, Juliana of Norwich, Margery Kempe, and the anonymous author of *The Cloud of Unknowing*. All these wrote works not merely of historical interest, but of permanent value for their religious insight. John Wycliffe*, as a prose writer, is more of historical interest as author of the first version of what was to become in early 17th C the great Authorized Version of the English Bible. One of the ablest handlers of prose expression in the century was John Trevisa, who translated from the Latin the *Polychronicon* (Universal History) by the contemporary monk, Ranulf Higden.

* *Bible in England.*

Fourteenth of July

The French annual national festival, dating from the storming of the Bastille, a state prison in Paris, on 14 July 1789. This was the first triumph of the French Revolution*, and marked the end of the Ancien Régime*.

Fourth Estate, The

Traditionally, and for political purposes, English society was thought until 20th C to have three estates: the lords spiritual, the lords temporal, the commons. Carlyle* alludes to a Fourth Estate, *ie* the press, implying that the newspapers have an essential role in the political functions of society. He attributed the phrase to the 18th-C statesman Edmund Burke*.

Fourth of July, The

Independence Day in the United States, dating from the Declaration of Independence* in 1776.

Fowling

Any form of hunting birds. Since 17th C shooting with guns has been the only common method, but previously shooting with the bow and arrow, trapping or hawking* were used. Guns (called bird- or fowling-pieces) began to make their appearance in 16th C, but the crossbow was still the more efficient weapon. Trapping was either by gins (using some kind of net) or by placing lime along the twigs of trees so that the bird's feet stuck to it on alighting. Hawking was the most aristocratic of these sports, until it gave place to shooting in 17th C.

* *Hunting.*

Fox, Charles James (1749–1806)

Principal leader of the Whig party from 1775 (the beginning of the American War of Independence) until his death. The crown was not then above politics, and the Tories, almost continuously in power during the same period, had the support of George III. Fox's fearless opposition in the House of Commons to the policies of the government in America, in Ireland, and in regard to the French Revolution*, caused the king to refuse his offer of

participation in the government in 1804, when he became convinced of the rightness of the war against France. Fox was dissolute in private life but set a high standard of political independence of mind. His principal political opponents were the Prime Ministers Lord North during the American war, and William Pitt* the Younger during the French one. Though powerful in opposition, he was less effective in office; but his service as Foreign Secretary in the Whig governments of 1782 and 1806 was too brief to show results.

* *Whig and Tory.*

Fox, George (1624–91)

Religious leader. He founded the Society of Friends (Quakers*), and left a journal of his spiritual experience, published in 1694. Apart from its religious importance, Fox's Journal is one of the classics amongst the English diaries*.

Fox-hunting

This sport began to reach its outstanding prestige in 18th-C England. Deer, the chief object of hunts in earlier centuries, were less available as land came increasingly under cultivation, but foxes did not diminish, and were just as much an enemy to farmers. Special packs of foxhounds were bred, and were given names – often taken from the great country houses where they were kept, such as the Quorn, the Pytchley, the Badminton – which became famous far beyond hunting circles. The 18th-C enclosures* of land into hedge-divided fields increased the danger and skill of 'riding to hounds', and this as much as anything steadily enhanced its popularity among the landed aristocracy who hunted for the sport and not merely to protect their poultry, like the farmers. To kill a fox by any method other than the approved one of hunting it with hounds and on horseback came to be regarded as little better than criminal; to be a Master of Hounds was to occupy a great social position; to misuse terminology (*eg* to call the hounds 'dogs') was to betray not merely laughable ignorance but a shameful sign of ill-breeding. The hunt 'liveries' (often, but not always, coats of brilliant 'hunting pink') worn by the hunt servants became a familiar feature of national pageantry, and 'hunt balls' were great social occasions. Fox-hunting takes place in winter, and fashionable families divided the year between the London 'season' in the summer, and winter visits to the famous fox-hunting regions. The most famous of these covers the counties of Leicester, Rutland, and Northampton, and is known as 'the shires'. Occasionally hunting takes place on foot, where the terrain is unsuitable for horses; the most famous English hunting song 'D'ye ken John Peel with his coat so grey' refers to an 18th-C huntsman who hunted his pack on foot in the Lake district.

It was in 19th C that fox-hunting flourished most. Railways, instead of reducing the sport, encouraged it by making the hunts more accessible from London. Robert Surtees* produced minor classics of hunting-field stories, such as *Handley Cross* (1843), and 'hunting prints' became a familiar ornament of the walls of English country inns. On the other hand, the urban intelligentsia later in the century sometimes revolted against 'hunting circles'. Oscar Wilde*, leader of the aesthetic* movement at the end of 19th C, defined fox-hunting as 'the pursuit of the uneatable by the unspeakable'.

* *Field Sports; Hunting.*

Foxe, John (1516–87) /foks/

Author of the *Book of Martyrs*; this was the title under which it was popularly known; the correct title of the 1st edition (1563) was *Acts and Monuments of these latter and perilous days.* Foxe was a Puritan* who first set out to write a history of Christian martyrdom in Latin. The first outline dealt chiefly with the 14th-C reformers, the English Wycliffe* and the Bohemian John Huss. In 1554 he went abroad to escape persecution under the Catholic Mary*, and completed his book there. The English version is fierce and eloquent, and had immense sales; for generations it inspired hatred for Catholicism in Britain, and was read alongside the Bible by simple folk who read little else. It is a classic of popular prose in the Elizabethan period.

* *Reformation.*

France and Britain: Literary Contacts

As in politics, and indeed almost all departments of life, literary relationships have been close and of long history. They can only be indicated in this note, and it is relevant only to consider the bearings of French literature on English, neglecting the counterflow.

[1] *Poetry.* In the Middle Ages, literary culture was less bound by frontiers than it became after 1500, and it is often difficult to distinguish what in English literature is nourished by specifically French influences from what belongs to the common European store. There is no doubt, however, of the impact of the French love romance and the fabliau, or comic verse tale, on the poet Chaucer*. He translated the *Roman de la Rose** from the French of Guillaume de Lorris and Jean de Meung, and he learnt a fluency and ease of movement from Guillaume de Machaut and his successors, substituting (though he did not originate the change) running metre with a regular count of syllables for the traditional English alliterative* and accentual pattern, gaining flexibility without sacrificing force. French influence on Chaucer then was distinct and marked, but it combined with Italian; this combined influence also affected English poetry of late 16th C – a Renaissance* movement later than in the Latin countries. Its lyric forms (especially the sonnet) were moulded by the *Pléiade* (Pleiades*) especially Ronsard* and Du Bellay. The influence here, however, was not so deep, and it is the minor writers that show it most.

French influence in 18th C was strong and profound: this was the age of classicism (the English Augustan* age) with its emphasis on clarity, elegance, wit and shapeliness. The poets were critics, even in their poetry, and Pope* and Johnson*, like Dryden* in the later 17th C, though men of thoroughly independent mind, took the canons of the 17th-C French critics – especially Boileau* and Rapin – as their starting-point. The Romantics* of early 19th C, owed something to the Germans but little to the French. Later in 19th C the Pre-Raphaelites* and the aesthetes* admired the French symbolists*, their contemporaries, without really understanding them; it was left to the two great 20th-C masters, W. B. Yeats* and even more T. S. Eliot*, to turn back to the French 19th C of Baudelaire, Mallarmé, Verlaine, and lesser figures, and find in them guidance for radical renewal of the English poetic movement.

[2] *Drama.* The Shakespearian age of English drama was unaffected by French influence, but the great French period of 17th C – the age of Corneille*, Racine* and Molière* – affected the lesser drama of the Restoration* period profoundly. English heroic drama (*eg* Dryden's) does not compare with that of Corneille and Racine; the English comedy of manners* (especially Congreve's*) is much better, but still inferior to Molière. On the whole it is in drama that the French mind has had least to say to the English, and here that the differences of national genius appear most clearly.

[3] *The novel.* The English novel developed in 18th C and for three-quarters of 19th C on independent principles; if there is a French influence, it is scarcely a contemporary one, but rather the effect of a 16th-C Frenchman, Rabelais*, on an 18th-C English novelist such as Sterne*. Late in 19th C, however, the Anglo-American novelist, Henry James*, studied the French novelists of 19th C – Balzac, Flaubert*, Zola* – and brought what they had to show of difference in range and formal treatment to bear on the English novel, which, till then, had received no systematic criticism. In consequence the masters of the English novel in the late 19th and early 20th C – James, Conrad*, Bennett*, Joyce* – all write with constant awareness of French formal technique and boldness in subject; the French novelist Proust in 20th C has made as strong an impression with his dense, close and subtle subjectivism.

French influence on all branches of English literary art has had a broadening, renewing, and disciplining effect on form; yet it has been largely absent in some of the phases of greatest English achievement: the drama of the Shakespearian age, the output of the Metaphysical* poets from 1590 to 1640, that of the Romantic poets from 1790 to 1830, and the Victorian* novel of the Dickens* age. But to consider only periods and literary forms is to limit the area of French influence. That of individual writers on thought, outlook, and feeling can only be indicated in separate entries: *see* Boileau; Descartes; Encyclopaedists; Montaigne; Pascal; Rousseau; Voltaire.

France and Britain: Politics

From 1066 until the time of writing relations have been close and complicated; for a simplified account it is convenient to divide them into phases:

[1] *1066–1327. Norman-French domination of England.* At the time of the Conquest*, France, though it had a king, lacked political unity. The provinces were effectively self-governing. William Duke of Normandy was, like his aristocracy, of Norse descent, though French-speaking and French in culture. The rule of the Norman* kings (1066–1154), and of the Angevin kings (Plantagenets*) until 14th C, was the rule of a French-cultured royalty through a French-cultured aristocracy. The language of the ruling class was French, and the kings of England ruled parts of France. Scotland was independent throughout, and Wales until its conquest in 1284.

[2] *1337–1453. Hundred Years' War**. The aristocracy came to think of itself as English, and was English-speaking. The wars were no longer merely rivalries between branches of a great feudal system but to some extent national contests, in which the peoples as well as the ruling classes were involved. France gradually ceased to be a merely geographical expression; it was indeed the English attempts at conquest that shaped it into a society with strong national feeling. Scotland was throughout an ally of France against England.

[3] *1453–1660. Disengagement and National Growth.* 'Disengagement' is a misleading term if the countries are thought of as having no close relationships; on the contrary, diplomatic dealings were always close, and there were short, sporadic wars. But English kings no longer ruled parts of France, except the town of Calais*, itself lost in 1558. France grew into a much larger and more powerful state than England, and, but for their greater common fear of Spain from 1500 to 1660, England itself would have been on the defensive against French ambitions. Scotland remained an

ally of France until the reign of Elizabeth I*, when there was a sudden reversal of alliances for religious reasons. (In 1603 Scotland and England were united under the same king.)

[4] *1660–1714. Resistance to Louis XIV of France.* French power was at its height. Charles II* of England restricted himself to an intricate game of diplomacy, now for, now against, the French, but the reigns of William III* and Anne (from 1689 to 1714) saw two great defensive wars in alliance with the Dutch against the expansionism of Louis XIV. This was the period of the great English general, John Churchill, Duke of Marlborough*.

[5] *1714–89. Rivalry in India and America.* Until 1743 there was peace. Then came the War of the Austrian Succession (1743–48) and the Seven Years War* (1756–63), the second of which was the more important. No longer so afraid of France as a direct danger, England sought to contain her enemy on the continent of Europe, and to defeat her as a competitor overseas. English command of sea-power now became all-important. In revenge, the French gave help to the American rebels in the War of Independence, 1775–83.

[6] *1793–1815. Wars of the French Revolution* and Napoleon*.* This was the bitterest contest of all. Again English sea-power was decisive. The English heroes were the admiral Nelson* (Battle of Trafalgar 1805) and the Anglo-Irish general, the Duke of Wellington* (Waterloo 1815).

[7] *1815–. Period of Alliances with France.* Relations have not always been good, but three wars have been fought with, instead of against, the French: Crimean War against Russia (1854–56), and two against Germany (1914–18; 1939–45).

Franchise

Normally understood as the right to vote for a representative in Parliament. From the reign of Edward I* when representatives of the commons* were first summoned to Parliament, until 1832, this right was possessed by landowners whose land was worth at least 40 shillings a year, and by the citizens of certain towns (parliamentary boroughs) in which the qualifications varied. The first Parliamentary Reform Bill of 1832 arranged a property qualification which enfranchised the middle classes uniformly throughout Britain. The Reform Bill of 1867 enfranchised the working classes of the towns, and the third, in 1884, extended the franchise to include men of all classes everywhere. In 1918 women were enfranchised on reaching the age of 30, and in 1928 they were accorded the vote, like men, at 21. The franchise today is said to be 'universal', *ie* it excludes only minors (*ie* people under 18), certified lunatics, criminals serving a sentence, or Peers of the Realm (*ie* holders of titles of nobility and Bishops, who are entitled to sit in the House of Lords).

* *Parliament; Reform Bills, Parliamentary.*

Franciscans

Members of an order of friars* founded by St Francis of Assisi in 1209. He was the son of a rich merchant of Assisi who vowed himself to a life of poverty, preaching, and service to the poor, and formed a body of companions who renounced their property. The movement so started spread rapidly through Europe, including England, where the order was known as the Grey Friars from the colour of their dress. In common with other religious orders, it was dissolved in England by Henry VIII*.

Frankenstein, or the Modern Prometheus (1818)

A philosophical romance which is also a tale of terror, by Mary Shelley, wife of the poet P. B. Shelley*. It belongs in part to the 'gothic' tradition of tales of terror popular at the time, and partly to a philosophical tradition going back to Rousseau*, concerned with themes of isolation, suffering, and social injustice. Mary Shelley originally wrote it to compete with the tales of terror being composed for their own amusement by her husband and their friend, the poet Lord Byron*. Frankenstein is a Swiss student of natural philosophy who constructs a monster and endows it with life. Its impulses are benevolent, but it is everywhere regarded with loathing and fear; its benevolence turns to hatred, and it destroys its creator and his bride. The view of man and society is in several ways typical of Shelley and his circle, and reflects the opinions of Mary's father, the philosopher William Godwin*.

* *Gothic Novels.*

Franklin's Tale, The

One of the verse tales in Chaucer's *Canterbury Tales**. A franklin was a freeholder, not a nobleman, but sometimes prosperous (like Chaucer's example) and not far in status from what by 18th C would be called a country squire*. He is thus midway in the social scale of Chaucer's pilgrims, and is represented as a man who enjoys life, is hospitable, fulfils social responsibilities, and has right values. Suitably, his tale is one of the most humane of the series. Dorigen laments the absence of her beloved husband Arveragus, and at the same time is courted by an ardent lover, Aurelius. To get rid of him, she promises to give herself if he can rid the coast of Brittany of the rocks which may shipwreck her returning husband. Aurelius finds a magician who, for a price, consents to perform the miracle, and Dorigen confesses to her husband the fearful dilemma which then faces her. Though sorrowful, he declares that she must keep her promise, but Aurelius is so touched by the good faith of Dorigen and Arveragus that he releases her of the bond, and in turn the magician releases him of the debt. The Franklin says that the story derives from an old British poem; similar stories are found in Boccaccio's *Filocolo* and *Decameron*.

Frazer, Sir James G. (1854–1941)

Anthropologist. His *Golden Bough* (1890–1915) is a vast study of ancient mythology; it has influenced 20th-C poetry such as T. S. Eliot's *Waste Land**. An abridged edition was published in 1922. Other publications include *Totemism* (1887); *Adonis, Attis, Osiris, Studies in the History of Oriental Religion* (1906); *Totemism and Exogamy* (1910); *Folklore in the Old Testament* (1918).

Free Trade

Nowadays the term is understood to mean trade between nations without restrictions either in the form of the prohibition of certain commodities or in duties (taxes) on their importation. The view that trade should be so conducted was expressed most influentially in Adam Smith's* *Wealth of Nations* (1776). In 19th C free trade particularly suited English industrialists, and it became a leading issue between the Whigs* who represented industrial interests and the Tories who wished to protect agricultural ones. The repeal of the Corn Laws*, which had imposed taxes on imported corn, was a decisive victory for the free-traders, though the policy of governments has always fluctuated, and trade has never been entirely free.

In early 17th C the term was used for trade unrestricted by the monopolies granted (for a price) by the Crown to certain individuals. In 18th C the term was a euphemism for smuggling.

Free Verse

A way of writing poetry without use of rhyme, stanza pattern, or metre. Free verse perhaps had French origins; at all events it is often referred to as vers libre. It was practised, especially in the first thirty years of this century, in an attempt to escape from the rather mechanical uses of rhyme and metre by the late romantics*. T. S. Eliot* attacked the whole concept of free verse, declaring that it could only be defined by negatives (*no* rhyme, etc.) and that a genuine form would have a positive definition (*Reflections on Vers Libre*, 1917); 'But the most interesting verse which has yet been written in our language has been done either by taking a very simple form, like the iambic pentameter, and constantly withdrawing from it, or taking no form at all, and constantly approximating to a very simple one.' Eliot himself was as bold as any of his contemporaries in rhythmic experimentation, but his methods are clearly one or other of the two which he here describes. These methods, however, do not seem to be those of D. H. Lawrence*, who is perhaps the most distinguished poet who wrote in (as he certainly thought) 'free verse'.

Freemasonry

An international society originating in England in 18th C and deriving from medieval guilds of building craftsmen. Some of its ritual is secret, and its purposes are obscure, but it is sometimes said to be influential owing to the distinction of its membership.

* *Craft Guilds.*

French Revolution (1789–94)

The immediate effect of the French Revolution was temporarily to abolish the French monarchy, to reduce for ever the rigid class divisions of French society, and to begin wars (lasting till 1815) which for the time being extensively altered the map of Europe. Its lasting effect was to inspire the European mind with the belief that change is historically inevitable and static order unnatural, and to imbue it with modern ideas of democracy, nationalism, and equality at least of opportunity.

The immediate effect on England was confusing, for many of the changes being brought about in France had already occurred here in 17th C, especially the establishment of the sovereignty of the elected representatives of the people in Parliament in 1688. Such changes had occurred here, however, without the same mental upheavals, partly because English society and politics had always been more fluid than in the other larger states of Europe, and though unjustified privileges and inequalities existed, there were few definable barriers to be overthrown. Politicians were divided between the Whigs* on the left who were neutral or sympathetic to the Revolution, and the Tories on the right who feared it from the start. Only when General Bonaparte took increasing charge of France and became Emperor Napoleon I* in 1804 did Britain become united in fear of French aggression. However, the great statesman and man of letters, Edmund Burke, published in 1790 his *Reflections on the Revolution in France**, one of the most eloquent documents of English political thinking, foretelling the disasters which the Revolution was to bring, and condemning it as ruthless surgery on the living organism of society. His opponent Tom Paine* answered him with *The Rights of Man* (1791), and the younger intellectuals agreed with Paine. Wordsworth* wrote later in *The Prelude** 'Bliss was it in that dawn to be alive', and William Blake* wore a revolutionary cockade in the streets; Southey* and Coleridge* planned the ideal communist society, Pantisocracy*; the philosophic novelist William Godwin* published *Political Justice* and *Caleb Williams* to prove that reason was the only guide to conduct and society needed by man. Later Wordsworth and Coleridge came round to a view closer to Burke's, and the younger generation, Byron* and Shelley*, saw them as traitors; the more so because the defeat of Napoleon at Waterloo introduced a phase of political and social repression everywhere. But the older generation (except perhaps Southey) did not so much go back on their earlier enthusiasms as think them out more deeply; the philosophical conservatism of the older Coleridge was as radical in its thinking as the Utilitarianism* of the philosophical radicals, Bentham* and the Mills*. In the 1840s the greatest conservative statesman of 19th C, Benjamin Disraeli*, was to show in his novels that conservatives could no more afford to rest on a static political philosophy than the radicals could.

* 1.4.3.

Freud, Sigmund (1856–1939) /froid/

Austrian scientist; inventor of psychoanalysis as a method of curing the mental diseases called neuroses. His discoveries were that the conscious mind is constantly subject to pressures from the unconscious mind, leading to the unconscious repression of disagreeable memories, and that the infant's attitude to its parents was affected by sexuality, causing daughters to be jealous of mothers, and sons of fathers. Freud clearly mapped what had hitherto only been intuitively guessed; the result was a new conception of the human personality which had extensive influence on imaginative literature.

Much behaviour which had formerly been thought rational was now seen as perhaps irrational in its motivations, and ideals which had been respected were now often suspected and found to be distorting and even perverting to the personality; sexuality assumed a larger importance, and much more of experience was found to be disguisedly sexual than had been supposed. Thus, firstly, novelists such as D. H. Lawrence* showed the integrating and disintegrating forces in the personality to be beyond the reach of the kind of depiction, on the social plane, which novelists had so far especially relied on. Secondly, it was realized that language could be used in new ways: to undermine the abstracting habits of the consciousness by presenting thought in continuous flow, in the 'stream of consciousness' technique of such novelists as James Joyce* and Virginia Woolf*; and to reach the unconscious layers of the mind by the dreamlike accumulation of meanings through images, as opposed to the logical progression of ideas. This became a way of using language which gave poetry a new kind of difficulty but also a new kind of concentration in, notably, the work of T. S. Eliot*. The use of imagery in prose and poetry acquired an even larger importance than it had had already, and it became more functional and less ornamental.

Not all this development is to be attributed merely to the influence of Freud; indeed, part of the interest of his work for writers was to see how imaginative writers had long before anticipated aspects of his thought, and he was himself only a manifestation of a larger movement of the European mind. Writers, however, found in him a confirmation and stimulus to the direction of their thought, to the extent that it is possible as a rule to distinguish writers of the post-Freudian age (roughly, from 1910) from their predecessors, by difference in treatment of subject matter.

* 3.5.

Frey, Freya

In Scandinavian myth, brother and sister deities: Frey was associated with fruitfulness, sunshine, rain; Freya, his sister, with love and night.

Friar

The friars were members of the mendicant orders of monasticism that originated in 13th C. Whereas monks lived in monasteries* which were corporate owners of property, friars were individually self-supporting either by their own labour or by begging – hence 'mendicant'. Friars answered important religious and social needs, since they were, unlike monks, free in their movements to go where they were most needed, working as poor men among the poor. Thus the orders spread rapidly throughout Europe after the deaths of their two main founders, St Dominic (d 1221), founder of the Dominicans*, and St Francis (d 1226), founder of the Franciscans*. These remained the dominant orders, though many others were introduced (some including both men and women) such as the Carmelites*, the Augustinian Hermits, and the Capuchins*.

Like other institutions, the friars tended to degenerate from their ideal. Just as the Monk in Chaucer's *Canterbury Tales** is a bad monk because he refuses to remain bound to his monastery, so the Friar is a bad friar, because as a 'limitor' or licensed beggar, he abuses his spiritual functions for money, and the friar in the *Summoner's Tale** is worse. The friars in Elizabethan plays, *eg* Friar Laurence in Shakespeare's *Romeo and Juliet**, are in general depicted from a distance, since England was by then a Protestant country with no friars; they represent 'wise men', often endowed with magical powers, and are not intended to be realistic.

* 2.1.1.1.

Friar Bacon and Friar Bungay

A romantic comedy by Robert Greene*, first acted in 1592. The title characters are based on historical figures: Franciscan* friars* of 13th C whom popular tradition had made into magicians; the play is based on a pamphlet of anecdotes about them. It has a double plot: one action concerns Bacon's manufacture of a brass head endowed (with the help of the devil) with power of speech, and the other is a pastoral* love-story about the rival loves of Prince Edward and Lord Lacy for Margaret, a village maiden. The play is Greene's best; his use of the double plot to present two aspects of a theme, and his treatment of romantic love, have relevance to the later development of Elizabethan* drama, including Shakespeare's.

* *Bacon, Roger.*

Friar's Tale, The

One of the comic verse tales in Chaucer's *Canterbury Tales**. The Friar uses his chance to mock the Summoner among the pilgrims, by describing how a summoner tries to extort money from a poor widow, and is carried off by the devil. The Summoner has his revenge by telling a tale against a friar. Both the narrators are shown by Chaucer to be as bad as the characters in the tales told against them.

* *Summoner's Tale, The.*

Froissart, Jean (1337?–1410)

A French chronicler whose vivid narrative of the Anglo-French wars of his time was translated into as vivid English prose by Lord Berners (1523–25).

Fuel

Fuel for heating in the Middle Ages was of course chiefly wood, though in some districts peat was used, but coal was mined in the north of England and brought from Newcastle to London by sea; hence it was called 'sea-coal'. It was used increasingly in 16th-C London owing to shortage of wood. The great increase of chimneys in Elizabethan houses was largely due to the need to carry away the disagreeable fumes from coal. In both England and Scotland the condition of coal-miners was wretched and humiliating. Conditions became in many ways worse in 18th C when deep mining became possible after the steam-pump was in-

vented (1712) to clear mines of water. Women and children were employed for hauling underground; it was not until the Mines Act of 1842 that this was forbidden. By this time, danger from explosions was greatly reduced by the invention of the safety-lamp by Sir Humphry Davy (1778–1829).

In transport, the revolutionary change was brought about by George Stephenson's invention of the steam locomotive in 1814. Railways spread rapidly over the country during the next twenty years. In literature, Charles Dickens's *Dombey and Son** gives an excellent impression of the impact on contemporary imagination.

* *Industrial Revolution.*

Funds, The; The Funded Debt; Fund-holders

From the reign of William III* the government sought to finance its wars by borrowing from private investors, issuing 'bonds' ('debentures') in acknowledgement of the loan, and paying regular interest. This is the National Debt*. It became the commonest investment for small investors, and was the source of many 'private incomes' in 19th C.

* *Bank of England.*

Furies, The

In Greek and Roman myth, the goddesses who pursued and punished evil-doers. The Romans called them *Furiae*; the Greeks *Erinyes* or, in propitiation, *Eumenides* (= the Friendly Ones). T. S. Eliot* uses them in his play *Family Reunion* (1939); they are the objectifications of the hero's mysterious but overpowering sense of guilt. When he discovers the causes of this guilt in his family history, and is able to accept its burden, his 'furies' become 'friendly'.

Furnishings and Furniture

1300–1600. Furniture was sparse and heavy: benches were the principal seating; chairs at first were few, and marks of rank. The commonest light furniture was the backless 'joint-stool', *ie* one put together by a carpenter or joiner. Heavy chests were used for books and clothes, and sometimes adapted for seating as 'settles'. Tables before 1500 were boards set on trestles, easily movable. Floor-coverings were commonly of rushes, not often changed. Walls were painted, or had painted cloth hangings, but by 16th C richer households used embroidered and woven hangings, and these also surrounded the great 'four poster' beds which were also used by the middle classes in 16th C. 'Court-cupboards' were used to store plate (not clothes) and heavy 'buffets' or sideboards were used by the rich for display of dishes and goblets of gold and silver. Cushions were widely used in 16th C. Display rather than comfort was the objective in all classes that could afford it; the poor were restricted to necessities: straw-stuffed sacks on benches or the earth floor for beds, and perhaps a trestle-table and a few stools.

1600–1800. These two centuries saw a steady advance towards modern standards of comfort. Carpets, formerly used, if at all, as wall-hangings or table coverings, found their way to the floor; walls were panelled in wood; chairs became plentiful in the second half of 17th C, and 18th was the great age of English furniture design: furniture of all kinds became light, graceful, adapted to the comfort of the users. Looking-glasses, still uncommon at the beginning of 17th C, were usual at the end of it. Wallpapers – known since 16th C – came into general use in 18th. Even the poor came by then to have the simplest comforts, including 'cottage' versions of the great 18th-C furniture designs – Chippendale*, Hepplewhite, Sheraton*.

After about 1830, 19th C saw the spreading of comfort amongst all classes in some degree – with the exception of the poorest agricultural labourers and the overcrowded slum-dwellers of the towns. Comfort rather than display was now the objective; or rather, a display of ornate comfort. Furniture became elaborate and much upholstered; window-curtains were heavy. Only beds became more rational, the four-poster going out of use as houses became better heated by more plentiful coal.

* **2.2.1.**

G

Gabriel

Archangel; the heavenly messenger, in the Bible sent to Daniel* to explain a vision (*Daniel* 8:16) and to foretell the births of John the Baptist and of Christ (*Luke* 1:19, 26).

* *Angel.*

Gadarene Swine, The Miracle of the

In the Bible (*Mark* 5:1–17), the demons who possessed the maniac were cast out by Christ but allowed to enter a herd of swine; these forthwith plunged into the sea.

Gael, Gaelic /geil/

The Scottish highland branch of the Celtic race (**Celts*), and its language. The words are sometimes used for the Scottish and Irish Celts together.

Galahad, Sir

In Malory's version of the Arthurian legend, *Morte D'Arthur**, Sir Galahad is the son of Lancelot*, and the knight whose perfect virtue enables him to succeed in the quest for the Holy Grail.

* *Arthur, King; Gawain; Grail, The Holy.*

Galatea /galəˈtiə/

In Greek myth, a sea nymph who loved the shepherd Acis, and was beloved by the Cyclops Polyphemus*. Polyphemus crushed Acis with a rock, and Galatea changed him into a river at the foot of Mount Etna in Sicily.

A different Galatea was the statue given life for Pygmalion*.

Galen (Claudius Galenus) (2nd C AD) /ˈgeilin/

Greek medical scientist; one of the most important anatomists and physiologists of the ancient world.

Galileo Galilei (1564–1642)

Italian astronomer; he was able, by improving the newly invented telescope, to confirm the theory of Copernicus* that the earth revolves round the sun, contrary to the theory of Ptolemy* that the earth is the centre of the solar system. The observation was made in 1610; in 1611 the English poet John Donne* wrote the *Anatomy of the World*;

And new Philosophy calls all in doubt,
The Element of fire is quite put out;
The Sun is lost, and th'earth, and no man's wit
Can well direct him where to look for it.

In fact the Church was disturbed at the implications of Galileo's discovery in regard to acceptance of the Holy Scriptures, and declared it a heresy. Nonetheless Galileo's view became slowly accepted. Milton, in his epic of the Creation of the World, *Paradise Lost**, uses the Ptolemaic theory, though he had met Galileo and alludes to him in the poem ('the Tuscan Artist' of Bk. I, lines 288–91); this, however, was for poetic convenience, and the discrepancy between Ptolemy and Copernicus did not affect the spiritual truths that Milton was concerned to inculcate.

Galsworthy, John (1867–1933) /ˈgoːlzwəːði/

Novelist and dramatist. As a novelist, his reputation was high in the first quarter of this century for his surveys of upper class English life, especially the *Forsyte Saga** sequence (1906–21) and *A Modern Comedy* (*The White Monkey*, 1924; *The Silver Spoon*, 1926; *Swan Song*, 1928). After World War I, Galsworthy underwent severe criticism by novelists of the new generation as different as Virginia Woolf* ('Modern Fiction' in *The Common Reader*, 1925) and D. H. Lawrence* ('John Galsworthy', 1927, in *Phoenix*). These novelist-critics were writing in a period of rich experiment in rendering the inwardness of human experience and in testing and renewing humane values in the social context; to them, Galsworthy was artistically an obstructive conservative, severely limited to a vision of the outside of social phenomena and to a merely social definition of human beings. From such attacks, Galsworthy's reputation has never recovered among the intelligentsia; however, the popularity of a televised serial version of the *Forsyte Saga* in 1967 suggests that he may still be favoured by at least the older generation of the general public. Other novels: *Jocelyn* (1898); *The Country House* (1907); *Fraternity* (1909); *The Patrician* (1911); *The Freelands* (1915); *Maid in Waiting* (1931); *Flowering Wilderness* (1932).

As a dramatist, Galsworthy was one of those in the first decade of the century who restored to the English theatre a substantiality of subject-matter which had long been missing from it. His plays dramatized ethical problems arising from social issues. These too, however, have lost prestige, partly because of weaknesses similar to those that his novels are supposed to suffer from. Another ground of criticism of the plays is that he brought to the theatre a novelist's vision rather than a dramatist's: during the last 40 years, British dramatists have believed that the drama requires an approach to the depiction of character and to the use of dialogue which is different to the vision of the novelist. Plays: *The Silver Box* (1906); *Joy* (1907); *Strife* (1909); *Justice* (1910); *The Pigeon* (1912); *The Eldest Son* (1912); *The Fugitive* (1913); *The Skin Game* (1920); *Loyalties* (1922); *The Forest* (1924).

* 4.5.2.

Bib: Marrott, H. W., *Life*; Parker, D., *Galsworthy*; Barker, D., *The Man of Principle.*

Galt, John (1779–1839)

Scottish writer of poems, travels, dramas and novels. He is chiefly remembered for his novels, especially *The Ayrshire Legatees* (1821), *Annals of the Parish*

(1821), *The Provost* (1822), and *The Entail* (1823). These are vivid, realistic, humorous accounts of Scottish provincial society.

Bib: Gordon, R. K., *John Galt;* Aberdein, J. W., *John Galt;* Parker, W. M., *Susan Ferrier and John Galt* (British Council).

Gambling (Gaming)

A favourite English pastime since the Middle Ages. The use of dice ('hazard') goes back to pre-Christian times. Playing cards were introduced in 15th C, and were early used for gambling by all classes in the towns. In the reign of Elizabeth I* gambling-houses (gaming-houses) had to be licensed by the Crown, and such licences were granted to courtiers. By 18th C, upper class society gambled extensively, and for high 'stakes' (sums of money to be lost or won). The London Clubs* were gambling rooms for men, and fashionable resorts such as Bath* and Tunbridge Wells used their assembly rooms primarily for gambling and dancing. The 18th-C Lord Sandwich is supposed to have invented 'sandwiches' so that he would not need to get up from the gaming-table for a meal. The dramatist Sheridan* ruined his finances by his heavy gambling.

Sport, especially horse-racing, has always had gambling as one of its main attractions; horse-races have appealed to rich and poor gamblers since the reign of Charles II* who first made them fashionable. Fights of all kinds – between cocks, dogs, or men – have always been used as pretexts for gambling. Among team games, cricket was such a pretext in 18th C, and in 20th C the most popular of all forms of gambling is conducted through 'football pools'.

The English have always been prepared to use any doubtful issue as an excuse for gambling; in 15th C appeals to the Pope by rival parties of churchmen, especially if these were composed of friars* and of parish priests, were gambling occasions. But the most serious of all forms of gambling has been the kind known as 'financial speculation', and is a product of the capitalist economic system. Already early in 17th C, adventurers known as 'projectors' were raising loans for investment in more or less illusory enterprises by encouraging the gambling spirit in country gentlemen; they and their foolish clients, known as 'gulls', were a common subject of Jacobean* comedies such as Ben Jonson's *The Alchemist** and *The Devil is an Ass**. Just over a hundred years later gambling speculations caused the major financial crisis known as the South Sea Bubble*, which brought Robert Walpole* to power as the 'first Prime Minister'. Debtors' prisons such as the Marshalsea* (the scene of much of Dickens's novel *Little Dorrit**) were filled with rash speculators until imprisonment for debt was abolished in mid-19th C.

In present-day Britain, gambling is as widespread as ever. The very popular gambling game of 'bingo' has led to the establishment of bingo clubs in nearly every town; these, and the widespread practice of gambling on football matches ('football pools') attract small gamblers in very large numbers, so that occasionally large sums of money are won though only small ones are lost. Speculating in shares (gambling on the Stock Exchange*) is now discouraged by heavy taxation, but the government profits from the national gambling instinct by the institution of Premium Bonds, which are similar to state lotteries in other countries. Legal restrictions on the transaction of ordinary bets have been relaxed, so that 'betting shops' are common in the towns of Britain. Whereas in 19th C gambling was either the fashionable activity of the rich, or the disgraceful one of the disreputable poor, it is now, in some of its forms, regarded as a legitimate pastime even for the respectable middle classes.

Game Laws

'Game' means animals suitable for hunting and protected in the breeding season to ensure that supplies should not fail. Such animals in England have been hares, foxes and deer. Other animals such as rats and rabbits are 'vermin' and may be killed at any time. Certain birds, especially pheasants and partridges, are 'game birds'. Game of all sorts on private estates and in royal forests was protected at all times by severe Game Laws from depredations by poachers, so that the owner of the land should enjoy the monopoly of hunting the game on his own land. As the magistrates* who enforced the laws were themselves the landowners who had secured their imposition in Parliament, there was until 19th C a fierce warfare between the landlords with their gamekeepers on the one side, and the poor who needed the game for food on the other; no part of the English penal system was so disproportionately severe.

Gamelyn, The Tale of /ˈgamilin/

An anonymous verse romance, about 1350. Gamelyn is the youngest of three brothers, and is robbed of his property and maltreated by his eldest brother. He takes to the forest and leads the life of an outlaw. He overthrows the forces of the law which side with his unjust brother, and himself becomes Chief Justice of the Free Forest. The tale has affinities with the Robin Hood* cycle of legends. It was used by Thomas Lodge* for his prose romance *Rosalynde* (1590), which Shakespeare used as his material for his comedy *As You Like It**. Chaucer intended to use it for his *Cook's Tale* (*Canterbury Tales**) of which he wrote only a small fragment.

Gammer Gurton's Needle

A slight but very lively verse comedy of uncertain authorship, first acted in 1566, and printed in 1575. Gammer = old woman. She loses her needle, which she had been using to mend her man's breeches. The whole village is upset, until the needle is found in the seat of the breeches.

Gamp, Sarah

A drunken nurse in Dickens's novel *Martin Chuzzlewit**. She always carried an umbrella, and her name 'gamp' has therefore come to mean umbrella in colloquial usage.

Ganymede /ˈganimi:d/

In Greek myth, a beautiful youth who was carried up to heaven on the back of an eagle and became cup-bearer to the gods.

In Shakespeare's *As You Like It**, Rosalind takes the name when she dresses as a boy to go to the Forest of Arden.

Garden

In the Middle Ages, the peasant kept his cottage garden for food, growing cabbages, beans, peas, onion, and garlic. Gardens also existed in the towns, and in 13th C were extensive in the suburbs. Monasteries* had larger gardens, mainly for use rather than ornament, and they included 'stew-ponds' with stocks of fish. By 15th C the upper classes were cultivating gardens in a more ornamental style, but it was in later 16th C that the real enthusiasm for gardening began. Bacon's* essay *Of Gardens* (1625) is the best known of many literary manifestations of it.

The gardens of the period were formal, with straight alleys; plentiful use was made of hedges of box and yew, for dividing flower-beds into ornamental geometrical shapes ('knot-gardens') for flanking alleys, for making 'mazes' such as the one which survives at Hampton Court*, for arbours (sheltered places) in which seats could be placed, and for the topiary work (cutting hedges and bushes into the shapes of birds, people, etc.) that Bacon despised. Utility was not ignored by rich gardeners, and their travel overseas made it possible for them to import new vegetables, such as the potato and the beetroot; these, however, were not cultivated as large crops until much later. Herbs such as marjoram, thyme, rosemary and others were valued both for adding savour to food and medicinally – as the Friar explains in Shakespeare's *Romeo and Juliet** II. ii. Rhubarb was also commonly used medicinally. Orchards were important; apples, pears, apricots, almonds, peaches, figs, cherries and currants were all cultivated. Botany and horticulture were studied enthusiastically.

The enthusiasm for gardening, especially during the period 1550–1650, coincided with widespread interest in the literary modes of pastoral*. In these, the garden is commonly used as an emblem for the innocence and freedom of unspoilt nature, in contrast to the corruption and anxiety of life in the towns and at court. Two traditions combined in the literary pastoral: the Bible-nourished Puritans* recalled the bliss of the original Garden of Eden* before the Fall of Man; and poet-scholars like Spenser (the Garden of Adonis in *The Faerie Queene** iii. 6) recalled the golden ages of Greek and Latin pastoral myth. Shakespeare uses a garden as an emblem of society in *Richard II** III. iv, and as an emblem of innocence in *The Winter's Tale*, IV. iii. Andrew Marvell* wrote several of his best poems on gardens as emblems of innocent and lavish happiness; the most famous of these is *The Garden* (about 1650).

The later 17th and the 18th C were periods in which comfort and elegance became important civilized values: buildings, to provide shelter from the unreliable British weather, began to ornament the grander gardens; orangeries, for instance, containing orange trees in tubs and galleries for sauntering out of the rain, were introduced in the reign of William III*. After 1725, gardens became means of escape from the formality of 18th-C civilization, and the old formal garden went out of fashion. Large gardens were designed increasingly with eyes that appreciated the wildness of 'picturesque'* landscape, a taste formed partly by 17th-C Italian and French landscape painters such as Salvator Rosa and Claude. Thus gardens became to some extent imitations of pictures; if the landscape were not wild enough, dead trees might be planted, *eg* in Kensington Gardens, London. Imitation Greek temples, such as occur in Claude's pictures, were erected at suitable viewpoints, for instance on an island in a probably artificially created lake. The poet Pope* was fond of carefully constructed caves ('grottos'). Later in the century, the taste for these architectural ornaments called 'follies' became more exotic: Chinese pagodas were built, and imitation ruins of medieval Gothic castles were very common.

The 18th-C taste for 'wild' gardens was closely related to the literature of the period; it was indeed stimulated by James Thomson's landscape poems the *Seasons**. Later 18th-C poets, such as Collins*, Cowper*, Gray* and others, wrote landscape poetry; much of it gives the impression of the poet enjoying a landscape from a distance, or from a sheltered spot, as the landed gentry enjoyed their landscape gardens from their drawing-room windows. Designers of landscape gardens became artists with great prestige. The poet William Shenstone (1714–63) devoted his life and his fortune mainly to the landscaping of his property Leasowes. The most famous designer was Lancelot Brown ('Capability' Brown, 1715–83), who refused to allow any merely useful building, such as stables, to remain in sight of the house. But comfort, if not convenience, was maintained: 18th- and early 19th-C novels frequently mention 'shrubberies' – picturesque, sheltered walks, where the ladies could walk out of the weather. At the very end of the century, the books on landscape gardening and on the picturesque in landscape by Repton were widely read, and coincided with the rise of the English school of landscape painters such as Cotman and Crome. Though the novelist Jane Austen* described surroundings very little, references to the taste for landscape recur in her books, and the whole fashion for landscape-gardening is satirized in Peacock's witty discussion novel, *Headlong Hall**.

After 1830, the taste for landscape gardening on the grand, artificial scale of 18th C declined. The most interesting development in the history of gardens in 19th C is the extension of the possession of them to all ranks of society; even the poor in the dense centres of the smoke-blackened towns commonly had 'allotments' provided for them at low rents in the suburbs. For Dickens*, the suburban cottage with its flowery bower or arbour becomes a setting for a new kind of pastoralism. Among the rich, the chief new feature was the large glass 'conservatory' for the cultivation of exotic plants; even these were adopted among the poor in the shape of the modest 'greenhouse'.

Public gardens and places of pleasure came in after the Restoration*, and allusions to such places, *eg* Vauxhall*, are common in 17th- and 18th-C literature.

Garden of Cyrus, The (1658)

A treatise on the quincunx, or shapes and patterns composed of five parts, by Sir Thomas Browne*. The essay is an example of Browne's delight in the pursuit of a theme through all its possible applications, in the manner of the contemporary Metaphysical poets*. It is written in Browne's characteristically relaxed and musical prose, and is less solemn than *Urn Burial** which was published together with it.

Gargantua /gaːˈgantjuə/

Chiefly known as the hero of François Rabelais'* romances *Gargantua* and *Pantagruel*, though he had a previous existence in French folklore connected with the Arthurian legends. He is mentioned in Shakespeare's *As You Like It** II.ii before Rabelais had been translated into English (1653), though Shakespeare may have read Rabelais in French. He is a giant with immense physical appetites and proportionately generous virtues. He is a product of the liberating forces of the Renaissance* spirit.

Garrick, David (1717–79)

Actor. His genius for acting combined with his great culture greatly enhanced the theatrical profession in social prestige. He was a leading member of Dr Johnson's* circle. He was manager of one of the three great London theatres, Drury Lane*, where he produced Shakespeare and acted in his plays frequently. He was himself a playwright, and *The Clandestine Marriage* (with Colman, – 1766) has been revived successfully.

* *Acting, The Profession of.*

Garter, The Order of the

An order of knighthood* instituted by Edward III* about 1344. The order was in imitation of the legendary one established by King Arthur*, and Edward III built the great round tower of Windsor Castle* as its meeting-place, relying on the authority of the French chronicler Froissart* that this was the spot on which King Arthur had had his palace, and the Round Table for his knights. The award of knighthood of the Garter is still one of the greatest honours in Britain, and its members are restricted in number.

Gascoigne, George (1525–77) /ˈgaskoin/

Elizabethan man of letters. He was one of the first of the gentry to use literature to help him in his career; though not outstanding as a writer he showed talent as an innovator. *Supposes* (1566) is the earliest surviving English comedy in prose, and his *Jocasta* (1575) the second earliest tragedy in blank verse*, unique in its time because derived from a Greek tragedy (by Euripides through the Italian) instead of a Roman one. He published at the same time *Certain Notes of Instruction concerning the making of verse*, the earliest English critical essay. His *Hundred Sundrie Flowers* (1573), a miscellany, contains *The Adventures of Master F. J.*, a story which anticipates 18th C in its realism. In lyric verse he was one of the few noteworthy successors to Wyatt* before Spenser* and Sidney*. His *Steel Glass* has sometimes been called the earliest English satire.

Bib: Prouty, C. T., *Life*.

Gaskell, Elizabeth Cleghorn (1810–65) /ˈgaskel/

Novelist and biographer. Her father and her husband were Unitarian* ministers. She spent her married life in Manchester. She and her husband first intended to write the annals of the Manchester poor, in the manner of George Crabbe*, and her first novel, *Mary Barton** (1848), presented the outlook of the industrial workers with justice and sympathy sufficient to anger some of the employers. The novel appealed to Dickens*, and she published her best known work *Cranford** (1851–3) in his periodical, *Household Words**. *Cranford* has been compared with the work of Jane Austen*; it is slighter, but has some of Jane Austen's ability to endow smallness of circumstance with large implications. It is a study of a small circle in a small town, modelled on Knutsford, Cheshire. *Ruth* (1853) is based on the same place. *North and South** (1855) is another study of industrial relations, centred this time on a south English heroine who comes to the north as to a foreign country. *Sylvia's Lovers* (1863) is more romantic than her previous work; in the same year appeared *A Dark Night's Work; Cousin Phyllis and other Tales*. Her masterpiece, *Wives and Daughters**, was not quite completed at her death. It belongs to the *Cranford* strain in her work, but has greater richness, substance, and variety. Her novels are an interesting connecting link between those of Jane Austen* and those of George Eliot*. She lacks the greatness of either, and her reputation has unfairly suffered by comparison with them, but her achievement is substantial and enduring.

Her biography* of her friend Charlotte Brontë*, published in 1857, is accounted one of the best in English.

* 4.4.3.

Bib: Hopkins, A. B., *Life*; Cecil, D., *Early Victorian Novelists*; Haldane, E., *Mrs Gaskell and her Friends*; Tillotson, K. (on *Mary Barton*) in *Novels of the Eighteen-Forties*.

Gawain /ˈgaːwein/

In Arthurian legend, nephew of King Arthur*. In the oldest tradition, he was most eminent of the Knights of the Round Table*, and hero of the quest for the Grail*. In later forms (notably Malory's *Morte D'Arthur**) he is often shown to be treacherous and mean, apparently owing to misunderstanding of some of his attributes in the old versions. His mysterious characteristic of increasing in strength till midday and thereafter declining may relate him to the sun and be derived from the pagan origins of the myth. As hero he is excelled in turn by Perceval*, Lancelot*, and Galahad*.

Gawain and the Green Knight, Sir

An anonymous narrative poem of 14th C, and one of the greatest long poems in English. It consists of 2,500 lines of alliterative* verse in the dialect of the north-west midlands. The story tells the ancient myth of the 'head-cutting' challenge, originally connected with the Irish hero Cuchulain*. A mysterious Green Knight visits the Court of King Arthur* on New Year's Eve, and challenges any knight to strike off his head, and in return, to come to the Green Chapel next Christmas Eve and submit to similar execution. Gawain accepts the challenge, and the beheaded Green Knight rides out of the Hall. In his search for the Green Chapel, Gawain at length takes refuge in the castle of Sir Bercilak de Born. Sir Bercilak goes hunting on three successive days, and on the same days his lady comes to tempt Gawain's virtue as he rests in bed. The temptation is a test not merely of his chastity and loyalty to his host, but a test of his courtesy, since chivalry demands that he shall not offend the lady. On the fourth day Gawain departs for the Green Chapel, where he discovers that the Green Knight is Sir Bercilak in another form. As Gawain has survived the temptations, except for secretly having accepted a girdle from the lady, Sir Bercilak spares his life. The episode of the girdle has caused scholars to think that the poem is connected with the founding of the knightly Order of the Garter* by Edward III in 1344.

For the general reader, it is an account, superbly related, of a symbolic trial of the medieval courtly virtues: Gawain stands for civilization against barbarism, and he undergoes the double temptation of surrendering either to the weaknesses implicit in civilization, or to the brutishness of its opposite.

4.1.2.

Gay, John (1685–1732)

Poet. His verse is light and witty in a style well suited to the heroic couplet* and the poetic diction of the period. He is now most remembered for the *Beggar's Opera** (1728). His *Fables* (1727; 1738) were immensely popular at the time, but modern criticial opinion about them varies. His *Trivia, or the Art of Walking the Streets of London* (1716) is a minor classic. Gay is famous for the epitaph, composed by himself, on his tomb in Westminster Abbey*:

Life is a jest, and all things show it;
I thought so once, and now I know it.

Bib: Johnson, S., in *Lives of the Poets*; Irving, W. H., *Gay, Favourite of the Wits*; Sutherland, J., in *Pope and his Contemporaries*.

Ge (Gaea) /dʒiː/

In Greek myth, the Earth, sister and wife of Uranus* the Sky. Her children were the Titans*

Gehenna /giˈhenə/

In ancient Jewish myth, the underworld, place of torment for the dead. Originally, a valley near Jerusalem and centre of the worship of the god Molech (or Moloch*). King Josiah (*2 Kings* 23:10) abolished this worship, and the place became a refuse dump for dead animals and criminals. Fires were kept burning to prevent infection.

Gemini

* *Castor and Pollux.*

Geneva

City in Switzerland and a canton of the Swiss confederation. In 16th C it became famous as the centre of the most extreme of the great Protestant* reformers, John Calvin*, founder of Calvinism. It became the centre of the League of Nations (1919) and, since the replacement of the League by United Nations, has remained an important centre of international organizations like the Red Cross, which was founded there in 1864.

* *Presbyterianism.*

Genghis Khan (1162–1227) /ˈdʒiŋgis ˈkaːn/

One of the great Mongol conquerors; ruler of an empire extending from the Pacific to the Black Sea.

Gentleman

The French 'gentil homme' meant 'nobleman', man of aristocratic descent. The tradition of courtly love required, however, that a gentleman's behaviour should correspond to his birth, *eg* in Chaucer's* 14th-C translation of the *Roman de la Rose**: 'he is gentil bycause he doth as longeth to a gentylman'. By 15th C, a gentleman did not necessarily own land, and at no time in the Middle Ages was a coat of arms considered a necessary adjunct to the rank. By 16th C, however, the connection between the gentleman and the fighting man was established in the mind of society, and coats of arms, whose original function had been to distinguish a man for his followers and friends in battle, were regarded as indispensable. They could be obtained for money from the Heralds' College* (as Shakespeare's father obtained his in 1596), and as soldiering was not a profession for which there was much opportunity in a peaceful country, they were freely granted. English society was anyway very mixed, and the sons of long-established gentlemen became apprentices in the City. By 17th C the feeling that a gentleman was known by his behaviour more than by his birth was thus more firmly established, and James II* is said to have remarked that he could turn a man into a nobleman, but God Almighty could not turn him into a gentleman.

By 19th C the title was allowed to all men of the educated classes, though being occupied in trade was still regarded as a barrier; in this respect 19th C was perhaps less liberal than 16th, and though in theory it was behaviour that counted, appearances for most people counted still more, as is shown in Magwitch's notions of a gentleman in Dickens's novel *Great Expectations** Chap. 39. The public schools*, at least since 17th C had associated the idea of gentleman with education, especially a classical education in Greek and Latin literature; in 19th C the public schools were greatly increased in numbers, and the association of the rank of gentleman with a public school education persists to the present day.

Geoffrey of Monmouth (d 1154)

Chronicler. His *Historia Regum Britanniae* is one of the earliest written sources of the Arthurian legend, as well as a number of other important myths, for which later writers used him as a source book. Ultimately, Shakespeare owes to him the story of *King Lear**; from him, too, comes Ferrex and Porrex, the story of the earliest English tragedy, *Gorboduc**. He is the source of the myth that Britain was founded by Brut, descendant of Aeneas*. Most chroniclers between 1550 and 1650, including Holinshed*, Drayton* (*Poly-Olbion* 1613), and Milton* rely on him as an authority.

George

The name of six of the kings of England belonging to the Houses of Hanover and Windsor. George I (1714–27) was great-grandson of James I (1603–25) and ruler ('Elector') of the German principality of Hanover. He was invited to take the throne of Britain, thereby superseding the House of Stuart, because the surviving members of this family were Catholics. George II, 1727 – 60; George III, 1760–1820; George IV, 1820–30; George V, 1910–36; George VI, 1936–52.

* *Windsor, House of*

George, St

The patron saint of England. He is said to have been a native of Asia Minor under the Roman Empire, and to have been martyred as a Christian about AD 300. It is not clear how or why he killed a dragon. He is thought to have come to Britain under the Roman Emperor Diocletian, and to have protested against the persecution of Christians here. Edward III* made him patron of England, and his festival is 23 April.

Georgian Poetry

A series of verse anthologies of which five volumes appeared between 1912 and 1922. It was called 'Georgian' owing to the accession of George V (1910) and to imply a new start for English poetry, involving a degree of experiment and freshness of approach to the art. The poets represented in it included Rupert Brooke*, W. H. Davies, de la Mare*, D. H. Lawrence*, John Masefield*, and Robert Graves*. However, the contemporary work of W. B. Yeats*, Ezra Pound* and T. S. Eliot*, more original and more substantial than the work of the Georgian poets, quickly made their movement seem relatively unexciting. Since 1950 there has been some revival of interest in it. It was lyrical, colloquial, emancipated from some of the dead poetic convention left over from the decadent romanticism of the previous century, but it lacked the strength and boldness of thought which marked the work of Yeats, Eliot and Pound.

Georgian

A term for the architectural style of the period 1714–1810, under George I, II and III. Georgian architecture was severe but perfectly balanced in its proportions. It was influenced partly by the Palladian style of Inigo Jones* and partly by the direct experience of English travellers who made the Grand Tour of Italy and admired its classical buildings. The term is not usually applied to 18th C literature; in other arts its suggestion of elegance and proportion is often modified by a taste for satire and caricature, as in Hogarth's* paintings. It was followed by the Regency* style.

Georgics, The

A poem on agricultural life by the Latin poet Virgil*; it describes the peasant's year, and contrasts the virtues of life in natural surroundings with the burdensomeness of urban luxury. The poem was of great influence on the tradition of pastoral* poetry from 16th to 18th C.

German Influence on English Literature

The continuous influence of German upon English literature begins early in 19th C. There were, however, both general cultural influences and isolated influences from individual writers before this date. The general influences were predominantly religious and mythological. For example, Old English (Anglo-Saxon*) literature before the Norman* Conquest shared the background of ancient Germanic mythology common to all the northern countries in pre-Christian times, and still evident after the conversion of the Anglo-Saxons to Christianity in 7th C. Again, the great religious reformer Martin Luther* exerted an important influence on the English religious Reformation* in 16th C and, in particular, his translation of the Bible into German was an inspiration for the various English translations which culminated in the great Authorized Version of 1611. One of the most notable individual German writers to impress English thought was the philosophical theologian Jacob Boehme* – often called 'Behmen' in English – whose works were translated between 1644 and 1662. Religious societies called 'Behmenist' grew up in England and America, and his highly individual thinking was on lines which were especially congenial to the English poet William Blake*. A very different writer, J. J. C. von Grimmelshausen, author of the picaresque novel *Simplizissimus* (1669), influenced the 18th-C writers, Henry Fielding* and Tobias Smollett*.

The great age of German literature came comparatively late, in 18th and 19th C, and thus it was not until 19th C that German influence became a sustained one. Another factor which conditioned the influence of German writing upon English writing is the radical difference between the historical experience of the two nations. English history has been typically insular: protected from foreign interference by the sea, England has been able to develop its culture consistently since 11th C with relatively few drastic crises. The English mind has in consequence tended to become empirical, relying on its practical powers to adapt itself to change, and mistrusting theories and ideologies in the fear that extreme and highly systematized ideas are not likely to stand the test of application to changing circumstances. German history, on the contrary, has been typically continental: Germany was kept in fragments under the Holy Roman Empire*, and constantly suffered from conflicts among the states that constituted it; its immense land frontiers, moreover, lacked definition and were subjected to invasion. In 17th and early 18th C, Germany was dominated by the monolithic culture of France, so that it was not until the second half of 18th C that the Germans found sufficient strength (centred on the growing power of Prussia) to form coherent ideas of a culture of their own. This culture had then to be forged by radical thinking in order to undermine the firmly established French orthodoxy. Thus the German experience seemed to the English to be that of a culture in crisis, and it has appealed to the English especially whenever they have felt themselves to be in crisis.

So, for example, 18th-C Germany learnt new insights, unavailable to the English of his time, through the critic Lessing (1729–81) who renewed the meaning of classical culture by going beyond the French neo-classicists back to the ancient Greeks. Imaginative literature in the same century underwent the excitement of the 'Sturm und Drang' ('Storm and Stress') movement, which was led by the poets Herder (1744–1803), Goethe* and Schiller (1759–1805), and reached its climax in the 1770s. This was a movement which counteracted the rationalism and the cosmopolitan neo-classicism of French cultural leadership by laying emphasis on national tradition, historical change, and the conflict of the passions; it replaced the standards of Racine* and decorum by those of Shakespeare and Nature.

The English at the end of 18th C were facing not only the deep disturbance to their received ideas of the French Revolution*, but the peculiar and unprecedented problems of their own Industrial Revolution* in its earlier phases. They found that they lacked a tradition of thinking that was bold enough for this crisis, and the Germans began to absorb their attention. The Scots were in rather a different position: they had become, culturally and politically, assimilated by England, but their own history had been more turbulent than the English one, and their tradition of thought, thanks to Calvinism (Calvin*), had been in some respects more rigorous. It is thus perhaps no accident that it was a Scottish philosopher, David Hume*, who, in his *Treatise on Human Nature*, carried scepticism so far that it offered a challenge for reformulation by Immanuel Kant (*Critique of Pure Reason*, 1781) – a German philosopher of Scottish descent. Furthermore it was another Scot, Thomas Carlyle*, who did most to make German thought widely known in Britain.

The English critic Matthew Arnold*, in his essay 'The Function of Criticism' (in *Essays in Criticism** I, 1865), criticized the English Romantics because 'they did not know enough'; he meant by this, not that their learning was insufficiently wide but that they were insufficiently aware of the most central and decisive currents of thought and feeling in their time. For Arnold, as for Carlyle and many others, it was the German poet Goethe who had really embraced the spirit of the age, uniting all that was most fruitful in classicism, 'Sturm und Drang', and romanticism in his own comprehensive genius. Goethe's specific influence affected various writers in various ways; his novel *The Sorrows of Young Werther* (1774), a study of the lonely, inward-turning sensibility, instigated Byron's cultivation of the romantic individualist in his

*Childe Harold's Pilgrimage**, and Goethe's *Faust**, as a study of the striving and divided mind, offered inspiration to Clough* in his study of the Victorian* divided mind in *Dipsychus*. But these were only the chief among a number of minor works suggested by the German poet; Goethe's principal influence in 19th-C Britain was more that of a sage. Carlyle, in *Sartor Resartus**, instructed his readers to turn from the fascination of the tormented and anarchic Byron to that of Goethe himself as a criterion of modern greatness of spirit. It was this cultivation of the German poets and thinkers as 'sages' that characterized much of the influence that the Germans exercised on 19th-C Britain.

German 'higher' biblical criticism contributed to the growth of agnosticism among British intellectuals, notably Mary Ann Evans, the future novelist George Eliot*. She translated Strauss's *Life of Jesus* in 1846, and the more strongly agnostic (though deeply religious) *Essence of Christianity* by Feuerbach in 1853. Feuerbach, especially, supported her in her struggle to project the spirit without the doctrine of Christianity into art. Goethe also had some influence upon her, mainly through George Lewes*, whose *Life of Goethe* (1855) was the first to appear in any language. Both in scholarship and imagination, the Germans were felt to have gone beyond the English and the French in their insight into contemporary intellectual and emotional experience.

The first major English writer to understand and transmit German thought was the poet-critic-philosopher, Samuel Taylor Coleridge*, but his own ideas were so akin to those of the Germans that, as he himself remarked in his notebooks, it is difficult to distinguish German influences upon him from accidental resemblances. Nevertheless, it was chiefly through Coleridge that the German 'transcendental' philosophy first became known in England, and that Kant became an important shaper of 19th-C trends of thought, much as Locke* had been the shaper of 18th-C trends. Kant's 'transcendentalism' was the most subtle and profound of all the attempts to 'transcend' the 18th-C rationalist belief that the mind is merely the outcome of sense experience, and he is thus the starting-point of much of the thinking which struggles throughout 19th C to assert the reality of spiritual truth against the materialism of the science-dominated machine age.

Kantian idealism was succeeded by the idealism of Hegel as an important influence on English ideas; even more than Kant, however, he appealed chiefly to professional philosophers such as T. H. Green (1836–82), E. Caird (1835–1908) and F. H. Bradley* – though the last of these helped to form the intellect of one of the most philosophically trained of all the English poets, T. S. Eliot*. Another of Kant's successors, Schopenhauer (1788–1860), had more influence on imaginative writers, through his book *The World as Will and Idea* (1818). Schopenhauer was a pessimist who exalted Will as the driving force of Nature and Man, but interpreted it as essentially evil. To Schopenhauer is due some of the pessimism of the later-19th-C novelists, such as George Gissing*, in his view of the human spirit fighting vainly against materialism, and Thomas Hardy*, in his conception of the individual confronting the pitiless 'president of the Immortals'. Yet Schopenhauer's 'World Will' also made some contribution to the optimistic vision of 'creative evolution' in the work of the dramatist Bernard Shaw*, though Shaw depended more on the French philosopher, Bergson, and on another German, Friedrich Nietzsche*, from whom he took the concept of the Superman.

In verse drama, the work of Hugo von Hofmannsthal (1874–1929) served as a precedent for T. S. Eliot's experiments in reviving the lost tradition of poetic drama in England.

In 20th C, German militarism (especially National Socialism) reduced the prestige in Britain of German thought, apart from those great exceptions, Karl Marx* and Sigmund Freud*, both of whom had a powerful influence on English literature between the wars. The three imaginative writers who have been most admired in England during this century have been the poet Rainer Maria Rilke (1875–1926), the novelist Franz Kafka (1883–1924), and the dramatist Bertolt Brecht (1898–1956). Rilke, an important influence on English poets in the 1920s and 30s, appealed to British taste by his opposition to literary naturalism* – never a popular creed in Britain – which owed allegiance to the 19th-C biological sciences. Kafka influenced British novelists by his imaginative presentation of the individual frustrated and bewildered among the huge, impersonal organizations of the modern world. Brecht not only discovered new techniques in dramatic art, which have influenced serious dramatists from Auden* and Isherwood in the 1930s to John Arden* in the 1960s, but offered the most viable alternative in drama to the tragic vision of Ibsen*, Strindberg and Chekhov*.

* *Bible in England; English Language; Romantic Revival.*

Geryon /'gerɪən/

In Greek myth a triple-bodied monster who owned a herd of oxen guarded by the herdsman Eurytion and the hound Orthrus. The hero Hercules destroyed them and carried away the oxen. In Dante's *Inferno**, Geryon is the guardian of the 8th circle of hell.

Ghosts

'Ghost' in modern English nearly always denotes a spirit of a dead person appearing to the living, though the older sense remains in the religious use of 'Holy Ghost'. Belief in ghosts has always been especially strong in the Celtic parts of the British Isles. For literary purposes ghosts may be divided into five kinds.

[1] Earthbound spirits of popular tradition; they are not allowed to rest in the grave until a wrong done to them or by them has been set right, *e.g.* vengeance taken for murder. Hamlet's* father is such a ghost.

[2] Dream apparitions, commonly sent with a message or a warning to the sleeper, *eg* the murdered man appearing to his friend in Chaucer's *Nun's Priest's Tale** (Canterbury Tales), and perhaps the ghost of Caesar appearing to Brutus in Shakespeare's *Julius Caesar** IV. iii.

[3] Protestant* belief in 16th C was that a ghost might be a disguised emissary of the Devil; this is important in *Hamlet* – 'Be thou a spirit of health or goblin damn'd' etc. (*Hamlet*. I. iv. 41) – Hamlet does not know whether the ghost really is his father, or a devil with his father's appearance.

[4] On the other hand the ghost of Banquo (*Macbeth* III. iv) may be regarded as a hallucination born of Macbeth's guilty conscience; another common form of 'ghost'.

[5] Finally, there is the comic or melodramatic kind of ghost, a kind of literary caricature of the first type, common in Gothic* tales of 18th and early 19th C, and in more light-hearted Victorian tales, *eg* Dickens's *Christmas Carol**. Ghosts have rarely been used in serious literature of the last two hundred years; exceptions are Emily Brontë's *Wuthering Heights** and Henry James's *The Turn of the Screw**.

Giants

In Greek myth, the children of Ge*, the Earth, and sprung from the blood of Uranus, the Sky. They revolted against the gods under Zeus, and had to be put down by the hero Hercules (Heracles*), since the oracle* declared that they could be overcome only by a mortal. (They are not to be confused with the Titans*, who preceded them.) They are said to have heaped a mountain on a mountain, Pelion on Ossa, in order to reach the heavens.

Giants are common in other mythology, and seem to arise from a widespread belief that the human race has undergone physical degeneration. Hence giants frequently occur in folk myth in fairy stories such as Jack and the Beanstalk*.

Giaour, The (1813) /ˈdʒauə/

A narrative poem by Lord Byron*. The word was used by the Turks as a general term for non-Muslims, especially Christians. The poem is about the love of a Turkish slave Leila for a giaour; her master causes her to be thrown into the sea, and her lover avenges her death.

Gibbon, Edward (1737–94)

One of the greatest English historians, author of *The Decline and Fall of the Roman Empire** (1776–88). His reputation rests almost entirely on this work, but his *Memoirs* (1796), put together from fragments after his death, are one of the interesting biographies of 18th C. In 1761 he published in French his *Essai sur l'Etude de la Littérature*, translated into English in 1764; it was more successful abroad than at home. He was a Member of Parliament, 1774–81.

Bib: Low, D. M., *Edward Gibbon*; Young, G. M., *Gibbon*; Sainte-Beuve, C.-A., in *Causeries du Lundi* vol viii.

Gibraltar

A rock at the southernmost tip of Spain. Together with the opposing rock on the North African shore, it formed the 'Pillars of Hercules' for the ancient Greeks and Romans. It was acquired by the British under the Treaty of Utrecht (1713) at the end of the War of the Spanish Succession*.

Gifford, William (1756–1826) /ˈgifəd/

Journalist. He began as a shoemaker's apprentice, and rose to be an influential writer and editor of the right-wing press. He edited *The Anti-Jacobin* (1797–8) to counteract opinion sympathetic to the French Revolution*, and became editor of the famous Conservative *Quarterly Review** in 1809.

Gilbert, Sir William Schwenk (1836–1911)

Writer of light verse. He is chiefly known as the librettist of the Gilbert and Sullivan operas – an unusual case of a librettist being more famous than the composer. His *Bab Ballads* (1869–73) are also classics of comic verse.

Gilfil's Love-Story, Mr

One of George Eliot's *Scenes of Clerical Life**.

Gipsies

A nomadic race, dark-skinned, speaking their own langauge related to the Indian Hindi. They spread across Europe in 15th C and seem to have reached Britain about 1500. Owing to a belief that they came from Egypt, they were known as Egyptians, corrupted to Gipsies (Gypsies), but they called themselves Romanies. They commonly lived in caravans, and moved from place to place, making a living (in the English countryside) as tinkers and by begging. Among country people they had a bad reputation for lawlessness and stealing, including the kidnapping of children; but their exoticism caused them to be romanticized in 19th C, *eg* the gipsies in the novel *Guy Mannering* (1815) by Walter Scott*. George Borrow (1803–81) is the most notable romanticizer of gipsies (of whom he made almost a life study) in his rambling, often vivid semi-fictional autobiographical and travel books, such as *Lavengro* (1851), *The Romany Rye* (1857). In modern Britain, so-called gipsies are often merely vagrants with no gipsy ancestry. Centuries of intermittent persecution have done less than the modern Welfare State* is doing to make the gipsy existence difficult. For a 20th-C tale of a gipsy see *The Virgin and the Gypsy* by D. H. Lawrence*.

Gissing, George Robert (1857–1903) /ˈgisiŋ/

Novelist; author of: *Workers in the Dawn* (1880); *The Unclassed* (1884); *Demos* (1886); *A Life's Morning* (1888); *The Nether World* (1889); *The Emancipated* (1890); *New Grub Street** (1891); *Born in Exile* (1892); *The Odd Women* (1893); *The Town Traveller* (1898); *The Crown of Life* (1899); *Our Friend the Charlatan* (1901);

By the Ionian Sea (1901); *The Private Papers of Henry Ryecroft* (1903). Posthumous: the historical novel *Veranilda* (1904) and *Will Warburton* (1905). Of these, much the best known is *New Grub Street*, a study of literary life in late-19th-C London. Gissing saw with deep foreboding the spread of a commercialized culture which would so oppress the disinterested artist and so encourage the charlatan that, in his view, national culture was bound to deteriorate, with concomitant effects on the quality of civilization as a whole. The partial fulfilment of his predictions has given this novel in particular a greatly revived prestige. His vision was serious and sombre, and he depicted the enclosed, deprived world of the poor of his time in *Demos* and *The Nether World*. *Thyrza* and *Henry Ryecroft* are other novels which are singled out from his work. He was deeply interested in Dickens*, and his study of that novelist (1898) is among the best on the subject; but he had also been affected by the austere, scrupulous artistry of the French 19th-C novelists Flaubert* and Zola*. His best work often has a strong autobiographical content, characteristic of some of his contemporaries, such as William Hale White* and Samuel Butler*.

Bib: Donnelly, M., *Gissing, Grave Comedian*; Korg, J., *Gissing*; Leavis, Q. D., 'Gissing and the English Novel' in *Scrutiny* VII; Roberts, M., *The Private Life of Henry Maitland* (novel based on Gissing's life).

Gladstone, William Ewart (1809–98) /'gladstən/

One of the principal British statesmen of 19th C and a leader, first of the Tories (Conservatives) and later, as Prime Minister four times, of the Liberals (formerly, Whigs*). His strength lay in finance – he was a great advocate of free trade* – and domestic reform; late in life he advocated and came near to bringing about self-government for Ireland (Irish Home Rule). His personality was impressive, and his ardour and energy very great, but he lacked the intimate charm and subtle wit of his opponent Disraeli*, whom he fought with almost religious dedication. Their rivalry is often recalled as a golden age of English parliamentarianism.

Gladstone was a man of deep culture, a classical scholar who published studies of ancient Greek literature. His reforms were important in removing abuses and improving justice and equality in the universities, the army, the franchise*, the right to form and maintain trade unions, and recruitment to the military and civil services.

Glastonbury

A town in the west of England, where there are the ruins of one of the greatest of the English Benedictine* monasteries. By tradition, it was the site of the first church in Britain, founded by Joseph of Arimathaea*, the rich man who had buried Jesus Christ in his own sepulchre (Matthew 27); his staff was planted and considered to survive in the shape of a thorn tree which flowers at Christmas. The abbey is also associated with the Arthurian legend; it was said by Giraldus Cambrensis (a 12th-C chronicler) to be the Avalon*, or Isle of the Blessed, to which Arthur was borne on his death; the town was no doubt often surrounded by water as it is in low-lying country, and in prehistoric times was a lake-village.

* *Arthur, King*.

Glaucus

The name of various characters in Greek myth. The meaning of the word suggests the colour of the sea. Hence:

[1] A sea-god worshipped by sailors and fishermen. He had been a mortal fisherman himelf, but was changed into a triton after tasting a certain herb and jumping into the sea.

[2] Son of Sisyphus* and Merope; torn to pieces by his own mares.

[3] Son of Minos* and Pasiphae; he was drowned in a jar of honey but was restored to life by a herb which had restored a dead serpent.

[4] Grandson of Bellerophon*. He met the Greek Diomedes in battle but exchanged armour with him instead of fighting; his armour being of gold and Diomedes' being bronze, a Glaucus swap is a bad exchange. Glaucus, in Keats's *Endymion** Book III, is doomed to a living death by Circe* under the sea, till Endymion rescues him.

Glencoe /glen'kəu/

A valley in Scotland, where in 1692 the Campbell clan massacred a branch of the Macdonald clan. The Macdonald chief (out of pride) had delayed taking the oath of allegiance to King William III*, and this was the pretext for the massacre, the real motive being clan warfare. William III's Scottish administrator shared the guilt because he authorized the action.

Glendower, Owen (1359?–1415) /glen'dauə/

A Welsh chieftain who rebelled against Henry IV* of England, and for a time ruled Wales. He was eventually defeated by Henry's son, the future Henry V*. Glendower is a character in Shakespeare's play *1 Henry IV** as an ally of the English rebel Hotspur. He is there presented as a boastful poet and mystic, such being reputed qualities of the Welsh.

Globe Theatre

The theatre used by the Lord Chamberlain's Company*; Shakespeare's plays were performed there, he acted in it, and was one of the shareholders. It was built by Richard Burbage* in 1598 out of the materials of 'The Theatre' erected in 1576; the new site was at Bankside on the south bank of the Thames in Southwark. It was built of wood, open in the centre, and the surrounding galleries ('this wooden O' – Prologue, *Henry V**) were roofed with thatch. It is thought to have held about 1,200 spectators. From the roof flew a flag, depicting Atlas carrying a globe with a Latin inscription equivalent to 'All the world's a stage' (*As You Like It* II.vii.138). The theatre was burnt down in 1613 during a performance of *Henry*

*VIII**, rebuilt, and finally pulled down in 1644. Much of the information about the Globe comes from the contract for the Fortune Theatre (built in 1599) the structure of which is specified as resembling the Globe, except that the Fortune was square. A panoramic view of London dated 1616 gives a view of the Globe among other theatres. In the main, the structure of the Globe, like that of its contemporaries, derived from that of the typical inn-yard where plays were commonly performed when theatres were not available.

* *Theatres.*

Gloriana

The Faerie Queene* of Spenser's poem; she represents Queen Elizabeth I*.

Gnome

A kind of fairy, said to live underground; usually represented as hooded and bearded dwarfs; said to guard hidden treasure.

Godiva /gəˈdaivə/

In English legend, the wife of Leofric, Earl of Mercia, under King Edward the Confessor* (11th C). She opposed her husband's intention to tax the people of the town of Coventry; he promised not to do so if she rode naked through the streets. She accepted the challenge, and the people shut themselves up in their houses in order not to expose her to shame. The only exception, 'Peeping Tom', was struck blind. The Earl withdrew the taxes.

Godwin, William (1756–1836)

Philosopher and novelist. His central belief was that reason alone was sufficient to guide the conduct not merely of individuals but also of all society. His principal work was *The Inquiry concerning Political Justice* (1793). Man he believed to be innately good and, under guidance of reason, capable of living without laws or control. Punishments he declared (at a time when the English penal system* was one of the severest in Europe) to be unjust; also the accumulation of property and the institution of marriage. The Prime Minister, William Pitt* (the Younger), decided that the book was too expensive to be dangerous. Godwin's best-known novel came out in 1794: *Caleb Williams* was written to demonstrate the power for injustice accessible to the privileged classes. Godwin was a brave man, not merely with the pen; but his naivety as a thinker would have left him without influence if his opinions had not agreed so well with the more extreme currents of feeling provoked by the contemporary French Revolution*. As it was, he influenced a number of better minds, including, for a very short time, the poet Coleridge* and, for a much longer period, Shelley*, who became his son-in-law. Mrs Godwin had been Mary Wollstonecraft, an early propagandist for the rights of women and authoress of *A Vindication of the Rights of Woman* (1792).

* 3.4.1.

Goethe, Johann Wolfgang von (1749–1832) /ˈgəːtə/

German poet; the greatest European man of letters of his time. His fame was due not only to the wide scope of his imaginative creation, but to the many-sidedness and massive independence of his personality. From 1770 to 1788 he was an inaugurator and leader of the passionate outbreak known in German as the *Sturm und Drang* – 'storm and stress' – movement, but from 1788 (after his visit to Italy) he represented to the world a balanced harmony inspired by the classicism he had found there. But he did not lose his sense that the spirit is free to find its own fulfilment according to its own principle of growth. At the same time, from 1775 he was prominent in the affairs of the German principality of Weimar (whose prince was his friend) concerning himself with practical sciences useful to the state, and thence with a serious study of botany and other natural and physical sciences to the point of making significant contributions to scientific thought. His commanding mind was admired in France, England, and Italy, with whose literatures Goethe was in touch; he corresponded with Byron*; Scott* translated his *Goetz von Berlichingen*, which dated from the romantic phase of Goethe's career; he encouraged the young Carlyle*. For Carlyle (*Sartor Resartus**) Goethe was the spirit of affirmation that the age needed, to be set against the spirit of denial and withdrawal which he saw manifested in Byron. For Matthew Arnold*, the greatest critic of the mid-century, Goethe's serene and responsible detachment represented the needed outlook for the practice of criticism.

Goethe is most famous for his double drama of *Faust**, but other works that became famous in England include the romantic drama already mentioned; a psychological novel *Wilhelm Meister*; the epic *Hermann and Dorothea*; a study in romantic sensibility *The Sorrows of Young Werther*, and a large body of lyrical verse.

Golden Age

* *Ages, Golden, Silver, etc.*

Golden Bowl, The (1904)

A novel by Henry James*. The theme is the relationship of four people: the American millionaire collector, Adam Verver; his daughter, Maggie; the Italian prince, Amerigo, whom Adam Verver acquires as a husband for his daughter; and Charlotte Stant, whom Maggie acquires as a wife for her widowed father. To the grief of the father and the daughter Charlotte seduces the prince into becoming her lover; the story is about the defeat of Charlotte, and Maggie's recovery of the prince's affections.

The novel belongs to James's last phase, which some critics consider to be his best, and others consider to show the narrowing of his originally more spacious genius. The writing is chiefly in dialogue, and very condensed. The language of the characters is charged with feeling and yet disciplined by their civilized restraint and their fear of degrading themselves and one another by damaging explicitness. It is a measure of their indirectness that the affair between the prince and Charlotte is never actually mentioned between the father and the daughter. Behind the conflict of personalities there is the theme of the clash between European and American kinds of value and consciousness; this theme is conspicuous in James's early novels, and he returned to it in his last period after a middle phase in which he was chiefly concerned with the European, and particularly the English, scene.

Golden Fleece, The

[1] In Greek myth, the quest of Jason* and the Argonauts*.

[2] An order of knighthood instituted by Philip, Duke of Burgundy in 1429.

Golden Hind

* *Drake.*

Golden Legend, The

A medieval collection of lives of the saints, sermons, religious commentaries, etc., begun in 13th C. It was printed by the first English printer, William Caxton*.

Golden Treasury

* *Anthology.*

Golding, William (b 1911)

Novelist: *Lord of the Flies* (1954 – filmed 1963); *The Inheritors* (1955); *Pincher Martin* (1956); *Free Fall* (1959); *The Spire* (1964); *The Pyramid* (1967); *The Scorpion God* (1971). He has also written a play, *The Brass Butterfly* (1958), and published a collection of essays, *The Hot Gates* (1965).

No novelist who started his career since 1945 has achieved more prestige, and this was acquired very quickly on the publication of his first book. Its fame has no doubt been in part due to its pessimistic vision of human nature as inherently violent, reflecting the mood of the post-war and post-Hitler years; it also epitomizes mid-20th-C disillusionment with 19th-C optimism about human nature. Golding's father (see 'The Ladder and the Tree' in *The Hot Gates*) was a schoolmaster with radical convictions in politics, a belief that religion is outmoded superstition, and a strong faith in science. Golding's own work is strongly, but not explicitly, religious, in the Puritan* tradition which emphasizes Original Sin. In 'Fable' (*The Hot Gates*) he explains how his first novel arose from his insights in the last war: 'Anyone who moved through those years without understanding that man produces evil as a bee produces honey, must have been blind or wrong in the head.' The book is also meant to counteract what may be called 'the desert island myth' in English literature, deriving from Defoe's *Robinson Crusoe**, and particularly evident in a famous book for boys, *The Coral Island* (1857) by R. M. Ballantyne. This myth nourished the belief that human beings in isolation from civilized restraints will sustain their humanity by innate virtues. Most of the boys in *Lord of the Flies* quickly degenerate into savages, and the process is made more horrifying by the convincing delineation of their character: Golding, like his father, has been a schoolmaster. His later novels have shown variety of theme and treatment, but similar preoccupation with fundamental corruption and contradiction in human nature. They show likewise Golding's most conspicuous literary qualities: great inventiveness in realistic fantasy, and a disposition to use the novel form as fable. For instance, *The Inheritors* is science fiction* about the remote human past: the elimination of innocent Neanderthal Man by the arrival of rapacious Homo Sapiens – a new version of the myth of the Fall. *Pincher Martin* is a dramatization of this rapacity in an individual, and a spectacular example of fantasy presented within the conventions of realism. *The Spire* shows comparable ingenuity used quite differently: it describes the building of the spire of Salisbury Cathedral and dramatizes the conflict between faith and reason.

Bib: Gregor, I., and Kinkead-Weekes, M., *William Golding: a Critical Study*; Pemberton, C., *William Golding* (*Writers and their Work*).

Goldsmith, Oliver (1730–74)

Novelist, poet, essayist, dramatist. His unusual versatility in different modes of writing is testified by his masterpieces: a novel, *The Vicar of Wakefield**; a poem, *The Deserted Village**; a play, *She Stoops to Conquer* (1773); his essays, *The Citizen of the World* (1762). This versatility is partly accounted for by exigency: Goldsmith had to write hard for a living, trying his hand at everything. Moreover he never achieved a really great work, despite his continuing popularity. In his own time he was esteemed for the qualities of his writing described by his friend Dr Johnson* as 'clarity and elegance'; later generations have repeatedly praised his literary 'charm', a quality made up of humour, modesty, generosity, and graceful lucidity. These he combined with the firm Augustan* virtues of judiciousness, balance, and proportion.

Among his other works, these are notable: the poem, *The Traveller* (1764), which first brought him public success; his first play *The Good-natur'd Man* (1768); his life of Beau Nash (1762), and the essays in his short-lived periodical *The Bee* (1759). He wrote much else, including histories of England, Greece, and Rome, and biographies of Voltaire, Bolingbroke and Parnell. He figures largely in Boswell's* *Life of Johnson.*

*** 5.2.2; 6.3.1.**

Bib: Wardle, R. M., *Life*; Balderston, K. C., *Letters*; Ford, B., in Pelican Guide iv, *From Dryden to Johnson.*

Goliardic /gəuli'a:dik/

A term applied in the first place to a kind of vigorous verse satire, often at the expense of the Church, practised and popular in 13th C. By 14th C, *eg* in Langland's *Piers Plowman**, a goliard was a wandering minstrel. Goliards were originally themselves churchmen inasmuch as they were student clerks at universities, and wrote in Latin.

Goliath /gə'laiəθ/

The giant* of the Philistines killed by the shepherd boy David*, in the Bible, *1 Samuel* 17. Goliath came out from the Philistine army day after day challenging anyone from the Hebrew army to single combat. At last David persuaded King Saul to allow him to accept the challenge and thereupon killed Goliath with a stone from his sling. The Philistine army fled.

Gorboduc, or Ferrex and Porrex /'go:bədʌk/

A tragic drama by Thomas Norton (1552–84) and Thomas Sackville*. The story is taken from British legendary history; the immediate source is Grafton's *Chronicle* (1556), but this in turn derives from the 12th-C *Historia Regum Britanniae* (History of the Kings of Britain) by Geoffrey of Monmouth*. It is the first play to be written in blank verse*, and it is modelled on the tragedies of Seneca*.

Gorboduc is a king of Britain. His reign has been a prosperous one, when he decides to retire from government and to divide his kingdom between his two sons, Ferrex and Porrex. He carries out the division against the advice of his wisest councillor. Jealousy and distrust between the two brothers break into civil war, which ends in the death of both, and a rising of the whole people, who slay Gorboduc and his queen. The country is only saved from final ruin by Fergus, Duke of Albany, who, with the aid of other nobles, succeeds in restoring order under single sovereignty.

The drama has slight literary value of its own, but it has considerable historical significance. Sackville and Norton were eminent politicians who forsaw great dangers to the kingdom if Queen Elizabeth I* should die without heirs. The play was first acted before the Queen in 1562, and is plainly designed as a warning to her against leaving her kingdom exposed to disunity. The authors are thus using history (or legend, which was not clearly distinguished from history) as later and greater dramatists were to use it, notably Shakespeare: that is to say, as a storehouse of political lessons which could be applied to the politics of their own time. The theme of the divided kingdom resembles one of the greatest of Shakespeare's tragedies, *King Lear**, which deals with the situation in far profounder terms. The Senecan model also anticipates later Elizabethan taste, and the use of blank verse* was the starting-point for the rich development of the medium by Marlowe* and Shakespeare. Apart from Seneca, a literary influence upon the writers is the collection of tragic tales, *A Mirror for Magistrates** (1559), to which Sackville made the most memorable contribution. This also used legend and history, recounted in a solemn style, to warn and edify contemporary courtiers and public men. The Senecan solemnity and formality of *Gorboduc* gave it peculiar dignity for the contemporary public, raising it above the (often much more lively) style of the familiar interludes* and comedies of the day, and giving it the requisite impressiveness to influence the Queen. It is not known what she thought of it, but Sir Philip Sidney* excepted it from his general condemnation of the English drama of his day, and wrote in his *Apology for Poetry*: 'it is full of stately speeches, and well sounding phrases, climbing to the height of Seneca's style, and as full of notable morality . . .' However he goes on to complain of its failure to observe the so-called Aristotelian unities of space and time.

* *Unities.*

Gordon Riots, The

Riots in London in 1780, led by Lord George Gordon against a law passed in 1778 to relieve the condition of Roman Catholics. The riots form the climax of Dickens's novel *Barnaby Rudge**.

Gorgons

In Greek myth, three hideous winged sisters – Stheno, Euryale, and Medusa. They had hideous faces, and writhing serpents instead of hair. Of the three, only Medusa was mortal, and she was decapitated by the hero Perseus*. The head turned all beholders to stone.

Gosse, Edmund (1849–1928) /gos/

Critic, biographer and poet. He is especiallly known for his autobiography *Father and Son* (1907) – one of the classic works for interpreting the Victorian age. As a critic, he was one of the first to introduce the Norwegian dramatist Ibsen* to the English public. He also wrote a number of studies of 17th C literature and a life (1917) of his friend and contemporary the poet Swinburne*.

Goth /goθ/

The Goths were Germanic tribes which invaded the Roman Empire in 3rd-5th C and eventually overthrew it. The western Goths were called Visigoths and conquered Spain; the eastern Goths were the Ostrogoths who conquered Italy. 'A Goth' is a term for an uncultivated person. The Goths had nothing to do with originating the style of architecture known as Gothic, which began in France in 12th C when the word was no longer in use as a contemporary racial description.

Gotham, Wise Men of /ˈgəʊtəm/

Gotham is a village near Nottingham in the English midlands. It had a reputation not for wisdom but for folly. The story is that the villagers simulated stupidity when King John* proposed to come and stay among them, since royal courts were burdensome to country neighbourhoods owing to their exactions of provisions and unpaid services from the countryside. When the king's commissioners came to inspect the place, they found the villagers trying to drown an eel in the village pond. King John is said to have seen through the villagers' tactics, and to have remarked 'More fools pass through Gotham than live there.'

Gothic /ˈgoθik/

A term for the style of architecture which dominated western Europe in the Middle Ages. Its main features were the pointed arch and the ribbed vault. In England, this period is divided into three: Early English (13th C), Decorated (14th), and Perpendicular (15th-16th). The finest example of the last is King's College Chapel, Cambridge.

*** 2.3.**

Gothic Novels

The 18th C stressed the supreme value of Reason, and the values that go with reason; despite the imaginative richness of Pope* and Swift*, this emphasis tended to repress emotion and the more mysterious forces in the personality, which were thought of as barbaric, and therefore medieval and Gothic. Gothic thus became associated with all that was felt to be fantastic, grotesque, wild, savage, mysterious, and capable of strong appeal to the emotions without restraint by the reason. Later in the century, the scepticism that resulted from the value attached to reason led to the belief that reason itself was limited in its capacity to express experience; sentiment began to be cultivated for its own sake, and Gothic art and literature exerted a fascination. Hence a form of literature grew up to satisfy this fascination.

The first Gothic novel was Horace Walpole's *Castle of Otranto** (1764), set in Italy during the Middle Ages. Other very popular examples were 'Monk' Lewis's* *The Monk* (1796), and Ann Radcliffe's *The Mysteries of Udolpho** (1794) which was satirized by Jane Austen in *Northanger Abbey**. It was natural that Gothic tales should often be set in Europe during the Middle Ages, since Gothic implies this setting, but the term was used for almost any sensational form of literature, whatever the setting or period. Thus, one of the best of them, *Vathek* (1786) by William Beckford, was set in 9th-C Arabia, and Mary Shelley's *Frankenstein** had a contemporary European setting.

The Byronic 'hero', especially in Byron's dramas, *eg Manfred**, is Gothic in spirit, but by this time the Gothic vogue was being taken much more seriously. Searching into the mysteries of the human passions was the serious occupation of such Romantics as Byron* and Shelley*, for the French Revolution* and the dramatic wars of Napoleon had seriously disturbed all the 18th-C assumptions about the rational order of man and society. Moreover, Sir Walter Scott* was giving the Gothic novel an entirely new kind of interest. He wrote as a Scotsman and as an antiquarian. As a Scotsman, he was the native of a country which was scenically more wild and socially more savage than England, so that his Scottish novels were both Gothic and realistic; as an antiquarian, he took the Middle Ages in both England and Scotland quite seriously, and taught his readers no longer to see them as a phase of history which was fascinating merely because anything pleasantly shocking or fantastic was likely to happen in it.

After 1840, the term Gothic ceased to be applicable to literature, in the sense of special kinds of appeal which were sensational and mysterious at the same time. These kinds of appeal, of course, still existed in Victorian fiction, but such effects were no longer characteristic of special kinds of fiction. The Gothic Revival* prevailed, so that to cultivate the Middle Ages was as normal as the cultivation of Greece and Rome ('classical' taste) had been in 18th C. Moreover the exploration of low life by Dickens (*eg* in *Oliver Twist**) exceeded Gothic in its vigour and excitement.

Gothic Revival

An architectural style now chiefly associated with the reign of Queen Victoria* (1837–1901). A taste for Gothic had in fact started in the 18th C; its starting point is associated with Horace Walpole's* design of his home, Strawberry Hill (1747). The taste for Gothic spread between 1750 and 1830; as an artistic style it remained a minority cult, but as a sentiment it grew with the popularity of the sensationalism of the Gothic novels* and with the rise of the Romantic cultivation of the sensibility. In the 18th C, the taste for Gothic tended to be fanciful and sensational rather than deeply serious, although it gained seriousness from such a publication as Percy's *Reliques**; the 19th-C Romantic Revival*, especially the novels of Walter Scott*, produced a deeper and much more genuine feeling for the Middle Ages. From about 1830, the Gothic revival became a genuine cultural re-direction; in literature it was advanced by Thomas Carlyle*

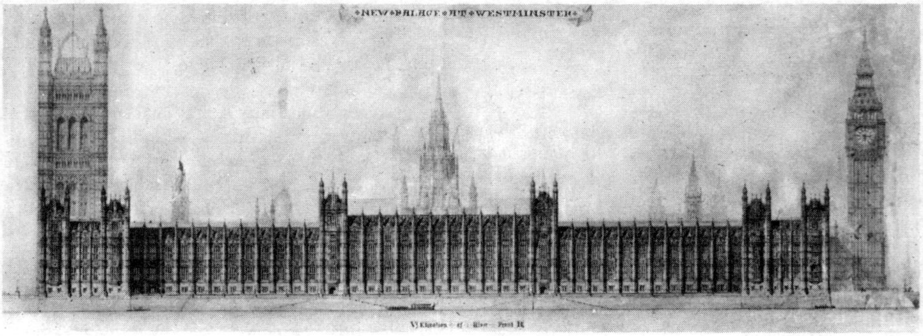

(*Past and Present*) and by John Ruskin* (*The Stones of Venice*); in religion by the Oxford Movement*; in architecture and painting by the Catholic architect Pugin (through his writings rather than his buildings) and the Pre-Raphaelites*. Ruskin, especially in his famous essay 'The Nature of Gothic', was the most eloquent of these exponents; he used the spirit of Gothic to challenge the materialistic spirit of the time consequent to the mass production methods of the Industrial Revolution*. Nonetheless, in architecture and design the Victorian Gothic Revival was partly vitiated by the facile technology of the new industrial methods, which elaborated Gothic ornament mechanically instead of with genuine feeling. In poetry and fiction, Tennyson's* revival of Arthurian* legend in *Idylls of the King*, Browning's* delight in elaborate descriptive detail, and Dickens's* vivid idiosyncrasies in the presentation of character and environment, can all be ascribed to a prevailing neo-Gothic appeal to the imagination. But in the 1870s, a reaction set in: neo-Gothic architectural styles were succeeded by a return to classicism, generally known as the new 'Queen Anne' style, though in reality it was much more eclectic and exuberant. Eclecticism in fact took over artistic taste in both the plastic arts and literature until the emergence of radical experiment (often assumed in the term Modernism*) in the 20th C.

Gower, John (1330?–1408) /ˈgauə/

Poet; a contemporary and friend of Chaucer*. He had great competence but small originality. His best known work is *Confessio Amantis**, an allegorical* romance in English, but he also wrote in French and Latin.

Bib: Ker, W. P., in *Essays on Medieval Literature*; Lewis, C. S., in *The Allegory of Love*.

Grace Abounding to the Chief of Sinners (1666)

The spiritual autobiography of John Bunyan*, author of *The Pilgrim's Progress**. The torments undergone by Christian in the latter book are substantially those of Bunyan in the earlier one. Bunyan had a similar spiritual awakening to Christian's, being aroused by a book; he suffers the terrible conviction of sin, like Christian's; he believes himself to commit the sin of blasphemy as Christian thinks he does in the Valley of the Shadow of Death; at last he achieves confidence in God's mercy. Much of the narrative is an account of painful mental conflict; but Bunyan never lost the sanity of perception into the fanaticism and mental morbidity of others, such as the old man who told him that he had certainly committed the sin against the Holy Ghost (for which there is no forgiveness). The book records how he developed that compassionate understanding of other men's spiritual conflicts which makes *Pilgrim's Progress* the antecedent of the great English novels.

Grail, The Holy /greil/

The mysterious object of quest by King Arthur's* Knights of the Round Table*. In the late form of the legend, Malory's *Morte D'Arthur**, the hero who eventually finds it is Sir Galahad*, son of Sir Lancelot*. The Holy Grail was the cup used by Jesus Christ in celebrating the Last Supper before the Crucifixion (in the Bible, *Matthew* 26 : 27; *Luke* 22 : 20). In older French and German versions, following the unfinished account by the French Chrétien de Troyes*, the hero was Sir Perceval*. A character in the earlier versions known as the Fisher King sickens, and his country grows infertile with him; he has to drink blood from the grail for both himself and his country to revive. This resembles myths about the ancient Assyrian Tammuz, the Egyptian Attis, and the Greek Adonis; the grail symbol is used in association with such world myths by T. S. Eliot as the basis of his poem *The Waste Land**.

Grammar Schools

* *Schools in England.*

Grand Guignol

A term denoting an entertainment relying merely on sensational horror for its effect; after an old French puppet show.

Grand National, The

One of the principal English horse-races; it is a steeplechase, over hedges, fences, and water. It was started in 1839, and is run at Aintree near Liverpool. The course is 4½ miles and includes 30 jumps.

Grand Siècle, Le

The Great Century in France – the 17th, especially the reign of Louis XIV (1643–1715). France was at her greatest politically (except for the First Empire, 1804–15) and had one of her greatest periods in literature, painting and music.

Granville-Barker, Harley (1877–1946)

Actor, producer, dramatist, dramatic critic. He began as an actor in 1891, but he achieved fame as a producer (1904–21). He favoured the modern drama of Ibsen*, Shaw* and Galsworthy* and did much to educate the public into accepting its often scandalizing themes drawn from contemporary social issues; in this he was much influenced by his close friendship with Shaw. However his chief fame as a producer was in his production of Shakespeare. The previous generation of Shakespeare production, dominated by Henry Irving*, had relied on the personalities of star actors, and Irving was continuing a tradition which went back to the 18th C. Granville-Barker concentrated on the production of the whole work, transferring the emphasis from the leading roles onto the speech and action of the entire cast. His own plays were in the Ibsen-Shaw tradition; the best known are *The Voysey Inheritance* (1905), *Waste* (which was forbidden by the censor) (1907), and *The Madras House* (1910).

In 1923 he became Editor of *The Players' Shakespeare* for which he wrote prefaces to individual plays. The series was discontinued, but the prefaces were published, and because they have Granville-Barker's unique stage experience as a basis, they now constitute the crown of his reputation. However he was also a lifelong publicist for the idea of a National Theatre, which was not to be established until 1976.

Graves, Robert (b. 1895)

Poet, critic, novelist. His poetry has been among the more important work of the last forty years, and belongs to a distinctively English strain of lyrical verse which has been overshadowed by the more ambitious and more massive work of the Anglo-Irish W. B. Yeats* and the American-born T. S. Eliot*. Earlier representatives of this kind of verse were Thomas Hardy*, Edward Thomas* and the war poets such as Wilfred Owen*, Siegfried Sassoon*, and Isaac Rosenberg*. The development of Graves's work was decisively affected by his experiences as an officer in World War I, and understanding of it is helped by a reading of Owen and Sassoon. Such poetry was partly a means of preserving sanity in the face of extreme horror, partly a desire to awaken in the reader a distrust of attitudes imposed on him by convention, or adopted by himself to help him preserve his own illusions. Graves published his first poems during the First World War, but he is not primarily one of the war poets; he extended the vision aroused by the war into the post-war world of human relations, especially those between the sexes, and into the impulses to self-deceive and to escape the realities of inner experience, especially by choosing to dull its image. He has always written lyrics with skilful and precise rhythm and often poignant or pungent rhymes, and an austere yet lively, colloquial diction – latest collected edition: 1965.

As a critic he was at first a self-conscious modernist; *A Survey of Modernist Poetry* (1927), written with his wife Laura Riding, educated the public in new kinds of poetic expression by a pioneering critical interest in subtleties and ambiguities of language. His later criticism has been less influential; it includes *The Common Asphodel* (1949), *The Crowning Privilege* (1955).

Graves has engaged extensively in historical and anthropological enquiry; this has resulted in work on primitive religion, *eg The White Goddess* (1948), which aroused controversy, and in historical fiction of great popularity, *eg I, Claudius* and *Claudius the God* (1934). By far the most important of his prose works, however, was his autobiography recounting his experiences in the First World War – *Good-bye to All That* (1929).

Bib: Seymour Smith, M., *Swifter than Reason* (1964).

Gray, Thomas (1716–71)

Poet. From 1744 he lived as a Fellow at Cambridge, and in 1768 was appointed professor of history and modern languages. His career was that of a shy reserved scholar, distinguished for his learning in ancient Greek and for fastidious taste in the arts, and informed in European literature. His poetry is strongly marked by the taste for sentiment controlled by classical ideals of restraint and composure that characterized the later Augustans*, without the inward emotional exploration displayed by the Romantics of the 1790–1820 generation: he shows sensitive response to natural environment without the sense of its organic union with human nature to be found in Wordsworth*. He was in his own time distinctive as a practitioner of poetic form by reason of his abandonment of the close discipline of the heroic couplet* for the greater rhetorical freedom of the Pindaric Ode (*Ode), and his odes (1742–57) are among his most famous work: *On the Spring*, *Eton College*, *The Progress of Poesy*, *The Bard*, *The Pleasure Arising from Vicissitude*. He was also interested in the English folk ballad, and had strong sentiment for the simple ways of life that went with it. This kind of taste for simplicity inspires his *Elegy in a Country Churchyard** (1750), one of the most quoted poems in the English language. His study of Norse literature led to his two *Norse Odes* (1761), and his interest in Celtic literature provided inspiration for the more famous *The Bard*. Because he had some affinity with the Romantics, his choice of diction was an interesting test case for them, and one of his sonnets is for this reason selected for critical examination by Wordsworth in his Preface to the *Lyrical Ballads** and is further examined, to throw light on Wordsworth's theory of poetic diction, in Chapter 18 of Coleridge's *Biographia Literaria**.

Bib: Ketton-Cremer, R. W., *Life*; Powell Jones, W., *Thomas Gray, Scholar*; Johnson, S., in *Lives of the Poets*; Arnold, M., in *Essays in Criticism* (*2nd series*); Tillotson, G., in *Augustan Studies*;

Leavis, F. R., in *Revaluation*; Martin, R., *Essai sur Thomas Gray*; Cecil, D., 'The Poetry of Thomas Gray' in *Poets and Story-tellers.*

Gray's Inn

* *Inns of Court.*

Great Expectations (1860–61)

A novel by Charles Dickens. Its title refers to expectations resulting from wealth anonymously donated to Philip Pirrip (shortened to Pip) who has been brought up in humble obscurity by his half-sister and her husband, the village blacksmith, Joe Gargery. His 'expectations' are to be made a 'gentleman'* – understood in social terms as holding privilege without responsibility. He supposes his money to be the gift of the rich and lonely Miss Havisham, who has frozen herself into vindictive hatred of the male sex, and has in fact merely used him as an experimental victim on whom her ward, Estella, is to exert her charm with the aim of breaking his heart. Pip's great crisis comes when he discovers his real benefactor to be the convict Magwitch, whom he had helped in an attempted escape when he was a child. Magwitch, who had been made into a criminal by the callousness of society in his own childhood, has built up a fortune in Australia (to which he was deported – see *Penal System**) and has tried the experiment of 'making a gentleman' out of another child. His assumption is essentially that of society as a whole, that appearances, and the money that makes them, are what matters. Magwitch returns to England illegally to see the fruit of his ambition, and Pip has to decide whether he will be responsible for his unwanted benefactor, or escape from him. His decision to protect Magwitch and help him to escape again produces a revolution in Pip's nature: instead of assuming privilege without responsibility he now undertakes responsibility without reward, since he will also divest himself of his money. 'Expectations' are important in other senses for other characters: Estella expects to become a rich lady dominating humiliated admirers, but she becomes enslaved to a brutal husband; Pip's friend, Herbert Pocket, dreams of becoming a powerful industrialist, but he has no capital until Pip (anonymously) provides it; Wopsle, the parish clerk in Pip's village, imagines himself a great actor and becomes a stage hack; Miss Havisham is surrounded by relatives whom she despises, and who nonetheless live in expectation of legacies after her death; Miss Havisham herself, and Magwitch also, live for expectations (in Estella and Pip) which are frustrated – in these instances fortunately. In its largest implications, *Great Expectations* is concerned with the futility of a society in which individuals live by desires powered by illusion. This view of the novel gives emphasis to those characters who are free of illusion: the lawyer Jaggers who exerts power by his cynical expectation of human folly; his clerk, Wemmick, who divides his life sharply between the harshness demanded by his profession and the tenderness of his domestic affections; Joe Gargery and his second wife Biddy, survivals from an older social tradition, who remain content with their own naive wisdom of the heart. Dickens was persuaded by his friend Bulwer Lytton to change the end of the novel: in the first version Pip and Estella, older and wiser, meet again only to separate permanently; in the revised one, Dickens leaves it open to the reader to believe that they will be permanently united.

Greek Literature

Until Greece was conquered by the Romans in 146 BC, it was a country of small states, mixed racial stock, and cultural origins from all round the eastern Mediterranean. These states attained a high level of self-conscious political and artistic culture, which later immensely enriched the Roman Empire, and was thence transmitted to medieval and modern Europe.

The beginnings of Greek literature cannot be dated, but its first period ended about 500 BC. The period contains Homer's great heroic epics, the *Iliad** and the *Odyssey**, and the poems of Hesiod. Homer's epics are the real starting-point of European imaginative literature; Hesiod's *Theogony* is one of the principal sources of our knowledge of the Greek religious system. In English literature since 18th C, the term elegy* has implied narrower limits of subject and treatment than it had for the Greeks and the Romans, but the Greek evolution of the elegy and the lyric* in this period has shaped our ideas of the character and resources of the short poem. An important variety of the lyric (whose principal characteristic was originally that it was intended to have musical accompaniment) was the 'Pindaric ode', so called after its most famous practitioner, Pindar*; this was much imitated by English poets from 17th to 19th C.

The second period (500–300 BC) is called the 'Attic Period', because it centred on the greatest of the Greek cities, Athens*, capital of the state of Attica. The outstanding imaginative achievement of the Athenians was the creation of dramatic literature. The 'choral lyric', sung by choirs on religious occasions, and especially on the festival of the wine-god Dionysus*, was developed into a dialogue by Thespis* in 6th C. In 5th C this was further developed into dramatic tragedy by three writers whose works have a fundamental influence on all our ideas of the theatre: Aeschylus*, Sophocles* and Euripides*. The primitive religion of the Greeks, based on the worship of the gods as the all-powerful forces of nature, was the origin of Greek tragedy; it was also the origin of comedy, of which the greatest Greek writer was Aristophanes*. Tragedy and comedy originally expressed the destructive and the recreative aspects of Nature; these dramatists already saw them as two ways of looking at human experience, and as such they have remained fundamental concepts for the European imagination. Athens, in this period, also developed Greek prose literature, in the works of the first of the great historians, Herodotus*, in the immensely influential philosophies of Plato* and Aristotle*, and in political oratory, especially that of Demosthenes*.

Demosthenes achieved fame by his efforts to

sustain the Greeks in their wars (357–338) against Philip of Macedon, a state to the north of Greece. The war ended with the Macedonians making themselves the dominant power in Greece. They did not actually destroy the independence of the states, but the intensity and many-sidedness of Greek city life diminshed. However, Philip's son Alexander the Great (ruled 336–323) took Greek culture with him in his rapid conquests, round the eastern Mediterranean and as far east as north-west India. The result was the 'Hellenistic Period' (**Hellas*) lasting until the Roman conquest, after which it did not cease but went into a new phase. The culture of Greece now became a climate of civilization shared by many lands; it was no longer even centred in Greece, but in the great university city of Alexandria in Egypt. The price paid for this expansion was that without the sustenance of the vigorous Greek city life, the literature lost its force, depth, and originality, though it retained its secondary qualities such as grace and sophistication. The best known imaginative works of this period are the 'pastoral' peoms by Theocritus* and others; they influenced the great Roman poet Virgil*, and were extensively used as models by Renaissance* poets in 16th and 17th C.

In the Graeco-Roman period (146 BC–AD 500), the Greeks were the teachers and cultural allies of their conquerors, the Romans. Latin literature written under Greek influence now excelled what continued to be written in Greek. Yet Renaissance Europe felt so much closer to the Romans than to the Greeks that it was the Greek writers of this period who influenced it more deeply than the earlier Greeks did. The historian and biographer Plutarch*, for instance, was widely read in England in the age of Shakespeare, who used him as a source-book for his plays. The Greek romances, the best known of which is *Daphnis and Chloe* by Longus (2nd C AD), were imitated by 16th-C writers such as Sidney in his *Arcadia**. To this period also belongs one of the most influential pieces of Greek literary criticism, the treatise *On the Sublime* by Longinus*.

In considering the influence of Greek literature on European, and in particular on English, literature, we have to distinguish between the influence of Greek philosophy and that of Greek imaginative writing. Plato and Aristotle had profound effects on Christian thought. Plato was made dominant by St Augustine of Hippo (4th–5th C), until St Thomas Aquinas* replaced his influence by that of Aristotle. In 16th C, Plato again became most important, but now as a source of humanist* as well as of religious ideas. Aristotle remained dominant as the first philosopher of literature for three centuries, and together they are still regarded as the important starting-points of European philosophy. Greek imaginative writing, on the other hand, made its impression on European, and especially English, imaginative writing chiefly through its assimilation by Roman writers. It was not, for example, the unexcelled Greek dramatists who impressed themselves on the equally unexcelled English dramatists of the age of Shakespeare, but the comparatively inferior Roman ones, Plautus* in comedy and Seneca* in tragedy. Only in the 30 years of the Romantic Revival* that followed the French Revolution* did English writers (partly under German influence) really discriminate between Greek and Roman literature, and value the Greeks more highly. Even then, such a poet as Shelley* valued Greek culture as sentiment rather than as a deep influence. For such as him, the Greeks stood for freedom of spirit and of intellect, whereas Latin culture was associated with the pre-revolutionary authoritarian 'old regime' to which he and others of his generation were so much opposed.

* *Classical Education; Classical Mythology; Latin Literature; Pastoral, Classical; Platonism and Neo-Platonism.*

Green, Henry (b 1905)

Pen-name for H. V. Yorke, one of the most original of living English novelists. *Blindness* (1926); *Living* (1929); *Party-Going* (1939); *Pack my Bag* (1940); *Caught* (1943); *Loving* (1945); *Back* (1946); *Concluding* (1948); *Nothing* (1950); *Doting* (1952). Of these, possibly the most distinguished are: *Living*, with an industrial working-class setting; *Loving*, about servants in an anachronistic great house in Ireland during World War II; *Concluding*, set in the future, about an institution for educating women civil servants, and *Party-Going*, a novel in which the events have only a few hours' duration and take place in a fog-bound London railway station. His style is condensed and poetically expressive; events are caught in movement, with a cinematic use of flash-backs to bring the past into relationship with the present. In the autobiographical *Pack my Bag* he wrote: 'Prose should be a long intimacy between strangers with no direct appeal to what both may have known. It should slowly appeal to feelings unexpressed, it should in the end draw tears out of the stone.' The later novels show increasing reliance on dialogue, after the example of the novels of Ivy Compton-Burnett*. The technique of Green's novels also has resemblances to that of Virginia Woolf*, and he has professed admiration for the work of the French writer, Céline.

Bib: Stokes, E., *The Novels of Henry Green.*

Greene, Henry Graham (b 1904)

Novelist. The son of a schoolmaster. He went to Balliol College, Oxford, and then became a journalist (1926–30) on *The Times**. He was converted to Catholicism in 1926. His first novel, *The Man Within*, appeared in 1929. It was followed by a steady succession of novels, of which the fourth, *Stamboul Train* (1932) made him well known. It was nonetheless one of the books he called 'entertainments', meaning that they were among his less serious works; this group also includes *A Gun for Sale* (1936), *The Confidential Agent* (1939), *The Ministry of Fear* (1943), and *Our Man in Havana* (1958). In 1934 he published *It's a Battlefield*, and a volume of stories the title story of which, *The Basement Room*, was later adapted into the film, *The Fallen Idol* (1950). In 1935 came *England Made Me*. In the same year he travelled in Liberia, on which he based his travel book *Journey Without Maps* (1936). He now became film critic for the weekly journal *The Spectator* (of which he was made literary editor in 1940). His next novel, *Brighton Rock* (1938) was the first in which there was clear evidence of Catholicism in his work. In the same year he was commissioned to visit Mexico and report on the religious persecution there; the result was another travel book, *The Lawless Roads* (1939) and one of his most famous novels, *The Power and the Glory* (1940). During World War II he worked for the Foreign Office, and again visited West Africa. After the war he became a publisher. Later fiction: *Nineteen Stories* (1947, including eight in *The Basement Room* volume); *The Heart of the Matter* (1948); *The Third Man* (1950, also made into a film); *The End of the Affair* (1951); *The Quiet American* (1956); *A Burnt-Out Case* (1961); *A Sense of Reality* (four stories, 1963); *The Comedians* (1967); *Travels with My Aunt* (1969); *A Sort of Life* (1971); *The Honorary Consul* (1973); *Lord Rochester's Monkey* (1974).

He has also written plays (*The Living Room*, 1953, *The Potting Shed*, 1959, *The Complaisant Lover*, 1959), and a book of critical essays, *The Lost Childhood*, 1951.

Graham Greene's high reputation is partly due to his exploration of emotions that are particularly strong in the middle of 20th C: the sense of guilt and frustration, impulses to violence and fear of it, pity, including self-pity. He has strong gifts for narrative and for the evocation of atmosphere, especially the atmosphere of squalid surroundings which convey deprivation and despair. His Catholicism counteracts the misery in his books by its implications of spiritual dignity remaining intact even amid degradation and abject suffering.

Bib: Allott, K., and Farris, M., *The Art of Greene*.

Greene, Robert (1558–92)

Dramatist and pamphleteer. He was one of the University Wits*, having himself been at Cambridge. Four plays by Greene, apart from collaborations, have survived: *Alphonsus, King of Aragon* (?1587); *Friar Bacon and Friar Bungay** (acted 1592); *History of Orlando Furioso* (acted 1592); *The Scottish History of James IV* (acted 1594). Of these the best known are the second and the fourth, and in them both the melodious and fluent handling of the blank verse and the appealing portrayal of the heroines anticipate Shakespeare's romantic comedies of the 1590s.

Greene is more notable for his prose. This includes romances written in emulation of Lyly's *Euphues** and Sidney's *Arcadia**, including *Pandosto, The Triumph of Time** from which Shakspeare derived *The Winter's Tale* (1610). More distinctive and very lively reading are his 'cony-catching pamphlets' (*ie* booklets about criminal practices in the London underworld), *A Notable Discovery of Cosenage* (*ie* 'cozenage' or criminal fraud, 1591) and *The Blacke Booke's Messenger* (1591) – both excellent examples of Elizabethan popular prose. A semi-fictional autobiography, *Greene's Groatsworth of Wit bought with a Million of Repentance* is notorious for containing the earliest reference to Shakespeare as a dramatist and actor, though it is an oblique one. The object of the pamphlet is ostensibly a warning to three others of the University Wits – probably Peele, Marlowe and Nashe – to amend their lives. The allusion to Shakespeare – 'an upstart crow beautified with our feathers . . . in his owne conceyt the onely shake-scene in a countrey' – comes by way of a charge of plagiarism. Thirty-five prose works, most of them short, and many containing lyrics of great charm, are ascribed to Greene.

* 5.1.2.4.

Bib: Pruvost, R., *A Study of Greene's romances*; Judges, A. V., *The Elizabethan Underworld*.

Greenwich Hospital /'grinidʒ/

From 1447 to 1705, a royal palace; from 1705 to 1869, a place of retirement for seamen, and since 1873 a Royal Naval College. The present buildings are mainly the design of Inigo Jones* and Christopher Wren*; it is on the south-bank of the Thames in the south-eastern quarter of London.

Greenwich Observatory

Erected by the order of Charles II in 1675 to advance nautical astronomy. Charles also inaugurated the office of Astronomer Royal. The longitudinal meridian passes through the Observatory from Pole to Pole. Greenwich time is time based on this meridian. In 1946 the observatory was moved to Herstmonceux in Sussex to escape the smoke and bright lights of London.

Greville, Sir Fulke (1st Baron Brooke) (1554–1628) /'grevil/

Writer of dramas of a philosophical kind, *eg Mustapha* and *Alaham*, and of *Caelica*, a collection of lyrics. He has been described as a Calvinist Stoic. He was a friend and contemporary of Sir Philip Sidney, of whom he wrote a life.

Bib: Rees, J., *Fulke Greville*.

Grey Friars

* *Franciscans*.

Griffin (Griffon, Gryphon)

In Greek myth, a monster with four legs, wings, and a beak – part eagle and part lion. It was consecrated to the sun, and watched over gold mines.

Grimm's Fairy Tales

German folk-tales collected by the brothers Jacob and Wilhelm Grimm, published 1812–15, and translated into English in 1823. They have been retold by many writers and continue to be very popular children's stories in England.

Grocyn, William (1446?–1519) /'grəusin/

English humanist*, and one of the earliest propagators of the study of ancient Greek in England; taught at Oxford.

Grub Street

A street in London frequented in 18th C by hacks, *ie* writers gaining a living by any sort of literary work they could get. Hence 'Grub-street' means literature or journalism of a low order. This is the reference in the title of Gissing's novel *New Grub Street**. The street in question is now called Milton Street.

Grundy, Mrs

A symbol of narrow-minded, intolerant, out-of-date moral censoriousness. The symbol derives from a character in an otherwise forgotten play; *Speed the Plough* (1798) by Thomas Morton. Mrs Grundy herself never appears, but her neighbour, Mrs Ashfield, is constantly worried about what Mrs Grundy's opinion will be about this or that incident or piece of behaviour.

Guelphs and Ghibellines /gwelfs – 'gibilainz/

Rival political parties in medieval Italy, the former supporting the influence of the Popes and the latter that of the German (Holy Roman*) Emperor. Hence, sometimes used for any two contending bodies of opinion.

Guild

* *Capitalism; Craft Guilds.*

Guildhall

In medieval times, the building where the Merchant Guild of a town held its meetings; now, often the name of a building where the town council meets, and especially the 15th-C town hall of the City of London.

Guinevere, Queen /'gwiniviə/

Wife of King Arthur*, in the Arthurian legend. According to Malory's *Morte d'Arthur**, the best-known English version of this legend, she and Sir Lancelot* developed a tragic love affair. This account goes back to the French of Chrétien de Troyes* and belongs to the class of medieval romances of courtly love, which commonly have a theme of adulterous love.

Gulliver's Travels (1726)

A satirical fable by Jonathan Swift*. It exploits the contemporary interest in accounts of voyages, *eg* William Dampier's *New Voyage* (1697). Daniel Defoe's* fictional account of Robinson Crusoe's voyages had been published in 1719, and had achieved great popularity; this was partly due to Defoe's strictly factual presentation, such that his book could quite well pass for a true account. Swift makes his hero, Lemuel Gulliver, recount his adventures with the same sober precision for the effect of accuracy, causing him, as Defoe caused Crusoe, to follow the philosopher Locke* in describing only the primary qualities of his strange environments – *ie* the objective, measurable ones – ignoring the secondary qualities of colour, beauty, etc. which are more subjective, less verifiable, and so more likely to arouse a reader's disbelief. Swift's intention in doing this was of course not to deceive his readers into supposing that Gulliver's fantastic adventures were true, but to make them realize the absurdity, and worse, of accepted human characteristics when they are looked at from an unfamiliar point of view. Thus in Part I, *Lilliput*, Gulliver is wrecked on an island where human beings are little bigger than insects, and their self-importance is clearly laughable, but in Part II, *Brobdingnag*, he is himself an insect in a land of giants, and made to feel his own pettiness. In Part III, contemporary scientists of the Royal Society are held up for ridicule: science is shown to be futile unless it is applicable to human betterment – the science of Swift's day had not yet reached the stage of technology. Part IV is about the land of the Houyhnhnms, where horses are endowed with reason but human beings are not; the point here is that the horses recognize that Gulliver has reason, unlike the Yahoos of the island which he so much resembles, but they succeed in demonstrating to him that human reason is woefully inadequate for the conduct of life because of the mischievousness of the human mind. Swift was, after all, a Christian, and believed that Man would destroy himself without divine aid.

Swift was such a good story-teller that his fable became popular for the sake of the narrative, and though it was in no ordinary sense a novel, his close attention to factual detail (the way in which, especially in Parts I and II, Gulliver is continuously under the pressure of his environment) takes a long stride in the advance of novelistic art.

* 4.3.1; *Travel Literature.*

Gunpowder Plot (1605)

A conspiracy by a section of English Roman Catholics to destroy the Protestant government of James I* by blowing up the Houses of Parliament at a time when the King, and the members of the Houses of Lords and Commons were all in the building. The plot was inspired by the Jesuits and led by Robert Catesby, but undertaken by Guy Fawkes. The date was fixed for 5 November, and the explosives were all laid; but the plot was betrayed, and Fawkes was arrested on the threshold of the cellar on 4 November. The day has since been celebrated annually with fireworks and bonfires on which Guy Fawkes is burnt in effigy.

Guy Fawkes

* *Gunpowder Plot.*

Guy Mannering (1815)

A novel by Sir Walter Scott*. It is set in the south of Scotland near the English border during 18th C. The plot concerns the attempt of a criminal lawyer, Glossin, to deprive Harry Bertram, the heir to the Scottish estate of Ellangowan, of his property. Bertram is kidnapped as a child by smugglers in Glossin's pay, and carried abroad. He returns to Scotland as a young man and recovers his estate with the help of a gipsy who lives on it, Meg

Merrilies*. Mannering is an English officer under whom Bertram has served in the army, and with whose daughter Julia he is in love. The novel is notable partly for its romantic scene painting, and partly for the characterization which is markedly more vivid in the lower social orders – the gipsies*, the farmer Dandy Dinmont, the tutor Dominie Sampson – than in its ladies and gentlemen. There are also very good descriptions of Edinburgh*.

Gypsies
* *Gipsies.*

H

Habeas Corpus /'heibjəs 'ko:pəs/
A legal writ which begins with these Latin words (= 'thou shalt have the body . . .'). The purpose is to order that a person should be brought before a judge. It has been most commonly used in instances of persons imprisoned without trial, so that a judge may decide the cause of imprisonment and arrange for a trial to take place. The writ was used in the Middle Ages as far back as 12th C, but its use was defined by Parliament in the Habeas Corpus Act of 1679. It has long been considered one of the foundations of English liberties.

Hades
In Greek myth, the god of the underworld; his Latin name is Pluto. He was brother of Zeus*, the king of the gods, and of Poseidon*. His name is often used for the underworld itself. It was mainly a gloomy world of shadowy existence bounded by the rivers Styx* and Acheron; one region, Tartarus*, was reserved for the punishment of those who had offended the gods, while another, the fields of Asphodel, was reserved for those who deserved neither reward nor punishment. The virtuous dead went elsewhere to Elysium*, though Virgil* regards Elysium too as part of the underworld.

Hakluyt, Richard (1553?–1616) /'haklu:t/
Geographer. In 1589 and 1598 he published his *Principal Navigations, Voyages and Discoveries of the English Nation*, being a record of English explorations, which had lagged behind those of the French, Spanish, Portuguese and Dutch until the middle of the century, and then made prodigious progress with the energy characteristic of England in the reign of Elizabeth I*.
* *Travel Literature.*

Hall, Edward (1498?–1547)
Chronicler; author of *The Union of the Noble and Illustrious Families of Lancaster and York* (1542; enlarged 1548, 1550). This tells of the bitter rivalries of the two branches of the House of Anjou (Plantagenets) from the death of the childless Richard II* in 1400, and the accession of Henry IV*, first of the House of Lancaster, to the death of the last of the House of York, Richard III*, in 1485, and the accession of Henry Tudor as Henry VII*. He idealizes Henry VII and Henry VIII*, partly because they re-established dynastic harmony, and partly because, as a Protestant*, Hall was strongly sympathetic to Henry VIII's reform of the Church. The Chronicle was one of Shakespeare's two main source-books for his English history plays, the other being Holinshed*.
* *Histories and Chronicles; Lancaster, House of; Wars of the Roses.*

Hall, Joseph (1574–1656)
Satirist; 'character'* writer; religious controversialist; Bishop, 1627–47. He published his *Virgidemiae* ('Harvest of Rods', *ie* for chastisement) in 1597–8; he claimed to be the first English satirist, but Donne* and Marston* were writing at the same time, not to mention Spenser's *Mother Hubberd's Tale**. He may have considered himself more truly a satirist than his rivals inasmuch as he was stricter in following classical Latin models, notably of Juvenal*. Like Juvenal, he attacked what he saw as contemporary vices. His *Characters of Virtues and Vices* (1608) was likewise in classical tradition, this time modelled on the Greek Theophrastus*, and was also intended for the moral improvement of the age.
Bib: Bush, D., in *English Literature in the Early Seventeenth Century.*

Hamlet
A tragedy by Shakespeare, written in about 1601. Three early versions of it exist: the imperfect quarto* of 1603, the superior quarto of 1604, and the version in the First Folio* of 1623, which omits some of the material in the 1604 quarto. The story was a widespread legend in northern Europe. Shakespeare's immediate source is likely to have been Belleforest's *Histoires Tragiques* (1559), and Belleforest's own version came from a 13th-C Danish chronicler, Saxo Grammaticus. But Shakespeare also had another source: a play of the same name already existed when he wrote, and is thought to have been a lost play by Thomas Kyd*. It is referred to without mention of the author by Nashe* in a letter accompanying Greene's* *Menaphon* (1589), by Henslowe* in his Diary (1594), and by Lodge* in *Wit's Misery* (1596). There are also parallels between Shakespeare's play and Kyd's *Spanish Tragedy**: both have ghosts and a play within the play; Kyd's tragedy is about a father seeking vengeance for his son, and Shakespeare's is about a son avenging his father. In both plays there are obstacles to the vengeance: in Kyd's play, the obstacle is a straightforward one, of how to bring retribution upon an offender who is so powerful as to be beyond the law; in Shakespeare it is so subtle that Hamlet's hesitations have been among the most discussed subjects in criticism.

Certain features of Shakespeare's play require special attention in assessing the play.

[1] The basic situation is that Hamlet's uncle, Claudius*, has married Hamlet's mother, Gertrude, only a month after the death of her husband, old Hamlet. Claudius has, moreover, ascended the throne ignoring the claim of his nephew and with the consent of the court. This thoroughly distasteful situation reflects badly not only on Claudius and Gertrude, but on the court as well, and it has already plunged Hamlet into disgust at the opening of the play. We need also to remember that marriage to a sister-in-law was of at least doubtful validity: it constituted Henry VIII's legal ground for divorce from Katharine of Aragon*.

[2] It is only later that Hamlet learns from his father's ghost that old Hamlet was murdered by Claudius. The revelation does not lead directly to action, but to Hamlet feigning madness, and to the 'play within the play', before which Claudius, in the audience, betrays his guilt.

[3] Claudius's self-betrayal, however, is only incriminating to Hamlet and his friend Horatio, who have already learned the facts. Either Hamlet mistrusts the Ghost who may not have been truly the spirit of his father, or it is part of his vengeance to inform Claudius that his guilt is known. One of the beliefs about ghosts* current in Shakespeare's time was that they were sometimes evil spirits assuming the disguise of dead men.

[4] Hamlet's hostility extends not merely to Claudius, but to the whole court, in so far as they are or may be subservient to Claudius. Thus Hamlet behaves brutally to Ophelia (the girl whom he loves) because he suspects (although she is entirely innocent) that she is used as a kind of decoy by Claudius and by her father, Polonius.

[5] Laertes, Ophelia's brother, is a contrast to Hamlet in being a straightforward revenger: he immediately seeks the death of Hamlet for causing the deaths of his father and sister. But his impetuosity puts him on the side of evil, for it causes him to connive with Claudius.

[6] Claudius is an unusual villain for the drama of the time, for he is not *seen* to be evil on the stage; we know of his guilt indirectly. Even his conspiracy against Hamlet's life can be excused as action in self-defence.

These features of the play suggest that Shakespeare was exposing traditional beliefs about revenge as over-simplified. Revenge is difficult if we do not feel the guilty man to be guilty: 'One may smile, and smile and be a villain' (I. v. 108). Further, revenge does not solve evil, if evil lies in a complex situation: 'The time is out of joint; O cursed spite / That ever I was born to set it right.' (V. i. 189–90). Finally, revenge itself may be morally wrong: what *was* the Ghost? Many of the difficulties of the play are discussed interestingly by J. D. Wilson in his book *What Happens in Hamlet.*

* 5.1.3.2. *Revenge Tragedy.*

Hampton Court

A palace on the Thames built by Cardinal Wolsey* and a principal royal residence in 16th and 17th C. It has an addition designed by Christopher Wren*.

Handel, George Frederick (1685–1759)

Composer. Born in Germany, he was appointed chief musician to George, Elector of Hanover, who became George I of Britain (1714–27). Handel visited England in 1710, and settled there in 1712; he became a naturalized British citizen in 1726. He had studied in Italy and was deeply experienced in French music, but in many respects his genius was in harmony with the English tradition, whose last great master, Henry Purcell*, had died in 1695. Nonetheless, Handel at first had an uneven career in England. He first attempted to establish opera in the Italian style; his opera *Rinaldo* was a success in 1711. Yet opera in the end reduced him to bankruptcy, and he became the great exponent of the art of oratorio, which he transformed from its original religious feeling and setting into a much more theatrical form. His first oratorio, *Esther* (1720), resembled the masques* that had been popular in fashionable circles since early in the previous century. *Semele*, *Susanna*, and *Judas Maccabeus*, to mention a few of the sixteen oratorios that followed, are choral dramas. His masterpiece was *The Messiah*, first performed in Dublin, 1741. Handel established the oratorio as the most popular English musical form for the next two centuries. Others of his choral works included his choral settings for Dryden's* poems, *Ode on St Cecilia's Day*, and *Alexander's Feast*.

Handel was a man of European culture, but, although he never properly mastered the English language, his combination of dramatic energy and majestic formal balance made him one of the greatest representatives of the English Augustan Age*.

Bib: Deutsch, O. E., *Handel: A Documentary Biography.*

Hanover, House of

* *George; Windsor, House of.*

Hansard /'hansa:d/

The official report of meetings of both Houses of Parliament, so called after an 18th-C printer employed by the government.

Hard Times (1854)

A novel by Charles Dickens*. It is the only one by him not at least partly set in London. The scene is an imaginary industrial town called Coketown. One of the main characters, Thomas Gradgrind, is based on the Utilitarian* leader James Mill (1773–1836); as such, he is an educationist who believes that education should be merely practical and hence factual, allowing no place for imagination or emotion. He marries his daughter Louisa to a ruthless manufacturer, Josiah Bounderby, who puts Gradgrind's philosophy into practice in that he has no place for humane feeling in the conduct of his business. Louisa accepts him in order to be in a position to help her brother Tom who becomes, under the influence of his upbringing, callous, unscrupulous, and meanly calculating. Louisa is nearly seduced by a visiting politician, James

Harthouse, who is cynically concerned only to find amusement in a place with no other charms. The opposition to this world of calculating selfishness is a travelling circus called 'the horse-riding' owned by Sleary. Cissy Jupe, a product of the circus and the human fellowship that it engenders, is found ineducable by Gradgrind, whose dependant she becomes, but she has the inner assurance required to face Harthouse and compel him to leave the town. Gradgrind's world falls apart when he discovers that he has ruined his daughter's happiness and turned his son into a criminal. A subplot concerns a working-man, Stephen Blackpool, a victim of the Gradgrind-Bounderby system, and of young Gradgrind's heartless criminality.

*** 2.1.1.3.**

Hardy, Thomas (1840–1928)

Novelist and poet. He was the son of a village builder in Dorset; thus he was close to the country peasantry by his origins, and he never lost feeling for them. As he grew up, he underwent the painful loss of faith so common among intellectuals in England in the second half of 19th C; this led him to a tragic philosophy that human beings are the victims of indifferent forces. At the same time he witnessed the steady weakening from within and erosion from without of the part of rural England with which he was so much identified. This region is the six south-western counties of England, approximately coterminous with the 6th-C Saxon kingdom of Wessex*, by which name he calls them in his 'Novels of Character and Environment'. These novels are by far this best known: *Under the Greenwood Tree** (1872); *Far from the Madding Crowd** (1874); *The Return of the Native** (1878); *The Mayor of Casterbridge** (1886); *The Woodlanders** (1887); *Tess of the D'Urbervilles** (1891); *Jude the Obscure** (1895). Two volumes of stories are *Wessex Tales* (1888) and *Life's Little Ironies* (1894). Hardy's originality was his discernment of the intimate relationship of character and environment, and his characters nearly always become less convincing when this relationship loses closeness, *ie* in his socially higher, more sophisticated characters. This may account for the fact that the other two groups of his novels have much less prestige. He called them 'Romances and Fantasies' (*A Pair of Blue Eyes*, 1873; *The Trumpet-Major*, 1880; *Two on a Tower*, 1882; *A Group of Noble Dames*, 1891; *The Well-Beloved*, 1897) and 'Novels of Ingenuity' (*Desperate Remedies*, 1871; *The Hand of Ethelberta*, 1876; *A Laodicean*, 1881).

Hardy's poetry is as distinguished as his novels; some critics would say more – that verse was his vocation, and that he turned to prose fiction because this promised a larger public. Though he wrote it from the beginning of his career, his best verse was chiefly the fruit of his later years when he had abandoned novels. It is in some respects very traditional – ballads such as *The Trampwoman's Tragedy*, and tuneful, rhyming lyrics. But though traditional – in touch with folksong and ballad – Hardy was never conventional. His diction is distinctive, and the singing rhythms subtly respond to the movement of his intense feelings; the consequent poignance and sincerity has brought him the admiration of poets since 1945, who seem especially sensitive to dishonesty of feeling. His lyrics have the peculiarity that they nearly always centre on incident, in a way that gives them dramatic sharpness. Amongst the most admired are some that he wrote to his dead first wife, included in *Satires of Circumstance* (1914). The *Collected Poems* (1932) are uneven in merit; the Penguin Books selection, edited W. E. Williams, is a good one.

*** 4.4.2; 6.4.2.**

Bib: Hardy, E., *Life*; Brown, D., *Thomas Hardy*; Weber, C. J., *Hardy of Wessex*.

Harley Street

A street in the West End of London largely occupied by medical specialists.

Harpies

In Greek myths, personifications – half bird and half woman – of storm winds. They snatched food from tables and caused hunger, hence Ariel's role as a harpy in *The Tempest** III. iii.

Harrow School

One of the great public schools*. It was founded in 1571 for poor children of the neighbourhood. After 1660 the school took children from the whole country, and in 18th and 19th C it became immensely fashionable. In 19th C the Eton v. Harrow cricket match became one of the most fashionable social occasions of the London season.

Hartley, David (1705–57)

Philosopher. He is important for his theory of association of ideas, based on the thought of Sir Isaac Newton* and of John Locke* in 17th C. In his *Observations on Man* (1749) he denied that moral ideas were inborn in man, holding that they derived from associations of pleasure and pain with certain behaviour. The higher pleasures derive from the lower, and culminate in the love of God. This philosophy of mechanistic psychology was very influential in the first half of 19th C, especially on the Utilitarian* school of thinkers. Coleridge* was at first strongly under Hartley's influence, but later rejected it, asserting that the human personality was active in its growth, not passive as Hartley's theory implied. Wordsworth* based much of his feeling for nature's creative influence on human personality on Hartley.

Hartley, L. P. (b 1895)

Novelist. Novels and stories: *Night Fears* (1924): *Simonetta Perkins* (1925); *The Killing Bottle* (1932); a trilogy – *The Shrimp and the Anemone* (1944), *The Sixth Heaven* (1946) and *Eustace and Hilda* (1947); *The Travelling Grave* (1948); *The Boat* (1949); *My Fellow Devils* (1951); *The Go-Between* (1953); *The White Wand* (1954); *A Perfect Woman* (1955); *The Hireling* (1957); *Facial Justice* (1960); *Two for the River* (1961); *The Brickfield* (1964), and *The Betrayal* (1966). His reputation rests at present chiefly on the trilogy (especially *The Shrimp and the Anemone*) and *The Go-Between*. These both contain very sensitive child studies, and relate the influence of childhood experiences on the development of the adult. Hartley is in the tradition of Henry James*, whom he resembles in his presentation of delicate but crucial personal inter-relationships; the effect of the psychologist Sigmund Freud* has intervened to give Hartley a different kind of psychological depth, more concerned with the recovery of the self buried in the forgotten experiences of the past than with the self buried under the false assumptions of society.

Bib: Brit. Council Pamphlet by Bernard Bergonzi; Allen, W., in *The Novel Today*.

Harvey, Gabriel (1545?–1630)

Man of letters and scholar; friend of Edmund Spenser* who presents him as Hobbinol in his *Shepherd's Calendar**. He argued vigorously for substituting Latin quantitative metres (based on length of syllables) for the English accentual rhythms which rely on accent. Otherwise he is chiefly known for his violent quarrels (especially with Thomas Nashe* and Robert Greene*) which cause his name to figure prominently in the pamphlets of the time.

Hatter, The Mad

A character in Lewis Carroll's* children's classic *Alice's Adventures in Wonderland* (1865). He is the friend of the March Hare – also mad – and the tea-party which they attend with Alice and the dormouse is one of the memorable scenes in the book. The reference, as with a good many characters and incidents in *Alice*, is to a popular saying: 'as mad as a hatter', itself a reference to a particular 17th-C hatmaker.

Hawking (Falconry)

The sport of using birds of prey (hawks, falcons, etc.) for the pursuit of other birds and of small mammals such as rabbits and hares. In England as in every other European country it was both a popular and a fashionable sport until in 17th C it was driven out by the use of the gun. Different species were considered appropriate to the various ranks of society, *eg* the eagle for emperors, gerfalcons for kings, peregrines for earls, goshawks for yeomen, sparrow-hawks for priests, kestrels for servants. The hawk was kept on the wrist of the falconer, and released when the prey or 'quarry' came into view. The training of the hawk, *eg* not to fly away with its prey, is a long and complicated

process. A good many hawking terms passed into common speech in the Middle Ages and 16th C; the following is a selection of terms that occur in writings:

Bate. A hawk 'bates' when it flutters up from the wrist of the falconer and returns to it.

Check. A hawk flies at 'check' when it makes an attempt at the wrong quarry.

Eyas. A hawk which is being trained from the nest.

Eyry. The nest of a hawk.

Haggard. A female hawk, caught and tamed from the adult wild state.

Hood. A covering for the eyes of a hawk, so that it should not look about while on the wrist.

Jesses. Strips of leather that remain fastened to a hawk's legs.

Leash. A leather thong about 3 feet long, used to keep a hawk secured to the wrist.

Lure. A piece of meat or other object used for summoning a hawk.

Mantle. A hawk 'mantles' when it hides its quarry by spreading out wings and tailfeathers over it.

Mew. A hawk 'mews' when it loses its feathers or moults.

Pitch. The height to which a hawk rises in the air.

Pounces. A hawk's claws.

Quarry. The prey or object of pursuit.

Seeling. The closing of the eyes of a hawk by drawing a fine thread through each eyelid, and twisting the threads above its head.

Stoop (swoop). The swift descent of a hawk on its quarry.

Tiercel (tarcel, tassel, tercel). The male of several species of falcon, *ie* long-winged hawk.

Haymarket

A short London street in the West End containing two famous theatres. The first of these was the opera house designed for his own use by Vanbrugh*, opened in 1705 as the Queen's Theatre and now called Her Majesty's. The other is the Haymarket Theatre, opened in 1720 without patent or licence. Fielding* took it over in 1735 and his attacks there on royalty and other personages and institutions led to the 1737 Licensing Act (*Theatres), which kept it closed for only a brief period before legal loopholes were found which enabled it to function unlicensed.

Hazlitt, William (1778–1830) /'heizlit/

Essayist and critic. He was the son of a Unitarian* minister with strong radical views, and himself took the liberal side in politics throughout his life; though he wrote for many papers and periodicals, he is most associated with John and Leigh Hunt's radical weekly, *The Examiner**. He was the early admirer and friend of Coleridge* and Wordsworth* (see one of his best essays, *My First Acquaintance with Poets*, 1823), and though he later resented what he considered their betrayal of the liberal cause, he continued to admire especially Wordsworth's early poetry for its integrity and disinterestedness, qualities which he exemplified in his own life. However, he did not share the simplifying, materialistic outlook of many of the radicals *eg* the Utilitarians*; his best work, *The Spirit of the Age* (1825) – studies of the leading minds of the time, including Bentham* and Wordsworth – shows his feeling that rational theorists like the former were really remoter from reality, though they claimed to base all their thought on experience, than were the poets who gave form to their experience directly. This regard for whole truth shows in his best criticism, especially of Shakespeare, (*Characters of Shakespeare's Plays*, 1817–18), and makes him, with Coleridge, one of the first critics to show understanding of Shakespeare's imaginative method. Other critical work: *Lectures on the English Poets* (1818–19); *English Comic Writers* (1819); *Dramatic Literature of the Age of Elizabeth*, 1820; *Table Talk, or Original Essays on Men and Manners*, 1821–2.

Though nowadays especially admired for his criticism, Hazlitt has always had a larger public for his miscellaneous essays, such as *On Going a Journey*, *Going to a Fight*, etc. His graphic, terse, energetic style often gives this part of his work strong character. Its detailed description and interest in mood anticipates some characteristics of the great age of the English novel which opened with the work of Dickens.

* 7.3; *Essay.*

Bib: Howe, P. P., *Life*; Baker, H., *Life*; Schneider, E., *The Aesthetics of Hazlitt*; Brinton C., *The Political Ideas of the English Romantics*; Stephen, L., in *Hours in a Library*; Saintsbury, G., in *Essays in English Literature.*

Headlong Hall (1816)

A novel by Thomas Love Peacock*. It is his first, and shows the main characteristics of his maturer work: witty, burlesque conversations and very little plot; the narrative interspersed with attractive lyrics and songs. As in his other novels, the characters are caricatures of contemporary types.

Heart of Midlothian, The (1818)

A novel by Sir Walter Scott*. Midlothian is a county in Scotland in which Edinburgh, the Scottish capital, is situated. The title refers to the old Tolbooth* prison in Edinburgh, so nicknamed. The central part of the story is Jeanie Deans's journey on foot to London in order to appeal to the Duke of Argyle – a Scottish nobleman high in royal favour – on behalf of her sister Effie who has been wrongfully charged with child murder. Argyle was a historical character, and the events are linked up with the attack on the Tolbooth – known as the Porteous riot – which actually took place, in 1736. As in other novels by Scott about 18th-C Scotland, the characterization is vigorous, *eg* of Madge Wildfire who has abducted the child whom Effie is supposed to have murdered, and Dumbiedikes, the silent suitor of Jeanie. It is commonly held to to be the best of Scott's novels.

Heartbreak House (1917)

A play by Bernard Shaw*. It is set in an English country house, and ends with the outbreak of the First World War. The guests are intellectuals, and the mood is one of disillusionment reminiscent of the plays of Chekhov* *eg The Cherry Orchard.* But Shaw typically exploits the conventional theatre of the later 19th C, introducing love rivalries which invite expectation of passionate climaxes, but end in calculated anticlimaxes. The Preface discusses the role of the English country house – either hunting or intellectual – in the English scene; the play brings out the frustration and disillusionment which burden the latter.

Heaven

The abode of God, in ancient Greek, Hebrew, Latin, and Christian religions. According to the cosmology of Ptolemy* the earth was surrounded by heavenly spheres, commonly seven of them. God resided in the seventh of these, hence the most blessed of all. Islamic and later Jewish cosmologies also recognized seven heavens.

Heavenly Twins

* *Castor and Pollux.*

Hecate /ˈhekəti/

In Greek myth, a goddess of the underworld. She was the queen of magic and witchcraft.

Hector

In Homer's *Iliad**, the most valiant of the sons of Priam, King of Troy, in the Trojan war. He was eventually killed by the Greek hero Achilles*, but in medieval and later literature he is commonly referred to as the principal hero of the epic.

Hecuba /ˈhekjubə/

In Homer's *Iliad**, wife of Priam, King of Troy, and mother of 19 of his 50 sons, including Hector* and Paris*. On the capture of Troy, she was made captive by the Greeks. There are various myths about her fate; she seems to have been changed into a dog.

Hegel, Georg Wilhelm Friedrich (1770–1831) /ˈheigl/

German philosopher and author of *Phenomenology of Mind* (1807) and *Logic* (1812–16).

* *German Influence on English Literature.*

Helen

In Greek myth, daughter of Zeus*, who disguised himself as a swan in order to achieve union with her earthly mother, Leda. Helen has always been regarded as the type of perfect female beauty. She became the wife of Menelaus, king of Sparta, but ran away with Paris*, son of Priam, king of Troy. She thus occasioned the siege of Troy by the Greeks, the subject of Homer's epic the *Iliad**. After the destruction of Troy, according to Virgil's *Aeneid**, she returned to Menelaus. Her brothers were Castor* and Pollux.

Hell

'Hel' was the underworld, or its goddess, of the pre-Christian Scandinavians. 'Hell' thence became the term for the Christian underworld of the Middle Ages, or the state of eternal torment for mortal sinners after death. In the Bible, it is used to translate the Greek Hades*, and the Hebrew Sheol* (Old Testament) or Gehenna* (New Testament).

Hellas /ˈhelas/

In Greek, the name of Greece. Hellenes were the Greeks. Hellenism: the influence of ancient Hellenic or Greek culture, especially in its ideals of intellectual enlightenment and the cultivation of beauty. Matthew Arnold* for example, in *Culture and Anarchy* (1869), contrasted Hellenism, in which he thought Victorian England was deficient, with Hebraism, or primary concern with right and wrong conduct, of which he thought she had quite enough.

Hellas is the title of a poetic drama by Shelley*; it was published in 1822 and inspired by the proclamation of Greek independence in 1821.

Hellespont /ˈhelispont/

The Dardanelles, the narrow strait separating Europe from Asia Minor and joining the Aegean Sea to the Sea of Marmara.

Helots /ˈhelәts/

The serfs in the ancient Greek state of Sparta*. They were enslaved by the Dorian invaders, who became the ruling military caste, before 1000 BC.

Heming, John (d 1630) and Condell, Henry (d 1627)

Acting colleagues of Shakespeare and editors of the first edition of his collected plays, known as the First Folio, 1623.

* *Folio.*

Hendecasyllabic /ˈhendekәsiˈlabik/

A metrical term meaning a line of verse having 11 syllables; decasyllabic = 10 syllables.

Hengist and Horsa /ˈheŋgist – ˈhoːsә/

Brothers who led the Jutes*, invaders of Britain. They were originally summoned by the British king Vortigern after the departure of the Romans (early 5th C) to help him resist the Pictish invaders from the north. They then quarrelled with their British allies, and seized what later became the county of Kent.

Henry I (1100–35)

The third Norman* king of England, fourth son of William I*.

Henry II (1154–89)

King of England. Son of Geoffrey Plantagenet, Count of Anjou, and Matilda, daughter of Henry I. Henry II was thus the first king of the House of Anjou, or Plantagenet*. By inheritance and marriage with Eleanor of Aquitaine he acquired all western France from Normandy to the Spanish border. In England, he was an extremely efficient ruler, especially in organization of the law courts, but this brought him into his famous conflict with Thomas à Becket*, Archbishop of Canterbury. His relationship with his wife was largely hostile, and later romancers made much of his love affair with Fair Rosamund* – Rosamund Clifford – *eg* Daniel* in his *Complaint of Rosamond.* The conquest of Ireland by the feudal nobility of England took place in his reign.

Henry III (1216–72)

King of England, fourth of the Plantagenet* line. His reign was much disturbed by internal conflict, especially the rebellion led by Simon de Montfort, who first secured the representation of the towns and the smaller landowners in the Great Council of the kingdom, from which Parliament has developed.

Henry IV (1399–1413)

King of England. He was called Bolingbroke from the name of his birthplace. His father, John of Gaunt*, Duke of Lancaster, was a younger son of Edward III*; his cousin Richard II* exiled Henry and confiscated his estates, in retaliation for which Henry succeeded in raising a rebellion and seizing the throne. Richard died mysteriously in prison. Henry thus became first of the three kings of the House of Lancaster*, really a junior branch of the Plantagenet* line. His reign was the subject of two plays by Shakespeare, *1 & 2 Henry IV.*

1 Henry IV

A history play by Shakespeare, performed about 1597 and printed in a quarto* edition, 1598. The central character is Prince Hal, the king's son and later Henry V*. The king is grieved first by the opposition of some of his nobles led by the Percy* family, notably Henry (Harry) Hotspur*, son of the Duke of Northumberland, and secondly by the dissolute conduct of his own son, who wastes his life in taverns instead of emulating Hotspur in a career of military honour. Hal's tavern companion is Sir John Falstaff*, one of the greatest of Shakespeare's comic characters. The contrast between Hotspur and Falstaff is the prominent feature of the play: Hotspur lives only for honour, without relating it to social responsibility; Falstaff, only for pleasure, in equal indifference to social consequences. Hotspur is thus passionate but inhuman, and Falstaff all too human in his passions. At the end of the play, Hal kills Hotspur at the battle of Shrewsbury, but Falstaff manages to steal the credit for Hotspur's death. The play is close to the Morality* tradition in its feeling and structure. Hotspur and Falstaff standing for 'honour' and 'riot' respectively; both in their different ways are rebels, the first in political terms against the state, and the second in spiritual terms against reason. Shakespeare's main sources were the chronicles of Hall* and Holinshed*.

* *History Plays.*

2 Henry IV
Quarto* edition 1600. A continuation of Shakespeare's *Henry IV*, Part 1, though independent in mood and dramatic structure. The Percy rebellion continues, though Hotspur is dead. A sick weariness is over the country, and the king is dying. Hal is still the central character, and again flanked by contrasting types: on the one side, Falstaff, pleasure-loving still but now aging and grasping for the power he expects when Hal becomes King Henry V; on the other side, the scrupulous and fearless Lord Chief Justice, who has faced his responsibilities so far as to send the Prince himself to prison for riot. However, when Hal becomes king at the end of the play, he unexpectedly upholds the Lord Chief Justice and dismisses Falstaff from favour. Again, the Morality* drama tradition is a strong influence: the just king upholds the principle of justice, and sets his face against riot and self-indulgence. Some of the best scenes are still comedy though the mood of Part 2 is grimmer than that of Part 1; the comedy is chiefly in Mistress Quickly's Boar's Head Tavern in London, and on the country estate of Justice Shallow. Shakespeare's sources were again the 16th-C chronicles of Hall* and Holinshed*.
  * *History Plays; 1 Henry IV.*

Henry V (1413–22)
King of England, and second of the House of Lancaster*. His brief reign is memorable for his brilliant victory over the French at Agincourt*. By the Treaty of Troyes (1420) he was recognized as heir to the throne of France, his claim to which had been the cause of the war. His dissolute youth (see Shakespeare's *Henry IV**) was a popular legend but is probably unfounded, though he was on bad terms with his father. He modelled himself on King Arthur*, the great heroes of the Crusades*, and the ideal of the Christian monarchy (the French war, in English eyes, was a just one) and in English tradition he became a national hero.
  * *Hundred Years' War.*

Henry V
A history play by Shakespeare performed in 1599; an imperfect version printed in 1600. It records the battle of Agincourt*, Henry's great victory in France; this is the triumphal conclusion to the series which had so far dramatized national disaster: *Richard II**, *1 & 2 Henry IV**. This play has been censured as too much a patriotic pageant with too little genuine dramatic interest. However, there is drama in the spectacle of a small national army united in moral purpose under a Christian king confronting a rich massive array of selfishly disunited nobility. The disintegrative elements on the English side are still present in the traitors Scroop and Grey, and in Falstaff's former cronies, Pistol, Bardolph and Nym. The union of the British Isles is forecast by the presence not only of the prominent Welsh officer, Fluellen, but of Irish and Scottish officers as well, though Scotland was in fact an ally of France at the time. The play is indeed primarily a patriotic drama, but it is by no means an uncritical one. There is, for instance, the obvious element of conflict in Henry between his dual aspects as King and as man, evident especially in his dialogue with Williams and his soliloquy in IV.i; modern critics (*eg* Traversi, *Approach to Shakespeare*) find many examples of irony at the expense of Henry in the play.
  * *History Plays.*

Henry VI (1422–61)
King of England, and last of the House of Lancaster*. He was strongly religious but no man of action, and his reign was darkened by the Wars of the Roses* and by the final defeat of England in the Hundred Years' War*.

1 2 & 3 Henry VI
Three very early history plays by Shakespeare, perhaps written between 1590 and 1592; Parts 2 and 3 were published in 1594–95 under different titles, but Part 1 not till 1623; it was possibly written, or revised, after the other two. Together they make the first three parts of a tetralogy ending with *Richard III** in which the spreading feuds, hatreds, crimes and vengeances finally concentrate all their force in the wickedness of one man. Part 1: the defeat of the English in the Hundred Years' War*, and the beginning of aristocratic feuds; Part 2: the marriage of Henry to the vigorous Margaret of Anjou*, Jack Cade's* popular rebellion, and the opening of the civil Wars of the Roses*; Part 3: Henry's final defeat and murder at the hands of the York branch of the Plantagenets*, Edward Earl of March (Edward IV, 1461–83) and his brother Richard of Gloucester (Richard III, 1483–5). The Henry VI plays have vivid and poignant episodes but are inferior to the masterly *Richard III*. The 16th-C chroniclers, Hall* and Holinshed*, are the sources of the plays.
  * *History Plays.*

Henry VII (1485–1509)
King of England. He was the first of the House of Tudor*, of Welsh origin and related to the House of Lancaster*; he defeated Richard III*, last of the House of York, at the battle of Bosworth (1485), with a mainly Welsh army. Henry connected his Welsh background with King Arthur*, and gave this name to his eldest son (d 1502). He was a notably able ruler, and was later paralleled with Henry V* as a restorer of national unity and order after civil war. At the end of Shakespeare's *Richard III** he makes an appearance as a national redeemer. Francis Bacon* wrote a life of him (1622).

Henry VIII (1509–47)
King of England. He was a powerful and talented man, entitled Defender of the Faith by the Pope for his pamphlet against Luther*, but he replaced Papal authority by his own by the Act of Supremacy*, 1534. His religious opinions remained otherwise conservative. He is notorious for having had six wives, two of whom he executed and two divorced. His personal power was great but he generally exerted it through Parliament, which has

caused a historian to designate him 'the greatest Parliamentarian who ever sat on the English throne'.

* *Tudor, House of.*

Henry VIII

A history play written (probably) by John Fletcher* and Shakespeare*. (For a view that the play is entirely Shakespeare's, see G. Wilson Knight: *The Shakespearian Tempest.*) Its main episodes concern the divorce of Katherine of Aragon*, the downfall of Cardinal Wolsey*, and the triumph of Thomas Cranmer*. The play ends with the triumphal christening of Henry's daughter, Princess Elizabeth, the future queen. In 1613 a performance of the play at the Globe Theatre* caused the destruction of the building by fire.

Henryson, Robert (1425?–1500?)

Scottish poet. His important works are his *Morall Fabillis* (Moral Fables) and his *Testament of Cresseid.* The former are a retelling of certain of Aesop's* Fables, fresh and original in style, and the latter, a great poem, is a continuation of Chaucer's *Troilus and Criseyde**. He also wrote *Orpheus and Eurydice* and a pastoral dialogue *Robene and Makyne.* Like others of the Scottish 15th-C poets, he is sometimes said to belong to 'the school of Chaucer'; most modern critics consider this description misleading and implying an under-estimate.

* *Cresseid, the Testament of; Fifteenth-century Literature; Scottish Literature.*

Bib: Stearns, M.W., *Robert Henryson*; Tillyard, E.M.W., *Testament of Cresseid* in *Five poems.*

Henslowe, Philip (d 1616) /'henzləu/

Theatre owner and builder. The Rose, the Hope, and the Fortune Theatres were all at least partly owned by him. His son-in-law was the famous actor Edward Alleyn* of the Admiral's Men*, whose finances he looked after. His Diary, 1592–1609, is a main source for the theatrical history of the age.

* *Theatres.*

Hephaestus /hi'fi:stəs/

(Vulcan.) In Greek myth, the god of fire, and the metal-worker of the gods. He was lame and ugly but his wife is represented as either Charis, a Spring goddess, or Aphrodite*.

Heptarchy /'hepta:ki/

From 5th to 9th C England was divided into a number of kingdoms, considered by 16th-C historians to have been seven (hence heptarchy, for seven kingdoms). These were: Northumbria in the north, Mercia in the midlands, East Anglia and Essex in the east, Kent in the south-east, Sussex and Wessex in the south and south-west. Such kingdoms certainly existed, but in fact the number was sometimes larger than seven, sometimes smaller. Essex (= East Saxons), Sussex (= South Saxons), and Kent have survived into modern England as counties. Wessex was a geographical term revived by Thomas Hardy* in his regional

novels. East Anglia is still used for the counties of Norfolk (= North folk) and Suffolk (= South folk) together. Northumberland remains as the nucleus of the former much larger Northumbria. The term Mercia is never used, Midlands having replaced it.

Hera /'hi:rə/

(Latin, Juno.) Sister and wife of Zeus*. She was closely associated with the phases of female life and with childbirth: sacred to her were the crow, the cuckoo and the peacock. She was a jealous wife and harried her husband's mortal mistresses.

Heracles /'herəkli:z/

(Latin, Hercules.) In Greek myth, the most celebrated of all heroes. He was the son of Zeus* and Alcmene, a mortal woman. Zeus's queen, Hera, in jealousy, sent two serpents to destroy him in his cradle but he strangled them – the first evidence of his prodigious strength. Later, she succeeded in driving him mad so that he killed his children. In penance for this, he undertook the twelve Labours of Hercules:

[1] The killing of the Nemean lion.

[2] The killing of a nine-headed serpent called the Lernaean Hydra.

[3] The capture of the wild boar of Erymanthus.

[4] The destruction of the man-eating birds of Stymphalus.

[5] The capture of the hind with the golden horns and brass hooves on Mount Ceryneia.

[6] The cleansing of the stables of Augeas.

[7] The capture of the Cretan mad bull.

[8] The capture of the man-eating mares of Diomedes.

[9] The capture of the precious girdle of Hippolyta*, Queen of the Amazons.

[10] The destruction of the three-bodied monster Geryon* and the capture of his herds.

[11] The bringing of the golden apples from the garden of the Hesperides*, at the western extreme of the world.

[12] The bringing from Hell of the three-headed dog, Cerberus*. Each labour involved a number of formidable subsidiary adventures. He met his death in a shirt soaked in the blood of the Centaur* Nessus whom he had killed; the shirt caused him intolerable agony, and he caused his friend Poeas to consume him with flames on his funeral pyre. He was received by the gods, reconciled to Hera, and married to her daughter Hebe, goddess of youth. A number of other tales are told of his strenuous life on earth.

Heraclitus (6th C BC) /herə'klaitəs/

Greek philosopher. He taught that the primary element is fire, and that all being is, despite appearances, the process of 'becoming', by the harmonious interaction of opposites (hot, cold; dark, light; good, evil, etc.). 'The law of things is a law of Reason universal; but most men behave as though they had a wisdom of their own.' His mysticism

and his sombre view of human nature caused him to be designated 'the dark philosopher'.
* *Elements, The.*

Heralds' College

A royal corporation, also called the College of Arms, founded in 1483 to regulate coats of arms, *ie* special formal designs originally worn by gentlemen in battle (before the days of military uniforms) to distinguish them for their followers. By 16th C the possession of these 'armorial bearings' was equivalent to the right to call oneself a gentleman, and their function in battle fell into disuse. The College grants armorial bearings for a fee. A modern function of the College is to trace and record family descent.
* *Gentleman.*

Herbert, Edward (Lord Herbert of Cherbury) (1583–1648)

Poet, philosopher, diplomatist. He was brother to the more famous poet, George Herbert*; they were members of an eminent noble family into which Sir Philip Sidney's* sister had married. His poetry is between the Metaphysical* school of his brother George and John Donne* – thoughtful, reasoning, imaginative – and that of the Cavalier Poets* such as Lovelace* and Suckling*, with their greater emphasis on lucidity and elegance of wit. In philosophy he has been called the 'father of deism', since he maintained the existence of a 'natural religion' common to mankind, and that belief in God was instinctive: *De Veritate* (Concerning the Truth, 1624). He wrote his autobiography in his old age, and a life of Henry VIII*.
* *Deism.*

Bib: Cruttwell, P., in *The Shakespearian Moment*; Williamson, G., in *The Donne Tradition*; Rossi, M.M., *Life* (in Italian).

Herbert, George (1593–1633)

One of the best poets of the Metaphysical* school. He came of an eminent family, and was younger brother of Lord Herbert of Cherbury, poet and philosopher. He won distinction at Cambridge University, and was a favourite at the court of James I*; yet in 1625 (the year of James's death) he renounced worldly ambitions, and became clergyman in a small parish (Bemerton) near Salisbury.

His poems, almost all of which were included in *The Temple; Sacred Poems and Private Ejaculations*, were published soon after his death. They are deeply religious; Herbert's Anglican* Christianity was strong and deep. The imagery is simple and concrete, and owes much to the popular emblem-books*. In the work of a less distinguished poet, such as the widely read Francis Quarles*, 'emblem' poems of this kind sometimes became commonplace exercises in moralizing ingenuity, with little deep relevance to human experience. Herbert, however, made them the means of active thought and sensitive and profound feeling. His poems combine elements which are not often found together: he uses the direct, unassuming language of the common man, and yet unites it with philosophical insight, sensuous response, and courtly graciousness. Despite this courtliness, he despised and rejected the amorous and artificial pastoral* mode of writing of the sophisticated courtier-poets like Suckling* and Lovelace*. Coleridge, in *Biographia Literaria**, cites him as the master of the 'neutral style' which he considered Wordsworth to be requiring in his Preface to the *Lyrical Ballads**: a poetic diction based on 'a selection of language really used by men'. In Herbert, the 'metaphysical' imagery is used much less to express the tortured kind of emotion so often found in Donne*, although some of the poems are about painful emotional and spiritual conflict. For poets writing since 1920, he is a fine example of the unity of thought and feeling which existed, according to Eliot's* theory of the 'dissociation of sensibility'*, before 1660, and which modern poets have tried to recover.

Izaak Walton* published a short life of Herbert in 1670; it ranks high among early English biographical studies.

Bib: Tuve, R., *A Reading of George Herbert*; Bottrall, M., *George Herbert*; Summers, J. H., *George Herbert*; Eliot, T. S., 'The Metaphysical Poets' in *Selected Essays*; Knights, L. C., in *Explorations*; Leishman, J. B., in *The Metaphysical Poets*; Coleridge, S. T., in *Biographia Literaria*.

Hercules

* *Heracles.*

Heresy

* *Inquisition, The.*

Hereward the Wake (11th C) /ˈherəwəd/

A half legendary Anglo-Saxon hero who, after the Battle of Hastings (1066), held out against William the Conqueror* in the fen-surrounded town of Ely, which was captured in 1070. His fame depends a good deal on Kingsley's novel *Hereward the Wake* (1865).

Hermaphroditus /hə:mafrəˈdaitəs/

In Greek myth, son of Hermes* and Aphrodite*. The nymph of the fountain of Salmacis loved him and prayed that they should be combined in one body – hence a 'hermaphrodite', having physical characteristics of both sexes.

Hermes /he:mi:z/

(Identifiable with Roman Mercury.) In Greek myth, the messenger of the gods; patron of travellers and of trade (honest or dishonest); bringer of dreams; conductor of the souls of the dead to the underworld. He is commonly depicted with a winged hat, winged sandals, and carrying a winged staff entwined with serpents (his caduceus*). He was celebrated for his cunning and trickery.

Hermes Trismegistus

(The thrice greatest Hermes.) The god Thoth of the ancient Egyptians, later identified with the Greek god Hermes. He was the scribe of the gods and supposed to be the author of certain sacred writings known by the Greeks as the 'hermetic books'. In 3rd C AD he was associated with a body of philosophy, partly oriental and partly Stoic*, which greatly interested western Platonist thinkers in 16th and 17th C.

Hero and Leander

Characters of a Greek myth used by several English writers, especially in a poem so entitled, left unfinished by Christopher Marlowe* and completed by George Chapman* (1598). Hero was a priestess of Aphrodite*, and lived at Sestos on the European shore of the Hellespont*. A youth called Leander, who loved her and lived at Abydos on the opposite shore, used to swim across to her at night, until he was drowned in a storm. Marlowe's poem is one of the finest narrative poems of his period.

Herod the Great

King of Judaea under the Romans in the time of Christ. According to the Bible (*Matthew* 2), in order to eliminate the infant Christ, he ordered the slaughter of all the young children in the village of Bethlehem. This made him the villain of the medieval Mystery* plays dealing with the subject. In these, he is always shown as an arrogant, boisterous, bullying character. Hence Hamlet's phrase 'it out-herods Herod' (*Hamlet* III.ii), referring to acting in a violent and exaggerated manner.

Herodias /he'rəudias/

In the Bible (*Mark* 6), wife of Herod Antipas, the son of Herod the Great. She persuaded him, through her daughter Salome*, to behead John the Baptist, prophet of Jesus Christ.

Herodotus (5th C BC) /he'rodətəs/

Greek historian. His main theme is the wars of the Persians against the Greeks and other nations.

Heroic Couplet

* *Couplet.*

Heroic Poetry

A term used, especially in 17th C, for epic* poetry.

Herrick, Robert (1591–1674) /'herik/

Poet and clergyman. Author of *Hesperides* (1648), a volume of love lyrics and pastoral poems, with some religious poems under the title *Noble Numbers.* He strongly admired the lyrical style of Ben Jonson* and therefore of the Latin lyrists such as Catullus* and Horace*. He lacked the tightness of form of Jonson, and his poems are without depth, but his grace and gaiety make an immediate appeal so that he has long been one of the most popular of 17th-C poets. Amongst the poets of the first half of 17th C he is much closer to the Cavalier* poets than to the Metaphysicals* such as Donne* and Herbert*.

Bib: Moorman, F. W., *Robert Herrick, A Biography and Critical Study*; Delattre, F., *Robert Herrick* (in French).

Hesperides /hes'peridi:z/

[1] In Greek myth, nymphs who guarded the golden apples in a garden across the western ocean. The apples had been the gift of Ge, the earth mother, to Hera*. They were also guarded by a dragon. It was one of the Labours of Hercules* to obtain them.

[2] A volume of poems by Robert Herrick*.

Hesperus /'hespərəs/

(Latin: Vesper.) In Greek myth, the evening star, *ie* the planet Venus, so called because it is already bright in early evening. Hesperus was son or brother of the giant Atlas*, and distinguished from Phosphorus (Latin: Lucifer), the morning star, though both are the same planet.

Hexameter /hek'samitə/

A line of verse having six metrical feet.

* *Metre.*

Heywood, John (1497?–1580?)

Playwright. He wrote highly entertaining short plays of the kind known as interludes*, *eg Play of the Weather* (1533), *A Play of Love* (1534), and *The Four P's** (1568).

Bib: Maxwell, I., *French Farce and John Heywood*; Bolwell, R. G. W., *Life and Works.*

Heywood, Thomas (1570?–1641)

Dramatist. His field was especially the drama of sentiment with middle-class characters, and to this belong his best-known plays, *A Woman Killed with Kindness*, and *The English Traveller.* His blank verse*, though not great poetry, benefits by the influences of a great age, and though plain, sometimes achieves poignancy. His first play may have been *The Four Prentices of London*, obviously appealing to a citizen (as distinct from a court) audience by its combination of romance and idealization of the middle class. This was perhaps acted as early as 1592. He has been admired for his sense of the theatre, *eg* by T. S. Eliot*. His many plays include: *The Fair Maid of the West*; *Edward IV*; *The Wise Woman of Hogsdon.* He also wrote pamphlets and non-dramatic verse.

Bib: Boas, F. S., *Thomas Heywood*; Clark, A. M., *Thomas Heywood*; Eliot, T. S., in *Selected Essays.*

Hibernia /hai'bə:njə/

The Latin name for Ireland; used poetically.

Highlands (of Scotland), The

The name given to the north and west of Scotland*. As a region, it is distinctive not merely because it is more mountainous than the Lowlands of the south and east, but for reasons of race, language and history. The Highlands are predominantly Celtic (*Celts*), and the Celtic language of Gaelic used to prevail there, although it is now gradually dying out. Socially, the Highlanders until 18th C lived under the semi-tribal 'clan' system, which again was never characteristic of most of the Lowlands. Economically, the Highlands have always been behind the Lowlands, which possess highly developed industry and agriculture. This is the main distinction between the two regions today: the Highlands, despite gradual afforestation, are chiefly given over to sheep and game.

Highwaymen

Robbers on the highways, usually on horseback. They became common in 18th C, when travel greatly increased, owing to improvements in roads and in vehicles, and policing was still very inadequate. Especially mail coaches were robbed, the practice being for the masked highwayman to stop the coach by pointing a pistol at the coachman. Highwaymen usually acted individually, not in gangs, but often with the assistance of inn-servants who passed on to them information about rich travellers. In 19th C, as the danger of highwaymen decreased, so they tended to be romanticized as 'gentlemen of the road'; this coincided with a fashion for tales about great criminals in the 1830s. Thus Harrison Ainsworth* in *Rookwood* (1834) popularized Dick Turpin*, an 18th-C highwayman, in consequence of which he has become something of a folk-hero like Robin Hood*, though the evidence is that he was a commonplace criminal.

Hind and the Panther, The (1687)

A didactic poem in heroic couplets* by John Dryden*. He wrote it after his conversion to Catholicism in 1685. It is a dialogue between the Church of Rome (the Hind) and the Church of England (the Panther). The fable form of the work is thin, since in most of the long speeches it is impossible to remember that it is beasts that are supposed to be conversing. The poem is to some extent a counteraction to *Religio Laici* (1682), a defence of the Church of England written before Dryden's conversion.

Hippocrates (5th–4th C BC) /hi'pokrəti:z/

Greek physician – known as 'the father of medicine'. Reputed author of writings called the Hippocratic Collection, including the Hippocratic Oath whereby confidential information given to doctors is not to be disclosed. The theory of humours* is attributed to him.

Hippocrene /hipə'kri:ni, 'hipəkri:n/

A spring on Mount Helicon in Greece, said in Greek myth to be sacred to the goddesses of the arts, the nine Muses.

* *Muses, The.*

Hippolyta /hi'politə/

In Greek myth, the queen of the Amazons*. Heracles* conquers her and gives her in marriage to Theseus* of Athens. She appears as the bride of Theseus in Shakespeare's *A Midsummer Night's Dream**.

Historical Fiction

Properly understood, this form of literature requires a 'historical imagination' – an awareness of the differences of outlook, customs and environment of any given period of the past. Such a faculty is the outcome of work by historians and historical biographers with a scientific approach to the past, *ie* a disinterested desire to discover the real truth about it. Until 17th C, Britain had no historians with this approach, but only chroniclers such as the 16th-C Holinshed* and Hall*, who did not see the past as inherently different from the present, and could not distinguish fact from myth. Thus Shakespeare's history plays, fictions based on those chroniclers, are not reconstructions of the English Middle Ages, but dramatizations of episodes in them in the spirit of his own day. A partial exception to this is the Roman plays: the gap in time between Augustan Rome and medieval England, and the records of Plutarch and of Roman historians (Livy, Tacitus, Sallust etc.), combined to give the Elizabethans a sense of historical difference and distance from their Roman subject matter. Thus, despite some anachronisms such as striking clocks in ancient Rome, Shakespeare's *Julius Caesar** and *Coriolanus** do read almost as if they were attempts at reconstruction of Roman civilization; the attempt is still more convincing in the case of a very scholarly drama such as Ben Jonson's *Sejanus**.

The 17th C saw the beginnings of history, biography, and historical biography (*eg* Francis Bacon's* *Henry VII*), and 18th C was the first age of great British historians (*eg* Robertson's *History of Scotland*, 1759; Hume's* *History of England*, 1757; and especially Gibbon's *Decline and Fall of the Roman Empire**, 1788); it was also marked by the foundation of the Society of Antiquaries (1718), with its periodical *Archaeologia* (from 1770). This spirit of the age led to the beginnings of a passion for historical fiction, linked with a largely non-historical mania for what was conceived as 'Gothic' (**Gothic Novels*). Sir Walter Scott*, a romantic poet with a passion for antiquities, combined the two tastes in his historical novels of the Middle Ages, *eg Ivanhoe** (1819). However, his medieval tales were by no means his best work, which comprised novels about 17th- and 18th-C Scotland, *eg Waverley**, *Old Mortality**, *The Heart of Midlothian**. The reason seems to be that 17th and 18th C were great formative centuries for Scotland, with important bearings on the society of Scott's own day; he therefore had an imaginative bond with that period, of much greater force than anything he felt for the medieval centuries. What is true for Scott seems to be true for all later historical fiction, and perhaps accounts for the scarcity of major works among the large number of historical novels written during the last 150 years. Thus Thackeray's *Esmond** is distinguished, because Thackeray's emotional bond with 18th-C England gives his historical reconstruction conviction and force, but George Eliot's *Romola** is usually regarded as the dullest of her books because the close historical reconstruction of 15th-C Florence is too external and lacks the life which can only come from the intuitive imaginative sympathy of the novelist.

Histories and Chronicles

Histories and chronicles are important in the study of literature in two ways: as sources for imaginative material, and as literature in their own right. However, with the exception of the Venerable Bede*, it was not until 17th C that English historians began to achieve the status of major writers.

Geoffrey of Monmouth* (d 1154) is the most important amongst a number of medieval historians for originating two national myths in his *Historia Regum Britanniae*: the myth that Brutus (Brut*), great-grandson of Aeneas, was the founder of the British race, and the myth of King Arthur* as the great defender of British Christianity. Both had importance in nourishing nascent English patriotism. When England became a centralized state under the Tudor* monarchs, Henry VII* chose the name Arthur for his eldest son. It was the main task of Tudor chroniclers both to heighten patriotism and to identify it with loyalty to the ruling family. This was the purpose of the Latin history of England by the Italian Polydore Vergil, in the service of Henry VII and Henry VIII. More important was Edward Hall's* *The Union of the two Noble and Illustrious Families of Lancaster and York* (1548), which showed the House of Tudor to be the saviour of the nation after the civil Wars of the Roses* in 15th C. Raphael Holinshed's* *Chronicles of England, Scotland and Ireland* (1578) was a compilation from various sources, including Geoffrey of Monmouth, and begins in ancient biblical times. The belief of the time was that history was useful as the means by which the present could learn from the past as a source of warnings, precepts and examples. The imaginative writers used the material of the chronicles in this spirit. Geoffrey of Monmouth, Hall and Holinshed were sources for many of the historical dramas of the reign of Elizabeth* including those of Shakespeare, and also for narrative poets such as those who contributed to *A Mirror for Magistrates* (1559), Daniel* (*Civil Wars*, 1595–1609), and Drayton* (*The Barons' Wars*, 1603). Much of this new interest in history arose from the Renaissance* transference of attention from heavenly destinies to earthly ones; thus the period 1500–1650 also produced the first eminent antiquarians, notably William Camden (1551–1623), and the first historical biographies: Thomas More's* *Richard III* (written 1513), George Cavendish's life of Cardinal Wolsey* (written shortly after the Cardinal's death but not published in full until 1667), Francis Bacon's* life of Henry VII (1622) and Lord Herbert's* life of Henry VIII (1648).

The True Historical Narrative of the Rebellion and Civil Wars in England by Edward Hyde, Earl of Clarendon*, is the first major historical work to rank as distinguished literature in English. Clarendon began it in 1646, but it was not published until 1702–4. It is told from the point of view of an important participator in the events and is notable especially for its portraits of other participators. Clarendon was a royalist; his younger contemporary, Gilbert Burnet (1643–1715), told the story of the second half of the century from the opposing political viewpoint in his most important work, *The History of My Own Time*. Burnet was more of a professional historian than Clarendon (who was primarily a statesman who took to history partly in self-justification) and he initiated historical writing as a major branch of literary activity and scholarship. The distinguished historical writing of William Robertson (*History of Scotland during the Reigns of Queen Mary and James VI*, 1759, and *Charles V*, 1769), of David Hume* the philosopher (*History of Great Britain*, pub 1754–61) and the lighter histories of England by the novelist Smollett* (1756) and by Goldsmith* (1764) have been superseded by later work, but Edward Gibbon's *Decline and Fall of the Roman Empire** (1776–88) is a very great work not only of history but of English literature, and, in the quality of its outlook on civilization, a great 18th-C monument.

The 18th C was the one in which antiquarian scholarship became thoroughly established; the antiquarians were interested by the nature of their studies in the detailed life of the past. Walter Scott* was one of them, and his historical novels, though very uneven in quality, are important as a new kind of history as well as a new kind of imaginative literature. It was his re-creation of the daily life of the past that was one of the influences upon Thomas Carlyle*, whose historical works (the most notable of which is his *French Revolution*, 1837) are more imaginative than factual. T. B. Macaulay* was a better historian and not inferior as an imaginative writer; *Macaulay's History of England** is the only historical work which comes near Gibbon's *Decline and Fall* in reputation, and Macaulay was responsible for the so-called 'Whig view of history' as steady progress in material welfare and political advance. Other eminent 19th-C English historians were J. A. Froude, who is, however, notorious for his prejudices in *A History of England from the Fall of Wolsey to the Spanish Armada* (1856–70), and J. R. Green whose *Short History of the English People* (1874) was for some time a popular classic owing to the breadth of Green's social sympathies. It was, however, in 19th C that the controversy about history as an art or as a science developed, and other distinguished historians of the period tended to become comparatively specialized scholars without the breadth of appeal of such men as Gibbon and Macaulay. The latter's great-nephew, G. M. Trevelyan (1876–1962), continued the broader humane tradition of historical writing, and Arnold Toynbee's *A Study of History* (1934–61), though the subject of scholarly controversy, is perhaps the most impressive investigation in this century of the origin and nature of civilizations.

History Plays (Chronicle Plays)

These are especially a phenomenon of the last two decades of 16th C, when they may have accounted for more than one-fifth of the plays written in a very prolific period of the drama. The history play is distinct from what is ordinarily called historical drama, which is a phenomenon of 19th and 20th C, and, like the historical novel of the same period, involves reconstructing another period of history in awareness of its differences in customs, habits, outlook, etc. Absence of 'scientific' history in 16th C debarred dramatists from a historical sense. On the other hand they were familiar with the dramatization of biblical events relevant to the Fall and Redemption of Man in the religious Mystery* plays: in a similar way history was to them and their audiences a collection of tales about the past, many of which were relevant to contemporary national predicaments. Thus in 16th C the English Church and state had cut loose from the Roman Catholic Church, and there was consequent interest in the reign of John* (1199–1216) when there had been a comparable quarrel between king and Pope; in the reign of Elizabeth I* men were alarmed at the possible consequences of the Queen's dying without a direct heir, and this caused them to be interested in the reign of Richard II*, etc. The Morality* plays also influenced the histories: until 16th C Moralities had concerned themselves with the spiritual destinies of men in general, but the growth of national consciousness, the splintering off of national churches in 16th C and the increased importance of the national ruler in deciding human destinies, all caused Morality dramatists to extend their interest to politics and to draw on history for their subject matter. Thus John Bale, supporter of Henry VIII in his emancipation of the English Church from Rome, wrote *King John* (?1547) to make his case for Henry's policy. The Morality content of Bale's play gives it coherent structure, but the chronicles of the 1580s, *eg The Famous Victories of Henry V* (?1588) relied chiefly on the eventfulness of their episodes. It was Marlowe* (*Edward II*, ?1593) and Shakespeare in his two great tetralogies ([1] *1, 2 & 3 Henry VI* and *Richard III*; [2] *Richard II, 1 & 2 Henry IV* and *Henry V*) and *King John*, who gave psychological and intellectual substance to the history play form. Marlowe did little more than bring his characters vividly to his audience, but Shakespeare brought deep insights to bear on the nature of political society and its problems. His two tetralogies have been called a great national dramatic epic covering the years 1377–1485; unfortunately, it is the second half of the period (from 1422 to 1485, the reigns of Henry VI, Edward IV, and Richard III) which constitutes his earlier work (perhaps 1590–93) while the plays concerning the first half (Richard II, Henry IV, Henry V) are relatively mature work (perhaps 1596–99). *King John* (?1596) is between the tetralogies in regard to maturity of style.

It becomes difficult, in the maturer Shakespeare, to draw a clear line between history plays and tragedy. *Julius Caesar** follows the Greek historian Plutarch* closely and is commonly called a history play, but it is also a tragedy; and *King Lear** derives from the chronicler Holinshed* as does *Henry V**, though the former is not history. The history plays and tragedies in fact merge into each other; both contain politics, and both present tragic catastrophe.

Hobbes, Thomas (1588–1679) /hobz/

The most important English philosopher between Francis Bacon* and John Locke*; his great work, *Leviathan** (1651) appears midway between Bacon's *Advancement of Learning** (1605) and Locke's *Essay concerning Human Understanding** (1690). He had in common with them a strong interest in physical science, and the belief that human knowledge begins with the senses. His important contribution to thought was in political and social organization. He lived in an age when Christianity and its doctrines had divided up among numerous conflicting and intolerant Christian sects, and when traditional political authority had been disrupted by the Civil Wars* of 1642–51; the medieval ethics of commerce were being rapidly replaced by the vigorous individualistic pursuit of wealth of the middle and upper classes. He concludes that men left to themselves would be anarchic, and their lives 'nasty, brutish and short'. He advocates as the only solution a strong, centralized state (commonwealth) under a single sovereign. His ideas were too uncompromising and radical to please his contemporaries; he shocked both the Royalists and the Parliamentarians. However, his thinking was so clear-sighted and thorough that he not only made a strong impression outside England as well as within it, but influenced the 19th-C Utilitarian* school of thinkers, in their practical, materialistic attempts to devise efficient state and social machinery. Hobbes's narrow rationalism involved a rigid theory of language and a contempt for the imagination, which he described as 'the decay of sense'.

* 3.3.1.

Bib: Bowle, J., *Hobbes and his Critics*; James, D. G., *The Life of Reason*; Aubrey, J., in *Lives*; Warrender, H., *The Political Philosophy of Hobbes*.

Hobbinol

* *Harvey, Gabriel.*

Hobgoblin

A mischievous fairy spirit, or a devil. Hob is a shortened form of Robin, a common name for mischievous fairies, *eg* Robin Goodfellow.

Hocktide

From 12th to 18th C, a general holiday held in the week after Easter week. Games were played to raise money for church and parish expenses.

Hogarth, William (1697–1764) /ˈhəuga:θ/

Painter. He excelled in the depiction of social life, especially the heartlessness of the richer classes permeated by social arrogance and commercial greed, with the consequent neglect of the poor. He painted sequences, each following a theme, a technique which is a pictorial equivalent of a stage drama: 'I wished to compose pictures on canvas, similar to representations on the stage; . . . I have endeavoured to treat my subjects as a dramatic writer; my picture is my stage, and men and women are my players. . . .' His art became an extremely popular one, because he made engravings of his oil paintings, and they were to be found on the walls of inns and cottages, not merely in great country houses. In his breadth of appeal and his realism, he is in strong contrast to the fashionable portrait painters of 18th C, Reynolds* and Gainsborough, and in the quality of his social indignation and his concern with unprivileged humanity he anticipates the poet-engraver William Blake*. Some of his great series of what he called 'pictur'd Morals' are: *A Harlot's Progress* (1731); *A Rake's Progress* (1735); *Marriage à la Mode* (1743–5); *The Four Stages of Cruelty*, *Beer Street* and *Gin Lane* (1751) (**2.2.3**) and *Election* (1754–66).

Hogarth's literary connections were close. Swift* invokes him as natural collaborator in his own kind of savage satire in his poem *The Legion Club* (1736), and his friendship with the novelists Richardson* and Fielding* influenced the visual element which gives their novels an advantage over those of Defoe* (*see* R. E. Moore, *Hogarth's Literary Relationships*).

* **2.3.**

Hogg, James (1770–1835)

A minor poet, nicknamed the Ettrick Shepherd because he had been a shepherd in Ettrick Forest in southern Scotland until his poetic talent was discovered by Sir Walter Scott*. He is now perhaps better known for his prose, especially *The Confessions of a Justified Sinner* (1824).

Hogmanay /'hogmənei/

A name in Scotland and the north of England for the last day of the year. Gifts of small cakes are made to children.

Holinshed, Raphael (d 1580?) /'holinʃed/

Chronicler: *Chronicles of England, Scotland, and Ireland* (1578). The history of England was written by Holinshed himself, but a vivid *Description of England* added to the history is by William Harrison. The history of Scotland is a translation of a Scottish work written in Latin – *Scotorum historiae* (1527) by Hector Boece, and the account of Ireland is by Richard Stanyhurst and Edward Campion, and others. Shakespeare and other Elizabethan dramatists used the Chronicles as a principal source book for history plays; Shakespeare also used them for *Macbeth**, *King Lear** and *Cymbeline**.

* *Histories and Chronicles.*

Holland House, Kensington

A great mansion to the west of Hyde Park in London. Built early in 17th C, in 1767 it was acquired by Henry Fox, Lord Holland, the father of the famous statesman, Charles James Fox*. From then until 1840 it was an important literary centre. The house was destroyed in air-raids in World War II.

Holmes, Sherlock

* *Detective Fiction; Doyle, Sir Arthur Conan.*

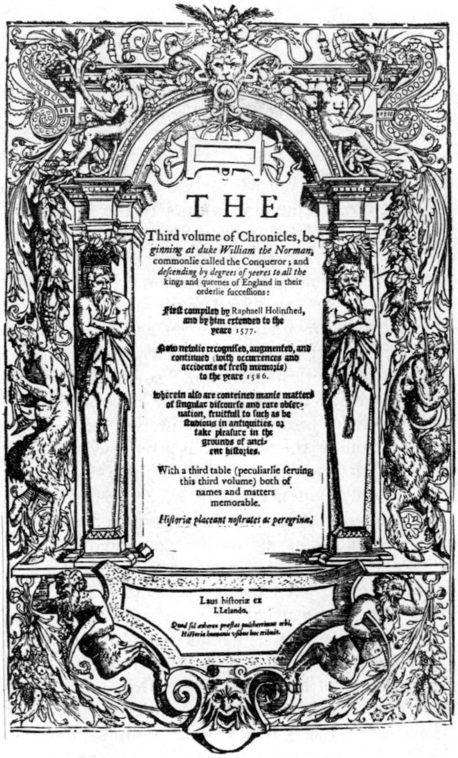

THE

Third volume of Chronicles, beginning at duke William the Norman, commonlie called the Conqueror; and descending by degrees of yeeres to all the kings and queenes of England in their orderlie successions:

First compiled by Raphaell Holinshed, and by him extended to the yeare 1577.

Now newlie recognised, augmented, and continued (with occurrences and accidents of fresh memorie) to the yeare 1586.

Wherein also are conteined manie matters of singular discourse and rare obseruation, fruitfull to such as be studious in antiquities, or take pleasure in the grounds of ancient histories.

With a third table (peculiarlie seruing this third volume) both of names and matters memorable.

Historiæ placeant nostrates ac peregrinæ.

Laus historiæ ex I. Lelando.

Title page from Holinshed's 'Chronicles'

Holy Roman Empire

Claiming to be the continuance of the Roman Empire of the West, the Holy Roman Empire lasted from the crowning of the Emperor Charlemagne by the Pope in AD 800 to its downfall in 1806 during the Napoleonic Wars. 'Holy' was added in 12th C to emphasize that the Empire was the political counterpart of the Pope's spiritual authority over Christendom; in truth, much of European history in 12th and 13th C sprang from rivalry between the two. Under Charlemagne, the Empire covered nearly all Europe. Thereafter its frontiers shrank, but its effective core was always the German-speaking lands. The Emperor was supposed to be elected by certain German princes (hence the title Elector, *eg* Elector of Hanover) but from 1493 the Empire remained with the Austrian Habsburg family. Even in Germany the Emperor's authority was by no means always effective; by 18th C the Holy Roman Empire merited Voltaire's gibe that it was neither holy, nor Roman, nor an empire.

Holy War, The (1682)

An allegory* by John Bunyan*. Its subject is the fall and redemption of man. The city of Mansoul has fallen into the hands of Diabolus (the Devil) and has to be recaptured by Emmanuel (Jesus Christ), who besieges it.

Home Rule

The term used in the second half of 19th C and until 1920 for the movement seeking to obtain a separate Irish parliament, to replace Irish representation in the London Parliament.

* *Ireland.*

Homer

Ancient Greek epic poet, author of the *Iliad** and the *Odyssey**, basic works for Greek literature, and therefore for the literature of all Europe. Ancient traditions exist about Homer, for instance that latterly he was blind, and that seven cities claimed to be his birthplace, but nothing is known about him. Archaeological investigation has disclosed that the destruction of Troy, following the siege described in the *Iliad*, took place in 12th C BC; linguistic, historical, and literary analysis of the poems show them to date as artistic wholes from perhaps 8th C BC. That they are artistic wholes is in fact the only evidence for the existence of Homer; efforts to show that they are compilations by a number of poets have proved unconvincing, though it is clear that Homer himself was using the work of other poets between the Trojan war and his own time. Part of the artistic consistency which proves the existence of a single genius behind the poems is the distinction of their style, and the difficulty of conveying its quality in translation. The critic Matthew Arnold* in his essay *On Translating Homer* (1861) says that Homer is rapid in movement, plain in diction, simple in ideas, and noble in manner; and that the translation of three eminent English poets, Chapman* (16th C) and Pope* and Cowper* (18th C), all fail in one or more of these qualities, however fine their verse is in other respects. The same qualities represent a touchstone of human greatness, and have caused the Homeric epic to be regarded as the crown of creative achievement in the history of European literature from the days of the ancient Greeks to modern times.

Hood, Robin

* *Robin Hood.*

Hood, Thomas (1799–1845)

Poet. His serious poetry shows strongly the influence of Keats*, but he is known chiefly for his comic and topical verse; the latter includes grim but haunting poems about contemporary social abuses, *eg The Song of the Shirt* (1843), a kind of poetic poster art which does not bear close examination but is extremely effective on first reading. In his comic verse, he was notorious for his puns (**Play on Words*) which he used obtrusively but often wittily.

Bib: Jerrold, W., *Life*; Reid, J. C., a critical study.

Hooker, Richard (1553–1600)

Theologian. His great work was *Laws of Ecclesiastical Polity* (1593–97). This was the first outstanding polemic expounding the Church of England* viewpoint, and its main purpose was to defend the Church against attacks by other Protestant* reformers. Such reformers (the Puritans*) trusted only the Bible as authority on matters of religion, since only the Bible was acknowledged to be inspired by God. They criticized the Church of England for being too near the Roman Catholic Church in its organization (*eg* in its retention of the authority of bishops) and for resembling the Roman Church in its excessive reliance on other kinds of authority. Hooker considered that the Puritans were making major issues out of inessentials, and that their attacks were dangerous both socially and religiously, since the state was indissolubly bound up with the Church, and it was essential for both to adapt themselves to historical change and requirement, and to draw upon the Law of Nature as well as upon the Holy Scriptures for guidance. Law he regarded as inherent in created nature, and as the same principle whether seen in the aspect of natural order, social order, or divine order. In this view of Law, Hooker is essentially a conservative thinker, inheriting from the Middle Ages the view of the universe as a system of related degrees ranging from God down to the four elements of hot, cold, moist and dry, as the basis of matter. Though conservative, the outlook was not reactionary; it was the most widely accepted assumption of the time, implicit in the imaginative literature, see *eg* the speech of Ulysses in Shakespeare's *Troilus and Cressida** I.iii.75. Hooker's was the noblest expression of it in the prose literature of the time. The biographer Izaak Walton* published a life of Hooker in 1665.

* 3.2.2.1.

Bib: Lewis, C. S., *English Literature in the Sixteenth Century*; Morris, C., *Political Thought in England: Tyndale to Hooker*; Krapp, G. P., *The Rise of English Literary Prose*; Carré, M. H., *Phases of Thought in England*, Chap. 6; D'Entrèves, A. P., *The Medieval Contribution to Political Thought*, Chap. 6; Walton, I., *Life*; Sisson, C. J., *The Judicious Marriage of Mr Hooker and the Birth of the Laws.*

Hop-o'-my-Thumb

The main character of a famous fairy tale taken from the French of Perrault* (17th C). He is a diminutive child who achieves great exploits by his cleverness. The name was used in English before the translation of the story, to indicate any very small person.

Hopkins, Gerard Manley (1844–89)

Poet. He was converted to Roman Catholicism in 1866, and entered the Jesuit Order in 1868. He then gave up poetry, but resumed writing in 1875 with *The Wreck of the Deutschland**, his first important poem. So unusual were Hopkins's poems that they were not published in his own lifetime; after his death they passed to his friend, Robert Bridges*, who delayed their publication until 1918, and even then Hopkins's fame did not become widespread until the second edition of 1930. One eminent critic then described him as the greatest of Victorian poets, but the date of his publication and the interest he shared with modern poets in the relationship between poetry and living experience has caused him to be thought of as belonging more to 20th C than to 19th. His 'sprung rhythm'* is a technical term meaning the combination of the usual regularity of stress patterns with freely varying numbers of syllables in each line. This was not new, but was contrary to the practice that had predominated in English poetry since Edmund Spenser*, which required a uniform pattern of syllabic counts as of stresses. In Hopkins's poetry, the rhythm of the verse could more easily combine with the flow and varying emphasis of spoken language, so that the two kinds of expressiveness unite. A kindred sort of concentration is obtained by his practice – natural to the spoken language but uncommon in writing – of inventing compound words, especially adjectives, *eg* 'dappled-with-damson west' for a sunset, 'lovely-asunder starlight' for stars scattered over the sky. Keats* was a strong influence upon him (as upon so many of the later Victorians) and Hopkins shared Keats's gift for evoking in words the physical response suitable to the thing they express. This was the more conspicuous in Hopkins because of his intense interest (for which he found support in the 13th-C philosopher Duns Scotus*) in the qualities which give any object its individual reality, distinguishing it from other objects of the same class. For these qualities he invented the term 'inscape'. He also invented 'instress' for the force of these qualities on the mind. This intensity of response to the reality and beauty of objects was akin to the intensity of his feeling about the relationship between God and man. All Hopkins's poetry is religious, and in quality recalls the early-17th-C devotional poets, John Donne* and George Herbert*; in his 'terrible sonnets', for instance, Hopkins engages in direct dialogue with God as does Donne in his *Holy Sonnets*, or Herbert in such a lyric as *The Collar*. Thus Hopkins unites the rhythmical freedom of the Middle Ages, the religious intensity of early 17th C, the response to nature of early 19th, and he anticipated 20th C in purifying the poetic medium of its merely conventional encumbrance.

*** 6.4.2; 7.4.**

Bib: Gardner, W. H., *Life*; Leavis, F. R., in *The Common Pursuit* and *New Bearings in English Poetry*; Richards, I. A., in *Practical Criticism*; Pick, J., *Hopkins, Priest and Poet*; Peters, W. A. M., *Gerard Manley Hopkins: A Critical essay*; Weygand, N., *Immortal Diamond: Studies in Hopkins*.

Horace (Quintus Horatius Flaccus, 65–8 BC) /ˈhɒrəs/

Roman poet of the Augustan* age. His work divides into three classes: his Satires*, Odes*, and Epistles. The last includes the *Ars Poetica* or *De Arte Poetica* (Concerning the Art of Poetry) which became an important critical document for Europe – for England particularly in 18th C. It emphasizes the importance of cultivating art in poetry; he lays down the principle that if you do not understand poetry it is better to leave it alone. Art means above all the cultivation of alert judgement: expression and form must be appropriate to theme; characterization and form must be consistent with the subject and with themselves; conciseness is a virtue in didacticism; adaptation of a writer is allowed but plagiarism is not; the poet must study to be wise as a man, and he must be his own severest critic; a just critic is a severe one. The age of Pope* and Johnson* took these principles to heart, and they also liked Horace's cultivation to the point of balance in prosperity between wealth and poverty: he had become the friend of the rich patron of letters, Maecenas*, who had provided him with a small estate in the Sabine hills. The English Augustans were acutely aware that mankind was situated midway between the extremes of the divine and the base, that its tendency was to strive too high and to fall catastrophically; their concern was to cultivate proportion and balance. Criticism and satire thus became important to them as correctives of inborn human tendencies, and they cultivated the congenial spirit of Horace as Horace himself had sought to practise the virtues of the Greeks. Thus the greatest 18th-C poet, Alexander Pope, entitled one of his best sequences of poems *Imitations of Horace**.

Horae /ˈhɔːreɪ/

In Greek and Latin mythology, the seasons; their dance symbolized orderly succession, and therefore law, justice and peace. When day and night came to be divided into 24 equal parts, each was given the name of hora – hour.

Hospitallers of St John of Jerusalem (Knights of St John)

A military religious order associated with the Crusades*. The Hospitallers were founded in 1099 to provide a hostel for pilgrims to Jerusalem. Driven from Jerusalem, they eventually settled in Malta in 1530. They had a branch in England which was suppressed in 16th C. The modern British order was founded in 19th C and exists for hospital work similar to that of the Red Cross.

Hotspur (Sir Henry Percy, 1364–1403) /ˈhɒtspəː/

Eldest son of the first Earl of Northumberland. Shakespeare represented him in *1 Henry IV*, where he is shown as the generous, tempestuous warrior, devoted entirely to honour, but failing to relate it to any feeling for human good. He is thus, despite his magnificent qualities, a destructive force.

Houndsditch

A district of London, originally a suburb about the ditch outside the walls.

Hours, Book of

Certain hours of the day, called the Canonical Hours, are set aside for prayers by the Catholic Church. A Book of Hours contained the prayers to be said at the appropriate times; medieval editions were often illustrated ('illuminated') with great art and at great expense.

House of Fame, The
A comic fantasy in the form of a dream poem by Geoffrey Chaucer*. It was written towards the end of his second period, when he was writing under the influence of Italian poets – perhaps 1383–4, not long before the *Canterbury Tales**. It is written in 8-syllable rhymed couplets* and is about 2,000 lines long, and unfinished. In Book I he visits the Temple of Venus and sees depicted on the walls the tragic love affair of Dido and Aeneas, from Virgil's *Aeneid.** In II he is carried off by an eagle, with whom he has an airborne conversation, to the House of Fame. In III we leave him in the House of Rumour or false news. Despite its easy spirited humour, the poem also contains sombre observation of human foolishness; here it is coloured by the influence of Dante's *Divine Comedy.*

Houses of Parliament
The Lords and the Commons. 'Houses' here does not mean buildings, but the assemblies. Both assemblies meet in the building known as the Palace of Westminster* in the respective 'chambers' reserved for their use.
 * *Parliament.*

Household Words
A weekly periodical edited by Charles Dickens* from 1850 to 1859. It emulated the magazine tradition of *Blackwood's** (started 1817) but aimed at a wider public. Among works published in it were Dickens's novel *Hard Times** and Mrs Gaskell's *North and South**. It was followed by *All the Year Round**.
 * *Reviews and Periodicals.*

Housman, A. E. (1895–1936) /'hausmən/
A classical scholar who published two small volumes of lyrics of enormous popularity: *The Shropshire Lad* (1896) and *Last Poems* (1922). They are very pessimistic but have an immediate musical appeal, and several have in fact been set to music by a number of composers, *eg* Vaughan Williams. His lecture *The Name and Nature of Poetry*, in which he described poetic creation as an essentially physical experience, also achieved considerable fame.
Bib: Housman, L., *AEH: Some poems, some letters and a personal memoir*; Richards, G., *Housman 1879–1936*; Watson, G. L., *Housman: a divided life.*

Houyhnhnms, The /'hwinmz/
The horses endowed with reason in Part IV of Swift's *Gulliver's Travels**. The word imitates the whinnying of a horse. The enlightened horses are a purely reasonable aristocracy, inhabiting an island which also contains a race called Yahoos, who, not endowed with reason, typify brutish and degraded behaviour. Gulliver's Houyhnhnm host recognizes that Gulliver is unlike the Yahoos in his possession of the faculty of reason, but proves to him that owing to his other qualities, which are Yahoo-like, he can only use his reason destructively.

Howards End (1910)
A novel by E. M. Forster*. The theme is the relationship between the Schlegel family (Margaret, Helen, and their brother Tibby) who live on an unearned income and are liberal, enlightened, and cultivated, and the Wilcoxes, who work in the commercial world which the Schlegels are inclined to despise but from which they draw their income. The Wilcoxes are snobbish, prejudiced, insensitive, and philistine; in fact they have much in common with the middle classes as described by Matthew Arnold* in his critique of English culture – *Culture and Anarchy* (1869). Mrs Wilcox, however, who has brought her husband the old house, Howards End, belongs to the older, aristocratic continuity of English culture; never understood by her husband and children, on her death she bequeaths the house unexpectedly to Margaret Schlegel. Margaret comes into the inheritance at the end of the book, but only after she has married and subdued to her values Mrs Wilcox's former husband, and when she has rescued the child of a poor bank-clerk, Leonard Bast, who has been the victim of both the Schlegel and the Wilcox social illusions and mishandling.

Hudibras /'hju:dibras/
A satire by Samuel Butler* (1612–80) in 8-syllable rhymed couplets*, published in 3 Parts: I, 1663; II, 1664; III, 1678. The form is a parody of the 16th-C romantic epics of Ariosto* or Spenser*; the hero takes his name from a knight in Spenser's *Faerie Queene**, whose strength exceeds his wisdom and whose reputation is greater than his real achievements. He also represents a caricature of the hero of Cervantes' *Don Quixote** – itself a parody of romance if not of romantic epic. The intention of the poem is to ridicule the Puritans* who had ruled England during the Interregnum*. Sir Hudibras is a Presbyterian* and his squire Ralpho an Independent – the two principal sects which had successively occupied power. The chief vice with which the Puritans were charged was hypocrisy, and this is Hudibras's special characteristic, under the cloak of which he practises treachery, avarice, brutality and fraud. The nature of the intention is political, but the execution goes beyond the intention and makes the poem an exposure of the kinds of vice that hypocrisy conceals, in the manner of the exposure of various forms of human greed in Ben Jonson's Comedy of Humours*. Another aspect of the poem arises from Butler's interest in language and his hatred of ignorant, pretentious uses of language both among the Puritans (some of whom were notorious for it) and among pretenders to learning; misuse of language, in fact, becomes for him a leading symptom of general human folly. Butler's own use of language, in the homeliness of his diction and the ingenuity with which he employs it, recalls the Metaphysical* poets, of whom he is a late example. On the other hand, his scorn of extravagance and admiration for temperance put him among the new Augustan* poets, whose outlook he helped to form. In his colloquial, uninhibited vigour he belongs to the earlier part of his century; in the pungency of his satirical wit he anticipates 18th C.

* 4.2.2; *Satire.*
Bib: Jack, I., *Augustan Satire*; Gibson, D., in *Seventeenth Century Studies*, ed. R. Shafer; Veldkamp, J., *Samuel Butler, the Author of Hudibras*; Johnson, S., in *Lives*; Richards, E. A., *Hudibras in the Burlesque Tradition.*

Hughes, Ted (b 1930)

One of the liveliest poets writing in Britain since 1945. *The Hawk in the Rain* (1957); *Lupercal* (1960); two volumes of verse for children – *Meet My Folks* (1961) and *Earth Owl and Other Moon People* (1963); *Wodwo* (1967); *Crow* (1970). His rather violent poetry appeared when English verse was dominated by the poets of the Movement (**Larkin*); these were restrained, disillusioned, ironic, and often urban in the setting of their poems. Hughes was remarkable for his evocation of natural life, in particular of animals, presented as alien and opposed to the civilized human consciousness, and for that reason, as in the poetry and prose of D. H. Lawrence*, peculiarly close to the subrational instinct in human consciousness. This association is made explicit in his poem *The Thought-Fox.*

Poems (1971); *Eat Crow* (1971); *Prometheus on his Crag* (1973); *Spring Summer Autumn Winter* (1974).

* 6.5.

Hughes, Thomas

* *Rugby School.*

Humanism

The word has two distinct uses: [1] the intellectually liberating movements in western Europe in 15th and 16th C, associated with new attitudes to ancient Greek and Latin literature; [2] a modern movement for the advancement of humanity without reliance on supernatural religious beliefs.

[1] Humanism in its first and much more important sense had its beginnings in Italy as early as 14th C, when its pioneer was the poet and scholar Petrarch* (1304–74), and reached its height (greatly stimulated by the recovery of lost manuscripts after the fall of Constantinople in 1453) throughout western Europe in 16th C, when it first reached England. Its outstanding characteristic was a new kind of critical power. In the previous thousand years European civilization had above all been dominated – even created – by the Church, which had put the literatures of the preceding Latin and Greek cultures to its own uses, and had directed movements in thought and art through its authority over the religious orders and the universities. The humanists began by criticizing and evaluating the Latin and Greek authors in the light of Roman and Greek standards of civilization. This in itself implied intellectual independence, and it led naturally to speculation about man and his environment and an increasing ardour for research and experiment for their own sake. Some of the important consequences of humanism were these: the rediscovery of many ancient Greek and Latin works; the establishment of new standards in Greek and Latin scholarship; the assumption, which was to dominate English education until the present

century, that a thorough basis in at least Latin literature was indispensable to the civilized man; the beginnings of what we nowadays regard as 'scientific thinking'; the introduction of the term Middle Ages* for the period between the fall of the Roman Empire of the West (5th C AD) and the Renaissance*, meaning by it a period of partial and inferior civilization. The greatest of the European humanists was the Dutchman, Erasmus*, and the greatest of the earlier English humanists was his friend Sir Thomas More*. The Church was not at first hostile to humanism; indeed such a pope as Leo X (reigned 1513–21) was himself a humanist. When, in the second thirty years of 16th C, the critical spirit became an increasingly aggressive weapon in the hands of the religious reformers – the Renaissance branching into the Reformation* – the attitude of the Church hardened, and humanists in later 16th C found themselves restricted by the religious quarrels of Protestants* and Catholics, or obliged (like Montaigne*) to adopt a retiring and circumspect policy. In 17th and 18th C, humanism hardened into neo-classicism, the weak side of which was pedantic interpretation of humanistic scholarship.

[2] Modern humanism assumes that man's command of scientific knowledge has rendered religion largely redundant. Its central principle is that 'man is the measure of all things', and elsewhere in Europe it is sometimes called 'hominism' (Lat. homo = man).

'Humanism' is also used as a general expression for any philosophy that proposes the full development of human potentiality. In this sense, 'Christian humanism', since 16th C, has stood for the marriage of the humanist value attached to a conception of humanity based on reason with the Christian value based on Divine Revelation. An example of a Christian Humanist movement is that of the Cambridge Platonists* in 17th C.

* 3.2.1; *Classical Education.*

Hume, David (1711–76)

Philosopher. His first major work, *Treatise of Human Nature* (1739–40) did not arouse much interest. His *Enquiry concerning Human Understanding* (1748) and *Enquiry concerning the Principles of Morals* (1751) are revisions and developments of the first work. His theory of knowledge was distinct from those of Locke* and Berkeley*. Locke had said that ideas proceeded from sensations, *ie* from experience received through the senses, implying that we know mind only through matter; Berkeley that on the contrary we know matter only through our mental conceptions of it, and that this proves the primacy of mind. Hume said that we cannot know of the existence of mind, except as a collective term covering memories, perceptions and ideas. He further argued that there was no necessity in the law of cause and effect, except in mathematics; what we call that law is inferred but not observed, a customary association confirmed by experience but with no provable necessity in it. Thus if Locke had seemed to validate science at the expense of religion, and Berkeley the reverse, Hume seemed to drive at the roots of both. The graceful lucidity with which he expounded this extreme scepticism caused a wit to summarize his philosophy in the epigram: 'No mind! – It doesn't matter. No matter! – Never mind.' In his ethics, Hume held that virtue is what makes for happiness, both in ourselves and others, and that the two kinds of happiness are in accord with each other. This is in agreement with the 18th-C tendency to rely on reason but to extol the generous emotions; as rational scepticism increased, for instance in consequence of Hume's thinking, so, as the century wore on, increasing value was attached to feeling.

Hume also wrote the first systematic history of England, beginning, at first, with the reign of James I*, when, as he considered with reasonable justice, the political differences of his own day had their start. His historical view is, however, distorted by his political prejudices, and, since he was a Scotsman, by his suspicion of English motives towards Scotland. His *Essays Moral and Political* (1741), and later volumes, contain acute comments on contemporary society. He differed from Rousseau* by arguing against the long established hypothesis that society is based on a 'social contract'. His economic writings were a stimulus to Adam Smith*.

* 3.3.1; *Histories and Chronicles.*

Bib: Mossner, E. C., *The Life of Hume*;
Willey, B., *The Eighteenth Century Background*;
Smith, N. K., *The Philosophy of David Hume*;
Pears, D. F. (ed), *Hume: A Symposium.*

Humour

The original meaning was 'liquid'. Ancient Greek and Latin medicine passed on to the Middle Ages* the theory of four liquids (humours) in the human body: phlegm, blood, yellow bile or choler, and black bile or melancholy. Individual temperaments derived their quality from the predominance of one or other 'humour'; thus we still speak of 'phlegmatic' or very calm temperaments, 'sanguine' or ardent temperaments, 'choleric' or easily angered ones, and 'melancholy' or depressive temperaments. In later 16th C a man's humour was his characteristic disposition, whether or not related to the original four physical humours. It could also have other meanings: his mania or obsession; his caprice or whim; his passing mood.

All these uses can be found in Shakespeare and his contemporaries; *eg* in *Julius Caesar** II. i., Portia begs her husband Brutus not to risk his health in the 'humours' (moistures) 'of the dank morning', but in the same scene Decius has declared that he can induce Caesar to go to the Capitol by giving 'his humour the true bent', *ie* by exploiting Caesar's disposition to superstition. In the *Merchant of Venice** IV. i, Shylock suggests that if an explanation is required for his preferring a pound of Antonio's flesh to 3,000 ducats, it should be put down to his caprice – 'Say it is my humour'; in *As You Like It** IV. i, Rosalind speaks of being in a 'holiday humour', *ie* in a gay mood.

Ben Jonson in *Every Man in His Humour** III. i speaks of a humour as 'a monster bred in a man by self-love and affectation, and fed by folly' *ie* produced by egotism, encouraged by fashionable ostentation, and not restrained by good sense. This sense is the origin of the principal modern use of the word. Goldsmith* (*Present State of Learning*, 1759) has already gone beyond 'a humour = that which is ridiculous' to the meaning of a faculty for perceiving the ridiculous, and also the laughter-raising expression of the ridiculous, although this is not one of the definitions found in Johnson's *Dictionary**. Goldsmith and Hazlitt* (*English Comic Writers*, 1819) both distinguish this faculty from wit*, though differently.

The novelist George Meredith* (*The Idea of Comedy*, 1877) gives perhaps the most comprehensive definition in accordance with modern use, paraphrasable as an attitude of mind readily responsive to the incongruous and ridiculous, but preserving a feeling of sympathy with, kindliness for, the object of laughter. 'A sense of humour' has, in this sense, become the favourite virtue of the English; and it has often been a singularly limiting one. Its merit has been its identification with a 'sense of proportion' and a refusal to be unduly earnest about secondary matters; its fault is often to confuse seriousness with earnestness, and to ridicule what is original and superior under the impression that it is merely eccentric. The English preference for humour over wit – always distinguished as having an intellectual quality – tends to inhibit recognition of mental mediocrity; and the kindliness supposed to be the concomitant of humour dilutes satire into insipidity.

* *Humours, Comedy of; Satire; Wit.*

Humours, Comedy of

A form of drama especially associated with Ben Jonson*. Starting from the traditional psychology which explained a temperament as the product of its physical constitution, Jonson treats humour as the monstrous distortion of human nature by egotism and the self-regarding appetites, notably some form of greed. Partly timeless satire on human nature, the comedy of humours is also social satire since such personal extravagances are nourished by social tendencies; new prospects of wealth let loose unbounded lusts, as with Sir Epicure Mammon (*The Alchemist**); the rush of speculation on often fantastic 'projects' (*ie* financial enterprises requiring investment) encourages unlimited credulity in the foolish, *eg* Fitzdottrel in *The Devil is an Ass**; the prevalence of avarice causes adventurers to overreach themselves in their contempt for their victims and in their own megalomania (Volpone and Mosca in *Volpone**). Jonson's world is a jungle of predators and victims, free from the restraint of religion, reason, or respect for tradition. But the passions which Jonson exposes in their excess arise from human energies that are themselves fine and belong to that exhilaration in the scope for human fulfilment which is characteristic of the Renaissance*; Jonson's more massive characters, though they condemn themselves by the exorbitance of their language, make speeches of great poetic splendour and force. The hyperbole of

Christopher Marlowe* in *Tamburlaine** and *The Jew of Malta** provides the tradition for Jonson's eloquence. Jonson's great comedies are *Volpone* and *The Alchemist*. *The Devil is an Ass* is nearly as fine, and *Bartholomew Fair** and *Epicoene, or The Silent Woman** are memorable. The mode was first established by *Every Man in his Humour**. *Sejanus** is a satirical tragedy, with similarities to the great comedies.

Among Jonson's followers, Massinger (*A New Way to pay Old Debts**, and *The City Madam**) and Middleton (*A Chaste Maid in Cheapside**) are the best. But Jonson's vision was influential beyond the drama; its detachment, objectivity, and moral emphasis on the need to temper the passions with reason and reverence for virtue, are essentially classical and emerge again in Pope's *Essay on Man** Book II.

5.1.3.3.

Humphry Clinker, The Expedition of (1771)

A picaresque* novel by Tobias Smollett*, written in letters. It describes a tour of England and Scotland made by Mr Matthew Bramble and his family party – his sister Tabitha, his nephew and niece Jerry and Lydia, and the maid Winifred Jenkins. Humphry Clinker is an inn-servant who joins the party on the way, turns out to be Mr Bramble's illegitimate son, and marries Winifred. Characterization is strongly marked but superficial, the chief object being to characterize the society of the time realistically and with an often coarse humour. But this is usually held to be the most successful of Smollett's novels, and shows something of the humane sympathies of the 16th-C Spanish novelist Cervantes*, whose *Don Quixote** Smollett had himself translated in 1755.

Humpty Dumpty

A short round-shouldered plump person; egg-shaped. The well-known folk rhyme 'Humpty Dumpty sat on a wall' is a riddle the answer to which is an egg.

Hun

The Huns were Asian tribes which invaded Europe and ravaged it at the end of 4th C. During World War I the word was used as a term of abuse for the Germans.

Hundred Years' War

The name given to the succession of wars between the kings of England and France between 1338 and 1453. The causes were partly territorial and partly economic. The territorial causes were especially bound up with the possession by the English kings of the large duchy of Aquitaine, first acquired through marriage by Henry II* of England; as the French kings grew stronger, they increasingly coveted this large slice out of their territory. The economic causes were connected with Flanders; the Flemish cloth manufacturing towns were the importers of English wool, but they owed political allegiance to the French king; it was largely to divert this allegiance that Edward III* first laid claim to the French crown. To these causes may be added the restlessness of the English and French nobility, and the popularity of the war with them as a profitable and advantageous pursuit – it was the peasantry who were the main sufferers of the campaigns. Scotland was much of the time an ally of France, either sending troops to assist the French or fighting along her own border.

Militarily, the war was notable for the great importance of the infantry soldier, especially in the form of the English yeoman* archer. Hitherto the armoured knight on horseback had dominated the battlefield; the victory of the foot-soldiers at Crécy*, Poitiers (1356) and above all Agincourt* not only changed methods of warfare but looked forward to important social changes. The aristocracy were in future more dependent than hitherto on the support of the common people, and this in turn implied a rise of national feeling.

The outstanding phases of the struggle were three.

[1] That under Edward III until the Treaty of Brétigny (1360) went strongly to the English advantage, though Edward renounced his claim to the French crown.

[2] Under Henry V* the English had another period of brilliant success, and by the Treaty of Troyes (1420) Henry was recognized as heir to the French throne; his baby son was acknowledged king of France and England in 1422. Part of the English success was due to the assistance provided to Henry by the French Duke of Burgundy.

[3] In the last phase, however, the English were completely defeated and driven from France except for the port of Calais, retained until 1558. This was the phase which has become memorable for the exploits of the French peasant patriot, Joan of Arc* (Jeanne d'Arc), burned for heresy and sorcery at Rouen in 1431. The expulsion of the English from France is regarded as a blessing for both countries; had they remained, the superior size and wealth of France would certainly have hindered the development of a separate English national identity, while French national identity was hindered so long as a foreign power occupied so much French territory.

1.1.2; *Black Prince*.

Hunt, Leigh (1784–1859)

Journalist and poet. With his brother John, he edited the widely read and boldly radical *Examiner** until he gave up his share in it in 1821. His outspoken attack on the Prince Regent (future George IV) in 1813 brought two years' imprisonment for the brothers, but they continued to edit the paper in prison. For a short time he was joint editor with Byron* of the short-lived *Liberal*, a quarterly, and he edited or had a hand in several other periodicals. His occasional essays were mostly ephemeral and the cause of a bad habit among later imitators who produced graceful effusions about nothing that matters; but a few of them are memorable sketches of daily life.

John Keats* belonged to the Hunt literary circle, and Hunt did much to publicize the reputations of

both Keats and Shelley*. His *Autobiography* (1850) is one of his most memorable works. Hunt's poetry was fluent and rather facile; his most famous poem is *The Story of Rimini* (1816).

* *Reviews and Periodicals.*

Bib: Blunden, E., *Leigh Hunt's Examiner Examined*; Landré, L., *Life* (in French); Blunden, E., *Life*.

Hunting

In English, the word usually refers to the pursuit of animals on horseback and with hounds, in distinction from shooting, hawking, and other forms of pursuit on foot. The pursuit of deer, for example, is called deer-stalking in the Highlands of Scotland, where it is done on foot, but stag-hunting in the south-west of England, where it is done with horse and hound.

In the Middle Ages, the wolf, the boar, the stag and the fox were the chief objects of hunting, but the first two were virtually extinct by 16th C, and by 18th C improved agriculture restricted the territory of deer. This has left the fox as by far the most important beast of the chase for the last 200 years.

* *Fox-hunting.*

Huxley, Aldous (1894–1963)

Novelist and essayist. His novels are 'novels of ideas', involving conversations which disclose viewpoints rather than establish characters, and having a polemical rather than an imaginative theme. An early practitioner of the form was Peacock*, and it is his novels that Huxley's earlier ones recall: *Crome Yellow* (1921); *Antic Hay* (1923); *Those Barren Leaves* (1925). *Point Counter Point* (1928) is his best-known novel and is an attempt to convey a social image of the age with more imaginative depth and substance, but his polemical and inquisitorial mind was better suited to *Brave New World* (1932), in which a future society is presented so as to bring out the tendencies working in contemporary civilization and to show their disastrous consequences. Fastidious, abhorring what he saw to be the probable obliteration of human culture by 20th-C addiction to technology, but sceptical of religious solutions – he was the grandson of the great 19th-C agnostic biologist Thomas Huxley* – he turned in the 1930s to eastern religions such as Buddhism for spiritual support. This is shown in *Eyeless in Gaza* (1936). This and his last books – *After Many a Summer* (1939), *Ape and Essence* (1949), *Brave New World Revisited* (1959) – return to the discursive form of his earlier work. His novels and his essays (Collected Edition, 1960), are all concerned with how to resist the debasement of 'mass culture' and to sustain the identity of the human spirit without the aid of faith in supernatural religion of the Christian kind. It is perhaps for his essays that he is now most read and admired.

Bib: Brooke, J., *Aldous Huxley* (British Council Pamphlet); Gérard, A., *A la rencontre de Aldous Huxley*; Henderson, A. J., *Aldous Huxley*.

Huxley, Thomas Henry (1825–95)

Biologist. He was a supporter of Darwin's* theory of evolution and combined philosophical speculation with technical exposition. His many works, essays, lectures and articles included the influential publications: *Man's Place in Nature* (1863), *The Physical Basis of Life* (1868), *Science and Culture* (1881), and *Science and Morals* (1886). He held that scientific discoveries had neither given support to nor discredited religious faith, and he invented the term agnosticism* for this attitude to religion.

* **3.4.4.**

Hyde Park

An extensive public park in the west of London, originally belonging to Westminster Abbey, but passing to the Crown on the dissolution of the monasteries* in 1539. It includes the lake called the Serpentine (because its shape was deliberately made irregular) artificially created in 1733, and an enclosure for amateur orators known as Speakers' Corner. In 17th C it was used for horse-racing, and then and since for fashionable parade. A comedy of manners called *Hyde Park* (1632) by James Shirley* has the park for its setting in a number of scenes.

Hydra /ˈhaidrə/

A nine-headed monster in Greek myth. Its centre head was immortal, and the other heads grew again when they were severed. Heracles* and Iolaus, by burning out the root of the heads as they were severed and burying the immortal head under a rock, eventually destroyed the hydra. Hercules then dipped his arrows into the wounds of the hydra to make them deadly.

Hydriotaphia

* *Urn Burial.*

Hygeia /hai'dʒi:ə/

In Greek myth, the daughter of Aesculapius; they were worshipped together as the deities of health.

Hylas /'hailas/

In Greek myth, a beautiful youth to whom the hero Heracles* was devoted. He was carried off by water nymphs when drawing water at Kios in Mysia.

Hymen (Hymeneus) /'haimen/

In Greek myth, the son of Dionysus*, god of the vine, and Aphrodite*, goddess of sexual love; as such, he was a god of fruitfulness and especially of marriage. He was sometimes said to be son of Apollo and a muse.

Hymettus /hai'metəs/

A mountain in the region of Athens, famous for its honey and its marble.

Hymns

The word 'hymn' is of ancient Greek origin; it meant a song of praise to the gods. Such songs have been important in all the religions that have lain behind European culture; Latin hymns were composed and sung in the Christian churches from the earliest days of Christianity, and the Jewish hymns, or Psalms*, are shared by the Jewish and the Christian religions.

The English hymn began its history in the religious Reformation* under Edward VI* when the abandonment of the Latin form of service produced the need for hymns in English. The Psalms were the obvious resource, but they were translated into English prose. Accordingly, in 1549, the first or 'Old Version' of metrical Psalms was published; the authors were Sternhold and Hopkins. The most famous of this collection, and the only one now generally known, is the 'Old Hundredth' (Psalm 100): 'All people that on earth do dwell'. The Old Version of the metrical Psalms was replaced by the 'New Version' (1696) by Tate and Brady. From this book, two psalms are still familiar: 'Through all the changing scenes of life' and 'As pants the hart for cooling streams'.

The majority of hymns in English, however, were not metrical Psalms, but specially composed original poems. The great period of English hymn composition was 17th and 18th C. However, it is necessary to distinguish between short religious poems which have been adopted as hymns, and poems which were composed as hymns. Some of the best religious poets of 17th C, notably Herbert* and Vaughan*, produced work in the first group. But the first professional hymn writer (as distinct from the composers of the metrical Psalms) was the Anglican bishop, Thomas Ken (1637–1711). His best hymns, *eg* 'Awake my soul', and 'Glory to thee, my God, this night', are distinguished poetry.

It was, however, the Dissenters* – the Puritan movements excluded from the Church of England by the Act of Uniformity (1662) – and their Evangelical* sympathizers within the Church of England, rather than the orthodox Anglicans, who were at first most active in hymn-writing. The Church of England had a set form of worship in the Book of Common Prayer*; hymns (in addition to the prose versions of the Psalms) were allowed in this service, but no special provision was made for them. But the Dissenting sects had no set form of worship; hymns for this reason alone were important to them. They were important also for three other reasons: Dissent was strong among classes in touch with traditions of ballad and folk-song; most forms of Dissenting faith demanded strong participation by the congregation in the act of worship; in 17th C, Dissenters underwent persecution, and communal, militant hymn-singing encouraged their spirit of endurance. John Bunyan included hymns in his *Pilgrim's Progress**, written in prison; one of these – 'Who would true valour see' – is famous. But the greatest of the Dissenting hymn-writers is Isaac Watts*. His language combines the homeliness of the broadside ballads* of the city streets with the dignity and musical cadence of biblical English. Charles Wesley*, the brother of the Methodist leader John Wesley, had greater versatility than Watts, and was very prolific; his best hymns are impressive though without the power of the best by Watts. Other notable 18th-C hymn-writers were John Newton (1725–1807) and William Cowper*. All these had at least some of the force of common speech and spontaneous emotion in their hymns. Beside them, the hymns of the orthodox Anglican, Joseph Addison*, are cold, though dignified and sincere.

In 19th C, partly under the influence of the Oxford Movement*, the Church of England reversed its policy of discouraging the use of hymns in its forms of worship. Hymn-writers became numerous; 220 Church of England hymn-books were published between 1800 and 1880, including the official compilation, *Hymns Ancient and Modern* (1861). It was an age in which strong religious feeling struggled with bitter doubt, often in the same mind; the struggle is exemplified in 'Lead Kindly Light' by Cardinal Newman*. Unfortunately, it was also an age in which the art of verse was widely practised with dexterity and facility, and this excessive ease of writing produced many hymns which are more remarkable for their superficial sentiment than for their depth of feeling. 20th C has produced very few hymns; the explanation for this barrenness is not so much the decline of church-going and religious belief as a reaction against the 19th-C decadence. Some of the best 19th-C hymns are in the style of the carol*, – a much older tradition in English poetry than ordinary hymn-writing; examples of Christmas hymns in the carol tradition are Mrs Alexander's 'Once in royal David's city' and Christina Rossetti's 'In the bleak mid-winter'.

Hyperbole /hai'pə:bəli/

* *Figures of Speech.*

Hyperboreans /haipəbo:'riənz/

In Greek myth, a race that lived in the far north, and worshipped Apollo*. They were said to be happy and peaceful in a fertile, sunny land, and to have an individual life-span of a thousand years.

Hyperion /hai'piəriən/

In Greek myth, a Titan*, son of the sky god Uranus and the earth goddess Ge. He was one of the greatest of the Titans, and often identified with the sun, of whom in the original myth he was the father; the sun-god was Helios.

* *Hyperion by Keats.*

Hyperion

Poetry by John Keats*, written in 1818–19: two fragments of an epic*, the second (*The Fall of Hyperion*) unrevised. Keats's aim was to rival Milton* with a theme of divine conflict originating before the creation of man; Milton chose the Christian myth of the Fall of the Angels, and Keats the ancient Greek myth of the war of the Gods and the Titans*. The first *Hyperion* fragment presents Saturn, chief of the Titans, already deposed and mourning his lost power; Hyperion, the only Titan as yet unfallen; and Apollo, yet a child but destined to succeed him, and related by his nature to the arts and enlightenment. This fragment is strongly Miltonic in style, and Keats abandoned it for that reason: 'Miltonic verse cannot be written but in an artful or rather artist's humour. I wish to give myself up to other sensations.' (Letter 151, Sept. 1819); 'I prefer the native music of it to Milton's cut by feet.' (Letter 156, Sept. 1819). The second *Hyperion* (*Fall of Hyperion*) opens with a dream in which the poet finds himself in the temple of Moneta* (from Roman myth, Juno Moneta = the Counsellor or Warner, but Keats has identified her with Mnemosyne*, Memory, mother of the Muses*, a Titaness who survived the overthrow of the Titans). His entrance to the shrine is a supreme moral test, for

None can usurp this height . . .
But those to whom the miseries of the world
Are misery, and will not let them rest.

The style and approach to this version was perhaps influenced by Dante* (in place of Milton); Keats had been reading Cary's translation (1814).

Hypsipyle /hip'sipili/

In Greek myth, daughter of Thoas, king of the island of Lemnos. The women of the island rose and slaughtered the men, but she saved her father. She later welcomed Jason of the Argonauts, and bore him twin sons.

Hyrcania /hə:'keiniə/

A region of ancient Persia, near the Caspian Sea, also called the Hyrcanian. It was famous for its wild beasts.

I

Iambic foot (Iamb, Iambus) /ai'ambik/

The classical verse foot of a short syllable followed by a long one, which in English is an unaccented syllable followed by an accented one. The Alexandrine has six such feet. The form used by Shakespeare is sometimes called an iambic pentameter, but in fact only occasional lines follow the strict iambic pattern when spoken naturally.

And gent/lemen / in Eng/land now / a-bed
Shall think / themselves / accursed / they were / not here,
And hold / their man/hoods cheap, / whiles an/y speaks
That fought / with us / upon / Saint Cris/pin's day.

(Shakespeare's *Henry V*, IV. iii. 64)

Iapetus /aiə'pitəs/

In Greek myth, one of the Titans*, and father of Atlas* and Prometheus*.

Iberians

The name originally given by ancient Greek seamen to the population in and around the valley of the Ebro in Spain. Later it was extended to include small dark-haired peoples from Spain to Britain. In Britain the Iberians are thought of as the pre-Celtic population, and the modern Welsh, though Celtic-speaking, are supposed to have their physical characteristics. The race loosely known as 'ancient Britons' are spoken of as their Celtic conquerors.

Ibsen, Henrik (1828–1906) /'ibsn/

Norwegian dramatist; his working life (1850–1900) began in a period when the art of the theatre had fallen low everywhere in Europe, and perhaps lowest of all in Britain. By the end of the century Ibsen's example had revived interest in the drama everywhere and had profoundly influenced a number of other important dramatists, such as Strindberg in Sweden, Chekhov* in Russia, and Shaw* in Britain. Ibsen began by writing romantic and historical dramas. Then, in self-imposed exile, he wrote his two great poetic dramas, *Brand* (1866) and *Peer Gynt* (1867). About 10 years later he started on the prose dramas the sequence of which continued to 1900. The first group of these treated social problems with startling boldness: *Pillars of Society* (1877); *A Doll's House* (1879); *Ghosts* (1881); *An Enemy of the People* (1882). After this, his work became increasingly psychological, anticipating 20th C in the handling of inner conflicts, self-deceptions, and frustrations: *The Wild Duck* (1884); *Rosmersholm* (1886); *The Lady from the Sea* (1888); *Hedda Gabler* (1890). So far these plays had been extremely realistic, but the psychological phase showed a new and interesting dramatic use of symbols. In the last group of plays the symbolism takes precedence over the realism: *The Master Builder* (1892); *Little Eyolf* (1894); *John Gabriel Borkman* (1896), and *When We Dead Awaken* (1900). It was the social realist phase which most influenced Bernard Shaw, and it was Shaw who was the most eloquent introducer of Ibsen's art to the British public, particularly in his book *Quintessence of Ibsenism* (1891). The English dramatic revival of 1890–1914 (as distinct from the Anglo-Irish one by Yeats* and Synge* happening at the same time) thus consisted predominantly of realist plays dealing with social problems, by such writers as Shaw, Galsworthy*, Granville Barker. The psychological and symbolical phases of Ibsen's work have had, together with the writing of Chekhov and Strindberg, greater influence since 1920.

Icarus /'aikərəs/

In Greek myth, the son of Daedalus*, the inventor of wings made of wax. Together they took to the air from Crete on the way to Sicily. But Icarus flew too near the sun, which melted his wings, so that he fell into the sea. Daedalus reached Sicily.

Ichabod /'ikəbod/

In the Bible (*1 Samuel* 4:21), a name meaning 'inglorious' given to the grandson of the high priest Eli when the ark of God was captured by the Philistines and 'the glory is departed from Israel'.

Ichor /'aiko:/

In Greek myth, the fluid that served as blood in the veins of the gods.

Icknield Way

An ancient road, its origin probably preceding the Roman Conquest, which crosses England from the east (county of Norfolk) to the south-west (Cornwall).

Ida

A mountain in Asia Minor, near Troy, frequently mentioned in ancient Greek myth. From its summit, the gods watched the Trojan war. On its slopes Paris* lived with the nymph Oenone*, and passed judgement on the three goddesses, Athene*, Aphrodite*, Hera*. It was the home of the earth-mother Cybele*.

Idalia /ai'deiljə/

One of the names of Aphrodite*, goddess of sexual love, in Greek myth. It derives from the ancient town of Idalium in Cyprus, a centre of her worship.

Idealism

In philosophy, any form of thought which finds reality not in the mind of the perceiver (the subject), nor in the thing experienced (the object) but in the idea in which they meet. In its earliest form idealism was developed by Socrates* and his disciple Plato*. Their influence was important in the 16th-C Europe of the Renaissance*, *eg* on Edmund Spenser*. A modern idealist, F. H. Bradley*, had as strong an influence on the poet T. S. Eliot*.

In ordinary usage, idealism means the ability to conceive perfection as a standard by which ordinary behaviour and achievement is to be judged. This view is really an inheritance from Plato, who believed that earthly realities were imperfect derivatives of heavenly perfections. To 'idealize' a thing or person is to present the image of what ought to be, rather than what experience knows in ordinary life. In imaginative art we have come to consider this as a fault, but to a 16th-C critic such as Sir Philip Sidney* poetry existed for just such a purpose. This is not, however, the kind of influence which Bradley had on Eliot; Bradley maintained that no reality existed outside the spirit, and he influenced Eliot towards interpreting the phenomena and dilemmas of his age in religious terms.
* *Apology for Poetry*.

Ides /aidz/

A term used in the Roman calendar for the 15th day of March, May, July and October; and for the 13th day of other months.

Idler, The

Essays contributed weekly by Samuel Johnson* to the *Universal Chronicle*, or *Weekly Gazette* from April 1758 to April 1760. As compared to his *Rambler** papers, they contain more humour, and more flexible treatment of the fictional characters such as Dick Minim, but they have the same kind of emotional force and moral gravity which distinguish Johnson as a periodical essayist.

Idomeneus /ai'dominju:s/

In Greek myth, a king of Crete, and ally of the Greeks in the siege of Troy. In one version of his story, in a storm on his return journey he vowed to Poseidon*, god of the sea, a sacrifice of whatever he should first meet on landing. This proved to be his own son.

Idyll

In ancient Greek literature, it meant originally a short poem. The Greek poet Theocritus* called his poems about the rural life of Sicily idylls. When the term was revived in the Renaissance*, it was consequently used for a short pastoral* poem, similar to an eclogue* except that an eclogue was more likely to be in dialogue. As pastoral verse commonly presented happiness or virtue in pure and simplified terms, an idyll then came to be used loosely for any piece of writing presenting experience in such a way, often an episode from a longer work – such as that of Juan and Haidee in Canto II of Byron's *Don Juan**. The best-known use of the term is Tennyson's *Idylls of the King**.

Idylls of the King, The

A series of poems by Alfred Tennyson* on episodes from the legends of King Arthur*. The earliest and most famous fragment is the *Morte D'Arthur* (1842), but the series really begins in 1859 with *Enid*, *Vivien*, *Elaine*, *Guinevere*. Followed by (1869) *The Coming of Arthur*, *The Holy Grail*, *Pelleas and*

Ettare, The Passing of Arthur; (1871) *The Last Tournament*; (1872) *Gareth and Lynette*; (1885) *Balin and Balan. Enid* was later divided into *The Marriage of Geraint* and *Geraint and Enid. Morte D'Arthur* was included in *The Passing of Arthur*. The whole series was intended to have a loose epic* structure; single-minded virtue ideally conceived is gradually overcome by evil through the sinful passion of Lancelot* and Arthur's wife, Guinevere. Extremely popular at the time, the *Idylls* have chiefly harmed Tennyson's reputation since. They were written under the influence of the Pre-Raphaelite* movement with its romanticization of the Middle Ages*. Later the poems struck readers as bodiless, with the life neither of the Middle Ages nor of 19th C. However, parts of the *Idylls*, notably *Morte d'Arthur*, exemplify Tennyson's art at its best.

Igdrasil

Yggdrasil.

Igraine

In the legends of King Arthur*, wife of Uther Pendragon and mother of Arthur.

Iliad /ˈiliəd/

An epic* by the ancient Greek poet Homer*. Its subject is the siege of Troy* by an alliance of Greek states; the occasion of the war is the elopement of Helen, wife of Menelaus, king of the Greek state of Sparta, with Paris, a son of Priam king of Troy. The poem is in 24 books; it begins with the Greeks already besieging Troy. In Book I the chief Greek hero, Achilles, quarrels with the Greek commander-in-chief, Agamemnon, king of Argos and brother to Menelaus. Achilles withdraws from the fighting, and only returns to it in Book XIX after the killing of his friend Patroclus by the chief Trojan hero, Hector. Achilles kills Hector in XXII, and the poem ends with Hector's funeral in Troy. Hector is the principal hero of the epic, much of which is taken up with his exploits, as well as with those of other Greek and Trojan heroes and with the intervention of the gods on either side. There is much speculation about the date of the historical events and that of the poem respectively. Present opinion seems to be that the historical city of Troy fell early in 12th C BC and that the poem was written about 300 years later. The surviving text dates from 2nd C BC.

The *Iliad* has had an enormous influence on the literature of Europe. With Homer's *Odyssey**, it set the standard for epic poetry, which until 19th C was considered the noblest poetic form. Its first great successor was the *Aeneid** (1st C BC) by the Roman poet Virgil, in many ways a continuation of the *Iliad* since it tells the adventures of Aeneas, son-in-law of Priam, and in the second book describes the fall of the city of Troy. The poem has been several times translated into English verse; the most notable versions are those by George Chapman* (1611) and Alexander Pope* (1720).

Translation.

Ilium /ˈailiəm/

An alternative name for the city of Troy*.

Imagism

A poetic movement founded by a group led by Ezra Pound* in 1912; it published four anthologies – *Des Imagistes*, 1914; *Some Imagists*, 1915–16–17. The inspiration came from the ideas of T. E. Hulme (1886–1917) who was an anti-romantic, believing that words were being used by poets to obscure emotions instead of to clarify them. The kind of poet he had in mind was Swinburne*. The Imagist credo may be summarized as:

[1] Use the language of common speech, but use it exactly.
[2] Create new rhythms for new moods.
[3] Allow complete freedom in subject.
[4] Present an image, but avoid vagueness.
[5] Produce poetry that is hard and clear.
[6] Concentration is the essence of poetry.

Pound is an American, though he was then living in England; Imagism was an Anglo-American movement, with an English periodical, *The Egoist* (started 1914), and an American one, *Poetry* (from 1912). Pound was himself the most distinguished of the Imagists, though he separated from the movement in 1914. Notable contributors to the anthologies included D. H. Lawrence* and James Joyce*. The movement was more organized and distinct in its aims than most English literary movements, but on the whole of minor importance – a contribution to the growth of distinctively 20th-C poetry whose greatest figures (Yeats* and Eliot*) were not imagists, though traces of imagist influence can be found in their work, *eg* Eliot's *Waste Land**.

Imitations of Horace

Some of the best satirical verse by Alexander Pope*, written 1733–8, mainly adaptations of the satires and epistles of the Roman Horace*. Horace had already been found a convenient model for satire by Rochester* in 17th C and Swift* in 18th. The culture of Rome in 1st C BC under the Emperor Augustus was particularly congenial to the English 18th C (the Augustan age* of English poetry). Pope's imitations, like those of other imitators of the classics in 16th, 17th and 18th C were not merely to translate nor to mimic slavishly but to imagine what the Roman poet would have written had he lived in Pope's own day. The standards of the great age of Rome were brought to bear on England of 18th C, sometimes with the effect of irony, as when Pope imitates Horace's verse epistle to Augustus by identifying the Emperor with George II (1727–60). Some of the force of Pope's satires is against contemporary politics, some against literary and personal rivals. Despite the numerous detailed personal references, Pope's force of wit and aphorism much surpass the purely local and contemporary influence of the poems.

In Memoriam A.H.H.

A sequence of poems by Alfred Tennyson inspired by the death of Arthur Henry Hallam, at 22, in 1833. He was a brilliant young man of great promise and hopefulness; Tennyson, a year or two older, had found in friendship with Hallam a strong resource against his own disposition to despondency and scepticism. The death crystallized for him the difficulty of spiritual affirmation in an age of upheaval in established ideas. Science was already shaking traditional certainties and contributing to the feeling that the reality of nature itself was perpetual flux: there are echoes in *In Memoriam* of Lyell's* *Principles of Geology* (1830–3).

The poem was written between 1833 and 1850, and consists of 130 sections, each section being a lyric* in stanzas of four 8-syllable lines rhyming *abba*—a form used by Ben Jonson* in his elegy* 'Though Beauty be the Mark of praise'. The sequence is a single poem arranged in three sections divided by Christmas Odes, and the whole concluded by a marriage-song for the wedding of Tennyson's sister, who had been engaged to Hallam and was at first inconsolable at his death. Various moods of grief are expressed, and a reaching out to restored confidence and hope; in places Tennyson engages issues between religion and science. Despite much disagreement about the work as a whole, *In Memoriam* is usually acknowledged to be Tennyson's finest achievement.

Inca

A race in Peru which, at the time of their discovery (1533) by the Spanish explorer Pizarro, ruled a large and highly organized empire. The word is also used for the supreme ruler of the Incas.

Inchbald, Mrs Elizabeth (1753–1821)

Novelist, dramatist and actress. Among other plays she translated *Lovers' Vows* from the German of Kotzebue, and this is the play rehearsed in Jane Austen's *Mansfield Park**. This, and some of the other nineteen plays she wrote or adapted, was a popular success: Jane Austen assumes knowledge of it by the reader. However, her best works are her two novels: *A Simple Story* (1791) and *Nature and Art* (1796).

Bib: Littlewood, S. R., *Elizabeth Inchbald and her Circle*.

Independents

* *Congregationalism*.

Indulgences

Medieval documents bearing the seal of the Pope or of a bishop and granting the recipient remission of punishment in the next world for sins committed in this. They were freely sold in the Middle Ages* by licensed 'Pardoners', and were an easy way for the Church (and also for the pardoners) to raise money. The Church based the practice on the authority of a number of Biblical texts, such as the words addressed by Christ to St Peter, by tradition the source of all papal authority: 'And I will give unto thee the keys of the kingdom of heaven: and whatsoever thou shalt bind on earth shall be bound in heaven: and whatsoever thou shalt loose on earth shall be loosed in heaven.' (*Matthew* 16:19) Indulgences were not supposed to be effective unless the recipients were truly repentant, and they were not supposed to apply to future sins, should they commit any. Nonetheless, the pardoners were often unscrupulous, and used the indulgences to frighten and flatter simple-minded people, and thus gain huge profits. Reformers such as the Englishman Wycliffe* and the German Luther* were fiercely critical of them. Chaucer made grim comedy of them (*Pardoner's Tale**) and his contemporary Langland regarded them sceptically (*Piers Plowman**, Passus VII).

Industrial Revolution, The

An industrial revolution has been defined as 'the change that transforms a people with peasant occupations and local markets into an industrial society with world-wide connections' (*Encyclopaedia Britannica*). Clearly then many countries have industrial revolutions, and more than one; for example it is currently said that Britain is undergoing a new industrial revolution with the advent of automation in industrial processes. However, we understand *the* industrial revolution to mean the succession of changes which transformed England from a predominantly rural and agricultural country into a predominantly urban and manufacturing one in 18th and 19th C, and especially between 1750 and 1850. It was, moreover, the first such revolution in the modern world.

[1] *Causes*. Although not, apart from London, a country of great towns, England at the beginning of 18th C was already a great trading nation, with much private capital ready for investment. Not only was trade free to move throughout the British Isles, but there was considerable freedom of movement between the social classes, which were not rigidly defined almost into caste systems as in other European countries, *eg* France. English middle-class religion laid emphasis on the individual conscience as the guide to conduct, and also on the moral excellence of sober, industrious employment; these values encouraged self-reliance and enterprising initiative. Although some of this middle class (the Nonconformist or Dissenting sects which rejected the Church of England) were barred from political rights, and Parliament, controlled by the aristocracy, was far from truly representative, the political leaders of the country were extremely interested in commerce, which they were ready to participate in and profit from. The bent of the whole nation, from the days of Bacon in early 17th C, had been increasingly practical, and the steadily growing population provided a market which invited exploitation by various methods of improved production. Once the process started, it gathered its own momentum, which was increased by the existence of large supplies of convenient fuel in the country's coalfields. Agriculture also contributed to industrial growth: the landowners were zealous farmers, and their improved methods of cultivation not only freed much labour (**Enclosures*), which then became available for employment in the town factories, but increased the food supplies available for the towns. Finally, 18th C (in contrast to 17th) was a time of peace and stability in Britain, undisturbed by the wars in which her armies and money were engaged across the sea.

[2] *Process.* In the textile industry, already established since 15th C as the principal one, a number of machines were invented which increased production and reduced labour, but were too large for the cottages where the processes had hitherto been carried out. They therefore had to be housed in factories and mills where large numbers of employees worked together. These machines were at first operated by water power. In the iron industry, the principal fuel used hitherto had been charcoal, the supply of which was becoming exhausted. However, improved methods of smelting by coal were discovered, and ironmasters set up their blast furnaces in the neighbourhood of the coalfields in the north midlands and north of England. Most important of all, in 1769 James Watt* patented an adaptation of his steam-engine to the machines used in the textile industry; this consequently ceased to depend on water power, and concentrated itself in the north of England to be near the coalfields. An important result was the immense expansion in manufacture of cotton cloth. An extensive system of canals was constructed in 18th C for the transport of goods and fuel, and the modern methods of road and bridge building were introduced, but the decisive advance in communications was the invention of the steam rail locomotive by George Stephenson (1814); by 1850 a railway system covered the country. We cannot understand the process of the British Industrial Revolution if we do not appreciate that it was a period of epic excitement, especially in the development of rail transport. It produced great inventors and engineers such as Isambard Brunel (1806–59) who had to force their projects against established prejudice and ignorance. The other side of the epic story was the meteoric emergence of great financial speculators such as George Hudson (1800–71), the 'Railway King', who rose from being a York draper to control of a third of the railway system, and ended in disgrace. The social changes were unprecedentedly dramatic, in the rapid growth of the midland and northern industrial towns, and the opening of new opportunities for wealth among humble but ambitious men. This heroic aspect of industrialism has to be remembered as a great motive power in Victorian culture, counterbalancing the deleterious consequences of industrialism which hold such prominence in much of the literature.

[3] *Consequences.* Britain was by 1850 the 'workshop of the world'; no other country was yet ready to compete with her in industrial production. The towns were the source of her wealth, though the landowners retained their social prestige and often became much richer by ownership of coalfields. The north of England, until 18th C a backward region, was now the most advanced in Britain; its towns grew rapidly, unplanned, in ugliness and dirt. The economic motives outran the social conscience, and the new urban proletariat worked and lived in evil conditions under employers who had often risen themselves from poverty, and had the ruthlessness which was a consequence of the severity of their struggle. England was divided as never before; the industrial north from the agricultural south, the industrial working class from (sometimes) pitiless employers, and both from the long-established gentry, particularly of the south. Victorian novels are eloquent testimony to the social conditions; the title of Elizabeth Gaskell's novel, *North and South**, and the subtitle of Disraeli's *Sybil, or The Two Nations** are evidence in themselves. Josiah Bounderby in Dickens's *Hard Times** is a portrait of the unprincipled kind of industrial employer; Sir Leicester Dedlock and Rouncewell the ironmaster in *Bleak House** exemplify the old order's failure to understand the new.

* 1.4.3, 1.5.1.1; *Cloth manufacture.*

Inferno, The

The first section of the *Divine Comedy* by the Italian poet Dante Alighieri*. It is an account of Dante's visit to Hell through which he imagines himself guided by the spirit of Virgil*. Hell is conceived as conical, reaching to the centre of the earth. It has three great divisions in accordance with the classification of vices by Aristotle*: incontinence (lust, greed, wrath etc.); brutishness (including unbelievers, tyrants, suicides, perverts, usurers); and malice (including all kinds of fraud and treachery). At the very bottom is Satan* (Lucifer) himself; from him the two poets pass through the earth to its opposite surface, where they arrive at the foot of the Mount of Purgatory*. The great divisions are subdivided into Circles, of which there are nine in all, in each of which the appropriate subdivision of sinners receives the appropriate punishment. The first circle is reserved for pre-Christian pagans who had no chance of knowing the true Faith; among these Virgil himself belongs, and their only punishment is their hopeless desire for God. Outside this circle is a dark plain populated by those who did not deserve even Hell: they had lived 'without blame, without praise'.

* *Paradiso; Purgatorio*

Inns, Taverns, Alehouses

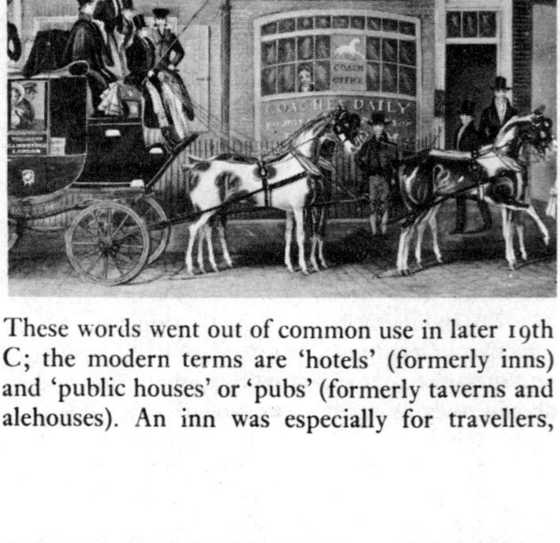

These words went out of common use in later 19th C; the modern terms are 'hotels' (formerly inns) and 'public houses' or 'pubs' (formerly taverns and alehouses). An inn was especially for travellers, who could eat, drink and sleep there; taverns existed chiefly in London and were drinking resorts; alehouses were a humbler form of tavern such as might be found in any village. From 16th C taverns and alehouses had to receive licences for their trade from magistrates, who could withdraw these if they became places of disorder. The word 'hostelry' is equivalent to 'inn' but is an older term still; similarly, 'hospital' originally stood for an institution offering 'hospitality' to travellers, but by 16th C was reserved for a refuge for the sick and aged; now, merely for the sick.

Until 14th C travel was comparatively rare, and shelter was provided chiefly by the monasteries*, which continued to serve the function of inns until their dissolution in 16th C. Already in 14th C, however, travel was becoming more common, and inns were growing up independently of monasteries; their number naturally increased after the monastic dissolution. One of the chief functions of the larger inns was to serve as 'post-houses' for mail-coaches which changed horses at them, and put down travellers who were using them.

Inns were identified by the coloured signs hanging outside them, still commonly found outside pubs and some hotels. Such signs often showed the coat of arms of the local great family, and the inn would be called, *eg* 'the Neville Arms'. Still commoner as a sign was the 'crest' or symbol (often an animal) that usually surmounted a coat of arms; hence the large numbers of inns called the Red Lion, the Black Bull, the White Hart, etc. Sometimes the sign represented a local trade or craft (the Carpenters' Arms, etc.), and the habit of old soldiers turning innkeeper led to many inns and taverns being called after famous generals, particularly if they had been popular, *eg* the Marquis of Granby, the Duke of Wellington.

* *Pub.*

Inns of Court

Institutions belonging to the legal profession, in London. There are now four, all dating from the Middle Ages: Lincoln's Inn; Gray's Inn; the Inner Temple and the Middle Temple. The buildings resemble those of Oxford and Cambridge colleges, and their function is to be responsible for the education of those students of the law who intend to become barristers, with the right to plead in the senior courts of law and – in the senior rank – the qualifications to be appointed judges. Each Inn is a separate society, governed by its senior members, called Benchers. The buildings are not exclusively occupied by barristers or their students, however; thus Furnivall's Inn (now pulled down) was for a time the home of Charles Dickens*, and one of his characters, Pip of *Great Expectations**, had rooms in Barnard's Inn, now part of a school.

Innuendo

* *Figures of Speech.*

Inquisition, The

An organization in the Roman Catholic Church, in the form of a judicial tribunal, whose task it was to detect and eliminate heresy, *ie* false religious doctrine. Officially it was known as the Holy Office, and survives today only for the identification of heretical literature. Its beginnings were in 13th C and it visited, or had branches in, the various European countries. In England it was unpopular even before the Reformation*, but in Spain its function of heresy hunting was not abolished until 1834. In the English Protestant mind, from 16th C, the Spanish Inquisition was identified with all that was conceived to be cruel and intolerant in the Catholic Church, and it was often confused with the Holy Office in Rome. Nonetheless, Protestantism* in Britain did not itself at first practise tolerance. The English law of 1401 that heretics must be burned alive was not abolished till 1676, though the practice had long ceased; in Scotland a young man accused of heresy was hanged in 1696.

Instauratio Magna (The Great Renewal)

The title of the great philosophical work projected by Francis Bacon*, and left incomplete. According to Bacon's plan of 1620, it was to have consisted of six parts: I. A review of existing sciences; *De Augmentis Scientiarum*, Latin translation of *The Advancement of Learning** (1605). II. Outline of a new inductive method; *Novum Organum** (The New Instrument). This exists in a compressed form, unfinished. III. A Natural History to be used as a basis for inductive conclusions. The tract *Parasceve* (Preparative) and the *Historia Ventorum* (History of the Winds); *Historia vitae et mortis* (History of Life and Death); *Sylva sylvarum* (Forest of Forests), a collection of facts and observations. IV. Examples of investigations by the new method. Of this there is only a small fragment, *Filum Labyrinthi* (The Thread of the Labyrinth). V. Hypotheses of Bacon's own, to be tested by inductive experiment. Of this part only a preface exists, though some other writings may have been intended to belong to it. VI. A synthesis of conclusions from the inductive method. No contribution to this exists.

Interludes

Short plays of a kind popular especially in 16th C before the great flowering of Elizabethan drama. In general they were more secular than Morality* plays, still being performed, but Moralities and interludes are not always clearly distinguishable, and indeed the term 'interlude' was applied to religious plays as early as 14th C. Nonetheless there is no other convenient term for such slight works as John Heywood's* *Play of the Weather* (1533) in which an emissary of the gods tries to find out the ideal weather for humanity, only to discover that opinions hopelessly conflict. The function of such a play seems to have been entertainment after a banquet in a nobleman's hall or in a college, or during the intervals of business of a town council, etc. That it was a performance during intervals of business or other kinds of entertainment, or perhaps of long, serious plays to provide light relief, has been assumed from the usual meaning of 'interlude' in ordinary speech; however, the word has also been surmised to mean merely 'a play between' performers taking parts. One of the best known examples is the interlude of *Pyramus and Thisbe* played before Theseus and his court in the last act of Shakespeare's *A Midsummer Night's Dream**.

* 5.1.2.3.

Interregnum

The term used for the period 1649–60, between the execution of Charles I* and the accession of his son Charles II – the Restoration*. It is divided into the period 1649–53, when England was ruled by the House of Commons and a Council of State, and the period 1653–8 when Oliver Cromwell* and for a brief time his son Richard were Protectors.

Intimations of Immortality from Recollections of Early Childhood

A poem by William Wordsworth*. Its main title is *Ode*; it is a pindaric ode* in 11 stanzas of varying length. The first four stanzas were composed in 1802; the rest of the poem was completed in 1806, and the whole was published in 1807.

This is one of Wordsworth's most controversial poems, as regards both its merit and its meaning. The part composed earlier is a deep, sad questioning of experience, from which the ardour that makes for poetic creation seems to have departed. In the longer and later part, the poet's confidence revives, but many readers are left with the impression that he is unnaturally 'forcing up' his spirits. However, the whole poem has great philosophical and psychological interest. Wordsworth makes use (stanza v) of the Platonic myth that the soul pre-exists the body – see Plato's* dialogue *Phaedo* – as an image to account for the intensity and purity of the responses of young children; in his own thought, these qualities of the child are infused into him by maternal love, and expand outwards towards all nature – see Wordsworth's *Prelude**, Book II, 232–65. His conclusion is that the child is a 'Mighty Prophet! Seer blest!' and that the vividness and purity of childhood experience not only shape the nature of the adult (see the poem *My heart leaps up*, composed 1802, pub 1807) but live on in the adult in a capacity for response that can never wholly be overlaid. The second half of the poem was evidently composed with Coleridge's *Dejection** in mind; both poets emphasize the creative fruitfulness of the state of joy.

Io /'aiəu/

In Greek myth, daughter of Inachus, first king of Argos. Zeus* loved her and changed her into a heifer to protect her from the jealousy of his wife Hera. Hera caught her and set the watch-dog Argus to guard her, but Zeus freed Io by having Argus killed. Hera then sent a gadfly to torment her; she crossed the Bosporus (passage of the ox) and the Ionian Sea, eventually reached Egypt and recovered her human shape.

Iphigenia /ifidʒi'naiə/

In Greek myth, the daughter of Agamemnon*, chief general of the Greeks in the Trojan war. On the way to Troy, the Greek fleet was windbound, because Agamemnon had offended the goddess Artemis; Iphigenia had to be sacrificed if the fleet was to be released. Artemis, however, relented and spirited her away to Tauris (Crimea) where she became the goddess's priestess, with the duty of sacrificing all strangers. Faced with the task of sacrificing her own brother, Orestes*, she planned an escape with him, taking with her the statue of Artemis. Plays about her have been written by Aeschylus*, Sophocles*, Euripides*, Racine* and Goethe*.

Ireland

A brief sketch of the confused and tormented history of this country must concentrate on its relations with England, and this account may conveniently be divided into phases.

[1] *1150–1600 – Period of Disorder.* Henry II* was the first English king to be acknowledged sovereign of Ireland, but at no time did the English succeed before 1600 in establishing an efficient central government. In 12th C, Ireland consisted of warring Celtic kingdoms, with a Norse settlement along the east coast. The conquest was not undertaken by Henry but by his Anglo-Norman nobility, notably Richard Strongbow, Earl of Pembroke, in alliance with the Irish king of Leinster. By 1500 Ireland was ruled by a mixed English and Irish aristocracy, the former regarded as English by the Irish and as Irish by the English. English law and speech were secure only in a narrow region known as the Pale*, centred on the capital city of Dublin. The first real crisis in relations between England and Ireland arose in 16th C, when the Irish refused to receive the English Protestant Reformation*. Fierce wars against Spanish armies which landed in Ireland with a view to invading England were followed by fierce suppression under Elizabeth I*, for instance under the governorship of Lord Grey de Wilton. The poet Edmund Spenser* was appointed his secretary (1580) and given a grant of land in the province of Munster as part of a plan to settle the country with Protestant overlords; his castle was burnt down in 1598, a year before his death. Spenser's singularly stern view of Justice in *The Faerie Queene** (Artegall, Bk. V) is a reflection of his Irish experiences. By 1600 Ireland was a nation of mixed English and Celtic people, with an English-speaking aristocracy, and firm identification with the Roman Catholic faith. The problem for England in the next two centuries was how to subdue the country to effective Protestant rule.

[2] *1600–1800 – Irish Protestant Ascendancy.* The policy of settling Protestants in Ireland was notably successful in one of the four provinces under James I* (1603–25) when Ulster became the Anglo-Scottish Protestant fortress which it has remained to this day. Oliver Cromwell* was savage in subjection of Catholic Ireland to his authority, and by extensive confiscations increased the class of Protestant landlords. In 18th C, penal laws further disabled Catholic landholders, refused political rights to Catholics, and barred them from most professions and from education. The only Irish university (founded by Elizabeth in

1591), Dublin, was a Protestant one. However, towards the end of 18th C, partly owing to the Irish patriotism of Anglo-Irish Protestants (including the satirist Swift* and the philosopher Berkeley*), the penal laws were reduced in severity, and in 1782 an Irish constitution was promulgated, by which the Irish Protestants were given political rights and limited powers in an Irish Parliament freed from Privy Council* control. The experiment was a failure, and in 1801 Ireland was united politically and in all other respects with England and Scotland, Irish Protestants receiving for the first time representation in the English Parliament.

[3] *1801–1921 – The Union.* 19th C was the age of steady emancipation of Irish Catholics and mounting Irish patriotism. The population at the beginning of the century was 4½ million, fewer than 1½ million being of English or Scottish Protestant descent. The Anglo-Irish were the social leaders of the country; the Scots were a middle class of business men and farmers; the native Irish were largely peasants. In 1829 Catholic Emancipation removed all the important restrictions on Catholics, notably the political ones. Henceforward there was a growing party of Irish Catholics in the English House of Commons, in the last quarter of the century known as the Home Rule Party from its intention to win national independence for Ireland. In the middle of the century reform was concentrated on land matters; this was the more necessary for the misery of the Irish peasantry whose sufferings were increased by the severe famines of the 1840s, leading to massive emigration to the United States. In 1841 the population was over 8 million, and it is now about 3 million; Ireland is thus one of the very few countries in the world whose population has actually diminished in the last 100 years. Attempts to obtain Home Rule through the English Parliament failed. A brief rebellion in 1916 was put down, but a severe one in 1919–21 resulted in independence within the Commonwealth. It was led by the Sinn Fein party, and the great bitterness of the fighting arose in part from their fanaticism and the brutality of the English auxiliary police (called 'Black and Tans' from their uniform) sent to suppress the rebels.

[4] *The Irish Free State.* This state was formed in 1922 and included the three provinces of Munster, Leinster and Connaught. The fourth province, Ulster, being mainly Protestant and Anglo-Scottish in population, has separate status as Northern Ireland, with its own government combined with representation in the English Parliament. The Irish Free State took the name of Eire (Ireland) in 1937, and is no longer a member of the Commonwealth. It is a republic with a president and two houses of parliament, the Dáil and the Seanad. The first official language is nominally Gaelic, but it is a minority language, since English has long been the majority language of the Irish educated classes.

* 1.5.3; *Irish Literature; Universities.*

Iris
In Greek myth, the messenger between the gods and mortals – an alternative to Hermes*. Her path to earth was the rainbow, with which she became identified.

Irish Literature
This exists in two forms: writings in the Celtic language of Gaelic, or Erse; English writing. The former does not concern English literature except in so far as it included myths used in the second.

[1] *Gaelic Literature.* Most of this is medieval (1100–1550). Two main cycles of myth are distinguished: the Ulster series, centring on Conchobar and Cuchulain*; that of Leinster and Munster centring on Finn* and Ossian (Oisin*). *Ulster Cycle*: Cuchulain was a great warrior in the court of Conchobar king of Ulster. Other characters are Ailill and Medb (Maeve), king and queen of Connaught, against whom Cuchulain defended Ulster; Fergus, the exiled king of Ulster; Deirdre*, brought up to be the bride of Conchobar, who killed her lover Naoise. Such legends were versified in the Middle Ages, but are thought to have originated in pre-Christian times, *ie* before 5th C AD. *Leinster-Munster Cycle*: in their best form, ballads; after 1250 these exceeded in popularity the Ulster legends. The events are supposed to take place in 3rd–5th C AD. Finn was a great warrior when Cormac was king of Ireland, and commanded a band called the Fenians. He was the father of the hero Ossian, who spent many years in a kind of fairyland, and was at last baptized Christian by St Patrick. Such myths were used by poets and dramatists of the Irish Nationalist movement in English, *eg* especially W. B. Yeats* and J. M. Synge*, between 1890 and 1910.

[2] *English Literature.* Until 19th C there was not much that was distinctively Irish about the English work produced by the Anglo-Irish. It is singular that nearly all the dramatists of note in 18th-19th C were English-speaking Irish, or Englishmen with strong Irish associations. The list includes Congreve* (though born in England), Farquhar*, Goldsmith*, Sheridan*, Wilde*, Shaw*, Yeats and Synge; but only Yeats and Synge were significantly Irish in viewpoint. Three of the greatest figures in 18th-C non-dramatic literature were Anglo-Irish: Swift*, Berkeley*, and Burke*. Perhaps the passionate feeling for justice in Swift and Burke, as also in the non-dramatic work of Goldsmith, has much to do with their origins in an unjustly oppressed country, though they themselves, like most of the great Irish writers till our own day, were of Protestant* background. The poet Thomas Moore* was more self-consciously Irish but a much lesser figure, though he had a European reputation in his own day. As 19th C went on, Irish writing became steadily more patriotic, but it remained principally of local interest until the 'Irish Renaissance' at the beginning of this century, which included as its major figures the great poet W. B. Yeats and the remarkable dramatist J. M. Synge. But Shaw, though he waved his Irishness in London faces and shows a style of rhetoric which is un-English, did not participate in the Irish movement, and the novelist James Joyce* turned his

back on it, taking refuge on the continent of Europe, though he continued to write about Ireland all his life.

The suffering generated by the unhappy relationships of Ireland with England fructified creatively; the literary production of Ireland since her independence in 1922 is chiefly of minor quality. Sean O'Casey* has been her most distinguished dramatist, except Samuel Beckett*, who lives and writes in France, often in French, though like his friend Joyce, with an abiding Irish preoccupation. O'Casey is certainly the outstanding Irish writer of the age.

* *Abbey Theatre.*

Irish National Theatre

* *Abbey Theatre; Yeats.*

Iron Duke, The

A popular name for the Duke of Wellington* because of his resolution as a general (in the Napoleonic Wars) and as a statesman afterwards.

Ironsides

An old English term for brave and enduring soldiers, and especially associated with the cavalry trained and used by Oliver Cromwell* in the Civil War*.

Irony

* *Figures of Speech.*

Irving, Sir Henry (1838–1905)

Actor. His original name was Brodribb, but he adopted the name of Irving when he gave up a commercial career for acting in 1856. For ten years he performed over 500 parts in provincial companies. He made his name in London in 1871 with the part of Mathias in the melodrama, *The Bells* by Leopold Lewis (adapted from *Le Juif Polonais* by Erckmann-Chatrian). This was at the Lyceum Theatre, which later became famous under his management. His reputation grew by his performance in a great variety of roles (including two in plays by the poet Tennyson*, *The Cup* and *Becket*), especially Shakespearian ones: his performances of Hamlet and Shylock became legendary. Irving's style was strongly romantic and powerfully eloquent; he and Ellen Terry, with whom he was associated at the Lyceum from 1878 to 1902, gave English theatre its main distinction at a time when contemporary literary contribution to the drama was undistinguished.

Isaac /ˈaizək/

In the Bible (*Genesis* 21-8 and 35) the second of the Patriarchs, *ie* ancient founders of the Jewish nation. He was the sole legitimate son and the heir of the first Patriarch, Abraham*, and the father of Jacob* and Esau. His name became interchangeable with Israel (*Amos* 7:9 & 16).

Isaiah /aiˈzaiə/

In the Bible, the greatest of the Old Testament prophetic books. The majority of it is dated towards the end of 8th C BC. It was a period of conflict among the western Asiatic powers, and the book includes a dramatic account of Sennacherib* of Assyria and his invasion of Judaea. He besieged Jerusalem, but his army was devastated by an epidemic of plague, and the city was saved. This is the subject of one of Byron's most famous lyrics – *The Destruction of Sennacherib.* Much of Isaiah consists of prophecies of great disaster to the Jews, of recovery, and of the coming of the Messiah*, *eg* Chapter 7; the early Christians judged the truth of the New Testament Gospels to a great extent as narratives showing the fulfilment of these prophecies, and the same is true of 16th- and 17th-C English Puritans*. Not all Isaiah is considered now to be by the same hand; in particular, Chapters 40–55 are said to be by a writer during the Babylonian exile in 6th C BC. The book contains some of the finest work of the 16th-17th-C translators into English in the Authorized Version.

* *Bible in England.*

Iseult (Isoud, Ysolde, Ysoude)

* *Tristram and Iseult.*

Ishmael /ˈiʃmeil/

In the Bible, (*Genesis* 16, 21, 25) the son of Abraham* and his concubine Hagar; Sarah, Abraham's wife, caused Hagar and Ishmael to be driven into the desert, where he grew up and became the ancestor of nomadic tribes. From this an Ishmael or Ishmaelite has become a term for an outcast and a wanderer.

Isis /ˈaisis/

In ancient Egyptian myth, a great nature goddess. She was sometimes identified with the moon, and her brother-husband Osiris* with the sun. Horus, the rising sun, was their son. The worship of Isis spread all over the eastern Mediterranean; the Greek historian Herodotus (5th C BC) identified her with Demeter* the corn goddess.

There is no connection between the goddess and Isis, the name given to the part of the river Thames which runs through Oxford.

Isocrates (436–338 BC) /aiˈsokrəti:z/

In ancient Greece, a great Athenian orator who advocated a united Greece for war against the states of Asia. He advanced Greek prose style by the artistic care he gave to his speeches.

Italy

Apart from the influence of Italian literature, Italy as a country was particularly important to England in 16th and early 17th C. The English attitude to Italy was complicated – a mixture of admiration, envy, intense interest, and disapproval amounting to abhorrence. The Italian cities were for Englishmen the centres and summits of civilization, and such centres in most periods are supposed to represent not only what is most advanced in thought and behaviour, but also what is most extravagant and corrupt.

Two Italian books of 16th C were immensely fascinating to Englishmen, and the English response to them explains much of the contradiction in English feeling. The first was Castiglione's* *Courtier* (1528, trans. 1561) which offered a model for the virtues and accomplishments of the perfect gentleman; this was greatly admired by English courtly figures such as Surrey*, Wyatt*, Sidney*, Raleigh* and Spenser*, and was approved even by such an anti-Italian as Queen Elizabeth's* private tutor, Roger Ascham*. The other was Machiavelli's* *Prince* (1513). This book was not translated into English until 1640, but many educated Englishmen knew Italian in 16th C; in any case, Gentillet's *Contre Machiavel* (Against Machiavelli, 1576) was widely known in England and translated in 1602. Machiavelli's object was to develop a political science capable of uniting Italy; this did not interest Englishmen, but they were deeply horrified by Machiavelli's demonstration that for such politics to be effective they had to disregard ordinary morality and good faith. The work no doubt impressed English statesmen such as Elizabeth's minister Cecil, but it made 'politics' – 'politic' – 'politician' into evil words for those not occupied by statecraft, and a Machiavellian was synonymous with an atheist, or with one who had taken the devil as his master. Such a man was Shakespeare's Richard III*, and it is Machiavelli who speaks the prologue to Marlowe's play about the evil Jew of Malta*. When Sir Andrew in Shakespeare's *Twelfth Night** says (III.ii) 'for policy I hate: I had as lief [would as soon] be a Brownist* as a politician' he is coupling a Puritan* sect hated by dramatists and playgoers with Machiavellians hated by the Puritans and anti-Puritans alike. More superficially, travel in Italy was supposed to induce folly and affectation and to corrupt morals. As Roger Ascham put it in *The Scholemaster* (1570) 'what the Italian saith of the Englishman . . . Englese Italianato, è un diavolo incarnato, that is to say, you remain men in shape and fashion, but become devils in life and condition.' Italians were poisoners, and seducers like Iachimo in Shakespeare's *Cymbeline**. It was not only because their fiction was popular that so many Elizabethan and Jacobean plays were based on Italian tales ('novelle'), but because Italy was the land where human nature was richest, darkest, and brightest.

The fact that Rome was the centre of the Catholic Church was of course bad enough for Protestant Englishmen after 1540; before that date, the image was brighter, and throughout the century Englishmen did not forget that Italy was the nation of such great scholars and philosophers as Pico della Mirandola (1463–94) whose works Sir Thomas More* partly translated, and whose ideas underlay the conception of the supremely wise man such as Prospero in Shakespeare's *Tempest**. It was the great independence of the best Italian minds that attracted the best English minds of 16th-17th C. The free-thinking Italian philosopher, Giordano Bruno (?1548–?1599), despised the stale traditions of the English universities on his visit (1583–5), but he admired Queen Elizabeth and made friends with men such as Sir Philip Sidney and Sir Walter Raleigh. The astronomer Galileo*, who, like Bruno, came into conflict with the Inquisition*, was studied by the poet John Donne*, and received visits from the sceptical philosopher Thomas Hobbes* and the Puritan John Milton*. Milton's visit to Italy (1638–9) enriched him with encounters with scholars and patrons of learning, while at the same time he felt in danger from the papal police because of his religious opinions; this is another example of the complicated relationships of Englishmen with Italy.

After 1650 Italy by no means lost its fascination for the English, but the great age of Italian culture was over, and it was Italy as a storehouse of the past, rather than a challenging present, that drew Englishmen. In 18th C the English invented tourism; what was called the 'Grand Tour' formed part of the education of upper class young men, and Italy was one of its principal objectives. They were drawn to the architectural and sculptural remains of the old Roman Empire, the framework of their literary education in Latin literature. In the second half of 19th C the great art critic John Ruskin* and the Pre-Raphaelite painters and poets turned interest to the Italian Middle Ages. Thus Italy still had a large place in the culture of English minds, but it was now very much a museum; only the Italian patriot Garibaldi and his struggle for Italian unification (1848–60) made Italy again vivid for England, but it was a relationship of popular sympathies rather than of intellects.

* *Renaissance*.

Ithaca /ˈiθəkə/

The kingdom of Odysseus* the hero of Homer's epic the *Odyssey**.

Itylus /ˈitiləs/

In Greek myth, the son of Zethus, king of Thebes, and his wife Aedon. He was killed by his mother in mistake for one of her nephews; she was then changed into the nightingale, whose song is a lament for Itylus. See the poem by Algernon Swinburne* in *Poems and Ballads*, First Series.

***Ivanhoe* (1819)** /ˈaivənhəu/

A historical novel by Sir Walter Scott*. It is set in the reign of Richard I*, who is one of the characters; the story concerns rivalry between the king and his wicked brother John* (king, 1199–1216), and between Saxons and the ruling Norman aristocracy. Locksley (the legendary outlaw, Robin Hood) aids Richard against his rebellious Normans, and helps to bring about the union of the Saxon hero and heroine, Wilfred of Ivanhoe and Rowena. It was the first novel by Scott to deal with an English (as distinct from a Scottish) subject, and is generally considered to be the beginning of his decline as novelist, though it was very popular in 19th C. This popularity is partly due to its being one of the first attempts to write a novel about the Middle Ages with a genuine regard for history.

Ivory Gate

* *Dreams, Gates of.*

Ixion /ik'saiən/

In Greek myth, son of Phlegyas, king of the Lapithae. He treacherously killed his father-in-law, and could not obtain purification from his crime. In compassion, Zeus* took him up to heaven, where Ixion abused divine hospitality by trying to seduce Hera*. Zeus then banished him to the underworld and condemned him to be bound eternally to a burning wheel.

J

Jack and the Beanstalk

A well-known fairy story based on a myth found all over the world. Jack exchanges his mother's cow for a hatful of beans. When thrown into the garden, the beans rapidly sprout stalks which reach above the clouds. Jack climbs one of the beanstalks and finds himself in a new land near the castle of a man-eating giant. Jack manages by cunning to steal the giant's wealth, and when the giant pursues him down the stalk, he fells it so that the giant falls and breaks his neck.

Jack Horner

A nursery rhyme* usually considered to derive from a story about one of the profiteers who acquired land from the monasteries when these were dissolved by Henry VIII*. Another old rhyme goes:

> *Hopton, Horner, Smyth and Thynne,*
> *When the abbots went out, they came in.*

Jack Sprat

A proverbial nursery rhyme* which has been traced back to 17th C. 'Jack Spratt' was a nickname for a dwarf, and there is some evidence that the rhyme was directed at a diminutive clergyman.

Jack the Giant-Killer

A traditional fairy tale, set in the time of King Arthur*, about episodes in the career of a boy who had a talent for killing giants by cunning.

* *Giants.*

Jacke Wilton

* *Unfortunate Traveller, The.*

Jacob

In the Bible, the grandson of Abraham*, son of Isaac*, father of Joseph*, and legendary ancestor of the Jews. He represented the pastoral way of life, while his brother Esau, ancestor of the tribes of Edom to the south of Israel, represented the hunting and raiding existence of the desert Arab. Though actually younger than Esau, Jacob gained the rights of seniority by a trick (*Genesis* 25 & 27). 'Jacob' in fact means 'supplanter', but he also bore the name Israel ('God rules').

Jacob's Ladder

A vision of Jacob* at Bethel ('House of God'). In a dream, he saw a ladder ascending from earth to heaven with angels climbing and descending it.

Jacobean /dʒakə'bi:ən/

Used to indicate the period of James I* (1603–25), and applied especially to the literature and style of architecture of his reign. In literature, it is most commonly a way of distinguishing the style of drama under James from the style that prevailed under Elizabeth*. Strictly, Elizabethan* drama is experimental, expansive, sometimes ingenuous, in fairly close touch with medieval tradition but energetic with the forces of Renaissance* optimism. It includes the work of the University wits* – Marlowe*, Kyd*, Robert Greene*, Peele* – and also earlier Shakespeare. Jacobean drama is thought of as critical, sombre, disillusioned; in style it is more sophisticated, and in substance it is more conscious of social abuses and rivalries. It includes mature and late Shakespeare, Jonson*, Tourneur*, Webster*, Middleton*, Beaumont* and Fletcher*. Artistically, it contains much of the greatest work of the great period of English drama, but it is also the beginning of decadence; dramatists (notably Beaumont and Fletcher) learn skilful techniques of theatrical effect without necessarily combining these with deep feeling or thought. The decadence continued in the Caroline* period associated with such figures as Massinger*, Ford*, and Shirley*. Courts were the centre of culture, and courts depended largely on the personality of monarchs; the difference between the courts of Elizabeth, James and Charles gives colour to the supposed cultural differences of their reigns, and so to differences of quality in the leading art form of drama. Elizabeth had strong personality and high personal culture; she was revered, and she was discriminating and severe about her favourites. James was a scholarly rather than cultured man of mean appearance, and he was undiscriminating about his favourites. Moreover, while the reign of Elizabeth was prosperous at home and (mainly) triumphant overseas, that of James saw increasing disagreement at home, and abroad was negative or even nationally humiliating. The reign of Charles I was yet more bitter in home dissensions, but his court was one of distinction and refinement. The mood of the drama varied with these differences in national fortune and court conduct. However, the labelling of literary periods is always to some extent simplifying and even falsifying; Jacobean sombreness might well have been the same if James had been a much greater man, and Caroline decadence might have continued even had Charles's reign been much more prosperous.

The Jacobean period was the first that was really

rich in prose, with writers like Bacon*, Donne* and Andrewes*. Their work contrasts especially with Restoration* prose, which sacrificed the poetic qualities of the Jacobean writing for the sake of grace and lucidity.

* *Periods of English Literature; Seventeenth-century Literature.*

Jacobin

Originally a name given to Dominican* friars in France, because their first convent was in the Rue St Jacques in Paris. The name was transferred to a political society which rented a room in the convent in the first year of the French Revolution*. The society developed into a highly organized political party, led by Robespierre*, who became practically dictator of France in 1793. The club was closed after the fall of Robespierre in 1794. The Jacobins were extreme in asserting the principle of equality and in their opposition to privilege. Later, when conservative reaction had set in, 'Jacobin' was used loosely for anyone with politically liberal tendencies in England as well as in France; *eg* the paper *The Anti-Jacobin* was founded to combat English liberal opinion in 1797.

Jacobite

From Jacobus, the Latin form of James. James II*, of the House of Stuart*, was deposed in 1688 because, as a convert to Catholicism, he was considered to be conspiring against the established Protestant* religion and against Parliament*. His supporters were called Jacobites, and this name continued for the supporters of his Catholic son and grandsons. After the crown passed to the House of Hanover, a German Protestant family, in 1714, British Jacobites conspired to restore the House of Stuart. The Jacobite Rebellions of 1715 and 1745 were the two most formidable attempts; both had principally Scottish support, partly because the Stuarts had originally been a Scottish royal family. The 'Forty-five' rebellion quickly became a romantic legend chiefly because of the gallantry and charm of its leader, Charles Edward Stuart, grandson of James II – 'Bonnie Prince Charlie' to his Scottish supporters, and the 'Young Pretender' to his opponents. After the failure of the 'Forty-five' Jacobitism became increasingly a matter of sentiment which even persists to the present day, though the direct line of the Stuarts died out in 1807.

James I, King of Scotland (1406–37)

He was not actually crowned until 1424, owing to a long period of exile in England. His literary importance is his poetry; he is generally regarded as the author of *The King's Quair**, a love poem which may be autobiographical. It employs the 7-line stanza known as the rhyme-royal* perhaps because of James's use of it, though he derived it from Chaucer.

James I of England and VI of Scotland

A member of the Scottish House of Stuart*, he ruled over Scotland alone (1566–1603) and then over England as well (1603–25). He was the first sovereign ever to reign over the whole of the British Isles. His accession to the throne of England was due to the death without children of his cousin Elizabeth I*, last of the English House of Tudor*. The literature and architecture of his era is known as Jacobean*, a term transferred, especially in architecture, to the greater part of 17th C.

James II of England and VII of Scotland (1685–88)

King of Great Britain and Ireland. He was deposed because, as a Catholic, he was threatening the security of the Church of England* and at the same time weakening the power of Parliament*. He was succeeded by his Protestant* daughter Mary II* in conjunction with her Dutch husband, William III*.

* *Jacobites; Revolution of 1688, The.*

James, Henry (1843–1916)

Novelist. Born in New York; his father was an original writer on philosophy and theology, and his brother became one of the most distinguished philosophers and psychologists of his day. His education was divided between America and Europe. Europe drew him strongly, and he finally settled in Europe in 1875 after a series of long visits. Towards both continents, however, he had mixed emotions. As to America, he belonged to the eastern seaboard, New England, which had its own well-established traditions originating in English Puritanism*, and he was out of sympathy with the American ardour for commercial enterprise and westward expansion. As to Europe, he was fascinated by the richness of its ancient societies and culture, but he brought an American, and especially a New England, eye to the corruption which such advanced development generated. The conflict was fruitful for his development as an artist, and it was not the only one; he was also conscious of the contrast between the contemplativeness of his father's mind and the practical adventurousness characteristic of his brother's outlook and of Americans in general. And in his close study of the art of the novel, he felt the difference between the intense interest in form of the French tradition and the deeper moral interest to be found in the English tradition.

In the first period of his work, his theme is preponderantly the clash between the European and the American outlooks: *Roderick Hudson** (1875); *The American* (1877); *The Europeans* (1878); *Daisy Miller** (1879); *Portrait of a Lady** (1881). To this period also belong two novels about American life: *Washington Square* (1881); *The Bostonians* (1886); and two restricted to English life, *The Tragic Muse* (1890); *The Princess Casamassima** (1886). His second period shows a much more concentrated and difficult style of treatment, and it concerns English society only: *The Spoils of Poynton* and *What Maisie Knew** (1897); *The Awkward Age** (1899). Between his first and second periods (1889–95) he experimented in drama; this was his least successful episode, but the experiment helped him to develop a dramatic technique in the writing of his novels. He wrote twelve plays in all. In his last period, the most intensive and subtle in style, James returned to the theme of American and European contrast: *The Wings of the Dove** (1902); *The Ambassadors** (1903); *The Golden Bowl** (1904). On his death he left unfinished *The Ivory Tower* and *The Sense of the Past*. Some of his best fiction is to be found among his short stories, and he was particularly fond of the 'nouvelle' (*Short Story) form – between a story and a usual novel in length; *The Europeans* and *Washington Square* come into this class, and so does his well-known ghost story, *The Turn of the Screw** (1898).

In his criticism, James is important as the first distinguished writer in English to give the novel and its form concentrated critical attention. His essays have been collected under the title *The House of Fiction*, edited by Lionel Edel. He also wrote books of travel, the most notable of which is *The American Scene* (1907), and autobiographical pieces – *A Small Boy and Others* (1913); *Notes of a Son and a Brother* (1914) and *Terminations* (1917). (The last is also the title of a story published in 1895.)

Henry James was naturalized British in 1915.

* **4.5.1; 7.4.**

Bib: Edel, L., *Henry James*; Matthiessen, F. O., *Henry James: The Major Phase;* Anderson, Q., *The American Henry James*; Leavis, F. R., in *The Great Tradition*; Dupee, F. W., *Henry James* and (ed.) *The Question of Henry James: a Collection of Critical Essays*; Bewley, M., in *The Complex Fate* and in *The Eccentric Design*; Wilson, E., in *The Triple Thinkers*; Krook, D., *The Ordeal of Consciousness in James*; Gard, R. (ed), *James: the Critical Heritage.*

Jane Eyre (1847)

A novel by Charlotte Brontë*. It is in the form of a fictional autobiography, with some authentic autobiographical experience. The experiences of the penniless, unattractive child at first in the household of her unfeeling aunt Mrs Reed and later at Lowood Asylum – a charitable school – are the subject of the earlier and most generally admired part of the book. Later she becomes governess to the ward of a rich landowner, Mr Rochester, whose terrible secret is his mad wife; this part of the story is a mixture of romantic love, romantic horror, and social naivety, together with a truthfulness to feeling which still keeps the heroine convincing and interesting. In the third section, Jane is sought in marriage by a clergyman, St John Rivers, a man of rigorous honour and ideals, whom she refuses because, unlike the passionate but morally imperfect Rochester, he does not love her. Her marriage to Rochester at the end of the book is again oddly compounded of naivety, romanticism, self-deception, and truthfulness. The novel was in more than one respect an innovation: it ran contrary to the puritanic tradition that a good woman did not need to feel physical passion or require it in her lover; it presented a romantic heroine whose nature and appearance it is impossible to sentimentalize or idealize; it is the first novel told in the first person in which the narrator's personality is not just a window through which the events are seen, but also defines the quality of the events as we experience them through her mind.

Janet's Repentance

One of George Eliot's *Scenes of Clerical Life**.

Janus /ˈdʒeinəs/

In Roman myth, the god of doorways and guardian of the city during war; he also presided over the first hour of the day, the first day of the month, and the first month of the year (January).

Japheth /ˈdʒeifiθ/

In the Bible (*Genesis* 9) one of the sons of Noah, and with the rest of his family, a survivor of the Flood which destroyed the remainder of mankind. By tradition, the ancestor of the northern races.

Jason

In Greek myth, son of Aeson, king of Iolchos; the kingdom was seized by his uncle Pelias, and he was brought up by the centaur*, Cheiron. His uncle agreed to return the kingdom if he brought back the Golden Fleece, which he obtained with the help of the princess Medea* of Colchis. He married her, but later abandoned her for Glauce (or Creusa). In revenge, Medea slew his children.

* *Argonauts.*

Jefferies, Richard (1848–87)

Essayist and novelist. He wrote about the English countryside and its life; unlike many other writers of his time who chose the same subject, he knew it familiarly from within, and not as a townsman writing for a town public. In consequence, he did not sentimentalize or romanticize it, but presented it plainly, without affection but with force. This has caused his reputation to rise in 20th C, with its intensified interest in preserving natural surroundings and in understanding their environmental influence on society. He is well known for his volumes of essays: *Gamekeeper at Home* (1878); *Wild Life in a Southern County* (1879); *Round about a Great Estate* (1880); *Wood Magic* (1881); *The Life of the Fields* (1884). His novels are esteemed by some critics for their vigour despite their fragmentary structure: *Greene Ferne Farm* (1880); *The Dewy Morn* (1884); *Amaryllis at the Fair* (1887). His romance *After London, or Wild England* (1885) is a remarkable account of the country after a hypothetical cataclysm. His best-known books are probably *Bevis* (1882), a children's story, and his autobiography, *The Story of my Heart* (1883).

Bib: Thomas, E., *Life*; Leavis, Q. D., in *Scrutiny* Vol. vi; Looker, S. J., *The Worthing Cavalcade*; Thom, A. F., *The Life Worship of Richard Jefferies*; Thomas, E., *Jefferies.*

Jeffrey, Francis (1773–1850)

Critic and editor (1803–29) of the influential *Edinburgh Review** which he helped to found in

1802. His poetic taste was conservative, and he was unsympathetic to the Lake Poets*, Wordsworth and Coleridge; he was, however, serious and thorough in his assessments, and, according to his lights, a just critic. His adverse review of Wordsworth's *Excursion** in 1814 has been confirmed rather than otherwise by later opinion, and in 1820 he judiciously encouraged Keats for his *Endymion**, which had been unfairly condemned by *Blackwoods** and the *Quarterly**. His weakness as a critic was not his conservatism but his susceptibility to verse of second-rate appeal such as that of Campbell and of Rogers.

If not a great critic, Jeffrey was a great editor; he gave the *Edinburgh* authority proportionate to its intellectual independence, and its sales reached nearly 14,000 in 1818 – a high figure at any time for a periodical of such intellectual seriousness. In politics, Jeffrey was Whig* – that is to say he belonged to the liberal wing which was unpopular during the first quarter of 19th C – and his journal was the mouthpiece of responsible Whig opinion.

His profession was the law, in which he excelled and was eventually made a judge.

* *Edinburgh Review; Reviews and Periodicals.*

Jeffreys, Judge

* *Bloody Assizes; Sedgemoor.*

Jehovah

In the English version of the Bible, the representation of the ancient Jewish principal name for God.

Jehu /ˈdʒiːhjuː/

In the Bible, *2 Kings* 9, a king of Israel, noted as a fast charioteer. Hence, a term for any driver, especially a fast one. It was Jehu who destroyed the wicked queen Jezebel*.

Jekyll and Hyde

From a novel *The Strange Case of Dr Jekyll and Mr Hyde* (1886) by Robert Louis Stevenson*. Dr Jekyll discovers a drug that can reduce his personality to an embodiment of his merely evil impulses – *ie* Mr Hyde. The phrase 'a Jekyll and Hyde personality' is sometimes used to describe any character with sharply distinct qualities, good as against bad.

Jephthah /ˈdʒefθə/

In the Old Testament of the Bible (*Judges* 11) one of the judges or leaders of Israel, before the days of its kings. Before fighting the Ammonites, he vowed that in return for victory he would sacrifice whatever came out of his house to greet him at his homecoming. This proved to be his daughter.

Jeremiah /dʒeriˈmaiə/

In the Old Testament of the Bible, a prophet in a particularly disastrous period of Israelite history, culminating in the temporary destruction of the Jewish kingdom (585 BC). His book is full of lamentations and warnings, from which comes the word 'jeremiad' *ie* a sorrowful complaint.

Jerusalem

The chief city of the ancient Jews, and a holy city for Jews, Muslims, and Christians. In medieval geography, which, like medieval cosmology, was governed by theology, Jerusalem was regarded as the centre of the land mass of the earth. Its capture by the Muslims led to the Crusades*. All the more for being in the power of an alien religion, Jerusalem represented a spiritual reality for medieval Europe, and in *Revelation* in the Bible the New Jerusalem had already been used as a term for Heaven. The most famous imaginative work concerned with the Crusades is the Italian romantic epic *Jerusalem Delivered* (1581) by Torquato Tasso*. William Blake* wrote a prophetic poem *Jerusalem*, using it as a symbol of mankind redeemed by the spiritual energies of the imagination; he did so again in his conception of a redeemed England in his famous lyric 'And did those feet in ancient time'.

Jesse /ˈdʒesi/

In the Bible, the father of David* (*1 Samuel* 16); therefore the ancestor of the predicted Messiah* (*Isaiah* 11), and so the reputed ancestor of Christ. The 'tree of Jesse' was a pictorial representation of this ancestry, and was often used in windows, sculptures, branched candlesticks, etc. in medieval churches.

Jesuit

A member of the Society of Jesus, a religious order founded by Ignatius Loyola, and approved by the Pope in 1540. The Jesuits were in the forefront in combating Protestantism*, and were much dreaded by Protestants as their most dangerous enemies. In the reign of Elizabeth I* they led, or were reputed to lead, the various conspiracies against her on behalf of the Catholic claimant to the English throne, Mary Queen of Scots*; they were therefore regarded as national as well as religious enemies. Their advanced training made them skilled debaters and subtle negotiators, as a result of which the term 'Jesuit' is to this day often applied to a person who (whether or not in the order or even a Catholic) is deceitful and unscrupulous in obtaining his object. In 18th C, when religious conflicts had subsided, Jesuits were no longer feared in England; but their activities in Europe led to their expulsion even from Catholic lands like France and Spain, and for 41 years they were totally suppressed by the Pope. Of later members of the order the most celebrated in English literature is the poet, Gerard Manley Hopkins*.

Jew of Malta, The

A blank verse* drama by Christopher Marlowe*, written and performed about 1590; published 1633. An actor impersonating the Italian political philosopher Machiavelli* speaks the prologue and thereby sets the tone of the play, since to the English of Marlowe's time Machiavelli, who had sought to conduct politics amorally by scientific methods, was a godless monster. We thus expect a play dominated by evil. However, a comic tradition for the presentation of godless monsters had come down to Marlowe from the medieval Mystery plays* which had presented such figures as Herod* and Satan as grotesque caricatures, frightening but funny at the same time. So the Machiavellian central character, Barabas the Jew, boasting that his wealth has been acquired iniquitously, is made too impressive to be taken lightly and yet too extravagant to be taken soberly. His only philosophy is the art of gaining advantage. In the first half of the play he tries to outwit the Christians of Malta, who, scarcely less Machiavellian than himself, try to deprive him of his wealth. He eventually betrays the island to the Turks, and proceeds to try to outwit them, but he falls victim to his own plot. In a famous essay on Marlowe (*Selected Essays*) T. S. Eliot* described the play as an example of 'the farce of the old English humour, the terribly serious, even savage comic humour'; in his essay on Jonson* Eliot points to *The Jew of Malta* as the forebear of Jonson's Comedy of Humours*.

Jews in England

The Jews first settled in England after the Norman* Conquest and, as elsewhere, undertook the occupation of lending money on interest which in the earlier Middle Ages was forbidden to Christians. They were expelled from England by King Edward I* in 1290. Neither in the Middle Ages nor later was anti-Semitism as strong in England as in some other countries, but the baseless myth that the Jews made ritual sacrifices of Christian boys is exemplified by the Prioress's Tale* in Chaucer's *Canterbury Tales*. Between 1290 and 1655, when they were readmitted by Cromwell*, a few Jews were admitted by special licence, and a number of rich Jews were living in London in the reign of Elizabeth I*. However, the wicked Jews of Marlowe's *The Jew of Malta** and Shakespeare's *The Merchant of Venice** are not products of popular anti-Semitism; Barabas and Shylock are typed as Jews because Marlowe and Shakespeare wanted each in his own way to dramatize the consequences of ignoring Christian morality, and the Jews were the most convenient class of people for the purpose.

Jews returned to England after 1655 in fair numbers; by the end of 18th C there were about 20,000 living in London. Anti-Semitism was inconspicuous – this fact has been attributed to the assiduous Bible-reading of the English middle classes – but unless they renounced their religion they suffered restrictions on political rights and entry into certain professions (*eg* the Law) similar to those of other denominations outside the Church of England*. These restrictions were not entirely removed until the middle of 19th C, although by that time Benjamin Disraeli*, a Jew who had been received into the Church of England, was already one of the country's leading statesmen. In 19th-C fiction Jews are commonly depicted in extremes of good or bad, but chiefly the former; as against the evil criminal Fagin of Dickens's *Oliver Twist** there is his Riah of *Our Mutual Friend**, George Eliot's idealized Daniel Deronda*, the godlike Sidonia in Disraeli's *Coningsby**, and Rebecca, the secondary heroine of Scott's *Ivanhoe**. In 20th C, Leopold Bloom in James Joyce's *Ulysses** is partly a representation of the myth of the Wandering Jew*.

* *Zionism*.

Jezebel /ˈdʒezəbel/

In the Bible, the fierce and arrogant wife of Ahab, king of Israel, and his accomplice in opposing the worship of Jehovah*. She persecuted the prophets of Jehovah (*1 Kings* 18) and caused Naboth* to be put to death in order to obtain his vineyard for Ahab (*1 Kings* 21). Her equally fierce opponent was the prophet Elijah* who caused the destruction of her prophets (*1 Kings* 20) in one of the most dramatic passages of the Old Testament. For her treatment of Naboth, Elijah cursed Ahab and Jezebel; in fulfilment of the curse, she is destroyed by Jehu* (*2 Kings* 9) who becomes king in place of her son. Before encountering Jehu she is described as adorning herself and painting her face; 'a painted Jezebel' thus became a term for a shameless woman.

Jig

A country dance, with equivalents in many countries. In England at the end of 16th C comic actors introduced the jig to the London theatre, where it was combined with singing and miming to make up a dramatic performance amounting to comic opera. Jigs were often performed at the ends of plays, particularly to lighten the effect of tragedies.

Joan of Arc (Jeanne d'Arc) (1412–31)

A French national heroine for the leading part she played in turning the Hundred Years' War* finally against the English invaders of France.

Politically the position was that Henry V* of England had succeeded by the Treaty of Troyes (1420) in getting his son recognized as the next king of France in succession to Charles VI (1380–1422). His son was in fact proclaimed king of France in 1422 in Paris, but the English controlled only the north and east of France, and the French were still fighting, although Charles VI's son, Charles the Dauphin, had no appetite for war. The English, in alliance with the Burgundians, continued to win victories.

In 1429 Joan, daughter of a French farmer, came forward declaring that heavenly voices had directed her to relieve the city of Orleans, besieged by the English, and to lead the Dauphin to Rheims to be crowned King Charles VII. She carried out both promises and attempted to relieve Paris, which was in English hands. She was, however, taken prisoner by the Burgundians, who delivered her to the English. She was by this time regarded as a heaven-sent inspiration to the French, and the English were determined to discredit her; accordingly they secured that she was condemned for heresy by a Church court, and then burnt alive in Rouen. The war continued to go against them, however, and by 1453 they were driven from France. In 1456 the condemnation of Joan for heresy was annulled by the Church, and in 1920 she was declared a saint*.

For some time the English continued to remember her as a witch, and she is so represented in the early play by Shakespeare, *1 Henry VI*, where she appears under her French nickname of 'La Pucelle' – the Maid. By far the most striking representation of her career in English is the play *Saint Joan* (1924) by Bernard Shaw*.

Job /dʒəub/

In the Bible, the central character of a book of the same name in the Old Testament. Job is a rich man whose faith in God is tested by the infliction of great suffering. Much of the book consists of dialogues with his friends, who declare that his misfortunes must be the consequence of his sins; hence the expression 'Job's comforters', used about friends whose attempts at comforting a sufferer are the reverse of successful. Job, however, continues to affirm his innocence, and he is forced into the position of questioning God's justice. Finally God speaks out of a whirlwind, justifies Job, and restores his fortune. The translation in the Authorized Version of the Bible is an example of some of the noblest English in the Old Testament. The New English Bible endeavours to present in English the flavour of the original poetic-rhetorical expression of folk wisdom.

John

King of England, 1199–1216. His reign was particularly disturbed; he succeeded in raising against him both his own nobles and the Church, as well as losing his father's French possessions. In 1215 the alliance of nobles and Church successfully imposed on him the Magna Carta* by which he agreed not to infringe the rights of the Church or of his subjects.

His quarrel with the Church caused him to be regarded favourably in 16th C when the Tudors were occupied in reducing the Church from a supranational into a national institution; thus he is idealized in the play *King John* (1547) by Bishop Bale. In Shakespeare's play *King John**, his crime is the death of his nephew Arthur, and sympathy is still with him against the Church; there is no mention of Magna Carta. It was in the 17th-C quarrels between the kings and parliaments that this document became important, as seeming to justify parliamentary resistance to the Crown. Since then, Magna Carta has been popularly regarded as the foundation of English liberties, and King John as the type of a bad king.

John Bull

A personification of England, dating from a political allegory *The History of John Bull* (1712) by John Arbuthnot. The character is there described as honest but quarrelsome, his temper depending on the weather; he understands business and is fond of drinking and the society of his friends. He is intended to represent the national character.

John of Gaunt, Duke of Lancaster

Fourth son of Edward III*. He derived the name 'Gaunt' from his birthplace, the town of Ghent in

Flanders. By marrying the only daughter of the Duke of Lancaster he inherited the title and became the greatest lord in England. He is chiefly remembered [1] as the ancestor of the Lancastrian line of kings, beginning with his son Henry IV*; [2] as the protector of the religious reformer John Wycliffe*; [3] as the patron of the poet Geoffrey Chaucer*, whose wife's sister he married; [4] for the representation of him by Shakespeare in *Richard II**.

* *Lancaster, House of.*

Johnson, Pamela Hansford (b 1912)

Novelist. Perhaps her best known work is the trilogy composed of *Too Dear for my Possessing* (1940), *An Avenue of Stone* (1947) and *A Summer to Decide* (1949). These extend from the late twenties of this century to the late forties, and combine observation on events and society with the study of intricate relationships arising from the attractions for each other of unlike characters. The formal quality reflects the influence of Proust, on whom Pamela Hansford Johnson has composed a series of radio programmes, *Six Proust Reconstructions* (1958). Some of her later novels have been more comic and satirical (*eg Night and Silence*, 1963, and *Cork Street*, 1965) but *An Error of Judgement* (1962) concerns the problem of apparently motiveless evil in modern society, and relates to her non-fictional investigation of the Moors Murder case which raises the problem of dangerous assumptions in our so-called 'permissive society': *On Iniquity* (1961). Pamela Hansford Johnson is the wife of the novelist C. P. Snow*. More recent novels: *The Survival of the Fittest* (1968); *The Honours Board* (1970); *The Holiday Friend* (1972); *The Good Listener* (1975).

Bib: Allen, W., in *Tradition and Dream*; Burgess, A., *The Novel Now*.

Johnson, Samuel (1709–84)

Critic, poet, lexicographer, essayist. He is the greatest representative of the later Augustan* age, as Alexander Pope* and Jonathan Swift* are the greatest of its earlier phase. The son of a country bookseller, he began life in poverty and with great personal disadvantages of physical awkwardness, poor sight, facial disfigurement, and tendencies to severe depression. Yet by the age of fifty he had the greatest prestige of any man of letters in English society. He achieved this eminence by the force of his intellect, the breadth and depth of his moral feeling, and by the weightiness and terseness of his literary style which communicated his personal qualities to the public so as to express what was best and strongest in the civilization of the time. He was, moreover, a magnificent talker and much of his influence was conveyed by his conversation. The Club (founded in 1764 and later known as The Literary Club), over which he presided, indicates by its membership the breadth of Johnson's influence; it included Joshua Reynolds*, the most celebrated painter of the period; the political thinker and statesman Edmund Burke*;

David Garrick*, the great actor; the writer Oliver Goldsmith*; several distinguished scholars and men eminent in fashionable life, and James Boswell*, whose life of Johnson was to be the greatest biography in English literature.

As a critic, Johnson is best known for his Preface to his edition of Shakespeare (1765) and for his *Lives of the Poets** (1779–81) in which he displays not only his critical powers but his biographical talents. It is easy to see that Johnson's literary criticism betrays special limitations characteristic of his century; he has often been condemned, for instance, for his complete failure to appreciate Milton's *Lycidas** and to distinguish what have since been discerned as among the outstanding qualities of Shakespeare's genius. On the other hand modern critics are more inclined to remark on the independence and conviction with which he applied the standards characteristic of his own time, and on the value of these standards as a corrective to some of the distortions of later criticism. As a biographer, Johnson is excellent in narrative and humane in sympathy; his life of Savage, included in the *Lives of the Poets* but first published in 1744, is his biographical masterpiece.

Johnson's poetic output was small, but it includes his satire *London** (1738) which first brought him to public notice, and *The Vanity of Human Wishes* (1749) which has been described as one of the few great poems of the Augustan period; it exhibits Johnson's strength as a moralist. Some of his shorter poems are greatly admired, notably *On the Death of Dr Robert Levett* (1782). In his best poetry he combines the strength of Augustan clarity and assurance with his peculiarly personal qualities of deep seriousness and humane sympathy.

It is in his essays for *The Rambler** (a periodical almost entirely written by him – 1750–52) and (in a series entitled 'The Idler'* – 1758–60) for the *Weekly Gazette*, and in his philosophical romance *Rasselas** (1759) that Johnson is most evidently the great moralist. The periodicals were emulations of Addison's famous *Spectator**, but they lack Addison's suavity which makes his essays particularly readable. On the other hand Johnson's virtue is his assumption that the reader shares his own deep seriousness and that he has the will and capacity to give himself with integrity to the gravest reflections. He was a devout Anglican* and some of the best essays are among the noblest expressions of Augustan religious feeling. *Rasselas* has been called a prose *Vanity of Human Wishes*; it is not intended as a work of realistic fiction but as a parable in which representative figures discourse on the fundamentals of human conduct, regarded, in typically Augustan fashion, in the light of social relationships. The *Journey to the Western Islands of Scotland* (1775), a record of a visit with his friend Boswell to some of the remotest and materially most backward regions of the British Isles, is highly interesting for Johnson's views on underdeveloped society in comparison with his native environment of highly developed society in southern England.

Johnson's *A Dictionary of the English Language* (1755) is the first great work of its kind in English. Johnson excelled in verbal definition and exemplification, though he was weak in understanding the derivations of words. It is imbued with a characteristic dedication to the service of the language, by purifying usage and setting standards of clarity.

* 3.3.2.; 6.3.1; 7.2.

Bib: Boswell, J., *Life*; Clifford, J. L., *Young Sam Johnson*; Raleigh, W., *Six Essays on Johnson*; Wimsatt, W. K., *The Prose Style of Samuel Johnson*; Hagstrum, J. H., *Samuel Johnson's Literary Criticism*; Greene, D. J., *The Politics of Samuel Johnson*; Hilles, F. W. (ed.), *New Light on Dr Johnson*; Brown, J. E., *Critical Opinions of Samuel Johnson*; Leavis, F. R., 'Johnson and Augustanism' in *The Common Pursuit*; Houston, P. H., *Dr Johnson: a Study in Eighteenth-century Humanism*.

Johnson, The Life of Samuel (1791)

* *Boswell.*

Johnson's Dictionary

* *Dictionary of the English Language, A.*

Joint Stock

* *Companies, Joint Stock.*

Jonah

In the Old Testament of the Bible, a Jewish prophet and hero of the narrative in the book of *Jonah*. Jonah is ordered by God to go and preach to the wicked city of Nineveh. He is, however, so callous as to fear that the city may repent and thus escape Divine destruction. He thus tries to evade the order by taking ship to Tarshish. On the way a storm arises, and to appease God's wrath he asks to be thrown into the sea, where he is swallowed by a whale. Three days later, the whale vomits him safely on to dry land, and Jonah proceeds to Nineveh to obey God's will. The city repents, at first to Jonah's disgust, but through further episodes God teaches him the virtue of pity.

A 'Jonah' is a bringer of ill-luck, since the sailors so regarded the prophet when the storm at sea arose on his account.

Jonathan Wild the Great, The Life of (1743)

A satirical romance by Henry Fielding*. His purpose was to ridicule 'greatness' by telling the story of a 'great' criminal in apparently admiring terms; the subject makes clear that the admiration is ironical, but the reader is reminded that eminent statesmen and other 'respectable' men of power – all those, in fact, who are normally regarded as great – commonly pursue their aims with as little scruple. Wild was a historical character who had been executed in 1725, and made the subject of a narrative by Defoe*.

In Fielding's fictional satire, Wild begins his career by being baptized by Titus Oates* – also a criminal character – and takes to a career of crime in childhood. He becomes the leader of a gang of thieves, among whom he keeps discipline by threatening them with denunciation, while

himself avoiding incrimination. The vilest of his crimes is the systematic ruin of his former school-friend, the jeweller Heartfree, whom he nearly succeeds in having executed. In the end it is Wild who is executed, but he is sent to his death with the same mock-heroic impressiveness as has characterized Fielding's treatment of him throughout.

* *Picaresque.*

Jones, Henry Arthur (1851–1929)

Dramatist. He wrote some 60 plays, and is notable for beginning an English dramatic revival in the later years of the 19th C, along with T. W. Robertson*, Arthur Pinero* and Bernard Shaw*. For instance *Saints and Sinners** (1884) was not only a dramatic success, but aroused controversy by discussing religious issues in a study of middle class provincial life. Other plays of comparable note: *The Middleman* (1889) and *Judah* (1890). His lectures and essays on drama were collected in *The Renascence of the English Drama* (1895).

Bib: Jones, A. D., *Life*; Archer, W., *The Old Drama and the New*; Cordell, R. A., *Henry Arthur Jones and the Modern Drama.*

Jones, Inigo (1573–1651)

Architect and stage designer. He is sometimes called 'the English Palladio' because he was strongly influenced by the Italian architect of that name, and he was in fact the first important classical (Palladian) architect in English architecture. Outstanding buildings of his design include the Banqueting Hall in Whitehall and St Paul's church in Covent Garden, both in London. He also designed sets for masques*, to which words were contributed by Ben Jonson*, Samuel Daniel* and other poets among his contemporaries. Scenery and music were as important in the masque as was poetry, and the fusion led to bitter rivalry between Jones and Jonson, who satirized him as In-and-In Medlay in *Tale of a Tub.*

* 2.3; *Palladio.*

Jonson, Benjamin (1572–1637)

Dramatist and poet; always known as Ben Jonson. In drama, he was Shakespeare's most distinguished rival, but they differed greatly in gifts and achievement. Sixteen of his plays, not including masques, have survived; fourteen comedies and two tragedies. Their merits vary greatly: his universally acknowledged masterpieces are the comedies *Volpone** (1605 or 1606) and *The Alchemist** (1610), to which some distinguished critics add the satirical tragedy *Sejanus** (1603). In the second rank of importance, the following are usually included: *The Devil is an Ass** (1616), of great satirical power but less dramatic concentration; *Epicoene, or The Silent Woman** (1609) and *Bartholomew Fair** (1614), slighter in content but vigorous entertainments; and *Every Man in his Humour** (1598), the first of the comedies of humours* with which his name is identified. Although all Jonson's work contains passages of interest, his remaining plays have faults (such as excessive academicism, diffuseness of treatment, or narrowness of satirical range) which usually restrict their interest to scholars. They are: *Every Man out of his Humour** (1599); *Cynthia's Revels* (1600); *The Poetaster* (1601); *Catiline** (a tragedy, 1611); *The Staple of News* (1625); *The New Inn* (1629); *The Magnetic Lady* (1632); *The Tale of a Tub* (1633); *The Case is Altered* (an early work, before he had discovered his characteristic comic medium, 1597). He left unfinished a pastoral drama *The Sad Shepherd.*

Jonson was both very much a man of his age and a strong traditionalist. Society was undergoing radical changes; the unsettlement of accustomed moral values gave scope to extravagance and folly. He himself was a man of strong appetites and vitality, but he understood and deeply cared for the restraining and directing qualities of civilization. His conception of civilization derived partly from his typically Renaissance* admiration for ancient Roman culture, which he thoroughly assimilated through Latin literature, and partly from the traditional virtues of English society, which economic and religious changes were confusing. He was thus a moral satirist, who delighted in animal vitality and human aspiration but made it his business to chasten the 'humours' (or, as we might say, 'manias') to which society was liable when it escaped the control of civilized discipline and reason. This made him a self-conscious artist in matters of literary form, and his plays, his prose miscellany (*Timber; or Discoveries made upon Men and Matter*, pub 1640), and his conversations reported by the Scottish poet Drummond, contain much critical comment on the virtues of poetic and dramatic discipline – often at the expense of his contemporaries including Shakespeare. At the same time he was a highly independent writer who showed no disposition to subject his work to the restriction of a code of rules.

In his non-dramatic poetry, Jonson produced a body of fine poetry which influenced the form of later lyric verse. His poems have neither the emotional extravagance of the idealizing love poets of the age, nor the rough texture of a realist like Donne*; they combine the grace of manner of the former with the masculine strength of the latter, and fuse a vitality which is personal to Jonson with an intellectual control which he learnt from Latin poets such as Catullus*. Andrew Marvell* was to learn from Jonson an incisiveness to temper the imaginative ingeniousness he learnt from Donne, and the school of Cavalier Poets* of the reign of Charles I* got from him much of their grace and poise.

Jonson had considerable importance as a personality who exercised influence by his talk. He was not born into the aristocratic circles of a poet like Sidney*, and his proud and independent attitude to his noble patrons helped to enhance respect for the independence of the literary profession. His meetings and discussions with other poets at the Mermaid Tavern* were commemorated by Francis Beaumont* in *Francis Beaumont to Ben Jonson* and much later by John Keats* in *Lines on the Mermaid Tavern* (1818) and in his old age he had a school of disciples who called themselves 'the sons of Ben'. They included such poets as Carew* and Herrick*.

* **5.1.3.2–3; 6.2.4; 7.1.**

Bib: Knights, L. C., *Drama and Society in the Age of Jonson*; Herford and Simpson, 'The Man and his Work' in *The Works of Ben Jonson*; Eliot, T. S., in *Selected Essays*; Barish, J. A., on Jonson's dramatic prose and (ed.) critical essays; Partridge, E. B., *The Broken Compass: A Study of the Major Comedies.*

Joseph

The husband of Mary the mother of Jesus, and betrothed to her at the time of the birth. Christian tradition maintains (in accordance with the accounts in *Matthew* and *Luke*) that he was not the father of Jesus whom Mary delivered by the Virgin Birth. He was, however, descended from King David, in agreement with Old Testament predictions that the Messiah* would belong to 'the house of David'.

Joseph

In the Old Testament of the Bible, the son of Jacob* and Rachel, and one of the principal ancestors of the twelve tribes which were later to make up the kingdoms of Israel and Judaea; the descent of the others was reckoned from his brothers, who, except for Benjamin, were the sons of Jacob but not of Rachel. Joseph was the son of Jacob's true wife Rachel, and consequently had special favour from his father. The jealousy of his brothers drove Joseph into exile in Egypt, where he rose high in the king's favour as a soothsayer. Later, famine drove Jacob's other sons to Egypt, and Joseph, as one of the king's ministers, received them, but they failed to recognize him. Joseph at first pretended to treat them harshly except for Benjamin, but he later settled them and Jacob prosperously in the province called the Land of Goshen. The story is told in *Genesis* 37–50. The escape of the Jews from Egypt, after the Egyptians had turned against them, is described in the Book of *Exodus*.

Joseph Andrews (1742)

A novel by Henry Fielding*. It was begun as a parody of Richardson's novel *Pamela**. In Richardson's novel the heroine, Pamela Andrews, is a chaste servant girl who resists seduction by her master, Mr B, and eventually forces him to accept her in marriage. Fielding ridicules Richardson by opening his novel with an account of the resistance by Pamela's brother Joseph to seduction by his employer, the aunt of Mr B, whose name Fielding maliciously extends to Booby (= clumsy fool). Joseph is dismissed for his obstinate virtue, and sets out in search of his own sweetheart. On the journey he is befriended by his old acquaintance, a clergyman, Parson Adams. At this point Fielding seems to have changed the plan of his novel; Adams, instead of Joseph, becomes the central character on whom all the interest centres. With the change, the novel becomes something like an English *Don Quixote**, since Adams is a learned but simple-hearted, single-minded Christian whose trust in the goodness of human nature leads him into constant embarrassments. Social satire thus takes the place of literary parody with great advantage to the interest of the book.

* 4.3.2.

Joseph of Arimathaea

In the New Testament, according to all four of the Gospels, the rich Jew who provided a tomb for Jesus Christ after the Crucifixion. According to a medieval English tradition (found in the works of William Malmesbury, 12th C, but possibly inserted by someone else) he later came to Britain to preach Christianity, founded Glastonbury* Abbey, and was buried there; his planted staff became the miraculous 'Glastonbury thorn' which flowered at Christmas. Later Arthurian legend attributes to him the Holy Grail* (in earlier legend a pagan symbol) as a vessel in which he caught the blood of Christ at the Crucifixion.

* *Arthur, King; Grail, The Holy.*

Joshua /ˈdʒɒʃwə/

Sixth book of the Old Testament of the Bible. Joshua, son of Nun, succeeded Moses* as leader of the Jews in their escape from Egypt. Chapters 1–11 concern the conquest of Canaan; the remainder deals with the organization of the conquered territory.

Journal of the Plague Year, A (1722)
A description, presented as if it were an eye-witness account, of the Great Plague of London* (1664–65) by Daniel Defoe*. He himself was a small child at the time of the epidemic, so that direct personal experience cannot have contributed significantly to the account. Nonetheless, the fiction gives a convincing effect of being a direct record of the events, and the work ranks as one of the first and most gifted pieces of historical reconstruction. It is important in the history of journalism*, and also in the history of the novel*, since it shows the care for persistent record of the detail of daily life which was to become one of the most distinguishing characteristics of the novel form.

Journalism
The profession of providing newspapers and periodicals with regular supplies of reading matter, consisting especially of news and comment. The distinction between journalism and literature is not always clear, and before the rise of the modern newspaper with its mass circulation in the second half of 19th C, the two forms of writing were even more difficult to distinguish than they are today. The most superficial but also the most observable difference has always been that journalism puts immediacy of interest before permanency of interest, and easy readability before considered qualities of style. But of course what is written for the attention of the hour may prove to be of permanent value; a good example is William Cobbett's *Rural Rides** in his weekly *Political Register* in early 19th C.

The 'pamphlets' of writers such as Thomas Nashe* and Thomas Dekker* in the 1590s, and those on the controversial religious matters of the day such as the Marprelate* pamphlets, are no doubt the earliest work with the stamp of journalism in English. However, the profession began to take shape with the wider reading public and the regular periodicals of early 18th C. In that period we can see that it was the attitude to writing that made the difference – at least on the surface – between the journalist and the serious man of letters. Addison* might regard himself as a journalist because he was one 'whose business it is to write for a public journal', but he considered himself a serious man of letters, whereas Defoe*, writing incessantly on matters of practical interest without concerning himself with subtleties and elegance of style, is more our idea of a journalist. The 18th C was inclined to disparage such writing as Grub-street*, though this term included all kinds of inferior, merely imitative 'literature' such as we would not accept as journalism. Defoe thoroughly understood the practical nature of journalism, and that it was a trade like any other – 'a very considerable Branch of the English Commerce'. The trade, however, taught him the realism that went into his fiction: the origins of the modern novel and of journalism are in fact bound up with each other. A good example of the combination is his *A Journal of the Plague Year** (1722) which is both a fine example of journalistic reporting (from other people's accounts) and a fine achievement in imaginative realism.

Defoe in 18th C and Cobbett in 19th C both assumed that the main function of their writing was to *enlighten* their readers; the persistence of this assumption among journalists until the last decade of 19th C makes it impossible to make more than a superficial distinction between journalism and literature until then. In the 1890s, however, the 'popular press' arose; newspaper proprietors realized that the consequence of universal literacy made possible by the Education* Act of 1870 was that a vast public existed without any critical standards, since the mass of people had been taught to read without receiving much of any other kind of education. The proprietors saw that immense profits could be made by *entertaining* this mass in the cheapest and most ephemeral ways, without any attempt at enlightenment. It is in this way that, in 20th C, journalism is often understood as the opposite of literature. Nonetheless it is true now as it was in the days of Defoe that the serious journalist is only distinguishable from other kinds of serious writer by being more concerned with 'news' – the events and preoccupations of the immediate present.

* **2.2.4.2**; *Newspapers; Reviews and Periodicals.*

Journeyman
A trained craftsman, originally one who worked by the day (French: *journée*). In the Middle Ages, a journeyman worked under a master who owned the business, and who also employed apprentices, *ie* craftsmen undergoing training. In 13th C, master, apprentices and journeymen were socially equal and all members of the craft guild; by later 14th C the richer masters were drawing away from the journeymen, most of whom, in the richer guilds, could no longer hope to become masters. A social cleavage thus developed between the class of masters and the class of journeymen, and this grew sharper as modern capitalism developed (especially in the clothing industry) during 15th and 16th C.

* *Apprenticeship; Capitalism; Craft Guilds; Master Craftsman.*

Jove
* *Zeus.*

Joyce, James (1882–1941)
Novelist. He was Irish, and born at a time when Irish nationalism was moving into its fiercest, most desperate phase. Moreover, unlike nearly all major Irish writers, who have been Protestant* at least by ancestry, Joyce was born into a Catholic family, was educated by the Jesuits*, and seemed destined for the Catholic priesthood. Yet he turned away from the priesthood, renounced Catholicism, and in 1904 left Ireland to live and work abroad for the rest of his life. But although he took no part in the movement for Irish liberation, he did not renounce Ireland; the setting for all his fiction is the capital city (and his home town) of Dublin. This and his own family relationships were always his centres, and from them he drew in-

creasingly ambitious imaginative conceptions which eventually extended to the whole history of European culture.

His first important work was a volume of stories, *Dubliners**, published after long delay in 1914. The collection has artistic unity given to it by Joyce's intention 'to write a chapter of the moral history of my country . . . under four of its aspects: childhood, adolescence, maturity and public life'. The method is objectively realistic and based on Joyce's idea of 'epiphanies' – experiences, often apparently trivial, presenting to the observer deep and true insights. His first novel, *A Portrait of the Artist as a Young Man** (1916), is largely autobiographical and describes how, abandoning his religion and leaving his country, he discovered his artistic vocation. Its original method of narration causes the reader to share the hero's experience by having it presented to him with a verbal equipment which grows with the hero's development, from infancy to young manhood.

The next novel, *Ulysses** (1922), is still more original in the use of language. Its subject is apparently small – a single day in the life of three Dubliners – but Joyce's treatment of it makes it vast. The characters are made to correspond to the three main characters of Homer's *Odyssey**, and the 18 episodes are parallels to the episodes in that epic. The past is thus made to reflect forward on to the present, and the present back on to the past, revealing both with comic irony and endowing the apparently trivial present with tragic depth. In this book, modern man in the modern city is presented with unprecedented thoroughness and candour.

In his last book, *Finnegans Wake** (1939), Joyce attempts an image of modern 'Everyman' with all the forces of his experience released – in other words it concerns one night of a character who, because he never fully wakes up, is not restricted by the inhibitions of normal daylight consciousness. To express this night consciousness Joyce uses a special dream language by which words are fused together to give instantaneous multiple allusiveness; the same technique had been used by the mid-19th-C children's writer Lewis Carroll* in the poem called 'Jabberwocky' (*Through the Looking-Glass*, 1872). However, because Joyce wishes to use the public-house keeper who is his hero as the representative of modern European man, he often fuses English words with those of other European languages, thus increasing the difficulty for the reader. Critics have pointed out that in *Finnegans Wake* the dream comes mainly through the ear; Joyce, like Milton* with whose mastery of language his own has been compared, had poor sight, and his imagination worked especially through the sense of hearing.

Joyce's *Collected Poems* (1936) are comparatively unremarkable, but they show his sense of poignant verbal beauty. His single play, *Exiles* (1918) is interesting chiefly for showing his admiration for the Norwegian dramatist, Ibsen*. An early version of his *Portrait of the Artist* was published in 1944 (enlarged 1955) as *Stephen Hero*.

* 4.5.4; *Epiphany; Ireland.*

Bib: Ellmann, R., *Life*; Joyce, S., *My Brother's Keeper*; Levin, H., *Joyce: a Critical Introduction*; Kenner, H., *Dublin's Joyce*; Magalaner, M., Kain, R. M., *Joyce: the Man, the Work, the Reputation*; Budgen, F., *James Joyce and the Making of Ulysses*; Gilbert, S., *James Joyce's Ulysses: a Study*; Campbell and Robinson, *A Skeleton Key to Finnegans Wake*; Denning, R. H. (ed.), *Joyce: The Critical Heritage*

Juan, Don

* *Don Juan.*

Judas Iscariot

The disciple of Jesus who betrayed him to the Jewish authorities (*Matthew* 26) for thirty pieces of silver. He later repented, returned the money, and hanged himself (*Matthew* 27). In another version (*Acts* 1:18) he fell down and burst asunder. A 'Judas' is a traitor; a 'Judas kiss' a treacherous act of friendship, since Judas betrayed the identity of Jesus by kissing him. In medieval tradition he was supposed (like Cain, the first murderer) to have had red hair, hence 'Judas-coloured'.

Judas Maccabaeus (2nd C BC)

A Jewish leader who led the revolt against the alien government of Antiochus Epiphanes the Syrian.

Jude the Obscure (1895)

The last novel by Thomas Hardy*. In Hardy's words the theme is the 'deadly war . . . between flesh and spirit' and 'the contrast between the ideal life a man wished to lead and the squalid real life he was fated to lead'. Jude Fawley is a village mason (like Hardy's father) who has intellectual aspirations. He is seduced into marriage by the 'female animal' Arabella Donn; when she abandons him, he turns back to learning, but falls in love with Sue Bridehead, whose contradictory nature seeks freedom and yet frustrates her own desire. She runs away from her schoolmaster husband, Phillotson, who disgusts her, and joins with Jude in an illicit union. Their children die at the hands of Jude's only child by Arabella, who takes his own and their lives because he believes that he and they had no right to be born. Sue returns in remorse to Phillotson, while Jude is beguiled back by Arabella, who deserts him on his deathbed.

The setting and the four main characters are so representative that the novel is almost an allegory. Jude's native place is Marygreen, a run-down village which is a kind of emblem of decayed rural England. His ambition is to enter the university of Christminster, which is Oxford*, but so named as a reminder by Hardy that the way of learning had once also been a goal of the spirit. Jude uproots himself from Marygreen but is unable to enter the university because of his social origins, though he lives in the town (where he meets Sue) and works there as a mason. Hardy's point is not so much the social one that the old universities of Oxford and Cambridge were all but closed to working-men; he is more concerned to show that the decay of spiritual goals in the England of his day matches the decay of the countryside. Jude himself is a complete man – physically virile as well as spiritually aspiring; it is his very completeness which the modern world, both Marygreen and Christchurch, is unable to accept. Sue Bridehead represents the 'new woman' of the day, emancipated in her own theory but not in body. Sue is all mind; Arabella all body, and Phillotson a kind of walking death – a man of the best intentions who is nonetheless helplessly destructive in consequence of his lack of both physical and spiritual vitality. The novel epitomizes Hardy's longing for spiritual values and his despair of them; its pessimism has strong poetic quality, and after completing it he gave himself entirely to poetry. Like many of Hardy's novels, *Jude the Obscure* is set in the recent past – about twenty years before the time of writing.

Judith

In the Apocrypha* of the Bible, the heroine of the book entitled by her name. Holofernes, general to Nebuchadnezzar king of Assyria, besieges the Jewish town of Bethulia. Judith, a beautiful Jewish widow, contrives to attract him and to spend the night in his tent. While he is asleep, she cuts off his head, and escapes with it back to the town. The Jews then succeed in driving off the Assyrians.

Julian the Apostate

Roman Emperor AD 361–3. Christianity was the official religion of the Roman Empire, but Julian renounced it and attempted to restore paganism. According to (unfounded) legend he was killed by a Christian, and, in dying, exclaimed 'Vicisti Galilaee' – 'Thou hast conquered, O Galilean' – thus acknowledging the victory of Christ.

Juliana of Norwich (Mother Julian) (?1343–after 1413)

Mystical writer; author of two accounts of revelations which she experienced during illness: *Comfortable Words* and *Revelations of Divine Love*. They are among the few works of memorable English prose from 14th C.

* *Fourteenth-century Literature*.

Bib: Knowles, M. D., *The English Mystics*; Underhill, E., *Medieval Mysticism*.

Julius Caesar

A historical tragedy by Shakespeare* based on the events of 44 BC, when Caesar was assassinated on suspicion of seeking to overthrow the Roman republic and make himself king. The conspiracy against him is led by Brutus, descendant of the Brutus who, according to legend, had first established the republic by throwing out the Tarquin line of kings in 6th C. Brutus is a friend of Caesar, and his motive in organizing Caesar's assassination is his disinterested love of Rome; his chief associate, Cassius, on the other hand, is motivated by personal envy and resentment. The third outstanding character in the drama is Caesar's friend Mark Antony, who, after the assassination, treacherously but most successfully turns the Roman mob against Brutus and Cassius and drives them out of Rome. Acts IV and V show the defeat of Brutus and Cassius at the battle of Philippi (42 BC). Caesar himself plays a comparatively small part although he is, alive and dead, the centre of the drama. The dramatic interest arises from the interplay between the characters of Brutus, Cassius, and Antony, and from the conflicts in the mind of Brutus who, as a good man, finds himself in the tragic dilemma of having to commit a horrible crime against a man he loves for the sake of the nation. Shakespeare based the events, with some interesting alterations, on Plutarch* whose *Lives* had been translated into English by Thomas North* (1579). The play belongs to his middle period, and dates from about 1599.

* *Caesar, Gaius Julius*.

Jung, Carl (1875–1961)

Swiss psychologist. He began as a disciple of Freud*, but came to disagree with Freud about the nature of the unconscious in the personality, and the role it played. Freud understood the unconscious as a region of suppressed desires and impulses; these manifested themselves in dreams, myths, and various forms of art and religion; he interpreted them as originating in sexual and family relationships. For Freud, the unconscious was therefore above all a source of mental illness. Jung came to see the unconscious as essentially the source of creativity rather than disease, and emphasized the need for co-operation between the conscious and unconscious parts of the personality. Mental disease arose out of their disordered relationship, and was not necessarily sexual in origin. Other well-known features of Jung's psychology are his division of types of personality into extroverted and introverted (outward-turning and inward-turning); and his classification of the four functions of the mind into thinking, feeling, sensation and intuition.

Junius /ˈdʒuːnjəs/

The pen-name of a political polemicist who published celebrated letters attacking the government of the day in the London newspaper *Public Advertiser*, 1769–72. The letters were fiercely satirical against the ministers of George III, and were notable for their unusual eloquence. The name 'Junius' was chosen from Lucius Junius Brutus, who, in legend, overthrew the Tarquin kings of Rome in 6th C BC. Their style shows the influence of Swift* and of the Latin historian Tacitus*. The real author has long been a mystery, but is now generally considered to have been Sir Philip Francis (1740–1818), a politician of the Whig* party who supported the rights and privileges of Parliament against what they considered to be dangerous encroachments by the king and his supporters.

Juno

* *Hera*.

Jupiter

* *Zeus*.

Jury System

A body of citizens without legal training who are summoned before a court of law and given the task, under the guidance of a judge, of ascertaining the facts of a case. If the case before the court concerns a crime, the most important fact for them to ascertain is whether the accused is guilty or not guilty. Hence it is the jury, not the judge, that tries the accused ('trial by jury') and its decision is called 'the verdict', in accordance with which the judge has to release the prisoner or decide the penalty appropriate to his offence.

The system originated in 12th C and reached its present form by 15th. It was often a defence against tyranny, although juries could be prejudiced (*eg* the jury in the town of Vanity Fair, in Bunyan's *Pilgrim's Progress**) or 'packed', *ie* deliberately made up from enemies of the accused man; or they could be intimidated, when the accused man was a great and powerful one.

Juries trying criminal or civil cases were technically called Petty Juries; Grand Juries (no longer in use) had the function of presenting men suspected of crime before the royal judges on their visits to the region. Small crimes have never been tried by juries but (since early 14th C) by Justices of the Peace (Magistrates).

* *Courts of Law; Magistrates.*

Justices of the Peace

* *Magistrates.*

Justinian I (AD 527–65) /dʒʌs'tiniən/

Emperor of the Byzantine (Eastern Roman) Empire whose capital was Constantinople*. He arranged the codification of Roman law, which became the basis of law all over Europe, including Scotland but not England.

Jutes

The earliest of the three Germanic tribes to invade Britain after the downfall of the Roman Empire. They were summoned by the Britons in 5th C (according to tradition) to help them resist the Pictish invasions from the north. Their leaders are said to have been Hengist* and Horsa. They established themselves permanently in Kent in the south-east, and in Hampshire and the Isle of Wight in the south. The other two invading tribes were the Angles* and the Saxons*.

Juvenal (Decimus Junius Juvenalis) (AD 60?–130?) /'dʒu:vinl/

Roman satirical poet. His sixteen satires describe the society of his time and denounce its vices. Satire*, as a literary form, is usually regarded as being a Roman invention, but Juvenal was the first of the Romans to associate it altogether with denunciation; his great predecessor, Horace*, had used it for ironic comment and discussion but was only intermittently denunciatory with the moral conviction associated with Juvenal. Like Horace, Juvenal had a strong influence on English poetry from 1590 until 1800; during these two centuries satire was increasingly practised, and Horace, Juvenal, or Horace's disciple Persius were taken as models. Both Thomas Nashe* and John Oldham (1653–83) have been described as 'the English Juvenal', but the greatest of his conscious followers is probably Samuel Johnson* in his two poems *London** and *The Vanity of Human Wishes*, imitations of Juvenal's third and tenth satires respectively. It is interesting to compare these with Pope's *Imitations of Horace**, which Johnson was emulating. The spirit of Juvenal is also strongly present in the satirical comedies of Ben Jonson* who used Juvenal in his great satirical tragedy *Sejanus**. John Dryden* translated Juvenal (1692).

K

Kant, Immanuel (1724–1804) /kant/

German philosopher of Scottish descent. His important works are: *Critique of Pure Reason* (1781 and 1787); *Prolegomena to every future Metaphysic* (1783); *Foundation for the Metaphysic of Ethic* (1785); *Metaphysical Rudiments of Natural Philosophy* (1757); *Critique of Practical Reason* (1788); *Critique of Judgement* (1790). He counteracted the scepticism of David Hume* by asserting the 'transcendence' of the human mind over time and space (hence 'transcendental philosophy'). Time and space are forms of our consciousness: we can know by appearances but we cannot know 'things in themselves'. On the other hand, it is in the nature of our consciousness to have inherent in it an awareness of design in nature, and of moral and aesthetic value under a Divine moral law. His philosophy, continued and modified by other German philosophers (Fichte, Schelling, Hegel) profoundly influenced the poet and philosopher Coleridge*; through Coleridge, it provided a line of thought which, in 19th-C England, rivalled the sceptical materialistically inclined tradition stemming from Locke*, Hume* and Bentham*. See *German Influence on English Literature.*

Katharine of Aragon

First wife of Henry VIII*. She was previously married to Henry's elder brother, Arthur, who had died in 1502. Politically, it was convenient for her to be married next to Henry, now heir to the throne, but marriage with a brother-in-law was forbidden as incestuous. The Pope gave a dispensation to make the marriage possible; there was some doubt, however, whether he was entitled to do so. Katharine's children died in infancy, except for a girl (later Mary I*), and a male heir was held to be essential. Henry accordingly used the doubtful legality of his marriage to serve as a pretext for a divorce. The Pope was in the power of Katharine's nephew, Charles V of Spain, and dared not allow one. His refusal was used by Henry as a further pretext for separating the English Church from papal domination (Act of Supremacy*, 1534). Katharine's dignity in the face of her suffering is movingly portrayed in the play *Henry VIII**.

Kean, Edmund (1787–1833)

Actor. Despite his small stature and lameness due to breaking both legs by a fall at the circus as a boy, he became the greatest Shakespearian actor of his time, famous in the roles of Richard III, Othello, Hamlet, Lear, Shylock and Macbeth. Coleridge* said of him that 'Seeing him act was like reading Shakespeare by flashes of lightning'. He also excelled in the part of Overreach in Massinger's *A New Way to Pay Old Debts**. His last role was Othello to his son's Iago. At the words 'Villain, be sure' (III, iii) he cried out 'O God, I am dying. Speak to them Charles', and collapsed into his son's arms. He actually died two months later.

Keats, John (1795–1821) /ki:ts/

Poet. He was the contemporary of Byron* and Shelley*, but of humbler social background. Like them, he was influenced by the older poets Wordsworth* and Coleridge*, and also critical of them; but unlike Byron and Shelley he was not active in the expression of his radical political sympathies. He belonged, however, to the radical circle centred on Leigh Hunt*, editor of *The Examiner**, and it was partly for this reason that his first ambitious poem *Endymion** (1818) was so severely criticized by the right wing periodicals *Quarterly** and *Blackwood's Magazine**. Byron gave currency to the legend that these attacks hastened Keats's death, but Byron knew nothing of the toughness of Keats's temperament, nor of the severity of his own self-criticism. Before *Endymion* Keats had already published *Poems by John Keats* (1817) in which the most interesting poem is *Sleep and Poetry*. His great year, however, was 1819, during which he produced all the work on which his high reputation now rests: the narrative poems *The Eve of St Agnes**, *la Belle Dame sans Merci*, *Lamia**, *Eve of St Mark*, *Isabella*, *Hyperion**; and the great odes* – *To a Nightingale*, *On a Grecian Urn*, *On Melancholy*, *To Psyche*, *To Autumn*. These were published in *Lamia and other Poems* in 1820. In the same year Keats, very ill with tuberculosis, took ship for Rome, where he died. Shelley wrote *Adonais** in his honour, and thereby achieved one of his own masterpieces.

Apart from the imaginative liberation for which Keats's generation was indebted to Wordsworth and Coleridge, the most important influences upon him were the poetry of Spenser*, Milton*, and Shakespeare*. Spenser is most apparent in the 1817–18 poems, and Milton in his most ambitious narrative, *Hyperion*. Both influences, as he came to realize, tended to encourage the faults to which his exuberant temperament was inclined; moreover his temperament was not merely strongly sensual but deeply reflective. Spenser's sweetness and rapture led him to poetic self-indulgence; Milton's sonorousness encouraged him in false rhetoric; Shakespeare's influence was especially congenial to his gift for vitalizing language through all the senses, and at the same time enriching it with the darker tones of experience. His second version of *Hyperion* (unrevised and published posthumously) shows a new austerity which Keats perhaps owed to his reading of Dante* in translation.

His letters are among the finest in English. They show the richness and spontaneity of his nature, the rapidity of his intellectual and moral development, and his fine powers of discrimination.

* 6.3.4; 7.3; *Romantic Revival*.

Bib: Colvin, S., *Life*; Ward, A., *John Keats*; Gittings, R., *The Living Year*; Bate, W. J., *Keats*; Murry, J. M., *Keats and Shakespeare*; Thorpe, C. D., *The Mind of Keats*; Ford, G. H., *Keats and the Victorians*; Rollins, H. E., *The Keats Circle*; Ridley, M. R., *Keats' Craftsmanship*; Leavis, F. R. in *Revaluation*; Trilling, L., in *The Opposing Self*; Gittings, R., *John Keats*; Jack, I., *Keats and the Mirror of Art*.

Keble, John (1792–1866)

Poet and scholar. He was a Fellow of Oriel College with Newman* and Pusey, and it was his sermon in 1833 in the University Church that was the first impulse for the Oxford ('Tractarian' or Puseyite) Movement. His verse was religious; he wrote a number of the most famous English hymns: *The Christian Year* (1827); *Lyra Innocentium* (1846); *Miscellaneous Poems* (1869). As Oxford Professor of Poetry (1831–41) he delivered lectures entitled *De Poeticae Vi Medica* in which he distinguished poets who wrote to relieve their emotions (Homer, Lucretius, Burns, Scott) from those who wrote with a less impulsive motive (Euripides, Dryden, Milton).

Bib: Irwin, E. F. L. W., *John Keble*; Ingram, K., *John Keble*; Battiscombe, G., *John Keble: a study in limitations*; Beck, W. J. A. M., *John Keble's Literary and Religious Contribution to the Oxford Movement*.

Kelpie /'kelpi/

In Scottish folklore, a water spirit which takes various shapes, commonly that of a horse. It lures travellers into the water and drowns them.

Kemp, William

A famous comic actor, contemporary with Shakespeare. He acted parts such as Peter, the comic servant of the Nurse in Shakespeare's *Romeo and Juliet**, and the muddle-headed constable Dogberry* in *Much Ado About Nothing**, and excelled at jigs*. His most famous exploit was dancing from London to Norwich (over a hundred miles) for a bet. He and Tarlton* established a national reputation for themselves as comic actors, as Burbage* and Alleyn* did as tragic ones.

Kenilworth (1821)

A historical novel by Sir Walter Scott*. It takes place in the reign of Elizabeth I*, and is based on traditions about the tragic death of a girl called Amy Robsart who is enticed into secret marriage with the Earl of Leicester, the Queen's favourite. Amy compels the Earl to acknowledge the marriage before the Queen at Kenilworth Castle, and so to incur Elizabeth's anger. Leicester is tricked into ordering his wicked intermediary, Richard Varney, to put his wife secretly to death. In historical fact, Leicester's marriage to Amy was not secret, although they lived much apart after he had been received into the Queen's favour. He seems to have maintained her generously, and her death was probably an accident. The Queen's visit to Kenilworth occurred fifteen years later.

Kensington

A western district of London. Originally a village several miles from the City, it became a fashionable suburb when William III* established his court at the great house which ever since has been known as Kensington Palace. By 19th C Kensington was fully integrated with London. By then the principal royal residence had become Buckingham Palace* further east, and Kensington became the quarter for rich business men.

Kensington Gardens

One of the Royal Parks in London. It was designed as the park of Kensington Palace, one of the royal residences since William III*, but it has been open to the public since 18th C.

Ketch, Jack (John), (d 1686)

A public executioner who made a name for himself in popular folklore, so that later executioners bore his name as a nickname. He was notorious for the clumsy brutality of his executions, which took place in public.

Kew Gardens

In 18th C the gardens of a royal residence which still stands. The gardens are situated on the River Thames, 9 miles west of the centre of London. They have long contained a particularly fine collection of plants and trees, and are officially known as the Royal Botanic Gardens.

Kilt

The heavily pleated skirt-like garment worn by Highland Scotsmen and reaching from the waist to the knees. Before 17th C it was the lower part of the plaid, or large woollen cloth in which the Highland Scotsmen wrapped themselves; the kilt was the part that hung down below the belt. Plaid and kilt are now separate. The term 'kilt' is often used for the whole costume, and is regarded as the Scottish national dress. In fact, it was only worn by Highlanders of the lower classes, and was forbidden in the middle of 18th C as part of a policy of destroying Highland ways of life by the British

government. Since then, apart from its use in Highland regiments, the kilt has been revived for romantic and sentimental reasons, and is worn by Scotsmen of all classes, especially on ceremonial occasions.

* *Scotland; Tartan.*

Kilvert, Robert Francis (1840–79)

Diarist. He was curate in the village of Clyro, Radnorshire. His candour and responsiveness to people and environment make his diaries valuable records of rural environment in the mid-Victorian era. Selections were published in 1938–40, edited by William Plomer.

Kim (1901)

A novel by Rudyard Kipling*. Kim, whose real name is Kimball O'Hara, is the orphan son of an Irish soldier in India, and he spends his childhood as a waif in the city of Lahore. He meets a Tibetan holy man in search of a mystical river, and accompanies him on his journey. Kim falls in with his father's old regiment, and is adopted by them, eventually becoming an agent of the British secret service under the guidance of an Indian, Hurree Babu. In spite of the ingenuousness of Kipling's British chauvinism, conspicuous in the later part of the book, the earlier part is an intimate and graphic picture of the humbler reaches of Indian life.

King, Henry (1591–1669)

Poet. He became Bishop of Chichester. He was a friend of John Donne* and belonged to the same Metaphysical* school of poets. His finest poem, by which he is chiefly known, is *The Exequy* on the death of his wife.

Bib: Mason, L., *Life* (Transactions of Connecticut Academy xviii); Williamson, G., in *The Donne Tradition.*

King John

A history play (*The Life and Death of King John*) by Shakespeare*, perhaps derived from the anonymous *Troublesome Reign of King John*, and written before the great history plays, *1 & 2 Henry IV*, which first exhibit his genius in maturity. Anticipations of this maturity show themselves in the central character, Philip Faulconbridge, illegitimate son of the previous king, Richard I*. The reign of the historical king John* (1199–1216) was very unsettled; in the play, the disturbance arises from John's having usurped the throne from his nephew Arthur, whose cause is taken up by the king of France, the Church, and his nobles. Philip, 'the Bastard', is excluded by his illegitimacy from the privileges and status of the class into which he is born, and he at first enters the king's service in a spirit of cynicism, like that of Shakespeare's other bastard, Edmund in *King Lear**. By degrees he takes to heart the dangers to the nation of the disorderly passions among the great men, and he acquires a political conscience. He is presented substantially, and stands out from the relatively flat background of the rest of the characters. However the theme that has given the play most of such popularity as it possesses centres not on the Bastard but on the child Arthur, whose pathos persuades his gaoler Hubert to spare his life. Arthur later dies from a fall in an attempt to escape.

Historically, the best-known fact about the reign of John is Magna Carta*, the Great Charter which the nobles and Stephen Langton, Archbishop of Canterbury, forced the king to accept as a guarantee against tyrannical interference with the rights of the subject. Shakespeare does not mention this; it only came into prominence for the national imagination in the next reign during the quarrels between King James I* and his Parliaments.

* *History Plays.*

King Lear (?1605–6)

A tragedy by Shakespeare*. Modern editions are compiled from two quartos* (1608, 1619) and the folio* version of 1623. The main plot about Lear is based on an ancient legend about a mythical British king which Shakespeare found in the Chronicles of Holinshed*; the subplot about Gloucester comes from Book II of Sidney's *Arcadia** – the story about the king of Paphlagonia. Shakespeare probably also knew a previous dramatization of the Lear legend called *The True Chronicle History of King Leir and his Three Daughters.*

The main plot proceeds from Lear's division of his kingdom between his two wicked daughters, Goneril and Regan. His third daughter, Cordelia, truly loves her father but she refuses to flatter him, and so gets nothing. The subplot arises from the relationships of the Earl of Gloucester with his two sons, the legitimate Edgar and the bastard Edmund; Edgar is traduced by Edmund and has to flee from his father's wrath. The plots combine: Gloucester takes pity on Lear when the latter is cruelly treated by his daughters, and has his eyes put out as penalty by Regan and her evil husband Cornwall. Edgar, disguised, protects his blinded father and eventually assumes leadership of the Lear–Cordelia party; Edmund, on the other hand, becomes leader of the Goneril–Regan party until he is slain by Edgar at the end of the play. Edgar and the cause of good are victorious, but Lear and Cordelia are dead.

The play shows Shakespeare at the height of his powers, and some eminent judges consider it to be his greatest. It has been described as his 'great exploratory allegory' (L. C. Knights, *Pelican Guide to English Literature*, vol. II) on the meaning of Nature. By dividing his kingdom in accordance with his daughters' professions of their 'natural' love for him, Lear unconsciously raises the fundamental question of how the natural passions really operate: in regard to Goneril, Regan, Cornwall and Edmund, he finds himself confronted by wild beasts; against them are ranged the no less 'natural' forces of good in Cordelia, Edgar, the Earl of Kent, and Goneril's husband the Duke of Albany. The conflict is also the course of Lear's spiritual pilgrimage from arrogance into humiliation, misery, madness, and finally a rebirth into a childlike simplicity and humility. Yet it is just at this point, when he seems to have earned an innocent happiness, that his tragic suffering culminates, since Cordelia meets her death in the very hour of victory.

King Lear is one of Shakespeare's longest plays, and the difficulty of producing it arises largely from the unusual number of roles in it that demand high acting ability: Lear himself is certainly the most testing of all Shakespeare's central characters, and Kent, Edgar, Edmund, Cordelia, Goneril, Regan, and Lear's Fool are all major parts.

King-maker, The

The nickname of Richard Neville, Earl of Warwick (1428–71). He was one of the most powerful English nobles during the civil wars known as the Wars of the Roses*. In the early 1460s he was from time to time in a position to control the destinies of the rival claimants to the throne – Henry VI* (of the House of Lancaster*) and Edward IV* (of York*).

King's Evil, The

A skin disease: scrofula. An ancient tradition maintained that kings could cure it by 'touching' the sufferer. In England the tradition goes back to king Edward the Confessor*; his miraculous healing power is described by the English Doctor in Shakespeare's *Macbeth** (IV.iii). The poet and critic Samuel Johnson* suffered from the disease, and was 'touched' for it as a child in 1712 by Queen Anne, the last reigning sovereign to practise the rite. Her nephew Prince Charles also used it during the Jacobite* Rebellion of 1745: since the power was supposed to inhere in the true royal line, the exercise of it was of propaganda value to him in his campaign for the English throne.

King's Friends

George III (1760–1820) tried to revive the power of monarchical government in England against the Whig* aristocracy which, since the accession to the throne of the House of Hanover in 1714, had controlled the country through Parliament. Since the institution of Parliament was too strong for the king to ignore it, he tried to carry his purpose by securing (largely through various forms of bribery) a party to support his policies and ministers from within Parliament. These became known as the King's Friends or the New Tories.

King's Quair, The

(Quair = book). A medieval allegorical love poem of 200 7-line stanzas in rhyme-royal*. It is usually considered to have been written by James I of Scotland* during his detention in England. Modern critics are not agreed on whether the poem is about the lady whom he married – Lady Jane Beaufort. It is an accomplished and graceful though not very original work in the style of medieval courtly love, and strongly influenced by Chaucer, especially *The Knight's Tale**.

* *Courtly Literature and Romantic Love.*

Kingship

The British tradition of kingship has two sources: the Germanic view was that the king was the father of his people, with no particular sacredness about the authority he exercised; the Latin tradition was that the king's powers were sacred, and after Christianity became the official religion of the Roman Empire (4th C AD) the Emperor represented the earthly side of the authority delegated by God to the Holy Church. The two aspects became united when the Frankish king Charlemagne* was crowned Emperor of the West in 800. Medieval English kings only nominally recognized the authority of the Holy Roman Emperors who succeeded Charlemagne, but they took to themselves the same status; a king on being crowned was anointed by holy oils, and a crime against him was a crime against God. In early times kings were elected, though the elected king was traditionally of the same family as the dead king, but by degrees the nearest surviving relative assumed the crown as a matter of course and eventually by right. (In Shakespeare's *Hamlet** and *Macbeth** neither young Hamlet nor Malcolm is the *inevitable* heir to the Danish and the Scottish thrones respectively.)

Until 17th C, peace, law and order depended on the king's authority. In the reign of Henry II*, for example, the king's judges imposed a universal 'Common Law' over the selfish interests of the competing barons, and the peace of the country was called 'the king's peace'. Everything depended on the king being universally acknowledged and respected; every kind of disaster followed when the king lost his authority like John*, ceased to be respected like Richard II*, was a tyrant like Richard III*, was a usurper like Henry IV*, or died without direct heir, leaving the succession uncertain, as seemed likely to happen after Elizabeth I*. The House of Tudor* had brought England stability and prosperity after a century of civil wars between the competing families of York* and Lancaster*, and of kings (Richard II, Henry IV, Henry VI, Richard III) who had almost all exhibited one or another of the disadvantages mentioned. The reign of Elizabeth, last of the Tudors, was particularly prosperous, but her childlessness and the changefulness of the times caused the nation to look to the future with foreboding. This accounts for the interest of the dramatists, and in particular of Shakespeare, in politics and especially in the politics of kings. Of his ten history plays* (1590–1600), all but one (*King John**) deal with the century before the accession of Elizabeth's grandfather, the first Tudor, in 1485, and all but the last (*Henry V**) deal with disturbed reigns.

The anxiety of Shakespeare and his contemporaries proved justified, though not as soon as they feared. James VI of Scotland succeeded peacefully as James I of England*, but almost at once his quarrels with Parliament and with the country began. James exaggerated the sacredness of kingship into the doctrine of 'the Divine Right of Kings', according to which the King was responsible to God alone; this made adjustment between royal policy and national interests difficult, and Parliament raised up Magna Carta* from the reign of King John to prove the right of the people to restrain royal power. No method had yet been discovered, however, of securing stable government except through a strong king, and under James's successor, Charles I*, civil war* broke out, culminating in the execution of the king. It took the remainder of 17th C and the whole of 18th to work out the modern system of 'constitutional monarchy', in accordance with which the king or queen reigns but does not rule, and government is conducted through an elected and truly representative parliament to which, and not to the crown, the ministers are responsible. The office of kingship remained sacred, but became merely symbolic.

Kingsley, Charles (1819–75)

Novelist; clergyman; reformer. He belonged to a movement known as Christian Socialism, led by F. D. Maurice. He is now remembered chiefly for his children's book, *The Water Babies** (1863). His novels *Yeast* (1848) and *Alton Locke* (1850) are concerned with the theme of social injustice. *Hypatia* (1853), *Westward Ho!* (1855), and *Hereward the Wake* (1865), are historical novels. His retelling for the young of Greek myths, *The Heroes* (1856), is still well known.

Bib: Pope-Hennessy, U., *Canon Charles Kingsley*; Martin, R. B., *The Dust of Combat: A Life of Kingsley*; Stephen, L., in *Hours in a Library*, Series 3; Thorp, M. F., *Life*; Barry, J. D., in *Victorian Fiction* (ed L. Stevenson).

Kipling, Rudyard (1865–1936)

Poet, short-story writer, novelist. He was born in India, educated in England, and returned to India at 17 as a journalist. In 1889 he came to England to live.

Kipling's poetry is striking for his success in using, vividly and musically, popular forms of speech, sometimes in the Browning tradition of the dramatic monologue*, *eg McAndrew's Hymn*, or in the ballad* tradition, *eg Barrack-Room Ballads* (1892). He was also able to write poetry appropriate to public occasions and capable of stirring the feelings of a large public beyond any other modern poetry, *eg* his famous *Recessional* (1897). His poetry is generally simple in its components but, when it rises above the level of doggerel, strong in its impact. It needs to be read in selection: *A Choice of Kipling's Verse* ed. T. S. Eliot, with a very good introductory essay.

His stories brought him fame, and, partly under French influence, he gave close attention to perfecting the art of the short story*. The volumes include *Plain Tales from the Hills* (1887), *Life's Handicap* (1891); *Many Inventions* (1893); *The Day's Work* (1898); *Traffics and Discoveries* (1904); *Actions and Reactions* (1909); *A Diversity of Creatures* (1917); *Debits and Credits* (1926) and *Limits and Renewals*. The early stories in particular show Kipling's capacity to feel with the humble (common soldiers, Indian peasants) and the suffering. But he admired action, power, and efficiency; this side of his character brought out much of the best and the worst in his writing. Some of his best stories show his enthusiasm for the triumphs of technology, and are about machines rather than people, *eg* in *The Day's Work*. On the other hand he was inclined to be crudely chauvinistic, and to show unpleasant arrogance towards peoples ruled by or hostile to Britain, though he also emphasized British responsibility for the welfare of the governed peoples. Yet again, he sometimes engaged in delicate if sentimental fantasy, as in *They* and *The Brushwood Boy* (1925); some of his later stories show a sensitive and sometimes morbid insight into abnormal states of mind, *eg Mary Postgate* (1917). The stories, like the poems, are best read in selection: *A Choice of Kipling's Prose*, ed. Somerset Maugham.

Kipling is not outstanding as a full-length novelist. His best novel is *Kim** (1901), based on his childhood in India; *Stalky and Co* (1899) is well-known as a tale about an English public school, and is based on Kipling's own schooldays at the United Services College. *The Light that Failed* (1890) shows his more sensitive and sombre aspect.

Kipling's children's stories are minor classics of their kind: *The Jungle Books* (1894–5); *Just So Stories* (1902); *Puck of Pook's Hill* (1906). *Rewards and Fairies* (1910) is less celebrated.

Bib: Carrington, C. E., *Life*; Brown, H., *Kipling*; Dobree, B., *Kipling*; Shanks, E., *Kipling: a Study in Literature and Political Ideas*; Orwell, G., in *Critical Essays*; Wilson, E., in *The Wound and the Bow*; Rutherford, A., *Kipling's Mind and Art*; Green, R. L. (ed), *Kipling: The Critical Heritage*.

Kipps (1905)

A novel by H. G. Wells*. It describes the social rise of a shop-assistant through an unexpected legacy, his engagement to a vulgarly snobbish young lady who has hitherto been out of his reach, and his painful acquisition of the false standards and cares which are forced upon him. He escapes the marriage by marrying suddenly a girl of his

own former class, but he only escapes his worries when he loses his money. The book contains acute social observation and comedy in the Dickens tradition, though Wells's style is quite his own.

Kit-Cat Club

Founded early in 18th C by leading Whig* men of letters and politicians; its members included Marlborough*, Walpole*, Steele*, Addison*, Congreve* and Vanbrugh*. It met at the house of a pastry-cook called Christopher Cat. Their portraits by Sir Godfrey Kneller hang in the National Portrait Gallery.

* *Clubs*.

Knight of the Burning Pestle, The (1609)

A comedy by Francis Beaumont*. It mocks the London middle-class taste for extravagant romances in the Spanish tradition about the adventures of wandering knights ('knight-errantry'), and parodies a contemporary play, *The Four Prentices of London* by Thomas Heywood*, who flattered this taste. It seems to owe something to Cervantes' *Don Quixote** (Pt I, 1605), itself a parody of the Spanish romances; this, however, was not translated until 1612.

The play at first purports to be called *The London Merchant* but a grocer and his wife, sitting in the audience, become worried that this may turn out to be a satire on London citizens. They are determined to have something to flatter their vanity, and force their son, Ralph, up on to the stage to perform the role of a 'grocer errant'; he wears on his shield the sign of a burning pestle, *ie* an implement used by shopkeepers for pounding etc. The play of 'The London Merchant' proceeds together with Ralph's Quixote-like adventures, and the grocer and his wife, still in the audience, interpose appreciative comments.

The comedy shows the great theatrical dexterity achieved by English dramatists at the height of the Shakespearian period. A main part of this dramatic skill is the intermingling of styles – song, comic rhyme, serious blank verse*, and colloquial prose.

Knight's Tale, The

The first tale to follow the *Prologue** in Geoffrey Chaucer's *Canterbury Tales**. It is over 2,000 lines long, in ten-syllable rhymed couplets* (heroic couplets). The story is a shortened version of *Teseide* by the 14th-C Italian poet Boccaccio*. Earlier fragmentary versions by Chaucer are *Palamon and Arcite* and *Anelida and Arcite*.

Palamon and Arcite, prisoners of Theseus of Athens, are rival lovers of Emilia, sister of Theseus' wife Hippolyta, queen of the Amazons. They compete for her in a tournament after seeking the favour of the gods, whose help Emilia also seeks. Arcite, favoured by Mars, is victorious; Saturn and Venus, however, cause him to be thrown from his horse and killed. As he dies, Arcite recommends his rival to Emilia, and after a period of mourning Palamon and Emilia are married.

The Knight's Tale is one of the great poems in the medieval courtly love tradition, and one of the most celebrated among Chaucer's masterpieces.

* *Courtly Literature and Romantic Love.*

Knights of the Shire

A term used in 14th and 15th C for small landowners who elected representatives to Parliament*. They were not necessarily knights in the usual sense of having had the honour of knighthood* conferred on them.

Knighthood

The origins of knighthood are obscure; knights became important in the Middle Ages, when they were horsed warriors recruited by the king for military service; hence 'chivalry' (from French 'cheval' = horse) used both as a collective term for knights and as the code of conduct for knights to follow. Knighthood was conferred as an honour by the king upon individuals, and never became hereditary. Originally it was acquired by prowess in battle, and was restricted to those of good family; a young nobleman was first a 'page' and then a 'squire', until he 'won his spurs' and received knighthood either by a brief ceremony known as receiving the accolade, or by a longer one involving religious ritual. Religion, at least ideally, played a strong part in knighthood and the code of chivalry; it was especially bound up with the cult of the Virgin Mary whose image, according to the 12th-C chronicler Geoffrey of Monmouth*, King Arthur* – the legendary pattern of all knights – always wore on his shield. The cult of Our Lady was bound up with the knight's chivalrous duty to revere and protect all women and all others who were weak and defenceless. Hence began the legends and romances of 'knights-errant' or wandering knights who went about dealing out justice and righting wrongs. Such legends began with King Arthur's Knights of the Round Table*, and developed into extravagant imitations which, in more or less vulgarized form, were popular reading among all literate classes in 16th and 17th C. Bunyan's *Pilgrim's Progress**, with its episodes of Christian fighting Apollyon, and Greatheart overthrowing the castle of Giant Despair, shows the impression on the popular mind from such romances. The Spanish writer Cervantes made fun of them in his *Don Quixote**, but he was not the first; Chaucer in *The Canterbury Tales** contrasts an image of a realistic knight of his time (14th C) with his own parody of knight-errantry in *Sir Thopas**.

However, Chaucer's contemporary William Langland, in his poem *Piers Plowman** was already complaining that knighthoods could be bought by merchants, and such knights were not, of course, likely to go to war. In the time of Shakespeare the term 'carpet-knight' was used in derision for knights who had never seen and would never see military service; in fact, soon after his time, knighthood ceased to have any necessary connection with war, except in memory and legend. The armoured knight on horseback had been made obsolete by the 16th-C musketeer on foot, but whereas in other countries the institution of knighthood gradually died out in consequence, in England it has been retained till the present day, and is conferred for many kinds of service to the state. Knights are still accorded the title 'Sir' before their first names; this title is now restricted to knights and to baronets – a hereditary title – whereas in Shakespeare's day it might be used as a term of respect, *eg* for clergymen, like Sir Oliver Martext in *As You Like It**. They may also belong to one of various orders of knighthood, analogous to Arthur's Order of the Round Table. Most of these, however, have been founded since the Middle Ages, the exception being the Order of the Garter*.

* *Heralds' College; Squire.*

Knightsbridge

A district of the west end of London. Since mid-19th C it has been a fashionable neighbourhood, but at the time of Congreve's comedy *Love for Love** (1695) it had a bad reputation.

Knox, John (1505–72) /noks/

Scottish religious reformer. More than anyone else, he was responsible for the conversion of Scotland from Catholic to Calvinist Christianity, and the eventual establishment of the national Presbyterian* Church there. This brought him into conflict with Mary Queen of Scots*, but he was out of the country when rebellion forced her to abdicate in 1567 and seek the protection of Elizabeth* of England. His *History of the Reformation of Religion within the realme of Scotland* includes an account of his celebrated controversy with the Queen.

Kotzebue, August von (1761–1819)

German dramatist. He wrote over 200 plays, some of which were translated or adapted into English and became very popular, *eg Menschenhass und Reue* presented by Sheridan* as *The Stranger* in 1798. Another, *Das Kind der Liebe* ('The Child of Love'), was adapted by Mrs Inchbald (actress, playwright, novelist) as *Lovers' Vows.* It remains famous in English because Jane Austen* made extensive use of it in her novel *Mansfield Park**. Agatha Friburg has long ago been seduced by Baron Wildenhaim. The play opens with the discovery of her by their son Frederic, who has hitherto been ignorant of his parentage; they have a passionate recognition scene. Wildenhaim has meanwhile acquired a legitimate daughter, Amelia, who is in love with the family chaplain, Anhalt, although her father wants her to marry the foolish Count Cassell. In one dialogue, she manages to induce Anhalt to acknowledge that he loves her in turn. In *Mansfield Park*, Maria Bertram is conducting a flirtation with Henry Crawford although she is engaged to Mr Rushworth; she takes the part of Agatha while Henry takes that of Frederic, and Rushworth – as foolish in real life as he is in his role – performs Cassell. Mary Crawford is in love with Edmund Bertram (a prospective clergyman) and they play the parts of Amelia and Anhalt respectively. The heroine, Fanny Price, herself in love with Edmund, is forced to help them rehearse the dialogue in which they confess love for each other.

Kubla Khan /'kublə 'ka:n/

One of the three famous 'supernatural' poems by Samuel Taylor Coleridge*. Coleridge recorded that the poem came to him, in 1797, as he lay asleep after reading an old book of travels, *Purchas his Pilgrimage* (1613). Unfortunately he was interrupted in writing down the poem, and when his visitor had left, he found the remainder of it had escaped his memory. Nonetheless some critics maintain that the fragment is artistically complete – see Lionel Trilling in *Beyond Culture*. J. L. Lowes in *The Road to Xanadu* uses the poem as a demonstration of how the subconscious mind works in imaginative creation.

Kyd, Thomas (1558–95) /kid/

Dramatist. He is associated with the group known as the University Wits*. His only known and important contribution to the output of the group is the *Spanish Tragedy** (?1589), extremely popular in its own time and the first important revenge tragedy*. He was probably also the author of a lost play on Hamlet, used by Shakespeare as the basis of his own; even without this, it is clear that Shakespeare developed the revenge theme from Kyd's first handling of it. Kyd's own starting-point was the tragedies of the Roman dramatist Seneca* whose *Ten Tragedies* had been published in translation (1559–81). He was not interested in Senecan form, but in Seneca's mingling of dramatic horror and the stern restraints of Stoic* philosophy, both of which were congenial to the Elizabethan age. Kyd's other surviving tragedies are only attributed to him and are much less important: *Soliman and Perseda* (?1588) and *Cornelia* (?1593), an adaptation of a Senecan tragedy by the French dramatist Robert Garnier.

Kyd was a friend of Marlowe*, and was arrested in 1593 on the accusation of atheistic pronouncements which he declared, under torture, to be really Marlowe's; he was released after Marlowe's death by murder in the same year, and seems to have died soon afterwards in poverty.

* 5.1.2.4.

Bib: Boas, F. S., *Works*; Bowers, F. T., *Elizabethan Revenge Tragedy*;
Carrère, F., *Le Théâtre de Kyd*.

L

Labour Party

Since 1923, one of the two main political parties in Britain, the other being the Conservative Party. The Labour Party was founded in 1900, and was called the Labour Representation Committee until 1906, when it took its present name. It claims to represent the interests of the working classes, and it favours state ownership of the means of production and distribution (state socialism) but it is not committed to complete socialization of the economy. The majority of its supporters are working-class, but it also has fairly extensive middle-class support among intellectuals.

Origins of the Labour Party:

[1] 19th-C working-class movements. The most important of these was the growth of trade unions*, which began a process of confederation in 1866; it was in consequence of a resolution by the Trades Union Congress (TUC) in 1899 that the Party was founded. Earlier movements which contributed to the origins of the party were those of the socialist Robert Owen*; the Chartist Movement* which, though it failed in its objectives, educated the working-class in political consciousness; the Philosophical Radicals or Utilitarians*, led by John Stuart Mill*, who appealed to intellectuals among the workers, and elsewhere.

[2] The Liberal Party. Throughout 19th C the Liberals (formerly the Whigs) claimed to be the party of reform, although important social reforms were often initiated by Conservatives (Tories) such as Shaftesbury* and Disraeli*. It was in alliance with the Liberal Party that the workmen Members first entered Parliament in the last 20 years of 19th C. The Liberals, however, received much support and money from employers of labour in the towns, so that a split caused by workers leaving the Liberal Party became inevitable.

[3] The Nonconformist sects. The Protestant churches which refused conformity with the Church of England included Baptists, Congregationalists, Presbyterians, Quakers, Unitarians and Methodists. Most of their support was from the lower social classes, and, though they were predominantly non-political, they inevitably encouraged thoughtful discussion of political questions, especially social justice; they also assisted by helping to educate their members in social co-operation.

[4] The Fabian Society*. This was a society of socialist intellectuals, founded in 1884. It was led by some brilliant minds, including Bernard Shaw* and Beatrice Webb*, and became very influential.

[5] Marx* and the growth of Social Democracy in Europe. The European Social Democratic Federation was founded in 1881. However, although the British Labour Party has always had affinities with Social Democracy, in its origins it was not predominantly Marxist; its socialism derived more from earlier thinkers such as Owen*.

[6] The leadership of the Scottish Labour Movement – Keir Hardie. Scotland was not so bound by tradition to the existing political parties as England was, and the Scottish working class was on the whole better educated. The Scotsman Keir Hardie was the greatest of the British Labour leaders at the time of the foundation of the party.

* 1.5.1.5; *Parties, Political.*

Labours of Hercules

* *Heracles.*

Lady Bountiful

A character in Farquhar's* play *The Beaux' Stratagem*. She is a rich country lady who devotes her time to helping her less fortunate neighbours. She has become a proverbial figure. Farquhar portrays her satirically.

Lady Chatterley's Lover (1928)

D. H. Lawrence's* last novel. Constance Reid ('Connie') is the daughter of late-Victorian, highly cultured parents with advanced views. She marries Sir Clifford Chatterley in 1917, when he is on leave from the army; soon afterwards he is wounded, and permanently crippled from the waist down. Connie finds herself half alive, as though she has not been fully awakened; her dissatisfaction, however, does not proceed merely from her husband's disability, but from the impotence of civilization which the disability symbolizes. She is rescued from it by her husband's gamekeeper, Mellors, who fulfils her as a lover and as a human being. For Lawrence, the sexual relationship was potentially the profoundest human relationship: to treat it lightly was to trivialize the whole human being, and to regard it with shame was to repress essential human energies in other activities besides the sexual one. He saw that 'advanced' young people took the former attitude, and that the older generation took the latter; he regarded both attitudes as leading symptoms of decadence in our civilization. He did not suppose that the sexual relationship could in itself constitute a renewal of civilization, but he considered that such a renewal depended on the revitalization of relationships, and that this revitalization could never take place without the recovery of a true and healthy sexual morality. 'I want men and women to be able to think sex, fully, completely, honestly and cleanly.' (*Apropos of Lady Chatterley's Lover*, 1930.)

This aim led Lawrence to use unprecedentedly explicit language in conveying the love affair between Connie and Mellors, and the novel thus acquired unfortunate notoriety. In Britain, the full version was suppressed for immorality, but an expurgated version was published in 1928. An unabridged edition came out in Paris (1929); the first British unabridged edition was published by Penguin Books in 1959. Its suppression in 1928 caused critics to fly to Lawrence's defence, and it has been hailed as his masterpiece, *eg* by Antony West. The best-known critic of Lawrence (F. R. Leavis) attaches less importance to it. There is more agreement however, in the judgment that Lawrence's defence of the novel, *Apropos of Lady Chatterley's Lover*, is one of the finest of his essays.

Lady Day

In the Church calendar, the feast of the Annunciation to the Virgin Mary, celebrating the prediction of the Birth of Christ by the Angel Gabriel* (*Luke* I). It is observed on 25 March, which is also a Quarter Day*, *ie* it marks the end of the first quarter of the year on which bills, etc. have to be paid. In the Middle Ages there were other Lady Days commemorating other events in the life of the Virgin Mary.

Lady of Shalott, The (1832) /ʃə'lot/

One of the best-known poems by Alfred Tennyson*. The story is an episode from the Arthurian legend of Sir Lancelot*, and is to be found in Malory's *Morte d'Arthur** and in the 13th-C French romance *Lancelot*. In the original legends 'Shalott' was 'Ascolot' or 'Astolat' – identified as the town of Guildford to the south of London. Tennyson's poem is popular as an example of his extremely musical verse; it is also an example of his recurrent theme of withdrawal from deathly reality into a world of reverie. He expanded the story in his *Lancelot and Elaine* (1859), one of the *Idylls of the King**.

Lady of the Lake, The

In the legends of King Arthur*, a mysterious half-supernatural character, who may be derived from Rhiannon, a queen of ancient Celtic myth. In Malory's *Morte d'Arthur** she gives Arthur the miraculous sword, Excalibur*, and she is one of the three queens who bear him away to be healed of his wounds after the last battle. She rids herself of the magician Merlin*, when he becomes infatuated with her, by burying him under a large rock. She has been identified with the enchantress Morgan le Fay*, Arthur's evil sister who tries to kill him, and with Nimue who saves him from danger. She is thus associated with supernatural powers which are sometimes maleficent and sometimes beneficent. She also goes under the name of Vivien, mother of Sir Lancelot.

Lady of the Lake, The (1810)

A narrative poem by Sir Walter Scott* about the Scotland of James V (1513–42).

Laestrygones /li:s'traigəni:z/

In Greek myth, a race of giant cannibals who inhabited Sicily. In Book X of Homer's *Odyssey**, they destroy 11 of Odysseus' 12 ships and devour the crews.

Lagado

In Swift's *Gulliver's Travels** (Pt III) capital of the island of Balnibarbi, and its neighbouring flying island Laputa.

Lake Poets

A term originating in the *Edinburgh Review** (Oct. 1807) to include Coleridge*, Southey*, and Wordsworth*, who for a time had lived in close association in the mountainous Lake District in the north-west of England. Their community of literary and social outlook in their earlier work made it natural to speak of them as a group, but in fact it was only Wordsworth who was profoundly influenced by the locality and its inhabitants.

Lallans (Lowland Scots) /'lalənz/

The Scottish word for the language spoken in the Lowlands of Scotland, *ie* the southern and eastern regions of the country as opposed to the north-western region which is called the Highlands. Historically, the Highlands are Celtic, and though the region is now largely English-speaking, its original language was Gaelic. The Lowlands, on the contrary, have a predominantly Germanic population which has never spoken a Celtic language. Although Lallans is close to English grammatically, and has many words in common, it is not usually considered a mere dialect of English comparable, for instance, to the Cockney spoken by Londoners. It has its own distinguished poetic tradition, which includes such poets as King James I of Scotland*, Dunbar* and Henryson* (16th C), Robert Burns* (18th C), and Hugh MacDiarmid* (20th C). The language of these poets is distinguished from English by its vocabulary, which has different word-forms, different borrowings from French and Latin, and more intimate associations with the concrete and forceful diction of peasant ways of life. It is the last peculiarity which gives the poems of Burns and MacDiarmid their special strength. In prose, Lowland writers chiefly used Latin until the first half of 17th C, and then adopted southern English; there is thus very little Lallans prose of importance.

* *Scotland; Scottish Literature.*

Lamb, Charles (1775–1834)

Essayist and critic. His best-known work is his two volumes of the *Essays of Elia** (1823 and 1833), in which he discourses about his life and times. His *Specimens of English Dramatic Poets who lived about the Time of Shakespeare* directed interest towards Shakespeare's contemporaries, who had been somewhat neglected in 18th C, although perhaps not so much ignored as Lamb thought. His friends included many of the best writers of his time, and this fact gives a special interest to his letters. He collaborated with his sister Mary in adapting Shakespeare's plays into stories for children – *Tales from Shakespeare* (1807). His poems are unimportant, but one or two, *eg The Old Familiar Faces* (1798) and the prose-poem, *Dream Children*, recur in anthologies. Lamb seems to have been a man of unusual charm, and of gifts which he never allowed himself to display fully and energetically, perhaps because he was haunted by the fear of insanity, to which both he and his sister were subject.

* 7.3.

Bib: Lucas, E. V., ***Life***; Tillyard, E. M. W. (ed.), ***Lamb's Criticism***; Blunden, E., ***Charles Lamb and his Contemporaries.***

Lambeth

A district of London south of the Thames; it includes Lambeth Palace, official residence of the Archbishop of Canterbury since 12th C.

Lamia (1819) /ˈleimjə/

A narrative poem in heroic couplets* by John Keats*. In Roman myth a lamia was a female demon, one of whose practices was to entice young men in order to devour them. In Keats's poem, a lamia is transformed from a serpent into a beautiful girl who fascinates a young Corinthian, Lycius. He takes her into his home and makes a bridal feast, which is attended by the philosopher Apollonius. Apollonius recognizes the lamia and calls her by her true name, whereupon she vanishes. Keats clearly intends to contrast the illusiveness of sensual apprehension and the piercing truthfulness of which the mind is capable. He obtained the story from Burton's *Anatomy of Melancholy** III.ii. Burton got it in turn from *De Vita Apollonii* by Philostratus (2nd–3rd C AD).

Lammas /ˈlaməs/

In Old English, 'loaf mass'; used formerly in the Church as a thanksgiving for harvest, or harvest festival, celebrated on 1 August. It was also (and in Scotland still is) a Quarter Day* for the payment of bills, etc.

Lampoon

A personal attack in the form of a verse satire*, usually motivated by mere malevolence. It was common in later-17th and 18th C.

Lancaster

The county town (*ie* administrative centre) of the county of Lancashire in the north of England, and in the Middle Ages the name of the whole county. In 14th C, when John of Gaunt, 4th son of Edward III*, became Duke of Lancaster, the county was given 'palatinate' status, *ie* it was given an unusual degree of administrative and legal independence under its Duke. A relic of this is the survival of the ministerial office of the Chancellorship of the Duchy of Lancaster in the British government. Lancashire no longer has any special status legally and administratively, however, and the office survives as a ministry without portfolio, *ie* with duties allotted by the Prime Minister according to his convenience. The title of Duke of Lancaster became united with the crown when John of Gaunt's son became king as Henry IV*, and it remains one of the titles of the sovereign.

* *Lancaster, House of.*

Lancaster, House of

A branch of the Plantagenet* family, or House of Anjou. The Lancastrian branch ruled over England from 1399 to 1461. It acquired the throne owing to a successful rebellion by Henry Bolingbroke, son of John Duke of Lancaster (John of Gaunt), against the reigning king, Richard II*, Henry's cousin. Henry became Henry IV*, and was succeeded by his son Henry V*, and his grandson Henry VI*. Henry VI was, in turn, deposed by his cousin, Edward, first king of the House of York*.

* *Wars of the Roses.*

Lancelot, Sir

The most famous of King Arthur's* Knights of the Round Table*. His prominence is due mainly to the lateness of his arrival in the cycle when courtly versions (in English, Malory's *Morte d'Arthur**) overlaid the older, more popular traditions. In older versions, Sir Gawain*, or Sir Perceval*, were the pre-eminent knights. In Malory, and in the 14th-C English poem *Morte Arthur*, he is the lover of Guinevere, Arthur's Queen. In Malory, he seeks the Holy Grail* (by then a purely Christian symbol) but is unable to do more than glimpse it because of his sins. He represents a phase in the development of the Arthurian legend when the original pagan elements had been entirely Christianized, and when the taste for the tragic passions of courtly love had replaced the symbolic themes of nature myth, traces of which have been explored by such scholars as Jessie L. Weston (*From Ritual to Romance*).

* *Courtly Literature and Romantic Love.*

Landor, Walter Savage (1775–1864) /'lando:/

Poet. Author of the blank-verse* epic* *Gebir* (1798), the tragedy *Count Julian* (1812); in prose, *Imaginary Conversations* (1824–7). His collected poems have been edited by S. Wheeler (1937), and selections made by G. Grigson (1964). He was a fine Latin scholar, and produced a Latin version of his epic *Gebir*. He belonged to no literary group, and is now chiefly remembered for *Imaginary Conversations* between such figures of the past as Dante* and Beatrice, and Elizabeth* and Mary* Tudor. This device of imaginative reconstruction has had its imitators, especially on the radio. In life he was a quarrelsome but generous personality, characterized by Dickens in Boythorn, in the novel *Bleak House**. Landor, like Byron*, is an example of the sort of English writer who is aristocratic in background and radical in principle. His strongly traditional classical education made him familiar with traditional epic and dramatic forms. He experimented in these without possessing the originality necessary for renewing their vigour, until he found in the *Conversations* the form suited to his individual talent.

Bib: Forster, J., *Life*; Elwin, M., a critical study; Super, R. H., *The Publication of Landor's Works*, and in *The English Romantic Poets and Essayists: a Review of Research and Criticism*, ed. Houtchens, C. W. and L. H.; *Landor: a Biography*.

Lanfranc (d 1089) /'lanfraŋk/

Archbishop of Canterbury, 1070–89, under William I*, first of the Norman kings. The English Church under the previous archbishop, Stigand, had been degenerate and had departed from the rules ordained by the Roman papacy. Lanfranc, an Italian by origin, corrected and reformed its ways, and yet helped the king to resist papal interference. It was characteristic of the absence of national frontier in 11th C that England, with its predominantly Germanic population, had an Italian as the leader of its Church.

Langland, William (?1330–?1400) /'laŋlənd/

Usually accepted as the sole author of the long 14th-C poem *Piers Plowman**, one of the greatest of English medieval works. According to some scholars, the poem is by various hands. Nothing is known of the author (whether or not his name was Langland) apart from internal evidence in the poem. From this, he seems to have been born in Shropshire in the west of England, the son of a franklin or farmer; he would in other words have belonged to the middle class of rural society. He obviously received an education and may have entered minor priestly orders, becoming a 'clerk' (**Clergy*). He is thought also to have been the author of an incomplete poem, *Richard the Redeless* (1399), but *Pierce Ploughman's Creed* is considered to be by another hand.

Bib: Donaldson, E. T., *Piers Plowman: the C-text and its Poet*; Coghill, N. K., *The Character of Piers Plowman Considered from the B-text*; Dawson, C., *Medieval Religion and other essays*; Owst, G. R., *Literature and Pulpit in Medieval England*; Lawlor, J., a critical study; Salter, E., *Piers Plowman: an Introduction*.

Laocoon /lei'okəuon/

In Greek myth, a priest of Apollo in Troy*; he profaned Apollo's temple, and (in vain) warned the Trojans of the dangers of the wooden horse which the Greeks had left behind them. As a punishment for the profanation and for trying to frustrate the course of fate, two serpents came up from the sea while he was sacrificing to Poseidon, god of the ocean, and strangled him and his two sons. The incident is described by the Roman poet, Virgil, in the *Aeneid**, Bk. II.

Laodamia /leiədə'maiə/

In Greek legend, the wife of the hero Protesilaus, killed by Hector before Troy. She was visited by her husband's ghost, and, unable to part from him, followed him to the underworld. This is the subject of Wordsworth's* poem *Laodamia* (1814).

Laodicean /leiədi'siən/

In the Bible (*Revelation* 3:15–16) a reference to the weakness of the Church of Laodicea, one of the oldest of the Christian communities; they were accused of indifference – 'I know thy works, that thou art neither cold nor hot: I would thou wert cold or hot.' The term is thence applied to indifferentism in politics or religion.

Lapithae /'lapıθi:/

In Greek myth a race of men in Thessaly, who warred against the centaurs*.

Laputa /lə'pju:tə/

In Swift's *Gulliver's Travels**, the flying island in the satire against the natural philosophers* of Part III.

Lares /'leəri:z/

In Roman myth, guardian deities of the home, and similar to the Penates.

Larkin, Philip (b 1922)

Poet. He is the most eminent of the group known as the 'New Lines' poets (from an anthology of that name, 1956, ed. by Robert Conquest) otherwise called the Movement, the dominant group of poets

in Britain since 1945. Many of them hold posts in universities, and their work is characterized by thoughtfulness, irony, self-doubt, humility, and the search for completely honest feeling. These qualities are in accord with the imaginative temper of Thomas Hardy's* poetry; Larkin, who greatly admires Hardy, has also been compared to Auden*. He resembles Auden in the political radicalism of his content, combined with conservatism of form; both are contrasts to Eliot*, who is conservative in his political and social content, but radically experimental in form. Books: *The North Ship* (1945); *The Less Deceived* (1955); *The Whitsun Weddings* (1964); *High Windows* (1974); Editor *Oxford Book of Twentieth Century Verse* (1973).
* 6.5.

Last Chronicle of Barset, The (1867)

The last of the Barsetshire* novels, about the politics of the imaginary cathedral town of Barchester, by Anthony Trollope*. It centres on one of Trollope's best characters – the Reverend Josiah Crawley, the curate of Hogglestock. A poor, proud, isolated man with rigorous standards, he is accused of theft, and persecuted by the arrogant Mrs Proudie, wife of the bishop. A minor theme is the engagement of Major Grantly to Mr Crawley's daughter, Grace, in defiance of the wishes of his father the Archdeacon. It is often considered to be the best of Trollope's novels.

Latimer, Hugh (?1490–1555)

One of the chief English Protestant* reformers. He was favoured by Henry VIII* and supported the king's separation of the English Church from papal authority. However, he went further than Henry in his independence of thought, and in 1539 he resigned the bishopric of Worcester because he could not accept Henry's conservative statement of doctrine, the Act of Six Articles. Under the more Protestant regime of Edward VI* he became a very popular preacher, but in 1555 he was burnt alive as a heretic under the Catholic Queen Mary I*. His words to his fellow victim, Nicholas Ridley*, are famous: 'Be of good comfort, Master Ridley, and play the man; we shall this day light such a candle in England as (I trust) shall never be put out.' The idiom is characteristic of Latimer's famous sermons. Among his memorable works is his letter to Henry VIII (1530) urging the free circulation of the Bible in translation.
* *Reformation.*

Latin Literature

Rome began as a small Italian city state, and grew to an empire that surrounded the Mediterranean and extended as far north as the borderland between England and Scotland. Politically, she established the framework out of which modern Europe grew. Culturally, in part by native genius and in part by her assimilation and transmission of the older and richer culture of Greece, her literature became the basis of European imaginative values, and especially those values that arise from the individual's relationship to his society.

Between 300 and 100 BC, Rome began to display her native tendencies in literature, and at the same time, after her conquest of the rich Greek colonies in southern Italy, to expand her imaginative and intellectual vision and to increase and refine the expressiveness of the Latin language through the study of Greek literature*. Primitive Roman literature had been of two kinds: that of the recording and examination of public life and conduct in annals of eminent men and in oratory, and that of the distinctively Roman art of satirical comedy. These centuries saw the production of the comic dramas of Plautus* and of Terence*. The orator and historian Cato the Censor* upheld the virtues of Roman severity against Greek sophistication and luxury; the dominant figure, however, was the poet Ennius (239–169) who preserved a balance between Greek and Latin values by emulating Homer* in a patriotic epic in Latin idiom and Greek metre, the *Annales*.

The first half of the first century BC was the last great period of the Roman Republic. Active participation in politics was still one of the principal concerns of Roman aristocrats, and by this time Romans had studied and profited from the lessons in depth and force of thinking that Greece was able to teach them. Cicero* was the great persuasive orator of public debate; such was the power of his eloquence that the period is often known as the Ciceronian age. Julius Caesar's* terse, practical account of his wars in Gaul and invasion of Britain shows a different kind of prose excellence, and the vividness of Sallust's* histories of episodes in recent Roman history is different again. It was thus a great age of prose, but it included one of the finest of all philosophical poems, the *De Rerum Natura* ('Concerning the Nature of Things') of Lucretius*, who expounded the thought of the Greek philosopher Epicurus*. It included also the passionate love poems of Catullus*, who gave new vitality to Greek mythology.

Julius Caesar's great-nephew, Augustus Caesar, became the first Emperor in 27 BC, and he ruled till his death in AD 14. The Republic ended, and with it the kind of moral thought and eloquence which had made Cicero so famous. Roman literature, however, entered upon its most famous period – the Augustan Age*. If the Empire had not quite reached its greatest extent, its power was nonetheless at its peak; the old traditions of austerity and masculine energy were not yet extinct; civilization, wealth and sophistication had not yet overbalanced into decadence resulting from excessive luxury. Augustus himself was a patron of letters. In prose, the outstanding writer was the historian Livy*, but it was above all an age of poetry. The greatest of Roman poets, Virgil*, celebrated great traditions, looked back to by a stable society, in which active political participation had become difficult or unimportant. His contemporary, Horace*, celebrated the values of civilized private life. Tibullus, Propertius, and above all Ovid* were poets of pleasure appealing to the refined taste of an elegant society.

The last great period of Roman literature lasted approximately a hundred years from the death of Augustus. The Emperors were bad, the great idea of Rome was losing much of its force, society was showing symptoms of decadence. The mood of the best writers consequently became more detached from and more critical of Roman society. In the philosophy and drama of Seneca*, the heroic poetry of Lucan*, the satire of Persius (34–62), the Greek philosophy of Stoicism* seemed the strongest defence of human dignity against social oppression and distress. The greatest work, however, was the savage satire of Juvenal* and the sombre history of his time by Tacitus*.

Literature in Latin did not of course end with the great period, nor did it end with the Roman Empire in 5th C AD. Latin became the language of the Roman Catholic Church, and therefore of the early medieval educated classes. It remained a living, growing language till its style was fixed by Renaissance* scholars in 16th C. Even in 17th C, Francis Bacon* wrote much of his philosophy in Latin, and Milton* wrote Latin poetry. Classical Latin was read and admired in medieval England, but knowledge of it was incomplete and inaccurate; much of this knowledge was obtained (for instance, by Chaucer*) from contemporary French and Italian writers whose traditions were closer to classical Latin. Virgil retained great prestige, and Terence was studied in the monasteries for the purity of his style. After 1500, the Renaissance caused English writers to study and emulate the classical writers. Writers modelled themselves on styles of classical prose; the terse manner of Seneca and Tacitus was imitated by Bacon, whereas the eloquent flow of Cicero was emulated by Edmund Burke*. More important than the study of styles was the way in which English writers again and again measured themselves against their own society by placing themselves in the position of Roman writers, and then assessed their society from a Roman standpoint. So, in late 16th C, Donne* modelled his elegies on those of Ovid, and a little later Ben Jonson* rewrote the lyrics of Catullus; in 17th C Milton emulated Virgil as Virgil had once emulated Homer; in 18th C Pope* took the standpoint of Horace, and Samuel Johnson* adopted that of Juvenal.

* *Classical Education.*

Latona

* *Leto.*

Laud, William (1573–1645) /lo:d/

Archbishop of Canterbury under Charles I*. He firmly resisted the desire for further reform among the religious extremists, and even tried to impose religious uniformity upon Scotland. His rigour was more than anything else responsible for the discontent which led to the outbreak of the Civil War* in 1642. Parliament, which had already secured his imprisonment in 1641, ordered his execution in 1645.

Laura

* *Petrarch.*

Laurence, Friar

A character in Shakespeare's play *Romeo and Juliet**. He marries the lovers secretly and devises the plot by which they are to escape together from Verona, where the feud between their respective families, the Montagues and the Capulets, makes it impossible for the marriage to become public. Like other friars in Elizabethan plays, he is presented more as a wise man, learned in medical lore, than as a holy one.

Lawrence, David Herbert (1885–1930)

Novelist, poet, critic. The son of a coal-miner, he passed through University College, Nottingham, and for a time worked as a teacher. He eloped to Italy with Frieda, the German wife of a Nottingham professor, in 1912, and married her in 1914. His hatred of the war, together with the German origins of his wife, caused them unhappiness in 1914–18; after the war they travelled about the world, visiting especially Australia and New Mexico. Lawrence died at Vence in France in 1930. His reputation has grown gradually, and he is likely always to remain a controversial figure.

Lawrence's life, art, criticism, poetry, and teaching were all so closely related that it is unusually difficult to distinguish one aspect of his achievement from all the others. Misunderstandings about his supposed obsession with sexuality and the needless legal action for obscenity in connection with two of his novels (*The Rainbow** and *Lady Chatterley's Lover**) have distorted judgement with vulgar scandal. On the other hand, he has been the subject of irrelevant hero-worship which is equally distorting, and which he would have repudiated. He was a deeply religious – though not a Christian – writer who believed that modern man is perverting his nature by the wilful divorce of his consciousness from his spontaneous feelings. He has been accused of social prejudice. It is true that he was keenly critical of society; but he was the first major English novelist to have truly working-class origins, and this, together with his wide range of friendships with men and women of all classes, gave him unusual perceptiveness into the contradictions of English society.

Novels: *The White Peacock* (1911); *The Trespasser* (1912); *Sons and Lovers** (1913), an autobiographical novel, was his first distinguished work, and it was followed by what are generally regarded as his two masterpieces, *The Rainbow* (1915) and *Women in Love** (1921); *The Lost Girl* (1920); *Aaron's Rod* (1922); *Kangaroo* (1923) about Australia; *The Plumed Serpent* (1926) about New Mexico; *Lady Chatterley's Lover* (1928), banned except for an expurgated edition until 1959. He also wrote several volumes of short stories and 'nouvelles' which include much of his best fiction. Among the best known of these are *St Mawr*, *The Daughters of the Vicar*, *The Horse Dealer's Daughter*, *The Captain's Doll*, *The Prussian Officer*, *The Virgin and the Gipsy*.

One of Lawrence's most distinguishing features as an artist in fiction is his use of natural surroundings and animals realistically and yet symbolically, to express states of experience which elude direct

There was an Old Man who said, "Hush! I perceive a young bird in this bush!"
When they said, "Is it small?" he replied, "Not at all!
It is four times as big as the bush!"

description. This 'poetic' element in his fiction is reflected in much of his verse; some of this is in rhymed, metrical stanzas, but a great deal of it is free of verse conventions and close to the more condensed passages of his prose. Lawrence began writing poetry at the time when Imagism* was seeking more concrete expression, and he contributed to Imagist anthologies. Some critics (*eg* A. Alvarez, *The Shaping Spirit*) are inclined to see his poetry as among the most important produced in the century, deserving to be set alongside the work of T. S. Eliot* and W. B. Yeats*.

Lawrence's descriptive, didactic, and critical prose is also important. His psychological essays, *Psychoanalysis and the Unconscious* (1921) and *Fantasia of the Unconscious* (1922) are imaginative, not scientific works, and contribute to the understanding of his creative mind. His descriptive volumes, *Sea and Sardinia* (1921), *Mornings in Mexico* (1927) show his outstanding powers of presenting scenes with sensuous immediacy, and his characteristic concentration of all his interest – moral and social, as well as aesthetic – on to natural environment. The same concentration is to be seen in his critical and didactic writing; he brought moral, aesthetic, and social judgements into play together. Much of his best critical writing is contained in the posthumous volumes *Phoenix* I and II.

Lawrence wrote three plays: *The Widowing of Mrs Holroyd* (1914); *Touch and Go* (1920); *David* (1926). These have never received the attention accorded the rest of his work. He was an excellent letter-writer: *Letters* ed. Aldous Huxley.

4.5.3; 7.5

Bib: Leavis, F. R., *D. H. Lawrence, Novelist*; E. T., *D. H. Lawrence, a Personal Record*; Lawrence, F., *Not I, but the Wind*; Moore, H. T., *The Intelligent Heart*; Nehls, E., (ed.) *Lawrence: a Corporate Biography*; Arnold, A., *D. H. Lawrence and America*; Spilka, M., *The Love Ethic of D. H. Lawrence*; Tiverton, W., *D. H. Lawrence and Human Existence*; Draper, R. P., *Lawrence: The Critical Heritage*.

Lawrence, Thomas Edward (1888–1935)

Archaeologist, soldier, author of *The Seven Pillars of Wisdom* (1926). This book is an account of the dramatic role he played in helping King Feisal in the Arab resistance to the Turks during World War I. He had acquired his close understanding of the Arabs during his archaeological studies in the Middle East before the war. He considered that Arab interests were betrayed at the Paris Peace Conference in 1919, and renounced any part in it. Instead of retiring to the world of university scholarship, which had seemed to be his natural vocation, he joined the Royal Air Force in 1922 as a mechanic. In 1927 he changed his name to Shaw. In 1935 he was killed in a motorcycling accident. Since his death, Lawrence's personality has become a legend: he belongs to the class of poetic men of action who include such figures as Sidney*, Raleigh*, and Byron*.

Bib: Aldington, R., *Lawrence of Arabia*; Lawrence, A. W., (ed) *Lawrence by his Friends*.

Lay

A lyrical or narrative poem, such as was recited or sung to music by medieval minstrels. In 19th C, when the Middle Ages became a cult, a number of poets wrote romantic poems described as 'lays', *eg The Lay of the Last Minstrel* by Scott*, and *Lays of Ancient Rome* by Macaulay*. A lay resembles a ballad but is less simplified in its form and diction.

Lear

* *King Lear*.

Lear, Edward (1812–88)

Comic poet. He wrote *The Book of Nonsense* (1846) and *Nonsense Songs, Stories, and Botany* (1870) for the grandchildren of the Earl of Derby. Like Lewis Carroll*, who wrote the *Alice* books for children, Lear's poems for children show remarkable freedom of fantasy; in consequence, 20th C, with its new science of psycho-analysis, has seen in them unsuspected depths of interest. The poems in any case show great skill, and manage to combine grotesque comedy with haunting melancholy. He did much to popularize the limerick*. He illustrated the poems himself with extremely witty line drawings. Lear was by profession a landscape painter, but his elaborate landscape paintings have much less distinction than his drawings and sketches.

* *Nonsense Literature.*

Bib: Davidson, A., *Life*; Noakes, V., *Life*; Sewell, E., *The Field of Nonsense.*

Leavis, Frank Raymond (b 1895) /'li:vis/
Critic. From 1932 till 1953 he edited *Scrutiny**, a literary review with exceptionally high critical standards, and pervaded by his personality. It maintained that the values of a society in all its activities derive from its culture, and that central to British culture is English literature; that a literature can only be sustained by discriminating readers, and therefore by a body of highly trained critics working together, especially in the collaborative circumstances of a university (*Education and the University*, 1943). The need for the testing of judgements by collaborative discussion is important in Leavis's view of criticism, and it was a large part of the excellence of *Scrutiny* that it partly realized this ideal. Unfortunately, collaboration may become uncritical discipleship, and this was one of the two unfortunate consequences of the exceptional force of Leavis's personality. The other unfortunate consequence was the hostility which this force of personality aroused in many critics who were not among his collaborators and followers. He maintained that true critical discernment can only be achieved by a total response of the mind – intellectual, imaginative, and moral; thus a critical judgement reflects not only the work of literature being judged, but the worth of the personality that makes the judgement, so that Leavis's censure of critics with whom he strongly disagreed was sometimes extraordinarily vehement, as in his *Two Cultures?: The Significance of C. P. Snow* (1962). However this vehemence was a price paid for his determination to sustain a living tradition of literature not only by assessing contemporary writers with the utmost rigour, but by reassessing fearlessly the writers of the past, distinguishing those with a vital relevance for the modern sensibility from those that stand as mere monuments in academic museums. Such rigorousness caused him to be widely regarded as a destructive critic; his attack on the three-centuries-long prestige of Milton* (*Revaluation* 1936 and *The Common Pursuit* 1952) gave particular offence. But a fair reading of Leavis's work shows that he repeatedly risked his reputation by positive assessments of neglected writers, as in his early essays on D. H. Lawrence* (later reinforced by *D. H. Lawrence: Novelist*, 1955) and E. M. Forster*, and his remarks on Hopkins*, Empson* and Bottrall in *New Bearings in English Poetry*, 1932.

Leavis and his collaborators in *Scrutiny** considered that the living tradition of British culture is very seriously menaced by huge forces for degradation and inertia, partly by the insufficiently guided spread of commercialism and mass communications, and still more by the failure of universities and cultural élites to sustain the tradition. They were particularly hostile to 'coteries' which claim to be élites, but tend to be merely fashionable or exclusive, such as the Bloomsbury Group* of the 1920s and distinguished writers associated with it, *eg* T. S. Eliot* in his later criticism. (The relationship between Leavis, *Scrutiny*, and the Bloomsbury tradition, is an important theme of modern literary history that remains to be written.) This sense of cultural crisis caused Leavis and his colleagues to emphasize the importance of English in education; their influence in education to the present day has been very great in both Britain and America, and from the primary school to the university level.

Leavis's intense concern with the relationship between the kind of sensibility nourished by a literary culture and the quality of a society as a whole has a historical background that extends to the beginning of 19th C. It first appears in Wordsworth's *Preface* to the *Lyrical Ballads** (1800), is to be felt in the writings of the 19th-C philosopher John Stuart Mill* (see *Mill on Bentham and Coleridge*, ed. by Leavis, 1950), and is explicit in Matthew Arnold's* writings, especially *Culture and Anarchy* (1869). Later the theme is taken up by the novelists, *eg* in Gissing's *New Grub Street** and, both in his novels and in his criticism, D. H. Lawrence*. The outstanding importance of novels in connection with the theme has caused Leavis to be pre-eminently a critic of the novel; perhaps his most important single book is *The Great Tradition: George Eliot, Henry James, Joseph Conrad* (1948), but this should be read in conjunction with his books on Lawrence and (with Q. D. Leavis) on *Dickens the Novelist* (1971).

* 7.5.

Leech-Gatherer, The
Popular name of a poem (*Resolution and Independence*) in 20 6-line stanzas by William Wordsworth*; composed 1802, published 1807, and subsequently revised. The title refers to an old man whom the poet encounters in the poem. A leech is a blood-sucking worm that inhabits ponds; in Wordsworth's day, leeches were in demand for medical use.

The subject of the poem is the vulnerability of the poetic character, and the stability that belongs to an opposed kind of character. The state of mind of Wordsworth at the beginning of the poem reflects his feelings a few weeks before his marriage. From an exalted delight in his surroundings, he falls into sudden deep despondency; the spontaneity of the poetic nature goes with a heedlessness of worldly needs, and he remembers the tragic ends of recent poets, Chatterton* and Burns*. In this depression he encounters the old leech-gatherer, deformed by age and hardship, but standing with rock-like stillness as he scrutinizes a moorland pond for leeches. The leech-gatherer's grotesqueness, loneliness and stillness at first impress the poet as inhuman, but when the old man speaks, his dignity, simplicity and indefatigable endurance begin to counteract the volatility of the poet's own mind, and the wave of despair that has overwhelmed it. Wordsworth had relied for the resources of his own spirit upon nature – see his poem *Tintern Abbey** – and at the beginning of *The Leech-Gatherer*, nature seems to have betrayed him, but the leech-gatherer's moral strength affects him as itself a natural force. The poem is commonly considered to be an answer to Coleridge's *Dejection**.

Legend of Good Women, The

A poem by Geoffrey Chaucer*, written after *Troilus and Criseyde** and before *The Canterbury Tales**. The Prologue (of which there are two versions) takes the form of a dreamed vision, a form very often used in the Middle Ages and which recurs in Sackville's* *Induction* to *The Mirror for Magistrates**; other examples of it by Chaucer are the *Romaunt of the Rose* and *The Parliament of Fowls**. The poet dreams that he meets the god of love walking with a lady. The god rebukes him for only writing about false women (in the *Romaunt* and *Troilus and Criseyde*), but the lady is prepared to pardon him on condition that he makes amends by writing in praise of women. Consequently, when he wakes, the poet sets about writing the stories (derived directly or indirectly from Ovid*) of nine good women: Cleopatra, Thisbe, Dido, Hypsipyle and Medea, Lucrece, Ariadne, Philomela, Phyllis and Hypermnestra. These are 'good' inasmuch as they are faithful in love. The poem is Chaucer's first use of the heroic couplet*, which was to be his principal verse medium in *The Canterbury Tales*.

Leicester, Robert Dudley, Earl of (?1531–88)

One of the principal favourites of Elizabeth I* and for some time expected to become her husband. He was also the uncle of Sir Philip Sidney*, killed at Zutphen during Leicester's campaign to assist the Netherlands in their resistance to Spain. Leicester had the brilliance which Elizabeth liked in her personal favourites, although for her statesmen she preferred more sober types such as Cecil and Walsingham. Scandalous stories were rumoured about his relationships with women, and in particular about his early marriage with Amy Robsart, but Scott's treatment of this in his novel *Kenilworth** is fiction.

Lemnos /ˈlemnos/

One of the largest islands off the coast of Greece in the Aegean Sea. In Greek myth, Hephaestus*, the artificer of the gods, was hurled down upon it by Zeus, from Mount Olympus. In the legend of the Argonauts*, it was said to be peopled by women who had slain their husbands. Their queen was Hypsipyle*.

Lemures /ˈlemjuriːz/

In Roman myth, the spirits of the wicked dead who were supposed to haunt the living. The Roman festival of Lemuralia was supposed to placate them.

Lent

The period of 40 days' fasting before Easter, which commemorates the Crucifixion and Resurrection of Christ.

Leprechaun /ˈleprəkoːn/

In Irish folklore, a shoemaker to the fairies, and one who knows the secrets of hidden treasure.

Lesbos /ˈlezbos/

An island off the coast of Greece, famous in 7th–6th C BC for its school of poets, the chief of whom was the woman poet Sappho*.

Lessing, Doris (b 1919)

Novelist. Brought up in (Southern) Rhodesia; came to England in 1949. Her first novel was *The Grass is Singing* (1949). Her novel sequence *Children of Violence* came out as follows: *Martha Quest* (1952); *A Proper Marriage* (1954), *A Ripple from the Storm* (1958), *Landlocked* (1965), *The Fourgated City* (1969). She has also written stories (*The Habit of Loving*, 1957, *African Stories*, 1964, and *A Man and Two Women*, 1963) and plays, *Each His Own Wilderness* (1959) and *Play with a Tiger*. Her novel *The Golden Notebook* (1962) is probably the richest and most original work of fiction to have appeared in Britain since 1945. *Going Home* (1959) is a study of (Southern) Rhodesia, and *In Pursuit of the English* (1960) a study of contemporary England. Her most recent novel is *Briefing for a Descent into Hell* (1971).

Lesson of the Master, The (1892)

A story by Henry James*. Its theme is the barrier set up against the true artist by supposedly cultivated society, which can understand nothing about the artist's dedication, and can therefore only hinder him by its unintelligent praise based on false standards.

Lethe /ˈliːθi/

In Greek myth, one of the rivers of the underworld; the spirits of the dead drank from it, and forgot their lives on earth. The word means 'oblivion'.

Leto /ˈliːtəu/

A Titaness (Latin: Latona) beloved by Zeus*. Pregnant by him, and pursued by the jealousy of his wife Hera*, she wandered about until she gave birth to Apollo* and Artemis* on the island of Delos.

Letter-writing

This is clearly an important branch of literature even when the interest of the letters is essentially historical (*eg* the Paston Letters*) or biographical. Letters may also be, by intention or by consequence of genius, works of intrinsic literary value. 18th C (the age of the epistolary novel) was more than any other the period when letter-writing was cultivated as an art: see, above all, the letters of Horace

Walpole*, and those to his son by Lord Chesterfield* – the former a record of events, and the latter consisting of moral reflections. Earlier than 18th C, postal services were not sufficiently organized to encourage regular letter-writing, and the art of familiar prose was inadequately cultivated; by mid-19th-C, communications had improved enough to make frequent and full letter-writing redundant. By then letters had intrinsic literary interest chiefly by virtue of the writers' talent for literary expression in other modes of writing, added to the accident that they found letters a congenial means of communication. The letters of the poet G. M. Hopkins* and the novelist D. H. Lawrence* are examples. In the first 30 years of 19th C the romantic habit of introspection resulted in a quantity of extremely good letters: those of Keats* are outstanding; those of Byron*, Coleridge*, and of Lamb* of great interest.

Lever, Charles James (1806–72)

Irish novelist. Famous in 19th C for his vigorous comic novels about Irish country life and life in the army, *eg Harry Lorrequer* (1837), *Charles O'Malley* (1841), *Tom Burke of Ours* (1843). He was criticized for perpetuating the Englishman's comic notion of the Irish character—the 'stage Irishman' caricature, but Thackeray*, who was a friend of Lever and parodied him in *Novels by Eminent Hands*, declared (in *A Box of Novels*) that Lever was true to Irish nature in being superficially humorous but sad at heart.

Leviathan

In the Bible, the name of a vast marine animal of varying character; in *Job* 41:15 it seems to be the crocodile, in *Isaiah* 27:1 a sea-serpent, in the *Psalms* 104:26 a dragon. Elsewhere than in the Bible, it is often used for the whale.

Leviathan (1651)

A work on political philosophy by Thomas Hobbes*. Its full title was *The Leviathan, or the Matter, Form, and Power of a Commonwealth Ecclesiastical and Civil.* By 'commonwealth' he meant the state, and by 'leviathan'* the sovereign (governing) power. He argues that left to itself in a state of nature, humanity is not co-operative but competitive, and lives (or would live) in an unending state of war. This is contrary to the traditional view derived from the Greek philosopher Aristotle*, who had considered that man was naturally a social being. Hobbes thought that on the contrary society is unnatural, and a contrivance to which men are compelled to resort in order to escape the intolerable conditions of the state of nature. Having contracted to form a society and thereby keep the peace among themselves, men have to choose a government, either of a single person such as a king, or of a body of people such as the English parliament. Whatever is chosen, the government's authority must not be divided; the king cannot share power with a parliament, or civil war will result, as had happened in England in Hobbes's own lifetime. Nor can any supreme power rest with a Church, which must also be subjected to this man-created monster, Leviathan, the sovereign power. Such a government must not be responsible to the people its subjects, though it is to be responsible to God. On the other hand, there is nothing sacred about Leviathan, which will be forcibly removed by society when it ceases to be able to protect it, or when it no longer chooses to do so.

The fearless realism of the argument and the clarity and vigour of the prose made *Leviathan* an epoch-making work in the development of English rationalism, though later writers (such as Locke* and Hume*) considered that Hobbes was too pessimistic in his conception of human nature, and too uncompromising in his belief in the totality of power with which he held that an efficient government should be entrusted.

* *Hobbes.*

Lewes, George Henry (1817-78)

Philosopher and critic. He wrote on a wide variety of subjects, but his most remembered work is his *Life of Goethe* (1855). Other works include *The Biographical History of Philosophy* (1845–6), studies in biology such as *Studies in Animal Life* (1862), two novels—*Ranthrope* (1847) and *Rose, Blanche and Violet* (1848), critical essays on the novel and the theatre, and, his most important philosophical book, *Problems of Life and Mind* (1873–8). He collaborated with Thornton Leigh Hunt in founding the *Leader* and was first editor of the *Fortnightly Review* 1865–6. In 1854 he left his wife, who had had three sons by Hunt, and lived with Mary Ann Evans (George Eliot*) until his death.

Bib: Kitchell, A. T., *George Lewes and George Eliot.*

Lewis, Cecil Day (b 1904)

Poet and critic. Day Lewis was one of the small group of poets (with Auden* and Spender*) which made a considerable impact in the 1930s under the poetic influence of T. S. Eliot* and the political influence of Marx*. In some near-propagandist poetry of that time, especially on the Republican side in the Spanish Civil War, he used with effect the sprung rhythm* and alliteration* of Gerard Manley Hopkins*. World War II broke up the group and tempered Day Lewis's political aims. His later work shows the versatility which caused him to be chosen as Poet Laureate* in 1968. Most recent *Collected Poems* 1953. Since then: *Pegasus* (1957); *The Buried Day* (1960); *The Gate* (1962). Critical essays: *A Hope for Poetry* (1936) and *The Poetic Image* (1946). Also detective fiction* under the pen-name Nicholas Blake.

Lewis, Clive Staples (1898–1963)

Literary critic and fabulist. As a critic he was chiefly distinguished for his work on the Renaissance* and the period leading up to it, especially *The Allegory of Love* (1936), subtitled 'A Study of Medieval Tradition' and concluding with an examination of Spenser's *The Faerie Queene**. He defended Milton* against contemporary critical attacks in *A Preface to Paradise Lost*. Other critical works: *Rehabilitations* (1939); *English Literature in the 16th Century*, excluding drama, (1954 – vol III of the *Oxford History of English Literature*); *Studies in Words* (1960); *An Experiment in Criticism* (1961); *The Discarded Image* (1964). His criticism was strongly influenced by his deep religious feelings, and he describes his conversion in his autobiography *Surprised by Joy* (1955). His religion also inspired a number of fables for adults: *The Pilgrim's Regress* (1933); the science fiction* trilogy *Out of the Silent Planet* (1938), *Perelandra* (1943), *That Hideous Strength* (1945); *The Screwtape Letters* (1942); and his books for children which include *The Lion, The Witch and the Wardrobe*, *Prince Caspian*, *The Voyage of the Dawn Treader*, *The Silver Chair*, and *The Horse and his Boy*. In all his fables and children's stories he was strongly influenced by the 19th-C novelist and writer for children George MacDonald.

* *Children's Books.*

Lewis, Percy Wyndham (1884–1957)

Painter, novelist, critic and polemical journalist. Before 1914 he was leader of the Vorticist movement in painting, which demanded clear analysis of pictorial forms rather in the manner of the French Cubist movement. This clarity of the eye he carried over into advocacy of clarity of mind when he took to literature. He took a boldly independent attitude to modern culture, rather like that of the poet Ezra Pound* with whom he edited the review *Blast* (1914–15), and asserted the right and the power of the intellect to take command in the cultural crisis. He was opposed to domination by political ideology (though he wrote favourably of Hitler in 1931), by psychological cults and by the bureaucratic and welfare state; he made it his principal aim to expose the confusion of mind which he considered to be overwhelming 20th-C man, and the hollowness of humanity which he believed to be the consequence of encroaching mechanization. He had something in common with his friend T. S. Eliot* (of *The Waste Land**) but never became a Christian; with D. H. Lawrence* (of *St Mawr*) whose mysticism he nevertheless despised; with James Joyce*, though he was strongly opposed to his subjective 'stream of consciousness'* technique; with Leavis* and the other *Scrutiny** critics, who, however, rejected him as brutally negative. He prided himself on his very distinctive style of expression, which is energetic and concentrates on presenting the externals of human nature with pitiless clarity.

His outstanding writings are probably his novels and stories: *Tarr* (1918); *The Wild Body* (stories, 1927); *The Apes of God* (1930 – a satire); *Snooty Baronet* (1932); *The Revenge for Love* (1937 – considered by some critics to be his best novel); *The Vulgar Streak* (1941); *Rotting Hill* (1951 – stories); *Self Condemned* (1954); and the four-part fable *The Human Age – The Childermass* (1928), *Monstre Gai* (1955), *Malign Fiesta* (1955) to have been completed by *The Trial of Man* which he did not live to finish.

His ideas are expounded in his philosophical work *Time and Western Man* (1927) and his autobiographies *Blasting and Bombardiering* (1937) and *Rude Assignment* (1950). He wrote notable literary criticism in *The Lion and the Fox: the Role of Hero in the Plays of Shakespeare* (1927), *Men without Art* (1934) and *The Writer and the Absolute* (1952).

Bib: Grigson, G., *A Study of Wyndham Lewis*; Handley-Read, C., *The Art of Wyndham Lewis*; Tomlin, E. W. F., *Wyndham Lewis* (British Council Pamphlet); Kenner, H., *Wyndham Lewis*; Wagner, G., *Portrait of the Artist as Enemy*.

Liberal Party

The name of the third and smallest of the three main political parties at present occupying seats in Parliament*, the other two being the much larger Labour and Conservative parties.

The Liberals are the successors of the former Whig* Party; the change of name came about gradually after 1830 owing to a change in the composition of the party's supporters. In its political sense, the word 'Liberal' was an importation from Spain and France. After the end of the Napoleonic Wars (1815) it was first applied to what were considered to be extreme or even revolutionary reformers. Byron* and Leigh Hunt*, both famous for the boldness of their politics, collaborated to found the short-lived *Liberal* magazine in 1822. In the meantime, the Philosophical Radicals, led by Bentham* and the Mills*, were collaborating with the Whigs to secure the passing of the first Parliamentary Reform Bill*, which was to extend the right to vote to a larger proportion of the population. When this Bill was passed into law (1832) the Whigs, who had formerly consisted preponderantly of landed aristocracy, found themselves supported by the newly enfranchised industrial middle class, and it became increasingly

clear that a new name had to be adopted to cover the former Whigs, the Radicals, and the industrialists. By the end of the 1830s the Whigs were increasingly calling themselves Liberals, and it became the accepted name for the party by the 1860s. Until 1923 the Liberals and the Conservatives were the principal political parties in Britain. The differences between them changed from decade to decade, but the Liberals were always more representative of town and industrial interests, and more inclined to strive for reform, whereas the Conservatives stood more for the countryside and sought stability. The disastrous decline of Liberal strength since 1923 has been due to a realignment of social interests (upper classes, now preponderantly Conservative, as against the working classes) and the consequent rise of the Labour Party.
I.5.I.5.

Liberty, On (1859)
A political essay by John Stuart Mill*. Mill discusses how far and in what ways the state is entitled to interfere with the liberty of individuals. He concludes that in general this interference should be restricted to the protection of other individuals, and of individuals collectively considered as society. Mill was mainly alarmed lest a new tyranny should arise from democratic majorities who might be indifferent to minority rights.

Licensing Act
* *Theatres.*

Lichas /ˈlaikəs/
The servant of Heracles*. When Heracles put on the poisoned shirt of Nessus, in the agony of the poison he hurled Lichas into the sea where he was changed into a rock.

Lilliput /ˈlilipʌt/
The island in Part I of Swift's *Gulliver's Travels**; the Lilliputians are diminutive in body, and their corresponding pettiness of mind is intended as satirical comment on the pettiness of contemporary English politics and society.

Lily, William (1468?–1522)
Scholar; a pioneer of Greek studies, and part-author with Colet of a famous textbook on Latin; it was still in use in 19th C.

Limbo
In medieval tradition, a region on the borders of Hell, supposed to be inhabited by the unbaptized: the souls of those who died before the coming of Christ, and infants who died too soon for baptism.

Limehouse
A district in the east end of London; in 19th and earlier 20th C it was poor and known for its population of immigrant labourers, especially Chinese.

Limerick
A kind of comic verse epigram* which hardly ever varies from the following form:

There was a faith-healer of Deal
Who said, 'Although pain isn't real,
If I sit on a pin
And it punctures my skin
I dislike what I fancy I feel!'

The form was popularized by the comic poet Edward Lear*, though he was not its inventor. Whatever the derivation of its name, it seems to have no traceable connection with the town and county of Limerick in Ireland.

Linacre, Thomas (1460?–1524) /ˈlinəkə/
Physician, and a pioneer in Greek and Latin scholarship. He was chiefly responsible for founding the College of Physicians in 1518, and translated into excellent Latin some of the works of the Greek physician Galen*. He is, however, less famous for his literary work than for the nobility of his character and for his zeal in promoting the study of medicine at Oxford and Cambridge.

Lincoln's Inn
* *Inns of Court.*

Lindsay (Lyndsay), Sir David (1490–1555)
Scottish poet. He was above all a satirist who rebuked social abuses in an accepted medieval tradition, but his standpoint was increasingly Protestant*; he is thus a transitional writer between the Middle Ages and the Reformation*. His best-known work is his *Satire of the Three Estates* (1540) which characteristically combines the form of medieval 'morality' drama with secular qualities belonging to a Renaissance* outlook. Other works: *The Dream* (1528); *The Complaint* (1529); *The Testament of the Papingo* (1530); *William Meldrum* (1550); and – his most ambitious work – *The Monarchy* (1552). Lindsay was the last of the line of fine 15th- and 16th-C Scottish poets.
* *Scottish Literature.*
Bib: Speirs, J., *The Scots Literary Tradition.*

Lion, The British
The national emblem, perhaps from its representation on the coats of arms of medieval kings. The first literary mention of the British Lion is in Dryden's poem *The Hind and the Panther**.

Litotes /ˈlaitəuti:z/
* *Figures of Speech.*

Little Dorrit (1855–57)
A novel by Charles Dickens. It centres on the theme of imprisonment, both literal and symbolic. William Dorrit (with his children and his brother Frederick) has been so long in the Marshalsea* Prison for debtors that he is known as 'the Father of the Marshalsea' – a title that gives him a spurious social prestige. Arthur Clennam, who befriends him in the belief that the Dorrit family have been victimized by the commercial interests of his own family, is eventually confined in the same prison. But outside, the characters inhabit prisons without visible walls: William Dorrit inherits a fortune, and he and his family are constricted by social ambition under the gaolership of Mrs General who instructs

them in fashionable ways; Mrs Clennam, Arthur's supposed mother, inhabits a gloomy house, confined to her chair and her bad conscience, under the gaolership of her servant Flintwinch who knows her guilty secrets; Merdle, the financier of reputedly enormous wealth, is the prisoner of his false position, and his gaolers are his fashionable wife and his arrogant butler; the servant girl, Tattycoram, is at first the prisoner of the well-intentioned but misguided Mr and Mrs Meagles, and then escapes to the worse prison of Miss Wade, herself a prisoner of her self-inflicted loneliness and perversion. The nation is under the imprisoning control of a government department, the Circumlocution Office, which exists to gratify the interests of the enormous Barnacle family. Three characters stand out in independence of this conspiracy to confine and frustrate: Frederick Dorrit, who lives out an existence of passive misery by refusing to share (in or out of the Marshalsea) the self-deceptions of his brother William; Amy ('Little Dorrit') who consistently follows the compassion of her affections and the duties this imposes on her; and Daniel Doyce, the engineer whose enterprise is baffled by the Circumlocution Office but who perseveres in his vocation in humble and disinterested reverence for the demands that it makes on him. The self-interested Circumlocution Office at the top of society is balanced by the inhabitants of Bleeding Heart Yard, people who are themselves prisoners of the exorbitant property owner, Casby, but who live in the freedom of their own equal and open-hearted society. The blackmailer Rigaud is a figure of menacing evil and a dramatic counterpart to Mrs Clennam's hypocrisy and pretence, which is at the heart of the imaginative scheme of the novel. *Little Dorrit* is often regarded as Dickens's greatest work, both in dramatic impressiveness and in psychological richness of insight.

Little Gidding

A small religious community founded by the Anglican theologian Nicholas Ferrar (1592–1637) at a manor house in Huntingdonshire in 1625. It was dispersed, and the buildings were destroyed, by Parliamentary soldiers at the end of the Civil War* (1646). King Charles I* visited the community in 1633, and according to tradition he came again after his final defeat at the battle of Naseby (1645). The community is the starting point of one of T. S. Eliot's* finest poems which takes its title from it (in *Four Quartets**), and an account of it comes into the remarkable historical novel *John Inglesant* (1881) by J. H. Shorthouse.

Little John

In the Robin Hood* cycle of legends, the principal lieutenant of the popular outlaw, Robin Hood. Originally John Little, his names were reversed ironically owing to his great size and strength.

Lives of the Poets, The (1779–81)

A collection of critical and biographical essays by Samuel Johnson*. He was originally invited by a group of London booksellers to undertake prefatory notes for a projected edition of English poets from Chaucer* onwards. The project was truncated so as to exclude poets before Abraham Cowley*, and Johnson's commentaries were so ample that in the event they were published without the poems. The booksellers chose 48 of the poets discussed, and Johnson added another 4 – Blackmore, Pomfret, Yalden and Watts. The choice is illustrative of the scope and limitations of 18th-C taste, and of Johnson's own. It is true that he dismisses many of the poets with terse contempt, but, apart from Chaucer and Spenser* who may have been omitted because they preceded Cowley, Johnson did not recommend the addition of outstanding figures such as Herrick* and Marvell*, who were Cowley's contemporaries. The reason no doubt is that Cowley's style of wit made him a more convenient starting-point for a study in the phase of poetry with which Johnson and his public felt most at home. Johnson's great achievement was that, in spite of these obvious limitations, he nonetheless wrote a great critical classic which is a monument to Augustan* taste at its best. Several of the essays are also classics of brief biography, notably the life of Savage, first published in 1744.

Each essay begins with the facts of the poet's life and a portrait of his character, and concludes with a critical estimate of his work. The best essays are those on the greatest poets – Milton*, Dryden*, and Pope* – but even the shortest essays on the trivial poets are forceful and witty. Together with the Preface to his edition of Shakespeare, *The Lives of the Poets* is Johnson's critical masterpiece.

*** 7.2.**

Livy (Titus Livius) (59 BC–AD 17) /'livi/

Roman historian. He wrote the history of Rome in 142 books, 35 of which have survived, with summaries of most of the rest. His aims were partly to ensure that the achievements of 'the chiefest people of the world' should be remembered, and partly to provide material for future political guidance. He has been a principal writer for study in the classical education* provided by English schools since 16th C.

* *Latin Literature.*

Lloyd's

An association of shipowners and other business men concerned with shipping. Its activities are primarily the insurance of ships and cargoes, and the dissemination of shipping information. It arose from a coffee-house* kept by an Edward Lloyd in London early in 18th C; this was frequented by merchants and insurers of ships who eventually formed their own association. It still has its main offices in London.

Locke, John (1632–1704)

Philosopher. He follows Thomas Hobbes* in his sceptical rationalism*, but he is the direct opposite of Hobbes in his optimistic view of human nature and in the moderation and flexibility of his social and political ideas. Hobbes was born in the year of the attempted invasion by the Armada* and was painfully aware of the human propensity to violence from the decade of civil wars* (1642–52); Locke's sympathies were identified with the moderation of the bloodless Revolution of 1688* and the climate of reasonableness which followed it.

In his two *Treatises of Government* (1690), Locke, like Hobbes, presupposes a state of nature preceding a social contract which was the basis of political society. But whereas Hobbes saw the state of nature as a state of war, Locke saw it as a peaceful condition in which the Law of Nature and of Reason was spontaneously observed; his idea of the social contract was not, as for Hobbes, that human existence was intolerable without it, but that it merely provided additional assurance that life and property would be respected. For Hobbes sovereignty had to be single and absolute, but for Locke it was merely a public service always responsible to society which may at any time remove it. Similarly, in his *Letters concerning Toleration* (1689, 1690, 1692, and a fourth published posthumously) Locke, unlike Hobbes, held that the state has no right to interfere in religious matters, and that it was oppression of religion by governments which caused religion to be a source of civil violence.

Locke's advocacy of religious toleration was consistent with his sceptical attitude to faith and knowledge. Man must first discover what he can know before he persecutes others for publishing false beliefs, and this inquiry he conducts in his *Essay concerning Human Understanding** (1690). This shows man's capacity for knowledge to be distinctly limited, but the existence of God turns out to be a necessary hypothesis discoverable by reason. Christianity therefore is inherently reasonable (*Reasonableness of Christianity*, 1695), and faith by revelation is indispensable only because the use of reason is unavailable to the majority of mankind; 'nothing that is contrary to . . . reason has a right to be urged or assented to as a matter of faith' (*Human Understanding*, Bk. IV).

In his *Thoughts on Education* Locke extols reason at the expense of imagination, and therefore (by implication) of the imaginative arts. When he applies his philosophy to politics or education, Locke is always guided by standards of practical utility, and in his abstract speculation he refrains from carrying his reasoning so far (as Hume* was to seem to do) that the logical basis for the conduct of practical life by the light of reason was undermined. His philosophy dominated 18th C, and is at the back of such 19th-C rationalist movements as Utilitarianism*.

3.3.1.

Bib: Cranston, M., *Life*; MacLean, K., *John Locke and English Literature in the Eighteenth Century*; Willey, B., *The Seventeenth Century Background*; *English Moralists*; James, D. G., *The Life of Reason: Hobbes, Locke, Bolingbroke.*

Lodge, Thomas (1558?–1625)

Poet and man of letters. He was one of the group now known as the University Wits*, university scholars who used their learning to make a career as professional writers for the expanding reading public of late 16th C. In many ways his career is representative of this new kind of Elizabethan* professional writer.

He was the son of Sir Thomas Lodge, a Lord Mayor of London, and was educated at Merchant Taylors School and Trinity College, Oxford. He then became a student of law at Lincoln's Inn, London, in 1578. The law students of the Inns of Court* in the reign of Elizabeth were a leading element of the literary public, and others besides Lodge found these law colleges a nursery for literary rather than legal talent. During the next twenty years he practised all the kinds of writing which were popular at the time. His first work (1580) was a pamphlet* entitled *A Defence of Plays*, written in answer to Stephen Gosson's attack on theatrical literature, *School of Abuse* (1580). Besides other pamphlets, he wrote prose romances interspersed with lyrics (*eg Rosalynde, Euphues Golden Legacy**, 1590, and *A Marguerite of America*, 1596), verse romances (*eg Scilla's Metamorphosis*, 1589, reissued as *Glaucus and Scilla*, 1610), a sonnet sequence (*Phillis*, 1593), and a collection of epistles and satires in imitation of the Roman poet Horace*, *A Fig for Momus* (1595). He also wrote plays, or at least collaborated with playwrights, *eg* a chronicle play *The Wounds of Civil War* (printed 1594), and, probably with Greene*, *A Looking Glass for London and England* (1594). Besides this writing activity, he joined two piratical expeditions against Spain, the first to the Canary Isles in 1588, and the second to Brazil in 1591. It was on the first that he wrote his most famous work, *Rosalynde*, later used by Shakespeare as the story for *As You Like It**, and on the second that he wrote *A Marguerite of America*. After 1596, when he published the penitential and satirical pamphlets (*Wit's Misery* and *World's Madness*), he became converted to Roman Catholicism and took to the study of medicine, receiving the degree of

M.D. from Oxford University in 1603. His literary works during the remainder of his life were serious and chiefly translations, (*eg* of Josephus (1602) and Seneca* (1614)), and religious and medical treatises.

Lodge's literary reputation rests chiefly on his romances *Rosalynde* and *A Marguerite of America*, which are among the best examples of the Elizabethan romance.

* 5.1.2.4.

Bib: Gosse, E. (ed.), *Complete Works of Lodge*; Gosse, E., in *Seventeenth-century Studies*; Sisson, C. J., *Lodge and Other Elizabethans*; Paradise, N. B., *Thomas Lodge.*

Loki

In Scandinavian myth, one of the gods, though evil and mischievous. He is both friend and enemy of the other gods, and this twofold nature has led him to be associated with fire. He has been compared to the Greek god Hephaestus*, to the Titan Prometheus*, and to Lucifer*.

Lollards

14th-C followers of Wycliffe*.

Lombard Street

In the City of London; for centuries a centre for financial and commercial transactions. Its name derives from the settlement of Italian merchants from Lombardy (north Italy) in the Middle Ages. To bet 'All Lombard Street to a China orange' would show great confidence.

London

The capital of Great Britain and, in particular, the capital of England. The original core of London is called 'the City'; it is the financial capital of Britain, and now has only a small residential population. Its Lord Mayor is still a figure of great prestige, as a kind of symbolic representative of the financial and commercial interests of the country. From early 18th C, London expanded rapidly outwards from the City so as to absorb the surrounding villages which until 1965 retained their identity as districts within the administrative county of Greater London.

London has always had a great cultural dominance in England, partly because from 12th C its neighbourhood was the main centre of the royal court, and partly because of its great superiority in size and wealth over other English towns. In the Middle Ages the chief royal residences were the Palace of Westminster and the Tower (respectively to the west and east of the City); in 16th C, Hampton Court; in 17th C, Whitehall in Westminster and (at the end of 17th C) Kensington Palace; since the middle of 18th C, Buckingham Palace. Windsor Castle, a royal palace and stronghold since 14th C, is not far to the west of London. London's superiority in size can be shown by the fact that in 1700 it had a population of about 600,000, whereas the cities next to it in size, Norwich and Bristol, had only about 30,000 each. A century before, in the time of Shakespeare, London's estimated population was a quarter of a million, and it was already one of the largest towns in Europe.

Districts west of the City (the 'West End') such as Westminster, Kensington, Chelsea, have always tended to be rich and fashionable; those to the east (the 'East End') the poorer areas.

The neighbourhood of the royal court was not the only cause of London's importance as the literary centre of national life. The Inns of Court* – colleges of legal education originating in 13th C – were equivalent to a university in fostering intellectual life, especially from 15th to 17th C. In later 15th C, the proximity of lawyers, courtiers, politicians, merchants, and churchmen, at a time when every aspect of English society was in a critical phase of growth, gave London a peculiar vitality which expressed itself in the Elizabethan drama and in the building of the first theatres. London had virtually a monopoly of the drama until 18th C; it was not until then that other towns began to build their own theatres. In the same century, the importance of the court as a cultural centre markedly declined. Intellectuals and men of letters met in the coffee-houses* – equivalent to the cafés of 19th-C Paris – and in the town mansions of the aristocracy and richer merchants. By 19th C, the population of London had enormously enlarged, and in consequence artistic and intellectual activity tended to concentrate in certain districts of it. Thus the great British Museum Library made Bloomsbury (part of Holborn) a centre of scholarship, and London University (founded 1828) has its Senate House near by; Chelsea became a home of painters, and Fleet Street the headquarters of national journalism. See maps on next page.

London (1738)

A poem by Samuel Johnson* in heroic couplets*, written in imitation of the *Third Satire* by Juvenal*. In the spirit of Juvenal, Johnson satirizes (through the character of Thales) the degenerate sophistication, the social injustice, and the crime and licence of the so-called civilization of London. The style has Johnson's typical compression and force, and the satire is more impersonal than that of his chief predecessors, Dryden* and Pope* who followed the more relaxed and personal style of Horace*. Juvenal is not imitated slavishly but interpreted with discernment and used as a criterion for emulation.

* *Satire*

London Bridge

The famous bridge of this name, between the City and Southwark, was completed in 1209, and until 1750 it was the only bridge across the Thames at London. It was built of stone and had twenty piers; the narrow arches caused the river to flow through them in violent and dangerous currents. The bridge was 20 feet (6·1 m) wide with a 12 ft (3·7 m) roadway between houses and shops which projected over the water on each side. Over the widest, centre arch there was a chapel dedicated to St Thomas à Becket* of Canterbury. It was the approach to the City from the south and it bore two gates, on the northernmost of which the heads of traitors were exposed. The bridge was

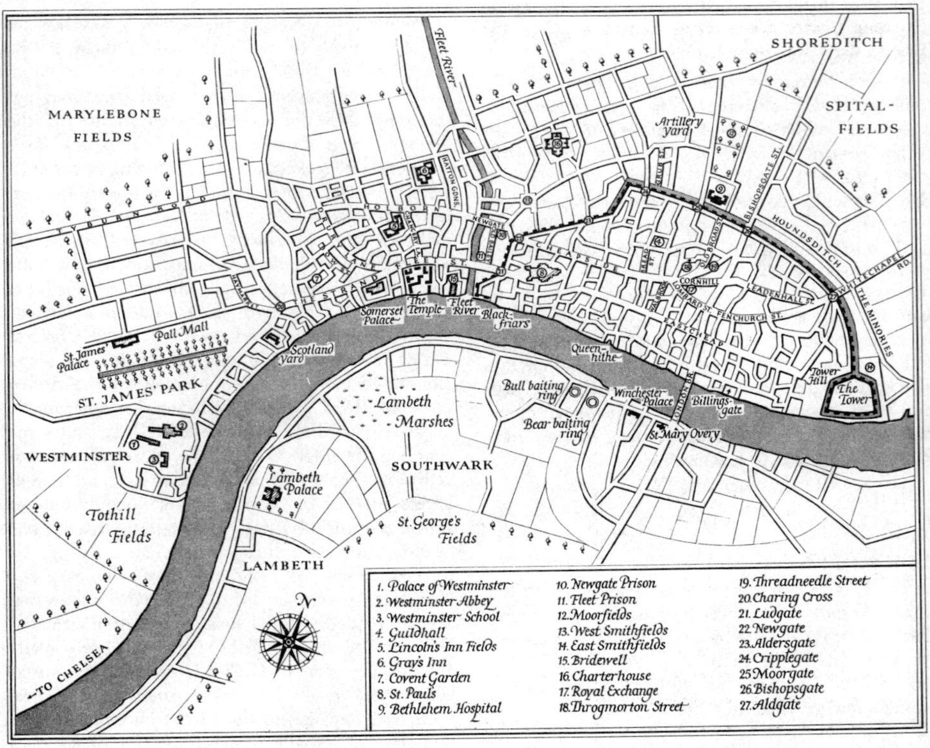

London: about 1660 (*above*); about 1860 (*below*).

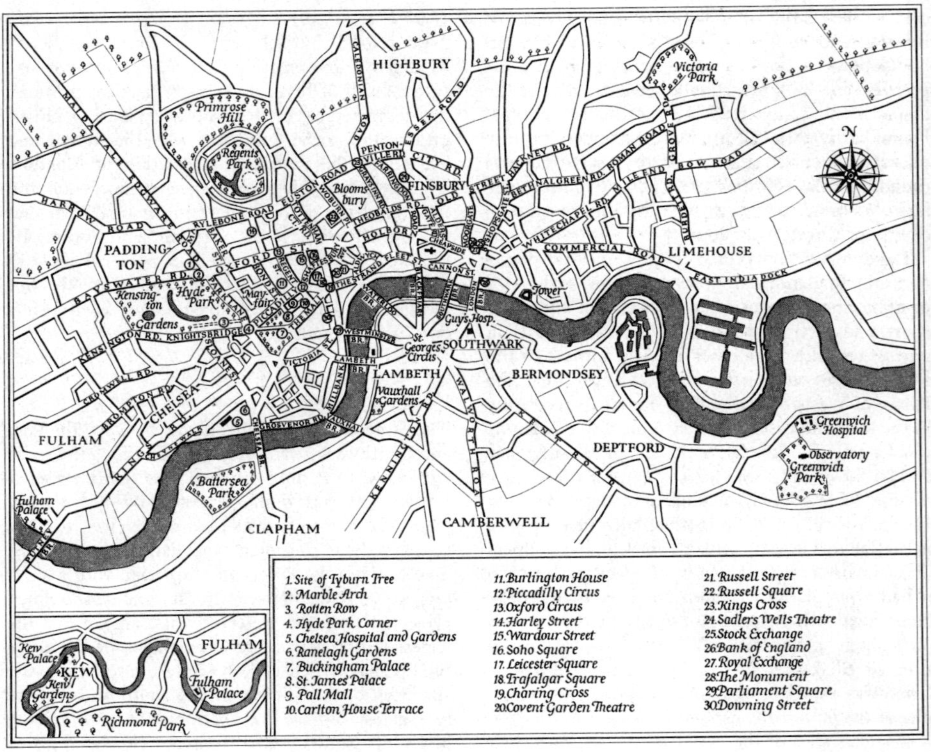

a great source of civic pride, but a great inconvenience to shipping. In the second half of 18th C two more bridges were built, and the houses on London Bridge were taken down; in 1831 the bridge itself was demolished and replaced.

London Magazine, The

Three periodicals of this name have existed: the first ran 1732–1785; the second, 1820–29; and the third, founded in 1954, still exists. The second is the most famous. It was founded as the political opponent of the right wing *Blackwood's Magazine**, and its first editor, John Scott, was killed in a duel in consequence of the rivalry. It had unusual literary distinction, with Lamb*, Hazlitt*, Hood* and De Quincey* on its staff; it published the first version of De Quincey's *Confessions of an English Opium-Eater**.

* *Reviews and Periodicals.*

Long Parliament, The

A parliament which was summoned by Charles I* in 1640 and continued until 1653, when it was dissolved by Oliver Cromwell*. It was this parliament that broke with the king and started the Civil War* in 1642. In 1648 those of its members who were disposed to come to terms with the king were expelled by Colonel Pride ('Pride's Purge'), and the remainder continued to sit under the nickname of 'the Rump'. After dissolving it, Cromwell called parliaments of his own, but after his death in 1658 it reassembled, and in 1660, the year of the Restoration* of the Monarchy, it dissolved itself to make way for a new parliament under the restored king, Charles II*. His government did not recognize the legality of Cromwell's parliaments, so that in law the Long Parliament was considered to have sat continuously from 1640 to 1660.

Longinus, Dionysius Cassius (1st C AD) /lonˈdʒainəs/

Greek critic. Most of his works have perished, but he is the reputed author of the extremely influential treatise *On the Sublime*. This is about literary style; 'the Sublime', though the traditional rendering of the Greek title, is usually regarded as misleading. The author is concerned with the qualities of expression that make for true impressiveness, relates them to greatness of mind in the writer, and discusses faults that arise from fallacious ideas of eloquence. The French critic, Boileau*, made a famous translation of the treatise in 1674, and through him it influenced 18th-C English ideas on style.

Lord's Cricket Ground

One of the principal centres for the English national game, situated near Regent's Park in London. It was founded at the end of 18th C by a certain Thomas Lord, and is the headquarters of the Marylebone Cricket Club, the most authoritative body for the regulation of the game.

* *Cricket.*

Lords, House of

Technically the Upper House of the two Houses of Parliament, the British legislature. It sits under the presidency of the Lord Chancellor*, who is minister for justice and the head of the judicial system. When he sits alone with seven specially appointed judges, the Lords of Appeal in Ordinary, the House of Lords constitutes the highest court of appeal in Britain.

The House of Lords is the direct descendant of the medieval Great Council, to which the king summoned his chief landholders (the nobles, or 'peers of the realm') and the leaders of the Church. The House still consists of hereditary peers in a majority, though a small number of life peers (created under the Life Peerages Act of 1958) have been added to the number of non-hereditary members, the Lords of Appeal and the Lords Spiritual (the two Archbishops and 24 other bishops of the Church of England*). In theory this makes the House of Lords a very large body with about 1,060 members; in fact only those peers who are politicians normally attend, so that in practice it is a smaller body than the House of Commons, and much less anachronistic than its composition makes it seem.

Until 1911 the legal power of the House of Lords was about equal to that of the House of Commons, though the latter had become politically the more important as early as 17th C. The Parliament Act of 1911 greatly reduced its powers, however, and it rarely shows opposition to the majority decisions of the Lower House. A Bill for the further reform of the House of Lords was dropped by the Labour government in 1968–69.

* *Parliament.*

Lorris, Guillaume de

* *Roman de la Rose.*

Lotos-Eaters, The /ˈləutəsi:təz/

A poem by Alfred Tennyson*, first published in the 1833 volume, which contains much of his most distinguished work. Its subject is the ancient Greek myth of the *lotophagi* ('lotus-eaters' – Tennyson used the Greek spelling, 'lotos') who occur in Homer's *Odyssey**. Those who visit the land where the lotus fruit grows and eat some of it lose all desire to return home. The theme of Tennyson's poem is the temptation to reject the world of activity, change, and stress, in favour of a trancelike existence measured only by the more languorous rhythms of nature. It is in the tradition of Spenser* and the more luxuriant Keats*: the rhythms have hypnotic music, and the imagery is strongly but lullingly sensuous. It opens in Spenserian stanzas*; the song of the lotus-eaters is in the free but complex style of an ancient Greek choric ode*.

Love for Love (1695)

A comedy by William Congreve*. The plot centres on an intrigue to frustrate an uncharitable father, Sir Sampson, who wishes to disinherit his extravagant elder son, Valentine, in favour of the younger brother, Ben, a hearty but ludicrous sailor. The intrigue is managed by Angelica, a rich and spirited girl in love with Valentine. A minor plot concerns

Sir Sampson's attempt to marry Ben off to an equally awkward country girl, Miss Prue, the daughter of a superstitious astrologer, Foresight. The rustic embarrassment of Ben and Prue, neither of whom wants to marry the other, nicely contrasts with the wit and grace of Valentine and Angelica. The play is one of the chief masterpieces of Restoration* comedy, especially by reason of its skilful and witty prose dialogue.

Love's Labour's Lost (1594–95)

A comedy by William Shakespeare*, published in a quarto edition in 1598. It is a play for court taste, recalling the comedies of John Lyly*; the plot is light and fantastic, and a pretext for dextrously witty dialogue and poetic flights of fancy. But the graceful artificiality is enriched by freshness that arises from elements of rural life, both in the imagery employed by the courtiers and in some of the characters. As in later comedies written by Shakespeare in the decade 1590–1600 (*A Midsummer Night's Dream**, *As You Like It**, *Twelfth Night**) the witty courtiers end by making fools of themselves in their own way, much as the clowns and simple-minded pedants do – predictably – in theirs.

The king of Navarre and three of his lords vow to shut themselves away from pleasure and ladies in order to devote themselves to study. They quickly find excuses to break the vow when the king is visited by the princess of France and three of her ladies on an embassy. A subplot concerns a group of ludicrous characters – the proud but seedy Spaniard, Don Armado; the pedantic schoolmaster Holofernes; Sir Nathaniel, the country clergyman, and Costard the rustic – who attempt to entertain the lords and ladies with a performance of the interlude* of 'the Nine Worthies'. The courting of the princess and her ladies by the king and his lords is abruptly ended by the announcement of the death of the princess's father. The play ends with the ladies imposing a year's ordeal on their suitors.

Some scholars have seen in the play a light satire on the School of Night*. Some of the characters are identified with living contemporaries, for instance Armado with Raleigh*, who is said to have been a member of the School.

Lovelace, Richard (1618–58) /ˈlʌvleis/

One of the Cavalier Poets*. He is known for his lyrics, which at their best combine the freshness and exuberance of his background as a country gentleman with the refinement and grace that characterized the court of Charles I*. His poetry is uneven in quality. He died a poor man having consumed his wealth in the cause of Charles I during the Civil War* of 1642–46. Parliament imprisoned him for his opposition in 1642, where he wrote one of his best known lyrics 'Stone walls do not a prison make'. He was again imprisoned in 1648 and during this time he prepared for publication his book *Lucasta: Epodes, Odes, Sonnets, Songs etc.* His remaining lyrics – *Lucasta: Posthume Poems* – were published after his death.

Bib: Hartman, C. H., *The Cavalier Spirit and its Influence on the Life and Work of Richard Lovelace.*

Lowry, Malcolm (1909–57) /ˈlauəri/

Novelist. He was educated in England, but spent most of his later life in Mexico, the United States, and British Columbia. His first novel, *Ultramarine*, was published in 1933. His reputation chiefly rests on his second and only other novel, *Under the Volcano* (1947). The central character, Geoffrey Firmin, is British Consul in a Mexican city situated under two volcanoes, just as in ancient times the Underworld, Tartarus, was supposed to be situated beneath the Sicilian volcano, Etna. Firmin is a dipsomaniac who has rejected the love of his wife and his friends and taken to alcohol as escape from the inhumanity of the modern world (the events take place in 1938). The novel is elaborately symbolical, and shows the influence of Joseph Conrad* and James Joyce*. It has been described as the most distinguished work of fiction produced by an English novelist since 1945.

Loyola, Ignatius

* *Jesuits.*

Lucan (Marcus Annaeus Lucanus) (AD 39–65) /ˈluːkn/

A Roman poet; author of the poem *Pharsalia* about the struggle for power between Julius Caesar* and Pompey*. Christopher Marlowe* translated the first book (1600). The translation by Rowe (1718) was greatly praised by Samuel Johnson*. In ancient times Lucan was noted for his florid style, and for his gift for epigram*.

Lucian (2nd C AD) /ˈluːsiən/

Greek satirist. He is especially known for his satirical dialogues and for his *True History* – an account of imaginary voyages which Swift may have used as a model for his *Gulliver's Travels**.

Lucifer

A Latin name meaning 'the light-bearer', originally used for the planet Venus as the 'morning star', when it appears in the east just before sunrise. In the Bible, *Isaiah* 14:12, the name is used to translate the Hebrew 'shining one' in allusion to the fall of the King of Babylon: 'How art thou fallen from heaven, O Lucifer, son of the morning!' (Authorized Version). In *Luke* 10:18, Jesus says: 'I beheld Satan fallen as lightning from heaven'. Early Christian scholars believed Jesus to be referring to the text in *Isaiah*; hence 'Lucifer' became one of the names for Satan, regarded as the brightest of the angels before his fall.

Lucina /luːˈsainə/

'She who brings to light'; the ancient Roman goddess of childbirth. She was sometimes identified with Juno, and sometimes with Diana.

Lucrece (Lucretia) /luːˈkriːs/

A Roman lady of outstanding virtue and beauty. She was the wife of Tarquinius Collatinus, but Sextus, the son of Tarquin, King of Rome tried to seduce her, and when she resisted, committed rape upon her. She told her father and her husband of the outrage, and exacted an oath of vengeance from them, after which she killed herself. In consequence, a relative of her husband, Lucius Junius Brutus, led a rebellion against the Tarquin monarchy and expelled them from the city. Lucrece was thus traditionally the occasion for the foundation of the ancient Roman Republic. Shakespeare wrote a narrative poem, *The Rape of Lucrece* (1594), and the story has also been made the subject of an opera by Benjamin Britten, with a libretto by Ronald Duncan.

Lucretius (Titus Lucretius Carus) (1st C BC) /luːˈkriːʃjəs/

Roman poet; author of the great didactic poem *De Rerum Natura* ('Concerning the Nature of Things'). It outlines the philosophy of the Greek thinker Epicurus*, which is based on the atomic theory of Democritus. The poet seeks to expound that all reality is material. The gods exist, but they also are material, though immortal, and they are not concerned with the affairs of men; the soul exists, but it, too, is material, and mortal like the body, dissolving into its original atoms after death. Lucretius is not, however, a cynical poet; he testifies to the beauty of the natural world, and the poem opens with an eloquent invocation to Venus, the conception of whom is followed by Spenser in *Faerie Queene** Bk. IV. x, stanza 44 onwards. Lucretius' love of the natural world and his reverence for reason caused him to be greatly admired during the Renaissance* and the succeeding two centuries; parts of the poem were finely translated by Dryden*.

Lucretius is a late dramatic monologue* by Tennyson*, in which the poet philosopher expounds his dying vision of the world.

Lucy

The subject of a small group of lyrics by Wordsworth*, composed between 1799 and 1801, though not as a sequence. There is no clear evidence that they were inspired by an actual person; Lucy may have been his sister Dorothy. They are: *Strange fits of passion have I known*; *Three years she grew*; *She dwelt among the untrodden ways*; *A slumber did my spirit seal*; *I travelled among unknown men.*

Lud /lʌd/

A mythical king of the ancient Britons, originally a god. He was supposed to have been the first to build walls round the City of London, and one of the medieval gates – Ludgate, still the name of the street that once led to it – was perhaps called after him.

Luddites

A name used for destroyers of machines, 1811–16. They were craftsmen who feared unemployment if the machines became established, and were so called after a mythical leader, Ned Ludd. Nowadays the term 'new Luddites' is sometimes misleadingly used for those who fear modern technological development, for whatever reason.

Luggnagg

A country in Part III of Swift's *Gulliver's Travels**. It is inhabited by the Struldbrugs who have immortality, and find it a curse.

Lupercal /ˈluːpəkal/

A cave in ancient Rome, sacred to Lupercus, a wolf-god, connected with the myth that the founders of the city, Romulus and Remus, were suckled by a she-wolf. The Lupercalia was the feast of this god, accompanied by rites which were supposed to induce fertility in women.

Luther, Martin (1483–1546) /ˈluːθə/

German religious reformer, and the chief figure in the European movement known as the Reformation*. The beginning of this is often dated from 1517, when Luther fixed on the church door at Wittenberg his 95 'Theses', against the sale of 'indulgences'; a consequence of this was his condemnation by the Pope at the Diet of Worms (1521).

Luther's influence on the English Reformation is a matter of dispute. Before he separated the English church from the authority of the Pope, Henry VIII* wrote a treatise against Luther, for which the Pope awarded him the title of Defender of the Faith (Fidei Defensor), still used by English monarchs. Lutheran influences were felt by humanists such as Colet and More*, and inspired Tyndale's* translation of the Bible, the first of several in 16th C. They certainly operated on the doctrines represented by the second Prayer Book, introduced by Archbishop Cranmer* under Edward VI*. However, reformist influences had been more or less current in England since Wycliffe* in 14th C.

Luther is the subject of a play, *Martin Luther* (1961) by the English playwright, John Osborne*.

Lycidas /ˈlisidas/

A pastoral* elegy* by John Milton*, written in 1637. It is in the form of a monody, *ie* modelled on the odes sung by a single actor in ancient Greek tragedy. Line lengths vary between three and five feet, and the rhymes follow no regular pattern, but the mournful, majestic sonority is consistently sustained. Milton is lamenting the death of his college friend Edward King, a gifted young man who was drowned at sea, but it is not a poem of personal loss. The theme is the tragic loss of promise: King is seen as a young man of talent and serious endeavour in an age whose spiritual laxity requires the reforming zeal of such a spirit. Greek pastoral imagery is used – gods, muses, nymphs, including Camus, invented for the occasion as the god of the river that flows through Cambridge where Milton and King had studied. More important, however, is the pastoralism of the Bible: King was a good shepherd; the clergy are spiritual shepherds by their function but mostly bad ones. The most eloquent passage in the poem is spoken by St Peter – 'Pilot of the Galilean Lake' – as a condemnation of the clergy of Archbishop Laud* who, as Milton believed, were debasing the English Church with Roman Catholic tendencies, emphasizing ceremonial at the expense of the true spirit of religion. This use of pastoral for religious polemic recalls Spenser's *Shepherd's Calendar** (7th and 9th Eclogues).

Lycurgus (?9th C BC) /lai'kɔ:gəs/
In ancient Greek history, the reputed founder of the political system of the state of Sparta*. He is often referred to as the ideal type of great lawgiver.

Lydgate, John (?1373–?1450) /'lidgeit/
Poet. He was a prolific writer, and also a prolix one; very popular in 15th C, he is nowadays considered to represent many of the literary weaknesses of the Middle Ages, as Chaucer* had exhibited many of its greatest virtues. His popularity was partly due to the large number of tales he made available. Some of his works: *Troy Book* (1412–20); *The Story of Thebes* (1420); *Falls of Princes* (1430–8, founded on *De Casibus Virorum Illustrium* by the Italian poet Boccaccio*); *The Pilgrimage of Man*, translated from the French of Deguileville, an allegorical work; and two other allegories, *Complaint of the Black Knight* and *Temple of Glass*.
Bib: Hammond, E. P., *English Verse between Chaucer and Surrey*.

Lyell, Sir Charles (1797–1875) /'laiəl/
Geologist. His principal work, *The Principles of Geology* (1830–33) revolutionized ideas about the age of the earth, and was a challenge to current theological thinking only less than Darwin's* *Origin of Species* (1859) was to be. He also contributed the idea of change as continuous and ceaseless instead of sudden, intermittent, and catastrophic, which had been the prevailing view. This added to the sense of flux and instability which haunted such contemporary imaginative writers as Arnold*, Clough* and Tennyson*, whose *In Memoriam** shows traces of Lyell's influence.
* 3.4.4.

Lyly, John (1554–1606) /'lili/
Poet, writer of romances, dramatist. He was a writer for the cultivated society of court and university circles, and amongst these he was immensely popular.

His prose romances, *Euphues, or the Anatomy of Wit** (1578) and *Euphues and his England* (1580) contain little story and are mainly pretexts for sophisticated discussion of contemporary manners and modes in a style whose graceful ornateness is really an end in itself. Its artificiality, now regarded as its fault, was at the time regarded as a virtue of high cultivation. It was much imitated in the last 20 years of 16th C, and it was also parodied *eg* by Shakespeare in his early comedies and, through Falstaff, here and there in *1 Henry IV**.

Lyly's comedies are in the same elaborately sophisticated style, and are in fact the first *socially* sophisticated comedies in English. The plays were performed by boy actors in private theatres; they were not intended for the socially mixed audiences of the public theatres such as the Globe*. *The Woman in the Moon* (before 1584) was the only one of these in verse. He followed it with prose plays interspersed with graceful lyrics: *Sappho and Phao* (1584); *Alexander and Campaspe* (1584); *Endymion* (1591); *Midas* (1592); *Galathea* (1592); *Mother Bombie* (1594), and *Love's Metamorphosis* (published 1601). The best-known of these are *Campaspe*, *Endymion* and *Mother Bombie*. They have grace and wit, and were closer to popular taste than was Restoration* comedy a century later.
* 5.1.2.4; *Theatres*.
Bib: Hunter, G. K., *John Lyly: The Humanist as Courtier*.

Lyonesse /laiə'nes/
In the legends of King Arthur*, a country which is supposed to have extended from Cornwall, in the south-west of England, to the adjacent Scilly Isles. In the legend of Tristram and Iseult*, it was Tristram's birthplace. Lyonesse is said to have been submerged by the sea.

Lyric Poetry
In ancient Greece, the kind of poem which could be sung to a lyre or other musical instrument, as opposed to epic* poetry. In modern English usage, the expression covers most forms of short poetry, whether or not intended to be sung, though it is also used technically in popular musical plays and light reviews for the parts that are to be sung as distinct from those to be spoken.

From the Middle Ages until about 1590, most short poems seem to have been composed with music in mind, and often explicitly for musical accompaniment. Certain stanza forms, however, were clearly less suitable for music than others, for instance the sonnet form so popular among poets in the last decade of 16th C. English music reached a high point of sophistication at this time, and the fusion of words and music was a refined art about which poets were generally well informed. It is possible to distinguish from this time onwards between poems composed to be spoken and those intended to be sung. For example some of the *Songs and Sonnets* of John Donne* are really songs ('Go and catch a falling star') and others (*The Ecstasy*) invite plain speech, by using inflections of phrasing which recall the poetic drama rather than song. There is an equally clear difference in George Herbert's* *The Temple* (1633) between *Virtue*, which is clearly a song, and *Redemption* which is clearly not.

Apart from its association with music, the lyric, especially in 19th C came to be thought of as a brief expression of intense feeling. The Romantic* generation of poets between 1790 and 1830 no longer had the constant and sensitive awareness of music which had been usual among the poets of 16th and earlier 17th C; if they had other arts in mind as they wrote, it is more likely to have been the pictorial ones, and Blake* (although he called his lyrics 'songs'), Wordsworth*, Coleridge*, Shelley*, Byron* and Keats* clearly wrote nearly all their lyrics on the assumption that they would be spoken. The value they attached to intense and spontaneous feeling really gave the form a new meaning; the 'lyrical impulse' is a phrase which suggests that spontaneity should have priority over art, whereas in 16th and 17th C art had the priority, even in such apparently impulsive lyrics as some of Donne's. 20th-C poets have been inclined to return to the self-critical and deliberate approach of 16th and 17th C.

Lyrical Ballads with a Few other Poems

A volume published jointly and anonymously by William Wordsworth* and Samuel Taylor Coleridge* in 1798. Most of the poems were by Wordsworth; Coleridge's contributions were *The Rime of the Ancient Mariner**, the longest in the book, *The Foster Mother's Tale*, *To the Nightingale*, and *The Dungeon*. In 1800 the second edition had Wordsworth's name on the title-page, and included his famous Preface and his poem *Michael*. Another change was the addition of Coleridge's poem *Love* in place of Wordsworth's *The Convict*. In the third edition of 1802 the Preface was enlarged. The fourth and final edition was published in 1805.

In chapter XIV of his *Biographia Literaria**, Coleridge describes how the collaboration came about. He and Wordsworth had been discussing 'two cardinal points of poetry, the power of exciting the sympathy of the reader by a faithful adherence to the truth of nature, and the power of giving the interest of novelty by the modifying colours of the imagination'. From this they projected a volume in which Coleridge should direct himself to characters 'supernatural or at least romantic, yet so as to transfer from our inward nature a human interest ... sufficient to procure ... that willing suspension of disbelief for the moment, which constitutes poetic faith'. Wordsworth's object would be to 'excite a feeling analogous to the supernatural' for everyday things the beauty of which was normally concealed by the 'film of familiarity'.

Wordsworth's Preface is a poetic manifesto and explains the intention of the book. He considers that the typical poetry of his day is too much inclined to 'gaudy and inane phraseology', and too remote from the deepest and purest truths of human experience. For this reason, he and Coleridge use the simplest and plainest diction, and 'Humble and rustic life was generally chosen . . . because in that condition of life our elementary feelings co-exist in a state of greater simplicity, and, consequently, may be more accurately contemplated, and more forcibly communicated . . .'

At first Coleridge felt entirely at one with Wordsworth's Preface, but by 1802 he began to have doubts about Wordsworth's theories of poetic language. These doubts were formulated as extended criticism in *Biographia Literaria*, chapters XVII–XX.

The finest poems in the first edition were undoubtedly *The Ancient Mariner* and Wordsworth's *Tintern Abbey*. The first edition was received with mild interest and little antagonism, though there was some hostility to the obscurity of *The Ancient Mariner*. It seems to have been on this account and at Coleridge's request that his name was kept off the title-page of the second edition. The third just preceded Jeffrey's attack in the new *Edinburgh Review*; in it he coined the phrase 'the Lake school of poetry', which became familiar in the critical controversies of the next thirty years.

* 7.3.

Lytton, Edward George Earle Lytton Bulwer- (1st Baron Lytton) (1803-73)

Novelist. He was the son of General Bulwer, and added his mother's surname of Lytton on inheriting her estate in 1843. He was educated at Trinity and Trinity Hall, Cambridge, and was made a Baron in 1866. His novels were very famous in his lifetime, and their range is an indication of the literary variety and changes in the Victorian period. His political outlook was radical when he was young; he was then a friend of the radical philosopher William Godwin* whose influence is evident in his early novels, *Paul Clifford* (1830) and *Eugene Aram* (1832). On the other hand, he was a member of fashionable society, and his first success (*Pelham*, 1828) is closer to Disraeli's* political novels of high society, for example *Coningsby*. Then in mid-career, under the influence of the strict Victorian moral code, he wrote domestic novels such as *The Caxtons – A Family Picture* (1848). He showed the influence of Sir Walter Scott* on the Victorians in his historical novels such as *The Last Days of Pompeii* (1834), *Rienzi* (1835), and *The Last of the Barons* (1843), and the current German influence in the didacticism of his early novels and in fantasies such as *The Pilgrims of the Rhine* (1834). Bulwer-Lytton was a friend of Charles Dickens* (see the biography of Dickens by Jack Lindsay) and satirized Lord Tennyson in his poem *The New Timon* (1846). He wrote some successful plays – *The Lady of Lyons* (1838), *Richelieu* (1838) and *Money* (1840). Like Disraeli, he combined his literary with a political career, for which he was rewarded with a peerage as Baron Knebworth (his mother's estate), but in his case literature had priority. His work is now little respected (he is considered as neither sincere nor original) but he is regarded as interestingly representative of his period.

M

M.C.C. (Marylebone Cricket Club)

The society, founded in 18th C, which controls the rules and conduct of the game of cricket*.

Mabinogion /mabi'nəudʒən/

A collection of medieval Welsh tales, some from the 14th-C *Red Book of Hergest*. A 'mabinog' was a bard's apprentice. 11 tales were translated by Lady Charlotte Guest (1838); four of these are versions of still older Celtic myths and are called the 'Four Branches of the Mabinogi'. These are the true 'Mabinogion'. The others are old British tales of Roman times, British tales of King Arthur*, and later tales of medieval romance.

* *Wales.*

Macaulay, Thomas Babington (1800–59)

Historian, essayist, politician, and poet. He was actively on the Whig* side politically; that is to say, without being a radical reformer, he had strong faith in the virtue of British parliamentary institutions. He was, from the publication of his essay on Milton in 1825, a constant contributor to the main Whig periodical, the *Edinburgh Review**, and his *History of England* (1848 and 1855) is strongly marked by his political convictions. He was trained as a lawyer and became an eloquent orator; his writing has corresponding qualities of persuasiveness and vividness. As a historian he was best at impressionistic reconstruction of the past, and the same gift served him in his biographical essays on Bunyan*, Goldsmith*, Johnson*, Fanny Burney*, and the younger Pitt*. He represented the most optimistic strain of feeling in mid-19th-C England – its faith in the march of progress.

Macaulay's *Lays of Ancient Rome* (1842) were an attempt to reconstruct legendary Roman history in a way that might resemble the lost ballad poetry of ancient Rome. Though not major poetry, they are very vigorous verse with the kind of appeal that is to be found in effective ballad poetry.

Macaulay was raised to the peerage in 1857.

* *Histories; Macaulay's History of England.*

Bib: Trevelyan, G. M., *Life and Letters*; Bryant, A., *Macaulay*; Firth, C., *A Commentary on Macaulay's History of England*; Trevelyan, G. M. in *Clio: a Muse*; Stephen, L., in *Hours in a Library*.

Macaulay's History of England from the Accession of James II

The history (Vols. 1 & 2 1848; 3 & 4 1855; 5 1861) is a thorough, detailed account of two reigns: James II* and William III*. It is unfinished and was originally intended to extend to the time of George I (1714–27): and further. The period covered is perhaps the most crucial for English political development: James II, a Catholic, tried to enforce his will in the Catholic interest against Parliament, which frustrated him and expelled him from the throne in the Revolution of 1688*. Parliament then summoned William from Holland to reign jointly with his wife, who was also James's daughter, Mary II (1689–94). William was the great champion of the Protestant cause in Europe, and Mary was also Protestant.

Macaulay's politics were strongly in the Whig* parliamentary tradition, and his history is an epic of the triumph of the ideas which to him gave meaning to English history. Considered as history, the work is accordingly one-sided, much more a work of historical art than of historical science; it represents what historians have come to call 'the Whig interpretation of history'. Nonetheless it is a learned book, based on extensive scholarship, and Macaulay was gifted with an eloquent style of prose. He was especially talented at the reconstruction of the intimate social texture of the past, and his famous Chapter III on England in 1688 is published as a separate volume, complete in itself.

Macbeth

A tragedy by Shakespeare*; it probably dates from 1605–6, and was first printed in the first folio* edition of Shakespeare's collected works, 1623.

The material for the tragedy comes from Raphael Holinshed's* *Chronicle of Scottish History* (1578). Macbeth was an historical king of Scotland who reigned approximately 1040–58. He seems to have been a capable and beneficent sovereign in spite of his usurpation of the throne and sundry acts of cruelty, and Holinshed so records him. Shakespeare blackens his character, elevates his predecessor Duncan into a kind of saint, and makes a virtuous figure out of Macbeth's associate Banquo. Banquo was the legendary ancestor of James VI of Scotland, who ascended the English throne as James I* in 1603. The relative idealization of Banquo, the prominence of witchcraft – a subject which was one of King James's hobbies – and other indications show that the play was written to appeal to the king's interest. They are all put to artistic purpose by Shakespeare, however, and enhance rather than deflect from his imaginative intention.

The tragedy is the conversion of a good man into a wholly evil one. Macbeth begins as the heroic warrior who defends Scotland against a triple enemy: the king of Norway has invaded Scotland in alliance with the open rebel Macdonwald and the secret rebel Cawdor. After his victory, Macbeth is confronted by a triple enemy assailing his own soul: the witches; his own evil desires; and his wife, who reinforces these desires. He first encounters the witches, who predict that he is to be king of Scotland, after being made Thane (Lord) of Cawdor. As Macbeth knows nothing of Cawdor's part in the rebellion and invasion, both prophecies are to him equally incredible. The second is, however, immediately confirmed by emissaries from Duncan, king of Scotland. Macbeth is now also Cawdor and finds himself haunted by thoughts of bloodthirsty ambition: he becomes his soul's own secret enemy. The witches and his own desire would not in the end have been sufficient to cause him to murder the king, but Lady Macbeth dedicates herself to reinforcing his ambition. Macbeth is thus brought to murder Duncan, though in a state of horror at the deed, and becomes king on the flight of Duncan's son Malcolm. After the murder, however, he becomes a hardened man though a restless and desperate one; he proceeds to the murder of Banquo, whose children the witches have predicted will succeed him on the throne, and then degenerates into massacre and tyranny. The play exemplifies one of the beliefs of Shakespeare's time: that the soul of man is the pattern of the state, and that where evil breaks into the soul of a king it will extend over the state he rules.

Macbeth was written in Shakespeare's maturest period; together with *Othello**, *King Lear**, and *Antony and Cleopatra**, it is accounted one of his greatest tragedies.

MacDiarmid, Hugh (Christopher Murray Grieve) (b 1892)

Poet and critic. A Marxist, and a leading Scottish nationalist. His outstanding contribution has been the revival of the Lowland Scottish branch of English (once called Inglis, now for literary purposes, Lallans*, and still the medium of speech) as a poetic medium. The language had a distinguished literary phase about 1500, and reached another peak in the work of Robert Burns* in 18th C, but thereafter was overwhelmed by southern English. In the earlier and greater period, Scots poetry was part of the wide European tradition; Burns's excellence drew from the surviving vigour of Lowland Scots culture. MacDiarmid's success has arisen from his ability to follow the example of Burns in far less promising conditions, and to resist southern English modes by his awareness of the wider context of Europe. His best-known poem in Lallans is *A Drunk Man Looks at the Thistle.* He has also written in southern English. A collected edition of his poems, incomplete, appeared in 1962, and another in 1967.

* *Scottish Literature.*

Bib: Glen, D., *Hugh MacDiarmid and the Scottish Renaissance*; a critical study by Kenneth Buthlay.

Mac Flecknoe, or a Satyr upon the True-Blew-Protestant Poet, T.S.

A verse satire by John Dryden*, written about 1678 and published in 1682.

'Mac' is a Scottish prefix meaning 'son of'; 'T.S.' are the initials of Dryden's enemy, Thomas Shadwell. The poem is thus an attack on Shadwell, who is designated as the son of (successor to) Flecknoe, a Catholic poet who had been satirized by Andrew Marvell* in *Fleckno, An English Priest at Rome.* Dryden may have disliked Flecknoe for his attacks on the English stage, for which Dryden was one of the leading writers. His hostility to Shadwell – his main objective – is partly literary and partly political. Dryden had written a political verse satire, *The Medal**, against Lord Shaftesbury, the leader of the Whig* party. Shadwell had replied with *Medal of John Bayes*, accusing Dryden of atheism. Dryden countered by attacking Shadwell politically in *Absalom and Achitophel**, Part II, and as a writer in *Mac Flecknoe.* It is written in heroic couplets*.

Machiavelli, Niccolo di Bernardo dei (1469–1527) /makiə'veli/

Italian writer, statesman, and political thinker. He is especially famous for his political treatise *The Prince* (1513), and it is for the influence of this work on English writers, particularly between 1580 and 1620, that he is important in English literature.

Machiavelli's aim was the unification of Italy, and he saw no hope of this taking place except under a powerful despot, whose success would depend on his capacity to see politics realistically, subordinating all moral principles to the expediency of the most effective political methods. He thus made a distinction between righteousness and 'effectual truth' which was of practical importance to statesmen and in line with the scientific thinking of such men as Francis Bacon*, but deeply disturbing to ordinary men and to the imaginative artists, who saw life and morality as inseparable. Politic, policy, and politician became bad words in the drama of the age of Shakespeare, implying ruthlessness, cunning, and diabolic indifference to the moral tradition.

The Prince was not translated into English until 1640, but educated Englishmen of 16th C commonly knew Italian. Still more knew French and read the treatise against Machiavelli by the French Protestant Gentillet (1576); this was translated into English in 1602. One reason why the Elizabethan English regarded Machiavelli with such horror may have been that he was widely known only through Gentillet's attack on him, and justice was not done to the patriotic motives that inspired his book.

For the majority of Elizabethan Englishmen who knew his name, Machiavelli was probably more an evil legend than a real man, and as such he was fascinating as well as abhorrent. The unruly energies of the time found embodiment in representations of him, as in Marlowe's Tamburlaine*, and his Barabas in *The Jew of Malta** – a play for which 'Machiavel' is made to speak the Prologue. The combination of abhorrent wickedness and splendid energy made for a natural association between the Machiavellian villain and the embodied Vice of the old Morality* play tradition; Shakespeare's Richard of Gloucester (Richard III), for example, compares himself to both (*3 Henry VI* III. ii and *Richard III* III. i).

Mackenzie, Compton (b 1883)

Novelist. Son of a British actor-manager and an American actress. A very prolific writer of great popularity; his best known novels are probably *Sinister Street* (1913–14) and *The Four Winds of Love*—a sequence composed of *The East Wind* (1937), *The South Wind* (1937), *The West Wind* (1940), *West to North* (1940), *The North Wind* (1944–45). When he began writing, Henry James* regarded him as one of the most promising of younger novelists, and Ford Madox Ford* thought *Sinister Street* perhaps a work of genius. However, serious critics have rarely given him extensive attention.

Bib: Robertson, L., *Compton Mackenzie: An Appraisal of his Literary Works.*

MacNeice, Louis (1907–63)

Poet. He was born in Northern Ireland, the son of an Anglican clergyman who became a bishop. During the 1930s he was associated by the reading public with a group of left wing poets led by W. H. Auden*. They were certainly his friends, but, although he had socialist sympathies, he never committed himself politically; in politics, as in religion, he was agnostic. He excelled in witty, sensuous verse of rhythmical versatility and with a strong element of caustic pessimism. He also wrote criticism, notably *The Poetry of W. B. Yeats* (1941), numerous plays for radio, and translated the *Agamemnon* of Aeschylus (1936) and Goethe's *Faust* (1951). He collaborated with Auden in *Letters from Iceland* (1937).

Bib: Fraser, G. S., in *Vision and Rhetoric*;
Thwaite, A., *Essays on Contemporary English Poetry*.

Madrigal /ˈmadrigəl/

A poem composed to be sung, with or without instrumental accompaniment. It derived from the Italian 'canzone', and flourished in England especially between 1580 and 1630. It was sung chorally, and had three forms:

[1] The Ayre. This had a melody composed for the top voice, which was accompanied by the other voices to the same melody.

[2] The Ballet. This resembled the ayre, but was distinguished by its dance-like melody and refrain.

[3] The Madrigal proper. This had different 'parts', *ie* melodies, for the individual voices, and was so composed that the melodies interwove. The parts were sometimes composed with the effect of dramatic contrast, *eg* by Thomas Weelkes (1575?–1623). Great attention was paid by composers to bringing out the meaning of the words, so that poets and musicians worked in close collaboration. Only Thomas Campion* is known to have composed music for his own words, but others are believed to have done so. Ayres and madrigals are common in the plays of the period, and most of the poets wrote them. Famous composers, besides those mentioned, included Dowland, Morley, Byrd, Gibbons and Tomkins.

Maecenas, Gaius Cilnius (1st C BC) /miˈsi:nas/

A Roman patron of literature. He had great wealth, and as a statesman enjoyed the special favour of Augustus Caesar, the first of the Roman Emperors. He used his influence to exalt the prestige of literature, and was the protector and benefactor of Horace* and Virgil*. 'A Maecenas' has become synonymous with 'patron of art and letters'.

Magazine

Originally meaning 'storehouse', the word has also denoted, since 18th C, a periodical containing miscellaneous material, *eg* the *Gentleman's Magazine* (founded 1731): 'a Monthly Collection to store up, as in a Magazine, the most remarkable pieces on the subjects above-mentioned' (from the introduction to the first number). In 18th and early 19th C magazines only differed from other serious periodicals (*eg* the *Edinburgh Review** and the *Quarterly**) in having greater variety of content and being open to imaginative writing. Distinguished magazines of this kind include *Blackwood's** and the second *London Magazine** (1820–29). Later in 19th C, magazines became predominantly popular periodicals devoted principally to fiction. However, serious magazines still exist, *eg* the current *London Magazine*, the third to bear the name.

* *Reviews and Periodicals.*

Magi /ˈmeidʒai/

[1] A priestly caste in ancient Persian religion.

[2] Supremely wise men or magicians, according to 16th-C neo-Platonic mysticism.

[3] In the Bible (*Matthew* 2) the three wise men from the east who came to worship at the cradle of the child Jesus; they are also traditionally known as the Three Kings, and bear the names of Caspar, Melchior, and Balthazar.

Magistrates

In England and Wales, magistrates (also known as Justices of the Peace, or J.P.s) are primarily minor judges, who try small offences and examine more serious charges in order to decide whether they should be taken to a senior court. Most magistrates are private citizens, and the ordinary Magistrates' Court is composed of a panel of J.P.s, never fewer than two; they are assisted by a Clerk who is a qualified lawyer, but they themselves are unpaid. Their meetings are Petty Sessions, and appeal from them lies to Quarter Sessions. There are also Stipendiary Magistrates' Courts, originally set up to cover the Metropolitan Police District of London and therefore known popularly as Police Courts, a term now commonly applied to any Magistrates' Court. Stipendiary Magistrates are qualified lawyers and receive a salary; they may sit alone.

In the past, however, magistrates have had much wider functions, and they have played an important part in English social and political life. The office dates from 13th C, when petty landowners were appointed as magistrates to help the sheriffs maintain order in their districts, but until 16th C their importance was comparatively slight. The great feudal lords and the abbots of the great monasteries were the real powers outside London and the districts adjacent to it. But by 16th C the feudal nobility were weakened, displaced, or overthrown, and in 1536–39 King Henry VIII* closed the monasteries. The Tudor sovereigns relied on the magistrates to enforce governmental policy in their districts, and supervised them carefully through the Privy Council*. Not only did the magistrates have to execute the Poor Laws*, maintain the roads, and enforce law and order, but they had to carry out functions formerly exercised by the town trade guilds (now greatly weakened) such as the regulation of wages, prices, and the rules of apprenticeship*. The middle class of landed gentry, from which magistrates were appointed, was the class most loyal to Tudor policies, and therefore provided the most effective allies of the ruling family. These magistrates were often to some extent qualified for the legal parts of their functions by education in law at one of the Inns of Court*; law was more a field for general (as distinct from professional) education than it is in modern England.

Magistrates continued to be drawn from the same class, and to have comparably wide functions, throughout 17th, 18th and much of 19th C, but their relationship to the Crown changed in political fact, although not in nominal allegiance. James II* lost the support of the class to which they belonged by his policy of re-establishing Roman Catholicism, and the Revolution of 1688* was carried out bloodlessly in England largely for this reason. In 18th C they were only nominally servants of the Crown; in reality, they and their class controlled the government through Parliament. However, it was in this century that the legal authority of the amateur magistrate first met competition from professional lawyers in the function of suppressing crime.

The Reform Bill* of 1832 put an end to much of the political influence of the magistrates and their class, and the Local Government Act of 1888, which set up County Councils, deprived them of their governing functions in their districts. In this century, magistrates have been chosen more democratically from all social classes; they are appointed by the Lord Chancellor* on advice from local committees.

Magistrates were satirized at the height of their power, *eg* by Shakespeare (Justice Shallow in *2 Henry IV**) and by the 18th-C novelists Fielding* and Smollett*. They were often regarded as inefficient, untrained in social as well as legal experience, and selfish in their interests, especially in their stern penalizing of offences against the game laws*. It is clear, however, that they exercised their functions with considerable responsibility, and that the magisterial function was itself valuable training in public affairs for the class which, by its preponderance of wealth; was in any case the most influential body in the country.

In 16th C the term 'Magistrate' was sometimes synonymous with 'Prince' or 'Ruler'; the anthology *A Mirror for Magistrates** shows this use.

* *Courts of Law.*

Magna Carta /ˈmagnəˈkaːtə/

The Great Charter which King John* was forced by his barons to accept in 1215. It has long been popularly regarded as the foundation of English liberties, guaranteeing such rights as freedom from arbitrary imprisonment. However, 16th-C plays on King John, *eg* Shakespeare's*, omit mention of the Charter, which came to have its modern symbolic importance only in consequence of the conflicts between kings and parliaments in 17th C.

Maia /ˈmaiə/

In Greek myth, eldest of the seven daughters (Pleiades*) of the Titan, Atlas*; she became the mother, by Zeus*, of Hermes*.

Maid Marian

A character in the Robin Hood* legend. She is unimportant in the earlier versions, but always had a place in the traditional morris dances* which represented characters from the story. In a late (17th-C?) ballad she disguises herself as a page to seek Robin Hood in the Forest, where she fights with him for an hour before she recognizes him.

Maid Marian (1822)

Thomas Love Peacock's* parody of medieval romances (such as Scott's *Ivanhoe**, 1819) fashionable in early 19th C. It contains very good songs in comic opera style.

Maid's Tragedy, The (1619)

A play by Beaumont* and Fletcher*. It takes place in the town of Rhodes, and the story concerns the attempt of the king to conceal his relationship with his mistress, Evadne, by forcing one of his most loyal courtiers, Amintor, to marry her. Aspasia, the 'maid' of the tragedy, is the girl whom Amintor has to give up. Evadne's brother, Melantius, discovers the unhappy secret and compels his sister to murder the king; she then commits suicide on finding that Amintor will not forgive her.

The tragedy is generally considered to be Beaumont and Fletcher's masterpiece. It is typical of later Jacobean* tragedy in relying for its effectiveness on individual scenes rather than on its totality, which is unconvincing. It is typical of Beaumont and Fletcher in the accomplished melody of its blank verse* and the skill of its theatrical craftsmanship.

Malaprop, Mrs /ˈmaləprop/

A character in Sheridan's comedy *The Rivals**. She is the aunt and guardian of the heroine, Lydia Languish. Her principal comic effect is her habit of misusing words; this has given rise to the term 'malapropism'.

Malcontent, The (1604)

A tragi-comedy by John Marston*, with additions by John Webster*.

An intrigue engineered by the villainous lord Mendoza has caused the deposition of Giovanni Altofronte, the noble Duke of Genoa, and substituted the weak Pietro Jacomo, who is married to Aurelia, daughter of the Duke of Florence. Altofronte, however, has returned to his own court in disguise as Malevole (the 'malcontent'). He is tolerated as a witty though sour court jester and commentator on the times and its corrupt manners. Meanwhile he awaits his chance for revenge and the recovery of his dukedom. Mendoza continues to conspire against the new Duke, whose wife is Mendoza's mistress, and Malevole in turn conspires against Mendoza. In the end, Mendoza is exposed, and Pietro and Aurelia penitently resign the duchy back to the rightful Duke.

The play is part satire* and part revenge play*, midway between Jonson's comedies of humours* (*eg Volpone**) and Tourneur's *Revenger's Tragedy**. The malcontent role of bitter commentator on society is a common one in Jacobean drama; Bosola in Webster's *Duchess of Malfi** is a well-known example, but Hamlet*, Iago (in *Othello**) and Thersites in *Troilus and Cressida** all have some aspects of the malcontent in their parts. The essence of the role is that the malcontent is somehow frustrated from satisfying his ambitions or being accepted by the rest of society; such exclusion gives him the motives (morally acceptable or otherwise) and the detachment for his satire.

Mall, The /mal/

A street in London forming a processional avenue from Trafalgar Square to Buckingham Palace. It was a fashionable promenade in 17th and 18th C, and owed its name to the game of 'pall mall'.
* *Pall Mall.*

Mallock, W. H. (1849-1923)

A Catholic controversialist now best known for his satirical novel *The New Republic*, portraying leading members of the Victorian intelligentsia, including Ruskin*, Arnold*, Pater* and Huxley. He wrote a number of books on social questions against socialism. His *Memoirs of Life and Literature* was published in 1920.
Bib: Adams, A. B., *The Novels of W. H. Mallock*; Woodring, C. R., *Notes on Mallock's The New Republic* in *Nineteenth Century Fiction* VI.

Malmsey wine

A strong sweet wine, originally from Napoli di Malvasia in Greece; in medieval Latin the name was corrupted to 'malmasia', hence the English 'malmsey'. Another English form is 'malvoisie'.

Malory, Sir Thomas (d 1471) /ˈmaləri/

Author of *Morte d'Arthur**. Probably the son of a Warwickshire gentleman. He was Member of Parliament for Warwickshire in 1445, led a lawless life, and died in prison.
Bib: Vinaver, E., *Sir Thomas Malory*; Bennett, J. A. W., (ed.) *Essays on Malory*.

Malthus, Thomas Robert (1766–1834) /ˈmalθəs/

Economist; particularly famous for his *Essay on Population* (1798), which he reissued in an expanded and altered form in 1803. Its original title was: *An Essay on the Principle of Population as it affects the Future Improvement of Society, with Remarks on the Speculations of Mr Godwin, M. Condorcet, and other Writers.*

The essence of his view was that social progress tends to be limited by the fact that population increases more rapidly than means of subsistence, and always reaches the limits of subsistence, so that a substantial part of society is doomed to live beyond the margin of poverty. The 'natural checks' which prevent population increase from exceeding the means of subsistence are war, famine, and pestilence, to which he added human misery and vice. In the second edition he added a further possible check by 'moral restraint', *ie* late marriages and sexual continence. These arguments made a strong impression on public opinion; an important practical consequence of them was the replacement of the existing haphazard methods of poor relief by the harsh but reasoned and systematic Poor Law* system of 1834.

Malthus's relentless and pitiless reasoning led to political economy becoming known as the 'gloomy science'. His conclusions were contested by humanitarians, and later seemed belied by factors he did not foresee, such as cheap imports of food from newly exploited colonies like Canada. Since 1918 'Malthusian' theories of the dangers of over-population have revived.
* 3.4.2.

Mammon

In the Bible, an Aramaic word for 'riches' – *Matthew* 6:24; *Luke* 16:9–13. In the Middle Ages, Mammon was personified as the devil of covetousness, and is so used by Spenser in the Cave of Mammon episode (*Faerie Queene** II, vii) and by Milton in *Paradise Lost** (i, 678 and ii, 228).

Man in Black, The

A character in the collection of essays by Oliver Goldsmith* entitled *The Citizen of the World* (1762). He is prodigiously generous, but his sensibility causes him to conceal this virtue by pretending to be mean.

Man in the Moon, The

In English folklore, a tradition that the marks on the moon represent a man with faggots on his back; he was supposed to have been banished there for gathering sticks on the Sabbath day – see Bible, *Numbers* 15:32.

Man of Law's Tale, The

One of Chaucer's *Canterbury Tales**. Written in rhyme-royal*, it tells the tale of the Christian princess, Constance, who is married to the Soldan (Sultan) on condition that he becomes a Christian. To prevent this conversion of her son, the Soldan's mother sets Constance adrift on the sea. After many ordeals in which Constance proves her constancy to the faith, she is reunited to her father, the Christian Roman Emperor. The story is also told in Book II of Gower's *Confessio Amantis**, and in an anonymous medieval poem of 14th C, *Emaré*.

Man of Mode, The (1676)

The third and last play by the Restoration* dramatist, Sir George Etherege*, generally held to be his best. The play has very little plot, but concerns the amorous intrigues of the main character, Dorimant, who is probably a portrait of the poet Lord Rochester*. The play is subtitled *Sir Fopling Flutter*, but Fopling Flutter, who is in the extreme of fashion based on Paris, is in fact a minor character and does not appear till Act III. The success of the play depends on the nimbleness of its dialogue with occasional glimpses through the prevailing heartlessness into tender sentiment, and on occasional wittily satirized situations. Basically it is a comedy of fashionable life which has gone to the opposite extreme from the ideals of courtly chivalry, and its tone is cynical rather than satirical.

Manchester Massacre, The

* *Peterloo Massacre, The.*

Manchester School, The

A group of politicians in the 1840s, led by Richard Cobden and John Bright; they advocated the reduction or abolition of import duties (Free Trade*) and the prevention of all political interference in the development of commerce ('Laissez-faire'). The heart of the movement was in the rapidly growing industrial towns of the north, of which Manchester was one of the chief. The name was first applied to the group by their opponent, the Conservative politician Benjamin Disraeli*.

Manciple's Tale, The

One of Chaucer's *Canterbury Tales**, in 10-syllable rhymed couplets*. The story is taken from Ovid's *Metamorphoses**. Originally the crow was a white bird; one such crow, owned by a man called Phebus, is able to imitate human speech, and betrays to Phebus his wife's infidelity. Phebus kills his wife in his rage, and then, in remorse, plucks out the crow's white feathers, and drives it forth 'unto the devil'; since then, crows have been black and deprived of speech.

Mandeville, Sir John

* *Travel Literature.*

Manes /ˈmaːneiz/

In Roman myth, the ghosts of the dead, who were propitiated in various rituals.

Manfred (1817)

A dramatic poem by Lord Byron*, in blank verse*.

The scene is the Alps. Manfred is an outcast, guilty of an unnamed inexpiable crime. He desires only oblivion, but the Spirits of earth and air, which by his occult powers he is able to conjure up, are unable to grant it; the Witch of the Alps refuses to grant it, because Manfred will not swear obedience to the supernatural powers which he has commanded. He encounters the Destinies and Nemesis, under the command of Arimanes (Ahriman, in ancient Persian – Zoroastrian – mysticism); they raise up Astarte, the spirit of the woman whom he has loved. She predicts his death on the following day. As he dies, Manfred defies the evil spirits who claim his soul, asserting his spiritual independence in isolation.

The poem is interesting as a document of the Romantic* movement, and of the romantic aspect of Byron's personality, *ie* as the demonstration of an attitude.

Manners, Comedy of

A form in which laughter is provoked by exaggerations of fashionable behaviour, absurdities in fashion itself, or departures from what is considered to be civilized normality of behaviour. Thus a comedy of manners can only arise in a highly developed society, in which there is a leisured class which not only has standards of politeness and good sense in human relationships but tends to give such standards first importance in social life. The Comedy of Humours* of Ben Jonson and his younger contemporaries dealt with fundamental human appetites, and was therefore concerned with much more than what was regarded as civilized behaviour by fashionable society, though that was often included in their purview. In the court of the French king Louis XIV in the second half of 17th C, a highly civilized society held to a code of behaviour which was also a code of morals; the comedies of Molière* were the first true examples of the Comedy of Manners, and had profundity as well as surface brilliance. His comedy influenced dramatists in England, but the English Comedy of Manners was a slighter affair. The intelligent, witty, but often cynical court of Charles II* was a small, smart set, unlike the contemporary French court which felt itself to be the summit of a great nation in one of its greatest periods. The humour of Etherege*, Wycherley*, and Vanbrugh* often depended more on coarseness than on wit; on the other hand, English prose had a new fluency without losing all the rich substance of the days of Jonson, and the work of Congreve* shows incisive dialogue with sometimes even poetic force.

The Comedy of Manners remained the only significant theatrical comedy until the polemical comedy of Bernard Shaw* at the end of 19th C. However, as standards of polite and rational behaviour extended through society, it tended to become more middle class and to show more propriety. Its masters in 18th C were Goldsmith* (*She Stoops to Conquer**) and Sheridan* (*The Rivals**, *The School for Scandal**). At the end of 19th C the Comedy of Manners had a last flare in the brilliant verbal wit of Oscar Wilde* (especially *The Importance of being Earnest*, 1895).

* 5.2.2.

Mansfield, Katherine (1888–1923)

Short story writer. Born (Katherine Mansfield Beauchamp) in Wellington, New Zealand; married the critic John Middleton Murry* in 1913. *In a German Pension* (1911); *Bliss* (1920); *The Garden Party* (1922); *The Dove's Nest* (1923). Her *Journal* (1927, enlarged edition 1954) and *Letters* (1928) were edited by Murry. The stories resemble in their form those of the Russian writer Chekhov, and Joyce's *Dubliners**; they do not have a distinct plot with a definite beginning and ending and a self-sufficient action, conveying instead an impression of continuity with ordinary life, and depending for their unity on delicate balance of detail and feeling.

Bib: Mantz, R. E. and Murry, J. M., *Life*;
Alpers, A., *Katherine Mansfield* (critical study);
Gordon, I., *Katherine Mansfield* (British Council Booklet).

Mansfield Park (1814)

A novel by Jane Austen. The theme is the conflict between three different styles of moral feeling. The first is that of Sir Thomas Bertram, owner of Mansfield Park; it stands for a system of conservative, orderly principle, a tradition inherited from the 18th C, emphasizing stability and discounting the feelings. The second style of moral feeling is embodied in Fanny Price, Sir Thomas's niece whom he takes into his household because her parents are poor and their family too large; although she is timid, withdrawn and overawed by her new surroundings, she possesses a highly developed sensibility and capacity for affection both of which are foreign to the Bertrams, except to the younger son, Edmund, who to some degree appreciates her. The third style is represented by Henry and Mary Crawford, half-brother and half-sister to the wife of the village parson. They are rich, independent, attractive; they do not share Sir Thomas's cold theories, and they do possess Fanny's capacity for ardent feeling; on the other hand, they are without Sir Thomas's dedication to conscience, and without Fanny's reverence for consistency of moral with affectionate and aesthetic sensibilities. The difference between the three styles of life becomes overt while Sir Thomas is absent in the West Indies; the Crawfords virtually take over Mansfield Park in order to rehearse, with the Bertram children and two guests, a performance of Kotzebue's* *Lovers' Vows*. Henry Crawford is by this time conducting a flirtation with Maria Bertram, who is engaged to one of the guests, Mr Rushworth, and Mary Crawford is in love with Edmund; these relationships are in effect parodied in the play (popular in Jane Austen's time) so that the characters can perform on the stage what they desire to enact in real life. Fanny, knowing that Sir Thomas would disapprove of amateur acting, refuses to take part, but the situation is painful to her because she is secretly in love with Edmund herself. The rehearsals are stopped by Sir Thomas's sudden return, but a new crisis occurs in Fanny's life when Henry, awakened to the reality of her diffident charms, proposes marriage to her. She refuses him, much to Sir Thomas's uncomprehending disapproval, and is not in a position to explain to him the grounds of her refusal: that she disapproves of Henry morally, and is in love with his son. She is exiled to her own family at Portsmouth, where disorder and strong emotion, often reduced to callous bad temper by poverty and overcrowding, are the rule. Henry is for a time constant, but he disgraces himself, the Bertrams and his sister by eloping with Maria after she has married. By degrees, both Sir Thomas and Edmund come to appreciate Fanny at her true value, and at the end of the novel she is to become mistress of Mansfield Park as Edmund's wife.

Of Jane Austen's completed works *Mansfield Park* is the most direct criticism of the Regency style of sensibility (represented by the Crawfords), with its tendency to reject continuity with the best elements of the past; at the same time the criticism is balanced by a recognition of the importance of the sensibility if morality is to receive true life from the feelings. It is also a bold challenge to the romantic style of fiction: Mary Crawford, antagonist to the heroine Fanny, is not only shown as friendly to her and in all but the deepest sense appreciative of her; she is also the possessor of genuine social attractions which Fanny lacks. The reader is made to like both her and her brother, and at the same time obliged to acknowledge Fanny's ultimate human superiority.

Marcus Aurelius Antoninus (AD 121–180) /ˈmaːkəs ɔːˈriːljəs/

Roman Emperor (AD 161–180) and Stoic* philosopher, famous for his *Meditations*, in Greek.

Margaret of Anjou (1430–82)

The queen of King Henry VI*. Owing to the weakness of her husband, it was she who was the effective leader of the Lancastrian party in the Wars of the Roses*. She became famous for her determined leadership, the ferocity with which she defended the rights of her husband and son, and her pitiless vengefulness. She is a prominent character in the three *Henry VI** plays by Shakespeare, and reappears in his *Richard III** IV. iv, where she joins with the Yorkist ladies in a common lament for the dead of both families, since Richard has now laid waste his own, as well as contributing to the destruction of the Lancastrians.

Mariana

A character in Shakespeare's *Measure for Measure**; she was betrothed to Angelo, the deputy of the Duke of Vienna, and after being cast off by him she lives forsaken in 'the moated grange' until the Duke compels Angelo to marry her. She is the subject of one of the most famous poems by Alfred Tennyson* – *Mariana*.

Marina

A character in *Pericles, Prince of Tyre**, a play written wholly or in part by Shakespeare*. She is the daughter of king Pericles, who loses her at sea and later recovers her (V.i) in a scene described by T. S. Eliot* as one of the most beautiful by Shakespeare. She is the subject of one of Eliot's Ariel Poems, *Marina*.

Marlborough, John Churchill, Duke of (1650–1722) /ˈmoːlbərə/

Son of Winston Churchill, a minor country gentleman. At fifteen he became a page of honour to James, Duke of York, and in 1667 he received an officer's commission in the Guards. In 1672 he showed distinction in various sieges in the Netherlands in a campaign in which the English were allied with the French against the Dutch, and in 1685 he was made a Baron and promoted to the rank of Major General. It was largely due to his efficiency that the Monmouth* rebellion against James II* (formerly the Duke of York) was defeated at the Battle of Sedgemoor*. When William of Orange landed in England in 1688, however, Marlborough deserted James, and thus facilitated the bloodless Revolution by which William became King William III*. Churchill was made Duke of Marlborough on the accession of Queen Anne in 1702, and his wife, Sarah, was the Queen's chief favourite. On the outbreak of the War of the Spanish Succession* in the same year, Marlborough commanded the armies of the allied states against France, and won brilliant victories at Blenheim* (1704), Ramillies (1706), Oudenarde (1708) and Malplaquet (1709). The country was tiring of the war, however, and the Queen was tiring of the Duchess. Marlborough was relieved of his command in 1711. In the meantime the great mansion of Blenheim Palace had been built for him in honour of his first and most remarkable victory in the war. The architect was Sir John Vanbrugh*.

Marlborough's military successes were due to the high intelligence of his strategy and his daring. His biography has been written by his descendant, Sir Winston Churchill.

Marlowe, Christopher (1564–93)

Dramatist and poet. Son of a Canterbury shoemaker; educated at King's School, Canterbury, and Corpus Christi College, Cambridge. He probably began writing plays on leaving Cambridge. They were produced by the Earl of Nottingham's Company (the Lord Admiral's Men*). Marlowe probably became a government agent, and his mysterious death in a fight in a tavern at Deptford – nominally about who should pay the bill – may have had a political cause. When he died, he was under shadow of charges of atheism* on the evidence of his fellow dramatist, Thomas Kyd.*

His four major plays were written between 1587 and 1593: *Tamburlaine the Great**, *Parts 1 and 2*; *The Jew of Malta**; *The Tragical History of Dr Faustus*; *Edward II*. *Dido, Queen of Carthage* (with Nashe*, 1594) and *The Massacre at Paris* (1593) are attributed to him. His non-dramatic poetry is famous for the narrative *Hero and Leander**, based on the Greek of Musaeus (5th C AD) and completed by Chapman*, and the lyric *The Passionate Shepherd*. Little else has survived, apart from his translation of Ovid's* *Amores* (printed 1596) and of *The First Book of Lucan* (printed 1600). It has been suggested without evidence that he had a share in the writing of a number of other plays, including Shakespeare's *Henry VI**, *Titus Andronicus**, and *Richard III**.

Marlowe was much the greatest dramatic writer in 16th C apart from Shakespeare, and much the most important influence upon Shakespeare. His importance is due to the energy with which he endowed the blank verse* line, which in his hands developed an unprecedented suppleness and power. His plays have great intensity, but they show a genius which is epic rather than dramatic – at least in *Tamburlaine* and *Faustus* which are his acknowledged masterpieces; his best constructed piece of theatre, *Edward II*, is also the least typical of his poetic genius. On the other hand the final scene of *Dr Faustus* is one of the most intensely dramatic in English literature. In the musical handling and control of the ten-syllable line, he learned from Spenser*, and contributed to Milton* as well as to Shakespeare.

*** 5.1.2.4; 6.2.2.**

Bib: Bakeless, J., *The Tragical History of Christopher Marlowe*; Boas, F. S., *Christopher Marlowe*; Kocher, P. H., *Christopher Marlowe: a Study of his Thought, Learning and Character*; Poirier, M., *Christopher Marlowe*; Levin, H., *The Overreacher*; Steane, J. B., *Marlowe: a critical study*; Leech, C. (ed.) *Essays on Marlowe*; Eliot, T. S., in *Selected Essays*.

Marmion, A Tale of Flodden Field (1808)

A narrative poem by Sir Walter Scott* in six cantos. It is a romantic tale, set in 1513, the year of the catastrophic defeat of James IV of Scotland by an English army. Lord Marmion is fictitious; the story concerns his attempts to marry the rich Lady Clare, and to get rid of her lover by false charges of treason. He is eventually killed in the battle and the lovers are reunited.

Marprelate, Martin /ˈmaːprelɪt/

The pen-name for an anonymous author or authors of a series of pamphlets which appeared 1588–90. They were written from a Presbyterian* standpoint denying the validity of bishops, and they attacked the religious establishment, by which the Church was governed by crown-appointed bishops. The bishops were satirized so vigorously in such expressive, popular prose that the authorities were alarmed into commissioning such gifted writers as Nashe*, Lyly*, and Greene* to reply to them. The leaders of the movement, including Penry from whose secret press the pamphlets were issued, were arrested in 1593, and the government of Elizabeth I* imposed severe restrictions on sermons and on the press. (Marprelate: mar = damage, ruin; prelate = bishop.)

Marriage of Heaven and Hell, The

A composition mainly in prose by William Blake*. It was engraved, with designs interwoven with the text, in about 1790, in Blake's revolutionary phase, when he was at work on *The Songs of Experience**. The text opens with 'The Argument' in free verse, and continues with a series of aphorisms and 'Memorable Fancies', which are mystical anecdotes expressed tersely with caustic humour. The most famous section consists of seventy aphorisms entitled 'Proverbs of Hell'.

Blake's essential thesis, influenced by the thought of Swedenborg*, is that 18th-C Reason, typified by the philosophy of Locke*, inhibited the most vital energies of the human spirit by condemning them as hostile to order. He presents Hell as the region of these dangerous but living energies, and Heaven, without them, as a lifeless abstraction. 'Without Contraries is no progression,' Blake writes. Energy is of the body, Reason of the soul, 'and Reason is the bound or outward circumference of Energy'. It is important to remember that Blake, at least in this phase of his thought, considered the body itself as spiritual, 'for that call'd Body is a portion of Soul discern'd by the five Senses, the chief inlets of Soul in this age'.

* 3.4.1.

Marryat, Frederick, Captain (1792–1848) /'mariət/

Novelist. He was a Captain in the Royal Navy. His novels are chiefly about the sea. The best known of them are: *Frank Mildmay* (1829); *Peter Simple* (1834); *Jacob Faithful* (1834); *Mr Midshipman Easy* (1836). *Japhet in Search of a Father* (1836) is the story of a child of unknown parents who eventually achieves prosperity. Others of his books were intended for boys; the best-known of these is *Masterman Ready* (1841). Marryat continued the 18th-C realistic tradition of narrative, the most famous examples of which are the novels of Smollett*.

* *Realism.*

Bib: Marryat, F., *Life and Letters of Captain Marryat*; Conrad, J., 'Tales of the Sea' in *Notes on Life and Letters*; Warner, O., *Captain Marryat: a Rediscovery.*

Mars

* *Ares.*

Marshalsea /'ma:ʃlsi/

A prison in Southwark, London. It was opened in 13th C as a prison for the Marshalsea Court, which dealt with cases involving a member of the royal household. After the Restoration* it was kept for petty debtors. Dickens's father was imprisoned there for debt, and it is described in *Little Dorrit** (1858). The prison was abolished in 1849.

Marston, John (1575?–1634)

Satirist and dramatist. His father was a lawyer. John Marston was educated at Brasenose College, Oxford; lectured in the Middle Temple (one of the Inns of Court*); entered the Church, 1609. His writing life runs from 1598 to 1607. During this period he engaged in literary warfare with Ben Jonson* ('the war of the theatres') who satirized Marston and Dekker* in *The Poetaster* (1601) and elsewhere. The two men were, however, intermittently friends, and collaborated (with Chapman*) in writing *Eastward Hoe* (1605) for which they were imprisoned for offending the king's Scottish friends.

In 1598 Marston published *The Metamorphosis of Pygmalion's Image* and, under the pen-name of W. Kinsayder, a collection of satires entitled *Scourge of Villainie*. The satires were modelled on those of the Roman poet Persius. Their language is coarse and vigorous, and the violence and disgust they exhibit become a feature of Marston's dramatic writing. His plays are his most successful work, but they are very uneven. *Antonio and Mellida* and *Antonio's Revenge* (1599 – **Antonio*) are revenge plays* in the tradition of Kyd's *Spanish Tragedy**, and exhibit a mixture of stoic* idealism and melodramatic sensationalism, with passages of intense poetry. *The Malcontent** is a tragi-comedy and usually considered to be Marston's most effective work; its satirical qualities and the role of the central character suggest comparisons with Shakespeare's *Measure for Measure** and *Hamlet**. *The Dutch Courtezan* (1604), *The Parasitaster, or the Fawne* (1606) and *What You Will* (1607) are comedies; *Sophonisba, Wonder of Women* and *The Insatiate Countess* (both 1606?) are tragedies.

It was Marston's lack of critical control and the bad taste of his extravagance which caused the satirical attacks on him by Jonson; a critic has spoken of his inability 'to bridge the gap between rhetorical idealism and rhetorical disgust' (L. G. Salingar in *Pelican Guide 2*, p. 341). His violent revulsion from sensuality and worldly vice is characteristic of some of his contemporaries – Chapman, Webster*, Tourneur* – and, as in their plays, it inspires some of his best passages as well as his worst ones. T. S. Eliot* (*Selected Essays*) remarks on Marston's 'positive, powerful and unique personality', which asserts itself even through his faults.

Bib: Axelrad, A. José, *Un Malcontent Elizabéthain*; Eliot, T. S., in *Selected Essays*; Ellis-Fermor, U. M., *The Jacobean Drama*; Caputi, A., *John Marston, Satirist.*

Martin Chuzzlewit, The Life and Adventures of (1843-44)

A novel by Charles Dickens*. The Chuzzlewit family includes old Martin, a rich man grown misanthropic owing to the selfishness and greed of the rest of his family; young Martin, his grandson, who begins with the family selfishness, but is eventually purified by hardship and the good influence of his servant, Mark Tapley; Anthony, old Martin's avaricious brother, and Jonas, Anthony's son, who, by the end of the book, has become a figure of the blackest evil; Pecksniff, at first a trusted friend of old Martin, is one of Dickens's most effective hypocrites; Mrs Gamp, the disreputable nurse, is one of his most famous comic creations. The novel is divided rather sharply by the episode in which young Martin temporarily emigrates to America. This episode is a self-sufficient satire on American life; moreover, not only is young Martin's character radically changed by it, but the story thereafter takes on a denser substance. Pecksniff, Jonas, and the fraudulent financier Tigg Montague cease to be merely comic and become substantially evil. These changes mark the transition from the earlier Dickens, the comic entertainer, into the later Dickens, of sombre power. The novel is thus a transitional work, but it is also, as his comic masterpiece, the climax of Dickens's first phase.

Marvell, Andrew (1621–78) /'ma:vəl/

Poet. He was educated at Hull Grammar School (where his father was master) and Trinity College, Cambridge. He travelled in Europe, and in 1650 became tutor to the daughter of Lord Fairfax, the Civil War* Parliamentary general. In 1653 he became tutor to Cromwell's* ward, and in 1657 Milton's* assistant in the foreign secretaryship. In 1659 he became Member of Parliament for Hull, which he continued to represent after the Restoration* of the monarchy in 1660, apart from a period in which he was secretary to Lord Carlisle, an ambassador. Though Marvell is associated with the Puritan* side in the great political divisions of the time, his political sympathies varied; yet he was no time-server. He valued good government more than political persons; this made it possible for him to write his *Horatian Ode* in praise of Cromwell, and to include in it a magnificent tribute to King Charles I*. He welcomed the Restoration, but later he bitterly criticized the disorder of Charles II's* government in verse satires and in prose pamphlets which influenced Swift.* It was said by Milton's nephew that Milton owed his safety after the Restoration to Marvell's influence in Parliament.

As a poet, Marvell is one of the central figures of 17th C. In the boldness of his wit in his similitudes he is of the school of Donne*, and one of the outstanding Metaphysicals*; the grace and economy of his form show the influence of Jonson*; his ability to assimilate both influences anticipates the energy and economy of Dryden*; his admiration for Milton's blank verse is expressed in his lines *On Mr Milton's Paradise Lost.* His total output of verse was small, but it includes some of the most famous poems in the language, for instance *To his Coy Mistress*, *The Definition of Love*, *The Garden* and *An Horatian Ode upon Cromwell's Return from Ireland.* He was perhaps the last English poet to exhibit the most impressive single quality of the age of Shakespeare: the fusion of high intellectual subtlety with strong sensuous immediacy. Most of his poems were not published till 1681; the satires not until 1689 – after the Revolution of 1688* – but the lyrics and the satires certainly circulated privately in manuscript.

Bib: Legouis, P., *André Marvell, Poète, Puritain, Patriote* (translated into English in a shortened version); Eliot, T. S., in *Selected Essays*; Bradbrook, M. C., and Lloyd Thomas, M. G., *Andrew Marvell*; Cruttwell, P., in *The Shakespearian Moment*; Leavis, F. R., in *Revaluation*; Walton, G., *Metaphysical to Augustan*; Williamson, G., *The Donne Tradition*; Toliver, H. E., *Marvell's Ironic Vision*; Leishman, J. B., a critical study.

Marx, Karl Heinrich (1818–83) /ma:ks/

German socialist philosopher. As a newspaper editor, he was expelled twice from Germany for his opinions, and he was given permission to settle in France only under conditions of restraint. Accordingly he moved to London in 1849, where he remained for the rest of his life; he was buried in the suburb of Highgate. His best known works are the brief *Communist Manifesto* and his great treatise *Das Kapital* (*Capital*) which he wrote in London, and which was completed by his friend and collaborator, Friedrich Engels. These are the principal bases of Communist doctrine throughout the world.

The essence of his teaching is that political and social institutions derive from the system of production and distribution. A given system will require domination by a given social class, and the state will represent and secure the interests of this class. When economic conditions change, the social structure will change with it, but as the hitherto dominant class will not willingly renounce its privileges, such changes will only come about by class war, culminating in revolution. Thus, capitalism, or the private ownership of the means of production and supply, was in Marx's opinion becoming obsolete and therefore oppressive. The proletariat (a term which Marx applied only to the class of industrial workers which capitalism had brought into being to serve its needs) was becoming organized and educated; it would soon be able to overthrow the capitalist class and replace private ownership of the means of production by state ownership, or socialism. Philosophically, Marx based his analysis on an inversion of the idealist doctrines of the German thinker, Hegel. Hegel had taught that history is really the record of the conflict of ideas; each idea calls into being its own opposite, and out of their conflict a new idea arises (thesis, antithesis, synthesis), and the process repeats itself. Marx substituted for ideas the battle of economic forces; thus the capitalist class had called into being the proletariat, and out of their conflict a classless (communist) society would eventually come into being.

Marxism was one of several kinds of socialist influence on 19th- and early-20th-C English imaginative writers, of whom Bernard Shaw* is the most important. It became a dominant influence only between 1920 and 1940, and especially in the 1930s. At that time the poet W. H. Auden* used Marxism as an instrument for exploring the insincerities of English middle-class social conventions, just as he used Freud* to analyse the sickness of the middle-class psyche; his associates, Stephen Spender* and Cecil Day Lewis*, had an even more distinctly Marxist phase. This was a period in which English (and American) liberal traditions were in confusion, and intellectuals required a firm if simplified base from which to confront German and Italian fascism. Marxism tended to be a superficial positive influence, however, and it was an evanescent one. It was more important negatively. On the one hand, writers of the right, such as T. S. Eliot*, Wyndham Lewis*, and W. B. Yeats*, tended to confirm their attitudes by opposition to Marxism; on the other hand, just as the psychology of Freud destroyed the possibility of ever again assuming certain forms of emotional idealism, so Marxism undermined for good certain forms of social assumption. In this, however, the secondary influence of Shaw was particularly important. Post-1945 Stalinism did most to destroy Marxist influences after the war, and the satire of George Orwell* (*Animal Farm* and *1984*) helped the process. The Auden school of poets underwent a conversion away from Marxism analogous to the conversion of Wordsworth* and Coleridge* away from the radical politics of the French Revolution*.

* 3.4.5.

Mary [in the Bible]

Four women named Mary are mentioned in the Gospels:

[1] Mary, the Mother of Jesus. The chief mentions of her are in *Matthew* 1 & 2, *Luke* 1 & 2, *John* 2 & 19. She is also mentioned in *Acts* 1 as praying with the Apostles in the interval between the Ascension and Pentecost. Later apocryphal writings placed more emphasis upon her, and she was given importance in the Church system of belief from about the time of the Council of Ephesus (413). Three doctrines about her were especially held: she was regarded as being perpetually virgin; she was absolutely sinless; she had supreme powers of intercession with God on behalf of man. Often referred to as 'the Holy Virgin', 'Our Lady', and 'Mother of God', she is constantly mentioned in medieval literature. After the Reformation*, however, these beliefs about her were held to be superstitions, and, apart from the Anglo-Catholic section of belief within the Church of England*, she was regarded by Protestants with much less reverence.

[2] Mary Magdalene. One of the women disciples of Jesus. The name 'Magdalene' refers to her town of origin, Magdala. She was frequently identified with the unnamed woman who washed the feet of Jesus with her tears, in *Luke* 7:37, and thus tradition held her to be a repentant prostitute. The tears of Mary Magdalene thus became a symbol of the cleansing powers of repentance. She is mentioned in each of the Gospels as being present at the open tomb after the crucifixion, and hearing the tidings of the resurrection.

[3] Mary of Bethany, sister of Martha (*Luke* 10: 38–42) and of Lazarus, whom Jesus raised from the dead (*John* 11). She is often confused with Mary Magdalene.

[4] Mary the mother of James and Joses, mentioned in *Matthew* 27 & 28 *Mark* 16, *Luke* 24 as accompanying Mary Magdalene to the tomb.

Mary I (1553–58)

Queen of England. She was the eldest child of Henry VIII* who had used his divorce from her mother, Katharine of Aragon*, as a pretext for taking the control of the English Church out of the hands of the Pope and into his own. Under her brother Edward VI* England had swung further into Protestantism*, but Mary restored the Roman Catholic religion of her mother. In 1554 she married the most fanatically Catholic sovereign in Europe, Philip II of Spain; this involved her in wars with France and the loss of the last English possession there – the town of Calais. Her reign, not bloodthirsty by comparison with that of Philip in his own dominions, was nonetheless severely repressive of Protestantism, and some 300 English Protestants were burnt alive, including Cranmer* and the eloquent Bishop Latimer*. John Foxe's* *Book of Martyrs* (1563) consigned her memory to national hatred, and she has come down in school books as 'Bloody Mary'. Her sister and successor Elizabeth I* restored a moderate form of Protestantism.

* *Tudor, House of.*

Mary II (1689–94)

Queen of Great Britain. She was the daughter of James II* by his first wife, and was educated in Protestant doctrine, which she retained when her father became converted to Catholicism. She married William of Orange, ruler of the Netherlands, in 1677. When James was removed from the throne in the Revolution of 1688* Mary was summoned to rule the nation jointly with her husband, who assumed the throne as William III*.

* *Stuart, House of.*

Mary Barton (1848)

The first novel by Elizabeth Gaskell*. Written while she was in deep distress over the death of her infant son, it is a plea for greater understanding between the employing class and the industrial proletariat of the north. It is set in Manchester in the decade in which she wrote; this was known as 'the hungry forties' because of the distress among the working classes. The best character creation is John Barton, a sober and intelligent workman, whose perception of the social injustice which surrounds him and of which he is a victim drives him into bitter resentment. A group of workers draw lots to assassinate Henry Carson, one of the younger and most callous of the employers, as a warning to the rest of the class. The lot falls on Barton, who commits the murder. Suspicion, however, falls on his daughter's lover, Jem Wilson, who is brought to trial and only saved from the death penalty by Mary Barton's strenuous efforts. John Barton confesses to the murder to Henry Carson's father, who forgives him on his deathbed. Despite implausibilities, the novel is one of the most sensitive studies of industrial working-class life in Victorian fiction; as such, it suffered angry criticism from some of the employing class whom it was intended to convert.

Mary Queen of Scots (1542–67)

Queen of Scotland. She was born a few days before the death of her father, James V. In 1548, when she was five years old, she was betrothed to Francis, heir to the French throne, and was sent to France. She returned to Scotland only after the death of her husband in 1560; she was Catholic, but in the meantime the Scottish Protestants with English help had overthrown the Catholic establishment in their country. Mary in consequence found herself opposed to her people, led by the reformer John Knox*. She was dangerously involved in English politics, both because she would be heir to the English throne should Elizabeth of England die childless, and because in the eyes of Catholics she was already legitimate Queen of England, since the Catholic Church did not recognize the legality of the marriage between Elizabeth's father, Henry VIII*, and her mother. For diplomatic reasons, Mary married her cousin, Lord Darnley, a worthless young man who treated her abominably. In 1567 Darnley was murdered. The evidence for Mary's complicity in the murder is in the so-called 'casket letters', but their authenticity is uncertain. However, three months later she married his murderer, Lord Bothwell. Her subjects rebelled, and Mary was imprisoned but escaped and fled to England. Elizabeth gave her shelter, but the succession of plots against her on Mary's behalf eventually drove the English Queen to authorize the Scottish Queen's execution. Her son, already recognized as James VI in Scotland, became in 1603, on the death of Elizabeth, James I* of England as well.

Owing to her charm, beauty, intelligence and misfortune, Mary became a legend in Europe. The greatest imaginative work about her is the tragedy *Maria Stuart* by the German poet Schiller; in English literature she is the subject of a dramatic trilogy by Swinburne* and of Walter Scott's* novel, *The Abbot* (1820).

Marylebone /ˈmarələbən/

A district in the west of London, north of Hyde Park. In 18th C, Marylebone Gardens were a fashionable resort.

Masefield, John (1878–1967)

Poet and novelist. He went to sea in 1893, and published his first volume of poems, *Salt-Water Ballads* in 1902. He was a prolific poet; the first edition of his *Collected Poems* came out in 1923, and the collection increased steadily until 1964. His work has immediate appeal, and is strongest in narrative verse: *The Everlasting Mercy* (1911); *The Widow in the Bye Street* (1912); *Dauber* (1913); *The Daffodil Fields* (1913); *Reynard the Fox* (1919). He was chosen as Poet Laureate* in 1930. His novels have romantic charm, *eg Sard Harker* (1924); *Odtaa* (1926). *The Midnight Folk* (1927) is a classic of children's literature.
Bib: A critical study by Muriel Spark.

Mask of Anarchy, The

A poem by Percy Bysshe Shelley*, written in 1819, when he heard the news of the Manchester Massacre, otherwise known as Peterloo*, when soldiers fired on a peaceful demonstration in favour of parliamentary reform. The poem consists of 91 quatrains and five-line stanzas, and differs from Shelley's usual style in its savage terseness and roughness of style; it was intended for popular reading and Shelley thus used a form similar to that of the popular ballad*. Shelley identifies Anarchy with lawless tyranny, and exhibits the leaders of the government as Anarchy's minions. He sent the poem to Leigh Hunt* for publication in his radical periodical *The Examiner**, but Leigh Hunt thought that its effect on the public might be more destructive than inspiring, and withheld publication until 1832.

Masque /ma:sk/

A form of dramatic entertainment which combined verse, music, dancing, and scenic effect in about equal proportions. In England it flourished between 1580 and 1630, and was essentially an aristocratic style of entertainment, especially popular at the royal court. The actors were commonly amateurs, often ladies and gentlemen of the court, although professional actors might take part with them. The subject was often symbolic – a conflict between virtue and vice (as in Milton's *Comus**) – or ceremonial, celebrating a great personage, *eg* Milton's *Arcades* in honour of the Countess of Derby. The masque was sometimes followed by an anti-masque, the content of which was comic and often satirical; the anti-masque was performed by professional actors.

Although masques were sophisticated entertainments for carefully selected audiences, they were in keeping with many forms of imaginative expression of the age, and may be regarded as a synthesis of them. First of all, the visual sense had been highly developed by the great Renaissance* schools of painting and architecture in Italy and France, and a favourite activity of artists was to translate into visual terms the allegorical vision that the Renaissance had inherited from the Middle Ages. This visual allegory influenced the poets; much of the best of Spenser's *Faerie Queene** consists of brilliantly visualized allegorical scenes, such as the House of Busirane (Bk. III, Canto 12). Secondly, the age attached great importance to spectacles such as Pageants* (*ie* ceremonial processions) which often contained symbolic, masque-like features; a famous example (which still survives) was the annual Lord Mayor's Pageant in the City of London, for which the dramatist George Peele* was more than once employed as designer. Thirdly, masques appealed to the contemporary taste for imaginative extravagance, delighting in the fairytales of English folk-lore and in classical mythology as well as in grand pageantry. Fourthly, the unrealistic styles of many Elizabethan plays – attributable partly to popular taste and partly to the explorations of humanist* scholars – made them either akin to masques (*eg* Greene's* *James IV*, Peele's* *The Old Wives' Tale*, Lyly's* *Mother Bombie*), or capable of including masques as part of the dramatic ingredient, *eg* Shakespeare's *Love's Labour's Lost** and *The Tempest**. Finally, it was an age of close musical and literary collaboration, and masques provided opportunities for musicians and poets to collaborate on a large scale, just as they already collaborated on a small scale in the madrigal*.

Dramatists who were eminent for their composition of masques included Chapman*, Fletcher* and Shirley*, but the greatest of them – in his own estimation and probably that of others – was Ben Jonson*. He collaborated with the composer Alfonso Ferrabosco the younger, and the great architect Inigo Jones*; with the latter he had bitter quarrels as to which of them had artistic control of the production. Amongst Jonson's most celebrated masques are *Masque of Blackness* (1606), *Masque of Beauty* (1608), and *Masque of Queens* (1609). The most famous of all masques, however, is Milton's *Comus*, composed for the Earl of Bridgewater, whose children acted the main parts, when he was installed as Lord President of Wales. Part of the fame of *Comus* is due to its untypical quality of containing much larger speaking parts than most masques did; thus Milton allowed himself more poetic scope than was usual. For this reason, some critics prefer to call *Comus* a pastoral* drama, like Jonson's *The Sad Shepherd* (1637) and Fletcher's *The Faithful Shepherdess* (1610). However, pastoral dramas and masques had much in common; both were symbolic rather than dramatic, and appealed to the spectacular element of theatre.

John Dryden* celebrated the end of 17th C with *The Secular Masque* (1700), but after the Restoration*, the masque tended to be submerged in the kindred form of opera*.

Massinger, Philip (1583–1640) /ˈmasindʒə/

Dramatist. His father was in the service of the great Herbert family. He left Oxford without a degree in 1606. He has been suspected of Catholic sympathies, largely on the strength of three plays: *The Virgin Martyr* (1620), *The Maid of Honour* (1621), and *The Renegado* (1624). He collaborated extensively with other dramatists, especially Fletcher*, but sixteen or eighteen plays are attributed to him alone; of these, the two usually regarded as being of the most enduring value are the comedies, *A New Way to Pay Old Debts** (1625) and *The City Madam** (1632). He himself regarded his tragedy *The Roman Actor* (1626) as his masterpiece. The dates of these plays show them to belong to the last, or Caroline*, phase of what is commonly called Elizabethan drama because it started in the reign of Elizabeth I. They belong, therefore, to the decadence, and tragedy declined faster than comedy. The comedies mentioned still show a lively influence from Ben Jonson*, whereas Massinger's tragedies have been accused of a lack of that intensity which gave grandeur to the work not only of Shakespeare but of Chapman*, Tourneur*, and Webster*. Massinger's blank verse* is in the late Shakespeare tradition, but grown so flexible as almost to have lost its rhythms into prose. However, he handled his sustained periods skilfully and sometimes impressively, anticipating the great verse paragraphs of Milton* without Miltonic grandeur.

* 5.1.3.3; 5.1.4; 6.2.2

Bib: Eliot, T. S., in *Selected Essays*; Knights, L. C., *Drama and Society in the Age of Jonson*; Dunn, T. A., *Massinger*; Stephen, L., in *Hours in a Library*; Chelli, M., *Le Drame de Massinger*.

Master Craftsman

In the Middle Ages, a full member of a Craft Guild* and usually an employer of apprentices* and journeymen*. Originally every apprentice could theoretically hope to become 'a master' after a specified period of 'apprenticeship' or training and the production of a 'masterpiece' to prove his skill in the craft. By 14th C, however, the master craftsmen of the guilds were already becoming a comparatively rich class of employers of labour, which the apprentices could not hope to enter unless they themselves had money, or married the master's daughter. Most apprentices could by then only hope to become fully trained journeymen.

* *Capitalism.*

Master Humphrey's Clock

The title of what Dickens* intended to be an inclusive serial linking distinct tales – *The Old Curiosity Shop** and *Barnaby Rudge**. Master Humphrey is the narrator of the early pages of the former, but Dickens abandoned the idea.

Maturin, Charles Robert (1782–1824)

Irish novelist and dramatist. Like 'Monk' Lewis and Mrs Radcliffe* he belonged to the school of writers who exploited the emotions of terror and love of mystery among readers in late 18th and early 19th C. *The Fatal Revenge, or The Family of Montorio* (1807), *The Wild Irish Boy* (1808) and *The Milesian Chief* (1812) were ridiculed but admired for their power by Walter Scott. Scott and Byron secured the production of Maturin's tragedy *Bertram* in 1816, which was a great success. His other tragedies were less successful, and he returned to the novel. The best of his later novels is *Melmoth* (1820), to which the French novelist Balzac wrote a sequel *Melmoth réconcilié à l'église* (1835).

Maud (1855)

One of the best-known poems by Alfred Tennyson*. It is called 'A Monodrama', and is in fact an example of the dramatic monologue*, a form particularly characteristic of Victorian poetry, especially in the work of Browning* and Tennyson.

It is in three parts. Part I tells of the mysterious death of the narrator's father, who has been ruined by the contrivances of 'that old man, now lord of the broad estate and the Hall'. But the narrator gradually falls in love with the old lord's daughter, and here occurs the famous lyric 'Come into the garden, Maud'. The young lord, her brother, treats him with contempt, however, and Part II opens with their duel and the death of the brother. The narrator flies abroad, and falls into the depths of morbid despair. In Part III he recovers, and seeks salvation through the service of his country in war: the poem was written in the year in which the Crimean War broke out.

Maud contains some of Tennyson's most distinguished lines, and it also displays some of his worst faults. It exemplifies the versatility of his craftsmanship by the variety of its metrical and stanzaic form, and the brilliant distinctness of his vision in some of the imagery. It contains bitter criticism of the temper of the age. But much of the young man's morbidity is dishonestly presented; the poet is using it as a screen for melodramatic indulgence. The spiritual rescue by war in Part III is unconvincing. The poem has been held to betray Tennyson's confusion about his age; criticizing it, yet swimming with its tide.

Maugham, William Somerset (1874–1965) /mo:m/

Novelist and dramatist. Educated at King's School, Canterbury, and Heidelberg University; he then studied medicine in London. His first novel, *Liza of Lambeth* (1897) shows the influence of Zola*, an example of the growing importance of French influence on English fiction at the end of 19th C. His semi-autobiographical novel *Of Human Bondage* (1915) made his name. Other novels: *The Hero* (1901); *The Moon and Sixpence* (1919); *The Trembling of a Leaf* (1921); *On a Chinese Screen* (1922); *The Painted Veil* (1925); *The Casuarina Tree* (1926); *Cakes and Ale* (1930); *The Mixture as Before* (1940). The professional accomplishment of his novels gave him a wide foreign public, and after 1930 his reputation abroad was greater than at home, though interest in him revived here towards his 80th birthday. He celebrated his 80th year by the special republication of *Cakes and Ale*, a novel which satirizes the English propensity for admiring the 'Grand Old Men' among their writers. Some of his best fiction is in his short stories.

His plays were successful, but have lost interest now. They include: *Caesar's Wife* (1919); *East of Suez* (1922); *Our Betters* (1923); *The Constant Wife* (1927); *The Letter* (1927); *The Breadwinner* (1930); *Sheppey* (1933).

Bib: Jonas, K. W., *The Maugham Enigma*; Critical studies by R. A. Cordell and by L. Brander; British Council Booklet by J. Brophy; Maugham, R., *Somerset and All the Maughams*.

May Day

1 May. A great festival* in England until the middle of 17th C. Its symbol was the maypole, painted in spiral stripes and decorated with flowers; it was carried in procession and then set into the ground for the people to dance round. The origins of the maypole seem to be in ancient pagan vegetation worship, marking the end of winter and the beginning of summer, and had their analogy in the ancient Roman festival of Floralia, held in the same month. A May queen (Queen of the May), and sometimes a May king, were chosen, to preside over the festival in each locality and the May games and morris dances* were performed, with representations of characters from the legend-cycle of Robin Hood*. The 16th and 17th-C Puritans* strongly disapproved of the festival, and after they came to power in the Civil War*, maypoles were forbidden by Parliament. They were revived at the Restoration*, and their use survived in some country districts until much later. May Day was revived as Labour Day by the International Socialist Congress in 1889.

Mayfair

A district in the west of London, bounded by Oxford Street, Regent Street, Piccadilly and Hyde Park. It is so called after a great May fair held there in 17th and 18th C. In 19th C and first quarter of 20th it was the most fashionable area of London. It is now much more commercial, but it still contains the most fashionable shops in Bond Street and its neighbourhood.

Mayflower, The

* *Pilgrim Fathers.*

Mayor of Casterbridge, The (1886)

A novel by Thomas Hardy*. Its hero is the country labourer, Michael Henchard. At the beginning of the book, when times are hard, he gets drunk at a fair and sells his wife and child to a sailor called Newson. He bitterly repents, and renounces strong drink for twenty years. His wife returns after 18 years, supposing Newson to be drowned, and by this time Henchard has prospered so far as to have become Mayor of Casterbridge (Dorchester). At the same time as her return, Henchard takes on as his assistant in his business of corn-dealing a wandering Scotsman, Donald Farfrae. The rest of the novel is the story of the rivalry between Farfrae and Henchard. Farfrae is never deliberately his enemy, yet merely by virtue of living in the same town he deprives Henchard of everything, and the latter leaves the place at the end of the novel as poor as when he started, and far more wretched. Hardy seems to have intended a kind of Darwinian study of the survival of the fittest among human beings. Henchard is a monolithic character, who puts all his energy and passion into every relationship and activity; Farfrae has a flexible personality, and is able to devote to every predicament exactly what it demands, without excess. Henchard's crowning sadness is the loss of the girl he has supposed to be his daughter, but who is in fact Newson's; he loves her nonetheless, but Newson returns and claims her.

Hardy regarded the book as his best, and it is certainly one of his two or three masterpieces.

Measure for Measure

A play by Shakespeare*. It was probably written in 1603–4, and was first printed in the First Folio* of 1623. Its plot derives from *Promos and Cassandra* (1578), the translation by Whetstone of a tale by the Italian Cinthio. In the Folio it is grouped with the comedies, but modern critics are inclined to call it a problem play*, a modern classification that includes *Troilus and Cressida**, *All's Well that Ends Well**, and sometimes *Hamlet**.

Vincentio, Duke of Vienna, is faced with the difficulty of enforcing severe laws against unchastity after they have fallen into disuse; he finds that the claims of justice and virtue conflict with those of mercy and compassion. He makes the experiment of pretending to leave the country so as to depute the task to Angelo, a man of austere life and rigid principle. In fact, the Duke remains on the scene, disguised as a friar, to watch the experiment. Angelo condemns Claudio to death for seducing his betrothed before marriage. Claudio's sister, Isabella, a novitiate nun, comes to plead for her brother's life, urged on by Lucio, a man of loose life but a friend of Claudio's. Angelo is appalled to find that his lust is aroused for Isabella. His strict principle is transformed into brutal hypocrisy when he attempts to blackmail Isabella into surrendering herself in return for her brother's life. The disguised Duke induces her to pretend to consent, while he substitutes for her Mariana, whom Angelo has cold-heartedly discarded in spite of his engagement to her. Even after Isabella's apparent consent, Angelo orders Claudio's execution, in order that no witness of his brutal conspiracy shall survive. This is prevented by another ruse. The Duke in the last scene reveals himself, and exposes his deputy, but spares his life on the appeals of Isabella and Mariana.

It is necessary to remember the biblical text (*Matthew* 7:1) from which the title is taken: 'Judge not, that ye be not judged. For with what judgement ye judge, ye shall be judged: and with what measure ye mete, it shall be measured to you again.' The three main problems that perplex critics are as follows.

[1] The Duke is evidently intended to be a virtuous ruler, who even plays the role of God, the invisible witness of our most secret thoughts and actions. Viewed realistically, however, he escapes from his duty and then plays the role of a mean spy on Angelo's actions. The mistake here is to confuse the conventions of modern, realistic drama with the conventions of Shakespeare's drama. The latter saw character in terms of role, or social function, first, and in terms of individual psychology only second. Vincentio is a ruler as God is the Ruler; by taking on the rule of the omnipresent witness who has ultimate power of judgement, he is extending his function, not escaping from it.

[2] Isabella is presented as a virtuous woman, and yet she seems inexcusably callous in her refusal to put her brother's life before her own chastity. This is not a problem if we understand that Isabella's religious vocation is the meaning of life to her (I. iv); she has to be educated into seeing that virtue can never retain its value if it is segregated from life, just as law can never operate wisely if it is isolated from knowledge of the human heart; this is Angelo's mistake.

[3] Although the death penalty on Claudio is cruel, no one disputes that he has committed an offence, and yet later Angelo (by the contrivance of the Duke) is made to commit the same offence with Mariana, for which neither of them is held guilty. An answer to this is the difference between Claudio's and Angelo's actions. Claudio had offended against the law, but not against his bethrothed, Juliet, whereas Angelo had previously offended against Mariana by renouncing his engagement to her, though not against the law. Morally, the play shows that Angelo's offence is the worse, and is in fact made good by his 'sin' of the Duke's contrivance.

For an adverse view of the play, see A. P. Rossiter in *Angel with Horns*; for favourable ones, see F. R. Leavis in *The Common Pursuit* and Wilson Knight in *The Wheel of Fire*.

Mecca /'mekə/

The birthplace of the Prophet Muhammad, and the chief goal of pilgrimage for Muslims. In English, the word is also used for any place that one is determined to reach.

Medal, The (1682)

A satirical poem by John Dryden* against Lord Shaftesbury*. Shaftesbury, the leader of the Whig* party which was trying to prevent James Duke of York from being accepted as heir to the throne, had been acquitted by a grand jury on the charge of treason. The Whigs celebrated this with a medal inscribed 'Laetamur' (We rejoice). The poem, in heroic couplets*, is directed against the methods and principles of demagogy, on which Shaftesbury relied.

* *Absalom and Achitophel*; James II.

Medea /mi'diə/

In Greek myth, a celebrated sorceress. She was the

daughter of Aeetes, king of Colchis, possessor of the Golden Fleece. She helped Jason* of Iolchos to steal it, and fled with him to Corinth. There, Jason abandoned her for Glauce, daughter of the king. In revenge, Medea destroyed her own two children by Jason, and Glauce as well. She was worshipped as a goddess in Corinth. Other tales about her show her as destroyer or renewer of life; she destroyed her brother to distract pursuit of herself and Jason by her father, restored Jason's father to youth by magic, caused the daughters of King Pelias of Iolchos to kill their father, and plotted to kill Theseus of Athens after marrying his father, King Aegeus.

Medes /mi:dz/

Inhabitants of ancient Persia; the Persians subjected them in 6th C BC. A reference in the Bible (*Daniel* 6:8) has caused the Law of the Medes and Persians to stand proverbially for that which is unalterable.

Medusa

**Gorgons.*

Meiosis /maiˈəusis/

* *Figures of Speech.*

Melchior

* *Magi.*

Meleager /meliˈeigə/

In Greek myth, the son of Oeneus king of Calydon and his wife Althea. The goddess Artemis* sent a giant boar to ravage the kingdom, because Oeneus had been neglectful in his worship. Meleager killed it, and gave its head to Atalanta* who had first wounded it. His uncles objected, and he slew them. His mother had once been warned by the Fates (Parcae*) that Meleager would live until a log then on the fire was consumed; she had removed the log, and preserved it carefully; now, to avenge her brothers, she threw it again on the fire, and her son perished.

Melibeus, The Tale of /meliˈbiəs/

One of the two prose narratives in Chaucer's *Canterbury Tales**. It is supposed to be the poet's own contribution to the series, after the Host has refused to listen to his doggerel romance *Sir Thopas**. Chaucer then goes to the other extreme, and tells this moral tale in the form of a discussion between Melibeus and his wife Prudence on the right way to treat those who have done one an injury. It is a translation of a French romance.

Melincourt, or Sir Oran Haut-ton (1817) /ˈmelinko:t – ˈo:ranˈəuton/

A novel by Thomas Love Peacock*. Sir Oran Haut-ton is an orang-outang of delightful manners and a good flute-player for whom the young philosopher, Mr Sylvan Forester, has bought the title of baronet and a seat in Parliament. 'Haut ton' is a French phrase then used in English for 'high tone', *ie* fashionable, refined, and aristocratic. Peacock is developing the idea of Lord Monboddo (1714–99), an early anthropologist, who describes such a creature in his books, as an example of 'the infantine state of our species'; Peacock's ape, however, compares favourably with the aristocracy. The book is predominantly a satire at the expense of the right-wing (Tory) establishment, and especially those writers who had once been Radicals but now favoured it: Southey* (Mr Feathernest); Wordsworth* (Mr Paperstamp); Coleridge* (Mr Mystic). Mr Vamp and Mr Killthedead are Tory reviewers, and Mr Fax may represent Malthus. Sylvan Forester may be the poet Shelley*; and Simon Sarcastic, Peacock himself.

Melodrama

The prefix 'melo-' derives from the Greek 'melos', music. Originally, melodrama was a play in which there was no singing but the dialogue had a musical accompaniment; the first example is said to be Rousseau's* *Pygmalion* (1775). The musical accompaniment gradually ceased; the word came to denote romantic plays of extravagantly violent action, and it is now applied to sensational action without adequate psychological motivation, in any work of fiction.

The word has also been used to denote popular ballad operas such as Gay's *Beggar's Opera**, in which spoken dialogue is used extensively. This use, however, is much less common.

Melpomene /melˈpomini/

In Greek myth, the Muse* of tragedy.

Memnon /ˈmemnon/

In Greek myth, the king of the Ethiopians, and the son of Tithonus and Eos (Lat. Aurora) the goddess of dawn. He came to help his uncle, Priam*, in the siege of Troy*, and was killed by the Greek hero Achilles*. Early morning dew was said to be the tears of his mother weeping for him. A giant statue near Thebes in Egypt was traditionally said to represent him; when it was touched by the rays of the rising sun, it emitted musical notes, which were said to be the spirit of Memnon responding to his mother Eos.

Memoirs of a Cavalier (1724)

A work of fiction by Daniel Defoe*, but it was thought that the memoirs were possibly genuine. They describe the career of a professional soldier, Colonel Andrew Newport, born in 1608. He sees military service in Europe during the Thirty Years War*, and then joins the English Royalist army in the Civil War*.

Men and Women (1855)

A volume of poems by Robert Browning*. It contained 50 pieces, all in dramatic monologue*, a form in which a character soliloquizes about himself, his predicament, or his relationship with another. The book contains much of Browning's best-known work, such as *Any Wife to Any Husband*, *The Bishop Orders his Tomb*, *Fra Lippo Lippi*. In the *Collected Works* of 1868, the poems were dispersed, and only 13 remained under the title *Men and Women*.

Menaechmi /me'neikmi/

A comedy by the Roman poet Plautus*, used by Shakespeare as the basis for his early *Comedy of Errors**.

Mendicant Orders

* *Friars*.

Menelaus /meni'leiəs/

In Greek legend, king of Sparta* and brother of Agamemnon*, leader of the Greek forces in the siege of Troy*. The wife of Menelaus was Helen*, the beautiful daughter of Leda and Zeus. When Paris*, son of Priam of Troy, stole Helen from Menelaus, the latter summoned all the princes who had sought her in marriage and had bound themselves to defend her; they united against Troy until the city was destroyed, and Menelaus and Helen were reunited.

Mentor

In Greek legend, the faithful friend of the hero Odysseus* (Ulysses). When Odysseus was lost on his return from the Trojan war, his son Telemachus* went in search of him, accompanied by the goddess Athene disguised as Mentor. The name has passed into English as a common noun: a mentor = an adviser.

Mephistopheles /mefis'tofili:z/

An evil spirit whose name first occurs in the German *Faustbuch* (1587), a collection of tales about the necromancer Johann Faust*. He is one of the seven great princes of hell. The word is variously spelt; *eg* in Marlowe's *Dr Faustus* (1592?) it is Mephostophilis.

Mercantile System

A term used by the economist Adam Smith* (*Wealth of Nations*, 1776) and later writers to denote the assumptions behind the practice of commerce from the later Middle Ages until 18th C. In its extreme form, it identified wealth with money so that the main object of governments was to accumulate large stocks of precious metals. Smith advocated a contrary theory of the free circulation of trade, which became the dominant policy by the middle of 19th C.

Merchant Adventurers

* *Companies, Joint Stock*.

Merchant of Venice, The

A comedy by Shakespeare*. It is dated by external evidence 1596–7. Its two outstanding incidents – the winning of a bride by undergoing a test, and the demanding of a pound of human flesh by the usurer – occur in a number of earlier narratives, but Shakespeare seems to have depended principally on a collection of Italian novels called *Il Pecorone* (*The Blockhead*) and the *Gesta Romanorum* (Tales of the Romans). Quarto* edition, 1600; included in the First Folio* (1623).

The play has a double plot.

[1] An impoverished young Venetian, Bassanio, seeks to marry a wealthy heiress, Portia of Belmont. For the expenses of the courtship he has to borrow 3,000 ducats from his friend, the merchant Antonio. When Bassanio and Portia meet, they fall in love at first sight, but before she can surrender herself, Bassanio has to pass the test of the caskets, ordained by her dead father. The test is to choose between a gold, a silver, and a lead casket; the right casket contains her portrait. He passes the test, but their rejoicing is interrupted by the arrival of a letter from Antonio.

[2] Antonio's money is all invested in mercantile expeditions, so that to help Bassanio he has had to borrow from the Jewish usurer, Shylock. Shylock has made the strange stipulation that Antonio will have to surrender a pound of his flesh in default of repayment. Antonio's letter now relates that his voyaging ships have all been lost, he is penniless, and will have to pay the pound of flesh. The two plots join in the trial scene of IV.i. The issue has come before a court of law at which Portia appears disguised as a young lawyer instructed to judge the case. She appeals to Shylock to show mercy, but when he insists on the letter of the law she lets him have it: he may take his pound of flesh, but there is no mention of blood in the bond; if he sheds any, the law of Venice is clear: his lands and goods are to become the property of the state. Antonio is saved, and Shylock has to undergo certain severe penalties, including compulsory conversion to Christianity. Act V concludes the play with light comedy and the lyrical union of several pairs of lovers.

Like others of Shakespeare's earlier comedies, the play is a mixture of courtly sophistication, light fantasy, and moving realism. The plot belongs to fable and fairy story, and the love affairs to the tradition of courtly romance. On the other hand, Shylock is a very powerful, sombre figure. His revolting bond is counterbalanced by Antonio's arrogant treatment of him and the eloquent irony with which Shylock protests against it. The trial scene is one of the elements of fable in the play: in real terms, Shylock is being treated with gross injustice, but the real theme is the contrast between Mercy and the Law. It is the function of mere Law to be merciless; he who refuses mercy and insists on law must abide by the consequences.

* *Usury*.

Merchant's Tale, The

One of Chaucer's *Canterbury Tales**. It is about an old man with a young wife – January and May. May is beloved by a young squire Damian. January goes blind, and Damian and May make love in a pear-tree. At the critical moment Pluto restores January's sight, but Proserpine befriends May and enables her to outwit him. The story is not so immoral as it seems; the description of the old man and his lust is one of the brilliant realistic passages in the Tales.

Mercia /ˈmɜ:ʃjə/

One of the ancient Anglo-Saxon* kingdoms 6th–9th C. From 10th C to the Norman* Conquest (1066) it was an earldom in the kingdom of England. It roughly corresponded to the modern Midlands.
 * *Heptarchy.*

Mercury

 * *Hermes.*

Mercutio /mɜ:kju:ʃjəu/

The friend of Romeo and related to the Prince in Shakespeare's tragedy *Romeo and Juliet**. He makes the celebrated speech about Queen Mab in I. iv. His quarrelsomeness leads to his death at the hands of Tybalt, the cousin of Juliet, followed by Romeo's fatal duel with Tybalt.

Meredith, George (1828–1909)

Novelist and poet. Born at Portsmouth, the son of a tailor and naval outfitter; his grandfather, Melchizedeck, had had the same business and is the basis of the character Old Mel in the novel *Evan Harrington*. George Meredith was educated in Germany, and his writings were influenced by Germans, especially the novelist Jean Paul Richter (1763–1825), who stimulated his conception of comedy. Meredith was even closer to French culture, however, especially the radical thinking of the 18th-C Philosophes (**Encyclopaedists*). On his return to England he began to study law, but soon took to journalism, and then to serious literature.

He began by publishing verse: *Poems* (1851). In 1855 he published his eastern romance *Shaving of Shagpat*, and in 1857 a romance in German style, *Farina, a Legend of Cologne*. *The Ordeal of Richard Feverel** (1859) was his first real novel, followed by *Evan Harrington* (1861), which is now regarded as one of his best. In 1862 he produced his most famous volume of poems, *Modern Love*. Other publications included: *Sandra Belloni* (1864; originally called *Emilia in England*); *Rhoda Fleming* (1865); *Vittoria* (1867 – a sequel to *Sandra*); *The Adventures of Harry Richmond* (1871); *Beauchamp's Career* (1875 – his own favourite); *The Idea of Comedy* (1877 – a critical essay, important for understanding his work); *The Egoist** (1879 – one of his best known novels); *The Tragic Comedians* (1880); *Poems and Lyrics of the Joy of Earth* (1883); *Diana of the Crossways* (1885 – the first of his novels to reach a wide public); *Ballads and Poems of Tragic Life* (1887); *A Reading of Earth* (1888 – verse); *One of Our Conquerors* (1891); *The Empty Purse* (1892 – a poem); *Lord Ormont and his Aminta* (1894); *The Amazing Marriage* (1895). His concluding works were all poetry: *Odes in Contribution to the Song of French History* (1898); *A Reading of Life* (1901); *Last Poems* (pub. in 1910 after his death). His unfinished novel, *Celt and Saxon*, was also published posthumously.

Meredith's reputation at present rests chiefly on his novels but, like Hardy*, he seems to have been a novelist who preferred poetry. His prose is poetic in its use of metaphor and symbolism, and both his poetry and his prose are often expressed in concentrated and difficult language which invites comparison with Browning*. The impulsiveness and ruggedness of his prose also recalls Carlyle*, whom Meredith resembled in his hostility to the mechanistic qualities of his age. Of all the Victorian novelists who ever had a major reputation, his has perhaps sunk the lowest in this century: both his prose and his poetry tends to be regarded as intolerably mannered, and he is accused of fixing his attention on style as an end, instead of using it as a medium. Nonetheless, his intense interest in psychological exploration (again recalling Browning), his use of metaphor and symbol from the natural world to express states of mind, and the freshness of some of his characters (especially women) were all original in his own time and keep him from being forgotten.

Bib: Stevenson, L., *Life*; Lindsay, L., *Life*; Trevelyan, G. M., *Poetry and Philosophy of George Meredith*; Sassoon, S., *Meredith*; Sitwell, O., *Novels of Meredith*; Lees, F. N., in *Pelican Guide* 6: *Dickens to Hardy*; Cline, C. L., *Letters*; Woolf, V., in *Common Reader*.

Meres, Francis (1565–1647) /mɪəz/

Author of *Palladis Tamia, Wit's Treasury* (1598), a book of moral and critical reflections. One chapter is an account of English writers, and is valuable to Shakespeare scholars for the list of Shakespeare's plays* that it includes: *Gentlemen of Verona*, *Comedy of Errors*, *Love's Labour's Lost*, *Love's Labours Won* (*ie* perhaps an early version of *All's Well that Ends Well*), *Midsummer Night's Dream*, *Merchant of Venice*, *Richard II*, *Richard III*, *Henry IV*, *King John*, *Titus Andronicus*, and *Romeo and Juliet*. The list is not regarded as complete (*eg* there is no mention of *Henry V*), but at least scholars know that these plays were written before 1598. Only *Titus* was published before 1597, the year before Meres's book; in 1597, *Romeo and Juliet*, *Richard II*, and *Richard III* were published. Meres also mentions *Venus* and *Adonis**, *Lucrece**, and the still unprinted sonnets*. His comments are interesting for estimating Shakespeare's reputation at the time: Meres regards him as the equal of the ancient Greek and Latin poets (the highest praise a 16th-C scholar could offer) and compares him specifically to Ovid*.

Merlin

Best known as the great enchanter in the legends of King Arthur*. In the literature of the Welsh language, there are old poems about a bard, Merlin, referred to in Shakespeare (*1 Henry IV* III. i; *Lear* III. ii). The chronicler Nennius (8th C) mentions a boy with prophetic powers who predicts that the Celts will expel the Anglo-Saxons from Britain; Geoffrey of Monmouth* identifies this boy with Merlin, and describes him as instrumental in bringing about the union of Arthur's parents. Other medieval legends describe him as the child of a demon, and narrate his love for Nimiane (Nimue, Vivien) who, to escape him, contrives his

confinement under a great rock. According to Malory's *Morte d'Arthur**, Merlin built the Round Table*; in Spenser's *Faerie Queene** iii, 3, his mother was a nun; Tennyson retells Merlin's unhappy love affair in *The Idylls of the King**.
* *Lady of the Lake, The*

Mermaid Tavern
A 16th-C tavern in London's Bread Street. According to legend the Bread Street, or Friday Night, Club was founded by Sir Walter Raleigh*, and was one of the earliest English clubs. It was famous as a meeting-place of men of letters – Shakespeare*, Donne*, Beaumont*, Fletcher*, Jonson*. See Beaumont's *Master Francis Beaumont to Ben Jonson*, and Keats's* *Lines on the Mermaid Tavern* (1818). However, modern research has demonstrated that there is no historical evidence for this Club, at least not as an association of writers.
* *Clubs; Inns, Taverns, Alehouses.*

Mermaids and Mermen
In the folklore of many races, half-human creatures of the sea, able to live above its surface. In British folklore, they always have fish-tails, but this is not universal. They often had supernatural powers, and beguiled men down to their submarine world. They resemble, among other such creatures in ancient myths, the sirens* and the tritons of Greek myth.

Merry Monarch, The
King Charles II*, because he was pleasure-loving and witty.

Merry Wives of Windsor, The
A comedy by Shakespeare*, probably written 1600–1; an imperfect edition came out in 1602, and a corrected version was published in the First Folio* of 1623. The critic John Dennis (1657–1734) states that it was written at the request of Queen Elizabeth I*, who wanted a play about Sir John Falstaff in love. Falstaff had been a great popular success in the two *Henry IV** plays. It has also been suggested that Shakespeare was emulating the realistic comedy of Thomas Dekker (*Shoemaker's Holiday**, 1600) and Ben Jonson (*Every Man in his Humour**, 1598; *Every Man out of his Humour**, 1599). *The Merry Wives* is the only play by Shakespeare to be written predominantly in prose.

Falstaff makes love to two married women, the wives of Ford and Page; but the wives and their husbands finally expose him in Windsor Forest, after he has been beset by neighbours disguised as fairies. A subordinate plot concerns the wooing of Anne Page by three suitors, and how she and Fenton, the suitor she prefers, contrive their elopement.

Apart from Falstaff, other characters recur from the Henry IV and V plays: Nym, Pistol, Slender, Mistress Quickly. The Falstaff of *The Merry Wives*, however, bears little resemblance to the massive creation of the earlier plays.

Messiah
In Hebrew, the title – meaning 'the anointed' – of the great deliverer who was expected, and who would raise up the Jewish nation: *Daniel* 9:25–6. In the New Testament, the Messiah (Messias) is identified with Jesus Christ (*John* 1:41).

Metamorphoses /metə'mo:fəsi:z/
Poems in Latin by Ovid*. They are a series of mythological tales whose common subject is miraculous transformation of shape, beginning with Chaos into Cosmos, ending with Julius Caesar into a star, and including such tales as Baucis and Philemon, the peasants who unawares gave hospitality to the gods, who granted them immortality as a pair of trees. They were popular in medieval Europe and afterwards, up till 19th C, and have often been translated, in whole or in part, into English, *eg* by Arthur Golding in 16th C, George Sandys and John Dryden* in 17th, and Pope* in 18th.

Metaphor /'metəfə/
* *Figures of Speech.*

Metaphysical Conceit
* *Figures of Speech.*

Metaphysical Poets /metə'fizikl/
The accepted designation of a succession of 17th-C poets, of whom the following are the principal names: John Donne*, George Herbert*, Richard Crashaw*, Andrew Marvell*, Henry Vaughan*, Abraham Cowley*. The term came to be applied to them in a special sense; that is to say, they were not so described because their subject was the relationship of spirit to matter or the ultimate nature of reality; this is true of Lucretius*, Milton*, and Dante*, who have little else in common. It is true that some of them – Donne, Herbert, Vaughan, and Crashaw especially – were metaphysical in this generally accepted sense, but the adjective is applied to them to indicate not merely subject matter, but qualities of expression in relation to subject matter.

Samuel Johnson* was the first so to classify these poets: 'The metaphysical poets were men of learning, and to show their learning was their whole endeavour' – essay on Cowley, in *Lives of the Poets**. The sentence shows that he is using the term disparagingly, and this disparagement had already been expressed by Dryden*: 'Donne affects the metaphysics not only in his satires but in his amorous verses . . . [he] perplexes the mind of the fair sex with nice speculations of philosophy' (*Discourse concerning the Original and Progress of Satire*, 1693). Dryden and Johnson were anatagonistic to Donne and his followers because they valued above all the assurance, clarity, restraint and shapeliness of the great Augustan* poets of ancient Rome. Critics and poets of 20th C have on the contrary immensely admired Donne, Herbert, and Marvell, but they still use 'Metaphysical' as the term under which to group them. H. J. C. Grierson (Introduction, *Metaphysical Poetry: Donne to Butler*) justifies it because it indicates 'the peculiar blend of passion and thought, feeling and ratiocination which is their greatest achievement.' However, they have also been labelled *'The Fantasticks'* (an anthology edited by W. S. Scott) and Professor Martz has suggested *The Poetry of Meditation* (the title of his book). The first of these alternative designations suggests resemblance between the English poets and their so-called 'baroque' contemporaries in Italy (Marino), Spain (Góngora), and France (Théophile de Viau and Saint-Amant); the second emphasizes the difference – the greater balance and control among the English poets; it may be said that Crashaw, at one extreme, belongs more to the former, and Herbert, at the other extreme, is much better described as 'meditative'.

The distinctiveness of the Metaphysicals was their use of the so-called 'metaphysical conceit' – *ie* paradoxical metaphor causing a shock to the mind by the unlikeness of the association, *eg* Donne's

her pure and eloquent blood
Spoke in her cheeks, and so distinctly wrought,
That one might almost say, her body thought.

(*Second Anniversary.*)

or Herbert's

Only a sweet and virtuous soul,
Like season'd timber, never gives;
But though the whole world turn to coal
Then chiefly lives.

(*Virtue.*)

At its best, this kind of image unites disparate experiences in a single impact on the imagination. In its more decadent forms (in Crashaw and Cowley) it is often a mere exhibition of ingenuity, and deserves Johnson's censure in his important essay on Cowley: 'The most heterogeneous ideas are yoked by violence together.' Both Johnson and Dryden, however, admired the faculty of 'wit' which forged these conceits. Wit* is here used with more substantial meaning than it possesses today.

* *Conceit.*

Methodism

A religious movement founded by John Wesley*. The name was at first applied derisively to himself and his associates when he was a student at Oxford in 1729, referring to the strict rules that they made for themselves in order to follow a religious life; however, he early accepted the designation. From 1739 the movement spread rapidly among the poor all over England, and it became particularly strong in the industrial towns. This spread of Methodist enthusiasm among the poor was due to the coolness of the religious temper in the Church of England, and even in the older Nonconformist (former Puritan*) sects. The Church offered little to the poor in the way of spiritual compensation for the hardness of their material circumstances. Wesley himself had no desire to separate Methodism from the Anglican Church, but the demands on his energies forced him to ordain preachers whom the Church felt it could not accept as clergymen; consequently the Methodists developed an independent organization. According to the French historian Halévy (*A History of the English People in the Nineteenth Century*) Methodism had great political importance after 1800, since its religious fervour absorbed emotional energy which might otherwise have become directed towards social revolution.

The later movement divided into a number of distinct organizations. It spread abroad, especially to the U.S.A. where the membership numbers about 13 million, as compared with rather more than half a million in Britain.

* 1.5.1.2; 3.4.3

Methuselah /mi'θju:zələ/

In the Bible (*Genesis* 5:27) the grandfather of Noah, *ie* a so-called 'antediluvian' because he lived before the Flood. He lived 969 years, hence the phrase 'as old as Methuselah'.

Metonymy

* *Figures of Speech.*

Metre

From the Greek word meaning 'measure'. In poetry, metre is the measure of the rhythm of a line of verse, when the line is rhythmically systematic, *ie* can be divided into units of 'metrical feet'. The names for these feet all derive from ancient Greek verse. The commonest feet in use in English are as follows:

Iambus *eg* the words 'again', 'revenge', 'delight'.
'Iambics march from short to long'.

Trochee *eg* the words 'never', 'happy', 'heartless'.
'Trochee trips from long to short'.

Anapaest *eg* the words 'entertain', 'supersede', 'engineer'.
'With a leap and a bound the swift anapaests throng'.

Spondee *eg* the words 'maintain', 'heartbreak', 'wineglass'
'Slow spondee stalks, strong foot...'

Dactyl *eg* the words 'melody', 'happiness', 'sorrowful'.
'... yet ill able
'Ever to come up with dactyl
trisyllable.'

The illustrative lines are taken from Coleridge's* mnemonic rhyme 'Metrical Feet' (the dactyl example in particular being a joke).

It is important to remember three points when analysing ('scanning') English verse:

[1] Despite Coleridge's use of 'long' and 'short' for iambic and trochaic feet, these words are inappropriate to English metrical feet, which are composed of accented and unaccented syllables (two accented ones in the case of the spondee) irrespective of their length.

[2] Except in the case of the iambus, it is unusual to find lines of verse entirely composed of the same foot; this is especially true of the spondee and the dactyl.

[3] It is unwise to think of metre at all when reading a great deal of English verse. Old and Middle English alliterative* verse was not metrical. Chaucer's* is metrical, but not consistently so; his verse depends more on the natural rhythms of the English speaking voice. This is also true of Wyatt* in early 16th C, of the mature dramatic verse of Shakespeare* and his contemporaries, of Donne*, of Hopkins* in 19th C, and of a number of 20th-C poets, especially Eliot* and Pound*. Spenser* is perhaps the most metrically musical of all English poets, and Milton* uses metre with subtle variations. The late-17th-C and 18th-C poets, especially Dryden* and Pope*, brought regular metre into closest accord with natural speech. The 19th-C Romantic* poets, especially Tennyson*, were much influenced by Spenser and Milton.

Verse lines have names according to the number of feet they contain; much the commonest English line is the iambic pentameter (five feet). The hexameter has six feet, and is called an Alexandrine* when they are iambic. Other lengths: monometer = one foot; dimeter = two feet; trimeter = three feet; tetrameter = four feet; heptameter = seven feet; octameter = eight feet. Some minor 16th-C poets used lines of fourteen syllables known as 'fourteeners'; a couplet consisting of a fourteener and an Alexandrine, first used by Wyatt in some poems, is known as the poulter's measure*.

* 6. *Introduction; Blank Verse; Free Verse; Ode; Sonnet; Spenserian Stanza.*

Mews

A lane in London (on the site of Trafalgar Square) where the king's falcons were kept while they were 'mewing', *ie* moulting, or losing their feathers seasonally. Later the lane was used for stables for the royal horses. Thus a mews became the name of any lane giving access to the stables and coach-houses behind the houses in the richer parts of London. In 20th C the stables were converted into garages, and later the coachmen's rooms over them were converted into smart flats.

Michael (1800)

A narrative poem by William Wordsworth*. It is about the austere life of a shepherd in the Lake District of England. His moral simplicity and physical strength are of a piece with the noble austerity of his environment, with which he is closely identified, but the main object of his devotion, and of his wife's, is their only son Luke. Luke goes away to work in town, and meets disgrace; he then disappears. The tragedy for Michael and his wife is that the only meaning that the future possesses for them is lost with their son. The poem is a masterpiece of Wordsworth's best period. It is in blank verse*.

Michael, Saint

In the Bible (*Revelation*, 12:7) the leader of the angels* against the dragon, *ie* the Devil. In Milton's *Paradise Lost** (vi, 44) he is the Prince of the heavenly armies.

Michaelmas

The feast of St Michael, 29 September. Also, the name for the last term (September to December) in law-courts and universities. 29 September is a quarter day* from which leases are dated, servants used to be hired, etc.

Microcosmographie

* *Characters, Theophrastian.*

Midas /'maidas/

In Greek myth, a king of Phrygia, of whom two particularly well-known tales are told:

[1] For a service to the god Dionysus, he was granted the power to turn all he touched into gold. He nearly starved to death, and asked for the gift to be withdrawn; he was told to bathe in the river Pactolus, which has had golden sands ever since.

[2] Asked to judge between Apollo, god of the arts, and Pan, god of shepherds, as flute players, he preferred Pan. To punish him, Apollo gave him ass's ears. He concealed these under a cap, so that the secret was known only to his barber. The barber found the secret too great a burden and whispered it to the reeds, which in turn betrayed it to the world whenever the wind disturbed them. In some versions, Pan is replaced by Marsyas, who discovered the flute (or oboe) after its inventor, Athene, had thrown it away because it distorted her features. Marsyas acquired skill in playing it, and competed against Apollo on his lyre.

Middle Ages, The

A term used by historians to cover the period between the fall of the Roman Empire of the West (end of 5th C) and the beginning of the Renaissance*, conventionally dated from the extinction of the Roman Empire of the East (Byzantine Empire) in 1453. The expression dates from 16th C when it is found in the Latin writings of a number of humanists* – 'media aetas', 'medium aevum'. The conception in 16th C was that civilization was renewing itself by rediscovery of the ancient civilizations of Greece and Rome; scholars considered that the centuries between 5th and 15th were a relatively dark period of ignorance and cultural backwardness. For long after 16th C modern history was commonly assumed to have begun with the 15th-C Renaissance. Modern scholars are inclined to think this view mistaken; many of them also consider that the so-called Middle Ages had much more continuity with classical history than the men of the Renaissance supposed. The term Middle Ages is thus a misleading and erroneous one, but its use has become habitual and cannot be dispensed with. Moreover the Renaissance of 15th–16th C was a major fact of history, however one interprets it, and it is still useful to have a term to designate the centuries which preceded it.

In English history, it is common to think of the Middle Ages as extending from the Norman* Conquest of 1066 until the end of the Wars of the Roses* and the accession of Henry VII* (first of the House of Tudor*) in 1485. The period from 5th to 11th C is called loosely the Anglo-Saxon period. The English term Middle Ages was first used by John Donne* in a sermon in 1621.

* *English Language.*

Middle English

* *English Language.*

Middlemarch, a Study of Provincial Life (1871–72)

A novel by George Eliot*. The events it describes occur just before the Reform* Bill of 1832, but its content of ideas is more relevant to the mid-Victorian period when it was written. The material was originally intended for two novels, one centred on Dorothea Brooke, and the other a study of provincial life in the town of Middlemarch, based on Coventry. Unity is achieved by the fusion of the two senses of 'provincial': the geographical sense of 'situated outside the capital', and the cultural one of 'ignorant of the central current of ideas'. Dorothea, the daughter of a country gentleman, aspires to a high spiritual conduct of life; she is however isolated geographically, socially and intellectually, like most girls of her time, and she finds no scope for her ambitions. In consequence she is led into an infatuation with Mr Casaubon, an elderly parson-scholar whose life work is the writing of his 'Key to all Mythologies', in which he expects to demonstrate the centrality of the Christian scriptures among human beliefs. Unfortunately, his work is reduced to futility by his ignorance of the leading (German) scholarship in his field, and his egotism and narrowness of human experience prevent him from appreciating the quality of Dorothea's ardour and potentiality. Dorothea finds her marriage a total disillusionment. This marital failure runs parallel to that of Tertius Lydgate and Rosamund Vincy. Lydgate, a young medical scientist, is engaged in equally radical research into the possible existence of a 'basic tissue'. Unlike Casaubon, he is alert to the intellectual centre of his thought (Paris), and he has chosen to live in a provincial town only because he supposes that by so doing he can escape the social involvements and professional rivalries of the metropolis. But Rosamund, the daughter of a Middlemarch manufacturer who has the typically provincial ambition to raise his family to the level of metropolitan fashion, has been attracted to Lydgate only because he has aristocratic relations. Rosamund has no understanding of her husband's intellectual promise, and does nothing but frustrate it. Moreover he has been beguiled into the marriage by his own emotional immaturity, which has misled him into assuming that a beautiful wife is a mere ornament to the life of an intellectual man, without a will of her own; his mistake, in fact, is a youthful equivalent of Casaubon's when the latter marries Dorothea. Lydgate is also mistaken in supposing that the provincialism of Middlemarch will leave him free to conduct his own affairs: he becomes unwittingly involved in the intrigues of the chairman of the Hospital Board, Nicholas Bulstrode, a banker and a bigoted Dissenter* who supposes himself to have a divine mission to direct the lives of others, and a heavenly dispensation which enables him to balance his moral accounts with God as his clients balance their financial accounts with himself. Bulstrode is ruined by the consequences of his own criminal past, and his ruin nearly drags down Lydgate, already faced with financial disgrace by the expensive tastes of his wife.

These are the novel's themes of public failure arising from individual inadequacies which are a result of a personal blindness in the characters and their failure to discern the central truths of their life and work. The themes of failure are counterbalanced by those of fulfilment. Dorothea loses her spiritual arrogance by learning from her own mistakes; after the death of her husband, she acquires a capacity for humble and open-minded human sympathy, which helps to save Lydgate and even momentarily redeems Rosamund. Her frustration is released by the gradual awakening of sexual love between herself and Casaubon's young relative, Will Ladislaw, who differs from the other characters by being essentially cosmopolitan in his background and outlook. Another centre of judgement is that of the Garth family, who acknowledge their provinciality and by avoiding illusions achieve balanced insights and clear directions for their energies in ways that are really less provincial than those of their superiors in wealth and social status. Mary Garth manages to rescue Fred Vincy, Rosamund's brother, from the unreal values which obsess his family. A comparatively minor character but one who is central to George Eliot's valuations is the free-thinking parson Farebrother, condemned to a life of self-sacrifice by external causes, and yet able to live it not only without either bitterness or unctuousness, but also without any narrowing down of his capacity for human sympathy.

At first sight *Middlemarch* seems to be as narrow in its environmental setting as it is complex in its structure, but George Eliot touches upon so many aspects of 19th-C intellectual and social experience as to make it one of the richest and most spacious of all English novels.

Middleton, Thomas (1580–1627)

Dramatist. Little is known about his life; he may have been a student of law in London and in the 1590s he was at Oxford. Later he was often employed to write pageants* to celebrate civic occasions, and in 1620 he was appointed city chronologer (historian).

His masterpeices were two tragedies: *Women*

Beware Women (1621?) and *The Changeling** (1623) with a subplot by William Rowley. The latter play is one of the finest tragedies in English since Shakespeare. In his comedies he was one of the two notable successors to Ben Jonson*, the other being Massinger*. His best are probably: *A Trick to Catch the Old-one* (1608), *The Roaring Girl* (with Dekker*, 1611), and above all *A Chaste Maid in Cheapside** (1611). These, like others of his comedies, are 'citizen comedies'* *ie* about London middle class life like the comedies of Dekker, but presented with more substantial realism. *A Game at Chess* (1624) was a political satire provoked by the king's failure to marry his son to a Spanish princess; its performance was stopped by the protest of the Spanish ambassador. *The Witch*, a revenge play* of uncertain date, may have influenced Shakespeare's *Macbeth** but was more probably influenced by it, and Middleton has been thought by some to have contributed Act III, Sc. v in *Macbeth*.

With Rowley, Middleton also wrote *A Fair Quarrel* (1617); *The World Tost at Tennis* (1620); *The Spanish Gipsy* (1623). Plays ascribed to Middleton alone: *The Old Law* (1599); *Blurt, Master-Constable* (1601–2); *Michaelmas Term* (praised by Swinburne* – 1606?); *The Phoenix* (1607); *The Family of Love* (1607?); *A Mad World, my Masters* (1606?); *Your Five Gallants* (1607?); *No Wit, No Help like a Woman's* (1613?); *Anything for a Quiet Life* (1617?); *More Dissemblers besides Women* (before 1622); *The Widow* (uncertain date). Eleven of his masques* have survived. He also wrote some poetry and prose pamphlets* of small account.

Bib: Bradbrook, M. C., *Elizabethan Tragedy*; Knights, L. C., *Drama and Society in the Age of Jonson*; Eliot, T. S., in *Selected Essays*; Schoenbaum, S., on Middleton's tragedies; Dunkel, W. D., on his comedies; Barker, R. H., *Thomas Middleton*.

Midsummer Night's Dream, A

A comedy by Shakespeare*. From internal evidence it has been dated about 1595; it was printed in 1600. The title refers to the fantastic quality of events, resembling a dream on Midsummer night, when fantastic dreams were supposed to be commonly experienced.

The characters are in four distinct groups. The background is the court of a character from Greek mythology, king Theseus of Athens, on the eve of his marriage to Hippolyta, queen of the Amazons. The four lovers whose confusions form the bulk of the action, Helena and Demetrius, Hermia and Lysander (as they are eventually paired) have classical names, but their story is a typical comedy of Renaissance* romantic love, in which they are the victims of blind passion. The third group is made from the Athenian artisans whose names – Bottom, Quince, Snout, Flute and Starveling – show them to be English types of Shakespeare's own day. They celebrate Theseus' wedding night (and that of the other lovers) by performing the interlude* *Pyramus and Thisbe* – intended to be tragic but, as they carry it out, decidedly comic. The fourth group is the fairies. In general (especially Puck, or Robin Goodfellow) these are drawn from English folklore, but their king, Oberon, comes from *Huon de Bordeaux* (a medieval French romance) and Titania from Ovid's *Metamorphoses**. Oberon, through Puck, confuses the lovers as they wander through the wood near Athens, and causes Titania to fall in love with Bottom, who, for the night, is given an ass's head. The fantasy is one of the most deftly contrived of Shakespeare's early plays.

Mill, John Stuart (1806–73)

Writer on economics, politics, psychology, logic and ethics. He did not invent the word Utilitarian*, but was the first to apply it to the reform movement which had been started by his father's friend, Jeremy Bentham*, and of which his father, James Mill, was one of the leaders. The movement derived from 18th-C rationalism*, and the group were known as 'the philosophical radicals' because of the intellectual thoroughness with which they reasoned out their political and social standpoints. James Mill educated his son strenuously from a very early age, but the education, wide as it was, ignored the imaginative and emotional needs of his son's character. J. S. Mill describes in his *Autobiography* (1873) how this neglect produced in him a spiritual crisis when he was 21, after he had already made a brilliant start to his career. He discovered that he was emotionally indifferent to the ends for which he was working. He recovered partly through his discovery of the poetry of Wordsworth*, and the crisis enabled him to develop a far more sympathetic and balanced outlook on human needs than had been possessed by his father or Bentham.

Mill's literary output was very large, and his influence on his time was great, though much of his writing (for instance his psychology, which he based on 18th-C associationism – *Hartley) has now been superseded by subsequent thinking. However, his *Autobiography* and a number of his essays have permanent value, for instance his essay *On Liberty** (1859) and those on Bentham (1838) and Coleridge* (1840), whom he described as the two great formative influences of his age. His most massive work was his *Principles of Political Economy* (1848). He was an early leader of the movement for the emancipation of women, and published *The Subjection of Women* (1869). His *Utilitarianism* (1863) was a reasoned defence of his philosophy.

A peculiarity of his upbringing, considering its period, is that he was educated against the Christian faith.

* 3.4.2; 7.4.

Bib: Packe, M. St J., *Life*; Leavis, F. R., *Mill on Bentham and Coleridge*; Wishy, B., *Preface to Liberty*; Halévy, E., *The Growth of Philosophic Radicalism*; Abrams, M. H., *The Mirror and the Lamp*; Anschutz, R. P., *The Philosophy of J. S. Mill*; Bain, A., *J. S. Mill: a Criticism*; Stephen, L., *Utilitarianism*; Neff, E., *Carlyle and Mill*; Britton, K. W., *Mill*.

Mill on the Floss, The (1860)

A novel by George Eliot*. It is set in the English midlands, and its central character is Maggie Tulliver, the daughter of a miller. She is intelligent and richly imaginative beyond the understanding of her relatives, and in particular of her brother, Tom, a boy of limited intelligence and sympathies to whom she is devoted. The novel is divided into seven parts; the first three lead up to Mr Tulliver's bankruptcy, and make a rich and comic study of English country life in mid-19th C with deep insights into the psychology of the rural middle class. The last three deal with the tragic love of Maggie for Philip Wakem, the deformed son of the lawyer through whom Mr Tulliver has been ruined, the compromising of her reputation by the educated and agreeable Stephen Guest, and her alienation from her brother, with whom she is, however, reconciled by means of the flood which drowns them both. The earlier part of the book contains some of George Eliot's best writing; the later part is more open to criticism, and the end is arbitrary.

Miller's Tale, The

One of Chaucer's *Canterbury Tales*. In ten-syllable couplets. It is a fabliau* or comic tale about the deception of a husband, a superstitious carpenter, whose faith in astrology is exploited by his wife and her lover. The tale is directed against the Reeve* (a carpenter) who retaliates in his tale by narrating the deception of a miller.

Milne, A. A. (1882–1956)

Novelist, dramatist, children's writer. He was for many years assistant editor of *Punch*, and he became widely popular as the author of light comedies and novels. His earliest play is *Wurzel-Flummery* (1917) and his best known *Mr Pim Passes By* (1920). However he achieved fame by four children's books, centring on his son, Christopher Robin. Two of these are verse: *When We Were Very Young* (1924) and *Now We Are Six* (1927). The other two are prose stories, with Christopher Robin's teddy bear Winnie the Pooh as hero: *Winnie the Pooh* (1926); *The House at Pooh Corner* (1928). They have been translated into many languages; *Winnie the Pooh*, rather to its advantage, into Latin.

Milton, John (1608–74)

Poet and prose polemicist. He was born in London, the son of a scrivener and musician whose own father had in his youth disinherited him for becoming a Protestant. John Milton was educated at St Paul's School in London and Christ's College, Cambridge, where the fastidiousness of his morals and perhaps a feminine quality in his personal appearance caused him to be nicknamed 'the Lady of Christ's'. He left Cambridge in 1632, and in 1638 set out on a course of foreign travel through Paris, Genoa, Florence, Rome, to Naples, meeting a number of distinguished men of learning including the astronomer Galileo*. In Naples he heard of the approaching outbreak of the Civil War* in England, and decided to return. His sympathies were already engaged on the side of Parliament on religious grounds; he had declined to enter the Church on leaving Cambridge owing to his disapproval of the religious policy of King Charles I* and Archbishop Laud*, which he regarded as too near Roman Catholic authoritarianism. From 1641 he abandoned poetry – reluctantly, for he took the vocation very seriously – for prose polemics on behalf of the Parliamentary and Puritan* causes. Not all his writing performed this function, however; in 1643 he married the daughter of a Royalist family who almost immediately abandoned him, and this led to the first of his pamphlets in favour of divorce. This in turn led to his quarrel with the Stationers* Company, since he had published the work without their licence. Parliament supported the Stationers, whereupon Milton published his *Areopagitica**, one of the noblest appeals for freedom of expression ever written. In 1649, the year of the king's execution, he was appointed Latin Secretary to the Commonwealth for the purpose of corresponding with foreign governments, a post he continued to hold until the Restoration*. In addition, he continued his prose propaganda on behalf of the republican Commonwealth and Oliver Cromwell*; he was defending the republican system in print only a month before the Restoration. Nonetheless, the restored monarch left him in freedom, perhaps owing to the influence in Parliament of his fellow-poet Andrew Marvell*, and at court to that of the Earl of Anglesey. Milton, though he was now blind, was left in peace to produce his most ambitious poetic works. In the meantime, his domestic life had been varied; his first wife had returned to him after the defeat of the king's forces in 1646, but had died in 1653, leaving him three daughters. His second wife died 15 months after their marriage in 1656, but his third wife whom he married in 1662 looked after him devotedly to the end.

His literary career divides sharply into three periods. During the first (1625–40) he wrote a considerable quantity of verse in Latin. In English: *Ode on the Morning of Christ's Nativity* (1629); *L'Allegro** and *Il Penseroso** (1632), the masque *Comus** (1634), and the elegy *Lycidas** (1637). There were lesser works, including a short poem on Shakespeare (1630), included in the second folio* edition of Shakespeare's works in 1632. In the second period – 1640–60 – Milton wrote little verse but produced a large quantity of prose treatises and pamphlets. Apart from *Areopagitica, a Speech for the Liberty of Unlicensed Printing* (1644) and the Treatise on Education (1644), these are mostly of historical rather than literary interest. The massacre of the Protestant Waldensians by the Duke of Savoy in 1655 caused his noble sonnet in protest *On the Late Massacre in Piedmont*. In the last period – 1660–74 – Milton produced all his ambitious poetry, on which his fame chiefly rests. The epic *Paradise Lost** was published in 1667, and brought him great prestige. Its sequel *Paradise Regained** and the tragedy on the Greek model *Samson Agonistes** were published together in 1671. The most important influence upon him in English was Spenser*, but the earlier poetry shows the influence of Elizabethan dramatists (in *Comus*) and of the Metaphysical* poets (in the early *Ode*).

Milton has been the subject of more controversy among modern critics than any other of the great poets. The scope of his own great later work is still acknowledged, but his large influence on later poets is often considered to have been a limiting one – see under *Paradise Lost*.

* 4.2.1; 6.3.1

Bib: Parker, W. R., *Life*; Hanford, J. H., *A Milton Handbook*; Stevens, H. D., *Reference Guide to Milton*; Leavis, F. R., in *Revaluation*; Eliot, T. S., in *Selected Essays*; Waldock, A. J. A., *Paradise Lost and its Critics*; Tillyard, E. M. W., *Milton* and *The Miltonic Setting*; Lewis, C. S., *Preface to Paradise Lost*; Empson, W., *Milton's God*; Kermode, F., (ed.) *The Living Milton*; Ricks, C., *Style in Paradise Lost*.

Mime

In modern usage, acting with movements and gestures but without speech. In Shakespeare's day, a brief mimed performance of a play sometimes preceded the real performance so that the more ignorant members of the audience might be able to follow the latter more easily. In the ancient Greek and Roman theatre, mime was a kind of comedy of low life; speech was used, but exaggerated and simplified gestures were probably important.

* *Pantomime.*

Minerva

* *Athene.*

Minim, Dick

A character in Samuel Johnson's 'Idler'* essays for the *Weekly Gazette*. Dick Minim is a satirical representation of the kind of person who seeks a reputation for critical acumen by praising what is in fashion and sneering at what is unfamiliar.

Minories, The

A street in London, so called because it ran near the convent of the 'Minoresses' or Poor Clares.

* *Clare, Order of St.*

Minos /ˈmainos/

In Greek myth, a wise king of Crete whose justice was such that after his death he was made supreme judge in the underworld. However, another tradition saw him as a cruel tyrant who had subdued Athens, and caused seven youths and seven maidens to be sacrificed to the Minotaur*. He is also supposed to have imprisoned Daedalus* in a labyrinth.

Minotaur /ˈmainəto:/

In Greek myth, a monster with the head of a bull and the body of a man. King Minos* refused to sacrifice a certain white bull to the sea-god Poseidon, who punished him by causing his wife to fall in love with the animal, so that she gave birth to the Minotaur. It was kept in the labyrinth constructed by Daedalus* for Minos.

Miracle Plays

* *Mystery Plays.*

Mirror for Magistrates, A (1559)

A collection of tales in verse by different writers; in each a historical character tells of his downfall. The book was popular, and was republished several times. The only parts of it now admired are the *Induction* and *Complaint of the Duke of Buckingham* by Thomas Sackville*. The contemporary appeal may partly have been patriotic: all the characters come from English history, whereas previous collections of a similar kind – Boccaccio's* *De Casibus Virorum Illustrium*, translated by Lydgate* as *Falls of Princes*, and Chaucer's *Monk's Tale** – had concerned foreign heroes. The reign of Elizabeth I* was one of rapidly growing national consciousness in England.

Misrule, Lord of

In the Middle Ages* and 16th C, it was the practice of royal courts and noble households, etc. to appoint a master of the revels for the twelve days of the Christmas feast. In Scotland they were called 'the abbots of unreason'. The origin of the practice is thought to be pagan: in ancient Rome the festival of Saturnalia* was also held in December; the festival had its king, and it was marked by unusual licensed disorder. In Shakespeare's *Twelfth Night** Sir Toby Belch is a kind of Lord of Misrule.

Mistletoe

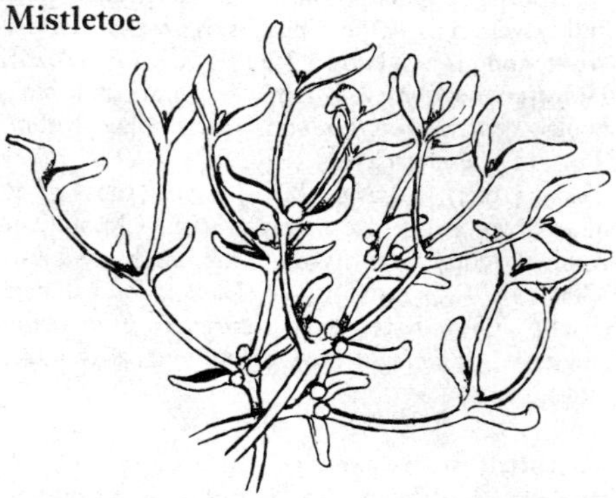

A small bush with white berries which grows on other trees and shrubs. In pagan times it was widely regarded as sacred in Europe, especially when it grew on the oak (see J. G. Frazer, *The Golden Bough*). According to the Roman historian Pliny* the Celtic Druids* ceremonially cut it at the beginning of the year with a golden sickle. It is one of the pagan symbols which has survived into the celebration of the modern Christmas: a girl standing under a sprig of mistletoe hanging in the house may be kissed without her permission.

Mitre

A ceremonial head-dress worn by bishops of the Catholic and Anglican Churches. The mitre was also a common inn-sign. Two famous taverns called the Mitre stood in Fleet Street*, London; one was a reputed meeting-place of poets in the days of Shakespeare*, and the other was frequented by Doctor Johnson* in 18th C.

Mnemosyne /ni:'mozini:/

In Greek myth, the mother of the nine Muses*. The name means Memory. She was one of the race of Titans*.

Mock Heroic in Literature

A kind of satire* in which a type of character or behaviour is shown to deserve contempt by the method of using heroic or romantic terms to describe facts which are quite evidently the reverse of heroic or romantic. The mock heroic style is thus chiefly cultivated in a society in which heroic literature is familiar and admired; it often takes the form of some kind of parody, and operates through irony. Cervantes' *Don Quixote** is mock heroic because the hero undertakes romantic adventures in a prosaic countryside, and it depends for its effect partly on the popularity of romances of knight-errantry based on the King Arthur* legends. The irony always implicit in mock heroism may, however, depend on the contrast of appearances and reality without any special literary model for parody; thus an excellent medieval example of the mock heroic is Chaucer's *Nun's Priest's Tale** in which the cock looks, behaves, and feels like a prince, although he is merely the property of a poor widow who has barely enough to live on.

The best period for mock heroic literature is that between 1660 and 1760. In this hundred years, classical epic (essentially a heroic form) was regarded as the summit of literary achievement, and John Milton* revived it very impressively in *Paradise Lost**. It was also the period when the French heroic drama of Corneille* and Racine* strongly influenced English drama, and was imitated by English dramatists such as Dryden*. At the same time, writers were trained in a new respect for fact by the philosophy of the Royal Society* (founded 1662), and the difference between the facts of human society and the high level of conduct imaged in its fiction forced itself poignantly on writers' attention.

Don Quixote had long been popular; it was a model for Samuel Butler's* exposure of the lofty ethical pretensions of the Puritans in his mock-epic, *Hudibras**. Its narrative is in the style of the 16th-C romantic epic, but the behaviour of its hero is consistently dishonest and contemptible. Dryden, in his *Absalom and Achitophel**, uses an epic hero, based on the contemporary politician Shaftesbury*, whose energies are truly heroic, but who uses them wastefully and destructively, and thus constitutes a warning to mankind instead of serving as a model. In *Mac Flecknoe**, on the other hand, he writes of a hero-poet (Shadwell) who excels only in what is the opposite of excellent for a poet, that is to say, dullness. This is again the theme of the greatest mock epic of the whole period: Pope's *Dunciad**, in which the mock hero is again a poet (Colley Cibber*) but the real theme is the destructiveness of the forces of mediocrity and frivolity at work in society. Pope's epic style is superlatively grand, but the material is mean, and the combination of heroic eloquence and mean subject convey the sense of the terrible power of what is inherently contemptible. In his earlier poem, *The Rape of the Lock**, Pope uses a different mock heroic technique. He is here concerned not with the dull mediocrity of fashionable culture so much as with its pettiness; he consequently uses a parody of the epic machinery of supernatural forces operating on human destiny by using the tiny spirits of Rosicrucian* mythology (instead of gods and goddesses, like Homer*, or angels and devils, like Milton*) and making them hover round the destiny of a lock of hair.

The great 18th-C prose master of mock heroic is Jonathan Swift*, especially in *Gulliver's Travels**. In Lilliput, Gulliver gravely describes the proud society of midgets whose values are proportionate to their size and the size of their toy country, while Swift allows the reader to see that Lilliputian ideals are not inherently more petty than those of ordinary human beings. In Brobdingnag, Gulliver, still self-consciously assured of his high civilization, is exposed as himself a midget among a race of giants with truly large and generous ideas such as are not at all characteristc of human societies.

Mock heroic almost depends on a strongly felt scale of values, and the downfall of 18th-C rationalism* in the romantic* period, with the overthrow of such a coherent value structure, made the mock heroic style much less natural to writers. It is used, however, by Thomas Love Peacock* in his discussion novels which satirize romantic sensibility, *eg Nightmare Abbey**. The greatest modern exemplar of mock heroic is undoubtedly James Joyce* in his *Ulysses**. *Ulysses*, however, is much more than mock heroic; its carefully worked-out parallels with Homer's *Odyssey** are not merely intended to expose the meanness of modern life by comparison with the greatness of the past, but to demonstrate the continuance under extremely different guises of certain features of human experience.

* *Epic; Epic, Mock.*

Modern Love (1862)

A series of 16-line poems resembling sonnets*, by George Meredith*. The poems tell the story of the breakdown of a marriage ending in the suicide of the wife. The tone is strongly emotional, and the attitude to the emotions is self-scrutinizing; in these ways Meredith's *Modern Love* suggest comparison with the dramatic monologues* of Browning* and Tennyson*, for example Browning's *Any Wife to Any Husband* and Tennyson's *Maud**.

Modest Proposal, A (1729)

A satirical pamphlet* by Jonathan Swift*, written when he was Dean of St Patrick's Cathedral, Dublin. The full title is *A Modest Proposal for Preventing Children of Poor People from being a Burden to their Parents or the Country.* Indignant at the extreme misery of the Irish poor under

English government, Swift, in the guise of an economic 'projector', calmly recommends that it would be more humane to breed up their children as food for the rich. The pamphlet is an example of the controlled but extreme savagery of Swift's irony, and the fierceness of his humanitarianism.

Mohammed (570?–632 AD)

(Sometimes 'Mahomet', but more correctly Muhammad.) Founder of the religion correctly called Islam, but commonly known in English as Mohammedanism. He was born at Mecca in the Arabian peninsula; this is consequently the principal holy place of the Islamic religion. He established monotheism (the worship of the one God, Allah) in Arabia, and the religion rapidly spread through the Middle East and across North Africa. In particular, the Muslims captured Jerusalem*, the Christian Holy City, in 637. They constituted the principal threat to Christendom throughout the Middle Ages, and it was against them that the Crusades*, or holy wars, were organized. They ruled southern Spain until 1492 and south-east Europe (the Balkans) until 19th C. Meanwhile Muslim pirates, the Barbary corsairs, preyed on Mediterranean trade. Chesterton's* poem *Lepanto* describes a famous sea-battle between Christian and Muslim forces. Since the fall of the Turkish Empire, the two faiths have existed together in peace.

Mohocks /ˈməuhoks/

The nickname for disorderly and violent young aristocrats who roamed London early in 18th C. It derives from Mohawk, a warrior tribe of North American Indians.

Molière (pseudonym of Jean Baptiste Poquelin) (1622–73) /ˈmolieə/

French dramatist. Born in the middle class, the son of an upholsterer, he became one of the most favoured playwrights at the court of Louis XIV. With one exception his plays are comedies – the finest stage comedies in European literature, and a basic influence behind English comedy from 1660 to 1800. His *Les Précieuses Ridicules* (1659), a satire upon an extremely fashionable, excessively sophisticated circle in contemporary Paris, marks the beginning of the Comedy of Manners* tradition in which the English dramatists, Etherege* Wycherley*, Vanbrugh*, Congreve* and Sheridan* all worked. He wrote over 30 plays, of which the best known are: *Sganarelle* (1660); *L'Ecole des Maris* (The School for Husbands, 1661); *L'Ecole des Femmes* (The School for Wives, 1662); *Tartuffe* (1664); *Le Festin de Pierre* (Don Juan, 1665); *Le Misanthrope* (The Misanthropist, 1666); *Le Médecin malgré lui* (The Reluctant Physician, 1666); *L'Avare* (The Miser, 1668); *Le Bourgeois Gentilhomme* (The Middle-Class Nobleman, 1670); *Les Femmes Savantes* (The Learned Women, 1672); *Le Malade imaginaire* (The Hypochondriac, 1673).

Molière wrote for the most sophisticated society Europe had yet seen, and the one in which the arts of civilization were the most diligently cultivated. He had the great qualities of this society, and shared its sceptical, critical, inquiring bent. In addition, he brought to bear on his theme the robust insight of his middle-class descent, and humane sympathies of wider reach than those demanded by the pomp and elegance of the court. The powerful simplifications of earlier comedy (such as the English Comedy of Humours*) were replaced by Molière with flexible, living personalities which were not only lively on the surface but (unlike the English Comedy of Manners) existed in depth. His nearest equivalent on the English stage is William Congreve*, but the only achievement in English literature comparable with Molière's kind of excellence is in the Augustan satire of Dryden* (*Absalom and Achitophel**) and Pope*, and the novels of Jane Austen*.

Moll Flanders (1722)

A novel by Daniel Defoe*, and his most famous, after *Robinson Crusoe* (1719). Its full title was *The Fortunes and Misfortunes of the Famous Moll Flanders*, and its substance is the adventures of an orphan girl from her early seduction through her various love affairs and her career of crime, to her transportation to Virginia and her final prosperity there. It is a realistic, episodic narrative with keen social and psychological perception in certain incidents. The book has no unifying structure, however, and none of the characters is fully established imaginatively. The conclusion is an example of Defoe's crude and superficial morality, Puritan* in its tradition, but much less profound and subtle than that of his predecessor Bunyan*. The Puritanism has become simplified to commercialism, especially evident in Moll's final 'repentance'.

* *Picaresque.*

Moloch /ˈməulok/

In the Bible, the name of a deity to which the people of Israel occasionally sacrificed their children: *Leviticus* 18:21; *2 Kings* 23:10. The worship of Moloch seems to have been a sporadic return to a religion of fear. In Milton's *Paradise Lost** (i.392) Moloch is one of the fallen angels*, and the name is elsewhere used to represent any brutal force which requires unnatural sacrifices.

* *Gehenna.*

Moly /ˈməuli/

In Homer's *Odyssey** a magical herb which the god Hermes* gives to Odysseus to save him from the enchantments of the sorceress Circe*.

Momus /ˈməuməs/

In Greek myth, the professional mocker among the gods, eventually expelled from Heaven for his fault-finding.

Monasteries and Monasticism

The practice of monasticism arose in the lands about the eastern Mediterranean in the early centuries of Christianity, and was inspired by the

belief that the holy life could be lived only in isolation from the practical interests of worldly society. This early monasticism consisted of hermits each living in his own cell, and Irish monasticism of 6th–8th C had similar characteristics. However, in 6th C St Benedict founded in Italy the Benedictine* order which, during the Middle Ages*, dominated western Europe including the British Isles, and had immense consequences for Western civilization; the monks lived in community, and followed a regular rule of life which included a great deal of practical activity. They were artists, architects, scholars and writers – especially historians, such as the Venerable Bede*, Geoffrey of Monmouth*, and Matthew Paris (13th C); monasteries such as the Cathedral Priory at Canterbury were seats of learning which rivalled universities such as Paris and Oxford, and they were both the soil from which the universities grew and an important power within them even when the secular (non-monastic, as opposed to the monastic 'regular') clergy began to take over from them in 14th C. Corporately, the monasteries were great landowners, and some of the abbots (heads of the abbeys or monasteries) managed these estates with great constructive efficiency; an example is the 12th-C Abbot Samson of Bury St Edmund's, – see Carlyle's* fine study of him in *Past and Present*, Bk. II (1843). The Cistercian Order, a reformed version of the Benedictine, planted their monasteries in the wild places in England, *eg* the Cotswold hills and the Yorkshire dales, and set up sheep farms which were a large part of the basis of the great English wool industry. In medieval England the monasteries were the only source of poor relief, and they were the only inns and hospitals until 14th C. Politically, the great abbots ranked with the Bishops in the Great Council of the realm; in 12th and 13th C monks were the intelligentsia, owners of at least 10% of the national income, and the largest employers of labour.

By 14th C monasteries were losing their value. The secular clergy, especially the very loosely definable part of it known as 'clerks', were not only keenly jealous of the regulars, but much better educated than they had been, and able to compete in learning and literature. Laymen, such as Geoffrey Chaucer*, were the equals of the clergy in their culture. Some of the social functions of the monasteries, such as hospitality to travellers, were now performed by laymen like the Host of the Tabard Inn in Chaucer's *Canterbury Tales**. Moreover, the monasteries were becoming lax and worldly, and monks were often useless parasites like the Monk in Chaucer's *Prologue**. It is only Chaucer's secular clergyman, the Poor Parson, who is true to his spiritual vocation; the Monk, Friar and Prioress are all regulars, and all have lapsed into worldliness. The abbots were no longer exemplars of good estate management, but leased their land to laymen or left its care to lay 'reeves' or stewards, while the practical labour was undertaken by an army of lay employees. However, it must be remembered that Chaucer was a native of south-eastern England, which was in all respects more advanced than the north and west; when Henry VIII* dissolved the monasteries (1536–9) the measure met with no resistance in the south-east but it provoked the rebellion known as the Pilgrimage of Grace* in the north.

There were no monasteries in Britain after the middle of 16th C, but since the second half of 19th C some have been re-established.

* 2.1.1.1; *Nuns and Nunneries.*

Moneta /mo'niːtə/

Juno Moneta (the admonisher) was the Roman goddess whose sacred geese had once saved Rome by the cackling they had set up, betraying the approach of the enemy. Her temple was the building in which money was made – hence the derivations, mint, monetary, money.

* *Hyperion by Keats.*

'Monk' Lewis

Matthew Gregory Lewis, whose sensational novel *The Monk* (1796) had such success in its day that he was nicknamed after it.

* *Gothic Novels.*

Monk's Tale, The

One of Chaucer's *Canterbury Tales**. It is written in 8-line stanzas, and is preceded by a Prologue in which the Monk gives the usual medieval definition of tragedy as the story of a man who has fallen from 'high degree' into the depth of misfortune. He then tells in brief the stories of Lucifer*, Adam*, Samson, Hercules, Nebuchadnezzar, Balthasar, Zenobia, Peter of Spain, Peter of Cyprus, Barnabus of Lombardy, Hugo of Pisa, the Emperor Nero, Holofernes, Antiochus, Alexander the Great, Julius Caesar, and King Croesus. At this point, the

Knight breaks in to declare that he has had as much as he can endure. The Monk's stories are taken from various authors and are modelled on Boccaccio's* *De Casibus Virorum Illustrium* ('Concerning the fortunes of famous men').

Monmouth, James Scott, Duke of (1649–85) /ˈmonməθ/

An illegitimate son of Charles II*. Charles had no legitimate son, and the heir to the throne was consequently James, Duke of York, his brother. James, however, was an open Catholic, and fear of Catholicism in England and Scotland was still very strong. Thus a strong movement arose in both countries to persuade Charles to exclude James from the succession, and to recognize Monmouth, who had been educated a Protestant*. Exclusion Bills to secure this change were introduced into Parliament, where the Exclusionists were led by Lord Shaftesbury*. Charles, however, resisted the movement, and in 1681 a reaction of opinion in the country came to the support of the King and his brother. In 1685, Charles died, and James succeeded him as James II*. Some of his more fanatical Protestant opponents, such as the Scottish Duke of Argyll, persuaded Monmouth to attempt rebellion. The Monmouth Rebellion was defeated at the single battle of Sedgemoor* (1685) and Monmouth himself was executed. Sedgemoor was the last battle to be fought on English soil.

* *Absalom and Achitophel; Bloody Assizes.*

Montagu, Mrs Elizabeth

* *Bluestocking.*

Montagu, Lady Mary Wortley (1689–1762) /ˈmontəgjuː/

Letter-writer. As the daughter of a duke and the wife of Edward Wortley Montagu who was at one time British ambassador to Turkey, she moved in the 'great world', and her letters are famous for their vividness. She also had a tendency to make enemies; the poet Pope* insulted her in his verse repeatedly, and Horace Walpole* – the best-known letter writer in the golden age of letter-writing – talked scandal about her.

* *Letter-writing.*

Bib: Halsband, R., *Life.*

Montagues /ˈmontəgjuːz/

The family of which Romeo is a member, and the sworn enemies of Juliet's family the Capulets, in Shakespeare's play *Romeo and Juliet**.

Montaigne, Michel de (1533–92) /monˈtein/

French essayist, and inventor of the essay* form. His life was lived partly at court, or performing the office of magistrate in the city of Bordeaux, and partly in retirement. During retirement, he wrote his *Essais* ('experiments'), the first two volumes of which were published in 1580, and the third in 1588. He was a scholar, well-read in humanist* literature and in the works of the ancient Greeks and Romans. His favourite author was the Greek biographer, Plutarch*.

The Essays seem to have been begun as commentaries on his reading, perhaps to assist his exceptionally bad memory. From this grew a desire to arrive at a complete image of man; as a means to this, he tried to develop a portrait of himself, since 'each man bears the complete stamp of the human condition'. The sentence shows the still-prevailing view of his time, that human beings followed general principles in the structure of their personalities – a view quite unlike the view that grew up in 18th C and came to predominate in 19th, that each individual is unique (see Rousseau*). He recognized, however, the difficulties in arriving at conclusive ideas about human nature, and the essays are characterized by the scepticism with which he weighs evident contradictions and opposing views.

Montaigne was translated into English by Florio* in 1603. The essays had an extensive influence upon English literature. Whether the long essay entitled *Apologie de Raimond de Sebond* had an important influence on Shakespeare's *Hamlet** is a controversial question; but Gonzalo in Shakespeare's *Tempest** quotes from Montaigne's *Des Cannibales* in II.i.143 ('I' th' commonwealth . . .') to 160. More important were the emulators of Montaigne in the essay form. Montaigne's sceptical, searching, flexible mind resembles those of Robert Burton* (*Anatomy of Melancholy**) and Sir Thomas Browne* (*Religio Medici**). These however, were not essayists; the Montaigne tradition of essay writing was taken up later in the century by Abraham Cowley* (*Essays in Verse and Prose*, 1668), Sir William Temple* (*Miscellanea*, 1680, 1692, 1701) and, after the more formal period of 18th C, Charles Lamb's *Essays of Elia** (1823).

Montrose, James Graham, Marquess of (1612–50) /monˈtrəuz/

Scottish patriot, general, and statesman. He was one of the noblest and most gifted of Charles I's* supporters in and after the Civil War*. After spasmodic but brilliant successes, he was caught by Parliament forces and executed. Walter Scott's* novel *A Legend of Montrose* (1819) concerns his career, and a notable biography was written of him by John Buchan.

Monument, The

In London. A massive pillar designed by Christopher Wren* and erected 1671–7 in commemoration of the Great Fire of London*. Its erection occurred in a time of strong anti-Catholic feeling, and the inscription at the base attributed the fire to the Catholics. Its summit is surrounded by a collar of gold spikes representing flames.

Moonstone, The (1868)

A novel by Wilkie Collins*. It is one of the earliest stories of detection and concerns the mysterious disappearance of a valuable diamond, formerly sacred to the Moon-god in one of the Indian temples. The novel is told in the first person by various participants in the events; it is plotted with skill, psychological ingenuity, and a typically Victorian delight in characterization. Sergeant Cuff, the first detective in English fiction, appears in it.

Moore, George (1852–1933) /muə/

Irish novelist. He combined an aestheticism* in tune with the aesthetic movement at the end of 19th C, and the Celtic revivalism that went with a part of it, with a naturalism* which showed the influence of late-19th-C French literature, especially from the novelist Zola.* His most famous novels: *A Mummer's Wife* (1885); *Esther Waters* (1894); *Evelyn Innes* (1898); *Sister Theresa* (1901); *The Brook Kerith* (1916); *Héloïse and Abélard* (1921). He was equally well known for his autobiographical studies: *Confessions of a Young Man* (1888); *Avowals* (1919, 1926); *Hail and Farewell* (1911–14) and *Conversations in Ebury Street* (1924). His carefully worked style was more admired in his own day than it is now.

* *Celtic Twilight.*

Bib: Korg, J., in *Victorian Fiction* (ed. L. Stevenson); Brown, M. J., *Moore: a Reconsideration*; Sechler, R. P., *George Moore: 'a Disciple of Walter Pater'*; Yeats, W. B., in *Dramatis Personae*; Hough, G., in *Image and Experience.*

Moore, G. E. (1873–1958)

Philosopher. He lectured on philosophy at Cambridge from 1911 to 1925, when he became Professor. His principal book is *Principia Ethica* (1903); he also wrote *Ethics* (1912) and *Philosophical Studies* (1922). His philosophy was that of the 'New Realism', in opposition to the idealism of F. H. Bradley* who was in the tradition of Hegel*. Where the Idealists* tended to a poetic conception of truth and ethics, rhetorically expressed and appealing to the emotions as much as to the reason, Moore appealed to the reason only, basing his arguments on common sense, and holding it to be the function of philosophy to clarify statements and arrive at fully intelligible definitions. At the same time, he argued that all experience is to be enjoyed, and that the richest possessions are aesthetic experience and personal friendship. He consequently had two kinds of influence, philosophical and literary. Philosophically, he was one of the starting points of Russell* and the Logical Positivists such as A. J. Ayer, but in literary circles he had considerable personal influence on the Bloomsbury Group*, centred on the novelist Virginia Woolf* and her husband Leonard. The Bloomsbury Group owed its cohesiveness to a cult of personal relations such as Moore advocated, and it regarded the state of mind of perfect aesthetic appreciation as one of the aims of life.

* 3.5

Bib: Schilpp, P. A., *The Philosophy of Moore*; Johnstone, J. K., *The Bloomsbury Group.*

Moore, Thomas (1779–1852)

Irish poet, especially famous for his musical lyrics (*Irish Melodies*, 1807 and after). His fame in his own day equalled that of his friend Byron*; he received 3,000 guineas for his series of oriental verse tales, *Lalla Rookh* (1817). Byron called him 'Anacreon Moore' because he translated the Odes of Anacreon into English verse (1800).

* *Anacreontics.*

Bib: Strong, L. A. G., *The Minstrel Boy*; Gwynn, S., *Life*; Jones, H. M., *Life*.
Hazlitt, W., in *The Spirit of the Age*; Saintsbury, G., in *Essays in English Literature.*

Moral Essays (1731–5)

Four poems by Alexander Pope* in imitation of

Horace*; they are written, like nearly all Pope's verse, in ten-syllable rhymed couplets*. The poems are called Epistles. Epistle I, addressed to Sir William Temple, concerns the characters of men, the difficulties in understanding them, and the importance of the principle of 'the ruling passion' as a clue. Epistle II, more flippant and satirical, concerns the characters of women, and is addressed to his friend Martha Blount. Various famous women pass under scrutiny – Chloe for Lady Suffolk, and Philomede for the Duchess of Marlborough. Epistle III treats the right use of riches, and is addressed to Lord Bathurst; it extols John Kyrle, the 'Man of Ross', a celebrated philanthropist. Epistle IV, addressed to Lord Burlington, satirizes the wrong use of wealth. All four poems are masterpieces of Augustan* poetry, and show its characteristic qualities of strong social feeling, the spirit of criticism expressed with imaginative intensity, and epigrammatic wit.

Morality Plays

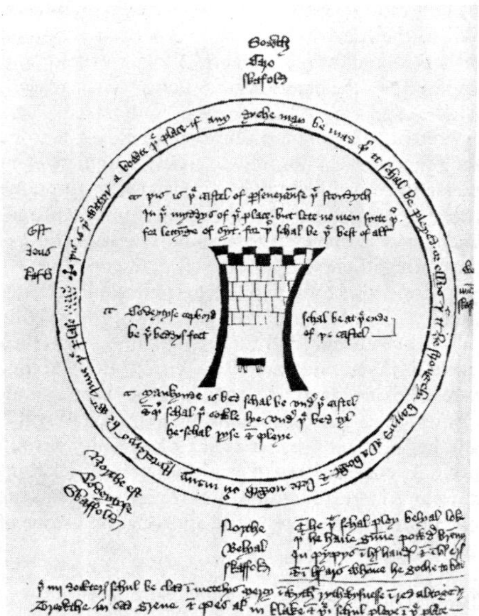

A form of religious allegorical drama, dating from 15th C. No doubt the form arose from the same allegorizing sermons from which Bunyan* in 17th C derived *Pilgrim's Progress**, and from allegorical poems such as William Langland's *Piers Plowman**. They may also have been encouraged by churchmen as more edifying entertainments than the popular Mystery plays*, which became mixed with worldly and semi-pagan elements. Moralities differed from Mysteries in that whereas the latter dramatized known episodes from the Bible or from the lives of the saints, the former dramatized the life of man by personifying the forces of good and evil, such as the seven deadly sins* and the corresponding virtues, or some representative crisis in his life such as his encounter with the fact of death. An example of the first kind of Morality is *The Castle of Perseverance* (1425?), and of the second kind, *Everyman**, which is the only real literary masterpiece among the true Morality plays.

The true Morality continued throughout 16th C, but the religious divisions caused by the Reformation* in that century, the rise of national politics, and the proliferation of interests in spheres such as education, led to derivatives from the main stream, such as Skelton's* *Magnificence* (1516); the Scottish political Morality, David Lindsay's *Satire of the Three Estates* (1540); and John Bale's *King John* (1547) which dramatizes the issue of national sovereignty over the Church. The influence of Moralities on the drama of Shakespeare's time is plain. Marlowe's* *Doctor Faustus* (1592?) is the most interesting drama which is evidently close to the tradition, and Jonson's Comedy of Humours* is a development of personification of the Morality type. More subtly, it is possible to trace Morality influence behind Shakespeare's plays about Henry IV*: Prince Hal is flanked in *1 Henry IV* by Hotspur who stands for Honour and by Falstaff as the Flesh; in *2 Henry IV*, Falstaff confronts the Lord Chief Justice who is wholly identified with his office.

* 5.1.1.3

Mordred (Modred) /'mo:drid/

In Arthurian legend, the nephew (sometimes the son) of King Arthur*. He was treacherous, and seized the kingdom during Arthur's absence; it was against him that Arthur fought the last battle – see Tennyson's* poem, *Morte d'Arthur* (1842).

More, Hannah (1745–1833)

A friend of Mrs Montagu and other Bluestockings*, and in the circle of Dr Johnson*, Burke*, Reynolds*, and Horace Walpole*, she wrote a number of successful plays which were produced by Garrick*. In later life she turned her attention to social conditions and the work of reformers such as Wilberforce*, who was the recipient of some of her great output of letters. Tracts written by her on such subjects as *Village Politics* attracted considerable attention and led to the formation of a Religious Tract Society. Her most famous book was *Coelebs in Search of a Wife* (1809), a moral tract about the ideal woman disguised as a novel.

* *Women, Status of.*

More, Sir Thomas (1478–1535)

Scholar, thinker, and statesman. He was the leading humanist* of his day, and a friend of Erasmus*. For some time he was a particular favourite of Henry VIII*, who raised him to the Lord Chancellorship*, the highest office in the state. However, More firmly refused to recognize the king's divorce from Queen Katharine and the Act of Supremacy* (1534). For this the king executed him, and the Catholic Church canonized him exactly 400 years later.

More's *History of King Richard III* (1513) has been called the first masterpiece of history and biography in English, but his principal work

*Utopia** (1516) was in Latin, translated into English in 1551. He was famous as a patron of letters and the arts, and invited the painter Holbein to England.

Bib: Chambers, R. W., *Life*; Marc'hadour, G., *L'Univers de Thomas More*; Mason, H. A., *Humanism and Poetry in the Early Tudor Period*; Hexter, J. H., study of *Utopia*; Bolt, R., *A Man for All Seasons* (play).

Morgan le Fay

A sister of King Arthur* and a sorceress. She is one of the three queens who carried Arthur away after the last battle to heal him of his wounds; she also tried to contrive his death earlier in the story (according to Malory*) by sending his sword, Excalibur*, to her lover, Sir Accolon. In the 14th-C *Sir Gawain and the Green Knight** it is her conspiracy to disgrace the Court of King Arthur that lies behind the testing of Sir Gawain.

* *Lady of the Lake; Morte d'Arthur.*

Morning Chronicle

A London Whig newspaper founded in 1769; its contributors included Sheridan*, Lamb*, James Mill, John Stuart Mill*, Dickens* and Thackeray*. It came to an end in 1862.

* *Newspapers.*

Morning Herald, The

A London newspaper, 1780–1869. It had a large circulation, and published police cases, illustrated by the famous artist George Cruikshank, illustrator of Dickens's novel *Oliver Twist**.

* *Newspapers.*

Morning Post, The

An extremely conservative but highly independent London newspaper, founded 1772, ceased 1936. Wordsworth*, Coleridge* and Southey* contributed to it.

* *Newspapers.*

Morning Star of the Reformation, The

The reformer John Wycliffe* was so called because his doctrines anticipated the Reformation* by 200 years.

Morris, William (1834–96)

Poet, socialist thinker, designer and printer. He was one of the leading artists of his day, associated with though not a member of the Pre-Raphaelite Brotherhood*, which sought to recover the cultural unity of medieval society. It is as a designer of textiles and wallpapers that he is most admired today. His aim was to counteract the industrial squalor of Victorian England, and to correct the major social injustice by which the proletariat were cut off from beauty of any sort by the nature of their environment: 'I don't want art for a few, any more than education for a few, or freedom for a few.' Unfortunately his campaign against aesthetic barbarism went with rejection of the machine and insistence on handwork, which cut him off from the realities of his age.

This withdrawal from hard realities is in keeping with his poetry which expresses withdrawal into the romances of the Middle Ages (*Defence of Guinevere*, 1858; *Earthly Paradise*, 1868–70), into ancient Greek epic (*Life and Death of Jason*, 1867; translation of Virgil's *Aeneid**, 1875, and of Homer's *Odyssey**, 1887), and into Icelandic epic (*Sigurd the Volsung*, 1876). His verse (the majority of it translation) was voluminous, fluent, decorative and musical in the Spenserian tradition current in the Victorian period.

Nonetheless, his socialism was a reality. He was one of the founders of the Socialist League (1884) and edited its monthly periodical *Commonweal*, until in 1890 the Anarchist wing of the movement drove him out. His *News from Nowhere* (1891 – previously contributed to *Commonweal*) is a prose 'utopia' describing England at a future date after the establishment of socialism. It is one of the most read of his works today. Another work of socialist inspiration, in mixed prose and verse is *The Dream of John Ball* (1888). He published a number of prose romances.

Morris had some influence on the young W. B. Yeats*, whose remark about him is revealing: 'The dream-world of Morris was as much the antithesis of daily life as with other men of genius, but he was never conscious of the antithesis and so knew nothing of intellectual suffering.' (*Autobiographies*, 1955).

* 3.4.5.

Bib: Henderson, P., *Life*; Mackail, J. W., *Life*; Hough, G., *The Last Romantics*; Jackson, H., *Morris: Craftsman-Socialist*; Thompson, E. P., *Morris: Romantic to Revolutionary*; Lewis, C. S., in *Rehabilitations*.

Morris Dance

A kind of dance popular in England from 14th to 16th C. It is said to have been introduced from Spain ('Morris' from 'Morisco' or Moorish). By 16th C it played a major part in village festivities. It was danced by a group accompanied by two musicians; the dancers adopted the characters of the Robin Hood* legends. The Puritans* abolished the dance in mid-17th C and it never flourished after the Restoration*.

* *May Day.*

Morte d'Arthur (1469–70) /ˈmɔːtˈdaːθə/

A collection of late versions of the legends of King Arthur*, translated from the French by Sir Thomas Malory*. It was among the earliest printed books in English (by Caxton*, 1485). The finest part is the last four books, comprising the unlawful love of Guinevere* and Lancelot* and the destruction of the fellowship of the Round Table*, all in keeping with the contemporary downfall of medieval England in the Wars of the Roses*. The rest of the book is episodic, in beautifully cadenced prose, but without the impact of earlier versions, *eg Sir Gawain and the Green Knight**.

This is also the title of part of Tennyson's *Idylls of the King*.

Moses

The great Jewish lawgiver, prophet and judge who

led the Israelites out of slavery in Egypt and through 40 years' wandering in the wilderness. References in English literature include his adoption by Pharaoh's daughter, who found the infant Moses floating in an ark on the Nile; his demand for freedom for the Jews, and the plagues which afflicted the Egyptians on their refusal; his leading the Jews to safety through the Red Sea; his striking the rock for water; his receiving from God the Ten Commandments, and his promulgation of a complete code of laws as contained in the first five books of the Bible, the Pentateuch*.

Mother Hubbard

The nursery rhyme* *Old Mother Hubbard* seems to date no further back than 1805, but the character was well known in 16th C. She was a folk-tale character, but the story has been lost.

* *Mother Hubberd's Tale.*

Mother Hubberd's Tale, or Prosopopeia

A verse satire by Edmund Spenser*, in 10-syllable couplets*, presented in the form of a fable; 'Prosopopoeia' means 'endowing things or animals with personalities'. It was published with other poems in *Complaints* (1591) but written at about the same time as *The Shepherd's Calendar** (1579). It was written at a time when Queen Elizabeth* seemed inclined to marry the Duke of Anjou, brother of Henry III of France. He was hated by the more convinced Protestants* in England (of whom Spenser was one) because he was a Catholic, and a member of the family responsible for the Massacre of St Bartholomew, 1572, in which French Protestants had been slaughtered. The fable tells how the ape and the fox steal the lion's crown while he sleeps. The ape is Anjou, and the fox is William Cecil, Lord Burleigh, Spenser's enemy.

Mothering Sunday

A festival derived from the worship of Cybele* (Rhea), Great Mother of the Gods, in ancient Rome. Under Christianity it was converted into worship of 'Mother Church', and it was also set aside as a day on which children paid special honour to their parents. It occurred in Mid-Lent (*ie* some time in March) but its secular descendant in the U.S.A. is fixed on the second Sunday in May. Commercialism has added father's days, etc.

Movement, The

* 6.5; *Larkin, Philip.*

Mr Polly, The History of (1910)

A novel by H. G. Wells*. Mr Polly is an imaginative little man oppressed by the meannesses of lower-middle-class circumstances. He begins as an unhappy shop-assistant, and then receives a small legacy which traps him in an unhappy marriage. He runs a little shop until he sees failure approaching; then he sets fire to it. He escapes, and settles down happily as assistant to the landlady of a country inn, first justifying himself by ridding it of the brutal nephew who terrorizes her. The first part of the book has excellent comedy in the Dickens* tradition, and acute social insight. The conclusion is a pleasant piece of pastoral* sentimentality.

Much Ado about Nothing

A comedy by Shakespeare. It was acted in 1598, and printed in 1600. The main plot is drawn from *Orlando Furioso** (Bk V) and from a novel by Bandello. The scene is Messina, at the court of the governor, Leonato, who receives a visit from the Prince of Aragon, his evil-minded brother, Don John, and the Prince's friend, Claudio. The main plot concerns Claudio's indirect courtship of Hero, Leonato's daughter, the frustration of their marriage by Don John who plants a slander on Hero, the eventual exposure of the slander, and the reconciliation. A sub-plot concerns the relationship between Benedick and Beatrice, who are famous in the court for their war of wits in which they declare mutual detestation; a plot is devised which enables each to recognize that their war is really a mask disguising their real love, and they acknowledge this to each other. The subplot joins the main plot when Beatrice tests Benedick's feelings for her by demanding that he challenge Claudio (his friend) to a duel for slandering Hero. The play is more famous for its subplot (and for Dogberry and Verges, the comic constables) than for its main plot, owing to the vividness of the characters in the former and the comparative colourlessness of those in the latter. However the comedy has more unity and impressiveness once the reader sees in it a strong current of satire. The court, like other Renaissance courts, is an environment in which witticism is valued without regard to true feeling, disguise of some sort is normal, artifice has more prestige than nature, and carefully cultivated appearances take the place of reality. In such a world, it is natural that Claudio should be a superficial lover easily deceived by a stratagem and that a mere game played in mockery of Beatrice and Benedick should lead to their stumbling on the truth. Their moment of truth stands out with dramatic poignancy. Similarly, Dogberry's naive stumbling over language is an appropriate contrast to the courtiers' artificial perversion of it.

Muir, Edwin (1887–1959) /mjuə/

Autobiographer, critic, poet, and novelist. He spent his childhood on a farm in the Orkney Islands, from which his father was compelled by economic hardship to move to Glasgow. For several years Muir struggled to earn his living in Glasgow as a clerk in various businesses; he became interested in socialism, and started writing. In 1919 he married, moved to London, and became a journalist. Thereafter, he travelled widely in Europe, and held a number of teaching posts. In 1940 he produced the first version of his autobiography, *The Story and the Fable*, expanded, revised and republished as *Autobiography* in 1954. The experiences of his own lifetime afforded him deep insight – social,

cultural, spiritual. He had moved from a pre-industrial society in Orkney to 20th-C industrialism at its grimmest in Glasgow. He was deeply aware of the Scottish roots of his culture, and was liberated from their limitations partly through German* literature and thought – Nietzsche*, Heine, Hölderlin; in the 1930s he and his wife Willa translated Kafka. Experience of psycho-analysis liberated the deeper levels of his imagination, and led him, through illumination about the relationship of man to his natural environment, to strong and unusually lucid religious feeling. His *Autobiography* is thus one of the classic works of modern English literature.

His birthplace, Orkney, has had some measure of detachment from the history of the rest of Scotland*, and it is partly this that enabled him to show some of the most penetrating perceptions about modern Scottish culture in *Scottish Journey* (1935) and *Scott and Scotland* (1936). His *The Structure of the Novel* (1928) is one of the few really valuable general surveys of the art of the novel in English criticism. Other critical works: *Latitudes* (1924); *Transition* (1926); *The Present Age* (1939); *Essays on Literature and Society* (1949).

Poetry: *First Poems* (1925); *Chorus of the Newly Dead* (1926); *Variations on a Time Theme* (1934); *Journeys and Places* (1937); *The Narrow Place* (1943); *The Voyage* (1946); *The Labyrinth* (1949); *Prometheus* (1954); *One Foot in Eden* (1956). He came to writing poetry late, through urgency of personal feeling rather than a professionally poetic concern with the medium. Nonetheless his later volumes embody some of his most moving insights, *eg* 'The Combat' from *The Labyrinth*.

Novels: *The Marionette* (1927); *The Three Brothers* (1931); *Poor Tom* (1932). Biography: *John Knox* (1929).

* *Autobiography*.

Bib: A Critical study by P. H. Butter; British Council Pamphlet by J. C. Hall.

Mummers

On various medieval festivals, especially Christmas, men and women dressed up in fantastic clothes and animal masks, and danced, sang, and performed before their neighbours. 'Mum' meant to mutter, and also to be silent, and 'mumming' is probably related to 'miming', the comic acting, often mainly through gesture, derived from the ancient Roman festival of Saturnalia*. The mummers also performed primitive folk plays about St George, etc. The performance of such plays continued in rural districts into 19th C – see Thomas Hardy's novel *The Return of the Native** (1878).

* 5.1.1.1

Munchausen, Baron (1720–97) /mʌn'tʃo:zn/

A German adventurer, who on his retirement made it his chief occupation to tell fantastic and implausible stories about his experiences. These were used by a German living in England, Rudolph Erich Raspe, for a book entitled *Baron Munchausen's Narrative of his Marvellous Travels and Campaigns in Russia* (1785). This was a great success, and later editions were supplemented by other writers, all purporting to be about Munchausen, but in fact derived from many sources going back to ancient Roman times.

Murdoch, Iris (b 1919) /'mə:dok/

Novelist. Works: *Under the Net* (1954); *Flight from the Enchanter* (1955); *The Sandcastle* (1957); *The Bell* (1958); *A Severed Head* (1961, dramatized 1963); *An Unofficial Rose* (1962); *The Unicorn* (1963); *The Italian Girl* (1964); *The Red and the Green* (1965); *The Time of the Angels* (1966); *Bruno's Dream* (1969); *A Fairly Honourable Defeat* (1970).

Iris Murdoch has also written a book on the French Existentialist* philosopher J. P. Sartre (*Sartre: Romantic Rationalist*, 1953), and a short philosophical work, *The Sovereignty of Good* (1970).

Her novels are characterized by their conspicuous symbolism, vivid narrative, grotesque comedy, and strong often macabre atmosphere, recalling early-19th-C Gothic* romances. They seem to be intended as philosophic fables, highlighting tormented extremes of modern experience.

Murry, John Middleton (1889–1957)

Critic. His own struggles to achieve personal integration, his close relationship with D. H. Lawrence*, and his marriage to the story-writer Katherine Mansfield*, led him to write about a number of writers relating their personal lives to

their art: *Dostoevsky* (1916), *Keats and Shakespeare* (1925), *Studies in Keats* (1930), *William Blake* (1933), *Shakespeare* (1936), *Jonathan Swift* (1954). He is perhaps best known for his controversial study of D. H. Lawrence, *Son of Woman* (1931), but in the last thirty years there has been a reaction against the biographical approach to criticism, and perhaps his most generally esteemed work is *The Problem of Style* (1922), which demonstrated that style is not a mere surface handling of words, but the expression of the writer's whole personality – a basic assumption of most criticism since.
Bib: Mairet, P., *John Middleton Murry* (British Council).

Muses, The

The nine daughters of Zeus and Mnemosyne (Memory) in Greek myth. Each presided over a separate art: Clio – history; Euterpe – lyric poetry; Thalia – comedy; Melpomene – tragedy; Terpsichore – the dance; Erato – love poetry; Polyhymnia – sacred songs; Urania – astronomy; Calliope (who ranked first) – epic poetry and eloquence. They may have originally been water deities, and various springs were associated with them – Castalia, Hippocrene, Aganippe. Water has always been associated with inspiration, and hence their later role as inspirers of the artist. They were also originally 'the mindful ones' through association with their mother, the goddess of Memory. Variations through the centuries have caused writers to attribute to them functions differing from the list given above.

Musgrove /ˈmʌzgrəuv/

Charles, Henrietta, Louisa – characters in Jane Austen's novel *Persuasion**. Charles is husband to the heroine's sister, and Louisa temporarily distracts Captain Wentworth from the heroine, who loves him.

Myers, Leopold Hamilton (1881–1944) /ˈmaiəz/

Novelist. His father, F. W. H. Myers (1843–1901) was a characteristic product of the 19th-C agnosticism so prominent among the educated classes; his reaction against it took the form of attempts to prove the existence of the soul by scientific experiment; he was one of the founders of the Society for Psychical Research. The son's concern with the spiritual life took the form of seeking answers to the question 'Why do men choose to live?'. His chief opponents in his pursuit of the answer were not scientific rationalists in the tradition of T. H. Huxley*, the associate of Darwin*, but aesthetes of the Bloomsbury tradition, who left moral experience to look after itself while they cultivated enjoyment of 'states of mind'. He also regarded the great influence on English writing of the French novelist, Marcel Proust (1871–1922) as pernicious, because Proust likewise esteemed experience aesthetically and not morally. Myers considered that this led to the trivializing of life, and his novels dramatize the opposition between those who interpret experience through moral discrimination and those who vulgarize it by regarding it as a means to aesthetic experience only; from the latter evil arises. He regarded civilized society as he knew it as corrupted by its moral indifference.

His first novel, *The Orissers* (1923) presents the issue in bare terms, but his principal work was the sequence of novels about 16th-C India, published together as *The Near and the Far* in 1929. Myers chose the remote setting of India under the Emperor Akbar because he wanted to escape from the secondary preoccupations of daily life in modern England, and to treat moral and spiritual issues with the large scope which the India of that date, with its multiplying religions and philosophies, afforded him. Evil is represented in the novel through Akbar's son Prince Daniyal, intelligent, artistic, but morally nihilistic, and rival of his merely stupid brother Salim for succession to the throne. Good is expressed through the character of the Guru (teacher) of the last section (*The Pool of Vishnu*): 'All communion', he says, 'is through the Centre. When the relation of man and man is not through the Centre it corrupts and destroys itself.'

* *Bloomsbury Group*.
Bib: Bantock, G. H., *L. H. Myers: A Critical Study*; Simon, I., *The Novels of L. H. Myers* (pub. Brussels).

Myrmidons /ˈməːmidənz/

In Greek legend, a race of warriors who followed the leadership of Achilles* in the Trojan war.

Mysteries of Udolpho, The (1794)

A novel by Mrs Ann Radcliffe*. It achieved great fame in its own day, and is often cited as the typical Gothic* novel. It is mainly set in a sombre castle in the Apennine mountains in Italy. The atmosphere is of secret plots, concealed passages, abductions, and the supernatural. Jane Austen* satirized the taste for such sensational literature in *Northanger Abbey**.

Mystery (Miracle) Plays

Cycles of religious plays performed in the Middle Ages* during the great Church festivals*, especially Corpus Christi* in June. The material came either from the Bible or from the lives of the saints. The attempt to distinguish Mysteries, as concerning the former, from Miracles, as about the latter, has not been accepted; the terms are synonymous.

The Mystery plays arose out of the performance of the Mass; this is itself already dramatic, and at Christmas and Easter there were sometimes dialogue interpolations illustrating the three shepherds at the cradle of Christ, and the three Maries at the tomb. Such playlets were performed by the priests in Latin, but there was in addition a strong lay contribution to the development of the form. Dancing and semi-dramatic performances were a pre-Christian phenomenon among the common people and they survived in Christian times (*eg* Morris dances* and May games) at seasonal celebrations – midwinter, spring and high summer.

The pagan nature worship expressed through these seasonal festivities was linked with Christianity in the popular mind, and the dating of the Church festivals* corresponded to the seasonal ones: the birth of the Christ-child symbolized hope in the darkness and dearth of the New Year; Christ's resurrection accorded with the earth's resurrection in spring, and the promise of human redemption by God with the promise of harvest at midsummer. Thus the people took increasing part in these special dramatic rituals, until by 14th C they were taken out of the hands of the clergy by the trade guilds of the towns, and were infused with elements about which the Church felt uneasy, though the predominant features remained Christian.

By the time the plays became completely secularized, the texts were in English. They commonly consisted of episodes from the Old and New Testaments illustrating God's justice and mercy. Each craft guild* made itself responsible for an episode, and often the episode was appropriate to the craft; thus the watermen of Chester presented the Flood, the goldbeaters of Newcastle presented the Magi* with their precious gifts to the Christ-child, and the painters and pinners (whose work was construction) presented the Crucifixion at York. Usually the performances took place on 'pageants'* or wagons which circulated the town so that all the episodes could be seen successively at given stations. Performances might begin at dawn, and continue all day, until all the selected stations had been visited by all the pageants.

There is evidence the Mystery plays were performed all over England from 14th to 16th C, and that many cycles must have existed. Four have survived: from York (48 episodes – **York Mystery Plays*); from Wakefield (32 episodes – **Wakefield Plays*); from Chester (25 episodes); and from Coventry (42 episodes). The Wakefield plays are sometimes called the Towneley cycle from the name of the family into whose possession the texts came. The Coventry plays were probably not performed at Coventry but perhaps went on tour. In addition to these whole cycles there are fragments from Norwich, Newcastle, and Beverley.

The texts of the surviving plays are 15th-C documents but they may be identical with earlier ones. Authorship is unknown, but two outstanding masters have been distinguished by their style: the 'Wakefield Master' who used a 9-line stanza and wrote five of the best Wakefield plays, and the 'York Realist', responsible for the magnificent Crucifixion. Certain features of such plays are perpetuated in Elizabethan drama, notably the juxtaposition of comedy and tragedy (*eg* the York Crucifixion – compare the comedy of the Porter's scene, *Macbeth* II. iii) and the presentation of evil through grim humour – minor devils and 'vices' in the mysteries anticipate clowns in the Elizabethans, and major representations of evil such as Herod* foreshadow monstrosities such as Shakespeare's *Richard III**. Though the Reformation* frowned on Mystery plays in general, they did in fact continue to Shakespeare's day – a record of a performance of the Chester Cycle in 1594 survives.

* 5.1.1.2; *Morality Plays; Vice, The.*

N

Nabob /'neibob/

In its original sense, a Muslim government official in 17th-C India, akin to 'Nawab'. In English 19th-C usage, it was a term for a rich man who had made his fortune in India.

Naboth's Vineyard /'neiboθ/

In the Bible – *1 Kings* 21. The wicked queen, Jezebel*, caused Naboth to be put to death in order that King Ahab of Israel should have his vineyard.

Naiads

* *Nymphs.*

Napoleon I (Napoleon Bonaparte, originally Buonaparte, 1769–1821)

A Corsican whose unique career began in the French Revolution*, when he joined the French army defending the first French Republic against European alliances. His military successes brought him to dictatorship in 1799, with the title of First Consul, and in 1804 he became Emperor. His armies dominated the greater part of Europe until 1812, when his campaign against Russia failed. His final defeat at the hands of the British and the Prussians under Wellington* and Blucher at Waterloo* (1815) led to his exile on the Atlantic island of St Helena, where he died.

His unprecedented success aroused contrasted feelings amongst the British. For the great majority he was a nightmare figure; mothers used his name to frighten naughty children into discipline. To a man like Wordsworth* he was the tyrant who revealed the illusoriness of the ideals of universal freedom which the Revolution had seemed to express. For Byron* and Shelley* he was the first man in Europe to have risen to the summit of power by intrinsic merit and not at least partly through privilege; his downfall and the restoration of the traditional kinds of government that he had overthrown was for them a defeat of the new hopes for mankind. Byron described him memorably in *Childe Harold** Canto iii, stanzas 36–44.

Napoleon III (lived 1808–73)

The nephew of Napoleon I*. He became Emperor of the French in 1852, after previously being elected to the office of President of the second French Republic in 1848. His revival of the Napoleonic title caused him to take the title of Napoleon III, out of respect for his uncle's dead son who had in fact never succeeded to the title. He was without his uncle's genius in war and statecraft, but among the British the mere fact of his succession to power renewed fears of French aggression. His regime was overthrown by the Germans in the Franco-Prussian war of 1870, and he died in England.

Narcissus

In Greek myth, a youth of exceptional beauty. He rejected the love of the nymph Echo, and to punish him Aphrodite* caused him to fall in love with his own reflection in water. He was changed into the flower which bears his name.

Nashe, Thomas (1567–1601) /naʃ/

Pamphleteer, poet and playwright. He spent six years at St John's College, Cambridge, and is numbered among the University Wits* who made the decade 1590–1600 an unusually lively period in literature. Two features of this liveliness were satire* and the prose romance (sometimes misleadingly called 'the Elizabethan novel'). Nashe contributed to both: his best known work, *The Unfortunate Traveller, or the Life of Jacke Wilton** (1594), is one of the outstanding romances of the decade, and it includes some of his best satire, often in the form of parody of some of the contemporary styles of fine writing. Most of the rest of his satire was also in prose. *Pierce Penniless, His Supplication to the Devil* (1592) is a satire in the tradition of the allegorical Morality plays*; an attack on the qualities that made for success in the London of his day, and a denunciation of them as new versions of the Seven Deadly Sins*; the method looks forward to Jonson's Comedy of Humours*. His last work, *Lenten Stuff* (1599), is a comic extravaganza on Yarmouth, a fishing town, and the red herring. Other prose work includes his early pamphlets attacking the Puritan* side in the Marprelate* controversy and vigorous disagreement with Gabriel Harvey* on literary and moral questions between 1593 and 1596. His *Christ's Tears over Jerusalem* (1593) records his repentance for religious doubts.

Nashe was sent to prison in 1597 for an attack on abuses in his play *The Isle of Dogs*, which has been lost. The only play of his sole authorship which survives is *Summer's Last Will and Testament* (1592). This defends the traditional festivities of the countryside against Puritan condemnation of them, and at the same time attacks the useless extravagance of courtiers. It includes some very fine lyrics, especially *In Plague Time* and *Autumn*.

Nashe is chiefly known as a prose writer; his prose is notable for the abundance of its energy which compensates for the confusion of its organization. His gift for parody and the rapidity and vividness of his expression show that the greater coherence and lucidity which English prose was to achieve in 17th C was not all gain. The freedom and zest of his comic writing owe something to earlier Renaissance* writers – the Italian poet and comedian Aretino* and the great French satirist Rabelais*.

* 5.1.2.4

Bib: Hibbard, G. R., *Thomas Nashe*; Krapp, G. P., *The Rise of English Literary Prose*.

National Anthem, The British

'God Save the King', sung as a national anthem, dates back to 1745, when the throne of George II was threatened by the second Jacobite* Rebellion in Scotland on behalf of the Stuart claimant. It consists of four verses of which the first only is normally sung, and the last (calling for suppression of the Scots) has been entirely forgotten. The tune has commonly been attributed to the composer John Bull (?1563–1628); alternatively, the words and the tune are said to have been the composition of the poet Henry Carey (d 1743), but there is no certainty.

National Debt

The system by which a government finances itself by borrowing money from its citizens, in addition to taxing them; the lenders in effect invest money in the state as in a business enterprise. In Britain this system originated in the reign of William III* and the Bank of England* was founded in order to operate it.

Nationalism

The emotion or the doctrine according to which human egotism and its passions are expanded so as to become identical with the nation state. As a widespread phenomenon it is usually dated from the American War of Independence (1775–83) and from the French Revolution* and the wars that followed it. This makes it an especially 19th-20th-C phenomenon, which it undoubtedly is, but on the other hand intense national self-consciousness existed among the older European nations before, though without the fanaticism which has been characteristic of it since 1790. Thus strong national feeling arose in England and France, in consequence of the Hundred Years War* in 15th C; it arose again in 16th and 17th C under the English queen Elizabeth I* and the French king Louis XIV respectively. Possibly these earlier emotions should be distinguished as patriotism, but the distinction is vague.

Nationalism is often culturally and artistically liberating; the reigns of Elizabeth and Louis in England and France are evidence of this, and so is the Irish nationalist movement at the end of 19th and the beginning of 20th C. New literatures, whether in English or other languages, among the new nations of the Commonwealth in 20th C may also be evidence of the creative influences of nationalism.

Natural Law

According to theologians (*eg* Richard Hooker*), that part of the Divine Will that manifests itself in the order of the material world: distinguishable from but of a piece with human and divine law. Modern scientists define it as the principles of uniformity discernible in the behaviour of phenomena, making such behaviour predictable. For 18th C, the existence of Natural Law was important as the basis for Natural Religion*.

Natural Philosophy

In 17th and 18th C, the study of physics and kindred sciences. Interest in Natural Philosophy became organized and heightened with the establishment in 1662 of the Royal Society*, which took the whole of knowledge as its province. The natural philosophers included such eminent men as Isaac Newton*, the chemist Robert Boyle (1627–91), and the naturalist John Ray (1627–1705). They were religious men who made their religion accord with their science. However, in spite of the respect accorded to some of them, especially Newton, men of letters in the period 1660–1730 tended to react against natural philosophy with angry contempt. They were provoked not so much by the fear of the injury such thought might do to religious faith – this was much more a 19th-C reaction – as by disgust at the triviality of much scientific inquiry, the technical fruits of which were slow to appear. The most notable satire was Swift's 'Laputa' in Part III of *Gulliver's Travels**. Other examples were Samuel Butler's *Elephant in the Moon*, some of the *Spectator** essays of Addison and Steele, and the *Memoirs of Martinus Scriblerus*, published with the works of Pope* in 1741, though the principal author seems to have been John Arbuthnot (1667–1735).

Natural Religion

A belief first taught by Lord Herbert* of Cherbury; according to him, belief in God and right conduct are planted in human instincts. This Christian doctrine was the basis for deistic thought (**Deism*) in the later 17th and 18th C, and contributed to the growth of religious toleration, though also to passivity of religious feeling and hence to indifference. Herbert's aim was to resolve the doubts arising out of the religious conflicts of his time – see *eg* Donne's* *Third Satire*. For the reaction against Deism, see William Blake's* propositions *There is No Natural Religion* (1788).

Naturalism

In literature, a school of thought especially associated with the novelist Emile Zola*. It was a development of Realism*. The Naturalists believed that imaginative literature (especially the novel) should be based on scientific knowledge, and that imaginative writers should be scientifically objective and exploratory in their approach to their work. This meant that environment should be exactly treated, and that character should be related to physiological heredity. Influential in France and Germany, the movement counts for little in Britain; the novelists George Gissing* and Arnold Bennett* show traces of its influence in the treatment of environment in relation to character.

Nature

The word is used throughout English literature with meanings that vary constantly according to period or to mode of expression, *eg* philosophic, religious or personal. This note is intended to guide the student by showing some of the basic approaches to the idea.

[1] *Creation and the Fall*. Fundamental to all conceptions of Nature is traditional Christian doctrine. This influences English writers even when they are using a more or less agnostic or atheistic approach. The doctrine is that Nature is God's creation, but by the fall of man, symbolized by the story of Adam's disobedience in the book of *Genesis*, earthly nature is self-willed and destructive though not to the extent that the Divine Will and Order is obliterated in it.

[2] *All-embracing Nature*. Nature is sometimes seen as the whole of reality so far as earthly experience goes. For instance, the opening 18 lines of Chaucer's Prologue* to the *Canterbury Tales* show Nature as the great reviver of life. This use of the word has a different kind of significance in 18th C when scientific Reason has replaced the religious imagination as the familiar vehicle for the interpretation of reality. See [4] Nature and Truth.

[3] *Nature and God*. In line with traditional Christian doctrine, Natural Law is linked to Human Law and Divine Law as a manifestation of the Divine Will, in such works as Hooker's* *Laws of Ecclesiastical Polity* (1597). However, from the beginning of 17th C, there was a new interest in the function of human reason as an instrument for the acquisition of knowledge independently of religious feeling. Men like Raleigh* (*History of the World*, 1614) and Bacon* (*The Advancement of Learning**) began to ask what, given that God was the Primary Cause of Nature, were the Secondary, or Immediate, Causes of natural phenomena. Newton's* work on gravitation (*Principia Mathematica*, 1687) and Locke's *Essay Concerning Human Understanding** seemed to solve the problem, causing people to see God as the Divine Artificer whose Reason could be discerned in the government of even the smallest phenomena, as well as in the great original act of Creation.

[4] *Nature and Truth*. Nature is in 18th C Truth scientifically considered. 'To follow Nature' (*eg* in works of imaginative literature) may mean: (i) to present things and people (*eg* an imagined character) as they really are; (ii) to reveal truths that lie beneath appearances; (iii) to follow rational principles. It was the attempt to 'follow Nature' in these ways that constituted the main discipline of the novelists Defoe*, Richardson*, Fielding*, Smollett*.

[5] *Nature as Moral Paradox*. The Christian conception of Nature as both God-created and spoilt by the fall of man led at various times to the problem that Nature is both good and evil. According to the medieval conception, maintained until the middle of 17th C, human society was itself the outcome of the Divine Natural Order, so that it was by Natural Law that children should honour their parents, subjects their sovereigns, etc. On the other hand, the natural passions of men and beasts, unrestrained by reason, were the source of rapacity and ruin. Thus Shakespeare's King Lear* begins by relying on the former conception of Nature, but he is exposed to the reality of the latter. In Shakespeare's time, man was the pattern of society, and as kings were necessary in society so Reason must be king over the passions in man. The 'kingly virtues' were conceived to be hereditable, so that in Shakespeare's *Cymbeline** Guiderius and Arviragus exhibit them though they have

never known their father and have been brought up in the wild; the same is true of Perdita in *The Winter's Tale**. Caliban in *The Tempest** is the product of mere ineducable nature and a violent animal; Miranda in the same play combines the ideal simplicities of nature enhanced by kingly descent and refined by 'nurture'; the 'Salvage Man' in Spenser's *Faerie Queene**, Bk. VI is good in a primitive way because he has noble blood.

19th-C natural science revived the feeling that Nature was essentially destructive, and hostile or at best indifferent to men; this is the 'Nature red in tooth and claw' image of Tennyson's *In Memoriam**, set against the idea of the love of God. The atheistic Thomas Hardy* saw men as subjected to the irony of indifferent fates, and the natural environment as governed in the same way.

[6] *Nature for Man's Use*. Implicit in Christian doctrine was the belief that Nature was created *for* man; that it was his birthright to exploit and use it. This begins with the conception of Nature as the Great Mother, originating in pre-Christian times but pervasive in medieval verse and later, *eg* in much Elizabethan pastoral* poetry. It took a more active significance when the 17th- and 18th-C 'natural philosophers' from Bacon* onwards sought methods by which man could increase his power over Nature; 18th-C poetry commonly shows Nature as beautiful when she is productive under the ingenuity of human exploitation.

[7] *Nature and Art*. 'Art' in earlier contexts often includes technology, *eg* in Polixenes' remarks on cultivation to Perdita in *The Winter's Tale* IV. iii; here art is seen as itself a product of nature. But art was often set against nature in Shakespeare's time and afterwards, *eg* in Sidney's *Apology for Poetry**: 'Her (*ie* Nature's) world is brazen; the Poets only deliver a golden'; here the function of imaginative art seems to be the opposite of the 18th-C poets' and novelists' conception of 'truth to nature', but Sidney meant that poetry should improve on Nature, not falsify it; the creation must be ideal but consistent with Nature.

[8] *Nature opposed to Court and City*. 'Art', however, was not necessarily an improvement. The city and the court, in Shakespeare's time, were the centres of new financial forces generating intrigue and 'unnatural' (*ie* inhuman) behaviour. The Elizabethan pastoral* literature of Sidney*, Spenser, Shakespeare, etc. was a way of simplifying human relations by seeing them in idealized rural surroundings without the complications of urban and court actualities. The setting and characters were in the tradition of ancient Roman pastorals, but commonly invigorated by elements from the rural life of the England of the day, *eg* in *The Winter's Tale* IV. iii. There was also a kind of pastoral made by idealizing the life of the great country houses, *eg* Ben Jonson's* *Penshurst*. In 18th C poets like James Thomson* wrote about natural surroundings for their own sake, and sometimes included wild nature as their subject, but it was Wordsworth who gave to wild nature its importance as the principal subject of what later came to be known as 'nature' poetry.

[9] *Nature in Communion with the Individual*. Wordsworth was to some extent anticipated in 18th C by such a poet as William Cowper*, and his teacher was especially Jean-Jacques Rousseau*. It was Wordsworth above all, however, who gave to Nature its modern most familiar sense – as the non-urban, preferably wild environment of man, to which the depths of his own nature always respond. Here he finds a communion which refreshes the loneliness of his spirit in a relationship which underlies and gives meaning to his human relationships.

Nausicaa /no:ˈsikiə/

In Homer's *Odyssey**, vi, the daughter of Alcinous, king of the Phaeacians in the island of Scheria. When Odysseus was shipwrecked and swam ashore there, she took him to her father, who gave him hospitality.

Nebuchadnezzar /nebjukədˈnezə/

King of Babylon, 605–562 BC. He conquered Israel. The first four chapters of the book of *Daniel* in the Bible tell of his dream that was correctly interpreted by Daniel; of his erection of a golden image which he ordered the people to worship; of the refusal of Shadrach, Meshach and Abed-nego to obey, and their survival from the fiery furnace into which they were cast by his orders; and of his eventual madness, in which he became like the cattle of the fields.

Nectar and Ambrosia

In ancient Greek myth, the fragrant drink and food of the gods. Both had fragrance, and were sometimes referred to as perfumes. Nectar was usually the drink and ambrosia the food, but they were considered to be honey-like substances and more or less interchangeable.

Nelson, Horatio, Viscount (1758–1805)

English admiral, and a national hero. His naval successes against Napoleon culminated in the Battle of Trafalgar* (1805) at which he lost his life in gaining victory over the combined French and Spanish fleets, thus saving England from French invasion. As an officer he was strongly independent and unconventional; one of the famous anecdotes about him tells how he put his telescope to his blind eye at the battle of Copenhagen in 1801 in order not to see his superior officer's signal ordering him to withdraw. Equally famous are the signal to his ships before Trafalgar: 'England expects every man to do his duty', and his dying words: 'Now I am satisfied; thank God I have done my duty.' His love affair with the beautiful Lady Hamilton was a notorious romance. In 1813 the poet Robert Southey* published his life, one of the best known of English biographies.

Neo-Classicism

This term can be understood for the purposes of English literary culture in two senses: (1) the broad sense, which refers to the Renaissance* of Classical culture and its influence on English literature down to the end of the 18th C. This influence operated mainly by the cultivation of Latin culture, and was mediated first by Italy and later by France. (2) the narrow sense of neo-classicism refers to a European artistic movement which originated in Germany and lasted approximately from 1750 until 1830.

In the first sense, neo-classical culture affected English literature in two phases:

[1] In 16th C England developed a fine school of classical scholars, of whom the greatest was Thomas More*. Through travellers and scholars such as Sir Thomas Wyatt* and Henry Howard, Earl of Surrey*, poetry and prose received strong influences from Italian writers such as Petrarch* and French ones such as Ronsard* who already belonged to the classical revival. A critic like Sidney* showed the influence of Italian critics who in turn were developing 'rules' out of classical writers for dramatic construction, etc. All these influences matured in the last decade of 16th C but their effect was uneven; the greatest of the rising dramatists, Shakespeare*, ignored the neo-classical rules for dramatic construction, whereas Ben Jonson*, his chief rival in the theatre by 1600, was deeply affected by classical principles and classical culture generally. Pastoral* poems, deriving from Italian influences and more directly from Virgil, were numerous from Spenser's *Shepherd's Calendar** (1579) onwards, and in the 1590s there was a widespread production of sonnets* under the influence of Petrarch. Much of the classical influence was on the level of ornament, however, as it was in English architecture in the same period. Jonson was outstanding in his absorption of classical influence to a deep level, and it was deeper in his lyrical work than in his drama. He is, in fact, an important link with the next phase of English neo-classicism – that which began in 1660 and lasted throughout 18th C.

[2] The second phase was much influenced by contemporary French literature, which was passing through its greatest age. English culture was entering a relatively aristocratic period by reaction from the Republican decade of the 1650s; it was also undergoing an increasingly strong revulsion against religious and political passions such as produced the Civil War*. The result was admiration for philosophy, reason, scepticism, wit and refinement – all qualities conducive to neo-classic culture. Significantly this was also the first important period of English criticism. Yet thoroughly neo-classic critics like Thomas Rymer* were the exception. The restlessness of English society, the increasing importance of the middle class, the difficulty of making such a large exception to neo-classic principles as Shakespeare, and the hostility the English literary tradition has always shown to authoritative doctrines, all help to explain the refusal of the leading critics, Dryden* and Samuel Johnson* to adopt neo-classic theory unquestioningly. Nonetheless, such a figure as the French neo-classicist Boileau* was deeply respected, and the best poets and essayists (though hardly the novelists) – Addison*, Swift*, Pope*, Johnson – all exhibited the neo-classic virtues of clarity, order, reason, wit, and balance.

Neo-classicism in the narrow sense was the cultivation of Greek culture in opposition to Roman

culture, and originated partly in the German movement to emancipate German culture from France. It can be said that whereas Renaissance classicism sought to emulate the culture of Rome, this 'New Humanism' sought inspiration in the originality of the Greeks. This difference enabled the new Neo-Classicism to merge with Romanticism*, whose progenitor was above all Rousseau*. In England, it is thus impossible to distinguish Neo-classic from Romantic writers in the period 1790–1830. It is clear, however, that William Blake* shows neo-classic inspiration in his graphic art, and that the poems by Keats* on classical themes (Endymion* and the two Hyperions*) are in a romantic-classical style, very different from Augustan* classicism of the previous century. Neo-classicism is more distinguishable in the architectural style known as Regency*, and in the sculpture of an artist such as Flaxman (as well as in costume*), than in imaginative literature.

* *Classic, Classics, Classical; Unities.*

Neo-Platonism

* *Platonism.*

Neoptolemus (Pyrrhus) /niːəp'tolimǝs/

In Greek legend, the son of Achilles*, the principal Greek hero of the Trojan wars. He was brought there after the death of his father, owing to a prediction that Troy would not fall without him, and distinguished himself in its capture. Later he married Hermione, daughter of Menelaus, and was slain by her cousin Orestes, to whom she had been betrothed.

Nepenthe /ne'penθi/

In Greek myth, a drug which caused forgetfulness of grief.

Neptune

* *Poseidon.*

Nereids

* *Nymphs.*

Nero (AD 37–68) /'niərəu/

Roman Emperor 54–68, and notorious for his tyrannous cruelty, the result of insane suspicion. In 64 Rome was burnt, according to many accounts by his secret orders. Legend says that he enjoyed the spectacle, and played music while he watched the conflagration – hence the proverb 'to fiddle while Rome burns', *ie* to be frivolous during a disastrous happening. At all events he had a highly developed aesthetic sensibility. Eventually his subjects revolted against his tyranny and he is reported to have died by his own hands with the words: 'What an artist dies with me!'

Nestor /'nestoː/

In Greek legend, one of the Greek kings who besieged Troy; he was an old man and full of wisdom.

New Atlantis, The
A philosophical tale by Francis Bacon*, in the tradition of Sir Thomas More's *Utopia**. It was left unfinished at Bacon's death, and published in 1626. The title is an allusion to the mythical island described by Plato* in his dialogue *Timaeus*. Bacon's island is called Bensalem (*ie* an analogous place to Salem or Jerusalem, the holy city) and its chief glory is its university, 'Solomon's House'. Unlike the English universities of Bacon's day, this is devoted to scientific research – 'the knowledge of causes, and secret motions of things; and the enlarging of the bounds of human empire, to the effecting of all things possible'.

New Grub Street (1891)
A novel by George Gissing*. The title refers to Grub Street*, which was inhabited in 18th C by journalists of a low order, who wrote to gain a living without seriousness of intention or artistic standards. The living they earned was generally a mean one, but since 1875 the new periodicals and newspapers had found a way to achieve massive circulations by printing material which had an immediate appeal although its intrinsic quality was trivial or merely sensational. This commercialization of journalism had spread to the production of books. Gissing's novel is about the difficulties of the serious literary artist faced by successful competition from the now very well rewarded commercial writer without scruples, either moral or artistic. The serious writer in the book is Edwin Reardon (a self-portrait) and his successful competitor is Jasper Milvain. Commercial success is also illustrated by Whelpdale, editor of the magazine *Chit-Chat* (based on the actual magazine *Titbits* founded in 1881) which never publishes articles longer than two inches in length. At the other extreme is the novelist Biffen, who has the artistic fastidiousness of the French novelist Flaubert* and writes the same kind of book. Biffen and Reardon both end in failure, but Gissing's novel was fairly popular, which perhaps argues against the extreme pessimism of his thesis.

* *Journalism*; *Newspapers*.

New Learning, The
Study of the Bible and the Greek classics* in the original languages instead of through Latin versions. This study in 15th-16th C was an important influence in the Renaissance* and the Reformation*.

New Model Army, The
Formed by Parliament in 1645 towards the end of the Civil War* between itself and King Charles I*. The war had so far been indecisive owing to the amateurish soldiering on both sides. Parliament now secured that its own army should be highly professional. The result was the decisive victory of Naseby in June 1645. The commander was Sir Thomas Fairfax, but its most gifted general was Oliver Cromwell*, who between 1646 and 1660 made the English army one of the most formidable in Europe. Cromwell's special contribution was his highly trained force of cavalry, the Ironsides.

New Statesman, The
The leading left-wing weekly periodical of the intelligentsia. It was founded in 1913; its Conservative counterpart is *The Spectator**. In politics it has always followed a general line of Fabian* socialism.

New Testament
The second and shorter part of the Bible, containing the sacred books of the Christians. It is divided into books, on the pattern of the Old Testament*, and dates as a whole collection from the end of 2nd C AD. It is customary to divide the books into four groups.

[1] The three Synoptic (*ie* 'summary narrative') Gospels of Saints Matthew, Mark and Luke, and the *Acts of the Apostles*. The Gospels are narratives about Jesus Christ, and *Acts* is the narrative of the missionary careers of the apostles (including St Paul) after Christ's death.

[2] The Epistles (letters) of St Paul. The four shortest of these are addressed to individuals: two to Timothy, and one each to Titus and to Philemon. The remainder are addressed to various early Christian communities from Rome to the eastern end of the Mediterranean. These are the Epistles to the Romans, Galatians, Ephesians, Philippians, Colossians, two to the Corinthians, and two to the Thessalonians. The Epistle to the Hebrews has been ascribed to Paul, but is nowadays considered to be by a disciple of his.

[3] The Catholic Epistles, so called because they were directed to Christians generally. Two of these are ascribed to St Peter, and one each to James and Jude.

[4] The Johannine writings, ascribed to the Apostle John. These are the Gospel of St John, distinguished from the Synoptic Gospels as probably not intended as a historical narrative, the Epistles of John, and the poetic, visionary narrative called the *Apocalypse*, or *Revelation*.

* *Bible in England*.

New Way to Pay Old Debts, A (1625)
The best-known comedy by Philip Massinger*. The main character is Sir Giles Overreach, a man of powerful energy and unlimited rapacity, who has no scruples in his schemes to increase his own wealth and social greatness. He is, however, outwitted by those very social superiors, Lord Lovell and Lady Allworth, whom he tries to flatter and use; they take the side of the young people whom he tries to victimize, his nephew Wellborn and his daughter Margaret. Overreach thus 'overreaches' himself, in the manner of Ben Jonson's* characters, and he is in fact the last vigorous representative of the Comedy of Humours* tradition. The weakness of the play is that Overreach's opponents are colourless characters, so that the play is artistically unbalanced in Overreach's favour. Massinger's use of blank verse* is extremely flexible to the

point sometimes of insipidity although in the best passages it regains much of the concentrated force of Ben Jonson himself. Overreach is based on a contemporary profiteer, Sir Giles Mompesson.

Newcomes, The (1853–5) /ˈnju:kəmz/

A novel by William Makepeace Thackeray*; it was published in instalments. The characters are drawn from the middle and upper classes, and the book is a study of the vices and virtues of such mid-19th-C society. The vices are shown in the worldly cynicism of Lady Kew who seeks for a fashionable marriage for her grand-daughter Ethel Newcome; in the mean snobbery of Ethel's brother Barnes, who frustrates her marriage with her cousin Clive Newcome; in the hypocrisy, intrigue and viciousness of Clive's eventual mother-in-law Mrs Mackenzie, and in the philistinism and arrogance of the social world as a whole. The virtues are less successfully presented. Clive Newcome's father, Colonel Newcome, is the honourable, single-minded soldier who loses his fortune and is subjected to the tyranny of Mrs Mackenzie. Thackeray was inclined to see decency as overwhelmed by materialism.

Newgate /ˈnju:git/

In the Middle Ages, the principal west gate of the City of London. The gate-house was a prison from 12th C, enlarged in 15th C and burnt down in the Gordon Riots* in 1780. Its destruction is described in Dickens's novel *Barnaby Rudge**. It was rebuilt and finally demolished in 1902, when the present Central Criminal Court (Old Bailey) was built on its site.

The 'Newgate school of novelists' in the 1830s and 40s were such writers as Harrison Ainsworth* and Bulwer Lytton, who tended to idealize famous criminals such as the highwayman Turpin*. They were attacked by Thackeray who satirized the mode in his novel *Barry Lyndon* (1844).

* *Oliver Twist.*

Newman, John Henry (1801–90)

Writer on religion and education. From 1833 to 1842 he was one of the most influential and controversial leaders of the Church of England, but in 1845 he was received into the Roman Catholic Church. As a Catholic convert he was even more influential, and he was made a Cardinal in 1879.

His first period of activity (1833–42) was as leader of the Tractarian Movement – more or less identical with the Oxford Movement* – whose aim was to defend the Church of England against encroachments by the state on the one hand, and against adulteration of its doctrines by the Broad Church tendencies on the other. The Church of England was founded in 16th C on a central position between the Catholicism of Rome and the whole-hearted Protestantism* of Luther* and Calvin*. This had always been both its strength and its weakness; it was able to accommodate a variety of believers, but it was inclined to lose itself in vagueness and become subservient to the state. Newman's *Tracts for the Times* tried to secure a firm basis for Anglican doctrine and discipline, as against supporters of the Broad Church party (such as Thomas Arnold) who cared less for doctrine than for social ethics. Newman's tracts led him steadily towards Roman Catholicism, however, until his *Tract XC* went so far as to say that the Anglican 39 Articles – which all clergy had to accept – were not incompatible with essential Roman Catholic beliefs, but only with distortions and exaggerations of them.

As a Roman Catholic, Newman's first valuable literary work was *The Scope & Nature of University Education* (1852), a collection of lectures to the new Catholic University of Dublin, of which he became Rector in 1854. These were combined with further lectures delivered in 1859 to make *The Idea of a University Defined* (1873). His spiritual autobiography, defending the sincerity of his Catholic beliefs against the accusations by the Broad Churchman, Charles Kingsley*, came out with the title *Apologia pro Vita sua* (Defence of his Life) in 1864. It was not only very persuasive in convincing the public of the genuineness of his faith; it was also an eloquent and lucid presentation of the nature of religious belief at a time when much religious thinking in English was muddled, superficial, and entangled in irrelevant controversies with scientific agnostics such as T. H. Huxley*. His *Grammar of Assent* (1870) was a more strictly philosophical account of religious belief.

Newman also wrote some minor poetry, including the famous hymn *Lead Kindly Light*, and the dramatic monologue* *The Dream of Gerontius*, better known for the music set to it by Elgar. He also wrote two religious novels – *Loss and Gain* (1848) and *Callista* (1856).

As a writer he is famous for the lucidity and grace of his style, which expresses the single-mindedness and depth of his thought and feeling. His wide influence, still very powerful, arose from his ability to understand the tragic extremity of the emotional and intellectual bewilderment of his contemporaries, while refusing to compromise his beliefs.

* 3.4.3; *Agnosticism.*

Bib: Harrold, C. F., *Newman: an Expository and Critical Study of his Mind, Thought and Art;*

Houghton, W. E., *The Art of Newman's Apologia*; Trevor, M., *Pillar of the Cloud* and *Light in Winter* (biography).

Newspapers

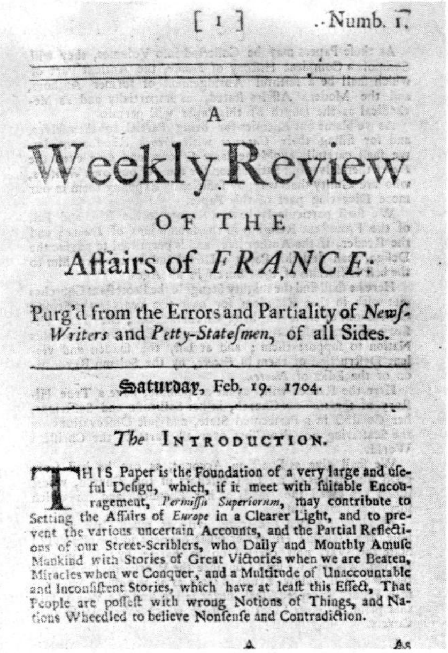

[1] ..Numb. 1.

A
Weekly Review
OF THE
Affairs of *FRANCE*:
Purg'd from the Errors and Partiality of *News-Writers* and *Petty-Statesmen*, of all Sides.

Saturday, Feb. 19. 1704.

The INTRODUCTION.

THIS Paper is the Foundation of a very large and useful Design, which, if it meet with suitable Encouragement, *Permissu Superiorum*, may contribute to Setting the Affairs of *Europe* in a Clearer Light, and to prevent the various uncertain Accounts, and the Partial Reflections of our Street-Scriblers, who Daily and Monthly Amuse Mankind with Stories of Great Victories when we are Beaten, Miracles when we Conquer, and a Multitude of Unaccountable and Inconsistent Stories, which have at least this Effect, That People are possest with wrong Notions of Things, and Nations Wheedled to believe Nonsense and Contradiction.

A As

Periodicals resembling newspapers began in a small way in the reign of James I*; in the decades of the Civil War* and the Interregnum* they increased in number owing to the need of either side to engage in propaganda. From 1695 press censorship* was abandoned; newspapers and weekly periodicals began to flourish.

The first English daily, the *Daily Courant*, a mere news-sheet, began in 1702, but in the earlier part of 18th C papers more nearly resembling what we now know as the weekly reviews were of greater importance, and leading writers conducted them, *eg* Defoe's* *The Review* (thrice weekly – 1704–13); Steele's* *Tatler** (thrice weekly – started 1709); Steele and Addison's* *Spectator** (daily – started 1711); and the *Examiner* (started 1710), to which the chief contributor was Jonathan Swift*. Samuel Johnson's* *Rambler** (1750) was of the same kind. Of these men, only Defoe resembled fairly closely what we nowadays regard as a journalist as distinct from a man of letters.

The first attempt to reach a mass circulation was made through this kind of periodical by William Cobbett* with his *Weekly Political Register* (started 1802), and in 1808 Leigh Hunt's* weekly *Examiner**, directed to a more educated public though with less remarkable literary merit, began to rival Cobbett's paper as a medium of radical comment and criticism.

Of daily papers founded in 18th C, the *Morning Post** (started 1772) survived until 1936, and *The Times** (started 1785) is today the daily with the greatest prestige, though it has a comparatively small circulation. Other important dailies with a shorter life were the *Morning Chronicle** (1769–1862), and the *Morning Herald** (1780–1869). Both reached peak circulations of about 6,000. To reach the very large circulations of today, newspapers had to await the abolition of the stamp duty – a tax on newspapers – in 1855. The Stamp Tax was started in 1712. It was a method of restricting circulations by raising the prices of newspapers. The government of the day resented criticism of its policies but did not dare revive the Licensing Act, the lapsing of which in 1695 was really the start of the British freedom of the press. The abolition of the tax, together with the advent of cheap paper and a nationwide potential public thanks to universal literacy, led to a new kind of newspaper at the end of 19th C. Alfred and Harold Harmsworth, later Lord Northcliffe and Lord Rothermere, founded the *Daily Mail* in 1896; by 1901 it was selling a million copies. Other popular newspapers followed it with steadily increasing circulations.

Several bad consequences have followed this development:

[1] Much journalism* has degenerated into mere commerce, so that news is regarded as what is most saleable, *ie* what appeals most readily to the baser and more easily roused human appetites.

[2] Newspapers, in order to keep their prices down, have come to rely on advertising revenue, which is attracted chiefly to those with very large circulations so that some with smaller circulations have been eliminated.

[3] The British newspapers have divided rather sharply into the serious ones with a large influence but a small circulation, and the popular ones, which often achieve their large circulations by irresponsible appeals to the baser public tastes. Finally, modern newspapers, as great capitalistic enterprises, tend to be right wing politically, so that left-wing opinion is underrepresented in the daily press. However, British newspapers are jealous of their independence: they are quick to resist any tendency by the government to check their freedom of expression. Since the war, the Press Council has been established for the purpose of limiting the abuse of this freedom by, for instance, the infringement of personal privacy; however, its powers are limited to public rebuke, and it has no power to penalize or censor newspapers.

The 20th-C weekly reviews have seldom been able to compete with the daily papers in the size of their circulations. However, the strong tradition of weekly journalism inherited from 18th and 19th C ensures that the 'weeklies' have large influence among the intelligentsia. The oldest of the influential weeklies is the *Spectator* which has no connection with Addison's periodical, but was founded in 1828. It is conservative and is counterbalanced by *The Statesman** on the left. The most authoritative literary periodical in Britain is *The Times Literary Supplement*, a weekly which is published by *The Times* newspaper.

* 2.2.4.2

Newton, Sir Isaac (1642–1727)

Mathematician and natural philosopher. He

entered Trinity College, Cambridge, in 1661, became a fellow of the college in 1667, and Professor of Mathematics in the university in 1669. He resigned the professorship in 1701; in 1703 he was made President of the Royal Society*, and was re-elected annually until his death. Queen Anne knighted him in 1705.

His principal work was *Philosophiae Naturalis Principia Mathematica* (1687), written in Latin. By the application of mathematical calculation, it explained the force of gravity in its operation through the solar system. His book on *Optics* (1704) was less important, but it aroused new interest in vision and colour and influenced descriptive writing throughout 18th C. His scientific and mathematical discoveries did not shake his religious convictions, which were very strong, and he also wrote on theology and biblical chronology. On the other hand, he did not understand and had no use for the imaginative faculty, and, like Locke (whose *Essay concerning Human Understanding** was published in 1690) he dismissed poetry as an unimportant and irrelevant activity.

Despite this indifference to poetic literature, Newton's discoveries, combined as they were with his religious piety, had a great influence on 18th-C poets. He caused them to revere Reason in both Man and God, who, seen through Newton's writings, became the Divine Artist of the Universe. Pope's *Essay on Man** was a restatement of the traditional vision of the natural order newly shaped to accord with Newton's rational harmony, and it was Pope who composed for Newton the famous epitaph:

> *Nature and Nature's laws lay hid in night:*
> *God said*, 'Let Newton be!' *and all was Light.*

The most famous poet of the natural scene in 18th C, James Thomson*, wrote his *Seasons** in accordance with Newtonian principles. In the revised *Prelude** (1850) Wordsworth wrote of the statue in Trinity College:

> *Of Newton with his prism and silent face,*
> *The marble index of a mind for ever*
> *Voyaging through strange seas of Thought, alone.*

Wordsworth thus chooses to emphasize the mysteriousness of science, whereas Pope had emphasized its power to clarify mystery. In general, 19th-C poets, having discovered the force of the irrational in human experience, lost respect for Newton; for William Blake* he stood for a deathly narrowing of experience:

> *May God us keep*
> *From Single vision & Newton's sleep!*
>
> (Letter to Butts 1802)

Bib: Nicolson, M. H., *Newton Demands the Muse.*

Nibelungs /ˈniːbəluŋz/

In German and Norse myth a race of dwarfs who dwelt in Norway.

Nicholas, Saint

An early Christian bishop (early 4th C AD) of Myra in Asia Minor. His festival is celebrated on 6 December. Very little is known of him, but legends accumulated round him, and in the Middle Ages* he became an extremely popular saint. In art he is frequently depicted beside three children standing in a tub; the legendary basis for this seems to be that he restored three youths to life after they had been murdered and concealed in a salting tub by an innkeeper. He is also said to have secretly found dowries for three impoverished girls, thus enabling them to marry. These legends led to St Nicholas becoming associated with children, and the practice grew of secretly giving presents on the eve of his festival. This practice was in time transferred to Christmas*, and St Nicholas was always supposed to be the mysterious giver. In the United States, the Dutch form of his name 'San Nicolaas' was corrupted to 'Santa Claus', but in England he is identified with 'Father Christmas', although 'Santa Claus' is also used.

Nicholas Nickleby (1838–9)

A novel by Charles Dickens*; like his other novels, it was first published in serial parts. Nicholas, his sister Kate, and their mother are left penniless, and struggle for a living under the oppressive guardianship of Ralph Nickleby, an avaricious financier, the dead Mr Nickleby's brother. Morally, the tale is in black and white; Nicholas stands for ardent and youthful virtue, Ralph for meanness and cruelty. Nicholas is sent to teach at Dotheboys Hall, an iniquitous school run by Wackford Squeers to whom Nicholas gives a vigorous thrashing. Kate is apprenticed to Madame Mantalini, a dressmaker, where she is exposed to the vicious advances of Ralph's associate, Sir Mulberry Hawk. Nicholas beats him too. Ralph's evil intentions are eventually exposed by his eccentric but right-minded clerk, Newman Noggs, and the Nickleby family are befriended by the Cheeryble brothers. The novel is in Dickens's early, episodic and melodramatic style, but many of the episodes are presented with great vividness and comedy.

Nick, Old

* *Old Nick.*

Nietzsche, Friedrich Wilhelm (1844–1900) /ˈniːtʃə/

German philosopher. He challenged the concepts of 'the good, the true, and the beautiful' as, in their existing form of abstract values, a decadent system at the mercy of the common man's will to level distinctions of all kinds. He set his hope on the will to power of a new race of men who would 'live dangerously' and develop aristocratic virtues by asserting their own spiritual identities. Among his more famous works are a book on the philosopher Schopenhauer and the composer Wagner, whom he regarded as his own teachers: *Unzeitgemässe Betrachtungen* ('Thoughts out of Season', 1876); *Die Fröhliche Wissenschaft* ('The Joyful Wisdom', 1882); *Also sprach Zarathustra* ('Thus spake Zarathustra', 1891).

Nietzsche was one of the important progenitors

of Existentialism*, and he had a considerable influence on some of the major English writers in the first quarter of this century. His ideas inspired Shaw* in the latter's belief in the Superman-hero as the spearhead of progress, *eg* his conception of Joan of Arc in his play *Saint Joan*, and D. H. Lawrence wrote in Nietzsche's spirit in his affirmation of spontaneous living from deep sources of energy in the individual – human 'disquality' (see *Women in Love*, ch. 8) as opposed to democratic egalitarianism. The Irish poet W. B. Yeats also affirmed a natural aristocracy of the human spirit, and saw in Nietzsche a continuation of the message of the poet William Blake*, who preached the transcendence of the human 'identity' over the 'self', which is defined and limited by the material environment. After 1930, Nietzsche's influence declined because he was seen as a prophet of the more vicious forms of fascism*.

* *German Influence on English Literature.*

Night Thoughts on Life, Death, and Immortality, The Complaint or

A blank verse* meditation by Edward Young (1683–1765), published 1742–5. It is in nine parts and has about 10,000 lines. Its eloquence is in the tradition of Milton*; its argument in the rational tradition of Pope's *Essay on Man**. Its thought is not original, but its melancholy sentiment is perhaps the starting-point of the cultivation of the sensibility which became increasingly characteristic of the later 18th C, and Young's apt and concentrated expression gave some passages proverbial force. This and the quality of the emotion brought the poem great celebrity. Boswell* quotes Johnson* (*Life* 1791): 'Particular lines are not to be regarded; the power is in the whole; and in the whole . . . there is the magnificence of vast extent and endless diversity.' Boswell adds that the poem has 'a power of the Pathetick beyond almost any example I have seen'. In the next century George Eliot*, in *Worldliness and Other-worldliness* (*Essays and Leaves from a Notebook*, 1884), demolishes the structure of religious ideas in the poem.

Bib: Wicker, C. V., *Edward Young and the Fear of Death.*

Nightingale, Ode to a

* *Odes, Keats's.*

Nightmare Abbey (1818)

A novel by Thomas Love Peacock*. It is a satire on the current taste for Gothic* mystery and romantic despair. Mr Glowry and his son Scythrop own the Abbey; Scythrop is in love with two girls, like Peacock's friend, the poet Shelley*. Mr Flosky is a satirical portrait of Coleridge* in his aspect as a transcendental mystic, and Mr Cypress represents Byron's* self-centredness. There are other characters of cheerful temperament to counteract the romantic sombreness of these. The plot is slight, but the comic fantasy is sustained by it and by the conversations which are always the greater part of a Peacock novel.

Nimrod /'nimrod/

In the Bible (*Genesis* 10:9) he is described as 'a mighty hunter before the Lord'.

Nine Worthies of the World

Caxton's list in his preface to Malory's *Morte d'Arthur** was of three 'Paynims' (Hector, Alexander, Julius Caesar), three Jews (Joshua, David, Judas Maccabaeus), and three Christians (Arthur, Charlemagne, Godfrey of Bouillon). The 'ostentation' in Shakespeare's *Love's Labour's Lost** (V. i & ii) varies in some cases from this list.

Nineteenth Century in English Literature

The period opened with a great revival of poetic expression, after a prose century in which the poets themselves had often attempted to emulate the virtues of prose. The first generation of the new poets – William Blake*, William Wordsworth*, Samuel Taylor Coleridge* – all began under the inspiration of deep spiritual disturbances, the historical manifestation of which was the French Revolution*. Against this Wordsworth and Coleridge reacted in disillusionment when they saw it transformed by Napoleon Bonaparte. On the other hand, the second generation of outstanding poets – Lord Byron*, P. B. Shelley*, John Keats* (he was the least touched by politics) felt the bitterness of anticlimax after the overthrow of Napoleon in 1815, and intensely resented the restoration of the old oppressive regimes. These six poets differed from one another greatly, although all except Blake felt the influence of Wordsworth, and they were not the only poetic geniuses, nor, except for Byron, were they amongst the most popular. Several of the more popular ones are now almost forgotten, *eg* Thomas Moore*; Scott* is more remembered for his novels, but his poetry is important in that he did most to express the new liberation of feeling through old ballad styles and in medieval settings. Crabbe* continued 18th-C poetic style with a 19th-C awareness of the common people and sensitiveness to the influence of environment.

But a sharp change occurred in the dominant form of literary expression after 1830. Despite the popularity of the poetry of Tennyson* in the mid-century, and (later) that of Browning*, it was the novel, particularly adapted as it was to the rapid social transformations of the Industrial Revolution*, which became the representative medium. The first mature English novelist, Jane Austen*, was already dead, and Scott had already made the new form of historical fiction with a coherent social vision enormously popular. However 1830 marks the beginning of the career of Dickens*, and his lifetime was almost to coincide with the first great phase of the English novel; in addition to himself, the leading names are George Eliot*, Emily Brontë*, Charlotte Brontë, and William Makepeace Thackeray*. Novelists of marked talent but lesser rank include Elizabeth Gaskell*, Anthony Trollope*, and Benjamin Disraeli*. The last quarter of the century saw the second great phase of the novel in Henry James* and Joseph Conrad*, who wrote with much more awareness of foreign influences; with their more radical questioning of social and cultural assumptions they became also the first great figures of the 20th-C novel. Thomas Hardy* is almost as prominent a figure, but as a regional novelist he stands apart from the other two, who were notably cosmopolitan: his insight is profound, but, in his best work, it is expressed through a specific environment.

An important aspect of 19th-C literature is its autobiographical inclination. Some outstanding works during the century were autobiographies (*eg* De Quincey's *Confessions of an English Opium-Eater**), but the tendency was even more important as a diffused approach to imaginative art, in poetry (*eg* Wordsworth's *Prelude**) and in the novel (*eg* Charlotte Brontë's *Villette**). It was, if anything, even more important in non-fictional prose, both that of the early 19th-C periodical essayists such as Hazlitt* and Lamb*, and that of the Victorian 'sages' - the polemicists of the middle and later century, who commonly expressed their deep concern with society (its changes, and its dangers and potentiality for the human consciousness) in autobiographical and semi-autobiographical form. Examples are Carlyle's *Sartor Resartus**, Newman's* *Apologia*, and Mill's* *Autobiography*. The autobiographical habit of mind is bound up with great changes in prevailing attitudes to the nature of the human personality, but the literary practice derives from a French 18th-C work, the *Confessions* of Rousseau*.

19th-C literary criticism also shows urgent concern with the social and spiritual questions of the age. The great critics are Wordsworth, Coleridge (whose chief critical work is characteristically in part autobiography – *Biographia Literaria**) and Matthew Arnold*. By the end of the century, Henry James had become the first important systematic critic of the novel.

It is common to think of 19th C as the century of Romanticism (**Romance*), in contrast to 18th C as the 'Age of Reason'. This is too simple, however. Firstly, Romanticism had its beginnings in 18th C; secondly, continuity with 18th-C rationalism was an important aspect of 19th-C thought and feeling, *eg* in Utilitarianism*; and finally, Romanticism is a difficult term in relation to English literature, and needs separate treatment.

* *Victorian Period.*

Nisus /ˈnaisəs/

[1] In Virgil's *Aeneid**, a Trojan hero whose friendship with Euryalus was proverbial for its devotion. They both accompanied Aeneas in his emigration from Troy to Italy, and were killed together fighting the Rutulians.

[2] In Greek myth, son of Pandion of Megara. This Nisus had a purple lock of hair, and while it grew on his head, Megara was safe. His daughter was bribed to cut off the lock by King Minos when he was besieging the city. Nisus perished while the city was being sacked and was turned into a sea-eagle.

Nixie

In Germanic and Norse myth, a female water spirit; the male was a Nix. They were akin to the Scottish kelpie*.

Noble (Coin)

A former gold coin first issued in 14th C. It was engraved with the image of the king (originally Edward III*) in a ship. Its value was 33p. Edward IV reissued it with the new design of the archangel Michael killing a dragon, and it became known as the Angel-noble or Angel. He also issued a new coin, worth 50p, adding a Yorkist rose to the old design of the king and ship; this was called the Rose-noble.

Nocturnal upon St Lucy's Day

One of the finest, and also the most difficult, of Donne's* *Songs and Sonnets.* There is much uncertainty as to the person to whom it is addressed, and consequently about the date on which it was written. It may be addressed to Lucy, Countess of Bedford, who was at the point of death in 1612, though she did not in fact die until later. It may on the other hand concern Donne's wife, whose name was not Lucy but Ann. If it is about Ann, it may refer to her actual death in 1617 or to a prior illness, for instance one that occurred in 1611. St Lucy's Day is 13 December. According to the Old Julian Calendar, in use in Britain until 1752, this was somewhere near, though never actually, the shortest day; yet Donne's original full title was *A Nocturnal upon Saint Lucy's Day; being the Shortest Day.*

The poem is in five 9-line stanzas. The theme is deprivation, and what lies beyond it. The death of the year is like human death, but the poet's sense of death goes beyond this seasonal death (stanza 1). In stanza 2 he refers to the revival of the year and of lovers in the spring. But he has not only been reduced to death but revived by the alchemy of love to a state beyond death: 're-begot/Of absence, darkness, death; thin things which are not'. Of these he is the 'quintessence' (line 14), an alchemical term, originally supposed to be the substance of the heavenly bodies. In stanza 3 he describes himself as 'the grave/Of all that's nothing'. In life, the lovers became chaoses if their affections ever wandered from each other, and became 'carcases' in each other's absence, but (stanza 4) her death has reduced him to a death beyond that of ordinary dead things, such as stones. Thus (stanza 5) while other lovers renew their loves when the sun renews his life, he will use the darkest night of the year to devote himself to preparing his spirit to meet hers in the resurrection that lies beyond death.

The alchemical image or 'conceit'* used by Donne to evoke the idea of an existence on the other side of death is typically metaphysical*. Typical of Donne is the rough yet strong rhythm which gives a feeling of actuality and solemnity to the poem, and the use of homely images such as 'Whither, as to the bed's-feet, life is shrunk' (stanza 1, line 7) combined with abstruse terms such as 'quintessence'. The poem is capable of much more complex interpretation than the surface one given here; see for instance Richard Sleight in *Interpretations*, ed. John Wain.

* *Alchemy.*

Noh Plays /nəu/

A kind of drama practised in Japan since 15th C. It is highly formal, austere, and ritualistic, making a great part of its effect through symbolism. Its artistic economy and symbolism have greatly interested some Western writers in 20th C – see the book *Noh, or Accomplishment* by Fenollosa and Pound. The poet W. B. Yeats* imitated the form in some of his experiments to revive the verse drama, *eg At the Hawk's Well* (1917).

Noll; Old Noll

Nicknames for Oliver Cromwell*. Noll was the diminutive form of the name Oliver.

Nominalism

One of the two main schools of medieval philosophy, the other being Realism*. The nominalists argued that terms naming things according to their kinds ('animal', 'vegetable', etc.) and abstract terms ('beauty', 'goodness', etc). are merely names describing the qualities of things and do not refer to things that have reality in themselves. The realists argued that on the contrary such 'universals' alone have an ultimate reality, and that the reality of individual objects depends upon them. The nominalist viewpoint is represented in modern philosophy by such thinkers as John Stuart Mill* and other 'empiricist' philosophers who reason that reality can only be known by particular experience of it, and argue against any theory of implanted ideas such as the Deists believed in.

* *Deism*; *Ockham.*

Nonconformists

* *Dissenters*; *Puritanism.*

Nonsense Literature

This covers several kinds of literature, which have in common that they all in some way deliberately defy logic, or common sense, or both. In English folk literature, many nursery rhymes* come into the category. The most important kind, however, is undoubtedly in children's literature, especially the poems of Edward Lear* and the *Alice* stories by Lewis Carroll*, both of which are to be taken seriously as literature. Both writers are Victorian*, and this perhaps accounts for their imaginative depth; they wrote in a period of great mental restlessness, in that respect similar to ours, but before the time of Freud* and his psychology of the unconscious mind. Thus they gave themselves wholly to their fantasies, undisturbed by the idea that they might be betraying secrets of their own nature. Modern writers, *eg* Joyce in his *Finnegans Wake**, will as fearlessly reveal their depths, but it will not be to children. Another reason why nonsense literature reached its peak in the Victorian period is perhaps that this was almost the earliest period when intelligent minds considered that children were worth writing for, merely in order to amuse them, and not to elevate their minds. 20th C writers in plenty have thought children worth amusing, but the child-public is now a recognized one, whereas Lear and Carroll wrote for a few young friends; they were thus as much concerned with their own interest and amusement as with that of their audience, whereas the modern writer has to sell his book.

Norman

Historically, the period of English history following the Norman Conquest (1066) when England was ruled by William, Duke of Normandy, and his descendants, *ie* William I*, 1066–87; William II* 1087–1100; Henry I, 1100–1135, and Stephen, 1135–54. The Normans were originally 'Norsemen' from Norway, who had conquered the province of northern France called after them. By the time they conquered England, however, they had become entirely French in culture, spoke French, and had French names. The 'Norman Conquest', therefore, was in effect a French conquest, and the imposition upon England of a ruling French aristocracy. In consequence, English became a lower-class language, and it was not until 14th C that it again became the language of the richer and the cultured classes.

A 'Norman family', and being 'of Norman descent', when such phrases were used later in English history, meant 'coming over with the Conqueror' and implied the most indefeasible claim to 'true' aristocratic descent.

At the time of the Conquest, English architecture in stone was very undeveloped, whereas the Normans, under the influence of the French, had become great builders. They introduced the style called 'Romanesque' because it derived from the style (characterized by the round arch) employed by the ancient Romans. Such a style (in old churches, etc.) is commonly called 'Norman' in England.

North, Sir Thomas (1535?–1601?)

Translator. He is especially known as the translator of Plutarch's* *Lives* of the ancient Greek and Roman heroes. The translation was from the French of Amyot, and was published in 1579. It was not close, but very clear and vigorous, and constituted one of the masterpieces of English prose. It was widely read in Shakespeare's day, and was used by Shakespeare himself as the basis for his plays *Julius Caesar**, *Antony and Cleopatra**, and *Coriolanus**. Other translations by him were: the *Dial of Princes* (from *Reloj de Príncipes* by Guevara) published in 1557, which set the fashion for ornate writing culminating in Lyly's *Euphues**; and *The Moral Philosophy of Doni* (1570), an Italian collection of eastern fables.

North and South

A novel by Elizabeth Gaskell* published serially (1854–5) by Dickens in his periodical *Household Words**. The heroine, Margaret Hale, moves from the rural south of England to the industrial north, Lancashire. The sharp contrast between the two halves of England is equalled by the misunderstandings and savage opposition between employers and employees in the northern town. Margaret becomes involved in the affairs of one of the employers, John Thornton, with whom she too has deep misunderstanding. Suffering eventually brings them together, and teaches Thornton the necessity of treating his workers as human beings and not merely as factors in industrial calculation. Like her earlier *Mary Barton**, this novel is a courageous penetration of the industrial jungle which she knew at first hand; both are attempts, like Dickens's *Hard Times**, to modify the harshness of the industrial world with humane values.

North-West Passage

In the reign of Queen Elizabeth I* English trade with Eastern Asia through the Indian and the Pacific Oceans was made difficult by opposition from England's national enemies, especially Spain. It was believed that a practicable passage existed by sea to the north of North America. Several attempts were made in Elizabeth's reign without success. When the route was discovered in 19th C it was found to be commercially useless.

Northanger Abbey /nɔː'θaŋgə/

A novel by Jane Austen*. It was written much earlier, and incompletely revised when it was published (in 1818 after her death) with her last completed novel, *Persuasion**.

The book is in part a satire on the sensational and sentimental literature of the time, particularly of the enormously popular *Mysteries of Udolpho** by Mrs Radcliffe. The heroine is an ingenuous young girl, Catherine Morland, who visits the fashionable resort of Bath, and afterwards, with some friends she has made there, the country house of Northanger Abbey. She is healthy-minded and trusting but very suggestible; on the one hand she is entirely deceived by the worldly flattery of her scheming friend, Isabella Thorpe, who tries to marry Catherine's brother under the mistaken impression that he is very rich, and on the other hand, she suspects (under the influence of Mrs Radcliffe's novel) that Northanger Abbey conceals terrible secrets. Its owner, General Tilney, is the father of the man she loves, and is in fact almost as cold-hearted and inhumane as she suspects him of being, but in quite a different way; he has not, as she at first suspected, murdered his wife, but he turns Catherine out of the house at very short notice from purely mercenary motives. The theme of the book is partly the danger of confusing literature and life, a theme to which Jane Austen returns in *Sense and Sensibility** and *Emma**; it is also that life is as surprising and remorseless as the most romantic literature but in quite a different way.

Northcliffe, Alfred Harmsworth, Viscount (1865–1922)

One of the principal founders of the 'popular press' with its very large circulation, and in particular of the *Daily Mail* (1896).

* *Newspapers*.

Northumbria; Northumberland

From 6th to 9th C, Northumbria was one of the most important of the Anglo-Saxon* kingdoms; it extended from the northern bank of the River Humber (hence its name) to the Firth of Forth. In 9th C, the kings were reduced to the status of Earls, owing allegiance to the Kings of Wessex who had now become Kings of England. Early in 11th C, the Scots annexed the northern part of the earldom of Northumbria, between the Firth of Forth and the River Tweed.

Northumberland is a county in north-eastern England, consisting of part of the former kingdom of Northumbria. The post-Conquest earldom of Northumberland was in a chronic state of conflict with Scottish chieftains on its north-eastern frontier. The earls from 14th to 18th C (with brief intervals) were of the Percy* family, prominent in Shakespeare's history plays about Richard II* and Henry IV*. This conflict ceased on the union of the Crowns of England and Scotland with the accession of James VI of Scotland to the English throne as James I*. The modern Dukes of Northumberland descend from another family, which took the name of Percy in 18th C.

Nostromo (1904) /nos'trəuməu/

A novel by Joseph Conrad*. The setting is imaginary; all the events occur in or near Sulaco, capital city of the Occidental Province in Costaguana, a fictional South American state. At the beginning of the novel, Costaguana is ruled by a brutal and corrupt dictator after a short period of enlightened and liberal rule. The Occidental Province, however, remains a refuge of enlightenment and comparative prosperity, thanks partly to its geographical isolation from the rest of the country, and mainly to the existence of a large silver mine, run by an Englishman, Charles Gould, who secures the financial support of an American millionaire. In outline, the story is the history of how the Occidental Republic establishes its independence of the rest of the country, but at the same time loses the ideals which inspired it in the struggle.

The imaginary geography of Sulaco and its neighbourhood is as important as the historical background. Sulaco is a port at the head of a large gulf, the Golfo Placido, famous for the stillness of its waters; behind it rises a high range of mountains, one of which, Higuerota, contains the silver mine. Both the gulf and the mountain act as important symbols throughout the book. The population of the province is characteristic of that of other Latin American countries: there is a lower class of Indian peasants with a Spanish admixture, an upper class of landowners of pure Spanish descent, and, between the two, a cosmopolitan middle class, drawn from various European countries, especially Britain and Italy.

The characters are chiefly taken from this cosmopolitan middle class. Each is the focus of a strand of narrative, and the strands link up into images of the history of the country.

[1] Charles Gould (nicknamed 'King of Sulaco'), in his struggles to save the mine from ruin by the corrupt government, becomes the centre of the party of freedom and justice; but he becomes increasingly dehumanized by his preoccupations, and estranged from his wife, whose values of humaneness and compassion are betrayed, despite the eventual triumph of her husband's party.

[2] Captain Mitchell, the Harbourmaster, is another Englishman; stupid, but honest and courageous, he is unable to see beneath the surface of events, and is used by Conrad to record these deceptive appearances.

[3] Gian'Battista Fidanza, the Italian chief of the dockworkers, is universally known as 'Nostromo' ('Our Man'). He has a romantic pride in the devotion of his men, and in the knowledge that Mitchell, Gould, and their associates have complete confidence in his integrity. His spiritual downfall, unknown to any but himself, is due to his desire to preserve the appearance of integrity while yielding to secret dishonesty.

[4] Giorgio Viola keeps an inn by the harbour; he is an Italian patriot and political exile, whose disinterested and fiery idealism dissociates him from realities, an alienation symbolized by his accidental shooting of Nostromo at the end of the book.

[5] Martin Decoud is the journalist of the Sulacan revolution; he is totally French by education and culture, though not by descent. He is cynically entertained by the spectacle of Costaguaneran politics, but romantically attached to Antonia Avellanos, daughter of José, a Sulacan scholar and liberal politician. He dies of the physical isolation brought upon him by circumstances, since his highly cultivated consciousness is incapable of sustaining a sense of his own reality when the spectacle of events and the woman he loves are removed from him.

[6] Dr Monygham is an Irishman, embittered by his self-contempt arising from his betrayal, under torture, of his political associates. His humanity is preserved by his devotion to Mrs Gould, who is for him the uncontaminated embodiment of what is good in human nature.

These are only the chief characters, and they do not exhaust the novel's large cast. They are united by the theme of individual isolation even in co-operation with one another, and by a discrete pattern of symbols, of which the chief is the silver of the mine. This operates at first as an instrument of liberation, and later as a force of corruption; all the time it is a symbol of the illusiveness of human idealism.

Nostromo is usually regarded as Conrad's masterpiece. Conrad often based his tales on his experiences during his travels, or on the lands he knew in his childhood and youth. This novel seems to have had a starting-point in his brief acquaintance with Venezuela 'in 1875 or '76' (see Author's Note).

Nouvelle

* *Short Story.*

Novel, The

A work of narrative fiction of some length, nearly always in prose, and bearing a close resemblance to daily life in psychology, environment, and time scale.

In Britain it arose as a distinct literary form in 18th C out of multiple causes, social, philosophical, and literary:

[1] In its social origins, the novel was the product of the rise of the middle class in 17th C, providing a new and large reading public with its own characteristic preoccupations and attitude to life. Economic individualism, with each man having to earn his living by his own efforts, was more natural to such a class than the order of traditional, inherited status, and gave the new interest of uncertainty to personal destinies. At the same time, the growth in economic importance of the middle class, and the comparatively open relationships among the classes in England, resulted in a cohesion of interests among them and increasing aspirations after improvement of status, so that the world of the gentry in the countryside was not a separate one, but rather an extension of the middle-class world of the towns. These were some of the social factors which encouraged the novel and resulted in a broad public for it.

[2] Philosophically, the abatement of passionate religious feeling, and the rise of 'natural philosophers' like John Locke* concentrated attention on people's social destinies, and at the same time aroused a new interest in facts and circumstances of the social world – the field of the novel.

[3] The Restoration* Comedy of Congreve*, Vanbrugh*, etc., developed great skill in the realistic presentation of the surface of social life – the Comedy of Manners* – between 1660 and 1710, and in the first 15 years of 18th C the periodical essayists such as Addison* and Steele* extended this kind of representation into their character sketches, such as Sir Roger de Coverley, and their descriptions and discussions of the social scene. The journalism of Daniel Defoe*

encouraged the taste for accounts drawn from human experience in more or less extraordinary circumstances – *Robinson Crusoe** and the *Journal of the Plague Year**. Defoe's works of fiction were perhaps the first novels; at all events they were among the tributaries to the main stream. There was, finally, the 18th-C addiction to letter-writing.

Samuel Richardson's* *Pamela** (1740) is usually considered to be the first English novel; it has more structure than Defoe's tales, and, in the form of letters, it more consistently explores individual psychological states. But 'the novelist's vision' formed itself gradually through a number of writers. A pre-novel such as Bunyan's *Pilgrim's Progress** already had some of its characteristics, and yet in 18th C Richardson, Fielding*, Sterne*, Smollett* and Fanny Burney*, whatever their other merits as writers, were all defective as practitioners of the novel form. It is fair to say that Richardson, in his central characters, idealized them excessively through the desire to edify his public; Fielding was insufficiently interested in the psychology of his heroes and heroines; Sterne is fantastic, and Smollett and Fanny Burney in their different ways are narrow. But Jane Austen*, learning especially from Richardson and Fanny Burney, acquired remarkable precision in discerning the scope and direction of the art. After her time, the novel was to take many shapes; later novelists were able to use the form for wider purposes than Jane Austen, but they learned from her strictness what they could not do with it.

The 'great century' of the English novel was 1830–1930; see under Nineteenth Century in English Literature. The most massive achievements are now generally recognized to be the work of Charles Dickens* and George Eliot* between 1830 and 1880; that of Henry James* and Joseph Conrad* between 1880 and 1914, and that of D. H. Lawrence* between 1914 and 1930. (See F. R. Leavis: *The Great Tradition* and *D. H. Lawrence*.) Foreign influences counted for little before 1880; thereafter, the influences of the French and Russian novelists were important, especially on Conrad and James.

* *Twentieth-century Literature.*

Novum Organum (1620) /ˈnəuvəm ˈɔːgənəm/

A philosophical treatise ('The New Instrument') by Francis Bacon*, written in Latin. His aim was to describe a method of gaining power over nature through a complete and correctly founded system of knowledge. Knowledge must be acquired by experience and experiment, *ie* inductively. The obstacles to true knowledge are false assumptions which Bacon calls 'Idols'. These are of four kinds: the Idols of the Tribe are common human weaknesses such as allowing the emotions to interfere with the reason; the Idols of the Cave are individual weaknesses arising from individual upbringing; Idols of the Market-place arise from erroneous uses of language, such as using names for non-existent things, or for concepts which have been inadequately defined; Idols of the Theatre are caused by false philosophical principles and by incorrect reasoning. The object of speculative science must be to discover the true 'forms' of things, beginning with the forms of 'simple natures', *ie* the true manifestations of the most elemental phenomena such as heat and light. By inductive experiment certain axioms will be made of increasing generality and abstractness. Thus Bacon sought a method of recognizing what he called 'an alphabet of nature' so that a reliable language could be built up from it. The method of discovery proved too slow to be scientifically useful in the coming centuries, but his approach was an advance from the too exclusively deductive methods of medieval thought towards the modern scientific combination of deduction and experiment.

Nun's Priest's Tale, The

One of Chaucer's *Canterbury Tales**. It is told by one of the priests attached to the Prioress, and is in ten-syllable rhymed couplets*. It is an animal fable, perhaps derived from the French cycle about Reynard the Fox*. A cock of enormous vanity is beguiled by a fox who pretends to admire his crowing. The fox, however, turns out to have as much vanity about his own defiant roguery, and by counter-flattery the cock manages to outwit him. The comedy is enhanced by the long dialogue between the cock (Chantecleer) and his favourite hen Pertelote on the subject of dreams, in which his arrogance as a male creature overlays without cancelling his nature as a common fowl, the property of a poor old peasant woman. The absurdity of his pride in circumstances which from a human point of view are mean is thus an additional and more subtle fable, pointing to the analogous absurdity of human pride in the relative meanness of earthly circumstances. The tale is one of Chaucer's comic masterpieces.

Nuns and Nunneries

Monastic orders in the Middle Ages had female as well as male branches; most English nuns belonged to the Benedictine* Order. They lived in 'nunneries', later increasingly known as 'convents', though originally a convent might house either sex. They were ruled by elected prioresses or abbesses. Until 14th C, nuns were usually from aristocratic families; among the lower classes it was generally possible for a woman to work (though the status of Chaucer's Wife of Bath who has her own clothing business is perhaps unusual) but in the upper classes, a nunnery was the only alternative to marriage. Before the Norman* Conquest (1066) nunneries compared with monasteries as places of learning, but afterwards the nuns were seldom learned, though they excelled in such accomplishments as embroidery. From 14th C merchants' daughters as well as girls from noble families were increasingly admitted. Nunneries were sometimes used as places of confinement for disobedient girls who refused to marry the husbands of their parents' choice, etc. Manual work was neglected from 13th C and conducted by lay servants, as in monasteries, but nunneries sometimes ran small schools for the children of well-to-do families. Nuns who wished to live a life dedicated to solitary meditation were called 'anchoresses'; such was the mystical writer Juliana of Norwich*. The number of nuns probably never exceeded 2,000.

Nursery Rhymes

Simon was sent to market,
To buy a joint of meat,
He tied it to his horse's tail,
To keep it clean and sweet.

He went to slide upon the ice,
Before the ice would bear,
Then he plunged in above his knees,
Which made poor Simon stare.

He went to shoot a wild duck,
But the duck flew away,
Says Simon I can't hit him,
Because he would not stay.

Then Simple Simon went a hunting,
For to catch a hare,
He rode an ass about the street,
But could not find one there.

He went for water in a seive,
But soon it all run through,
And went all o'er his clothes,
Which made poor Simon rue.

He washed himself with blacking ball,
Because he had no soap,
And then said to his mother
I'm a beauty now I hope.

He went to eat some honey,
Out of the mustard pot,
It bit his tongue until he cried,
That was all the good he got.

Simple Simon cutting his mother's bellows open to see where the wind lay.

A body of folk verse, some of it very ancient, some of it being concealed comment on political events, some of it apparently never having had any meaning. The description 'nursery' refers to the fact that whether intended originally for children or not, most such rhymes are considered suitable 'for the nursery'.

Nut-Brown Maid, The

A 15th-C poem by an anonymous writer, first printed in 1502. It is in 30 12-line stanzas, spoken by the young man and the girl alternately, with the respective refrains 'Alone a banished man' and 'I love but you alone'. The argument is about the faithfulness of women; the nut-brown maid exemplifies it, since she is true to her lover though she believes him to be an outlaw. The poem has the tunefulness and simplicity of a ballad* and the artistry of court poetry (*Courtly Literature*); it is probably an example of the latter and shows the openness of the sophisticated poetry of the time to popular influences.

The poem had enduring popularity, and was paraphrased by Matthew Prior* as *Henry and Emma* in the very different classical style of his period. The original was included in Percy's *Reliques**.

Nymph

In Greek myth the nymphs were a race of minor female deities, often attendant on the major deities of both sexes. The word derives from the Greek for marriageable woman, and nymphs seem to have been associated with fertility. They were subdivided according to their various habitats: Naiads belonged to rivers, springs and lakes; Oceanids or Nereids lived in the sea; Oreads inhabited mountains and rocky places; Dryads and Hamadryads, forests and trees.

Nymphidia (1627) /nim'fidia/

A poem by Michael Drayton* in 78 8-line stanzas. It is a comic fairy tale in the Spenserian tradition, and has the same kind of wit and delicacy as Mercutio's speech on Queen Mab* in *Romeo and Juliet** I. iv. Nymphidia is the fairy attendant on Queen Mab, and tells the story. A character called Pigwiggin steals the queen, to King Oberon's frenzy; he and Puck make search for her. The climax is a duel between Pigwiggin and Oberon, mounted on earwigs; Proserpina, goddess of fairyland, makes peace.

O

Oak Trees

Slow-growing deciduous trees of very long life and particularly valuable as timber. In pagan times Europe had very large oak forests and the tree was almost universally regarded as sacred, especially in conjunction with the parasitic plant mistletoe* that grew upon it. For this reason, the oak tree plays an important part in European mythology. In Britain, where one of the largest and best timber-producing varieties is found, the tree became one of the national emblems owing to the fact that it was the best timber for building ships, on which the national safety and prosperity depended.

Oates, Titus (1649–1705)

An English conspirator. He was the son of a Puritan* preacher, and himself professed to stand for the defence of Protestantism* against supposed Catholic dangers, but he was really a disreputable adventurer who used the religious passions of the time for his personal advantage. In 1678 he fabricated the Popish Plot, by which he pretended without factual basis to expose a Catholic conspiracy against the Church of England*. Popular suspicion of Charles II*, and the fact that the Queen and his brother James were avowed Roman Catholics, caused a national panic, and a large number of Catholics were put to death. His evidence was eventually proved false, and he was imprisoned. He is satirized under the name of Corah in Dryden's *Absalom and Achitophel** and occurs in Scott's* novel *Peveril of the Peak* (1822).

Oberon /'əubərən/

In Germanic myth, king of the elves, or fairies. A French 13th-C romance, *Huon of Bordeaux*, in which he occurs, was translated into English in 1534. From this, Greene* introduced him into his romantic play *James IV* (1594), and Shakespeare into his comedy *A Midsummer Night's Dream*. He was used thereafter in a number of works, including a masque* by Ben Jonson* and the poem *Nymphidia** by Drayton.

* *Fairies.*

Objective Correlative

An expression first used by the critic and poet T. S. Eliot*, in his essay on *Hamlet* (1919). Eliot describes Shakespeare's play as an artistic failure because it 'is full of some stuff that the writer could not drag to life, contemplate, or manipulate into art'. He goes on: 'The only way of expressing emotion in the form of art is by finding an "objective correlative"; in other words, a set of objects, a situation, a chain of events which shall be the formula of that *particular* emotion; such that when the external facts . . . are given, the emotion is immediately evoked'. He then instances the sleep-walking scene in *Macbeth** as a successful 'objective correlative', and adds: 'The artistic "inevitability" lies in this complete adequacy of the external [*ie* the event on the stage as witnessed by the audience] to the emotion; and this is precisely what is deficient in *Hamlet*.'

Eliot's adverse judgment of *Hamlet* has not been widely accepted, but the term 'objective correlative' has passed into critical currency.

Observer, The

A newspaper* published only on Sundays, started in 1792. It is central in its politics, and aims to appeal to the thoughtful, better-educated public.

O'Casey, Sean (1884–1964) /'ʃɔ:n əu'keisi/

Irish dramatist, born in Dublin. He had little formal education, and worked for some time as a labourer and as a shop-assistant. His play *The Shadow of a Gunman* was produced at Dublin's Abbey Theatre* in 1923; it was followed by his most famous play, *Juno and the Paycock* (1924) and *The Plough and the Stars*. He then moved to London where *The Silver Tassie* (1928) was produced. Later plays: *Within the Gates* (1933); *The Star Turns Red* (1940); *Red Roses For Me* (1942); *Drums Under The Windows* (1945); *Oak Leaves and Lavender* (1948); *Cock-a-doodle Dandy* (1949); *Rose and Crown* (1952); *The Bishop's Bonfire* (1955). *Pictures in the Hallway* is an autobiography.

Ockham (Occam), William of (1300?–1349?) /'okəm/

Philosopher and Franciscan* friar. He was one of the leaders of the Nominalist school of philosophy, according to which individual things were considered to be real, but the names for kinds and classes referred to qualities of individuals only, and not to independent realities. This prepared the way for the thought of Francis Bacon* which was in itself the starting point of modern scientific thinking, since Ockham's ideas implied building generalizations from the knowledge of individual objects instead of arguing from pre-established generalizations, as the more typically medieval Realists had reasoned.

The principle known as 'Ockham's Razor' lays down that 'entities' must not be unnecessarily invented, implying that abstractions must be somehow proved to have a necessary relationship with known realities. The principle makes for exact thinking, and also for scepticism. He went so far as to say that the existence of God could not be proved, though he did not mean by this that God did not exist.

* *Nominalism*; *Realism*.

O'Connor, Frank (pen name of Michael O'Donovan) (1903–66)

Irish writer, especially famous for his short stories. He was born in Cork, and received little education. For some time he worked as a librarian in Cork and Dublin. He was encouraged to write by the Irish poet AE (George Russell), and his publisher, Harold Macmillan (later the English Conservative Party leader) influenced him in deciding for a literary career. He participated in the Irish Rebellion after World War I. His first volume of short stories, *Guests of the Nation*, was published in 1931. Other volumes: *Bone of Contention* (1936), *Three Tales* (1941), *Crab Apple Jelly* (1944), *The Common Chord* (1948), *Traveller's Samples* (1951), *My Oedipus Complex* (1963). His translations of poetry and legends from the Irish are also famous: *A Golden Treasury of Irish Poetry* (1967). He wrote two novels which have less repute than his short stories: *The Saint and Mary Kate* (1932) and *Dutch Interior* (1966). His critical works include one of the best studies of the art of the short story, *The Lonely Voice*, and a study of the novel, *The Mirror in the Roadway*. He also published two volumes of an uncompleted autobiography, *An Only Child* and *My Father's Son*. From 1952 he taught in an American university.

O'Connor's stories are remarkable for their insight, comedy, pathos and compassion. His field was the lower ranges of Irish society, which he understood profoundly, and which he universalized by his generous intelligence and sympathies in a way that recalls Chekhov's treatment of Russian life.

Bib: Sheehy, Maurice, (ed.) *Michael/Frank*.

Octavia /ok'teivjə/

Half-sister of Octavius Caesar, who became the first Roman Emperor, Augustus (ruled 27 BC–AD 14). She married her brother's rival, Mark Antony, and occurs as a character in Shakespeare's tragedy *Antony and Cleopatra** and in Dryden's tragedy *All For Love**.

Ode

In ancient Greek literature, an elaborate lyrical poem, distinguished from the ordinary lyric by being composed for a chorus to chant and to dance to. Like the ordinary lyric, it was accompanied by instrumental music. It was divided into strophes, *ie* units of verse in a certain rhythmic pattern, and chanted by one half of the chorus; antistrophes, corresponding to the strophes but sung by the other half of the chorus; and epodes, sung by the chorus at a standstill. The greatest Greek writer of odes was Pindar*, who used very elaborate patterns, later wrongly supposed to be irregular. The 'Pindaric' form later came also to be known as the 'greater' ode. In content the ode was solemn and dignified, often religious. Pindar's were mostly on athletic subjects.

The most famous Roman writer of odes is Horace*, but his poems were not choral; they are called odes by virtue of their solemn content, moral or patriotic. The Horatian form came to be known as the 'lesser' ode.

In English poetry, both the Pindaric and the Horatian ode have been imitated. The terms 'strophe', 'antistrophe' are still sometimes used (*eg* in Shelley's* *Ode to Naples*, 1820), but generally the divisions become identical with stanzas, held together by rhyme schemes. Spenser's great marriage poems, *Epithalamion* (1594) and *Prothalamion* (1596) resemble Greek odes, though not specifically the Pindaric form. Cowley's* *Pindaric Odes* (1656) started a fashion for the 'free' interpretation of Pindar's form, and Dryden* wrote notable poems in this style, *eg A Song for St Cecilia's Day* (1687). Congreve* made a study of the subject (1705) and so did Gilbert West (1703–56); in consequence Gray* wrote poems nearer the strict Pindaric style, *eg Progress of Poetry* (1754) and *The Bard* (1757). Wordsworth's *Intimations of Immortality** and Coleridge's *Dejection: an Ode** are in the free Pindaric style, and Keats's great odes (**Odes, Keats's*) are lyrics in long stanzas suggested by the Pindaric form. Tennyson's* *Ode on the Death of the Duke of Wellington* (1852) is again a fine example of free Pindaric, and Swinburne* wrote in both styles. Sometimes the solemnity of the Pindaric ode was inverted into comedy, *eg* Gray's *Ode on the Death of a Favourite Cat.*

The Lesser or Horatian Ode was imitated splendidly by Andrew Marvell* in *An Horatian Ode upon Cromwell's Return from Ireland* (written 1650?) and Collins* used this measure to exquisite effect in his *Ode to Evening* (1747), though he also wrote in other forms of the Greek Ode less familiar than the Pindaric and Horatian forms. Shelley's* *Ode to the West Wind* (1819) is an example of the use of the word to suggest majesty of theme without strict reference to specific traditions of form, though he also tried the Pindaric form according to his conception of it (*eg Naples* already mentioned).

* **6.3.4**

Ode: Intimations of Immortality

* *Intimations.*

Odes, Keats's

The six important Odes by John Keats* were all written in 1819; they represent his maturest art, and his high poetic reputation rests principally upon them. Their titles are *On Indolence*, *On a Grecian Urn*, *On Melancholy*, *To Psyche*, *To a Nightingale*, and *To Autumn.* Keats's most evident quality in his early poetry had been the lavishness with which he had exploited the sensuous appeal of language, but his letters show that his outstanding quality as a man was the courage, sanity, and intelligence with which he faced the tragic side of human experience. This insight and strength of character was bound up with his intense devotion to poetic art, which he steadily disciplined into a medium for complex expression of both sides of his nature. The Odes were written in the order in which they have been listed, and they show a steadily increasing depth, richness, and coherence; the last two are least questionably the masterpieces of his short poetic career. They are not strictly odes in the ancient Greek sense, but the supple and abundant Pindaric form, especially in the 'free' interpretation of it by many English poets, incited him to the construction of long, rhymed stanzas which are flexible enough to be a vehicle for the variety of his emotion and disciplined enough to concentrate this emotion into a unified impact.

* **6.3.4**; *Keats; Ode.*

Odin /'əudin/

The principal god of the pagan religions of northern Europe; he presided over war and wisdom. In England he was called 'Woden', and his name is preserved in 'Wednesday'. The Angles and Saxons, before their conversion to Christianity, believed him to be the ancestor of their kings.

Odysseus /ə'di:sju:s/

The Greek hero and king of Ithaca in the *Odyssey**, an epic by Homer. In Latin he was known as Ulixes, which has been converted into Ulysses. He also occurs in Homer's *Iliad**, where he is famous among the Greek leaders for his wise advice. In the dramas of Sophocles* and Euripides* his wisdom shows as mere cunning, but Shakespeare (in *Troilus and Cressida**) shows him as the sane politician, making the best of a bad Greek world. For Tennyson* (*Ulysses* 1842) he is the heroic wanderer, setting out for a final voyage after his return to Ithaca; Tennyson got this conception of him from Dante's *Inferno**. See Stanford, W. B., *The Ulysses Theme.*

Odyssey /'odisi/

An epic* by the ancient Greek poet Homer*, author also of the *Iliad**. The hero, Odysseus King of Ithaca, is on his way home after the Trojan war, but he is blown off course and the return journey takes him ten years. The principal episodes of his voyage are as follows:

[1] The land of the Lotus-Eaters. Those who eat of the lotus plant forget their homeland.

[2] The land of the Cyclopes. These are a race of one-eyed giants. Odysseus puts out the eye of the Cyclops Polyphemus, who is son of Poseidon, god of the sea; it is to punish him for this that Poseidon sends him wandering for ten years.

[3] The Isle of Aeolus, king of the winds. Odysseus steals from him the bag in which the winds are contained, but his companions open it too soon, and the winds escape.

[4] Telepylus, the city of the cannibal Laestrygonians. They destroy his fleet except one ship, in which he escapes.

[5] The Isle of Circe*. She transforms his men

into swine, but with the aid of the god Hermes*, he resists her enchantments, compels her to restore his men, and remains in the island as her lover for a year.

[6] He visits the Underworld, Hades, to learn from the prophet Tiresias* the way home. Tiresias warns him against harming the cattle of the sun-god, Helios.

[7] He evades the enchanting songs of the Sirens*, who try to lure him on to the rocks.

[8] He passes through the strait of Scylla* and Charybdis – a treacherous rock and a whirlpool.

[9] He comes to the Island of Thrinacia (Sicily) where the cattle of Helios live, which the ghost of Tiresias has warned him not to harm, but overcome by hunger, his companions devour them.

[10] In punishment, his ship is wrecked and all his men perish, but Odysseus reaches the island of the goddess Calypso*, who keeps him prisoner for seven years as her lover. He eventually escapes, with the aid of the goddess Athene, and reaches the lands of the Phaeacians where Nausicaa and her father, the king of the country, befriend him. The narrative of all the above events comes to the reader through Odysseus, who tells them to the king. The king helps him back to Ithaca. There, with the help of his son Telemachus, he kills the suitors who have been pestering the chaste Penelope, his queen.

Oedipus /ˈiːdipəs/

In Greek myth, a character first mentioned by Homer* as having (unknown to himself) killed his own father and married his own mother. In later versions the story was filled out: his father, King Laius of Thebes, was warned by an oracle* that his son would kill him, and ordered that the child Oedipus should be destroyed; he was accordingly exposed in a waste place, but a shepherd rescued him; ignorant of his parentage, he later returned to Thebes, and on the way there, killed his father in consequence of a wayside quarrel; on his arrival at Thebes, he saved the city from the Sphinx* and married his mother, Jocasta. One of the greatest of the Greek tragedies, Sophocles'* *Oedipus the King*, tells of his subsequent discovery of his parentage and the consequences of this discovery; Sophocles also dramatized Oedipus' death in *Oedipus at Colonus*.

The 'Oedipus Complex' is the name for a discovery by the psychoanalyst Sigmund Freud* that children tend to feel sexual attraction to the parent of the opposite sex, and corresponding jealousy towards the parent of the same sex.

Oenone /iːˈnəuni/

In Greek Myth, a nymph* who was the wife of Paris*, son of Priam of Troy. Paris deserted her to run off with Helen, and in the subsequent siege of Troy he died of a wound which Oenone refused to heal, knowing that she alone could do so. Oenone had in the meantime repented of her refusal and hurried after him; when she found she was too late, she took her own life.

Tennyson* wrote one of his finest early poems about her – *Oenone*; later he wrote another called *The Death of Oenone*. Her story is also told in *The Death of Paris* by William Morris*, in his *Earthly Paradise*.

O'Faolain, Sean (b 1900) /ˈʃɔːn əuˈfeiəlin/

Irish novelist and writer of short stories. He was born in Dublin and attended the National University of Ireland and Harvard University in the United States. He participated in the Irish Rebellion following World War I, and later lived in England as a teacher. He is regarded as the most distinguished Irish novelist writing since 1930; the novels include *A Nest of Simple Folk* (1933) and *Bird Alone* (1936). His first volume of stories, *Midsummer Night Madness* (1932) vividly reflect the atmosphere of the Irish disturbances. A collected edition of the stories was published in 1958, and in 1966 he published a further volume, *The Heat of the Sun*. Among his other writings are two biographies which are studies of Irish leaders, one on Daniel O'Connell entitled *King of the Beggars* (1938), and *The Great O'Neill* (1942). His critical work includes *The Short Story* (1948). His autobiography *Vive Moi!* appeared in 1965. He was made Director of the Arts Council of Ireland in 1957.

O'Flaherty, Liam (b 1897) /ˈliəm əuˈfleəti/

Irish novelist and writer of short stories. Born in the Aran Islands he was educated for the Roman Catholic priesthood, but did not enter it. He fought in World War I, and settled in England in 1922. His first volume of stories, *Spring Sowing*, was published in 1926; it contains stories of Irish peasant life and wild nature. At his best, his stories have the intensity of fine lyric poetry, and he is peculiarly gifted at representing the exhilaration and poignancy of life directly exposed to natural forces. Other volumes of stories include: *The Mountain Tavern* (1929), *The Wild Swan* (1932), *Two Lovely Beasts* (1948). His novels include *The Informer* (1925 – made into a famous film in 1935) and the historical *Famine* (1937). His autobiography is entitled *Shame the Devil* (1934).

Og, king of Bashan

In the Bible, the last of 'the remnant of the giants' (*Deuteronomy* 3) killed by Moses and the Israelites. Dryden used him to represent his literary and political enemy Thomas Shadwell in his political satire *Absalom and Achitophel**.

Ogre

A man-eating giant or monster.

Ogygia /əˈdʒidʒiə/

The island inhabited by the goddess Calypso* in Homer's epic the *Odyssey**.

Oisin /uˈʃiːn/

Also known as Ossian. In 1760–63, James Macpherson published a series of blank verse epics which he attributed to Ossian and claimed to have translated from the Gaelic. His version had an immense success and a wide influence; however, Macpherson was later proved not to have translated the poems, but to have synthesized them from a number of genuine Celtic legends, in which the hero Oisin occurs. Dr Johnson* was among the earliest sceptics; when asked whether he thought any man 'of the modern age' could have written the poems, he replied: 'Yes, Sir, many men, many women, and many children.'

W. B. Yeats* wrote a narrative poem *The Wanderings of Oisin* (1889), the earliest of his attempts to create a new literature out of Celtic mythology. In the ancient legends Oisin bridged the gap between the heroic pagan age and Irish Christianity; his longevity was due to a long sojourn in Fairyland.

* *Celtic Twilight*; *Irish Literature*.

Old Bailey

The Central Criminal Court in London. It owes its name to the fact that it stands within the former bailey of the City of London. A bailey is an open space enclosed by fortifications, in this case between Lud Gate and New Gate.

Old Curiosity Shop, The

A novel by Charles Dickens*; it was serialized as a part of *Master Humphrey's Clock** in 1840–41 (published in book form in 1848).

The Curiosity Shop (a shop which sells second-hand goods of ornamental or rarity value) is kept by the grandfather of little Nell Trent. The old man has been impoverished by the extravagances of his son-in-law and those of Fred Trent, Nell's brother. He is forced to borrow money from Quilp, a grotesque and malevolent dwarf, who believes the old man to be a miser with a hidden store of wealth. Quilp gets possession of the shop, and Nell and her grandfather take to wandering about the countryside. Eventually Nell dies, too late to be saved by her grandfather's brother, who has returned from abroad and finds them after a long search. Quilp is drowned while attempting to escape arrest. Other characters include Sampson Brass, Quilp's unscrupulous lawyer, his sister Sally, and 'the Marchioness', a child whom the Brasses keep as a servant in vile conditions.

The novel shows Dickens's extraordinary vitality of imagination, and also exemplifies the vulgarity which was part of his vitality. This vulgarity tended to display itself in melodrama and in sentimentality, here exhibited in the characters of Quilp and Little Nell respectively. The death of Little Nell is often regarded as Dickens's most notorious sentimental indulgence, but she is nonetheless a memorable child portrait; so is 'the Marchioness'.

Old English

* *English Language*.

Old Lady of Threadneedle Street

A nickname for the Bank of England, situated in a street of that name in the City of London. The nickname dates from 18th C. The street itself probably owes its name to its earlier association with tailors.

Old Man of the Mountains, The

The translation of the title of a fanatical leader of a religious sect whose beliefs were compounded from Islam and ancient Persian religion. The sect was founded in 11th C in Persia, and transferred to the Lebanon. The members of the sect made a practice of the secret assassination of their enemies, and before doing so they intoxicated themselves with the drug hashish, from which 'assassin' is derived.

Old Moore

Francis Moore (1657–1715), doctor and astrologer, used to sell 'almanacs' containing spaces for diaries, miscellaneous information, and predictions of the weather. The practice continued, and today a number of Old Moore's Almanacs are sold with astrological predictions covering every side of life.

Old Mortality (1816)

A novel by Walter Scott,* one of the first of the series called *Tales of my Landlord*. Its title refers to a nickname for Robert Paterson, who in late 18th C. made it his business to keep in repair the tombs of the Covenanters* of the century before, when they had died resisting religious oppression. The story is based on his anecdotes, and concerns the period 1679–90, from the military operations against the Covenanters under Grahame of Claverhouse to the beginning of toleration under William III*. Mixed up with the historical events is a love-romance in which the hero, Henry Morton, one of the leaders of the Covenanters, is the rival of Lord Evansdale, one of Claverhouse's officers, for the possession of Edith Bellenden.

The novel concerns a phase of Scottish history which was of great importance in the formation of the Scotland of Scott's own day; its interest lies in the vigorous representation of the common people, and in Scott's talent for showing a whole society passing through a phase of history. It is usually regarded as one of his most successful novels.

Old Nick

A popular expression for the devil, dating back to 17th C.

Old Pretender, The

James Francis Edward Stuart (1688–1766), son of King James II* who had been deposed for reasons connected with his Catholicism. He was a pretender to (*ie* he claimed) the British throne on the death of his half-sister Queen Anne in 1714, but his claim was rejected because like his father he was a Catholic. Instead, George of Hanover became king as George I. In 1715, James led a rebellion on his own behalf in Scotland, but this failed. His followers were called Jacobites* from the Latin Jacobus = James, and he was termed the 'Old' Pretender to distinguish him from his son, Charles Edward Stuart, the Young Pretender, who attempted a similar Scottish rebellion in 1745.

* *Stuart*, *House of*.

Old Testament

The first and larger part of the Bible, consisting of

the sacred writings of the Jews. It concerns the peculiar, divinely ordained destiny of the Jewish race from earliest times, and it is considered by Christians to expound the divine promise which the New Testament fulfils not merely for the Jews but for the whole of mankind. The Old Testament is divided into books which are grouped by Jews into three main sections, as follows:

[1] The Torah ('Law', otherwise called the Pentateuch), consisting of five books, as follows: *Genesis*, *Exodus*, *Leviticus*, *Numbers*, *Deuteronomy*. They are called 'the five books of Moses', and were ascribed to the authorship of this ancient Jewish lawgiver. The first two are narrative and descriptive, and move from the creation of the world to the escape of the Jews from slavery in Egypt. The remainder contain laws and discourses.

[2] The Prophets. This section is divided into two in the Hebrew Bible: the 'Former Prophets', consisting of *Joshua*, *Judges*, the two books of *Samuel* and the two books of *Kings*; and the 'Latter Prophets', consisting of *Isaiah*, *Jeremiah*, *Ezekiel*, and the Minor Prophets. The books of the Former Prophets are mainly historical, telling the story of the establishment of the Jews in the kingdom of Israel, and their subsequent history. The Latter Prophets contain history together with prophetic discourses.

[3] The Sacred Writings, or Hagiographa, which are divided into three sections: (i) the Poetical books, consisting of *Psalms*, *Proverbs*, *Job*; (ii) the five 'Rolls', which are read at special seasons in the Jewish year: *Song of Songs*, *Ruth*, *Lamentations*, *Ecclesiastes*, *Esther* – of these *Esther* and *Ruth* are narratives; the other three are poetic meditations; (iii) *Daniel*, *Ezra*, *Nehemiah*, and *Chronicles*, all consisting mainly of historical narrative.

* *Apocrypha*; *Bible in England*; *New Testament*.

Old Vic Theatre

A theatre on the south bank of the Thames in London, founded in 1818, and given the name of Victoria in 1833. The district was poor, and until 1880 it presented entertainment of the kind enjoyed by uneducated Londoners in 19th C. In 1912 Lilian Bayliss took it for the production of Shakespeare. The performances became increasingly successful, and 'the Old Vic Company' became recognized unofficially as the English National Theatre Company, long before it was officially established as such in 1963.

* *Theatres*.

Old Wives' Tale, The (1908)

A novel by Arnold Bennett*. Two sisters, Constance and Sophia Baines, are the daughters of a shopkeeper in Burslem (one of the Five Towns*, and called Bursley in the novel). Constance marries one of the salesmen, Samuel Povey, and spends her whole life in the same town. Sophia runs off with an unscrupulous commercial traveller, Gerald Scales, who takes her to Paris and abandons her. She struggles for her living as a lodging-house keeper, and endures the siege of 1870. In the end, the sisters are reunited. The lives are chronicled with a multiplicity of factual detail according to the naturalist tradition, and Bennett intends to show that both lives are equally interesting when their total pattern is seen. The book shows the influences of Maupassant and Zola*, French novelists of the Naturalist school.

* *Naturalism*.

Oliver Twist

A novel by Charles Dickens*, published in instalments in 1837–39. Oliver is a child of unknown parents, born in a workhouse* where he leads a miserable existence under the tyranny of Bumble, a beadle, *ie* a parish council official. He runs away to London and becomes mixed up in a gang of thieves led by Fagin, and including the brutal burglar, Bill Sikes, Nancy his whore, and a young pickpocket called the 'Artful Dodger'. He is temporarily rescued by the benevolent Mr Brownlow, but a mysterious character called Monks, who has an interest in keeping Oliver's parentage a secret, induces the gang to kidnap him. He is finally rescued through the action of Nancy, who in consequence is brutally murdered by Sikes.

The novel shows the mixture of sentimentality and melodrama characteristic of early Dickens, but in Bumble especially he exhibits keen social satire, and the London underworld is presented vividly. It was written at a time when a number of novelists (*eg* the 'Newgate School', especially Harrison Ainsworth*) had written romances about crime, but Dickens was realistic enough to startle the educated public into a new consciousness of the unprivileged and the criminal level of society, and shows how lack of compassion in the more privileged helped to make poverty a nursery of crime

Olney Hymns (1779) /ˈəulni/

Religious poems by the Rev. John Newton and William Cowper*, so called from the village of Olney where they lived.

Olympus

The name of a number of mountains in Greece and Asia Minor, but especially of one which the ancient Greeks considered to be the home of the gods. It is situated on the border of Thessaly and Macedonia in Greece, and is about 10,000 feet high, with a massive and precipitous appearance.

Omar Khayyam

* *Rubaiyat of Omar Khayyam, The*.

Ombre /ˈombə/

A card game introduced from Spain into England in 17th C, and very popular throughout 18th C. Its appeal lay in its demand on the intelligence of the players, and it was later superseded in popularity by whist and then bridge, games which make a similar demand. The name is from the Spanish for 'Man'. Ombre is the game played in Pope's famous poem, *The Rape of the Lock**.

Omphale /ˈomfəli/

In Greek myth, the queen of Lydia whom the hero Heracles* served as a slave for three years in penance for having killed his friend Iphitus in a fit of insanity. He fell in love with the queen, and sat spinning among her women wearing women's clothes while she wore his lion-skin.

Onomatopoeia /onəmatə'piːə/

The use of verbal sound to evoke the sound of what the word represents. Thus a cuckoo is a bird whose song resembles the two syllables of its name, which is therefore onomatopoeic. The device is often used in poetry, *eg* in Keats's *Ode to Autumn*:

Then in a wailful choir the small gnats mourn

to express the sound of a swarm of small insects. 'Wailful' and 'mourn' are the two specifically onomatopoeic words.

Open Field System

That system of land use especially typical of medieval English agriculture. Land under cultivation was divided into strips, and distributed among the peasants of the village or manor. The strips were not surrounded by hedges or fences, so that good farmers suffered from the effects of the bad farming of their immediate neighbours. The system began to be replaced in 16th C, when landowners preferred sheep-farming, and it was effectually abolished in 18th C when, in the course of 'the agricultural revolution', the open fields were enclosed in larger arable units by the landlords.

* *Enclosures.*

Opera in England

There have been two periods in which English opera has been a truly living art: the second half of 17th C, and the 20th C.

The first of these was a period of beginnings, without later development. Opera, as an independent art form, had started in Italy in late 16th C, but the first English opera, *The Siege of Rhodes*, with words by William Davenant* and music (which has been lost) by Matthew Locke and others, was not performed until 1656. The reasons for this delayed beginning of opera may partly be that the stage play and the masque* were already firmly established. The theatre public, used to a highly developed idiom of dramatic speech, did not take well to a drama in which speech was sung; on the other hand the masque, essentially a court entertainment, already included music as a leading element, but its conventions were not dramatic enough to allow its transformation into opera. Davenant's experiment seems to have been an attempt to circumvent the law of 1642 which had closed the theatres and prohibited stage plays. His *Siege of Rhodes* production in 1656 is historically memorable not only because it was the first production of an opera, but because of the appearance of an actress on the English stage for the first time since the Middle Ages.

When the theatres reopened after 1660, approaches towards opera were made by the addition of musical interludes to stage plays, particularly those of Shakespeare, which in many instances already contained songs and episodes that required a musical accompaniment. Thus Henry Purcell* composed music for *The Tempest** and for Restoration* dramas, for instance Dryden's* *Amphitryon* (1690). His *The Fairy Queen* (1693), an adaptation of *A Midsummer Night's Dream**, and *King Arthur* (1691), in which he collaborated with Dryden, are more nearly operatic, but the music is still dramatically peripheral to the stage dialogue. His true opera was *Dido and Aeneas* (1689) with words by Nahum Tate, which is fully sung, following the example of John Blow's *Venus and Adonis* (1685). Dryden was seriously interested in opera, and if he had begun his collaboration with Purcell sooner, they might together have achieved major works. After Purcell's death, however, opera went into decline. 18th C opened with a fashion for opera in the Italian style, but Handel*, who settled in England in 1712, nearly ruined himself with his own operas in the style; he established the oratorio as a popular national form. Addison*, who later derided opera in the *Spectator**, wrote a libretto for an opera, *Rosamond* (1706 – music by Clayton), about the legendary love affair between Henry II* and Fair Rosamund*, but it was a failure.

A native tradition of 'ballad opera' did, however, establish itself with *The Beggar's Opera** (1728). The words by John Gay* were written for traditional tunes arranged by the German, Pepustch. It has remained extraordinarily popular and has been re-arranged from time to time, most notably by Benjamin Britten in 1948. Other ballad operas followed, and the famous Gilbert* and Sullivan operas (1875–96) belong to the tradition. They established an urban popular song which became a kind of urban folk art, and led outside opera to the Music Hall tradition of 19th C. The other native tradition of opera in 19th C, the romantic operas, especially those of William Balfe (1808–70), of whose numerous works only *The Bohemian Girl* (1843) is well-known, is much less distinctive.

English opera in 18th C suffered partly from the lack of Court patronage which helped opera elsewhere. Vanbrugh's* opera house in the Haymarket, opened in 1705, and Covent Garden since 1858 have been the chief urban centres of opera, but these places were exclusive rather than popular resorts. In 1880, however, the Old Vic theatre was opened in a poor part of London, and spread the taste for serious opera as well as for great plays to other classes than the relatively rich, especially after the Sadler's Wells theatre was opened in association with it in 1931. In 20th C a number of distinguished British composers began to write operas, for example Rutland Boughton (*The Immortal Hour*, 1914) and Vaughan Williams (*Hugh the Drover*, 1924). In 1945 Benjamin Britten, the most eminent of all British opera composers, began his career with *Peter Grimes** (librettist Hugh Slater). This was followed by *The Rape of Lucretia* (1946, librettist Ronald Duncan), *Albert Herring* (1947), *Billy Budd* (1951, librettist E. M. Forster*), and *The Turn of the Screw** (1954). His later works have included an operatic version of *A Midsummer Night's Dream*, based closely on Shakespeare's play, and the 'fable operas' *The Curlew River*, *The Prodigal Son*, and *The Burning Fiery Furnace*.

Ophir /ˈəufə/

In the Bible, the place from which King Solomon* obtained his gold and jewels (*1 Kings* 10:11). Its situation is unknown, but is thought to have been on the southern coast of the Arabian peninsula.

Ops

In Roman myth, the goddess of earth's riches, and wife of Saturn*.

Oracle

In ancient Greek religion, a place where an inspired priest gave answers to the questions put to him by worshippers about their destinies or the outcome of a crisis. The most famous was the oracle of Delphi, sacred to Apollo*. Here the mouthpiece of the oracle was a priestess known as the Pythia, who gave ambiguous replies in verse.

Orange, House of; Orange Free State; Orangemen

The town of Orange in southern France was originally an independent principality. Philibert of Orange (1502–30) was rewarded by the Emperor Charles V (who ruled the Netherlands amongst his other territories) with large estates in the Netherlands for his help in statesmanship and war. The Princes of Orange thus became great Dutch nobles, and later William 'the Silent' of Orange established the Dutch (Netherlands) Republic by defeating the armies of the territory's former ruler, Philip II of Spain. William's leadership, and the importance of the Orange family in the Netherlands, gave the House of Orange special eminence in the Republic, and successive members of it held the high office of Stadtholder. They twice married into the Stuart* family reigning in Britain: William II married Mary, daughter of Charles I*, and in 1677 their son, William III, married Mary, daughter of James II*. William and Mary became joint sovereigns of Britain in 1689 after the expulsion of James II. After William III's death in 1702, the family continued to be pre-eminent in Dutch politics, and were kings of Holland (the Netherlands) from 1814. In the same year the Dutch colony in South Africa was ceded to Britain; in 1836 some of the Dutch colonists, fleeing from British sovereignty, set up the Orange Free State Republic to the north of the colony.

Throughout 17th C the House of Orange were champions of Protestantism* against the Catholic powers, first of Spain and then of France; the religious conflict was also a fight for Dutch national survival, and from 1690–1700 it was in addition one for the survival of the British system of politics. The issue was then felt most keenly in Ireland*, where the northern province of Ulster was Protestant, and the southern three provinces were Catholic. Religious hostility between the north and the south continued throughout 18th C, when it died down in most of Europe, and it is still a political issue at the present day. In 1795 'Orange Societies' were founded in Ulster, in memory of the great Protestant king William III, who had saved Ulster from being overrun by the Catholic south by defeating James II's army at the Battle of the Boyne (1690). Orangemen (*ie* members of these societies) are still an important political force in Northern Ireland, although the societies are nominally religious and not political.

Oranges and Lemons

A nursery rhyme* based on the church bells of London. Each chime is given its distinctive utterance – *eg* 'Oranges and lemons say the bells of St Clement's' – culminating in 'the great bell of Bow'. The earliest record of the rhyme is 1744. It is also the basis of an old children's game.

Ordeal of Richard Feverel, The (1859)

A novel by George Meredith*. Sir Austin Feverel prides himself on the 'system' which he has devised for the upbringing and education of his motherless son, Richard; he is, however, a self-satisfied egotist who lacks disinterested understanding of his son's character. The 'system' breaks down in Richard's adolescence, when the boy falls in love with Lucy Desborough, a girl of lower social background than Sir Austin's ideal for his son's bride. They are secretly married but Sir Austin manages to separate them by egotistically exploiting Richard's love for him. Richard becomes involved with a beautiful woman of loose morals; he begins this new relationship with characteristically romantic and idealistic motives of redeeming her, but he partly falls under her spell. Lord Mountfalcon, who is interested in permanently separating Lucy and Richard, is chiefly responsible for Richard's betrayal of her, and in remorse for his infidelity Richard fights a duel with him, and is wounded. Lucy has meanwhile become reconciled with Sir Austin, but the shock of the duel kills her. The novel – Meredith's first important one – exemplifies his combination of romantic intensity with psychological analysis.

Orders in Council

Laws or regulations made by the king or queen in conjunction with the Privy Council*; in practice this means that the Prime Minister and his Cabinet advise the sovereign to issue them, and they are then accountable to Parliament* for the action. Orders in Council were often used in emergency, especially in wartime. Modern Orders in Council are usually administrative regulations limited by relevant Acts of Parliament.

Orestes /oˈresti:z/

In Greek legend, the son of Agamemnon* and Clytemnestra*. He is the hero of the *Oresteia* – three tragedies by Aeschylus*: *Agamemnon*, *Choephori*, *Eumenides*. In the second, Orestes kills his mother in vengeance for her murder of his father. To be purified of this crime, the god Apollo sends him to plead his cause before the Areopagus, the highest judicial court of Athens; the Erinyes (Furies*) demand him as their rightful victim, but in the last play they are placated by a new ritual by which they are worshipped under the title of the Eumenides (Friendly Ones). The legend was further developed by Sophocles* and by Euripides* with emphasis on the roles of Orestes' sister Electra* and his friend Pylades. The legends in their dramatized forms illustrate the growing fear of bloodshed, the rising interest in cases of conscience, and the new belief that cases of vengeance should be conducted by the state. English revenge tragedy* in the age of Shakespeare (Kyd's* *Spanish Tragedy* and Shakespeare's *Hamlet**) illustrates analogous developments of feeling.

Orfeo, Sir **(14th C)** /ˈɔːfiəu/

A popular English version of the ancient Greek Orpheus* and Eurydice myth. In this version Orfeo is an English king, son of 'King Pluto' and 'Queen Juno', *ie* a Roman god and goddess. His queen, Heurodys, is carried off to Fairyland, and pursued by Orfeo disguised as a minstrel. By his musical genius he is able to bring her back. The poem is one of the best English metrical romances. The ballad *King Orfeo* was a later version of the legend.

Orgoglio /ɔːˈgoljəu/

A character representing Arrogance in Spenser's *Faerie Queene**. He occurs in Bk. I, Canto vii, viii; he captures the Red Cross Knight and is slain by Prince Arthur. The name derives from the Italian for Pride.

Oriana /oriˈaːnə/

A name sometimes used for Queen Elizabeth I* by Elizabethan poets. It comes from the 15th C Spanish-Portuguese romance *Amadis de Gaula*; in which Oriana is a British princess beloved by the hero, Amadis.

Origin of Species, The

* *Darwin.*

Orion

In Greek myth, a giant of whom several tales occur, famous as a hunter. He was the son of Poseidon, god of the sea, by some accounts; by others he sprang from the earth. Eos, the dawn-goddess, carried him off to the Island of Delos, but he was killed by the arrows of Artemis, goddess of hunters. After death he was changed into a constellation of stars.

Orlando

The Italian form of the name Roland, hero of the French 12th-C epic, *Chanson de Roland* ('Song of Roland'). From the Italian 16th-C romantic epics by Ariosto*, the name passed into English romances, for instance for the hero of Shakespeare's romantic comedy, *As You Like It**.

Orlando **(1928)**

A fantasy by Virginia Woolf* in which the evolution of poetic genius is traced through the Sackville family and their country mansion of Knowle from Thomas Sackville* (1536–1608) to the poet Victoria Sackville-West (1892–1962). This is done through an immortal character Orlando, representing the poetic genius of the family; he changes sex in 19th C (when it became common for women to take to literature) and throughout he meets a number of the great poets of English literature. The book is a combination of historical novel and biographical fantasy.

Orlando Furioso **(1532)** /ɔːˈlandəu ˈfjuəriˈəuzəu/

A romantic epic by the Italian poet Ariosto*. It is in a tradition of Italian developments of the legends centring on the French hero Roland, who in the reign of Charlemagne (768–814) repelled the Muslim invasion of Europe. Ariosto invents fantastic episodes and introduces plenty of romantic love. Orlando goes mad because his lady, Angelica, marries a Moorish youth, but he is cured in time to defeat Agramante, king of Africa, who has been besieging Paris. Many linked tales and episodes accompany this central theme, as is usual in 16th-C romantic epic, of which Ariosto is the chief master, and Spenser* (*Faerie Queene**) one of his chief emulators.

Orpheus /ˈɔːfjuːs/

In Greek myth, the son of the muse* Calliope and Apollo*, from whom he received a lyre on which he played so beautifully that the wild beasts came to listen to him. When his wife, Eurydice, was killed by snakebite, he descended to the underworld to bring her back. His music charmed the deities there so much that they permitted him to return to earth with her on the condition that he never looked back at her during the journey. When they were nearly at the gates, however, he could not resist the temptation to see whether she was following him, and so she was lost to him for ever. According to some versions, he was later torn to pieces by the Thracian women, because after this second loss of his wife he cared for women no more. Orpheus was the centre of an ancient religious cult, Orphism. He is also connected with the Argonaut* legend; his singing subdued the various natural and supernatural dangers which threatened the ship Argo, and it lulled into acquiescence the dragon that guarded the Golden Fleece.

* *Orfeo, Sir.*

Orwell, George (pseudonym of Eric Blair) (1903–50) /ɔːwel/

Journalist, critic and novelist. Born into a poor but proud middle-class family, he was sent to a private school, from where he won a scholarship to Eton. His snobbish upbringing, and the uneasiness he felt in living with boys richer than himself, gave him a distaste for middle-class values and, in relation to the working-classes, a sense of guilt which was intensified by the large unemployment of the 1930s. He served in the Burma Police (1922–7), and then resigned from dislike of what he interpreted as imperialist oppression – *Burmese Days* (1934). He then tried to appease his sense of social guilt by living for 18 months in the utmost destitution – *Down and Out in London and Paris* (1933). At the height of the economic depression in the 1930s, he was commissioned by a left-wing publisher, Gollancz, to make a personal investigation of conditions in the north of England – *The Road to Wigan Pier* (1937). By the time of its publication, Orwell was fighting for the Republicans in Spain, where he was wounded in the throat – *Homage to Catalonia* (1938). During the war 1939–45, he was rejected for the army on medical grounds, and worked for the Indian service of the B.B.C. In 1945 he published his masterpiece, the fable *Animal Farm*, a satire on Stalinism. After the war, he wrote a gloomy prognosis of western civilization, calling it *1984* (*Nineteen Eighty-Four*) (1949), which presents a world under dictatorships of the Stalinist style (not necessarily Communist ones).

Other novels: *A Clergyman's Daughter* (1935); *Keep the Aspidistra Flying* (1936); *Coming Up For Air* (1939). Among his best works are his social and literary critical essays: *Inside the Whale* (1940); *The Lion and the Unicorn* (1941 – subtitled *Socialism and the English Genius*); *Critical Essays* (1946); *Shooting an Elephant* (1950). Orwell's independence of mind, and his intellectual, moral and physical courage have given him a kind of heroic status among modern writers.

Bib: Studies by Laurence Brander; John Atkins; Christopher Hollis; Tom Hopkinson; Lewis, P. W., in *The Writer and the Absolute*; Wain, J., in *Essays on Literature and Ideas*.

Osborne, Dorothy (1627–95)

Wife of Sir William Temple*, statesman, diplomatist and author. Their marriage was delayed for seven years owing to the disapproval of her family, and her letters to him during a part of this time are famous social documents.

Osborne, John (b 1929)

Dramatist. He is widely thought of as the leader of the dramatic revival which started in the 1950s, through the great popular success of *Look Back in Anger* (1956), which found an infectious contemporary idiom for the frustration of the younger British generation since World War II, and for their rejection of the traditional values of 'the Establishment'*. The play gave currency for a decade to the term 'the angry young men'. Later plays: *The Entertainer: Epitaph for George Dillon* (1957); *World of Paul Slickey* (1959); *Luther* (1961); *The Blood of the Bambergs* (1962); *Under Plain Cover* (1962); *Inadmissible Evidence* (1965); *A Patriot for Me* (1965); *A Bond Honoured* (1966); *Time Present* (1967); *West of Suez* (1972); *A Sense of Detachment* (1972); *A Place Calling Itself Detachment* (1972); *The Picture of Dorian Gray* (1973); *Watch It Come Down* (1975).

* 5.3.3

Bib: Allsop, K., *The Angry Decade*.

Osiris /əu'saiəris/

In ancient Egyptian myth, at first a nature god who died with the harvest and was reborn with the sprouting grain; later the god of the dead. The Greeks identified him with Dionysus*, their vine god, and with Hades, their god of their dead; Osiris used music to subdue violence. He was assassinated by his evil brother Set; his sister-wife Isis brought him to life again, but he preferred to reign over the dead and the souls of the just.

Osmond, Gilbert

A principal character in Henry James's novel, *Portrait of a Lady**; he is a poor, expatriate American dilettante living in Italy, and secures in marriage the rich young heroine, Isabel Archer, whose life he then ruins by his moral triviality and cold-heartedness.

Ossian

* *Oisin.*

Othello /ə'θeləu/

A tragedy by Shakespeare*, first acted in 1604. It was based on an Italian tale in *Hecatommithi* by Giraldi Cinthio (1565 – translated into French 1584).

The full title of the play is *Othello, the Moor of Venice*: the extended title emphasizes Othello's position as commander of Venetian forces against the Turks, and it is a clue to the understanding of his tragedy. Othello is fighting for Christians against Moslems, and yet he himself belongs to a Moslem race, though not the Turkish one. He is highly valued by the Venetians for his military prowess, but he is not a member of Venetian society; he is first and last a soldier, a member of a military community, trusting and trusted by his brother officers. Consequently it is as astonishing to him when Desdemona, a conventional Venetian aristocratic girl, leaves her home to marry him, as it is outrageous to her indignant father, Brabantio. Venice urgently needs Othello to defend Cyprus against the Turks, so that Brabantio is forced to accept the match; however he warns Othello that a girl who has behaved so unpredictably once may prove as unreliable a wife as she has been a daughter. Othello is in rapture; his bliss is the greater for its incredibility, so that he naively imagines himself transported into a heaven on earth. But his junior officer, Iago, has motives of resentment against him; the most concrete of these is that the Florentine, Cassio, has been promoted over his head. Moreover he is himself a cynic who has a low opinion of human nature and of the scope for genuine happiness. Partly as a double revenge against Othello and against Cassio, partly as a cynical game the object of which is to bring Othello down to his own level of reality, he contrives first to disgrace Cassio temporarily, and then to insinuate into Othello's mind the suspicion, mounting by degrees to certainty, that Cassio and Desdemona are conducting a secret love affair. In Othello's mind the circumstances make this affair more than plausible: he has the habit of trusting Iago as his confidential officer; Desdemona has come to him out of a foreign society; Cassio is the sort of man who would have been considered an eligible husband for her. Until their marriage, Othello had had a single-minded dedication to his military vocation;

the marriage has enriched this dedication, since it has been Desdemona's admiration for him as a soldier that has attracted her to him; he now finds that his jealousy has divided his single-mindedness and is destroying his integrity. Accordingly he murders her, in the belief that heavenly justice is on his side. Desdemona, however, has been presented as one of the most innocent of all Shakespeare's heroines, for whom adultery is unimaginable, and her innocent goodness has won the heart of her lady companion, Emilia, who is Iago's wife. Emilia, who has been ignorant of Iago's plot but has unintentionally assisted him in it, realizes his guilt and publicly exposes him; Othello, restored to his dignity, makes a final speech of self-assessment, and kills himself.

Othello follows *Hamlet** in the sequence of Shakespeare's tragedies and is another masterpiece in the tradition of Revenge Tragedy*. It is psychologically much more lucid, though perhaps not a greater play, than *Hamlet*, and one of the most eloquent of Shakespeare's poetic dramas.

Ottava rima /əu'ta:və'ri':mə/

An Italian stanza of 8 lines rhyming *a b a b a b c c*. It was used by Boccaccio* in the 14th C. Pulci in 15th C used it for the mock-heroic, ironic style with which the stanza is chiefly associated in English through Byron's *Don Juan** and his *Vision of Judgement*.

Otterbourne, The Battle of /'otəbə:n/

A famous medieval ballad* about a battle fought in 1388 between the English and the Scots near the English castle of that name. The English commander was Henry Hotspur*, Lord Percy, and the Scottish one, James Earl of Douglas. The Percy* family and the Douglases were the chief rival families on either side of the Scottish-English border in the later Middle Ages. The battle was a Scottish victory, but Douglas was killed; Hotspur was taken prisoner. Another version of the battle is the ballad *Chevy Chase**.

The Hotspur of the ballad is the same as the character in Shakespeare's *1 Henry IV*; the Douglas in that play is another member of that family, whom Hotspur had just taken prisoner in the battle of Homildon Hill (1402).

Otway, Thomas (1652–85) /'otwei/

Dramatist. He is remembered for his blank verse* tragedy, *Venice Preserved* (1682), which had great contemporary fame and a high theatrical reputation until 19th C. His other drama of note was *The Orphan* (1680), a domestic tragedy. They are still considered as two of the best English tragedies in the second half of 17th C, a period now famous almost entirely for its comedy. Otway's other plays and his poems have no modern reputation. He died young in extreme poverty.

Bib: Taylor, A. M., in *Next to Shakespeare*; Dobree, B., in *Restoration Tragedy*; Ham, R. G., *Life*; Johnson, S. in *Lives of the Poets*; Ham, R. G., *Otway and Lee*.

Our Mutual Friend

The last complete novel by Charles Dickens*, published serially 1864–65.

The principal plot starts from the will of a deceased refuse-collector, Old Harmon, who bequeaths his fortune to his son, John Harmon, on condition that he marries a certain girl, Bella Wilfer. Young Harmon wishes to discover what she is like before he discloses himself. He intends to adopt a disguise, but his identity is obscured beyond his intention when circumstances point to his death by murder. Since he is believed dead, the father's property goes instead to Mr Boffin, old Harmon's foreman. Boffin adopts Bella, and young Harmon, disguising himself as John Rokesmith, becomes engaged as Boffin's secretary. Bella becomes spoilt by wealth, and contemptuously rejects Rokesmith-Harmon as a lover; she is, however, reformed by Boffin, who pretends himself to undergo complete debasement of character through his accession of wealth, and thus gives Bella, who has been devoted to him, a violent distaste for the evils of money. Rokesmith's true identity as young Harmon is at length brought to light. With this main plot goes a minor story of Silas Wegg's attempt to blackmail Boffin. In addition there is a parallel main plot concerning the rival lovers of Lizzie Hexam, daughter of a Thames boatman; one of her lovers is the aristocratic young barrister, Eugene Wrayburn, and the other the embittered schoolmaster of low social origins, Bradley Headstone. Headstone tries to murder Wrayburn and nearly succeeds, but he is drowned in a struggle with Rogue Riderhood, another waterman who is also a blackmailer. Wrayburn, physically wrecked, marries Lizzie for whom he at last comes to have a real need. The two main plots are linked through the waterside characters who are connected with young Harmon's supposed murder at the beginning of the book. The novel extends through the Wrayburn-Lizzie story into upper middle class circles which include the arrogant Podsnaps, the Veneerings who attempt to climb into wealthy society and fall out of it again, the fraudulent social adventurers Mr and Mrs Lammle, the mean and ruthless financier, Fledgeby. Through Fledgeby on the one side and Lizzie on the other the lower social circles include Riah, the benevolent Jew, and Jenny Wren*, the bitter-sweet doll's dressmaker. The book is thus given an unusually wide variety of character and social environment, even for Dickens, and it is pervaded by a rich symbolism arising from the use made of the River Thames and the dust-heaps out of which the Harmon fortunes have been made. The motive of special social reform, more characteristic of early Dickens (*eg Oliver Twist**, 1838) is evident in the episode of Betty Higden, the poor woman who dies by the roadside sooner than enter a workhouse.

Overbury, Sir Thomas (1581–1613) /'əuvəbəri/

Essayist and poet; as a writer he is chiefly remembered as the author of one of the most widely read collections of 'Theophrastian' character-sketches, published in 1614; Webster*, Dekker*,

Donne* and others made additions to subsequent issues of the collection between 1614 and 1622.

Overbury was also the victim of one of the most sensational murders in English history. He tried to oppose a love intrigue between James I's royal favourite, Thomas Carr, Earl of Somerset, and the young Countess of Essex. The lovers conspired to have Overbury poisoned; the crime came to light, and the prosecution was conducted by Francis Bacon*. Carr and the Countess were convicted and disgraced, but their agents who actually administered the poison were hanged.

* *Characters, Theophrastian.*

Ovid (Publius Ovidius Naso) (43 BC–AD 17) /'ovid/

Roman poet, and the last of the greatest period of Latin poetry, the Augustan Age*. He wrote for the sophisticated and elegant society of the capital of the Empire, but the immorality of his *Ars Amatoria* ('Art of Love') offended the Emperor Augustus who (for this and some other more mysterious offence) exiled him to the Black Sea about AD 9. The works by which Ovid is principally known are: the *Amores*, love poems in what is called the 'elegiac' couplet; the *Ars Amatoria*; the *Remedia Amoris*, in which he tries to redeem himself for the offence he caused by the *Ars Amatoria*; the *Heroides*, in which he makes the heroines of myth give tongue to their misfortunes; the *Metamorphoses*, a collection of tales about miraculous transformation of shape; the *Fasti*, a poetic account of the Roman calendar; and the *Tristia*, verse epistles in which he laments his exile.

Ovid was one of the most read and influential poets in later centuries; in England this is especially true from 16th to 18th C. His most popular work was the *Metamorphoses*; these were repeatedly imitated and translated, memorably by Golding in 16th C and by Sandys and Dryden* in 17th. Shakespeare* was called in 1598 'the English Ovid' because the source of his *Venus and Adonis* was the *Metamorphoses* and that of *The Rape of Lucrece* was the *Fasti*; moreover the quality of these two poems was felt to be Ovidian. Marlowe* translated Ovid's love elegies, and the freedom and vigour of his kind of love poem influenced Donne* in his Elegies. As early as 14th C Chaucer* got the tales in his *Legend of Good Women** from the *Heroides*, and these poems set a tradition in 'Heroic Epistles' which began with Drayton* in early 17th C and culminated in Pope's *Eloisa to Abelard**. Ovid's influence is traceable repeatedly in the work of Spenser* and touched Milton*. Thus he may be said to have affected, either in subject matter or in style, almost all the major poets from Chaucer to Pope, and his influence was equally extensive among lesser figures. The influence was not always deep, however, and it can be ascribed partly to his being the liveliest and most beguiling of the Roman poets who were regarded as the basis of a cultured understanding of literature.

* *Elegy.*

Owen, Robert (1771–1858)

Social reformer, and a leading socialist thinker in early 19th C. He became part-owner of the New Lanark Cotton Mills in 1800, and found that its workers were living in the degraded and nearly desperate conditions common in the earlier phase of the Industrial Revolution*. He set about improving their housing and working conditions, and established infant schools. His reforms were a success, but his expenditure on them caused resentment among his partners, and in 1813 he established a new firm, with Jeremy Bentham* as one of his partners. In the same year he published a volume of essays, *A New View of Society*, in which he sought to prove that the human character is entirely created by its environment. In 1817, in a report to the House of Commons, Owen pointed out that the existing social misery was caused by men competing unsuccessfully with machines, and he recommended the establishment of socialist working communities in the country; they were to vary from 500 to 3,000 in size, and were to be partly industrial. His views were received favourably by, among other people, the Duke of Kent, the father of Queen Victoria, but Owen spoilt his case with public opinion in general by mixing his proposals with anti-religious propaganda. Nonetheless two experiments were attempted in 1825, one in England and one in America; both failed in under two years. Owen now became the leader of a socialist-secular movement, through which he sought to replace the emphasis on political reform by emphasis on economic action. His influence led to the Grand National Consolidated Trades Union in 1833, but this also failed owing to bad organization. The word 'socialism' originated through discussions centred on the Association of all Classes of all Nations, which Owen founded in 1835. The only permanent success among Owen's experiments was his establishment of the Cooperative Movement, which nowadays is affiliated to the Labour Party*.

* 3.4.2

Owen, Wilfred (1893–1918)

The best known of the so-called 'War Poets' of World War I: *Poems* (1920). He served as an infantry officer, was awarded a decoration for bravery, and was killed a week before the armistice. Before the war he was already writing mildly sensuous poetry influenced by Keats*; for some time during the war he contined to write in the sensuous, late romantic tradition, but he then adapted his technique so as to express the intensity of the suffering of the Western Front, deliberately introducing elements of discordance and harshness into his style especially by the use of 'para-rhyme', *ie* the repetition of consonants but changing the vowels, as in the words 'hall'-'hell'. The best known of his poems is *Strange Meeting* – a dream about an encounter with an enemy soldier who is, humanly, a friend, in surroundings which are both those of the war and of hell. Owen's poems have been used by the composer Benjamin Britten in one of his major musical compositions, *War Requiem*.

* *War Poets.*

Bib: Owen, H., *Life*; critical study by D. S. R. Welland.

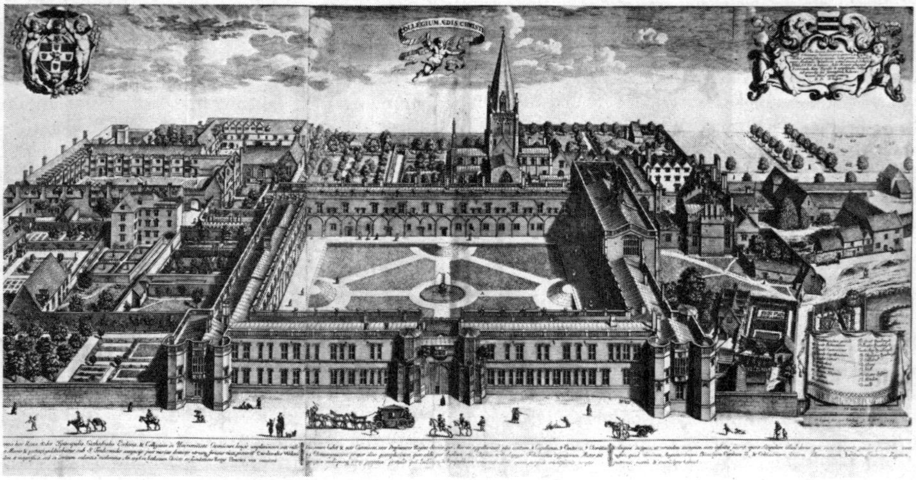

Oxford Groups (Buchmanism)

A religious movement in Britain during the 1930s, inspired and led by the American evangelist Frank Buchman. It was organized in small groups, whose members met to discuss their problems under Divine Guidance received in answer to prayer, a procedure similar to that employed by the the 18th-C Methodists and the 17th-C Quakers. Opponents alleged that Divine Guidance was unduly right wing; the movement was concerned about the spread of atheism through Communist cells throughout Europe. It was largely despised by intellectuals, but had wide influence especially among the upper classes. Since World War II the movement has been re-formed under the title MRA – Moral Rearmament. MRA seems to have many of the same characteristics as the Groups, but to be more international in its scope. To left-wing intellectuals, both the Groups and MRA represent a kind of 'Fascism' (**Fascist*).

Oxford Movement (Tractarian Movement)

A religious movement within the Church of England*; it had its origin and main centre in Oxford and ran from 1833, when it began with a sermon by Keble*, until 1845 when its most eloquent leader, John Newman*, entered the Roman Catholic Church. Some of the leaders of the Church of England realized (especially after the Act of Catholic Emancipation, 1829) that the Church was by its constitution largely at the mercy of the state, and was in danger of becoming in essentials a department of the state. The Oxford Movement preached that the Church had its independent, spiritual status, was in direct descent from the medieval Catholic Church, and represented a 'middle way' between post-Reformation* Catholicism and Protestantism*. The movement's propaganda was conducted through tracts*, many of them by John Newman, and culminated in *Tract XC* which asserted that the Thirty-nine Articles*, on which Anglican* doctrine is based, are compatible with Roman Catholic doctrine. The tracts divided Anglican opinion severely, and Newman's secession to the Church of Rome, followed by the secession of other High Anglican clergy, brought the movement into discredit with the majority of Anglican opinion. Edward Pusey, Professor of Hebrew at Oxford, was the leader of the Oxford Movement, which was in consequence often called Puseyite. An indirect result of the movement was to focus attention on the medieval background of the Church, and to encourage that strong sentiment for the Middle Ages which emerged in much Victorian literature, in the artistic movement known as Pre-Raphaelitism*, and in Victorian neo-Gothic architecture.

* 3.4.3

Oxford Street

One of the principal streets in the West End of London, running from the vicinity of the City westwards, as far as Marble Arch, the site of Tyburn*, where public executions once took place. Until early in 18th C it was called Tyburn Road; it was renamed after Edward Harley, Earl of Oxford, a leading statesman in Queen Anne's reign. It is now one of the main shopping streets.

Oxford University

The oldest of the English Universities. It was started by students from the still older University of Paris in 12th C, and the colleges which give it (and Cambridge) its distinctive character began to be founded in 13th C, as a means of housing students and keeping order among them. The colleges are not controlled by the University, but are self-governing institutions, though their members usually (always in the case of senior members) hold university appointments as well. Oxford provided the students who early in 13th C started Cambridge University*, but Oxford remained of superior importance until 15th C, by which time it was infected by Wycliffite heresies, and the great patrons (especially the Crown) began to distribute to Cambridge at least an equal share of the wealth in endowments.

Oxford produced some of the intellectual leaders of medieval Europe: in 13th C Roger Bacon* and Duns Scotus*, in 14th C Wycliffe*. The New Learning* of the Renaissance* began in 16th C under the leadership of Erasmus*, Thomas More*, Grocyn* and Colet to oust medieval scholasticism*. Since then Oxford has retained its status as one of the two main channels through which men of thought and letters have received their education.

* *Universities.*

Oxymoron /oksi'mo:ron/

* *Figures of Speech.*

Ozymandias /əuzi'mandiəs/

One of the famous short poems by P. B. Shelley*. The ancient Greek historian Didorus Siculus (1st C BC) calls the tomb of the great Egyptian Pharaoh Rameses II the tomb of Ozymandias.

P

Paean /'pi:ən/

In ancient Greece, a hymn of thanksgiving, obscurely linked with the god of health (or perhaps Apollo* in one of his aspects), perhaps through the practice of chanting sacred healing spells.

Pageant

The word derives from the name of a kind of stage used in medieval Mystery plays* which moved in procession to prearranged positions in the town and exhibited scenes from the Bible dramatizing the fall of man and his redemption by Christ. In modern England, a pageant is a display, commonly in the form of a procession, celebrating a historical or legendary event, usually with patriotic significance. This sense of the word 'pageant' has clear relationship with the Mystery plays, and illustrates a particular dramatic viewpoint. The Mysteries were dramatic inasmuch as they represented conflicts between good and evil, but the stories and their outcome were fully known to the audience, so that there was small place for the unexpected. The modern pageant is an undramatic spectacle, and such pageants existed in 16th C symbolizing non-biblical legends of patriotic significance like the story of St George* and the Dragon. Thus the traditions of the pageant are twofold: in one sense it is merely spectacle, but in another it may be a spectacle combined with the narrative of a conflict, which is dramatic only because the conflict is symbolic of a permanent truth of human experience. This second sense of the pageant tradition is important for understanding Elizabethan* history plays*, especially those of Shakespeare. Thus, in *1 Henry IV** the modern audience is inclined to see the drama as a conflict for the soul of Prince Hal, who on the one hand is faced with the temptations of self-indulgence through Falstaff, and on the other with the task of winning 'honour' from Hotspur. Yet the audience is misled by this approach, since in I. ii Prince Hal declares that he is in no danger of yielding to Falstaff, and his acquisition of honour is also foreknown through the historical fact of the battle of Agincourt*; Hal is thus not the hero of an inner moral and an outer physical conflict at least in the sense that there is the smallest uncertainty in the audience's mind about the outcome. On the other hand, Falstaff and Hotspur – the self-indulgent favourite and the self-centred politician – are dangers to which any nation is everlastingly exposed. Thus the dramatic interest of the play is not Hal but the nation, and the play is essentially the re-enactment of a conflict to which the nation is perpetually exposed – a dramatic pageant in the Mystery and Morality* tradition.

Paine, Thomas (1737–1809)

Political author. The son of a small farmer, his early career in England as an official ended in failure, and he sailed for America in 1774. In 1776 he published the republican pamphlet *Common Sense*, which set the colonists openly on the road to independence. After the opening of the American War of Independence, he maintained the morale of the rebels with a series of pamphlets called *The Crisis* (1776–83). The opening sentence was 'These are the times that try men's souls' – words which became a battle-cry.

In 1787 he returned to Europe to carry on his fight for republican democracy. When Burke published his *Reflections on the Revolution in France** in 1790, Paine replied with Part I of his *Rights of Man* (1791). The Government was setting on foot his trial for treason in 1792 when the poet William Blake* got him out of the country to France, where the French revolutionary government had elected him a member of the republican Convention. In France he published his *Age of Reason* (1793) which defended a rational, abstract form of deism* against orthodox Christianity. This caused him to lose his popularity in England and in America. He also lost favour with the French for his injudicious criticisms, and for a time he was imprisoned, though he was later restored to his seat in the Convention. In 1802 he returned to America to find that he had lost his influence there. In 1819 the English radical William Cobbett* returned to England with Tom Paine's bones. For some time his works remained a text-book for English radicalism*.

Palace of Pleasure

An anthology of tales translated from the Italian and Latin, compiled by William Painter (1540?–94) and published 1566–7. Writers include Bandello, Boccaccio*, Herodotus*, and Livy*. It was used as a source-book for plots by Elizabethan dramatists, including Shakespeare who drew on it, at least to some extent, for *All's Well that Ends Well**, and perhaps some other plays.

Palace of Westminster

* *Westminster, The Palace of.*

Palamon and Arcite

/'paləmən – 'a:sait/

Rivals for the love of Emilia in Chaucer's *Knight's Tale**, the first of the *Canterbury Tales**. Dryden* paraphrased Chaucer's tale as *Palamon and Arcite*, published in his *Fables Ancient and Modern* (1699).

Pale, The English

An area round Dublin on the eastern coast of Ireland in which, from 12th to 16th C, English authority was well established; the rest of the country, though nominally under the English Crown, was not governed effectively by it. The Pale was larger or smaller according to the degree of English strength, and it disappeared in the reign of Elizabeth I* when Ireland was for the first time thoroughly subdued. The idiom 'beyond the Pale' means 'uncivilized', or merely 'unacceptable in civilized society'.

Palgrave

* *Anthology.*

Palindrome

/'palindrəum/

* *Figures of Speech.*

Palinode

/'palinəud/

The withdrawal in a piece of writing of ideas or attitudes expressed in another by the same writer; or the expression in one work of ideas which are in direct opposition to those which the author has expressed in a previous one. Thus in Spenser's* *Four Hymns* his *Hymn of Heavenly Love* is a palinode of his *Hymn of Love*, and Blake's* *Songs of Experience* (1794) are a palinode of his *Songs of Innocence* (1789).

* *Songs of Innocence and Experience.*

Palinurus

/pali'njuərəs/

In Virgil's *Aeneid**, the pilot of Aeneas' ship; he went to sleep and fell overboard, reached a savage shore, and was murdered by the natives.

Pall Mall

/'pal'mal/

A street in the west end of London; it is famous for its distinguished men's clubs*, such as the Athenaeum*, Reform, and Junior Carlton. The name derives from the game called in French *pallemaille* played in the street in its humbler days in 17th C.

Palladio, Andrea (1518–80)

/pa'ladjəu/

An Italian architect who built in a formal, stately style derived from ancient Rome. His ideas strongly interested the first great classical architect in England, Inigo Jones*, and in 18th C many of the great English country mansions were designed according to Palladian principles. The balanced symmetry, formal dignity, care for proportion, and stateliness of this style is in accord with the classical virtues of much 18th-C literature, *eg* the poetry of Pope* and Johnson*.

* 2.3

Palm Sunday

The Sunday before Easter, on which Christ's ceremonial entry to Jerusalem is celebrated; see the Bible, *John* 12:13. The day was formerly celebrated by the carrying of palm branches in procession.

Pamela, or Virtue Rewarded (1740–41)

A novel by Samuel Richardson*. It is in epistolary form, *ie* it consists of a series of letters describing the events, written by the heroine, Pamela Andrews, to her parents. Part I tells how Pamela resists attempts by her employer to seduce her, and how he, Mr B., eventually abandons his dishonourable conduct and agrees to marry her, though she is only his servant. Part II (1741) is about her married life.

Pamela is commonly credited with being the first true novel in English, because it is a minute and sustained representation of the day-to-day behaviour and psychology of the chief characters. The book arose from a suggestion put to Richardson that he should prepare 'a little volume of letters, in a common style, on such subjects as might be of use to country readers' – a volume which appeared independently in 1741 with the additional aim of instructing readers 'how to think and act justly and prudently in the common concerns of human life'. It was this secondary intention which inspired Richardson to write *Pamela*, which is intended to be as much a moral treatise or 'conduct book' as a narrative. Its success as a narrative was very great, not only in Britain but elsewhere in Europe, especially France and Germany. As a work of moral instruction, however, it aroused some derision: Pamela's willingness to marry the man who has behaved so badly to her too clearly suggests that she is not so much motivated by good morals as by social ambition. *Pamela* thus provoked parodies, of which the most important were *An Apology for the Life of Mrs Shamela Andrews* (1741), probably by Fielding, and the more famous *Joseph Andrews** (1742), which is certainly his. The rivalry between the novelists was continued in their respective masterpieces, Richardson's *Clarissa Harlowe** (1747–8) and Fielding's *Tom Jones** (1749).

* 4.3.2

Pamphlet

Any short treatise published separately, usually without hard covers. The word derives from a popular 12th-C love poem, written in Latin and entitled *Pamphilus, seu de Amore*, the name of the hero becoming adapted to Pamphilet, and in 14th C applied in its modern sense. A 'pamphleteer' is a writer of pamphlets. They are usually polemical, *ie* written to defend or attack some body of ideas, especially religious or political ones. In 16th C and especially towards the end of the reign of Elizabeth I* pamphleteering became a widespread literary industry, the beginning of journalism. Thomas Nashe* and Thomas Dekker* were amongst the most famous pamphleteers, and the Marprelate* controversy was the most famous of the 'pamphlet wars'. In 17th C Milton was the most famous writer of pamphlets, and his *Areopagitica** is his masterpiece. In 18th C some of Swift's* finest prose was in pamphlet form, *eg A Modest Proposal* (1729), and Defoe* was a prolific pamphleteer. 18th C, however, saw the rise of the weekly periodicals, which reduced the need for the pamphlet form of literature.

* *Journalism.*

Pan

In Greek myth, the god of shepherds and huntsmen, and therefore associated with animals and wild places. He is represented with horns, with the legs and feet of a goat, and as playing on the seven-reed shepherd's pipe. He was worshipped chiefly in the pastoral state of Arcadia*. According to the Greek historian Plutarch*, some travellers heard a voice calling the pilot of their ship and bidding him to tell the news that 'great Pan was dead'. The incident was never explained, but in Christian legend it has been supposed to signify the beginning of the reign of Christ. The word 'panic' derives from Pan, owing to the sudden fear that overcomes wanderers in wild and lonely places.

The nymph Syrinx was turned into a reed so that she could escape pursuit by Pan, who commemorated her by calling his flute by her name.

Pandemonium

In Milton's *Paradise Lost** I, the capital city of Hell, constructed from the precious minerals dug out by Mammon*.

Pandora /pan'do:rə/

In Greek myth, the first woman. She was sent as a calamity to men by Zeus*, who was enraged by the theft of fire by Prometheus*, acting for mankind. Zeus sent her as a gift to Epimetheus, the brother of Prometheus, and she brought with her a vase ('Pandora's box'). When she opened the vase, all the calamities from which mankind suffers spread over the world; only Hope remained in the vase to comfort mankind.

Pandosto (1588) /pan'dostəu/

A prose romance by Robert Greene*, used by Shakespeare as the basis for his late play, *The Winter's Tale**.

Panjandrum /pan'dʒandrəm/

The word first occurs in a sentence devised by the actor-playwright Samuel Foote (1720–77) to test the memory of another actor-playwright, Charles Macklin (d 1797): '. . . and there were present the Picninnies, and the Joblillies, and the Garyulies, and the Grand Panjandrum himself, with the little round button at top.' The word came to be used for any pompous person, or for someone of supposed power.

Panope /'panəpi/

In Greek myth, a nereid or sea-nymph, for whose aid sailors used to call in a storm.

Pantagruel

A comic romance by François Rabelais*, published in its first version in 1532. Pantagruel is the son of Gargantua*.

Pantaloon

A character in old Italian popular comedy. He represented a Venetian, and the name derived from the Venetian saint, San Pantaleone. He became a popular figure in international pantomime*, and appears as a stupid old man wearing spectacles, slippers, and clumsy trousers or pantaloons, from which comes 'pants'. Pantaloon used also to be a term for any feeble-minded old man, *eg* in Shakespeare's *As You Like It** II. vii. 158.

Pantheism

A term used to cover a variety of religious and philosophical beliefs, which have in common that God is present in Nature, and not separable from it in the sense in which a cause is separable from its effect, or a creator from his creation. Pantheism is implicit in doctrines derived from Plato*, *eg* in some of the neo-Platonists of 16th C, and in some poetry inspired by the natural environment. Amongst English poets, the most famous example is Wordsworth* in his earlier phase (1797–1807), notably in the first two books of his 1805 version of *The Prelude**. In his revised version of this autobiographical poem, Wordsworth tried to eliminate the pantheistic tendencies, since they are not in accordance with most forms of Christian doctrine.

Pantheon

In ancient Rome, a building with niches for seven gods, erected in 27 BC. In Europe (*eg* the Pantheon in Paris) imitations of the Roman institution have been set up for the purpose of enshrining national heroes. A building of this name in 18th-C London was merely a pleasure-resort, including a theatre and a promenade. It was burnt down in 1792, and rebuilt, but was never again so fashionable.

Pantisocracy /panti'sokrəsi/

A visionary conception of a communistic form of society, to which the poets Coleridge* and Southey* devoted themselves in 1794–5. The idea was originally Southey's, and was inspired by the French Revolution*. The pair hoped to establish a community in which motives of gain would be replaced by brotherly love; its site was to be the banks of the River Susquehanna in the United States. They were unable to raise money, however, and abandoned the idea. The derivation is from Greek words meaning government by all in equality.

Pantomime

Originally, in ancient Rome, a representation by masked actors, using gestures and dance, of religious or warlike episodes. One actor played many parts, male and female, with changes of mask and costume. It was often accompanied by music. It was used for episodes in medieval religious drama, and as the 16th-C Italian *commedia dell'arte** it became a form of popular drama that spread all over Europe together with a number of traditional characters such as Harlequin and the Clown. In 18th C it established itself in England. Nowadays the children's pantomimes performed in Britain after Christmas are usually musical plays representing traditional folk-tales (*Puss in Boots*, *Dick Whittington*, etc.) in a vulgarized form, but sometimes introducing traditional characters from the *commedia dell'arte*. Certain conventions are peculiar to it: the hero of the story or 'principal boy' is always performed by an actress, and a comic character known as the 'pantomime dame' is performed by an actor.

Paolo and Francesca /'pauləu – fran'seskə/

A pair of medieval lovers, chiefly famous through their representation by Dante in the 5th canto of the *Inferno**; their story was among the great medieval tragic love romances. The lovers lived in Italy in 13th C. Francesca was given in marriage to Giovanni Malatesta of Rimini, but fell in love with Paolo, his brother. When the affair was discovered they were put to death. In Dante's poem, Francesca tells the poet that she had been corrupted by reading the tale of Lancelot* and Guinevere in the legends of King Arthur*. Leigh Hunt's* *The Story of Rimini* (1816), a poem on the subject, had some contemporary fame and impressed the young John Keats*.

Paphos /'peifos/

A city in Cyprus and, in the period of ancient Greece, a centre for the worship of Aphrodite* (originally of a similar goddess who became identified with her). As she was the goddess of sexual love, a 'Paphian' became a synonym for a prostitute.

Paracelsus (Theophrast Bombast von Hohenheim, 1493–1541) /parə'selsəs/

A Swiss doctor and medical theorist, who made great, though largely baseless pretensions to scientific knowledge. He is the subject of a long early poem (1835) by Robert Browning*.

Paraclete /'parəkli:t/

The Holy Spirit of Christian theology. The word derives from the Greek for 'intercessor'.

Paradise

In the Old Testament of the Bible, especially in the Book of Genesis, the Garden of Eden* when the world was in its golden age before the fall of man; in the New Testament it is identified with Heaven, or some part of it.

Paradise Lost **(1667)**

An epic poem by John Milton*; originally in ten books it was rearranged in twelve. It is in blank verse*.

Milton had long intended to write an epic* to rival the ancient Roman *Aeneid** by Virgil, and the still more ancient Greek *Iliad** and *Odyssey** by Homer, whom Virgil was himself emulating. At length he chose the great Christian theme of the Fall of Man, binding it up with the mythical Fall of the Angels* which had preceded it. He follows Virgil's epic construction closely, but the opening 'exordium' or introductory passage makes it clear that he regards himself as engaged on a far more difficult enterprise, since he is concerned with ultimate truth, and with the ambition to 'justify the ways of God to men'. 'Justify' is used not in the philosophical sense of 'making clear to men's reason' but in the religious sense of communicating with men's spiritual faculties; as the Greeks and Romans began their epic endeavours with appeals for inspiration from the muses, so Milton declares he cannot achieve his enterprise without the aid of the Holy Spirit.

Book I: Satan lies prostrate in Hell, having been cast down from Heaven after the failure of his great war against God; around him lie the fallen angels who have shared in his defeat. Book II: In a council of war, the strategy of continuing the war against the reign of God is debated; it is decided that a campaign is to be conducted against the new creation – the Earth; Satan sets out on a voyage of discovery of the Earth, first passing through the gates of Hell, guarded by Sin and Death, and then voyaging through Chaos. Book III: God foretells Satan's assault on the Earth and the consequent fall of man; the Son offers himself as man's ransom; Satan alights on the Earth. Book IV: The Garden of Eden is described; Satan spies on Adam and Eve, and learns about the forbidden fruit of the Tree of Knowledge. Book V: The archangel Raphael is sent to the Earth, and relates to Adam how Satan, through pride, was incited to rebel against God. Book VI: Raphael continues his account of the War in Heaven, and describes how the Son of God drove the rebellious angels out of Heaven. Book VII: The creation of Earth is described by Raphael. Book VIII: Further conversation between Adam and Raphael, about the construction of the Universe, and about Adam's relationship with Eve. Book IX: Satan, entering into the Serpent, persuades Eve to eat of the forbidden fruit of the Tree of Knowledge; Adam in despair at losing her, follows her example. Book X: The Son comes to judge Adam and Eve for their sin, and Sin and Death make their way upward to the Earth; Satan returns in triumph to Hell. Book XI: The Archangel Michael is sent to expel Adam and Eve from the Garden; an Angel shows them the future of man until the Flood. Book XII: Michael foretells the Messiah, the history of the Church and its corruption, and the Second Coming.

The especial greatness of the epic is not primarily due to Milton's technical achievement in emulating Virgilian epic in structure and in elevation of tone. Firstly it is his fusing in the poem of the two great warring traditions in the culture of his time: that of the Renaissance*, which emphasized the grandeur of the created world and of the works of Man, and that of the Reformation*, which emphasized the authority of the Scriptures, exclusive of all other influences, over the mind of Man. No other imaginative writer was so aware of the conflict between these traditions and of the necessity of reconciling them. The most poignant episode from this point of view is in Book IX, where Adam meets Eve returning from the Tree of Knowledge and recognizes in her the falling apart of beauty and virtue, never to be reunited until the Second Coming. Secondly, Milton had deep insight into the basic contradiction in human nature between the instinctive assertiveness of the Will and openness to Divine Grace. Satan is here the central figure: he is human as well as superhuman, and not so much the embodiment of evil as the vehicle through which evil enters the universe: defiance of the Divine Will is indispensable to the continuance of his identity, a predicament which raises him to tragic status.

For the next two centuries, the poem had an immense influence on English poetry. Its scope was vast, and its style sonorous, fixing for English readers their conception of what was meant by the word 'sublime' in poetry. Addison* in early 18th C and Johnson* in mid-18th C, praised it rather ambiguously, Addison declaring that 'Our language sunk under him [Milton]', and Johnson that 'None ever wished it longer than it is'. Keats* imitated the Miltonic style in his own unfinished epic, *Hyperion**, and then abandoned it, declaring that 'English ought to be kept up', in allusion to the Latin syntax of Milton's sentences. Blake*, one of whose prophetic books was *Milton* (1804), declared in *Marriage of Heaven and Hell** that Milton 'was of the Devil's party without knowing it', in allusion to the enigma that the first two books of the epic – usually accounted the finest – present Satan in terms which command admiration, whereas his God is a dim and tedious figure. Nonetheless, Milton was accepted as second only to Shakespeare until 20th C, largely on account of *Paradise Lost*. On account of this same masterpiece, Milton lost heavily with leading 20th-C critics when a reassessment of English poetic values became necessary in the light of the poetry of Eliot* and Yeats*. Milton's heavy, sonorous music, his Latin syntax, the monumental quality of his epic style divorced from the liveliness of spoken idiom, cause him to be seen as a false guide to English poets in 18th and 19th C. As his reputation and that of Spenser* (who influenced him and shared some of his more artificial qualities) sank, so the reputations of his contemporaries, the Metaphysical poets*, rose because they were found to possess the qualities that Milton lacked. *Paradise Lost* is too great a poem ever to lose respect, but the general refusal to see it any longer as an achievement which almost equals Shakespeare's tragedies is the major revolution of poetic taste in 20th C.

* 4.2.1; 6.3.1.

Paradise Regained (1671)

An epic* poem in four books, written in blank verse*, by John Milton*. It is a sequel to *Paradise Lost**; as Eve, by yielding to Satan's temptation and thus withdrawing her submission to the Divine Will, had brought about the fall of man, so Christ, by resisting the temptation by Satan, regained the promise of Paradise for man. In both epics, the events are drawn from the Bible; in *Paradise Regained*, from *Luke* 4.

Book I: Christ is baptized by John the Baptist, and a voice from Heaven proclaims him to be the Son of God; Satan undertakes the temptation of Christ; Christ is led into the desert, where, after 40 days, Satan approaches him in the disguise of an old man and challenges him to turn the stones of the desert into bread, but Christ says, as in the Bible, 'Man lives not by bread alone'; Satan is repulsed. Book II: Christ is again tempted through his hunger, and then through the offers of wealth and power. Book III: When these temptations also fail, Satan suggests to Christ the possibility of political leadership. Book IV: the political arguments also fail, and so do suggestions of command through art and knowledge; the final temptation is that Christ should cast himself down from the pinnacle of the temple in Jerusalem, to prove his divinity by causing himself to be borne up by his angels; Satan receives the abrupt answer, 'Thou shalt not tempt the Lord thy God'; Satan retires in final defeat. The temptations are made vivid by Satan's conjuring up of panoramic visions of the world of the Roman Empire and of the civilization of Greece, but the style is subdued by comparison with the eloquent sweep which characterizes *Paradise Lost*. This is appropriate, since it is Christ himself who refuses the epic role; the refusal shows austerity and dignity, and these are the qualities of the verse.

Paradiso

The third and final section of Dante's* great religious epic, *Divina Commedia*. It is written in terza rima*, and has 33 cantos.

Dante has been led through Hell and Purgatory by the spirit of the Roman poet, Virgil*; Virgil, however, was a pagan on earth and cannot enter the confines of the Christian Heaven. Dante's guide is from now on Beatrice, the girl whose earthly beauty had so inspired him, and who now signifies Theology. As Hell had been divided into circles, so Heaven is divided into spheres: the sphere of the Moon, of Mercury, Venus, the Sun, Mars, Jupiter, Saturn, the Fixed Stars, and the Primum Mobile, or First Mover. Each sphere contains the kind of spirit which the ancient Greek and Roman myths had caused to be associated with it: Mars, the Christian warriors and martyrs; Jupiter, the just rulers; Saturn, the holy contemplatives, etc. The spheres are in ascending order of merit, and culminate in Dante's remote, ecstatic vision of God Himself. In each, Dante has conversations on philosophical and spiritual matters with the men and women from history whom he conceives to have been assigned there.

* *Inferno; Purgatorio.*

Paradox

* *Figures of Speech.*

Parcae /'pa:si:/

In Roman and Greek myth, the Fates; the Greek name for them being Moirae. They were three daughters of Night: Clotho, who spun the thread of life; Lachesis, who represented chance and fortune, and Atropos, who brought life to an end by cutting the thread.

Pardoner's Prologue and Tale, The

In Chaucer's *Canterbury Tales**, written in ten syllable couplets*. The profession of a pardoner was to raise money for the Church by selling the holy relics of saints, and documents called Indulgences* which 'pardoned' sins and enabled the perpetrators to escape divine punishment for them in after-life. The Church's doctrine about indulgences was not, at least originally, as crude as this use of them makes it appear, but the system was clearly open to abuse; pardoners were inclined to be unscrupulous individuals who exploited the superstitions of simple people in order to get their money. Chaucer's Pardoner is one of these; his prologue resembles that of the Wife of Bath* in being a full and exulting 'confession' to the other pilgrims about his own wickedness. He describes how he preaches a sermon to the people on the sin of avarice in order to make them surrender up their money to him – avarice being his own especial sin. He also speaks of the sins of fleshly indulgence such as drunkenness and lechery (to both of which he is himself openly addicted), and his Tale is a grim allegory about the attempt of three 'rioters', *ie* dissolute characters, to seek out and destroy 'Death'. A mysterious old man who himself longs to die but cannot, directs them to a place where there is a pile of gold; over this the rioters fight, and end by killing one another. The Pardoner winds up with a rhetorical condemnation of gluttony, and then apparently forgetting how he has exposed himself, he tries to sell some pardons and relics to the pilgrims, beginning with the Host, whose reply is printable only because it is in Middle English.

Paris

In Greek myth, the son (sometimes called Alexander) of King Priam* of Troy* and his queen, Hecuba. Because, during pregnancy, Hecuba dreamed that he would bring destruction on Troy, Priam ordered that the baby should be exposed on Mount Ida. Shepherds found him, however, and brought him up as one of themselves. He and the nymph Oenone* fell in love and lived happily together, until the episode of the golden Apple of Discord. This had been thrown among the gods and goddesses when they were assembled, and was inscribed 'For the fairest'. The goddesses Hera, Athene and Aphrodite disputed for its possession, until it was decided that Paris should judge between them. Each tried to bribe him to decide in her favour, but Aphrodite won the apple by promising him the possession of the most beautiful woman on earth.

Paris abandoned Oenone, and went to Troy, where Priam acknowledged him as his son. He then visited the court of Menelaus, king of Sparta, who was married to Helen*, the most beautiful woman in the world. They eloped to Troy, but Menelaus and his brother Agamemnon raised a great army from all the Greek princes who had ever courted Helen, and began the siege of Troy which ended with the destruction of the City. Paris was mortally wounded by an arrow shot from the bow of Philoctetes*, and he sought out Oenone, whom he had abandoned, but who alone could cure him. In resentment, she refused to treat him until it was too late, when she took her own life from grief.

Parker, Matthew (1504–75)

Became Archbishop of Canterbury on the accession of Elizabeth I*, and her main ally in her policy of keeping the Church of England* on its unique midway course between the Roman Catholic Church and the more decidedly Protestant* sects such as the Lutherans and Calvinists, represented in England by the Puritans*. He was a notable scholar, and promoted the 'Bishops' Bible' (1568) which became the basis for the 'Authorized Version' of 1611.

* *Anglican ; Bible in England ; Reformation.*

Parliament

The name of the supreme law-making body of Great Britain and Northern Ireland. It has two parts – the House of Commons, whose members are elected, and the House of Lords, the majority of whose members still sit by hereditary right. 'House' in these expressions does not refer to a building, but is equivalent to 'assembly'; the Lords and Commons meet in different chambers of the same building, officially called the Palace of Westminster* but colloquially known as the Houses of Parliament.

Parliament is a direct descendant of the medieval Magnum Concilium or Great Council, composed until the end of 13th C of the chief landowners (nobility) of the realm, together with the bishops and principal abbots. To these Edward I* added representatives of the Commons, *ie* elected members from the towns and smaller landowners; his purpose was to facilitate the imposition and collection of taxes. At first the Commons assembled with the nobility or lords, but in 14th C they began to sit as separate assemblies.

In 16th C the great nations of western Europe became despotisms; the kings of France and Spain ceased to summon their national assemblies, which under different names were equivalent to the English Parliament. In England, Henry VIII*, though no less a despot, found his Parliament useful as an instrument in asserting the independence of the Church of England*, since the authority of the Pope had long been unpopular in England. The growth in wealth of the English middle class and the financial weakness of the Crown combined with religious disagreements inherited from the Reformation* to make 17th C a period of epic struggle for power between Parliament and the kings. The successive stages of this conflict – open disagreement on policy under James I*, the Civil Wars* under Charles I*, the republican interregnum followed by the restoration of the monarchy – culminated in the complete victory for Parliament (in which the Commons were now taking the leading role) following the deposition of James II* in the Revolution of 1688*.

This did not mean, however, that England became a parliamentary democracy; methods of election were corrupt, and the system did not correspond to the distribution of the population, with the result that throughout 18th C power remained in the hands of the landed aristocracy, which controlled both Houses and usually tied the hands of the kings, but retained an alliance and close connections with the middle class. In 19th C steady movements were made towards democracy through the succession of laws widening and modernizing the electoral system: the passing of the Reform Bill* of 1832 extended the vote to all the richer middle class; the Act of 1867 gave it to industrial workers, and the Act of 1884 to agricultural workers. (Women had to wait for laws passed in 1918 and 1928 to receive the vote.) These changes in 19th C were brought about by the Industrial Revolution*, which enormously increased the populations of the towns, some of which had hitherto been unrepresented in Parliament, and brought about a cleavage of interest between the urban industrialists and the landowners; the same set of causes encouraged the working classes to organize themselves so that they could no longer be ignored as a separate body of opinion.

Scotland had her own Parliament until the Union of Parliaments in 1707, since when she has sent representatives to Westminster; Ireland sent members from 1801, when her own parliament was abolished; Wales never had her own parliament but has sent members to Westminster since union in 1535. In 1922, Irish representation at Westminster was reduced to Ulster, or Northern Ireland, since the rest of the country became an independent republic.

Since 17th C, the Commons has been unquestionably the more important House; since the Parliament Act (1911) the legal powers of the House of Lords have been severely reduced, by that law and by later legislation.

Parliament of Fowls, The
A verse fable* by Chaucer* in which the characters are birds. It is about 700 lines long and is composed in rhyme-royal*. It dates from about 1380. The fable celebrates St Valentine's Day, popularly regarded as the festival of lovers. The poet has a vision of the Court of Nature where the fowls have attended to choose their mates. Three male ('tercel') eagles are competing for a female ('formel'), and the fowls debate their claims. Each speaks in character, the less noble (the duck, the cuckoo, the goose) offering ignoble counsel, and the aristocrats (the hawks and falcons) affirming the principles of humble devotion prescribed by the doctrines of courtly love. The debate is informal and enlivened by laughter and ridicule in the tradition of the flyting*. Nature decides that the formel shall make her own choice, and the formel asks for a year to decide.

Parliament of the Three Ages, The
An anonymous alliterative* poem in a west English dialect, dating from near the middle of 14th C. It is a flyting* poem – a debate between Youth, Middle Age, and Old Age. It uses the dream convention, *ie* the poet falls asleep while hunting and after slaying a deer – often a preliminary to visionary dreams in medieval legends, since the deer was regarded as an emissary from fairyland. Each of the Ages represents the characteristic weaknesses of his time of life: Youth shows Pride; Middle Age, Avarice; Old Age, Envy and Wrath. Middle Age attacks Youth for his improvidence; Youth disdains Middle Age for his life of anxiety and worry; Old Age (Elde) shows them that they equally mislead themselves with vanities, but by displaying his own shortcomings he leaves the younger men and their positive values a share of victory in the debate. The allegory* is a means of expressing concrete experience in vivid terms, and the poem is one of the masterpieces of 14th-C poetry.

Parmenides of Elea /paː'menidiːz/
Greek philosopher, living in Italy in 6th C BC. He held reality to be indivisible, continuous throughout the universe, and changeless; all the phenomena that change and discontinue are unreal, and exist only in their illusory appearances. Plato* reconstructs this philosopher in his dialogue *Parmenides*, and treats him as a forerunner of his own idealism.

Parnassus /paː'nasəs/
A mountain near Delphi in Greece. Originally sacred to Dionysus, it was later regarded as the dwelling of Apollo* and the nine Muses*, and hence particularly associated with poetry. The Castalian spring* rises there, and drinking from it was said to give inspiration.

Parnell, Charles Stewart (1846–91) /paː'nel/
Irish political leader. He entered Parliament in 1875, and led the Home Rule* party in its fight for Irish self-government. He converted Gladstone* and the Liberal Party to the support of Home Rule, but was politically ruined by becoming involved in a scandal with the wife of Captain O'Shea in 1890. His success was the more remarkable because he was a Protestant*; the scandal finally turned the Catholic Church in Ireland against him. His downfall caused a deep split among the Irish nationalists.

Parnell, Thomas (1679–1718) /'paːnəl/
Poet. He was of the Augustan* school, and the author of reflective poems – *The Night Piece on Death*, *The Hymn to Contentment*, *The Hermit*, and satirical verse, especially *Homer's Battle of the Frogs and Mice* satirising the critics Theobald and Dennis.
Bib: Johnson, S., in *Lives of the Poets*.

Parody
A literary form which constitutes a comic imitation of a serious work, or of a serious literary form. Thus Fielding's *Joseph Andrews** is partly a parody of Richardson's *Pamela**, and Pope's *Rape of the Lock** is a parody of grand epic* in the style of Homer* and Virgil*. These examples show two uses of parody: Fielding was concerned to ridicule Richardson's novel, but Pope was concerned to ridicule the subjects of his poem rather than the epic form itself, by using epic machinery in miniature (*Epic, Mock) in order to expose the ridiculous over-seriousness of fashionable preoccupations and grievances. Minor examples of parody are numerous, *eg* Max Beerbohm's *A Christmas Garland* (1912), a collection of parodies of Wells*, Bennett*, Conrad*, Chesterton*, James* etc. It is difficult to draw a line between parody and burlesque*; the latter is more obviously comic in its style of imitation; Gay's *The Beggar's Opera** is a burlesque of Italian opera, fashionable at the time. An element of parody may enter into literature which is not primarily parody, *eg* Bernard Shaw* tended to introduce into his plays episodes and characters which would have been taken seriously in the contemporary theatre when presented as straightforward melodrama or sentimentality, but which he then developed ironically so as to defeat expectations.

Paronomasia /parənə'meizjə/
Figures of Speech, Play on Words.*

Parthenon /'paːθinən/
The ruined temple to the ancient Greek goddess Athene in Athens. It is one of the noblest examples of ancient Greek architecture.

Parthia
A kingdom situated south-east of the Caspian Sea; it flourished between 250 BC and AD 226. The population was a mixture of an Iranian tribe (the Parthians) and a Scythian aristocracy. They were formidable enemies of the Roman Empire, and in war were famous for their mounted archers who eluded close engagement with the enemy. The

expression 'a Parthian shot' is used for a sarcasm inflicted in the moment of parting, like an arrow shot by a retreating horseman. One of their most powerful rulers was Mithridates VI (c. 115–63 BC).

Parties, Political

The English political scene has been dominated by political parties since mid-17th C. It was not till 19th C that political parties became highly organized, and though there have seldom been more than two important ones, these have not always been the same. Nonetheless, there has been a continuity in the history of parties sufficient to give a long history to political loyalties. The principal phases of party development are summarized as follows:

[1] 1640–1660: the Civil War* and Interregnum*. Parliament*, especially the House of Commons*, successfully led a rebellion against the king, and established a republic. The division was partly religious (Puritan* against Anglican*), and partly economic (the commercially progressive south and east against the more traditional north and west). A minority of the House of Commons and a majority of the House of Lords sided with the king against the rest of Parliament; the supporters of the former were known as Royalists or Cavaliers, and the supporters of the latter as Parliament Men, or Roundheads.

[2] 1660–1714: rivalry of Tories and Whigs. The basic opposition represented by the Civil War continued after the Restoration*. The Tories were strong upholders of the monarchy and of the Church of England; the Whigs, without opposing the continuance of either as institutions, laid emphasis on the rights of Parliament and the dangers of a re-establishment of Roman Catholicism with monarchical despotism. The Whigs were twice victorious – at the bloodless Revolution of 1688* when they succeeded in deposing James II* in consequence of his Roman Catholicism, and in 1714 when they prevented the succession of his son as James III, on the same grounds. (**Whig and Tory* – for the origin of these names.)

[3] 1714–1832: the Whig Oligarchy and the Tory Revival. Tories virtually disappeared from the political scene until the accession of George III in 1760. During this period Parliament dominated the monarchy, but the Whigs divided up into a number of family alliances and political coteries. After 1760, George III tried to revive royal power by creating a party in Parliament to support it; these were called the King's Friends or New Tories. The victory of the colonists in the American War of Independence (1776–83) and the king's insanity destroyed his ambitions for reviving royal power, but other issues confirmed the Tories in power from 1783 to 1830. Chief among these new issues dividing the nation were: (i) the French Revolution*, which influenced the Whigs in the direction of political reform and the Tories in the direction of resistance to change; (ii) the English Industrial Revolution*, which was rapidly expanding an urban middle class which lacked political rights owing to the anachronistic parliamentary electoral system; and (iii) new social problems arising from the growth of a large urban proletariat. The Reform Bill* of 1832 was another Whig victory, greatly increasing the power of the urban middle class.

[4] 1832–1918: the evolution of the modern parties; Liberals, Conservatives and, finally, Labour. The parties became more self-conscious and closely organized; Whigs came to call themselves Liberals, and Tories changed their name to Conservatives. Until 1846, the division was between the agricultural interest (Conservative) and the industrial interest (Liberal), and the old religious divisions survived, so that the Conservatives were the guardians of the Church of England, and the more decidedly Protestant sects – now called Nonconformists – voted Liberal. In the second half of 19th C the upper classes of both towns and countryside tended to vote Conservative, and the Liberals depended increasingly on the urban working-class vote. However, the Liberals, by their traditions, could never become a predominantly working-class party; hence the Labour Party was founded in 1900. The chief issue over which Liberals and Conservatives fought in the mid-19th C was Free Trade* against Protection (by import taxes) of English agriculture. Later the Tories became the imperialist party, resisting Irish and South African Dutch nationalism – issues on which some Liberals took a more liberal view.

[5] 1918–Present Day. After World War I, social discontents caused the Labour Party to succeed the Liberal Party as one of the two greatest in the country. Since 1923, the Liberals have been reduced to a very small though not insignificant Parliamentary body. The Labour Party, on the other hand, owes as much to the great 19th-C Liberal traditions as to the doctrinaire socialism of Marx*.

Pascal, Blaise (1623–62) /pas'ka:l/

French religious philosopher and mathematician. In 1646 he became a devout adherent of the Jansenist movement which had its headquarters at the nunnery of Port-Royal near Paris. Jansenism (started by Cornelius Jansen, 1585–1638) maintained, like the Protestant predestinarians, that salvation through the love of God was possible only for those whom God pleased to love, *ie* an individual was predestined to salvation or to damnation; however it also emphasized the necessity of belonging to the Roman Catholic Church. The movement was strongly attacked by the Jesuit* Order, and when its leading exponent, Antoine Arnauld, was being threatened with dismissal from his academic post, Pascal wrote *Provincial Letters* (1656) in his defence. This was his first important work, a masterpiece of lucid, ironical controversy; in particular, Pascal advocated moral austerity and criticized Jesuit libertinism. His *Pensées* ('Thoughts' – pub 1670) is his more famous work; it consists of notes for a book on religion intended to demonstrate the necessity of the religious life. Though fragmentary, the notes have great aphoristic power; with an intellect as powerful and a style as lucid as that of Descartes*, Pascal criticizes the earlier philosopher's notion of the supreme power of human reason, and shows the limitations of reason in dealing with ultimate mysteries.

* *Predestination.*

Passage to India, A (1924)

A novel by E. M. Forster*. It had originally been planned ten years earlier, and its picture of India belongs partly to that period. The scene is the city of Chandrapore on the banks of the Ganges, and India is under British rule. The background characters consist mainly of the British officials and their wives, and the local Indian intelligentsia. The main characters are as follows: Aziz, a Muslim Indian doctor; Godbole, a Hindu professor; Fielding, the British Education Officer of the district; Ronald Heaslop, another of the British officials; and two visitors from Britain, Mrs Moore, the mother of Heaslop by her first marriage, and Adela Quested, who is engaged to him. Both women have strong liberal principles, and make friends easily with Fielding, the only liberal in the resident British colony. Fielding is also a friend of Aziz, and a colleague of Godbole. Aziz issues an impulsive invitation to the British visitors to visit the local Marabar Caves; these have a strong significance for the Hindus, although Godbole, when he is asked about them, is unable to explain it. The climax of the book occurs when this visit takes place. Heat, discomfort, and the caves themselves cause Mrs Moore and Adela to suffer traumatic experiences. Mrs Moore loses all her faith and idealism; Adela has an attack of hysteria which temporarily convinces her that Aziz has attempted to rape her. This supposed rape brings the already strained relations between the British and the Indians to a crisis, but the crisis is resolved (not without disgracing the more reactionary British officials) by Adela's return to sanity in the witness-box. Mrs Moore, although she is now selfish, hard and disillusioned whereas before she had been generous, kind and idealistic, is in touch with a new kind of truthfulness which helps Adela's restoration. Only Mrs Moore and Godbole understand the true nature of Adela's experience in the caves, and they understand it from opposite, though complementary points of view.

The novel has psychological, political, and religious dimensions, and it is the last of these that is the most important. The Christianity, or the sceptical liberalism, of the British is shown to be adequate for normal relationships and practical affairs, but they have become too shallow for the interpretation of deeper human experience; Aziz's Muslim faith is stronger, but it is more an aesthetic and cultural tradition than a binding spiritual faith. Godbole's Hinduism, on the other hand, is profound and intelligent, though it is no guide to the daily conduct of affairs. This religious dimension is presented by constant symbolism, ranging in character from unobtrusive (though often important) details, to the conspicuous and manifold suggestive image of the caves themselves. *A Passage to India* is usually regarded as Forster's masterpiece, and is certainly one of the finest English novels of 20th C.

Passionate Pilgrim (1599)

An anthology of poetry containing odes by Richard Barnfield (1564–1627) formerly attributed to Shakespeare.

Passover

A Jewish religious feast held in the spring; it commemorates the event narrated in the Bible (*Exodus* 12) when the angel of the Lord passed over the houses of the Jews but slew the eldest child of each Egyptian family as a punishment to Pharaoh for not releasing the Jews from captivity. Pharaoh then released the Jews.

Pasteur, Louis (1822–95) /pas'tɜː/

French chemist, famous for his work in preventive medicine, especially in the use of inoculation.

Paston Letters /'pastən/

A collection of correspondence between members of the Paston family of Norfolk and others, from 1422 to 1509. The Pastons were a rising family, but the letters cover an exceptionally disturbed period of English history – the reigns of Henry VI*, Edward IV*, and Richard III* – the period which includes the civil Wars of the Roses*. The reign of Henry VII* was more peaceful, so that the letters which conclude the collection are less exciting. The collection is perhaps the finest historical record of England in the Middle Ages*, and is an early example of good, informal English prose.

Pastoral, Classical

A form of literature originally developed by the ancient Greeks and Romans in the idylls* of the former (*eg* Theocritus'*) and the eclogues* of the latter (*eg* Virgil's*). Ancient pastoral idealized the Greek state of Arcadia* which had a rustic population of shepherds and herdsmen. The Renaissance* of 16th C, deeply interested in the literature of the Greeks and the Romans, revived the pastoral mode; the earliest forms of it date back in Italian literature to 15th C, but it was the romance *Arcadia* (1504), by the Italian poet Sannazaro, which was particularly influential throughout Europe. The appeal of the pastoral kind of literature was partly to human wishfulness – the desire to conceive of circumstances in which the complexity of human problems could be reduced to its simplest elements: the shepherds and shepherdesses of pastoral are imagined as having no worries, and they live in an ideal climate with no serious physical calamities; love and death, and making songs and music about these experiences, are their only preoccupations. Another function of pastoral, however, was as a vehicle of moral criticisms; the shepherds and shepherdesses sought the pleasures of nature and despised or were innocent of the corrupting luxury of courts and cities. Finally, pastoral presented a means of offering, allegorically, thinly disguised tributes of praise and flattery to real people whom the poet admired or wanted to please. The satirical, moral, and eulogistic functions of Renaissance pastoral all tended to make it allegorical, since it was through allegory that the poet could most safely make his criticisms felt, and could most eloquently convey his praise. Allegory also suited the neo-Platonic, idealizing cast of mind so characteristic of 16th-C writers. When we remember that the tradition of romantic love was one of the most ardently pursued inheritances from the Middle Ages*, and that the circumstances of pastoral lent themselves to its expression, it is not surprising that the pastoral mode was so extensively cultivated in 16th-C Europe. To England it came late, by way of influences from France, Spain and Italy, but it lasted longer; it was especially pervasive in the last quarter of 16th C, and continued till mid-17th; there was a minor revival early in 18th C.

The first important English pastoral poem is Edmund Spenser's *Shepherd's Calendar** which consists of an eclogue for each month of the year; the tone is morally didactic in some, satirical in others, and eulogistic of the queen in a third group. Sidney's *The Arcadia** (1580) is a pastoral romance whose purpose is entertainment, but it idealizes the courtly virtues, as does Book VI of Spenser's *Faerie Queene**, about Sir Calidore, the Knight of Courtesy. The University Wits*, Peele*, Lyly*, Greene*, and Lodge*, wrote pastoral dramas in verse and romances in prose, and one of the best pastoral works of the 1590s is Shakespeare's *As You Like It**, based on Lodge's romance *Rosalynde* (1590). Shakespeare dramatized the pastoral mode, however, with a difference: the fanciful world of pastoral romance is contrasted with the world of common sense, and the fairyland pastoral country of shepherds and shepherdesses with Greek names is juxtaposed to the real English countryside and its commonplace peasants, so that his pastoral romance is also antipastoral. It was not unusual, however, to salt pastoral with elements from real country life – Spenser does it in *The Shepherd's Calendar*, and Shakespeare does it most skilfully in *The Winter's Tale** IV. iii. More conventional pastoral dramas were John Fletcher's* *Faithful Shepherdess* (1610) and Ben Jonson's* *The Sad Shepherd* (1635). The artificiality of pastoral lent itself to the masque* form which combined music, poetry, dancing, and decor in equal proportions; Jonson, the master of masque, wrote a number of pastorals for it, but by far the most famous pastoral masque is Milton's *Comus**.

Of the various forms of pastoral, the prose romance had the shortest life, and ended with 16th C; the last pastoral drama was Elkanah Settle's *Pastor Fido* (1677). In non-dramatic poetry, pastoral lasted much longer. Michael Drayton* is the next pastoral poet of note after Spenser with *Idea : The Shepherd's Garland* (1593) and *Endimion and Phoebe* (1595); Marlowe's* famous pastoral lyric *Come Live With Me* was first printed in 1599, and pastoral lyric writers in the tradition of Spenser were numerous from 1590 up to 1650; they included Nicholas Breton (1545?–1626?), George Wither (1588–1667), William Browne (1591–1643), and above all Robert Herrick*. However, the most famous poems in 17th-C pastoral are Milton's: *L'Allegro** and *Il Penseroso** and his elegy *Lycidas**. In 18th C, Pope's* early *Pastorals* (1709) were a small masterpiece influenced by Virgil, but his *Windsor Forest* (1713) is a more impressive work, using pastoral to extol the Peace of Utrecht (1713) which ended the long War of the Spanish Succession*, and to celebrate peace, prosperity and civilization.

Classical pastoral has not been practised notably since the first half of 18th C. Great works were never produced in it except when it was being used for purposes beyond itself – the moral allegory of Spenser, and of Milton in *Comus* and *Lycidas*, or in contrast with reality, as in Shakespeare. However, pastoralism is to some extent a basic human impulse in so far as we always wish for artificial simplification of experiences which are too hard for us; modern critics, notably William Empson* (*Some Versions of Pastoral*, 1935) sometimes use the term more widely than classical pastoral denotes. Pastoral – even of the non-classical kind – is not synonymous with 'nature poetry' or poetry of country life: Wordsworth*, Clare*, Hardy*, Blunden* are not writers of pastoral in any usually accepted sense.

Patch

Originally the name of Cardinal Wolsey's* Fool; later a name applied to any household or court fool.
* *Fools.*

Pater, Walter Horatio (1839–94) /'peitə/

Scholar, essayist and critic. He was elected to a fellowship in Brasenose College, Oxford, in 1864. He was connected with the Pre-Raphaelite* group, shared their idealistic worship of beauty, and became an important influence in the cult of art which led to the Aesthetic* Movement at the end of the century. His most important work was *Studies in the History of the Renaissance* (1873), a collection of essays on Italian painters and writers from 14th to 16th C; the Conclusion to these essays, in which he advocates a fusion of psychic, moral, and sensuous ecstasy, became a kind of manifesto of the aesthetic movement. His next most famous work is the philosophic romance *Marius the Epicurean* (1885). Other works: *Imaginary Portraits* (1887); *Appreciations with an Essay on Style* (1889); *Plato and Platonism* (1893); *The Child in the House* (1894); *Greek Studies* and *Miscellaneous Studies* (1895); an unfinished romance, *Gaston de Latour* (1896). Pater wrote with immense care for beauty of style, which became for him an end in itself. The feeling among moderns that that is not the purpose of style has been one of the principal reasons for the decline of interest in his writing in this century.

* 7.4.

Paternoster /ˈpatəˈnostə/

The Latin term for the Lord's Prayer; the first two words in the Latin Vulgate edition of the Bible are *Pater Noster* ('Our Father ...'). The prayer is the one commended by Christ to the disciples in *Luke* 11, and hence a standard prayer for Christians.

Pathetic Fallacy

* *Figures of Speech.*

Patience

An alliterative*, unrhymed poem of 14th C, about 500 lines long. Its subject is the adventures of the Prophet Jonah in the Old Testament of the Bible. From its merit and the fact that it survived on a single manuscript which also included *Purity**, and the more famous *Pearl** and *Sir Gawain and the Green Knight**, scholars conjecture that all these poems may be by the same unknown poet.

Patmore, Coventry Kersey Dighton (1823–96) /ˈpatmoː/

Poet. He contributed to the Pre-Raphaelite* periodical *The Germ*; in 1864 he became a Catholic. The two books by which he is most remembered are *The Angel in the House* (comprising *The Betrothed*, 1854; *The Espousals*, 1856; *Faithful for Ever*, 1860; *The Victories of Love*, 1862) and *The Unknown Eros* (1877). The former is about his first marriage and celebrates married love; the latter, consisting of 42 irregular odes*, is on a similar theme but more mystical. Both poems are examples of philosophizing in verse characteristic of William Wordsworth's* famous *Prelude**. Patmore had independent ideas on poetic technique, and has been considered by some critics to bear resemblance to the 17th-C Metaphysical* poets. As much as for his own poetry, he is known today for being the friend and correspondent of the greater Catholic poet G. M. Hopkins*, whose work, however, he seems not to have properly appreciated. Other works: *Amelia* (1878), which was his own favourite among his poems; the critical essays *English Metrical Law* (1878); *Principle in Art* (1879); *Religio Poetae* (1893); the religious meditations *Rod, Root and Flower* (1895).

Bib: Patmore, D., *Life*; Oliver, E. J., *Life*; Page, F., *Patmore: a Study in Poetry*; Reid, J. C., *The Mind and Art of Coventry Patmore*; Hopkins, G. M., (ed Abbott, C. C.) *Further Letters*

Patmos

A Greek island in the Aegean Sea. It was the place of banishment of the evangelist St John, in AD 95. According to legend, he wrote the *Apocalypse* (*Revelation*) during his banishment there.

Patrick, Saint

The patron saint of Ireland; he seems to have been of Welsh birth, and was born about 389. He was early carried off to Ireland by Irish raiders, but later he escaped and for a few years studied at the French monastery of Lérins. He then returned to Britain, and was there inspired with the vocation to convert Ireland to Christianity.

Patroclus /pəˈtrokləs/

In Greek legend, the intimate friend of Achilles*, the principal Greek hero in the siege of Troy*. Patroclus was killed by Hector*, the Trojan prince, and Achilles avenged him by killing Hector in turn.

Patronage in Literature

A system by which the king or a nobleman afforded protection and livelihood to an artist, in return for which the artist paid him special honour, or returned him service in the form of entertaining his household and his guests. The great period for this system was 16th C, but patronage continued to be an important cultural and social institution until the end of 18th C. In the Middle Ages* the writer or scholar might work under the protection of a religious order, but already Chaucer* was dependent on the patronage of John of Gaunt. After 18th C, through circulating libraries and wide circulation of periodicals, writers could rely on support from the general public; from 16th to 18th C failure to secure a patron might mean oblivion, or at least starvation, as in the case of Chatterton*. In 16th C patronage was a natural institution since noblemen still kept large households and it was assumed that these would include entertainers (such as a band of actors) and scholars who performed educational and secretarial functions. In this century actors ('players') who were not attached to some household were regarded as vagabonds liable to punishment or shutting up in houses of correction by the public authorities; by the end of the century, however, the Lord Chamberlain's Company*, the Lord Admiral's Men* etc. were attached to their patrons only in name, and they performed in public theatres or at court. The Earl of Essex (patron of Ben Jonson*), the Earl of Southampton (patron of Shakespeare*), and Sidney's* sister, Margaret Countess of Pembroke*, were among the great patrons in the reign of Elizabeth I*, but the most valuable patron was the sovereign. Disagreeable results of patronage were the flattering 'dedications' which commonly preceded works of literature, and poems written specially to honour or gratify the patron, such as Donne's* *First* and *Second Anniversary* commemorating the death of Elizabeth Drury, daughter of his patron Sir Robert Drury – though Donne's poems are evidence that such work was by no means necessarily bad or insincere. The status of men of letters steadily gained in esteem, moreover, freeing the writer of the necessity of servility, and Ben Jonson was one of the most vigorous in upholding its dignity and independence. Nonetheless, it tended to be true under Elizabeth and her successor, James I*, that writers were either 'gentlemen amateurs' like Sidney and Raleigh*, able to work independently, or professional writers like Jonson and Shakespeare, for whom patronage was important, if not indispensable. By 18th C, thanks largely to the increased reading public and the growth of periodicals like Addison's *Spectator** and Johnson's *Rambler**, patronage was obsolescent, and chiefly required when a writer of slender means, such as Samuel Johnson*, attempted a major task, such as his Dictionary. Johnson's famous letter to Lord Chesterfield is a classic example of rebuke to a neglectful patron. Political parties and leaders by this time provided extensive patronage, *eg* Harley and the Tories to Defoe*. Many writers gained a livelihood through the system by which the universities and landlords inherited from the monasteries (dissolved in the 1530s) the right to appoint parish priests; one example among many is the poet Crabbe*, whose verse tale *The Patron* (*Tales* of 1812) illustrates the unhappy side of patronage.

Patterne, Sir Willoughby

The character referred to in the title of George Meredith's novel *The Egoist**. The name is an ironical reference to his conception of himself as the 'pattern' of gentlemen; he is a parody of Samuel Richardson's* Sir Charles Grandison.

Paul's Cathedral, St

The cathedral of the City of London, and its principal church. The old cathedral was burnt down in the Great Fire of London* (1666) and the present one was built according to the design of Sir Christopher Wren*. Until 18th C not only the churchyard but the building itself was a public meeting-place for much besides Christian worship; news was exchanged there, servants were hired, and business was conducted. The central aisle was called Paul's Walk, and a Paul's Man was a term for one of its frequenters.

Paul's, Children of St

A company of boy actors, chosen from the choirboys of St Paul's Cathedral, who were very popular with audiences at the end of 16th C. Their chief rivals among boy-actors were the Children of the Chapel Royal. Both were to some extent serious rivals of the adult actors – see Shakespeare's *Hamlet* II. ii. The boy companies were used especially for pastoral* plays, such as those of Lyly* and Peele*.

* *Acting, The Profession of.*

St Paul's Cathedral

Paul's, Covent Garden, St

A church overlooking Covent Garden* Market in London. Built in 1635 by Inigo Jones*, it was burnt down in 1795 and then rebuilt according to the original design.

Peachum

In John Gay's *Beggar's Opera**; he is the 'fence' or receiver of stolen goods, whose daughter falls in love with the highwayman, Macheath. His name derives from underworld slang – to 'peach' on someone, *ie* to betray them to the authorities. Peachum keeps his gang of thieves in order by threats to do this.

Peacock, Thomas Love (1785–1866)

Novelist and poet. After unsuccessful attempts in poetry and the theatre, he found his special form in the 'discussion novel': *Headlong Hall* (1816); *Melincourt** (1817); *Nightmare Abbey** (1818); *Maid Marian** (1822); *The Misfortunes of Elphin* (1829); *Crotchet Castle** (1831); *Gryll Grange* (1861). These consist almost entirely of conversation and have very little plot; the characters represent outlooks, ideas, and attitudes such as arouse Peacock's derision, and the prevailing tone is comic and satirical. The conversations are interspersed with songs, often of great charm, and hilarious and extravagant episodes. Peacock's point of view is more 18th C than romantic, emphasizing common sense and proportion but also radicalism* in politics. The comedy is zestful and humane; it is as much opposed to the sterility of the political economists as to the morbidity and eccentricity of poets such as Shelley*, who was his close friend. The form is said to have more resemblance to French 18th-C polemicists and novelists such as Diderot and Voltaire* than to English predecessors, but his son-in-law, the novelist George Meredith*, resembles him in his exuberant humour and vivacious satire, and the novelist Aldous Huxley* continues his mode of sharp caricature and his method of discussion. His sceptical essay *The Four Ages of Poetry* (1820) provoked Shelley's famous *Defence of Poetry* (1821).

Bib: Van Doren, Carl, *Life*; Priestley, J. B., *Life*; Able, A. H., *Meredith and Peacock – A Study in Literary Influence*; House, H., in *All in Due Time*; Brett-Smith, H. F. B. (ed), *Life* in *Works*, Vol I; Mayoux, J. J., *Un Epicurien Anglais: Peacock*; Jack, I., Chap VII in *Oxford History of English Literature*.

Pearl

One of the finest of the great 14th-C alliterative* poems. The author is unknown, but is conjectured to be the same as that of *Sir Gawain and the Green Knight**, *Patience*,* and *Purity**. It is in the same dialect of the north-west Midlands, and is composed in 12-line stanzas of 8-syllable lines. The poet dreams of his dead child, and has a vision of her in Heaven; she rebukes him for his grief and demonstrates that she is in bliss. He plunges into the stream which runs between them in order to reach her, and instantly wakes, resigned to her loss, and in peace of mind.

Peasants' Revolt, The

A great popular uprising that occurred in 1381. The ultimate cause of it was the Black Death* which struck England in 1349 and reduced the population by between a third and a half, causing a serious shortage of labour. Free labourers in consequence demanded higher wages, and non-wage-earning serfs either broke their bondage or had it commuted into free-labouring status. Some became outlaws in the woods, thus adding to popular currency of the folk legends of Robin Hood*; it is no doubt significant that the first mention in literature of this folk hero occurs in Langland's 1377 version of *Piers Plowman** (Passus V – the speech by Sloth). Parliament tried to prevent the rise of wages by the Statute of Labourers (1363), but the attempt to enforce this only increased popular resentment. The immediate cause of the rising was an attempt to raise a tax per head of the population, known as the Poll Tax (poll = head). The rebellion was a truly social one, directed against the rich clergy and the lawyers as well as against the landowners. Peasants from the counties surrounding London invaded the city, broke into the Tower and executed the Archbishop of Canterbury. A rebel leader, Wat Tyler*, was killed by the Lord Mayor. The rebels were eventually dispersed, partly by a show of force, but more by promises to amend their grievances. The promises were not kept, and a bloody revenge on the peasants was taken by the lords who were ruling England on behalf of the boy-king, Richard II*.

* 2.1.1.1; *Ball, John*.

Peel, John (1776–1854)

The hero of a famous English hunting song, *D'ye ken John Peel*. He ran a pack of foxhounds in the Lake District. The words are by John Woodcock Graves.

Peele, George (1558–97)

Poet and dramatist. He was one of the University Wits*. Peele was educated at Christ's Hospital and Oxford. His work comprised various forms of dramatic entertainment characteristic of the taste of the time. His best-known plays are the pastoral play *The Arraignment of Paris* (1584?), acted by the Children of the Royal Chapel, and *The Old Wives' Tale* (1593?), which is something like a dramatized folk-tale. He also wrote a biblical play, *The Love of King David and Fair Bethsabe* (1588?), and patriotic history plays, *The Famous Chronicle of King Edward I* (printed 1593) and *The Battle of Alcazar with the Death of Captain Stukeley* (1588?), and in 1585 and 1591 he designed pageants for the London Lord Mayor's Show. Other plays have been attributed to him. As a precursor of Shakespeare he has a similar importance to Greene*; he helped to give greater smoothness and flexibility to the use of the blank verse* line, and to combine elements appealing to popular taste with qualities of courtly refinement, thus contributing to the rich variety of tone for which the greater Elizabethan drama is unique.

* 5.1.2.4.

Bib: Prouty, C. T., *Life and Works*; Cheffaud, P. H., *George Peele*.

Peerages

* *Titles of Nobility*.

Pegasus /ˈpegəsəs/

In Greek myth, a winged horse which sprang from the body of Medusa (**Gorgons*) when Perseus* had beheaded her. Ovid* makes Perseus ride Pegasus when he slays the monster that threatens Andromeda*. It was with the aid of Pegasus that Bellerophon* slew another monster, the Chimaera*. The spring Hippocrene*, on Mount Helicon, sacred to the Muses*, is said to have sprung from the hillside at a blow of his hoof, and Pegasus is hence associated with the Muses and especially with poetry.

Peisistratus /paiˈsistrətəs/

In ancient Greek history, a ruler of Athens* in 6th C BC. He enriched the city with public buildings, and was a notable patron of the arts, especially poetry.

Pelagian /pəˈleidʒjən/

The adjective from Pelagius, the Latin name of an early British theologian (4th-5th C AD). He is associated with a doctrine ('the Pelagian heresy') held to be false by most branches of the Christian

Church – that it is within human power to be good; this is contrary to the Christian doctrine of 'Original Sin', according to which human beings relying on their own efforts must inevitably sooner or later do wrong, since moral goodness depends on the aid of Divine Grace.

Peleus /ˈpiːljuːs/

In Greek myth, the son of Aeacus, king of Aegina, and father of Achilles* by the nymph* Thetis. It was at their wedding feast that Eris, goddess of discord, threw the 'apple of discord' among the assembled gods and goddesses, an incident which led to the 'judgement of Paris'.

* *Paris.*

Pelion and Ossa, Mounts /ˈpiːljən – ˈosə/

Mountains in Greece. In ancient Greek myth, the Giants*, in their war against the gods, piled Pelion on to Ossa in order to reach Heaven. Pelion was the home of the Centaurs*.

Pelleas, Sir

One of the knights of King Arthur's* court; in Malory's *Morte d'Arthur** he is described as marrying Nimue, the Lady of the Lake. He may be developed from the ancient British god of the underworld, Pwyll, and she from Rhiannon, a fertility goddess. Tennyson's poem (one of the *Idylls of the King**) *Pelleas and Ettare* is about his unhappy earlier love for Ettare, a type of feminine heartlessness and vanity.

Peloponnesian War /peləpəˈniːʃn/

Between the ancient Greek states of Athens* and Sparta* (431–404 BC). It ended with the victory of Sparta, which succeeded Athens as the leading state of Greece. The Peloponnese is that part of Greece south of the Isthmus of Corinth; in the Middle Ages it was known as the Morea.

Pelops /ˈpiːlops/

In Greek myth, the grandson of Zeus* and the son of Tantalus*, who boiled him, cut him into pieces, and served him up to the gods. They realized the crime and none of them took of the dish except Demeter who ate his shoulder. Hermes* restored him to life and gave him an ivory shoulder.

Later, Pelops won his bride Hippodameia by bribing her father's charioteer, Myrtilus, not to defeat him in a chariot-race, but when Myrtilus claimed his reward, Pelops threw him into the sea. Myrtilus cursed him and his posterity with his dying breath. Hence arose the grim tragedies afflicting his sons Atreus and Thyestes*, and his grandson Agamemnon*.

Pembroke, Mary Herbert, Countess of (1561–1621) /ˈpembruk/

Sister of the poet, Sir Philip Sidney* and a famous patroness of literature. Sidney wrote his prose romance *The Arcadia** for her, and she edited this and prepared it and his poems for publication in 1590–1. Spenser* refers to her under the name of Clorinda in his poem in honour of the dead Sidney, *Astrophel*, and he dedicated to her his *Ruins of Time*. She assisted the poet Samuel Daniel* who was tutor to her son, as well as other poets including Ben Jonson*. She was one of the most enlightened patrons in an age in which literature depended greatly on enlightened patronage.

* *Patronage in Literature.*

Penal System

As in most societies without efficient police forces, punishments were severe in England until the establishment of the Metropolitan Police by Robert Peel and his reform of the penal system between 1823 and 1827. They tended to become more severe as society became more settled and prosperous, in order to deter crime, especially robbery, by terror, so that by 1800 there were 200 offences punishable by hanging. However, the penal laws were not consistently formulated or applied. Until the reign of Henry VIII* the privilege known as 'Benefit of Clergy', according to which those in any kind of priestly orders could not be punished by lay courts, was apt to be interpreted in such a way that educated people were treated leniently. Later, juries would return verdicts of 'Not Guilty' when they were moved to compassion, or magistrates would interpret the accusation mercifully. The normal form of capital punishment was by hanging, though decapitation, as more dignified, was used for the aristocracy. In 17th C, when the colonies in America had become established, transportation was often used instead; after the loss of the colonies in 1783, Australia was substituted. Transportation was finally abolished in 1864. Execution was public, and watching it a favourite amusement, until in mid-19th C public hanging was abolished. In 16th C burning was used for religious heretics and for witches*; for a short time boiling was used as a capital punishment for poisoning.

For minor offences, whipping was a common punishment, and it too was public until 19th C, to increase the disgrace. Confinement in the stocks or the pillory* – wooden structures with holes for the head, the legs and the arms – was used for some offences, and there were also, of course, imprisonment and fines. Ducking in a pond or river was reserved for bad-tempered wives.

By 1861, crimes punishable by hanging had been reduced to four (murder, treason, piracy, arson) and in 1965 capital punishment was abolished. Corporal punishment was abolished in 1948 except for attacks on warders in prison.

Torture was legal to extract evidence until it was abolished in 18th C. Mutilation – cutting out the tongue or cutting off the ears, nose or hand – was a penalty for certain offences, especially of a treasonable nature, and it survived in law until 1870, but it was not used after 17th C.

* *Prisons.*

Pendennis, The History of

A novel by William Makepeace Thackeray*, published serially 1848–50. It is about worldly upper class society in London, and the fortunes of a young man, Arthur Pendennis, whose 'bad angels' are his cynical, materialistic uncle, Major

Pendennis, and the pretty but selfish Blanche Amory whom he nearly marries. Blanche's father, an escaped convict who is thought to be dead but is in fact – as Major Pendennis knows – still alive, haunts the book in the guise of Colonel Altamont. Arthur's 'good angels' are his widowed mother, Helen; Laura Bell, whom he eventually marries and whom his mother has adopted; and George Warrington, a friend with whom he shares rooms. The good influences are, however, less imaginatively presented than the bad ones, and the distinctiveness of the novel depends on its amusing portrayal of the vulgarity, intrigue, and materialism of London society and the journalistic and literary world of Fleet Street*.

Pendragon /pen'dragən/

An ancient British title for a chieftain, meaning 'chief dragon'. The dragon was the war standard, and is today the unofficial crest of the Welsh nation. As a name, it is chiefly known as that of the father of King Arthur*, Uther Pendragon.

Penelope /pə'neləpi/

In Homer's *Odyssey**, the wife of Odysseus*, king of Ithaca. During his long absence, she is pestered by numerous suitors who seek her in marriage on the assumption that he will never return. She puts them off by telling them that they must wait until she has woven a winding-sheet for Laertes, the father of Odysseus. She weaves all day, but every night she unweaves the day's work, so that it never draws to completion. Eventually the trick is exposed by her maids. Odysseus returns after an absence of 20 years, and slays the suitors.

***Penseroso, Il* (1632)**

A poem by John Milton*. It celebrates the pleasures of the studious and retired life, and is written as a companion to *L'Allegro**. The title is Italian (slightly inaccurate) and means 'the reflective man'.

Pentameter /pen'tamitə/

In English verse, usually five iambic feet, *ie* with the stress coming on every second syllable. The line has been the commonest in use since Chaucer*, *eg* the *Prologue to the Canterbury Tales*:

He knew the taverns well in every town.

The commonest English uses of the iambic pentameter are in blank verse* and in heroic couplets* (as in the *Prologue*).

* *Metre.*

Pentateuch /'pentətju:k/

In the Bible, the first five books of the Old Testament: *Genesis*, *Exodus*, *Leviticus*, *Numbers*, *Deuteronomy*. They were traditionally ascribed to the authorship of Moses*.

Pentecost /'pentikost/

A Jewish feast, corresponding to the Christian harvest festival, but also a Christian feast celebrating the descent of the Holy Spirit on Christ's disciples (in the Bible, *Acts* 2) – an event which took place during the feast of Pentecost. In Britain, the day is known as Whit-Sunday. It occurs on the seventh Sunday after Easter*.

Penthesilea /penθesi'li:ə/

In Greek myth, the daughter of Ares*, god of war, and an Amazon queen; as herself the queen of the Amazons, she led her race of female warriors against the Greeks in the siege of Troy*, in which she was killed by Achilles. Achilles mourned her perished youth and beauty and killed Thersites* for mocking him.

Pentonville Prison

Built 1840–2, in London; it was part of a scheme to substitute imprisonment for transportation to the colonies for criminal offences.

* *Penal System.*

Pepys, Samuel (1633–1703) /pi:ps/

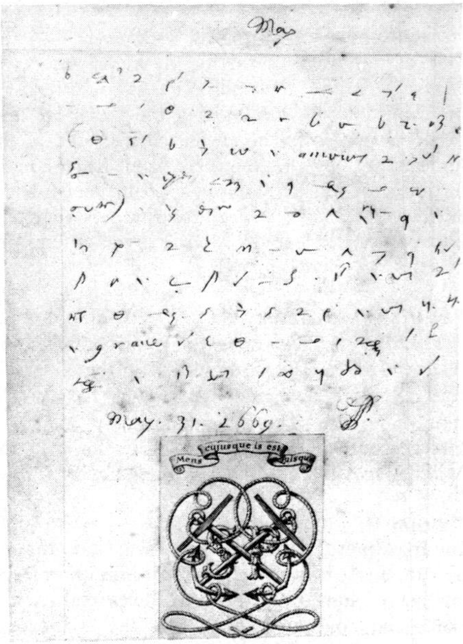

Diarist. He was an industrious and highly efficient official in the Admiralty Office, and a man who had musical culture and persistent if amateurish scientific and literary interests. As secretary to his cousin, Edward Montagu, Earl of Sandwich, he was aboard the fleet which brought Charles II* back to England at the Restoration* in 1660. His official position in the Admiralty gave him the confidence of the king's brother, James Duke of York, who was Lord High Admiral, and an opportunity for direct observation of court life. He was elected to Parliament and knew the world of politics, was a friend of a number of leading writers and musicians, and held distinguished appointments in the City of London. He was thus centrally placed to observe his age, and with all his seriousness he was pleasure-loving and witty.

His diary (kept 1660–9) is a unique document not only because he brought to it these qualities and advantages (many of which were shared by his friend the diarist John Evelyn*) but because he kept it for his eye alone, and consequently wrote with unusual candour and objectivity. To prevent his servants and family from prying into it, he used a kind of shorthand cypher, which was not interpreted until 1825, when part of the diary was first published. The first more or less complete edition was in 1896. Of all diaries in English, it has the greatest appeal to the general reader, as well as having outstanding value for the historian.

* *Diaries.*

Bib: Lives by J. R. Tanner, Arthur Bryant, and J. H. Wilson. Letters edited by J. R. Tanner, Arthur Bryant, and J. H. Wilson. Marburg, C., *Mr Pepys and Mr Evelyn*; *Diary* ed Robert Latham.

Perceval /ˈpɜːsivl/

The hero of an ancient Celtic folk-legend on the theme of the child of noble origin who is brought up primitively in ignorance of his high birth, and later recovers his noble status by excelling in some adventure in the presence of aristocracy and princes. This kind of story has been classified as 'the Aryan Expulsion and Return Formula', and other examples of it are the Greek myth of Perseus*, and the Latin one of Romulus* and Remus (*Encyclopaedia Britannica*). In the 12th-C French romance of *Perceval* by Chrétien de Troyes* and the German *Parzival* by Wolfram von Eschenbach, Perceval becomes one of the knights of King Arthur* and succeeds Gawain* as the hero of the quest for the Holy Grail*, as he himself was later displaced by Sir Galahad*. The English 14th-C romance tells of his childhood and adventures as a knight of King Arthur, but does not mention the Grail. In 15th C Malory describes, in his *Morte d'Arthur**, how Perceval, Galahad, and Bors eventually discover the Grail.

Percy

The name of a noble family closely connected with Northumberland*, and famous in history, ballad*, and Shakespeare's dramas *1 & 2 Henry IV**. They are especially famous for their border warfare with the Scots, and in particular with the Scottish border family of Douglas.

The English history of the family originates with William de Perci, a follower of William I*. A descendant, Henry Percy, was one of the English commanders in the attempt of Edward I* to conquer Scotland, but he was driven out by the Scottish leader Robert the Bruce*; he built the great family fortress of Alnwick in the north of England. His son captured the Scottish king David II at the battle of Neville's Cross (1346).

Later in 14th C come the two Percies who are famous in ballad and Shakespeare's drama – Henry Percy, 1st Earl of Northumberland, and his son Sir Henry, nicknamed Hotspur. The ballads *Chevy Chase** and *Otterbourne** describe the battle of Hotspur and his brother against the Scots under Douglas by the River Otterbourne in 1388; Douglas was killed, but the Percies were taken prisoner. Later Hotspur and his father assisted Henry Bolingbroke to seize the throne from Richard II* in 1399 – the theme of Shakespeare's *Richard II**. In 1402, Hotspur fought the battle of Homildon Hill against the Scots under another Douglas, and it was now Douglas who was taken prisoner. In the meantime, relationships with Henry IV had been deteriorating, and Hotspur broke into open rebellion over rights to possession of the Scottish prisoners. In 1403, in alliance with the Welsh chieftain Glendower and the Scottish Douglas, he met the king's forces at the Battle of Shrewsbury, and was defeated and killed; this is the subject of Shakespeare's *1 Henry IV*. His father, the Earl, was killed at the battle of Bramham Moor (1408). The Percies were deprived of their lands, but these were restored to them by the next king, Henry V*.

The Percies continued to be important in English history, but they cease to have prominence in literature. In 18th C the male line died out, but the name of Percy was taken by the family which succeeded to the lands and titles.

Percy's Reliques of Ancient English Poetry /ˈreliks/

A very influential anthology of old English ballad* poetry published in 1765 by Thomas Percy (1729–1811), later Bishop of Dromore. In making the collection he was partly inspired by the success of James Macpherson's rewriting of Scottish Gaelic legends especially those alleged to be by the mythical poet Ossian (**Oisin*). Macpherson's poems were in fact largely of his own composition; Percy only 'civilized' his English poems, so that his versions are usually somewhat changed from the originals. Nonetheless their simplicity and power survived Percy's editing, and counteracted the rather forced and artificial style of eloquence which the educated public of 18th C were becoming used to. This audience now recovered its ear for a very different voice, one which poets like Chatterton*, Scott*, and Coleridge* all used with varying degrees of talent. Percy gave the ballad a resurrected interest and life which has lasted it to the present day. He was not, however, quite first in the field: Addison* had already praised *Chevy Chase** in the *Spectator**, and the poet Gray* had already written in imitation of primitive poetry. Part of the success of the *Reliques* was a consequence of the characteristically 18th-C interest in archaeology; the modern Society of Antiquaries was founded in 1718.

* 4.1.3

Peregrine Pickle, The Adventures of (1751)

A novel by Tobias Smollett*. The hero is an adventurer seeking his fortune in England and on the Continent. Its form is a succession of episodes without a uniting structure, depending for its interest on the vigour of depiction of the characters and incidents. It contains famous eccentric characters, especially the retired sailor and his associates, Commodore Trunnion, Lieutenant Hatchway, and Tom Pipes. The episodes give opportunity for much social and political satire, from English village life upwards, and shows an awareness of social structure like that found in Fielding's novels. Trunnion and his circle were an inspiration to Laurence Sterne's* Uncle Toby in *Tristram Shandy**.

Perfectibilism

The optimistic doctrine that individuals and society are capable of achieving perfection in living. The French Revolution*, with its reliance on reason for the solution of all human problems, encouraged perfectibilism, and the philosopher William Godwin* was an English example. Peacock*, in *Headlong Hall* (1816), presents a humorous version of a perfectibilist in Mr Foster.

Peri /ˈpiəri/

In Persian myth, a supernatural being, resembling a European fairy.

Pericles /ˈperikli:z/

In Greek history, a leading statesman of Athens* in 5th C BC. His period of power (460–429) was that when Athens was at her greatest, politically and artistically. The Peloponnesian War*, which ended in her defeat by Sparta*, began in 431. At the end of that year Pericles made his great funeral oration, which included a survey of Athenian greatness and appealed to the national pride of the Athenians. It is recorded by the 5th-C Athenian historian Thucydides*.

Pericles, Prince of Tyre

A play, Acts III–V of which are considered to be by Shakespeare*; Acts I–II are mainly or entirely by another hand. The play was published in 1609 in an untrustworthy edition, but it was not included in a collected edition of Shakespeare's works until (in the same version) the third folio* of 1664.The story is based on a well-known late classical romance, Apollonius of Tyre, used by John Gower* in his 14th-C cycle of poems *Confessio Amantis** (Book 8). Gower appears in the play to speak the chorus, but the play does not follow his version in all respects; another source book was Lawrence Twine's *The Pattern of Painful Adventures*, first published in 1576.

In the first two acts, the play has a very rambling structure, but from Act III it follows a pattern characteristic of Shakespeare's last four plays; though in each the pattern is varied, they have in common a central relationship between a prince and his daughter – in this case Pericles and Marina. Pericles is separated from her and is led to believe that both she and her mother Thaisa are dead. By the end of the play, however, he recovers them both, and the recovery restores him to happiness and health. The scene (V. i) in which Marina, at first unrecognizing of and unrecognized by her father, restores him from his stupor of sorrow, is of remarkable beauty, and recalls the scene in *King Lear* (IV. vii) in which Cordelia restores her father.

* *Reconciliation Plays of Shakespeare.*

Periodicals

* *Reviews and Periodicals.*

Periods of English Literature

These are often designated rather loosely. The following is an alphabetical list of terms for different periods, with an indication of the kinds of literature to which they chiefly apply.

*Augustan**. This refers to the period in which English literature was dominated by neo-classical ideas on literature and culture; standards were taken from ancient Greece and Rome, and in particular from the finest period of Latin poetry under the first Roman Emperor, Augustus Caesar (reigned 27 BC–AD 14). In English literature the Augustan period is in its briefest limits more or less coterminous with the lifetime of the poet Alexander Pope* (1688–1744), but it is commonly broadened to include the entire 18th C. It is chiefly used in reference to poetry (Dryden*, Pope, Johnson* etc.) but includes the essay and prose satire (Addison*, Swift*, Johnson, Gibbon*, Goldsmith* etc.). The novel (Defoe*, Richardson*, Fielding*) less obviously shows neo-classic qualities – the Romans had no novelists – and the term is not so often made to include novels written within the same period.

*Caroline**. The reign of Charles I* (1625–49). The term is above all used for lyric poets both of the Cavalier* school (Lovelace*, Suckling*, Carew* etc.) and of the later Metaphysical* school (Vaughan*, Crashaw*, Cowley*). But it is also used for the last phase of the Elizabethan blank-verse drama – Ford*, Massinger*, Shirley* – and for some prose, *eg* the earlier work of Sir Thomas Browne*. 'Caroline' characterizes qualities of wit, grace and refinement associated with the court of Charles I.

*Edwardian**. Used to characterize the cultural qualities of the reign of Edward VII* (1901–10). It is less often applied to literature than to art, architecture, and social history. However, it is associated with the earlier and best work of the novelists Wells*, Bennett*, Galsworthy*, and a kind of witty paradoxical writing practised by Shaw*, Chesterton* and Belloc*. Some of the best work of Forster* and of Conrad* also comes within the period, although, perhaps because their reputations now stand higher, they are less often restricted by this period term. 'Edwardian' is often extended to the outbreak of World War I in 1914 – but see under Georgian Poetry*.

Elizabethan. The reign of Elizabeth I* (1558–1603). Elizabethan literature is that of the rich decade 1590–1600, and the term applies particularly to forms flourishing in that decade, *eg* the so-called Elizabethan novel* (really a kind of prose romance), and the sonnet*. It is also, of course, applied to the poetic drama, but in regard to this it is used varyingly. It may refer to the first decade and a half of the great movement of English poetic drama, *ie* the work of Kyd*, Greene*, Peele*, Marlowe*, and the early Shakespeare; or it may be used to cover the period of the whole movement – from 1580 to 1640.

Georgian. Used for the reigns of George I (accession 1714) to George IV (d 1830). It is sometimes used more narrowly to cover 18th C from 1714. The term is used for architecture rather than literature.

*Georgian Poets**. This refers to successive volumes of verse anthologies, of which 5 appeared 1912–22. The term 'Georgian' refers to the reign of George V* (1910–36), but it is now used generally in reference to the kind of poetry published in these anthologies – short, musical poems, with strong sentiment but not making strong demands on the intellect.

*Jacobean**. The reign of James I* (1603–25). The term applies to the poetic drama, *ie* later Shakespeare, Ben Jonson*, Middleton*, Webster*, Tourneur* etc. Whether applied to the drama or to non-dramatic poetry (*eg* the earlier Metaphysicals, notably Donne*) 'Jacobean' often denotes the strength, ruggedness and profundity of much of the writing of the reign. However it was a complex period; the most popular dramatists were Beaumont* and Fletcher*, who were neither rugged nor profound, and the lyrical poems of Ben Jonson were strong but shapely. The Jacobean prose writers included notable sermon writers (Donne, Andrewes*) and the rationalistic Bacon*.

Medieval. Literally, 'of the Middle Ages', especially from the Norman Conquest (1066) to the accession of the House of Tudor* (Henry VII 1485–1509). More especially, the term is used for the poetry and prose of 14th and 15th C – Langland*, Chaucer*, Malory* etc, since these were the centuries of important literary production. It was in 14th C that English once more became the literary language throughout English society. Medieval literature is often designated linguistically as 'Middle English'.

Modern Literature. When this does not refer merely to literature currently being published, it is made to include works of the past which are the immediate shaping forces of the present. Thus, in the novel, 'modern' is often made to include Joseph Conrad* (working life from 1895), Henry James* (from 1870), James Joyce* (from 1904) and D. H. Lawrence* (from 1914). In poetry, 'modern' often goes back to the mid-point of the career of W. B. Yeats* (about 1914) and the early work of T. S. Eliot* (1917). The poetry of G. M. Hopkins* (1844–89) is often included as modern, because it was not published until 1918, and then had a large influence. 'Modern literature' sometimes refers to narrower limits, however, *eg* writing since 1945.

Old English. Literature of the earlier Middle Ages, *ie* Anglo-Saxon* writing from before the Conquest of 1066.

Queen Anne. 1702–14: the earlier Augustan period, including the early poetry of Pope, some of the prose of Swift, and the essays of Addison and Steele, etc.

*Regency**. Strictly, this refers to the period when the Prince of Wales (later George IV) became Prince Regent during the final illness of his father, George III, *ie* the years 1811–20. In fact, it is often used to cover the first 20 years of 19th C; it includes the work of the great romantic poets (Wordsworth*, Coleridge*, Shelley*, Keats*, and Byron*) as well as the work of writers still dominated by classical influences, *eg* the poet Crabbe* and the novelist Jane Austen*.

*Renaissance**. This is a vague term for English literature. It may be said to begin with the first English humanists* (More, Colet, Grocyn, Linacre) in the reigns of Henry VII* (1485–1509) and VIII* (1509–47), and to extend throughout 16th C, reaching its high point under Elizabeth I*; it is even made to extend to the middle of 17th C. The term refers to that period when classical influences of ancient Greek and especially Latin literature began to affect English writing in a new, more scholarly way than in the past; at its peak, it applies to the period (approx. 1580–1620) when these classical influences combined with contemporary French, Italian and Spanish influences to strengthen the native English tradition to the peculiar excellence of the age of Shakespeare. The Renaissance ceases to be applicable as a period term when, after 1660, the fertilizing classical influences became consolidated in the neo-classic Augustan period. A useful starting-point for the English Renaissance may be taken as Caxton's* introduction of the printing press (1476).

Romantic. The English romantics are usually identified with six poets: Blake*, Wordsworth, Coleridge, Byron, Shelley and Keats. The Romantic period may be thought of as beginning with Blake's *Songs of Innocence** in 1789 – a convenient date also because the nature of Romanticism is bound up with the French Revolution* which began in the same year. However, a far better known and more influential book was Wordsworth and Coleridge's *Lyrical Ballads** of 1798, which may be accepted as the effective opening of the Romantic period. By 1830, all these poets except Wordsworth and Coleridge were dead; Coleridge died in 1834, and Wordsworth's most creative life was past. Thus the Romantic period proper lasted for the first 30 years of 19th C. The term 'late romantics', however, may extend over the rest of 19th C.

*Stuart**. The Stuart sovereigns reigned over Britain from 1603 to 1714, but the term is not usually applied to the last of the reigns – that of Queen Anne (1702–14).

*Tudor**. The Tudor sovereigns reigned from 1485 to 1603; however, since the reign of Elizabeth I* is commonly regarded separately as 'the Elizabethan period', such terms as 'the Tudor poets' usually refer to 16th-C poets before her reign, notably Skelton*, Wyatt*, and Surrey*.

*Victorian**. Queen Victoria reigned 1837–1901. The term 'Victorian' covers all forms of literature in this period, especially the novel, poetry, and the essays of such writers as J. S. Mill*, Carlyle*, Ruskin*, and Macaulay*.

Periphrasis /pəˈrifrəsis/

The use of a phrase or group of words in the place

of a single word, *eg* Wordsworth's* 'feathered tenants of the flood' instead of 'duck'.

Perrault, Charles (1628–1703) /'perəu/

French author, chiefly known in England for his collection of fairy tales published in 1697, *Histoires et Contes du Temps Passé* ('Stories and Tales from the Past') subtitled *Contes de ma Mère l'Oie* '(Tales of Mother Goose'). They were translated into English by Robert Samber (1729), and have remained the best known fairy tales among English children. They were retold by Perrault from popular sources, and are as follows: *Sleeping Beauty*; *Red Riding Hood*; *Blue Beard*; *Puss in Boots*; *The Fairy*; *Cinderella*; *Riquet with the Tuft*; *Hop o' my Thumb*. Several of them provide the themes for modern Christmas pantomimes*.

* *Fairies.*

Persephone (Proserpine) /pə:'sefəni/

In Greek myth, the daughter of the corn-goddess, Demeter*, and Zeus. Hades, god of the underworld, carried her off while she was gathering flowers, and Demeter wandered in search of her while the earth went barren. To save the life of the earth, Zeus persuaded Hades to surrender Persephone, but as she had consumed a pomegranate seed in the underworld, she was forced to spend half the year only on the surface of the earth with her mother, and to return to Hades for the other half. Persephone is thus the spring and autumn goddess: the spring announces her return, and the autumn, her departure.

Persepolis /pə:'sepəlis/

The greatest city of ancient Persia, and the burial-place of her kings; it was partially destroyed by Alexander the Great (331 BC).

Perseus /'pə:sju:s/

In Greek myth, the son of Danae* and the god Zeus*. The legend about him has the following episodes:

[1] Zeus caused Danae to conceive him by pouring into her as a shower of gold. Acrisius, father of Danae, learnt that her son was destined to kill him; to prevent the fulfilment of this prophecy he caused the mother and son to be launched into the sea in a chest. They were rescued by Polydectes, king of Seriphos.

[2] Polydectes fell in love with Danae, and tried to rid himself of Perseus by sending him to fetch the head of Medusa*, the sight of whom turned men to stone. Perseus discovered the whereabouts of the Gorgons*, of whom Medusa was one, from the Graeae. These were three ancient women who shared a single eye and a single tooth among them; by stealing the eye and the tooth, Perseus persuaded them to give him the information he needed. He also stole from the Graeae a magic bag and a helmet that made him invisible. In some versions of the story, the goddess Athene* gave him a shield as highly polished as a mirror, the god Hermes* gave him wings for his shoes and a sword, and he got the helmet from Hades*, god of the underworld.

[3] With the aid of this equipment, Perseus beheaded Medusa, from whose body sprang the winged horse, Pegasus*. He passed through the country of Ethiopia, where he learnt that Andromeda*, daughter of King Cepheus, was in the act of being sacrificed to a sea-monster sent by the sea-god Poseidon, whom Cepheus' queen, Cassiopeia*, had offended. He rescued Andromeda by slaying the monster, and married her.

[4] In some versions, another adventure on his return from slaying the Medusa was to turn into stone the giant Atlas*, who supported the heavens, or perhaps the world on his shoulders; Atlas thus became the great mountain chain (in North Africa) which bears his name today.

[5] Perseus then returned to Seriphos, where he rescued his mother from the undesired attentions of Polydectes by petrifying him with Medusa's head. He then offered the head to the goddess Athene, who henceforth wore it on her shield.

[6] He next returned to his birth-country, Argos, where the prophecy was fulfilled that he would one day kill his grandfather. This happened accidentally when Perseus was throwing the discus at funeral games. Unwilling to succeed to the throne of the man whom he had killed, Perseus reigned over Tyryns and Mycenae, where he established the family which was destined to produce Heracles.

Personification

* *Figures of Speech.*

Persuasion

The last completed novel by Jane Austen*; it was published, incompletely revised, in 1818, the year following her death. The theme is the coming together of the heroine, Anne Elliot, and the hero, Captain Wentworth, in spite of social obstacles, the selfishness and foolishness of her father (Sir Walter) and sisters, and the rival attraction of the more obviously seductive Musgrove sisters. Anne, before the novel begins, had already refused Wentworth on the counsel of Lady Russell, who stands in place of mother to her; Lady Russell had misunderstood Wentworth's character and feared his poverty. Anne's personality is diffident and humble, but at the opening of the story she has begun to realize that the refusal was a mistake, likely to ruin her happiness. The renewal of Wentworth's love and his eventual marriage to Anne is a victory: their strong and distinctive but quiet and reticent qualities overcome the cruder and shallower social characteristics of their circumstances.

Peter Bell

A poem in ballad form by William Wordsworth* published in 1819 but written in 1798. Peter's lawlessness is redeemed by his experiences when he goes in search of the widow of a drowned man whom he has found. The poem contained some of the ridiculously flat passages that marred Wordsworth's poetry; these caused it to be parodied. Shelley*, in his *Peter Bell the Third* (1819, published 1839), made the poem an excuse for an

attack on Wordsworth, although he had only read a review of it.

Peter Grimes

A verse tale in 10-syllable couplets* by George Crabbe*; it is *Letter XXII* in the series composing *The Borough* (1810). Peter is the son of a poor fisherman who tries to bring him up kindly and religiously. However, the boy is violent and wilful, and causes the death of his father by ill-treatment. He then lives a solitary life, distrusted and feared by the neighbourhood, with only a boy from an orphanage for company. He treats the boy brutally until the latter dies from ill-treatment, after which he misuses two other boys in the same way. He is then forbidden by the magistrates to employ any more pauper boys as apprentices. He lives a still more solitary life, until he is found drifting distractedly along the desolate coast in his boat, and is taken to the parish hospital. There as he lies dying, he tells how he has been haunted by the ghosts of his dead father and the three boys, who never leave him, and ceaselessly condemn him to an eternity of such lonely drifting. The story was used by Benjamin Britten for his opera*, *Peter Grimes*, 1945.

Peter Pan

A children's play by J. M. Barrie*, originally called *Peter Pan, or the Boy who wouldn't grow up*. It became, and remains, extremely popular for its whimsical charm and its ingenious use of some traditional features of children's romances, such as Red Indians, the pirate Captain Hook who lives in fear of a crocodile which has already consumed one of his arms, and the fairy Tinkerbell.

Peter the Hermit (1050–1115)

A monk whose preaching led to the first Crusade (1096) to recapture the Holy Land from the Muslims.

* *Crusades, The.*

Peter's Pence

A medieval tax paid by England to the Pope until it was abolished by Henry VIII* in 16th C. Its origins are obscure. It survives as a voluntary contribution by English Roman Catholics.

Peterloo Massacre, The

At a political meeting advocating the reform of parliamentary elections at St Peter's Field, Manchester, in 1819, the magistrates took alarm and ordered soldiers to attack the crowd. A small number of people were killed, and a large number were injured. The event caused intense resentment against the government of the time, and was nicknamed 'Peterloo' in ironic reference to the Anglo-Prussian victory over Napoleon at Waterloo* in 1815. It provoked Shelley's fierce poem *The Mask of Anarchy**. It was also one of the causes of the establishment of the Metropolitan Police Force by Robert Peel in 1829, so that there should be a possibility of keeping order among crowds without the use of soldiers and firearms.

* *Reform Bills, Parliamentary.*

Petition of Right

A demand leading to a law forced on King Charles I* by Parliament* in 1628; it ended imprisonment without trial, the raising of taxes without parliamentary authorization, martial law (*ie* legal judgements enforced under military authority), and the billeting of troops on private houses as an indirect means of forcing political obedience. It was the first major clash between Charles and Parliament in the conflict which ended in the Civil War* of 1642–46.

Petrarch (Francesco Petrarca) (1304–74) /ˈpetra:k/

Italian poet and scholar. He was famous outside Italy even in his lifetime; Chaucer* certainly admired him, but does not show his influence. This influence was very strong on English poets in 16th C. Petrarch was the first great practitioner of the sonnet*; the idealism of his sonnets to Laura set a tradition for this kind of poem in Italy and France, which English sonneteers – Wyatt*, Sidney*, Spenser* – partly emulated. Petrarch was important as a scholar throughout Europe; his collection of ancient Greek and Latin manuscripts and his use of classical writers as models made him one of the great initiators of the Renaissance*.

Phaeacians /fiːˈeiʃənz/

In Homer's *Odyssey**, the inhabitants of the island Scheria which Odysseus reached after leaving Calypso*; it was ruled over by Alcinous, the father of Nausicaa*.

Phaedra /ˈfiːdrə/

In Greek myth, the daughter of Minos* and the wife of Theseus* of Athens. She fell in love with Theseus' son Hippolytus; when he rejected her, she accused him to Theseus of trying to seduce her, thus causing his death. She is the subject of tragedies by Euripides*, Seneca*, and Racine*.

Phaeton /ˈfeitən/

In Greek myth, son of the sun-god Helios and the nymph Clymene. The sun was envisaged as a burning chariot that drove round the earth; Phaeton took charge of his father's chariot, but, losing control of his father's horses, he drove it too near the earth. To save the earth from being consumed by fire, Zeus* slew Phaeton with a thunderbolt, and he fell into the river Eridanus (the Po in Italy). He was buried by the nymphs, and his sisters, who came to weep at his tomb, were changed into poplar trees. Their tears were said to form the amber which was plentiful by this river.

In 19th C, the name 'phaeton' was given to a kind of light carriage.

Pharisees /ˈfarisiːz/

An ancient Jewish sect, composed especially of religious teachers. They adhered to the doctrine that the Jews were a separate and privileged race by virtue of their special relationship with God; and they regarded as Jews all who, whatever their racial descent, were obedient to the law of Moses*. Because of their rigid adherence to this law, they are often, though not invariably, represented in the New Testament as hypocrites who attached more importance to external behaviour than to inner righteousness. Hence in English, 'pharisee' is often synonymous with 'hypocrite'.

Pheidias (Phidias) /ˈfaidias/

In ancient Greece, a famous sculptor of 5th-C BC Athens, during the rule of Pericles*.

Philaster, or Love lies a-bleeding /fiˈlastə/

A romantic play by Francis Beaumont* and John Fletcher*; it was produced in 1611, and is in blank verse*. It is the first in a style of tragicomedy* which became characteristic of the English theatre during the next 30 years. Of all Beaumont and Fletcher's collaborations, it is perhaps the most famous; it derives from the prose romances of chivalry popular in France and Spain, and to some extent (*eg* Sidney's *Arcadia**) in England. The plot is characteristic: Philaster is rightful king of Sicily, but his throne has been usurped by the king of Calabria, with whose daughter, Arethusa, he is in love. He keeps communication with her through his page, Bellario. Her father wants her to marry Pharamond of Spain, and to avoid this she reveals to him the love affair between Pharamond and Megra, a lady of her father's court. In revenge Megra makes out that Arethusa has been having an affair with Bellario, whom Philaster accordingly dismisses. It then turns out that Bellario is a girl disguised as a page for love of Philaster. This situation seems to be borrowed from Shakespeare's *Twelfth Night**, but Shakespeare combined poignant truth to natural feelings with the romantic extravagance of the plot. Beaumont and Fletcher's emotion is obviously 'poetic' but not convincing.

* 5.1.3.3.

Philemon and Baucis /fiˈliːmon – ˈboːsis/

A tale by the Roman poet Ovid*, from the eighth book of his *Metamorphoses**. They are an aged peasant couple and very poor, but they give hospitality to the gods Zeus* and Hermes*, disguised as travellers. In reward, their cottage is transformed into a temple, of which they are made priest and priestess; they are also permitted to die in the same hour, and after death they are transformed into trees with intertwining boughs. Dryden's version (1693) of Ovid's poem is one of his best translations*; Swift* also wrote a poem on the subject (1709).

Philistines /ˈfilistainz/

In the original sense, a race inhabiting the coast of Palestine in biblical times; their epic wars of survival against the Jews are described in the Old Testament, especially in the books of *Samuel* and *Joshua*.

In a secondary meaning, the term is applied to those who are indifferent or actively hostile to artistic and cultural values. This common use was introduced by Matthew Arnold* (*Culture and Anarchy* 1869; *Essays in Criticism** I – essay on Heine). Arnold divided the English society of his day into three classes of cultural indifference: the upper class were barbarians; the middle class, philistines; the working class, the populace. By this he meant that the upper class underestimated cultural values, the middle class ignored them, and the populace was ignorant of them. Arnold had derived this use of 'philistines' from the Germans, who applied it to townspeople as opposed to students in university towns.

Philoctetes /filəkˈtiːtiːz/

In Greek legend, a great archer and the possessor of a deadly bow and arrows given to his father by

Heracles*. During the siege of Troy*, he was abandoned on the isle of Lemnos owing to a snake-bite that refused to heal. However, the Greeks were told by an oracle* that victory was impossible to them without the weapons of Philoctetes. Accordingly, Odysseus* and Diomedes* were sent to fetch him from the island; he arrived before Troy in the tenth year of the war, and was cured of his wound. He then slew Paris*, the son of Priam king of Troy, and the original cause of the war. Soon after that, Troy was destroyed by the Greeks. He is the subject of a tragedy, *Philoctetes*, by the Greek poet, Sophocles*.

Philomela /filəu'mi:lə/

In Greek myth, the daughter of Pandion, a king of Athens. She was raped by her brother-in-law, Tereus king of Thrace, who also cut out her tongue. Nevertheless, she communicated the crime by a piece of tapestry to her sister, Procne, the wife of Tereus. In revenge, Procne killed her son, Itys, cooked him, and served him to Tereus for dinner. In the act of drawing his sword on the sisters, Tereus was transformed into a hoopoe. At the same time, Procne became a swallow and Philomela a nightingale. Itys was reconstituted into a goldfinch.

Philosophes

* *Encyclopaedists.*

Phiz (Browne, Hablot Knight) (1815–82)

Illustrator. He was the principal illustrator for the novels of Dickens* (especially *David Copperfield*, *Pickwick*, *Dombey and Son*, *Martin Chuzzlewit*, *Bleak House*). He also illustrated the works of other Victorian novelists, notably Harrison Ainsworth*, and Charles Lever*. (See opening illustration to Chapter I.)

Phoebe

* *Artemis.*

Phoebus

* *Apollo.*

Phoenix /'fi:niks/

A mythical bird. Belief in it seems to have been widespread both in Greece and all round the eastern Mediterranean in the centuries before Christ. It was the only one of its kind, and was always male; it had an immensely long life – according to most accounts 500 years but according to some, much longer. It met its death by consuming itself by fire, and from its ashes a new phoenix was born. The new bird always deposited the body of its father on the altar of the Sun in Heliopolis in Egypt.

Phoenix and the Turtle, The

A poem by Shakespeare* included in an anthology *Love's Martyr* (1601) assembled by Robert Chester. The book includes other poems on the love and death of the phoenix and the turtle (turtle-dove); some of these are anonymous and others (including Shakespeare's, and verses by Ben Jonson*, George Chapman*, and John Marston*) are signed. The book also contains other matter, including treatises on British history, herbs and precious stones, to which the phoenix and the turtle myth is supposed to be symbolically related.

Shakespeare's poem consists of thirteen quatrains followed by five triplets (stanzas of three lines) as a concluding 'threnos' (*ie* threnody, or song of lament). The phoenix represents Beauty, and the turtle, Truth; they are united by love; by their death, Reason (personified as the singer of the threnos) declares that the world has been deprived of real truth and real beauty:

> *Truth may seem, but cannot be;*
> *Beauty brag, but 'tis not she;*
> *Truth and beauty buried be.*

Beauty and Truth, the poem says, have therefore no meaning separable from Love. The poem is idealist in the style of Renaissance* Platonism*; it is also metaphysical in its concepts, but not in the style of the Metaphysical Poets* who owe their name to ways of thinking rather than to the concepts they invoke.

Physiocrats

A school of 18th-C French economists and philosophers. They believed: [1] that the Law of Nature, derived from Divine Law, set the pattern to which human society and its institutions should conform; [2] that society was composed of individuals each of whom possessed the same natural rights; [3] in consequence, the individual had an inalienable right to the fruits of his labour in his property; [4] that agriculture (and mining) were the means of acquiring natural wealth, and that commerce and industry merely distributed wealth or gave a new form to it without markedly increasing it; [5] that, consequently, the state should base its taxation on the only true source of wealth, *ie* the land. Their partiality for land and their views on human rights gave them influence among those who were promoting the revolutionary spirit, though the physiocrats themselves favoured enlightened despotism as the most efficient form of government, rather in the spirit of the English 17th-C philosopher, Thomas Hobbes*. The British thinker on whom they had most effective impact was Adam Smith* (*Wealth of Nations*, 1776), although he disagreed with their doctrine that land was the sole real source of wealth. The leader of the physiocrats was François Quesnay (1694–1774).

* *Natural Law*

Picaresque /pikə'resk/

From the Spanish *picaro* 'rogue'. The term is especially applied to a form of prose fiction originating in Spain in the 16th C, dealing with the adventures of rogues. The extension of the term to English literature is very loose, and not at all strictly in accordance with Spanish picaresque. As used by English critics, a picaresque narrative is an episodic story in which the hero is thrown out of, or has never possessed, a stable position in society so that he is forced to seek his own fortune as chance and his enterprise may provide it for him. Such a hero or heroine is often daring and unscrupulous; he may be an individualist by choice, but he is likely also to suffer from social injustice or at least misfortune. The first distinctive example in English is Thomas Nashe's *Unfortunate Traveller** (1594). The growth of middle-class individualism in 17th C gave a new social stimulus to English picaresque; a notable example is Defoe's *Moll Flanders**. Fielding's *Jonathan Wild the Great** and Smollett's* *Ferdinand Count Fathom* are other instances, but the long episodic novel in 18th C did not depend on picaresque alone. There was, for instance, the mock romance of knight-errantry, deriving again from a Spanish source, Cervantes's *Don Quixote**, which was an equally important tradition for other novels by Fielding and Smollett, especially their best: Fielding's *Tom Jones** and Smollett's *Humphry Clinker**. There was also the old tradition of the religious pilgrimage (Bunyan's *Pilgrim's Progress**) to which Fielding's *Joseph Andrews** can be related. The distinctiveness of the picaresque among the other traditions was the variety, comedy, and savage realism which its convention of a not too scrupulous hero afforded. However it also conduced to moral simplification and excessive dependence on mere incident; consequently when the novel form matured in the 19th C the picaresque element disappeared, though other kinds of episodic form persisted.

Piccadilly

An important street in the west end of London; it runs between Piccadilly Circus and Hyde Park.

Pickwick Papers, The

The first novel by Charles Dickens*, published serially 1836–7. The story is the adventures of Mr Pickwick and his friends Tupman, Snodgrass, and Winkle, who go on a journey of observation of men and manners on behalf of the Pickwick Club, of which Mr Pickwick is the founder and the chairman. The episodes are predominantly comic, and Mr Pickwick seems at first to be intended as a mere figure of fun, destined always to be made a fool of owing to his extreme innocence of the ways of the world. Fairly early on, however, he acquires a servant, Sam Weller. Sam is the ideal servant; he is practical, good-humoured, resourceful, and devoted. Pickwick now begins to be endowed with a new dignity; still very innocent, he is no longer a mere figure of fun, for he is also shown to have positive moral qualities, such as a determination to stand by the values of truth and justice. He becomes, in fact, a kind of 19th-C English middle-class Don Quixote* with Sam Weller as a Sancho Panza*, without any of the ridiculousness of Sancho, but with a great deal of comedy derived from his highly developed and typically Cockney sense of humour. At first there is a story but no plot; about half-way through, however, a semblance of a plot develops with Mrs Bardell's conspiracy to obtain £750 from Mr Pickwick for breach of promise of marriage. Assisted by a firm of unscrupulous lawyers, she is at first successful, and Mr Pickwick goes to prison. This is the beginning of Dickens's constant preoccupation with prison and with the parasitic qualities of the legal profession. Various episodes illustrate the kinds of social viciousness which Dickens was to enjoy ridiculing or dramatizing – the cheerful roguery of Mr Jingle; the hypocrisy of the 'shepherd', Mr Stiggins; the demagogic Mr Potts in the parliamentary election at Eatanswill, etc. By contrast, Mr Wardle represents the opulent philanthropy and cordial 'religion of Christmas' which were also to figure in Dickens's novels to the end, but especially in the earlier ones. In the outcome, Mr Pickwick and Sam Weller emerge as a kind of ideal alliance between the middle and working classes – complete sincerity and integrity in moral guidance on Pickwick's part, total devotion and most useful practical capacity on Weller's side. The values of the book are representative of the older rural England; Dickens has not yet entered the darkness, mystery, and dramatic evil of 19th-C urban civilization.

* *Surtees* (for the inception of Dickens's idea)

Picturesque, The Cult of the

A phase of taste in late 18th and early 19th C for wild landscape. It was part of the cultivation of the sensibilities, in reaction against the Augustan* reliance on reason. It was nourished by poets such as James Thomson* (*The Seasons** and *The Castle of Indolence**) and by Macpherson's Ossianic poems (* *Oisin*), and was related to the interest in Gothic* architecture associated most strongly with Horace Walpole*. 'Picturesque' implies the kind of beauty that composes into good pictures: landowners employed landscape gardeners such as 'Capability' Brown and Repton to lay out their estates into vistas and perspectives of 'wild nature', including the artificial construction of classical and Gothic ruins known as 'follies'. The writer most identified with the movement was William Gilpin (1724–1804) who wrote a series of illustrated picturesque tours: *The Wye and South Wales* (1782), *The Lakes* (1789), *Forest Scenery* (1791), and *The West of England and the Isle of Wight* (1798). These were parodied by William Combe in his verse narratives *Dr Syntax in Search of the Picturesque* (1809), *The Second Tour of Dr Syntax in search of Consolation* (for the loss of his wife – 1820) and *The Third Tour of Dr Syntax in search of a Wife* (1821). The cult of the picturesque was a mental climate in which the poets Wordsworth* and Coleridge* made serious discoveries which permanently altered the national attitude to nature. See illustration opposite.

Pied Piper of Hamelin, The

A poem by Robert Browning*, published 1845. It retells an ancient legend: a piper promises to rid the town of Hamelin in Germany of its plague of rats in return for a thousand guilders from the Council. The rats follow the music of his pipe as far as the river Weser, where they are drowned. The Council, however, refuses to pay the piper, whereupon he similarly plays the children out of town and into the side of a mountain which opens

to receive them. The origin of the legend may be the Children's Crusade of 1212, when thousands of young people were persuaded to join an expedition to the Holy Land, and many of them perished on the journey.

Pierrot /ˈpiərəu/
A character in French pantomime* plays, familiar also in English pantomimes and similar entertainments. His face and dress are always white, and the dress is loose like that of a circus clown. Originally he was a comic, playful figure, but he is often made to perform pathetic or romantic roles.

Piers Plowman /ˈpiəz ˈplaumən/
An alliterative* allegorical* poem which exists in three versions (known as the A, B, and C texts), the earliest of which was written soon after 1360, and the latest in the late 1390s. B and C are expansions of A, and there is some doubt whether they are entirely by the same hand, but William Langland* is the accepted author of A, which he is generally supposed to have amplified himself. The language is the West Midland dialect. Text A is 2,500 lines long and Text C, 7,300; each text is divided into sections called 'Passus' (= 'steps' or 'stages').

The form is that of the typical medieval convention of the dream or vision; the substance is a survey of society, the extent to which it has fallen away from the spiritual standards to which it nominally conforms, and the ways in which it can be restored. The corruption of the world is figured in Lady Meed, who stands for Reward, and her prospective marriage to False Fickletongue (*ie* who lives merely for his material advantage); jointly they will have dominion over the Seven Deadly Sins*. The king, on the other hand, wants her to marry Conscience, and he sends for Reason to give him advice. Lady Meed is contrasted to Piers Plowman, at first the honest, unpretentious countryman, later the expounder of the great simplicities of Christian teaching, and finally identified with Christ himself. The ways in which the world can be redeemed are figured in the three visions of Do Well, Do Better, and Do Best. The first is the state in which men do their work and their duty conscientiously; the second enriches the first by spiritual insight; Do Best, finally, is the total dedication of the self to the will of God and the teaching of Christ. The idiom of the poem is close to the allegorical style of the medieval sermon, and expresses concretely the mind of the suffering common people in a time of growing luxury and materialism among the rich; 14th C saw the devastations of the Black Death*, the profiteering of the Hundred Years' War*, and the Peasants' Revolt* of 1381. However, though fierce in its criticism of both Church and State, *Piers Plowman* is not a revolutionary poem in the usual sense; that is, it does not advocate change in the structure of society, but only that its various ranks and professions should conform to the true teaching of Christ.

Piers Plowman is a more uneven work than some of the other masterpieces of 14th C, *eg Sir Gawain and the Green Knight** and the poems of Chaucer*, but it is an achievement of genius and perhaps the major example of the medieval use of allegory, in which the symbols are as concrete as the actualities they represent.

* 4.1.2.

Pilate, Pontius /ˈponʃəs ˈpailət/
Roman Governor of Judea, AD 26–36. His action of handing over Jesus Christ to the Jews is mentioned in each of the Gospels: *Matthew* 27; *Mark* 15; *Luke* 23; *John* 18 and 19. Each account suggests that he acted with reluctance, and the degree of his responsibility for the Crucifixion has been much debated throughout the Christian Churches. The

early Church tended to exonerate him, and he is even held a saint by the Abyssinian Church. The Medieval Church regarded him much more severely; see for instance the Wakefield* play of the Crucifixion.

Pilgrim Fathers, The

The earliest settlers in the 'New England' section of the east coast of the U.S.A. They left England in 1620 in the ship *Mayflower* in order to escape political persecution for their faith. This was the Independent (Congregational*) kind of Protestantism*, which in England resisted the authority of the Bishops of the Church of England.

Pilgrim's Progress, The

A prose allegory* by John Bunyan*. *The Pilgrim's Progress from this World to that which is to come* is in two parts: Part I (1678) tells of the religious conversion of Christian, and of his religious life – conceived as a pilgrimage – in this world, until he comes to the River of Death, and the Heavenly City which lies beyond it; Part II (1684) describes the subsequent conversion of his wife Christiana and their children, and their similar journey with a group of friends.

Both parts contain episodes which symbolize real life experiences: thus, Christian, soon after the way has been pointed out to him, falls into the Slough of Despond – a bog which represents the depression which overcomes the new convert when he has passed the stage of first enthusiasm; later he has to pass through phases of spiritual despair and terror, symbolized by the Valleys of Humiliation and the Shadow of Death; he has to face the derision and anger of public opinion in the town of Vanity Fair, etc. Christiana and the children have an easier time; perhaps Bunyan wished to show that God in his mercy shields the weaker pilgrims, or perhaps that public opinion is harsher to pioneers than to those that follow them.

The 'pioneer pilgrims' – Christian and his associates – belong to the Puritan* sects, of one of which Bunyan was himself a member, who were undergoing persecution in the reign of Charles II*, especially during the earlier years of it, when English society was in strong reaction against the previous Puritan regime of Oliver Cromwell*. Yet *The Pilgrim's Progress* is much more than merely a dramatization of the Puritan spirit. By its allegorical content, it is related to the tradition of the allegorical sermon which, in village churches, survived the Reformation* of 16th C, and some of the adventures (Christian's fight with Apollyon, the Castle of Giant Despair, the character of Greatheart) are related in spirit to popular versions of medieval and 16th-C romances, surviving in the chapbooks*. These aspects give it a close relation with popular traditions of culture to an extent unequalled by any other major literary work. Another element of popular culture shows in Bunyan's assimilation of the English translation of the Bible*, and this reminds us that for many households the Bible was the only book constantly read, and that during the next century Bunyan's allegory took its place beside it. Still more important than these links with the past is Bunyan's anticipation of the kind of vision of human nature which in 18th and 19th C was to find its scope in the novel: his allegorized characters do not, as in past allegories, merely simplify human virtues and vices, but reveal how an individual destiny can be shaped by the predominance in a personality of an outstanding quality, good or bad; the adventures of the pilgrims are conditioned by the differences of these qualities. Thus, Christian and Faithful, fellow pilgrims, have radically different temperaments and correspondingly different experiences.

* 4.2.3.

Pilgrimage of Grace, The

A rebellion provoked by the closing of the monasteries* in 1536. It arose in and was chiefly supported by the north of England, and this fact shows that it had a social and political basis, as well as a religious one. The south of England was economically and socially much more advanced, and more closely in touch with movements of religious reform on the continent of Europe; in consequence, monasteries were not only becoming redundant there in their social functions, but were to some extent actively resented. In the north of England they were more respected on religious grounds, and still served social functions of poor relief and large employment of labour. In addition to these causes which were directly related to monastic institutions there were other social causes bound up with the resentment of the old landed nobility of the north for the newer nobility of the south who were encouraged and advanced in public service by King Henry VIII*; the closing of the monasteries was a pretext for rebellion such as the northern nobility had been looking for. The rebellion was formidable, and the government, through its representative the Duke of Norfolk, had to come to terms; the terms, however, were not kept, and once the rebel army had dispersed, its leaders were executed.

Pillory and Stocks

The pillory was a form of punishment in use for small offences from the early Middle Ages until its abolition in 1837. It consisted of a rectangular wooden frame raised above the ground; the pilloried man stood behind the frame, and his head and hands were thrust through holes in the horizontal bar at the top. He was often made to stand in the pillory throughout the day, and was the target for insults and missiles.

The stocks were a similar instrument. The victim was seated behind the frame, and his legs were thrust through holes in a bar along the bottom of it. Sometimes his head and hands were also exposed through holes in another horizontal bar higher up. The stocks survived longer than the pillory; they were last used in 1865.

* Penal system.

Pindar (5th C BC) /ˈpində/

Greek poet. He is famous for his lyrical odes*, *ie* poems to be sung to the accompaniment of musical

Pillory

instruments and dancing. The odes had a strong religious tone and were designed for solemn occasions, including sporting celebrations. The fact that their composition was influenced by their musical and dance accompaniment gives the odes an appearance of irregularity. This, and the loftiness of their emotion, made them tempting models, from 17th to 19th C, for English poets when they were writing on themes of deep emotional power and felt the need of an ample form which would allow them considerable licence in the treatment of the subject. Pindar's odes were not really as unsystematic as they seemed, however, and many English poems in 'Pindarics' have only a superficial resemblance to the kind of ode that Pindar wrote. Notable examples are Dryden's* *Alexander's Feast*, and *Ode to the Memory of Anne Killigrew*.

Pindarics

* *Pindar*.

Pinero, Sir Arthur (1855–1934)

Dramatist. His earliest plays were farces, but in 1889 *The Profligate* showed great advance in seriousness over earlier plays in the century, when the English theatre had been practically bankrupt of contemporary drama of interest. At about this time, largely owing to the influence of Ibsen*, drama was stirring to life all over Europe. Pinero's *The Second Mrs Tanqueray* (1893) was at the time of its production a conspicuous contribution to the new movement; it was translated into French, German and Italian, and attracted the leading European actress of the age, Eleonora Duse. Pinero followed this success with other plays which sustained his reputation in Britain at least, such as *Trelawny of the Wells* (1898) and *The Gay Lord Quex* (1899). He was in fact a prolific writer, publishing 39 plays between 1891 and 1930. His plays are now seldom produced and little studied: in wit and dramatic ingenuity he was soon excelled by Shaw*, and many other 20th-C dramatists have opened up far richer themes. Like Robertson* before him, his brilliance was like that of a candle in the dark: he was conspicuous in contrast to the dullness that preceded him.

Bib: Dunkel, W. D., *Life*; Boas, F. S., *From Richardson to Pinero*.

Pinter, Harold (b 1930) /ˈpintə/

Dramatist. *The Room*; *The Birthday Party*; *The Dumb Waiter* (1957); *A Slight Ache* (radio 1958, stage 1961); *A Night Out*; *The Caretaker* (1960); *The Homecoming* (1964); *Old Times* (1971); *No Man's Land* (1975).

His distinctiveness among contemporary dramatists, among whom he is perhaps the most remarkable, arises from his use of dialogue. Words are used less for communication than for justification by the speaker's self to himself, and as weapons against others who exist not for relationship but in order that each may find assurance that he exists himself. The characters live in constant mistrust and fear, requiring refuge and assurance from their physical environment, and expecting mysterious invasions. When strong emotion actually brings about relationship through words, however inarticulately, the effect is dramatically poignant. Pinter's characters have been compared to Samuel Beckett's*, but the resemblance is probably superficial; Beckett's characters exist in dissolving relationship, whereas Pinter's require social bond. The idiom, however, of both dramatists seems to derive from dramatists working at the end of 19th C – the Swedish Strindberg, the Russian Chekhov*, and the Belgian Maeterlinck.

Bib: Esslin, M., *The Theatre of the Absurd*; Taylor, J. R., *Anger and After*.

Pip

The central character of Dickens's novel *Great Expectations**. The name is a contraction of his first and second names, Philip Pirrip.

Pitt (the Elder), William, Earl of Chatham (1708–78)

English politician. He led the government during the major part of the Seven Years' War*, during which the British won Canada from the French, and established themselves as the dominant political influence on the subcontinent of India. The brilliant successes of this war are usually attributed to the genius of Pitt's statesmanship.

Pitt (the Younger), William

Politician. The son of William Pitt, Earl of Chatham. He led the government from 1783 to 1801, and again in the years 1804–6. He first became Prime Minister when he was only 24, at a time when George III's government had been deeply discredited by defeat in the American War of Independence, brought to an end by the Treaty of Versailles, 1783. Moreover, politics were thoroughly corrupted by various systems of bribery, and Parliament no longer represented the interests of the nation, but only of various sections of the privileged classes. Pitt was as prudent a statesman as his father had been a dynamic one, and he was famous for his strict integrity. His first ministry was one of cautious reconstruction such as Britain needed for the long wars with France (War of the French Revolution, 1793–1801, and the Napoleonic War, 1803–15). Politically he was conservative ('Tory'), but he was the first political leader to rely on public opinion as expressed in the electoral constituencies instead of on more or less bribed backing among Members of Parliament.

* 1.4.2.2.

Plague of London, The Great

A particularly severe epidemic of bubonic plague which struck London in 1664–5. Epidemics had been frequent, either of the bubonic plague or of equally deadly diseases, ever since the Black Death* of 14th C, and several times caused the compulsory closing of theatres (for fear of infection) during the lifetime of Shakespeare, but this epidemic, at its height, killed over 68,000 of London's population of 460,000 in one year. It was already declining when the Great Fire of London* in 1666 helped to end it.

* *Journal of the Plague Year, A.*

Plague Year, A Journal of the

* *Journal of the Plague Year, A.*

Plantagenet (Anjou), House of

A medieval royal family which reigned over England from 1154 until 1399: Henry II* 1154–89; Richard I* 1189–99; John* 1199–1216; Henry III* 1216–72; Edward I* 1272–1307; Edward II* 1307–27; Edward III* 1327–1377; Richard II* 1377–99. The first of the line, Henry II, succeeded to the English throne through his mother, Mathilda, daughter of the last Norman* king, Henry I. Henry II's father was Geoffrey, Count of Anjou, a province in France; hence the family was known either as the House of Anjou or as Plantagenet, from the plant broom (in Latin, *planta genista*) which Geoffrey used to wear in his cap. The families of Lancaster* and York*, which ruled England successively in 15th C, were junior branches of the Plantagenet family.

Plath, Sylvia (1932–63) /plaθ/

Poet and novelist. She was brought up in the United States; her father, who died when she was 9, was of Prussian origin and her mother Austrian. Her university education was at Smith College, Massachussetts, and Newnham College, Cambridge. She married the English poet, Ted Hughes, in 1956. For a time she taught at Smith College, but in 1959 she settled in England. In 1960 she published her first volume of poetry, *The Colossus*, and in 1963 her only novel, *The Bell Jar*, under the pen-name of Victoria Lucas. Her reputation derives chiefly from her posthumous book of poetry, *Ariel* (1965). This volume aroused more interest in Britain than any other since Dylan Thomas's *Deaths and Entrances* (1946). The poems combine bold imagery and original rhythms with strenuous artistic control; their themes concern states of mind in extremity. In a commentary recorded for the British Council, she declared: 'One should be able to control and manipulate experiences, even the most terrifying . . . with an informed and intelligent mind.'

Bib: Alvarez, A., in *Beyond All This Fiddle.*

Plato (428?–348? BC) /ˈpleitəu/

Greek philosopher. He was a follower of the Athenian philosopher Socrates*, and his dialogues represent conversations in which Socrates takes the lead. The most famous of these 'Socratic' dialogues are *Protagoras*, *Gorgias*, *Phaedo*, *Symposium*, *Republic**, *Phaedrus*, *Timaeus*. His longest work, the *Laws*, does not include Socrates as a character. His central conception is that beyond the world of transient material phenomena lies another eternal world of ideal forms which the material world represents in the form of imitations. His figure for this in the *Republic* is that men in the material world are like people watching shadows moving on the wall of a cave; they see only these shadows and not the realities which cast the shadows. Plato is one of the two most influential philosophers in European thought, the other one being Aristotle*, who was at first his pupil.

* *Platonism.*

Platonic Love

A kind of love superior to sexual desire and not including it. This conception originates in Plato's* dialogue the *Symposium*; its first use as a term in English is in William Davenant's* play *The Platonic Lovers* (1536). Shakespeare's poem *The Phoenix and the Turtle** is the most eloquent succinct expression of 'platonic love'.

Platonism and Neo-Platonism

The term 'Platonism' is applied to the school of thought derived immediately from the Greek philosopher Plato*. 'Neo-Platonism' names schools of thought which adapted his philosophy by adding to or modifying it. Two main periods of revival of

Plato's thought are described as neo-Platonism: [1] that initiated by the pagan Plotinus (3rd C AD) in Rome, and at first a revival of Christianity, into which it was to some extent carried by St Augustine of Hippo (345–430) when he was converted; [2] that which Marsilio Ficino initiated by his studies of Platonic philosophy in Florence (15th C). The 17th-C group known as the Cambridge Platonists were true Platonists rather than Neo-Platonists.

[1] Plato had taught that beyond the world of transient phenomena that surrounds us is that of permanent and imperishable ideas, but he relied on logical reason for the development of his philosophy. Neo-Platonism added a religious aspect which depended on revelation; it derived this influence from other philosophies and from eastern religions. The elements that St Augustine transferred to Christianity remained dominant until 13th C when Platonic influence was succeeded by that of Aristotle*.

[2] 16th-C neo-Platonism in Italy revived the ancient neo-Platonist conception that the universe was peopled by many supernatural beings, and maintained that these existed in addition to the angels and devils allowed by Christian doctrine. It also sometimes taught that men, being essentially spirits, could, by the acquisition of wisdom and virtue, immensely increase their power and knowledge, and could control for their good and wise purposes the non-human supernatural spirits. Thus arose the idea of 'the Mage', or master of high magic; in Shakespeare's *The Tempest**, Prospero is such a neo-Platonic Mage, and Ariel is a spirit such as the neo-Platonists believed could be controlled and used. Neo-Platonism also influenced poetic conceptions, such as that the beloved lady of a sonnet sequence (*eg* Sidney's *Astrophil and Stella**) was a sublime image of her ideal soul, and that the virtues (*eg* those allegorized by Spenser in his *Faerie Queene**) could exist as ideal realities. In criticism, Sidney shows neo-Platonic influence in his conception that poetry should not merely represent but improve on nature, in accordance with the Platonic idea that the world of ordinary realities was an inferior imitation of the eternal idealities. This outlook emphasized the importance of the imagination, as the faculty that could create ideal images and not merely imitate the general qualities common to classes of actual objects, in accordance with Aristotle's critical theory.

Platonists, The Cambridge

A group of thinkers at Cambridge University in mid-17th-C. Their aim was to combine reason with revealed religion, and to counteract the religiously destructive tendencies of the thought of Descartes* and Thomas Hobbes*. Their concern with true religion was combined with a care for clarity of thought and for religious tolerance. Their chief representatives were Henry More (1614–87), Ralph Cudworth (1617–88), Benjamin Whichcote (1609–83), and John Smith (1618–52).

* 3.3.2; *Platonism and Neo-Platonism.*

Plautus, Titus Maccius (254?–184 BC) /'plo:təs/

Roman comic dramatist. His comedies are based on situation and intrigue; they had a high reputation in his own time, but unlike the other outstanding Roman comedian, Terence*, he was ignored during the Middle Ages. In 16th C his reputation revived, and his style of comedy was emulated throughout Western Europe. The play which is often called the first English comedy, Nicholas Udall's *Ralph Roister Doister**, is based on Plautus' *Miles Gloriosus* ('The Boastful Soldier') and Shakespeare's *Comedy of Errors** on Plautus' *Menaechmi*, which, using a confusion between twins, may also have influenced Shakespeare's *Twelfth Night**. Again, Shakespeare's *Taming of the Shrew** may be partly based on Plautus' *Mostellaria*, and the last act of Jonson's *The Alchemist** is also endebted to it. Certain of Plautus' comic characters, such as that of the boastful soldier as in Udall's play, started a tradition, exemplified by Captain Bobadill in Jonson's *Every Man in his Humour** and Parolles in Shakespeare's *All's Well that Ends Well**. These are the most important examples, but traces, at least, of Plautus in the background of English plays can be found in other work of Ben Jonson, and in plays by Thomas Heywood,* Dryden* and Fielding*.

Play on Words

* *Figures of Speech.*

Plays for Puritans

The title of a volume of three plays by Bernard Shaw*, published in 1901: *The Devil's Disciple*; *Caesar and Cleopatra**; *Captain Brassbound's Conversion.* Shaw was himself a declared Puritan* in the sense that he shared the Puritan insistence on the importance above all of a sensitive conscience, but he was concerned that the public should be clear-thinking about it. Hence each of these plays treats the conscience and its workings from an original and ironic angle.

Plays Pleasant and Unpleasant

A collection of seven plays by Bernard Shaw*, published in 1898. The four 'pleasant' plays are comedies with serious themes (the character of the true soldier, what constitutes moral strength, the nature of greatness etc.) but nothing likely to dismay or shock the conventional moral sense of the audiences of the day. These are: *Arms and the Man*, *Candida*, *The Man of Destiny*, *You Never Can Tell.* The three 'unpleasant' plays dealt with social topics (sexual morality and the ownership of slum property) such as were generally felt to be unsuitable for presentation in the theatre. These are *Widowers' Houses*, *The Philanderer*, *Mrs Warren's Profession.* This collection of plays made history: Shaw wrote them with elaborate stage directions, so that they could be read as novels are read. He was thus the first dramatist in English literature to write for a reading public as well as for production in the theatre.

Playboy of the Western World, The (1907)

A play by John Millington Synge*. The scene is a remote part of rural Ireland. The hero, Christy Mahon, arrives at a village inn in flight from the law, since he believes himself to have killed his tyrannical father. Instead of being handed over to the police or regarded with abhorrence, he is treated with admiration, and the innkeeper's daughter, Pegeen Mike, falls in love with him. He is at first a miserable youth with no belief in himself, but the universal admiration and Pegeen's love build up his confidence, until he feels himself and behaves like, a true hero. This fiction is destroyed momentarily when his father, who has merely been injured, suddenly appears on the scene. The assault on the father is then suddenly removed from fiction into fact, and the village, including Pegeen, turn against Christy. However, Christy turns into yet a third type of person; he defies the village, through sheer desperation at the idea of sinking back into subservience to his father, and makes his departure in the bullying style which has always been his father's character. The play is thus a mixture of ironic comedy, poetic tragedy, and exuberant farce.

The language is that of the superstitious Irish peasantry, musical and imaginative in its idiom, and though the dialogue is prose, it reaches an intensity that is unique in drama in the English language since the days of Shakespeare. Irish nationalist opinion was deeply angered by Synge's refusal to idealize the Irish character, and its early performances at Yeats's Abbey Theatre* in Dublin caused riots. Nonetheless it remains the play which more than any other made that theatre the most famous in the British Isles since Shakespeare's Globe.

* 5.3.2; *Irish Literature.*

Pleiades /ˈplaiədi:z/

In Greek myth, the seven daughters of the Titan, Atlas*. All except one – Merope – had gods for lovers; Merope was beloved by the mortal, Sisyphus*. They were pursued by the giant Orion, and called upon Zeus for help; Zeus changed them into doves, and then into stars. Of the cluster, Merope shines faintest because she had no god for a lover.

In French literature the name Pléiade was used more than once for a brilliant group of writers. The most famous of these is the group of 16th-C poets led by Ronsard* and Du Bellay; they abandoned medieval forms of lyric verse such as the ballade and the rondeau, and cultivated the sonnet*, thus stimulating the great English writers of the sonnet – Sidney*, Spenser*, Shakespeare* etc. – in the last decade. They also established the twelve-syllable alexandrine* as the staple of French verse.

Pleonasm /ˈpliənazm/

The use of unnecessary words in the expression of a meaning, *eg* in the phrase 'a deceitful fraud', 'deceitful' is pleonastic, since a fraud is by definition a kind of deceit.

Pliny /ˈplini/

There were two Roman writers of this name. Pliny the elder (1st C AD) was the author of a famous *Natural History*, in which fantastic myths about animals are mixed up with some sound early science. His nephew, Pliny the younger, was the author of letters which are an interesting source of information on the ancient Roman world under the Emperor Trajan, especially about the treatment of Christians.

Plotinus

* *Platonism and Neo-Platonism*

Plutarch (AD 46–120?) /ˈplu:ta:k/

Greek biographer and moralist. He is chiefly famous for his 46 *Parallel Lives* in which he matches 23 famous men from Greek history with 23 famous Romans. The *Lives* were presented in an English version by Sir Thomas North* in 1579; North did not translate them from the original Greek but from the French version by Jacques Amyot. North's book was as popular and influential in England as Amyot's was in France; Plutarch's conception of the great and many-sided man was in harmony with the 16th-C conception of the public virtues and personal accomplishments that should go to make the full man and the perfect courtier. The *Lives*, in North's version, were used as a source-book by dramatists – notably by Shakespeare in *Julius Caesar**, *Antony and Cleopatra**, and *Coriolanus**. Plutarch also wrote a number of treatises on moral and physical subjects known as the *Moralia* – a precedent for the essays of Bacon* as well as the very different ones of the great French essayist, Montaigne*.

* *Translation.*

Pluto

* *Hades.*

Plymouth Brethren

A Christian community founded in Plymouth in 1830. It is in the Puritan* tradition, and more famous for the narrow strictness of its moral teaching than for its doctrines.

Poet Laureate

The laurel, also known as the bay, is a tree which was sacred to Apollo, the god most associated with the arts. The Greeks honoured Olympic victors, triumphant generals, and winners of all kinds by crowning them with a wreath of laurel leaves. Oxford and Cambridge gave the title 'laureate', meaning worthy of laurels, to various poets (*eg* Skelton*) in 15th C. It was later given to court poets like Jonson*, but the first to hold the official title as a paid member of the royal household was Dryden*, in 1670. The office of Poet Laureate has unfortunately suffered in public respect from the inferiority of the poets chosen; politics, or other irrelevant considerations, have too often influenced the appointment. Since Dryden, the only really eminent poets chosen have been Southey*,

Wordsworth*, and Tennyson* in 19th C, and perhaps Robert Bridges*, John Masefield* and the present holder Cecil Day Lewis* in 20th. Wordsworth was the first to make his acceptance conditional on his not being obliged to honour official occasions with specially composed poems, but Tennyson wrote a number of such poems, some of them good.

Poetics

A treatise on poetry by the Greek philosopher Aristotle*. He had already written a dialogue *On the Poets*, which has only survived in fragments, and a treatise on Rhetoric; knowledge of both is to some extent assumed in the *Poetics*. The *Poetics* is considered to have been an unpublished work, resembling notes for lectures addressed to students rather than a fully worked-up treatise for the general public, like the *Rhetoric*. This accounts for its fragmentary character. Thus Aristotle distinguishes Tragedy, Epic and Comedy as the chief kinds of poetry, but Comedy is practically omitted from fuller discussion. Lyric, though it is referred to, is not included among the chief kinds, either because Aristotle considered it to be part of music or because he considered it to be taken up into Tragedy. The main part of the work is therefore concerned with Tragedy and Epic – the former more extensively than the latter. Aristotle's method is essentially descriptive rather than prescriptive; that is to say, he is more concerned with what had been done by acknowledged masters such as Homer* and Sophocles*, than with what ought to be done according to so-called 'rules'.

Nonetheless, the *Poetics* became the most authoritatively influential of all critical works. Its dominance in European critical thought from 16th to 18th C was partly due to its influence on the most widely read of the Roman critics, Horace*, and partly because it was rediscovered at the end of 15th C when the Renaissance* was at its height, and the spirit of the Greek and Latin writers was felt to be civilization itself. Critics such as the 16th-C Italian Scaliger took what are mere hints in Aristotle and erected them into important rules of art, such as the 'neo-Aristotelian' unities* of time and place. In England, the important critics, such as Dryden* and Johnson*, regarded Aristotle and neo-Aristotelianism with strong respect rather than total reverence, but the complete submission of minor critics such as Thomas Rymer* is exemplified by his obtuse treatment of Shakespeare's *Othello* in the essay *Short View of Tragedy* (1692). Neo-Aristotelianism was set aside by the Romantics, who cultivated literary virtues which are different from Aristotelian shapeliness and order, but the influence of the *Poetics* is still evident in Wordsworth's Preface to the *Lyrical Ballads**.

Today the *Poetics* remains one of the most outstanding works of European thought. Critics still use Aristotle's terminology in classifying poetic forms; his theory of art as imitation (different from Plato's*) is still the starting-point of much aesthetic discussion; such terms as 'harmatia', for the element in human nature which makes it vulnerable to tragedy, 'peripeteia' for the reversal of fortunes common in tragic narrative, and 'katharsis' for the effect of tragedy on the mind of the audience, have permanent usefulness.

* 7.1.

Political Register, The

A weekly journal started by William Cobbett* in 1802, and continued until the year of his death, 1835. It was singularly bold and independent in opinion, and had a wide circulation especially among the poor of rural England. In 1803, Cobbett was fined £500 for his criticism of the government's Irish policy, and in 1809 he was sent to prison for two years for his criticism of military punishments. He continued to edit the paper from prison. Later he made a series of tours of inspection about the countryside and published his reports in the journal; they were collected under the title of *Rural Rides** in 1830, and have remained a literary classic for the excellence of their description.

* *Journalism*.

Polo, Marco (1254?–1324?) /ˈmaːkəu ˈpəuləu/

Italian traveller. At a time when Europe was in almost total ignorance of the majority of Asia, he travelled from Venice across central Asia as far as China where he remained for 17 years. On his return to Italy after an absence of 24 years, he wrote an account of his journeys. This became very popular, particularly in 16th C, when contacts with eastern Asia were renewed. The book was first translated into English in 1579.

Polycrates (6th C BC) /poˈlikrətiːz/

In ancient Greek history, the ruler of the island of Samos and famous for his acts of piracy by which he became extraordinarily rich. A legend tells that his ally, the king of Egypt, became alarmed at Polycrates' unfailing good fortune, and considered that it would inevitably sooner or later be punished by the gods. He advised Polycrates to throw away an object of exceptional value to appease the jealousy of the gods, and the latter accordingly cast a valuable ring into the sea. Soon afterwards, Polycrates recovered the ring from the belly of a fish which was presented to him.

Polyphemus /poliˈfiːməs/

In Greek myth and Homer's epic the *Odyssey**, a Cyclops*. He captured Odysseus and twelve of his companions, and shut them up in his cave. He daily devoured two of them but Odysseus escaped by putting out Polyphemus' single eye after making him drunk, and then escaping by tying himself and his remaining companions to the bellies of the giant's huge rams when they were let out of the cave to graze. Polyphemus also loved the nymph Galatea*, who however, preferred the shepherd, Acis; the giant crushed his rival with a rock, and Acis was changed by the gods into a river.

Pomona /pəˈməunə/

In ancient Italian myth, a goddess of orchards and gardens.

Pompadour, Marquise de (1721–64) /ˈpompəduə/

The mistress of Louis XV, king of France. She was a woman of strong personality and exceptional talent, and left a strong impression on both the politics and the culture of the time; hence the use of her name in connection with many items of fashionable life in England as well as in France.

Pompey (Gnaeus Pompeius) (106–48 BC) /ˈpompi/

A Roman general in the period when the republican system of government was weakening. In the social struggles he was a leader of the aristocratic party, and he was very successful in wars of Roman expansion on the eastern seaboard of the Mediterranean. At the height of his power he was, with Crassus and Julius Caesar*, a member of the triumvirate which ruled the Empire. Later, Pompey and Caesar quarrelled, and Caesar decisively defeated him at the Battle of Pharsalus in 48. Soon after the battle he was assassinated by one of his officers.

Poor Laws

Laws which gave public relief to those among the poor who could not earn their own living and were not supported by others. The first great Poor Law was that of 1601, under Elizabeth I*. The dissolution of monasteries* and other Church institutions which had undertaken the care of the destitute, together with a number of causes of unemployment (*eg* enclosures*) caused a series of poor laws to be passed in 16th C, of which the law of 1601 was the climax. Every parish was required to appoint overseers, whose task it was to provide work for the able-bodied unemployed, and relief (through a local tax called a 'poor rate') for those who were unable to work. The law survived until 19th C, when problems of poor relief had become too great for it to be an efficient solution. Local magistrates employed a method known as the 'Speenhamland System', from the place of its origin, by which the unemployed were given enough money to enable them to survive; the disadvantage of this system was that it demoralized those who were employed in very hard labour but unable to earn more than the unemployed who were given relief. In 1834, the New Poor Law was passed. Parishes were grouped into Unions under Boards of Guardians. The main principle of this was that the able-bodied poor were only given relief in workhouses*, and that these were not to be so agreeable as to make them inviting to such unemployed as were merely lazy and unwilling to work. The workhouses were in consequence often very disagreeable places, and bitterly unpopular. This law was replaced in 1925 by a more complicated and humane system. In the 1930s, when there was extensive unemployment in Britain, the most unpopular feature of relief to the unemployed was the 'Means Test', involving detailed investigation into whatever means a family might possess to support itself without state aid. The system of National Insurance, set up by the Labour Government of 1945–50, avoided this cause of resentment by making relief available to everyone whatever their income, in return for a universal weekly payment.

Pope, Alexander (1688–1744)

Poet. He was the son of a Catholic linen-draper in London. He was born in the year of the 'Glorious Revolution' – the Revolution* of 1688. The nature of this smooth revolution characterized the cultural temper of the age which was now well established. The care of educated men was for civilization interpreted as order, peace, refinement, and the arts that went with these. These qualities were not interpreted passively but regarded as high ideals which could be achieved only by strenuously emulating high models and maintaining strict standards. A model was found in Roman civilization of the Augustan* age, and the standards were those demonstrated by the classicism of French literature then at its height. Passion did not go out of English literature, but became both conservative and constructive; clarity, balance, proportion and concentration were valued above invention and exploration. Dryden* had been the chief shaping force of these ideals in English poetry, and Milton's great epic *Paradise Lost**, Puritan* but at the same time classical, by its vast scope prevented the poetic spirit from interpreting its values too narrowly. Pope was Dryden's disciple, but Milton's poetic personality was too strong for either of them to ignore.

Pope's poetic ambitions began early, and his youthful work shows experiments in various forms: *Pastorals* (1709); *Essay on Criticism** (1711), and *Windsor Forest* (1713) – the last a patriotic poem with strong pastoral elements. *The Rape of the Lock** (1714) was his first masterpiece, a satire in the form of a mock epic*. By this time his reputation was rising high, and it was established by his translation of Homer's *Iliad**, published in instalments, 1715–20. During this early period he had at first associated with Addison*, the chief man of letters of the time, but in 1713, with Swift*, Gay*, Arbuthnot and Congreve*, he formed the lively Scriblerus Club* whose object was to 'ridicule all false tastes in learning'. In 1717 he produced two further masterpieces, the subject of both of them being great passion: *Eloisa to Abelard**, and *Elegy to the Memory of an Unfortunate Lady*. In 1725–6 he completed his translation of Homer with the *Odyssey**. His major satirical work, the *Dunciad** first appeared in 1728, but the great fourth book was not published until 1742. In 1733–4 he published his philosophical poem *An Essay on Man** and the *Moral Essays** – on the characters of men, the characters of women, and the use of riches. Between 1733 and 1738 he published his satires, *Imitations of Horace**, and in 1735 the *Epistle to Dr Arbuthnot* which was also the prologue to the Horatian satires. Pope's modern reputation depends especially on the *Moral Essays*, *The Rape of the Lock*, the *Epistle to Dr Arbuthnot*, and the fourth book of the *Dunciad*. It is in these poems that Pope was most concrete and composed the brilliant analytical portraits which show his art at its most concentrated.

Dryden had used the heroic couplet*, which in its original form had been introduced by Chaucer in 14th C. Pope brought this metrical medium to perfection; in his hands it was, as he chose, terse and pungent, subtle and delicate, sonorous and imposing, or combinations of these qualities. It was particularly effective as a satirical weapon, and Pope's satire focused on his personal enemies; this has done his reputation harm since, in the words of a modern critic, it has led to too much concern *with* his victims as well as too much concern *for* them. The importance of his satire is that, even when he was satisfying personal resentment, his imaginative genius enabled him to express the moral and aesthetic vision of his age at its finest.

* 4.2.2; 6.3.1; 7.2; *Augustan Age.*

Bib: Sherburn, G., *The Early Career of Alexander Pope*; Johnson, S., in *Lives of the Poets*; Tillotson, G., *On the Poetry of Pope*; Williams, A. L., *Pope's Dunciad*; Mack, M., *44 Essential Articles on Pope*; Leavis, F. R., in *Revaluations*; Blanchard, R. A., *Discussions of Pope.*

Popish Plot

* *Oates, Titus.*

Port-Royal

* *Pascal.*

Port Wine

A sweet red wine, often fortified with brandy, very widely drunk in upper class English society in 18th and 19th C. Port was drunk at table when the meal was over; the ladies withdrew to the 'Withdrawing' (drawing-) room, and the gentlemen circulated the bottle clockwise amongst themselves.

Portrait of a Lady, The (1881)

A novel by Henry James*. The heroine, Isabel Archer, is brought from America to England by her aunt, Mrs Touchett, the wife of a retired American banker. Isabel has the candour and freedom conspicuous among American girls of the period; she also has beauty, intelligence, and a spirit of adventure and responsiveness to life. She refuses offers of marriage from both Lord Warburton, a 'prince' of the English aristocracy, and Caspar Goodwood, a 'prince' of American industry. In the meantime her cousin, Ralph Touchett, has fallen in love with her, but he is slowly dying of consumption and dare not become her suitor. Instead, he tries to play the 'fairy godmother' by persuading his father to leave her the money which would have been due to himself. His action has two unfortunate results: it awakens Isabel's New England puritan conscience through the sense of responsibility which the possession of wealth entails, and it attracts the rapacious Madame Merle, whose guilty secret is that she is looking for a rich stepmother for her daughter by her former lover, Gilbert Osmond. Osmond (like Madame Merle herself) is an artistic but cold-blooded and totally self-centred expatriate American; Isabel in her humility is easily made to feel her own cultural inferiority to the exquisite exterior qualities of Osmond, whom she sees as the prince she has been looking for – a man deprived of noble potentialities by the unjust circumstance of his poverty. She marries him, only to discover his hollowness, and that her marriage is imprisonment in the ogre's castle.

The novel, sometimes regarded as James's masterpiece, shows his conception of the relationship of the American and European consciousnesses; the Americans have integrity, the will to live, and good will towards humanity, but they lack richness of tradition and are restricted by the limitations of the New England puritan inhibitions; the Europeans (especially some of the American expatriates) have rich cultural awareness but this commonly corrupts their integrity, and instead of good will they have immense rapacity. On the other hand the best kind of American expatriate (Ralph Touchett) combines the best of both worlds. Critics (*eg* F. R. Leavis* in *The Great Tradition*) have remarked that James's theme – of the young girl exposed to the complexities of a society whose motives she lacks the experience of life to discern – resembles George Eliot's* treatment of Gwendolen Harleth, the heroine of her novel *Daniel Deronda**, but that Gwendolen is created from within by a woman novelist, whereas Isabel Archer is created from without by a man.

Portrait of the Artist as a Young Man, A (1916)

An autobiographical novel by James Joyce*. The theme is the life of a middle-class Irish boy, Stephen Dedalus, from his infancy in the strongly Catholic, intensely nationalistic environment of Dublin in the 1880s to his departure from Ireland some twenty years later. In his boyhood he sees his elders bitterly divided in consequence of the Church's rejection of Parnell*, the nationalist leader, owing to the scandal of his private life. As he grows up he is repelled by the pettiness, treacheries and vindictiveness of Irish nationalism, and for a time is drawn towards the rich spirituality of the Catholic tradition. The Irish Catholic Church, however, also suffered from provincialism and narrowness, and a moment of revelation on the seashore shows him that the largeness of an artistic vocation will alone suffice for him to harmonize the spiritual and fleshly sides of his nature, and enable him to rise above the vulgarity of his environment; but the choice brings with it the decision to leave Ireland.

The originality of the novel consists in its presentation of the hero's experience from within his own consciousness. The language gradually expands from the fragmentary diction of an infant on the first page through the connected but limited range of expression characteristic of a schoolboy to the sophistication of a fully articulate university student.

Poseidon /poˈsaidən/

In Greek myth, the god of the sea, identifiable with the Roman Neptune. He was the son of Cronus and

Rhea, and brother of Zeus and Hades. His character was generally wild and cruel, and his symbol was the trident with which he lashed the sea into storm; he was also supposed to cause earthquakes. In the siege of Troy* he favoured the Greeks because the Trojan king had defrauded him of his reward for building their walls. Like another violent god, Ares*, he was the enemy of the goddess of wisdom, Athene*.

Positivism

* *Comte*

Poulter's Measure

A verse metre* used by some 16th-C poets; it consisted of a 12-syllable line (Alexandrine*) alternating with a 14-syllable one. 'Poulter' = 'poulterer' – an allusion to variations in the number making up a dozen in the poultry trade. It was used by Wyatt*, Surrey*, and less distinguished poets.

When Dido feasted first the wand'ring Trojan knight,
Whom Juno's wrath with storms did force in Lybic sands to light,
That mighty Atlas did teach, the supper lasted long,
With crispéd locks, on golden harp, Jopas sang in his song.

[Wyatt: Jopas' Song]

Pound, Ezra (b 1885)

American poet. He came to Europe in 1907, and made London his home during the period 1908–20. His influence on English poetry during this period, especially on that of his fellow-American, T. S. Eliot*, was very great. English poets had become narrow and insular, and they tended (with some exceptions) to occupy themselves with a marginal field of experience left over to them by the novelists, abstaining from the issues that were central to the destiny of their thoroughly industrialized society. They also restricted themselves to a limited diction, consecrated as 'poetic', with an obvious emotional appeal. The recent British poets who interested Pound were Robert Browning* for his direct and 'unpoetic' address to the reader, and the Irish poet W. B. Yeats*, for his austere seriousness and energy. In his campaign to reform diction he became the leader of the Imagist* Movement, though he later abandoned it; this phase is illustrated by his *Personae* (1909) and *Ripostes* (1912). It also drew him to Chinese poetry, from which he made excellent English verse although his are not such accurate translations as those of his contemporary Arthur Waley.

In his campaign to free English poetry from insularity, Pound had the ability, which he shared with some other American writers (*eg* Henry James* and T. S. Eliot), to see European culture as a whole, not segmented into national cultures. Thus he offered fresh insights into French and Italian poetry back to the Middle Ages* (see his critical essays, *Make It New*) and into the Latin classics. In his poetry he used the diction of everyday speech with a subtle ear for its rhythms. Like Eliot, he abandoned the logical continuity of prose in favour of a juxtaposition of ideas and images whose continuity appears through their psychological association. Also like Eliot, he used quotation frequently, thereby relating his treatment of his themes with the treatment accorded by past poets to similar themes, and thus illuminating the fundamental alterations in outlook and assumption brought about in the course of history. This technique of quotation is conspicuous in Eliot's poem *The Waste Land**, which Pound heavily revised. A comparable poem by Pound is *Hugh Selwyn Mauberley* (1920), which heralded his departure from Britain by offering an assessment of the state of culture there at the time. He moved to Paris, and in 1924 to Italy, where he became increasingly sympathetic to Fascism partly in consequence of his strongly held and eccentric economic theories (see his *ABC of Economics*). He has spent much of the remainder of his life on a very long poem, the *Cantos*, in which these theories play a prominent part. His central critical position is that it is the function of the writer to sustain the vitality of language, without which civilization decays in all its aspects.

Bib: Kenner, H., *The Poetry of Ezra Pound*;
Russell P., *An Examination of Ezra Pound*;
Davie D., in *The Pelican Guide: The Modern Age*.

Powell, Anthony (b 1905) /ˈpəuəl/

Novelist. He writes sophisticated comedy of upper class life in England since 1920; his approach may be compared with the different treatment of the same society by Aldous Huxley*, Evelyn Waugh*, and by D. H. Lawrence* in *St Mawr*. Early novels: *Afternoon Men* (1931); *Venusberg* (1932); *From a View to a Death* (1933); *Agents and Patients* (1936); *What's Become of Waring* (1939).

In 1948 he produced a study of John Aubrey*, the 17th-C anecdotal biographer, author of *Brief Lives*. He then began his major work which, it has been suggested, owes something to Aubrey as it clearly does to the sequence *A la Recherche du Temps Perdu* by the early 20th-C French novelist Marcel Proust. Powell's sequence of novels is called *The Music of Time*. The narrator, whose personality is kept in detachment but not eliminated, is an upper-class young man with whose life various circles of friends intertwine in a kind of dance, and in a way that is only conceivable in the upper levels of any society. The characters make a pattern of contrasts, the most serious and interesting being that of the man of distinction – Stringham – who evokes the high style of Elizabethan courtier such as Raleigh*, but who is in the worldly sense a failure, and Widmerpool, the man of grotesque and crude manners and feeling, who is yet a worldly success owing to his insensibility and the force of his ambition. Novels completing *The Music of Time*: *A Question of Upbringing* (1951); *A Buyer's Market* (1952); *The Acceptance World* (1955); *At Lady Molly's* (1957); *Casanova's Chinese Restaurant* (1960); *The Kindly Ones* (1962); *The Valley of Bones* (1964); *The Soldier's Art* (1966); *The Military Philosophers*

(1968); *Books Do Furnish a Room* (1971); *Temporary Kings* (1973); *Hearing Secret Harmonies* (1975). The sequence begins in 1921 at the narrator's public school; it ends after the war with the death of Widmerpool in circumstances of sinister pathos.
Bib: Brit. Council Pamphlet by Bernard Bergonzi; *The Novel Today* by Walter Allen.

Powys, John Cowper (1872-1963) /'pəuis/

Novelist and essayist. Principal novels: *Wolf Solent* (1929); *A Glastonbury Romance* (1933); *Jobber Skald* (1935); *Maiden Castle* (1936); *Owen Glendower* (1941); *Porius* (1951). Works of criticism and thought: *Visions and Revisions* (1915, revised 1935); *Psychoanalysis and Morality* (1923); *The Religion of a Sceptic* (1925); *The Meaning of Culture* (1929); *In Defence of Sensuality* (1930); *The Pleasures of Literature* (1938); *The Art of Happiness* (1946). See British Council pamphlet 'Writers and their Works' 150 (R. C. Churchill: *The Powys Brothers*) for a fuller bibliography. One of his most famous books is his *Autobiography* (1934), developed from his contribution to the *Confessions of Two Brothers* (1916) written with Llewelyn Powys. He has also written verse.

Like his brother, T. F. Powys*, his fiction is impressed by his background in the English west country, but his prose is contrasted with his brother's by its expansiveness and diffuseness. His writing combines a strongly physical sensationalism with a fascination for the intangible and mysterious reaches of human experience.
Bib: Derry, W. C., *John Cowper Powys;* Ward, R. H., *The Powys Brothers.*

Powys, Theodore Francis (1875–1953) /'pəuis/

Novelist. His novels and fables were set in the rural south-west of England; the characters are presented with a simplicity and poetry resembling the style of the Old Testament of the Bible, but the individuality of the expression is too distinct for the resemblance to be obvious, and the tone is naïve on the surface but sophisticated in its pagan, often cynical implications. At its best, *eg* in *Mr Weston's Good Wine* (1927) and *Fables* (1929), Powys's art rose to exquisite tragic poetry; at its worst it descended to brutality and cruelty. His fiction is a very late and unusual example in English of a writer using purely rural traditions and environment; the tragic pessimism, less humane and more sophisticated than Hardy's*, is perhaps a reflection of the disappearing vitality of that way of life. Some other works: *Mr Tasker's Gods* (1924); *Kindness in a Corner* (1930); *Mark Only* (1924). *Fables* was republished as *No Painted Plumage* in 1934.
Bib: Coombes, H., *T. F. Powys*; Hunter, W., *The Novels and Stories of T. F. Powys.*

Praxiteles (4th C BC) /prak'sitəli:z/

Greek sculptor; he worked at the period in which Greek sculpture achieved its greatest sophistication in representing the human form, and his name is made to stand for this achievement at its best. However, his work survives only in one undisputed figure – the statue of Hermes carrying the child Dionysus; it is otherwise known only in copies.

Predestination

A theological doctrine which was the subject of dispute from early Christian times, and caused a major division among Protestants* in 16th C. The essence of the doctrine is that since God in his eternal wisdom has foreknown the events of time since before the creation of the world, therefore he has foreseen and chosen those individuals who are damned and those who are saved for eternal life after death. Those who are saved are called 'the elect', and those who are damned 'the reprobate'. The Puritans*, especially the Presbyterians* who were followers of the French reformer Calvin*, accepted Predestination, and tended to believe that a sign of election was that men were granted prosperity in their lawful worldly pursuits, whereas the 'reprobates' tended to fail in them, and of course their pursuits were commonly unlawful. According to R. H. Tawney (*Religion and the Rise of Capitalism*) this is why Calvinism was particularly congenial to the industrious middle classes of the towns. On the other hand the Dutch Protestant James Arminius (d 1609) believed that men could be saved by Divine Grace, and that whether they were saved depended not on predestination but on the use they made of Grace. The Church of England accepted the Arminian view in the first half of 17th C, and thus Predestination became a dominant issue between the orthodox Anglicans* and the majority of Puritans during this period.

* 3.2.2.2.

Prelude, or Growth of a Poet's Mind, The

A blank verse* autobiographical poem by William Wordsworth*. In its first version, written between 1799 and 1805, it contained 13 Books; instead of publishing this, however, he continued to revise the poem at intervals throughout his life, and it was eventually published, divided into 14 Books, in 1850 after his death.

Wordsworth, under the influence of his friend Coleridge*, originally hoped to achieve a great philosophical poem 'on man, on nature, and on human life', and *The Prelude* was to be preliminary to it; of the philosophical poem itself, only one part, *The Excursion**, was written. *The Prelude*, a taking stock by Wordsworth of his experience and resources, was unprecedented in English as an autobiographical experiment, but it had behind it the prose *Confessions* of the French writer Jean-Jacques Rousseau* (published 1782–9) and it opened a century in which autobiography was to be a very important medium. The material of the poem is indicated by the titles of the books in the final version (which differ from the first in the inclusion of an extra book on his life in France): I-II Childhood and School time; III Residence at Cambridge; IV Summer Vacation; V Books; VI Cambridge and the Alps; VII Residence in London; IX-X-XI Residence in France; XII-XIII Imagination and Taste, how Impaired and Restored; XIV Conclusion.

The long poem is uneven in quality, but the

first two Books and passages throughout the remaining ones are examples of Wordsworth's art at its best, and constitute the finest introduction to the rest of his poetry. The revisions which he undertook after the completion of the first version in 1805 are generally regarded as improvements in one sense and unfortunate in another: on the one hand, though Wordsworth's inspiration failed him later in his life, his poetic judgement did not, and the revisions often make for greater concentration and clarity of effect. On the other hand, his later Christian orthodoxy caused him to modify the marvellous immediacy of his original ideas about the influences on the human mind of communion with natural environment, since these laid him open to the charge of pantheism*. Both the 1805 and the 1850 versions of the poem are now in print; the 1805 one was first published in 1926. The edition by E. de Selincourt has both versions in parallel.

* *Autobiography; French Revolution.*

Pre-Raphaelite Brotherhood /ˈpriːˈrafəlait/

A movement of painters and poets which began just before 1850; it was more important in painting than in poetry, but one of its leading members, Dante Gabriel Rossetti*, was equally famous in both arts. The essence of the movement was opposition to technical skill without inspiration. This made it anti-Victorian, inasmuch as industrial techniques (illustrated by the Great Exhibition* of 1851) were producing vast quantities of work which were products of mere engineering. Technical skill without inspiration had been an aspect of the neo-classical art of 18th C, against which the Romantics* had already protested, and behind neo-classicism lay the 16th-C Renaissance* of Greek and Roman art, and the paintings of the Italian artist Raphael (1483–1520), who had produced religious pictures of extraordinary perfection in technique but (in the opinion of the Pre-Raphaelites) with an almost cynical disregard of spiritual feeling. This tenderness of the spirit, medieval art had possessed; hence the Brotherhood, by no means hostile to highly polished technique, cultivated the artistic spirit of the Middle Ages*. The principal painters of the Brotherhood were Rossetti, John Millais, and Holman Hunt; its poets were Rossetti and his sister Christina, and, a little later, William Morris*.

The movement drew for its poetical inspiration on the ardour of the Romantic poet, John Keats*, who had also cultivated the Middle Ages, and it greatly revered the contemporary poet, Alfred Tennyson*, whose art owed much to Keats. But Pre-Raphaelitism was not merely an aesthetic movement; a great influence upon it was the work of the art critic, John Ruskin*, who had a strong social consciousness about the duty of art to society, and especially of the duty of redeeming the squalid life of the urban working classes. Less close to the movement, but still in harmony with it, was the poet and critic Matthew Arnold*, with his attack on the philistinism of the middle classes and the barbarism of the upper classes. Finally, the ground of Pre-Raphaelitism had been prepared religiously by the Oxford Movement* in the Church of England; this had cried 'Hands off!' to the interfering state, and by its cultivation of ritual in religious worship had brought beauty back into religion.

However, Keats had not been dismayed by the world of his time so much as by the inevitability of desperate suffering as part of the human lot in every age. Arnold and Tennyson, in their poetry, were dismayed by the surface hideousness and the apparently irremediable injustices of their society. They had tended to write a 'poetry of withdrawal', creating an inner world of unassailable dreams (Tennyson) or a transcendent fortress of lofty feeling (Arnold). The Pre-Raphaelites followed this example. The poetry of D. G. Rossetti and of Morris is a 'literary' art, *ie* it depends on the proved poetic stimulus of a special 'poetic' language and imagery which was alien to the ordinary man of the age, and had no relationship to the engineering genius of the age itself. (The intensely pious Christina Rossetti had a more authentic, religious inspiration, but even in her work the feeling is subjectively personal as compared to the work of a 17th-C religious poet such as George Herbert*, whom in some respects she resembled.) Thus, whatever the social consciences of Rossetti and Morris, they tended to take poetry to be an autonomous activity, largely independent of the political and social issues of the time. It was as though they moved upwards, while the age was moving horizontally: the poets and history were going in different directions. The poet Algernon Swinburne* had the courage to take this autonomy seriously; with him, 'art for art's sake' was born, and the aesthetic movement (**Aestheticism*). The only poetry which was moving strongly in another direction was that of G. M. Hopkins* from 1865 to 1889, and he was regarded as unpublishable. Another poet, W. B. Yeats*, owed much to the Pre-Raphaelites and especially to Morris, but the bitter realities of Irish politics made him, in the next century, one of the leaders of the reaction against the whole direction of art as the worship of Beauty. This reaction has lasted to the present day. The Pre-Raphaelites had their own periodical – *The Germ*; it first appeared in January 1850, and ran for only four numbers.

* 2.3.

Presbyterianism

A doctrine of church organization maintained by an important group of Protestants*. 'Presbyter' comes from a Greek word meaning 'elder', and Presbyterianism is a system of church government by councils of elders. The system was devised by Calvin*. The elders represented their churches at Presbytery meetings, which then sent representatives to a General Assembly. This system became dominant in Scotland under the leadership of John Knox* and had wide support in England from about 1570. It was, however, essentially anti-episcopalian (*ie* opposed to government through bishops) and its democratic spirit made it greatly feared by James VI of Scotland who became James I of England in 1603. In 1604, James held the Hampton Court Conference with the Puritans*, amongst whom the Presbyterians were one of the most influential sects; he agreed to their demand for the authorized translation of the Bible, but flatly refused their demand for the abolition of bishops, with the pronouncement 'No bishop, no king!' The importance of Scottish aid to the Parliamentary cause in the Civil War* of 1642–6 led to the increased power of Presbyterianism in England, but the Scots later made a treaty with Charles I, thus dividing puritanism. The result was the civil war of 1648–51, which was essentially a war between the Anglo-Scottish Presbyterians and the English Parliamentary forces, amongst whom the Puritan Independents (Congregationalists*) led by Oliver Cromwell* were the strong nucleus. Cromwell was victorious, but Presbyterianism survived in Scotland, where it is still the national Church. In England, Presbyterians seceded extensively to Unitarianism* under the influence of 18th-C rationalism*, and it is now a comparatively small religious group.

* 3.2.2.2.

Press Council, The

A body recently established by the British Government to maintain good and responsible standards of journalism*. When newspapers seem to abuse their powers by interfering with private life and liberty, complaints may be made to the Council which can then, if it thinks the abuse is genuine, administer a public rebuke to the newspaper concerned. It has no powers of censorship or of penalizing newspapers in any other way.

Pretender

* *Old Pretender, The; Jacobite.*

Priam /ˈpraiəm/

In Greek legend and Homer's *Iliad**, the last king of Troy*. He was the son of Laomedon, and his queen was Hecuba. He had fifty sons and twelve daughters. Among the most famous of the former were Hector*, Troilus*, and Paris* whose theft of Helen* caused the Trojan war. The most famous of his daughters was the prophetess, Cassandra*. The death of Priam and the destruction of Troy are described in Book II of Virgil's *Aeneid**. The translation of this work is one of the masterpieces of the English poet John Dryden*; another masterpiece of verse translation is the version by Gavin Douglas*.

Priapus /praiˈeipəs/

In Greek myth, a son of Aphrodite*, the goddess of sexual love. Owing to the jealousy felt by the goddess Hera*, he was born with a deformity, and abandoned by his mother to the shepherds. He became a nature god, similar to Pan*, and was a god of licentious love for the Romans.

Pride and Prejudice (1813)

A novel by Jane Austen*. Mr and Mrs Bennet belong to the minor gentry, and live at Longbourne near London. Mr Bennet is witty and intelligent, and bored with his foolish wife. They have five daughters, whose marriage prospects are Mrs Bennet's chief interest in life, since the estate is 'entailed' – *ie* by the law of the period it will go on Mr Bennet's death to his nearest male relation, an absurd clergyman called Mr Collins. The main part of the story is concerned with the relationship between the witty and attractive Elizabeth Bennet and the haughty and fastidious Fitzwilliam Darcy, who at first considers her beneath his notice, and later, on coming to the point of asking her to marry him, finds that she is resolutely prejudiced against him. His friend Charles Bingley is in love with the eldest daughter, Jane, but they are kept apart by the jealous snobbishness of his sisters and (at first) the fastidious disapproval of Darcy. Meanwhile, Elizabeth is subjected to an insolent offer of marriage by Mr Collins and the arrogant condescension of his patroness, Lady Catherine de Bourgh, Darcy's aunt. Those who regard the Bennet family as foolish and vulgar have their opinion justified when Lydia Bennet elopes with an irresponsible young officer, George Wickham; by this time, however, Darcy has been chastened by finding in Elizabeth a fastidiousness and pride that exceed his own, and, despite the family scandal, they are united.

The novel has always been one of the most liked of Jane Austen's, and it contains excellent social comedy, but in some respects it stands apart from her other work. She herself said of it 'The work is rather too light, and bright, and sparkling; it wants to be stretched out here and there with a long chapter of sense.'

Pride's Purge

* *Long Parliament, The.*

Priestley, Joseph (1733–1804)

A nonconformist minister, scientist, and teacher. He was partly educated at a nonconformist academy at Daventry; such academies existed in

18th C to give a university education to nonconformists, who for their religious views were not admitted to the recognized universities of Oxford and Cambridge. They were commonly more advanced scientifically than the real universities; Priestley eventually became the first chemist to isolate oxygen. In 1768 he published his *Essay on the First Principles of Government*, advocating 'the happiness of the majority' as the criterion by which government must be judged. This line of thought was developed by Jeremy Bentham* and his 19th-C followers, the Utilitarians*. Priestley's house in Birmingham was destroyed by the mob in 1791 owing to his well-known sympathy with the French Revolution*, and in 1794 he emigrated to the United States.

Prime Minister

Since 18th C the office of greatest power in the British political system. It arose in consequence of the struggles for power between king and parliament in 17th C. Parliament was victorious, inasmuch as it became difficult for the king to lead the country politically without the approval of Parliament at every major step. This could only be managed by a politician who was himself a member of the parliamentary body, as the king was not; moreover George I (1714–27) and George II (1727–60), the first two kings of the House of Hanover (**George*) had the additional disadvantage of being foreigners in the nation they were supposed to govern. Thus the 18th-C art of 'managing' parliaments grew up; the first politician to be a master of the art was Robert Walpole*, whose period of power ran from 1721–42. He is usually regarded as 'the first Prime Minister' in English history, though he objected to the title. Walpole's 'management' was politically unsatisfactory, however, since it depended too much on the bribery of Members of Parliament, and exploitation of the confusion of the out-of-date system for electing them. After his downfall, the parliamentary system went through an unsatisfactory period of about 40 years during which aristocratic coteries intrigued for power, and George III (1760–1820) made an ultimately unsuccessful attempt to recover royal political initiative. Then William Pitt* the younger took over the government with the king's approval, and retained power from 1783 to 1801. He insisted that he should have complete control; his personal integrity placed him above the suspicion of exercising it dishonestly; he based his authority on public opinion. For these three reasons he did more even than Walpole to establish the office of prime ministership, although Parliament had to undergo the reform of 1832 before this office could achieve a strong basis in national acceptance.

A Prime Minister now usually has a seat in the House of Commons* and is in the first place elected as an ordinary Member of Parliament, but it is nearly always understood that he is the leader of one of the contending parties, and that the sovereign will call on him to 'form a government' if the party in question has a majority of members in the House of Commons.

* 1.4.1.2.

Primrose League

A Conservative political society founded in memory of Benjamin Disraeli*, Lord Beaconsfield, whose favourite flower was said to be the primrose. The society was founded in 1883 and achieved large membership; it was one of the earliest successful attempts at permanent organization of public opinion in support of a political party.

Princes in the Tower, The

The two sons of King Edward IV*: the 13-year old king Edward V*, and his younger brother Richard of York. They were shut up by their uncle Richard Duke of Gloucester who thereupon made himself King Richard III*. According to Sir Thomas More's* *History of King Richard III*, he then had the princes murdered. This became accepted as historical fact, and is the version of events in Shakespeare's drama *Richard III**. Moreover the discovery of the bones of two boys of about the same age buried at the foot of a staircase in the Tower is important evidence that they were murdered. But there is no proof that the murder was ordered by Richard, whose character Tudor historians were naturally inclined to blacken.

Princess Casamassima (1886)

/ka:zə'masi:mə/

A novel by Henry James*. Its theme is social revolution, and the moral issues involved in it. Hyacinth Robinson is the orphan son of an English lord and a working-woman; brought up by a dressmaker, he comes under the influence of the anarchist Anastasius Vetch and a French communist bookseller, Monsieur Poupin. His interest in radical politics bring him into relationship with the Princess Casamassima, a rich young widow who tries to achieve a sense of reality by playing with the idea of revolutionary politics, and Paul Muniment, a highly intelligent working-man, who is really motivated by the self-interested desire for power. Both of them condescend to Hyacinth, whose sensitivity and youth seem to disqualify him from a serious political role; nonetheless, it is Hyacinth, not they, who is trusted by the secret authorities of the international revolutionary organization to which they belong. Hyacinth is enabled to travel in Europe, where his eyes are opened to the richness of European culture; he does not lose his compassion for social misery, but he is now prepared 'to fight for art' which the revolutionaries in general do not understand and leave out of their calculations. He is eventually commanded to commit a political assassination, but shoots himself instead.

The novel has often been criticized for its absence of political realism; the American critic, Lionel Trilling, takes the opposite view – see his essay in *The Liberal Imagination*.

Prior, Matthew (1664–1721)

Poet and diplomat. As diplomat, he played an important part in bringing about the end of the War of the Spanish Succession* by his secret

negotiations with the French government leading in 1713 to the Treaty of Utrecht – popularly known as 'Matt's Peace'. As a poet he was particularly favoured by the Tory Party in its period of power, 1710–14. His verse shows the graceful, witty elegance and light, easy tone of the refined society of his day, and owes as much to the French tradition of 17th-C neo-classicism as to English models. His reputation chiefly survives through his short poems, though he also wrote ambitious long ones, *eg Alma; or the Progress of the Mind*, a humorous philosophical poem, and *Solomon on the Vanity of the World*, both published in 1718. Other works: The Story of the *Country and City Mouse* (with Charles Montague, 1687 – a burlesque of Dryden's *The Hind and the Panther**); *Henry and Emma*, based on the old ballad* *The Nut-Brown Maid**; *Carmen Saeculare* in honour of William III*; *Down-Hall, a Ballad*; and *The Secretary*, about his early diplomatic experiences.
Bib: Eves, C. K., *Life*; Johnson, S., in *Lives of the Poets*; Legg, L. G. W., *Prior: His Public Career*.

Prioress's Tale, The

One of Chaucer's *Canterbury Tales**. It recounts the legend of St Hugh of Lincoln. St Hugh is a widow's son who insists on walking through the Jewish ghetto on his way to school, singing a Christian hymn while he does so. In resentment, the Jews murder him, but the body is discovered because the dead boy miraculously continues to sing even after his throat has been cut. The tale is in rhyme-royal*, and is one of the shortest in the series.

Prisoner of Chillon, The (1816) /ˈʃilon/

A narrative poem of 392 lines by Lord Byron*; in 8-syllable rhyming couplets* varied by quatrains. The subject is the imprisonment of François de Bonnivard, a patriot of Geneva, by the Duke of Savoy. The imprisonment lasted from 1530 to 1536, when he was rescued.

Prisons

In 11th and 12th C dungeons (underground cells) in castles were the prisons of those who displeased powerful barons or the king, and for long afterwards the Tower of London – fortress, palace, and prison – was used for important political prisoners. In London were the royal prisons of Newgate*, the Marshalsea* and the Fleet*, which all lasted till Victorian times. In 16th C houses of correction were set up for the incarceration of vagrants, who were regarded as a menace to the peace; these were modelled on the first to be established at Bridewell*, London, in 1552, and were called 'Bridewells' after it. They were at first intended as 'workhouses' for the unemployed, but they beacme prisons in all but name. Prisoners were also kept in prison ships or 'hulks'.

Conditions in the prisons were very bad until 19th C. Three principal reasons for this were:

[1] Prisons were not considered to be the responsibility of the authorities but of the gaolers; there was thus no supervision or maintenance of even the lowest standards of decency and hygiene, or of other aspects of living conditions.

[2] The gaolers were not regarded as officials, but as though they kept lodging-houses as tenants of the local or central authorities; they were paid no salaries, and drew their incomes from the prisoners who had to pay for privileges, and from whom the gaolers often extorted money by abominable treatment.

[3] Public attention to the necessity of a secure but humane prison system was delayed by the practice of 'transporting' criminals convicted of the more serious crimes to the American colonies or, after 1783, to Australia; transportation only ceased in the 1840s.

John Howard in 18th C and Elizabeth Fry in 19th were the leaders of the movement of reform in the prison system, which only made real advance after 1850. Jeremy Bentham* was also influential in making prison organization more efficient and rational. The best known of all the writers who publicized the need for reform was Charles Dickens*; he repeatedly used prison themes and episodes in his novels.

* *Penal System; (particular prisons) Fleet, Marshalsea, Newgate, Pentonville.*

Privy Council

With a history going back to the king's council which in 13th C gave the sovereign private ('privy') advice on the government of the country, this is now a body with largely formal work, mainly carried out by committees since the membership – now conferred as a special honour – is large. The former powers of the Privy Council are now exercised by the Cabinet.

* **I.2.1.1.**

Problem Plays (of Shakespeare)

A term first used in late 19th C by critics of Shakespeare to designate a group of his plays written between 1600 and 1604. These are: *Hamlet**, *Troilus and Cressida**, *All's Well that Ends Well** and *Measure for Measure**. What makes these all 'problem plays' in the view of some critics is that it is difficult to discern the author's intention. In the case of *Hamlet* this difficulty lies in Hamlet's mysterious hesitation in carrying out revenge for the murder of his father, especially in view of the fact that he carries out several other killings without apparent remorse. *Troilus* is regarded as a problem because, while the Trojans are shown to be intrinsically nobler than the Greeks, they are also shown to be wrong, although the Greeks are not conclusively shown to be right in their outlook. Thus no positive value is preached by the play, nor does it seem to be light-hearted enough to be a mere comedy. *All's Well*, the slightest of the four, is a problem because the noble heroine uses means which we should nowadays despise to gain her lover, who does not, in any case, seem to be worth her trouble. The play is thus a 'romantic comedy' but one in which the romance has gone sour. *Measure for Measure* is a comedy which, in the opinion of some critics, is both too serious and too cynical in some of its characteristics to be successful either as a comedy or as a serious critique of society. Not every critic agrees that all these plays, or any of them, are really 'problematic'. For a general discussion of the group, see E. M. W. Tillyard: *Shakespeare's Problem Plays.*

Procrustes /prəu'krʌsti:z/

In Greek myth, a giant. He lived by robbery, and kept a famous bed on which he tied travellers; if it was too short for them, he cut off their overlapping limbs, and if too long, he stretched them to the right length. He was killed by the hero Theseus* of Athens.

Professor, The

The first novel by Charlotte Brontë*. She offered it for publication in 1846, but it was refused and not published until 1857 after her death. In the meantime she recast the material, which was based on her experience as a teacher in Brussels in 1843, and made it into *Villette**, which came out in 1853. *The Professor* has a man, William Crimsworth, for its central character, whereas *Villette* has a young woman, Lucy Snowe. William Crimsworth has a love affair with an Anglo-Swiss woman teacher analogous to Lucy's with Monsieur Paul Emmanuel, but the relationship is less intricate and profound.

Prologue to the Canterbury Tales

This poem, by Geoffrey Chaucer*, opens *The Canterbury Tales**; it is in 10-syllable couplets*, and is 858 lines long. It begins with a passage which associates the stirrings of Spring in nature with the the impulse among people to go on pilgrimages. Chaucer then describes how he put up at the Tabard Inn* in Southwark and found there a mixed company of men and woman prepared for the pilgrimage to the shrine of St Thomas at Canterbury. The pilgrims are then described, most of them in individual pen-portraits, but a few merchants and clergy are merely mentioned as a group. Chaucer then describes how the Host of the Inn welcomes them, and proposes to accompany them. He suggests that each of the party shall tell two stories on the way to Canterbury and two on the return journey. The Host himself is to be judge of the best tales, and the prize to the winner will be a supper at the Tabard, paid for by the rest of the pilgrims. Everyone agrees to this, and it is decided that the Knight shall begin.

The Prologue is especially famous for its portraits of the characters of the pilgrims. These are lively and sometimes satirical, but are always presented with a generous sympathy for the springs of vitality in each individual, whether he is righteous or sinful. They are an important source of information for social historians of medieval life, but this is the least of their merit. The personalities of the pilgrims remain important throughout the series of the Tales, and they mainly tell stories that are congruous with their characters.

Prometheus /prə'mi:θju:s/

In Greek myth, one of the Titans*.

In the war between the gods and the Titans, he remained neutral, and was still on terms with Zeus* when the gods were victorious. He was, however, very cunning, and skilled at outwitting the enemy of his race.

At a meeting of gods and men to decide what portion of sacrificed animals was due to the gods, Prometheus arranged two piles; in one of these the good flesh was concealed beneath the offal, and in the other, the animal's fat concealed merely its bones. Zeus chose the second pile, and in his rage at the deception he deprived mankind of fire. Prometheus, however, stole fire from the gods, and gave it to man. Zeus then tried to punish man by sending the first woman (Pandora*) with her jar of misfortunes; Hope, however, was left to man when the misfortunes were released to plague humanity. Zeus now tried to drown the human race in a great flood. According to one tradition, Prometheus succeeded in saving humanity by getting his son Deucalion to trick Zeus into granting a prayer; according to another, he recreated humanity with the help of the goddess Athene. To punish Prometheus for repeatedly outwitting him, Zeus had him bound to Mount Caucasus, and sent an eagle which gnawed incessantly at his liver. Prometheus, however, refused to ask pardon, and withheld a secret affecting Zeus's destiny. Eventually, Zeus allowed Heracles* to free the Titan, who told the secret, and enabled Zeus to save himself. Prometheus was mortal, and on his death descended to the underworld. However, at the prayer of the centaur, Cheiron, he was eventually released, and permitted by Zeus to join the company of the gods.

Prometheus Unbound (1819)

A verse drama by P. B. Shelley*, written to correspond to the final lost play of the Promethean trilogy by the Greek poet, Aeschylus*. Shelley does not, however, attempt to imitate the form of a Greek tragedy, or to use the same assumptions as the Greek myth, nor does he attempt to fit the drama to stage requirements – it is essentially to be read. The poem is an expression of Shelley's revolutionary idealism, and is divided into 4 acts. Instead of ending, as in the Aeschylus trilogy, with the reconciliation of Jupiter (Zeus*) and Prometheus, Jupiter is overthrown in Act III by Demogorgon*, whom Shelley conceives to be the ultimate destiny governing the world. Act IV shows the reign of love, peace and freedom which immediately follows, since Shelley believed that evil, in the form of oppression and cruelty, was an irrelevant accident in human experience, and could be overthrown by a supreme act of will. The figures in the poem thus make an allegorical pattern as follows: Prometheus stands for all that is finest in humanity and for the spirit of patient and heroic resistance to oppression; Jupiter stands for this oppression; the Earth is the mother of Prometheus, and Asia, or nature, is his bride.

Proserpine

* *Persephone.*

Protestant Succession

The belief that the throne should not pass to a Roman Catholic. The arguments about the royal succession became bitter when Charles II* was succeeded by his brother James II*. James's Catholicism was only one reason for the Revolution of 1688* but the fear of a return of James or of later succession by other Catholics caused further controversy and led to the Act of Settlement of 1701 and later Acts which made it impossible for a Catholic to succeed to the throne.

* *Protestantism.*

Protestantism

A term used for all varieties of Christian belief which broke away from Roman Catholicism during the Reformation* in 16th C, or for religious communities not in agreement with Roman Catholicism but originating since the Reformation. It was first used in regard to those who protested against the Empire Charles V's condemnation of the reformers in Germany at the Diet of Spires, 1529. Protestants in Britain include Anglicans*, Presbyterians*, Methodists*, and Baptists*.

* 3.2.2.

Proteus /ˈprəutjuːs/

In Greek myth, a sea spirit, whose task it was to care for the herds of the sea (*ie* seals, etc.) He had prophetic power, but those who wished to consult him had to catch him and bind him when he came ashore for his midday sleep. This was no easy task, since Proteus was able to turn himself into any shape he pleased.

Prothalamion

* *Ode*; *Spenser.*

Proust, Marcel (1871–1922)

French novelist, author of *A la Recherche du Temps Perdu*, of which a celebrated English translation was made by C. K. Scott-Moncrieff under the title of 'Remembrance of Things Past'. It was originally published in eight parts from 1913 until 1927: *Du Côté de Chez Swann* ('Swann's Way'); *A l'Ombre des Jeunes Filles en Fleurs* ('Within a Budding Grove'); *Le Côté de Guermantes* I ('The Guermantes Way'); *Le Côté de Guermantes* II and *Sodome et Gomorrhe* I ('The Cities of the Plain'); *Sodome et Gomorrhe* II; *La Prisonnière* ('The Captive)'; *Albertine Disparue* ('The Sweet Cheat Gone'); *Le Temps Retrouvé* ('Time Regained'). The eighth part was translated by Stephen Hudson. Proust had to publish the first part at his own expense because he could not find a publisher, but the second received the Prix Goncourt.

Proust was the son of a fashionable Parisian doctor and a Jewish mother. The family was rich, and his youth was spent circulating among the most distinguished aristocratic and intellectual circles in Paris. After the death of his mother in 1905, he retired into a solitude which he dedicated to the writing of his novel. This is a portrait of the society among which he had moved seen through the mind of his first person narrator, Marcel; his mind occupies the foreground of the narrative to the extent of becoming its real subject. We are no longer provided with a coherent plot structure as we are by most 19th-C novelists: the form of events is that afforded by the growth of his consciousness through his personal relationships, and still more, through the accumulation of intimate sensations which, from childhood onwards, build up his sense of identity. Proust uses the faculty of memory in a new way: instead of being subjected to a moral or social idea of what is worth remembering, and consequently sifted for its relevancies, it becomes the keystone of the other faculties, enabling them to compose themselves into unique artistic coherence.

Proust's novel achieved great prestige in British literary circles, partly because it was the most advanced realization of a new kind of literary art in which other novelists and some poets were also experimenting. His subtle minuteness in rendering the human consciousness subjectively, for example, recalls both Henry James* and James Joyce*. His perception that the insignificance of an incident at the time of experiencing it may contrast with the importance it may come to have in the memory anticipates Virginia Woolf* in *eg To the Lighthouse**. His artistic design by which personal relationships amplify through a lifetime into a pattern like that of themes in a musical composition became a new artistic form emulated, for instance, by Anthony Powell* in *The Music of Time.* On the other hand, other 20th-C novelists, such as D. H. Lawrence* and L. H. Myers*, approaching human experience from quite different assumptions, have rejected Proust on the grounds that the principles of his art are merely aesthetic; that he ignores ranges of moral and spiritual values which shape human nature.

Psalms, The /saːmz/

A book of the Old Testament composed of the sacred songs of the ancient Jewish religion. In ancient Hebrew, they were called 'praise-songs', indicating the predominant function of the collection, though other functions – lament, meditation imprecation etc. – were included. Authorship was traditionally attributed to King David*, but it is evident that the psalms either date from after the Babylonian Captivity* (6th C BC) or were re-edited then; in any case they originated at different periods. A predominant theme is the power of God to rescue from misfortune, and his special care for his special city, Jerusalem. Though they are above all hymns affirming God's concern for the Jews, there is little that is so specific in their language as to limit their relevance for other people, especially if Jerusalem is interpreted symbolically; thus the psalms continued as the principal instrument of Christian worship, as well as Jewish.

In 16th C under the inspiration of the Protestant Reformation*, the psalms were translated into English. The task presented the usual problems of translating poetry: in the ancient Hebrew they were rhythmical but unrhymed, and this sound pattern could not be reproduced in English;

however, they also had a rhetorical pattern of parallel statement, and this could be conveyed in either prose or verse. Both were tried. There are two prose versions in official use in the Church of England: that of the Authorized Version of the Bible of 1611, and the older translation in the Book of Common Prayer* dating from 1549. Both include some of the well-known masterpieces of English prose of the Renaissance*. In addition, there are the metrical and rhymed versions especially favoured by the more extreme Protestants. The so-called 'Old Version' by Sternhold and Hopkins was published in its complete form in 1562, and some of their psalms became battle-hymns of the Puritans*, *eg* 'the Old Hundredth': 'All people that on earth do dwell'. Another version, principally the work of Francis Rouse, came into general use in Scotland in mid-17th C, and in 1696 Nicholas Brady and Nahum Tate produced the so-called 'New Version'. The metrical versions depart farther from the original Hebrew than do the prose translations, and with a few exceptions such as 'the Old Hundredth' they lack distinction as poetry. More distinguished attempts to versify the prose psalms were made in 16th C by Sir Philip Sidney* and his sister the Countess of Pembroke*; in 17th, by George Sandys, George Wither, and John Milton*; in 19th, by John Keble.

Psyche /ˈsaiki/

In Greek myth, a personification of the human soul. She was a girl so beautiful that she aroused the jealousy of Aphrodite*, the goddess of sexual love. She told her son Eros, the god of love, to punish Psyche for her beauty by causing her to fall in love with base men. However, Eros fell in love with her himself, and kept her in a magnificent palace where he visited her only at night. She thus never saw him face to face, and did not know his true identity; he warned her that should she try to see him or discover who he was, he would leave her for ever. However, her curiosity was too great for her, and one night she lit a lamp to see him; he awoke, and departed. The palace vanished, and Psyche became the victim of a series of terrible ordeals imposed on her by Aphrodite; however, she survived these, thanks to the invisible protection of Eros, who finally persuaded Zeus to allow Psyche to be admitted among the gods. Psyche has been the subject of a number of poems in English, the most famous of which is the *Ode to Psyche* (1819) by John Keats*.

* *Odes, Keats's.*

Ptolemy (Claudius Ptolemaeus) (2nd C AD) /ˈtolimi/

Astronomer, geographer, and mathematician. He was a native of the Egyptian city of Alexandria, and may have been of Greek origin. His theory of the structure of the universe, according to which the planets, sun and stars all revolved round the earth, remained the accepted opinion until replaced by the theory of Copernicus* in 16th C and the observations of Galileo* early in 17th. This is the Ptolemaic System summarized in the *Almagest*, his treatise on astronomy.

'Pub' (Public House)

A house which is licensed to sell intoxicating drinks to be enjoyed on the premises, essentially the same as a 'tavern' – a word which is now seldom used but is sometimes assumed by a pub which wishes to appear picturesque. Licensing laws controlling the sale of drink go back to 1551, when it first became necessary to obtain permission from a magistrate* to open a tavern. This long history is not so much evidence of English Puritanism as of the reputation the nation had, and kept until 20th C, for the vice of drunkenness. Pubs since 1910 have been allowed to open only at certain hours; hence the phrase 'opening time' when they open their doors. Socially, the English pub has the peculiarity that it is commonly divided into different bars: the 'public bar' where the beer is slightly cheaper, and the 'saloon bar'. Some pubs, especially the old-fashioned ones, are further divided into the 'lounge bar', the 'private bar', the 'jug and bottle' (where patrons are served when they wish to take drink to their homes), and even a 'ladies' bar'. This segmentation probably derives from the time when drunkenness was more common, and gentlemanly customers did not wish to associate with drunken working-men. Until recently it was a social principle that no woman 'who called herself a lady' ever entered a pub unaccompanied by one of the male sex, and this tradition still has some force. Most pubs are 'tied houses', *ie* they are owned by particular brewers who stock them with their own beers; a 'free house' is one not so owned, and free to buy its beer where it chooses. Beer is the principal drink consumed in pubs, but they also sell distilled spirits and wines.

* *Inns, Taverns, Alehouses.*

Public Schools

In Britain these are not and have never been either schools under the state, or entirely non-feepaying schools. They are distinguished from 'private' schools in not being run for private profit by individual owners; like the colleges of Oxford and Cambridge, they were founded and endowed for the public good, often for poor scholars. Until the Education Act of 1944, they were often hard to distinguish from endowed Grammar Schools; the latter were, however, more likely to draw on the immediate locality for their pupils, whereas the public schools drew on the whole nation, with varying provision for 'poor scholars'. Since, until 19th C, education was largely restricted to study of the classics – ancient Greek and Latin language and literature – they tended to attract, in the Middle Ages*, those who were to enter the Church and the learned professions; from 16th C it became increasingly regarded as indispensable to 'a gentleman' that he should possess a firm classical culture, and from 18th C, public schools began to be aristocratic educational institutions. The middle classes often had little use for the education they provided, or they were excluded as Dissenters and went to a Dissenting Academy instead, where in any case the education was wider and more practical. A change came in 19th C when the middle classes had enormously increased in wealth and numbers and many of them aspired to be or regarded themselves as 'gentlemen' and required a 'gentleman's education' for their sons. Several other causes extended public school education to much of the middle class: Dissenting Academies declined and public school education broadened; Thomas Arnold* as headmaster of Rugby* (1828–42) imbued it with strong religious and moral feeling, suited to the traditions of the middle classes, in which Puritanism was a large element; the country needed a large governing class for its rapidly growing empire. Now that this empire has gone, various motives, creditable and less creditable, cause the English upper and middle classes to maintain the public schools; sometimes the motive may be snobbery, but it is often the great educational prestige that some public schools have acquired. The nature of this prestige varies greatly, since 20th-C public schools do not conform to a model. In 19th C the inspiration of Arnold tended to make the public schools somewhat narrow; leadership and fair-mindedness were cultivated at the expense of wide culture and intellectual flexibility. When Arnold's son, the poet and critic Matthew Arnold*, described the English upper classes as 'barbarians', he was thinking of the products of the great public schools.

Some public schools date from 19th C, but those with greatest prestige are usually much older: Winchester (founded 1382); Westminster (1560); Eton (1440); Harrow (1571); Rugby (1567). Some characteristics shared by most public schools are these: they are usually boarding-schools, and of one sex only; boys' schools use the 'prefect system' by which discipline is maintained by specially appointed senior boys who have authority (very often) to inflict punishment by beating; strong emphasis is placed on games as a means of education. Even these few generalizations are not safely made for all modern public schools. Many criticisms have been levelled at the system; the arguments, for and against, are too often clouded by prejudice.

The public school system is 'English' rather than 'British', since it has flourished mainly in England, and has never become characteristic of Scotland, Wales or Ireland, though distinguished public schools exist in those countries. It was at one time a predominantly masculine system, although there are now a large number of girls' public schools.

* **2.1.2.3**; *Schools in England.*

Puck

In Old English, an evil spirit; from 16th C a mischievous fairy, as in Shakespeare's *A Midsummer Night's Dream**.

* *Fairies.*

Pun

* *Figures of Speech.*

Punch

A weekly comic periodical, founded in 1841.

Hood* and Thackeray* were early members of its staff, and it employed a number of distinguished illustrators in 19th C including Leech, Tenniel, Keene, and Du Maurier. From 1849 for a century it kept the same cover picture – of Punch* of the puppet-shows. It was at first a radical paper, but as it became more and more an upper class 'institution', so in politics, tone and taste it began to represent an influential but increasingly narrow section of the upper middle class. Since 1945, it has once more become comparatively radical.

Punch and Judy

The principal characters of a popular puppet-show. There are allusions to Punch in the diaries of Pepys* and Evelyn*, and the show can still be seen, especially at seaside resorts. Punch is hook-nosed, humpbacked, violent and cunning; he is always represented with his wife Judy, who is not particularly grotesque, and a little dog Toby – usually real. Punch kills his wife and the dog, beats the doctor who comes to visit him, hangs the hangman who is supposed to execute him, and eventually outwits the devil.

* *Mime: Pantomime.*

Purcell, Henry (1658–95) /ˈpəːsl/

Composer. His father and uncle held musical appointments at the Chapel Royal, and his father was also master of the choristers of Westminster Abbey. He himself became a chorister in the Chapel Royal as a young boy, and as a young man was made 'composer in ordinary to the king' and organist at the Abbey. He composed some instrumental pieces, but is especially famous for his choral compositions. Some of these were church music, *eg* the *Te Deum and Jubilate* (1694), which was the first English religious work to be scored for both strings and brass. His official appointments also caused him to set choral odes written for official occasions, such as the odes to St Cecilia. In addition, he collaborated with a number of Restoration* dramatists in writing for the theatre including a musical setting for a masque* in Betterton's drama *Diocletian* and musical numbers in several dramas by Dryden*: *Tyrannic Love* (1687), *Amphitryon* (1690), *King Arthur* (1691). This work for the theatre included a musical version of Shakespeare's *Midsummer Night's Dream*, entitled *The Fairy Queen* (1693). His masterpiece was his opera *Dido and Aeneas* (1689), with a libretto by Nahum Tate.

Purcell's career concluded the great period of English music which had begun in mid-16th C. In his youth one of his principal teachers had been the English composer John Blow, but he was also a close student of French and Italian musical development. As a composer he had great freedom of imagination and strong gifts for dramatic writing.

* *Opera in England.*

Purgatorio

The second book of the *Divine Comedy* by the 14th-C Italian poet Dante*. Still guided by Virgil*, the poet, having emerged from Inferno* or Hell, follows a spiral road up the Mount of Purgatory, where the souls of the dead are purged of their sins while they await release into Heaven (Paradiso*). The mountain is divided into seven terraces, corresponding to the Seven Deadly Sins*. On its summit is the Earthly Paradise, where the poet meets Beatrice, who is to guide him through the spheres of Heaven.

* *Purgatory.*

Purgatory

According to Catholic faith, a state in which the souls of the dead undergo purification from their sins on earth. These sins must be 'venial' not 'mortal', *ie* not so serious as to cause the soul damnation in Hell, yet too serious for them to attain the spiritual perfection that enjoys the eternal bliss of Heaven. It is believed that the prayers of the living on earth can shorten the duration of Purgatory. The Protestant Churches, with the exception of Anglo-Catholic members of the Church of England, do not accept the doctrine of Purgatory.

Puritanism

The term is used in a narrow sense of religious practice and attitudes, and in a broad sense of an ethical outlook which is much less easy to define.

[1] In its strict sense, 'Puritan' was applied to those Protestant reformers who rejected Queen Elizabeth's religious settlement of 1560. This settlement sought a middle way between Roman Catholicism and the extreme spirit of reform of Geneva*. The Puritans, influenced by Geneva, Zurich, and other continental centres, objected to the retention of bishops and to any appearance of what they regarded as superstition in church worship – the wearing of vestments by the priests, and any kind of religious image. Apart from their united opposition to Roman Catholicism and their insistence on simplicity in religious forms, Puritans disagreed among themselves on questions of doctrine and church organization. The principal sects were: Presbyterians*, Independents (at first called Brownists*, and later Congregationalists*), Baptists*, and (later) Quakers*. They were strong in the towns, especially in London, and in the University of Cambridge, and socially they were widespread, and included members of the aristocracy and of the working classes, as well as the middle, commercial classes where they had their chief strength. Puritanism was very strong in the first half of 17th C and reached its peak of power after the Civil War* of 1642–6 – a war which was ostensibly religious, although it was also political. Matters of church government were much involved with matters of state government, since Presbyterians and Independents, who believed in popular control of the church, were not likely to tolerate royal control of Parliament's political affairs. Puritanism was both religiously and politically supreme in the decade 1650–60, but on the Restoration* of the monarchy Puritans were denied participation in the Church of England, and refused rights of free religious worship. The last was granted them by the Toleration Act of 1689, and during 18th C both Puritanism and the official attitude to it were modified under the influence of Rationalism. Nonetheless, the Methodist* movement of that century had many of the characteristics of the older Puritan sects. It was, moreover, only in 1829 that Nonconformists (as they were now called) were allowed to offer themselves as candidates for seats in Parliament, and only in 1871 did the Universities of Oxford and Cambridge cease to be the monopoly of the Church of England.

[2] In the broader sense of a whole way of life, puritanism has always represented strict obedience to the dictates of conscience and strong emphasis on the virtue of self-denial. In this sense individuals can be described as 'puritan' whether or not they belong to one of the recognized Puritan sects, or even if they are atheists.

The word 'Puritan' is often thought to imply hostility to the arts, but this is not necessarily true. In the reign of Elizabeth I* poets such as Spenser* and Sidney* combined a strong puritan moral tone (without any Puritan doctrine in the sectarian sense) with an intense delight in artistic form; in 17th C John Milton was an ardent Puritan, but his poetry is one of the great climaxes of English Renaissance* art. However, it is true that the strict Puritans of the age of Shakespeare were commonly opponents of the art of the theatre; this was partly because the theatres were sometimes scenes of moral licentiousness and disorder, and partly because the strict Puritan, in his intense love of truth, was very inclined to confuse fiction with lying. Thus in later 17th C Bunyan was criticized by some of his Puritan comrades for writing fiction in his allegory, *Pilgrim's Progress**, and in early 18th C Defoe* had to defend his *Robinson Crusoe** against similar charges. Nonetheless, in 18th and 19th C, Puritanism, or attitudes derived from it, did tend to encourage 'philistinism', or contempt for culture. This was because Puritanism had always encouraged an essentially practical attitude to worldly affairs, and when religion slackened as a driving force, the practical virtues came to be regarded as the principal, if not the only ones. Art, on the other hand, encourages the contemplative virtues, which the practical man of Puritan tradition was inclined to regard as unnecessary, therefore frivolous, and so, in a puritan sense, 'sinful'. There is continuity of development from Priestley, the 18th-C scientist and preacher, through the practical philosophy of Bentham*, to James Mill, the Utilitarian* leader, who was an atheist.

What is called the 'Puritan conscience', on the other hand, had an important influence on one kind of art form – the novel. Puritans believed that the good life could only be lived by 'the inner light' – the voice of God in the heart – and to discern this light it was necessary to conduct the most scrupulous self-enquiry. This produced the kind of spiritual autobiography that was common in mid-17th C, and of which the best example is Bunyan's *Grace Abounding**. Such self-knowledge had two important consequences: it increased interest in, and understanding of, the human heart in others as well as the self, and the first results of this are apparent in Bunyan's *Pilgrim's Progress*; but it also encouraged a sense of the loneliness of the individual – a sense that was supported by the growing economic individualism of the later 17th C. These are important constituents of the novelist's vision, and when one adds to them the preoccupation with moral values with which Puritanism is so bound up, and which are such a permanent feature of the English novel, it is possible to think that without Puritanism the novel form would never have developed indigenously in England.

* 1.3.1.1; 3.2.2.2; *Reformation.*

Purity

A medieval alliterative* poem of 14th C; it has survived on the same manuscript as *Sir Gawain and the Green Knight**, *Patience**, and *Pearl**. This fact, together with the fact that all four poems are written in the same north-western dialect and share some similarities of style, has led scholars to suppose that they may be by the same poet. *Purity* is a narrative about the Fall of the Angels, the Angels' Visit to Abraham, the Feast of Balthazar, and the Fall of Nebuchadnezzar. Though it is a poem of relatively high quality, it is not usually considered to equal the outstanding merit of *Sir Gawain* and *Pearl.*

Puss in Boots

A folk tale, translated into English in 1729 from the French collection by Charles Perrault*. The cat is the property of a poor man, the third son of a miller. By the animal's ingenuity, the miller's son marries the king's daughter. The story is a popular theme of Christmas pantomimes*.

Puttenham, George (d 1590) /ˈpʌtənəm/

The reputed author of *The Art of English Poesy* (1589). The book is a thorough treatise on English poetic technique at the time, on the threshold of one of the great decades of English short poems. It discusses the various forms of metrical verse, discusses – without deciding between them – the rival merits of metrical and non-metrical forms, and presents an enlightened review of English verse. With Sidney's *Apology for Poetry**, Puttenham's book is one of the two most important critical works of the Elizabethan* period. It is more scholarly, if less eloquent, than Sidney's essay, but like Sidney, Puttenham is trying to establish civilized standards for the composition of poetry, and is opposed to the 'vulgar', popular traditions of a poet such as Skelton*.

* 7.1.

Pygmalion /pigˈmeiljən/

In Greek myth, a king of Cyprus famous for his sculpture. He made an ivory statue of a woman, so beautiful that he fell in love with it, and was in despair because the statue could not return his love. Aphrodite* took pity on him, and brought the statue to life.

Pygmalion (1912)

A play by George Bernard Shaw*. The theme is the transformation of an impoverished, illiterate and wretchedly neglected London girl into the image of a fashionable lady who can make an imposing appearance at an ambassador's reception. The transformation is contrived by the phonetician Higgins, who undertakes it as a scientific experiment; he resembles the sculptor Pygmalion in bringing into existence a being of great beauty, but, like Pygmalion's statue, Lizzie possesses no life, in this case because Higgins has invested no feelings in her, merely using her as an instrument of his research. The play has always had great success, though it is one of the least convincing of Shaw's plays: the real transformation of Lizzie could not have been made by changing Lizzie's speech sounds, and Shaw falls a victim to the same fallacy that he exposes in Higgins, inasmuch as he, too, fails to understand the true nature of his own creation.

Pygmies

A race of people who had very small stature, frequently referred to as living in Africa and fighting wars with giant birds (cranes), by ancient Greek writers. They were probably the ancestors of the modern Pygmies of Central Africa.

Pyramus and Thisbe /ˈpirəməs – ˈθizbi/

The hero and heroine of a love story by the Roman poet Ovid* (*Metamorphoses** iv). The lovers are forbidden marriage by their parents, but they exchange vows through a hole in the wall that separates their respective houses. They agree to meet outside Babylon at the tomb of Ninus, but Thisbe, who arrives first, is frightened by a lion and hides in a cave, the lion meanwhile covering her dropped veil with blood. When Pyramus arrives and finds the bloody veil, he supposes

Thisbe to be dead, and kills himself; Thisbe follows his example. In Shakespeare's play *A Midsummer Night's Dream** the artisans give a comically bungled performance of the tragedy before King Theseus of Athens.

Pyrrhus (318–272 BC) /'pirəs/

A King of Epirus, in northern Greece. He made war against the Romans, the Greeks of Southern Italy, and the Carthaginians. After a victory over the Greeks and Romans at Heraclea, his own losses were so heavy that he declared: 'One more such victory, and we are lost.' This is the origin of the phrase 'a Pyrrhic victory', meaning one gained at too great a cost.

Pytchley /'paitʃli/

The name of a famous 'hunt', *ie* pack of foxhounds, in the Midlands of England.

* *Fox-hunting.*

Pythagoras (6th C BC) /pai'θagərəs/

Greek philosopher. He is important in the histories of religion, mathematics, and astronomy. In religion he founded the Pythagorean brotherhood, which believed in the immortality of the soul and its migration into another body, perhaps that of an animal, after death; for this reason they practised vegetarianism. In mathematics, he discovered the mathematical relations of musical intervals; he or his followers believed that the sun and the planets were divided by comparable intervals – hence the tradition of 'the music of the spheres' inaudible to earthly hearing. In geometry, he is credited with the theorem called after him, that the square on the hypotenuse of a right-angled triangle is equal to the sum of the squares on the other two sides. In astronomy, he discovered that day and night are caused by the revolution of the earth about its own axis.

Many legends grew up round Pythagoras, amongst others that he was of extraordinary beauty and had golden thighs. Historically, his ascetic philosophy, based on the belief that the body was the tomb of the soul and that denial of the flesh was the way to its final release, is considered to foreshadow Platonism*.

Pythia /'piθiə/

In Greek myth, the python was a great snake slain by the god Apollo* at Delphi*, and the source of the Delphic oracle. It was the child of Earth, and there was said to be an oracle of Earth before Apollo took possession of Delphi. The Pythia or the Pythoness was the priestess of Apollo who delivered the oracle. The Pythian Games were held in honour of Apollo's victory over the Python.

* *Oracle.*

Q

Quadrille

[1] A game of cards which replaced ombre* in fashion about 1726, to be succeeded about twenty years later by whist.

[2] A dance of French origin; it was first used in ballet, and then became popular in the ballroom. Introduced into England in late 18th C.

Quadrivium and Trivium /kwo'driviəm – 'triviəm/

In medieval education, the 'seven liberal arts' were divided into the Trivium – grammar, rhetoric, logic – followed by the Quadrivium – arithmetic, geometry, astronomy, music.

Quakers

Originally a derisive name for the members of a religious society properly called the Society of Friends; the Friends are still known as Quakers, but the term has lost its contemptuous significance. The Society was founded by George Fox*, who began his preaching career in 1647. He preached that the truth came from an inner spiritual light, and declared that no special class of men (*ie* priests) or buildings (*ie* churches) should be set apart for religious purposes. This individualism at first attracted a number of mentally disturbed followers whose ecstasies are perhaps responsible for the nickname 'Quaker', though Fox himself declared that it was first used in 1650 because he taught his followers to 'Tremble at the Word of the Lord'. They held the view, unusual among Puritans*, that it was possible to gain complete victory over sin in this life. Such a doctrine, in addition to their refusal to accept those religious institutions that the other Puritans accepted, made them intensely unpopular for the first 10 years of their existence. Later they became influential far beyond their numbers, which have remained comparatively few. Owing to the freedom of mind which is the essence of the movement, it is difficult to define their doctrine, which seems to vary greatly among individuals. On the other hand they are well known for a range of characteristic virtues: humanitarianism (they were amongst the first to protest against slavery – 1688); non-resistance to violence; respect for individuals regardless of race, sex, or religion; sobriety of conduct and tranquillity of mind. One of the most important of their early members was William Penn (1644–1718), the founder of the American colony of Pennsylvania. Like other Puritans, they were prominent in commerce, but took care to engage in activities that were not harmful; in consequence Quaker names are particularly well known in connection with the manufacture of chocolate. However, in 18th C their outstanding importance was in banking: their sober-mindedness and strictness of morality counteracted the speculative manias of the time, and did much to establish secure financial foundations for the rapid expansion of British trade.

Quarles, Francis (1592–1644) /kwa:lz/

A minor poet of the Metaphysical* School, chiefly famous for his *Emblems* (1635), verse meditations in connection with visual illustrations, in the tradition of the emblem-books*. His facility of expression without complexity of thought made him very popular in 17th and 18th C amongst the less well educated.

Quarter Days

Days which mark the division of the year into four quarters. They are used especially for the payments of rents, and for entering or leaving houses that have been bought or sold. Festival* days were chosen as quarter days, and these were originally Whitsuntide (50 days after Easter), Lammas (1 August), Martinmas (11 November), and Candlemas (2 February). These were later changed to Lady Day (25 March), Midsummer Day (24 June), Michaelmas (29 September), and Christmas (25 December). Scotland keeps the old quarter days.

Quarterly Review, The

A Tory review, founded in 1809 in opposition to the Whig* *Edinburgh Review*. Walter Scott* was one of its most famous early supporters and contributors; its first editor was William Gifford*, and he was succeeded by Scott's son-in-law, John Lockhart, and Coleridge's* nephew, Sir John Coleridge. In 1818 the *Quarterly* published a very severe review of the poem *Endymion** by John Keats, and (in the opinion of Lord Byron) is supposed thereby to have hastened Keats's death in 1821. However, Keats, in a letter of October 1818, wrote that he was severer as a critic of himself than the *Quarterly* was. The review was not entirely unjust, but it was meanly based on political prejudice more than on literary grounds: Keats was a friend of Leigh Hunt*, the editor of the formidable radical* weekly paper, *The Examiner**. To balance the attack on Keats, it should be remembered that the *Quarterly* published one of the first favourable reviews of Jane Austen*, by Walter Scott.

Quarto /'kwo:təu/

A term used in publishing to designate a size of volume, made by folding the standard paper twice instead of only once (folio* size). The quarto editions of Shakespeare's* plays are those published in his lifetime, as distinct from the folio collected editions after his death. Twenty of his plays appeared in separate quarto editions.

* *Shakespeare – History of Textual Study.*

Quatrain /'kwotrein/

A stanza of four lines, usually rhyming *a b a b* or *a b c b*.

Queen Mab

A name for the Queen of the fairies used in Shakespeare's *Romeo and Juliet** (I. iv), Drayton's *Nymphidia**, and Shelley's* polemical poem *Queen Mab* (1813).

Queen of Hearts, The

[1] A character in an English nursery rhyme* based on the figures in a pack of cards.

[2] A character in *Alice's Adventures in Wonderland* by Lewis Carroll*, based on the nursery-rhyme character.

[3] A nickname of Elizabeth of Bohemia, daughter of King James I* and grandmother of George I.

Queen of the May

* *May Day.*

Queen's Maries (or Marys), The

Mary Queen of Scots* is supposed to have had four ladies attendant on her, all with the first name of Mary –

There was Mary Beaton, and Mary Seaton,
Mary Carmichael, and me.

These lines come from a ballad referring to 18th-C events, but were later transferred to Mary's ladies. The names are given variously in Scottish ballads*, the fourth name being Livingstone, Fleming, or Hamilton.

Queenhithe /'kwi:nhaið/

One of the former quays of the City of London; it was situated near London Bridge.

Quorn /kwo:n/

A famous pack of fox-hounds in the Midlands of England.

* *Fox-hunting.*

R

Rabelais, François (1495?–1553) /'rabəlei/

French humanist* and satirist. He began his career as a Franciscan* friar, then became a Benedictine* monk, and finally abandoned the religious life and became a physician, credited with being the first to practise dissection. His famous works are *Pantagruel** (1533) and *Gargantua** (1535); these were later reversed in order, since Gargantua was the father of Pantagruel. These satirical romances were continued with the *Third Book* (1545) and the *Fourth Book* (with the other three) in 1552. There was also a *Fifth Book*, which is not certainly his.

Gargantua, the giant, and Pantagruel, were heroes of popular medieval romance, linked with the legends of King Arthur*. Rabelais drops King Arthur, and uses the characters and their adventures to satirize the rigidity of education in his time and to advocate a free and abundant expression of the human intellect and appetites. Gargantua has immense capacities of eating and drinking (hence 'a Gargantuan appetite') and his other capacities for fullness of life are in proportion. He founds the abbey of Thelema, which is the opposite in all its characteristics to the abbeys that Rabelais knew:

it is free and luxurious with no rules but 'Do what you will.' *Pantagruel* introduces the character of Panurge, who possesses immense talents but no morality; his investigations of the desirability of marriage and his voyages in search of the Oracle of the Holy Bottle are the subject of Books 3 and 4 ending with the bottle's advice which is 'Drink.'

Rabelais's style is exuberant, and his humour is uninhibited. In English tradition, the adjective 'Rabelaisian' is often used as the opposite of 'Puritan'. Puritanism* implies moral introspection, self-denial, and the sensitive conscience; its bad sides are a tendency to replace sympathy by censure, narrowness in judging behaviour, and self-complacency amounting to hypocrisy. Any writer exhibiting opposing qualities to these defects, and especially writers who are uninhibited in the expression of the human appetites, is apt to be called 'Rabelaisian' in English literature. Jonathan Swift* had Rabelais's generous indignation, but his furious disgust is un-Rabelaisian. Laurence Sterne* had much of Rabelais's emancipation, but he also possessed a sly pruriency which is contrary to Rabelais's candour. The Elizabethan journalist Thomas Nashe* shares much of the French writer's energy; Robert Burton's *Anatomy of Melancholy** has a comparable amplitude of language; and Samuel Butler's bitter attack on the Puritans, the mock epic* *Hudibras**, is Rabelaisian in its coarse, bitter humour. Nashe, Burton and Butler were all consciously indebted to Rabelais; amongst 20th-C writers, so was James Joyce in *Ulysses** and *Finnegans Wake**. Rabelais was notably translated by the Scotsman Thomas Urquhart (Bks. I–II, 1653; Bk. III, 1693).

Racine, Jean (1639–99) /ra'si:n/

French dramatist; he was the greatest exemplar of the French ideal of 'pure' tragedy. The noble, disciplined rhetoric of his poetry was in accordance with French neo-classicism*, which was not, as in England, a largely alien regimentation imposed on the native culture, but a natural product of an essentially classical culture centring on a formal, ordered, magnificent royal court and an aristocracy which was more rigidly defined than its English counterpart but was highly cultivated. Racine (like his predecessor Corneille*) exercised a powerful influence on his English contemporaries, notably the writers of 'heroic drama', Dryden* and Otway*, who emulated him without ever approaching his greatness. His greatest plays were: *Andromaque* (1667); *Britannicus* (1669); *Bérénice* (1670); *Mithridate* (1673); *Iphigénie* (1674); *Phèdre* (1677); *Athalie* (1690).

Radcliffe, Mrs Ann (1764–1823)

Novelist. She was one of the most famous of the writers of Gothic novels*, who sought to gain their effect through mystery and the supernatural in a setting of grand scenic description. She was immensely popular in her own day for her four novels: *The Sicilian Romance* (1790); *The Romance of the Forest* (1791); *The Mysteries of Udolpho** (1794), and *The Italian* (1797). *Udolpho* is the most remembered, owing to satirization through an account of its effect on a young girl in Jane Austen's *Northanger Abbey**.

Radicalism

The political views of Radicals, who believe in the need for thorough reform going right to the roots (the meaning of 'radical') and origins of undemocratic abuses. The term probably originated in 1797 with the declaration of Charles James Fox that 'radical reform' was necessary. In early 19th C it had the pejorative connotation that 'extremist' has today.

Rainbow, The (1915)

A novel by D. H. Lawrence*. It is set in Lawrence's own background, the English Midlands; the subject is three generations of the Brangwen family extending from the middle of the last century to the early years of the present one.

The Brangwens are a family of farmers and have for generations lived on their own land which, by the time at which the novel begins, is near an encroaching industrial area. The men of the family are depicted as concentrating their minds earthwards, on their work and surroundings; the women have tended to look outwards to society, and to emulate their social superiors. Tom Brangwen, the first of the main characters, is sent to a grammar school (**Schools in England*) by his ambitious mother; the experience both frustrates him and arouses him. His awakened need for what is strange and mysterious attracts him to Lydia Lensky, an aristocratic but impoverished Polish exile, a widow, and the mother of a small daughter. Their marriage meets difficulties but becomes a happy one: Lydia and Tom remain ignorant of much in each other's nature, but Lydia finds confidence in Tom's established way of life, while he finds enlargement precisely in what, for him, is mysterious in his wife. Tom's stepdaughter, Anna, is attracted to his nephew, Will Brangwen, who has had an urban upbringing and has a strong artistic imagination and profound religious instincts inherited from his forefathers. This marriage is much less happy. Anna is suspicious and jealous of her husband's religious spirit, and since he himself cannot relate it to a way of life, she succeeds in destroying it. In doing so, she unintentionally transforms him from an original artist into a mere craftsman in the William Morris* style. They are united in a passionate night-time sensuality, but have no daylight union. Their daughter, Ursula, belongs to the first generation of the modern woman: she sets out to be a teacher, and after an intense struggle in one of the characteristically inhuman English board schools, she succeeds in affirming her independence. But her love affair with Skrebensky, a thoroughly Anglicized descendant of another Polish exile, ends in frustration. She inherits from her mother a capacity for passion which expresses her full nature, whereas his nature is divided between a dead conformity to society and a sensuality which is incapable of real passion. Ursula tries to compromise by suppressing her instincts, but a concluding scene, in which she is exposed at night to the menace of restless horses, on to which she projects her disturbed emotions, shows that she is wrong in attempting this solution. The title of the novel signifies the binding power which unites otherwise unrelated natures; another form of the symbol is the arch which denotes the relationship of Tom and Lydia at the end of Chapter III.

The novel was for a time suppressed on grounds of immorality, but is now regarded as one of Lawrence's greatest achievements.

* 4.5.3.

Raleigh, Sir Walter (1552?–1618) /'ro:li, 'rali/

Poet, historian, courtier. His stormy and varied life has made him a legend; his personal distinction and versatile gifts make him memorable as an example of the humanist conception of the many-sided 'Renaissance* man'. He served in the French Protestant Huguenot army in France (1569), took a part in the policy of settling Ireland with Protestant colonists, and engaged in numerous adventures in North and South America – he was half-brother of the explorer, Sir Humphrey Gilbert. During the reign of Elizabeth I* he was for much of the time one of the Queen's principal favourites; the well-known story of his spreading out his costly cloak over a puddle for the Queen to step on it without wetting her feet illustrates his reputation as the perfect courtier. As the Queen's favourite he was the rival of the Earl of Essex, but he shared Essex's triumph in the capture of Cadiz (1596). His anti-Spanish record made him unpopular with Elizabeth's successor, James I*, and from 1603 until 1616 he was a prisoner in the Tower of London*. Then James released him on his promise to find gold in South America without antagonizing the Spaniards; the feat was impossible, and he returned to be executed – as James had promised the Spanish ambassador – in 1618.

Raleigh was one of the best writers of shorter poems in the decade 1590–1600. Many of his poems have been lost, but sufficient survive to give him a high reputation. One side of his character was the opposite of the outward-turning adventurer, and was responsive to spiritual teachings about the hollowness of worldly rewards. This comes out in the harshness of *The Lie* and the traditional religious idiom of *The Passionate Man's Pilgrimage: supposed to be written by one at the point of death* – and possibly written when he was imprisoned in 1603, perhaps expecting death. His *Cynthia, the Lady of the Sea*, left uncompleted, expresses his devotion to Elizabeth. His poetry has more personal feeling in it than was characteristic of much of the verse of the time, while it possesses much of the freshness for which the Elizabethan short poem is famous, as well as the force of older tradition that gives the best examples of it solemnity and weight.

As a prose writer, Raleigh is particularly known for his *History of the World* (1614), written in the Tower. The title alone is a sign of the ideal of all-inclusiveness in intellectual conceptions which was typical of the Renaissance, and some of the matter, *eg* on human uncertainty about immediate causes, is characteristic of its sceptical side. Only one volume of the History was completed, down to 130 BC.

Raleigh was a friend of Spenser*, and figures as the Shepherd from the Sea in Spenser's poem, *Colin Clout's Come Home Again**.

Bib: Studies by Oakeshott, W.; Rowse, A. L.; Edwards, P.; Bradbrook, M. C., *The School of Night*; Firth, C., *Raleigh's History*.

Ralph Roister Doister

A comedy by Nicholas Udall, printed in 1566, and written in about 1551. It is sometimes called 'the first English comedy', presumably because the earlier 'comic interludes' notably by John Heywood (*eg The Play of the Weather* and *the Four P's**) were too slight to count, whereas Udall's play, which may have been written for the boys of Westminster School, is an adaptation of the *Miles Gloriosus* ('The Boastful Soldier') by Plautus*. The basic situation is the same in both plays: a vain but foolish and boastful soldier makes love to a respectable woman (Christian Custance in Udall's play) who is betrothed to a merchant, Gawin Goodluck, and Ralph is encouraged in his misguided enterprise by a mischievous associate, Matthew Merygreek. But the play has a kind of farcical humour which has more in common with the popular Interludes* and even the May Games of English country life, and it reads as a thoroughly native product. The rhymed verse is rather primitive, but the dialogue has realistic freshness. The comedy is an example of humanistic learning married to popular entertainment, a union which 40 years later was to give rise to the beginnings of the great period of English drama.

* 5.1.2.3.

Rambler, The

A twice-weekly periodical produced by Dr Samuel Johnson* from March 1750 to March 1752. All except five were written by Johnson himself. The papers were in the tradition of the *Tatler** and *Spectator** essays by Addison and Steele 40 years before, but Johnson is weightier and less concerned to entertain, and the essays are less suitable for periodical publication; it was only when they appeared in volume form that they had real success, running into 10 editions in the next 30 years. Johnson was not, as Addison had been, concerned with the detailed events of daily life, since, as he pointed out (in No. 4), these were now the field of the novel; his essays are mainly occupied with the terse and sincere expression of the great commonplaces of human experience. His strong personality gives them distinguished individuality nonetheless, and the best (*eg* No. 77 on the duties of authors and 185 on forgiveness) are masterpieces of the reflective essay in English.

* *Essay; Reviews and Periodicals.*

Ranelagh /ˈranələ/

One of the 18th-C pleasure gardens. The land, now part of Chelsea Hospital Gardens, was acquired by Lord Ranelagh in 1690, and in 1742 the gardens were opened to the public. A circular building called the Rotunda, where concerts were held, was erected in the centre. By 1803 the gardens had gone out of fashion and were closed.

Later in 19th C a new Ranelagh was established in the suburbs of London; it was a centre for the game of polo, which had been introduced from India and had become fashionable.

Rape of the Lock, The

A poem in ten-syllable rhymed couplets* by Alexander Pope*. In its first published version (1712) it comprised two cantos; in 1714 it was enlarged to five cantos, and about 750 lines.

The poem was occasioned by a ridiculous incident which had disrupted the friendly relationships of two aristocratic families with whom Pope was acquainted. Lord Petre had cut off a lock from the hair of Miss Arabella Fermor, and she regarded herself as gravely insulted. Pope wrote the poem to end the quarrel by showing the triviality of its cause in true perspective. The incident is narrated in the form of a mock epic*; its triviality is faithfully depicted, and so is the disproportionate anger that it excites, but the language is in the tradition of Homer's *Iliad** expressing the anger occasioned by the rape of Helen. In the expanded form of the poem Pope used supernatural machinery borrowed from Rosicrucian* doctrines so as to exhibit a miniature analogy to the gods and goddesses of Homer's poem. Pope's poem is more than a witty joke; it is also an exquisite image of the selfishness and triviality of fashionable society which obscure real human values by overlaying them with a surface of artificial manners and ostentation arising from petty vanities. The mock epic is suited to the tradition of neo-classicism*, and Pope is following the example of Nicolas Boileau's* *Le Lutrin* ('The Lectern', 1674), a mock epic about an ecclesiastical quarrel over the placing of a lectern.

Raphael the Archangel

* *Angels.*

Raphael the Painter

* *Pre-Raphaelite*

Rasselas, Prince of Abyssinia, The History of (1759) /ˈrasiləs/

An oriental tale by Samuel Johnson*. Rasselas, son of the Emperor of Abyssinia, escapes from the surroundings in which he is completely protected from all that is disagreeable, and, in company with his sister Nekayah and the philosopher Imlac, he seeks the active principle of happiness. They discover the illusoriness of philosophy and of power and the enduring peace of an arduous life in the pursuit of virtue. The principle on which the tale is composed is implied by Imlac: 'The business of the poet is to examine not the individual but the species, to remark general properties and large appearances: he does not number the streaks of the tulip.' This is characteristic of the Augustan* tradition of which Johnson is one of the most distinguished representatives. What the tale loses by sacrificing particularity in incident and character is counterbalanced by Johnson's grand, disinterested vision and the spaciousness of his moral scheme, and it is saved from superficiality and vagueness by the force of conviction expressed in the style.

Rationalism

[1] In philosophy, the belief that reason, rather than sensation, is the only certain guide to knowledge.

[2] In religion, the practice of seeking explanations which satisfy reason for what had been accepted as supernatural.

Realism

A term used in various senses, both in philosophy and in literary criticism. Three principal meanings, two of them philosophical and one literary, are particularly worth distinction.

[1] In medieval philosophy, the realists were opposed to the nominalists*. Realism here means that classes of things ('universals') have reality whereas individuals have not, or at least have less: *eg* individual birds take their reality from the classification 'bird'. The nominalists considered that only the individual bird has reality, and that the classification 'bird' is only a formulation in the mind.

[2] Since the Middle Ages, realism has become opposed to idealism*. Here realism means that reality exists apart from ideas about it in the mind,

and idealism represents the view that we can know nothing that is not in our minds.

[3] Literary realism is a 19th-C conception, related to [2]. In general, it means the use of the imagination to represent things as they are. It does not apply only to 19th-C literature; Defoe* is commonly called a realist because of his factual description and narration. 19th-C realism in literature arose, however, from a reaction against 19th-C romanticism, and it is related to naturalism*. Realism is also used in modern literature in opposition to what is regarded as sentimentalism – the disposition to represent feelings (*eg* the various forms of love) as nicer than we know them to be; an illogical extension of this use of the term is sometimes to apply it to literature that represents experience as nastier than we know it to be. Finally, realism in literature is sometimes related to nominalism, *ie* the realist writer is he who represents individuals rather than types; in this sense, modern literary realism is the opposite of the realism of medieval philosophy.

Rebellion, The Great

* *Civil Wars.*

Recluse, The

* *Excursion, The.*

Reconciliation Plays of Shakespeare

A term used by some modern critics to express the character of Shakespeare's last four plays: *Pericles** (1608–9); *Cymbeline** (1609–10); *The Winter's Tale** (1610–11); *The Tempest** (1611–12). These plays have some distinctive qualities that mark them off from Shakespeare's earlier work; 19th-C critics commonly referred to them as 'the Romances', but this indicates their quality less specifically and is somewhat confusing since much of Shakespeare's work in the 1590s had been distinctly 'romantic'.

The following are some of the qualities that distinguish these plays:

[1] Extravagance of incident. Shakespeare abandons the comparatively realistic presentation characteristic of his tragic period, 1604–8. Events are extraordinary, and in *Pericles* and *The Winter's Tale* they are widespread in place and time; in *Pericles* and *Cymbeline* they are loosely related in plot. In *Cymbeline* and *The Winter's Tale* there is no consistency of period, and classical history mingles with 16th-C social settings. In *The Tempest* Shakespeare makes a freer use of magic than in any of his other plays, but in its strict unity of time and place this play is otherwise in contrast to the other three plays of the group.

[2] Although *The Tempest* is again here to some extent a contrast to the others, the group belongs to a category known as 'tragicomedy'; that is to say *Pericles*, *Cymbeline*, *The Winter's Tale* each deepen into tragedy which reaches climax midway in the story, and then lighten towards a happy conclusion. *The Tempest* is different in that the tragedy has all taken place before the play has begun; the whole play is thus devoted to restoring happiness out of a tragedy already accomplished.

[3] In each play the theme concerns an ordeal undergone by the main character; in this respect, however, the plays show a progression. Pericles does no wrong; he is a passive sufferer, with no power of his own to relieve his suffering. Cymbeline commits errors, and the tragedy arises from them, but he is not called on to act in order that the errors shall be redeemed. Leontes' error amounts to terrible crime, and this has to be expiated by a long period of unremitting repentance. Prospero, in *The Tempest*, has committed no error beyond severing himself from his worldly responsibilities; he is a powerful and virtuous man who could wreak vengeance on his enemies but chooses instead to reconcile himself to them by acts of godlike mercy.

[4] In the first three plays, the ordeal of the hero is characterized by the loss of his family, and in each of them it is a daughter who is chiefly instrumental in bringing about the reunion which constitutes the happy ending. *The Tempest* is again somewhat different from the others; here father and daughter remain together, but they are both cast off from the rest of the world; it is again the daughter who is instrumental in the final reunion.

The theme of this final group stands in contrast to the theme common to several of the more sombre examples of Shakespeare's early dramas – the English history plays of the 1590s, *Titus Andronicus*, and, from his maturer phase, *Hamlet*. These had been much concerned with the opposite of reconciliation – with vengeance and retribution.

* 5.1.3.3.

Recusancy

A term used under Elizabeth 1* for refusal to attend religious worship in the Church of England*; this was an offence in law punishable by a fine of 1 shilling. A 'recusant' was usually a Roman Catholic, but refusal was sometimes based on other grounds; arrests for debt commonly took place when people assembled at church, and a debtor seeking to escape arrest often became a recusant. This seems to have been the fact about Shakespeare's father, who was fined for recusancy. The recusancy law continued to exist until the Toleration Act (1689) which permitted freedom of worship.

Red Cross Knight, The

The central figure of Book I of Spenser's *Faerie Queene**. He represents Holiness, the Church of England, and St George*, whose red cross on a white ground is the national emblem of England. His adventures are connected with two women: Una, the true religion from which he is separated, and Duessa, the Roman Catholic Church, which beguiles him. He is eventually united to Una with the assistance of Prince Arthur* who rescues him from the House of Pride.

Red Riding Hood, Little

A popular fairy tale, originally derived from the French version by Perrault*, translated into English 1729. The little girl is so called because of the red hood that she wears. A wolf meets her in the forest while she is on her way to her grandmother. Having discovered the purpose of her journey, he goes on ahead and eats the grandmother and takes her place in bed; when Red Riding Hood arrives he eats her as well. In modern versions, she and her grandmother are subsequently cut out of the wolf's stomach, alive and well, by her father, a woodcutter.

Reeve's Tale, The

One of Chaucer's *Canterbury Tales**. It is in 10-syllable rhymed couplets* and is based on a French fabliau* – *De Gombert et ses deux Clers*. The Reeve tells it in revenge against the Miller, who has told a comically insulting story against a carpenter – a usual secondary employment of a reeve, who was a land steward. The incident takes place at a mill at the village of Trumpington, near Cambridge. Two students (clerks) are cheated by the miller, who in turn is cheated by them; they devise an opportunity to make love to his wife and daughter.

* *Miller's Tale*.

Reflections on the Revolution in France (1790)

A political treatise by Edmund Burke*. Burke attacks the principles on which the French Revolution* was being conducted, denies that the English Revolution of 1688* was based on the same principles, and insists that a society is an organic growth like a tree, requiring the same kind of careful surgery in accordance with its principles of growth. The book was provoked by a sermon in praise of the French Revolution, preached by a nonconformist minister, Dr Price; Burke is in effect not merely attacking the French revolutionaries, but the reverence for abstract, rational, scientific enlightenment which, during 18th C, had increasingly transformed the 17th-C Puritans* into the 18th-C rationalistic dissenters or nonconformists, and had found disciples among many others of the educated classes. The *Reflections* is a great work of conservative political philosophy, as well as a masterpiece of polemical prose; its tradition of thought was carried on in 19th C by the poet and philosopher S. T. Coleridge*, while the tradition of 18th-C 'enlightenment' was continued by the Utilitarian* school of thought.

Reform Bills, Parliamentary

In English history, a succession of laws passed in 19th and 20th C for the reform of the system of election of Members of Parliament. The system has always been based on towns and rural districts, grouped into constituencies, each electing one or (until recently) sometimes more than one candidate as Member. The most important Reform Bill was the first, passed through Parliament in 1832, because it reduced the electoral confusion into a rational system. Most constituencies had remained unchanged since the Middle Ages*; in consequence, some towns had grown to great size with inadequate representation in Parliament, or none at all, while others were represented by more than one Member although they had sunk into insignificance or even, in a few cases, had ceased to exist. This meant great power for the landed aristocracy, and great deprivation of power for the large and growing middle class. Some boroughs ('towns' – but often mere villages) were called 'pocket boroughs' because they were virtually owned by one landlord, who had them 'in his pocket', *ie* caused them to elect the Members of his choice; others were called 'rotten boroughs' because few inhabitants possessed the right to vote, and they were easily and habitually bribed. The law of 1832 redistributed Members of Parliament so as to correspond to the great centres of population, but limited the franchise (right to vote) to those who possessed a level of income such as ensured that electors belonged at least to the middle class.

The Reform Bill of 1867 extended the franchise to all male members of the working class in the towns, and that of 1884 to the rural working class. The delay in extending the franchise to the working class was bound up with the absence of any official state system of education; this was introduced in 1870. The town working classes received the vote before the rural ones owing to their greater experience in organization gained through trade unions* and the running of Nonconformist (Dissenting*) chapels.

The vote was now possessed by all men over 21 (with few exceptions, such as lunatics, criminals, and peers who had seats in the House of Lords) but not by women. Women over 30 were enfranchised in 1918 thanks to the campaigning by Suffragette movements and the services performed by women in World War I. Women over 21 received the vote in 1928. The same laws enabled women to stand for Parliament. A 1969 Act lowered the voting age for both men and women to 18.

Much of the intimidation and corruption of voters was a consequence of votes being made openly; secret voting, or 'voting by ballot', was introduced in 1872.

* 1.5.1.4; *Parliament*.

Reformation

A great religious movement in 16th C; its aim was to protest in a variety of ways against the conduct of the Catholic Church, which had hitherto remained undivided. The outcome was division: the Roman Catholics remained dominant in the countries bordering on the western Mediterranean and in south Germany; the new Protestant* churches became supreme in northern Europe. The causes of the movement were political (the rise of the new nation-state); moral (resentment at the low example set by many of the clergy); and doctrinal (disagreement, stimulated by the new critical spirit of the Renaissance*, over points of doctrine hitherto imposed by the authority of the Church).

The reformation in England proceeded in three phases.

[1] Henry VIII* carried out the first in merely political terms. His desire to divorce Katharine of Aragon was merely a pretext; he himself sought

complete control over the Church in England, and needed money; he resented the authority of the Pope in Rome and the internationalism of the monastic orders; he welcomed the opportunity to increase his wealth by confiscating their property. He declared himself Supreme Head of the Church in England by the Act of Supremacy*, supported by Parliament and passed by it in 1533; he dissolved the monasteries in 1536–39. On the other hand, his Six Articles* of 1539 tried to keep the Church fully Catholic on all points except that of papal sovereignty. As the support by Parliament showed, he had popular opinion behind him, at least in southern England; the English Church had long been restive against the sovereignty of the Pope, particularly when, in 14th C, he had reigned from Avignon in France, the home of the national enemy.

[2] The second phase, under his son Edward VI*, went further and aroused more national disagreement. The clergy were permitted to marry, and the Book of Common Prayer* included 42 articles of faith (later reduced to 39) which defined the doctrine of the Church of England in Protestant terms; there was extensive destruction of religious images in churches throughout the country. Henry's daughter Mary I* undertook a complete reaction back to Catholicism, but her persecution of the Protestants and her subservience to her husband, Philip II of Spain, the most fanatical of the Catholic sovereigns, confirmed the country in a Protestant direction.

[3] Henry's remaining daughter Elizabeth I* contrived a religious settlement that was a careful compromise between the reforms of her father and those of her brother. The intention was to be inclusive: Catholics were not to be driven out of the Church of England if she could help it, and she wanted to keep as many of her Protestant subjects within it as possible. The result, however, was disunion: Catholics could not subscribe to the Church of England after the Pope had excommunicated the Queen in 1571, and the more extreme Protestants were constantly pressing for further reforms, especially in the structure of church government (they mostly wanted the abolition of rule through bishops) and in the conduct of worship, which they wanted in full austerity. These Puritans*, as they were called by their enemies, eventually established their own religious organizations, but not until after 1660. The vagueness of the Elizabethan settlement also gave rise to disagreement within the Church of England, and this has lasted until the present day: the High Church is the section which emphasizes the more Catholic interpretation of the settlement (*ie* more in keeping with Henry VIII's intentions), and the Low Church is the section which insists that the Church of England is essentially Protestant. This disagreement, however, has never disrupted the organization of the Church, which, under the headship of the sovereign, is still that of the Catholic church of medieval England.

The reformation in Scotland proceeded side by side with the Elizabethan phase in England, and helped to bring about a reconciliation of the two nations which had been hostile to each other for 3 centuries. The Scottish reformation, however, was extreme, under the leadership of John Knox*, a disciple of the French reformer Calvin*. The national Church of Scotland has remained Calvinist (Presbyterian*) to this day. Ireland remained Catholic, and in consequence suffered severe persecution by its English rulers in 16th and 17th C. The only excuse for this tyranny was the real danger that Ireland might become a base for one of England's more powerful Catholic enemies – France or Spain.

* 1.2.2; 3.2.2.

Regency

In English history, the period 1811–20 when George, Prince of Wales, later George IV (1820–30), took the title of Prince Regent during the final illness of his father, George III (1760–1820). In British cultural history, the term is often applied to cover the first 20 years of 19th C during which a certain style of taste in art and architecture prevailed. It was inspired by the taste of the first French Empire (Napoleon I*) which itself arose from French revolutionary cultivation of ancient Greece, especially the republic of Athens. Architecture was austerely classical (the 'Greek style'), and dress was similarly modelled on long, graceful lines suitable for men and women with slender figures.

In literature, the term covers the working life of the second generation of romantic poets (Byron*, Shelley* and Keats*), the work of the essayists Lamb* and Hazlitt*, and that of the novelists Jane Austen* and Walter Scott*. The best work of the essentially Augustan poet Crabbe* also comes into the Regency period. Thus 'Regency' expresses, for literature, a blending of romantic and classical taste. The word is applied, however, more to architecture, dress, and furniture than to literature, the principal architects being John Nash (1752–1835) and John Soane (1753–1837), architect of the Bank of England.

Regent Street

One of the principal streets in the west end of London; it runs through Oxford Circus and Piccadilly Circus, and continues down to Carlton House Terrace. It was originally designed by the order of the Prince Regent (**Regency*) in 1813 to unite the royal Regent's Park to his residence, Carlton House, and was the noble conception of the architect John Nash. It was rebuilt in its present form in 1922–26.

Regent's Park

One of the great parks in the west end of London, about one mile north of Hyde Park. It was originally laid out by the architect John Nash, and was called after the Prince Regent (**Regency*). The intended royal palace at its centre was never built, but it is surrounded by a circle of terraces which were also designed by Nash. It contains the London Zoological Gardens.

Regicides

(From Latin, meaning 'king killers'.) In English

history, the group of men responsible for the execution of King Charles I*. The king was tried on a charge of treason, a distinction being made between the institution of the Crown and Charles himself, who was king. Eighty-four people, including the executioners, were said to be responsible for his trial and death. When his son was restored to the throne in 1660 as Charles II*, the regicides were tried, and 10 of them were executed; some of them, however, had already escaped abroad.
* *Restoration.*

Religio Medici

A true and full coppy of that which was most imperfectly and Surreptitiously printed before under the name of: **Religio Medici.**
Printed for Andrew Crooke 1645.

(The Religion of a Physician) A work of spiritual and autobiographical reflection by Sir Thomas Browne*. It was written in about 1635, when Browne was 30, and was not intended for publication. However, it was published without his permission in 1642, reissued with his authority in 1643, and subsequently translated into French, Dutch, German and Latin. The book consists of a succession of essays* in which the leading theme is the nature of the author's religious faith, expressed as a distinctively personal viewpoint, and elaborated with a wide variety of out-of-the-way scholarship. The prose is mannered but beautifully cadenced, and shows much of the delight in ingenious and fantastic wit that characterized contemporary poets of the Metaphysical* school, such as Vaughan* and Crashaw*. Browne was an Anglican* but not at all bigoted; in particular he shows a strong attraction to Roman Catholicism. He anticipates 18th C by his scepticism which inclines him to tolerance of viewpoints different from his own, but he delights in the exercise of his faith in defiance of his reason. This attitude gives the book a place in the history of English thought midway between the work of Francis Bacon*, who had taken faith for granted and emphasized the scientific uses of reason, and that of John Locke*, who found a basis for faith in God only in the incapacity of reason to interpret the world fully.

Reliques

* *Percy's Reliques.*

Renaissance in England, The /rə'neisəns/

'Renaissance' (or 'Renascence') derives from Latin 'renascentia' = 'rebirth'. The word was first used by Italian scholars in mid-16th C to express the rediscovery of ancient Roman and Greek culture, which was now studied for its own sake and not used merely to enhance the authority of the Church. Modern scholars are more inclined to use the term to express a great variety of interdependent changes which Europe underwent politically, economically, and culturally between 1450 (although the starting-points were much earlier) and 1600. The religious outcome of these changes is expressed through the terms Reformation* and Counter-reformation*, a sequence of events which were closely bound up with the Renaissance.

In England, the Renaissance is usually thought of as beginning with the accession of the House of Tudor* to the throne in 1485. Politically, this marks the end of the period of civil war amongst the old feudal aristocracy (the Wars of the Roses*) in mid-15th C, and the establishment of something like a modern, efficient, centralized state; technically, the date is close to that of the introduction of printing into England – an invention without which the great cultural changes of the Renaissance could not have occurred. Culturally, the first important period in England was the reign of the second Tudor monarch, Henry VIII*. This was the period of the English humanists* More*, Grocyn*, Linacre*, and the poet Sir Thomas Wyatt*.

Several distinctive features characterize the English Renaissance. The first is the lateness of its impact; Italian, French, German, Dutch and Spanish scholars had already worked hard on the ancient Greek and Latin writers, and had produced works of their own inspired by the classics; in consequence, English culture was revitalized not so much directly by the classics as by contemporary Europeans under the influence of the classics. Castiglione's* *The Courtier*, Machiavelli's* *The Prince*, Ariosto's* *Orlando*, were as important in the English Renaissance as Virgil's *Aeneid** or the plays of Seneca*, and it was characteristic that North* translated Plutarch's* *Lives* not from the original Greek but from a French version. Such an influx of foreign influences, both contemporary and ancient, might have overwhelmed the native English literary tradition but for two more distinctive features: England as an insular country followed a course of social and political history which was to a great extent independent of the course of history elsewhere in Europe, for example in the peculiarity of the English Reformation, and this assisted the country in preserving its cultural independence; and owing to the great genius of the 14th-C poet Chaucer*, the native literature was sufficiently vigorous and experienced in assimilating foreign influences without being subjected by them. A fourth characteristic of English Renaissance literature is that it is primarily artistic, rather than philosophical and scholarly, and a fifth is the coinciding of the Renaissance and the Reformation in England, in contrast to the rest of the Europe where the Reformation (or, in countries that remained Roman Catholic, the Counter-reformation) succeeded the Renaissance as a consequence of the emancipated and critical spirit which was one of its characteristics.

The English Renaissance was largely literary, and achieved its finest expression in the so-called Elizabethan drama which began to excel only in the last decade of 16th C and reached its height in the first 15 years of 17th; its finest exponents were Christopher Marlowe*, Ben Jonson*, and William Shakespeare*. Non-dramatic poetry was also extremely rich, and reached its peak in the same period in the work of Edmund Spenser*, Philip Sidney*, Shakespeare and John Donne*, but it is typical of the lateness of the Renaissance in England that its most ambitious product, John Milton's epic *Paradise Lost**, was published as late as 1667. Native English prose shaped itself more slowly than poetry; More wrote his great work *Utopia** in Latin, which was the vehicle of some other writers including Francis Bacon* (in much of his work) owing to its advantages (for international circulation) over English, at a time when the latter was little learned in other countries. Nonetheless English prose developed with great vigour in native English writers such as Roger Ascham*, Thomas North, Richard Hooker*, in the English works of Francis Bacon, and in the translators of the Bible*.

*.1.2.3; 3.2.1.

Republic, Plato's

A philosophical dialogue by the Greek philosopher Plato*. Socrates* discusses with his friends the nature of justice, and the conversation leads to an outline of the ideal state. Public life must exhibit the highest virtues of private life, and justice is achieved if the classes work together to contribute to society the virtues in which each excels. Democracy (the rule of the people), oligarchy (the rule of a small powerful group), and timocracy (the rule of men of property) are in turn rejected, in favour of aristocracy – the rule of the best, trained by an exacting system of education. The aristocrat will seek wisdom, whereas the man of action seeks honour, and the merchant gratifies his appetites. Wisdom is a direct apprehension of the good conceived as a system of ideal forms; Book VII contains the famous parable of men sitting with their backs to these forms (the only substantial reality) watching the shadows on the wall of the cavern – *ie* phenomena apprehended by the senses – and supposing these shadows to be the only reality. Book X contains Plato's notorious rejection of poetry: poets must be expelled, though with honour, because they frustrate the pursuit of true wisdom by extolling the illusory phenomena of this world, and weaken the mind by stimulating wasteful sympathy with the misfortunes of men.

Resolution and Independence

* *Leech-Gatherer, The*.

Restoration, The

The word is used in two senses: the re-establishment of the Stuart monarchy in the person of King Charles II* after the republican experiment of 1649–60; and as a period designation, often to cover the last 40 years of 17th C, *ie* not only the reign of Charles II* but that of his brother James II*, and that of William III* and Mary II. This period was marked by special cultural characteristics which were promoted by the political fact of the restoration of the monarchy, and the triumph of reason and tolerance over religious and political passion which this fact symbolized. In this sense the term is most commonly used to identify three principal literary products: [1] Restoration prose; [2] Restoration drama (especially comedy); [3] Restoration poetry.

[1] Restoration prose is marked by a very conscious determination by leading writers to use prose as a vehicle of reason. It had of course already been used in this way by, for instance, Francis Bacon, but even Bacon did not distinguish the virtues of prose for such a vehicle. It was one of the aims of the new Royal Society* to cultivate these virtues, which were described by Thomas Sprat in his *History of the Royal Society* (1667): '. . . a close, naked, natural way of speaking; positive expressions; clear senses; a native easiness; bringing all things as near the Mathematical plainness, as they can: and preferring the language of Artisans, Countrymen, and Merchants before that of Wits, or Scholars.' Sprat thus describes what have been considered the normal qualities of good prose ever since, and the Restoration period is indeed the first age of modern English prose writing. Its great master was the poet, John Dryden*, in his prose criticism, for instance his *Essay on Dramatic Poesy* (1668).

[2] Restoration drama. This period is sometimes described as 'the silver age' of English drama, by comparison with the 'golden' age of Shakespeare. Owing to the hostility of the Puritans* to drama, the art had practically ceased to be practised in the period of their power, 1642–60; it was then continued with ardour, but in less promising circumstances than in the 'golden' age. The decline had indeed already been evident before the close of the theatres in 1642, and a dramatist such as James Shirley*, writing in the 1630s, exhibits many of the characteristic virtues and weaknesses of the Restoration. The audience had already ceased to be one drawn from all classes, and was restricted to people of fashion and refinement; wit, elegance of speech, skilful stage technique were the qualities which were sought after, and they implied a drama

of greater superficiality than that of Shakespeare and his contemporaries, which was intended to please alike the learned and the simple, the profound and the frivolous. After 1660, the French drama of Molière* in comedy and of Corneille* and Racine* in tragedy were the dominating influences of the English stage, but English society was not so constructed as to be able to emulate the greatness of the French 'golden' age. English 'heroic' tragedy, with the exception of a few plays by Dryden and Otway*, lacked the conviction of French tragedy in a comparable style, and the comedy of Etherege*, Wycherley*, Vanbrugh*, Farquhar*, and even of Congreve*, is slight and superficial by comparison with that of Molière. However, Restoration comedy is in prose, unlike most of the tragedy, and the virtues of Restoration dramatists are especially in the wit, grace and poise of their prose dialogue; the comedies are still successful and even popular on the English stage, whereas few of the tragedies are ever performed.

[3] Restoration (non-dramatic) poetry. This, especially the poetry of Dryden, is really the beginning of Augustan* poetry. The virtues admired in the prose of the time reigned also over the poetry, so that a 'close, naked, natural way of speaking' is as evident in the verse as in the prose of Dryden. Besides him, Samuel Butler* and the Earl of Rochester* are the principal names classifiable as 'Restoration poets', but the greatest poet of the reign of Charles II, John Milton*, cannot be so classified. The Restoration poets excelled in satire whereas Milton, in his epics and his one tragedy in so different a style from the neo-classic French tragedies, is a late product of the English Renaissance, profoundly modified by Puritanism.

* 1.3.3.

Resurrection Man; Resurrectionist

A term in use in late 18th and early 19th C for one who made a living by digging up dead bodies and selling them to anatomists to use for dissection; such a person is Jerry Cruncher in Dickens's novel about the French Revolution, *A Tale of Two Cities**.

Return of the Native, The (1878)

A novel by Thomas Hardy*. Its setting is Egdon Heath, a wild tract of country in Dorset, in the south-west of England. The atmosphere of the Heath prevails over the whole book; as an environment, it repels some and absorbs others of the characters; those who are absorbed achieve a sombre integration with it, but those who are repelled and rebel suffer disaster. The central character – 'the Native' – is Clym Yeobright, a Paris diamond merchant who has returned to the Heath in revulsion from the futility of his urban life and occupation. He intends to become a schoolmaster and marries the restless, self-seeking Eustacia Vye who is unfaithful to him; her affair with the unscrupulous Damon Wildeve leads to the death of both. Other characters include Thomasin Yeobright whom Wildeve marries, to her misfortune and the grief of Diggory Venn, the travelling sheep-dyer (or 'reddleman') who represents a primitive sincerity and truthfulness, and Mrs Yeobright, Clym's mother, whom Eustacia estranges from her son. Clym becomes a furze-cutter on the Heath, and eventually a travelling preacher. The novel is an example of Hardy's preoccupation with the relationship of characters with natural environment, but it suffers from a weak conception of the central character, Clym.

Revels, Master of the

An official at the royal court in 16th and 17th C; his function was responsibility for court entertainments, *eg* masques*.

Revenge Tragedy

A kind of tragedy which was particularly popular during and just after the lifetime of Shakespeare, *ie* 1590–1620. The plot of such plays was commonly the murder by a person in power of a near relative, wife, or husband of the central character, who is then faced with the problem of how, or sometimes whether, to carry out revenge against a murderer who, because of his social importance, is out of reach of ordinary justice. The literary inspiration for this kind of play came from the plays of the Roman poet Seneca* whose *Ten Tragedies* were translated into English between 1559 and 1581. Seneca's plays would doubtless have been insufficient in themselves, however, to set going the great English series of revenge tragedies, if the theme had not been relevant to English society. This society was in a stage midway between primitive lawlessness, in which justice is beyond the reach of the weak and unprivileged, and the modern state, in which justice is impartial and police are numerous and efficient. The tradition that revenge for an injury to a member of his family was a duty for the individual was still widely maintained; against it, the state maintained that revenge not carried out as due punishment through a court of law was a crime, and the Church taught that it was a sin. On the other hand, the law was unreliable, though not helpless, against the powerful and the powerfully protected, and in the face of the religious prohibition, the revenger might consider himself to be the instrument of Divine Vengeance.

This state of conflict in the Elizabethan conscience made for different styles of revenge play. The first of those offering straightforward treatment of the theme was Thomas Kyd's *Spanish Tragedy**; Shakespeare's early history plays, *1, 2 & 3 Henry VI* and *Richard III**, are revenge plays as well, and another early example by Shakespeare is his *Titus Andronicus**. Later examples: *The Revenger's Tragedy** by Cyril Tourneur (or perhaps Thomas Middleton) and Thomas Middleton's *Women Beware Women* (1621?), to mention only plays of distinction. Another style might be called the 'anti-revenge' drama, in which the hero is too enlightened to seek revenge – examples are Tourneur's *The Atheist's Tragedy* and Chapman's* *Revenge of Bussy d'Ambois*, both about 1611. The greatest of all tragedies of revenge, Shakespeare's *Hamlet**, is between the two styles, inasmuch as the hero both accepts the obligation to revenge and has to fight against his revulsion from it. A third style might rather be called the tragedy of retribution, inasmuch as a crime is avenged but the drama is not centred on a specific avenger; such plays include Webster's *The White Devil** and *The Duchess of Malfi** and Middleton's masterpiece *The Changeling**. Revenge and retribution are of course akin, and the importance of revenge tragedy, apart from its intrinsic interest, is that it is the starting point for the development of some of Shakespeare's greatest tragic themes, *eg* his *Othello** and *Macbeth**, though these are not usually placed in the same category.

* 5.1.3.2.

Revenger's Tragedy, The (1607)

A drama in blank verse attributed to Cyril Tourneur*, although modern scholars incline increasingly to prefer to attribute it to Thomas Middleton*. The scene is a dissolute Renaissance* court in Italy. The sensual Duke has a vicious legitimate son, Lussurioso, by his first wife; the Duchess, his second wife, is in love with his illegitimate son, Spurio, who uses his bastardy as a pretext for general sensual rapacity; her own sons, Ambitioso and Supervacuo are consumed with envy, and she herself is totally without moral restraint. This evil family is not so much a group of characters in the ordinary, realistic sense as an array of allegorical representations of the fleshly vices ; their Italianate names suggest their allegories – Lussurioso = Luxury, Spurio = falseness, etc. They are predatory on one another, and the downfall of the whole family is plotted by Vindice (= Revenger), whose betrothed has been poisoned by the Duke; he is assisted by his brother Hippolito. Disguised as Piato, Vindice enters the service of Lussorioso, and pretends to procure his own sister, Castiza (= Chastity) as mistress for his master; he finds to his horror that their own mother is prepared to sell her for the price of becoming a court lady. Vindice carries out his revenge on the Duke in a scene of great emblematic ferocity, and eventually contrives the bloodthirsty destruction of the whole family. He himself, however, is sent to his death by the Duke's virtuous successor: a Revenger, in however just a cause, is a criminal too dangerous to leave alive.

The violence of the action is redeemed from crudity by the energy, compression, and conviction of the language, and by the way in which Tourneur fuses three modes of feeling into original art. One of these is the tradition of medieval allegory*, which was becoming diluted and abstract in much Renaissance poetry, but in this play keeps its old power of condensing emotion into powerful images. Tourneur uses the allegorical form to substantiate Puritan* detestation of sensual vice, which was the evil extreme of the Renaissance liberation of the physical appetites. At the same time, both these vices and Vindice's vindictiveness are expressed with an energy that is itself a rich manifestation of Renaissance feeling. In uniting these disparate resources, the play is one of the masterpieces of Jacobean* drama.

* *Revenge Tragedy.*

Reviews and Periodicals

The English periodical press arose gradually from the controversial religious and political pamphleteering of late 16th and 17th C. It became established as a recognized institution early in 18th C, and it was also in 18th C that the review, which expresses opinion, became distinguished from the newspaper, which gives priority to information on current events. The great age for the periodical press was, however, 1800–1914; this was the period when the quarterlies and the monthlies had their widest influence, and the weeklies their largest circulation proportionately to the size of the reading public. Since 1914, the influence of the quarterlies and monthlies has declined; the weeklies have remained important, but they have had to compete on the one side with the tendency of newspapers to include a large amount of material originally restricted to reviews, and on the other with the medium of broadcasting. The following is a list, in chronological order, of periodicals from 1700 to 1914 which are of importance in the study of literature.

Published weekly or more frequently

The Review. 1704–13. Three times weekly. Written by Daniel Defoe*. Politically impartial; it expressed Defoe's opinion on current political events, and also on literature and manners. Defoe has been called the inventor of the leading article, a feature of modern newspapers.

*The Tatler** 1709–11. Edited and written by Richard Steele* with the collaboration of Addison*. Essays on current manners and civilization.

The Examiner 1710–11. A right-wing (Tory) journal, started by Lord Bolingbroke and conducted by Jonathan Swift*. Engaged in controversy with the left wing (Whig*) writers, Addison and Steele.

*The Spectator** 1711–12; 1714. Largely written by Addison and Steele. Similar to, but more celebrated than, *The Tatler*.

*The Rambler** 1750–52. Written by Samuel Johnson*. Deeply considered essays on moral themes.

The North Briton 1762. A radical political weekly written by John Wilkes* and Charles Churchill. It opposed the government of George III* and his Prime Minister, the Scotsman Lord Bute, and was aimed particularly against Bute's journal *The Briton*, edited by the Scottish novelist, Tobias Smollett*. After 45 issues it was suppressed.

*The Political Register** 1802–35. A boldly radical journal written in the popular, and especially the rural, interest by William Cobbett*. Especially famous for his surveys republished as *Rural Rides**.

*The Examiner** 1808–80. Founded by John and Leigh Hunt*, with a policy of strong opposition to the oppressive Tory government of the period 1808–20.

The Athenaeum 1828–1921. One of the most enlightened periodicals of 19th C. It was honest and independent in literary criticism, and a leader of the movement to spread education among the working classes. In 1831 it reduced its price by half in order to reach this wider public, and in consequence increased its circulation 6 times. It was also very progressive in social reform. In 1921 it was incorporated in the *Nation and Athenaeum*, which in turn was merged in 1931 with the socialist weekly, *The New Statesman**.

*The Spectator** begun in 1828, and continuing. It was more concerned with reporting events and affairs than *The Athenaeum*, but its literary criticism had prestige. It is today the leading Conservative review.

*Household Words** 1850–59. A magazine founded and edited by Charles Dickens; it was intended to appeal to more popular taste than such well-established magazines as *Blackwood's*. In it and its successor, *All the Year Round** (1859–70), he published serially Elizabeth Gaskell's *Cranford**, Wilkie Collins's* *Woman in White* and his own *Great Expectations**.

Saturday Review 1855–1931. It was noted for the brilliance of its contributors and the severity of its criticism; regular contributors to it were known as 'the Saturday revilers'. It tried and to some extent succeeded in achieving an authoritative voice on cultural matters.

Published monthly and quarterly

The Gentleman's Magazine 1731–1907. The first to call itself a 'magazine'. It included, as later magazines were to do, a wider variety of material than the Reviews, including political reports which, in 1739–44, were contributed by Samuel Johnson.

*Edinburgh Review** 1802–1929. A serious review of moderate left (Whig) principles; it had very great influence in 19th C. After 1830 it grew markedly less literary.

*Quarterly Review**. Founded in 1809 as a right-wing (Tory) opponent to the *Edinburgh*. It exercised a comparable influence. Like its rival, it took less interest in literature after 1830.

New Monthly Magazine 1814–84. It had editors of considerable literary note such as the poets Thomas Campbell and Thomas Hood*, the novelists Harrison Ainsworth* and Bulwer Lytton, and the essayist Theodore Hook. It gave considerable space to criticism.

*Blackwood's Magazine** founded in 1817. Like the *Quarterly*, it was strongly Conservative, and noted for its violent attacks on the young radical writers, particularly such as were in the circle of Leigh Hunt*, like John Keats*. Later it became almost wholly a journal for stories and serialized fiction such as George Eliot's *Scenes of Clerical Life**.

*London Magazine** 1819–29. It had a brilliant literary period until 1825, during which it published the work of contemporary writers such as Lamb*, Hazlitt* and De Quincey* (*Confessions of an English Opium-Eater**). In 1825 its editor, John Scott, was killed in consequence of a quarrel with *Blackwood's*, whose policy in literature and politics were at the opposite and Conservative extreme. During its last few years it followed the principles of the Utilitarian* thinker, Jeremy Bentham*. A magazine with the same title was started in 1954.

Westminster Review 1823–1913. It was founded as a vehicle for the Benthamite (otherwise known as the Philosophical Radical or Utilitarian*) school of thought, and at first kept severely to its principles. Its politics of ruthless, scientific institutional reform made it not only a strong opponent of the Tory *Quarterly* but put it well to the left of the *Edinburgh*. It appealed to a narrower public, and tended, in the Utilitarian manner, to regard the arts with disdain. In 1836 it combined with the now livelier Utilitarian *London Review*, and continued as the *London and Westminster Review*, under the editorship of the distinguished Utilitarian John Stuart Mill*. Mill wanted to broaden Utilitarian thinking, and writers who were not followers of the movement were brought in, such as Carlyle* and the novelist George Eliot, who was assistant editor 1851–54. Later contributors varied as greatly as Walter Pater*, father of the Aesthetic* movement, and the positivist Frederic Harrison. It continued to advocate scientific progress, and by the end of the century it ceased to be literary.

Fraser's Magazine 1830–82. It started Conservatively, as an imitator of *Blackwood's*, but after mid-19th C it became Liberal. It published Carlyle's *Sartor Resartus** in 1833–34; at this time it was under the influence of Coleridge's* Conservative philosophy. In 1848 it was publishing Charles Kingsley's* novel of idealistic reform, *Yeast*. The historian J. A. Froude was its editor 1861–74, and tried to publish Ruskin's* radical treatise on the nature of wealth, *Munera Pulveris* (1862–63), but this proved unpopular with the public, and the treatise was left unfinished.

Macmillan's Magazine 1859–1907. This included among its contributors Alfred Tennyson*, Matthew Arnold*, Henry James*, and Thomas Hardy*.

*Cornhill Magazine** founded in 1860. It was the most distinguished and successful of the magazines and quarterlies of the second half of 19th C. The novelist Thackeray* was its first editor, and it published his last two novels *Philip* and *Denis Duval*. It also published Mrs Gaskell's masterpiece *Wives and Daughters**, George Eliot's *Romola**, and novels by Trollope*, Wilkie Collins, Thomas Hardy, and Henry James. Matthew Arnold contributed most of his *Culture and Anarchy* – his major single work – as well as other essays, and Ruskin part of his *Unto this Last**. Its first number sold 110,000 copies; its circulation later declined, but the editorship of Leslie Stephen* (1871–82) brought it to the respectable figure of 12,000.

Fortnightly Review. Founded in 1865 by, among others, the novelist Anthony Trollope. It was a vehicle of advanced liberal opinion, and included amongst its contributors the scientist T. H. Huxley*, the political scientist Walter Bagehot*, the positivist philosopher Frederic Harrison, the critics Matthew Arnold and Leslie Stephen, the novelists George Eliot and George Meredith*, the poets D. G. Rossetti* and Algernon Swinburne*, and Walter Pater and William Morris*, both of them leaders of social and critical thought.

The Nineteenth Century (renamed *The Nineteenth Century and After* in 1900, and *The Twentieth*

Century in 1950). It was distinguished for bringing together leading antagonists of opposing views. Other Victorian reviews which ought to be mentioned are: *The Contemporary Review*, founded 1866, whose most famous editor was Percy Bunting; and the *North British Review* (1844–1871). The *Wellesley Index of Periodicals* is useful for reference.

Though some of the above monthlies and quarterlies have continued to exist, their influence has much declined. One 20th-C literary quarterly, however, deserves mention for its extensive influence in reshaping critical and educational thought; this is *Scrutiny**, 1932–53.

2.2.4.2; 7.3.

Revolution of 1688, The

A name given to the removal by Parliament* of King James II* (1685–88) and the substitution of his daughter Mary II* and her husband William III*. The reason for the quarrel between James and Parliament was not so much that James was a Catholic as that he was using every means in his power to assert the superiority of royal power (in the name of his religion) over the power of Parliament. His policy united the whole nation against him, except for a very small minority of Catholics, and the success of Parliament finally settled the question of whether sovereign power lay with the king or with Parliament; this problem had been left unsolved when the period of republican rule (1649–60) had been succeeded by the Restoration* of the monarchy. In 1688 the Revolution was a bloodless one, though there was subsequently some fighting in Ireland and Scotland. The consequences of the event were that the passionate religious and political disagreements which had so divided the nation since the beginning of 17th C were greatly lessened, and a new temper of reasonable debate and tolerant inquiry took their place; the change is typified by the *Letters concerning Toleration* (begun 1689) by the philosopher John Locke*.

* 1.3.4.

Reynard the Fox

The hero of a cycle of animal fables or bestiaries*, begun about 1200, and very popular during the Middle Ages. The animals stand for basic characteristics of human nature, especially as it betrays itself in social relationships. Reynard is the cunning self-seeking individualist who betrays everyone and preys on society, always escaping justice. Caxton* published an English translation of a Flemish version of the tales in 1481, but there is no native version of the cycle in English. The most famous work in which Reynard makes an appearance is Chaucer's *Nun's Priest's Tale**, one of the *Canterbury Tales*.

Reynolds, Sir Joshua (1723–92) /'renldz/

One of the leading portrait painters of 18th C, the great age of English portrait painting. He was the first President of the Royal Academy*, and the author of *Discourses*, *ie* lectures, delivered to its students between 1769 and 1790, on the principles of art. The friend of Samuel Johnson*, he was a founder-member of the Literary Club of which

Johnson was the centre. Reynolds was strongly representative of 18th-C aristocratic taste, and in the opinion of William Blake*, writing about 1808, 'This man was Hired to Depress Art'. However, his *Discourses* were admired by the greatest 19th-C English art critic, John Ruskin*.

* 2.3.

Rhadamanthus /radə'manθəs/

In Greek myth, the son of Zeus* and Europa*, and brother of Minos* of Crete. Such was his strictness of justice in life that after death the gods appointed him one of the judges of the underworld, together with Minos and Aeacus.

Rhapsody

In ancient Greek poetry, a 'rhapsode' or 'rhapsodist' was an epic* poet who sang his own poetry. The word meant 'one who stitches together a song'. In Shakespearian times a rhapsody was an incoherent but eloquent succession of words or lines. It is now used for any form of enthusiastic literary or musical expression.

Rhea

* *Cybele*.

Rhodope (7th C BC) /'rodəpi/

In ancient Greece, a famous courtesan with whom the brother of the poetess Sappho* fell in love and whom he married. A legend tells that an eagle flew away with one of her sandals when she was bathing, and dropped it near Psammeticus, king of Egypt. Psammeticus was so enraptured by the beauty of the sandal, that he sought out its owner, and married her.

Rhyme

* *Figures of Speech*.

Rhyme-royal

A 7-line stanza of 10-syllable lines, rhyming *ababbcc*. It was first used in English by Chaucer* in his *Complaint unto Pity*, and it is the stanza of his *Troilus and Criseyde**, and *The Man of Law's Tale** in the *Canterbury Tales*. An example from *Troilus* Book II, stanza 124:

'Loke up, I seye, and tel me what she is
Anoon, that I may goon aboute thy nede;
Knowe ich hir oughte? for my love, tel me this;
Than wolde I hopen rather for to spede.'
Tho gan the veyne of Troilus to blede,
For he was hit, and wex all reed for shame;
'A ha!' quod Pandare, 'here biginneth game!'

Shakespeare used the measure in his *Lucrece**, but it is mainly a medieval stanza. It is called 'royal' because of its use by James I of Scotland* in the poem of which he is the alleged author, *The King's Quair*.

Rialto

A bridge over the Grand Canal, Venice, and the centre of the commercial district of the city.

Richard I Coeur de Lion (Lionheart) (1189–99)

King of England. He spent most of his reign out of the country, engaged in various wars, especially the third Crusade*. His exploits made him into a figure of romance and legend, and as such he appears in two very popular novels by Walter Scott*: *Ivanhoe** and *The Talisman* (1825). He belonged to the House of Plantagenet* (Anjou) and was the son of his predecessor Henry II* and the brother of his successor, John*.

Richard II (1377–99)

King of England, and last of the direct line in the House of Plantagenet* (Anjou). He was the son of the Black Prince* and the grandson of his predecessor, Edward III*. His neglect of the war against France, his youthfulness (he came to the throne at the age of 11), and his capricious, inconsistent character all helped to make his reign a period of disorder; the throne was eventually usurped by his cousin, Henry Bolingbroke, who became first king of the House of Lancaster* as Henry IV*. Richard had an expensive court, and was a patron of the arts in so far as he intermittently showed favour to the poets Chaucer* and Gower*.

Richard II, King

A historical drama in blank verse* by Shakespeare*, based on the Chronicles of Holinshed*. First performed in 1595, and published in a 1st Quarto* in 1597, it is the first of the second tetralogy of history plays* by Shakespeare, the other three being *1 & 2 Henry IV** and *Henry V**

The theme of all four is kingship; Richard II* is treated as a king whose sacred claim to the throne is beyond doubt, but tragically unaccompanied by any capacity to rule. The leading story is about his relationship with his cousin, Henry Bolingbroke; he drives Henry (not altogether without justification) into exile, and then quite unlawfully confiscates Henry's land. Henry returns to England to defend his right, and receives so much support that he is driven to making himself king. Usurpers, however, were considered to be opposing God, since kings held the throne by God's authority, and so Henry does his best to persuade Richard to abdicate publicly. Richard does so, but he skilfully makes it clear to all the witnesses that his abdication is involuntary (IV. i), so that the public abdication only emphasizes, instead of relieving, Henry's guilt. Concerned as it is with the ritualistic aspect of monarchy – the ceremonies that are the signs of the sacredness of the office – the whole play has been observed by critics to have a ritualistic style, in the formal patterning of much of the verse and the pageant-like ceremony of a number of the important scenes. Richard is imprisoned in the Tower, and later – not by Henry's orders – he is assassinated; thus the effect of criminality in Henry's action in seizing the throne is confirmed.

Richard III (1483–85)

Last king of England in the House of York, which seized the throne from the House of Lancaster* in 1461. The first of the short line was Edward IV* (1461–83), Richard's brother; he was succeeded by his son, the boy king Edward V*, whose throne Richard usurped. He was himself defeated and killed at the Battle of Bosworth (1485) by Henry Tudor, who succeeded as Henry VII* the first sovereign of the Tudor* line. It was very much in the Tudor interest to blacken the character of Richard III, and 16th-C historians (Polydore Vergil, Thomas More*, Holinshed*) depict him as satanically evil. Modern historians have found it difficult to discover whether this account is just, and there have been some attempts to whitewash his character. One of the chief charges against him is the murder of his two nephews Edward V and Richard of York, the 'princes in the Tower'. That they were murdered is almost certain, but there is no proof that Richard was guilty. His portrait shows a distinguished face, but he was hunchbacked and had a withered arm.

* *Histories and Chronicles.*

Richard III (1593?)

A historical drama in blank verse* by Shakespeare* based on Holinshed's* Chronicles, and the last of Shakespeare's first historical tetralogy, the other plays in which are the three parts of *Henry VI**. The Henry VI plays are about the Wars of the Roses*, and the accumulation of hatred, vengefulness and crime which those wars brought about. *Richard III* opens in the reign of Edward IV*, Richard's brother, and shows the attempts of the king to induce his nobles to be reconciled. Fear and war-weariness make them comply, but Richard is still filled with ambition and cold-blooded cruelty. In spite of his appearance – he is a hunchback and has a withered arm – he has a magnetic personality and manages to win friends to help him in his conspiracies. By consistent treachery and ruthlessness he acquires the throne, but is shortly after defeated and killed by Henry Tudor (Henry VII*), who is shown in the play to have right and divine aid on his side. Though totally evil, Richard is presented as a character of energy and wit, the source of much sardonic comedy. Dramatically he is both in the tradition of Machiavelli's* *Prince* – a treatise of evil for Englishmen of Shakespeare's day – and in that of Herod* in the medieval Mystery plays*. The play is the masterpiece of the earliest group of Shakespeare's plays, *ie* those probably written before 1594.

Richard Feverel

* *Ordeal of Richard Feverel.*

Richards, I. A. (b 1893)

Critic. His approach to poetry has been philosophic, linguistic, and psychological. One of his important insights is that we are inevitably influenced by some kind of 'poetry', even if it is only that of bad films and magazine covers, or advertisements. In *Principles of Literary Criticism* (1924) and *Science and Poetry* (1926) he discusses what kind of truth is the subject-matter of poetry, the place of poetry in the context of the rest of life, and what is the nature of critical judgements of poetry. He works to his conclusion on Benthamite (Utilitarian*) lines, of asking what is 'the use' of poetry, but his conclusion is not far from that of Matthew Arnold*, that poetry's function in the modern world is that formerly provided by religion – to provide a 'touchstone' of value, and hence, if only indirectly, a guide to living. (See Arnold's 'Study of Poetry', in *Essays in Criticism**, 2nd Series, 1888.) This view resembles the judgements of other writers of the 1920s and 30s, such as Pound*, Wyndham Lewis*, Eliot*, Leavis*, though each of them arrives at his judgement by a different approach. Richards's *Practical Criticism* (1929) is a teaching manual for the study of poetry with the aim of training students to judge poems presented anonymously, without being influenced by the author's reputation; its ideas have been extensively followed in English and American schools and universities. Much of his later work has been purely linguistic, *eg Basic English and its Uses* (1943). A good study of Richards is contained in *The Armed Vision* by Stanley Hyman. Other works: *The Meaning of Meaning* (with Ogden, 1923); *Coleridge on Imagination* (1934); *The Philosophy of Rhetoric* (1936); *Basic English and its Uses* (1943); *Speculative Instruments* (1955); *Goodbye Earth and other poems* (1959); *The Screens* (1961).

* 7.5.

Richardson, Samuel (1689–1761)

Novelist. He was of humble middle-class origin, and his father – a furniture-maker – seems to have been involved in the Monmouth* Rebellion of 1685, the last Puritan* rising. This gives him the same kind of background as the novelist Defoe* who also took part in the Monmouth Rebellion, but he belongs to the next generation, when Puritan violence and violence against Puritans were alike extinguished, and the very word 'Puritan' was obsolete. Nonetheless, the tradition remained and Richardson belonged to it, though it had undergone changes corresponding to the social assimilation of the class in which Puritan attitudes were so strong. Without the religious passions which had made for heroic qualities in the great 17th-C Puritans like Bunyan*, the Puritan virtues were such as Addison* in his *Spectator** had shown to be compatible with aristocratic wit and refinement of taste: the prudential virtues which make for success in worldly life; for instance it was held that honesty is the best policy, chastity will win a good husband, and economy is the most substantial virtue in a good wife. These are some of the qualities which Richardson wrote his novels to extol, but he was endowed with a creative imagination which was much greater than the narrow principles to which he was restricted in the middle class world where he conducted a prosperous business as a printer.

Richardson wrote three long novels, each in the epistolary form: *Pamela** (1740–41); *Clarissa Harlowe** (1747–48); and *Sir Charles Grandison** (1753–54). Their length causes them to be neglected by the general reader today, but the second is one of the great masterpieces of prose fiction, and the sustained psychological coherence of all three permanently influenced the form the novel* was to take as a branch of literary art, not only in Britain but throughout western Europe. In his realism, Richardson follows Defoe, but Defoe's novels, like his life, were episodic and depended on successive dramatic incidents without distinct psychological relationship; Richardson was able to live a settled and consistent life, and his novels reveal this consistency, making up in psychological intensity what they lack (by comparison with Defoe's) in the quantity of exciting incidents. He also advances on Defoe in his visual intensity, a quality for which he was perhaps indebted to his friend, the great realist painter, William Hogarth*. His career as a novelist runs parallel to and in rivalry with that of Henry Fielding*. *Pamela* provoked *Joseph Andrews**; *Clarissa*, a novel about a virtuous heroine pursued by a villainous rake, was answered in part by Fielding's *Tom Jones**, a novel in which the reader is invited to respond with affection and indulgence to the rakish hero; *Sir Charles Grandison*, the portrait of a gentleman of incomparable virtue, is a further answer. Fielding was a generous-hearted, cultivated aristocrat, well able to see the limitations of Richardson's narrow middle-class morality, but he was artist enough to appreciate the greatness of *Clarissa*. Fielding's comic genius and talent for lively incident make him much the more popular of the two novelists among modern readers, but Richardson shows the more original genius.

* 4.3.2.

Bib: Eaves and Kimpel: *Life*; McKillop, A. D., *Richardson, Printer and Novelist*; Watt, Ian, in *The Rise of the Novel*; Kettle, A., in *An Introduction to the English Novel*; Pritchett, V. S., in *The Living Novel*; Daiches, D., in *Literary Essays*; Downs, B. W., *Samual Richardson*; Stephen, L., in *Hours in a Library*; Sale, W. M., *Richardson, Master Printer.*

Ridley, Nicholas (1500?–55)

One of the leading religious reformers in the reign

of Henry VIII* and, with Cranmer* and Latimer*, one of the three principal martyrs in 1555 under the Roman Catholic reaction of Mary I. He helped Cranmer compile the Books of Common Prayer* of 1549 and 1552, and thus contributed to one of the first English prose masterpieces. He became Bishop of London in 1549.

Ridolfi Plot (1570)

Organized by an Italian Roberto di Ridolfi against Elizabeth I*. He planned to marry the Catholic Mary Queen of Scots* to the Duke of Norfolk, and place her on the throne of England with Spanish help. The plot was discovered by Elizabeth's spies, but Ridolfi was himself in safety in Paris.

Ridotto /ri'dotəu/

A kind of public social gathering, with dancing and music, introduced into England in 1722, and very popular in 18th C.

Rights of Man

* *Paine.*

Rimmon /'rimən/

A god of ancient Assyria, mentioned in the Bible: '... when I bow down myself in the house of Rimmon, the Lord pardon thy servant in this thing' (*2 Kings* 5:18.). He is one of Milton's fallen angels – *Paradise Lost** i. 467.

* *Angels, Fallen.*

Risorgimento /ri'so:dʒi'mentəu/

Italian for 'resurrection'. The name given to the movement for the unification of Italy in mid-19th C, led by Victor Emmanuel, king of Sardinia, his Prime Minister Cavour, the agitator Mazzini, and the soldier Garibaldi. In 1847 Cavour founded a newspaper called 'Risorgimento'. The movement appealed to English sympathies, which were strongly liberal at that time; references to it are common in mid-19th-C literature.

Rivals, The (1775)

A prose comedy by Richard Brinsley Sheridan*. It is set in the fashionable city of Bath, and the plot concerns parents and guardians at cross purposes with their children. The central situation is that the young and sentimental Lydia Languish, a great novel reader, prefers the idea of marrying a young, penniless officer to the possibility of a rich young heir as a husband. Captain Absolute is such an heir and genuinely in love with her, but to win her affections he disguises himself as the penniless Ensign Beverley. His father, Sir Anthony Absolute, a rich baronet, is determined to make an unromantic marriage of convenience between his son and Lydia, but the Captain dare not disclose his disguise and so seems to be disobeying his father's wishes. Mrs Malaprop, Lydia's guardian, is equally anxious for the worldly match and disapproves of Beverley, but at the same time she is making love by letter to the aggressive Irishman, Sir Lucius O'Trigger, who supposes that the letters come from Lydia, and is one of her suitors. An additional complication is that the so-called Beverley and Sir Lucius have as another rival an absurd young country squire, Bob Acres. A sub-plot of very little worth is another love affair between Julia Melville and the morbidly jealous Faulkland. This sub-plot is a concession to the sentimental drama initiated by Colley Cibber* half a century before.

Sheridan's comedies – of which *The Rivals* is the first – are, like those of Goldsmith* at about the same time, above all a reaction against the sentimental tradition, and recall the wit and theatrical deftness of Restoration* drama without its licentiousness.

* 5.2.2.

Roaring Boys

A common term from 16th to 18th C for disorderly young men who terrorized the London streets at night. The 18th-C Mohocks were similar but more aristocratic. Thomas Middleton* wrote with Dekker* a play, produced in 1611, called *The Roaring Girl, or Moll Cut-Purse.*

Robertson, T. W. (1829–71)

Dramatist. Plays: *Society* (1865), *Ours* (1866), *Caste* (1867), *Play* (1868), *M.P.* (1870). He is memorable chiefly for restoring to the drama some degree of relevance to contemporary social life at a time when contemporary plays had very little serious interest. His best-known play is the social comedy *Caste.*

Bib: Nicoll, A., in *A History of Late Nineteenth Century Drama 1850–1900.*

Rob Roy (1817)

A novel by Walter Scott*, giving a picture of Scotland just before the first Jacobite* rebellion of 1715. The plot concerns the rivalry in love of the cousins Francis and Rashleigh Osbaldistone for Diana Vernon. Rashleigh, the villain, is involved in Jacobite intrigue. Their adventures are interwoven with the fortunes of Rob Roy Macgregor, a historical character whom Scott romanticizes. He is the chief of the Clan Macgregor in the Scottish Highlands*, and a convicted outlaw who lives by plunder. In the novel he acts on the side of the hero, Francis, at Diana's earnest appeal. As usual in Scott's novels, the notable parts are those which concern Scottish common life, and such characters as Bailie Nicol Jarvie and Francis's servant Andrew Fairservice.

Robespierre, Isidore Maximilien de (1758–94) /'rəubzpjeə/

A leader of the extremist Jacobins* during the French Revolution*. He exercised virtual dictatorship from July 1793 to July 1794, during which he conducted the Reign of Terror and tried to establish the worship of the deistic Supreme Being in opposition to Catholicism on the one side and atheism on the other. His reputation for fanatical integrity caused him to be known as the Incorruptible.

* *Deism.*

Robin Goodfellow

* *Fairies.*

Robin Hood

The hero of popular ballads* from 14th to 16th C. The earliest surviving reference to him is in Langland's *Piers Plowman** (Passus 5) where Sloth, seventh of the Seven Deadly Sins*, says:

I can noughte perfitly my pater noster as the prest it syngeth
But I can rymes of Robin Hood and Randolf erle of Chestre

As a popular hero, he was to some extent the counterpart of King Arthur*, the ideal of the noble class. Robin Hood lived in the forest of Sherwood near Nottingham in the midlands; he was an expert archer and huntsman, stole from the rich in order to give to the poor, was the enemy of the rich churchmen but not a pagan. He is sometimes represented as a Saxon* hero resisting the Norman-French aristocracy, but the period at which he was supposed to live varies from 12th to 14th C; Scott's novel *Ivanhoe** sets him (as Locksley) in the reign of Richard I* which is also the time of the Randolf Earl of Chester in Langland's reference.

The ballads about him do not have great literary merit, and the surviving texts do not date further back than 15th C; the most important is *A Lytell Geste of Robyn Hode* (1510). He and some other characters in the legends (Friar Tuck*, Maid Marian*, Little John*) were enacted in the morris dances* and May games performed until mid-17th C. The stories, however, have had vitality enough to survive into modern children's versions and films.

Robinson, Henry Crabb (1775–1867)

A lawyer whose wide acquaintance with the leading writers of his time has made his diary* and letters a rich source for the literary history of the early years of 19th C. Among his friends were Wordsworth*, Coleridge*, Lamb* and Hazlitt*. He helped to found the Athenaeum* Club and University College, London. He worked for the *Times* newspaper in Spain, 1800–9, as a war reporter.

Robinson Crusoe, The Life and strange surprising Adventures of (1719)

A novel by Daniel Defoe*. The first part was based on the experiences of a sailor, Alexander Selkirk, who went ashore on the uninhabited island of Juan Fernandez in 1704, and remained there until he was rescued in 1709. Crusoe runs away to sea (as Selkirk had done) and after a number of adventures is wrecked on an uninhabited island, where he remains for 20 years. Defoe describes the industrious and methodical way in which he builds up a life for himself, how he is endangered by the periodical visits of a race of cannibals, how he tames one of them into an ideal servant, Man Friday. The island is eventually visited by a ship in the hands of mutinous sailors; he subdues the mutineers and rescues the officers, who take him back to England, leaving the repentant mutineers

behind as a colony, together with some Spaniards whom he had previously rescued from the cannibals.

In *The Farther Adventures of Robinson Crusoe* published in the same year Crusoe revisits the colony and relates its fortunes; he also travels elsewhere, visits China, and returns to England across Siberia and Russia. The third part, *The Serious Reflections of Robinson Crusoe* (1720), consists of moral essays in which Defoe represents the book as an allegory of his own life. This was partly a defence against the disapproval of his fellow Puritans* who regarded fiction as hardly distinguishable from lies; on the other hand, Defoe's tale is certainly an image of the loneliness and arduousness of the life of individual economic enterprise which was becoming increasingly typical of society; Crusoe is made to say that he has been more lonely since his return to London than he ever was on his island.

Modern critics have noticed how Crusoe sees human beings merely in terms of their economic virtues. The book has always been praised for its detailed verisimilitude, which caused it to be received at first as an authentic account; the descriptions are almost entirely in terms of what the philosopher John Locke* had distinguished as the objectively discernible 'primary qualities' (*Essay Concerning Human Understanding**) as opposed to the subjectively experienced 'secondary qualities' (colour, beauty, etc.) which it is difficult to verify. The style of the writing is extremely plain, in keeping with the principles that Thomas Sprat had laid down for the Royal Society* in 1667 (*History of the Royal Society*): 'the language of Artisans, Countrymen, and Merchants'. That Crusoe appears much less religious than Defoe means him to is also often remarked; on the other hand, if there is a principle of unity in the long, episodic narrative, it is the function of God as the basic Providence, subjecting chaos so that man may use his constructive virtues for the building of an orderly world.

* 4.3.1.

Roc

In Arabian myth, an enormous bird, which appears in the story of Sinbad the Sailor in the *Arabian Nights**. It was reputed to feed its young on elephants.

Rochester, John Wilmot, Second Earl of (1648–80) /ˈrotʃistə/

Poet. He belonged to a brilliant group of writers, courtiers, and wits (including Buckingham, Etherege*, Wycherley*, Sedley) at the Court of Charles II*. Like the others, he owed much to the refined, rational, neo-classical* culture of contemporary France, especially to the criticism and poetry of Nicolas Boileau* (1636–1711). He shared, too, their sceptical, even cynical reaction against the spiritual earnestness of the preceding generation – the generation which had been deeply affected by the Civil War* with its religious issues. He was influenced by the clear-sighted, practical vision of the philosopher Thomas Hobbes*, who tended to reduce the meaning of life to immediately apprehensible pleasures and pains. But he was remarkable in his generation for the seriousness with which he followed the life of pleasure, and for the seriousness with which he accepted the disillusionment which pleasure entailed. His short love poems are often sincere as well as witty, and his poem *A Satire against Mankind* (1675) shows strong conviction in its bitterness. He and his circle were building up the tradition of worldly Augustanism*, but he wrote with an individual voice, and saw clearly that it would be a limited and unsatisfying structure in the long run. Contemporary religious tradition, on the other hand, did not satisfy his intelligence, until he came under the influence of the keenly intellectual Bishop Burnet. According to Burnet, Rochester was moving towards religious conversion, and planned to devote himself to 'Divine Poetry', when he died. Burnet wrote a memoir of him.

Bib: Pinto, V. de S., *Life*; Leavis, F. R., in *Revaluation*; Johnson, S., in *Lives of the Poets*; Wilson, J. H., *Restoration Court Wits*; Burnet, G., *Some Passages of the Life and Death of Rochester* (1680).

Roderick Hudson (1875)

The second novel by Henry James*. The hero is a young American who leaves America and sets up as a sculptor in Rome. The theme is an aspect of the problem of success and failure in art, and the nature of the eventual failure of the hero.

Roderick Random (1748)

A novel by Tobias Smollett*. It is based on Smollett's own experience as a naval doctor at the siege of Cartagena in 1741; it is episodic in form, and vivid but somewhat brutal in manner. In the Preface, the author pays tribute to the comic genius of Cervantes, author of *Don Quixote**.

Rolls-Royce

A make of expensive car, first manufactured in 1906. The possession of one has ever since been a symbol of wealth and luxury. Since World War I the firm has also made aircraft engines.

Roman de la Rose; Romaunt of the Rose

A French allegorical romance dating from 13th C. The first 4,000 lines were by Guillaume de Lorris, and the remaining 16,000 were completed by Jean de Meung. The two parts are quite distinct in character; the first is a gracious narrative in symbolic terms of a courtship, and the second is much harsher, consisting of long satiric dialogues.

Before 1373, Chaucer* made a version of part of the poem in English – the *Romaunt of the Rose*. He translated and amplified the first part, and added about a sixth of the second, all in 8-syllable rhymed couplets*. Characteristically for medieval love poetry, the story is in the form of a dream; the poet visits the Garden of Mirth, where he finds allegorical figures, including the God of Love, dancing. He sees the reflection in a clear spring of a rose-bud, which he falls in love with and desires to pick. His attempts to do so are assisted or frustrated by more allegorical figures; Bialacoil (Welcome, from French Bel Accueil) is his friend, but such figures as Shame and Danger are his enemies. The lover is made the servant of the God of Love who helps him, but Jealousy builds a castle round the rose-tree and shuts him out. The significance of the allegory is that possession of the bud represents possession of the lady, and the figures that surround it are aspects of herself or representatives of her family; since she is well brought up, her natural courtesy befriends the lover, while her chastity causes her to defend her honour, and her kinsfolk resist the lover from their own motives. The poem amounts to a classic statement of romantic love in symbolic terms; Chaucer was later to translate the symbolism into realistic terms in the narrative poem *Troilus and Criseyde**. Of the two poets he was translating, Guillaume de Lorris was to leave his mark on such works as *The Book of the Duchess*, *The Legend of Good Women** and the *Squire's Tale**, while the sardonic humour of Jean de Meung has affinities with the *Parliament of Fowls** and the fabliaux* of the *Canterbury Tales*; *Troilus* shows a blend of the two.

Roman Wall

A wall built across the north of England by the Roman Emperor Hadrian (reigned AD 117–38) and strengthened or reconstructed by the Emperor Severus in 3rd C. Its purpose was to provide a line of fortifications against the tribes of Picts and Scots to the north, and hence to protect the province of Britannia (corresponding to modern England and Wales) from invasion. Substantial sections of the wall, which runs south of the Scottish border, still survive.

Romance

Originally a tale in one of the Romance languages, *ie* one of the forms of the Latin language spoken round the shores of the western Mediterranean in the earlier Middle Ages*, and especially southern French. Such tales developed special characteristics, such as loose, episodic construction, extravagant incident, and miraculous occurrences. From 11th–12th C the heroic adventures of knights following their vocation of dealing justice and protecting the weak become prominent in the tradition, as in the cycle of legends about the court of King Arthur*; so do tales of passionate lovers who defy all circumstances and other loyalties for the sake of the one reality of their love for each other – hence the phrase 'romantic love'. Such tales passed from France to England, and both they and native stories (such as the legends of Robin Hood) came to be known as 'romances' independently of the original meaning of the word as a linguistic classification, which survives.

In 18th C 'romantic' was used in connection with disorderly construction or extravagant feeling and behaviour, and the word usually had a disparaging implication. What is now called the 'Romantic movement' in the England of early 19th C was quite unaware of itself as romantic, and the word continued to have its 18th-C sense until after 1830. In France and Germany, however, the sense of contrast between the freedom of imagination in romances and the restraint and discipline which was thought to have been characteristic of classical (*ie* ancient Greek and Roman) literature, led to discussions about similar contrasts in contemporary literature. Hence began the well-known use of the terms 'classical' and 'romantic', which from mid-19th C became familiar in England as well.

* 3.4.1; 4.1.2; *Romantic Revival.*

Romanesque

* *Norman.*

Romantic Revival

A term used in Germany and France at the end of 18th and beginning of 19th C to classify a new movement in literature, especially in poetry. According to Goethe*, it originated in discussions between himself and Schiller, but the German critic A. W. Schlegel (1767–1845) and the French writer Madame de Stael (1766–1817), had most to do with its popularization.

The English romantic revival is supposed to be the work of a number of writers between 1790 and 1830, especially the six poets William Blake*, William Wordsworth*, Samuel Taylor Coleridge*, Lord Byron*, Percy Bysshe Shelley* and John Keats*. These are commonly known as the Romantic Movement, but the term is unfortunate and misleading in certain respects:

[1] The writers were individualists, and did not cohere in a movement. It is true that the influence of Wordsworth to some extent affected all the others except Blake, that Wordsworth and Coleridge were closely associated in their most vital poetic years, and that a friendship existed between Shelley and Byron, but there was, over the whole period, more disagreement and even dissension amongst the six than collaboration or even sympathy.

[2] These poets did not think of themselves as romantic, and would probably not have appreciated the term; Byron, commonly regarded as an extreme romantic, was a strong admirer of the 18th-C poet Pope*, one of the most 'classical' of all English poets, and (writing in 1820) expressed his disapproval of the 'classical versus romantic' controversies that he found going on in Germany and Italy, and his hope that they would not arise in England.

On the other hand, it is to be admitted that these 6 poets had certain qualities in common, which set them apart at least from their predecessors of 18th C.

[1] They cultivated imaginative freedom, though in very various ways, and this encouraged them to use a variety of sometimes very loose poetic forms.

[2] Each tended to express the feelings of man in solitude as opposed to those of man in society (but this was also true of some 18th-C so-called 'romantic precursors' such as Collins*).

[3] They shared a tendency to be 'inward turning' rather than outward-looking; but again the extent of this tendency varied greatly from Coleridge at one extreme to Byron whose best poetry – the satires – are as outward-looking as (though more individualistic than) any 18th-C work.

[4] All, except perhaps Blake, responded vividly to natural environment.

[5] They tended to use language with more freedom and informality than the 18th-C poets.

[6] They were all, but in different ways, profoundly affected by the great historical fact of the French Revolution*, and by its various immediate consequences, especially the career of Napoleon*; Blake, Wordsworth, Coleridge began as warm revolutionary sympathizers, but the Napoleonic wars caused Blake to withdraw and turned the other two into convinced Conservatives; Byron and Shelley were aristocratic revolutionaries, and Keats was non-political but radical in his sympathies.

[7] All these poets were deeply interested in problems of growth and process, both in life and in art; it has been said that the most interesting poems of the period were about writing poetry. Some of these qualities – *eg* looseness of form, reliance on the imagination, and introversion – are commonly accepted as 'romantic', but the term is more darkening to the understanding than enlightening as a general description of these six poets. However, no other term is available.

* 3.4.1; 7.3.

Romanticism

* *Romance.*

Romany

* *Gipsies.*

Romaunt of the Rose

Chaucer's* translation of the *Roman de la Rose**.

Romeo and Juliet

A romantic tragedy by Shakespeare*. It was published in quarto* in a corrupt form in 1597, and in a better edition in 1599. The story is an old one; Shakespeare's version is based on a poem *Romeus and Juliet* (1562) by Arthur Brooke, itself based on a French version (by Boiastuau) of an Italian tale by Bandello (1554). The story is of the romantic love of Romeo, belonging to the family of Montague, and Juliet, of the Capulet family, both living in the Italian city of Verona. The affair has to be kept secret owing to the bitter hostility of the two families, and only Juliet's Nurse and Friar Laurence, who marries them, know of it. Even so the affair is not allowed to continue peacefully; Juliet's cousin Tybalt provokes an affray which leads not only to his own death but to that of Mercutio, friend of Romeo and relative of the Prince of Verona, with the result that Romeo is exiled from the city. Moreover, Juliet's father, in ignorance of his daughter's secret marriage, proposes to marry her off in haste to a young nobleman, Paris. To enable her to escape this, Friar Laurence gives Juliet a potion which sends her into a profound sleep and causes her family to suppose her dead; the Friar's design is that she shall be placed in the family burial vault, and that meanwhile a message is to be sent to Romeo directing him to come by night and steal her away. However, by an accident the message is not sent, and Romeo hears only of her death; he returns to Verona, but only to take poison and die by her side. A moment later, the effect of the potion passes away and Juliet recovers; she sees her lover dead beside her, and kills herself in turn.

The play is one of Shakespeare's early masterpieces, and is famous for its exquisite poetry and the dramatic excellence of some of its scenes (*eg* II. i where the lovers declare their love to each other in the 'balcony scene') and of three of its characters, namely Juliet, her nurse, and Romeo's friend Mercutio. It is not, however, a tragedy in the sense in which we understand the term 'Shakespearian tragedy', in regard to the plays written after 1600. In these plays, tragedy is the outcome of the nature and situation of the central character (*eg* Othello*), whereas in *Romeo and Juliet* the unhappy ending is more the result of accident – notably the failure to send the message to Romeo. On the other hand, it is possible that the usual response to the play is more sentimental than Shakespeare intended: Brooke's poem is puritanical and reproves the lovers for their passion; Shakespeare presents them sympathetically, but there are signs – *eg* the Friar's soliloquy opening II. iii – that he intended the passion to be regarded as a misfortune in itself. Whatever one's views on this, the excellence of the play arises above all from the actuality with which Shakespeare presents Juliet: the tradition of courtly romance is brought, as in Chaucer's *Troilus and Criseyde**, closely into relationship with real life.

* *Courtly Literature and Romantic Love.*

Romola (1863) /ˈromələ/

A historical novel by George Eliot*, serialized in *Cornhill Magazine* (1862–3). It is set in late-15th-C Florence at the time of the predominance of the reforming monk Savonarola*. Romola is a high-minded girl who marries a self-indulgent and unscrupulous Greek, Tito Melma. Repelled by her husband and disillusioned by the course of Savonarola's career, she eventually finds her salvation in self-denial. In writing the novel, George Eliot was putting forward the principle that it is as important to actualize the society in which the characters move as to give reality to the characters themselves. The novel has been praised for the thoroughness of research which established the Florentine scene; on the other hand, by comparison with the later novels (*Middlemarch* and *Daniel Deronda*) set in England, modern readers feel that medieval Florence did not touch the author in the sense that she participated imaginatively in its life, with the result that of all her novels, *Romola* is probably the least read.

Romulus /ˈromjuləs/

The legendary founder of the city of Rome. He and his twin brother Remus were the children of Mars, the god of war, and Ilia, daughter of Numitor, the king of Alba. As infants, they were thrown into the river Tiber by the order of their uncle, Amulius. They were, however, saved and nurtured by a she-wolf. They grew up to revenge themselves on their uncle, and to lay the foundations of the city of Rome. The omens favoured Romulus for this task, and Remus, in jealousy, showed his contempt by leaping over them. Romulus killed his brother in resentment. He filled his city with fugitives and criminals, and conquered the Sabines.

Rondeau /'rondəu/

A form of short poem originated in 16th-C France. It consisted of 13 8- or 10-syllabled lines, divided into stanzas of unequal length, with the addition of short refrains, and only two rhymes throughout. The form was little used in England until late 19th C when a taste developed for the more artificial forms of short poem among poets like Swinburne*, *eg* his *Century of Roundels*.

Rondel /'rondl/

A form of short poem similar to the rondeau, but consisting of 14 lines instead of 13, and with a somewhat different rhyme scheme. It was not much used in English until the end of 19th C in the work of such poets as Bridges*, Dobson and Henley. It originated in France in 14th C.

Ronsard, Pierre de (1524–85) /ron'sa:/

French poet, leader of the group known as the *Pléiade* (**Pleiades*). He was one of the chief lyric poets of 16th C, and is particularly famous for his sonnets*, in which form he was influential among the English sonneteers of the last decade, *eg* Constable and Daniel*.

Rosalind, Rosalynde

[1] The central character in Shakespeare's comedy *As You Like It**. She is based on the heroine of Thomas Lodge's* romance *Rosalynde, Euphues Golden Legacy* (1590).

[2] A character in *January*, the first month of Spenser's *Shepherd's Calendar**; she has been thought to represent Rosa Daniel, the sister of the poet Samuel Daniel*, and wife of John Florio*, translator of the Essays of Montaigne*.

Rosamund, Fair

Rosamund Clifford, the mistress of Henry II*, and the subject of a number of later legends. These relate that Henry built a labyrinthine house for her at Woodstock, and guided himself to her chamber by a clue of thread; Henry's queen, Eleanor of Aquitaine, is said to have found her way by the same thread, and to have poisoned Rosamund. The legend has a clear basis in the ancient Greek myth of the labyrinth of Crete, where Theseus*, guided by Ariadne's* thread, found and killed the Minotaur*. The story, baseless in fact, is used by Samuel Daniel* in his poem *The Complaint of Rosamond* (1592) and by Thomas Deloney* in a ballad.

Roscius (Quintus Roscius Gallus) (126?–62 BC) /'roʃiəs/

A famous Roman comic actor. He wrote a treatise comparing acting and oratory, and the great orator Cicero took lessons from him. It became a habit to praise actors by comparing them to Roscius; thus Ben Jonson* compared Edward Alleyn* to him.

Rose Tavern

A public house near Covent Garden* at the end of 17th C and beginning of 18th. It was a favourite pleasure resort.

Rose Theatre

Opened by the theatre manager, Philip Henslowe*, in 1592 on Bankside* in Southwark. Shakespeare was a member of his company at the time. Henslowe managed the theatre together with his son-in-law, Edward Alleyn*, until 1603.

* *Theatres*.

Rosenberg, Isaac (1890–1918) /'rəuzənbə:g/

Poet. He was born in Bristol, and educated at an elementary school in London. He then became apprenticed to an engraver, and entered the Slade School of Art in 1911. He joined the army in 1915, serving as a private soldier, and was killed in action. He was the most original of all the 'war poets'. His work is full of rhythmic energy, less sombre than Wilfred Owen's*, and bolder in imagery. Owen reacted with indignation and compassion against the war; in the Preface to his poems he wrote: 'Above all I am not concerned with Poetry. My subject is War, and the pity of War. The Poetry is in the pity.' Rosenberg wrote in a letter (1916): 'I will not leave a corner of my consciousness covered up but saturate myself with the strange and extraordinary new conditions of this life, and it will all refine itself into poetry later on.' Works: *Night and Day* (1912); *Youth* (1915); *Poems* (edited by G. Bottomley, with a Memoir by L. Binyon, 1922). *Collected Poems* (ed. G. Bottomley and D. Harding, 1937).

* *War Poets*.

Roses, Wars of the

* *Wars of the Roses*.

Rosetta Stone

A stone bearing an inscription in Egyptian hieroglyphics, and in the simplified form of hieroglyphics known as 'demotic', and in Greek. The combination made it possible to interpret Egyptian hieroglyphics. It was found by the Nile by soldiers of Napoleon, and is now in the British Museum, London.

Rosicrucianism /rəuzi'kru:ʃjənizm/

A system of philosophical and mystical beliefs professed by an organization known as the Ancient Mystic Order of Rosa Crucis (the red cross). Its origins are obscure; it is first mentioned in 1614. Part of its doctrine has consisted in the belief that the universe contains a hierarchy of spirits governing the various elements. Pope, in his second version of *The Rape of the Lock**, used this system for satirical purposes; he needed for his mock epic* a supernatural system comparable to the ancient Greek gods and goddesses of Homer's *Iliad**, but adapted, as they would not be, to the pettiness of his theme. He used the Rosicrucian system because it provided spirits of all degrees of importance.

Rosinante /rosi'nantei/

Don Quixote's* horse; though he imagined it to be worthy of the knight of romance that he supposed himself to be, it was in fact a wretched, lean and starved animal.

Rossetti, Christina Georgina (1830–94) /ro'seti/

Poet. She was the youngest child of Gabriele Rossetti, an Italian political refugee who came to England in 1824. Her brothers were the poet and painter, D. G. Rossetti*, and the critic William Michael Rossetti; her sister, Maria Francesca, entered an Anglican* convent, and is known for a book on Dante*. Christina was also a deeply religious Anglo-Catholic, and her poetry is suffused with piety; she modelled herself on the 17th-C spiritual poet George Herbert* in this respect. She was also associated with the Pre-Raphaelite Brotherhood* led by D. G. Rossetti, contributing to its journal *The Germ* edited by her other brother, William Michael; she shared the Pre-Raphaelite taste for beautiful but sad and rather languid imagery, but her diction is remarkable for its simplicity and sincerity. This simplicity attracted her to children as an audience, but her bad health and the frustration of her love affairs through religious causes made her poems too sad to be popular with children. Her religious appeal, in contrast to Herbert, is also limited by the narrowness of High Anglicanism in relation to the rest of the society of her time. Her most famous book of verse, *Goblin Market and other Poems* came out in 1862. Other volumes: *The Prince's Progress* (1866); *Sing-Song* (1872); *A Pageant and other Poems* (1881); *New Poems* (1896). She also published works of religious prose, and *Time Flies, a Reading Diary* (1883) combines prose and verse. Christina Rossetti was one of the finer products of the Oxford Movement*, and in spite of the serious limitations in her work, it is still admired by 20th-C critics for simplicity and sincerity unusual in poetry of the second half of 19th C.

* *Church of England.*

Bib: Bell, M., *Life*; Sandars, M. F., *Life*; Bald, M. A., in *Women Writers of the Nineteenth Century*; Birkhead, E., *Christina Rossetti and her Poetry*; Zativenska, M., *Christina Rossetti: a Portrait with a Background*; Packer, L. M., *Christina Rossetti.*

Rossetti, Dante Gabriel (1828–82) /ro'seti/

Poet and painter; the son of an Italian political refugee and an English mother. In 1848 he started the Pre-Raphaelite Brotherhood* with a number of fellow-painters, but the inspiration of his painting as of his poetry was essentially literary. The poetry is a continuation of the English romantic* movement, particularly the work of Keats*, inasmuch as its central impulse is the sensuous response to beauty, and the inspiration of the Pre-Raphaelites was the direct appeal of detail in medieval painting. Rossetti also inherited, however, the feeling for the mysteriousness of the Middle Ages* which both he and Keats shared with the taste for 'Gothic' which was an aspect of romanticism at the beginning of the century. In addition, he inherited some of the feeling for aestheticism* in sanctity which had been part of the Oxford Movement* in the Church of England during the 1830s and 40s. However, Keats had responded to 'Beauty' as fullness of life, and had accompanied his search for it with fearless scrutiny of his relationships with people and his own intellectual and moral growth. Since his death (in 1821), the triumph of English industrialism, with its admiration for technology and its disregard of values which were not practical ones, had tended to throw poets, who required values that were ends in themselves, into something like despair. (Arnold* is an example, *eg* in *The Scholar Gipsy**.) Thus poets like Rossetti were tempted to use their poetry as a dream world of refuge from external squalor and commercial struggle so that the explorations of men like Keats were replaced by self-regarding nostalgia that led naturally to the aestheticism of the end of the century. This meant that fields of inspiration such as the Middle Ages and religion are not so much expressed in their own reality as used as a defence against other, objectionable realities; Rossetti is accused of being 'religiose' rather than 'religious', and of having falsified the past. On the other hand Rossetti's poetry, within these limitations, is sumptuous and melodious. He was at first much better known for his paintings, but his poem *The Blessed Damozel* was published in the Pre-Raphaelite journal *The Germ* in 1850. Later came his translations from Dante*, *The Early Italian Poets* (1861); *Poems by D. G. Rossetti* (1870); *Ballads and Sonnets* (1881), including a sonnet sequence, *The House of Life*, which was expanded from a version in the 1870 volume, and is sometimes called his masterpiece.

Bib: Doughty, O., *A Victorian Romantic*; Winwar, F., *Poor Splendid Wings*; Holman Hunt, W., *Pre-Raphaelitism and the Pre-Raphaelite Brotherhood*; Boas, H. O. B., *Rossetti and his Poetry*; Cary, E. L., *The Rossettis*; Pater, W., in *Appreciations.*

Rotten Row

An earth-covered track extending three-quarters round Hyde Park in London. It is a fashionable resort for exercise on horseback.

Round Table, The

In Arthurian legend, King Arthur* devised a round table about which his knights were to sit at banquet. Its advantage was supposed to be that its shape prevented disputes as to precedence, since a rectangular table always has a 'head'. The knights were hence known as 'the Knights of the Round Table'. A special seat called the 'siege perilous' was reserved for the knight who should find the Holy Grail*.

Roundheads

A name for Puritan* supporters of the Parliamentary* party in the Civil Wars* of 1642–51. They were so called because they habitually cut their hair close to their heads, whereas the Royalists

(Cavaliers*) wore their hair ornamentally long. This Cavalier habit was regarded by the Puritans as a symptom of worldliness. The word has been traced back to 1641, when a Cavalier officer was quoted as declaring that he would 'cut the throats of those round-headed dogs that bawled against bishops'. Earlier than this, a pamphlet against long hair was published under the title of 'The unloveliness of lovelocks.'

Rousseau, Jean-Jacques (1712–78) /ˈru:səu/ French-Swiss thinker. His chief works were: *Discourse on the Influence of Learning and Art* (1750), in which he argues that progress in these has not improved human morals; *Discourse on Inequality* (1754), in which society is considered to have spoilt the liberty and virtue natural to primitive peoples; a novel, *The New Héloise* (1761), in which the return to primitive nature is considered in relation to the relationships of the sexes and the family; *The Social Contract** (1761), a political treatise with the theme that the basis of society is artificial, not binding on individuals when society ceases to serve their interests; *Emile* (1762), advocating education through the evocation of the natural impulses and interests of the child, and the *Confessions*, an autobiography which was self-revealing without precedent, published after his death.

Rousseau was immensely influential, not only in France but throughout Europe. His praise of Nature and protests against Society have always been thought significant contributions to the creation of a revolutionary state of mind, culminating in the French Revolution* of 1789. Education from Nature, his conception of Nature as a life-giving force, was of great importance in the background of Wordsworth*, and through Wordsworth, of much of English 19th-C imaginative thinking, and linked with his devotion to Nature was his equally influential reverence for childhood. As an autobiographer, Rousseau was one of the first to base the importance of individual experience on its uniqueness, not on its moral excellence or intellectual attainment. This was quite contrary to the characteristic 18th-C view, expressed in works like Samuel Johnson's *Rasselas**, in which the valuable experience was conceived to be only that which was true of and for humanity at large. Rousseau's feeling for the uniqueness of the individual has governed imaginative art, especially in the novel, until 20th C.

* *Autobiography.*

***Roxana, or The Fortunate Mistress* (1724)** /rokˈsa:nə/
A novel by Daniel Defoe*. It is the fictional autobiography of Mademoiselle Beleau, the daughter of French Protestant refugees. Her first husband, a London brewer, deserts her, leaving her destitute, and she takes to a life of prostitution in England, France and Holland, in the course of which she becomes prosperous. After a second marriage to a Dutch merchant, she finds herself a widow and again impoverished, deprived of the social importance and stability which she had enjoyed with him. She is imprisoned for debt, but ends in a state of penitence. The story is told with Defoe's characteristic effect of solid realism, and contains vivid episodes.

Royal Academy of Arts

Founded with the approval of King George III in 1768 'for the purpose of cultivating and improving the arts of painting, sculpture and architecture'. The first President (P.R.A.) was the portrait painter Sir Joshua Reynolds*; an elected council of 40 Royal Academicians are entitled to place R.A. after their names, and a further number of Associates bear the letters A.R.A. The Royal Academy runs schools of art and holds an annual exhibition of about 1,000 works submitted to it and approved by it; the opening is an important social occasion. The Academy is further the manager of financial trusts on behalf of artists, and organizes exhibitions of foreign artists. Until mid-19th C the Academy included distinguished artists amongst its number, such as the landscape painter, Turner, but for the last 100 years its policy has been conservative to the point of mediocrity, so that the livelier movements of English art have occurred without its patronage. Nonetheless, apart from the Royal Society*, it is the only official institution in the arts to have achieved national prestige. It has occupied its present site, Burlington House, Piccadilly, London, since 1869.

* 2.3.

Royal Exchange, The
The principal London centre for international monetary transactions, founded by Sir Thomas Gresham in 1566. The original building was destroyed in the Great Fire of London* in 1666; the present one dates from 1844.

* *Stock Exchange.*

Royal Martyr, The
Charles I*, so called by his supporters in consequence of his trial and execution by the revolutionary Parliament* of 1649. Charles was devout,

and the Civil Wars* broke out for reasons which were partly and ostensibly religious; the victory of Parliament was also that of the Puritans*, and entailed the temporary overthrow of the Church of England*. Charles was consequently not only regarded as a martyr for the Anglican Church, but even by some as a saint, and a few churches exist dedicated to King Charles the Martyr.

The Royal Martyr is also the subtitle of a play otherwise called *Tyrannic Love* (1669) by John Dryden*.

Royal Society, The

Founded with the authority of Charles II* in 1662; its full name was 'The Royal Society of London for Promoting Natural Knowledge'. It grew out of a philosophical society started in 1645 and composed of 'divers worthy persons, inquisitive into natural philosophy and other parts of human learning, and particularly of what hath been called the New Philosophy or Experimental Philosophy', in other words, of men whose minds were moving in the way opened up by Francis Bacon*. The Society took the whole field of knowledge for exploration; one of its aims was to encourage the virtue of intellectual lucidity in the writing of prose, and Thomas Sprat, writing the *History of the Royal Society* in 1667 defined the standards which writers were to emulate. The Royal Society was thus central in the culture of its time; it was promoted not only by scientists such as the chemist Boyle, but by poets – Cowley*, Dryden*, Waller* –, the biographer Aubrey*, and the diarists Evelyn* and Pepys*. Since its foundation, the Society has become increasingly scientific; the title Fellow of the Royal Society is today one of the greatest honours to be conferred on a scientist. Part of its functions is to advise the government on problems which require scientific elucidation. Its original meeting place was Gresham College, which since its foundation by Sir Thomas Gresham in 1597 had always served more practical branches of knowledge than the universities of Oxford and Cambridge; since 1857 it has been situated at Burlington House, premises which it shares with the Royal Academy*.

* 3.3.1.

Rubaiyat of Omar Khayyam, The

/ˈru:baijet – ˈɔuma: kaiˈjam/

Verses by Omar Khayyam, a Persian scholar and poet who died in 1123. He was an outstanding mathematician and astronomer, but is still more famous for his verse epigrams written in 'rubai', *ie* four lines the first, second and fourth of which have the same rhyme while the third is usually rhymeless. The rubai had been invented for the epitomizing of subtle thoughts on Islamic belief, but Omar used them to satirize religious bigotry with a free-thinking irony. This has caused him to be referred to as 'the Voltaire of the East'.

The English poet Edward FitzGerald* published a translation of the Rubaiyat in 1859 (75 verses); he enlarged this to 110 verses in a new edition in 1868, and issued other versions (101 verses) in 1872 and 1879. FitzGerald emphasizes the pleasure-loving aspect of the Persian poet, and the poem was extremely popular in Victorian* England both for its musicality and for its expression of a liberated way of life which contrasted with the narrow and bigoted codes of mid-Victorian respectability. The poet Robert Graves* has published a new translation of the Rubaiyat.

Rubicon

/ˈru:bikən/

In ancient Italy, the name of a small river which divided Italy from Cisalpine Gaul. When Julius Caesar* crossed it with his army in 49 BC, he was leaving the province assigned to his care and taking the fateful step of declaring war on the Roman Senate led by Pompey*. Hence the phrase 'crossing the Rubicon' has come to mean taking a critical decision.

Rugby School

One of the most famous of the English Public Schools*. It was founded in 1567, but its importance begins with the headmastership of Thomas Arnold (father of the poet and critic Matthew Arnold*) from 1828 to 1842. Hitherto, the ancient Public Schools had imparted education (chiefly in the Greek and Latin languages and literatures) but without any consistent moral instruction. Arnold was a man of strong moral and religious character, and under his management Rugby became a pioneer of 'character-building', which came to be regarded as the most typical quality of the English 'public school tradition'. The virtues were supposed to be those of physical and moral discipline, leadership, and fair-mindedness. A large number of public schools were founded in the second half of 19th C, and they were modelled on Arnold's ideals. Since the large Empire of which Britain was the centre required an extensive class of administrators, these ideals were eminently useful in producing them. A once popular novel, *Tom Brown's Schooldays* (1857) by Thomas Hughes, describes life at Rugby under Arnold.

There is a tradition that the game of rugby football was invented at Rugby in 1823.

Ruined Cottage, The

A narrative poem in blank verse* by William Wordsworth*. It was written in 1797, with the alternative title *The Story of Margaret*, and was later made into Book I of *The Excursion** (1814). The poem tells the story of a poor woman who struggles to survive the disappearance of her husband who has joined the army and not been heard of again. Eventually grief and poverty take her life, and the cottage is overgrown by the surrounding vegetation. The simplicity, poignancy, and ultimate serenity of the poem make it one of Wordsworth's finest achievements.

Rule Britannia

A patriotic poem by James Thomson (1700–48), occurring in the masque *Alfred* (1740) by Thomson and David Mallet. It was set to music by Thomas Arne (1710–78), and became almost equivalent to a national anthem.

Rumpelstiltzkin /rʌmpl'stiltskin/
One of Grimm's* fairy tales, about a dwarf who enables a girl to become a king's bride by undertaking a number of impossible tasks for her. In return she has to guess his name. When she succeeds in this most unlikely task of all through hearing him say it, he tears himself in two with rage.

Runnymede /'rʌnimi:d/
The place on the south bank of the Thames, where the Barons forced King John* to accept Magna Carta* in 1215.

Rupert, Prince (Count Palatine of the Rhine and Duke of Bavaria) (1619–82)
Son of Frederick of the Palatinate and James I's* daughter Elizabeth. Rupert was an able cavalry commander on the Royalist side in the Civil Wars*, and after the Restoration*, an enthusiastic supporter of the Royal Society*.

Rural Rides
Reports of rural conditions by William Cobbett*. He disapproved of certain remedies proposed by an official body to the Government for agricultural distress resulting from the Napoleonic War. He decided to make a number of tours on horseback in order to find out the facts for himself, and published his impressions in his journal, the *Political Register**, between 1820 and 1830, when they were collected into book form. The essays are in vivid, direct prose, full of acute comments, lively incident, and strong if prejudiced argument. They are early examples of direct journalistic reporting and are raised to permanent value as literature by the energy of Cobbett's conviction and the simplicity and vigour of his prose, which he had modelled on the writings of Swift*.

* *Journalism.*

Ruritania /ruəri'teinjə/
An imaginary country in central Europe, the setting of Anthony Hope's popular romances, *Prisoner of Zenda* (1894) and *Rupert of Hentzau*. The tales are full of colourful politics and extravagant incident; any kingdom, real or imaginary, which exhibits comparable qualities is called a 'Ruritania'.

Ruskin, John (1819–1900) /'rʌskin/
Writer on art and on its relationship with society. His central inspiration was the force of his idea that great art is moral, and the corollary that the working men of industrial England were spiritually impoverished. Like the Pre-Raphaelites* (he was a patron of D. G. Rossetti*, their leader), he found the contrast to the England of his day in the freedom of individual response to environment among the medieval artists, and he expressed this view in the famous chapter called 'The Nature of Gothic' in *The Stones of Venice*.

The latter part of his life was much concerned with attacks on the social philosophies of political economists, such as John Stuart Mill*, to whom he did less than justice, and in endeavours to awaken the working classes to the nature of their combined artistic and moral impoverishment. He wrote his artistic books in a style of elaborate but precise and delicate eloquence, but his social gospel had more concentrated and direct fervour. His puritanical mother (he was an only child) had given him a concentrated education in the Bible, and though his religious views as an adult were not explicit, his conception of art as fundamentally spiritual arose out of the intensity of his early religious training. Though a supporter of the Pre-Raphaelites, Ruskin did not lean like them towards 'art for art's sake' but towards 'art for the spiritual health of man'. In his campaign against the mediocre aspects of industrial culture, he was a disciple and admirer of Carlyle*, but he extended Carlyle's vision of greatness, and has proved to be a writer of more permanent interest. Nonetheless, he wrote so voluminously that, like Carlyle, he is best read in selections.

His principal works are: *Modern Painters* (1843–60) in which he champions Turner, one of the greatest of English painters, and at the time one of the most controversial; *The Seven Lamps of Architecture* (1849) leading to *The Stones of Venice* (1851–3) in which he makes his discovery of 'the Nature of Gothic'; this took him towards problems about the nature of civilized society in *The Political Economy of Art* (1857), *The Two Paths* (1859) and, one of his most famous books, *Unto This Last** (1862). *Sesame and Lilies* (1865), *Ethics of the Dust* (1866), *The Crown of Wild Olive* (1866) are essays in criticism on the age, and *Fors Clavigera* (1871–84) is composed of ninety-six letters to an educated artisan in which he shows himself distrustful of liberal democracy. *Praeterita* (1885–89) is one of the celebrated autobiographies* in English, although it is fragmentary and incomplete. Its most famous section is the first, in which Ruskin describes his unusual, in some ways unnatural, yet fertilizing childhood.

3.4.4; 7.4; *Gothic.*

Bib: Selections by Quennell, P.; Clark, K.; Rosenberg, J. D.; Leon, D., *Life*; Evans, J., *Life*; Ladd, H., *The Victorian Morality of Art*; Rosenberg, J. D., *The Darkening Glass*; Wilenski, R. H., *John Ruskin*; Lippincott, B., *Victorian Critics of Democracy*.

Russell, Bertrand Arthur William, Lord (1872–1970)
Philosopher. He belonged to one of the great aristocratic families elevated by the Tudors* in 16th C, which in large measure took over power from the English feudal aristocracy of the Middle Ages. Such families, by their control of Parliament*, became effective rulers of the country in 18th C; the 19th-C politician-novelist Disraeli* called them a 'Venetian Oligarchy'; to the present day, they retain great prestige and influence. Their importance raised them above fear and insecurity, and individual members have sometimes been radical* in their social and political thinking; an example is the Prime Minister Lord John Russell, Bertrand Russell's grandfather.

Bertrand Russell was true to this radical tradition both in his social and in his abstract philosophy though he declared that there was no connection between these branches of his thought. As an abstract philosopher he is in the sceptical tradition of the 18th-C philosopher, David Hume*, abandoning metaphysics; his linguistic analysis of the operation of statements, and his investigation of the relationship of modern physics and behaviourist psychology to philosophical thinking, lie behind the ideas of younger thinkers – Wittgenstein, Gilbert Ryle, A. J. Ayer – and have also had indirect influence on important literary critics, such as I. A. Richards* and William Empson*.

Russell's social philosophy was related to his political activity, which was energetic. His first book was *German Social Democracy* (1896). In World War I he was imprisoned for 6 months as a pacifist, and in his old age he was a powerful propagandist for nuclear disarmament.

Some works of abstract philosophy: *Principia Mathematica* (with Whitehead) (1910–13); *An Introduction to Mathematical Philosophy* (1919); *What I Believe* (1925); *An Outline of Philosophy* (1927); *Religion and Science* (1935); *Physics and Experience* (1946); *Human Knowledge, Its Scope and Its Limits* (1948). Some books on society and politics: *Principles of Social Reconstruction* (1916); *The Conquest of Happiness* (1930); *Education and the Social Order* (1932); *Education for Democracy* (1937); *Authority and the Individual* (1949).

A notable characteristic of Russell's writing is its lucidity and vitality. In this he resembles other British philosophers in the same sceptical tradition, for instance Hume, and his older contemporary, G. E. Moore*.

* 3.5.

Bib: Schilpp, P. A. (ed), *The Philosophy of Russell.*

Russell Square

One of the large squares in the district of London known as Bloomsbury. It was built in early 19th C on land belonging to the Russells, who were Dukes of Bedford. In mid-19th C it was inhabited by rich business men (as in Thackeray's novel *Vanity Fair**). It is now mainly composed of offices.

Russian Influence on English Literature

The international importance of Russian literature belongs chiefly to its achievements in the 19th C. Until the middle of the 19th C, the influence was chiefly from Britain upon Russia: Sterne*, Scott*, Byron*, and, later, Dickens* all made an important impression on Russian writers. Since about 1850, however, the balance of influence has been in the opposite direction, although Russian literature has chiefly been known in translation, which has limited extensive public knowledge to prose works, especially the novels. These have been widely read, especially in the famous translations by Constance Garnett, who translated Tolstoy, Dostoevski, Turgenev, Chekhov and Gogol in the decades before and after 1900.

Tolstoy and Turgenev were the first Russian novelists to receive wide acclaim in Britain; Tolstoy is still considered the supreme novelist, and a novelist cannot receive a greater tribute than to be described as 'Tolstoyan'. His reputation in Britain owed much to Matthew Arnold*, whose essay in praise of Tolstoy appeared in 1887, and is included in *Essays in Criticism, Second Series** in 1888. His tribute is the more noticeable because he otherwise ignored novelists in his criticism, and it made its mark because he was the most influential critic of his day. However, other critics contributed their admiration for the Russians in the last quarter of the 19th C. This interest was awakened by the feeling that the Russians, besides the French, were the only nation to produce a range of major novelists comparable to those writing in English, and that, unlike the French, they shared with the British and Americans a great moral concern with human nature in society. There was also the feeling that the Russian novelists went beyond the British and Americans, excelling in their rendering of religious experience, though the full force of this was not felt until Constance Garnett produced her translation of Dostoevski's *Brothers Karamazov* in 1912.

In America, interest in Russian writing seems to have gone deeper, because of a feeling that these two great continental nations shared comparable experiences in the disorderly variety of their rapid growth. It was not merely this, however, that made the great Anglo-American novelist Henry James* a lifelong admirer of Turgenev. Turgenev was already well known in England from the middle of the century when he became the friend of George Eliot*. These two novelists were the predominant influences on James's own work. He admired both for the depth of their moral insights, but he admired Turgenev for what he saw as his superior artistic strictness in handling the elusive novel form. Turgenev thus combined for James the virtues of the great French novelists with those of the English novelist he most admired. Gilbert Phelps, in *The Russian Novel in English Fiction* (1956), traces Turgenev's influence in some of the detail of James's novels, and suggests his further influence on Gissing*, Moore*, Bennett*, Galsworthy* and Conrad*. Conrad is the most doubtful instance of these writers showing the Russian influence; as a Pole, he felt antagonistic to Russia and he did not know Russian, and yet it is impossible not to think of both Turgenev and Dostoevski when reading *Under Western Eyes**.

Chekhov's influence on the short story and on the drama seems evident, although it may be that the distinctive development of the short story* in English (for instance in Joyce's *Dubliners** and in Katherine Mansfield*) is as much an example of parallel development in the form as owing to Chekhov's initiation. In the drama, Chekhov's original handling of human speech as a medium which involuntarily expresses the character of the speaker has been developed in the works of Beckett* and Pinter*.

The prestige of Russian literature in mid-20th C remains very high in Britain, especially Boris Pasternak's *Doctor Zhivago* and the works of

Alexander Solzhenitsyn. What is admired is the rendering of human experience on an heroic scale missing in English fiction since the death of D. H. Lawrence. Lawrence himself underwent 'the Russian fever' early in his career – 'I thought them the greatest writers of all time' (letter to Constance Garnett, 1916) – but he later reacted against the Russians, in the belief that they wrote of human experience in terms of what he called the 'social ego' (letter to Edward Garnett, June 1914) instead of finding the sources of its significance at deeper levels than any indicated directly by society.

Ruth

[1] A book of the Old Testament of the Bible; the central character, who is sympathetically and almost tenderly presented, is one of the tribe of Moabites. The story tells how she began by gleaning corn in the fields of the rich landowner, Boaz, and eventually married him, thus becoming the ancestress of King David*.

[2] The title of a novel by Elizabeth Gaskell*. Her *Ruth* (1853) is based, like her more successful *Cranford**, on the small town of Knutsford.

[3] The title of a poem by Wordsworth* in the *Lyrical Ballads** (1800).

Rutherford, Mark

* *White, William Hale.*

Rye House Plot (1683)

A plot led by the 1st Earl of Shaftesbury*, the leader of the Whig* Party, to kidnap Charles II* and force him to summon a parliament. The plot was discovered, and the consequent discredit of the Whigs, together with Charles II's popularity, caused a public reaction against them, and enabled James II* to succeed peacefully in 1685, in spite of his open Roman Catholicism.

Rymer, Thomas (1641–1713)

A rigid neo-classic* critic, chiefly known for his obtuse though witty and amusing *Short View of Tragedy* (1692) in which he condemned Shakespeare's tragedy *Othello**.

Ryswick, Treaty of (1697) /ˈrizwik/

A peace brought about between William III's* Grand Alliance of Britain, Holland, Austria, Spain on the one hand, and France under Louis XIV. The truce was only a preliminary to the more serious War of the Spanish Succession* (1701–13).

S

S.P.C.K.

* *Society for Promoting Christian Knowledge.*

Sabaeans /səˈbiːənz/

An ancient people of southern Arabia.

Sabaoth /saˈbeioθ/

A Hebrew word meaning 'hosts', *ie* 'armies'. In the Bible and elsewhere, 'the Lord of Sabaoth' = the Lord of Hosts – a way of alluding to the power and glory of God.

Sabbath

Among the Jews, the seventh and sacred day of the week. On the sabbath, conduct is regulated by strict rules, and all forms of work are forbidden. Among Christians, Sunday, the first day of the week, became the sacred one, in commemoration of the Resurrection of Christ. After the Reformation* more extreme British Protestants (Puritans*) frequently referred to Sunday as 'the Sabbath', and emulated ancient Jewish strictness in its observance. In modern Britain, a 'Sabbatarian' is one who wishes to continue the ideal of Sunday as a day on which only essential work is done, and places of entertainment are closed. In many families, from 17th to 18th C, Sunday was the only day available for serious reading, but reading was restricted to the Bible, *Pilgrim's Progress**, and volumes of sermons* and sacred verse such as the poems of Quarles* and Isaac Watts*. The freer kind of Sunday (on which shops are opened, etc.) is known as 'the Continental Sunday'.

Sabbath, Witches'

* *Witches.*

Sabians /ˈseibjənz/

A partly Christian religious sect of Babylonia, contemporary with the early Christian Church. They have often been confused with the Mandaeans who were a similar sect in the same region, and with the Neo-Platonic* Harranians, who called themselves Sabians to avert persecution by Muslims.

Sabines /ˈsabainz/

A tribe of central Italy, noted for their frugality and hardihood, contemporary with the ancient Roman Republic. In legend, they made war on the Romans, who took revenge by carrying off the Sabine women.

Sabrina

A poetic name for the River Severn, from a princess of ancient British legend. She was the daughter of King Locrine and his mistress, Estrildis; Sabrina and her mother were drowned in the river by Locrine's jealous queen, Gwendolen. The story is told by the chronicler Geoffrey of Monmouth* (*History of the Kings of Britain*), by Spenser in Book II, x of *The Faerie Queene**, and by Swinburne* in his drama *Locrine* (1887). The most famous representation of Sabrina is in Milton's masque *Comus**, where she appears as the nymph of the Severn.

Sack

Formerly a name for a variety of wines imported

from Spain and the Canary Islands. The word derives from the French 'sec' = dry, but 'Sack' also included sweet wines. It was often combined with a more specific name, *eg* sherry (sherris)-sack, canary-sack.

Sackville, Thomas (1536–1608)

Poet, statesman, diplomat; created 1st Earl of Dorset in 1604. He contributed the *Induction* and the *Complaint of Buckingham* in the verse compilation *Mirror for Magistrates**; the *Induction* is the main basis for his fame as a poet. He also collaborated with Thomas Norton in writing the first tragedy in blank verse*, *Gorboduc**. Historically, his poetic career falls between those of Wyatt* and Surrey* on the one hand, and those of Sidney* and Spenser* on the other; he is one of the most distinguished writers in this intervening period, and helped to prepare the way for the great concluding decade of the century.

Bib: Lewis, C. S., *English Literature in the Sixteenth Century*; Davie, D., in *Articulate Energy*.

Sacred Nine

A name for the Muses*.

Saddučees /'sadjusi:z/

A sect among the Jews at the time of Christ. They were opposed to the Pharisees* in that the Pharisees accepted oral as well as written traditions of the Law, whereas the more conservative Sadducees accepted the written Law only. According to *Acts* 23:8, they denied the existence of angels and spirits, and would not accept the doctrine of the resurrection of the dead. Their disbelief in these matters seems to have arisen from the absence of evidence for them in the written Law.

Sade, Donatien Alphonse, Marquis de (1740–1814) /sa:d/

French novelist and poet. His morbid addiction to cruelty caused his life and writings to become notorious, and originated the word 'sadism' = love of inflicting pain. His work had widespread influence, however, owing to his intelligence and insight into his own neurosis; his belief that his destructive impulses were uncontrollable and therefore part of his nature counterbalanced the doctrine of his French-Swiss contemporary, Jean-Jacques Rousseau, who preached that man left to himself (*ie* not distorted by social forces) was naturally good. The two ideas profoundly influenced the Romantic* Movement of 19th C: 'beauty tainted with pain, corruption, and death' (Mario Praz – *The Romantic Agony*) was the dark side of Romanticism (*eg* Shelley's *The Cenci**) and owed much to Sade, just as Rousseau's 'Man was born free and is everywhere in chains' lay behind Romanticism as a positive faith. Sade's influence, however, was less important in Britain than in other countries of Western Europe. Amongst British writers, Algernon Swinburne* was the most influenced of his more important admirers.

Sadler's Wells

Originally a health resort in north London, on account of its mineral spring. A theatre was built there in 18th C, and in 19th C this became – like the Old Vic* in south London – famous for its productions of Shakespeare. Since 1931 it has been used principally for ballet and opera. Both theatres are in unfashionable parts of London, and their policy of appealing to the poorer and less educated social classes has caused them to become the starting-point for a National Theatre.

Saga /'sa:gə/

An old Norse word meaning 'oral story'. The sagas were a body of Norwegian and Icelandic prose epics (11th–13th C). Some of these were translated by the English poet William Morris*.

Saint

In the New Testament, the saints were either simply Christian believers, or Christian martyrs, or souls enjoying eternal bliss. From about 6th C, 'saint' became a term of honour for dead Christians who deserved special reverence; sainthood was conferred by the Church by 'canonization'. Canonization was disused by the Protestant* Churches from the Reformation*, but English and Scottish Puritans* often referred to themselves as 'saints' in the original New Testament usage meaning 'true believers'.

Saint-Germain-en-Laye

A town on the River Seine in northern France; James II* held his exiled court there after his deposition at the Revolution of 1688*.

St James's Palace

One of the royal palaces in London, built in 16th C by Henry VIII*. In 18th C it superseded Whitehall* as the official royal residence; hence foreign ambassadors have ever since been officially accredited to 'the Court of St James', meaning the British government, although in the reign of Victoria* it was in turn superseded by Buckingham Palace* close by, and became the residence of the heir to the throne.

St James's Park

One of the royal parks of London, behind St James's Palace* and with Buckingham Palace* and Whitehall* at either end. It was originally laid out by Charles II*.

St Leger, The /snt'ledʒə/

A famous annual horse-race held at Doncaster. It was founded by Lieutenant-General St Leger in 1776.

St Stephen's Chapel

A chapel in the old Palace of Westminster*. It was used as the meeting-place of the House of Commons* from the reign of Edward VI* until 1834, when it was burnt down. The present chamber was then built on its site; the crypt of the original chapel still exists.

Saintsbury, George Edward Bateman (1845–1933)

Literary historian and critic. His works included: *Short History of French Literature* (1882); *A Short History of English Literature* (1898); *A History of Criticism* (1900–4); *A History of English Prosody* (1906–21); *The History of English Criticism* (1911); *History of the French Novel* (1917–19). He also wrote studies of Dryden*, Walter Scott*, and Matthew Arnold*. His treatment of literary study was historical; that is to say, principles of evaluation or critical theory were for him secondary to coherent narration. This is contrary to the mid-20th-C emphasis, which has gone to the opposite extreme of selecting the elements of literary tradition which are of most relevance to the present time, *eg* T. S. Eliot* (*Selected Essays*, 1932) and F. R. Leavis* on the novel in *The Great Tradition* (1948).

* 7.4.

Saladin (1138–93) /'salədin/

Sultan of Egypt. His conquest of the Christian Latin Kingdom of Jerusalem (1187) provoked the Third Crusade under Richard I* of England and Philip II of France, with whom he made a truce. He was famous for his fierce piety compounded with chivalrous generosity; in English history and legend these qualities are made to represent him as a suitable antagonist to Richard, himself a legend for his courage and chivalry. Their rivalry is the subject of Scott's* novel *The Talisman* (1825). Historically, Saladin is important for halting the invasion of the East by the Christian West, and starting a counter-movement against the West which lasted until 17th C.

* *Crusades.*

Salic Law /'salik/

A body of early French laws which include a prohibition against women inheriting property. This prohibition was once supposed to be the ground for disallowing the claims of English kings (from Edward III* in 14th C onwards) to have inherited the French throne through the female line; hence in the first act of Shakespeare's play *Henry V**, the Archbishop of Canterbury is made to refute the validity of the Salic Law at some length. Historically, however, the Salic Law seems not to have been invoked against the English claim.

Salisbury Plain /'sɔ:lzbəri/

A bare upland of chalk hills (not a plain but a plateau) to the north of the cathedral city of Salisbury in southern England. The Plain, because of its freedom from forest, was an important centre of activity in prehistoric times, and contains numerous prehistoric remains, the most notable of which is Stonehenge*.

Sallust (Gaius Sallustius Crispus) (86–34 BC) /'saləst/

Roman historian. He wrote the history of a Roman North African campaign (110–106 BC), and also of the Catiline conspiracy (63 BC).

Sally Lunn

A kind of sweet bun, apparently called after a young woman who sold them in Bath in late 18th C.

Salome /sə'ləumi/

[1] In the New Testament of the Bible, one of the women present at the crucifixion of Christ (*Mark* 15:40) and afterwards at the tomb (*Mark* 16:1).

[2] The damsel who danced before Herod and afterwards demanded the head of John the Baptist (*Matthew* 14:6–8 and *Mark* 6:17–25) is referred to as the 'daughter of Herodias' – another Salome. The latter was the subject of a drama by Oscar Wilde* – *Salome* (1893).

Salvation Army

Founded in the slums of the East End of London as the Christian Mission by William Booth in 1865; the organization took its present name in 1880, and was organized like an army, with military ranks. Its success in penetrating the most degraded areas of the big English cities caused it to spread widely throughout Britain and to other countries. Its meetings often take place in the open air to the accompaniment of brass bands, and the Army provides hostels for the destitute. The idiom and glamour of the Army had a strong appeal to the slum-dwellers of the big London boroughs, and influenced even the most brutalized of that population to an extent that excelled every other organization. In many ways its influence was parallel to that of the Methodists* of 18th C. Bernard Shaw's* play *Major Barbara* (1905) analyses the virtues and limitations of the Salvation Army approach to the problem of poverty, by comparison with the organization of material welfare by the 'social conscience'.

Samson Agonistes

A tragedy in blank verse* by John Milton*, published (with *Paradise Regained**) in 1671. It is an example of Milton's blended Puritan-biblical and Renaissance-classical inspiration: the subject is drawn from the Old Testament (*Judges* 16) and the form from the ancient Greek tragedy of Aeschylus* and Sophocles*.

Samson, the Jewish hero, has been betrayed by his Philistine wife, Dalila (spelt Delilah* in the Authorized Version of the Bible, where she is not his wife) to her people, who are the foes of the Jews. His hair, on which depended his exceptional, God-given strength, has been cut off; he has been blinded, and cast into prison in Gaza; here his hair is allowed to recover its former length and he is subjected to slavery by his enemies. The play opens while he is resting from his enormous labours, and he is approached by a chorus of lamenting Jews. In his mood of extreme despair, he is visited by his father Manoa, who hopes to negotiate his release from the Philistines; Samson, however, has the moral strength to refuse Manoa's suggestions, on the grounds that his lot is a consequence of his own moral weakness in betraying the secret of his strength to his wife. His next visitor is Dalila herself, who seeks his forgiveness in return for alleviation of his sufferings; he replies, however, that if he cannot pardon himself, her crime is still more unpardonable. This double moral victory heartens him enough to enable him to frighten away his third visitor, the Philistine giant Harapha, who comes to mock at him. Next a messenger arrives with an order that he is to come before the Philistine lords in order to entertain them with feats of his strength. To the dismay of the chorus, he accepts the order, but we learn from a messenger that it is only to destroy the entire assembly (including himself) by rooting up the two pillars which support the roof of the building. The chorus is left to chant praise of the hero and of the wisdom of God, who sustains his people.

Critics have complained that much of the dialogue is inert dramatically, and that the structure (*eg* in Doctor Johnson's* opinion) lacks dramatic movement. The latter criticism, however, seems to be a failure to see how Milton, through the successive visitors, shows Samson building himself up from despair to heroism through a succession of moral victories. The Old Testament grimness of the theme is in keeping not only with Milton's Puritan inspiration but with the desperation of the Puritans, since, when the play was written, their enemies had conquered: the drama shows the spirit of a resistance movement, and Milton's position, particularly when we remember his blindness, had resemblances to Samson's at the beginning of the play.

* 5.2.2.

Samuel

In the Old Testament of the Bible, an early prophet, after whom are named the two books which cover the history of Israel to the death of David*, the second king of the Jews. Samuel heard the voice of God calling him while he was a young child in the temple, and he was dedicated to the priesthood from then on. He became the ruler of the Jews as a national leader against the Philistines, and appointed the first king of Israel, Saul, who was later replaced by David.

Sancho Panza /ˈsantʃəuˈpanzə/

The servant and squire of Don Quixote*, in Cervantes' comic romance. While Quixote, the idealistic dreamer, imagines himself a wandering knight in the tradition of the legends of King Arthur*, Panza is a practical man of the people, very much concerned with his own material advantage, but ignorant and credulous whenever an appeal is made to his appetites; at the same time he remains loyal to his master when their adventures repeatedly end in disaster.

Sancho is a model for the comic loyal servant who follows a master (always of superior social position and contrasted character) in several English novels of 18th and earlier 19th C. Notable examples are Humphry Clinker* in the novel by Tobias Smollett (a translator of Cervantes); Partridge in Henry Fielding's *Tom Jones**, and, most famous of all, Sam Weller in Charles Dickens's *Pickwick Papers**. These all differ from Sancho in character, but exhibit a parallel contrast to their respective masters, and resemble him in their loyalty in discouraging circumstances.

Sandhurst

The popular name for the Royal Military Academy, founded in 1802 as the Royal Military College, for the training of officers for the British Army. The small town of Sandhurst in Berkshire, to which the College moved in 1813, gave its name to the establishment.

Sandringham

A country house belonging to the British royal family. It is situated in Norfolk, and was purchased by the future Edward VII in 1861.

Sanger, John (1816–89)

The founder of the most famous of the British travelling circuses. He began with a conjuring exhibition in Birmingham in 1845, and reached the height of his fame as a circus proprietor in the 1870s and 80s. In his later years he was known as Lord John Sanger, though he never received a peerage.

Sangreal /saŋˈgreil/

A name for the Holy Grail*.

Sanhedrin /ˈsanidrin/

The supreme judicial council of the Jews at the time of Christ.

Sansculottes

The name for recruits from the poorer classes to the French Revolutionary* army. The word means 'without breeches' – knee-breeches being then the wear of all but the poorest. The sansculottes wore loose trousers or 'pantalon'.

Santa Claus

* *Christmas.*

Sappho of Lesbos /ˈsafəu/

Greek woman poet of 6th C BC. The fragments that have survived are famous for their passion and simplicity. The term 'lesbian', for homosexual love among women, derives from her passionate poems referring to her women friends. According to legend, she died by throwing herself into the sea after being rejected in love by Phaon, the boatman whose ugliness had been changed to beauty by Aphrodite.

Saracens

A term used, chiefly in the Middle Ages*, for the Muslim Arabs against whom the Crusades* were waged. Its origin is obscure, but the ancient Greeks and Romans used 'Saraceni' as a name for nomadic Arabs.

Sardanapalus (7th C BC) /sa:dəˈnapələs/

In Greek legend, the last king of Assyria, famous for his luxury and effeminacy. He threw off his self-indulgence to defeat formidable rebels in a succession of battles. Eventually he had to face total defeat, and burnt up his wives and himself in his palace. This (with variations) is the subject of Byron's* tragedy *Sardanapalus* (1821).

Sargasso Sea

A region of the North Atlantic, covered by floating seaweed from which it is named. It was once believed that ships could be embedded in the weed and immobilized.

Sarmatia /sa:ˈmeiʃjə/

In ancient Roman geography, the name of a region of eastern Europe, extending from the River Vistula to the River Volga. In English poetry it is used as a name for Poland.

Sartor Resartus: The Life and Opinions of Herr Teufelsdröckh /ˈsa:to: riˈsa:təs/

A disguised spiritual autobiography* by Thomas Carlyle*. It was serialized (1833–4) in *Fraser's Magazine*, and published in book form in Boston, U.S.A., in 1836, and in Britain in 1838. Carlyle was under the influence of the German romantics, *eg* Jean Paul Richter. The title is Latin for 'the tailor re-patched': Carlyle offers the fable that human beliefs and institutions are like clothes and need renewing. Against Byron's* attitude of doubt, isolation, and suffering, Carlyle calls for the affirmativeness of the German poet Goethe*; heroic qualities such as sacrifice and devotion to duty must redeem the inner man, and, through men, the directionless age in which Carlyle felt himself to be living – the age of flux and the decay of unquestioning religious faith. Besides the drive of German influence, Carlyle felt the force of the old-fashioned Scottish Calvinism such as had animated his father. The three crucial chapters are 'The Everlasting No', 'Centre of Indifference', and 'The Everlasting Yea'. Despite the difficulty he had in getting the book published in Britain, it marks the beginning of his exposition of the creed of heroism, which made Carlyle an inspiring figure in commerce-dominated mid-19th-C Britain.

Sarum /ˈseərəm/

The old name for the Cathedral city of Salisbury. Old Sarum, 2 miles to the north of the present town, is the site of the original town. Though uninhabited, it still returned two members to Parliament until 19th C – a conspicuous example of the unreality of political representation in England up till the Reform Bill* of 1832.

Sassenach /ˈsasənak/

A Gaelic word, used by Gaelic-speaking Irishmen and Scottish highlanders for Germanic (Saxon*) inhabitants of Britain.

Sassoon, Siegfried (1886–1967) /səˈsu:n/

Poet and autobiographer. His *Memoirs of a Fox-hunting Man* (1928) and *Memoirs of an Infantry Officer* (1930) are accounts of his life as a country gentleman before World War I, and of his experiences during it. He also became famous for his savagely satirical poems written during his military service. He was a friend of Wilfred Owen*, and influenced Owen's writing. The two volumes of memoirs were put together as *The Complete Memoirs of George Sherston* (1937), which includes an addition section, *Sherston's Progress*. His poems, including volumes published since World War I, are in a collected edition (1961).

* *War Poets.*

Satan

A Hebrew word meaning 'adversary'; in the Christian tradition, one of the habitual names for the Devil. In *Job* (Old Testament), an older tradition is evident in 1:6–12 and 2:1–6. Satan is a servant of God, and his special function is to test the virtue of men by trials and suffering.

* *Lucifer.*

Satire

A form of attack through mockery; it may exist in any literary medium, but is often regarded as a medium in itself. The origins of the word help to explain the manifestations of satire. It derives from the Latin 'satura' = a vessel filled with the earliest agricultural produce of the year, used in seasonal festivals to celebrate harvest; a secondary meaning is 'miscellany of entertainment', implying merry-making at such festivals, probably including verbal warfare. This primitive humour gave rise to a highly cultivated form of literary attack in the poetry of Horace*, Persius (1st C AD) and Juvenal*. Thus from ancient Roman culture two ideas of satire have come down to us: the first expresses a basic instinct for comedy through mockery in human beings, and was not invented by the Romans; the second is a self-conscious medium, implying standards of civilized and moral rightness in the mind of the poet and hence a desire on his part to instruct his readers so as to reform their moral failings and absurdities. The two kinds of satire are inter-related, so that it is not possible to distinguish them sharply. Moreover it is not easy to distinguish strict satire in either of its original forms from other kinds of comedy.

[1] Strict satire, *ie* satire emulating the Roman poets. This was one of the outcomes of Renaissance* cultivation of ancient Latin literature. Between 1590 and 1625 several poets wrote deliberate satires with Juvenal, Persius and Horace in mind; the most important of these were Donne* and Ben Jonson*, but Joseph Hall* claimed to be the first, and another was Marston*. The great age of the strict satire was 18th C, notably in the work of Pope* who emulated the relatively genial satire of Horace, and Samuel Johnson*, who emulated the sombre style of Juvenal. Satire of this sort makes its object of attack the social forms and corruptions of the time, and its distinctive medium is the 10-syllable rhymed couplet, perfected by Pope, and used with different force by Johnson.

[2] Comedy of Humours* and Comedy of Manners*. These are the most easily distinguishable forms of dramatic satire. The former is associated chiefly with Ben Jonson, and has its roots in the older Morality* drama, which was only intermittently satirical. The 'humours' in Jonson's conception are the obsessions and manias to which the nature of human beings invites them to abandon themselves; they have a close relation to the medieval Seven Deadly Sins*, such as lust, avarice, and gluttony. The Comedy of Manners belongs to the period 1660–1800, and, especially, to the first forty years of it. Its most notable exponents are Congreve* at the end of 17th C and Sheridan* at the end of 18th. This comedy is less concerned with basic human dispositions and more with transient social ones; rational social behaviour is the standard in the mind of the dramatist. Both these forms of satire were taken over by novelists; the 18th-C novelist Fielding* began as a writer of dramatic comedies of manners, but Dickens in 19th C writes more distinctly in the tradition of the comedy of humours, with a strong addition of social indignation.

[3] Satire of Parody* and Irony. This includes the most skilful and powerful satire in the language; its greatest period is between 1660 and 1750. Parody at its most powerful implies the writer's complete respect for the serious form which he is using in a comic way; thus in this period (which included the very serious epic *Paradise Lost**) the prestige of the epic form was still high, and Dryden* (*Absalom and Achitophel**) and Pope (*The Rape of the Lock** and *The Dunciad**) used their appreciation of epic* to make ironic contrast between the grandeur of its style and the pettiness, meanness, and destructiveness of their chosen subject. Similarly Samuel Butler* used the mode of romantic epic to attack the Puritans* in *Hudibras**.

Irony does not necessarily use parody, but even when it does not, it operates in a similar way, by addressing the reader in terms which he has learnt to receive as acceptable at their face value, and then shocking him into recognition that something quite unacceptable is the real subject. Jonathan Swift* (*eg A Modest Proposal**) is the greatest ironist in the English language. *Gulliver's Travels** is partly a parody of the popular travel books of the time.

[4] Flytings*, and other traditional forms. The Middle Ages took from its popular festivals a strong tradition of verbal combat (flytings) and sardonic criticism of the established social order. One aspect of this emerges in popular ballads* (especially in the printed form of broadsides* which developed after the medieval period) and in the work of educated writers such as Langland* and Chaucer* – grimly in the former's *Piers Plowman**, and genially in the latter's *Canterbury Tales**. Dunbar* was another eminent practitioner of flytings, *eg* his *Flyting of Dunbar and Kennedy*.

[5] Novelistic satire. Much satire in novels from 18th to 20th C cannot be summed up under comedy of manners. The novels of Peacock*, for example, establish a tradition of comic discussions mocking at contemporary trends of thought; Peacock's example was partly followed by Meredith* and Aldous Huxley*. Another variant is the 'anti-utopia', using an imaginary country to satirize actual tendencies in contemporary Britain. The most notable examples of this are *Erewhon** by Samuel Butler*, *Brave New World* by Aldous Huxley*. Apart from these examples, it is difficult to find a novelist who does not use satire at least intermittently, usually as social comment. Eminent examples are: Fielding, Jane Austen*, Thackeray*, Dickens, Wells*, Forster*, and (among those still writing) Angus Wilson* and Antony Powell*.

* 4.2.2.

Saturn /ˈsatən/

In ancient Roman myth, an agricultural deity who was supposed to have ruled Italy in the golden age. Astrologically, however, the planet Saturn is associated with lead. Thus, confusingly, the name of Saturn is often mentioned in connection with these contrasting metals. The god Saturn of the Romans became identified with Cronos of the Greeks. Cronos was chief of the Titans in Greek myth, and warred with his off-spring, Zeus and his brothers. Thus, *eg* in Keats's poem *Hyperion**, Saturn is often made to play the role of Cronos in these wars in heaven. In this capacity, his defeat by Zeus helps the astrological conception of the planet Saturn as a deathly, baleful influence, *eg* in Chaucer's *Knight's Tale**.

* *Ages, Golden etc.*

Saturnalia /satə:ˈneiljə/

The Roman feast of Saturn; it began on 17 December and lasted 7 days. It commemorated the age of gold, and was a period of great licence, traditions of which came to influence the Christian tradition of Christmas.

* *Misrule, Lord of.*

Satyr /ˈsatə/

A woodland nature spirit or minor deity in Greek myth; the satyrs were companions of the wine god Dionysus (Bacchus). They had goatlike legs, horns and ears. In the English translation of the Bible (*Isaiah* 13:21 and 34:14) satyrs are mentioned in translation of the Hebrew word for he-goat, and Christian representations of minor devils closely resemble the ancient satyrs.

There is no connection between 'satyr' and 'satire', but confusion between them is natural, especially as ancient Greek mocking comedies represented casts of satyrs (*eg* the *Cyclops* of Euripides*).

Saul /so:l/

[1] In the Bible, the first king of Israel (*1 Samuel*), later succeeded by the great king David*.

[2] Saul (of Tarsus) was the first name of the apostle Paul (*Acts*).

Savonarola, Fra Girolamo (1452–98) /savonəˈrəulə/

In Italian history, a Florentine monk who led a revolt against the worldly excesses of the Renaissance*. His own reforms went to excess, and he was eventually condemned and executed as a heretic. George Eliot's novel *Romola** deals with his period of power.

Savoy

A 13th-C London palace, between the Strand and the river. It was burnt down in the Peasants' Rebellion* and replaced, in Henry VIII's* time, by a hospital. The site is now occupied by a famous hotel and restaurant and by the Savoy Theatre. Here the Gilbert* and Sullivan operas were produced from 1882 on, and were therefore called the Savoy Operas. The royal chapel of the Savoy, built by Henry VII*, is still in use.

Saxons

The name of a Germanic people which invaded southern Britain from their homeland around the mouth of the Elbe in 5th and 6th C, after the departure of the Roman occupying forces. They eventually shared what came to be known as England (Angle-land) with the Angles and the Jutes. Their principal kingdom was Wessex (*ie* West Saxons) in the south-west. Other Saxon kingdoms are commemorated in the names of modern English counties: Sussex (South Saxons); Middlesex (Middle Saxons, in London and the immediate north of it); and Essex (East Saxons). Wessex* itself has disappeared as a geographical name, except in the novels of Thomas Hardy*.

* *Anglo-Saxon.*

Scenes of Clerical Life

Three tales by George Eliot*, and her earliest work in fiction: *The Sad Fortunes of the Rev. Amos Barton*; *Mr Gilfil's Love-Story*; and *Janet's Repentance*. The hero of each is a clergyman. They were published first in *Blackwood's Magazine** in 1857 and collected as *Scenes of Clerical Life* in 1858.

Schism, The Great

The state of division in the western Church owing to the election of rival Popes. The Schism was ended by the Council of Constance in 1417, though it was not properly healed until 1448. The papacy had been forcibly transferred from Rome to Avignon in 1305, but in 1378 the Italians elected their own Pope in Rome. He was supported by Germany and England, while the French Pope was supported by Spain as well as by France.

Scholar Gipsy, The

A poem by Matthew Arnold*, first published in 1853. He took the subject from a legend reported by Joseph Glanvill in *The Vanity of Dogmatizing* (1661). The Scholar of the legend renounced the anxiety of seeking a career through his scholarship, and took to wandering with the gipsies, dedicating himself to learning their lore. Arnold regards him as an immortal figure, and uses him as the type of a man who has happily escaped the anguish of the 19th-C intellectual's loss of faith and controlling convictions. The poem is not always considered to be Arnold's best, but it is his most famous, since it expresses the distress and doubt that is widely evident in mid-Victorian writing. It is written in 25 10-line stanzas, resembling those of Keats's Odes*. It is like the Odes too in its sensuous evocation of natural surroundings, though Arnold's tone is more nostalgic than that of Keats. In 1867 Arnold published a companion-piece to *The Scholar Gipsy* entitled *Thyrsis*, an elegy to his friend Clough* who died in 1861.

Scholasticism

A term covering a variety of philosophical and theological forms of thought, dominant in the Western Church between 1100 and 1500. The name derives from the episcopal schools (*ie* schools under bishops) first set up under the French emperor Charlemagne in 8th C; followers of the philosophy taught in these schools were called 'schoolmen'. Their aim was to reconcile the logic of ancient Greek philosophy (especially Aristotle*) with the teachings of the Christian faith; thus human reason was not conceived as being able to operate independently of theology, which explains the contempt into which scholasticism fell during the Renaissance*. The first of the great scholastics was the 9th-C Irish philosopher, Scotus Erigena, who found Christian theology perfectly in keeping with thought in the tradition of Plato*, but St Thomas Aquinas* preferred the tradition of Aristotle. His contemporary, Duns Scotus*, however, began a process of challenging the possibility of achieving perfect harmony between faith and reason, and the 14th-C William of Occam (**Ockham*) carried the process further. This began the decay of scholastic philosophy; one of the characteristics of the Renaissance was to liberate philosophy from its status as 'the handmaid of theology'. At the same time interest in the philosophy of Plato greatly revived, but now for its own sake.

School for Scandal, The

A comedy by Richard Brinsley Sheridan*, first produced in 1777. Two of the central characters are brothers: Charles Surface, whose character is open-hearted but reckless and extravagant, and Joseph Surface, a mean-hearted hypocrite. The principal women are Lady Teazle, the young, gay wife of the elderly Sir Peter Teazle, and Maria, his ward, with whom Charles is in love and whom Joseph is trying to marry for her money, while he also makes love to Lady Teazle. Sir Oliver Surface, rich uncle to the two brothers, returns from India in disguise in order to spy on his nephews, thereby to discover their true characters. In the background, a group of scandal-lovers (Lady Sneerwell, Mrs Candour, Sir Benjamin Backbite) do their worst to damage as many reputations as possible. Sir Oliver satisfies himself, in scenes of extremely successful theatrical comedy, about which of his nephews truly deserves his affection; Charles marries Maria, and the deceitfulness of Joseph is exposed.

The comedy is Sheridan's masterpiece, and the last notable play in the tradition of the English Comedy of Manners* until Oscar Wilde* at the end of 19th C.

School of Night

A term used to designate a circle of intellectuals who centred on Sir Walter Raleigh* in the early 1590s. It derives from Shakespeare's play *Love's Labour's Lost**, IV. iii. 251–2. The courtier Biron has just been praising the lady Rosaline who has a dark complexion: 'No face is fair that is not full so black', whereupon the King breaks in –

O paradox! Black is the badge of hell,
The hue of dungeons and the School of Night.

'School of Night' has puzzled editors, who have variously emended it to 'scowl' and 'stole'. Some modern scholars, however (see especially the Cambridge Shakespeare edition, and M. C. Bradbrook's *The School of Night*) consider that Shakespeare was alluding to Raleigh's dark complexion and to the reputation of himself and his circle for atheism. At about the time the play was written (1594–5), Raleigh, in disgrace at court, had retired to his country house and declared his preference for a life of study over the active and public life. The rival claims of the studious and retired and the active and public life is the theme of *Love's Labour's Lost*.

Raleigh's circle seems to have consisted of himself, the famous mathematician Thomas Harriot, the poets Marlowe* and Chapman*, the Earls of Northumberland and Derby, and a few others. Marlowe and Harriot shared Raleigh's atheistic reputation, Chapman had highly developed philosophical interests, and Northumberland and Derby had esoteric interests in alchemy*. The truth is probably that neither Raleigh nor his circle were atheists, but that they were dedicated to free intellectual inquiry. If Shakespeare was in fact alluding to the Raleigh circle, his motive may have been that he belonged to the circle of the Earl of Essex, Raleigh's rival at court.

Schools in England

The following is an alphabetical list of most kinds of school mentioned in English literature.

Almonry schools. One of the forms of grammar school (see below) in the Middle Ages*; they were usually attached to monasteries*, and the boys followed the rules of monastic life.

Board schools. These got their names from the School Boards, *ie* committees responsible for education in a neighbourhood, set up by the Education Act of 1870, which provided for universal elementary education to the age of 11. The boards were abolished by the Education Act of 1902 and were replaced by the usual local authorities (County Councils, etc.).

Boarding schools. Schools where the pupils live during their terms of study, as opposed to Day Schools from which they return each evening.

Charity schools. Set up in 18th C for children (of both sexes) of the very poor. The schools were endowed or maintained by the churches, and gave only elementary education. They were widespread but their distribution was uneven, so that many villages were without one.

Comprehensive schools. A very large school giving secondary education of all types in one complex of buildings so that in theory there is equality of educational opportunity given to all pupils, there being no selection (as by an examination at the age of 11 or later) for grammar school, modern school, etc. (see below).

Dame schools. Characteristic of 18th and early 19th C, and so called because they were commonly owned and run by poor, single women to make a small income. Only reading and writing and the beginnings of arithmetic were taught.

Dissenters' schools and academies. In 18th C, Protestants who did not belong to the Church of England* (*ie* Dissenters or Nonconformists) were not allowed to attend its schools. They could enter Scottish but not English universities. They therefore set up their own educational institutions which provided efficient education, often more up-to-date than that in the schools attended by Anglicans*.

Dissenting schools and academies became steadily less important in 19th C, especially after London University was opened in 1828. (The last restrictions on non-Anglicans at Oxford and Cambridge were removed in 1871.)

Elementary schools. This is either a general term for schools of any period which taught nothing more than reading, writing and arithmetic, or for the state schools established by the Act of 1870 providing for education up to the age of 11. The term 'Elementary' was abandoned by the Education Act of 1944, and 'Primary' was substituted.

Finishing schools. Schools for girls, fairly common in 19th and 20th C. They cater for the richer classes and take adolescents. Emphasis is commonly laid on behaviour and artistic accomplishments, though the education is sometimes more thorough. They are often situated in France, Germany, Switzerland or Italy, to facilitate the learning of a foreign language.

Girls' schools. Until the dissolution of the monasteries in the 1530s, many convents of nuns ran schools for girls. In 16th and 17th C girls' schools for the wealthier classes were rather rare, and such girls received their education at home from private teachers, *ie* governesses. This was still usual in 18th C, though private boarding schools for girls were increasing in number. By mid-19th C girls were approaching equality with boys in opportunities for education in all classes.

Grammar schools. In the Middle Ages the various kinds of monastery school for older children had Latin grammar as their principal subject. This continued to be true when such schools were taken out of the hands of the Church between 1530 and 1560 and endowed by public funds or placed in the hands of town councils etc. An example is the Grammar School at Stratford-on-Avon, probably attended by the young Shakespeare. As time went on, the educational curriculum changed, but the term 'grammar school' remained for all schools providing an academic education up to university entrance standard, unless they were called 'public schools' – which were usually richer and drew their pupils from a wider area.

High schools. Until 1944, equivalent to grammar schools, but usually for girls. Nowadays the term is merely a survival.

Modern schools. Set up in 1944 to provide for education of children who are not attending a grammar school, attendance at one or another type of secondary school being then made compulsory till the age of 15.

National schools. Schools founded in 19th C by the Church of England 'National Society for Promoting the Education of the Poor in the Principles of the Established Church'. From 1833 it received a small grant from the government. The National Society had its complement in the British and Foreign School Society, which founded schools on behalf of the Dissenters. Until 1870, the National Society was responsible for most of the schools for the poor in 19th-C England. It gave a fairly intensive education in the Bible as well as elementary education of a general description.

Preparatory schools. In 19th and 20th C, schools which prepared the sons of the wealthier classes for public schools. They were and are nearly all privately owned. Boys pass from them to public schools at the age of 13.

Private schools. Used either for schools under private ownership (*ie* not endowed, and not run by public subscription or by the state), or as an alternative term for 'preparatory schools'.

Public schools. See separate entry. Here, it is relevant to point out that they are schools neither run by the state nor under private ownership.

State schools. Applicable to all schools, since 1870, run under the authority of the state.

Secondary schools. Applicable to state schools providing education over the age of 11.

Sunday schools. Started in 1780 for the education of poor children on the one day in the week on which they were likely to be free from employment. They are now wholly religious in their instruction.

Technical schools. In 2nd half of 19th C, places for training youth in industrial and craft skills; schools called 'polytechnics' and technical colleges became common. Since 1944, while polytechnics and technical colleges have continued and increased, the term 'technical school' has been restricted to alternatives to grammar schools and modern schools, providing a more technical education than either. Technical colleges receive only students over the age at which compulsory education ceases.

Voluntary schools. A term applicable to all schools supported by voluntary contributions.

* 2.1.2.

Schoolmen

* *Scholasticism.*

Schopenhauer, Arthur (1788–1860)

/ˈʃəupənhauə/

German philosopher and author of *The World as Will and Idea* (1818).

* *German Influence on English Literature.*

Science Fiction

In his book on the subject, *New Maps of Hell* (1960), Kingsley Amis* writes: 'Science fiction presents with verisimilitude the human effects of spectacular changes in our environment, changes either deliberately willed or involuntarily suffered.' Mr Amis points out that it has a long ancestry. Much of this overlaps with 'Utopian literature' and includes such works as Bacon's *New Atlantis** and Swift's *Gulliver's Travels**. It is clear, however, that science fiction began to develop as a distinct form when technology and scientific investigation were advancing so fast that they outran human ability to foresee their consequences even in the near future. The real beginnings are therefore in 19th C, and the first clearly identifiable science fiction writer is the Frenchman, Jules Verne (1828–1905), *eg Voyage to the Centre of the Earth* (1864), *Twenty Thousand Leagues under the Sea* (1869), and *Round the World* *in Eighty Days* (1873). In England, Richard Jefferies's* *After London* (1885) is in some respects a more studied and interesting speculation about the future than most science fiction offers, but it is an isolated work, and only really successful in its first part. The first notable British writer of science fiction is H. G. Wells*, for example *The Time Machine* (1895), *The War of the Worlds* (1898), *The First Men in the Moon* (1901), *The Country of the Blind* (1911). His successors (E. M. Forster*, Aldous Huxley*, George Orwell*) come under the heading of the Utopian* branch of this literature. After World War II, 'S.F.' became a popular cult in English-speaking countries, especially the U.S.A. Much of the enormous body of work in the 'S.F.' magazines is negligible, but there has been some serious writing. Mr Amis cites William Golding* as 'closer to being a writer of science fiction than any earlier figure of comparable stature'. This is especially true of *The Inheritors* (1955), a book which shows that science fiction may as naturally be concerned with the remote past as with the future. Golding collaborated with John Wyndham and Mervyn Peake in *Sometime, Never*. Wyndham is one of the more orthodox and more interesting practitioners of science fiction; his best known book is perhaps *The Day of the Triffids*. One of the most popular of the contemporary serious writers is Brian Aldiss: *Intangibles Inc. and other short stories*, *The Inner Landscape* (in collaboration with Mervyn Peake and J. G. Ballard), *A Hand Reared Boy*, *Report on Probability A*, and *Barefoot in the Head*.

Sciron /'skairon/

In Greek myth, a robber who compelled his captives to wash his feet. When they stooped to do so he kicked them into the sea, where they were devoured by a great turtle. He was killed by the hero Theseus*, who dashed him against a rock.

Scone /sku:n, skəun/

A town in Scotland, at which Scottish kings were crowned. 'The stone of destiny' or 'stone of Scone' on which they sat, was by ancient tradition that on which in the Bible (*Genesis* 28) Jacob rested his head and dreamt of the ladder ascending to Heaven. The English king Edward I* captured it, and ever since it has been kept under the English coronation chair in Westminster Abbey*.

Scotland

The northern kingdom of Great Britain. Geographically, racially, linguistically and culturally, it has two parts.

The northern and north-western half, known as the Highlands* and the Islands, is Celtic in race, with a Norse admixture. The native language was originally the Celtic one called Gaelic, but this is now spoken only by a small minority. Until the middle of 18th C its social structure was of the semi-tribal clan system under hereditary chieftains. Its culture was chiefly oral and Gaelic-speaking, and much of it has been lost. The so-called Scottish national dress, of the kilt* woven into chequered designs known as tartans*, was in fact peculiar to this region; it was forbidden after the second Jacobite* rebellion of 1745, when the British government started its policy of taming the Highlands, but it was revived in 19th C as a sentimental fashion for the upper classes. This region of Scotland, though extremely beautiful, has had a sad history; centuries of clan warfare were followed by a century and a half of economic neglect and depopulation, during which the small farms or 'crofts' were steadily replaced by 'grouse moors', preserved by rich landlords for hunting and shooting. In 20th C the economy has to some extent revived, thanks to the tourist industry and efforts by successive governments to cultivate forests.

The southern and eastern half of the country is called the Lowlands, and contains all the important cities including the capital, Edinburgh*, and the largest, Glasgow. These two cities are respectively at the east and west ends of the narrowest part of the country, and the plain between them is a rich coal-mining area. The Lowlands are geographically for the most part hilly, in spite of their name. Racially, the population is as Germanic in origin as that of most of England, and with small exceptions it has always been English-speaking. It has never been subjected to the clan system of the Highlands, although the great families along the border with England had, until 17th C, an influence comparable to that of the clan chieftains of the Celtic north. Economically and politically, the Lowlands have always been the richer and more important part of the country. When we speak of Scottish culture, we are nearly always thinking of the literature of the Lowlands; this has had its distinctive tradition, but it has become increasingly absorbed into English culture since 16th C.

Relations with England. Scotland remained a separate country under its own kings until 1603, when James VI of Scotland became also James I* of England. Thereafter the two countries retained separate governments under the same king until the Act of Union of 1707. By this treaty Scotland surrendered its parliament and agreed to send representatives to the English parliament in London; in return, it has retained its own legal system and state Presbyterian* Church – a more Calvinistic version of Protestantism than the Church of England.

Before the union of the crowns in 1603 the relationship between England and Scotland had been predominantly hostile. England, which has always been much the larger, richer, and more powerful of the two nations, made one attempt at systematic conquest of Scotland, 1296–1328, but this was resisted by William Wallace* and eventually defeated by Robert the Bruce* in the Scottish War of Independence. Thereafter, England became absorbed in two centuries of intermittent hostilities with France, and during this period (*ie* until about 1550) Scotland was consistently a French ally. Apart from frequent periods when Scotland and England were officially at war, there was almost uninterrupted unofficial warfare along the border between them. The English family of Percy* and the Scottish one of Douglas* were the principal antagonists, and their fighting is commemorated in epic ballads* such as *Chevy Chase** and *Otterbourne**.

Anglo-Scottish relationships were transformed half a century before the union of the crowns in 1603 by the religious Reformation*. Both England and Scotland became Protestant, the latter taking the extremer form of Calvinism (Presbyterianism*). Whereas, however, the English Reformation was conducted by the sovereigns of the country, though mainly with popular support, the Scottish one was a popular movement against the Crown which was then under the regency of the Frenchwoman Mary of Guise. The result was an alliance between the Scottish national leaders and Elizabeth I* of England in 1559, and with English help the French occupying forces were expelled. The rising against Mary Queen of Scots*, and her imprisonment in England by her cousin Elizabeth in 1568, completed the close alliance between the two countries. It was Mary's son who succeeded to the English throne in 1603, when Elizabeth died without direct heirs.

* *Scottish Literature.*

Scotland Yard

Now known as New Scotland Yard, the headquarters of the London Metropolitan Police.

Scott, Sir Walter (1771–1832)

Scottish poet and novelist. The son of an Edinburgh lawyer, he was descended from famous families on the Scottish side of the Border with England. This ancestry early attracted him to the drama and tragedy of Anglo-Scottish border history; he became an antiquarian, and a very romantic one. His romanticism was stimulated further by reading the poetry of the contemporary Germans, Bürger and Goethe*; he hoped to do for the Scottish border what they had done for the German Middle Ages, and make its past relive in modern romance. A widespread taste was already developed for the Middle Ages* and was manifesting itself in the Gothic novel*. He collaborated with the most famous of the Gothic novelists – 'Monk' Lewis* – in producing *Tales of Wonder* in 1801. A little later Coleridge's poem *Christabel**, which is written in 8-syllable couplets*, inspired him to write poems in the same metre, and between 1805 and 1815 he produced the succession of narrative poems which made him famous. He began to feel himself outdone as a narrative poet by Byron*, however, and from 1815 he devoted himself to the novels for which he is now better known. Publishing enterprises in which he had begun to involve himself in 1809 left him with a debt of £130,000 to pay off, when the London publisher Constable went bankrupt. Scott was immensely proud, and determined to pay off the debt by his own literary efforts. By writing very prolifically for the rest of his life, he nearly succeeded; he was by then a very sick man, and his efforts are a legend of literary heroism. They did not, however, make for good literature; opinions about his later work vary, but everyone agrees that its merit shows a general decline.

Scott's most famous poems are *The Lay* of the Last Minstrel* (1805); *Marmion** (1808), and *The Lady of the Lake* (1810). The first two are from Anglo-Scottish border history and legend; the third is about the equally bitter enmity of Scottish Highlander for Scottish Lowlander. The readability of these poems makes it easy to account for their popularity, but the kind of interest they offer – the dramatization of the life of a whole society – was not such as Scott was able to work out in the verse-narrative medium.

His novels (**Historical Fiction*) show a double interest: he was the first novelist in English to present characters as part of a society, and not merely against the background of a particular society, the nature of which is taken for granted; he was also the inventor of the true historical novel. The two achievements are related; he knew how to reconstruct the history of Lowland Scottish society in periods of the past that were directly relevant to that society as he knew it. When he wrote of a society he did not know, or of a past that had no direct relevance to his own time, the virtues of his writing are essentially negative: he was able to avoid the unrealities of the Gothic novelists by his antiquarianism, but he was not able to present characters and events with imaginative force. His best work is contained in the Waverley novels and in the first three series of *Tales of My Landlord**: *Waverley** (1814), *Guy Mannering** (1815), *The Antiquary** (1816), *Old Mortality** (1816), *Rob Roy** (1817), *The Heart of Midlothian** (1818), *The Bride of Lammermoor* and *The Legend of Montrose* (1819). All these concern 17th- and 18th-C Scotland, and the religious and dynastic struggles that shaped the nation as Scott knew it. From then onwards he was writing with excessive haste in order to pay off his debts, and he commonly chose English and medieval subjects, *eg Ivanhoe** (1819), *Kenilworth** (about English Elizabethan times – 1821), *Quentin Durward* (1823) and some 16 others, only one of which, *St Ronan's Well* (1823), was set in Scott's own time.

Not only was Scott's influence, both in Britain and Europe, very large in shaping literary taste, but he had an extensive influence in encouraging non-literary taste, such as that for wild landscape (especially of the Highlands) and more intelligent interest in the past. As a critic he was sometimes enlightened; he was among the first to recognize the genius of Jane Austen*. In politics he was strongly right wing (Tory), and he helped to found the great Tory review, the *Quarterly**, in 1809.

Bib: Lockhart, J. G., *Memoirs*; Buchan, J., *Life*; Muir, E., *Scott and Scotland*; Davie, D., *The Heyday of Sir Walter Scott*; Lewis, C. S., in *They Asked for a Paper*; Hillhouse, J. T., *The Waverley Novels and their Critics*; Hayden, J. O., *Scott: The Critical Heritage*.

Scottish Chaucerians

* *Fifteenth-century Literature.*

Scottish Literature

This belongs above all to the Lowlands (* *Scotland*);

it is a distinctive branch of literature in the English language, the Lowland Scottish form of which had originally a close resemblance to that spoken in the north of England. Racially, linguistically and culturally, Lowland Scottish ties with England were close, despite the constant wars between the two countries between late 13th and mid-16th C. In contrast, until the 18th-C destruction of Highland culture, the Lowlanders had little more than the political bond of a common sovereign with their Gaelic-speaking fellow-countrymen of the north. While it is not true to say that Scottish literature is merely a branch of English literature, nonetheless the two literatures have been closely related, whereas Lowland Scottish and Highland Gaelic cultures remained apart.

The first notable work was John Barbour's* *The Bruce* (1375–8), an epic* in 8-syllable couplets* about the war of independence against England (1296–1328). Written at a time when Scottish political fortunes were low, its intention is to inspire the national spirit, not by rhetorical eloquence but by the facts of the heroic struggle; it is one of the least fanciful of the more important medieval poems. Barbour was writing at the same time as Chaucer* in his early work. The next notable Scottish poem was strongly under Chaucer's influence – *The King's Quair**, probably by James I of Scotland*, part of whose reign was spent in imprisonment in England, where it was no doubt written. It is a tale of romantic love, echoing Chaucer's *Knight's Tale**. 15th C was a dull period for poetry in England, if we except the ballads* and some of the religious plays the surviving versions of which may date from it. In Scotland, on the contrary, it saw the beginning of a golden age, covering the careers of Robert Henryson*, William Dunbar*, Gavin Douglas*, and David Lindsay*. The climax of this period was the reign of the exceptionally able and enlightened King James IV (1488–1513), who produced an unusual state of order and civilization in the country. Henryson's masterpiece is the great *Testament of Cresseid**, a continuation of Chaucer's *Troilus and Criseyde**, but with a tragic quality which is quite un-Chaucerian. Dunbar wrote in contrasting styles – the courtly and the colloquial; his finest work is perhaps in the latter, notably, the *Tretis of the Tua Mariit Wemen and the Wedo* (Treatise of the Two Married Women and the Widow). Douglas's finest work is his translation of Virgil's *Aeneid**, and Lindsay is best known for his *Satire of the Three Estates* – a political morality play.

The flowering of high Scottish poetry was halted by the Scottish religious Reformation*, and all the political troubles attendant on it from 1550 till 1700. Such poets in this period as deserve attention (*eg* Drummond of Hawthornden, 1585–1649) were thoroughly anglicized. The native culture remained alive at popular level, however, especially in its fine ballad and folksong tradition, of which *Sir Patrick Spens** is one of the most notable examples. In 18th C a revival took place, the first noteworthy example being Allan Ramsay's *The Gentle Shepherd* (1725). Robert Burns* was the first great Scottish poet since 16th C. By now, however, the tide of English influence had moved strongly into Scotland; Walter Scott* collected Scottish ballads, and produced a few fine examples in the ballad tradition, but his longer poems belong to the history of English verse narrative, though their subject was often Scottish history and legend. Patriotic sentiment still seized on opportunities to resist the English pressure, however, and 20th C has seen a reassertion of the national idiom in the Lallans* (Lowland) renaissance, the most vigorous example of which is the work of Hugh MacDiarmid*. Wherever this idiom can be seen at its finest – in the work of Henryson, Dunbar, Douglas, Burns, MacDiarmid – the reasons for its periodic renewal after long periods of abeyance can be understood: it is concrete, sardonic, realistic, harsh and physical, all qualities of the common people in most countries, and notably among the Scots.

Gaelic literature of the Highlands had what is said to be a 'golden age' in later 18th C, just at the time when Gaelic culture was being destroyed by the English and the Lowland Scots for political reasons. The work in it (*eg* that of Alexander Macdonald, Duncan Ban, Dugald Buchanan) is little known outside the comparatively small number of Gaelic speakers in the Highlands, and does not belong to English literature. For the alleged translations of the Ossianic poems by James Macpherson (1736–96) see under Oisin.

It is not possible to speak of a Scottish prose literary tradition. Medieval philosophers such as Duns Scotus* and Renaissance humanists* such as George Buchanan (16th C) wrote principally in Latin. Thereafter the great Scottish writers (especially from 18th C) were thoroughly anglicized in their prose expression; David Hume* and Adam Smith* in the 18th C, Walter Scott and Thomas Carlyle* in 19th, to mention only the most famous names, had strong Scottish sentiments, but they belong to the history of English literature. The only partial exception is Walter Scott in his earlier novels; his work is often at its best in the vernacular dialogue of his Lowland characters.

* *Scotland.*

Scotus, Duns

* *Duns Scotus.*

Scriblerus Club /skrib'liərəs/

Formed by the poet Pope* and his friends, Swift*, Gay*, Parnell*, Congreve*, Arbuthnot, Atterbury, and Lord Oxford. Its aim was to satirize 'false tastes' by collaborating under the disguise of the memoirs of a fictional German scholar, *Martinus Scriblerus*. The club was formed in 1713; only the first volume of the memoirs was completed, and they were published in Pope's works in 1741. Pope sometimes used 'Scriblerus' as a pen-name, and so did the poet George Crabbe*.

Scrooge /skru:dʒ/

The main character of Dickens's tale *A Christmas Carol**. From his behaviour, 'a Scrooge' has entered the language as a term for a mean, avaricious person.

Scrutiny

A literary critical review published in Cambridge from 1932 to 1953; its principal editor was F. R. Leavis*. *Scrutiny* was famous for its intellectual energy, the coherence of outlook among its contributors, and the urgency and purposefulness of its tone. This purposefulness was a response to an analysis of the contemporary cultural scene which may be summarized as follows. The quality of Western (more particularly, British) civilization was deteriorating because of the influence upon it of commercial vulgarization. Such vulgarization could only end in the complete loss of those standards by which life in any organized society can be seen and felt to be valuable. The importance of a great literary tradition is that it constitutes a form of spiritual life that sustains high values and withstands vulgarization. However, such a tradition must itself be sustained by constant, sensitive and scrupulous critical activity carried on by alert and active intellects within the society. But the British literary tradition no longer possessed this kind of cultural leadership; the leading men of letters, on the contrary, with a few exceptions, regarded literature as an elegant pastime for a fashionable elite (such as the Bloomsbury Group*) and they employed slack and inadequate standards in their judgements. *Scrutiny*, therefore, was intended to demonstrate the exacting standards which are required of criticism if a lively and effective literary tradition is to be sustained. The example to be followed was that of the recently defunct review, *The Calendar of Modern Letters* (1925–27) edited by Edgell Rickword.

The strongest part of *Scrutiny's* critical attack was directed towards literary education. It sought to counteract the kind of academic inertia which tends to the passive acceptance of some literary reputations and the equally passive neglect of other writers. This policy led to an extensive revaluation of the writers of the past. In regard to poetry, this revaluation took the direction already pursued by T. S. Eliot* (*Selected Essays*, 1932); in regard to the novel, the dominant influences were those of F. R. Leavis himself, and his wife Q.D. Leavis. *Scrutiny* had a great influence in Britain and the United States, especially among teachers at all levels of education. The review has been republished in book form by the Cambridge University Press, which has also republished some of the most important essays from it in two volumes (paperback). Selections from *The Calendar of Modern Letters* have been published under the title of *Towards Standards of Criticism*, edited by F. R. Leavis.

* 7.5.

Scylla and Charybdis /ˈsilə – kəˈribdis/

The name of a monster (later identified with a rock) and a whirlpool respectively, situated, according to Greek myth, on either side of the Straits of Messina, the narrow channel that separates Italy from the island of Sicily. Scylla broke up passing ships if they came within her reach; Charybdis three times a day sucked in the sea, and three times vomited it forth again. Homer describes how Odysseus and his crew negotiated these dangers in the 12th book of the *Odyssey**.

Seasons, The

Four blank verse* poems by the 18th-C James Thomson*, published 1726–30: *Winter*, 1726; *Summer*, 1727; *Spring*, 1728; *Autumn*, 1730. A tradition of topographical and reflective poetry, represented by John Denham's *Cooper's Hill* (1642, pub 1668) and Pope's* *Windsor Forest* (1713), had come down from 17th C to 18th, but the predominant movement of 18th-C poetry had hitherto been satirical or artificially pastoral, *eg* Pope's *Pastorals* (1709). Thomson's work was more direct and stronger in feeling, but *The Seasons* are still very much poetry of the age: they are in the classical spirit of Virgil's *Georgics**, with a self-conscious sublimity which comes from Milton*; Thomson also sees nature in terms of the scientific classifications in which his age was so much interested, and the appeal of nature to him is typically its provision of livelihood to man. Yet the four poems are important as the first 18th-C example of the culture of the feelings in response to nature – the beginning of a tendency which was developed by such poets as Akenside, Collins*, Cowper*, and Gray*, and found its completeness in Wordsworth* at the very end of the century. The most admired of the four poems is *Winter*.

Second Nun's Tale, The

One of Chaucer's *Canterbury Tales**. Its subject is the martyrdom of St Cecilia* from the *Golden Legend** by Jacobus a Voragine. Written in rhyme-royal*.

Secret Agent, The (1907)

A novel by Joseph Conrad*. The subject is revolution and counter-revolution in Western Europe; the scene is London. The 'secret agent' is Mr Verloc, of mixed nationality. He is employed by the embassy of an unnamed foreign power (Czarist Russia) to mix with anarchist conspirators who have taken refuge on British soil, and to report their activities. Between the embassy and the conspirators are the London police, represented by Chief Inspector Heat, whose work is to watch the anarchists but not to interfere with them until they commit crimes. The embassy wishes to force the British government and its police to suppress the anarchist colony, and uses Verloc to organize a bomb outrage (against Greenwich Observatory) so as to incriminate them. The irony of this is that the tactics of the embassy suit not only the wishes of Heat, who would like any excuse to shoot the anarchists down, but also the wishes of the most ruthless of the anarchists, nicknamed the Professor. The Professor is disquieted by the inability of the British masses to see politics in terms of violence; if violence were used by the government, the masses would believe that counter-violence was their only hope, and a revolutionary situation would exist in Britain. In addition to this political level, the novel has a psychological one: if either revolution or counter-revolution is to be accomplished successfully, the human instruments must be disinterested, but in fact both the revolutionaries and their opponents are dominated by self-regard. The only characters capable of full disinterest are those who are so wretched as to be incapable of reflecting on their own condition. Mrs Verloc's half-witted brother Stevie rises to one idea only: 'bad life for poor people'. He thus becomes the willing tool of Mr Verloc, who charges him with the task of placing the bomb. In the event, Stevie causes no damage to the Observatory but he is himself blown up. Mrs Verloc, who has married Mr Verloc solely to provide support for Stevie, though her husband supposes her entirely devoted to himself, murders him from rage and grief. In contrast to Winnie Verloc and Stevie, characters simplified by misery and elementary development, is the Assistant Commissioner of Police, who neither acts disinterestedly nor has any belief that he can, but lives by the awareness that self-knowledge is the only antidote to the poison of self-regard. He solves the mystery of the outrage, and thus frustrates the destructive folly of Mr Vladimir, the ambassador. It is the Assistant Commissioner who stands nearest to the mentality of Conrad; his compassionate irony radiates the novel with sanity.

Sedan Chair /si'dan/

A Modern Belle going to the Rooms at Bath. Pub. H.H.

A portable covered chair, carried on two poles by chairmen, and with a trap in the roof so that the passenger could stand. It was introduced into England in 1634, and was much used as a way of getting about towns in 18th C.

Sedgemoor, Battle of (1685)

The culmination of a rising of west-of-England Puritans* against Charles II's openly Catholic brother James II*. It was led by Charles's illegitimate son, the Duke of Monmouth. The battle was won by the government troops, and was followed by the ferocious punishment of the rebels by Judge Jeffreys in his notorious *Bloody Assizes**. Sedgemoor was the last battle fought on English (as distinct from British) soil.

Sejanus (1603) /si'dʒeinəs/

A satirical tragedy by Ben Jonson*. The central character is a historical figure, a favourite of the Roman emperor Tiberius (reigned AD 14–37). The play is a study of a man driven by extreme ambition; he first eliminates all his rivals to power in the Senate, and then, exploiting the emperor's love of luxurious indolence and inclination for retirement, he conspires to murder Tiberius' heirs in order to occupy the throne himself. Tiberius, however, is too cunning for him; he employs Macro, a new favourite, to bring about the downfall of the old, and Sejanus ends by being torn to pieces by the Roman mob, leaving Macro, equally ambitious and unscrupulous, in his former seat of power. The sensuality of Tiberius and his court, and the violence of the politicians, are contrasted with a group of grim commentators led by Arruntius, remnants of the old stoical (* *Stoics*) Romans whose austere virtues had made Rome great. Ben Jonson presents through Sejanus one of the Renaissance* 'men of power', glorying in the consciousness of unlimited resources, the pattern for whom is Christopher Marlowe's Tamburlaine*. Sejanus is also the diabolical Machiavellian* politician, without conscience and capable of any crime, such as recurs in many Elizabethan and Jacobean dramas. Yet in his unbounded appetites, he is almost a grotesque figure, like the ludicrous sensualists in Jonson's great comedies, *Volpone** and *The Alchemist**. The play may have been an attempt to rival Shakespeare's *Julius Caesar** of a few years before; it is much more learned in its use of ancient authors, and dramatically it is perhaps the more impressive work.

* 5.1.3.2.

Selborne, Natural History and Antiquities of

* *White, Gilbert.*

Selene /si'li:ni/

In Greek myth, the original goddess of the moon, later identified with Artemis* and (in Roman myth) with Diana. The most famous legend about her is of her love for the mortal, Endymion* – see the poem by John Keats*.

Selkirk, Alexander (1676–1721) /'selkə:k/

A sailor, whose experiences on the uninhabited island of Juan Fernandez, where he was landed at his own request and remained from 1704 to 1709, are the basis of the desert island part of Defoe's *Robinson Crusoe**.

Semele /'semili/

In Greek myth, the daughter of Cadmus* and the mistress of Zeus*, who visited her in mortal disguise. Zeus' jealous queen, Hera*, put it into her mind to ask Zeus to appear in his full glory; he consented, with the result that Semele was consumed by his divine radiance, leaving behind the child whom he had fathered upon her, Dionysus*.

Semiramis (about 800 BC) /se'mirəmis/

Historically, an ancient queen or princess of Assyria, about whom little is known. In legend, she is said to have built great cities including Babylon, to have had wonderful beauty and many lovers. More than one queen has been nicknamed after her, notably Catherine II of Russia (1729–96).

Seneca, Lucius Annaeus (?4 BC–AD 65) /'senikə/

Roman philosopher and dramatist. He belonged to the Stoic* school of philosophy, which taught that men should seek virtue, not happiness, and that they should be superior to the influences of pleasure and pain. As an orator, he was famous for the weight and terseness of his expression – the 'Senecan style'. He was tutor to the emperor Nero* during the latter's boyhood, but later was suspected of being involved in a conspiracy against him; Nero accordingly ordered him to end his life which he did with true stoical dignity. His nine tragedies were modelled on those of Aeschylus*, Sophocles* and Euripides*, but there is much doubt whether they were ever intended to be performed in a theatre; they seem to be designed for declamation to small circles. They contain no action, though the subjects are of blood-thirsty revenge. Their titles: *Hercules Furens*; *Thyestes*; *Phoenissae*; *Phaedra* (*Hippolytus*); *Oedipus*; *Troades* (*Hecuba*); *Medea*; *Agamemnon*; *Hercules Oetaeus*. A tenth, *Octavia*, has been proved to be by another author.

Neither as a philosopher nor as a dramatist was Seneca one of the most important figures of the ancient Mediterranean world, but he had great importance for 16th-C Renaissance* Europe, and particularly for English poetic drama between 1560 and 1620. This influence was of three kinds: [1] Seneca's dramas provided inspiration for Elizabethan revenge tragedy* or 'tragedy of blood'; [2] at a time of English literature when there was keen interest in modes of expression but no settled standards about them, Senecan style was one of the favourite modes, both inside and outside the drama; [3] at a time when inherited ideas about the ordering of society and the ethical systems that should control it were undergoing alarming transformations, Senecan stoicism had an appeal for thoughtful men that harmonized with Protestant* strictness and individualism of conduct. The three influences were more related than might appear. The translator of Seneca's *Ten Tragedies* (1559–81) declares in his preface that their effect was 'to beat down sin', and Protestants were familiar with the vengefulness of Old Testament religion. Delight in bloodthirstiness combined in the Elizabethan mind with admiration for Senecan high seriousness, and both found suitable expression in weighty, eloquent Senecan style. Sensational drama could unite with serious social purpose, and thus mingle learned, sober conceptions of drama (*eg Gorboduc**) with the demands of popular taste, *eg* in Shakespeare's history plays on Henry VI* and Richard III*. Finally, Stoic love of virtue could be used either for the dramatic castigation of vice by the lonely, heroic individual (Tourneur's *Revenger's Tragedy**, or Chapman's* *Bussy d'Ambois*, 1607) or as a dramatic attitude to be taken by a hero rising morally above misfortune, like Othello* in his last speech, or Clermont in Chapman's *Revenge of Bussy d'Ambois*. Outside the drama, the terse sententiousness of Senecan style is best found in the *Essays* of Francis Bacon*.

Sennacherib /se'nakərib/

King of Assyria, 705–681 BC. He made extensive conquests, but one of the most eloquent narratives of the Old Testament of the Bible describes how his attempt to capture Jerusalem from Hezekiah, king of the Jews, was prevented by a sudden pestilence among his army (*2 Chronicles* 32). This is the subject of Byron's* poem, 'The destruction of Sennacherib' in *Hebrew Melodies* (1815).

Sense and Sensibility

A novel by Jane Austen*. A youthful version, *Elinor and Marianne*, has been lost. The revised novel was published in 1811.

The two heroines, Elinor and Marianne Dashwood, are fatherless sisters who live with their mother in comparative poverty, having been defrauded of more substantial income by their stepbrother, John Dashwood, and his arrogant and selfish wife. The title of the novel indicates the difference between the sisters: Elinor is practical and watches after the family affairs with sober good sense, and Marianne prides herself on the strength of her feelings and her contempt for material interests. Elinor is in love with a depressed and apparently dull young man, Edward Ferrars (brother of Mrs John Dashwood), while Marianne loves the handsome and glamorous John Willoughby. The superficial contrast between the sisters and their lovers is shown to be deceptive: Elinor's feelings are as deep as Marianne's, but her sense of responsibility is greater, and she keeps her sorrows to herself, whereas Marianne makes almost a virtue of the public exhibition of her grief, thus becoming a burden on her sister and her mother. In the end, the romantic-seeming Willoughby turns out to have given up Marianne from fear of losing a legacy, while the prosaic Edward gladly sacrifices the favour of a rich relative for the sake of marriage to Elinor. Much of the book is presented in terms of an answer to the question 'What is the right attitude to money?' A subsidiary theme is the way in which false ideas of feeling, derived from literature (Marianne is a great reader of the poet Cowper*), may confuse real life judgements.

Sentimental Journey through France and Italy, A

A narrative, part novel and part travel book, by Laurence Sterne* (under the pseudonym of 'Mr Yorick' – the name of a character in Sterne's *Tristram Shandy**), based on his stay in France, 1762–64. It was intended to be longer, but Sterne died after the publication of the first two volumes in 1768. It is an example of the frank liberation of sentiment characteristic of the second half of 18th C, but the sentiment is presented with constant irony in a way that is quite unlike 19th-C romanticism.

September Massacre

An episode of the French Revolution*, when fear of foreign invasion caused revolutionaries to massacre political prisoners between 2 and 5 September 1795.

Septuagint /ˈseptjuədʒint/

The oldest Greek translation of the Old Testament of the Bible, so called from the tradition that 72 translators were employed on it ('septuagint' derives from the Latin for 70). According to this tradition, the translation was made on the orders of Ptolemy II of Egypt (3rd C BC) on behalf of the Jews of the Egyptian city of Alexandria.

Seraph

* *Angels.*

Serapis /ˈserəpis/

In ancient Egyptian myth, a fusion of Apis, the bull-god of the sun, with Osiris*, king of the underworld. Serapis eventually came to be worshipped as god of the underworld, or world of the blessed dead, in preference to Osiris.

Serf

* *Village, The English.*

Sermons

The word 'sermon' is used in English to denote a speech from a church pulpit for the edification of the audience, always in this context called a 'congregation'. The sermon considered as a means of communication had a central importance in English life until 19th C, when universal literacy and the rise of the mass-circulation newspaper tended to eclipse it. At a popular level, it reached a larger audience than any other form of public communication. Chaucer's Pardoner in the *Canterbury Tales** demonstrates the power that a medieval preacher felt that he had over an ignorant and superstitious audience, but *The Pardoner's Tale** is partly a satire about how the sermon could be abused. Used positively, the sermon was the main means by which the traditional Christian faith was kept alive in the minds of the common people. At the level of the village pulpit, even the Reformation* had less force on traditional preaching than one might suppose: G. R. Owst, in his *Literature and Pulpit in Medieval England* (1933) has shown that

in 17th C Bunyan's knowledge of medieval allegory*, evident in *Pilgrim's Progress**, was probably acquired from village sermons heard in his youth.

Nonetheless, the Reformation had an important effect in producing preachers of national fame. The sermon was a necessary means of propaganda for the Protestant* faith, and one of the most central principles of that faith – that each man stands alone with his conscience before God – meant that the preacher's function as a spiritual guide and teacher became even more important. Doctrine, speculative philosophy, social criticism, and ethical problems of daily life were all within the sphere of the sermon, and interested all ranks of society in one way or another. Consequently the great preachers of 16th and 17th C belong to the main stream of English prose.

The most famous of the 16th-C preachers is Hugh Latimer*, who lived and died in the most dramatic phase of the English Reformation and whose sermons are some of the earliest examples in English of vivid prose in the popular and spoken idiom. By the end of the century the Church of England* had become firmly established, and the three famous preachers of the golden age of Anglicanism in the first half of 17th C have left sermons addressed to the Court or to other highly educated audiences. The best known of these is the poet John Donne*, who became Dean of St Paul's in 1621. His sermons have massive learning, but his style is richly personal and persuasive, with a depth of feeling comparable to that of his great religious verse. Lancelot Andrewes* was a subtle and elaborate analyst in language, and appealed more exclusively to the intellect, and Jeremy Taylor* was described by Coleridge* as the 'Spenser* of prose' because of his command of musical cadence and linguistic flow. All three men lived in an age when English prose still possessed the emotive power of poetic language, and at the same time had acquired a high degree of flexible expression of abstract thought.

The change that came over English in the middle of the century emphasized flexibility, control, and lucidity at the expense of poetic emotive power. It is heralded by John Wilkins's book on preaching, *Ecclesiastes* (1646), which teaches the virtue of strict method in organizing a sermon. The great Anglican preachers of the next hundred years, such as Robert South (1634–1716), notable for his succinctness and satire, Isaac Barrow (1630–77), whom Charles II* called 'the best scholar in England', John Tillotson (1630–94), famous for the elegance of his prose, and Joseph Butler (1692–1752), an acute thinker, were all central figures in the movement known as English Augustanism (**Augustan Age*). The virtues of this kind of sermon, and the vices that it sought to combat, are tersely expressed by Swift* (whose own sermons are exemplars of the ideal) in his *Letter to a Young Gentleman entered into Holy Orders* (1721). The best of the Puritan* preachers followed a similar course in a more popular idiom, for instance the Presbyterian Richard Baxter (1615–91) who declared 'The Plainest words are the profitablest oratory in the weightiest matters', and this is a criterion which Bunyan exemplifies at its noblest.

However, there is always a temptation to excite ignorant minds by fervour and frenzy, and this seems also to have been a Puritan tendency. South is severe on it, and Swift made a ferocious attack on it in his account of the Aeolists* in *A Tale of a Tub**. The sermon tradition enters into its first period of decline in 18th C, by becoming too rationalistic, and divorced from the feelings and idiom of the common people. The sermons of William Paley (1743–1805) owed their fame to his talents as a teacher, but they show mediocrity of thought and tepidity of feeling. Those of the novelist Laurence Sterne* (*Sermons of Mr Yorick*, 1760) and of the poet George Crabbe* have merit (especially Sterne's) as literary essays in ethics, but that is what they are, rather than spiritual discourses. The people hungered for something to touch their hearts in need, and the sermons of the founder of Methodism, John Wesley* gave it to them without false rhetoric. His eloquent rival George Whitefield (1714–70) was more inclined to this fault, and was accused by the fastidious Horace Walpole* in one of his letters of 'acting very vulgar enthusiasm'.

In 19th C there were still preachers of great influence, some on the popular level, such as the enormously popular Baptist clergyman, Charles Spurgeon*. But J. H. Newman*, the leader of the Oxford Movement* who later became a Catholic and a cardinal, was perhaps the last great preacher to be also a major literary figure. It was not merely the competition of the Press that displaced the sermon from its central influence in English life by the end of 19th C, but the growth of agnosticism among the intelligentsia and the corresponding decline in the prestige of the pulpit.

Bib: Henson, H., ed. *Selected English Sermons* (World's Classics); Sampson, A., ed. *Famous English Sermons.*

Set

In ancient Egyptian myth, the brother of Osiris* and god of evil.

Setebos /'setibos/

A god of the Patagonians in South America at the time when Shakespeare wrote *The Tempest**. In the play, he is the god worshipped by the witch Sycorax, mother of Caliban, the savage monster who is one of the characters. Shakespeare may have known of Setebos from Francis Fletcher's account of Drake's* voyage round the world, 1577–81. In his poem 'Caliban upon Setebos' (*Dramatis Personae*, 1864) Robert Browning* presents a savage's meditation on the creation of the world.

Seth /seθ/

In the Bible (*Genesis* 4:25) the youngest of Adam and Eve's three children, the others being Cain and Abel.

Seven Bishops, The

Sancroft, Archbishop of Canterbury, and six other bishops of the Church of England*, who respectfully protested in 1688 against James II's* Declaration of Indulgence, granting religious liberty to Dissenters* and Roman Catholics. James ordered the trial of the Bishops, but they were acquitted of the charge he brought against them, amid popular rejoicing.

Seven Champions of Christendom

In medieval tales, the guardian saints of European countries: Saint George of England, St Andrew of Scotland, St Patrick of Ireland, St David of Wales, St Denis of France, St James of Spain, and St Anthony of Italy.

Seven Deadly Sins

The sins for which, as the Church taught, the punishment was spiritual death (*ie* not a venial sin for which it was possible to obtain forgiveness). The list usually given is: Pride; Envy; Sloth; Gluttony (or intemperance); Avarice (or covetousness); Anger (ire, wrath); Lust. These sins were frequently personified, *eg* in the medieval morality plays* and in *Piers Plowman**, the Parson's Tale in Chaucer's *Canterbury Tales**, and Spenser's *Faerie Queene**.

Seven Dials

In 18th C, an impoverished district of London, just north of the Thames, extending over the area covered by Shaftesbury Avenue and Charing Cross Road. The name derives from a column in an open space where seven streets met; the column bore seven sun-dials.

Seven Seas

The Arctic, Antarctic, North Pacific, South Pacific, North Atlantic, South Atlantic, and Indian Oceans.

Seven Sisters, The
A name for the group of stars called the Pleiades*. Also, a line of high chalk cliffs on the south coast of England, near Newhaven.

Seven Sleepers of Ephesus, The
A Christian legend dating from 6th C. In 3rd C, seven young Christians, fleeing persecution by the Emperor Decius, took refuge in a cave. When they were discovered asleep there, the emperor ordered that the cave should be walled up. Their sleep was miraculously prolonged, and 187 years later they emerged to find Christianity everywhere triumphant. They told their story to the Christian emperor, Theodosius II, and then returned to their slumbers.

Seven Wonders of the World, The
A list dating from 2nd C BC of what were then considered to be the most remarkable productions by man in the known world: the Egyptian pyramids; the Mausoleum at Halicarnassus; the hanging gardens of Babylon*; the temple of Artemis* at Ephesus; the statue of Zeus* by Pheidias* at Olympia; the Colossus* at Rhodes, and the Pharos at Alexandria (for which the Walls of Babylon was substituted in another list).

Seven Years' War, The (1756–63)
Frederick the Great of Prussia, in alliance with Great Britain and Hanover, fought an alliance of France, Austria and Russia. Frederick kept his dominions by the Treaty of Hubertusberg. The importance of the war for Britain was that it left her predominant in North America and in India (Treaty of Paris, 1763). An indirect consequence of this was that the American colonists, no longer afraid of conquest by the French, now felt free to resist the British policy of taxing them without allowing them representation in Parliament; this led to the American War of Independence (1775–83) and the establishment of the United States.

The Seven Years' War produced three great war-leaders: in India, Robert Clive, victor of the battle of Plassey, 1757; in America, James Wolfe, captor of Quebec, 1759; and William Pitt the Elder*, Earl of Chatham, the minister who controlled the strategy of the Franco-British struggle.

Seventeenth-century Literature
17th C was certainly the richest period in the history of English literature, both for the greatness of achievement and for the variety of it. It also saw a revolution in the human mind, not only in Britain but elsewhere in Europe – a revolution which constitutes the birth of the modern outlook. We begin the century with writers like William Shakespeare* and John Donne*, whose language fused thought and feeling in both poetry and prose; we end it with John Dryden* and John Locke*, writers whose language was shaped by a new ideal of prose, who opposed 'judgement' to 'wit' – that is to say, the analytic to the synthetic powers of the mind. Another way of putting it is to say that the century opens with the greatest phase of one of the greatest periods of poetic drama in the whole history of Europe, and it closes with the first great period of English satire*, and the prose of fact which in the next century was to find its most ample form of expression in the novel*.

We are in the habit of using the term 'Elizabethan drama' for the greatest period of the English theatre, but in fact it was in the reign of James I*, the Jacobean* period, that this drama came to fruition. By 1600, Shakespeare was only approaching his best work, Ben Jonson* was just beginning his career, and the plays of the other important dramatists – Chapman*, Webster*, Tourneur* and Middleton* – were as yet unwritten. The greatest of this drama was the result of a precarious balance, which kept the long medieval past in mind together with the social and intellectual changes of the present, and communicated with the populace as well as with the court. Already by 1610, this balance was being upset; the elegant but superficial taste of the younger dramatists, Beaumont* and Fletcher*, was turning a national drama into an upper and middle class London theatre, which has remained dominant to the present day. By the time of the Caroline* drama of the reign of Charles I*, this transformation was nearing completeness in the plays of Massinger*, Ford*, and Shirley*. But in the meantime, the peculiar genius of the best dramatists, especially Shakespeare, had helped to produce among the lyric poets the school now so much admired under the name of the Metaphysicals*. The great Metaphysical poets (notably John Donne, George Herbert*, and Andrew Marvell*) owe their name to the possession of a quality which is central to Shakespeare's genius: the capacity to unite oppositions of thought and of feeling under the control of a flexible, open, but poised intelligence; their poetry, like Shakespeare's greatest work but in a smaller way, thus expresses a peculiarly rich body of experience, united from different levels of the mind.

But the Metaphysicals were not the only fertile school of poets in the first half of the century, nor was Shakespearian drama the only kind from which poets could learn. Shakespeare's rival, Ben Jonson, was, as a dramatist, in isolated opposition to the Shakespearian drama. The difference lay in conceptions of form. Whereas the Shakespearian dramatic form proceeded from the nucleus of the metaphor and opened outwards until the whole play is what Wilson Knight has called an 'expanded metaphor', Jonson imposed his form upon his matter: the confusion and violence of experience is shaped by a selective process which is a disciplining of the mind as well as a critical analysis of the subject. In his lyric poetry as well as in his dramas, this discipline shows itself in irony, proportion, and a union of strength with elegance. Jonson's example influenced the later Metaphysicals, notably Marvell, but it also led to a different school, not always to be sharply distinguished, which we know as the Cavalier Poets*, such as Carew*, Herrick*, and Lovelace*. Above all, Jonson's criteria anticipated the 'classicists' of the later part of the century, especially Dryden.

But yet another poet left an important legacy to 17th C. This was Edmund Spenser* who had perfected those qualities of musical cadence and sensuous imagery which many readers think of as essentially 'poetic'. He had his followers in the first 30 years of 17th C, though none of note, but it is to him that John Milton* owes most among his predecessors. In Milton, we have two very different 17th-C outlooks uneasily united: the love of all that is implied by the Renaissance*, that is to say the revaluation of classical literature and the discovery of the glories of earthly civilization as opposed to those of a heavenly destiny, and devotion to Puritanism*, implying the extreme Protestant belief that not only is all truth God's truth, but that the sole ultimate source of it is the Bible. This uneasy union produced in Milton the determination to impose on his society a Judaic-Christian conception of human destiny so grand that it compelled acceptance, and to use as his medium what was considered to be the grandest of all the ancient artistic forms, the epic*. *Paradise Lost** was so impressive as an attempt to realize this impossible ambition, and so imposing in its union of the classical form and the biblical subject, that it has won the reverence of three centuries. But Milton's sonorous eloquence, like Spenser's sensuous music, was a kind of magic that subdued the intellect rather than persuaded it. The unfortunate consequence was the common belief among 18th- and 19th-C poets that 'sublime' poetry should elevate the emotions while passing the intellect by. This Miltonic influence no doubt encouraged the exponents of reason like Locke* (*Essay concerning Human Understanding**) to believe that poetry belongs to an immature stage of mental development, before the mind has acquired reason and respect for facts, the best medium for which is prose.

From the beginning of the century, prose writers showed signs of seeing their function as clarifying the reason as opposed to enlarging the imagination. This turning away from the imagination went naturally with a gradual relegation of religion. Bacon*, in his *Advancement of Learning**, treats religion with respect and then ignores it, and he ends his few remarks on poetry with the sentence: 'But it is not good to stay too long in the theatre.' Shelley (in his *Defence of Poetry*) was nonetheless to consider Bacon himself to be a poet, but the vivid imagery which strikes out of his terse style is more functional than that of earlier prose writers. His main theme is the inductive method of acquiring knowledge through experiment, and all his prose, including his *Essays**, is essentially practical. Although the imaginative connotations are preserved, the dominant tendency in the first half of the century (*eg* in the 'character'* writers such as John Earle, and Robert Burton's* treatise on psychology, *The Anatomy of Melancholy**) is to use prose descriptively and analytically. Thomas Browne's *Religio Medici** is written, like his other works, in the most sonorous prose in the English language, but Browne is defending his religious faith just because it exceeds his reason, and his poetic style (in contrast to that of the great sermon writers like John Donne) is partly a conscious contrivance.

In the middle of the century, Thomas Hobbes* published his treatise on political philosophy, *Leviathan** in which, with pungent ruthlessness, he forced his readers to face the 'facts' of human nature in their grimmest interpretation. After the Restoration* of the Monarchy (1660), the historian of the Royal Society*, Bishop Sprat, laid down the new standards that were to guide the prose writer: 'a close, naked, natural way of speaking; positive expressions; clear senses; a native easiness'. This is the prose we find in the dialogue of Restoration comedy (Etherege*, Wycherley*, Vanbrugh*, and Congreve*), in the literary criticism of Dryden, and above all in the sceptical, reasonable philosophy of Locke. However, the spiritual life of the middle and lower classes was not yet permeated by this rationalism. The spirit of Puritanism, still biblical and poetic, is expressed in the spiritual autobiographies of the Puritan leaders, such as the Quaker George Fox* (*Journal*, 1694), and, at its most impressive, that great imaginative work *The Pilgrim's Progress**, by the Baptist tinsmith, John Bunyan. In this work, the old allegories* of the Middle Ages reach forward into the field of the novel, the new form which was to come into being in 18th C.

* *Dissociaton of Sensibility*; *Humours, Comedy of*; *Manners, Comedy of.*

Sèvres /seivr/

A town in France, near Paris, famous from 1756 for its manufacture of fine porcelain.

Shadwell, Thomas (1642?–92)

Dramatist. He was a disciple of Ben Jonson* and admirer of his contemporary French dramatist Molière*, on whose play *Les Facheux* he based *The Sullen Lovers* (1668). He wrote 17 plays, of which the best known are *Epsom Wells* (1672) and *Alsatia* (1688). (The latter refers to Whitefriars, a London district where those liable to arrest took sanctuary.)

Shadwell was not among the best Restoration* dramatists, but his plays have their characteristic liveliness of dialogue, and the merit, no doubt due to his emulation of Jonson, of penetrating further than his contemporaries to lower levels of the society of his time. However, Shadwell is now chiefly remembered for his quarrel with Dryden. At first the two men were on good terms, but they took opposite sides when Lord Shaftesbury* clashed with Charles II* on the issue of the Protestant succession to the throne. Dryden attacked Shaftesbury in *Absalom and Achitophel** and *The Medal*; Shadwell retorted with *The Medal of John Bayes: a Satire against Folly and Knavery* (1682), and Dryden stigmatized Shadwell in *Mac Flecknoe, or a Satire on the True Blue Protestant Poet* (1682). (Flecknoe was an Irish writer who had himself been satirized by *Andrew Marvell** in 1645.) Shadwell attempted counter-attack in an adaptation of Juvenal's* tenth satire, but it is Dryden who is still read. However Shadwell had some revenge by

superseding Dryden as Poet Laureate after the Protestant triumph in the Revolution of 1688*.
Bib: Borman, A. S., *Life*; Dobrée, B., *Restoration Comedy*.

Shaftesbury, Lord (Anthony Ashley Cooper, 1st Earl of Shaftesbury, 1621–83) /ˈʃa:ftsbəri/
Politician. He first took the side of the king in the Civil War* of 1642–46, but changed sides because he considered that Royalist policy threatened the Protestant religion. He later became a parliamentary opponent of Cromwell*, however, and after the Restoration* he became one of Charles II's* chief ministers. Charles II, however, was Catholic in sympathy, and Shaftesbury again went into opposition in 1673. By the Exclusion Bill, he tried to exclude Charles's openly Catholic brother, James Duke of York, from succession to the throne, advancing the claims of Charles's illegitimate son, the Duke of Monmouth*, in James's place. The alliance of Shaftesbury and Monmouth is satirized in Dryden's *Absalom and Achitophel**, one of the great satirical poems in the English language. Charles II's statesmanship outwitted Shaftesbury, who fled to Holland and died in exile.

Shaftesbury, Lord (Anthony Ashley Cooper, 3rd Earl of Shaftesbury, 1671–1713)
A moral philosopher, with great influence in the first half of 18th C. His main beliefs are contained in his *Characteristics of Men, Manners, Opinions, Times* (1711; revised edition, 1713). He was a Deist (* *Deism*), a Churchman, and a Platonic idealist. His optimistic philosophy was in direct opposition to that of Thomas Hobbes*, author of *Leviathan**. He believed that men have 'natural affections' which are capable of going beyond self-interest. The cultivation of disinterested affection for others will produce virtue and the true social morality. His concept of these 'natural affections' seemed to make the supernatural elements of Christian doctrine unnecessary to the acquirement of true religion. On this ground he was opposed by Bishop Butler in his *Analogy of True Religion* (1736). On a purely theoretical level, Shaftesbury anticipated the beliefs about Nature of the poet William Wordsworth*, and he encouraged the growing emphasis on sentiment and sensibility in criticism and poetry in 18th C.

* 3.3.2.
Bib: Willey, B., in *Eighteenth-century Background* and *The English Moralists*; Brett, R. L., *The Third Earl of Shaftesbury: a Study in Eighteenth-century Literary Theory*.

Shaftesbury, Lord (Anthony Ashley Cooper, 7th Earl of Shaftesbury, 1801–85)
Statesman and philanthropist. His politics were right wing, but he devoted his career to improving the condition of the working classes. It was largely owing to him that the Ten Hours Bill, restricting hours of work in factories became law in 1847, and in the same decade his efforts led to improvement in the mines. After 1846, he gave his attention to the London slums; clearance of the squalid district of Seven Dials* led to the building of Shaftesbury Avenue, called after him; the statue of Eros in Piccadilly Circus also commemorates him. Shaftesbury was an adherent of the religious revival known as the Evangelical Movement*, working against the Utilitarian* theories of the political economists (Adam Smith*, Jeremy Bentham*, Thomas Malthus*) in the shaping of the industrial changes and urban expansion of mid-19th C.

* *Industrial Revolution*.

Shakespeare, William (1564–1616) – Biography /ˈʃeikspiə/
Dramatist and poet. He was baptized on 26 April 1564; his birth is commemorated on 23 April, which happens also to be St George's Day, the festival of the patron saint of England. His father, John Shakespeare was a Stratford-on-Avon merchant who dealt in gloves and probably other goods; his grandfather, Richard Shakespeare, was a yeoman, *ie* small farmer, and his mother, Mary Arden, was the daughter of a local farmer who belonged to the local noble family of Arden, after whom the forest to the north of Stratford was called. John Shakespeare's affairs prospered at first, and in 1568 he was appointed to the highest office in the town – High Bailiff, equivalent to Mayor. A grammar school existed in Stratford, and since it was free to the sons of burgesses, it is generally assumed that William attended it. If he did, he probably received a good education in the Latin language; there is evidence that the sons of Stratford merchants were, or could be, well read and well educated. He married Anne Hathaway in 1582, and they had three children: Suzanna, born 1583, and the twin son and daughter, Hamnet and Judith, born 1585.

Thereafter Shakespeare's life is a blank, until we meet a reference to him in *A Groatsworth of Wit* (1592), an autobiographical pamphlet by the London playwright Robert Greene*, who accuses him of plagiarism. By 1592, therefore, Shakespeare was already successfully embarked as a dramatist in London, but there is no clear evidence of when he went there. From 1592 to 1594 the London theatres were closed owing to epidemics of plague, and Shakespeare seems to have used the opportunity to make a reputation for himself as a narrative poet: his *Venus and Adonis** was published in 1593, and *The Rape of Lucrece* (* *Lucrece*) a year later. Both were dedicated to Henry Wriothesley, Earl of Southampton. He continued to prosper as a dramatist, and in the winter of 1594 was a leading member of the Lord Chamberlain's Company with whom he remained for the rest of his career. In 1596 his father acquired a coat of arms – the sign of a Gentleman* – and in 1597 William bought New Place, the largest house in Stratford. There he probably established his father, who had been in financial difficulties since 1577. In 1592, John Shakespeare had been registered as a recusant (* *Recusancy*); this might mean that he was a Catholic, but is more likely to show that he was trying to escape arrest for debt.

In 1598, Francis Meres*, in his literary commentary *Palladis Tamia, Wit's Treasury*, mentions Shakespeare as one of the leading writers of the time, lists 12 of his plays, and mentions his sonnets* as circulating privately; they were published in 1609. The Lord Chamberlain's Company* opened the Globe* Theatre in 1598, and Shakespeare became a shareholder in it. After the accession of James I* the company came under royal patronage, and were called the King's Men; this gave Shakespeare a status in the royal household. He is known to have been an actor as well as a playwright, but tradition associates him with small parts: Adam in *As You Like It**, and the Ghost in *Hamlet**. He may have retired to New Place in Stratford in 1610, but he continued his connections with London, and purchased a house in Blackfriars in 1613. In the same year, the Globe theatre was burnt down during a performance of the last play with which his name is associated, *Henry VIII**. His will is dated less than a month from his death. The fact that he left his 'second-best bed' to his wife is no evidence that he was on bad terms with her; the best one would naturally go with his main property to his elder daughter, who had married John Hall; his younger daughter, who had married Thomas Quiney, was also provided for, but his son, Hamnet, had died in childhood. His last direct descendant, Lady Barnard, died in 1670.

Owing to the fact that the subject-matter of biography was restricted until mid-17th C to princes, statesmen and great soldiers, the documentary evidence of Shakespeare's life is, apart from the above facts, slight. His contemporaries, Christopher Marlowe* and Ben Jonson*, are in some respects better documented because they involved themselves more with political events. Many legends and traditions have grown up about Shakespeare since near his own day, but they are untrustworthy. He was certainly one of the most successful English writers of his time; his income has been estimated at about £200 a year, considerable earnings for those days. After the death of Marlowe in 1593, his greatest rival was Ben Jonson, who criticized his want of art (in *Discoveries* 1640), admired his character, and paid a noble tribute to him in the prefatory poem to the First Folio* collection of his plays (1623). There is no evidence that Shakespeare did not write the plays attributed to him and no reason why he should not have done so.

Bib: Halliday, F. E., *A Shakespeare Companion*; Halliwell-Phillipps, J. O., *Outlines of the Life of S.*; Lee, Sidney, *Life*; Chambers, E. K., *William Shakespeare*; Harrison, G. B., *Introducing Shakespeare*; Alexander, P., *Shakespeare*.

Shakespeare – Criticism

As with any author of the first greatness, different ages have appreciated different aspects of Shakespeare. In his own day, popular taste, according to Ben Jonson*, particularly enjoyed *Titus Andronicus**, now regarded as one of the least interesting of his plays. Dryden* (*Essay on Dramatic Poesy**), picked out *Richard II**; Johnson* (*Preface to Shakespeare*, 1765) admired the comedies. It is possible to understand these preferences: *Titus* is the most bloodthirsty of all the plays, and suited the more vulgar tastes of an age in which executions were popular spectacles. Dryden and Johnson both belonged to neo-classical* periods; Dryden accordingly liked a play which nowadays is considered comparatively lacking in depth and complexity, but which for him was stately and shapely; Johnson, like Dryden, was troubled by the differences in Shakespeare's tragedies from the formalism of ancient Greek and 17th-C tragedy which the spirit of their period encouraged them to admire, and Johnson's warm humanity caused him to respond to the plays which displayed wide human appeal while their mode permitted some licence of form. Both Johnson and Dryden rose superior to the limitations of their period in according Shakespeare high greatness; for an idea of neo-classicism at its narrowest, though wittily expressed, one should read Thomas Rymer's* *Short View of Tragedy* (1692). 19th-C romanticism appreciated Shakespeare's tragedy; Coleridge* (*Shakespearian Criticism*, ed. T. M. Raysor), and A. C. Bradley* (*Shakespearian Tragedy*, 1904) are the most important critics. In 20th C, more attention has been directed than ever before to Shakespeare's language and imagery; two generations of symbolist poets (French and English) have trained the taste of critics in appreciation of the late 'romances' – *Pericles**, *Cymbeline**, *The Winter's Tale**, and *The Tempest**. Modern critics tend nonetheless to agree with those of 19th C in judging the supreme work of Shakespeare to be the five great tragedies: *Othello**, *King Lear**, *Macbeth**, *Antony and Cleopatra**, and *Coriolanus**. Opinion varies whether *Hamlet** should be included with these five.

Wilson Knight (*The Wheel of Fire*, *The Imperial Theme*, *The Crown of Life*) is the most influential of the 20th-C critics. H. Granville-Barker (*Prefaces to Shakespeare*) combines deep insight with his practical experience as a theatrical producer and actor. Among the best recent introductions is D. A. Traversi's *Approach to Shakespeare*.

Other useful books: Halliday, F. E., *A Shakespeare Companion*; Smith, D. N., ed. *Shakespeare Criticism* (for earlier studies); Bradby, A., ed. *Shakespeare Criticism 1919–35 & 1935–60* (separate volumes); *Shakespeare Quarterly* and *Shakespeare Survey* (annual); Fluchère, H., *Shakespeare* (trans. from French); Eliot, T. S., on Shakespeare, on Seneca, and on *Hamlet* in *Selected Essays*; Leavis, F. R., on *Measure for Measure* and *Othello* in *The Common Pursuit*; Knights, L. C., on the Sonnets in *Explorations*; Stoll, E. E., *Shakespeare Studies*.

Shakespeare – History of Textual Study

Apart from a scene sometimes ascribed to Shakespeare in the play *Sir Thomas More* (1596), none of Shakespeare's work has survived in manuscript. In his own lifetime, eighteen of his plays were published in separate volumes (the Quartos*), but this was probably without the author's permission,

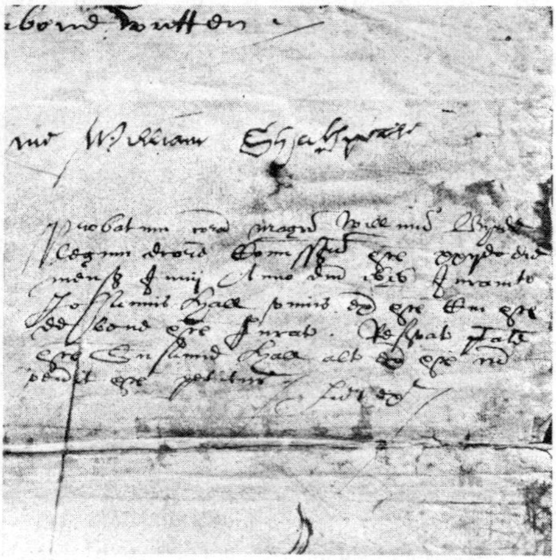

and therefore without his revisions and textual corrections. His non-dramatic poems, including the Sonnets*, were also published during his lifetime. After his death, his fellow-actors, Heming and Condell, published his collected plays (except *Pericles**) in the large, single volume known as the First Folio*, and this was succeeded by the Second Folio (1632), and the Third (two editions), and Fourth in 1663, 1664 and 1685. The Second Folio regularized the division of the plays into Acts and Scenes, and the second issue of the Third added *Pericles*, as well as other plays which are certainly not by Shakespeare. In several important respects the Folio editions were unsatisfactory:

[1] The texts of some (though not all) of the smaller quarto volumes of the plays published during the poet's lifetime differed materially from the text of even the First Folio, which in turn differed from the later folios.

[2] The First Folio arranged the plays according to their kinds (Comedies, Histories, or Tragedies) and gave no indication of the order in which the plays were written.

[3] There was no evidence that even the first editors had had access to the best manuscript texts, and there were evident errors in some passages, the fault of either the editors or their printers, and editors of the later Folios made alterations of their own. Consequently, there was plenty of work during the next two centuries for scholars to re-establish, as nearly as possible, Shakespeare's original text. Work also had to be done on the chronological order of the plays, discovery of the sources of their plots, philological investigations of linguistic peculiarities, and research into the conditions in which the plays were originally acted.

Two of the most eminent 18th-C writers published editions of the plays; these were Alexander Pope* (in 1725 and 1728), and Samuel Johnson* (in 1765). Neither, however, was a sound scholarly edition, though Johnson's was important for its critical Preface and annotations. Lewis Theobald (1688–1744) attacked Pope's poor scholarship in his *Shakespeare Restored* (1726), and published his own edition in 1734. He was the first enlightened editor, and did permanently useful work both in removing post-Shakespearian additions and alterations and in suggesting emendations of corrupt passages. After him came Steevens and Capell, who compared the original Quarto texts with the Folio ones, and Edmond Malone (1741–1812), the most eminent of the 18th-C Shakespeare scholars. In 1778 he made the first serious attempt to establish the chronological order of the plays, and in 1790 he brought out the best edition of them yet established.

Shakespearian scholarship in 18th C was more the work of individuals than a collaborative enterprise. They saw many of the problems involved in estimating the relative values of the early texts, the possibilities of scholarly emendation of corrupt passages, and the necessity of eliminating the errors of unscholarly 17th- and 18th-C editors. This work culminated in the publication of 'Variorum' editions of the plays, 1803–21. But the establishment of a really sound text required the study of wider subject-matter: Shakespeare's work had to be estimated as a whole so that his development could be understood; philological study of the state of the language in his time was needed; historical events had to be examined for their possible relevance; many sources for the plots remained to be discovered; theatrical conditions and the relationship of Shakespeare to dramatists contemporary with him needed exploration; even handwriting was important, for the detection of possible misprinting. All this was the work of the collaborative scholarship of 19th C. It was carried out by German scholars, by the English Shakespeare Societies led by Halliwell and Furnivall, and by the universities.

In later 18th C Shakespeare became an inspiration to the movement in Germany for the emancipation of German culture from its long subjection to French culture, represented by the very different genius of Racine*. A. W. Schlegel's remarkable translations (1797–1810) were fine enough to enable Germans to adopt Shakespeare as something like a national poet. German scholars such as Tieck, Ulrici, Gervinus and Franz adopted Shakespearian studies with thoroughness and enthusiasm. They stimulated the foundation of Shakespeare Societies in England, and in 1863–66 the Cambridge University Press was able to publish an edition of Shakespeare's works, which, in its revised form (1891–93), is substantially the text now generally in use.

In 20th C, the major English scholars have been John Dover Wilson, editor of the *New Shakespeare* (begun in 1921, rivalling the Arden edition begun earlier in the century), and Sir Edmund Chambers*. Chambers's books (*The Elizabethan Stage*, 1923, and *William Shakespeare*, 1930) were culminations of work on Shakespeare himself and on the theatre as it existed in his time. Important on textual problems: W. W. Grey's *The Editorial Problem in Shakespeare*.

The first serious attempt to produce a play in the theatrical conditions of Shakespeare's own day was made with *The Taming of the Shrew** in 1844. Most modern productions show some influence from research into Elizabethan stage conditions done since.

Shakespeare's Plays

Earliest publications. The first collected edition was the volume always known as the First Folio* (1623). This included all the plays now acknowledged to be by Shakespeare, with the exception of *Pericles*. It also includes *Henry VIII*, which most critics now consider to be mainly by John Fletcher*. Stationers* (the profession then combining bookselling and publishing) were glad to bring out individual plays in quarto editions in his lifetime, however, and since there was no law of copyright these were often 'pirated', *ie* published without the permission of the author. On the whole, Shakespeare's company (the Lord Chamberlain's Company*) did not want such publication, since printed editions enabled other acting companies to perform the plays in competition. Eighteen of Shakespeare's plays were published in this way, sometimes in more than one edition, and occasionally in editions that varied considerably. Since none of the plays has survived in the original manuscript, the task of modern editors is often to reconcile different quartos (where they exist) with each other, and any quartos that exist with corresponding versions in the First Folio. Shakespeare is not known to have revised any of his plays for publication. The following is a list of the separate editions of the plays, published while Shakespeare was alive or soon after his death, with dates of different editions where they substantially disagree with one another:

Titus Andronicus (1594)
2 Henry VI (1594)
3 Henry VI (1595)
Richard II (1597, 1608)
Richard III (1597)
Romeo and Juliet (1597, 1599)
Love's Labour's Lost (1598)
1 Henry IV (1598)
2 Henry IV (1600)
Henry V (1600)
A Midsummer Night's Dream (1600)
The Merchant of Venice (1600)
Much Ado About Nothing (1600)
The Merry Wives of Windsor (1602)
Hamlet (1603, 1604)
King Lear (1608)
Troilus and Cressida (1609)
Pericles (1609)
Othello (1622)

Order of composition. The First Folio does not print the plays in the order in which they were written. Scholars have had to work out their chronological order, on three main kinds of evidence: [1] external evidence (*eg* records of production, publication); [2] internal evidence (*eg* allusions to contemporary events); [3] stylistic evidence. The following, mainly the work of Sir Edmund Chambers*, is an approximate chronological arrangement, though in some instances there is no certainty:

1590–91	2, 3 Henry VI
1591–92	1 Henry VI
1592–93	Richard III
	Comedy of Errors
1593–94	Titus Andronicus
	Taming of the Shrew
1594–95	Two Gentlemen of Verona
	Love's Labour's Lost
	Romeo and Juliet
1595–96	Richard II
	Midsummer Night's Dream
1596–97	King John
	Merchant of Venice
1597–98	1, 2 Henry IV
1598–99	Much Ado about Nothing
	Henry V
1599–1600	Julius Caesar
	Merry Wives of Windsor
	As You Like It
	Twelfth Night
1600–1	Hamlet
1601–2	Troilus and Cressida
1602–3	All's Well that Ends Well
1604–5	Measure for Measure
	Othello
1605–6	Macbeth
	King Lear
1606–7	Antony and Cleopatra
1607–8	Coriolanus
	Timon of Athens
1608–9	Pericles
1609–10	Cymbeline

1610–11 Winter's Tale
1611–12 Tempest

Two doubtful plays, *Henry VIII* and *Two Noble Kinsmen*, are dated 1612–13. Shakespeare probably had a hand in both.

Phases of development. The settling (more or less) of the chronological order of the plays has enabled critics to discern a process of artistic development in Shakespeare's work. It is to some extent a guide to the student and may be summarized as follows. Shakespeare's development passed through five phases, the last two of which are more clearly distinguishable than the three preceding ones.

[1] From *Henry VI* to *Romeo and Juliet*: early work, in which the dramatist experiments in a number of different modes – histories, varieties of comedy, a revenge tragedy*, a romantic tragedy. The style mainly consists of end-stopped* blank verse*, with fairly plentiful rhyme in some, and no great complexity of imagery.

[2] From *Richard II* to *Twelfth Night*: Shakespeare gradually develops a fully mature style, flexible in syntax and rhythm, concentrated in imagery, increasingly forceful in characterization.

[3] From *Hamlet* to *Measure for Measure*: the 'problem plays'*, which set peculiar difficulties in regard to interpretation. *Hamlet* is a tragedy, but unlike all others of Shakespeare; the other three are comedies of remarkable sombreness.

[4] From *Othello* to the probably uncompleted *Timon of Athens*: the great tragedies, showing a now fully developed style, and a mode of tragic thought which is unlike either the great tragedies of ancient Greece or the cruder conceptions of the Middle Ages* and the Renaissance*.

[5] From the imperfect *Pericles* to the *Tempest*: the romances or 'reconciliation plays'*. They are romances because in them Shakespeare abandons the realism, or partial realism of the tragedies; they are reconciliation plays because tragedy is transmuted into reconciliation of the opposing elements.

* 5.1.3.1–3.

Shalott

* *Lady of Shalott*.

Shamrock

A plant whose leaf is divided into three segments; the leaf is used as the national emblem of Ireland. Legend says that St Patrick*, who converted Ireland to Christianity early in 5th C, used the leaf to exemplify the doctrine of the Trinity.

Shaw, George Bernard (1856–1950)

Dramatist, critic, social thinker. His family belonged to the Irish Protestant gentry. His father was an unsuccessful business man; his mother was a musician of talent. Apart from the musical education he received from her, he was practically self-educated. He came to London in 1876, and set to work as a novelist. The novel proved not to be his medium, but his efforts in the form were an apprenticeship for dramatic writing in which he excelled. He wrote five novels in all: the best known are *Cashel Byron's Profession* (pub 1885–6), and *The Admirable Bashville* (pub 1901). In 1884 he joined the newly formed socialist Fabian Society*, of which he became a leading member; he edited *Fabian Essays* (1887) which was influential in forming socialist opinion in Britain. Between 1885 and 1898 he wrote much criticism for a number of papers; he was the best music and dramatic critic of his time.

His career as a dramatist began in 1892 and lasted substantially until 1939, though he wrote his last play when he was over 90. Through Joseph Archer, the translator, he had come to know the work of the Norwegian dramatist Henrik Ibsen* and was profoundly impressed especially by Ibsen's plays of social criticism, *eg A Doll's House.* In 1891 came his study *The Quintessence of Ibsenism*, and then he embarked on plays of social purpose on his own account. Shaw's art is, however, very different from Ibsen's; whereas for Ibsen the characters are always more important than the ideas in a play, and the characters engage in convincing talk, in Shaw it is the ideas that really matter, and his characters don't talk – they make speeches. The speeches are composed in the operatic tradition of Mozart; Shaw once said that it was Mozart who taught him to write. As a dramatic critic and a student of Ibsen, he had learnt stagecraft thoroughly, and he knew how to achieve theatrical effect, to which his unique talent for wit, surprise, and paradox strongly contributed. In regard to ideas, he was concerned to shock his audiences out of their unthinking acceptance of social conventions, but he was careful (unlike Ibsen) never to scandalize them beyond their willingness to listen. Apart from socialism, his leading doctrine (derived partly from the French philosopher Bergson and partly from the German philosopher Nietzsche*) was his belief in the 'Life Force' – that the progress of humanity depends in every generation on the evolution of geniuses, who comprise the spearheads of advance but inevitably arouse the hostility of their contemporaries. He was the first dramatist to realize that the reading public for plays was now larger than the theatre-going public; accordingly he published his own plays with long prefaces, which are commonly as famous as the plays themselves, and with elaborate state directions intended not only for stage producers but for readers accustomed to the kind of detail provided by novels.

His most famous plays are probably *Man and Superman* (1903); *Major Barbara* (1905); *Pygmalion** (1912); *Heartbreak House** (1917); *Back to Methuselah* (1921); *Saint Joan* (1924); Other plays: in *Plays Pleasant and Unpleasant** (1898) – *Widowers' Houses* (first staged 1892); *The Philanderer*; *Mrs Warren's Profession*; *Arms and the Man**; *Candida**; *The Man of Destiny*; *You Never Can Tell.* In *Plays for Puritans** (1901) – *The Devil's Disciple*; *Caesar and Cleopatra**; *Captain Brassbound's Conversion.* Other plays before 1914: *John Bull's Other Island*; *How He Lied to Her Husband*; *Press Cuttings*; *The Doctor's Dilemma**;

Getting Married; *The Showing up of Blanco Posnet*; *Misalliance*; *Fanny's First Play*; *Androcles and the Lion**; *Overruled*; *Great Catherine*. After 1918: *The Apple Cart**; *In Good King Charles's Golden Days*.

Among Shaw's extensive political writings are his attack on the British government, *Common Sense about the War* (1914) and *The Intelligent Woman's Guide to Socialism and Capitalism* (1928).

* 3.4.5; 5.3.1.

Bib: Pearson, H., *Life*; Henderson, A., *Life*; Chesterton, G. K., *George Bernard Shaw*; Bentley, E., *George Bernard Shaw*; Meisel, M., *Shaw and the Nineteenth Century*.

She Stoops to Conquer

A comedy by Oliver Goldsmith*, first acted in 1773. The basic comedy is that of a morbidly shy man misled into a situation in which he behaves in a way such as to horrify him when he awakes to the true circumstances. The young man is Marlow, sent by his father to court in marriage the daughter of his friend Hardcastle. Marlow loses his way, and is deceived into supposing the Hardcastle house to be an inn. In a gentleman's house he is horribly embarrassed, but in an inn he is at ease; he proceeds to behave off-handedly to old Hardcastle as to a landlord, and to make love to his daughter, as to a waiting maid. The arrival of his father clears up the situation, and the mistake turns out to Marlow's advantage. The play is one of Goldsmith's best works, and an example of the brief revival of the comedy of manners* in the 1770s.

* 5.2.2.

Sheba, The Queen of /ˈʃiːbə/

In the Bible, the great queen from the south (southern Arabia?) who comes to visit and admire Solomon*, king of the Jews – *1 Kings* 10.

Shelley, Percy Bysshe (1792–1822) /ˈʃeli/

Poet. He belonged to an old aristocratic family, but grew up with violently revolutionary ideas, which contrasted with those of his father. After schooldays at Eton, he went to Oxford University, but was expelled on account of his pamphlet *The Necessity of Atheism* (1811). He eloped with and married Harriet Westbrook, and then joined the circle of the revolutionary philosopher, William Godwin*. Later he eloped abroad with Godwin's daughter, Mary Wollstonecraft Godwin, accompanied by her step-sister, Claire Clairmont. In Switzerland they met Byron*, with whom Shelley made a close friendship. Another important literary friend of Shelley's was Leigh Hunt*, the radical journalist, whom he helped to achieve collaboration with Byron in the short-lived *Liberal* periodical. Later, Shelley was drowned while sailing. His first wife had already committed suicide in the Serpentine in London, and he had married Mary Wollstonecraft Godwin.

Shelley believed that religion was an instrument of oppression, that the French Revolution* had been betrayed, that man was naturally good and only vitiated by social institutions, that love between the sexes was naturally, and should be actually, free. These opinions were in line with the beliefs of Godwin, who, however, ceased to approve of free love when it invaded his own household. Mary Wollstonecraft Godwin was the daughter of Godwin's first wife Mary Wollstonecraft, author of a celebrated work on women's emancipation called *Vindication of the Rights of Women* (1792).

Shelley's very early writings show him to have been strongly affected by the Gothic* school of writers, such as 'Monk' Lewis*. His first work of any note was his atheistic poem *Queen Mab* (written in 1813, and published without his permission in 1821) which he later disowned as juvenile. In 1816 he wrote the more notable *Alastor, or the Spirit of Solitude*, a condemnation of self-centred idealism; in 1817, *The Revolt of Islam*, preaching bloodless revolution; in 1818, *Julian and Maddalo*, a fine poem, about the power of man over his mind, describing a visit of himself and Byron to a madhouse. In 1819 he published *The Cenci**, a drama very much in the Elizabethan style, a study of evil, and composed *Prometheus Unbound**, his best long poem, expounding his imaginative philosophy of revolution. In 1819 he also wrote the best known of all his poems, *Ode to the West Wind*. It was followed by: *The Witch of Atlas*, *The Cloud*, *To a Skylark* (1820); then his famous elegy on Keats*, *Adonais**, the love poem, *Epipsychidion*, and the lyrical drama inspired by the struggle for Greek independence, *Hellas* (1821). He was working on *The Triumph of Life* when he died. Shelley was a prolific poet, and this list includes only his more ambitious poems, and some of the best known of his shorter ones. It is the shorter poems that are now chiefly read; a characteristic judgement on his longer ones is J. S. Mill's*: 'He had scarcely yet acquired the consecutiveness of thought necessary for a long poem; his more ambitious compositions too often resemble the scattered fragments of a mirror; colours brilliant as life, single images without end, but no picture.' An exception is *The Mask of Anarchy** (1819), an uncharacteristically harsh and clear poem inspired by the Peterloo* riots in Manchester.

Shelley's one distinguished piece of prose is his *Defence of Poetry* written in answer to his friend Peacock's* *The Four Ages of Poetry* which argued that poetry was an obsolete art.

* 6.3.4; 7.3.

Bib: White, N. I., *Life*; Cameron, K. N., *The Young Shelley: Genesis of a Radical*; Blunden, E., *Life*; Grabo, C., *The Magic Plant: the Growth of Shelley's Thought*; Butter, P. H., *Shelley's Idols of the Cave*; Rogers, N., *Shelley at Work*.

Sheol

Among the ancient Jews, the underworld of the dead; place of darkness.

Shepherd's Calendar, The [by Edmund Spenser]

A pastoral* poem by Spenser* in 12 parts, one for each month of the year, published in 1579. The series is written in the tradition of the 'eclogues' of

Virgil*, *ie* verse dialogues in a rural setting, with shepherds and shepherdesses with classical, French or (more frequently) English peasant names, *eg* Colin Clout (for Spenser himself) and Hobbinol (for his friend Gabriel Harvey). The intention is not that of 19th-C nature poetry (contrast Clare's *Shepherd's Calendar*) to give a description of the countryside as it actually is at any particular time of the year, but to use the simplified conditions of an ideal rural setting as a standpoint for commenting on life. Four of the dialogues ('January', 'June', 'November' and 'December') are complaints*, *ie* laments for such things as lost love ('January') or advancing age ('December'). Three of them are cheerful: 'March', in praise of love; 'April' in praise of Queen Elizabeth; and 'August', a shepherds' song competition, again in praise of love. 'February', 'May', 'July', 'September' and 'October' are 'moral' eclogues on such topics as respect for age ('February') or a Protestant* attack on Roman Catholicism ('May'). The three main themes are love, poetry and religion. The verse is sophisticated and varied, owing much to the examples of Virgil and Theocritus*, and also to the French 16th-C pastoralist Clement Marot, but paying tribute to Chaucer* as well and following the free rhythms of medieval English poetry. The poem set a fashion for pastoral in England, and inaugurated the great lyrical period of the last 20 years of 16th C.

*** 6.2.1.**

Shepherd's Calendar, The

[by John Clare]

A poem in 12 parts, one for each month of the year, published in 1827. Clare* has been called 'the best naturalist in English poetry', and these poems are perhaps the best example of his fresh, exact, detailed vision. His publisher, John Taylor, however, thought otherwise, and extensively cut and edited the work. This, and the poor reception of the book, was one of the causes of the decline in Clare's mental health. Each poem gives an account of the English countryside as it commonly appears in the corresponding time of year, but the observation is keen and particular, and the reader does not feel that he is reading what is merely general and representative. The poem has only recently (1964) been restored to the original version which Clare submitted to Taylor.

Sheraton, Thomas (1751–1806) /ˈʃerətn/

Next to Chippendale* the most famous English furniture designer. His reputation, which began about 1790, was built up on his severe and graceful style; later, under the influence of French Empire furniture, his designs became much more elaborate. He had many imitators, and the name 'Sheraton' is usually associated with a general style rather than with the works of the original master. It is the style that an English reader imagines as the background of Jane Austen's* novels.

A Sheraton chair

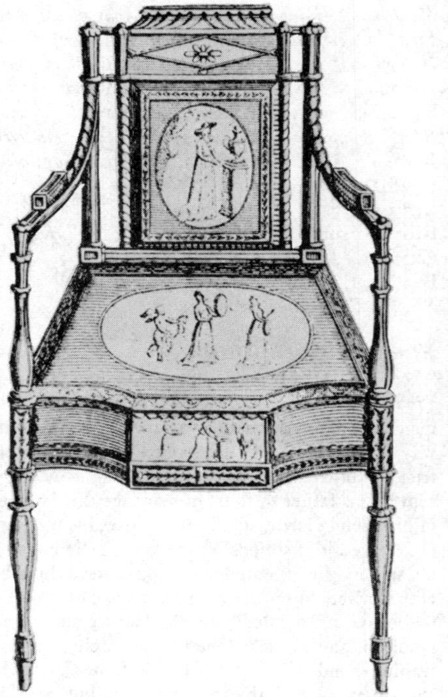

Sheridan, Richard Brinsley Butler (1751–1816) /ˈʃeridn/

Dramatist and politician. Like all dramatists of note writing in English during 18th and 19th C, he was of Irish extraction, born in Dublin. The romantic story of his marriage with the beautiful young Elizabeth Linley, began with his carrying her off to a French nunnery to save her from the attentions of a suitor to whom she objected; he returned to fight two duels with his rival; in 1773 his secret marriage to her in France was publicly recognized. In 1776 he became principal director and, a little later, sole proprietor of the Drury Lane* theatre in London; it was twice burnt down and rebuilt during his proprietorship. He entered Parliament in 1780, and was famous for his oratory there; his opposition to the American War of Independence caused the American Congress to offer him £20,000, which he refused. His most famous oratorical exploit was his impeachment of Warren Hastings in 1787. During the French Revolution*, he supported the Whig* leader, Fox*, in opposing military intervention against France. Later he held an independent position politically, but he was influential, partly owing to his friendship with the Prince Regent (later George IV). He ended his life deeply in debt.

His memorable plays are *The Rivals** (1775), *The School for Scandal** (1777), and *The Critic* (1779); they show a reaction against the sentimental comedy which had dominated the English theatre for most of 18th C, and the first two belong to a revival of the comedy of manners* which had been dominant at the beginning of it. They are still appreciated for the freshness of their dialogue and the ingenuity of their comic situations. Other plays:

St Patrick's Day (1775); *The Duenna* (a comic opera, 1775); *A Trip to Scarborough* (1777), an adaptation of Vanbrugh's *Relapse* (1696), and the tragedy *Pizarro* (1799).

* 5.2.2.

Bib: Sichel, W., *Life*; Nicoll, A., *A History of Late Eighteenth-century Drama*; Sadleir, T. H., *The Political Career of Sheridan*.

Sherry

A fortified wine, very popular in Britain since 16th C (Falstaff is eloquent about it in Shakespeare's play *2 Henry IV* IV. iii). It is nowadays taken chiefly before dinner. The name is a corruption of Xeres (now Jerez de la Frontera), a town in Spain near which it was originally made.

Ship Money

An ancient tax for providing ships to defend the country in time of war. Charles I* revived it in 1634 in time of peace and without the consent of Parliament*. His action caused great resentment, but 12 judges gave their verdict that it was legal. Nonetheless, repeated revivals of the tax aroused positive resistance, notably from John Hampden, and it was one of the contributory causes of the Civil War* that broke out in 1642. In 1641 Parliament passed a law declaring Ship Money an illegal tax.

Shipman's Tale, The

One of Chaucer's *Canterbury Tales**. It is in 10-syllable couplets*. There is internal evidence that Chaucer originally intended it to be told by a woman – probably the Wife of Bath. It is a fabliau* about the wife of a merchant who keeps her short of money. She seeks the money from a priest, who borrows it from her husband and then gives it to her in return for her favours. Later, when the husband asks the priest to return the money, the latter tells him that he has repaid it to the wife, who tells her husband that she repays him daily – a statement of their relations which the merchant is obliged to accept. Chaucer probably based the story on one by Boccaccio* in *Decameron* viii, 1.

Shirley, James (1596–1666) /ˈʃɜːli/

Dramatist. He was one of the last dramatists of the great Elizabethan–Jacobean–Caroline period of English drama, a period which lasted from 1580 to 1640 and included the career of Shakespeare*. Shirley wrote fluent, graceful blank verse* and is at his best in social comedy; in many ways he anticipates the Restoration* writers of comedies of manners* after 1660. His audience, as in Restoration comedy, was that of the elegant, refined court; it was not drawn from all social classes like the audiences for Shakespeare and Ben Jonson*, so that his plays have a comparatively narrow though sophisticated range of interests. He wrote over 40 plays, of which the best known are the tragedies *The Traitor* (1631) and *The Cardinal* (1641); and the comedies *Hyde Park* (1632) and *The Lady of Pleasure* (1635).

* 5.1.4.

Bib: Harbage, A., *Cavalier Drama*; Lynch, K. M., *The Social Mode of Restoration Comedy*.

Shirley (1849)

A novel by Charlotte Brontë*. It is set in the north of England, and deals with the bad labour relations of the time of the Napoleonic Wars (1803–15). A mill-owner, Robert Gérard Moore (half Belgian and half English), introduces labour-saving machinery against the opposition of his workers, who threaten to destroy the mill. He attempts to gain money by marrying the rich and proud Shirley Keeldar, who refuses him and eventually marries his brother Louis, opposed to Robert. The end of the war releases Robert from his financial difficulties, and he marries Caroline Helstone, whom he really loves and who loves him. The novel was characteristic of a number written during the 1840s and early 1850s (by Dickens*, Disraeli*, Mrs Gaskell*) on the social problems of class hostility, and it is this part of *Shirley* which is now generally admired; otherwise the novel is normally considered inferior to the other two novels of Charlotte Brontë's maturity, *Jane Eyre** and *Villette**. In the character of Shirley Keeldar, Charlotte portrayed her sister Emily Brontë*.

Shoemaker's Holiday, The

A comedy by Thomas Dekker*, published in 1600. It is a citizen comedy*, *ie* designed to appeal to the taste and sentiment of the London merchant class, with a strong romantic flavour. The time of the story is mid-15th C, and the principal character is Simon Eyre, shoemaker and, at the end of the play, Lord Mayor of London. The story concerns the courtship by the young nobleman, Rowland Lacy, of Rose, the daughter of the existing Lord Mayor. The courtship is opposed both by his uncle, the Earl of Lincoln, and by Rose's father. Lacy disguises himself as a shoemaker, takes employment with Simon Eyre, and eventually, with the support of the king, they are successfully married. The play is mainly in prose, with blank verse interspersed; it has no profundity but its mood of joyousness has kept it popular.

Shoreditch /ˈʃɔːditʃ/

A district of east London; it was the first to have a theatre (1576–77). According to legend, its name derives from Jane Shore, the mistress of Edward IV*; she is supposed to have died in a ditch there. In fact the name is older.

* *Theatres*.

Short Story

This very ancient kind of fiction was first taken seriously in 19th C as an independent literary form, making different demands on the writer and the reader from the demands of longer works of fiction such as the novel. Three writers originated this serious practice of the art of the short story: the American, Edgar Allan Poe (1809–49); the Frenchman, Poe's disciple, Guy de Maupassant (1850–93); and the Russian, Anton Chekhov*. These writers evolved the qualities especially associated with the short story: close texture, unity of mood, suggestive idiom, economy of means. Such qualities associate the short story with the short poem, and we find that in English the verse story anticipated the prose story in work such as the tales of George Crabbe* and Arthur Hugh Clough's* *Mari Magno* (1862). However, no relationship can be established between the verse of such writers and the prose of Rudyard Kipling*, with Maupassant behind him, or that of Katherine Mansfield*, who was strongly influenced by Anton Chekhov. These two wrote little else in prose except stories (Kipling wrote two novels), but the greatest masters of the short story form – Henry James*, Joseph Conrad*, James Joyce*, and D. H. Lawrence* – were predominantly novelists. Their stories were perhaps formed less by the example of the foreign writers mentioned than by the structure of their own novels. These had a less distinctly marked plot line than those of earlier novelists, and yet a closer coherence; chapters from them can be extracted showing many of the essential qualities of short stories (*eg* 'Rabbit' in Lawrence's *Women in Love**, or the Christmas dinner in Joyce's *Portrait of the Artist**) in spite of their relationship to their respective novels as wholes. It seems therefore that the best stories of these writers were by-products of their novels, which by their structure suggested the evolution of stories as separate entities.

It is difficult to make a clear distinction between the short story and the *nouvelle* (or novelette, or long story); it is difficult also to say at what point a *nouvelle* stops short of being a novel; on the whole the *nouvelle* or 'long short story' seems to share with the short story as generally understood a unity of mood which is not so likely to be found in a true novel, however short. All the masters of the short story who have been mentioned were also masters of the *nouvelle*, but not necessarily (*eg* Chekhov) of the novel form.

The period 1880–1930 was the flowering time of the short story in English; besides the English writers already mentioned, it included the early and best work of A. E. Coppard*, who was one of the few English fiction-writers of any note (Katherine Mansfield being another) who have restricted themselves to the short-story form. Later short-story writers have been numerous, but they have mostly practised the art as an alternative and often subsidiary form to that of the novel. In Ireland, where the art of the novel has scarcely taken root, the art of the short story has flourished more distinctively. It begins with the stories of George Moore* (*The Untilled Field*, 1903), but the Irish tradition becomes really outstanding in the first books of Liam O'Flaherty* (*Spring Sowing*, 1926), Sean O'Faolain* (*Midsummer Night Madness*, 1932), and Frank O'Connor* (*Guests of the Nation*, 1931). In his book on the art of the short story, *The Lonely Voice* (1964), O'Connor offers an explanation as to why the short story should be the more natural form of fiction for Irish literary culture.

Bib: Bates, H. E., *The Modern Short Story*; O'Faolain, S., *The Short Story*; O'Connor, F., *The Lonely Voice*; Bowen, E., Introduction to *The Faber Book of Short Stories*.

Shrovetide, Shrove Tuesday

The period, and in particular the day before, the six weeks of fast called Lent, which precedes Easter. The name derives from the verb 'to shrive', *ie* to absolve a person from his sins after he has confessed to a priest. Traditionally, it was a period of festivity before the period of fast; in England this festivity is now reduced to the eating of pancakes on the last day of shrovetide, *ie* Shrove Tuesday. The following day, Ash Wednesday, is the first day of Lent, during which luxuries are supposed to be renounced.

Sibyl /'sibil/

A proper name used, especially in ancient Greek myth, for women who were divinely inspired by the god Apollo* with the gift of prophecy. The original Sibylla is said (by Heraclitus*) to have lived at Marpessus, near Troy. She was supposed to be the author of the Sibylline Books which were kept in the temple of Jupiter Capitolinus at Rome. Apollo loved her, and granted her not only the gift of prophecy but as many years of life as grains of dust she could hold in her hand. However, she forgot to ask for eternal youth, and when, long after, some boys asked her what she wanted, she said that she wanted to die.

Sick Man of Europe, The

In the second half of 19th C, a way of referring to Turkey, regarding that country as one which was too large to ignore, yet too weak to be able to control its own conquered territories, so that it had become a subject of chronic international crisis. The phrase was originated by Tsar Nicholas I of Russia, in conversation with the British ambassador.

Siddons, Mrs Sarah (1755–1831)

The most famous of the 18th-C actresses. She encouraged the revival of interest in the performance of Shakespeare, notably by her role as Lady Macbeth. Other Shakespearian roles in which she achieved fame were Desdemona in *Othello*, Rosalind in *As You Like It*, Ophelia in *Hamlet*, and Katherine in *Henry VIII*. Contemporary plays, except for a few by Goldsmith* and Sheridan*, remained insignificant, but her acting excelled in some of them. Like David Garrick*, the most famous actor of the century, her genius tended to distract interest from the merit of plays to the merit of performances.

* *Acting, The Profession of*.

Sidney, Sir Philip (1554–86)

Poet, courtier, soldier and statesman. A member of a distinguished noble family, he was a fine example of the Renaissance* ideal of aristocracy in his ability to excel in all that was regarded as fitting for a nobleman. He thus became a pattern for his age, as is shown by the numerous elegies to him, including one by Spenser* (*Astrophel*) and one by James VI of Scotland. He was wounded at the battle of Zutphen in Flanders in characteristic circumstances, having discarded leg armour on finding that a comrade in arms had neglected to wear any; as he lay mortally wounded in the leg, he is reputed to have passed a cup of water to a dying soldier with the words, 'Thy need is greater than mine'.

Sidney's writings date mostly from the period 1580–83, when he was temporarily out of favour with Queen Elizabeth* for political reasons, and was living with his sister, Mary Countess of Pembroke* at Wilton House near Salisbury; they were published after his death. His most famous poetry, the sonnet* sequence, *Astrophil and Stella**, was published in 1591, and inspired the numerous other sonnet sequences of the 1590s, including Shakespeare's*. Apart from his sonnets, Sidney's poetic reputation rests on the verse interludes in *The Arcadia**, Sidney's prose romance, started in 1580 and published in 1590. His prose work also includes the most famous piece of Elizabethan criticism, the *Apology for Poetry**, published in 1595. A collaboration with his sister, the verse paraphrase of *The Psalms of David*, was not published till 1823. He also wrote two pastoral poems published in Davison's *Poetical Rhapsody* (1602) and partly translated from the French Du Plessis Mornay's *A Work Concerning the Trueness of the Christian Religion* (1587).

* 6.2.3; 7.1.

Bib: Lives by Malcolm W. Wallace, Mona Wilson, John Buxton; Myrick, K. O., *Sidney as a Literary Craftsman*; Davis, W. R., and Lanham, R. A. (jointly) on *Arcadia*; Smith, H., in *Elizabethan Poetry*; Atkins, J. W. H., in *English Literary Criticism: the Renascence.*

Silas Marner (1861)

A novel by George Eliot*. Silas is a weaver who has been driven out of a small community of dissenters* in a northern industrial town, in consequence of false information that he has stolen some of the community's funds. He emigrates to a midland village where he is in all essential respects 'a foreigner'. He sets up again as a weaver, but he has no relationship with his neighbours beyond the commercial one; having also lost his religious faith, he lives only for money and acquires a store of it. This is stolen from him by Dunstan Cass, son of the local squire*, but Silas's despair is later obliterated by the mysterious arrival in his cottage of a little girl, whom he adopts, calls Eppie, and devotes himself to. His love for her gradually brings to him the affection and respect of his neighbours. It turns out that Dunstan, who had vanished after the theft, had drowned immediately afterwards, and that Eppie is really the daughter of Dunstan's elder brother, Godfrey, by a low-class, drunken woman, now dead, to whom Godfrey was secretly married. Godfrey, now happily married but childless, claims Eppie when she is nearly grown up, but she refuses to part from Silas. The plot of the novel thus resembles a fable about living and deathly attachments, but it is a fable told with great realistic art, and as such is one of the perfect smaller masterpieces of the English novel.

Silenus /saiˈliːnəs/

In Greek myth, a minor woodland deity, usually depicted as drunk. He was generally represented as the son of Hermes* (sometimes Pan*) and Earth; the oldest satyr, he was also tutor to the wine god Dionysus* and one of his principal followers. He is usually depicted as a bald-headed fat old man riding on a donkey.

Sillitoe, Alan (b 1928) /ˈsilitəu/

Novelist and poet. The son of a labourer in a cycle factory, he left school at 14 to work in a similar factory. His birthplace was the midland town of Nottingham, near which D. H. Lawrence* was also brought up. Sillitoe, like Lawrence, writes from the standpoint of one whose origins are outside London and the middle classes, and he is the best known of a group of novelists that have arisen since the war with a similar background. The impress of Lawrence on these writers is inevitably strong, and especially so in the case of Sillitoe, but he presents a narrow spirit of social rebellion from which Lawrence is free. At present, his fame rests chiefly on his first novel, *Saturday Night and Sunday Morning* (1958), which has been filmed. The novel's hero, Arthur Seaton, has become a type-figure of post-1945 industrial, welfare state working man, born into an economic fabric against which his strong impulses rebel. More original and equally well known is the tale *The Loneliness of the Long-Distance Runner* (1959), a kind of fable of anarchic social rebellion. He has also written stories (*The Ragman's Daughter*, 1963); poems (*The Rats*, 1969; *A Falling Out of Love*, 1964); and more novels (*The General*, 1960, about the war in Malaya, in which Sillitoe served; *The Key to the Door*, 1961; *The Death of William Posters*, 1965); *A Tree on Fire* (1967); *A Start in Life* (1970); *Travels in Nihilon* (1971); *Raw Material* (1972); *The Flame of Life* (1974).

Simile

* *Figures of Speech.*

Simnel, Lambert (1477?–1525) /ˈsimnl/

An impostor, used by Yorkist opponents of Henry VII*, first king of the Tudor* family; they declared Simnel to be Edward, Earl of Warwick, whose father, George, Duke of Clarence, was the younger brother of Edward IV*. The true Earl of Warwick (1475–99) had been imprisoned by Henry VII. Simnel received extensive foreign support, but his army was defeated by Henry VII at Stoke-on-Trent in 1487. Henry spared Simnel's life, and made him a humble servant in the royal household.

Simple Simon

A character in nursery rhymes*, depicted as a comically stupid, simple-minded person.

Sinbad the Sailor /ˈsinbad/

The hero of one of the eastern tales called *Arabian Nights**. His best known adventure is that with the huge sea-bird called the Roc. (Also spelt Sindbad.)

Sir Charles Grandison, The History of (1754) /ˈgrandisn/

The last of the three novels presented through letters by Samuel Richardson*. It is an attempt to present the type of the perfect gentleman, just as its predecessor, *Clarissa Harlowe* (1748) had represented the perfect woman. It prescribes the kind of behaviour which Addison* had preached in his periodical *The Spectator**. However, it suffers much more than does *Clarissa* from the excessive idealization of its central character. The theme is right conduct in acute sentimental and ethical dilemma; Grandison is in love with Harriet Byron (whom he rescues from the vicious Sir Hargrave Pollexfen), but has obligations to Clementina Porretta, member of a noble Italian family. Among other lessons, Sir Charles shows how a gentleman can avoid fighting a duel without losing his honour. The book has some good minor characters, and is an interesting study in manners, though Richardson did not understand the Italian aristocracy of his period. As a psychological study, it is much inferior to *Clarissa* but it influenced the work of the first fully mature English novelist, Jane Austen*.

Sir Patrick Spens /spenz/

An old Scottish ballad* describing the loss at sea of a Scottish ship, its commander Sir Patrick, and all the crew. It exists in several versions; in the best and shortest, the ship puts to sea in bad weather at the order of the king, and Sir Patrick foresees the disaster – brought about, apparently, by royal vanity. In the longest version, the ship goes to Norway to bring back a princess, who may be based on the Maid of Norway who died at sea in 1290, or may be the Scandinavian queen of James VI (16th C); the Norwegian lords complain about the behaviour of the Scottish nobility, who leave suddenly, in bad weather, having taken offence. Both versions are fine examples of the art of the ballad, but the shortest exhibits that art at its most economical and dramatic. The first printed version is in *Percy's Reliques**. The best-known version is probably Scott's*.

Sir Thopas, Tale of /ˈtəupas/

One of Chaucer's *Canterbury Tales**. It is contributed by Chaucer himself, as one of the pilgrims. In this capacity he is supposed to be offering the tale quite seriously, but it is really intended as a satirical parody of contemporary popular rhyming romances. The 6-line stanzas have a mechanical, jerking rhythm, and the incidents succeed each other in a flat hackneyed style. Contemporary romances (*Sir Isenbras*, *Le Bel Inconnu*) are quoted and there are references to contemporary romantic heroes such as Sir Bevis. In the middle of the thirty-second stanza, the Host declares that he has had enough (' "This may wel be rym dogerel," quod he.') and Chaucer is obliged to start again. He tells the long Tale of *Melibeus** in prose.

Sirens

In Greek myth, nymphs who lived on a Mediterranean island (variously identified) and sang to passing ships so musically as to lure the sailors to destruction. Odysseus, in Homer's *Odyssey**, escaped by stopping the ears of his crew with wax and having himself bound to the mast. In the legend of the Argonauts*, Orpheus* sang in competition more beautifully still, and thus saved his crew. They are commonly represented as having a bird's body and a woman's head, in this resembling the ancient Egyptian human-headed hawk which also represented the souls of the dead.

Sisyphus /ˈsisifəs/

In Greek myth, the son of Aeolus*; because of his great cunning, he was in later myth said to be the father of Odysseus*. He was even able to cheat death, but his spirit was in the end subdued to the pains of the underworld. He is chiefly associated with the penalty he had to suffer there: he was condemned for eternity to roll a boulder up a slope; whenever it nearly reached the top, it rolled down again. Hence a 'Sisyphean labour' meaning one doomed to near success and eventual failure, both repeatedly recurring.

Sitwell, Edith (1887–1964), Sir Osbert (1892–1969), Sir Sacheverell (b 1897) /ˈsitwəl – səˈʃevərəl/

An eminent literary family, of whom Edith is best known as a poet, and her brothers (both of whom are also poets) as an autobiographer and a writer of travel books respectively.

Edith is the most celebrated of the three. Her poetry is distinctive for her interest in elaborately contrived sound effects, experiments in rhythm, and startling imagery. Her sequence *Façade* (1923) is her most popular work; it was set to music by the composer William Walton. Osbert Sitwell indicates its character in his autobiography, *Laughter in the Next Room*: 'The idea of *Façade* first entered our minds as the result of certain technical experiments at which my sister had recently been working: experiments in obtaining through the medium of words the rhythm of dance measures such as waltzes, polkas, foxtrots. These exercises were often experimental enquiries into the effect on rhythm, on speed, and on colour of the use of rhymes, assonances, dissonances, placed outwardly, at different places in the line, in most elaborate patterns'. The tone of *Façade* is lighthearted or satirical. From *The Sleeping Beauty* (1924) a more romantic tone predominated, and in 1929 *Gold Coast Customs* opened her most ambitious phase of philosophic verse with majestic themes. These include *Street Songs* (1942), *The Song of the Cold* (1945) and *The Shadow of Cain* (1947). Her prose works and criticism include a biography of Alexander Pope* (1930).

Bib: Megroz, R. L., *The Three Sitwells*; Powell, D., *Edith Sitwell*; Villa, J. G. (ed.) *Celebrations for Edith Sitwell*.

Six Articles

A law passed through Parliament on the authority of Henry VIII* in 1539. Having removed the

English Church from the authority of the Pope and abolished the monasteries*, Henry was concerned to prove himself a true Catholic 'without the Pope'. He therefore ordained that the traditional doctrines should be reaffirmed, especially 'the real presence' of Christ in the bread and wine taken in Holy Communion. Protestants*, by then numerous in southern England, disliked the law, which they called 'the whip with six strings'.

* *Reformation*.

Sixteenth-century Literature

In 16th C, great changes in English society ended with an extraordinary release of creative energies, particularly in the last decade. The powerful feudal aristocracy gave place to a new aristocracy, and a great improvement occurred in the standing both of the country gentleman and of the city merchant. The Church ceased to be part of an international organization, and became part of the national polity, under the authority of the Crown. The Renaissance* secularized learning entirely, and educated the aristocracy with the love of it. The nation fought a struggle for survival, and became fully conscious, delighting in itself as never before.

Yet in some respects the Middle Ages* died slowly in England. Lord Berners's translation (1525) of the 14th-C *Chronicles* of Froissart* belongs with the prose of Malory's *Morte d'Arthur**, and Sir Thomas More's principal work in English, *The History of King Richard III* (written 1513?), is medieval in spirit, though it is a new kind of work.

The language of prose made notable advances in 16th C. It is significant that much of the best prose was about education, such as Sir Thomas Elyot's* *Governor* (1531) and Roger Ascham's* *The Schoolmaster* (pub 1570), and some of it arose out of the religious changes, notably William Tyndale's* version of the New Testament, the Sermons of Latimer, and Cranmer's* noble *Book of Common Prayer**.

In poetry, we find the same tentative movement away from the Middle Ages, so that it is sometimes hard to say whether a poet from the earlier part of the century is medieval or of the Renaissance. John Skelton* has more vitality than the English (as distinct from Scottish) poets of 15th C. Thomas Wyatt* is a fine poet of strong individuality, but his rhythms, though often subtle, seem to be suspended between the roughness of 15th C and the smoothness which Chaucer* had introduced. Henry Howard, Earl of Surrey*, and Thomas Sackville* are less interesting than Wyatt, but superficially their work is moving closer to the smooth handling of language which the Elizabethans prized so much in the sonnets* of Sir Philip Sidney* (pub 1591) and in Spenser* from *The Shepherd's Calendar** (1579) to *The Faerie Queene** (1596). Such uncertainties in verse technique have small importance, however, except in so far as they betray uncertainty of purpose in a poet. The uncertainty of technique among the dramatists is more important.

The Morality Play* style of drama continued into 16th C although its content became less religious and more secular, as in Skelton's *Magnificence* (1516?) and the finer *Satire of the Three Estates* (1540) by the Scots poet David Lindsay*. A lighter kind of play called the Interlude* often had no didactic purpose (*eg* the plays of John Heywood*), and moved towards the first pure comedies, *Ralph Roister Doister** (written 1551?) and *Gammer Gurton's Needle** (1556). Meanwhile the Morality Play, having become secular and (often) political, tended to evolve into the historical drama, such as *Gorboduc** (1561) by Sackville and Norton, and *Cambyses* (1569) by Preston. Preston was a scholar; Sackville was an aristocrat. Now that the drama had lost its roots in the Church and the town rituals, it needed thoroughly professional writers, learned and yet in touch with the everyday world, to give it a fully developed form and life of its own. A group of just such writers – Thomas Kyd*, John Lyly*, George Peele*, Robert Greene* and Christopher Marlowe*, collectively known as the University Wits* – began work in the 1580s. None of them, except Marlowe, produced much work of inherent value, but they evolved among them a self-confident art of the theatre, and Shakespeare in his first decade (from *Henry VI* to *Hamlet*) was indebted to them.

These new writers, including Shakespeare himself, form a new social phenomenon: the professional man of letters, who was not a nobleman like Wyatt, Surrey or Sidney, practising literature as part of the aristocratic life, nor a scholar or churchman like Ascham or Tyndale, practising it as a by-product of his profession, nor a court poet as Chaucer had been and Spenser was, practising it partly with a view to receiving court emoluments, but a writer who depended on the 'great public', as writers do today. They contributed greatly to the extraordinary vitality of the 1590s, not only in the drama but in prose pamphleteering (the earliest form of journalism*) and the kind of romance known as the Elizabethan novel*, in which Thomas Nashe*, Thomas Lodge*, and Thomas Deloney* were among the foremost practitioners.

In the 1590s the drama, non-dramatic poetry of all kinds but notably the sonnet and the short poem for a musical setting, and prose including not merely the journalism of the 'novelists' and pamphleteers but the great philosophical writing of Richard Hooker* (*Laws of Ecclesiastical Polity*), reached a new mastery. The poetry has an extraordinary range of style, from the highly wrought music of Spenser's *Faerie Queene* (1596) to the strenuous thought of Donne's* *Songs and Sonnets**. Literary criticism has also made its beginnings with Puttenham's* *Art of English Poesy* (pub 1589) and Sidney's *Apology for Poetry** (pub 1598). The arrival of the critic on the scene of literature is evidence of the seriousness with which educated men had studied literature, and ideas which had a bearing upon it, throughout the century. Further evidence of this is the number of translations* in the period; Italian and French writing and thought, as well as the ancient classics (above all, the philosophy of Plato* and the critical theory of Horace* and, through the Italians, Aristotle*) contributed a large part of the English literary Renaissance. The rest came from the first full assertion of national self-consciousness.

Skelton, John (1460?–1529)

Poet. He was tutor to Prince Henry, later Henry VIII*, and a kind of unofficial poet laureate*. He was respected as a humanist* by the greatest of humanists, Erasmus*, but his work is chiefly comic and satirical, *eg Bowge of Court* (1509?), an allegory in the morality* tradition against court vices; *Colin Clout** (1519), a satire on the vices of the clergy, recalling in some respects Langland's *Piers Plowman**; *Magnificence*, a morality play on the evils of ambition. His *Book of Philip Sparrow* (1503–7) is a long poem, probably stimulated by the ancient Roman poet, Catullus*; it contains passages of charm and delicacy unusual in his work. His *Skelton Laureate against the Scots* is a patriotic poem celebrating the English victory at Flodden*. Though a minor poet, Skelton is the most vital English (as distinct from Scottish) one between Chaucer* and Wyatt*. Unlike the latter, however, his work looks backward to the Middle Ages* rather than forward to the English Renaissance* at the end of 16th C. By profession, he was a churchman, though his work carries few characteristics of one.

Bib: Nelson, W., *John Skelton, Laureate*; Edwards, H. L. R., *Skelton*; Fish, S. E., a critical study; Auden, W. H., in *The Great Tudors* ed. K. Garvin.

Sketches by Boz /boz, bəuz/

Early journalism by Charles Dickens*. The sketches, 'Illustrative of Everyday Life and Everyday People', were begun in 1833, published in various magazines, and collected into book form in 1836. Dickens was continuing the tradition of the periodical essay as it had been practised since Addison*, and in the previous thirty years by Charles Lamb*, William Hazlitt*, and Leigh Hunt*. But Dickens emphasizes the narrative element as opposed to the descriptive element of the periodic essay, and his material is much more that of common life. The subject-matter of the *Sketches* is, in fact, very much the subject-matter of the novels he was soon to begin.

Skimmington Ride

An ancient British custom (no longer in use) of ridiculing unfaithful or quarrelsome married partners by carrying effigies of them in a procession. Such a 'skimmington' is described in Hardy's novel *The Mayor of Casterbridge**. The origin of the term is unknown.

Sleeping Beauty, The

A famous fairy story in the collection made by Charles Perrault*, translated into English in 1729. A baby princess is doomed by a wicked fairy to prick herself in the finger and die, but a good fairy changes death into a hundred years' sleep, from which the princess is awakened by the kiss of a prince. The story is an ancient folktale and said to be a legend about the earth being awakened from its winter sleep by the sun.

Slough of Despond

A boggy place in John Bunyan's allegory *Pilgrim's Progress**. Christian sinks into it immediately after taking flight from the City of Destruction. It signifies the period of depression into which a convert is liable to fall after the first enthusiasm of his conversion.

Smart, Christopher (1722–71)

Poet. He early showed poetic gifts, and received support from the aristocratic Vane family, for whose estates his father was a steward. He developed a strong religious enthusiasm and was for a time locked up as insane. After his release he published (1763) his *Song to David*, a long, ecstatic poem in praise of David* as author of the Psalms* in the Bible. This boldly imaginative work, written while he was reputed insane, is now the chief work by which he is remembered. The poem is often regarded as uncharacteristic of 18th C, but it is in a long tradition of biblically inspired literature reinforced by the 17th- and 18th-C tradition of hymn writing, *eg* by Isaac Watts* and Charles Wesley*. He also wrote a satirical poem, *Hilliad* (1753) and a number of religious poems, including *Rejoice in the Lamb*.

Bib: Life and criticism by Ainsworth, E. G. and Noyes, C. E.; Devlin, C.

Smectymnuus

A name under which five Presbyterian* writers wrote against episcopacy – rule of the Church by bishops – in 17th C. The name was suggested by the initial letters of the names of the writers: Stephen Marshal, Edward Calamy, Thomas Young, and Matthew Newcomen. Their pamphlet* was attacked by Bishop Hall*, and was defended in two pamphlets by John Milton* in 1641 and 1642. Samuel Butler*, in his poetic satire *Hudibras**, written against the Puritans, calls the Presbyterians the 'Legion of Smec'.

Smiles, Samuel (1812–1904)

Journalist: philosopher of 'self-help'. Born at Haddington in Scotland, one of eleven children, his early life was a struggle dominated by the vigour of his widowed mother. He graduated in Medicine at Edinburgh University in 1832, and began practising as a doctor in his home village. Competition was severe however, and he exchanged medicine for journalism, becoming editor of the *Leeds Times*. He also became secretary to railway companies, and in this capacity he made acquaintance with George Stephenson, inventor of the steam railway engine. His *Life of Stephenson* was published in 1857, and was followed by the lives of other famous 19th-C engineers: *James Brindley* (1864); *Boulton and Watt* (1865); *Telford* (1867). But the book that made him famous was *Self-Help* (1859); it sold 20,000 copies in the first year, and was translated into at least 17 languages. He followed it by similar books, all demonstrating the worldly advantages of certain moral virtues: *Character* (1871); *Thrift* (1875); *Duty* (1880). The success of these books was due to their optimism, and to the simple, forceful, practical expression of his ideas. His international prestige is illustrated by his reception of the Order of St Sava from the King of Servia in 1897. Smiles represents the vigorous and hopeful aspect of the Industrial Revolution*, as it affected ordinary people, in contrast to the sceptical and sombre view of it taken by many of the imaginative writers.

Smith, Adam (1723–90)

Political economist. His important work was *An Enquiry into the Nature and Causes of the Wealth of Nations* – always referred to as *The Wealth of Nations* – published in 1776, at the outbreak of the rebellion of the American colonists, who, he predicted, 'will be one of the foremost nations of the world'. The especial influence of this book comes from his discussion of the function of the state in the degree and kind of control it should exercise over the activities of society, and in particular, of trade. He concluded that the traditional mercantile system* (nowadays called 'protection') was based on a misunderstanding of the nature of wealth, and that nations prospered to the extent that governments allowed trade to remain freely competitive, unrestrained by taxes intended to protect the economy of a nation from competition from other nations. His opinions became increasingly influential and eventually dominant in British economics during the first half of 19th C; his opposition to *unnecessary* interference by the government in trade and society became harmful in that it was interpreted by later governments as an excuse not to remedy social abuses arising from industrialism.

* *Free Trade*.

Smollett, Tobias George (1721–71) /'smolit/

Novelist. He was a Scotsman who (like many others in 18th C) came south to England, and suffered a number of rebuffs and hard struggles that embittered his temper. He failed as a dramatist, and took service as a surgeon's assistant in the navy in 1741 during the war against Spain, witnessing the siege of Cartagena. On his return he tried and failed to make a living as a surgeon, and took to writing. His first novel, *Roderick Random**, was published in 1748; it was followed by *Peregrine Pickle** (1751); *Ferdinand Count Fathom* (1753), *Sir Launcelot Greaves* (1760–2), and, his most famous work, *Humphry Clinker** (1771).

Smollett's novels are episodic; they owe much to two European traditions of episodic fiction, the picaresque* exemplified by Le Sage's *Gil Blas*, and that derived from Cervantes' mock epic *Don Quixote**. *Roderick Random* is based on Smollett's early life, his coming to England and experience at sea. *Peregrine Pickle* and *Ferdinand Count Fathom* are both about the careers of unscrupulous adventurers; *Sir Launcelot Greaves* has a comic but virtuous hero, in the style of Don Quixote. *Humphry Clinker* is mellower in its humour than the others, and centres on a gruff though sentimental humanitarian, Matthew Bramble, who has resemblances to Smollett himself in his old age. The weaknesses of these novels are obvious: their construction is very loose and the characterization lacks imaginative insight; moreover, though Smollett is essentially a comic novelist, he is (until *Humphry Clinker*) without the generous and sympathetic delight in human nature that distinguishes his contemporary, Fielding*. On the other hand, the novels have strong physical actuality, and the coarse comedy is vivid enough to have made many of the characters celebrated throughout 19th C, *eg* Tom Bowling (*Roderick Random*), Commodore Trunnion (*Peregrine Pickle*), and Matthew Bramble in *Humphry Clinker*. It is now the first and the last of his novels that are most read; of the others, only *Sir Launcelot Greaves* has never had a period of strong popularity. *Ferdinand* is said to have had a strong influence on the late-18th-C Gothic* novelists, 'Monk' Lewis* and Mrs Radcliffe*.

Smollett translated *Don Quixote* (1755) and *Gil Blas* (1749), wrote *Travels in France and Italy* (1766), for the ill temper of which the novelist Sterne* nicknamed him 'Smelfungus' (although in some respects Smollett was a sympathetic observer), attacked the government in a satire *The History and Adventures of an Atom* (1768), and edited a number of reviews, including *The Briton* in defence of Bute's ministry, provoking the much livelier *North Briton* by Wilkes*. He also wrote a farce, *The Reprisal* (1757), and parts of a *History of England* and a *Universal History*.

Bib: Martz, L. L., *Life*; Knapp, L. M., *Life*; Hazlitt, W., in *English Comic Writers*; Scott, W., in *Lives of the Novelists*; Thackeray, W. M., in

The English Humourists; Buck, H. S., *A study in Smollett*; Jones, C. E., *Smollett Studies.*

Snobs, The Book of (1848)

A collection of satirical sketches by the novelist William Makepeace Thackeray*, first published in the periodical *Punch** in 1846–47 as *The Snobs of England by one of themselves.* The sketches satirize the complacency and mediocrity of the middle classes, and show the point of view and style of humour which Thackeray was to develop in his novels, most of which concern the rich and powerful upper middle classes of mid-19th-C England. He based his title on a Cambridge student paper, *The Snob*, to which he contributed as an undergraduate in 1829.

Snow, Charles Percy (b 1905)

Novelist; author of the sequence *Strangers and Brothers* comprising *Strangers and Brothers*, *The Light and the Dark*, *Time of Hope*, *The Masters*, *The New Men*, *Homecomings*; *The Conscience of the Rich*; *The Affair*; *Corridors of Power* (1964); *The Sleep of Reason* (1968).

He has also played a large part in public affairs; he was created Baron (Life Peerage) in 1964, and served as a junior minister (Ministry of Technology) from 1964 till 1966. Trained as a scientist, he holds strong views about the intellectual cleavage between men trained in the sciences and those trained in liberal studies in the modern world. His Rede Lecture at Cambridge, *The Two Cultures and the Scientific Revolution* (1959) became famous, partly because it provoked an exceptionally ferocious retort from the critic F. R. Leavis*.

Bib: Cooper, W., *C. P. Snow* (British Council).

Social Contract

A doctrine about the origins of society especially associated with the English thinkers Thomas Hobbes* and John Locke*, and the French thinker Jean-Jacques Rousseau*. Hobbes (in *Leviathan**) argued that men were naturally violent and rapacious, and that they contracted to put themselves under strong government in order to make the continuance of life and property possible. Locke (*Treatise on Government*) thought the social contract was a convenience rather than a necessity, arguing that private property could have existed in pre-social humanity, but that men contracted to accept government to make themselves secure. Man for Locke was not necessarily violent, and government should be tolerant and humane. Rousseau (*Social Contract*) argued that primitive men were above all timid, and that they contracted to form governments which rested on the consent of the people, who should overthrow them if they were inefficient or tyrannical. Rousseau's view supported the action of the French revolutionaries and encouraged the growth of democratic ideas in 19th C. All three men opposed the beliefs maintained until mid-17th C everywhere, that rulers owed their authority to the will of God.

Socialism

* *Communism*; *Labour Party*; *Marx.*

Society for Promoting Christian Knowledge (S.P.C.K.)

Founded in 1698; it was then an unusual collaboration of all the Protestant* sects to help in the education of the poor by founding 'charity schools', and to extend religious education by the circulation of inexpensive Bibles and other religious literature. A subsidiary was the missionary Society for the Propagation of the Gospel in Foreign Parts, in 19th C a channel for the movement against slavery and the slave trade.

* *Schools in England.*

Socinianism /səu'siniənizm/

A theological doctrine associated with two 16th-C Italian theologians, Lelio and Fausto Sozzini (latinized to Socinus). They regarded Jesus Christ as wholly human (*ie* not a member of the Holy Trinity) but as divinely inspired. They were thus representative of that side of the Protestant Reformation* that sought to simplify and rationalize Christian doctrine; in Britain in 17th C 'Socinians' were substantially what in 18th C became known as Unitarians*.

Socrates (470?–399 BC) /'sokrəti:z/

Greek philosopher. He taught entirely by word of mouth, the so-called 'Socratic method' being the discovery of the truth by putting appropriate questions. Because he wrote nothing, all information about him depends on the writings of two contemporaries – the historian Xenophon* (*Memorabilia*) and the philosopher Plato*, who stands in relation to Socrates somewhat as St Paul does to Jesus Christ, except that Plato was personally taught by Socrates. Plato puts his own ideas into the mouth of Socrates in his philosophical dialogues, and it is of course difficult to know just how much and in what ways he expanded the Socratic philosophy. This philosophy declared for the first time that the true end of philosophy was not to discover the nature of the world but the nature of goodness and how to lead the good life; related to this is the doctrine of Forms, according to which reality is seen as fundamentally spiritual, and the real in man is his soul.

Socrates is said to have had a beautiful soul in an ugly body, and a quarrelsome wife called Xanthippe. He fell out of favour with the ruling party of Athens, his native city, because he befriended enemies of the party; he was accordingly made to put himself to death by drinking hemlock.

Sodom and Gomorrah /'sodəm – gə'morə/

In the Bible (*Genesis* 13, 14, 18, 19) the wicked 'cities of the plain', destroyed by a rain of 'fire and brimstone'. They were in the neighbourhood of the Dead Sea.

Soho /'səuhəu/

A district of London, east of Regent Street and west of Tottenham Court Road and Charing

Cross Road, now famous for its foreign restaurants and its international colony. It was fashionable in 17th C; Dryden*, Evelyn*, and the Duke of Monmouth* all lived there. The origin of the name is unknown.

Solemn League and Covenant

* *Covenant.*

Solomon

The third king of Israel; he was the son of David* and Bathsheba, and the dates of his reign are approximately 974–937 BC. His name means 'peaceful', and his reign was exceptionally peaceful and prosperous. He secured the friendship of Egypt by marrying Pharaoh's daughter, and expanded foreign trade with the assistance of the king of Tyre to the north. The reign is described in the first eleven chapters of *1 Kings* in the Bible, where special attention is given to his construction of a splendid palace and temple at Jerusalem, and to his wisdom as a ruler.

In the Bible, part of the book of *Proverbs* was traditionally ascribed to Solomon, as a kind of tribute to his reputation as an embodiment of wisdom. He was also supposed to be the author of *The Song of Solomon*, which Christians once interpreted as an allegorical expression of the union between God and the spiritual body of his Church; it is now agreed to be a human love drama, written much later than the reign of Solomon.

Solon (638?–558? BC) /'səulon/

In ancient Greece, a famous lawmaker of Athens*. He laid the foundation of Athenian democracy and contrived to readjust the economic structure of society in favour of the poor, many of whom were being reduced to slavery because of their inability to pay their debts.

Somerset House

A building on the north bank of the Thames, now housing state departments concerned with records of births, deaths, wills, marriages and income tax. The present building dates from 18th C; its name derives from a 16th-C palace on the same site, belonging to the Duke of Somerset.

Sompnour's Tale

* *Summoner's Tale.*

Songs and Sonnets

A volume of 55 love poems by John Donne*. They were first published in 1633, but they circulated widely in manuscript during his lifetime. According to Ben Jonson* (reported by Drummond of Hawthornden), Donne wrote all his best poems by the age of 25, but some of the finest of the *Songs and Sonnets* are from well after 1600, *eg A Nocturnal upon St Lucy's Day**. Despite the title, none of the poems are sonnets. Nearly all are written in stanzas, and only one stanza form (the quatrain* with 8-syllable lines and alternating rhymes) is used more than once. The tone varies from light-hearted contempt for women and love (*eg Go and catch a falling star*) to deeply serious declarations of devotion (*eg A Nocturnal, Valediction Forbidding Mourning*). The character of the poems is in strong contrast to much of the love poetry of the 1590s, such as Spenser's* *Amoretti*. Spenser and the other neo-Petrarchans (* *Petrarch*) wrote limpid, ceremonious, musically incantatory verse, whereas Donne's poems are abstruse, dramatic, and colloquial, and appear to owe much to the idiom of the contemporary playwrights. They are simultaneously strongly intellectual and intensely physical, but the physical sensations are conveyed through images of movement integrated with the strenuous rhythms rather than images that appeal to the ear and eye through colour and melody like those (notably) in the work of Spenser. Donne's *Songs and Sonnets* made a strong impression in the first half of 17th C, although the influence of his style is more evident on religious poets such as Herbert* and Vaughan* than on writers of love poetry, with the notable exception of Marvell*. In succeeding periods, largely owing to their difficulty, they were neglected, until in 20th C they won the admiration of major poets as different as Eliot* and Yeats*.

* *Metaphysical Poets.*

Songs and Sonnets (Tottel)

* *Tottel's Miscellany.*

Songs of Innocence and Experience

Two collections of short poems by William Blake*, engraved and illuminated by hand. *The Songs of Innocence* were completed in 1789, and *The Songs of Experience* were added in an enlarged edition in

1794; one of the latter, *To Tirzah*, was not added until 1801. The contrast between the two parts may represent the contrast between the hopes generated in Blake by the early phases of the French Revolution* and his disillusionment at its later phases after 1791, but in any case they are complementary, each based on a valid but partial viewpoint. The viewpoint in *Innocence* insists on the qualities in human nature that are the source of love – compassion and sympathy – and expresses the reaching out to life of the child, confident in the protective devotion of loving parents. *Experience* shows the ruthlessness in nature and injustice in society, expounds the subtle contrivances of human selfishness, and expresses the inevitability of suffering. *To Tirzah* shows yet a third viewpoint – the freeing of the soul from its physical bonds. The lyrics are uniquely simple in their diction, and the stanzas and rhythms derive from two popular sources – the hymns* of such writers as Isaac Watts*, and the 'broadside' ballads* sold in the London streets. Yet Blake uses these homely elements with refined art, and combines them with a symbolism which is profound though often perplexing.

*** 6.3.3.**

Sonnet /'sonit/

A short poem of 14 lines, and a rhyme scheme restricted by one or other of a variety of principles. The most famous pattern is called the 'Petrarchan sonnet', from its masterly use by the Italian poet Petrarch*. This divides naturally into an 8-line stanza (octave) rhyming *abba abba*, and a 6-line stanza in which two or three rhymes may occur; the two stanzas provide also for contrast in attitude to the theme. The origin of the sonnet is unknown, but its earliest examples date from 13th C in Europe, although it did not reach England until 16th C. The immense popularity of the form perhaps derives from its combination of discipline, musicality, and amplitude. The subject-matter is commonly love, but after 16th C it becomes, at least in England, much more varied.

The first writers of sonnets in England were Sir Thomas Wyatt*, and Henry Howard, Earl of Surrey*; the popular anthology *Tottel's Miscellany** (1559) made their experiments widely known, but neither of these poets produced his best work in the form. The first really fine sonnet sequence was Sir Philip Sidney's *Astrophil and Stella**. Its publication in 1591 set an eagerly followed fashion for its distinctively English form. This consisted of a single stanza of 14 lines concluding in a couplet*; it is thought that the comparative scarcity of rhyming words in the English language may be the explanation of the greater number of rhymes and freedom in the rhyming scheme in contrast to the Petrarchan form. The greatest of the succeeding sequences was undoubtedly Shakespeare's (* *Sonnets by Shakespeare*), but notable ones were produced by Daniel*, Drayton*, and Spenser*.

The sonnet form continued to be used after 1600, notably by Donne* and Milton*, but much less for amorous themes and more for religious ones (*eg* Donne's *Holy Sonnets*) or, (by Milton) for expressions of other forms of personal experience (*eg On his Blindness*) or for political declamation (*On the Late Massacre in Piedmont*). Milton used the Petrarchan rhyme scheme, but he kept the English form of using a single stanza. From mid-17th to mid-18th C the different style of thought and feeling suggested by the heroic couplet kept the sonnet out of use; the cult of sentiment by poets such as Gray* and Cowper* then brought it back, but a real revival had to wait for the first 30 years of 19th C in the work of the 'romantics' – especially Wordsworth*, who used it freely, Keats*, who wrote few but some of them among his best short poems, and Shelley* whose *Ozymandias** sonnet is one of the best of all his poems. The Romantic poets tended to follow the Miltonic example both in form and subject-matter. After 1830, the form continued to be popular in 19th C, notably in the work of Christina Rossetti*, Dante Gabriel Rossetti*, Elizabeth Barrett Browning* (*Sonnets from the Portuguese*, 1847). G. M. Hopkins* experimented very boldly in the form, and produced some of his best work in what he claimed to be sonnets, though they are often scarcely recognizable as such. In 20th C the sonnet has again lost favour.

*** 6.2.3.**

Sonnets, Shakespeare's

First published in 1609, but there is no clear evidence when they were written. They are commonly thought to date from 1595–99; Francis Meres* in *Palladis Tamia* (1598) mentions that Shakespeare wrote sonnets. There are 154 sonnets; numbers 1–126 are addressed to a man (126 is in fact not a sonnet but a 12-line poem) and the remainder are addressed to a woman – the so-called 'dark lady of the sonnets', since it is made clear that she is dark in hair and complexion. There has been much speculation about the dedication: 'To the only begetter of these ensuing sonnets Mr W. H. all happiness and that eternity promised by our everliving poet Wisheth the well-wishing adventurer in setting forth T.T.' 'T.T.' stands for Thomas Thorpe, the stationer (*ie* bookseller and publisher of the sonnets); speculation centres on what is meant by 'begetter' and who is meant by 'W.H.' W.H. may stand for the man (William Hughes?) who *procured* the manuscript of the sonnets for Thorpe, if that is what 'begetter' means. But if 'begetter' means 'inspirer', it has been conjectured that W.H. may be the inverted initials of Henry Wriothesley, 3rd Earl of Southampton*, to whom Shakespeare had dedicated his *Venus and Adonis** and *Lucrece**, or they may stand for William Herbert, Earl of Pembroke, or for someone else. Guesses have also been made as to the identity of the 'dark lady', who has been thought by some to be Mary Fitton, a Maid of Honour at Court who was a mistress of William Herbert. There is too little evidence for profitable conjecture on either subject.

Critics and scholars disagree about the extent to which the sonnets are autobiographical (and if so what they express) or whether they are 'literary exercises' without a personal theme. A middle view is that they are exploratory of personal relations in friendship and in love, and that some of them rehearse themes later dramatized in the plays – for instance 94 suggests the character of Angelo in *Measure for Measure**, and the recurrent concern with the destructiveness of time seems to look forward to *Troilus and Cressida** and the great tragedies. Since it is unknown whether the edition of 1609 is a reliable version, there is also some doubt whether the order of the sonnets in it is that intended by Shakespeare; most scholars see little reason to question it.

* 6.2.3.

Bib: Knights, L. C., in *Explorations*; Hotson, L., *Shakespeare's Sonnets Dated*; Empson, W., in *Some Versions of Pastoral*; Hubler, E., *The Riddle of Shakespeare's Sonnets*; Leishman, J. B., *Themes and Variations in Shakespeare's Sonnets*; Lever, J. W., *The Elizabethan Love Sonnet*; Schaar, C., *Elizabethan sonnet themes and the dating of Shakespeare's Sonnets*; Gittings, R., *Shakespeare's Rival*; Brown, I., *Dark Ladies*.

Sons and Lovers (1913)

The first of D. H. Lawrence's* important novels. It is based on his own early life in the midland coal-mining village of Eastwood (Nottinghamshire), on his relationship with his mother and with his father who was a mineworker, and on those with his early women friends.

Eastwood is called Bestwood in the novel; the character who corresponds to Lawrence himself is Paul Morel. The strongest relationship is the close tie between Mrs Morel and Paul, who has two brothers and a sister. Mrs Morel comes of a proud, Dissenting* middle-class family with memories of ancestors who fought against Charles I*. She inherits the uncompromising traditions of English Dissent, and, though her family has been impoverished, she has an inherent aristocracy of temperament derived from her family tradition of high standards. The father, Walter Morel, a miner, is a contrast to his wife, both in his background (he is the grandson of a French refugee and an English barmaid) and in his easy-going, pleasure-loving, spontaneous temperament. The marriage is an unhappy one: Mrs Morel's strictness and truthfulness are outraged by her husband's slackness and deceitfulness. In the war between them, the children take the side of the mother.

The closeness between Mrs Morel and Paul develops after the death of her eldest son, William, and Paul's own serious illness. He goes to work in a Nottingham factory, but he has his mother's intellectual seriousness and artistic sensitivity, and has ambitions to become an artist. Mrs Morel invests in him all her pride of life and the hopes and passions that her marriage has disappointed. She finds a rival in Miriam Leivers, the shy and intensely serious daughter of a local farmer, and bitterly opposes her friendship with Paul. He is affected by his mother's opposition, and at the same time he resents what he considers to be Miriam's emotional demands upon him, since he believes them to be a barrier to the sensual release for which he craves. He reacts against Miriam by engaging in a sensual love affair with Clara Dawes, a married woman who has quarrelled with her husband. This relationship is not opposed by Mrs Morel, since it is a physical one and does not compete with her own emotional possessiveness. Paul, on the other hand, finds that Clara affords him no more release than Miriam had done; he is unconsciously subjected, all the time, to his mother. The mother's protracted illness and death, and Paul's fight with Baxter Dawes, Clara's husband, are complementary climaxes of the novel. Both together constitute his release, although the death leaves him with a sense of complete dereliction: he has to face the choice of willing himself to live or surrendering to his own desire for death.

Lawrence had been studying Freud*, and the book was early regarded as a vivid presentation of the working of the Oedipus* Complex. It is in its own right a major novel, but it certainly constitutes Lawrence's attempt to release himself from the problems of his own early development. He later declared that his study of his father had been unfair and one-sided. Jessie Chambers, the woman on whom Miriam was based, wrote an excellent study of Lawrence as a young man: *D. H. Lawrence, A Personal Record* by E. T.

* 4.5.3.

Sophists /ˈsofists/

In ancient Greece of 5th C BC, professional educators, who claimed to train men for civic life, but not for any particular trade or profession. They differed from philosophers in that they professed to teach, whereas philosophers professed to know; it is the difference between victory by argument and discovery through argument. By degrees the Sophists fell into disrepute, and today the term 'sophistry' means an ingenious argument deliberately intended to mislead the audience.

Sophocles (495–406 BC) /ˈsofəkli:z/

One of the three great ancient Greek dramatists, the other two being Aeschylus* and Euripides*. He wrote about 100 dramas, of which only 7 survive: *Oedipus the King*; *Oedipus at Colonus*; *Antigone*; *Electra*; *Trachiniae*; *Ajax*; *Philoctetes*. His poetic language shows more flexibility than that of Aeschylus – their relationship in this respect has been compared to that of Shakespeare* and Marlowe* – and he used three actors on the stage instead of only two (not counting the Chorus). In his relationship to Euripides, he is quoted by Aristotle* as saying that he depicted men as they ought to be whereas Euripides depicted them as they were. The Irish poet W. B. Yeats* made free English renderings of his *Oedipus the King* (1928) and *Oedipus at Colonus* (1934).

Sophy, The /ˈsəufi/

Originally the surname of the ruling family of Persia (16th–18th C) and later adopted as a title of the ruler.

Sorbonne /so:ˈbon/

Originally the name of a college founded in Paris by Robert de Sorbon in 1256, then used for the theological faculty in the university of Paris, and finally extended to the whole university.

South Sea Bubble

The name given to a series of extensive speculations in 1720 involving the South Sea Company, founded in 1711. In 1720 individuals who had lent money to the government through the Bank of England were invited to exchange their claims for shares in the Company, which had a monopoly of trade with Spanish America and was very prosperous. This project led to irresponsible financial speculation in a number of dishonest companies, financial scandals in which ministers of the Crown were involved, and a major financial collapse in which thousands were ruined. The South Sea Company survived until 19th C. Its headquarters, South Sea House, was for a time the place of employment of the essayist Charles Lamb*, and is the subject of one of his essays.

Southampton, Henry Wriothesley, 3rd Earl of (1573–1624)

Chiefly famous as a patron of letters, and particularly as a patron of Shakespeare*. He was educated at St John's College, Cambridge, from 1585 to 1589, where he made friends with the chief favourite of Queen Elizabeth*, the Earl of Essex, and was shown special favour by the Queen herself. Shakespeare dedicated to him his poems *Venus and Adonis** (1593) and (in terms of warm devotion) *The Rape of Lucrece* (1594). There has long been much speculation about whether the young man in the Sonnets* is Southampton, and whether the initials of 'Mr W. H.' in the dedication ('To the Onlie Begetter of These Insuing Sonnets') stand for 'Henry Wriothesley' reversed. Southampton accompanied Essex on his two naval expeditions against Spain in 1596 (to Cadiz) and 1597 (to the Azores), and distinguished himself by his daring on the second of them. In 1598 he had to make a hasty marriage with Essex's cousin, Elizabeth Vernon, and this angered the Queen against him. He was later concerned in Essex's conspiracy against Elizabeth, and is thought to have arranged a special performance of Shakespeare's *Richard II** on the eve of the rebellion. In 1601 he was senteneced to death; however the sentence was commuted to life imprisonment, and when James I* acceded in 1603, Southampton returned to court. He died of a fever when serving, with his son, as a volunteer on the side of the Dutch in their war with Spain. Other writers with whom he was associated as patron included John Florio*, the translator of Montaigne, and Thomas Nashe*, who dedicated *The Unfortunate Traveller** to him.

Southcott, Joanna (1750–1814)

A religious fanatic who attracted a following of about 100,000 early in 19th C. She is particularly known for her sealed box, which she declared should be opened in the presence of the assembled bishops at a time of national crisis. It was opened in 1927, but was found to contain unimportant objects, perhaps because only one bishop was present.

Southey, Robert (1774–1843) /ˈsauði/

Poet and biographer. He was the friend of Coleridge* (they married sisters) and also of Wordsworth*. He shared their revolutionary ardour in the 1790s, but his opinions, like theirs, became conservative during the first decade of 19th C, and from the founding of the *Quarterly Review** in 1809 he became one of its leading contributors. He was made poet laureate* in 1813, 30 years before Wordsworth. In 1821 his poem *A Vision of Judgement*, describing the admission of George III into heaven, provoked the satire with almost the same title by Lord Byron* – one of Byron's masterpieces.

Southey wrote long heroic epics (*eg Thalaba*, 1801; *Madoc*, 1805; *Roderick*, 1814) which in their own day were much admired but are now unread. Poetically, he survives by a handful of short poems, of which the best known is *The Battle of Blenheim*. As a prose writer he has a higher reputation; his *Life of Nelson* (1813) is a minor classic. His personal reputation suffered badly from the thoroughness of his change in political opinion; he is featured as Mr Feathernest in Peacock's satirical novel *Melincourt** (1817). But his letters show him to have been a likable and in many ways admirable man.

Bib: Simmons, J., *Life*.

Southwark /ˈsʌðək/

A district of London south of the Thames, opposite the City, in distinction from which it is often referred to as 'the Borough'. In literary history it is famous for its ancient inns (*eg* the Tabard Inn* of Chaucer's *Canterbury Tales**, and the White Hart of Dickens's *Pickwick Papers**) and still more for the theatres that existed in it in Shakespeare's day – the Globe*, the Hope and the Rose*.

Southwell, Robert (1561?–1595) /ˈsauθwel/

Poet and Roman Catholic priest. He worked in England as a member of the Jesuit* Order at a time when this was illegal; in 1592 he was arrested and tortured for evidence of other priests, which he did not disclose. He was executed after three years in prison, where he wrote some fine religious poems (*St Peter's Complaint with Other Poems* and *Maeoniae*, 1595). His most famous poem is *The Burning Babe*. He also wrote a long poem *Fourfold Meditation of the Four Last Things* (1606) and a number of religious tracts, one of which, *Mary Magdalen's Tears*, was imitated by Thomas Nashe* in his *Christ's Tears over Jerusalem*.

Bib: Life by Devlin, C.; a study by Janelle, P.

Spanish Main

A term given to the seaboard of central America when it was under Spanish rule, especially between Panama and the River Orinoco in Venezuela.

Spanish Succession, War of the (1701–13)

A great European war which arose from Louis XIV's endeavour to support the claim of his grandson Philip to the throne of Spain. It was fought by an alliance of Britain, Holland, some German states, Austria, Denmark and Portugal on the one side, against France and Spain on the other. The aim of Britain and Holland was to reduce the dangerous power and ambitions of Louis XIV of France. The war was notable for the number of gifted generals on both sides, especially the Englishman John Churchill, Duke of Marlborough*, and Prince Eugene of Savoy, fighting in the Austrian service. Their principal victories were the battles of Blenheim* (1704), Ramillies (1706), Oudenarde (1708) and Malplaquet (1709). The war was closed by the Treaty of Utrecht (1713). The war party in Britain was the Whigs* but they were succeeded in power in 1710 by the Tories who were disposed to peace. The Tories were at first only able to slacken the pace of the war. Swift's* pamphlet *The Conduct of the Allies* (1711) was written to dispose the nation in favour of peace.

Spanish Tragedy, The

A drama by Thomas Kyd*, probably written before 1590. It is the earliest important Revenge Tragedy*, and both by date and by influence it is one of the principal starting-points of the great age of Elizabethan drama. The plot has no known source and is presumably Kyd's invention. The scene is Spain, just after the Spanish-Portuguese war of 1580. Andrea, a Spanish nobleman, has been unchivalrously killed in battle by Balthazar, a Portuguese prince, who in turn is captured by Lorenzo, nephew of the King of Spain, and Horatio, son of Hieronimo, Marshal of Spain. The ghost of Andrea and the spirit of Revenge sit above stage and watch the action throughout: Andrea is to witness how his death is to be avenged. This process is most intricate, and centres on Bel-imperia, Lorenzo's sister. She and Andrea have been lovers, and in consequence she detests Balthazar, who nonetheless seeks her in marriage with Lorenzo's support. She deliberately slights Balthazar by cultivating the affections of Horatio, who is in consequence murdered by Lorenzo and Balthazar. Hieronimo – hitherto a background figure – discovers the identity of his son's murderers; half crazed with grief, he seeks justice, but his pleading is brushed aside by the king. He eventually secures it by contriving a play (within the play) in which the guilty parties suffer real deaths instead of simulated ones. Hieronimo then takes his own life after biting out his tongue. Thus Andrea (after displaying some impatience) watches how his own death is avenged. The audience sees how justice is brought about when it is left to mere human motives: not as Heaven would bring it, cleanly and economically, but wastefully and brutally, hatred breeding hatred, and callous contrivance countered by contrivance still more ruthless. Only Lorenzo can be described as an evil character – a Machiavellian* schemer; the other characters are driven out of their natural virtue by vindictive bitterness. Hieronimo himself is momentarily checked by Biblical authority – 'Vindicta mihi': 'Justice is mine, saith the Lord' (Romans: 12; 19), but he is driven on by the energy of his grief.

Kyd's poetry is undistinguished, but the play is theatrically so effective that it remained popular for a generation. In 1602 the play was expanded by some more effective verse, probably by Ben Jonson, whom the theatre manager Philip Henslowe* paid for additions in 1602. However, these obscure rather than enhance Kyd's essential drama.

Kyd was certainly influenced by the plays of Seneca*, for instance in his use of stichomythia* and in the role of the ghost. Kyd's own influence was great, and can be seen in *Hamlet**. The dilemma of revenge, in one aspect seen to be a duty and in another an acknowledged sin, deeply preoccupied the Elizabethans. At the lowest level it was a pretext for the violence that appealed to them in the theatre – the 'tragedy of blood'; at a higher level is presented the problem of how it could be executed against evil-doers who were men of power or protected by such men; at a higher level still it was a natural vehicle for dramatizing the theme of the corrupted conscience which both Renaissance* and Reformation* ideas brought to the forefront of social attention. *The Spanish Tragedy* was effective on all these planes.

Spark, Muriel (1918–)

Before becoming a novelist, she was a poet (*Collected Poems*, 1967). Her first novel was *The Comforters* (1957), which she has described as 'a novel about writing a novel' *ie* an experiment in, and exploration of what it means to write fiction. At about the same time she became a convert to Roman Catholicism, and her novels since have tended to take a parabolic form (characteristic of other contemporary novelists, *eg* Iris Murdoch*, William Golding*) combining overt, often wittily satirical realism with implications of an extra-realist, spiritual dimension. *Robinson* (1958), *Memento Mori* (1959), *Ballad of Peckham Rye* (1960), *The Bachelors* (1960), *The Prime of Miss Jean Brodie* (1961), *The Girls of Slender Means* (1963), *The Mandelbaum Gate* (1965), *The Public Image* (1968), *The Driver's Seat* (1970), *Not to Disturb* (1971).

Other writings include a stage play *Doctors of Philosophy* (1963), radio plays collected in *Voices at Play* (1961) and short stories *Collected Stories* (1967).

Bib: Stanford, D., *Muriel Spark: A biographical and critical study*; Stubbs, P., *Muriel Spark* (Writers and their Work series).

Sparta /ˈspaːtə/

One of the two principal states of ancient Greece, the other being Athens*. Whereas Athens was famous for its material, artistic, and intellectual civilization, Sparta cultivated the austere, warlike virtues. The two states were allies against the Persian invaders at the beginning of 5th C BC, but they fought against each other in the Peloponnesian War* of 431–404 BC, which ended in the downfall of Athens as the greatest power of the Greek world. The Spartans had no civilized virtues, but have always been considered as exemplars of the virtues of courage, endurance, and austerity of life.

Spectator, The

The name of two periodicals, the first appearing daily (1711–12 and 14), and the second a weekly, founded in 1828 and still continuing. The earlier is the more famous of the two, owing to the contributions of its famous editors, Addison* and Steele*; it had an important influence on the manners and culture of the time. The later *Spectator* has also had a distinguished history, however; it began as a radical* journal, but is now the leading intellectual weekly periodical of the right.

* *Reviews and Periodicals.*

Spencer, Herbert (1820–1903)

Philosopher. He was representative of one aspect of the Victorian period in his faith in Darwin's* theory of evolution and his trust in scientific progress. Politically he was individualist, and ethically utilitarian*. Some of his more influential works were: *First Principles* (1862); *Principles of Biology* (1864); *Principles of Psychology* (1870–2); *Principles of Sociology* (1877–96); *Principles of Ethics* (1893).

Spender, Stephen (b 1909)

Poet and critic. Son of a distinguished journalist, J. A. Spender, who was editor of the liberal *Westminster Gazette*. Educated at University College School, London, and University College, Oxford. At Oxford, he became friendly with the poets W. H. Auden*, C. Day Lewis*, and Louis MacNeice. The four, together with the novelist Christopher Isherwood, formed an influential group of left-wing writers in the 1930s. His volumes of verse include *Nine Entertainments* (1928), *Twenty Poems* (1930), *The Still Centre* (1939), *Ruins and Visions* (1942). As a critic he has written two studies of modern literature: *The Destructive Element* (1935) and *The Creative Element* (1953). Autobiography: *World within World* (1951). In 1953 he became co-editor of *Encounter*, a monthly review of culture and world affairs. In 1969 he published a study of student politics: *The Year of the Young Rebels*. In 1970 he became Professor of English Language and Literature at University College, London.

Spens, Sir Patrick

* *Sir Patrick Spens.*

Spenser, Edmund (1552?–99)

Poet. He probably started life in poverty; his father was a journeyman clothmaker, though the poet later claimed to be related to the aristocratic family of the Spencers of Althorp, who acknowledged him. He nevertheless received a good education at Merchant Taylors School and at Pembroke College, Cambridge, where he made friends with the distinguished scholar Gabriel Harvey*. Cambridge was strongly Protestant*, and Spenser there absorbed the almost Puritan* cast of opinion which was later strengthened by his experiences in Ireland. By 1579 he was in the service of the Earl of Leicester*, Queen Elizabeth's* chief court favourite, but he made an enemy of her chief statesman, William Cecil, Lord Burleigh. Burleigh was believed to favour the projected marriage of the Queen and the Duke of Alençon, and Spenser, who feared the match because it meant a Catholic alliance, satirized both men as the Fox and the Ape in the poem which was later published as *Mother Hubberd's Tale**. Burleigh's hostility seems to have been the reason for Spenser never achieving the high position at court that he hoped for.

In 1580, he became secretary to Lord Grey, the newly appointed Lord Deputy (Viceroy) of Ireland. Spenser spent most of the rest of his life there, returning to London in 1589–91 and 1595–97 to arrange the publication of his long poem *The Faerie Queene**. The English policy was to counteract Irish rebellion by settling English landlords upon the country, and in 1586 Spenser received the large estate of Kilcolman Castle near Cork. In 1598 Tyrone's rebellion broke out, the castle was burnt down, and Spenser had to escape to England. He died in 1599 in poverty though he was buried with honour near Chaucer* in Westminster Abbey*.

Spenser began his poetic career while still at school, translating from French poets, Marot and du Bellay, and this kind of work prepared him for the virtuosity and artifice of his first important poems, *The Shepherd's Calendar** (1579). He began his *Faerie Queene* in the same year, and the first three books were published in 1590; three more in 1596, and fragments of the seventh in 1609. It is possible that more still was written and lost when Kilcolman Castle was burnt. His other poems include: *Astrophel*, an elegy for Sir Philip Sidney, killed in 1586; *Complaints*, and *Daphnaida* (1591); *Amoretti*, love sonnets in honour of his bride, Elizabeth Boyle, and *Epithalamion*, one of his most famous poems, celebrating their marriage, published in 1595; *Colin Clout's Come Home Again* (1595) about his visit to England in 1589; *Prothalamion*, for the marriage of the Earl of Worcester's daughters, and *Four Hymns*, in 1596.

Spenser had exceptional command of all kinds of verbal music, and his handling of the 10-syllable line was instructive to Marlowe* in the latter's evolution of blank verse* into a richly expressive medium. He came to be known as the 'poet's poet' from being the master of this kind of skill, and also for a more disparaging reason; it is from Spenser that poets and poetry readers learned the narrow significance of the word 'poetic', as the expression of exalted and dreamlike feeling which has brought poetry into discredit with practical people. His influence was strong on Milton* and on reflective poets of 18th C such as Thomson* and Gray*. It was still stronger in 19th C, especially at the beginning of it, for instance on Shelley. Keats's* early poems too show strong Spenserian influence, but the later ones throw it off. In his own day the poet, twenty years his junior, who was farthest from him in style, was John Donne*; it is not surprising that 20th-C poets, who have tried to keep Spenser at arm's length, have cultivated Donne intensively. Nonetheless, Spenser was in his day the greatest English poet since Chaucer, his ultimate master. His remoteness is in part that of a now unfamiliar way of feeling – the Platonism* characteristic of the Renaissance*.

4.1.4; 6.2.1.

Bib: Judson, A. C., *Life*; Jones, H. S. V., *Spenser Handbook*; Renwick, W. L., *Edmund Spenser: an essay on Renaissance Poetry*; Lewis, C. S., in *The Allegory of Love*; Nelson, W., ed. *Form and Convention in the Poetry of Spenser*; Hough, G., *Preface to the Faerie Queene*; Fowler, A., *Spenser and the Numbers of Time*; Cummings, R. N., *Critical Heritage*.

Spenserian Stanza /spen'siəriən/

A verse form devised by Edmund Spenser* for his poem *Faerie Queene**. It consists of 8 10-syllable lines, plus a ninth line of 12 syllables (alexandrine), an iambic rhythm and a rhyme scheme as follows: *a b a b b c b c c*. Example from *Faerie Queene*:

And as she looked about, she did behold,
How over that same door was likewise writ,
'Be bold, be bold,' and everywhere 'Be bold',
That much she mused, yet could not construe it
By any riddling skill, or common wit.
At last she spied at that room's upper end,
Another iron door, on which was writ,
'Be not too bold'; whereto though she did bend
Her earnest mind, yet wist not what it might intend.

(Bk III, Canto xi, 54)

The stanza was used by Spenser's poetic disciples, Giles and Phineas Fletcher*, early in 17th C. It was revived in 18th C by reflective poets such as Thomson* (*The Castle of Indolence**), Akenside (*Virtuoso*, 1737), Shenstone (*Schoolmistress*, 1742), Beattie (*Minstrel*, 1771). The Romantics used it more notably, *eg* Byron* in *Childe Harold**, though he was never quite at home with it; Shelley* in his elegy on Keats, *Adonais**, and Keats* himself in his *Eve of St Agnes*. Since then it has been rarely used; its use and disuse are a fair index of the periods of rise and decline in Spenser's influence.

* 6.2.1.

Sphinx /sfiŋks/

A mythical monster of ancient Egypt, Assyria, and Greece. It may have originated in Egypt, where the most famous effigy of a sphinx survives, near the Great Pyramid of Giza; it is male, with the body of a lion and the head of a man, and it represents the pharaoh identified with the sun-god Ra. Assyrian sphinxes are also male, but Greek sphinxes are female and winged. The most famous legend about a sphinx is the Greek one about the monster that laid waste the neighbourhood of the Greek city of Thebes. The Muses had taught her a riddle, the answer to which the Thebans had to guess: 'What is that which is four-footed in the morning, two-footed at noon, and three-footed in the evening?'; when they failed to guess, the sphinx devoured them. At last the answer was guessed by Oedipus*: a man goes on all fours in infancy, on his feet in maturity, and with the aid of a stick in old age. The sphinx then destroyed herself.

Spitalfields /'spitlfi:ldz/

A district in east London, so called because from 12th to 16th C, it belonged to the religious foundation called the Hospital of St Mary. Later the district was colonized by French Protestant refugee silk weavers.

Spondee /'spondi:/

In ancient Greek and Latin poetry, a unit of verse measure composed of two long syllables; in English verse, two accented syllables. Words like 'maintain', 'wineglass' in English may be spondees, just as 'again' is an iambus, and 'only' is a trochee. It is possible to find whole lines of verse in trochee (falling) rhythm, and usual to find lines in iambic (rising) rhythm, but whole lines in spondaic rhythm have to be artificially contrived, *eg*

Slow spon/dee stalks; / strong foot.

* *Metre.*

Sport

* *Field Sports.*

Spring Gardens

A fashionable place of amusement in 17th-C London, situated between what is now Trafalgar Square and St James's Park. Later in 17th C their popularity was displaced by the New Spring Gardens at Vauxhall*, further west.

Sprung Rhythm

A term used by the poet Gerard Manley Hopkins* to denote the method by which his verse is to be scanned. In his time most English verse was written in Running Rhythm, *ie* metres with regular stresses in the line:

Tonight the winds begin to rise

And roar from yonder dropping day

(Tennyson – *In Memoriam*)

Hopkins wished to free English verse from this rhythm, so as to bring verse into closer accord with common speech, to emancipate rhythm from the linear unit, and to achieve a freer range of emphasis. His theory of Sprung Rhythm (contained in the Preface to his Poems) is complicated, perhaps because he felt he had to justify himself to rather academic metricists like his friend Robert Bridges*. In fact he was reviving the rhythm of old English Alliterative* Verse (he cites Langland's *Piers Plowman** as being in Sprung Rhythm) and in folk poetry including many ballads* and nursery rhymes*. In Sprung Rhythm the number of stresses in each line is regular, but they do not occur at regular intervals, nor do the lines have a uniform number of syllables. The rhythm also drives through the stanza, and is not basically linear. The following is an example:

Súmmer énds now; now, barbarous in béauty, the
stóoks rise
Aróund; up abóve, what wind-walks! what
lóvely beháviour
Of sílk-sack clóuds! has wílder, wílful wávier
Méal-drift móulded éver and mélted across skíes?
(Hopkins – *Hurrahing in Harvest*)

Spurgeon, Charles Haddon (1834–92) /spəːdʒən/

An extremely popular Baptist* preacher, for whom the Metropolitan Tabernacle, Newington, London, was built to hold audiences of 6,000. His sermons were in the old Puritan* tradition, with strong appeals to the emotions and the conscience, but also varied by a bold and unusual kind of humour. In doctrine he was thoroughly traditional, and eventually he left the Baptists because of his distrust of the new biblical criticism.

Squire

In the middle ages, a young gentleman in training for knighthood, who acted as attendant to a knight. The term became synonymous with 'gentleman', particularly of the landowning sort, and a village squire would be the chief landowner in the neighbourhood or 'manor'; his house was often known as the 'manor house', and many of the inhabitants of the neighbourhood were likely to be tenants on his land. In English social history the 'squirearchy' is a term used for the class of medium landowners, more important than the yeoman freeholders, but less important than the landed nobility with great estates. An example of the older use of the term 'squire' is the knight's son in Chaucer's *Canterbury Tales**; an example of the later and more familiar use is Squire Western in Fielding's novel *Tom Jones**. Another form of the word is 'esquire' and the British habit of addressing envelopes, *eg* John Smith, Esq., is a polite assumption that the addressee is a gentleman.

The word is also used sometimes for a male escort of a lady, hence 'to squire (escort) a lady'.

Squire's Tale, The

One of Chaucer's *Canterbury Tales**, in 10-syllable rhymed couplets*. Its origin is unknown, and it is unfinished. Cambuscan, king of Tartary, is brought magic gifts from the king of Arabia, including a ring for his daughter Canace. The ring enables her to understand the language of birds, and she listens to a lament by a female falcon who has been deserted by the male 'tercelet' falcon. The tale is thus a romance of courtly love suited to the character of the teller. The franklin* (a middle-class landowner) compliments the squire at the end of it for the refined breeding that his choice of story shows him to have.

Stagirite, The /ˈstadʒirait/

The philosopher Aristotle*, from his birthplace, Stageira, in northern Greece.

Staple Inn

One of the old Inns of Court*, or places of residence for lawyers, in London. It may derive its name from originally being a place of exchange for the wool trade.

Star Chamber

A room in the old Palace of Westminster* with a ceiling ornamented with stars. From 14th C to 1641, it was used for meetings of the royal council, sometimes for judicial purposes. Judicial meetings of the Council came to be known as the Court of the Star Chamber; it was used to try accused men who were too powerful to be tried by an ordinary court of law with a jury. However it was 'a prerogative court', *ie* it depended directly on royal authority, unlike the Common Law* courts with which the king had very little, if any, power to interfere. Its oppressive role under James I* and Charles I* led to its abolition by Parliament* just before the outbreak of the Civil War.*

* *Courts of Law.*

Stars and Stripes, The

The national flag of the United States. The stars represent the states of the Union.

Stationers

In modern English, sellers of writing materials. In the Middle Ages* and until mid-17th C, however, they were booksellers, and were so called from their practice of taking up stalls or 'stations' at suitable places in cathedral towns (*eg* against the walls of St Paul's Cathedral in London) and universities. In 16th and early 17th C they not only sold books, but printed and published them as well. The absence of a law of copyright* (until 1709) made it lawful for stationers to publish authors' manuscripts whenever and however they could procure them, without the authors' permission. This kind of unauthorized publishing is now called 'pirating'. 18 of Shakespeare's plays were possibly pirated before the publication of the first collected edition of his plays in the First Folio* of 1623, and the fact has caused some difficulties to scholars; there is no assurance that their publication was authorized by the poet, that he had revised the plays for publication, or even that the stationer had procured a reliable version.

The Stationers' Company was formed in 1557 by royal charter; by this charter, no one not a member was entitled to publish a book except by special privilege, and all stationers had to record the titles of books they published; the Company's record of books is thus an important source of information for the literary historian, and particularly valuable evidence in dating many Elizabethan plays. The Company gradually lost its publishing monopoly in 17th C.

The modern institution, Her Majesty's Stationery Office, publishes official government documents.

Steele, Sir Richard (1672–1729)
Essayist and journalist. He was educated (with Addison*) at Charterhouse School; on leaving Oxford University he entered the army. His prose treatise *The Christian Hero* (1701) attracted the favour of King William III*, but caused Steele the inconvenience of finding that he was expected to live up to his own precepts. This his pleasure-loving nature did not find convenient, and he redressed the balance by his comedy *The Funeral* (1701). He wrote other comedies: *The Lying Lover* (1703); *The Tender Husband* (1705), an imitation of Molière's* *Sicilienne*; *The Conscious Lovers* (1722). It is not, however, for his comedies that he is now read, but for a new kind of periodical essay* of which he was practically the inventor, and which he published in *The Tatler**, started in 1709, and appearing three times weekly. Although since the lapsing of the Licensing Act in 1695 there was no active censorship* of political opinion, Steele found it safer to avoid politics at least after the Tory party came to power in 1710, since he was a consistent Whig*. His essays treated daily life, manners and behaviour, in a way calculated to educate middle-class readers and win the approval of people of virtue, and yet always to entertain them. These motives and the kind of interest that his essays inspired anticipate the character of later 18th-C novels, especially those of Richardson*. *The Tatler* was already a success when Addison started to collaborate with Steele, but they closed it down in 1711, and started the still more famous *Spectator** (1711–12). The crisis of succession to the throne grew intense in 1713–14: the Whigs favoured the Protestant House of Hanover and a powerful Tory faction was ready to support Anne's half-brother James if he would turn Protestant, though other Tories remained loyal to the Act of 1701 in favour of Hanover. Steele was consequently attacked by the Tory journalist, Swift*, both for his conduct of his next paper, *Guardian* (1713), and for his pamphlet* in favour of the Protestant succession, *The Crisis* (1714). In 1714 the Whigs returned to power and Steele's political fortunes revived; he was knighted in 1715, and received various official posts. In 1714 he produced his autobiographical *Apology for Himself and his Writings*; he also edited a number of other periodicals, all of them short-lived, and none with the fame of *Tatler* and *Spectator*: *Englishman*, *Reader*, *Town Talk*, *Tea-Table*, *Chit Chat*, *Plebeian*. The last, a political paper, led to a quarrel with Addison in 1718.
Bib: Aitken, G. A., *Life*; Hazlitt, W., *The English Comic Writers*; Dobree, B., *Variety of Ways*; Bateson, F. W., *English Comic Drama*, 1700–50.

Stella

[1] The name used by Sir Philip Sidney* for Penelope Devereux in his sonnet sequence *Astrophil and Stella** ('Star-lover and star') published in 1591; she married Lord Rich.

[2] The name used by Jonathan Swift* for Esther Johnson in his *Journal to Stella*, published in 1768.

Stentor /'stento:/
A Greek warrior in Homer's *Iliad**; his voice was as loud as the voices of fifty other men.

Stephen, Sir Leslie (1832–1904)
Critic and biographer. He began his career as a tutor at Trinity Hall, Cambridge, and university rules demanded that he should be in orders as an Anglican* clergyman. His philosophical studies led him to the religious scepticism so frequent among intellectuals of the middle and later 19th C, and he renounced his orders in 1875. From 1866 he contributed critical essays to the *Cornhill Magazine** and political ones for the *Nation*; he also wrote for the *Saturday Review* and helped to found the *Pall Mall Gazette* (1865). In 1871 he became editor of the *Cornhill*; the 11 years of his editorship made it one of the most distinguished literary reviews of later 19th C. His critical essays were published in book form in *Hours in a Library* (1874, 6, 9). He wrote philosophical essays, defining his agnostic position: *Essays on Free Thinking and Plain Speaking* (1873). He contributed a number of biographies to the *English Men of Letters* series: *Johnson* (1878); *Pope* (1880); *Swift* (1882); *George Eliot* (1902), and *Hobbes* (1904). His most distinguished work is firstly his editorship of the *Dictionary of National Biography*, started in 1882, to which he contributed many of the articles, and his book on *The English Utilitarians* (1900). His last book, *English Literature and Society in the Eighteenth Century*, was published on the day of his death.

Today, Stephen is second only to Matthew Arnold* as the most respected among critics of the later 19th C; the rigour and sincerity of his thinking make him exceptionally trustworthy, and he is one of the most distinguished links between the Victorians*, ourselves, and 18th-C rationalist traditions of thought which continued into 19th C in the Utilitarian* school of thinkers. He has twice been used as the basis of a character in the masterpieces of distinguished novelists: Vernon Whitford in *The Egoist** by Meredith*, and Mr Ramsay in *To the Lighthouse** by Virginia Woolf*, his daughter by his second wife. His first wife had been a daughter of the novelist William Makepeace Thackeray*.

* 7.4; *Agnosticism; Reviews and Periodicals.*
Bib: Lives by F. W. Maitland; Noel Annan

Sterne, Laurence (1713–68)
Novelist. The son of an army officer, he spent his childhood in camps and garrisons; after leaving Cambridge, he became an Anglican priest near York, where his great-grandfather had been Archbishop. His famous novel, *Tristram Shandy**, appeared in successive volumes from 1760 until 1767. Opinion is much divided about the merit of this book to this day, but Sterne's reputation rests principally upon it; he wrote few other works, and

the only other that is widely known is the account of his travels, *A Sentimental Journey through France and Italy** (1768). Both books have aroused distaste owing to the alleged prurience of their humour, and later opinion has been astonished at the broadmindedness of his age, which tolerated such licence in a clergyman. Yet Sterne also published his sermons (under the title of *Sermons of Yorick*, 1760–67–69) and in their way they show that he took his profession of priest seriously; they are not spiritual and they do not moralize, but they show a genuine concern with practical wisdom based on an understanding of human instinct.

Sterne's contribution to the shaping of the novelistic vision is distinctive; he derives from a different tradition of thinking and feeling from the mixed traditions of the other leading 18th-C novelists. Defoe* followed the practical realism of 17th-C Puritanism* as it showed itself in the commercial classes; Richardson* was also in the Puritan tradition. Both were affected by the rationalism of the philosopher John Locke*, and so were Fielding* and Smollett*, though they were not in the least Puritan. Sterne, on the other hand, is one of the leaders of the later 18th-C reaction towards a life of feeling and fantasy; he not only anticipates writers of the early 19th C such as the essayist Lamb*, but even 20th-C subjective novelists such as Virginia Woolf*. However, he is still strongly 18th C in the cool, ironic wit which accompanies his sentiment; this irony recalls Swift, but the boldness of Sterne's imaginative humour owes much to the 16th-C Frenchman, Rabelais*, and to the Spaniard, Cervantes*, writing in early 17th C. The *Essays* of Montaigne were perhaps another influence, anticipating Sterne's sceptical and searching investigation of individual psychology. Much of his interest to 20th C arises from the frankness with which Sterne faces the problems of writing a novel (*eg* where is it natural to start?) and these problems are in fact an important part of his subject.

* 4.3.3; *Eighteenth-century Literature*; *Novel*; *Sermons*.

Bib: Cross, W. L., *Life*; Traugott, J., *Sterne's Philosophical Rhetoric*; McKillop, A. D., in *Early Masters of English Fiction*; Fluchère, H., a general study in French (abridged English translation); Stephen, L., in *Hours in a Library*; Woolf, V., in *The Common Reader*.

Stevenson, Robert Louis Balfour (1850–94)

Novelist, essayist, poet. The son of an engineer, he intended to take up the same profession, for which he showed early talent, but bad health prevented this. Partly because of his health and partly for love of travel, he spent much of his life abroad, and some of his best writing is in essays of travel, *eg An Inland Voyage* (1878) and *Travels with a Donkey in the Cevennes* (1879). His most famous works, however, are the fantasy, so often used as an emblem of divided personality, *The Strange Case of Dr Jekyll and Mr Hyde* (1886 – * *Jekyll and Hyde*), and his boys' adventure story, *Treasure Island** (1883). Still well known are his Scottish historical romances, in the tradition of Walter Scott*: *Kidnapped* (1886), *The Master of Ballantrae* (1889), and *Catriona* (1893); it has been said that *Weir of Hermiston*, also in this style but left unfinished, would have been his masterpiece. Other works of fiction: *New Arabian Nights* (1882); *Prince Otto* (1885); *The Black Arrow* (1888); *The Wrong Box* (1889); *The Wrecker* (1892); *Island Nights Entertainments* (1893); *The Ebb Tide* (1894); *St Ives*, also left unfinished at his death. Essays: *Virginibus Puerisque* (1881); *Familiar Studies of Men and Books* (1882); *Vailima Letters* (1895). His *A Child's Garden of Verses* (1885) was for long considered a minor children's classic, and he published other poetry in *Underwoods* (1887). Stevenson was strongly influenced by French ideas of literary style, and his preoccupation with style apart from the substance that is being expressed was characteristic of the aestheticism* of the later 19th-C, and has lost favour now. He had too much love of the world of action and simplicity of mind, however, to make it possible to class him with the aesthetes.

Bib: Life by Graham Balfour; Daiches, D., *Robert Louis Stevenson*; Elwin, M., *The Strange Case of Stevenson*; Furnas, J. C., *Voyage to Windward* (life).

Stichomythia

A terse but artificial style of dramatic dialogue, used in disputes between two characters, each speaking in turn a single line of verse. It originated in ancient Greek tragedies; from them it passed to Seneca* whose influence caused it to be used by some of the early Elizabethans, *eg* Thomas Kyd in *The Spanish Tragedy* and Shakespeare in *Richard III* (III. ii):

King Richard:	*Wrong not her birth; she is of royal blood.*
Queen Elizabeth:	*To save her life, I'll say she is not so.*
Richard:	*Her life is safest only in her birth.*
Elizabeth:	*And only in that safety died her brothers.* (*&c.*)

Stock Exchange

An institution in London for the purchase and sale of investments in the form of shares, stocks, and bonds; it is the largest of its kind in the world. London stockbrokers once met at the Royal Exchange and elsewhere for the transaction of their business, but in 1802 they formed themselves into a society and built their own premises on the present site between Throgmorton Street and Old Broad Street.

Stoics /'stəuiks/

A school of philosophy founded by the Greek Zeno of Citium, 4th C BC. It later extended to Rome, where its leaders became Epictetus and Seneca* (both 1st C AD) and the Roman Emperor Marcus Aurelius (2nd C AD). They reasoned that all being is material, and therefore the soul is, and so are the virtues. The soul in man, however, is

Stonehenge

an active principle which sustains the body, and proceeds from God; only the active principle has significance, and the wise man is therefore indifferent to material suffering and cares only for virtue governed by his judgement which is in accordance with the principles of wisdom. Some of the ethical principles of Stoicism were in accordance with Christianity (which Marcus Aurelius nevertheless persecuted) and, abstracted from religious doctrine, they appealed to the Renaissance* ideal of the noble soul; hence the recurrence of Stoic attitudes in the drama of Shakespeare* and his contemporaries.

Stonehenge

Concentric circles of standing stones, some of them very large, situated on the chalk plateau called Salisbury Plain* in central southern England. They are prehistoric, dating perhaps from the second millenium BC, but their purpose is unknown; one theory ascribes it to sun-worship, and another to burial.

Storey, David (b 1933)

Novelist and dramatist. *This Sporting Life* (1960); *Flight into Camden* (1960); *Radcliffe* (1963); *Pasmore* (1972); *Saville* (1976).

Before he became a novelist and playwright he was an art student, and to pay for his studies in London he played at weekends in professional Rugby League football for a northern team. The son of a miner, Storey is the most interesting of a number of novelists in modern Britain who have in common that their social viewpoint is outside the middle class and centred geographically outside London. Their obvious antecedent is D. H. Lawrence*. He is distinguished from his contemporaries with a similar background by the absence of social belligerence and an ability to reach across from a provincial-industrial world denuded of art to a world of highly cultivated sensibility without playing false to the social experience that shaped him. His first novel, which has been filmed, is about his background world, in which sport is the principal cultural force; the next two are in different ways more ambitious and less successful, but their faults are interesting as the price paid for their serious experimental boldness. Storey's plays have originality and distinction: *The Restoration of Arnold Middleton* (1966); *In Celebration* (1969); *The Contractor* (1970); *Home* (1970); *The Changing Room* (1971); *The Farm* (1973); *Life Class* (1974).

Strachey, Giles Lytton (1880–1932)

/ˈstreitʃi/

Biographer. His best-known works are *Eminent Victorians* (1918) – short biographical studies of Cardinal Manning, Florence Nightingale, and General Gordon – and *Queen Victoria* (1921). He also wrote *Elizabeth and Essex* (1928), and criticism: *Landmarks in French Literature* (1912) and *Books and Characters* (1922).

Strachey regarded most biographies of 19th C as dull monuments to the subject, whereas he considered biography to be an art form, presenting the subject as a human being, and showing him or her from unexpected aspects.

Strachey was a prominent member of the Bloomsbury Group*.

* *Biography.*

Bib: Sanders, C. P., *Strachey: His Mind and Art*; Johnstone, J. K., *The Bloomsbury Group*. Holroyd, M., *Lytton Strachey*

Strafford, Sir Thomas Wentworth, first Earl of (1593–1641)

Statesman, and one of Charles I's* chief ministers. He began his career as an opponent of the king; as Member of Parliament for Yorkshire in 1625, he opposed the attempt of Charles's minister, the Earl of Buckingham, to raise taxes for war against Spain, and in 1627 he was imprisoned for refusing to contribute a forced loan to the king. His opposition to Charles was different in motive from that of other members; theirs was based on the desire to assert the power of Parliament*, whereas Wentworth's motive was to secure efficient government. Consequently when in 1628 Parliament asserted itself by forcing on the king the Petition of Right*, he changed sides. Charles in 1632 sent him to Ireland to reform the administration there; this he did very efficiently by his policy of 'Thorough'. He was by far the most efficient of the king's ministers, but Charles never consulted him on English affairs until the major crisis brought about by the defeat of the royal troops by the Scots in 1639. Wentworth was then recalled, and made Earl of Strafford in 1640; events, however, had gone so far that he could no longer help the king, and merely focused public hostility upon himself. Parliament condemned him to death by an Act of Attainder (*ie* a law effecting death of a subject without using the normal judicial process), and he was executed accordingly.

Strawberry Hill

* *Walpole, Horace.*

Strindberg, August (1849–1912)

Swedish dramatist and novelist. His father, a shipping agent, married his servant who had been his mistress during his first marriage. The unpromising circumstances of this parentage, intensified by his bad relations with his father, were the beginning of a psychologically tormented life for Strindberg; he was married and divorced three times, and had a mental breakdown in 1895–6, described in *Inferno*, one of several autobiographical fragments and a vivid document. Intellectually he was immensely versatile: a student of Chinese, botany, chemistry, alchemy and painting. He had comparable literary versatility, including radical journalism (1872–80), prose fiction (notably *The Red Room*, 1879), and his varied, original dramas. He is chiefly famous, at least outside Sweden, for the last. He wrote historical dramas (*Master Olof*, 1872; *Saga of the Folkungs*, *Gustavus Vasa*, *Eric XIV*, 1899) which show the influence of Shakespeare's History Plays*; naturalist tragedies influenced by Zola's* naturalism and the philosophy of Nietzsche*; fantasies (*Easter*, 1900; *Dream Play*, 1902) under the influence of the Belgian dramatist, Maeterlinck; and, at the end of his career, highly symbolic dramas often called 'expressionist', of which the best known is *The Ghost Sonata* (1907). Two partly autobiographic works, *To Damascus* (1898) and *The Great Highway* (1909–12) can also be grouped under this 'expressionist' heading.

Strindberg's dramatic inspiration was to epitomize human experience as fundamentally the experience of conflict, and he sought to dramatize this conflict at its deepest and most intense. This shows most clearly in his naturalist phase, especially the two plays by which he is best known in Britain: *The Father* (1887) and *Lady Julia* (1888). To these may be added the double play *The Dance of Death* (1901), a naturalist tragedy verging towards the expressionist symbolism of his later work. One of his strongest preoccupations at this period was the theme of conflict in the relationship of women with men, since he considered women to be undergoing a fundamental change in their nature in consequence of their struggle for emancipation. His parentage and experiences of marriage were clearly influences on him in this theme. He was strongly aware of the possibilities of the stage as a medium for dramatic experiment, and enhanced the visual as distinct from the dialogue constituent in drama. In dialogue he was also experimental, though not with such decisive success as his Russian contemporary, Anton Chekhov*.

In Britain (in contrast to America), Strindberg did not have an influence comparable to that of Ibsen* until after the Second World War. Since then, the outspokenness of such dramatists as John Osborne* and John Arden*, and the dialogue and stage experiments of Harold Pinter* and Samuel Beckett*, as well as new freedoms shown by many dramatists in the handling of stage sets and dramatic plots, all show his impact.

Strophe /ˈstrəufi/

A Greek word meaning 'turn'. It is used as a term in Greek versification, for example, the Pindaric Ode, for a passage which is sung and danced (or 'turned') by a chorus. When another passage succeeds it, to be danced and sung by another part of the chorus, this second passage is known as an 'antistrophe'.

* *Ode.*

Structuralism

A method of studying phenomena in terms of the relationship of their structures, on the assumption that this enables the assimilation of apparently dissimilar phenomena within an intelligible system. The method is especially associated with the French anthropologist Claude Levi-Strauss, whose investigations of widely separate societies and cultures have demonstrated common meanings relating their unlike institutions, social practices and mythologies. The structuralist method has spread to other disciplines, including the study of literature, partly because it affords an escape from excessive specialization within each discipline, and partly because it offers opportunities for comparing and associating hitherto distinct disciplines, such as literature and anthropology.

Literary structuralism has had other progenitors besides Levi-Strauss. These include the French linguist Saussure who conceived the possibility of a science of semiology based on the belief that all social behaviour is structured in codes, or sign-systems, of which language is the most important and most central. Semiology is thus a kind of structuralism; its best-known practitioner is the French critic Roland Barthes. The Russian 'Formalist' school of literary criticism, active between 1915 and 1930, were also structuralist precursors: they analysed narratives in terms of their supposed universal constituents and processes, thus employing what is essentially the structuralist method later elaborated by French and American critics such as the Canadian Northrop Frye in his *Anatomy of Criticism*.

The American, Robert Scholes, in *Structuralism in Literature*, traces the seeds of literary structuralism back to English Romantic critics. Coleridge* in his *Biographia Literaria*,* developing critical ideas from the philosophy of Kant*, conceptualized the human imagination as the power inherent in us of giving significant form to the flux of our experience of nature. Shelley*, in *Defence of Poetry*, developed from Coleridge the idea that the poet (broadly interpreted as the literary artist) shapes experience on behalf of his society, thus reaching his famous definition of the poet as 'the unacknowledged legislator of mankind'.

Literary structuralism has been very active in France and America in the 1970s. In Britain it is currently active in the universities, but it is not yet possible to say how fruitful it is likely to become in critical and imaginative literary achievement. Structuralism seems to enlarge knowledge of literature as a social and anthropological phenomenon; the best English critics have on the whole been evaluators.

Stuart (Stewart), House of /stju:ət/

The family from which came the sovereigns of Scotland between 1371 and 1603, and the sovereigns of Scotland, England, and Ireland between 1603 and 1714. The family originated in Brittany, from where they migrated to England in 11th C and to Scotland in 12th, where they acquired the surname 'Stuart' (variously spelt) by serving the kings of Scotland as Stewards. They came to the Scottish throne by intermarriage with the Bruce family, and the reigns until 1603 were as follows: Robert II (1371–90); Robert III (1390–1406); James I* (1406–37); James II (1437–60); James III (1460–88); James IV (1488–1513); James V (1513–42); Mary (1542, deposed 1567); James VI (1567–1603). In 1603 Elizabeth I* of England died childless, and James VI inherited the crown of England by virtue of his descent from Elizabeth's aunt Margaret, who had married James IV. James VI thus became also James I* of England, and ruled over the two countries until 1625. The succession continued as follows: Charles I* (1625–49), after whom there was an interregnum* until 1660 when the monarchy was restored in his son, Charles II* (1660–85); James II* (1685–88) was deposed in the Revolution of 1688* and was succeeded by his daughter Mary II* and her husband William III* reigning jointly. After the death without surviving children of Anne (1702–14), the Protestant line of the Stuarts died out, and Parliament* established the Protestant and German House of Hanover (descended from a daughter of James VI and I) on the throne of the United Kingdom. James II had left a Catholic descendant behind him, however, and the Catholic Stuarts twice attempted to regain the throne in the Jacobite* Rebellions of 1715 and 1745. The direct line of the House of Stuart died out in 1808.

* 1.3.1.2.

Styx /stiks/

A river of the underworld of the dead in Greek myth, generally its boundary, so that 'crossing the Styx' is synonymous with dying. An oath invoking the River Styx was binding on gods and mortals. It was crossed by Charon's* ferry.

* *Hades.*

Suckling, Sir John (1609–42)

A Cavalier poet*. He was one of the leaders of the Royalist party, and fled abroad after the failure of his attempt to devise the escape of Strafford* from the Tower of London in 1641. He had been a lavish and brilliant courtier at the Court of Charles I*, and his 17th-C biographer, John Aubrey*, declares that he committed suicide in fear of poverty. His verse has the lightness and wit of the Cavalier poets, and the character Millamant in Congreve's play *The Way of the World** describes him as 'natural, easy Suckling'. His *A Session of the Poets* describes a meeting of 'the sons of Ben', *ie* the circle surrounding Ben Jonson* – the poet with strongest influence on the Cavalier poets. His best known poem is *A Ballad upon a Wedding* (pub 1640). He also wrote four plays.

Bib: Aubrey, J., in *Brief Lives*.

Suffragette Movement

Colloquial term for the Women's Suffrage Movement which pursued violent action to secure political rights for women before and during the first World War. Specifically they wanted equal rights with men to have the vote (suffrage) in parliamentary elections and to be candidates for election. Among the famous leaders of the movement were Mrs Pankhurst and her two daughters, Sylvia and Christabel. The movement ended in 1918 when votes were given to women at the age of 30; in 1928 they received equal rights with men.

Summoner's Tale, The

One of Chaucer's *Canterbury Tales**, a fabliau* written in 10-syllable rhymed couplets*. A summoner was an official of a bishop's court, and responsible for bringing cases before it. As such, he was an unpopular figure in 14th-C England, as were begging friars whose function it was to acquire money for their order, possibly by extortion. The friar and the summoner among the Canterbury pilgrims are bitter enemies. When the summoner's turn comes to tell a tale, the friar has just told one about an extortionate summoner who has been carried off by the devil; the summoner retorts by describing how a begging friar is frustrated from extorting money from a woman whose husband is on a sick bed.

* *Friar's Tale.*

Supremacy, Acts of

[1] The law passed through Parliament* on the initiative of King Henry VIII* in 1534; it established the King as Supreme Head of the Church in England, and thus displaced the sovereignty of the Pope. The Act was the immediate consequence of Henry's dispute with the Pope over his attempt to divorce his Queen, Catherine of Aragon; however, this immediate cause was insufficient by itself to bring about the break. Deeper causes include the growth of national feeling; long-standing resentment against some forms of papal taxation; distrust of Roman Catholic doctrine, first roused by Wycliffe* and now reawakened by the German reformer, Luther*; growing dislike of the international religious orders of monks and friars who were ultimately subject to the Pope. Nonetheless, Henry was a conservative in doctrine, and the act did not entail doctrinal reformation.

[2] The similar law passed through Parliament on the initiative of Elizabeth I* in 1559. Since the

act of 1534, the English nation had undergone Protestant* doctrinal reformation* in the reign of Edward VI* and had reverted to full Roman Catholicism under headship of the Pope in the reign of Mary I*. Both the reformers and the counter-reformers had gone further than the nation wished; in consequence Elizabeth's Act of Supremacy was deliberately vague, so as to gain the widest possible national support, from both Protestant and Roman Catholic sympathizers. Elizabeth abandoned the title 'Supreme Head' and adopted that of 'Supreme Governor'.

Surrey, Henry Howard, Earl of (1517–47)
Poet. He was the son of the Duke of Norfolk, the senior nobleman of England. Surrey and his father were both arrested by Henry VIII* on a ridiculous charge of high treason. Surrey was executed, Henry's last victim; his father, also condemned to death, survived Henry and was reprieved. In character Surrey was a man of the Renaissance*, with the Renaissance conception of the courtier as the complete man in all worthy things – art, learning and action. His poetry was thus a cultivation of poetic ideals on the model of the poets of the Italian Renaissance, and he shares with his older contemporary, Sir Thomas Wyatt* the distinction of being the first poet to naturalize Renaissance poetic modes in English; their work was published by Tottel* in his *Miscellany* of 1557. Like Wyatt, Surrey cultivated the sonnet*, and he was the first poet to use blank verse*, in his translation of Virgil's *Aeneid**, Bks 2 and 3. However, Surrey was respected for these contributions more by past critics than he is by modern critics, who point out that the merit of his poetry is much slighter than Wyatt's, and that the flowering of the English short poem in the 1590s owes more to the sonnets of Sidney* (*Astrophil and Stella**) and to Spenser's pastorals *The Shepherd's Calendar** than to the work of either Wyatt or Surrey.
Bib: Casady, E., *Life*.

Surtees, Robert Smith (1803–64) /ˈsəːtiːz/
Novelist. In 1832 he helped to found the *New Sporting Magazine* which he edited for five years, and to which he contributed sketches collected in 1838 under the title of *Jorrocks's Jaunts and Jollities*. It was this book which suggested to the publishers, Chapman and Hall, the idea that Dickens* might write a similar series of sketches about a Nimrod Club of amateur sportsmen. Dickens adapted this idea to the Pickwick Club, and thus started *The Pickwick Papers**, issued in 20 parts in 1836–37 and published in book form in 1837. Surtees's most famous fox-hunting novel is probably *Handley Cross* (1843), still regarded as a minor classic. He published eight novels in all.

Swedenborg, Emanuel (1688–1772) /ˈswiːdnboːg/
Swedish scientist, philosopher, and theologian. The earlier part of his life was dedicated to the natural sciences, and his theories anticipate important discoveries in geology, cosmology, and especially in the physiology of the brain. Later he devoted himself to religion and had mystical experiences: his religious beliefs led to the founding of the New Jerusalem Church and the English Theosophical Society. According to Swedenborg's beliefs, God is Divine Man, whose essence is infinite love; there are correspondences between spiritual nature and material nature, but the former is alive and the latter is dead; both in God and in man and nature there are three degrees, those of love, wisdom and use, or end, cause and effect; by a love of each degree man comes into relation with them, and his end is to become the image of his Creator, God. Swedenborg's *Heaven and Hell* and *True Christian Religion* were translated into English in 1778 and 1781, and amongst his followers were the father of the poet William Blake*, and Blake's friend, the sculptor, John Flaxman. Swedenborg's doctrines are the starting point of much of Blake's thinking. But Blake, who wrote comments on Swedenborg's doctrines, came to disagree with the philosopher in important respects; for instance Swedenborg had written that there were two receptacles for God in man – the will, for divine love, and the understanding, for divine wisdom, whereas for Blake the will was always evil.

Swift, Jonathan (1667–1745)
Satirist. He was of an old English family, but his grandfather seems to have lost his fortune on the Cavalier side in the Civil Wars* of mid-17th C; the poet Dryden* was his cousin. Swift was educated in Ireland, where he had the future playwright Congreve* as a schoolfellow, and took his degree at Trinity College, Dublin. He began his working life as secretary to the statesman and writer Sir William Temple* in 1689, left him to take orders as a priest in the Church of England in 1694 (receiving a small ecclesiastical office in Ireland), and returned to remain in Temple's service until Temple's death in 1699. Throughout the reign of Queen Anne (1702–14) he played a large part in the literary and the political life of London, though he was dividing his time between England and Ireland. He contributed some numbers to Addison and Steele's journals, *The Tatler** and *The Spectator**, and together with Pope* and Arbuthnot founded the Scriblerus Club*. Politically he at first served the Whig* party, but in 1710 he changed over to the Tories, led by Edward Harley, Earl of Oxford, and the brilliant but unreliable Bolingbroke. He served the Tories by his pamphlet* *The Conduct of the Allies* (1711) advocating peace in the War of the Spanish Succession*, and by his conduct of the journal *The Examiner* (1710–11). His assistance was invaluable to the Tory party, who held power from 1711 until the death of the Queen; in 1713 Swift was rewarded by being made Dean of St Patrick's Cathedral, Dublin, an office which he at first held as an absentee. By this time, however, the Queen was dying, and Harley and Bolingbroke, divided over the succession to the throne, were opponents. Bolingbroke offered Swift great rewards for his support, but Swift preferred to remain with

Harley, who had lost power and for a time was even in danger of losing his life. In 1714 the Queen died, the Whigs returned to power, Bolingbroke fled, and George I came over from Germany as King. Swift left England for his Deanery in Ireland. At first he had few friends there, but between 1720 and 1730 he wrote a number of eloquent pamphlets in the interests of the oppressed Irish, and ended by achieving great popularity. The same decade saw the crisis of his relationships with the two women who loved him: Esther Johnson, the 'Stella' of his *Journal to Stella*, compiled 1710–13, and Esther Vanhomrigh, whom he called 'Vanessa'. The relationship with the latter was tragically concluded with her death in 1723; Stella died in 1728. Swift lived as a conscientious and efficient Dean almost to the end of his life, unselfishly disposing of most of his wealth for the poor, but he went out of his mind in 1742.

Swift wrote a great deal of prose, chiefly in the form of pamphlets, and not all of it is satire; *The Conduct of the Allies* is not, for instance, nor are his sermons*. However, his great reputation rests principally on his prose satire, and he is especially admired for the very subtle and powerful form of his irony. The surface of his prose is limpidly clear and beguilingly placid, but his use of it is to enforce by close logic an impossible and commonly very shocking proposition, which is driven home with distinct and startling imagery. His position is that of a sincere Christian who advocates reason; he despises alike the emptiness of the Deists* and the emotionalism of Puritans*. He is at the same time a strong humanitarian, who is revolted by injustices leading to so much suffering, but despairs of the capacity of the human race to rid itself of its tendency to bestiality and heartlessness. Though a believer in reason, he despised the pedantry of so many scholars, and the irrelevances of the 'natural philosophers'* in their pursuit of science. He has been censured on two grounds: first, the minor but undoubted one that his disgust at some aspects of human existence derived from his own morbidity, and secondly, the much more controversial one that his vision is in the end negative and destructive. His most famous works are as follows: *The Battle of the Books* (written 1697, published 1704), a contribution to the dispute between the relative merits of the ancients and the moderns in literature; *A Tale of a Tub** (1704), a satire on 'corruptions in religion and learning' and one of his masterpieces; *Argument against Abolishing Christianity* (1708), a satire on the irreligion of the time; *Drapier's Letters** (1724), against the monopoly granted by the English government to William Wood to provide the Irish with a copper coinage; *Gulliver's Travels** (1726); and *A Modest Proposal** (1729), a most forceful exposure of the conditions of the Irish poor.

Swift's poetry is much less well known; it is less in quantity and much of it lacks the immaculate art of his prose. His most admired poem is *On the Death of Dr Swift* (1731), a partly satirical poem in which he imagines public reaction to the news of his death, and then gives his own estimate of himself. His *Cadenus and Vanessa* gives the story of his love affairs with Esther Vanhomrigh, and was published at her request after her death: Cadenus is an anagram of Decanus = Dean.

* 3.3.2; 4.3.1; 7.2.

Bib: Ehrenpreis, I., *Life*; Quintana, R., *The Mind and Art of Jonathan Swift*; Williams, K., *Swift and the Age of Compromise*; Case, A. E., *Four Essays on Gulliver's Travels*; Traugott, J., ed. *Discussions of Swift*; Davis, H., *The Satire of Jonathan Swift*; Johnson, M., on the poetry of Swift; Price, M., on Swift's rhetoric; Leavis, F. R., in *The Common Pursuit*; Johnson, S., in *Lives of the Poets*; Williams, K., *Critical Heritage*.

Swinburne, Algernon Charles (1837–1909) /ˈswɪnbɜːn/

Poet and critic. His family background was aristocratic: his father was an admiral and his grandfather a baronet. He was educated at Eton and at Balliol College, Oxford. The English aristocracy has always been freer from subjection to social conventionality than the middle classes (as in the examples of Shelley* and Byron*) and Swinburne's opinions and tastes exemplify this aristocratic emancipation. The style of his poetry is very distinctive, and his literary sympathies were wide. In his first book, the dramas *The Queen Mother* and *Rosamond* (1860), he was, like most English 19th-C verse dramatists, in the Elizabethan* tradition, but his more famous *Atalanta in Calydon* (1865) as well as his much later *Erectheus* (1876) were in the style of the ancient Greek tragedy of Sophocles*. The eroticism of his lyrics in *Poems and Ballads* (1866) owed something to the Latin poet, Catullus*, and more to Pre-Raphaelite poetry of his own day, chiefly that of D. G. Rossetti*. In this book he is rebelling against the moral repressiveness of the dominant middle class attitude to sex; in the *Song of Italy* (1867) and *Songs before Sunrise* (1871) he is siding with Italian political revolt against oppression in the spirit of the French 19th-C poet Victor Hugo. *Chastelard* (1865) and *Bothwell* (1874) are the first two plays, again in Elizabethan style, on Mary Queen of Scots*, and were completed by *Mary Stuart* in 1881. A second series of *Poems and Ballads* in 1878 contains tributes to the contemporary French poets, Baudelaire and Théophile Gautier and translations of the medieval French poet François Villon. *Songs of the Springtides* and *Studies in Song* (1880) show the strong inspiration he drew from the sea, and the Arthurian legend *Tristram of Lyonesse* (1881) is a romance of the Middle Ages comparable to those of William Morris* and Alfred Tennyson*, amongst other mid-Victorians. In *Marino Falieri* (1887) he produced a drama on a theme drawn from medieval Venice already used by Byron (*Marino Falieri*, 1821); it was published with another drama, *Locrine*. Later works: the dramas *The Sisters* (in prose, 1892) and *Rosamund, Queen of the Lombards* (1899); poems – *Poems and Ballads*, 3rd series (1889); *Astrophel* (1894), *A Tale of Balen* (1896), *A Channel Passage* (1904), *The Duke of Gandia* (1908).

Swinburne was thus a poet who drew on a wide range of influences and interests, and was prolific in output. Yet the character of his work has come to seem narrow. The influence of the ancient Greeks and Romans, the Elizabethans, and the French both of the Middle Ages and of his own century, was in reality superficial; in reality he extended the much narrower range of mid-19th-C English romanticism, in verse that is extremely melodious and very varied in the handling of metre, but as vague and shallow in content as it is emotionally intense. Against the prejudices of his time, which declared that poets should be morally serviceable, he asserted the right to pursue the poetic vocation to express beauty, but this in itself isolated him from his age, which at its best was reaching beauty through the search for deeper moral experience in the novels of George Eliot* and Dickens*. He belongs, in the view of 20th-C critics, to the Spenserian strand of English poetry, and just as Spenser* in his own day invites contrast with his younger contemporary John Donne*, so modern critics are inclined to contrast Swinburne, to his own disadvantage, with his contemporary G. M. Hopkins*. The work of the latter was, however, not published until 20th C; Swinburne's own influence was strong on his younger contemporaries of the aesthetic* movement.

In his criticism, Swinburne is notable for studies of dramatists who were contemporaries of Shakespeare as well as of Shakespeare himself: *Study of Shakespeare* (1880); *The Age of Shakespeare* (1909). He also wrote a study of William Blake* (1868), *A Note on Charlotte Brontë* (1877), *A Study of Victor Hugo* (1886), amongst other criticism.

Swinburne also wrote novels, which are very little known; they have been praised by the distinguished American critic Edmund Wilson in *The Bit between my Teeth*. One of them, *Love's Cross-Currents*, was published in 1905. They show yet another influence upon him – that of the French 18th-C writer the Marquis de Sade*.

Bib: Gosse, E., *Life*; Lafourcade, G., *La Jeunesse de Swinburne*; literary biography (in English); Chew, S. C., *Swinburne* (critical study); Nicolson, H., *Swinburne*; Welby, T. E., *A Study of Swinburne*; Winwar, P., *The Rossettis and their Circle*; Eliot, T. S., 'Swinburne as a Poet' in *Selected Essays*; Hyder, C. K., *Critical Heritage*.

Swithin, St /ˈswiðin/

A bishop of Winchester who died in 862. William of Malmesbury (12th C) states that he requested to be buried 'where the rains of heaven might fall on him and he be trodden underfoot by those who entered the church'. This has led, obscurely, to a tradition expressed by the following lines:

St Swithin's day if thou dost rain
For forty days it will remain;
St Swithin's day if thou be fair
For forty days 'twill rain na mair (*no more*).

St Swithin's day is 15 July.

Sword-dance

A primitive dance-drama of the Middle Ages* introduced by rhyming speeches; one character is called the fool and is dressed in the skins of an animal, and another is a man dressed as a woman, called Bessy The dance is commonly within a framework of swords lying on the ground. Its significance is probably a dramatization of the coming of the New Year.

* *Mummers*.

Sybaris /ˈsibəris/

An ancient Greek town in southern Italy. In 6th C BC it was unrivalled among the Greek cities of the Mediterranean for its wealth, luxury and splendour – hence the term 'sybarite' for one who is addicted to luxury. Late in 6th C it was completely destroyed in consequence of civil war.

Sybil, or The Two Nations (1845) /ˈsibil/

A novel by Benjamin Disraeli*. The 'two nations' are the rich and the poor. The country is shown to be governed by the rich in the interests of the rich – *ie* the landlords and the employers. Sybil is the daughter of Gerard, a Chartist* leader; she is loved by an enlightened young aristocrat, Charles Egremont, younger brother of an oppressive landlord, Lord Marney. Disraeli gives romantic historical background to his theme by causing Sybil to belong to the same family as the last abbot of Marney, whose lands Lord Marney's ancestors had seized at the time of the dissolution of the monasteries* under Henry VIII*. The poor nation is likewise identified with the Anglo-Saxons*, despoiled of their land by the Norman* conquerors of 11th C. This novel, like *Coningsby** (1844) in which he had expounded the selfishness and sterility of the British political parties, is part of Disraeli's campaign to renew the Tory party through the Young England movement by inspiring it with a true and disinterested ideology. The novel combines a rather comic element of operatic romanticism with shrewd observation and social satire.

Syllepsis /ˈsiˈlepsis/

* *Figures of Speech*.

Sylphs /silfs/

According to the 16th-C Swiss physician, Paracelsus, they were spirits of the air, something between pure spirit and material being.

Symbolism

A name primarily associated with a school of French poets writing in the second half of 19th C. The movement grew out of the work of Baudelaire (1821–67) and is above all associated with Paul Verlaine (1844–96), Arthur Rimbaud (1854–91) and Stephane Mallarmé (1842–98). In addition to Baudelaire, the American writer Edgar Allan Poe (1809–49) and the German music-dramatist Richard Wagner (1813–83) contributed to the shaping of Symbolism. It constituted a development from Romanticism inasmuch as it was poetry of the feelings as opposed to the reason, but it was a reaction against it inasmuch as it was more intellectual in its conception of the way poetry operates. This intellectualism did not imply that the content of poetry should be one of what is ordinarily called ideas: Mallarmé's affirmation was that 'Poetry is not made with ideas; it is made with words'. This looks forward to much 20th-C thought in all the arts, requiring that the artist should above all have respect for the medium in which he has chosen to work; it also anticipates T. S. Eliot's* praise of the English 17th-C Metaphysical* poets that 'they were, at best, engaged in the task of trying to find the verbal equivalent for states of mind and feeling'. Since 'states of mind and feeling' are ultimately mysterious and elusive, the Symbolists emphasized the suggestiveness of poetic language, but though this emphasis on suggestiveness makes much of their poetry obscure, their care for the organization and operation of language kept it from vagueness, in the sense in which the poetry of their English contemporary, the late Romantic Algernon Swinburne*, is very commonly vague. Swinburne is also much concerned with the poetic medium of words, but in such a way that his verse subdues the reader into a state of passive receptivity, whereas the French Symbolists evoke active participation; Swinburne relies for his effect on stimulating emotions already latent in the reader, whereas the Symbolists incite extension of these emotions. T. S. Eliot's essay on Swinburne (in *Selected Essays*) is a help in elucidating the distinction.

The French Symbolists are particularly important in English literature for their decisive influence on the two most important poets writing in English in the first half of the 20th C: T. S. Eliot and W. B. Yeats*. Eliot's understanding of them was much the more intimate and profound, but A. Symons's *The Symbolist Movement in Literature* (1899) acted on them both.

Synecdoche /si'nekdəki/

* *Figures of Speech.*

Synge, John Millington (1871–1909) /siŋ/

Irish dramatist. He belonged to the Protestant Anglo-Irish segment of Irish Society, but at the suggestion of W. B. Yeats* in 1899, he devoted his career to interpreting Irish Celtic peasant life. From this proceeded his remarkable series of dramas which were the chief glory of the drama of the Irish literary renaissance, and of the Abbey Theatre* in Dublin (under the direction of Yeats) through which this movement expressed itself. Part of the Irish dramatic endeavour was to revive poetic drama; Synge wrote in prose, but he exploited with great sensitivity the poetic suggestiveness of the rhythms, diction, and imagery of Irish peasant speech. At the same time he avoided the sentimentalities of late-19th-C romanticism and the falsifications which Irish nationalistic vanity required; the result was that his masterpiece, *The Playboy of the Western World** (1907) was received with rage and uproar. Other plays: *The Shadow of the Glen* (1903); *Riders to the Sea* (1904); *The Well of the Saints* (1905); *The Tinker's Wedding* (1907), and his last play, drawn unlike the others from Irish myth – *Deirdre of the Sorrows*, published in 1910 after his death.

Synge also wrote descriptions of Irish peasant life in *The Aran Islands* (1907) and *In Wicklow* and *In County Kerry* (both published 1910).

* 5.3.2; *Irish Literature.*

Bib: Greene, D. H., and Stephens, E. M., *Life*; Price, F., *Synge and Anglo-Irish Drama.*

Synoptic Gospels

In the New Testament of the Bible, the Gospels of St Matthew, St Mark, and St Luke, so called because in their content and its treatment they have much in common so that they can be considered together, *ie* 'synoptically'. The Gospel of St John, on the other hand, is different in important respects from the other three, and requires separate study.

Syrinx /'siriŋks/

In Greek myth, a maiden pursued by the god Pan*; she threw herself into the river Ladon, where she was changed into a reed, from which Pan made his pipe. Her legend is retold by Pope* in his pastoral poem *Windsor Forest* (1713). In Spenser's *Shepherd's Calendar** for the month of April, Syrinx represents Anne Boleyn, mother of Elizabeth I*.

T

Tabard Inn

An inn on the south bank of the Thames, in the borough of Southwark*. It was here that Chaucer's pilgrims assembled before setting out to Canterbury in the *Canterbury Tales**. The inn was pulled down in 1875.

A tabard was a sleeveless coat worn by heralds and by knights over their armour. The coat was painted or embroidered with armorial bearings, *ie* the crest and emblems of the knight's family or the king whom the herald represented.

Tacitus, Cornelius (AD 55?–120?) /'tasitəs/

Roman historian. He was eminent in Roman political and social life, and the son-in-law of Gnaeus Julius Agricola, the governor of Britain who effectively transformed the island into an orderly Roman province. His surviving works are the *Dialogue on Orators*, consisting of conversations about the decay of Roman education; the *Life of Agricola*, including an account of Britain under the rule of his father-in-law; *Germany*, an account of the characteristics of the land and its people, contrasting their freedom and simplicity with the degeneracy of Rome; the *Histories*, a fragment of an account of the Roman Empire during the last thirty years of 1st C; the *Annals*, a fragment of a history of the Empire in the first half of the century.

Tacitus was a contemporary of the satirical poet

Juvenal*; together they represent the last great phase of classical Latin literature; both have a strong ethical concern with the condition of Roman civilization, and Tacitus reveres the austere virtues of the pre-imperial republic, though he accepts the Empire as a political necessity. His style is distinguished for its brevity, and his works were an outstanding constituent of English education from 16th to 19th C.

* *Classical Education.*

Tale of a Tub, A

A prose satire by Jonathan Swift*, first published in 1704. The title is the same as that of one of the last and least interesting comedies by Ben Jonson*, but Swift ironically explains it in his Preface as derived from the practice of sailors of tossing a tub to a whale in order to divert it from attacking the ship. The ship, Swift explains, is an image of the state, and the whale is *Leviathan*, Hobbes's* political treatise, from which the wits of the age drew their dangerous armament of scepticism and satire; he pretends that he has been employed to divert these attacks by his engaging nonsense. For the next edition, 1710, Swift added *An Apology*, in which he discloses his true aim – to satirize 'the numerous and gross corruptions in Religion and Learning'. The real meaning of the title is that Swift is beguiling the reader so as to expose him the more effectively to the ferocity of irony. The central fable of the *Tale* is the story of three brothers, Martin, Peter and Jack, who inherit three simple coats from their father, whose will enjoins that the coats must in no way be altered. Under the leadership of Peter, however, the brothers find it convenient to alter the coats beyond recognition to comply with fashion. Peter's authority eventually becomes so insanely domineering that Martin and Jack revolt against him; Martin tears off the ornaments to his coat, but stops before he altogether disfigures it; Jack, however, reduces his to a squalid rag. The fable is an allegory of the Reformation*: Peter represents the Church of Rome, Martin the Church of England, in which Swift was a priest, and Jack, the extremer Protestants, or Dissenters*; the coat is the Word of God as expressed in the New Testament. Swift's main object of attack is Jack, since he regarded the Dissenters, with their claim to receipt of divine inspiration and their resistance to authority, as the principal threat to the rule of right reason, true religion, and fine civilization in his time. The fable is interspersed with digressions, satirizing the arrogance of those who set up their private intellects or privileged inspiration as guides to their fellow-men; by Section XI the digressions come together with the fable, and Jack is declared to be the leader of the Aeolists*, who expounds their doctrines through 'wind', from Aeolus, Greek god of the winds. The satire is essentially an attack on the 'windiness' that Swift discerned in the more pretentious philosophical and religious teaching of his time.

Tale of Two Cities, A (1859)

A novel by Charles Dickens*. The cities are London and Paris, and the tale is a romance of the French Revolution*. The hero is a young French nobleman, Charles Darnay, who has renounced his status as nephew of the Marquis de St Evrémonde from hatred of the pre-revolutionary aristocratic oppression, exemplified by his uncle. He marries the daughter of Dr Manette, who at the beginning of the novel has just been released from the Paris prison of the Bastille, where he was confined 18 years before by the secret influence of the Marquis. Darnay, owing to his aristocratic descent, nearly falls victim to the Terror*, but he is saved by the dissolute Englishman, Sydney Carton, who redeems himself by sacrificing his life for Darnay; this is made possible because Carton and Darnay exactly resemble each other, so that the former is able to substitute himself for the latter. The novel is notable for its scenes of revolutionary violence, for which Dickens was indebted to Carlyle's* *History of the French Revolution* (1837). The revolutionaries Monsieur and Madame Defarge, and the English body-snatcher Jerry Cruncher, who makes a living by stealing corpses and selling them for medical dissection, are memorable characters.

Tales in Verse

* *Crabbe.*

Tales of a Grandfather

Two series, one of the history of Scotland (1827–29), and one of the history of France (1831), by Walter Scott*; they were originally intended for his grandson.

Tales of My Landlord

Four series of novels by Walter Scott*. Series 1: *The Black Dwarf, Old Mortality** (1816). Series 2: *The Heart of Midlothian** (1818). Series 3: *The Bride of Lammermoor*, *The Legend of Montrose* (1819). Series 4: *Count Robert of Paris*, *Castle Dangerous* (1832). *Old Mortality* and *The Heart of Midlothian* are among his acknowledged masterpieces, and *The Bride* has received strong praise, but the 4th series marks Scott's last stage of decline through illness and overwork.

Taliesin /tal'jesin/

A Welsh poet of 6th C AD. Various poems are attributed to him, of which the tales of Urien and Owein (in the legends of King Arthur* called Ryence and Yvain) may be genuine. Taliesin is a half-legendary figure. Peacock* introduces him into his parody of Arthurian romance, *The Misfortunes of Elphin* (1829), and Tennyson includes him as one of the Knights of the Round Table* in his *Idylls of the King**.

Talmud /'talmud/

A collection of Jewish religious law and teaching, developed from the scriptural law of the Old Testament. It was codified in 2nd–6th C AD.

Talus /ˈteiləs/

In Greek myth, a man of brass made by Hephaestus*, the smith of the gods. He protected the island of Crete, and received the Argonauts* with a shower of rocks.

In Book V of Spenser's *Faerie Queene** Talus is a character who acts as an instrument of punitive justice, represented by Sir Artegall. He disposes of criminals with an iron flail.

Tam o'Shanter /tamə'ʃantə/

One of Burns's* best-known poems, published in 1790. It is in rhyming couplets*, and in the Lowland* Scots language in which Burns wrote all his best poems. Tam is a drunken farmer; riding home late at night he passes a haunted church (the 'kirk of Alloway') which he sees lighted up, and a dance of witches and warlocks (male witches) going on inside, to the tune of the bagpipes played by Old Nick (the Devil). He admires one of the prettiest of the witches and in his excitement cries out: 'Weel done, Cutty Sark!' A 'sark' is a woman's undergarment or shift; 'cutty' means short. The witches come rushing after him, but he is able to reach the middle of the bridge over the River Doon, beyond which they can't follow him, though they wrench off his horse's tail.

Tamburlaine the Great, Parts 1 and 2 /ˈtambəlein/

Two dramas in blank verse* by Christopher Marlowe*, published in 1590. The subject is the life of the 14th-C central Asian, Timur, who rose by his conquests from obscurity to the position of one of the most powerful men in Asia. A life of Timur by Pedro Maxia was translated into English and published in 1571.

Part 1 is a drama of conquest. Tamburlaine is an obscure shepherd chieftain who defeats Mycetes, king of Persia, and subsequently the king's brother, Cosroe, as well. He is next victorious over Bajazet, Emperor of Turkey, and finally captures Damascus from the Soldan (Sultan) of Egypt. His victories are a triumph of immense natural energy and of ruthlessness over equally cruel but weak and decadent civilizations; however, Tamburlaine's barbarity is not merely brutish – he worships the potentialities of the human mind, and he falls passionately in love with his bride, Zenocrate, the daughter of the Soldan. Tamburlaine is, in fact, a product of Marlowe's characteristically Renaissance* imagination, fascinated by the earthly magnificence available to men of imaginative power who have the energy of their convictions. The play is essentially non-moral; Tamburlaine is not judged, but presented as though he were a natural force.

Part 2 was probably written in consequence of the success of Part 1, rather than foreseen as a sequel, though critics differ in their opinions about this. Tamburlaine is forced to face the truth that, though he feels his energies to be inexhaustible, he cannot triumph over death – first that of Zenocrate, and then his own. This play is therefore a tragedy, that man feels himself to be infinite but is nonetheless mortal.

The plays are a most important advance in the use of blank verse as a medium of drama. Hitherto it had been used stiffly and unimaginatively; Marlowe, for the first time in these plays, made blank verse eloquent.

* 5.1.3.1.

Taming of the Shrew, The

An early comedy by Shakespeare*; probably written 1593–94, and first published in the first folio* of 1623. It may be partly a recasting of an anonymous play, *The Taming of a Shrew* (of uncertain date), and both are based on George Gascoigne's* comedy *Supposes* (1566), itself a translation from the Italian of Ariosto's *Suppositi* (1509).

In a prologue or 'induction', a drunken tinker, Christopher Sly, is subjected to a practical joke; a nobleman picks him up in his stupor, brings him to his mansion, and causes his servants to explain to him that he is himself a great lord who has for some time been out of his wits. The play is then performed by the nobleman's actors for Sly's benefit. The scene is Verona, and the plot concerns the successful attempts of a gentleman, Petruchio, to tame into obedience and love the wilful and ferocious Katharina, thought to be unmarriageable because of her shrewishness. A subplot concerns the courting of Katharina's sister, Bianca, by Lucentio (who is successful) and by Hortensio, who marries a widow instead. At a feast that concludes the play, Petruchio proves that he has, after all, the most affectionate and docile wife of the three. The play is essentially a comedy of situation, and may be regarded as one of several experiments in different kinds of comic form by Shakespeare in the years 1592–95.

Tammuz

* *Thamuz*.

Tantalus /ˈtantələs/

In Greek myth, a king of Phrygia or of Lydia, condemned for crimes against the gods to an eternity of thirst and hunger in the underworld. He stood in water up to the chin, with a bough of delicious fruits within his reach; when he stooped to drink or stretched out his arm to pluck, the water or the branch always receded. This punishment is the origin of the word 'tantalize'.

Tarlton, Richard (d 1588) /ˈtaːltən/

A famous comic actor, mentioned in 1583 as one of the Queen's Players, and a favourite clown of Elizabeth 1*. He dressed as a rustic ('a clown' was originally a term for a simple-witted country peasant) and was gifted at composing the rough, comic kind of verse known as 'doggerel'; he popularized on the London stage the mixture of song and dance, something like light opera, called country jigs*. He wrote a comedy, *The Seven Deadly Sins*, for the Queen's Players, and after his death a number of volumes of popular humour – not necessarily his – were published under the title of *Tarlton's Jests*. He was one of the first actors to become a national figure. He was probably an innkeeper before he became an actor.

Tarot cards /ˈtarəu/

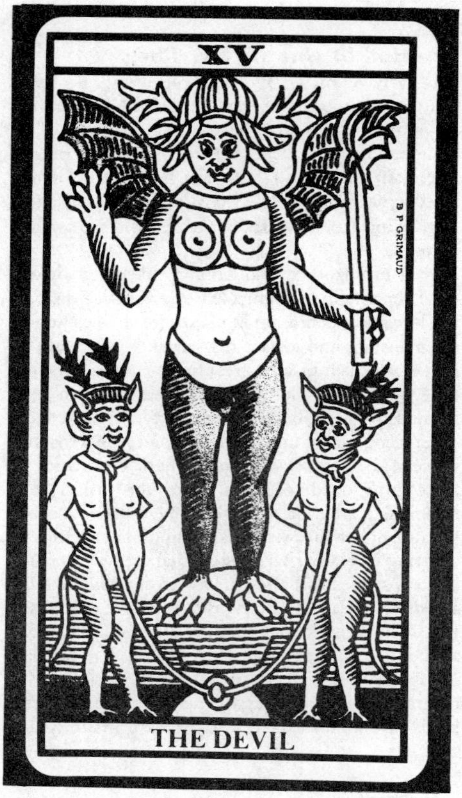

Playing cards bearing emblems such as sun, moon, hanged man etc. instead of the effigies of kings, queens, and knaves of usual cards. They were used in the middle ages; today they are associated chiefly with fortune-telling. The emblems may be vestiges of ancient myths.

Tarpeian Rock /taːˈpiːən/
A rock in ancient Rome; criminals were executed by being thrown from it. It derives its name from Tarpeia, daughter of a governor of the citadel during the Sabine wars in the early days of the Roman republic. The legend is that she offered to betray the citadel to the Sabines* in return for their bracelets; however, when she opened the gate to them, they killed her by piling upon her not merely their bracelets but their shields. The legend perhaps arose in order to account for the use of the rock as a place of execution.

Tarquin /ˈtaːkwin/
The family of seven legendary kings of ancient Rome; the last, Lucius Tarquinius Superbus, was expelled by a rising of the citizens in consequence of the rape of Lucrece* by his son in 510 BC.

Tartan
Cloth woven into chequered designs; this cloth was formerly the regional dress or 'plaid' in the Scottish Highlands*. The plaid was draped about the body and hung down below the belt as a skirt or kilt*. It is commonly believed that each Highland clan has always had its own tartan of distinctive colour and weave. The evidence that this was true before the prohibition of Highland national dress (which followed the Jacobite* Rebellion of 1745 and lasted until 1782) is uncertain. Undoubtedly many existing tartans ascribed to clans are the invention of 19th-C romanticism (especially stimulated by Sir Walter Scott*) and the tourist industry. However, tartan weaves certainly varied from region to region of the Scottish Highlands, and to this extent there must have been some degree of distinction among the clans.

Tartars (Tatars)
An Asian Mongol race which overran Asia and Eastern Europe in 13th C under the leadership of Genghis Khan*. They came to represent the essence of barbarism and ferocity for civilized Europeans.

Tartarus /ˈtaːtərəs/
In Greek myth, an underworld of punishment for the dead. Homer in the *Iliad** describes it as being as far below Hades* as Hades is below the earth. Virgil* describes it as surrounded by impenetrable walls and the burning waters of the Phlegethon. The Titans*, and others who defied Zeus* were confined there. In the oldest myths, Tartarus was the son of Aether and Ge – the sky-father and the earth-mother.

Task, The
* *Cowper*.

Tasso, Torquato (1544–95) /ˈtasəu/
Italian poet. He continued the tradition of the romantic epic*, already made famous by Ariosto's *Orlando Furioso** (1532), in his two major works, *Rinaldo* (1562) and *Jerusalem Delivered* (1581). Tasso's imagination was romantic, but in his literary ideal he was classical*, and the thought of the second poem is elevated by the high seriousness of the Catholic Counter-Reformation*. His seriousness made his work very attractive to the English romantic epic poet, Edmund Spenser*, whose very Protestant* *Faerie Queene** is also an attempt to rival Ariosto by a poem of similar form but imbued with strong religious feeling. Tasso's impress is strong on parts of *The Faerie Queene*, especially in its Platonism. *Jerusalem Delivered* was finely translated by Sir Edward Fairfax and published under the title of *Godfrey of Bulloigne or the Recovery of Jerusalem* in 1600 (**Translation*).

Tasso was locked up for insanity by Alphonso II, Prince of Ferrara, between 1579–86; subsequent legend attributed his imprisonment to a love affair with the Princess Leonora d'Este. This supposed love affair was the subject of a poem by Byron*, *The Lament of Tasso* (1817).

Tate Gallery, The
A public gallery for modern paintings and sculpture on the north bank of the Thames in London. It was established by a sugar-merchant, Sir Henry Tate, and opened in 1897.

Tatler, The
A periodical edited and largely written by Richard Steele* (and later by Addison*). It started in April 1709 and appeared three times weekly until it closed in January 1711, after which Addison and Steele replaced it by *The Spectator**. It was one of the most important early enterprises of English journalism*. At first it contained news of domestic and foreign affairs, but after 6 months this was replaced by essays discussing manners and social conduct, often in the form of sketches and stories. Steele took the pen-name of Bickerstaff, a contemporary astrologer who had become famous owing to the jokes at his expense in Jonathan Swift's* *Bickerstaff Papers* (1708).

* *Reviews and Periodicals.*

Taylor, Jeremy (1613–67)
Clergyman and religious writer. He was one of the great representatives of Anglicanism* in its greatest period, and his career shows the vicissitudes of the Church of England in 17th C. The son of a barber, he was educated at a Cambridge grammar school and in the University of Cambridge. His talent for preaching attracted the favour of Archbishop Laud*, to whom and to King Charles I* he became chaplain. In 1645 he was captured by Parliamentary troops, and until 1660, while the Church of England was in abeyance, he was private chaplain to the Earl of Carbery. It was during this period that he wrote much of his best work. Later, he was made Bishop of Dromore in Ireland, where, contrary to his inclination, he was obliged to discipline clergy who were hostile to the Anglican establishment. He thus stands in contrast to his former patron, the authoritarian Archbishop Laud, and the change marks not merely a difference in personalities but the growth in the spirit of Anglican tolerance in later 17th C. His *A Discourse of the Liberty of Prophesying* (1646) was a plea for religious toleration; his other outstanding works were his *The Rule and Exercises of Holy Living* (1650) and *The Rule and Exercises of Holy Dying* (1651). His expression is an example of the expansive, imaginative prose of his times, and he shows great sensitivity to the human condition.

* *Sermons.*

Bib: Stranks, C. J., *Jeremy Taylor*; Gosse, E., *Jeremy Taylor*; Smith, L. P., *The Golden Grove: Selected Passages from Jeremy Taylor*.

Te Deum /ˈtiːˈdiəm/
Opening words of a Latin hymn; Te Deum laudamus = We praise Thee, O Lord. The hymn dates from 4th C, but the authorship is uncertain. An English translation is sung every Sunday morning in churches of the Church of England*.

Teiresias
* *Tiresias.*

Telemachus /tiˈleməkəs/
In Greek legend (especially Homer's *Odyssey**, i–iv, xv–xxiv) the son of Odysseus*, and a child when his father embarked for the Trojan war. When his father's return was long delayed, he set out in search of him. On his return, he found that his father had reached home and was waiting in disguise to rid himself of the suitors who were persecuting his wife, Penelope, and conspiring to kill Telemachus himself. Father and son then contrive their destruction together.

Tellus /ˈteləs/
In Roman myth, the deity representing the earth, corresponding to the Greek Ge*.

Tempe, Vale of /ˈtempi/
A deep gorge in Greece, formed by the River Peneus, and running between Mount Olympus and Mount Ossa. It has always been famous for its beauty, and in ancient times it was sacred to the god Apollo*.

Tempest, The
A play by Shakespeare*, probably written in 1611, and generally regarded as the last completely by his own hand. The plot does not derive from any known principal source. The setting of the island with its aboriginal inhabitant Caliban, and the shipwreck with which the play opens, owe details to travel books of the time, especially a pamphlet* by Sir George Somers (1609) about his voyage to and shipwreck on the Bermudas.

Prospero, Duke of Milan, with his daughter Miranda, has been expelled from his duchy, where he had avoided the task of government for the sake of devoting himself to secret learning, by his wicked brother, Antonio. At the opening of the play Prospero and Miranda have lived on a lonely island for many years, served by the brutish savage Caliban, and the sprite Ariel. By his magic powers, Prospero contrives the shipwreck on the island of his enemies – his brother Antonio, Alonso king of Naples who had conspired with Antonio, Alonso's wicked brother Sebastian and a few courtiers. Also shipwrecked but separated from the others is Ferdinand, the virtuous son of Alonso; each believes the other to be drowned. The situation is such that Prospero, if he wishes, can use his supernatural powers to execute vengeance on his enemies; instead, he uses it to bring about reconciliation and forgiveness. Ferdinand, after a brief trial in which he is subjected to austere labours, is united with Miranda. Alonso's company is also subjected to trials, but finally reunited with Ferdinand and reconciled to Prospero, who discloses himself. A subplot concerns the farcical attempt of Trinculo and Stephano, Alonso's servants, to rob Prospero of his instruments of magic, with the aid of Caliban.

The play is the most symbolic of Shakespeare's plays. Prospero is in the tradition of the Platonic* mage, who, according to one line of Renaissance* thought, could achieve extraordinary power by uniting exceptional wisdom with exceptional virtue. Miranda unites the innocence of nature with the nobility of high breed; her union with Ferdinand and their restoration to a corrupt world symbolize the renewal of vital forces. Caliban, on the other hand, represents the unredeemably brutal side of nature, and also the inherently vicious propensities of the body: he can be forced to serve, but he cannot be elevated. The other characters represent degrees of redeemability: the 'good old lord' Gonzalo has always been virtuous though he has been made to serve evil ends; Alonso has done evil but is capable of repentance; Antonio and Sebastian do not repent and can only be intimidated; the rest are merely passive and, in Antonio's phrase 'take suggestion as a cat laps milk'.

The Tempest is the last of four plays sometimes called reconciliation plays*, the others being *Pericles**, *Cymbeline**, *The Winter's Tale**. An interesting feature of it is that while the other plays in the group are very loosely constructed in terms of time and place, *The Tempest* has the greatest unity in these respects of all Shakespeare's plays: the action is restricted to the island, and occupies only three hours.

Templars, The

The Knights Templars, or Poor Knights of Christ and the Temple of Solomon, were a religious military order founded in 12th C to protect pilgrims to the Holy City of Jerusalem, to defend the city itself, and to wage war against the Muslims who either threatened it or occupied it. They owed obedience to the Pope, and took vows of poverty and humility, but in the course of time they became powerful, rich and arrogant. This caused them to be suppressed early in 14th C – the English branch in 1308. The Grand Master of the Order, Jacques de Molay, was burnt as a heretic by the King of France in 1314.

Temple, The

A district of London on the north bank of the Thames; it receives its name from the Temple Church, formerly the property of the medieval order of the Knights Templars*. Churches in the west were commonly built in the shape of a cross and directed towards the east and the Holy City of Jerusalem; the church of the Holy Sepulchre in that city is round, and the London Temple is round in imitation of it. In 14th C the Temple and its surrounding buildings were transferred to the use of law students; the resulting Inns of Court* of the Inner and Middle Temple remain to this day.

Temple, Sir William (1628–99)

Statesman, diplomatist, essayist. In English literature he is especially known as the patron of Jonathan Swift*, who lived at his house (Moor Park) as Temple's secretary from 1689 to 1694, and again from 1696 till Temple's death. Temple's most famous essay* was his contribution to the controversy about the relative merits of ancient (*ie* Greek and Latin) and modern literature; the essay

was entitled *Of Ancient and Modern Learning*, and praised the Letters of Phalaris as a notable example of ancient work. Unfortunately the great scholar Bentley* exposed the Letters as a forgery. Temple's embarrassment provoked Swift to come to his aid with his first notable essay, *The Battle of the Books*. Temple was a model of the cultivated aristocracy of his time, and his essays (chiefly on political matters) were regarded as setting standards for correctness and elegance of expression. His wife's letters to him before their marriage (in 1655) were first published in 1888; her position resembled that of Samuel Richardson's* heroine in his novel *Clarissa**, inasmuch as her parents were opposed to the marriage. Temple's memoirs were published by Swift in 1709.

Bib: Lives by C. Marburg and H. E. Woodbridge.

Temple, Solomon's

The main centre of worship of the ancient Jews in Jerusalem. Erected by King Solomon* in 10th C BC, it was several times destroyed and restored in the course of Jewish history; its final destruction by the Romans took place in AD 70. Its original form is described in the Bible, *2 Chronicles* 3.

Temple Bar

Originally a gateway between the City of London and the City of Westminster, now marked by the effigy of a griffin on a pedestal, situated opposite the Law Courts, at the junction of Fleet Street and the Strand, near the Temple Church. A stone gateway was designed and erected by Sir Christopher Wren* in 1672; this was removed in 1878 and later re-erected at Theobald's Park, Hertfordshire. The heads of traitors used to be displayed on spikes on Temple Bar.

Tennyson, Alfred (1809–92) /'tenisn/

Poet, usually known, after he was made a baron in 1884, as Alfred, Lord Tennyson. Fourth of twelve children (two others of whom, Frederick and Charles, were also poets) of a Church of England clergyman. The family was long-established among Lincolnshire landowners, but the poet's father had been disinherited by his grandfather, and Alfred's childhood and youth were spent in comparative poverty; he was partly educated by his father, but later he went to Trinity College, Cambridge. His earliest work (*Poems by Two Brothers*, in which his brother collaborated) is unimportant, and he did not begin to win fame until the 1840s. Thereafter he achieved popularity unequalled by any other English poet in his own lifetime. In 1850 he was made Poet Laureate* (in succession to Wordsworth*) and in 1884 he was made a Baron – the only English poet ever to have been ennobled purely for his poetry. This popularity arose from two facts: he had, on the one hand, exquisite poetic skill; he was, on the other hand, in his mental and emotional outlook, very representative of his age. He had a characteristically Victorian* insular patriotism; he was both exhilarated and disturbed, like so many of his contemporaries, by the social and industrial changes of the age, and he was distressed by the shaking of traditional religious beliefs by the scientists – in his youth, the geologist Charles Lyell* (*The Principles of Geology*, 1830–33), and in his middle age, the biologist, Charles Darwin* (*The Origin of Species*, 1859). He countered this threat from the intellect by an emotional, sometimes sentimental, idealism which was extremely acceptable to the middle-class reading public. His idiom was that of the Romantics – Wordsworth*, Shelley*, especially Keats* – but his formal technique was as meticulous as that of the 18th C poets; the combination was both beguiling and reassuring. Tennyson was short-sighted, a defect which he turned to account by the exactness of his closely-observed detail. Physically and in his dress, he was imposing and romantic, and with this appearance he typified the great poet for the nation.

The first three books of his sole authorship (1830, 1832, 1842) include much of what is now considered his best work – *eg Mariana**, *The Lady of Shalott**, *Ulysses*, *Morte d'Arthur*, *The Lotos-Eaters**. In 1833 his great friend, Arthur Hallam, died, and the great grief of this loss produced the series of elegies which are usually considered to be his masterpiece – *In Memoriam**, eventually published in 1850. Queen Victoria* declared that she valued it next to the Bible; however, it was the mixture of picturesque romanticism and acceptable idealism in *The Princess* (1847) which greatly extended Tennyson's popularity with the general public. In 1852 he produced the most impressive of his public poems, *Ode on the Death of the Duke of Wellington*, and in 1854, the most popular of English patriotic poems, the *Charge of the Light Brigade**. *Maud** (1855) is one of the most singular of his works, and contains some of his best and worst poetry. Other works: his immensely popular but now largely unread cycle of tales, *Idylls of the King** (1859–72); dialect poems, *eg The Northern Farmer* (1864); narrative, in the tradition of Wordsworth, *Enoch Arden* (1864); ballads, notably *The Revenge* (1880), and a number of not outstanding verse dramas, of which the most successful is *Becket* (1884).

Taste in 20th C has on the whole turned against his poetry; the accusation of one of his earliest critics, John Stuart Mill*, (reviewing the 1832 volume) that Tennyson's poetry is deficient in power of thought anticipated modern opinion, which is attuned to T. S. Eliot* and the 17th-C Metaphysicals*. It is still admitted that he had an extraordinary ear for cadence and rhythm, but it is implied that this virtue does not compensate for the mediocrity of his intelligence. However, this tribute to his 'fine ear' amounts to acknowledgement that Tennyson was a fine artist – perhaps the truest artist among English Victorian poets until Hopkins* – and no true art can be without some kind of depth. His first three books and *In Memoriam* contain poems in which some of the deeper emotional conflicts of his time are beautifully articulated.

* 6.4.1.

Bib: Lives by his son, Hallam Tennyson, and his grandson, Charles Tennyson; Auden, W. H., *Tennyson, a Selection and Introduction*; Baum, P. F., *Tennyson Sixty Years After*; Bradley, A. C., in *A Miscellany*; Leavis, F. R., in *New Bearings in English Poetry* and *The Common Pursuit* (for comparison with Hopkins); Nicolson, H., *Tennyson: Aspects of his Life, Character and Poetry*; Willey, B., in *More Nineteenth-century Studies*; Johnson, E. D. H., *The Alien Vision*; Killham, J., ed. *Essays on Tennyson*; Jump, J. D., *Critical Heritage*.

Terence (Publius Terentius Afer, 190?–159? BC) /'terəns/

Latin dramatist. His six comedies are adaptations of older Greek comedies, especially those of Menander (342–291 BC). They have been praised for the purity of their Latin and criticized for their deficiency of comic power. They were known, read and imitated throughout the Middle Ages and afterwards, *eg* his *Heautontimorumenos* (163) was adapted by Chapman* into *All Fools* (1605), and his *Andria* (166) was adapted by Steele* into *The Conscious Lovers* (1722). Other dramatists such as Ben Jonson* used some of his themes and his comic devices such as the role of the crafty slave (*eg* in *Volpone**). The comedy is essentially that of manners and of situation.

Tereus

* *Philomela*

Termagant

An imaginary god. Medieval Christians thought that he was worshipped by Muslims, and represented him in Mystery Plays* as a violent and overbearing character. Hence the word came to mean a violently quarrelsome woman.

Terpsichore /tə:p'sikəri/

In Greek myth, the muse* of dancing.

Terror, The (Reign of)

The period in the French Revolution* from June 1793 to July 1794 under the dictatorship of Robespierre*, when many people were executed without trial merely because they were suspected of opposition to the Revolution. The term has since been applied to similar regimes in other periods and countries.

Terza Rima /'teətsə'ri:mə/

The pattern used by the Italian poet Dante* in his long poem the *Divine Comedy*. Each line is of 11 syllables, the last syllable unaccented, and the rhyme scheme follows the pattern *aba bcb cdc ded* etc. Examples in English are rare, and consist of 10-syllable lines. The following is an example from the opening of Shelley's* *The Triumph of Life*:

> *Swift as a spirit hastening to his task*
> *Of glory and of good, the Sun sprang forth*
> *Rejoicing in his splendour, and the mask*
>
> *Of darkness fell from the awakened Earth –*
> *The smokeless altars of the mountain snows*
> *Flamed above crimson clouds, and at the birth*
>
> *Of light, the Ocean's orison arose,*
> *To which the birds tempered their matin lay.*

One reason for the scarce use of *terza rima* in English is the paucity of rhyming words in the language, by comparison with Italian. Thus, in rhyming lines 2 and 4, Shelley has to be content with the half-rhymes 'forth', 'Earth'. The form was first used in English by Thomas Wyatt* in his *Satires* and paraphrases of the Psalms.

*** 6.3.4.**

Tess of the D'Urbervilles, A Pure Woman

A novel by Thomas Hardy*, published in 1891. The heroine is Tess Durbeyfield, daughter of a poor west country peasant who learns that he may be a descendant of the aristocratic D'Urbervilles. The novel is about her tragic predicament between her brutal seducer, Alec Stoke D'Urberville, and her husband Angel Clare. Both Alec and Angel are intruders into Tess's environment; Alec (who has no proper title to his aristocratic surname) is the son of a north country businessman who has bought his way into the class of gentry; Angel is the son of a conventional clergyman, and has dissociated himself from his background by acquiring vague liberal ideas. When Tess confesses to him her seduction, his old-fashioned prejudices overcome him, and he casts her off, repenting when it is too late. Forsaken by her husband, Tess is faced by renewed assaults from Alec, whom she murders. After a period of hiding with Angel, Tess is tried, condemned, and executed for murder. The finest passages of the book are the episodes set in the peaceful environment of Talbothays Dairy Farm where Tess meets Alec, and the grim surroundings of Flintcomb Ash, where she works when Angel has forsaken her. Tess is represented as the victim of cruel chance – an example of Hardy's belief that the world is governed by ironical fate – but as usual, in his work, it is the intruders who are the instruments of the destructive force.

Testament of Cresseid, The

A poem by the Scots poet, Robert Henryson* (15th C). It is written as a continuation of Chaucer's *Troilus and Criseyde** but is a work of individual genius. In Chaucer's poem, Criseyde abandons her Trojan lover, Troilus, for her Greek seducer Diomedes*. In Henryson's poem, Diomedes casts her off, and the gods deprive her of her beauty and strike her with disease. Troilus passes her on horseback while she sits begging by the wayside, but fails to recognize her, and her eyes are too dim to recognize him. He tosses her money and passes on. Later she learns who he was, and sends him a ring as token before she dies. The poem is one of the masterpieces of medieval literature.

Tethys /'teθis/

In Greek myth, one of the Titans*; daughter of Ge, the earth-mother, and Uranus, the sky-father, and wedded to her brother, Oceanus, she was the mother of the great rivers and of the nymphs* known as Oceanides.

Thackeray, William Makepeace (1811–63) /'θakəri/

Novelist. He had a conventional upper-class education at a public school – Charterhouse – and Cambridge University, which he left in 1830 without taking a degree. For the next sixteen years he worked as a comic illustrator and journalist, writing satirically humorous studies of London manners in *The Yellowplush Correspondence* (*Fraser's Magazine* 1837–38), and *Snob Papers* (*Punch** 1846–47) – later published as *The Book of Snobs**; parodies of the contemporary fashion for the criminal-hero (*Catherine*, 1839, and *Barry Lyndon*, 1844); humorous travel books (*The Paris Sketch-Book* and *The Irish Sketch-Book*, 1840 and 1843), tales of humour and pathos (*The Great Hoggarty Diamond*, 1841).

His first major novel, *Vanity Fair**, came out in the year 1848 (it was published serially, as were most of his novels, and the date given is that of completion); it was a social panorama of the English upper-middle classes, satirizing their heartlessness and pretentiousness at the height of their prosperity; it was followed by novels in a similar field: *Pendennis** (1850), and *The Newcomes** (1853–55). *Esmond** (1852), is a historical novel set in the reign of Queen Anne (1702–14), and represents Thackeray's strong taste for 18th C; *The Virginians* (1859) is its sequel in 18th-C England and America. The same taste for 18th-C England is expressed in his historical lectures, *The Four Georges*, published in 1860. In 1855 he published his comic-romantic children's story, *The Rose and the Ring*. In 1860 he became editor of the famous *Cornhill Magazine**, and contributed to it *The Adventures of Philip* (1861–62), his essays

Roundabout Papers, and the novel, unfinished at his death, *Denis Duval*.

Thackeray was once considered the great counterpart to Dickens* in the mid-Victorian novel (the years 1850–70). Dickens conveyed a panorama of the lower half of society, and Thackeray of the upper half; both were great humorists, with a strong bent for satire and a capacity for social indignation. In addition, Thackeray was credited with the greatest historical novel in English, in *Esmond*. However, he is now chiefly remembered for *Vanity Fair*. His imaginative intensity is seen to be far inferior to that of Dickens, and the sentimentality with which he counterbalanced his satire is the more conspicuous. Like Dickens, he opposed the heartless utilitarianism* of his age by an appeal to spontaneous affection, and he tried to counterbalance its vulgar extravagance by an appeal to 18th-C proportion and elegance, but he also felt impulses of romanticism which in Dickens are far more uninhibited.

Bib: Ray, G. N., *Life*; Tillotson, G., *Thackeray the Novelist*; Stevenson, L., *The Showman of Vanity Fair*; Stevenson, L., ed. in *Great Victorians*; Studies by J. Dodd, L. Ennis, J. Y. T. Greig and G. N. Ray; Tillotson, G., and Hawes, D. (eds.), *The Critical Heritage*.

Thales of Miletus (640–546 BC) /'θeili:z/

Ancient Greek philosopher, chief of the 'Seven Wise Men' of Greece. His fame is based on his prediction of a total eclipse of the sun in 585, and his invention of abstract geometry, or geometry of lines, enlarging on the Egyptian geometry of surfaces. Philosophically, he believed that all things proceeded from water. His philosophy was the basis of much later Greek philosophy, for instance of Parmenides* and Heraclitus*, who pursued the problem of the relationship between the one and the many, a problem implied by Thales in his derivation of variety from a single element.

Thalia /θə'laiə/

In Greek myth, the muse* of comedy.

Thames

The chief river of England. It rises in the Cotswold Hills in the west and runs through Oxford and Windsor to its estuary just beyond London. The name is Celtic, and Julius Caesar* in his book *De Bello Gallico* gives it as Tamesis; since 18th C the part that flows through Oxford has been known as the Isis, perhaps by derivation from the last two syllables.

Thamuz (Thammuz, Tammuz) /'tamuz/

The ancient Assyrian god of harvest; his death was caused by the love for him of the goddess Ishtar, associated with the planet Venus, and symbolized the arid weather succeeding the harvest season. Thamuz and Ishtar have their counterparts in Greek mythology – Adonis* and Aphrodite*.

Theatres

No special buildings were erected in England for dramatic performances until late in 16th C. The earliest form of regular drama in England was the Mystery Plays*, which began as interpolations in religious ritual in the churches. By 15th C these plays were being performed at religious festivals in towns on movable stages or pageants*, conveyed from point to point on wagons. In country districts at seasonal festivals such as May Day*, primitive dramas of pagan origin – jigs, May games, Morris dances – were performed in the open air. The absence of theatres did not indicate scarcity of drama, but its wide pervasion of ordinary life.

Secular dramas of entertainment, such as we know today, grew up in 16th C; they were performed in the courtyards of inns and in the great halls of country mansions, royal palaces, Oxford and Cambridge colleges, and the inns of court* of London. The performers were professional actors who were usually incorporated in companies attached to noble or royal households, but by degrees this attachment became increasingly nominal, and actors required places where they could work independently and permanently. Hence the first playhouse, known as The Theatre, was erected by James Burbage* in Shoreditch, outside the City of London, in 1576–77. It was followed by many others, including the Globe* (1598) which is the most famous owing to its association with Shakespeare. None of these theatres survived the middle of 17th C, but a contemporary sketch of one of them (the Swan, 1598) exists, and there is a detailed description in the contract for the Fortune (1600).

The designs owe nothing to those of ancient Greece and Rome (unlike contemporary Italian theatres) but seem to be based on a mixture of the typical inn-yard and the bear-pits, *ie* the arenas for fights between animals. The structures were usually of wood, and round or hexagonal, though they might be rectangular. The centre was an arena exposed to the open air, where the poorer spectators stood; the richer ones sat in galleries surrounding the arena. The stage was probably divided into two or three parts; the main ('apron') stage projected into the arena, so that spectators surrounded it on three sides. The wall at the back of this stage was flanked by doors for exits and entries, between which there was probably a rear stage, though the sketch of the Swan does not include this. Above the rear stage there was probably an upper stage (to represent *eg* a castle wall); above this again, possibly a musicians' gallery. A canopy may have extended partly across the apron stage. The projection of the apron stage – upon which spectators sometimes actually sat – shows that the theatre of Shakespeare's day was not adapted to convey illusion like the typical modern theatre; scenery was scarcely used, though 'props' (*ie* thrones, objects representing flowery banks, etc.) were brought on and off.

Such were the 'public theatres'; there were also 'private theatres' such as the Blackfriars which came into the hands of Shakespeare's company in 1608. Pictures or accounts of these do not survive, but they were roofed, probably used some kind of artificial lighting, and may have provided more opportunity for scenery. Scenic spectacle was certainly not unknown or despised by Shakespeare's contemporaries; in the reign of James I* there was a pronounced fashion for masques*, an early form of opera, in which a poet such as Ben Jonson* and a designer such as Inigo Jones* collaborated.

It was only after the Restoration* of the Monarchy in 1660 that the theatre began to assume its modern shape, with a proscenium arch dividing the audience from the stage, thus providing greater scope for scenery and illusion. One of the earliest English theatres of this style was Drury Lane*, which had already been a theatre in the reign of James I and was rebuilt in 1662. From this time the theatre became the special entertainment for the middle and upper classes, largely cut off from the mass of the people, that it has, on the whole, remained. It was still, however, a place of influence, and in 1737 the government found it convenient to pass a Licensing Act which had the effect of restricting the theatres in London to three – the Haymarket opera house, Drury Lane, and Covent Garden – until the act was repealed in 1843, though licences were issued for a few theatres in the provinces, at Bath, Bristol and Liverpool. The law greatly hindered the development of a creative drama in 18th-C England, though it was a period of great actors and actresses.

The repeal of the Licensing Act in 1843 was followed by widespread building of theatres, but there was no live taste for intelligent new plays until Bernard Shaw*, in the last decade of 19th C, began to create one. In 20th C there has been a sharp division between the commercial theatres which provide intellectually commonplace entertainment, and the theatres of the intelligentsia.

Two companies of the latter kind have an official national status. One of these, the Royal Shakespeare Company directed by Peter Hall, produces Shakespeare's plays at Stratford-on-Avon, and, since 1960, plays by other dramatists, including contemporaries, at the Aldwych Theatre in London. The other, the National Theatre directed by Laurence Olivier, opened in 1963 at the London Old Vic Theatre*; it produces the great classics of European drama. Among other London companies, the English Stage Company since 1956 has taken a lead in the production of serious modern drama at the Royal Court Theatre, and Theatre Workshop, under Joan Littlewood from 1953 to 1961, showed exceptional boldness and success in experiment. Such theatres are also numerous outside London; some of the most conspicuous are the Traverse in Edinburgh, the Nottingham Playhouse, and the Belgrade in Coventry. The Council of Repertory Companies (*ie* theatres with resident companies) has a membership of over 40 companies engaged in the production of serious drama. Such theatres have been a distinctively 20th-C phenomenon; the most famous of them all, the Dublin Abbey Theatre* founded by W. B. Yeats* in 1904, was one of the earliest. They used to be known as the 'Little Theatres' because scarcity of money caused the buildings to be small; nowadays the central government and the local authorities commonly provide some financial support for them. Their growth has been closely related to the dramatic renaissance in Britain since 1950. At the same time, all theatres, including the commercial ones, have suffered severely through competition from the cinema and from television and sound radio; these, on the other hand, provide new and different scope for the dramatists.

* 5.1.2.2; 5.2.1.

Thebes (Greece)

In ancient Greece, the capital of Boeotia. It was the setting of many famous Greek legends, *eg* those associated with Cadmus*, Oedipus*, Dionysus*, Heracles*.

Thebes (Egypt)

The Greek name for an ancient capital of Egypt, on the site of which Luxor now stands.

Theocritus /θi'okritəs/

A Greek poet of 3rd C BC. Little is known about him, but his importance is that he originated pastoral* poetry in his 'idylls' – short poems about shepherds and shepherdesses living in primitive simplicity in the rural parts of Sicily. He may have written these in the great Egyptian city of Alexandria for urban readers; one of the characteristics of pastoral has been that it has expressed the longing of town-dwellers for the beauty of country surroundings, the simplicity of country living, and the purity of country air. Theocritus was emulated by the Roman poet Virgil*, and both Theocritus and Virgil were taken as models by 16th-C Renaissance* poets in Western Europe, of whom the most notable English example is Edmund Spenser*.

Theophrastus /θiə'frastəs/

A Greek philosopher, follower of Aristotle*, of 4th C BC. Amongst other writings, he composed a series of descriptions of moral types called *Ethical Characters*. These were the original pattern for the minor literary form of character-writing, widely practised in England in early 17th C. The most notable example is John Earle's *Microcosmography* (1628). Other examples: Joseph Hall's* *Characters of Virtues and Vices* (1608); Thomas Overbury's* *Characters* (1614).

* *Characters, Theophrastian.*

Thermopylae /θə:'mopili:/

A pass between the mountains and the sea in Greece; in 480 BC a force of 300 Spartans under Leonidas defended it against a large army of Persians under Xerxes* until not one Spartan was left alive.

Thersites /θə:'saiti:z/

In Homer's *Iliad** (ii) the ugliest and most disagreeable of the Greek host besieging Troy. In Shakespeare's play *Troilus and Cressida** he is a kind of clown, who respects nobody and reviles everybody.

Theseus /'θi:sju:s/

In Greek myth, the principal hero of Athenian legend. His mother, Aethra, was jointly loved by Aegeus, king of Athens, and Poseidon, god of the sea; Theseus was thus credited with double, and partly divine, paternity. His principal adventures were as follows:

[1] Before leaving Troezen, the home of Aethra, Aegeus hid his sword and sandals under an enormous rock. At the age of 16, Theseus lifted the rock single-handed, put on his father's sword and sandals, and set out for Athens.

[2] On the way to Athens he accomplished a number of feats. He killed a dangerous bandit, Periphetes; he killed Sinis, a son of Poseidon, by tearing him apart on sprung pine trees, a torture which Sinis had inflicted on others; he killed the monstrous sow of Crommyon; he killed Sciron, who had waylaid travellers and kicked them into the sea to be eaten by a giant turtle; finally, he killed the giant Procrustes, who had tortured travellers by fitting them to his bed, either by stretching them if they were too short, or cutting them down to the right length if they were too tall. Eventually he arrived at Athens.

[3] His father, Aegeus, had married the witch, Medea*; jealous of Theseus, who was unrecognized, she tried to poison him. His father recognized him by his sword, however, and Theseus drove Medea and her children away from the court. He next overcame Aegeus' nephews, the Pallantids and destroyed the great wild bull that was devastating the land of Attica.

[4] His next, and most famous, adventure, was to slay the Minotaur*, the monster inhabiting the Labyrinth of Crete. To test his claim to be the son of Poseidon, Minos, the king of Crete, tossed a ring into the sea and told Theseus to reclaim it. Theseus dived in, and returned, not only with the ring but with a crown from Amphitrite, Poseidon's queen. He was guided through the Labyrinth by a thread provided by Ariadne, Minos' daughter, who had fallen in love with him. On his return to Athens he unintentionally caused his father's death by forgetting to substitute a white sail, the sign of victory, for the black one, the sign of defeat. When Aegeus saw the black sail approaching, he threw himself over the cliff in his grief.

[5] Theseus was now king of Athens; he instituted its basic social structure and established its principal religious festival in honour of the goddess Athene*, the Panathenaea.

[6] In his wars against the race of women warriors, the Amazons*, Theseus carried off Antiope, who bore him a son, Hippolytus. Later he repudiated Antiope, and married Phaedra*, who fell in love with her stepson. When Hippolytus rejected her, she made accusations against him to Theseus, who called down the vengeance of Poseidon on his son, who accordingly met his death by means of a sea-monster that caused his chariot horses to stampede.

[7] In grief at these tragedies, Theseus retired to the island of Scyros, whose king treacherously killed him from jealousy at his fame.

Thespis /'θespis/

A Greek poet of 6th C BC; he is usually regarded as the originator of tragic drama. Choric songs were already sung at festivals; Thespis is said to have introduced an actor who engaged in dialogue with the leader of the chorus.

Thetis /'θetis/

In Greek myth, a sea-goddess, and mother of the hero Achilles*.

Third Estate

From 13th C, three classes of society were said to participate in the work of politics in Parliament*: the Lords Spiritual (leaders of the Church) or first estate; the Lords Temporal (nobility) or second estate; and the Commons (common people) or third estate. This organization is still shown in modern Parliaments: Bishops of the Church of England and peers with the rank of baron and above sit in the House of Lords*; the rest of society is represented by Members of Parliament who sit in the House of Commons*.

Thirty Tyrants

A body of 30 magistrates imposed as rulers upon Athens* by Sparta* after the victory of the Spartans over the Athenians in the Peloponnesian war*.

Thirty Years' War

A great European religious war, lasting from 1618 to 1648, between nearly all the Catholic and Protestant nations of Europe. It was fought principally in Germany to the ruin of that country, and was concluded by the Peace of Westphalia. Britain was one of the few important countries which took hardly any part in it.

Thirty-nine Articles

The code of religious doctrine which all clergy of the Church of England* have to accept. In 1553 42 articles were laid down; these were reduced to 39 in 1571.

Thomas à Becket

* *Becket*.

Thomas, Dylan Marlais (1914–53) /'dilən 'toməs/

Poet. He was born in the Welsh town of Swansea; much of his work shows the impression on his early life of grim Welsh religious Puritanism contrasting with the equally Welsh characteristic of strong emotion combined with his own innate sensuality. His *18 Poems* (1934) and *Twenty-five Poems* (1936) bring together conflicting images in startling association, with pronounced and emotive verbal rhythms. The method has superficial resemblances to those of the 19th-C poet G. M. Hopkins* and the 17th-C Metaphysicals*, but it presents less access than they do for the analytical intellect. Thomas's theme is characteristically the relationship between the disorderliness of sexual impulses and the forces of growth in nature. *The Map of Love* (1939) is mixed prose and poetry; it includes one of his most remarkable poems, *After the Funeral*, in which the striking rhythm and images cohere round the figure of the woman for whose death the poem is an elegy. *Deaths and Entrances* (1946) contained most of Thomas's most famous work. The poems show the impression made on him by the war (during which he remained a civilian) in *A Refusal to Mourn*, a more overt use of religious emotion in *The Conversation of Prayer*, and delight in natural environment (*eg Poem in October*, *Fern Hill*). These poems are often less obscure than earlier ones, but the method remains a strong attack on the emotions, achieved by the shock of the imagery and the sweep of the rhythm.

Thomas also wrote prose works – notably the stories entitled *Portrait of the Artist as a Young Dog* (1940) and the play *Under Milk Wood* published after his death (1954). The prose has no obscurity and exhibits, as the poems do not, Thomas's strong humour. The play shows a mastery of the medium of drama for sound broadcasting which remains unexcelled.

Thomas's wide fame derives especially from three qualities: his unashamed appeal to latent emotionalism in the common reader, on whom he made a direct impact far greater than that of other modern poets except Yeats*; his remarkable talent as a public reader of verse; his personality, which became a legend during his own lifetime, especially in America. On the other hand, his exuberance ran counter, before the war, to the intellectual fastidiousness of T. S. Eliot* and the emotional scepticism of W. H. Auden*, the two poets with the greatest prestige amongst the intelligentsia in England during the 30s; again, he has been regarded with suspicion since 1945 by younger poets who have cultivated scrupulous honesty of feeling. No one doubts that Thomas had talent and used it remarkably; but critics often express doubt about the maturity of his mind and the sincerity of his feelings. It is possible that his reputation as a writer of comic prose may outlive his reputation as a poet.

*** 6.5.**

Bib: Maud, R., a critical study; Tedlock, ed. symposium, biographical and critical; Jones, T. H. critical study in *Writers and Critics* series; Fraser, G. S., in British Council *Writers and their Work* series; Holbrook, D., *Llaregyb Revisited*.

Thomas, Philip Edward (1878–1917)

Poet and essayist. He was educated at St Paul's School and Lincoln College, Oxford, and was killed at the battle of Arras. He made his living by writing a long series of prose works, beginning with *The Woodland Life* (1897) and including biography, criticism, and essays on natural surroundings. The last are in a tradition that extends back through Richard Jefferies*, about whom Thomas wrote a critical assessment (1909), to the poetry of Wordsworth*. It was not until 1914 that Thomas began to write poetry, under the influence of the American poet Robert Frost, whom he first met the year before. His poems are continuous with his prose studies of nature*, but it is by the poems rather than the prose that his reputation has grown since his death. English 'nature poetry' at its best has never been merely descriptive, but has concerned the power of the natural environment to elicit the purest human responses, not only to environment but to elemental human relationships, including the relationship of the poet with himself. Thomas's poems show great integrity of responsiveness and sensitivity to the language of his day; they are without the weakening nostalgia and sensibility which showed the decadence of the nature poetry tradition in some of his contemporaries. After his death, his poetic achievement was at first overshadowed by the reaction against the decadence of his contemporaries. Ezra Pound* and T. S. Eliot* led public taste away from the whole tradition, in both its good and its bad aspects, in which Thomas wrote. However, *New Bearings in English Poetry* (1932) by F. R. Leavis* contains intelligent reassessment of his work. Since 1945, Thomas's austere honesty and delicacy of perception have caused his work to appeal strongly to English poets striving for the same virtues; with Thomas Hardy*, he is seen as representative of distinctively English sensibilities in contrast to the partly alien sensibilities of Pound and Yeats*.

Bib: Lives by Eckert, R. P., Moore, J., Farjeon, E.; Thomas, H., *As It Was* and *World Without End*; Coombes, H., *Edward Thomas*; 'Hardy, De la Mare and Thomas' in *The Modern Age* (Pelican Guide); Leavis, F. R., *New Bearings in English Poetry*; Day Lewis, C., in *Essays by Divers Hands* (Transactions of the Royal Society of Literature Vol. XXVIII, 1956).

Thompson, Francis (1859–1907)

Poet. He gave up the study of medicine in Manchester to seek his fortune in London, where he nearly starved. He published his *Poems* in 1893. Thompson was a Catholic; the most famous of his poems (included in this volume) was the intensely religious *Hound of Heaven*. Its bold, extravagant style recalls the work of the 17th-C Catholic poet Richard Crashaw*, one of the English Metaphysicals*. On the other hand, Thompson was more in the tradition of his immediate predecessors in his employment of sensuous, ornate symbolism; in this he resembles the Pre-Raphaelites* of mid-19th C, and another Catholic poet – one of the first of his admirers – Coventry Patmore*. In this respect, a comparison of the *Hound of Heaven* with *The Wreck of the Deutschland* (1875) by yet another Catholic, G. M. Hopkins*, is instructive; Hopkins shows equal emotional intensity with much more of the intellectual rigour of the 17th-C poets. Thompson's other volumes were *Sister Songs* (1895) and *New Poems* (1897). His prose work includes his *Essay on Shelley* (1909).

Bib: Lives by Meynell, E., Meynell, V., and Thomson, P. van K. Critical studies by Reid, J. C., and Danchin, P. (in French).

Thomson, James (1700–48)

Poet. He was a Scotsman, born among the wild scenery of the Scottish border. In 1725 he travelled up to London with the first draft of a landscape poem, *Winter*, in his pocket. This was the first written of the four *Seasons**, in blank verse*, and one of the first poems in English to be devoted entirely to natural surroundings. Their novelty surprised contemporary taste, and Thomson filled them out with moral reflections based on contemporary natural philosophy which were very congenial to it. His blank verse is strongly Miltonic; his next most famous poem, *The Castle of Indolence** (1748) is a reflective poem, partly a burlesque, in the tradition of Spenser*. His other verse has proved less memorable, except for the ode *Rule Britannia** in the masque *Alfred* (1740). He published a long patriotic poem *Liberty* in 1736, and a number of not very successful blank verse tragedies: *Sophonisba* (1730); *Agamemnon* (1738); *Edward and Eleanora* (1739); *Tancred and Sigismunda* (1745); *Coriolanus* (1749).

* 6.3.2.

Bib: Grant, D., *Life*; Johnson, S., in *Lives of the Poets*; Van Tieghem, P., *Le Préromantisme*; Cohen, R., in *The Art of Discrimination.*

Thomson, James (1834–82)

Poet. He was the son of a sailor in the merchant service and of a deeply religious woman who belonged to one of the narrower protestant sects. He was an army schoolmaster, 1850–62, during which period he had a tragic love affair, and made friends with Charles Bradlaugh, who became a well-known atheist radical. Thomson is chiefly known for a long, sombre, atheistic poem, *The City of Dreadful Night* (1874), which expressed in the most uncompromising terms the darkest aspect of the loss of religious belief common among Victorian intellectuals. He was also capable of gaiety (*Vane's Story and Other Poems*, 1881). *A Voice from the Nile and other Poems* was published posthumously in 1884. He commonly wrote under the initials B. V. (Bysshe, from Percy Bysshe Shelley, and Vanolis, anagram for the German poet, Novalis).

Bib: Dobell, B., *The Laureate of Pessimism*; Walker, E. B., *James Thomson.*

Thopas, Sir

* *Sir Thopas.*

Thor

An ancient god of the Germans, Scandinavians, Icelanders, and possibly the Anglo-Saxons. The name means Thunder and his sign was a hammer. He has given his name to the day of the week, Thursday.

Thoth /θəuθ/

An ancient Egyptian god, sometimes represented with the head of an ibis, and sometimes as a dog-headed ape. He was the messenger of the gods (like the Greek Hermes*) and the arbiter in their disputes.

Thrale, Hester Lynch (1741–1821)

Wife of a wealthy brewer; she achieved fame by her close friendship with Samuel Johnson*. In 1786 she published *Anecdotes of the Late Samuel Johnson*, much disapproved of by Johnson's great biographer, James Boswell*. After the death of her first husband, she married a Gabriele Piozzi in 1784, the year of Johnson's death. Johnson found the marriage unforgivable and severed relations with her.

Threadneedle Street, The Old Lady of

A familiar term, dating from 18th C, for the Bank of England*, which stands in a street of that name. The name of the street seems to derive from its original occupation by tailors.

Through the Looking-Glass

* *Carroll, Lewis.*

Thucydides (5th-4th C BC) /θjuː'sididiːz/

Greek historian of the Peloponnesian war*. It is one of the earliest genuinely historical works in European literature in its distinct care for accuracy. Nearly a quarter of the book is devoted to political speeches, including the great Funeral Oration by Pericles*; these give an important insight into Greek attitudes to politics. Thucydides has been a principal text for English classical education*.

Thule /θjuːli/

The ancient Greek and Roman name for a land in the far north, first mentioned by the Greek navigator Pytheas (about 300 BC). It has been conjectured to be the Orkneys, the Shetlands, Iceland, or Norway. The Latin expression Ultima Thule (Farthest Thule) is used in modern English to mean the extreme point attainable.

Thunderer, The

* *Times.*

Thyestes /θai'estiːz/

In Greek myth, a king of Argos, son of Pelops*, and brother of Atreus. He seduced the wife of Atreus, who revenged himself by killing Thyestes' children and then inviting their father to a banquet where he gave him his own children as meat. After the banquet, Atreus disclosed the truth, and Thyestes responded by cursing Atreus and his descendants. Thyestes is the subject of a tragedy by the Roman poet, Seneca*.

Thyrsus /θəːsəs/

In ancient Greece, a rod or staff, tipped with a pine cone and wreathed with vine leaves or ivy, carried by the worshippers of the god Dionysus*.

Times, The

British newspaper. It was founded in 1785 as *The Daily Universal Register*, and took its present name in 1788. In 19th C it took the lead in contriving new methods of collecting news (notably through the employment of foreign correspondents), and its succession of distinguished editors and contributors gave it an outstanding status among British newspapers, which it has never lost. Though always in private ownership, it has always claimed to be an independent newspaper rather than a party one, and though its circulation (about half a million) is comparatively small for a British newspaper, it is commonly acknowledged to have that kind of prestige. The literary style of one of its staff writers caused it to be nicknamed 'The Thunderer' in 19th C; the novelist Anthony Trollope* con-

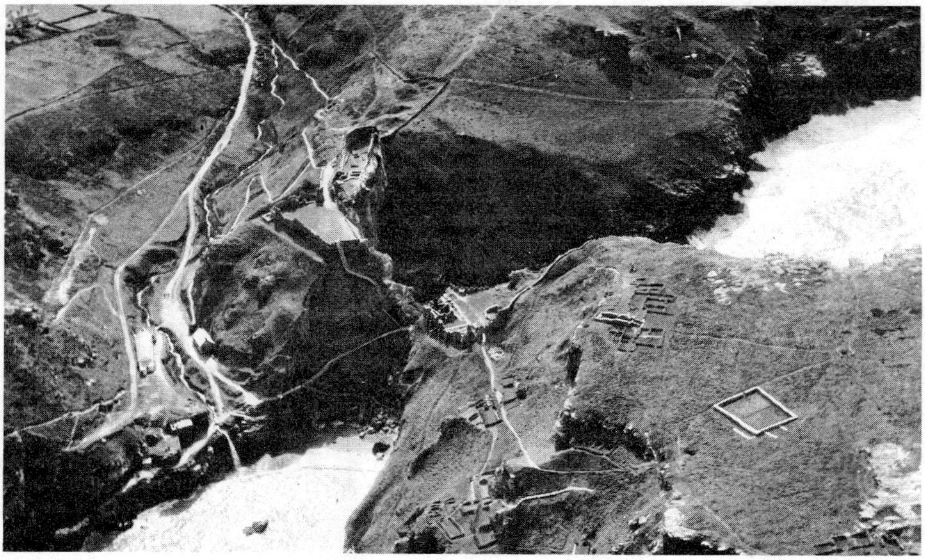

sequently refers to it as *The Jupiter* in his novels, since this king of the gods was known as the Thunderer by the ancient Romans. *The Times* publishes *The Times Literary Supplement* weekly; it is the leading British literary periodical.

* *Newspapers.*

Timon /ˈtaimən/

A rich citizen of Athens of 5th C BC; he was celebrated for his hatred of mankind. He is referred to by a number of ancient Greek writers including Aristophanes*, and notably by Plutarch*, in his life of Mark Antony, and by Lucian* in his dialogue *Misanthropos.* Shakespeare (*Timon of Athens**) makes him a rich, ostentatious philanthropist who becomes a misanthropist through disillusionment at men's ingratitude. Pope, in his *Moral Essays** (iv–1734) described a rich Timon of his own day – perhaps the Duke of Chandos – laying emphasis on tasteless ostentation and indifference to people rather than hatred of them.

Timon of Athens

A tragedy by Shakespeare*, written about 1607. The material is probably taken from Plutarch's* life of Mark Antony (written 1st C AD), Lucian's* dialogue *Misanthropos* (2nd C AD), and an anonymous play of Shakespeare's own day. Although the drama is carried through to its conclusion, most scholars consider that the play is an unrevised draft; the grounds for this judgement are chiefly the quality of the verse, which has the strength of mature Shakespeare combined with some signs of confusion and crudity, and the uncharacteristic bareness with which the theme is presented.

Timon is an Athenian nobleman who delights in the prodigal entertainment of his guests. In spite of his great wealth, he presently finds himself in debt; he is then outraged to discover that none of those to whom he has been so generous is prepared to help him. He invites his friends to one more banquet, but the steaming dishes, uncovered, contain only hot water; throwing the dishes and water at them, he drives his guests out of the house. In a frenzy of hatred, he then takes to a life of solitude in the wilderness, where he is visited by the cynical philosopher Apemantus, his devoted steward Flavius, the general Alcibiades who is rebelling against the meanness of the Athenian government, and other characters from his past life of opulence. This part of the play consists of a series of dialogues which leave Timon resolute in his hatred of humanity, though he is obliged to make an exception of his disinterestedly loyal steward. The dialogue with Apemantus is the most striking: Apemantus has always foreseen that Timon would be deceived by his friends, since he has a low opinion of human nature; Timon, however, retorts that Apemantus' cynicism is groundless except for the mean motive of jealousy, whereas he, Timon, has proved that humanity is inferior after testing it on the opposite hypothesis. Alcibiades is afflicted by the public meanness of the Athenian state, as Timon has been afflicted by private ingratitude; thus he regards Timon as an ally though he cannot persuade him to join forces with the rebels. The rebellion of Alcibiades is successful, and when Timon dies, the Athenian rulers penitently acknowledge their ill-treatment of him.

A few critics consider this to be among Shakespeare's noblest achievements: see Wilson Knight in *The Wheel of Fire.*

Tintagel /tinˈtadʒəl/

A ruined castle by the sea in Cornwall. By tradition it was the birthplace of King Arthur*; it is mentioned as such in Malory's *Morte d'Arthur**. The present castle dates from after the Norman Conquest* (1066), but there may have been a castle of sorts there in Celtic times.

Tintern Abbey /'tintən/

One of the most famous remains of the great medieval abbeys, dissolved by Henry VIII* in 1536–39. It stands in a particularly beautiful natural setting, in the valley of the River Wye, near the border of England and Wales. The poet William Wordsworth* used this setting for one of the best known of his early poems, *Lines Composed a Few Miles Above Tintern Abbey* (in *Lyrical Ballads**), in which he meditates on the influence of natural surroundings on the formation of his mind.

Tiresias (Teiresias) /tai'ri:sias/

In Greek myth, a sage of Thebes whom the gods afflicted with blindness but then compensated with the gift of prophecy. In the most familiar form of the legend, he spent part of his life as a woman, and his blindness was a punishment from Zeus* for declaring that women got more pleasure from sexual love than men. He lived to a great age, and even in Hades* (the underworld of the dead) was allowed to keep his earthly intelligence instead of becoming a mere shade.

Tennyson's* poem *Tiresias* is one of those dramatic monologues* which are now among the most admired of his poems; here, Tiresias speaks with the voice of the lonely, timeless sage. He also occurs in Part III of T. S. Eliot's poem *The Waste Land**; here he is more the impartial witness of the crises of the human mind, and is described in a note as 'the most important personage in the poem, uniting all the rest'.

Titania /ti'ta:njə/

In Shakespeare's *A Midsummer Night's Dream**, the Queen of the Fairies and wife of Oberon, the king. The name derives from Ovid*, who used it in his *Metamorphoses**, for a variety of female deities, especially woodland ones.

Titanic, The /tai'tanik/

The name of a great Atlantic liner which sank with the loss of over fifteen hundred lives in consequence of striking an iceberg on 15 April 1912. Thomas Hardy* described the event, which exemplified his fatalistic philosophy, in one of the finest of his narrative poems, *The Convergence of the Twain* (1914).

Titans

In ancient Greek myth, the first divine race, the children of Uranus*, the sky, and Ge (Gaea) the earth. The six male Titans were Oceanus, Coeus, Crius, Hyperion, Iapetus, and Cronos*; the six females – Thea, Rhea, Themis, Mnemosyne, Phoebe and Tethys. The brothers and sisters intermarried; for instance Iapetus and Themis produced Prometheus* and Epimetheus, and Cronos and Rhea produced Zeus* and the other gods of Mount Olympus*; Hyperion and Thea produced Helios, later the Sun, Selene, the Moon, and Eos, Dawn. Under the reign of the Titans a number of mythological beings were produced, symbolizing the creation of the world. Eventually Cronos and the other Titans were overthrown by Zeus and the other Olympians, thus bringing about the divine order which the Greeks (and later, the Romans) believed to be contemporary with themselves.

The English Romantic poets, Keats* and Shelley* used these myths for their own purposes. In the two versions of his unfinished epic *Hyperion**, Keats described the overthrow of the Titans to symbolize the replacing of old orders by new, and the consequent tragedy which he felt to be intrinsic to experience. Keats mingled Roman deities with Greek, giving Cronos the Roman name of Saturn; he opposed Hyperion to Apollo, instead of to Helios. Shelley invented a myth in *Prometheus Unbound**: Prometheus, son of the Titan Iapetus, witnesses, on behalf of Man, the downfall of the tyrant Zeus. Prometheus is represented as the child of Earth.

Tithes

A system for the maintenance of the parish clergy of the Church of England*, consisting, originally, of one-tenth of the produce of the parish farmers. It was replaced during 19th C by an annual rent and was abolished altogether by Parliament in 1936.

Tithonus /'tiθənəs/

In Greek myth, the son of Laomedon, king of Troy. Such was his beauty that Eos (Aurora), goddess of the dawn, fell in love with him and made him her husband. She secured for him from Zeus the gift of immortal life, but forgot to require also immortal youth. He became a hideous old man, physically helpless except for his speech, which 'flowed on incessantly'. Eos took pity on him and turned him into a cicada, whose voice flows like that of an old man.

Tennyson's* poem *Tithonus*, one of his finest early poems, is a dramatic monologue* representing Tithonus in the agony of his eternal old age.

Titles of Nobility

The main titles of nobility, or peerages, in Britain are as follows, from lowest to highest in order of seniority:

Baron. A title originating with the Norman aristocracy after the Conquest*.

Viscount. Originating in 1440.

Earl. As old as the title of baron, and equivalent to the title of Count in other countries of Europe. An earl's wife is known as a countess.

Marquess. Originating in 1385.

Duke. Originating in 1337, when the title Duke of Cornwall became a title regularly awarded the heir to the throne. The title of duke was restricted to the royal family until the end of 14th C.

All the above-mentioned titles are hereditary, with the exception of life peerages (always Baron or Baroness) originally awarded for political purposes. Whether inherited or awarded for the life of the holder, such a title carried with it the right to sit in the House of Lords*.

The title of knight or baronet (hereditary knighthood*) is not a title of nobility; the holder is, politically speaking, a commoner, *ie* represented in accordance with his vote in the House of Commons, and entitled to seek election as a member of it.

Titus Andronicus /ˈtaitəs anˈdronikəs/

A tragedy by Shakepeare*, published in 1594. The origin of the plot is not known; it may owe something to Ovid's* Procne and Tereus, one of his *Metamorphoses** translated by Golding, 1565–67, and to Seneca's* drama *Thyestes* translated between 1559 and 1581. It is in any case a violent revenge tragedy* of the kind that Shakespeare and his contemporaries derived from Seneca. The setting is Rome of the Empire; the plot concerns the revenge of Titus, a Roman general, for the atrocities committed by Tamora, the Queen of the Goths, against his family. She is aided by a villainous slave, Aaron the Moor. Much doubt has been expressed by scholars as to whether the play is entirely by Shakespeare, by Shakespeare in collaboration, or not by Shakespeare at all; the last opinion arises partly from the low esteem in which the play is usually held, although, according to Ben Jonson*, its popularity was great among the contemporary public.

To the Lighthouse (1927)

A novel by Virginia Woolf*. The setting is a house used for holidays by Mr and Mrs Ramsay. The household consists of themselves, their eight children, and a number of their friends, of whom the most important is the painter Lily Briscoe. The novel dispenses with plot and is organized into three parts, dominated by two symbols – the lighthouse out at sea, and Lily's painting of the house, with Mrs Ramsay sitting in the window with her son James. The parts are entitled 'The Window', 'Time Passes', and 'The Lighthouse'. The first part is dominated by Mrs Ramsay, who is intuitive, imaginative, and possesses a reassuring and vitalizing influence upon people and their emotions. The mysterious lighthouse flashing through the darkness is associated with her. In the interval represented by the second part of the novel, corresponding to the war years 1914–18, she dies, and the third part is dominated by Mr Ramsay who is intellectual, philosophical, and lonely. The lighthouse seen as a practical instrument, close at hand and by daylight, is associated with him. The middle section concerns the empty house, subject to the flux of time and its changes. Lily Briscoe, the artist, stands aloof from Mrs Ramsay's embracing influence and seeks to fix the constantly changing relationships of people and objects in a single composition; she completes the picture in the last sentence of the book, when the Ramsay son, James, achieves reconciliation with his father and with the lighthouse seen as fact.

The story is told through the flow of thought and feeling in the minds of the characters, especially James, Lily, and Mrs Ramsay. The novel, one of the most original of the many fictional experiments in the 1920s, is partly autobiographical, and based on Virginia Woolf's own family. Mr and Mrs Ramsay are her father and mother, Leslie Stephen* and his second wife.

Tobit

A book of the biblical Apocrypha*; in some ways it is like a light-hearted romance, and its charm as such accounts for its widespread popularity. Scholars are inclined to date it about 250 BC, and ascribe it to the authorship of an Egyptian Jew writing in Greek. The period of the story is the Jewish captivity in Babylon. Tobit, a Jew, sends his son Tobias (accompanied by his dog) to search for buried treasure. Tobias is assisted by the angel Raphael in disguise; with this assistance Tobias not only recovers the treasure but, with the aid of a magic fish that he catches in the River Tigris, he drives off the evil spirit, Asmodeus, who has been persecuting Sarah, daughter of Tobit's relative Raguel. Tobias marries Sarah, and cures his father of his blindness with the gall of his fish. Tobias's dog is probably the original of the dog Toby in the Punch and Judy* puppet shows.

* *Babylonian Captivity.*

Toby

The dog in the traditional puppet-show of Punch and Judy*. His name is probably derived from the apocryphal Book of Tobit*.

Tolbooth /ˈtolbu:θ/

Originally, a stall where tolls, *ie* taxes on merchandise, were collected. This then became identified with a town hall, perhaps with prison cells beneath it, and finally the term was applied, in Edinburgh, to the town prison.

Tolstoy, Count Leo Nikolaevitch (1828–1910) /ˈtolstoi/

Russian novelist, dramatist, and moral philosopher. What are usually considered his two greatest novels, *War and Peace* (1864–66) and *Anna Karenina* (1875–77), have a spaciousness, profundity, and balance of sanity which have caused them to be used as a standard by which the achievements of other novelists can be measured. This scale of greatness is to be accounted for not only by the depth of Tolstoy's mind but by the breadth of his experience, which in turn owes something to Tolstoy's position in Russian society, and the critical phase of history through which Russia was passing during his lifetime. He belonged to the class of Russian landed gentry, and was partly educated by French tutors, a fact which, taken with the sensitivity of the Russian intelligentsia to West European culture, gave him a broader understanding of the issues of civilization in his time than was characteristic of most Western novelists. Tolstoy frequented the intellectual and fashionable classes of Russian society, travelled abroad, and spent the years 1851–57 in the Russian army, seeing service in the Crimean War against Britain, France and Turkey. Two other absorbing aspects of his experience were the problems of Russia's vast peasantry, emancipated from serfdom in 1861, and the prominence of religion in Russian life.

Tolstoy was early influenced by the thought of Jean-Jacques Rousseau*, and this, combined with his own direct experience of peasant life, developed in him a strong faith in spontaneous, simple living in contrast to the sophisticated, fashionable, educated society which he also knew well. From 1876, disillusioned by worldliness and inspired by the example of the peasants, he thought increasingly about the religious interpretation of experience, but his thinking turned him away from the Russian Orthodox Church to a religion of his own, based on the words of Christ (in *Matthew* 5:39) 'that ye resist not evil'. Tolstoy's religion was thus pacifistic and on the side of self-abnegation; it did not admit the existence of life after death nor a personal God, his belief being that the kingdom of God is within man. He described his religion in *What I believe in* and *A Short Exposition of the Gospels*; a complete account of his conversion is given in *A Confession* (1844), and in the same year he published stories inspired by his inner life at the time, *The Memoirs of a Madman* and *The Death of Ivan Ilyich*. In *What is Art* (1896), he expounded his doctrine that good art works by re-creating in the reader the fine emotions of the writer, bad art by similarly conveying the bad ones.

Tom Brown's Schooldays

* *Rugby School.*

Tom Jones, a Foundling

A novel by Henry Fielding*, published in 1749. The central character begins life as a baby of unknown parentage (*ie* 'a foundling') who is discovered in the mansion of the enlightened landowner, Squire Allworthy. Allworthy adopts him, and he grows up a handsome and generous-hearted youth, whose weakness is his excess of animal spirits and inclination to fleshly lusts. He falls in love with Sophia Western, daughter of a neighbouring landowner, Squire Western, who is as gross, ignorant and self-willed as Allworthy is refined and enlightened. Western intends Sophia for Blifil, Allworthy's nephew, a mean and treacherously hypocritical character, who is supported against Tom by two members of Allworthy's household, the pedantic chaplain Thwackum and the pretentious philosopher, Square, who counterbalance each other. They succeed in disgracing Tom, whom Allworthy is persuaded to disown. The central part of the novel describes his travels and amorous adventures in the company of a comic follower, Partridge. Sophia also leaves home, to escape from Blifil, and nearly falls victim to a plot by Lady Bellaston, with whom Tom has become amorously entangled, to place her in the power of Lord Fellamar. Tom is eventually identified as the son of Allworthy's sister; the plots against him are brought to light; he is received again by Allworthy, and marries Sophia.

The novel, like its predecessor by Fielding, *Joseph Andrews**, is a 'comic epic', offering a wide range of social types of the age, all of whom are presented as permanent human types rather than as unique individuals, as 19th-C novelists would show them. Fielding's method is expository; he does not attempt to create illusions of characters with interior lives of their own, but expounds behaviour, with the aid of prefatory essays to his chapters, always light-heartedly, but always with a view to exhibiting basic human motives as they have always existed, rather in the manner of the 17th-C comedies of humours* and of manners*. He owes much to Cervantes' comic romance *Don Quixote** and to the studies of contemporary morals and manners by the painter William Hogarth*. To some extent the book was written in rivalry to Samuel Richardson's *Clarissa Harlowe**, a novel written in a tragic spirit and in a strenuous and idealistic moral tone. It was Fielding's tendency to 'correct' Richardson's idealism and partly self-deceiving moral rigour by reducing events to more usual human experience and interpreting this in the light of tolerant comedy instead of grand tragedy; for instance, Lovelace, in *Clarissa* is a human fiend (though also an interesting psychological study) where Tom is merely a healthy young man whose licentiousness is bound up with his virtue of outgoing sympathy and generosity. Thus, *Tom Jones* is both one of the first important English novels, a new kind of imaginative work, and one that embodies highly traditional values.

* 4.3.2.

Tom Thumb

An old folk-tale, several versions of which exist in northern Europe. Tom is (in the English version) the son of a ploughman living in the days of the legendary King Arthur*; he is Tom Thumb because he is no bigger than the ploughman's thumb. He has a number of absurd adventures consequent on his diminutive size, including being carried off by a crow, swallowed by a cow, and swallowed again by a giant.

Tophet (Topheth) /ˈtəufet/

In the Bible, a place near Gehenna*; both places were used for the consumption of rubbish by fire, and thus became symbolic of a fiery underworld where sinners were punished after death.

Torquemada, Tomas de (1420–98) /toːkiˈmaːdə/

A Dominican friar who was appointed in 1483 as the first Inquisitor-general to investigate religious heresies in Spain. His zeal has made him a symbol of cruelty in England.

* *Inquisition, The.*

Tory

* *Whig and Tory.*

Tottel's Miscellany (1557)

An influential anthology of verse published by Richard Tottel, a bookseller, and Nicholas Grimald, a translator and scholar. It was originally entitled *Songs and Sonnets*, and included the work of the Earl of Surrey* and Sir Thomas Wyatt*. Their poems, the first of any distinction in English to show characteristics of Renaissance* style, had never before been printed though they had circulated in manuscript, and the great popularity of the anthology helped to shape the short poem so much cultivated in the last 20 years of the century; their success led to the publication of many similar anthologies. Unfortunately the editors made alterations in Wyatt's rhythms to make them smoother, and thereby robbed some of his poems of some of their character.

* *Anthology.*

Tournament (Tourney)

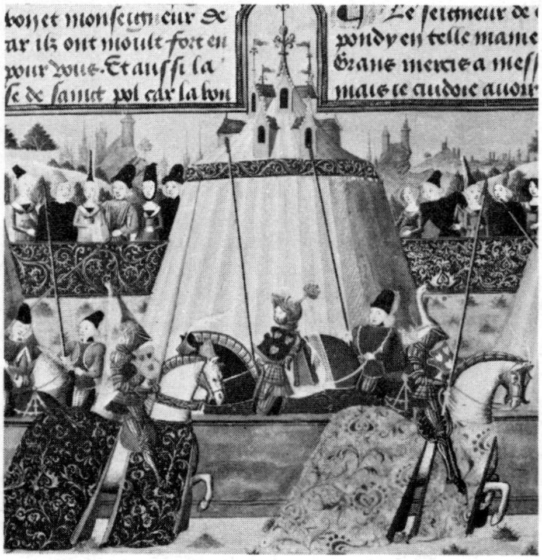

A kind of mock fight, popular among knights and men of noble birth in the Middle Ages*; it was also known as 'jousting'; the arenas were known as 'tilt-yards' or 'lists'. The sport originated in France, perhaps in 11th C, and it was exceedingly popular in England by 12th. At this time tournaments were often ill-organized and dangerous enough to cause injuries and deaths; both the Church and the Monarchy took steps to forbid or at least to restrict them. By 15th C, however, tournaments were better regulated, and became exhibitions of pageantry popular with the general public. During the reign of Elizabeth I*, pageantry predominated, and precautions were taken against injury. Then tournaments disappeared, to be revived again, in a spirit of entirely artificial romanticism, in early 19th C when the cult of the Middle Ages was at its height.

* *Knighthood.*

Tourneur, Cyril (1575?–1626) /'tə:nə/

Dramatist. Not much is known of his life, except that he was employed abroad in military and diplomatic service, and died in Ireland on the return of the unsuccessful naval expedition under Buckingham to capture Cadiz. He is well known for two plays, one of which, *The Revenger's Tragedy** (1606–7), is regarded as one of the finest achievements of the period, and is attributed by some scholars to another dramatist, Thomas Middleton*. The other, *The Atheist's Tragedy* (1611), an interesting anti-revenge play, is much less esteemed. The case for Tourneur being the author of the more admired of the two plays is partly based on the resemblance to an obscure religious poem by him, *The Transformed Metamorphosis* (1600). He also wrote a number of elegies*.

* 5.1.3.2; *Revenge Tragedy.*

Bib: Murray, P. B., *Tourneur*; Eliot, T. S., in *Selected Essays*; Bowers, F. T., in *Elizabethan Revenge Tragedy*; Bradbrook, M. C., in *Themes and Conventions of Elizabethan Tragedy*; Ellis-Fermor, U. M., in *The Jacobean Drama.*

Tower Hill

A slight eminence near the Tower of London* on the north bank of the Thames. It was used as a place of execution for aristocratic or otherwise eminent political prisoners, including Sir Thomas More* (beheaded there in 1535), the poet Earl of Surrey* (1547), the Earl of Strafford* (1641), and Archbishop Laud* (1645).

Tower of London

A medieval fortress, the central part of which – the White Tower – was built after the Norman Conquest* by William I* to subdue the City of London; it stands by the Thames at the south-east corner of the old City, and counterbalances the Palace of Westminster* (now the Houses of Parliament), also on the river, at the western end of the City. The Tower was extended later in the Middle Ages*, and incorporated a royal palace, which was pulled down in the 1650s by the order of Oliver Cromwell*. The frequent mention of the Tower in English history and literature is due to the imprisonment there (and often execution there or on the adjacent Tower Hill*) of numerous eminent men and women. For instance Edward V* and his brother were imprisoned in it by Richard III* and probably murdered there; other victims include two of the queens of Henry VIII*, Anne Boleyn and Catherine Howard, Sir Thomas More (beheaded in 1535), Sir Walter Raleigh (1618), and Charles II's illegitimate son, the Duke of Monmouth (1685). The Tower continued to be used as a prison until 19th C. It is now a museum, and contains 'the Crown Jewels', *ie* the regalia of the British monarchy. It is guarded by the Yeomen of the Guard (known as 'Beefeaters' – **Yeoman*) who wear 16th-C uniform.

Town and Gown

A term used in Oxford* and Cambridge*, to express the rivalry between citizens and students. The two parties were sporadically hostile, especially in 13th and 14th C, when the hostility led from time to time to dangerous riots, such as those early in 13th C which resulted in the emigration of many of the students from Oxford, and the consequent founding of the University of Cambridge.

Towneley Plays

* *Wakefield Plays.*

Tract

An essay or treatise, usually short but published singly; usually on a religious subject. The most famous in English are the *Tracts for the Times* (1833–41) by a group of devout Anglicans*, Hurrell Froude, Pusey, Keble*, and Newman*. Their purpose was to increase the spiritual dignity and independence of the Church of England* by the revival of doctrines stressed in 17th C but since then largely neglected, with the consequence, as the authors believed, that the Church was losing its spiritual identity and was exposing itself more and more to secular utilitarianism and domination by the state. Newman's was the predominating spirit in the group; he started the series, and he wrote *Tract XC*, which caused scandal by emphasizing the closeness of the Anglican to the older Catholic tradition, and thus ended it.

* *Oxford Movement.*

Tractarian Movement

* *Oxford Movement; Tract.*

Trade Union

The history of British trade unionism may be divided into four main phases.

[1] Impulses to start trade union associations arose naturally from the early development in England of capitalist industrialism and the congregation of workers in factories in later 18th C. At first workers associated chiefly in small ways for such purposes as mutual insurance against unemployment in what were known as 'Friendly Societies'. Nonetheless the movements were regarded with suspicion by the government as possible centres of revolution, especially after the French Revolution* of 1789–93. Consequently Parliament* passed the Combination Acts of 1799–1800 to forbid the formation of unions. These laws were repealed in 1824, and thereafter the activity of forming associations amongst employees was a lawful one, but this did not include striking.

[2] The next phase was a brief one, and ended in failure. An attempt was made, at first successfully, to form a national union of workers called the Grand National Consolidated Trades Union; this came to nothing after the trial and transportation of six Dorsetshire agricultural labourers in 1834 on the charge of administering false oaths; they are the so-called 'Tolpuddle Martyrs', whose memory is still revered.

[3] For 30 years industrial relationships remained stormy, but until 1850 working-class energies were taken up with other movements such as the Chartist Movement* and the Anti-Corn Law League. A respectable kind of Trade Unionism developed among skilled workers, such as the Amalgamated Society of Engineers. In the 1860s a number of outrages in the industrial north of England again alerted public suspicion of trade unions, and the government appointed an inquiry into their activities. This was so reassuring that unionism began to prosper. In 1868 the Trades Union Congress (T.U.C.) was started; thus began a new phase in which trade unionism again had a national organization capable of coordinating the interests of industrial workers.

[4] The last phase, since 1870, has been the development of Unionism to its present state of being one of the most powerful factors of national life. Two laws gave the movement new legal security; that of 1871 legalized action through strikes, and that of 1876 gave unions the right to exist as corporations, able to own property and to defend their rights corporatively (*ie* not as mere collections of individuals) in courts of law. Two important developments followed in the last 20 years of the century; the growth of unions where they were most needed, among unskilled workers; and the formation of a political party, the Labour Party*, which had union interests at heart and strong financial support from the T.U.C. Modern unions federated in the T.U.C. have a membership of over 10 million, and unions have tended to amalgamate, so that, while they are much larger than in 19th C, they are fewer in number. A common criticism of Unionism today is that it has too much power in the national economy and not enough responsibility; criticisms are especially made of the trade union official with direct contact with factory workers – the shop steward – who, it is alleged, is inclined to cause disputes and strikes with insufficient regard for national interest. On the other hand, the workers are inclined to complain that senior officials of large unions are mere bureaucrats with insufficient experience of actual problems, so that only by the action of 'wildcat strikes', *ie* unofficial ones not supported by the unions, can certain grievances be rectified. The Industrial Relations Act, which came into force in 1972, represents a move towards bringing the question of industrial action within a legal framework.

* 1.5.1.3; *Industrial Revolution.*

Trafalgar, Battle of (1805) /trə'falgə/

The chief sea-battle of the war against Napoleon*, in which the British fleet under Nelson* defeated a joint French and Spanish fleet under Villeneuve. The victory made impossible an invasion of Britain by the French army, but Nelson was killed in the action.

Tragedy

Tragedy as it is understood in Western Europe has its origins in the Greek dramas by the Athenian dramatists Aeschylus*, Sophocles* and Euripides*, in 6th–5th C BC. Essentially the spirit of this writing was that inevitable suffering overwhelms the characters, and yet the characters maintain their dignity in the face of this suffering, and prove their greatness (and the capacity of human beings for greatness) by doing so. Greek tragedy arose out of their religious interpretation of the nature of human destiny. When Christianity prevailed over Western Europe, a much more hopeful interpretation of human destiny dominated the thought of writers, and tragedy, in the Greek sense, became difficult to imagine and unnatural: if good men suffer in this world, they are rewarded in Heaven, and this is not tragic; wicked men who happen to suffer in this world may be damned in the next, but this is also not tragic because they are wicked. Hence medieval tragedy was on the whole reduced to the rather uninteresting conception of the Wheel of Fortune – that chance in this world is apt to take men from prosperity to misfortune, whatever their spiritual merits; an example is the Monk's Tale* in Chaucer's *Canterbury Tales.*

In late 16th C the tragic vision of human experience was rediscovered by some English dramatists, notably by Marlowe* and Shakespeare*. Insofar as it had a literary ancestry, this was not the great tragedy of the ancient Greeks, which was scarcely known, but the comparatively debased imitation of it by the Roman poet Seneca*, which helped to give rise to Elizabethan Revenge Tragedy* or 'Tragedy of Blood'. More interesting was the growth of conceptions of human destiny which did not usurp the Christian conception, but existed side by side with it, as an alternative, or perhaps rather as a complementary, vision. Thus perhaps the the first important English tragedy is Marlowe's *Doctor Faustus** in which the hero forgoes eternal happiness after death for the sake of earthly ecstasy; Marlowe sets in opposition the Christian doctrine of the soul and Renaissance* delight in earthly experience. *Hamlet**, in which Shakespeare for the first time makes the task of revenge a genuine moral dilemma, is perhaps the next. The greatest achievements of English tragic drama are Shakespeare's five plays: *Othello**, *Macbeth**, *King Lear**, *Antony and Cleopatra**, and *Coriolanus**. These cannot be summed up in a phrase, but they have in common that the hero's hope of some form of supreme earthly happiness collapses into terrible misery, brought about less by the hero's character than through the nature of earthly reality of which his character forms a part. Among Shakespeare's later contemporaries and his successors, several dramatists wrote distinguished plays in the tragic style, but critics disagree about which of these achieved a genuine tragic vision. There is least disagreement, perhaps, about Middleton's *The Changeling**; other notable examples are Webster's *The Duchess of Malfi** and *The White Devil** and Tourneur's (or Middleton's) *Revenger's Tragedy**.

This period, from 1590 till about 1625, was the only one in English literature in which there were more than isolated examples of distinguished theatrical tragedy. The single important example of a work written in the Greek style is Milton's *Samson Agonistes**, but critics disagree as to whether it can be called truly dramatic. Numerous attempts were made to write tragedy in the Greek style, or in the neoclassical French style of Corneille* and Racine*, after 1660, but they lacked conviction; perhaps the best is Dryden's *All for Love**. Various attempts were made by 19th-C poets to revive the Shakespearian mode of tragedy. Of these, Shelley's *The Cenci** is the only noteworthy example, but even that was only a minor success.

Some of the plays of Synge* and Yeats* were genuinely remarkable and original tragedies, but their scale is unambitious, and their scope is narrowed by their distinctively Irish setting.

Owing to the high example of the ancient Greeks, tragedy is generally thought of as a dramatic art, but the authentic tragic spirit may, of course, permeate other forms of narrative. Thus Chaucer's *Troilus and Criseyde** is considered by some critics to be a genuinely tragic poem although the same poet shows so limited a conception of tragedy in the Monk's tales. The English novel is on the whole averse to tragedy until near the end of 19th C, but notable exceptions are *Wuthering Heights** by Emily Brontë and the novels of Thomas Hardy*. In the late 19th and 20th C an authentic tragic spirit is implicit in the novels of Henry James* and Joseph Conrad*. It seems indeed that, at least in English, the novel became the successor to the stage drama as the vehicle for tragic vision. However, in the 1960s the work of such dramatists as Pinter*, Osborne*, and Arden* raises doubts about such a conclusion.

* 5.1.3.2.

Tragicomedy (Tragi-comedy)

Drama in which the elements of both tragedy* and comedy are present. Examples are the reconciliation plays* of Shakespeare, particularly *Pericles**, *Cymbeline**, and *The Winter's Tale**, each of which reaches a tragic climax half way through and then lightens towards a happy conclusion. A peculiarly English form of tragicomedy developed in the years 1610 to 1640, another early example being Beaumont and Fletcher's *Philaster** (1611).

* 5.1.3.3.

Traherne, Thomas (1634?–1674) /trəˈhɜːn/

Religious writer and poet. The son of a west country shoemaker, he became an Anglican* clergyman after leaving Oxford University. He later became private chaplain to Sir Orlando Bridgeman, who held government office under Charles II*. In 17th C the published works of Traherne were *Roman Forgeries* (1673), *Christian Ethics* (1675) and *A Serious and Pathetical Contemplation of the Mercies of God* (1699); however, his poems and his most famous prose work, the *Centuries of Meditation*, were not discovered until the end of 19th C. The poems were at first thought to be by Henry Vaughan*; they have a similar childlike response to experience and reverence for the innocence of childhood, together with a similar Platonic idealism and spiritual mysticism characteristic of the best period of Anglican thought – the first half of 17th C. The poetry has in fact a different character from that of Vaughan, who was one of the Metaphysical* poets. Like others of his group, Vaughan embodied his experience in concrete but surprising and far-reaching imagery, whereas Traherne's verse is much plainer, and in the opinion of most critics, less distinguished either than Vaughan's poetry or his own prose.

Bib: Wade, G. I., *Thomas Traherne*.

Transcendentalism

* *German Influence on English Literature.*

Transferred Epithet

* *Figures of Speech.*

Translation

The life of English literature has always issued from a combination of strong insular traditions and participation in wider European traditions. Translation has always been the principal means of assimilating European literatures into the English idiom, and it was particularly important before 18th C, when the main streams of European cultural life were flowing through other languages. The aim of translators was then less to make an accurate rendering than to make the substance of foreign work thoroughly intelligible to the English spirit; the character of the translation thus proceeded as much from the mind of the translator as from the mind of the original writer. If the translator had a strong personality, the translation often became a distinguished work of English literature in its own right. Translators with less individuality often produced work of historical importance because of its contemporary influence on English writing.

From 14th to 18th C, English writers were constantly absorbing the ancient and contemporary Mediterranean cultures of Europe, and worked on the literatures of France, ancient Rome, Italy, ancient Greece, and Spain. There is no distinct boundary between translation and adaptation; Chaucer* brought English poetry into accord with French and Italian poetry partly by freely adapting work in those languages. His outstanding work of translation is his version of Guillaume de Lorris' *Roman de la Rose**. French ceased to be the first language of the English upper classes in Chaucer's lifetime, but the English nobility continued to have strong ties with French aristocratic culture, and thus translations from French prose were in demand in 15th and 16th C. Caxton*, the first English printer, published many English versions of French romances. The outstanding 15th-C work of English prose was Malory's *Morte d'Arthur**, which Caxton published, and which is partly a translation and partly an adaptation. The work of translation was an important influence on the development of a fluent English prose medium, and this is evident in the difference between Wycliffe's* 14th-C translation of the Latin Bible and Tyndale's* version of the New Testament from the Greek (1525). Lord Berners's translation of Froissart's* *Chronicles* is another distinguished example of English prose development in 15th and early 16th C.

Printing, the Renaissance*, and the rise of new educated classes, all helped to expand translation in 16th C, which was the first great period for translation of classical writers. These had been of central importance in the Middle Ages* too (King Alfred and later Chaucer had translated Boethius' *De Consolatione Philosophiae*) but knowledge of them had now widened and standards of scholarship had advanced. The first important rendering in English of a great classical poem is that of Virgil's *Aeneid** by the Scots poet, Gavin Douglas* (1553). Chapman's* *Iliad** (1611) and *Odyssey** (1615) are impressive, but have less intrinsic merit as English literature. Ovid* had long been a favourite poet, and translations were made of his poems by Arthur Golding (1565–67) and Christopher Marlowe* (pub 1597). But in 17th and 18th C the best-known English version of Ovid was George Sandys's version of *Metamorphoses**, completed in 1626. Ovid had an extensive influence on poets, including Shakespeare; Seneca's* influence on the poetic drama, both as a philosopher and as a dramatist, was equally conspicuous, and it was no doubt helped by the historically important but otherwise undistinguished *Ten Tragedies*, translated by various hands and published between 1559 and 1581. Among the most distinguished prose translators of ancient literature in this period was Philemon Holland, remembered especially for his version of Pliny's* *Natural History*, which he published in 1601. The best known of all, especially for his value to Shakespeare but also for the quality of his writing, is Thomas North*, whose version (1579) of Plutarch's* *Lives* was made not from the original Greek but from the French of Jacques Amyot.

Translations from the contemporary European languages were also numerous in 16th and early 17th C, and indicate the constant interest of English writers in foreign literatures. Sir John Harington translated Ariosto's *Orlando Furioso** in 1591: Tasso's* *Jerusalem Delivered* was translated as *Godfrey of Bulloigne or The Recovery of Jerusalem* (1600); Castiglione's* very influential *Il Cortegiano* was translated by Sir Thomas Hoby (1561). The best known of all these contemporary works is John Florio's* rendering of the *Essays* of Montaigne, published in 1603. Part I of Cervantes' *Don Quixote** was translated in 1612 before Part II was written; the whole work was three times translated in 18th C, by Motteux (1712), Jarvis (1742) and Smollett* (1755). The first three books of Rabelais'* *Gargantua and Pantagruel* were translated notably by Thomas Urquhart; two were published in 1653, and the third in 1694. The fourth and fifth books were added by Motteux in 1708.

Many of the translations made before 1660, especially those in prose, were marked by a superabundance of words, characteristic of much English writing in 16th and 17th C; the originals tended to be amplified rather than closely rendered. After the Restoration* in 1660, writers attached importance to discipline and control, and to emulating these virtues as they were exemplified in the old Latin poets and in contemporary French writers of verse and prose. In consequence, John Dryden* accomplished some of his best work in translating Latin poetry, especially Ovid (*eg Philemon and Baucis**) and the *Aeneid* of Virgil, whose works he translated entire, completing them in 1697. Pope's* translations of Homer's *Iliad* and *Odyssey*, which appeared in 1720 and 1726, greatly enhanced his reputation, but despite the skill of the versification, they are obviously much further from the spirit of Homer than Dryden's renderings are from the Latin poets; the British Augustans* were much closer in feeling to the Roman Augustans than they were to the ancient Greeks. As the century went on, writers became restless under Augustan restraints, and became interested in literatures that had hitherto been ignored or despised; Thomas Gray* imitated Icelandic and Celtic verse. Macpherson's versions of Gaelic legends, which he alleged to be by the legendary poet Ossian (or Oisin*), were more inventions and adaptations than translations, but they probably had a wider influence in other countries than any other English work going under the name of translation, with the exception of the English Bible. Sir William Jones (1746–94), the first important British Oriental scholar, published in 1783 a version in English of the ancient Arabic poems called *Moallakat*, as well as other work from Persian and from Sanskrit.

Some of the more distinguished translations of the first 30 years of 19th C, such as Cary's translation in blank verse of Dante's* *Divine Comedy* (1805–12), Coleridge's* version of Schiller's *Wallenstein* (1800), and Shelley's* fragments of Goethe and Calderon, show the new kinds of influence on the Romantic writers. After 1830, translation became a kind of net for hauling in exotic writings, and its field became very wide, *eg* FitzGerald's* version of the Persian poem, *The Rubaiyat of Omar Khayyam** (1859), Richard Burton's *Arabian Nights** (1885–88), William Morris's* translation of the Icelandic Sagas (beginning in 1869), Swinburne's* versions of Villon, as well as many new versions of the ancient Greek and Latin authors. Two vices of the period were a tendency to make a foreign work express essentially English 19th-C sentiment (*eg* FitzGerald's *Rubaiyat*), and to use peculiarities of style under the mistaken impression that because they gave strangeness to the work, therefore they gave the translation an air of authenticity – a fault which Matthew Arnold* criticizes in his fine essay *On translating Homer* (1861). The really influential translations were more often of contemporary writers, such as those by Constance Garnett of the Russian novelists Tolstoy and Turgenev; William Archer's* translations of Ibsen*; and Scott Moncrieff's fine rendering of Proust's great novel, under the title of *Remembrance of Things Past*. These works bring us into 20th C, in which translation has been cultivated with a new sense of its importance and difficulties. Among the most eminent of modern translations are Arthur Waley's *Chinese Poems* (collected 1946), Ezra Pound's *Cathay* (also from the Chinese) and his version of the Anglo-Saxon *The Seafarer* (1912), Roy Campbell's* *Poems of St John of the Cross* (1951), and Willa and Edwin Muir's* translations of Kafka (1930–49).

One of the most important of all English translations has barely been mentioned in this account; this is the Bible, which is given a separate entry.

Transportation

* *Penal System.*

Travel Literature

This large branch of English literature may be conveniently discussed under these headings: [1] fantasy purporting to be fact; [2] factual accounts; [3] travel experiences regarded as material for art.

[1] *Literature of fantasy purporting to be fact.* So long as extensive travel was rarely undertaken, it was possible for writers to present accounts of fantasy journeys and to pass them off as fact without much fear of being accused of lying. Thus a 14th-C French writer wrote the *Travels of Sir John de Mandeville*, which is a work of fiction or compilation from narratives by other travellers, but purporting to be an account of genuine journeys written by Mandeville himself. The work was translated into English in 1377, became extremely popular, and was long regarded as genuine. Long after the extravagances of the story were seen to be falsehoods, Mandeville, a purely fictional English knight, was thought to be the genuine author.

[2] *Literature of fact.* By the second half of 16th C, the great Portuguese, Spanish and Italian explorers had discovered the Americas and greatly extended knowledge of eastern Asia. Liars could still find large, credulous audiences, but the facts were marvellous enough to require no distortion. Writers also began to feel strong motives for publishing truthful accounts. Thus Richard Hakluyt* published his *Principal Navigations, Voyages and Discoveries of the English Nation* in 1589, partly for patriotic reasons. The English had been slow to start on exploratory enterprises, although by this time they were extremely active. Hakluyt, finding that the reputation of his nation stood low among foreigners in this field, wanted to demonstrate the reality of the English achievement, and at the same time to stimulate his fellow-countrymen to further endeavours. His book is really a compilation of accounts by English explorers; an enlarged edition came out in 1598, and a still further enlarged edition was published under the title of *Hakluytus Posthumus, or Purchas his Pilgrims* by Samuel Purchas in 1625. The accounts vary from those by accomplished writers like Sir Walter Raleigh* to others by writers with little or no experience of writing; they constitute an anthology of early English descriptive writing in which the writers are concerned with the truthfulness of their accounts rather than with entertaining or deceiving the reader. Other examples of this new kind of honest and truthful handling of descriptive language are Captain John Smith's history of the founding of the colony of Virginia, *General History of Virginia, New England, and the Summer Isles* (1624). The contrast between this newer, plainer style and the extravagant and whimsical style more characteristic of the pamphleteers* can be seen in accounts of travels in Europe by Thomas Coryate (1577?–1617), author of *Coryate's Crudities*, and Fynes Morison (1556–1630), author of *Itinerary*: Coryate is deliberately strange and fanciful, though an acute observer, but Morison is much more straightforward.

The steady growth of English overseas trade kept alive a taste for accounts of great voyages throughout 17th and 18th C. At the end of 17th C Captain William Dampier published three books which influenced the imaginations of Defoe* and Swift*: *New Voyage Round the World* (1697), *Voyages and Descriptions* (1699), and *Voyage to New Holland* (1703). Dampier was an excellently direct and clear writer of his own books, but Lord George Anson's voyage round the world (1740–44) was written up from his journals by his chaplain, R. Waters, and depends on the singularly dramatic events for its force of interest. The last of these outstanding accounts of great voyages were the three undertaken by Captain James Cook, *A Voyage Round Cape Horn and the Cape of Good Hope* (1773), *A Voyage Towards the South Pole and Round the World* (1777), and *A Voyage to the Pacific Ocean* (1784). With the discovery of the coast-lines of Australia and New Zealand, the main outlines of world geography became known, and the interest of both explorers and their readers passed to the mysteries of the great undiscovered interiors of the continents. With this change in subject matter, a change also came over the style of travel literature.

[3] *Travel Literature as material for art*. Mungo Park's *Travels in Central Africa* preserves the plain, unaffected style of 18th-C travel literature, but subsequent work, for instance Richard Burton's book about India, *Scinde or the Unhappy Valley* (1851), and his later books about his exploration of East and Central Africa (*First Footsteps in East Africa*, 1856; *The Lake Region of Central Africa*, 1860) bear more of the stamp of the author's personal feelings and reactions. Partly, no doubt, this arose from the new importance attached to authorial personality due to Romanticism (**Romance*); also the contact with strange physical environments and peoples (in contrast to the emptiness and impersonality of the ocean) inevitably drew out authorial response. At all events, travel literature began to draw nearer to autobiography. Not only 'darkest Africa', but the Arabian peninsula fascinated writers. Burton was one of the first Englishmen to visit the holy city of Mecca, and wrote an account of it in *Pilgrimage to Al-Medinah and Mecca* (1855). Later Charles Doughty tried to restore the vividness of 16th-C language to 19th-C prose in his *Arabia Deserta* (1888), and T. E. Lawrence's* *Seven Pillars of Wisdom* (1926), an account of the Arab struggle against the Turks in World War I belongs to the same tradition of art made from travel in Arabia. George Borrow (1803–81) did not go so far for his material, but he went a stage further than these writers in combining travel literature and imaginative art, so that it is difficult to know whether or not to classify his books with the novel. They are full of personal encounters with individuals, chiefly among the common people; he was particularly interested in the Gipsies* (*The Gypsies in Spain*, 1841; *Lavengro*, 1851; *Romany Rye*, 1857) and he was talented at conveying the intimate texture of the life of a country (*The Bible in Spain*, 1843; *Wild Wales*, 1862). James Kinglake's account of his travels in the lands of the Eastern Mediterranean, *Eothen* (1844), and Lafcadio Hearn's *Glimpses of Unfamiliar Japan* (1894) are two other examples of travel literature which owe their classic status as much to the author's art and personality as to their subject matter. Thus travel literature became a natural subsidiary form for the novelists; it is among the best writing of R. L. Stevenson* and D. H. Lawrence*. Joseph Conrad*, who, as a sailor, was a professional traveller during the first part of his adult life, may be said to have completely assimilated the literature of travel into the art of the novel.

Treasure Island (1883)

A boy's romance by the novelist Robert Louis Stevenson*, and perhaps his best known work. It is set in 18th C, and the plot concerns the search for hidden treasure buried in a desert island by a historically actual 18th-C pirate, Captain Kidd. The story contains the basic elements of a traditional English boys' romance – treasure, pirates, a desert island – and belongs to a line of desert island literature descending from *Robinson Crusoe**, for long a favourite boy's book.

Treatise of Human Nature

* *Hume*.

Trianon

The name of two small palaces in the park of the great palace of the kings of France at Versailles*. Le Grand Trianon ('the Great Trianon') was built in 17th C by Louis XIV. Le Petit Trianon ('The Little Trianon') was built by his successor, Louis XV, in 18th C; its smallness and intimacy suited the spirit of withdrawal through which Marie Antoinette, queen of Louis XVI, sought to escape the complexity of public affairs which were driving France to the French Revolution*.

Tricoteuses /triːkoˈtəːz/

The 'knitters', from the French tricoter = to knit. A name given to the women who brought their knitting to the debates in political assemblies during the French Revolution*. In English fiction, Madame Defarge* in Dickens's novel *A Tale of Two Cities** knits the names of those who are to meet death by the guillotine into an endless scarf.

Trinity College

The largest of the colleges at Cambridge*. It was founded by King Henry VIII* in 1546 by amalgamating two older colleges. Distinguished writers who were students at it include the scientist Isaac Newton* and the philosopher Francis Bacon* in 17th C; the 17th-C poets Herbert*, Cowley*, Dryden*; the 19th-C poets Byron* and Tennyson*; the 19th-C novelist Thackeray*, and the historian Macaulay*. Architecturally it is one of the most distinguished of the Cambridge colleges and includes a library designed by the greatest English architect, Christopher Wren*.

There is also a Trinity College at Oxford, founded in 1555.

Trinity College, the one college constituting the University of Dublin, was founded in 1591. Among its students have been William Congreve*, Oliver Goldsmith*, Jeremy Taylor*, Edmund Burke*, Jonathan Swift*, and George Berkeley*.

Trinity House

On the north bank of the Thames, near the Tower of London*; the home of a corporation founded 1512–14 for the safeguard of shipping; its special function is to maintain a supply of pilots for ships and to ensure the safety of the coasts by lighthouses, buoys, and other warning systems. Lifeboats, however, are operated by a voluntary and unofficial service, and coastguards belong to a government department.

Triolet /ˈtraiəulet/

A graceful verse form of 8 lines and two rhymes with a rhyme scheme *abaaabab*. It was invented in France in 13th C, and was not used in England till 17th C. Like other verse forms which have little merit beyond their gracefulness, it has seldom been used in English except by minor poets, and those chiefly of late 19th and early 20th C. The following is an example by Austin Dobson (1840–1921):

I intended an Ode
And it turned out a Sonnet
It began à la mode,
I intended an Ode;
But Rose cross'd the road
In her latest new bonnet;
I intended an Ode;
And it turn'd out a Sonnet.

Triplet

In verse, three lines rhyming together, occasionally used among couplets* to introduce variety, *eg* by Dryden*:

For close designs and crooked counsels fit,
Sagacious, bold, and turbulent of wit.
Restless, unfixt in Principles and Place,
In power unpleased, impatient of disgrace;
A fiery soul, which working out its way,
Fretted the pigmy body to decay:
And o'er informed the tenement of clay.
(From *Absalom and Achitophel*, 152–8)

Tristram and Iseult /tristrəm – iːˈzuːlt/

A medieval romance of tragic love. It is included by Malory in his *Morte d'Arthur** as part of the Arthurian cycle of legends, but originally it was probably independent of them, and at least equally ancient. It is usually considered to be of British origin. Its original written version was probably 12th-C French by an Anglo-Norman poet, Thomas. Other versions succeeded this, and by the time the legend reached Malory it had become enlarged with a number of redundant episodes.

The salient points of the story are that Tristram is sent to Ireland by King Mark of Cornwall, his uncle, to bring back the king's bride, the princess Iseult. On the way back they accidentally drink a love potion intended by Iseult's mother to arouse undying love between Mark and Iseult. The secret love affair between Tristram and Iseult is eventually exposed to King Mark, and Tristram flees to Brittany, where he marries, but in name only, another Iseult ('of the White Hand'). He is wounded by a poisonous weapon and sends for Iseult of Ireland to come and cure him; if she consents, the ship that brings her is to bear a white sail; if not, a black one – compare the return of Theseus* from Crete in the Greek legend. His jealous wife lies to him, saying that the approaching ship bears a black sail, and Tristram turns to the wall and dies.

The most famous post-medieval version of the legend is Wagner's opera *Tristan and Isolde* (1865) with a libretto by the composer. In English, there are the poems *Tristram and Iseult* (1853) by Matthew Arnold*, and *Tristram of Lyonesse* (1882) by Swinburne*.

Tristram Shandy, the Life and Opinions of /ˈtristrəmˈ ʃandi/

A novel by Laurence Sterne*, published in successive volumes, i to ix, from 1760 to 1767. Of all famous novels, it is one of the most eccentric ever written. Tristram, the nominal hero, plays very little part in it; he is not born till vol. iv, and never gets beyond infancy. The circumstances attending and preceding his birth, on the other hand, are dealt with elaborately, and so are the talk and habits of his immediate relatives and their neighbours: his father, Walter Shandy of Shandy Hall; his Uncle Toby and Toby's servant, Corporal Trim, who are obsessed with military science; his mother (a comparatively minor character); the clergyman, Yorick; Dr Slop, and the Widow Wadman. These are the excuse for numerous digressions, and Sterne, in addition, plays jokes on the reader by tricks of typography. The effect on the reader is to suggest that the conventional notion of a biographical narrative, with a distinct beginning, sequence of events, and ending, is untrue to human experience which finds that beginnings do not really exist, and orderly sequences are frustrated by every kind of distraction. Critics have described *Tristram Shandy* as a 'novel about writing novels'. Philosophically, it is remarkable for its questioning of accepted ideas, especially of notions of time and theories about the association of ideas originating in the work of John Locke*.

* 4.3.3.

Trochee

* *Metre.*

Troilus and Cressida: the legend /ˈtrəuiləs – ˈkresidə/

This legend of tragic love is one of the great themes of medieval romantic literature, but its origins are obscure. Troilus is the son of King Priam* of Troy and his queen, Hecuba*, but in Homer's *Iliad** he is mentioned (xxiv. 257) only as having been slain before the poem begins. The legend originates in a Latin document, *Dictys Cretensis* of 4th C, which is supposed to be a translation of a Greek record of the Trojan war; it may therefore have a lost Greek ancestry. The forms of the story known to us are medieval, the most famous of which, outside English, is the 14th-C *Il Filostrato* by Boccaccio*. This, very much lengthened and altered, is the basis of Chaucer's *Troilus and Criseyde**. The name is variously spelt; Chaucer has Criseyde and Cryseyde.

Troilus and Cressida

A play by Shakespeare*, written 1601–2, and first printed in 1609. Its position in the first collected edition of Shakespeare's plays, the Folio* of 1623, is curious, inasmuch as it was placed by itself and not in one of the three groups of histories, tragedies, and comedies. Shakespeare used as sources Caxton's* *Recuyell of the Histories of Troy* (1474), translated from the French of Raoul leFebvre, Chaucer's *Troilus and Criseyde**, especially for Pandarus and the love story, Chapman's* translation of the *Iliad** (for Thersites) and possibly Lydgate's* *Troy-book*.

Troilus, son of King Priam of Troy, woos Cressida, with the help of her uncle, Pandarus. Meanwhile the war continues between the Trojans and the Greeks; the latter are doing badly, because their chief warrior, Achilles, is sulking in his tent. The subtle Ulysses contrives a plan to rouse Achilles by provoking his vanity; he chooses the brutishly stupid Ajax to fight the Trojan champion, Hector; the ruse is successful. A pact is made for an exchange of prisoners, and the Trojans consent to hand over Cressida, whose father has deserted to the Greeks; she and Troilus part, with many promises of fidelity, but she quickly becomes the mistress of the Greek Diomed, to the bewildered disillusionment of Troilus who sees her in Diomed's arms during a truce. The end of the play is a chaos of fighting, in which all higher emotions are lost in a rage of murderous hatred, and Hector, the noblest character in the play, is treacherously murdered by Achilles.

What bewilders critics is the hopelessness of the play. Two of the finest episodes are debating scenes, during the first of which (I. iii) the Greeks discuss their failure in the cold light of reason; in the second (II. ii) the Trojans defy reason for the sake of emotional dedication to 'honour'. But the play shows that reason alone conduces to ignobility and treachery, while honour alone is defeated by the facts of human nature. The voice of truth seems to be the mocking one of the Greek clown Thersites, who despises everybody and respects nothing. A possible view is that the much prized virtue of honour, so cultivated by Renaissance* courtiers, is an idealistic value, a literary growth in terms of which real life cannot be evaluated, whereas the 'reason' of politicians by itself destroys the value of living. This interpretation makes the play more an affair of lighthearted mockery than it is commonly taken to be; it is frequently interpreted as a grim and despairing satire.

* *Problem Plays* (*of Shakespeare*)

Troilus and Criseyde

A poem of tragic love by Geoffrey Chaucer*, written probably between 1372 and 1386, and one of his two masterpieces, the other being *The Canterbury Tales**. The poem is over 8,000 lines, in the 7-line stanzas known as rhyme-royal*. It is based on the Italian *Il Filostrato*, by Boccaccio*, but greatly lengthened, and changed in spirit. The chief characters are Troilus, son of King Priam of Troy; the young widow, Criseyde, with whom he falls in love; Pandarus, her uncle, who helps Troilus to win her, and Diomed, who seduces her among the Greeks, after she has been surrendered to them by the Trojans at the request of her father, Calchas, who has deserted Troy. To some extent, Chaucer seems to be mocking at the literary tradition of courtly love, which made of courtship a kind of game, according to which cunning and treachery were legitimate in winning the lady, though the gentleman had duties of fidelity to her afterwards. This scheme was apt to make romances of courtly love follow a standard course, with somewhat standardized characters who play roles rather than show convincingly complex human nature. In Chaucer's poem Troilus is the most conventional character; he behaves to the end like the typical romantic lover. Criseyde, on the other hand, is a lifelike heroine, who is shown to be prevented from resisting her lovers by her spontaneous courtesy, the consequence of her fine breeding. Pandarus is presented in warmly humorous terms, careful of his niece even while he betrays her, delighting in the sport for its own sake, and genuinely compassionate when, in the end, Troilus has lost. Diomed is a convincingly harsh, selfish soldier, caring for nothing but his own temporary satisfaction. Thus the literary quality of the courtly love theme is illuminated by reality, and Troilus, the 'literary' hero given just enough life to keep the reader's sympathies, is shown to be deluding himself about the ideality of his romance, not because Criseyde is treacherous, but because she is essentially human. Although later than Boccaccio's poem, Chaucer's poem is in many ways more medieval; in place of the shapeliness of Boccaccio's Renaissance* style of narrative, Chaucer uses characteristically medieval digressiveness and figures of rhetoric. And yet Chaucer's tale is, in its convincing treatment of character, remarkably modern and has been described as the first great English novel. In quality, it is probably the best sustained long poem in the English language.

* *Courtly Literature and Romantic Love*.

Trollope, Anthony (1815–82) /'troləp/

Novelist. The unbusinesslike qualities of his father, a barrister who forsook the law and ruined himself in farming, caused his childhood to be poverty-stricken, although his mother, Frances Trollope, kept her family from the worst hardships by writing over 50 novels. Trollope himself was a prolific novelist, and though he worked seriously his *Autobiography* (1883) deeply offended the taste of the time by his frank statement that the writing of novels was a craft and a business, like making shoes, with nothing exalted or inspired about it. He was a strong admirer of the novels of Thackeray* and shared Thackeray's contempt for the commercial arrogance of the British upper-middle classes. On the other hand, unlike Thackeray, Trollope had also strong faith in the traditional virtues and values of the English gentry, and several of his novels are about how the gentry class opened its ranks (through marriage, and after a struggle) to the best elements of less-privileged classes. His first novel was published in 1847, but it was in 1855 that he published the first of his most famous series, the Barsetshire* novels – *The Warden**. The series continued with *Barchester Towers*

(1857); *Dr Thorne* (1858); *Framley Parsonage* (1864); *The Small House at Allington* (1864); *The Last Chronicle of Barset** (1867). It is in these books that he displays his very conservative values most winningly and convincingly; they present a world of very solidly portrayed church dignitaries and landed gentry and show a loving care for fully-rounded characterization. The world he shows with such conviction was perhaps already passing, and in presenting it Trollope does not forget the weaker side of its values nor the assaults and encroachments upon it of political adventurers and the more vulgar of the middle class. His later work became more political, for instance *Phineas Finn* (1869); *The Eustace Diamonds* (1873); *Phineas Redux* (1874); *The Way We Live Now* (1875); *The Prime Minister* (1876); *The Duke's Children* (1880). Some critics consider that this group of his novels is unduly neglected; the setting is commonly London, which Trollope thought a source of evil, and the tone is more critical of society. *The Way We Live Now* reflects his disillusionment most strongly; it includes a powerful portrait of a fraudulent tycoon in Melmotte, and is not so much political as a devastating social study.

Trollope lost favour after his death, but regained strong popularity in mid-20th C. This was because this period of insecurity and war made Trollope's traditional world of values seem very reassuring. Yet critics seldom allow him rank equal to his contemporary George Eliot*; he does not even pretend to insight as deep, or tragic vision, though he is often subtle and fond of pathos.

Bib: Sadleir, M., *Life*; Bowen, E., *Trollope: a new Judgement*; Cockshut, A. O. J., *Anthony Trollope: a Critical Study*; Gerould, W. G. and J. T., *Guide to Trollope*; Smalley, D., (ed) *The Critical Heritage*.

Troubadours and Trouvères

/'tru:bəduəz – 'tru:'veəz/

Poets of southern and northern France respectively. They were court poets of 12th–14th C and their special theme was the refinement and idealization of love between the sexes, known as 'courtly love'. English kings were French speaking at the time, and Richard I* of England was one of the troubadours; his mother, Eleanor of Aquitaine, was the grand-daughter of another, and made her court the centre of them. The poets were often accompanied by apprentices called 'joglars' or 'jongleurs' who sang their songs, and perhaps composed their musical setting. The poets adapted the British legends of King Arthur*, and established the theme of courtly love as the predominating one for English as well as French poetry when the former had its great revival in 14th C; their influence, too, converted much pre-14th-C English verse-writing from the alliterative* mode to the metrical and rhymed mode, though the alliterative forms survived until the lifetime of Chaucer*.

* *Courtly Literature and Romantic Love.*

Troy

Ancient capital city of the Troad, a region on the north-west coast of Asia Minor; strictly, the capital was Ilium (in Homer's *Iliad**) and Troy and Ilium have become alternative names for the same city. Troy is the subject of legends which began in ancient Greek times and were added to by the Romans, and further expanded by medieval writers in Western Europe. Somewhere behind the legends is a background of historical fact, but this is very obscure.

[1] *Historical background.* Archaeologists and historians doubted whether a real city of Troy ever existed, until the German archaeologist Heinrich Schliemann discovered its remains near the modern Hissarlik, very near the traditional site. Subsequently, excavations uncovered nine cities in successive levels; the earliest (Troy 1) dates from 3000–2500 BC, and the latest (Troy 9) faded away in about 5th C AD. Opinion has been divided about whether the Trojan war was fought against Troy 6, which in fact was destroyed by earthquake and fire about 1800 BC, or the rebuilt city known as Troy 7A, destroyed by similar causes in about 1200 – nearer the traditional date of the Trojan War in which the city is supposed to have been destroyed by the alliance of Greek princes. The latter date is now favoured.

[2] *Greek myths of the founding of Troy.* These recount a succession of mythical princes, the earliest being of divine or semi-divine origin: Teucer, Dardanus, Ericthoneus, and Tros – from whom the name of the country and its people originated. Tros's son Ilus was the founder of the city of Ilion (Ilium) or Troy. In the reign of Laomedon, son of Ilus, the walls of Troy were built by the ocean god Poseidon, to whom Laomedon refused the agreed reward; he was in punishment killed, together with most of his family, by the hero Heracles*. One of his two surviving children was Priam*, who was king of Troy in the Trojan war and met his death after the capture of the city. Priam's children included: Hector*, the Trojan hero of Homer's *Iliad*; Paris*, whose elopement with Helen* was the cause of the war; Cassandra*, the sombre prophetess; and Troilus*, around whom legends were to be constructed in medieval times. Ilus' brother Assaracus was ancestor of another line of heroes who were to become more important in Roman and medieval European myth: this line of descent went through Capys, Anchises and Aeneas, who according to the Roman poet Virgil* was the ancestor of the Roman people.

[3] *Troy in epic.* The legendary Trojan war led to three epics: Homer's *Iliad*, about the siege; Homer's *Odyssey** about the wanderings of Odysseus after the siege; and Virgil's *Aeneid**, about the wanderings of Aeneas until he finds his destination in Italy. Homer's epics arise out of still more ancient legends, but their own date is uncertain, as, to some extent, is their authorship; scholars do not think that they can be later than 7th C BC. Virgil's poem dates from 1st C BC, and is a deliberate attempt to emulate Homer. The three poems are the pattern of a tradition of European epic* – *eg* Milton's *Paradise Lost**.

[4] *Trojan myth in western Europe to AD 1500.* The prestige of Homer and Virgil kept Trojan myth alive and growing in the Middle Ages* of

Europe, but these poets were not the only source of its growth. Two collections of writing, alleged to be records of the Trojan war, and to be by Dictys the Cretan and Dares the Phrygian, date from 4th–6th C AD, and are the source of new legends, including Troilus and Cressida. Virgil's view that the Romans were descendants of the Trojan Aeneas led to legends that other European nations have similar ancestry. For instance, *The History of the Britons* by the Welsh chronicler Nennius (8th–9th C) declares the ancestor of the British race to have been Brutus (* *Brut*), the great-grandson of Aeneas; this is repeated by the 12th-C Geoffrey of Monmouth*.

Tudor, House of /ˈtjuːdə/

The name of a family that ruled over England and Wales from 1485 until 1603. The succession was as follows: Henry VII*; his son, Henry VIII*; Henry VIII's three children, Edward VI*, Mary I* and Elizabeth I*. Elizabeth died childless, and the throne passed to the Scottish family of Stuart*, one of whom (James IV) had married a daughter of Henry VII.

The Tudors were of Welsh origin; Henry VII was the grandson of Owen Tudor, who married a member of the Lancastrian branch of the royal Plantagenet* family; Henry thus acquired the claim of the House of Lancaster* to the English throne, which he won at the Battle of Bosworth, the concluding battle of the Wars of the Roses*, where he defeated Richard III* of the House of York.

The Tudor family was notable for its abilities. Henry VII was a cautious ruler, who reconstructed the government's finances. Henry VIII started the Reformation* in England by founding the Church of England*, and this became distinctively Protestant* under the boy king Edward VI. Mary I was a Catholic, married Philip II of Spain, and re-established Catholicism in England, but she died childless, and Protestantism was restored by her sister Elizabeth, possibly the most successful sovereign ever to sit on the English throne. The last ten years of Elizabeth's reign saw the beginnings of the literary flowering known as the 'Elizabethan age'. Her reign was also remarkable for victory over Spain and the beginnings of English overseas enterprise.

* 1.2.1.

Tudor Myth

A term used by historians to express the 16th-C belief, encouraged by the royal House of Tudor*, that the Tudors were national saviours from the horrors of the Wars of the Roses* and restorers of legendary national greatness. The first Tudor, Henry VII*, took the throne from Richard III* in 1485 by force of conquest, and since usurpation of a kingdom from its rightful king was a deadly sin, it was important for the Tudors to prove that they had not been guilty of it. Henry maintained that his was the rightful claim, but this was too clearly open to doubt; on the other hand if Richard III was a proved tyrant, the usurpation was justified. 16th-C historians made it their business to blacken Richard's character, not only to please the Tudors, but in reflection of national relief that they had brought the civil wars to an end, with the consequence that Richard is the legendary evil man of English history. Such is the picture given by Thomas More's* *Richard III* (1513), Hall's* *Union of the Noble and Illustrious Families of Lancaster and York* (1548), and Holinshed's* *Chronicles* (1578). The Tudors also encouraged the belief that, as a Welsh line of princes, they could trace themselves back to King Arthur*, the hero of the mythical British golden age; Henry VII called his eldest son Arthur, but he did not live to succeed to the throne. The impress of the Tudor myth is strong on Shakespeare's* history plays*.

Tuileries, The /ˈtwiːləriː/

A royal palace in Paris, built in 16th C and destroyed by the mob in the Commune of 1871. It formerly divided the palace of the Louvre from the surviving Tuileries Gardens, and was the place of confinement for Louis XVI and his queen, Marie Antoinette, during the earlier phase of the French Revolution*.

Turn of the Screw, The

A 'nouvelle' (* *Short Story*) by Henry James*, published in *The Two Magics* (1898). It is a ghost story, about a governess given sole charge of two children, Miles and Flora, in a country house named Bly. She finds that she has to contend with the evil, ghostly influence of two dead servants, Peter Quint and Miss Jessell, over the children, who are ostensibly angelic but invisibly corrupted. The mental conflict caused by the good influence of the governess and the evil influence of the manservant leads to Miles's death. The story was used by Benjamin Britten (born 1913) for an opera of the same title.

Turpin, Richard (Dick) (1706–39)

A famous English highwayman* and thief, hanged at York for horse-stealing. He was greatly romanticized by the novelist Harrison Ainsworth* in his novel *Rookwood* (1834), in which Turpin's famous ride from London to York on his mare, Black Bess, is described. The ride, like other romantic episodes told about him, is fictional.

Tussaud, Marie (Madame Tussaud) (1760–1850) /təˈsɔːd/

A famous modeller in wax. During the French Revolution*, she made many portraits of revolutionary leaders and also of victims of the revolutionary Terror*. In 1800 she came to England and set up an exhibition in London. This was destroyed by fire in 1925, but a museum of waxwork effigies known as 'Madame Tussaud's' still exists in London. It contains lifelike figures of notable contemporaries, and a 'Chamber of Horrors' with figures of well-known criminals.

Tweedledum and Tweedledee /ˈtwiːdlˈdʌm – twiːdlˈdiː/

Characters in a popular English verse of the sort known as a nursery rhyme*. The rhyme occurs in

Lewis Carroll's* children's story *Through the Looking-Glass* (1872), but it is older than that. The first mention in print of the two characters is an epigram* about the rivalry of the German composer Handel* and his contemporary Bononcini, the last two lines of which go:

Strange that such high dispute should be
'Twixt Tweedledum and Tweedledee.

The implication is that the two composers are really very much alike. Either the epigrammatist (Pope*? Swift*? Byron?) was adapting an existing rhyme, or the nursery rhyme derived from the epigram. A version similar to Carroll's was published in a book of nursery rhymes in 1805.

Twelfth Night

* *Epiphany.*

Twelfth Night, or What You Will

A comedy by Shakespeare*, probably written 1599–1600 or possibly a little later. Its main source is a prose tale, *Apolonius and Silla* (1581) by Barnabe Rich, an English version of an Italian tale by Cinthio (* *Elizabethan Novels*). The comic situations arising from confusion between twins come down from *Menaechmi* by the Roman playwright Plautus*; Shakespeare had already adapted this play into *The Comedy of Errors**. Two 16th-C Italian plays, *Inganni* (Deceits) and *Gl'Ingannati* (The Deceived) have also been suggested as possible sources.

The setting is the court of Orsino, Duke of Illyria, and the house of the wealthy Countess Olivia, whom he is courting. He uses as a go-between his page Cesario, really a girl, Viola, disguised as a boy. The page has already fallen in love with Orsino, and expresses sentiments on love so eloquently to Olivia that the Countess believes herself in love, but with the page, not with the Duke. Meanwhile Viola's twin-brother, Sebastian, turns up, wearing the same style of clothes that his sister has chosen to wear as Cesario; he has been rescued from shipwreck by a sea-captain, Antonio, who feels a deep affection for him. The possibility of confusion is clearly various and great, and every possible confusion occurs. A subplot centres on Olivia's drunken kinsman, Sir Toby, and her conceited steward, Malvolio; Sir Toby takes revenge on Malvolio for an insult, and incidentally gets mixed up in the confusions occurring round Viola and Sebastian by playing a trick on his friend, Sir Andrew Aguecheek, who is also courting Olivia. Sir Toby's interference ends in a clearing-up of the confusions of identity, and a subsequent suitable pairing off of Orsino and Viola, Sebastian and Olivia.

The comedy can be regarded as about different forms of love, or imagining oneself to have fallen in love, and though the plot is bewildering in summary, it is deftly worked out theatrically and beautifully balanced, with finely cadenced poetry and a more unifying theme than any earlier comedy by Shakespeare. The title, like *A Midsummer Night's Dream** and *The Winter's Tale**, indicates the sort of occasion for which the story is suitable; Twelfth Night was the last night of the Christmas festival and a time of licensed disorder presided over by a Lord of Misrule*, such as Sir Toby Belch.

Twentieth-century Literature

This review begins at 1914, both because the year of the outbreak of World War I is more significant than 1901 as a point of departure, and because the Edwardian* period (1900–14) is described in a separate entry.

1914–20. The war years and those immediately following are especially interesting for the new attitudes to and styles of poetry which arose in them. These were partly due to the war itself. Britain had never before experienced a war in which so many of the population were engaged, and the public had hitherto entertained unreal, often sentimentally romantic views of war. The War Poets* were not merely poets who chose war as their subject, but poets who felt it as an unpredictable revelation of the unguessed horrors of human violence so far screened by the thick facade of civilization. Poetry had been in danger of becoming a minor pleasure of leisured people; the War Poets used it to discomfort and awaken the readers at home, by arousing their pity and indignation. Rosenberg*, indeed, expressed more than this; for him the war was a terrible but enriching enlargement of experience, and he was by far the most interesting of the War Poets in his development of the range of his poetic expression. He died, however, before he could fulfil his genius, and the other two notable War Poets, Wilfred Owen* and Siegfried Sassoon, modified the traditional language of poetry rather than extending it. The remoulding and revivifying of poetic expression was much more the work of three writers who were not personally involved in the fighting. The Irishman, W. B. Yeats*, was more affected by the rise of Irish nationalism to the crisis of civil war in 1919, and he developed in these years a stern and eloquent syntax which enriched the language with a new style of grandeur. The Americans, Ezra Pound* and T. S. Eliot*, brought from across the Atlantic a detached and comprehensive vision of Europe in a crisis so huge that the war was only a symptom of it, and they introduced into English poetry the influence of literary currents of which the insular poets were largely unaware. They entirely altered the range of poetic diction, and gave new intensity, as well as difficulty, to poetic forms; the reader found himself engaged intellectually by their poetry more than by almost any verse for a century.

1920–35. Poetically, the next fifteen years continued to be rich, thanks largely to the work of three writers. Pound went back to America, but Eliot published his most epoch-making, though not his greatest, poem, *The Waste Land**, in 1922. Yeats reached the height of his genius in *The Tower* (1928) and *The Winding Stair* (1933). The third writer to make a strong impression was G. M. Hopkins*, who had died in 1889, but whose work was not published as a whole until 1918, and did not really make its full impression until its second edition in 1929. Hopkins showed unsuspected strengths in the now generally despised movement of romanticism; readers realized that poetry could demand the intellectual concentration that was demanded by the work of Eliot or the 17th-C Metaphysicals*, and yet retain the strong sensuous appeal of Keats*.

But these fifteen years are still more memorable for the greatness and versatility of the novelists. Three in particular stand out for their depth and breadth of vision: E. M. Forster*, D. H. Lawrence* and James Joyce*. Forster published his finest novel, *A Passage to India** (1924). In his pre-war novels he had shown himself an acute and witty critic of British middle-class culture, partly by contrasting it with ways of life (usually foreign ones) which ignored its basic assumptions; in this novel he gave a new and much deeper perspective to this criticism by setting the British way of life against the vast, immensely confusing and mysterious culture of India. Lawrence was a greater novelist, whose masterpieces are usually considered to be *The Rainbow** (1915) and *Women in Love* (1921), and the last ten years of his life (1921–30) in some ways show a decline, caused by illness and stupid public hostility, into the kind of extravagance that produced his most notorious novel, *Lady Chatterley's Lover** (1928); but the decade also produced some of his most original and searching tales. Lawrence's aim was to achieve an entire vision of human nature and its potentialities, and he achieved it beyond most other European novelists of any period. The third of the outstanding novelists of the period was James Joyce, whose *Ulysses** was published in Paris in 1922. Joyce used extraordinary, elaborate and unfamiliar techniques to present an image of modern man with the detailed complexity characteristic of the novel form and at the same time with the different sort of scope hitherto associated with the epic*.

The period was also interesting for the variety and liveliness of its secondary figures. At the time, the novelists of distinction with the widest public were those who had already built up their reputations with more conventional styles and less searching themes. These included John Galsworthy* (*A Modern Comedy*, 1929), Arnold Bennett* (*Riceyman Steps*, 1923), H. G. Wells* (*The World of William Clissold*, 1926) and Somerset Maugham* (*eg Cakes and Ale*, 1930). These reached a wide public, and it was partly in reaction against them that Virginia Woolf* wrote her symbolic and poetic novels which show the abandonment of ordinary plot structure and traditional styles of character portrayal. Her most notable books were *To the Lighthouse** (1927) and *The Waves** (1931). Virginia Woolf was a novelist of the intelligentsia, conscious of belonging to a minority and resisting the current of the time. It was a time when the intelligentsia cultivated its sense of minority with proud and aristocratic self-consciousness: Virginia Woolf was the centre of an elite known as the Bloomsbury Group* (to which Lawrence was strongly opposed) but Bloomsbury was far from including all the minority elitists. Two who were outside it were Aldous Huxley* (*Point Counter Point*, 1928, and *Brave New World*, 1932) and Wyndham Lewis* (*The Apes of God*, 1930). Huxley revived the satirical 'discussion novel' of the early-19th-C novelist, Peacock*; Wyndham Lewis used a bold technique of pitiless and rather brutal satire to stigmatize what he considered to be the intellectual mediocrity of his time.

1935–Present Day. The first 35 years of 20th C produced one of the most vigorous and inventive periods of English literature. The next 35 years have undoubtedly been less great, but are much more difficult to summarize. The economic depression of the early 1930s, the War of 1939–45, the reduction of Britain's world power and her constant disorientation since, perhaps above all the rise of broadcasting in competition with the printed word, have combined to cause literary confusion, changes of direction, few of which have been carried far, and frequent depression of promising talent. Elitist minority culture of the Bloomsbury type seemed a luxury that could not be afforded by a society that had lost faith in its cultural leadership, and it was succeeded by the grimly serious minority culture of the *Scrutiny** group of critics, under the leadership of F. R. Leavis*, who sought by rigorous criticism of the highest standards to re-establish a reliable basis for literary culture. In poetry the difficult language of writers like Eliot, Pound and Lewis was succeeded by writing of a plainer style to reach wider audiences, sometimes with a sense of urgent message.

Probably the most interesting developments have been in the drama. The outstanding dramatist of the first thirty-five years had been Bernard Shaw*, but the character of his genius was such as to inhibit emulation and discipleship. No one else could use the highly individual 'Shavian' rhetoric, and his polemical comedy was felt to be a hindrance to the poetic and dramatic directions that the theatre might take. Thus the 1930s and 40s saw a number of considered experiments in verse drama, notably the plays of T. S. Eliot, *eg The Family Reunion* (1939) and *The Cocktail Party* (1950). But such experiments had very limited success; it seems that no verse idiom of the time could generate the kind of theatrical force which dramatic expression requires if it is to reach the central nerve of the age. Since 1950, another generation has arisen, whose three leading names are John Osborne* (*eg Look Back in Anger*, 1956, and *Luther*, 1961), John Arden* (*eg Sergeant Musgrave's Dance*, 1959, and *Armstrong's Last Good Night*, 1964) and Harold Pinter* (*eg The Caretaker*, 1960, and *Homecoming*, 1964). Each of these is intense and highly individual, but each has studied the leaders of modern European drama (Ibsen*, Strindberg, Chekhov*, Brecht, and the bilingual writer Beckett*) and has combined techniques from these with a kind of poetry of speech made out of current colloquial idiom. Each, moreover, has achieved some success on the most far-reaching of all modern media, television. They have so far created no masterpieces, but they speak for and to their time more convincingly than do writers in other literary forms.

In poetry, T. S. Eliot's masterpieces, *Four Quartets** (published as a collection in 1944), stand alone, both by their merit and in their kind. In the 1930s the conspicuous poets were a group led by W. H. Auden* who were strongly influenced by Eliot (and by Yeats in his last phase) in technique, but who worked on new themes from points of view that were opposed to his. Eliot's extraordinary achievement in the *Quartets* was to extend into 20th C an ancient, spiritual, contemplative tradition to which the modern world seemed largely inimical, and to make great modern poetry out of it. Auden and his school turned to Marx* and Freud*. They were concerned to be above all contemporary; their subject matter was the outer world of unemployment, class conflict and approaching war, and the inner world of the psychoneuroses. They were often brilliant and astringent commentators, but they failed to grow convictions strong enough for their distinctive character to survive the impact of World War II, which dispersed them as a group and changed their character; Auden, who had the strongest personality, was converted to Anglican* Christianity. They were always a minority group whose appeal was mainly to the intelligentsia, and in the 1940s they were almost eclipsed by the quite different, exuberant talent of Dylan Thomas*, who came nearest of all poets of the last 35 years to reaching a popular audience. His achievement was peculiar and personal, and owed much to a specially Celtic (as opposed to Anglo-Saxon) disposition to enjoy language as an uninhibited game with words and their emotional connotations. Auden had seemed to release poetry into the world of contemporary facts and ideologies, but he was still very introspective; Thomas seemed to release it again, using it for the outpouring of emotions through very strong rhythms and the boldest possible play with the meanings of words. But he did not establish a school although he had followers – the 'Apocalyptics' – and only a handful of his poems are really achieved works of art. Auden's work sometimes lays him open to the charge of intellectual pretentiousness, and Thomas's to the charge of irresponsible emotional extravagance. It was in reaction against both that 'the Movement' came into existence, of whom the leaders were D. J. Enright (b 1920), Donald Davie (b 1922), and Philip Larkin*. They cultivated restraint, simplicity of form, clarity of language, and honesty of tone. Though they no longer constitute a group, they are still writing, and Larkin is one of the best known of contemporary poets. Yet, beside them, there is a slightly younger, more adventurous group, of which the most conspicuous names are Thom Gunn (b 1929), Sylvia Plath* (1932–63), and Ted Hughes* (b 1930). These are more exciting, and perhaps more impressive. An indication of their difference is to measure the work of Larkin against that of Hughes: the former is an astute poetic commentator, but the latter (in ways that recall D. H. Lawrence) achieves a vision of the modern human being which is both radical and impersonal; the former offers a detachment as a starting-point for criticism, but the latter offers a detachment which is a starting-point for imaginative self-understanding.

The difficulty of finding images that embody the wholeness of human nature in the bewilderment of contemporary civilization has above all afflicted the novelists. Up to 1930, English novelists shared certain assumptions with their readers as a basis upon which they could build and enlarge their own fictive constructions. Since 1930, these shared assumptions about the forces that keep human nature coherent as a concept have extensively dissolved, and in consequence we have had novelists who may be grouped into six different classes. [1] There have been those who have sought to recover a unified human image, but have attempted it diffusely (Joyce Cary*) by an eclectic technique, or philosophically (L. H. Myers*) with insufficient art. [2] Those who have used change itself as a unifying theme in sequences of novels (Anthony Powell* and C. P. Snow*) in which design enters unexpectedly into the apparent confusion of temporal flux. [3] Those who have concerned themselves with the new social conditions characteristic of the post-war period, especially social mobility and the rise to affluence of the working class: John Wain*, Kingsley Amis*, Alan Sillitoe*, John Braine*, and David Storey* can be grouped among these, but there are many others. [4] Those who have adopted doctrinal standpoints which they use – explicitly or implicitly – as a means of diagnosing the spirit of the time. These include the Catholic novelists, Graham Greene* and Evelyn Waugh*, and the very Protestant, almost Old Testament in outlook, William Golding*. [5] Those who have evolved idiosyncratic techniques, or have chosen very special areas of life, for the sake of obtaining a fresh or eccentric angle of vision. This includes novelists as various as Ivy Compton-Burnett* (who has written about tightly enclosed Edwardian families almost entirely in dialogue), Iris Murdoch* (who uses a technique of symbolic extravaganza), and Laurence Durrell*, who cultivates an exotic style and writes about cosmopolitan society in the eastern Mediterranean. [6] Finally, there have been those who have sought a unifying theme in the ways in which the modern mind wrestles with the complex problems of and techniques for self-knowledge. These are best represented by Angus Wilson* (*eg No Laughing Matter*, 1968) and Doris Lessing* (*eg The Golden Notebook*, 1962). Such a classification is necessarily crude and provisional; it brings writers who are in important ways very unlike each other into association, and some of the writers mentioned belong to more than one of the groups. It may, however, be justified in so far as it indicates the variety of directions which modern writers have taken, and the nature of their difficulties.

Two Gentlemen of Verona, The

An early romantic comedy by Shakespeare*, probably written about 1594. The plot is a double love affair with complications; Proteus is in love with Julia, and Valentine with Silvia, but Proteus plays both Valentine and Julia false in his efforts to win Silvia. Julia follows Proteus, disguised as a page, while Valentine, by the contrivance of Proteus, has to flee and takes refuge as the captain of a band of robbers. Proteus in the end is confronted by both Valentine and Julia, and happiness is restored by his suitable repentance. In plot, poetry, and characterization the play is clearly very immature, though it has a limpid charm. There is an element of low-life comedy in the role of Launce, servant to Proteus, accompanied by his dog. Julia's disguise and the sentiment of the play look forward to the much more interesting *Twelfth Night**. Shakespeare's source seems to have been a Spanish tale, Montemayor's *Diana*.

Two Noble Kinsmen, The

A play of romantic love chiefly by John Fletcher*, perhaps in collaboration with Shakespeare*. It was probably written in 1612–13, and was printed in 1634. The plot derives from Chaucer's *Knight's Tale** about the tragic rivalry in love of Palamon and Arcite.

Tyburn /ˈtaibəːn/

The site of public executions by hanging until 1783. The gallows stood somewhere near the modern Marble Arch, at the end of Oxford Street and on the edge of Hyde Park, about three miles north-west of the old City of London.

Tyburnia

A wealthy district of London near the Tyburn gallows; often mentioned in the novels of Thackeray* and Trollope*. It later became less fashionable and less familiar as a district name than Belgravia, to the south of Hyde Park.

Tyler, Wat /ˈtailə/

The leader of the Peasants' Revolt* of 1381. He was killed in the street by the Lord Mayor of London in the presence of Richard II*.

* *Ball, John.*

Tyndale, William (1492?–1536) /ˈtindl/

A translator of the Bible; his version was a principal basis for the Authorized Version of 1611. He was a convinced Protestant*. His other works include: *Parable of the Wicked Mammon* (1528); *Obedience of a Christian Man* (1528), and *Practice of Prelates* (1530). These works influenced the forms that extreme Protestantism, Puritanism*, took in England. While on a visit to the Netherlands, he was arrested in 1535 and burned as a heretic.

* *Bible in England; Reformation.*

Typhoeus /tiˈfiːəs/

In Greek myth, a giant raised up by Ge, the Earth, to combat Zeus*. He had a hundred dragon heads, which breathed forth fire. Zeus eventually overwhelmed him with his thunderbolts and buried him under the volcano, Etna.

Typhon /ˈtifon/

In Greek myth, the son of Tartarus* and Ge*, he was the largest monster ever born. He almost defeated Zeus*, who finally hurled Mount Etna upon him, which accounts for the volcano's breathing fire and smoke. In another version, Typhon was a monster delivered by Hera*, queen of the gods, when she was consumed with jealousy at Zeus' giving birth to Athene* unaided.

U

Udall, Nicholas (1505–56) /juːdəl/

The writer of *Ralph Roister Doister**.

Ulysses

* *Odysseus.*

Ulysses /ˈjuːlisiːz/

A novel by James Joyce*. It was first published in Paris in 1922, but was banned in England for its alleged obscenity until 1936. In a number of ways the book is an innovation in methods of presenting human experience through the novel form, and it is also the most ambitiously comprehensive attempt to do so, except perhaps for Joyce's next book, *Finnegans Wake** (1939). [1] It is an attempt to present a character more completely than ever before. The story shows in immense detail the life of a man during a single day of 24 hours. The man is Leopold Bloom, a Jew of Hungarian origin living in Dublin; the day is 16 June 1904. [2] To do this requires a method of conveying the process of thinking; Joyce's method has become known as the 'stream of consciousness' technique, suggested to him by the work of a French novelist, Dujardin. [3] At the same time as seeking to create imaginatively 'a whole individual', Joyce seeks to make this individual representative, by setting him against the background of the oldest extended portrait of a man in European literature. He does this by making Bloom analogous with Homer's* Odysseus, and by dividing the book into episodes, each of which corresponds to one in the *Odyssey**, though not in the same order. [4] Joyce varies the technique of written expressions so as to make his language as close an analogy as possible to the modes of modern human experience. Thus in the fierce drunken episode 15 (Circe), the method is dramatic dialogue; in the fatigued anti-climax of 17 (Ithaca), the questionnaire is used; in the final episode 18 (Penelope), the stream of consciousness is used to the full, without punctuation.

No human experience is complete without relationship; Bloom is a lonely man, with numerous casual acquaintanceships. However, two deeper relationships dominate his story: there is the physical relationship with his wife, Molly, whose fidelity he more than mistrusts, and a spiritual affinity with Stephen Dedalus*, whom he does not meet till near the end, but who is a lonely young man unconsciously seeking a father, as Bloom is a lonely middle-aged man wanting a son. Molly is analogous to Penelope* in the *Odyssey* and Stephen relates to Telemachus, the wife and son respectively of Odysseus.

In some respects Joyce is carrying the artistic devotion of the French novelists to an extreme: *Ulysses* is an elaborate formal construction of immense seriousness, showing a dedication to art for its own sake comparable to that of the novelist Flaubert*; it is also a realistic exercise, carrying to extreme the naturalism of Zola*.

Umbriel

In Pope's *Rape of the Lock**, he is a melancholy sprite, part of Pope's mock epic* supernatural machinery. The name is derived from the Latin *umbra* 'shade' ironically combined with Ariel* of Shakespeare's *Tempest*.

Uncle Sam

In Britain, a name in popular use for the United States, corresponding to John Bull* for Britain. Both characters have been realized in consistent visual form by cartoonists: Bull is stout, peremptory and rubicund, and Sam is tall, lean, and wears a goatee beard; their clothes are usually patterned according to the flags of their respective countries. The origin of the name 'Uncle Sam' is unknown; it dates from the time of the Anglo-American war of 1812.

Uncommercial Traveller, The

A collection of tales, sketches, and essays, descriptive of places, society and manners, by Charles Dickens*. They were published in *All the Year Round** and reissued in book form in 1861 and 1868. A commercial traveller is a businessman who travels to sell goods to shops. Dickens indicates by his title that he is not at all commercial in his intentions.

Under the Greenwood Tree (1872)

The first of the Wessex* novels by Thomas Hardy*. The story is a village love affair between a schoolmistress, Fancy Day, and Dick Dewy, son of a 'tranter' or carrier of goods. It includes the theme of the rivalry of the village orchestra, who have hitherto played the music in church services, with Fancy, who takes over from them by substituting the harmonium. The story is thus slight and idyllic compared to Hardy's later Wessex stories, but it is written with delicacy and insight. The title is the first line of a song in Shakespeare's *As You Like It**.

Under Western Eyes (1911)

A novel by Joseph Conrad*. It is set in pre-revolutionary Russia and in Switzerland, and is told through the character of the English language teacher, who witnesses many of the events in Switzerland, and reconstructs those in Russia from the notebooks of the central character, Kyrilo Sidorovitch Razumov. Razumov is the illegitimate son of a Russian nobleman, and has been brought up in the household of a Russian priest. He is given to understand that if he behaves well, his real father will assist him in his career; accordingly he is studious at the university, and keeps himself rigorously isolated from student politics. His enigmatic silence on political subjects, however, is misinterpreted by the radical students as signifying that he is a strongly committed supporter of revolutionary activity; thus, when one of them, Victor Haldin, commits a political assassination and takes refuge with him, Razumov tries to disembarrass himself by betraying Haldin to the police. The police, however, will not allow him to return to his solitary studies; instead they send him to Switzerland, ostensibly as a revolutionary emissary, but actually to spy on the Russian revolutionaries in exile there. He finds them to be a circle composed partly of flamboyant or brutal self-seekers, such as Peter Ivanovitch, Madame de S., and Nikitin (nicknamed Necator, the killer). But there are also idealists of complete integrity, including Victor Haldin's sister, Nathalie Haldin. Nathalie is a pupil and friend of the English language teacher, who thus becomes involved in the story. She welcomes Razumov as a revolutionary hero, and the friend of her brother, for whose death he has in fact been responsible. Razumov is tormented by his guilt, his love and admiration for Nathalie, his horror and contempt of the debased elements among the revolutionaries, and the seeming impossibility of recovering his integrity and living otherwise than by false appearance. Eventually he confesses the truth to Nathalie and to the revolutionaries, and is reduced to total deafness by two blows from Nikitin. Nathalie is appalled, but understands him. She has told her English friend: 'You belong to a people which has made a bargain with fate, and wouldn't like to be rude to it.' The Western (British and Swiss) attitude to politics and the individual is such that fateful choices such as the one forced on Razumov are not demanded. His drama 'under the Western eyes' of the English language teacher is the drama of a nation where the individual is not permitted to withdraw from political decision into private life. Razumov spends the rest of his days as a sick man in Russia, respected by the best of the revolutionary circle whom he has known in Switzerland, and cared for devotedly by one of them.

Underwoods

A collection of short poems by Ben Jonson*, first published in 1640. It includes Jonson's famous elegy* to Shakespeare*. R. L. Stevenson* borrowed the title for a book of his own poems (1887).

Unfortunate Traveller, or the Life of Jacke Wilton, The

A romance by Thomas Nashe*, published in 1594. Wilton begins as a page in the court of Henry VIII*, and then travels through Europe as adventurer, soldier of fortune, and hanger-on of the poet Earl of Surrey*. It is one of the first notable picaresque* tales in English. Among other historical figures, apart from Surrey, Wilton meets Sir Thomas More*, Erasmus*, and Aretino*; he witnesses historical events such as the struggle between the Anabaptists of Munster and the emperor Charles V, and describes a plague in Rome. The book is extremely episodic, and Jacke himself has no consistent character. The narrative begins as a sequence of mischievous pranks in the manner of the popular 'jest-books' of Nashe's time, and at the other extreme goes into brutally realistic descriptions of rape and of the plague in Rome. Its merit is the exuberance of the vivid style, which itself varies in character from passage to passage; much of it consists in parody of the style of Nashe's contemporaries. English had not yet achieved a 'norm' of prose expression, as it was to do by the second half of 17th C.

* *Elizabethan Novels.*

Unicorn

A mythical beast, with a history that goes back to the ancient Greeks. It is commonly represented as a white horse with a straight, spiral horn projecting from its forehead. In the Middle Ages the unicorn was supposed to possess great strength and ferocity, perhaps owing to misunderstanding of the Hebrew word for wild ox in the Bible. It was also symbolic of chastity, and the horn was said to be an antidote to poison. In heraldry, the unicorn was used often as a 'supporter' of a shield bearing a coat of arms; until 1603, the Scottish royal coat of arms had two unicorns to support it; in that year the union of the kingdoms led to the modern coat of arms of Great Britain, bearing a lion (for England) on the right, and a unicorn (for Scotland) on the left. The old folk-rhyme (nursery rhyme*), 'The Lion and the Unicorn', obviously relates to the conflicts between the two nations, though it may earlier have had a seasonal symbolism.

Uniformity, Acts of

Laws passed by Parliament during and after the Reformation* to secure religious union in England. The first was that of 1549 (under Edward VI*) and the second and more important in 1559, under Elizabeth I*. Both required the common use in church worship of the Book of Common Prayer*. In 1662, under Charles II*, another Act of Uniformity insisted on its use by all clergy and schoolmasters, and marks the beginning of the dissenting* sects as formally separate religious bodies, distinct from the Church of England*.

Unionist

A name used by politicians from 1886 to express opposition to Home Rule* for Ireland, *ie* a separate Parliament for that country. The word at first united Conservatives with a number of Liberals who resisted the Home Rule policy of their leader, Gladstone*. Later 'Unionist' became synonymous with 'Conservative', and it is still used by members of that party, though it officially accepts the existence of the Irish Republic.

Union Jack

Flag of the United Kingdom of Great Britain and Ireland, combining the crosses of St George (patron saint of England), St Andrew (patron saint of Scotland), and St Patrick (patron saint of Ireland). The St George cross was rectangular, red, on a white ground. James VI of Scotland added the St Andrew's cross (diagonal, white, on a blue ground) after he became James I of England in 1603. St Patrick's cross (diagonal, red, on a white ground) was added in 1801 when Ireland was for the first time represented in Parliament at Westminster. 'Union' clearly originates in the uniting of the separate kingdoms; 'Jack' probably derives from the name of James I (Latin – Jacobus).

Unitarianism

A doctrine of religion that rejects the usual Christian doctrine of the Trinity, or three Persons in one God (the Father, the Son, and the Holy Ghost), in favour of a belief in the single person of God the Father. It originated in Britain in 18th C and was in accord with the rationalistic approach to religion of that century. The first Unitarian church opened in London in 1774; many English Presbyterians* (in 16th and 17th C one of the largest sects outside the Church of England) became Unitarians.

Unities, The Dramatic

An artistic doctrine supposed to be derived from Aristotle*, that Tragedy* should have one main action covering a single period not longer than the playing time of the tragedy, and occurring in a single place. Unity of action is in fact found in Aristotle's *Poetics**; he stated that Tragedy 'is based on a single action, one that is complete and whole in itself . . . with all the organic unity of a living creature'. Unity of place is not mentioned by Aristotle, and this and unity of time originate, as artistic rules, in the edition of his *Poetics* prepared by Castelvetro in 1570. Aristotle himself mentions the unity of time, but not so as to make it an artistic requirement. The English critic Philip Sidney* (*The Apology for Poetry**) and French 17th-C critics such as Corneille* nonetheless follow Castelvetro in giving the unities of time and place equal authority with that of action, and the belief that Aristotle insisted on all three unities has ever since been widespread.

Universities

Until 1828, England possessed only two universities, those of Oxford*, founded from Paris in 12th C, and of Cambridge*, founded largely by an emigration from Oxford in early 13th C. Scotland's first university was St Andrew's (1411), followed by Glasgow (1451), Aberdeen (two – 1494 and 1593) and Edinburgh (1582). That of Dublin (Trinity College) was opened in 1591. Medieval universities were in the hands of the clergy, which mattered little when the Church was undivided and Christian belief was almost universal. After the Reformation* in mid-16th-C, Catholics were excluded, and from 1660 (the Restoration*) all Protestants who were not members of the Church of England* were excluded from the English universities, though not

from the Scottish ones, since the Anglican Church was not established there.

Dissenters* established their own academies in 18th C, and in early 19th C a movement was started among prominent Dissenters to establish the University of London, which opened in 1828.

Since then, numerous universities have been founded, many of them since 1945; there is one in Wales, and there are forty-one in England, eight in Scotland, and two in Northern Ireland. The expected university population in 1973 is 218,000.

This rapid rise of new universities in recent years has reduced the pre-eminence of Oxford and Cambridge (sometimes referred to jointly as 'Oxbridge') which preserved their superior prestige at least until 1945. The universities of 19th and earlier 20th C were disdainfully designated 'provincial', and were popularly known as 'red-brick' in allusion to their ugly architecture in the cheapest Victorian building material.

Oxford and Cambridge, which became open to the members of all religious sects in 1871, represented an aristocracy of intellect, but their students were also drawn disproportionately from the richer classes, since, until 1945, state grants of money to poorer students were relatively few, and life at these ancient universities was comparatively expensive. Some of the Oxford and Cambridge colleges, in which the students live and are largely taught, for instance Trinity and King's in Cambridge and Christ Church and Magdalen in Oxford, have a renown equal to the fame of whole universities elsewhere. Attendance at such colleges, especially when preceded by attendance at one of the more important public schools* (*eg* Eton, Harrow, Winchester, Rugby) was regarded by many people as of even greater social than intellectual importance. This was not entirely due to snobbery, but was bound up with the complex tradition of the English gentleman*; nonetheless, it was not uncommon for commercial families (like the Vincys in George Eliot's *Middlemarch**) to send their sons to Oxford and Cambridge to acquire no more than the manners of their social superiors. In the 1960s, however, the prevailing radicalism among students led them to react violently against this kind of 'Oxbridge' appeal, and Oxford and Cambridge are themselves seeking to free their reputations from the suggestion of social privilege and conservatism.

Until the period since 1945, British universities have been singularly independent of state control; this independence is now threatened by their extensive dependence on government finance. The state grants are, however, distributed by a politically neutral body called the University Grants Committee.

* 3.1.2.

University Wits

A group of young men in the reign of Elizabeth I* who were educated at either Oxford or Cambridge University, and then embarked on careers as men of letters. Their names were John Lyly*, dramatist and writer of the kind of romance known as the Elizabethan novel*; George Peele*, dramatist; Robert Greene*, dramatist; Thomas Lodge*, who tried most of the branches of contemporary literature; Thomas Nashe*, novelist and pamphleteer*; Christopher Marlowe*, dramatist. To these, the name of Thomas Kyd* is sometimes added, although he is not known to have attended a university. Lyly was a writer for court circles, but the others were representative of a new kind of writer (of which Shakespeare* was also an example) who sought his fortune with the general public. Most of them had some kind of influence on, or relationship with, Shakespeare: Lyly used the kind of sophisticated diction which Shakespeare partly emulated and partly parodied in *Love's Labour's Lost** and elsewhere; Greene wrote a mellifluous blank verse* which anticipates some qualities in the earlier verse of Shakespeare, and was the author of the 'novel' *Pandosto*, source of *The Winter's Tale**; Lodge wrote *Rosalynde*, the source of *As You Like It**; Marlowe was the greatest architect of the dramatic blank verse medium; Kyd possibly wrote the first version of *Hamlet**.

* 5.1.2.4.

Unto This Last
Four essays on political economy by John Ruskin*. They were intended to be part of a larger treatise, but their publication (1860–2) in the *Cornhill Magazine** aroused so much hostility that the editor (Thackeray*) discontinued them. The reason for the anger was that Ruskin (an art critic) was, as it seemed to the public, stepping out of his professional function in order to attack the predominant economic theory of trading relationships, to do which he was considered by the middle-class public to be unqualified. The middle classes were inclined to believe that the subject had been reduced to the clear elements of a science by the political economists and utilitarian* thinkers of the first half of 19th C – men such as Bentham*, Ricardo, Malthus*, James and John Stuart Mill*. Ruskin pointed out that what was called 'political economy' was really 'commercial economy', and that it was untrue since it omitted facts of human nature, unjust since it unduly favoured the employing middle class, and uncivilized since it omitted the cultural values that ought to underly wealth. He found space to praise Dickens's novel *Hard Times**, itself an attack on Utilitarianism. In spite of the hostility and scorn of Ruskin's contemporaries, much of his thinking in these essays has been accepted by later sociologists and economists. The Indian leader Mahatma Gandhi admitted a debt to *Unto This Last*, as did a number of the early leaders of the British Labour Party.

* 3.4.4.

Urania; Uranian Aphrodite (Venus) /juə'reinjə/
[1] The muse* of astronomy in Greek myth.

[2] Uranian Aphrodite was the goddess of heavenly love, as opposed to Aphrodite Pandemos, the goddess of sexual love.

* *Aphrodite.*

Uranus /juə'reinəs/
In ancient Greek myth, the sky-god. He was the oldest of the Greek gods. By the union with Ge*, he produced the Titans*, who succeeded him in power, and were in turn overthrown by the Olympian gods, Zeus*, etc.

Uriel /'juəriəl/
In Christian and Jewish myth, one of the seven archangels; in Milton's *Paradise Lost**, the Regent of the Sun.

* *Angels.*

Urizen
In the 'prophetic books' by the poet William Blake*, a being who represents bondage to limitations, whether of the senses ('horizon'?), the reason ('your reason'?) or the Law; in the last respect he resembles Jehovah of the Old Testament. He occurs especially in *The Book of Urizen* (1794).

Urn Burial, or Hydriotaphia
A treatise by Sir Thomas Browne*, published in 1658. Its starting point is the discovery of ancient burial urns in Norfolk; this leads to an account of various ways of disposing of the dead, and meditations on death itself. The book is characteristic of Browne's practice of uniting factual curiosity with spiritual reflections; it is famous for his characteristically sonorous and poetic style.

Usury
Nowadays, demanding excessive interest in repayment of a loan. In the Middle Ages*, any charging of interest was at first considered wrong in principle, and was forbidden by the Church; since it was not forbidden by Jewish law, and Jews were in general forbidden to compete with Christians in other forms of trade, money-lending as a business became a Jewish speciality. The Christians soon found it convenient to relax their practice, however, and by 13th C Christians were competing with Jews in money-lending. The more commerce developed, the more necessary was it for capital to become fluid so that investment could increase, and investment could only increase if the payment of increase on loans became normal practice. Yet the feeling that *any* taking of interest was usurious remained, and it continued to be condemned on principle. The change to the modern view that demanding interest on loans is legitimate, and that it is only wrong to demand excessive interest, is illustrated by two laws passed by the English Parliament in 16th C: in 1552 an Act of Parliament forbade interest as 'a vice most odious and detestable'; in 1571 a new Act permitted the taking of interest up to 10%.

* *Capitalism; Jews in England.*

Uther Pendragon /'ju:θə pen'dragən/
In Arthurian legend, the father of King Arthur*. 'Pendragon' is Welsh for 'chief leader in war'.

Utilitarianism
A 19th-C political, economic, and social doctrine which based all values on utility, *ie* the usefulness of anything, measured by the extent to which it promotes the material happiness of the greatest number of people. It is especially associated with Jeremy Bentham*, at first a jurist concerned with legal reform, and later a social philosopher. Followers of the movement are thus often called 'Benthamites', but Bentham's disciple, John Stuart Mill* used the term 'Utilitarians'. Owing to their habit of criticizing social concepts and institutions on strictly rational tests, the leaders of the movement were also known as Philosophical Radicals.

Utilitarianism dominated 19th-C social thinking, but it had all its roots in various forms of 18th-C rationalism*. In moral philosophy, David Hume* had a strong influence on Bentham by his assumption that the supreme human virtue is benevolence, *ie* the disposition to increase the happiness of others. Psychologically, Bentham's principle that humans are governed by the impulses to seek pleasure and avoid pain derives from the associationism of David Hartley*. But Bentham and his associates believed that the virtue of benevolence, and human impulses towards pleasure, operate within social and economic laws which are scientifically demonstrable. Bentham accepted Adam Smith's* reasoning in *The Wealth of Nations* (1776) that material prosperity is governed by economic laws of supply and demand, the beneficial operation of which is only hindered by governmental interference. Malthus*, in his *Essay on the Principle of Population* (1798), maintained that it is mathematically demonstrable that population always tends to increase beyond the means of subsistence, and Ricardo, a friend of Bentham's, applied Malthus's principle to wages, arguing that as the population increases wages will necessarily get lower, since the increase is more rapid than that of the wealth available to support the workers. Smith, Malthus and Ricardo were masters of what was called the science of Political Economy, and the inhuman fatalism with which they endowed it caused it to be known as the dismal science*. However, it was not dismal for the industrial middle class of employers, whose interests it suited; they were already 'utilitarians' by self-interest, and thus willing converts to the theory.

Thus the operation of Utilitarianism in 19th C was paradoxical. It liberated society from laws which were inefficient survivals from the past (the Elizabethan Poor Laws*) but it replaced them by laws that often operated with cold inhumanity (*eg* the Poor Law of 1834). It reduced senseless government interference with society, but its concern with efficiency encouraged a bureaucratic civil service. It liberated the employers, but it was often unsympathetic to the interests of the employees. Its principle was benevolence, but its faith in reason often made it indifferent to individual suffering. The inhumanity of the creed, and its indifference to cultural values unless they could be shown to be materially useful, caused it to be vigorously attacked by leading writers between 1830 and 1870, including Carlyle*, Dickens*, Ruskin*, and Matthew Arnold*. But perhaps its sanest and most lucid critic was John Stuart Mill; though himself a Utilitarian to the end of his life, he saw the philosophical limitations of the movement and exposed them in his essays in 1838 on Bentham, and on Coleridge* whom he admired as the father of the opposing tendency of thought. Mill's essay *Utilitarianism* (1863) emphasized that some kinds of pleasure are better than others – a distinction Bentham failed to make – and that the highest virtue in humanity is 'the desire to be in unity with our fellow creatures'. Mill was aware, as Bentham had not been, of the importance of the artistic imagination, in particular of poetry, in a civilization.

Our society is still in many ways utilitarian, but as a systematic philosophy Utilitarianism did not outlast 19th C. The last important figures connected with the movement are the philosophers Herbert Spencer* and Leslie Stephen*.

* *Unto This Last.*

Utopia (1516) /juːˈtəupjə/

A political and philosophical treatise by Sir Thomas More*, in the form of an account of an imaginary, newly discovered country. It was written in Latin, and translated into English (after More's death) in 1551; it had already been translated into French (1530), and such was the European fame of the book that Italian, Spanish, and German versions also appeared.

The idea of a fictional country was no doubt stimulated by recent Italian, Portuguese, and Spanish exploration, and in particular by Amerigo* Vespucci's account of his travels (1507). Philosophically, the book is a pure product of Renaissance* humanism*, and like other products of that movement, it was inspired by the ancient Greek philosopher, Plato*. The land of Utopia is the Platonic ideal of a country, only to be realized on the assumption that man is basically good. Private property is replaced by communal ownership; there is complete freedom of thought; war is regarded as abominable, and to be used only in the last resort, when it should be waged as effectively as possible, even, if necessary, by unscrupulous means. Earthly happiness is glorified; the good life is the life of mental and physical fulfilment, rather than the medieval Christian life of self-denial and asceticism, but the Utopians are humane and benevolent, not self-indulgent. There is perfect mutual respect, and women receive the same education as men.

The Platonic idealism of the book is in some ways an indication of its weakness – a weakness characteristic of much Renaissance humanism: the very perfection of More's imagined society makes it so remote from the actual society of his own day that there can be no practical relationship between them. Thus, there are strong contrasts between the picture of Utopian practice as recounted by More's imaginary traveller, Raphael Hythloday, and More's private and public life in England. He was himself a devout Catholic, who, when he became Lord Chancellor, persecuted Protestants, and far from renouncing asceticism, he was a man who wore a hair shirt to subdue the pleasure-loving body for the sake of the soul.

More's *Utopia* is the only work of distinction in 16th-C England to be written purely in the spirit of the Renaissance; the fact that it was written in Latin shows that More intended it for an international society of humanist scholars rather than for the society of educated people, many of whom were not humanists, in his own country.

Utopian Literature

More's *Utopia** introduced into the English language the word 'utopian' = 'imaginary and ideal', and started a succession of 'utopias' in English literature. The idea of inventing an imaginary country to be used as a 'model' by which to judge earthly societies did not, however, originate with More, but with his master the Greek philosopher Plato*, who did the same in his dialogues *Timaeus* and the *Republic*. *Utopia's* most notable successors in 17th C were Bacon's unfinished *New Atlantis** (1626), in which science is offered as the solution for humanity, and James Harington's *Oceana* (1656), which put forward political ideas that were to have a powerful influence in America. In 20th C, H. G. Wells* was, in his earlier days, a vigorous Utopian: *Anticipations* (1901), *A Modern Utopia* (1905), and *New Worlds for Old* (1908). Just before Wells, William Morris's* *News from Nowhere* (1890) is a noteworthy socialistic utopia.

However, from 18th C, much utopian literature is satirical, intended to give warning of vicious tendencies of society rather than to exemplify ideals. An example of this is Mandeville's *Fable of the Bees* (1714), about the downfall of an ideal society through the viciousness of its inhabitants; and Swift's *Gulliver's Travels** (1726) can be put in the same class. In 19th C the best known examples are Samuel Butler's *Erewhon** (1872) and *Erewhon Revisited* (1901). In 20th C, fears for the future of mankind have predominated over the optimism about inevitable progress which was more typical of 19th C, and this has led to a new kind of utopian writing, portraying our own society set in the future, showing our fears realized. For this kind of work, the term 'dystopia' has been invented. The first striking example was Aldous Huxley's* *Brave New World* (1932), about the deadness of a civilization which has come to be dominated by scientific technology; E. M. Forster's* tale *The Machine Stops* has a similar theme, and both are written in reaction against H. G. Wells's optimism about technology. George Orwell's* *1984* is a nightmare about 20th-C political totalitarianism, the grimmer because Orwell brought the date of his anticipated society so close to the time of writing.

* *Science Fiction*.

Utrecht, Treaty of (1713)

* *Spanish Succession, War of the*.

V

Vagabonds and Vagrants

Generally known today as 'tramps'; men and women who have no settled residence or work, but live by begging or 'casual labour', wandering from place to place, finding shelter where they can or in Salvation Army* hostels or 'casual wards' in the towns.

The vagrant class probably began in 14th C owing to the breakdown of the status of serfdom. A serf was not a slave, but his labour was due to a specific employer – probably a landowner – and his residence was fixed to one place; that is to say, he could not 'sell' his labour wherever he could get the best wages, nor was he free to move about as he wished. The epidemic of Black Death* in mid-14th C reduced the population so much that there was a shortage of labour, and landowners were forced to find their labourers wherever they could. Nonetheless, wandering labourers were regarded with suspicion, and the government tried to stabilize the working population and relationships with them by the law known as the Statute of Labourers, which sought to fix wages regardless of economic change, and ensure that labourers did not move about. Any who did so became known as 'vagabonds', and were regarded as potential criminals.

16th C was a period when vagrancy was a critical problem, for special causes: the dissolution of the monasteries* (1536–39) caused unemployment among monastic servants and tradesmen; enclosures* of land for sheep-farming and parks evicted peasants from their farms. Some of the vagabonds (also called 'rogues') were wandering entertainers, including actors ('players') unattached to noble households; some were pedlars (like Autolycus in Shakespeare's *The Winter's Tale**) with goods for sale; a special class were the gipsies* who appeared in England early in 16th C. Many, more or less inevitably, became part of the underworld of crime, for which a large slang language of 'cant' grew up: Abraham men = pretended lunatics (Mad Tom, in Shakespeare's *King Lear**); 'hookers' or 'anglers' = thieves who extracted goods from houses with a hooked stick; 'rufflers' = highway robbers; 'priggers of prancers' = horse thieves. 'Prig' was at this time a common word for thief. This underworld was the subject of a class of popular literature known as 'rogue pamphlets', the most notable examples of which are Robert Greene's* 'conny-catching' pamphlets, 1591–92.

The government tried to deal with the problem of vagrancy by constructive legislation (*eg* the Poor Law* of 1601) and by severity – imprisonment, whipping, and, in 17th C, branding. The Poor Law of 1834 dealt with vagrants (such as were not proved criminals) by regulating workhouses, which were hated more than prison, so that Betty Higden in Dickens's *Our Mutual Friend** prefers to die by the roadside. Begging in modern England is illegal, and the tramp population is much reduced and treated, on the whole, humanely, but tramps are still suspected and may find themselves arrested for 'loitering with intent' to commit a crime.

Valentine's Day, St (14 February)

St Valentine is the name of two early Christian martyrs. It is also a festival of lovers, and has been this at least since 15th C. There appears to be no connection between lovers and either of the saints, and the association is probably an example of a Christian feast by chance coinciding with a pre-Christian, pagan one. 14 February is at the end of winter, when animals and birds begin to think of mating. 'A Valentine' was originally a chosen lover of either sex, but is nowadays a card or other token sent, often anonymously, to someone of one's choice of the other sex.

Valhalla /val'halə/

In Germanic myth, a great hall of Odin*, the chief of the gods, where he received the souls of brave warriors killed in battle.

Valkyries /val'kiəriz/

In Germanic myth, female messengers in the service of Odin*; they decided the issues of battles, and selected the heroes suitable for Valhalla*.

Valley of Humiliation; Valley of the Shadow of Death

Two places of trial through which pilgrims had to pass in Bunyan's *Pilgrim's Progress**. The Valley of the Shadow of Death is a reference to Psalm 23 in the Bible (Authorized Version).

Vanbrugh, Sir John (1664–1726) /'vanbrə/

Architect and dramatist. His chief plays are *The Relapse* (1696); *The Provok'd Wife* (1697); *The Confederacy* (1705 – adapted from the French of Dancourt's *Bourgeoises à la Mode*). As a dramatist he was said by his contemporary, Cibber*, to write as he talked, and he was casual also in plot construction. His usual subjects are unhappy marriage, or the predicament of needy younger sons. His plays have much gaiety, however.

As an architect he was more important. He was a pupil of Christopher Wren*, and an English example of the style that combines classical forms and proportions with bold display of ornament, known on the continent of Europe as Baroque. His well-known country mansions are Castle Howard and Seaton Delaval, both in the north of England, and the Duke of Marlborough's Blenheim Palace near Oxford. He designed the library and quadrangle of Queen's College, Oxford, and six churches in London.

* 2.3; 2.5.2; *Manners, Comedy of*; *Restoration*.

Bib: Whistler, L., *Sir John Vanbrugh, Architect and Dramatist*; Boas, F. S., in *An Introduction to Eighteenth-century Drama*; Dobrée, B., in *Restoration Comedy* and *Essays in Biography*; Palmer, J., in *The Comedy of Manners*; Perry, H. T. E., in *The Comic Spirit in Restoration Drama*.

Vandals

A Germanic group of tribes which in 4th-5th C AD overran Gaul, Spain, and North Africa, capturing Carthage, the third city of the Roman Empire, in 439, and Rome in 455. They took from Rome all its movable wealth, and this has led to their reputation for barbarous destructiveness, though they were not more destructive than other Germanic invaders of the Empire.

Vanessa

Swift's* name for Esther Vanhomrigh who was in love with him between the years 1708 and 1723.

Vanity Fair

A town through which the pilgrims pass in Bunyan's *Pilgrim's Progress**. It is a vivid representation of the pleasure-loving worldliness of society in the reign of Charles II*, seen from a Puritan* point of view. 'Vanity' in the Biblical sense is equivalent to triviality and worthlessness, and it includes all the good things of this world, when compared to the values of the heavenly world of the spirit: 'Vanity of vanities, saith the Preacher, vanity of vanities; all is vanity.' (*Ecclesiastes* 1:2). The town is a great market (fair) for these vanities; the townsmen are not only trivial but heartless, and also bitterly resentful when the pilgrims despise their vanities. Faithful is martyred there, but in Part II he has left disciples behind him and they are to some extent tolerated. Perhaps this is Bunyan's way of acknowledging that the spirit of his age was becoming more tolerant of the Puritans.

Vanity Fair

A historical novel by Thackeray* published in monthly issues, 1847–48. The title, borrowed from Bunyan's *Pilgrim's Progress**, shows that Thackeray's subject matter is the worldly, materialistic society of his time. It is not such a gay society as Bunyan's; in Thackeray's day, worldly goods weighed more heavily, and Thackeray has no spiritual solution to their oppressiveness. The 18 years before the novel was completed had been years in which religious forces had been energetic: they had seen the Oxford Movement* led by Newman*, and the conscience of the ruling classes, stirred by the evangelical* religious revival, had been engaged in the remedy of social abuses, under the leadership of Lord Shaftesbury*. Yet Thackeray shows his men of religion to be either hypocrites or deluded. Dissenters*, the descendants of Bunyan, include old Osborne, the arrogant, sombre and unfeeling businessman; evangelicalism is represented by the hypocritical Bute Crawley.

The novel is subtitled 'A Novel without a Hero', and there is in fact nothing heroic about the society that Thackeray presents. However, its heartlessness and snobbery are skilfully manipulated by the central character, Becky Sharp, an ingenious and vigorous adventuress of poor parentage. She begins her socially ambitious career with a friendship with Amelia Sedley, the soft-hearted, weakly sentimental heroine of the book. Becky tries to marry Jos Sedley, Amelia's brother, a foolish but rich 'nabob'*. Frustrated in this, and reduced to being a governess, she then makes love to the mean and avaricious Sir Pitt Crawley,

Vauxhall Gardens

but makes the mistake of marrying his second son, Rawdon, a gallant but ignorant and dissolute man who, despite his incapacity, is later made Governor of the unhealthy Coventry Islands. Her marriage does not prevent her from pursuing her social ambitions still further by becoming the mistress of the aristocratic and degenerate Lord Steyne. Her ambitions are eventually defeated, but she manages to end up as a respected member of society.

Amelia Sedley first marries the worthless young officer, George Osborne, who is killed at the battle of Waterloo. The only fine human values are characterized by his friend, Dobbin, an English gentleman in the moral rather than the social sense, who eventually becomes Amelia's second husband. The novel is an impressive, if negative, landscape of upper class society in the first half of 19th C; its best parts are those that concentrate on Becky Sharp and are written with a keen, sardonic humour. The novel is commonly regarded as Thackeray's most successful work.

Vanity of Human Wishes, The

* *Johnson, Samuel.*

Vaughan, Henry (1622–95) /vo:n/

Poet. He was of south Welsh origin, and is hence often known as 'the Silurist', after the Silures, an ancient British tribe of the region. He was one of the Metaphysical* poets, and the work by which his reputation stands, *Silex Scintillans: or Sacred Poems and Pious Ejaculations* (1650) is strongly influenced by George Herbert*. However, he had two qualities of his own that distinguish him from Herbert: a mystical fascination with the innocent apprehensions of the mind of childhood, which associates him with Thomas Traherne* and with William Wordsworth*, and a strong responsiveness to natural surroundings, which also anticipates Wordsworth. Vaughan's poem *The Retreat* has resemblances to Wordsworth's *Ode: Intimations of Immortality from Recollections of Early Childhood.* Other notable poems in this volume of Vaughan's are *Peace*, *Ascension Hymn*, *Quickness*, *Regeneration*, *The World.* He also wrote non-religious poetry – *Poems* (including a translation of a satire by Juvenal*) published in 1646, *Olor Iscanus* (1651) – as well as some religious prose.

Bib: Hutchinson, F. E., *Life*; Bennett, J., *Four Metaphysical Poets*; Holmes, E., *Vaughan and the Hermetic Philosophy*; Leishman, J. in *Metaphysical Poets*; Mahood, M. M., in *Poetry and Humanism*; White, H. C., in *The Metaphysical Poets*; studies by Ross Garner; E. C. Pettet; R. A. Durr.

Vauxhall Gardens /'voksho:l/

Pleasure gardens in London, laid out in 1661 and closed in 1859. They were at first called 'the New Spring Gardens', and were also known as 'Fox Hall Gardens', from the name of the manor on which they stood, Falkes Hall. They are frequently mentioned as a place of resort in 17th- and 18th-C writings.

* *Spring Gardens.*

Vehicles

The development of ways of travelling by vehicle in Britain may for convenience be divided into three phases.

[1] *Until 1550.* Travelling overland in the Middle Ages* was chiefly on foot (for the poor) or on horseback. The sick and aged would be carried by a man-handled bed known as a 'litter', suspended between horizontal poles; heavy goods went by ox- or horse-drawn wagons, of a design similar to the farmers' wagons still in use in the first half of 20th C, and light goods went by packhorse. Travel by barge along the rivers was common.

[2] *1550–1830.* The first coach in England was built in 1555, and in the next century and a half coaches came more and more into use among the nobility; in 17th C hackney coaches (*ie* coaches for hire) were already beginning to put the Thames watermen out of business. By 18th C the stage-coach was in use for general travel; it was so called because horses were changed at fixed 'stages' on the journey. More rapid travel was undertaken by

privately hired post-chaises. Movement about towns was by sedan-chair, resembling a light litter except that the traveller was seated. The great improvement in roads towards the end of 18th C led to a great increase in light private carriages of various designs; gigs and curricles were the lightest, favoured by young men.

[3] *1830–Present Day*. The first major revolution in transport was the invention of steam railways shortly before 1830; they spread rapidly over the country by 1850, soon eliminating stage coaches except in remoter districts. Private travel was still by carriage; a new style was invented in 1838 for Lord Brougham* and was called after him. In towns, the old kind of hackney carriage and the sedan chair were alike superseded by the hansom cab, invented in 1834. It resembled a more spacious sedan on wheels, with the driver seated above and behind the passengers. The pedal-bicycle came into general use in the 1870s, although primitive forms of it had been invented a hundred years before; it was the first private vehicle available to even the humblest. The motor car made its entry in the last decade of 19th C. By the next century the best makes – notably the Daimler and the Rolls-Royce – were becoming symbols of high social status.

* 2.2.2.

Veneerings, The

A pretentious, newly-rich husband and wife in Dickens's novel *Our Mutual Friend**. 'Veneer' is a thin coat of fine wood put on furniture of inferior wood to make it look superior. Mr and Mrs Veneering similarly cultivate social ostentation.

Venus

* *Aphrodite*.

Venus and Adonis (1593)

A narrative poem in six-lined stanzas by William Shakespeare*. It is dedicated to Henry Wriothesley, Earl of Southampton*. It is based on the Romano-Greek myth of the love of Venus (Aphrodite*), the goddess of sexual beauty, for the beautiful youth Adonis*. The poem probably emulates the love poem *Hero and Leander** by Marlowe (completed by Chapman) and is Shakespeare's earliest published work.

Vergil, Polydore

* *Histories and Chronicles*.

Verne, Jules

* *Science Fiction*.

Vers de Société

A kind of poetry originating in France in 17th C, distinguished by its content, and the treatment of it: light, graceful, witty comment on current manners. In England it was particularly characteristic of early 18th C – much of the work of Prior*, Gay* and Swift*. An example is Swift's *A Soldier and a Scholar* (1732).

Vers Libre

* *Free Verse*.

Versailles /veəˈsai/

A town near Paris where Louis XIV of France (1638–1715) built the most splendid of all the European royal palaces. It was also the scene of two important treaties: the Peace of Versailles (1783) which ended the American War of Independence, and the Treaty of Versailles (1919), concluding World War I.

Vertumnus /vəːˈtʌmnəs/

In Roman myth, a god of fruit trees like Pomona*, whom he courted in a number of disguises; one of his characteristics is a constant changing of form, presumably corresponding to the changing of the seasons.

Vesta and the Vestal Virgins

In Roman myth, Vesta was the goddess of the hearth-fire, and in general of domestic life, among the Lares* and Penates.

Vesta was served by dedicated women called the Vestal Virgins, chosen from noble families. They took vows of chastity, and were subjected to horrible penalties if they broke them.

Vicar of Bray, The

The title of an anonymous 18th-C song, about a parish priest who managed to keep his parish through every political and religious vicissitude. He may be based on Simon Aleyn, vicar of the village of Bray in Berkshire from about 1540 to 1588. Beginning as a Catholic, he became a moderate Protestant to suit Henry VIII*, a more pronounced Protestant under Edward VI*, a Catholic again under Mary I*, and a Protestant again under Elizabeth I*. A more recent vicar, who died in 1709, had similarly adapted himself during the political changes of the previous 42 years, and is the more likely subject of the ballad. The name is thus representative of time-servers, *ie* those who change their opinions and their beliefs whenever it suits their interests.

* *Reformation*.

Vicar of Christ

One of the titles of the Popes, first used by Innocent III (1198–1216).

Vicar of Wakefield, The

A novel by Oliver Goldsmith*, written 1761–62; the publisher did not expect it to be popular, and publication was delayed until 1766, when it was enthusiastically received. It has remained a popular classic ever since. Dr Primrose is an unworldly parish priest, comically innocent-minded, but devoted to his vocation and to his wife and six children. The Primroses live in circumstances of comfort though they are not rich; their way of life is like an idyll* in the pastoral* tradition. They have no vices except mild ones: Dr Primrose has some literary vanity, and his wife is rather snobbishly ambitious for their children. In spite of their blamelessness, a succession of disasters overcomes them and reduces them to ruin and disgrace.

Eventually they recover their prosperity through the friendship of a benefactor, Mr Burchell, who turns out to be Sir William Thornhill, uncle of the villainous squire who first precipitated their misfortunes. The story closely recalls that of Job* in the Bible; the Vicar endures all his troubles with a Job-like patience and a more than Job-like sweetness of temper. The narration is episodic, and includes an account of the eldest son's adventures on the continent of Europe, probably based on Goldsmith's own, and several famous poems including *Elegy on the Death of a Mad Dog* and *When lovely woman stoops to folly.*

The book is a compromise between a fable* and a novel*; it has the directness and didacticism of the former, and some of the circumstantial realism of the latter form. Considered merely as a novel, *The Vicar* is easily disparaged and added nothing to the development of the novel form in 18th C; considered as essentially a comic and sentimental fable, the book has a charm which easily explains its popularity.

Vice, The

In medieval Mystery Plays*, a comic devil who plays a role similar to the court Fools* and other comic characters in the plays of Shakespeare and his contemporaries – see Feste's song at the end of IV. ii in *Twelfth Night.* In the Mystery Plays he was often called Tutivillus or Titivil, a devil who, according to the monks, had the special function of carrying off to hell any words neglected through laziness or carelessness in the recitation of the church liturgy. Looking further back, the 'Vice' has a good deal in common with the role of the cunning slave in the comedies of the Roman dramatist, Terence*. Terence was a popular writer among the learned in the Middle Ages*. Thus the 'Vice' is a role that links the Middle Ages with the pagan Roman writers on the one hand, and with the Renaissance* on the other. The servant, Mosca, in Jonson's *Volpone**, is an example of a role which derives directly from Roman comedy.

Victoria

Queen of Britain, 1837–1901. She came to the throne at 17, and had the longest reign in British history. It was also a highly successful reign, for it re-established the prestige of the monarchy, which at her accession was neither popular nor respected. The political conflicts between the monarchy and Parliament between 1603 and 1714 had concluded with the victory of Parliament, and England was a constitutional monarchy, with the king reduced to symbolic status. However, Victoria's grandfather, George III (1760–1820) was insane for the last ten years of his life; her uncle George IV (1820–30) had disgusted the nation by his immoral conduct, thus leaving a bad impression which the reign of his successor and brother, William IV (1830–37), had been too short to redeem. The other members of the royal family, including Victoria's father, the Duke of Kent, were also in low esteem. Yet when Victoria died in 1901, the monarchy was more popular and respected than ever before, and she succeeded in establishing a model of behaviour for the sovereign which has preserved the popularity of royalty to the present day.

Victoria achieved this partly through her personality, which has become a legend, partly through her husband, and partly through historical circumstances. Though very short, she had great dignity and a fine sense of behaviour on public occasions; moreover, she could be pointed to as setting a standard for the domestic virtues of rectitude of personal conduct and devotion to her husband and family, virtues greatly esteemed by the middle classes at the period when these classes dominated national life. She married Prince Albert* of Saxe-Coburg-Gotha in 1840; he died in 1861, by which time they had had 9 children. Albert, the Prince Consort, was a conscientious man of intelligence, who discreetly educated Victoria's mind and political behaviour, to the extent that her public success was very largely his creation. Their court was dull, but it was dignified and decorous.

Thanks to her personality and to her husband, Victoria was able quite naturally to perform the role of a monumental symbol for the nation during the 60 years of the greatest prosperity, power and influence that it had ever known. During her reign the British Empire was built up to its greatest extent, and for an empire a monarchy is a much more effective symbolic head than a president. This her Prime Minister, Benjamin Disraeli*, well understood when he induced Victoria to adopt the title Empress of India in 1877. Her relationships with her ministers were not always as happy as they were with Disraeli, but the disagreements were mainly behind the scenes. Her jubilees of 1887 and 1897 were great national occasions, on which the sovereign was identified with the nation as never before since the reign of Elizabeth I*.

* *Victorian period.*

Victorian Period

The period coinciding with the reign of Queen Victoria (1837–1901) is commonly divided into three.

[1] *1837–1851: the Early Victorian period.* This was a time of struggle and growth; the age of the Chartist* Movement and the Anti-Corn Law League (* *Corn Laws*), but also of the building of railways. The 'hungry forties' ended with the Great Exhibition* in 1851, the culmination of the Industrial Revolution*, which Britain achieved earlier than any other nation.

[2] *1851–1870: the Mid-Victorian period.* Britain had passed the time of the worst popular discontents, and was at her height in wealth, power, and influence.

[3] *1870–1901: the Late Victorian Period.* A less fortunate period, when other nations (especially Germany and the United States) were competing with Britain industrially. Britain had not hitherto been deliberately 'imperialist', though she had acquired much territory in consequence of her pursuit of trade; she now became imperialist in her jealousy and mistrust of other imperialist nations,

and the period ended with the imperialist South African War (Boer War) of 1899–1901. Economically, Britain was becoming less the 'workshop of the world' than the world's banker. Domestically, partly in consequence of the second Parliamentary Reform Bill* (enfranchising the town workers – 1867) and the Education Act (establishing a state system of education – 1870) it was a time of popular political and social movements which included the building up of trade unions* and the formation of the Labour Party*.

Culturally, the Victorian period was the age when change rather than stability came first to be accepted as normal in the nature of human outlook. Ancient foundations of religious belief were eroded, among intellectuals, by scientific advances, especially the biological discoveries of Darwin* (**Agnosticism*). The educated classes and their leaders sought to establish guiding values for living; it was the period of the 'Victorian Sage' – Carlyle*, Mill*, Arnold*, Ruskin*, and Tennyson* – educating the social conscience. The relationship of the individual to himself, to other individuals, and to society at large is the study to which the novel* is admirably adapted; the English novel developed in the works of Gaskell*, Thackeray*, Trollope*, the Brontës*, Dickens*, George Eliot* and Henry James* into the great art form of the age. The immense technological developments of the time were rather inimical to the other arts: poetry, in spite of the popularity of Tennyson, or perhaps because of it, was rather a refuge from anxieties than an illumination of them; painting followed the direction of poetry. Architecture was inevitably prolific when the nation was so rich and growing so fast, but the very demands upon it threw taste into confusion, and its output was most uneven in merit. It is typified by the revival of the most undisciplined of styles, the Gothic (**Gothic Revival*), although other styles proliferated. Culturally and in many ways socially, the Victorian period saw the outset and display of the problems which 20th C has had to solve.

* *Writers mentioned*; *Agnosticism*; *Corn Laws*; *Chartism*; *Exhibition*; *Gothic Revival*; *Victoria, Queen*.

Victory, The

The flag-ship of Admiral Nelson* at the Battle of Trafalgar* (1805). It is preserved at Portsmouth as a national monument.

Vienna, The Congress of (1814–15)

A conference of governments at the end of the Napoleonic War to settle the national frontiers in Europe. Britain, Russia, Prussia and Austria were represented on the side of the allies, and Talleyrand was the French representative. The spirit of the Conference was such as to ignore or repress the nationalistic and democratic emotions aroused all over Europe by the French Revolution* and by Napoleon*; on the other hand, great attention was paid to the Balance of Power and the preservation of international peace. The consequence was a period of 40 years' international peace, but much popular unrest culminating in the civil wars of 1848, from which Britain was one of the few countries to be exempt.

Vikings

The name by which are known the Scandinavian (especially Danish and Norwegian) invaders of Western Europe from 9th to 11th C; they are also called 'Norsemen'. They overran the northern and western coasts and islands of Scotland, and established a kingdom, centred on Dublin, on the east coast of Ireland. They also conquered northern, central, and eastern England, but were then defeated by Alfred* of Wessex (reigned 871–901). In northern France they settled in what became known as the province of Normandy at about the same time; from this, two centuries later, they set out (no longer as Vikings but as Normans*) to conquer England. In neither England nor France did the Vikings make a strong original contribution to culture; they became absorbed by the Anglo-Saxon* and French cultures respectively, and in 11th C they imported their Norman French culture to England.

Village, The English

Before the Norman Conquest* of 1066, the Anglo-Saxon rural communities were the 'vils'; these became more or less identified with the Norman manor, the basic social and economic unit of the Middle Ages*. Each manor usually had a 'lord of the manor', or principal landowner, but it was common for one lord to hold several manors, and his authority in the village was then exercised (through the manor court or 'court leet') by his 'reeve' or steward. Most of the peasants were 'serfs'; that is to say, in return for their lord's protection, they were compelled to work on his land, owed him certain gifts on such occasions as the marriage of a daughter or the death of the head of a family, and were not allowed to leave their settlements. Their own land consisted of large open fields which were divded into strips for cultivation, each husbandman being awarded particular strips in the manor court. This is known as the open field system* of agriculture.. Beyond the arable fields was another area of pasture for grazing the peasants' cattle; this was held in common by all the villagers and was known as 'common land'.

The status of 'serf' could be 'commuted', if the lord agreed, by the payment of a sum of money in consequence of which the serf might become a landless labourer, free to work for wages, or a tenant farmer, paying rent. There were many degrees and kinds of serfdom, but in no case was the serf a mere slave; he owed his services to the lord, but the lord had no rights over his person. The lord could not usually impose his own will over the manor court which decided the domestic affairs of the village; its law was 'customary', *ie* decided by tradition and precedent, much as the Common Law* of England was. There were even cases when the lord was fined by the manorial court, like any of his serfs, for infringing the customary law. In addition to the lord and his steward or reeve, an important person in each village was the priest or parson (such as Chaucer describes in the *Canterbury Tales**), supported by 'tithes' or tenths of the agricultural produce of the villagers.

The first important change in this system came as a result of the devastations of the Black Death* epidemic of about 1348–49, which greatly reduced the population of serfs and the available labour on the manors. Lords found it convenient to hire labour, and by 16th C serfdom, with a few exceptions, had gone from England. The peasants were now tenant farmers paying rents to the lord of the manor, who farmed his own land by hired labourers. The next important change was the enclosure* of land by the landlords in 16th C. The profitability of sheep-farming was such as to make it worth the lord's while to deprive the peasants of their holdings in order to turn arable land over to grazing. Enclosures of land continued until 19th C for different motives, with the consequence that the small farmer ('yeoman'* or 'smallholder') ceased, at least from mid-18th C, to be typical of English rural society in the sense that he is typical, for instance, of French society. They remained, nonetheless, a substantial class, represented by Tom Brangwen in D. H. Lawrence's novel *The Rainbow**, which begins in mid-19th-C England.

The final important change in the English village was brought about by the rapid growth of towns in 19th and 20th C. The percentage of the population now directly engaged in agriculture is about 5%; the inhabitants of the villages are often town workers who go to their employment in the neighbouring town daily, and others are owners of 'weekend cottages' who live in the town and use the village merely as a holiday resort; farms are commonly large but so mechanized that they employ comparatively little human labour. A social problem that arises from these circumstances is that villages lose their independent life as real communities, and tend to become mere suburbs of the big towns. The traditional pattern of village life, so often described in 18th- and 19th-C novels, has gone. The Squire* (corresponding to the medieval lord of the manor) has often found it profitable to sell his land, and too expensive to maintain his manor house, for which, moreover, he has difficulty in finding servants. The village vicar (* *Clergy*) finds himself preaching to an empty church.

Villanelle /vilə'nel/

Originally a rustic song; made into a regular form of courtly grace and sweet tunefulness by the French poet Passerat (d 1602). The form was not much used in England until the period 1880–1910, when a fashion developed – chiefly among minor poets – for all such graceful forms (the ballade, rondeau, triolet, etc.). It consists of five three-line stanzas and a final four-line one; the first and third lines of the first stanza recur, alternately, as refrains, and make a concluding couplet to the last stanza. An example, by James Joyce, purporting to be by the character Stephen Dedalus in Joyce's novel *A Portrait of the Artist as a Young Man**:

Are you not weary of ardent ways,
Lure of the fallen seraphim?
Tell no more of enchanted days.

Your eyes have set man's heart ablaze
And you have had your will of him.
Are you not weary of ardent ways?

Above the flame the smoke of praise
Goes up from ocean rim to rim.
Tell no more of enchanted days.

Our broken cries and mournful lays
Rise in one eucharistic hymn.
Are you not weary of ardent ways?

While sacrificing hands upraise
The chalice flowering to the brim.
Tell no more of enchanted days.

And still you hold our longing gaze
With languorous look and lavish limb!
Are you not weary of ardent ways?
Tell no more of enchanted days.

Villette (1853) /vi'let/

A novel by Charlotte Brontë*. The title is the name by which the author disguises Brussels, capital of Belgium, where she had been employed as a teacher in a school kept by Monsieur and Madame Héger. The novel is based on her experiences, and is told in the first person by the central character, Lucy Snowe. Lucy is a young girl who begins life in secure circumstances, and then, as the result of disasters, finds herself deprived of family and means of financial support. After a period of living as companion to an old lady, who dies, she sets forth to seek her fortune in the foreign city of Villette, where she is first nursery governess to the children of Madame Beck, who keeps a school, and then one of the teachers. The main part of the novel is the story of her stormy love affair with Paul Emmanuel, Madame Beck's cousin and her colleague in running the school. She ends up with her own school, established by Monsieur Paul, and as his fiancée, but the conclusion is left uncertain. The novel is remarkable in three respects. First, like Charlotte Brontë's *Jane Eyre**, it is autobiographical in a new and interesting sense: the reader experiences the events entirely through the mind and feelings of Lucy, who thus provides the psychological atmosphere that the reader breathes, although at the same time the artistry is such that he can make his own judgements of these events independently of Lucy's prejudices, despite the fact that these are not only very strong but are clearly shared by the author. Secondly, the love affairs are so presented that they are shown to be a process of self-discovery by which the lovers learn to know themselves and thus enlarge their personalities. This is especially true of Lucy and Paul, but it is also true of secondary affairs in the book; only the trivial personalities fail to undergo this development, and are proved trivial by their failure. Thirdly, though it was probably not part of Charlotte Brontë's conscious intention, the novel shows the clash of two cultures – the Protestant Anglo-Saxon culture of Lucy Snowe, and the Latin, Catholic culture of Paul Emmanuel – and the ways in which the personalities of each transcend their differences so as to achieve mutual admiration and love, although their cultural opposition remains as strong at the end as at first. The novel is Charlotte Brontë's masterpiece.

* *Autobiography*.

Virgil (Publius Vergilius Maro) (70–19 BC) /ˈvɜːdʒil/

Roman poet. He was born on a farm not far from Mantua in northern Italy, and is thus quite often referred to as 'the Mantuan'. He greatly esteemed the farming section of society to which he belonged, and valued the farming way of life. He was not, from the place of his origin, of Roman descent, but belonged to the first generation of Italians who felt a consciousness of nationhood, with Rome as their capital. By 40 BC he was in Rome, under the patronage of the wealthy Roman patrician (nobleman), Maecenas. He wrote the first work for which he is famous, the *Eclogues* or *Bucolics* (* *Eclogue*), between 42 and 37 BC; their title merely means short, selected pieces, but his intention was to praise the Italian countryside as the Greek poet, Theocritus* had praised the countryside of Sicily. The *Georgics** (37–30 BC), written at the instigation of Maecenas to encourage a sense of the value of a stable and productive society, is devoted to the praise of the farming way of life. The *Aeneid** written during the remainder of his life, is an epic* about the travels of Aeneas the Trojan, and emulates Homer's *Odyssey**. Its purpose is not merely this, but to relate the Romans to the great civilization of the Greeks, on which their own civilization was so much based, by making Aeneas the ancestor of the Roman nation. The *Aeneid*, with the epics of Homer, is one of the basic poems in the culture of Europe and is taken as a standard for what was, perhaps until 19th C, regarded as the noblest form of literature.

Not even Homer exceeds Virgil in the extent of his influence and prestige in the 20 centuries of European culture. He did not, like all the Greek poets and many of the Roman ones, have to wait for the Renaissance* to 'discover' him, for he was esteemed in the Middle Ages*, when, indeed, he became a legend. This was partly owing to his *Fourth Eclogue* which celebrated the birth of a child who was to restore the Golden Age, a poem which in the Christian centuries was supposed to be a prophetic vision of the birth of Christ. He was thus regarded as more than merely a pagan poet, and Dante* chose him as his guide through Hell and Purgatory in his 13th-C Christian epic, the *Divine Comedy*. In direct literary influence, he was, even more than Theocritus, the pattern for pastoral* poetry, and even more than Homer, for the epic, although he was himself a student of both.

* *Translation*.

Virgin Queen

A name for Elizabeth I* of England, on account of the fact that she never married. The title enabled poets and other writers to associate her with Diana, the Roman goddess of chastity (* *Artemis*). The first English colony in America was called Virginia by Sir Walter Raleigh* in her honour.

Virtues, The

[1] In the Middle Ages, a name for one of the highest orders of Angel*. [2] In medieval philosophy, there were said to be three Theological Virtues of faith, hope and charity, and four Cardinal Virtues of justice, prudence, temperance and fortitude. The latter originate before the Middle Ages in Plato's *Republic**; the Church distinguished them from the Theological Virtues as natural, *ie* available to all men without the inspiration of revealed religion. The Scottish philosopher David Hume*, in 18th C, regarded none of these but the virtue of benevolence as the noblest virtue owing to its social value; the change is indicative of new attitudes to society since 18th C.

Vision of Judgement

A poem by Southey*, *A Vision of Judgement*, 1821, provoked a satirical reply by Byron*, *The Vision of Judgement*, 1822.

Vision of Piers Plowman, The

* *Piers Plowman*.

Volpone /volˈpəuni/

A comedy in blank verse* by Ben Jonson*; it was first acted in 1605 or 1606 and was printed in 1607, and is often considered Jonson's masterpiece. The names of the principal characters signify their roles in the comedy: Volpone = fox; his servant Mosca = fly, since he is a parasite who tries to take advantage of the vicious natures of everyone; the lawyer Voltore = vulture, Corbaccio = crow, and Corvino = raven, because all three birds feed on dead bodies, and all three men hope to gain from Volpone's will when he dies. Volpone is well aware of this, and pretends to be very ill in order to extract gifts from his so-called friends; Corvino, a jealous husband, is even prepared to sacrifice his wife, the pure-hearted Celia. Mosca tries to outdo his master by blackmailing Corvino, and this leads Voltore the lawyer to bring them both to judgement. A subplot concerns an absurd Englishman and his wife, Sir Politick and Lady Would-Be, who are on a visit to Venice (the scene of the play) and are satires on the contemporary English enthusiasm for financial speculation through fantastic 'projects'. The concentrated satire in the morality* tradition of the main plot rises to heights of great poetry: the play is not, as it first seems, a piece of savage cynicism, because the characters, especially Volpone, have a vivid zest for living which is morally condemned only because they carry it to the point of mania. The manias are what Jonson means by 'humours', and what Pope in *The Essay on Man** was to call 'the Ruling Passion'.

* *Humours, Comedy of*.

Voltaire (pseudonym of François Marie Arouet, 1694–1778) /ˈvolteə/

French writer. He wrote prolifically, and in his own day was regarded as above all a poet and a philosopher, but his international fame rests more on his prose work – satirical essays, and the ironical romance, *Candide* (1759). He is even better known as the pattern of humane intellectuals: he was the determined opponent of beliefs and institutions sanctified by tradition but really disguising the selfishness and inhumanity of privileged classes of society. His dictum 'Ecrasez l'Infâme' (Crush the Evil) is not, as it has often been thought to be, a slogan against religion as such, but against intolerance, superstition, and unjustified privileges supported by religious institutions. He stood for free thought and perfected a style of perfect lucidity which he combined with unique wit. He gained immense prestige all over Europe, and corresponded with Frederick II of Prussia and Catherine II of Russia. His nearest equivalent in English literature is perhaps Bernard Shaw*. *Candide* was published very near in date to *Rasselas* by Samuel Johnson, and Johnson himself remarked on the extraordinary similarity of their themes, although there was no direct exchange of ideas between the two men. In general, Voltaire had strong sympathies with English trends of thought, and his long visit to England (1726–29) was an important episode in his development. In his *Lettres sur les Anglais* he used his English experiences as a basis for his attack on the French establishment. Correspondingly, Voltaire was admired in England and his influence is pervasive in English 18th-C writing.

Vulcan

* *Hephaestus.*

Vulgate, The /'vʌlgit/

From the Latin 'vulgatus' = 'made public or common'. The name of St Jerome's Latin version of the Bible, completed in AD 405. For long it was the only authorized text for the Catholic Church. The Protestants* in 16th C insisted on extending Jerome's principle of making the Word of God common to all, by translating it into other languages, a principle now accepted by the Catholic Church itself.

* *Bible in England.*

W

Wain, John (b 1925)

Novelist, poet and critic. Prose fiction: *Hurry on Down* (1953); *Living in the Present* (1955); *The Contenders* (1958); *A Travelling Woman* (1959); *Nuncle and Other Stories* (1962); *The Young Visitors* (1965); *Death of the Hind Legs and Other Stories* (1966); *The Smaller Sky* (1967); *A Winter in the Hills* (1970); *The Life Guard* (1971). Verse: *A Word Carved on a Sill* (1956); *Weep Before God* (1961); *Wildtrack* (1965). Criticism: *Preliminary Essays* (1957); *Essays on Literature and Ideas* (1963); *The Living World of Shakespeare* (1964). His first novel showed him to be a leading member of the school of novelists who concern themselves with the changed surface and social texture of the post-war world. His novels are distinguished by unusual narrative force and economy, and his criticism by the clarity and forthrightness of his judgements.

Wakefield Plays

A cycle of medieval Mystery Plays*, probably dating from early 15th C. They are often called 'the Towneley Plays', because the texts were the property of a family of that name. The cycle consists of 32 plays, thought to have been performed by the guilds of the wool town of Wakefield in Yorkshire. All Mystery Plays are anonymous in authorship, and the various cycles seem to have borrowed individual plays from each other; some of the Wakefield plays, for instance, seem to be based on plays in the York Cycle. Sometimes, however, a master hand is evident; there is for instance a Wakefield Master. Five or six of the plays are attributed directly to him, and he probably undertook revision of the whole series. The plays thought to be entirely by his hand are written in 9-line stanzas, and of these the two Shepherds' Plays are outstanding. The second of these includes the comic episode of the exposure of Mak, the sheep stealer, and it has sometimes been called the first English comedy. The episode has nothing to do with the play's Christian theme, the visit of the shepherds to the infant Jesus (*Luke* 2), and seems at first to be a topical interpolation made for its own sake. However, there is reason to think that the episode represents a survival of a seasonal drama of pre-Christian origins. Mak conceals the stolen sheep in a cradle and he and his wife pretend to the intruding shepherds that it is their baby; when the shepherds look closely, however, they see that it has horns, and that the child is indeed a dead sheep. According to John Speirs (see 'The Towneley Shepherds' Plays' in *Pelican Guide – Age of Chaucer*) the dead sheep represents the pagan 'horned god', still secretly worshipped in medieval England as the fertility god who seasonally restores the cycle of birth and death. The shepherds proceed to Christ's cradle, so that the mock nativity is succeeded by the real one – an example of paganism and Christianity side by side in the medieval mind, and an explanation of why the medieval Church looked on the Mystery Plays in general with some mistrust. These plays are for us of far more than merely scholarly interest; they are amongst the first examples of living dramatic art.

* 5.1.1.2.

Walbrook /'wo:lbruk/

A street in the City of London which follows part of the course of a stream of the same name. St Stephen's Walbrook is one of the finest of the smaller churches by Christopher Wren*.

Wales

A mountainous country to the west of England; it

has been united to England politically since 1536, but it has preserved a national individuality and its native Celtic language, though this is now spoken by only about 30% of its 2½ million population. The geography of the country has always been a hindrance to its unity, and before the English conquest it tended to divide into separate northern and southern regions. Just before the Norman Conquest* of England (1066), however, a Welsh prince succeeded in uniting the country briefly, and Wales in consequence seemed formidable enough for the first Norman king of England, William I*, to establish three strong earldoms for the defence of England along the Welsh frontier; these earldoms correspond to the modern English counties of Hereford, Shropshire and Cheshire, long known as 'the Marches'.

After his conquest of Wales, Edward I* in 1301 gave his eldest son the title of Prince of Wales, as English monarchs have done ever since. However, until 16th C they did very little else to govern Wales. The Welsh were twice influential in English history: once they rebelled with considerable success under Owen Glendower* against Henry IV* (see Shakespeare's play *1 Henry IV*), and again it was a mainly Welsh army that won the Battle of Bosworth (1485) and thus established on the English throne a dynasty of Welsh descent, the Tudors*. The second king of this dynasty, Henry VIII*, passed an Act of Union in 1536 which united Wales administratively with England. Since then, the most notable differences between the two countries have been in language and religion.

The Reformation* made slower headway in Wales than in England, but it was effectively established by the end of 16th C. In 18th and 19th C, Methodism* became very strong in Wales, to the extent that the Church of England was disestablished (*ie* it ceased to be the state Church) by a law passed in 1914. The Welsh Nonconformist churches are thus not 'nonconforming' in the English sense; the country is divided among a number of religious denominations (of which Anglicanism is only one) none of which have any official pre-eminence over the others. The Methodist churches in particular have done much to keep the Welsh language alive and vital. Education is conducted in the Welsh language in state schools up to the age of 11 in those regions where the parents are predominantly Welsh-speaking, and the yearly cultural festival of the National Eisteddfod* exists to keep the literature alive and healthy; it is the main focus of Welsh nationalism. The chief opponent of this nationalism is not the English, but industrialism; the main industrial regions are in the south-east, around the capital city of Cardiff, and in the south around the port of Swansea; the main industry is that of the South Wales coal-mines. Where there are large towns and urban ways of life, the essentially rural and peasant characteristics of Welsh life tend to yield to anglicization.

Whereas, since 1350, the principal output of literature in Scotland and Ireland has been in English though with Scottish and Irish national colouring, Welsh literature has chiefly been in the native Welsh language. It is thus scarcely possible to say that English literature has been distinctively modified by the literature of Wales, as this can be said in speaking of the literatures of Scotland and Ireland. Occasionally a writer arises with a distinctively Welsh personality, and this is true of two 20th-C poets, though they are of very different character; Dylan Thomas*, and R. S. Thomas (b 1913). Nor is it common for an English writer to learn Welsh so as to receive influence from Welsh literature, though this is to some extent true of G. M. Hopkins*; unfortunately the strength of that literature is especially its poetry, and poetry is never fully translatable. Its best period was the Middle Ages. The majority of Arthurian legend (* *Arthur*) as we know it is of French, not Welsh, creation, but the oldest parts of it have their roots in Welsh myth, *eg* the figure of Gawain*.

Wall Street

In New York; the financial centre of the city.

Wallace, William Sir (1270?–1305) /ˈwolis/

A Scottish national hero of the Scottish War of Independence (1296–1328). He cleared most of the country of the English and then gained a major victory over them at the Battle of Stirling (1297), but he was defeated by Edward I* at Falkirk in 1298. Taken prisoner in 1305, he was brought to trial by the English as a traitor; he replied to this charge that he owed no allegiance to the English king, and therefore could not be a traitor to him. He was beheaded. Wallace was one of the first patriots in the modern sense in British history; he received comparatively little help from the Scottish nobility, who wanted to stand well with Edward. He is the subject of a long, not very interesting poem by Henry the Minstrel ('Blind Harry') written about 1461.

* *Scotland.*

Waller, Edmund (1606–87) /ˈwolə/

Poet. He belonged to the landed gentry, and spent much of his life as a Member of Parliament. During the Civil War* he became a Royalist, but in 1651 he made his peace with Cromwell*, and wrote a 'Panegyrick' to him. After the Restoration*, he wrote another to Charles II*. When the king asked him why the second was not so good as the first, he replied, 'Sir, we poets never succeed so well in writing truth as in fiction.' His first book of poems came out in 1645; one of his most famous lyrics, 'Go, lovely Rose' was printed in 1655. He was famous for the smoothness and musicality of his songs, and for his use of the 10-syllable rhyming couplet*, later perfected by Dryden* and Pope*. Dryden admired him for the simplicity of his syntax and the ease of his rhythms, and historically he is thought of as a transitional poet who substitutes for the imaginative paradoxes of the earlier part of the century the limpidity, clarity and shapeliness of the later part, though he is less interesting in this respect than his contemporary, Cowley*. A hundred years later, Johnson* wrote of him: 'The general character of his poetry is elegance and gaiety.'

* *Metaphysicals.*

Bib: Johnson, S., in *Lives of the Poets*; Bateson, F. W., in *English Poetry: a Critical Introduction*; critical study by Allison, A. W.

Walpole, Horace (1717–97) /ˈwɔːlpəul/

Letter writer, antiquarian, connoisseur. He was son of the powerful statesman, Robert Walpole*, and for a short time followed a political career, but he abandoned it, though he continued his interest in politics. His father's influence procured for him three sinecures (*ie* posts under the government which carried salaries though they required very little work) and these enabled him to pass his life as an assiduous spectator and man of pleasure. In an eminently classical age, he developed a strong taste for the Gothic style in all its forms, converting his house (Strawberry Hill, Twickenham, where he settled in 1747) into what he called 'a little Gothic castle', and writing the first of the Gothic novels*, *The Castle of Otranto** (1764). He is chiefly famous for his letters, however, and is regarded as one of the best correspondents in the best period of letter-writing*. Their main quality is their liveliness, humour, and vividness of observation.

Bib: Lives by Ketton-Cremer and Lewis, W. S.; Stephen, L., in *Hours in a Library*.

Walpole, Sir Robert (1676–1745)

Statesman. He is sometimes called 'the first Prime Minister', meaning that he was the first statesman to hold chief power in the state and at the same time to base this power on the House of Commons*. His practice of consulting his ministers in a private office or 'cabinet' and of insisting that they should comply with his policies or resign their posts has also caused him to be credited with the invention of the Cabinet system of government. In both, he is a figure of importance in the history of the development of the British constitution. He held power continuously from 1721 to 1742, and was enabled to do so partly by his financial ability (he came to office at the time of the South Sea Bubble* crisis), and partly by the incapacity of the German-born kings, George I (1714–27) and George II (1727–1760), to manage English politics.

Walton, Izaak (1593–1683) /ˈwɔːltən/

Biographer, and author of *The Compleat Angler** (1653). He is the first true biographer in English; previous biographies, such as More's* *Richard III* (1513) and Bacon's* *Henry VII* (1622) had been works of history, whereas Walton's lives of the poets Donne* and George Herbert* and of Wotton, Hooker* and Sanderson are true portraits of people in the modern biographical sense. He is best known, however, for his book on fishing, the first of the English sporting classics.

* *Biography.*

Wandering Jew, The

An old legend, first found in England in 13th-C chronicles by Matthew Paris. The story is that a Jew, following Christ when he was bearing his cross to the place of crucifixion, struck him and cried, 'Go faster, Jesus; why dost thou linger?' whereupon Christ replied, 'I indeed am going, but thou shalt tarry till I come.' The Jew thereafter was condemned to wander the earth, waiting for the Second Coming of Christ.

War Poets

A group of poets who served in the army in World War I, and made poetry out of the experience. The three who are most commonly thought of as 'War poets' are Wilfred Owen*, Siegfried Sassoon (1886–1967) and Isaac Rosenberg*. Rupert Brooke*, who wrote with feeling about the outbreak of war, died before he saw much action; his poetry does not in consequence reflect the shock and violence so evident in the other three. Edward Thomas* was killed in action, but little of his poetry is about the war. Edmund Blunden* and Robert Graves* both survived to write memorable prose works about the war, but their poetry was only indirectly affected by it.

The effect of the war on the verse of Owen, Sassoon and Rosenberg was to cause them to turn away from the rather tepid romanticism of much pre-war poetry, and to adapt their language to the new and terrible experiences. They thus played a significant part in the renewal of poetic language.

Wars of the Roses, The

A name for the civil wars that were waged intermittently between the two branches of the Plantagenet* family, the House of Lancaster* and the House of York, between 1455 and 1485. The name derives from the emblems chosen by either side: the Lancastrians chose the red rose, and the Yorkists chose the white. The Tudor* rose was a red and white emblem, to signify the reconciliation of the two sides by the marriage of Henry Tudor on the Lancastrian side (Henry VII*) with Elizabeth of York, daughter of Edward IV*.

The immediate causes of the war were dynastic; the underlying ones were social. Richard II*, the last Plantagenet king by direct succession, died without heirs, having lost his throne by usurpation to Henry IV*, his cousin and the first king of the Lancastrian line, so called because Henry was the son of John Duke of Lancaster (John of Gaunt*).

There was always some doubt whether the descendants of another of Richard's uncles, Edmund Duke of York, had not a better claim to the throne, and the disagreement broke into open war in 1455 owing to the drop in Lancastrian prestige when England was at last defeated in the Hundred Years' War* against France (1453). It is here that the social causes become important. In the first place, power in England was in the hands of a number of rich, self-interested and ambitious nobles, whose energies were now no longer taken up by the wars in France. They sought new outlets for their ambition by an attempt to dominate the government at home. Secondly, the ending of the French wars let loose upon England a mass of unemployed soldiers who urgently needed occupation. The interests of the majority of the common people were not deeply engaged, though the towns were disposed to be Yorkist and the rural areas to be Lancastrian. Consequently the Wars of the Roses were felt to be a profitless evil by the majority of the nation. A deep dislike of the profession of common soldier, which lasted till the early years of this century, was instilled into the people, and the reign of Elizabeth I* was haunted by the fear that civil wars might recur because the queen (like Richard II) had no direct heirs.

The House of Tudor was correspondingly revered because it brought the wars to an end. An important social consequence was that the great medieval nobility which was responsible for their outbreak was much weakened and discredited at the end of them. The Tudor sovereigns raised up their nobility from men of lesser family, from whom the aristocratic families of modern England, *eg* the Cecils and the Russells, commonly descended.

Shakespeare used the Wars of the Roses as the material for his first tetralogy of historical dramas, the three plays on Henry VI* and one on Richard III*. The first three are national tragedies of mounting conflict and destructive hatred; the last shows the evil which has afflicted the country concentrated in one king of diabolic proportions, with Henry Tudor presented in religious terms as the saviour of the people at the conclusion.

* *Tudor Myth.*

Warbeck, Perkin (1474–99)

The son of a poor citizen of Tournai in Flanders, he pretended to be Richard, Duke of York, one of Edward IV's two sons whom Richard III* had imprisoned in the Tower of London, and whose fate was unknown. He was supported by a number of enemies of Henry VII*, including Charles VIII of France and James IV of Scotland. Eventually he landed in the west of England in 1497, but was soon captured by Henry's troops and hanged. The dramatist John Ford* wrote a moving play about him, *Perkin Warbeck* (1634).

* *Princes in the Tower.*

Ward, Mrs Humphry (Mary Augusta) (1851–1920)

Novelist. Her father, Thomas Arnold, showed the religious restlessness characteristic of so many Victorian intellectuals, and, specifically, of his brother, the critic and poet Matthew Arnold*. Her own most famous novel, *Robert Elsmere* (1888), was a study of religious conflict. Elsmere is a clergyman who loses his faith through a study of the 'higher criticism' of Bible texts. (The novelist George Eliot* lost her faith in Christianity by the same influence). The purport of the book is that the revitalization of Christianity required more attention to the social obligations of the Church, and the abandonment of its supernatural—or at least its miraculous—constituents of belief. The book was very widely read in Britain and America, partly in consequence of a review of it in the *Nineteenth Century* by the statesman, W. E. Gladstone. In accordance with the ideas expressed in the novel, Mrs Ward was a very active philanthropist. She was also an active opponent of the Women's Suffrage Movement (the 'Suffragettes'*). She wrote a number of other novels, and translated Amiel's *Journal Intime* into English.

Warden, The (1855)

A novel by Anthony Trollope*. It was the first of his novels to be a success with the public, and the first of his Barsetshire* series.

The theme of the novel is the two aspects of the problem of the reform of public abuses. It shows how an office which brings to its holder an income much in excess of his duties may nonetheless be conducted usefully and with integrity, so that to abolish the office may be an act of personal injustice although the abolition may be justifiable on public grounds.

The novel is set in the cathedral city of Barchester in Barsetshire. A clergyman, the Reverend Septimus Harding, is Warden of Hiram's Hospital a long-established charitable institution for maintaining 12 poor old men in comfort. For this he draws an income which in the course of time has increased to £800 a year, although his actual duties are almost non-existent. However, he maintains with the old men affectionate relationships which are inestimable financially. The wardenship is attacked as a public abuse by John Bold, a Barchester surgeon, although Bold is in love with Harding's daughter Eleanor. Bold is opposed (on the wrong grounds) by the worldly churchman Archdeacon Grantly, who is Harding's son-in-law. Harding resigns his office as a matter of conscience, but the Bishop refuses to appoint a new Warden, and the old men of the Hospital lose in Dr Harding's relationships with them what in fact was the chief solace of their old age.

Wardour Street /ˈwɔːdə/

A street in London, formerly taken up by dealers in antique and imitation antique furniture. From this arose the expression 'Wardour Street English', for the diction of some historical novelists when they try to imitate the language of the past, and thus produce a kind of linguistic equivalent of imitation antique furniture. The street is nowadays associated with the film industry.

Washington, George (1732–99)

Leader of the American rebel forces in the War of

Independence (1775–83); president of the American convention, 1787; first President of the United States, 1789. He served in the British forces during the wars against the French and Indians in the 1750s and was a rich and efficient tobacco planter, but he did not play a leading part in American politics until relationships with Britain became critical in the 1770s. He was however noted as 'a young man of an extraordinary and exalted character'. Washington's great-grandfather had emigrated from Britain in 1657.

Waste Land, The (1922)

A poem by T. S. Eliot. It is 433 lines long, and is divided into five parts: I. *The Burial of the Dead*; II. *A Game of Chess*; III. *The Fire Sermon*; IV. *Death by Water*; V. *What the Thunder said.* There is no logical continuity between the parts, or within each part except for the very short Part IV. The lines vary in length and rhythm and are usually unrhymed, but the poem is not written in 'free verse'. The author contributed his own (often cryptic) explanatory notes.

The theme is the decay and fragmentation of Western culture, conceived in terms of the loss of natural fertility. Despite the absence of logical continuity, *The Waste Land* possesses artistic coherence brought about by four closely related methods.

[1] The use of symbols derived from two anthropologists: Jessie L. Weston (*From Ritual to Romance*) and James Frazer* (*The Golden Bough*). These books relate to ancient myths about the alternation of fertility and barrenness. Although study of them undoubtedly helps the reader to understand the poem, it is not entirely necessary; Eliot intended the symbols to be imaginatively convincing, by their own force, to a sufficiently responsive reader.

[2] The juxtaposition of passages with contrasting rhythms, diction, and imagery to accomplish 'a music of ideas . . . arranged not that they must tell us something, but that their effects in us may combine into a coherent whole of feeling and attitude' (I. A. Richards*. Compare Eliot in *Shakespeare and the Stoicism of Seneca*: 'The poet who "thinks" is merely the poet who can express the emotional equivalent of thought.')

[3] The use of past history in contrast to the present time, as a means of demonstrating the peculiarities of the present. This method is paralleled by James Joyce* in *Ulysses* and Ezra Pound* in his *Cantos.*

[4] The use of literary quotation and parody in order to bring out the contrasts of past and present states of culture. At least 35 writers are quoted or parodied in *The Waste Land.*

The poem caused great controversy when it was published, and is often considered to mark the effective beginning of a distinctively 20th-C kind of verse, although Eliot had already published verse in the new idiom with *The Love Song of J. Alfred Prufrock* (1915) and *Gerontion* (1920). *The Waste Land* is dedicated to Ezra Pound, and Eliot acknowledged that Pound's influence upon the writing of it was important; a recently rediscovered manuscript of it, with Pound's emendations, suggests that this influence may have been even greater than has hitherto been supposed.

* 6.4.1.

Water Babies, The (1863)

A moral fantasy for children, by Charles Kingsley*, subtitled *A Fairy Tale for a Landbaby.* The little boy Tom is employed as a chimney-sweep by the brutal Mr Grimes; he falls into the river, gets turned into a water baby and is carried down to the sea. He meets a number of fabulous creatures and undergoes ordeals which effect moral instruction. He emerges purified, on equal terms with Ellie, the little girl in whose house he once swept the chimneys. Grimes is sent away to a penance of sweeping out Etna. The book is partly an attack on the exploitation of child labour and on the brutalization of the poor, and partly a fable about their moral education. Some of the moralizing is offensive, socially and psychologically, to modern readers, but the book remains a children's classic for the sake of the ingenuity of its fantasy.

* *Child Labour*; *Children's Books.*

Waterloo, Battle of (1815)

An army of British, Dutch, Belgians and Germans under the Duke of Wellington* and the Prussian army under Blücher finally defeated a French army under Napoleon* and thus ended the Napoleonic War (1803–15). Waterloo is a village in Belgium to the south of Brussels. Wellington's army took up its position in squares, which the French attacked unavailingly all day, until Blücher's army came to Wellington's assistance. Wellington's own comment on the battle was that 'it was a damn near thing', and Napoleon's defeat is partly attributable to his failing health. He surrendered to the British and was exiled for the remainder of his life to the island of St Helena.

Watling Street

One of the great roads built by the Romans during their occupation of Britain (1st–5th C AD). It ran from Verulamium (modern St Albans) near London north-west to Viroconium (modern Wroxeter) near Shrewsbury. The road continued to be used by the Anglo-Saxons* after the Romans had departed, and the name is early English; a modern road follows nearly the same course. According to Chaucer* in his *House of Fame** (ii, 431) the name was also given to the configuration of stars otherwise called the Milky Way.

Watt, James (1736–1819)

Scottish engineer, inventor, and scientist. His outstanding achievement was the improvement of the steam engine, the principles of which (apart from ancient Greek experiments) had been discovered in 17th C. Newcomen's improvements on existing models in 1705 enabled it to be put to practical use, but it was Watt in 1763 who made it commercially successful and one of the main instruments of the Industrial Revolution*, the beginnings of which are sometimes dated from his time. Watt's engine made deep mining for coal possible when it was applied to pumping; it could be used for driving machines in factories, and it led in the 1820s to the invention of railway locomotives.

Watts, Isaac (1674–1748)

Hymn writer. He was a Puritan* (an Independent, *ie* Congregationalist*, clergyman) and in his best work he wrote with the eloquence and fervour of the best Metrical Psalms. Some of his hymns, *eg O God, our help in ages past* and *When I survey the wondrous Cross* are constantly sung in churches of different Protestant creeds, and are among the best known verses in the English language. His *Divine Songs for Children* (1715) also became a part of popular British culture, and influenced William Blake* in his *Songs of Innocence and Experience**.

* *Hymns; Psalms.*

Waugh, Evelyn (1903–66) /wo:/

Novelist. His early novels, *Decline and Fall* (1928), and *Vile Bodies* (1930), belong to the lively satire that was one of the characteristic features of the 1920s decade, but Waugh was considered by some to be too frivolously cynical and too mannered to be regarded as a serious satirist. World War II changed the character of his work; it became more explicitly Catholic, serious to the point of sombreness, and more three-dimensional in his portraval of his characters. The first novel to show these qualities was *Brideshead Revisited* (1945). In 1961 he completed his most considerable work, a trilogy about the war entitled *The Sword of Honour*. Among others of his novels that have achieved fame is *The Loved One* (1948), a satire on American commercialism, extending to the commercialization of death. All his work is marked by an exquisite sense of the ludicrous and a fine aptitude for exposing false attitudes. His comedy is closely dependent on the carefully calculated urbanity of his style.

Waugh also wrote travel books, selections from which have been collected under the title *When the Going Was Good* (1946), and biographies of the 19th-C poet and painter D. G. Rossetti*, and of the 16th-C Catholic martyr, Edmund Campion* (1935).

Bib: Bradbury, M., *Evelyn Waugh* (Writers and Critics Series); Hobson, C., *Evelyn Waugh* (British Council); Rutherford, A., on *The Sword of Honour* in *Imagined Worlds* ed. Maynard Mack and Ian Gregor.

Waverley (1814)

The first of Scott's* novels, subtitled *'Tis Sixty Years Since*. The hero, Edward Waverley, is a young English officer who visits the Highlands of Scotland just before the Jacobite* Rebellion of 1745. Here he falls in love with Flora, the Jacobite daughter of a Highland chieftain. He joins the Jacobite forces. When these are eventually defeated, Waverley is saved from execution by a senior English officer on the other side, whom he has saved in a battle. *Waverley* is the first historical novel of distinction in English literature, and Scott's vivid description of Scottish society and scenery caused it to be received with great enthusiasm.

* *Historical Fiction.*

Waves, The (1931)

A novel by Virginia Woolf*. It is the story of six characters, each of whom tells his own story in monologue, and reflects images of the others in his or her own mind. The monologues occur in groups, at different stages of their lives, and each group is preceded by a passage describing a time of day, from dawn to nightfall. *The Waves* is the climax of Virginia Woolf's experiments in fictional form.

Way of All Flesh, The

A novel by Samuel Butler*, written 1873–75, and published after his death, in 1903. It is one of the few purely satirical works of distinction of the Victorian* period; the satire is directed against the Victorian cult of the family as the sacred and blessed nucleus of society, and (as so often in Dickens*) the refuge from the harshness of the world. The arrogant, self-righteous, intolerant and stupid kind of Victorian parent is exemplified in the clergyman Theobald Pontifex, father of Ernest Pontifex. Victorian authoritarianism and repressiveness is also attacked in Theobald seen as a religious humbug, and in Dr Skinner, headmaster of the public school* that Ernest attends. The first 50 chapters of the book are autobiographical; Butler even includes actual letters in the text. The narrative is not told through Ernest (Butler as a boy), but in the first person through his friend the middle-aged Overton, who represents a more tolerant aspect of Butler; by this means, Butler conveys criticism of his intolerant younger self, in the person of Ernest.

* *Autobiography.*

Way of the World, The

A comedy by William Congreve*, produced in 1700. The plot is a complicated succession of intrigues which surround the love affair between the sparkling young rake, Mirabell (a hero in the tradition of Etherege's Dorimant in *The Man of Mode**), and the urbane and witty heroine, Millamant. Mirabell's aim is to trick or persuade Millamant's aunt, Lady Wishfort, into consenting to their marriage; and his efforts include pretending to make love to Lady Wishfort herself. This intrigue is frustrated by Mrs Marwood, embittered against Mirabell because he has previously rejected her. Mirabell then attempts further intrigue, and this leads to counter-intrigues by Mrs Marwood in alliance with Mirabell's treacherous friend Fainall, who combines them with conspiracies against his wife, a former mistress of Mirabell's, and blackmail of Lady Wishfort. Mirabell finally succeeds in defeating his enemies and saving Lady Wishfort from the threats against her; in gratitude, she consents to his marriage to Millamant. The intrigues serve as a framework for theatrically very successful comic scenes and imaginatively witty dialogue. The central relationship of Mirabell and Millamant stands out from the general tone of Restoration* comedy in rising clear of the heartlessness so usual to it, yet without losing wit and poise. Millamant's charm and independence have made her role a star part for great actresses, and supply a main reason for the play's reputation as the masterpiece of all Restoration Comedies.

* *Manners, Comedy of.*

Weak Ending

In blank verse* an unstressed syllable in the place of the normally stressed one at the end of a line; also, a word such as a conjunction or preposition which may bear metrical stress but cannot bear speech stress. An example is the conjunction 'and' in the following lines by Prospero (from Shakespeare's *The Tempest* IV. i):

Our revels now are ended. These our actors
As I foretold you, were all spirits, and
Are melted into air, into thin air.

In Shakespeare's later work he emphasized syntactical continuity in his speeches over the metrical rhythm of each line, so that weak endings become numerous. This is also characteristic of his younger contemporaries and successors, such as Fletcher*, Middleton*, Massinger*.

Wealth of Nations

* *Smith, Adam.*

Webb, Beatrice (1858–1943)

Sociologist. She was the daughter of Richard Potter, a railway director and friend of the philosopher, Herbert Spencer*, who exercised a guiding influence over her education. Her mother was a product of the 19th-C Utilitarian* school of thought. She early developed a strong social conscience, which led her to choose as her career the almost unprecedented one of 'social investigator'. Victorian sensitiveness to social abuses was strong amongst the intelligentsia, but she realized that constructive action was hampered by lack of exact information: 'The primary task is to observe and dissect facts.' In order to do so, she took bold steps for a Victorian girl of the prosperous middle class, such as disguising herself as a working girl and taking employment under a tailor in the East End of London. She and her husband were among the early members of the Fabian Society*, and among the founders of the Labour Party*. Her autobiographies* *My Apprenticeship* (1926) and *Our Partnership* (1948) are in the tradition of John Stuart Mill's* *Autobiography* (1873) in being essentially histories of the growth of opinions and ideas; *My Apprenticeship*, however, is very enlightening about social backgrounds in the 1880s, and a valuable addition to the Victorian novels, which, she said, were the only documents for the study of society available in her youth. She and her husband were among the founders of the weekly journal *New Statesman**, still the leading organ of the left-wing intelligentsia in Britain.

Webster, John (1580?–1625?)

Dramatist. The dates of his birth and death are very uncertain and little is known of his life. There are similar difficulties about what works can be ascribed to his sole authorship. *Devil's Law Case* (1619–20) is an undistinguished tragicomedy*; the other two ascribed confidently to him are among the best-known Jacobean* tragedies: *The White Devil** (1612) and *The Duchess of Malfi** (1613?).

* 5.1.3.2.

Wedgwood /ˈwedʒwud/

The name of a firm of distinguished manufacturers of china. The founder of the firm, Josiah Wedgwood (1730–95), was the son of a potter of Burslem. He perfected an English style of pottery called cream ware, and later Queen's ware. He then developed a new style of classical designs, inspired by contemporary interest in ancient Greek pottery and by the discovery of the Roman city of Pompeii in southern Italy. The most famous of the Wedgwood designers in this style was the friend of the poet William Blake*, John Flaxman. The Wedgwood factory near Hanley is called Etruria; the firm continues in production at the present day. Josiah's son, Thomas Wedgwood (1771–1805), was a generous patron to the poet Coleridge*.

The ceramics industry established by the Wedgwoods in Staffordshire is the basis of the industrial area known as the Five Towns*, and was to constitute the principal setting for the novels of Arnold Bennett*.

Welfare State

A term currently in use to describe the national system of social security brought into being by the Labour* government of 1945–50. The system depends on National Insurance payments which are obligatory for all adult members of the community apart from Old Age Pensioners and family dependants. In return for these payments, made weekly, the state grants financial assistance in the form of family allowances, payments made during sickness and unemployment and to maintain those who have been permanently incapacitated by injury, and pensions for the old. Medical attention is partly free and partly assisted. State education, from the nursery school level for children under five to university level, is also frequently assumed in the concept of the Welfare State.

The Welfare State is thus the opposite of the *laissez faire* concept of the state which prevailed in 19th C. According to the latter, the state was expected to allow society to develop freely according to 'natural' economic forces. Its function was merely to prevent interference with these in the shape of crime or insurrection. The *laissez faire* concept was never quite supreme; the state always assumed some responsibility for the very poor, for instance in the provision of workhouses*. Nevertheless, *laissez faire* ideas prevailed to the extent that the state was assumed to have no basic responsibility for the individual material welfare of its citizens. The opposite 'Welfare' concept of the state's duties arose partly from 19th-C religious thinking about society, and partly from the growth of socialist philosophies. The modern Welfare

State is generally considered to have had its beginnings under the Liberal* government of Campbell Bannerman and Asquith (1905–14); this introduced old-age pensions, some Unemployment and Health Insurance, and other measures.

* 1.5.4.

Wellington, Arthur Wellesley, 1st Duke of (1769–1852)

General and statesman. By origin, of Anglo-Irish aristocracy. He joined the army in 1787, and between 1796 and 1805 he had a distinguished military career in India, where his eldest brother was Governor-General. Arthur Wellesley then returned to Britain. Between 1808 and 1814 he gained fame for his resistance to the French armies of Napoleon* in the Spanish Peninsula. In 1815, with the Prussian general Blücher, he inflicted the final defeat on Napoleon at Waterloo*. He was created Duke in 1814.

He took part in the Congress of Vienna*, which made the peace treaty with France, and his influence did much to prevent the partition of the country. Thereafter, his career was in British politics, where he was one of the principal leaders of the Tory (Conservative) party. He gave way, however, over one issue, that of Catholic Emancipation (*ie* granting Catholics full political rights) because he understood its political inevitability; he was less clear-sighted about Parliamentary reform, and was forced to resign in 1830. He again held ministerial posts, though not that of Prime Minister, in 1834, and 1841–46, under the leadership of Robert Peel. After his death, Tennyson* commemorated him with one of his best poems, his *Ode on the Death of the Duke of Wellington*. He was popularly known as 'the Iron Duke', and used proudly to call his London mansion at Hyde Park Corner, 'Number One, London'.

Wells, Herbert George (1866–1946)

Novelist and journalist. He was brought up in the lower middle class, the son of a professional cricketer; in 1888 he took an excellent degree in science at London University. His social origins and his education explain much of his approach to life as a writer. The great novelist of the 19th-C lower middle classes is Dickens*, and some of H. G. Wells's best fiction is about the same field of society; novels such as *Kipps** (1905) and *The History of Mr Polly** (1910) are of this sort, and they have the kind of vigorous humour and sharp visualization that is characteristic of early Dickens. On the other hand, rising into the educated class at a time of rapid scientific and technical progress, he ignored the values of traditional culture and art, and became fascinated with the prospects that science offered, for good as well as for ill. This side of him produced a different kind of writing: Wells was one of the inventors of science fiction*, and possibly the best writer of it yet. *The Time Machine* (1895), *The Invisible Man* (1897), *The War of the Worlds* (1898) and *The First Men in the Moon* (1901) are examples of his fantasies. But his social experience and his interest in technology also drew him to writing fictional-sociological studies in which he surveyed and analysed, often with the same Dickensian humour, the society of his time; *Tono-Bungay* (1909) is perhaps the best of these. Other examples are *Ann Veronica* (1909) about the problems connected with newly emancipated women, *The New Machiavelli* (1911) about socialist thinking – Wells had joined the Fabians* in 1903 – and *Mr Britling Sees It Through* (1916) about World War I seen from the point of view of the 'Home Front'. But the interest in science also made him a utopian* optimist, and this point of view caused him to write such didactic works as *A Modern Utopia* (1905) and *New Worlds For Old* (1908). There was always a great deal of naivety in Wells's optimism, and later in his life he paid the penalty by reacting into excessive gloom, in *Mind at the End of its Tether* (1945). He declared that *The Open Conspiracy* (1928) contained the essence of his philosophy. He was never a deep thinker, however; his work lives by the vitality of his humour and by the urgency with which he pressed his ideas. This urgency necessarily made him a popularizer, and his most notable work of popularization was *The Outline of History* (1920).

In some ways Wells resembles his contemporary, the dramatist Bernard Shaw*; both were socialists, both felt the urgency to enlighten mankind as quickly as possible, and both cared more that their works should have immediate effect than that they should be works of art – Wells told the novelist Henry James* that he would rather be called a journalist than an artist. Possibly the most penetrating remark on Wells was that addressed to him by the novelist Joseph Conrad*: 'You don't really care for people, but you think they can be improved;. I do, but I know they can't.'

* 3.4.5; 4.5.2.

Bib: Critical studies by Bergonzi, B., (on the scientific romances) and Vallatin, A.; Belgion, M., *H. G. Wells*; Brome, V., in *Six Studies in Quarrelling*; Nicholson, N. C., *H. G. Wells*; Van Wyck Brooks, *The World of H. G. Wells*; Connes, G. A., *Etude sur la pensée de Wells*; Orwell, G., 'Wells, Hitler, and the World State' in *Critical Essays*.

Werewolf

According to an ancient superstition, a person capable of transforming himself into a wolf – sometimes into another animal, such as a hare, *eg* in Scotland. The superstition may have connection with a widespread belief that the corn-spirit sometimes embodied himself as a wolf. The superstition existed in England at least until 18th C.

Wesker, Arnold (b 1932)

Dramatist. Born in the East End of London, son of a Russian Jewish tailor. After military service, he became a professional pastry-cook, and then entered the London School of Film Technique. John Osborne's* *Look Back in Anger* (1956) influenced him to concentrate on the theatre. In 1961, he became Director of Centre Forty-two, intended to break down such barriers to popular appreciation of the arts as commercialism and intellectual and social snobbery, or social fragmentation due to restricted ways of life and inarticulacy in the shaping of goals. These obstacles to communication in the mass of society are the subject matter of his plays which are pervaded by a search for cordial understanding and sympathy. *Chicken Soup with Barley* (1959); *Roots* (1959); *The Kitchen* (1960); *I'm Talking about Jerusalem* (1960); *Chips with Everything* (1962); *The Four Seasons* (1966); *Their Very Own* and *Golden City* (1966); *The Friends* (1970).

Wesker has been one of the leaders of the post-war dramatic revival, together with John Osborne, Harold Pinter*, and John Arden*.

Bib: Taylor, J. R., *Anger and After*; Ribalow, H. U., *Arnold Wesker*; Leeming, Glenda, *Arnold Wesker* (Writers & their Work series).

Wesley, Charles (1707–88)

Hymn writer. He was the brother of the evangelist, John Wesley*, and the poet of the Wesleyan (Methodist*) movement. He wrote about 6,500 hymns of unequal merit; some of them are genuine poetry and very well known.

Wesley, John (1703–91)

Evangelist, and founder of the Methodist* religious movement. At Oxford, with his brother Charles, he became the centre of a society which regulated the lives of its members; this led to their being described as 'Methodists'. He was at first a strict Anglican*, conforming rigidly to Church of England liturgies and doctrines, but on a voyage to America in 1735 he became deeply impressed by the purity and undogmatic spirit of fellow-passengers belonging to the German sect known as the Moravians. On his return to England, Wesley preached up and down Britain. Both the Church of England and the Dissenters* who were heirs of the 17th-C Puritans* had by now relatively little to offer to the minds of the simple people; reaction against the violent conflicts of the previous century had caused the clergy of all denominations to obscure the sense of religion as a power in individual lives. Wesley taught both that every man was naturally a sinner, and that the power of God was available to all for spiritual salvation. In this he followed the Arminian tradition of religious belief, instead of the belief in Predestination* more prevalent among the 17th-C Puritans. Wesley's direct challenge to the hearts and the wills of his hearers caused deep psychological disturbances, and the Methodists were despised by many for the hysteria and emotionalism of their meetings. Nonetheless, the influence of Wesley was extensive and profound, and bore fruit in other religious revivals in 19th C. He was himself a highly cultivated man, courteous, and with a pleasant wit. When confronted by an arrogant opponent in a narrow street who declared 'I never make way for fools!', Wesley stood aside politely, replying: 'I always do.'

* *Sermons*.

Wessex

The kingdom of the West Saxons from 6th C till the reign of Alfred* at the end of 9th, after which it developed into the kingdom of England. The capital was the town of Winchester* in Hampshire, and the area also included Dorset, Somerset, Wiltshire, and Berkshire. The name of Wessex was revived by the novelist and poet Thomas Hardy* for his regional novels.

Westminster Abbey

Originally an abbey of monks on the bank of the Thames and to the west of the City of London. The abbey was dissolved by Henry VIII* in 1539, and the present building is the old abbey church. It was built by King Edward the Confessor* in 1065 and rebuilt by Henry III*, whose structure still stands. It has long been the state church of England; since William I* the sovereigns have been crowned in it, and many have been buried there. To be buried in Westminster Abbey is a national honour, and the church is in consequence lined with monuments. The Poets' Corner contains monuments to eminent writers, not all of whom are buried in the Abbey; they include Chaucer*, Spenser*, Shakespeare*, Ben Jonson* and Milton*.

Westminster School

Adjacent to Westminster Abbey; one of the most distinguished and most ancient of the great public schools*. It was originally maintained by the monks; after the dissolution of the abbey, Henry VIII* continued it, and Elizabeth I* re-founded it in 1560. Among the distinguished men educated there were the poets Ben Jonson*, John Dryden*, and William Cowper*; the historian Gibbon*; the philosophers Locke* and Bentham*, and the architect Wren*.

Westminster, The Palace of

Though it still officially bears this title, the building is more familiarly known as the Houses of Parliament*. It already existed as a palace under Edward the Confessor*. As such, it was the meeting-place of the House of Lords* and the House of Commons* in the Middle Ages. In 1512, the palace was damaged by fire and it has not been a royal residence since. In 1834, it was further and more seriously damaged, and all that now remains of the medieval palace is the great Hall built by William II in 1097 and reroofed by Richard II in 1399, and the crypt to the chapel of St Stephen's, under the present House of Commons. The rest of the present building dates 1840–67; it contains the two chambers of the House of Lords and the House of Commons. The latter was destroyed by a bomb during World War II, but it was afterwards reconstructed identically in every detail.

Westminster Hall has been the scene of many famous state trials including those of the Scottish patriot William Wallace*; the kings Richard II* and Charles I*; the Catholic martyrs Sir Thomas More* and Edmund Campion*; George IV's queen Caroline (1820), and the Governor-General of India, Warren Hastings, (1788–95).

What Maisie Knew (1897)

A novel by Henry James*. Its theme is the survival of innocence in a world of adult corruption, the influence of adults on a child, and her influence on them.

Maisie Farange is a small girl whose parents have divorced each other with equal guilt on both sides. The parents are heartless and indifferent to their daughter, except as a weapon against each other and in their farcical though not wholly vain struggles to maintain acceptable social appearances. Maisie is passed from one to the other, and each employs a governess to take responsibility for her welfare. Both parents marry again, and eventually relinquish Maisie herself. By the end of the book Maisie finds herself torn between two prospective 'step-parents', each formerly married to her real parents, divorced from them, and about to marry each other, Maisie herself having been the occasion of their coming together. Her 'stepfather', Sir Claude, is charming and sweet-natured, but weak and self-indulgent; her 'stepmother', Mrs Beale, is genuinely fond of Maisie (as Sir Claude is) but is basically selfish and rapacious. In addition, the child has a simple-minded, plain and elderly governess, Mrs Wix, who is herself in love with Sir Claude, and devoted to Maisie. The affection of none of them, however, is single-minded, as hers is for each one of them. The pathos of the novel arises from the warm responsiveness, deep need, and pure integrity of Maisie, from whose point of view all the events are seen. Its irony arises from the way in which the child's need for and dependence on adult care and love is transformed into responsibility for the adults themselves, who become dependent on her decisions. In the end these decisions lead her to choose life alone with Mrs Wix, who naively hopes to imbue her with a 'moral sense', unaware that beside Maisie's innocence her own idea of a moral sense represents modified corruption.

The novel is written in James's late, compressed and dramatic style, and is one of his masterpieces.

Whig and Tory /wig – 'to:ri/

Political terms distinguishing the two parties which were the forebears of the present Liberal and Conservative parties respectively. They were originally terms of abuse, provoked by the attempt of Lord Shaftesbury* in 1679 to exclude James Duke of York (later James II*) from succession to the throne because he was a Catholic. Shaftesbury and his party were called Whigs because their preference for the Protestant* religion over the law of hereditary succession caused their opponents to liken them to the Scottish Presbyterian* rebels of the time – called derisively 'whigs' from the nickname given to Scottish drovers. They retaliated by calling the supporters of James, 'tories', from the Irish term for robbers, implying that they no more cared about safeguarding the Protestant religion than did the Irish Catholic rebels. The Exclusion question was settled in favour of James, but not for long, since the Tories did in fact care greatly about the maintenance of the Church of England*, and when James II was clearly seen to be acting in Catholic interests, the Tories united with the Whigs in deposing him in 1688.

The political terms remained because, though not very consistently, the parties remained; and the parties survived because they represented distinct social interests in the country, though also not very consistently. The Whigs were especially the party of the landed aristocracy, who cared less for the institutions of the Crown and the Church of England than for their own power; since this was allied to the commercial interests of the country, they tended to gain support from the merchants of the towns, many of whom were Dissenters* opposed to the Church of England. The principal Tory support came from the smaller landed gentry, or squirearchy, whose interests were conservative, and whose fortunes seemed best protected by introducing as little change in the established institutions, whether of Church or of State, as possible. In the major crises the Tories were generally defeated, but they had extraordinary survival capacity by virtue of their willingness to accept changes once they had become inevitable. Their first major defeat was in 1714 when the Tory party was split between Bolingbroke's* anti-Hanoverian faction and those loyal to the 1701 Act of Settlement by which the throne went to the House of Hanover and not to Anne's Catholic half-brother.

Whigs were then supreme for forty years (though they disintegrated into rival groups), until after the accession of George III in 1760. George tried then to revive the power of the throne by securing supporters for his policies in Parliament; these supporters were known as 'the King's Friends' or 'New Tories'. This policy was also defeated, however, by their loss of prestige as a result of the victory of the American rebels in the War of American Independence (1775–83). The country was not then in a mood to see the return of the restless and corrupt Whigs, and Tory governments continued in power until 1832.

About 1830 the names Liberal and Conservative began to replace Whig and Tory in popular use, and these terms were officially adopted some 30 years later. 'Tory' survives, to some extent, as interchangeable with Conservative (it is shorter for newspaper headlines), but 'Whig' has been altogether superseded.

* 1.3.3.

Whistler, James Abbot McNeill (1834-1903)

American painter, who settled in England in 1863. He was influenced by Japanese colour prints, and made known his contempt for the very literary kind of painting that prevailed in England. His paintings grew in public favour as the taste for the French Impressionists grew. He was a witty and vigorous controversialist and a famous episode in his career was his verbal duel with the great art critic, John Ruskin*. In *Fors Clavigera* (1877) Ruskin wrote that one of Whistler's pictures was no better than 'a pot of paint thrown in the public face'. Whistler brought a libel action against Ruskin, for which he was awarded only a farthing damages. In 1890 he published *The Gentle Art of Making Enemies* in which he deals with the subject of his trial as well as attacking others of his critics.

Whistler was an important figure in the Aesthetic Movement*.

Whit-Sunday

The religious festival* of Pentecost, commemorating the descent of the Holy Ghost upon Christ's disciples – in the Bible, *Acts* 2. Whit = white, perhaps from the white garments of those who underwent baptism on the night before. Whit-Sunday occurs on the 7th Sunday after Easter*. Pentecost was originally a Jewish feast, when thanks were given for the first fruits of the earth, after the return of spring; the Christian feast shows thanks for the first fruits of the spirit, after the ascent of Christ to Heaven.

White, Gilbert (1720–93)

Writer on natural history. He was born at Selborne, a village in Hampshire. After spending some years as a Fellow of Oriel College, Oxford, he became a country curate, and spent the last nine years of his life in the village of his birth. His *Natural History of Selborne* (1789) is a record of the plant, animal, and bird life there, inspired by genuine scientific curiosity and showing great delicacy and charm of expression. The book has been described as the first to raise natural history to the level of literature, and is the fruit of the development of 17th- and 18th-C natural science, partly initiated by the greatest of English naturalists, John Ray (1627–1705), author of *The Wisdom of God Manifested in the Works of his Creation* (1691), a scientist who shared Newton's* intellectual curiosity and his religious awe at the spectacle of divine organization in the universe. Another tradition leading to White was the newly awakened sensibility for natural surroundings in the poetry of William Collins*, Goldsmith* and Cowper*. The poetic movement culminated in 19th C in the work of Wordsworth* and Clare*.

Bib: Holt-White, R., *Life and Letters*.

White, William Hale (1831–1913) (pseudonym: Mark Rutherford)

Novelist. His father was a Dissenter*, and intended his son to be a Dissenting clergyman. However, he could not reconcile his ideas and the religious doctrines that he was required to believe, and instead he had a civil service career in the Admiralty. His three famous novels were *The Autobiography of Mark Rutherford* (1881), *Mark Rutherford's Deliverance* (1885), and *The Revolution in Tanner's Lane* (1887). The first two are autobiographical and concerned with loss of faith. White makes Rutherford more outwardly unfortunate than he was himself, since he had a successful career both as a writer and as a civil servant; the reason seems to be that he makes his character represent not only his own loss of Christian faith but the sense of impoverishment that accompanied it. In his study of John Bunyan* (1905), he makes the statement: 'Religion is dead when imagination deserts it.' White's own questioning of his belief started from reading Wordsworth in *Lyrical Ballads** (1798–1800) and the subsequent feeling that nature stirred him as 'the God of the Church' could not. As studies of spiritual loss and contention with it, the Mark Rutherford novels have wide human relevance. The third novel is concerned with radical movements in early 19th C, and shows White's political intelligence which comes out directly in his pamphlet on the political franchise. His other novels are *Miriam's Schooling* (1890), *Catherine Furze* (1893), and *Clara Hopgood* (1896). Other works: *Pages from a Journal* and *More Pages from a Journal* (1900 and 1910); *Last Pages* (1915).

* *Agnosticism*.

Bib: Lives by Maclean, C. M. and Stone, W.; Stock, I., *William Hale White*.

White Devil, The

A tragedy* by John Webster*, published in 1612 with the subtitle *Vittoria Corrombona*, written in 1608–9. It is based on the story of the actual murder of Vittoria Accoromboni (1585) as told in William Painter's *Palace of Pleasure**. Vittoria is the wife of Camillo. The Duke of Brachiano, husband to Isabella, the sister of the Duke of Florence and of Cardinal Montecelso, falls in love with her and is assisted in winning her by her brother, Flamineo. Flamineo causes the death of Camillo, and Brachiano poisons his own wife. In Act III, Vittoria faces trial before Cardinal Montecelso for adultery and murder; she is proudly defiant, and condemned to confinement in a convent, where Brachiano continues to visit her, and whence he eventually steals her away and marries her. In Act V, Flamineo kills his brother, Marcello, who is upbraiding him for his wickedness, and their mother sings over her dead son the lovely dirge 'Call for the robin redbreast and the wren'. Florence's hireling, Lodovico, avenges the death of Isabella by killing Flamineo and Vittoria. 'My soul, like to a ship in a black storm, is driven, I know not whither.' The spirit of the stormy play is expressed by this line spoken by the dying Vittoria; it contains many passages of intense poetry, no virtuous characters among the outstanding ones, and a number of fine theatrical episodes which are difficult to perform because they are long drawn out. The unifying tone is of desperation produced by destructive and self-destroying passions.

White Friars

The Carmelites, an order founded in early 13th C. They were called White Friars in England because they wore a white mantle over a brown habit. Their convent in Fleet Street, London, caused the district to be known by their name.

* *Friars*.

White's Club

One of the important men's clubs in London. It arose out of White's Chocolate House (1698) and was originally the headquarters of the Tory party, but is now non-political.

* *Clubs*; *Whig and Tory*.

Whitechapel /ˈwaittʃapl/

A poor district in the East End of London. It has a

large Jewish population, and a celebrated art gallery.

Whitehall

A street in London that runs between Trafalgar Square and Parliament Square. It is mainly occupied by the buildings of government ministries, so that 'Whitehall' is often used as a term for the state bureaucracy. The name derives from the royal palace that formerly stood there, of which only Inigo Jones's* Banqueting Hall (erected under James I*) now remains. Until the fall of Cardinal Wolsey* (1530) it was called York Place, since he built the palace when he was Archbishop of York:

1ST GENTLEMAN: *Sir,*
You must no more call it York-place, that's past;
For, since the cardinal fell, that title's lost:
'Tis now the king's, and call'd Whitehall.

(*Henry VIII* IV. i. 94)

It was outside the Banqueting Hall that Charles I* was executed in 1649.

Whittington, Richard (d 1423) /ˈwitiŋtən/

A rich and famous Lord Mayor of London in 1397–98, 1406–7, and 1419–20. He made substantial loans of money to the kings Henry IV* and Henry V*, and used his wealth for public works, including a legacy for improving Newgate* Prison. His almshouses for the poor are still maintained. According to popular legend, he was originally a poor orphan and became the ill-treated servant of a rich merchant. He ran away from London, with his cat, until he heard Bow bells* calling him back:

Turn again, Dick Whittington,
Lord Mayor of London.

The legend is a popular subject of Christmas pantomimes*, in which the cat plays a principal part.

Who's Who

An annual biographical dictionary of eminent contemporary men and women. First published in 1849.

Wife of Bath's Prologue and Tale, The

In Chaucer's *Canterbury Tales**. The wife, Alisoun, describes her long experience of married life comprising five husbands: 'As three of hem were gode and two were badde'. The first three good ones were 'riche, and olde'; the two bad ones were young, when she herself was ageing. Her experience begins in fact like that of other women in the Tales (*eg The Miller's Tale**, *The Merchant's Tale**): she is married off to a rich husband, whom her parents would consider a good match because of the wealth he had accumulated during a long life, while she herself is a young girl. Her problem has always been to keep mastery over the husband; this she managed easily with the good, old husbands, but has naturally found more difficult with the lively young ones, who must have married her for the wealth she inherited from the first three. Thus her life has grown progressively more difficult and bitter, though she has enjoyed all of it; she has only just managed to defeat her fifth husband who partly destroyed her hearing by a blow on the ear. Her Tale is in a different style though on the same theme as her (much longer) Prologue. It is a romance, similar to that of Florent in Gower's *Confessio Amantis**, but the setting is the court of King Arthur*. To escape execution, a knight must find the answer to the question: What do women love most? He seeks the answer everywhere and at last obtains it from a foul old hag on condition that he will grant her desire. With the answer, which is 'Sovereignty', he gains his pardon from execution, and is then faced with the demand from the old woman that he marry her. On the marriage night he promises his bride freedom of choice, upon which she is immediately transformed into a beautiful young wife who moreover promises to be faithful to him. The contrast with the Prologue is typical of the medieval difference between the Fabliau* and the Romance*: the former is about real life, and often comic and brutal; the latter is a fiction of life as it is wished, not as it is.

Wilberforce, William (1759–1833) /ˈwilbəfoːş/

Philanthropist and politician. He devoted much of his life to the campaign to abolish the slave trade and slavery in overseas British territories. In 1807, the slave trade was made illegal, and so was slavery itself in the year of his death. He was leader of the Evangelical* movement, particularly of a group known as the Clapham Sect because it met in his house at Clapham.

Wilde, Oscar Fingal O'Flaherty Wills (1856–1900) /ˈoskə ˈwaild/

Dramatist, poet, novelist and essayist. He was the son of an eminent Irish surgeon and a literary mother. At Oxford University his style of life became notorious; he was a disciple of Pater*, the Oxford father of aestheticism*, and he carried the doctrine as far as to conduct his life as an aesthetic display – a direct challenge to the prevailing outlook of the society of his time, which was inclined to regard art with suspicion or disdain. In 1888 Oscar Wilde produced a volume of children's fairy tales very much in the melancholy and poetic style of the Danish writer Hans Christian Andersen* – *The Happy Prince*. He followed this with two other volumes of stories, and then the novel, *The Picture of Dorian Gray* (1891), whose hero is an embodiment of the aesthetic way of life. More durable in reputation than these were his comedies, *Lady Windermere's Fan* (1892), *A Woman of No Importance* (1893), *An Ideal Husband* (1895), and above all the witty *Importance of Being Earnest* (1895). The plays are apparently light-hearted, but they contain strong elements of serious feeling in their attack on a society whose code is intolerant, but whose intolerance is hypocritical. In 1895, by a libel action against the Marquis of Queensberry, he exposed himself to a countercharge of immoral homosexual conduct, and spent two years in prison. In 1898 he published his *Ballad of Reading Gaol* about his prison experiences, proving that he could write in the direct language of the ballad* tradition, as well as in the artificial style of his *Collected Poems* (1892). His *De Profundis* (1905) is an eloquent statement of his grief after his downfall, but modern critics are more impressed by the intelligence of his social essays, such as *The Critic as Artist* and *The Soul of Man under Socialism*. The paradox of Wilde is that, while for his contemporaries he represented degeneracy and weakness (and for later readers such decadence is only too evident in much of his aesthetic writing) there is nonetheless plenty of evidence that he was a brave man of remarkable strength of character who made an emphatic protest against the vulgarity of his age and yet, artistically, was himself subject to vulgarity of an opposite kind.

* 5.3.1.

Bib: Critical studies by Roditi, E., Ransome, A.; Lives by Lemmonier, L.; Ervine, St. J.; Pearson, H.; Bentley, E. R., in *The Playwright as Thinker*; Beckson, K., (ed) *The Critical Heritage*.

Wilkes, John (1727–97)

Journalist and politician. He was dissolute, and notorious for his membership of the scandalous Hell-Fire Club at Medmenham Abbey, with its motto 'Fay ce que voudras' = 'Do as you will'. Politically he was radical and courageous, and a popular hero. In 1762 he attacked George III's administration under Lord Bute in *The North Briton*, a periodical which countered *The Briton* edited by the novelist, Tobias Smollett*. As an M.P., he was twice expelled from the House of Commons for libel, and in 1769 he was three times elected to Parliament by the county of Middlesex, the election each time being annulled. He was allowed to sit in 1774, in which year he was Lord Mayor of London. His character was such as to win the respect of Dr Johnson*, a man of opposite moral and political principles: 'Jack has great variety of talk, Jack is a scholar, Jack has the manners of a gentleman.' (Quoted in Boswell's *Life of Johnson*.)

Will's Coffee-house

A literary resort in late 17th and early 18th C, frequented by the poets Dryden* and Pope*, the essayist Addison*, and the dramatists Wycherley* and Congreve*. It stood at the corner of Russell Street, London.

* *Coffee and Coffee-Houses*.

William I (1066–87) the Conqueror

As Duke of Normandy he came to power in 1035, and proved himself an effective soldier and ruler. In 1051, he may have received some sort of promise from Edward the Confessor*, his relative, that the English throne should pass to him, and Harold Earl of Wessex promised his support in 1064. When, nonetheless, Harold himself succeeded Edward, William invaded England and defeated Harold near Hastings in Sussex, 1066. By 1070 he had reduced the whole country. The invasion had behind it the authority of the Pope, since the English Church was in a decadent and heretical condition. William's government was remarkably thorough and efficient. There was an extensive redistribution of land, with the result that the Anglo-Saxon* nobility were largely dispossessed and England was subjected to a Norman-French aristocracy, French-speaking until 14th C when it became itself anglicized. At the same time, William so managed this redistribution that the royal authority could be more effectively maintained throughout the country than was usual in 11th-C Western Europe.

* *Domesday Book*; *Lanfranc*; *Norman*.

William II (1087–1100)

King of England. His nickname William Rufus arose from the reddish colour of his complexion and hair. He continued the policy of his father, William I, but was much more unpopular owing to his wilful tyrannies. According to legend he was killed while hunting in the New Forest by an arrow shot by Walter Tirel.

William III (1689–1702)

King of Britain, reigning jointly with his wife Mary until her death in 1694. As William of Orange, Stadtholder of Holland, he was leader of the European opposition to the power of Louis XIV, which also menaced Britain. His wife was the daughter of James II*, deposed for his Catholicism and his threat to the liberty of Parliament*. His reign was largely taken up with war against France, which he conducted with ability. The political power of Parliament was further increased by his foreign preoccupations, and by the fact that, as a foreigner, he lacked experience of English political affairs.

* *Revolution of 1688, The*.

William IV (1830–37)

He was brother of his predecessor, George IV*, and uncle to his successor, Victoria*. He was a well-meaning man of small ability, but the most popular member of a royal family which was otherwise very unpopular.

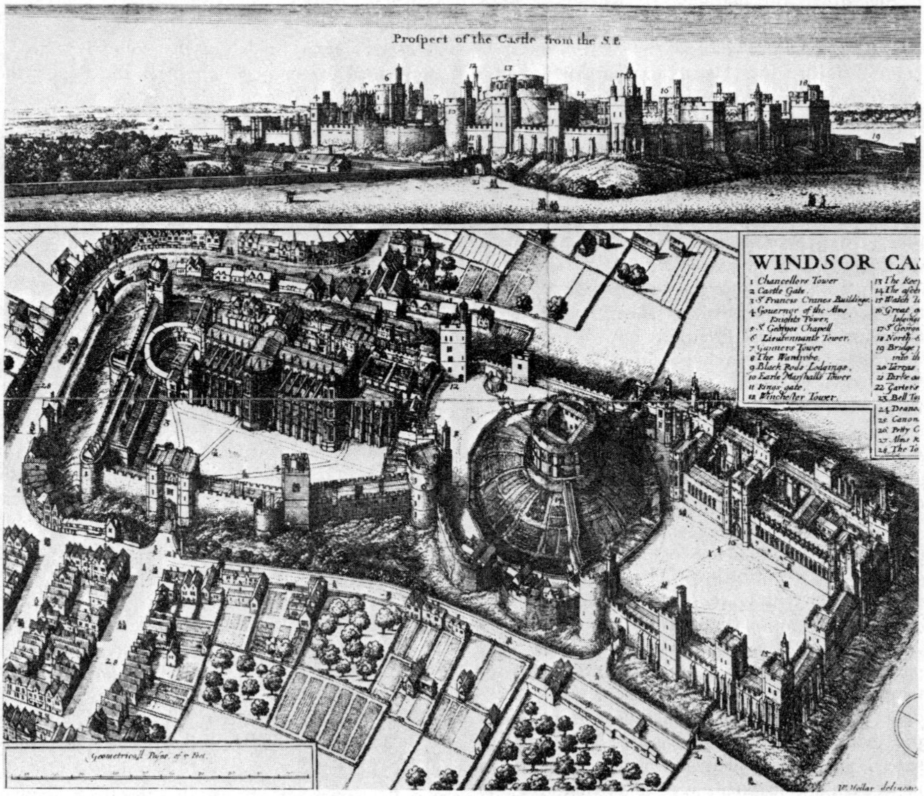

Wilmot

* *Rochester*.

Wilson, Angus (b 1913)

Novelist. He began to write in 1946, and this late start may account for his maturity of outlook and judgment, excelling those of most contemporary novelists. He is the sharpest and most effective satirist in post-war fiction. He brings to the modern scene standards which have their basis in pre-war liberalism, but to which he adds the weight of his personal, humane values. Stories: *The Wrong Set* (1949); *Such Darling Dodos* (1950). Novels: *Hemlock and After* (1952); *Anglo-Saxon Attitudes* (1956); *The Middle Age of Mrs Eliot* (1957); *The Old Men at the Zoo* (1961); *No Laughing Matter* (1968). The last of these has considerable originality of form; the narrative includes passages of straight narration, passages of theatrical farce, and others which resemble the 'stream of consciousness' technique of James Joyce*, the variation of method depending on the kind of experience which is being presented.

Angus Wilson has also written for sound broadcasting and television; his essay *Tempo* (1964) is about the impact of television on the arts. Criticism: *Emile Zola* (1950); *The Wild Garden* (1963).

Wilson, John (1785-1854)

Scottish journalist, chiefly known under the pseudonym 'Christopher North' which he used when writing for *Blackwood's Magazine**, for which he was the principal writer from 1817. He wrote very lively, semidramatic discussions called *Noctes Ambrosianae* which became famous. In 1820 he was elected to the professorship of moral philosophy in Edinburgh University. The election was politically motivated; he was a Tory* and had no special qualifications for the post, but was backed by Walter Scott*. Nonetheless he filled the post very effectively. He contributed much other journalism to Blackwood's, and was also a poet: *The Isle of Palms* (1812) and *The City of the Plague* (1816).

Bib: Swan, E., *Christopher North—John Wilson*.

Winchester

A town in Hampshire. It was the capital of the kingdom of Wessex* from 6th to 9th C, and after that held an equal status with London until late in 12th C. It is famous for its medieval cathedral and for its public school*, which was founded in 1382 and served as a pattern for later schools like Eton*.

Windsor Castle

The principal residence of the English royal family since 11th C. Its most conspicuous feature is the huge round tower at the summit of the hill on which the castle is built; it was constructed by Edward III* on the site where, according to the contemporary French chronicler Froissart*, King Arthur* had sat surrounded by his Knights of the

Round Table*; Edward, who had founded the knightly Order of the Garter*, still the most distinguished order of knighthood*, built the tower as a meeting-place for it, in emulation of Arthur. To the north of the castle is the River Thames, and beyond it, the most famous of English Public Schools*, Eton*; to the south and east is the enormous Windsor Park, and to the west, the little town of Windsor. The town and castle are just over 20 miles west of London.

Windsor, House of

Since 1917, the official designation of the British royal family, which, previously, had been known as the House of Hanover. The change was made by George V, in deference to British hostility to Germany during World War I.

* *George.*

Wine

This has always been rather a rich man's drink in England, though in 17th and 18th C, because beer and ale were considered low class, it was more frequently and widely drunk than it is today, when it has become more expensive because of the taxes levied on it. Home-grown British wines existed at least until 18th C, but as early as 14th C ships were sent in convoy to Bordeaux in south-west France to import claret. Spanish wines such as sherry and canary were drunk in 16th and 17th C; French burgundy is mentioned in 1672 in a play by Wycherley*; champagne is first mentioned in 1700, and the sweet Portuguese wine, port, in 1711. For a hundred and fifty years the last was above all the gentleman's drink, taken among the men as they sat round the table after dinner when the ladies had departed to the 'withdrawing room'. Rhenish wines from Germany were popular from 16th C. Until 18th C, wine was not allowed to mature, nor, until mid-17th C, were glass bottles used, and wine glasses were often imported from Venice. By 19th C, taste was much more sophisticated; gentlemen 'laid down' bottles to be drunk by their sons, and such a legacy was much prized.

* *Drinks.*

Wings of the Dove, The (1902)

A novel by Henry James*. The scene is principally London and Venice. Kate Croy and Merton Densher, a young journalist, are in love, but without the money to marry. Kate's rich aunt, Mrs Stringham, takes under her protection Milly Theale, a lonely American girl of great single-mindedness, eagerness for life, and capacity for affection, and also a millionairess. Mrs Stringham learns from Milly's doctor that the girl is suffering from a mortal illness, that her death cannot be long delayed, and that it can only be delayed at all if she achieves happiness. Mrs Stringham communicates this to Kate, who conceives a plot with a double purpose: Merton is to engage Milly's love, thus bringing her the happiness that she needs, and at the same time securing her money when she dies, so that Kate's own marriage to Merton can at last take place. Milly's love for Merton is very real; because of it, however, she refuses another suitor, Lord Mark, who knows Kate's plot and in revenge betrays it to Milly. She dies, broken-hearted, but she leaves Merton her money. Merton and Kate, however, find that they are for ever separated by the shadow of the dead Milly between them.

The story is an example of James's 'international theme': in this case, the openness and integrity which he saw as strengths of the American personality are opposed to the selfishness and deviousness which he saw as part of the decadent aspect of European culture. It is written in the condensed, allusive style which is characteristic also of *The Ambassadors** and *The Golden Bowl**.

Winner and Waster

A 14th-C alliterative poem of unknown authorship. It is a discussion, in the form of a debate, of current problems. Like *The Parliament of the Three Ages**, which may have been written at about the same time, and like the more important *Piers Plowman**, which they may have preceded, it uses a vision as the pretext for moral and critical reflections.

Winter's Tale, The

A play by Shakespeare*, dated 1610–11, and based on Robert Greene's *Pandósto**. Leontes, king of Sicilia, is married to Hermione, whom he deeply loves, and at the opening of the play is receiving a visit from Polixenes, king of Bohemia and the intimate friend of his childhood. Leontes becomes consumed by an insane jealousy, and is convinced that the child with which Hermione is pregnant has been fathered by Polixenes. He orders Camillo, a courtier, to poison Polixenes, but instead Camillo and Polixenes flee the country together. Leontes orders the trial of Hermione for adultery, and, to appease his indignant courtiers, he sends to the oracle of Delphi* in order to obtain what he believes will be confirmation of her guilt. The baby is born, but Leontes orders another courtier, Antigonus, to leave it in a waste place to perish. At this point a succession of catastrophes is heaped on Leontes: he learns from the oracle that his wife is innocent, from Paulina, wife of Antigonus, that Hermione has died, and that his little son has also died, of grief at the suffering of his mother. The last scene of Act III shows Antigonus depositing the baby on the coast of Bohemia and its discovery by two shepherds. Thus far the play is tragic; Acts IV and V show recovery. The baby grows up into a beautiful girl, Perdita, who believes herself to be a shepherd's daughter. Florizel, son of Polixenes, courts her at the shepherds' sheepshearing feast, but they have to flee to Sicilia to escape the anger of his father. Polixenes follows them, and at Leontes' court once more a great reconciliation takes place. Paulina discloses that Hermione is not dead, but has been kept in hiding until the return of Perdita, in accordance with the prediction of the oracle; in the last scene she is shown to Leontes as a statue of her supposedly dead self, but at the command of Paulina the statue gradually comes to life to the sound of music.

The summary shows that the play has no pretence to external realism; it is a fable about the destructiveness of the passions and the healing power of time. The symbolism is especially of the seasons: 'a winter's tale' is about deprivation, but the play ends in autumn, the season of recovered fulfilment, while the sheep-shearing scene (IV. iii) has springlike qualities, with Perdita reminding one of Persephone* in her lines about the spring flowers. The pastoral* aspect of the play shows pastoralism in a new light – not as an escape into daydream from change and decay, but as a phase of development which must be outgrown if capacity for growth is to be fulfilled. The process of growth implies desire, fear, and possessiveness which are the state of mind of the jealous Leontes at the beginning of the play, when he finds that he has outgrown his pastorally innocent friendship with Polixenes. From this false development, he can recover only by repentance.

* *Reconciliation Plays.*

Wit

This word has a number of distinct, though related, meanings. [1] The oldest meaning is identical with 'mind', as in Wycliffe's* 14th-C translation of the Bible: 'Who knew the wit of the Lord?' (*Romans* 11:34). This use of 'wit' rarely occurs in the literature of the last hundred years. [2] Another long-established meaning is 'a faculty of the mind'. This is still in use today, as when we speak of someone having 'lost his wits', *ie* lost the use of his mental faculties. [3] A common meaning in 17th and 18th C was the capacity to relate unlike ideas, as in Locke's* definition: 'Wit lying in the assemblage of ideas, and putting these together with quickness and variety wherein can be found any resemblance or congruity, thereby to make up pleasant pictures in the fancy' (*Essay concerning Human Understanding**, 1690). Cowley*, in his poem *Of Wit* (1656) wrote 'In a true piece of wit all things must be,/Yet all things there agree'. Johnson*, in his *Life of Cowley* (1779), wrote: 'It was about the time of Cowley that Wit, which had been till then used for Intellection, in contradistinction to Will, took the meaning, whatever it be, which it now bears.' Johnson here refers to the original meaning of wit as 'mind' or 'understanding', and points to the complex and important suggestiveness of the word in his own day. [4] During the same period, but chiefly in the 'Age of Reason' (about 1660–1800), wit was also thought of as meaning fine and clear expression: Dryden's* 'propriety of thoughts and words elegantly adapted to the subject' (*Heroic Poetry and Poetic Licence*, 1677), and Pope's* 'what oft was thought but ne'er so well expressed' (*Essay on Criticism**). Johnson went some way to reconciling interpretations [3] and [4] in his own definition: 'that which is at once natural and new, and that which though not obvious is upon its first production acknowledged to be just . . . that which he that never found it wondered how he missed it'. [5] Definition [3] points to the element of surprise in wit; this often induces laughter. Thus wit has also been considered, since 1600, to be one of the principal sources of comedy, and it is in this sense that it is chiefly used in 20th-C English. [6] In the personal sense, in later 17th and 18th C a wit was a man with clear insight into many aspects of life and manners, capable of summarizing and relating these aspects lucidly and forcefully. The term is often used disparagingly, however, for pretentious young men who try to achieve reputations for themselves by their superficial but fashionably clever talk. Nowadays, a wit is a person capable of expressing himself in concise and memorably amusing language.

Definition [3] in the above paragraph resembles Coleridge's* description of the poetic imagination at the end of Chapter xiv of his *Biographia Literaria**. What modern critics, such as F. R. Leavis*, describe as 'the line of wit' in English poetry, running from Donne* to Pope* is the phase in which imagination (as understood by 19th-C Romantics) combined with the intellectual alertness always associated with wit. Both poets and prose writers handled ideas simultaneously with feelings. In the first half of 17th C, Donne, Marvell* and Browne* used wit very seriously, though the first two modulated their seriousness with irony; Swift* and Pope, in early 18th C, used wit satirically, and Sterne* (in *Tristram Shandy**) used it for exuberant comedy. At the time of the Restoration* (1660) the line of wit was influenced by the new values attached by the natural philosophers* to the analytic use of reason, and the consequent preference for clarity, and kindred qualities such as elegance, over complexity. It was at this time that definition [4] began to supersede definition [3], although both definitions are appropriate to Pope's kind of wit.

In 17th and 18th C, wit (considered as the instrument of the imagination, or 'fancy', acting together and simultaneously with the reason) was the quality of the human mind at its most civilized. Yet it was a quality which many people criticized and distrusted even in those centuries. The writers who most valued it – Cowley, Pope and Swift – disliked the misuse of it by second-rate minds. One of the most famous wits, the Earl of Rochester*, wrote of the 'gibing, gingling Knack called wit' in his *Satire against Mankind* (1675). The Puritans* were especially suspicious of it. Steele*, who, with Addison*, made it his mission to draw together the respectable middle classes with their esteem for virtue and the fashionable circles with their esteem for intelligence, wrote: 'There is hardly that person to be found, who is not more concerned for the reputation of Wit and Sense, than Honesty and Virtue.' The serious middle classes, with their Puritan tradition, valued singleness of mind, which seemed incompatible with wit, though Addison and Steele tried to persuade them that it need not be. At the end of 18th C, Wordsworth's* admiration of the childlike mind, and the Romantic cult of the purity of the feelings, seemed even more incompatible with wit, and they eventually directed the taste of 19th C. In his essay on Gray (*Essays in Criticism**, 2nd series, 1888) Arnold* wrote of Dryden and Pope: 'Their poetry is conceived and composed in their wits, genuine poetry is conceived and composed in the soul.' However, the present century has seen a strong revival of admiration for 'the line of wit' led by the older Yeats* and T. S. Eliot*, as well as other poets and critics. 19th-C critics thought that the 'wit-writers' had been too narrow; the 20th-C critics consider that it was the 19th-C writers who were narrow, through having formed a narrow conception of wit.

It was partly the narrowing conceptions of wit that caused it, from later 18th C, to be repeatedly contrasted with humour*, as though they were both mainly sources of comedy. Goldsmith* (*Enquiry into the Present State of Polite Learning*, 1759) considered that humour, in contrast to wit, always arises from a subject inferior, by its nature, to the reader. Hazlitt* (*English Comic Writers*, 1819) thought that wit always required terms of comparison, whereas humour could arise from the subject considered by itself; Coleridge (*Wit and Humour*, 1831) said that wit always provokes surprise, and tends to be impersonal, whereas humour is a quality intrinsic to the subject that is found funny. All these distinctions suggest that there is in wit an element of intellectual quality that is absent in humour.

* 7.2.

Witches

People supposed to be in league with the devil, who gives them supernatural powers. The name 'witch' was sometimes used for both sexes, though witches were usually women. They commonly had 'familiars' in the form of spirits disguised as animals of bad or sinister reputation – toads or cats of certain colours. To work their magic, witches uttered 'spells' of specially devised words, or they used objects ('charms') supposed to have magical properties; witches used to gather in small communities known as 'covens', and they assembled on one day of the year (a 'witches' Sabbath') to worship the Devil.

The common scientific explanation of witchcraft is that, in Europe at least, it represents the long survival of pre-Christian pagan religions in which the gods were the embodiments of the powers of nature, usually in the forms of animals, often a goat, but in Britain commonly the bull, the dog, or the cat.

That witchcraft was common in the Middle Ages* is not surprising; it is at first sight surprising that it was conspicuous in later 16th and early 17th C, and that not merely the ignorant and uneducated but some of the learned believed in it. James VI of Scotland and I of England*, who has been called 'the greatest scholar who ever sat on the English throne', was himself deeply interested in it and wrote a denunciation of it – his *Daemonologie* (1599). The pamphlet *News from Scotland* (1591) describes his conversion from scepticism to belief in it, and seems to have been used by Shakespeare in the portrayal of the witches in *Macbeth**. James later, however, moved to a more sceptical position again. The first law making witchcraft an offence punishable by death in England was passed in 1603 (though causing death by witchcraft had been so punishable since 1563) and it was not repealed until 1736. Sir Thomas Browne declares his firm belief in it in *Religio Medici** (1643); the last learned defence of the belief was *Saducismus Triumphatus* (1681) by the scholar and clergyman Joseph Glanville. The belief seems to have been particularly strong among Puritans* and in Puritan countries, for instance in Scotland, 17th-C New England, and England under the Long Parliament*. Rare survivals of it have been found in 20th-C England. It has been suggested that the prevalence of the belief in 17th C and among Puritans is that their superstitious impulses were no longer satisfied by the Catholic system of mysteries (miracles, lives of the saints, etc.) which they had expelled from their faith by its 'purification'.

In the reign of James I, a number of plays besides *Macbeth* dealt with witchcraft, *eg* Dekker* and Ford's* *Witch of Edmonton* (1623) and Middleton's* *The Witch* (1615). William Golding's* *The Spire* (1964) deals with medieval pagan survival.

* 3.1.2.

Wives and Daughters

A novel by Mrs Gaskell*, published serially 1864–66 in *Cornhill Magazine**, and not completed at her death. It is a study of two families, the Gibsons and the Hamleys, in a small country town, and the relationships of the parents and the children in each. The central character is Molly Gibson, whose liberal, frank, sincere and deeply responsible nature is painfully tested by the marriage of her widowed father (a country doctor) to a silly, vain widow. The widow brings with her, however, her own daughter, Cynthia, a girl with her mother's outward charm but without her mother's silliness, and with feelings guided more by her discerning intelligence than by spontaneous loyalties. Cynthia at 16 has become engaged to a coarse but astute man, Mr Preston, who is a local land-agent. The two girls become involved with the two sons of Mr Hamley, the local squire. The elder boy, Osborne, is superficially brilliant and charming and much overestimated by his father. The younger son, Roger, has much less showy qualities but a deeper nature, and eventually wins the academic successes expected of but not achieved by the elder, who makes an unfortunate marriage, is cast off by the father, and dies young. The novel thus brings out the differences between superficial and deep natures, and the perils that result from consequent false estimates of character, made even by the intelligent.

Wolsey, Thomas (1475?–1530) /ˈwulzi/

Statesman and churchman. He was born of comparatively humble parents in Ipswich, but with the aid of various patrons he received rapid promotion in the Church. In 1507 he became chaplain to King Henry VII* who employed him on diplomatic affairs. In the next reign he was for 20 years practically the sole ruler of the country, having the full confidence of Henry VIII*. He became Bishop of Lincoln, Bishop of Tournai in France, Archbishop of York, Cardinal, within reach of becoming Pope. At home he was a firm and able administrator. His foreign policy was skilful, but his personal ambitions led to its ultimate failure. In his anxiety to become Pope, he sought the favour of the Emperor Charles V and allowed him to become too powerful in Europe. Charles was nephew to

Henry VIII's queen, Catherine of Aragon, whom in 1528 Henry wanted to divorce. Since Charles had Rome in his hands, the Pope could not consent, and in 1529 Wolsey lost the favour of the king; his downfall was the more complete because he had no other powerful supporters in the country. His life was written by a member of his household, George Cavendish, but it was not published until 1641. His downfall was finely dramatized by Fletcher and Shakespeare in *Henry VIII**.

Women, Education of

In the early medieval convents, nuns were often learned and received the same education as monks, but later the standard deteriorated. Thereafter, women's intellectual education was not widely provided for until later 19th C, though much would depend on their social rank, their parents, or their husbands. Thomas More in *Utopia** advocated equal education for both sexes, but this was a Platonic ideal; Swift* in the *Land of the Houyhnhnms* (*Gulliver's Travels**) causes his enlightened horse to scorn the human habit of educating only half mankind, and yet allowing the other half (*ie* the women) to bring up the children. On the other hand, in 16th C the enthusiasm for education caused some highly born women to be very highly educated; this is true of the two queens, Mary I* and Elizabeth I*, of the 'ten-days queen' Lady Jane Grey (whose education is described in Ascham's* *Schoolmaster*, 1570), and of the Countess of Pembroke*, Sidney's sister. In 17th C we see from Pepys's* Diary how he tried to educate his French wife, and Evelyn*, the other great diarist, describes his highly educated daughter. Well-bred women were expected to have social and some artistic accomplishments, but Pepys, for example did not expect his wife to share his scientific interests. Boarding schools for girls came into existence in 17th C and became more numerous in 18th, but either they were empty of real educational value or they were absurdly pretentious, like Miss Pinkerton's Academy described in Thackeray's *Vanity Fair** (1848); Mrs Malaprop in Sheridan's comedy *The Rivals** (1775) is a satire on the half-educated upper class woman. Upper class girls had governesses for general education, music masters, dancing masters, and teachers of 'deportment', *ie* in the bearing of the body; lower class women were illiterate, unless they learned to read and write at 'charity schools'. On the other hand they had a much wider range of domestic skills than is usual with modern women, and among the poor, a rich store of folklore. However, in 18th C there was already a shift in values. Swift, in his letter to a young lady about to enter marriage, points out that the way to keep a husband's affections was to grow in maturity of mind, and the blue-stocking* women of the middle of the century were entertainers of the intellectual elite of their society.

The big change dates from mid-19th C. Colleges were founded for the higher education of women (beginning with Queen's College, London, 1848), and schools (*eg* Cheltenham Ladies' College) comparable to the ancient great public schools* for boys were founded. The women's colleges Girton (1869) and Newnham (1875) were founded in Cambridge, and others followed at Oxford. Societies were also founded for the advancement of women's education. Since the commencement of state education in 1870, the status of women teachers has been brought equal to that of men teachers, and since 1902 equal secondary education has been provided for both sexes.

* **2.1.3**; *Schools in England.*

Women, Status of

Unmarried women had few prospects in Britain until the second half of 19th C. In the Middle Ages* they could enter convents and become nuns, but when in 1536–39 Henry VIII* closed the convents and the monasteries, no alternative opened to them. Widows like Chaucer's Wife of Bath in *The Canterbury Tales** might inherit a business (in her case that of a clothier) and run it efficiently, or like Mistress Quickly in Shakespeare's *2 Henry IV** they might run inns. The profession of acting was opened to women from the Restoration* of the Monarchy in 1660, and literature began to be acceptable as a career from the end of 18th C – the period of Fanny Burney* and Hannah More*. At about the same time, the increase of interest in education for girls led to extensive employment of governesses to teach the children in private families; such a position might be peaceful and pleasant, like Mrs Weston's experience in the Woodhouse family in Jane Austen's *Emma**, but it was at least as likely to be unpleasant, underpaid, and despised, as the novelist Charlotte Brontë found. Nursing was also open to women, but nurses had no training and were commonly a low class of woman like Betsey Prig and Mrs Gamp in Dickens's *Martin Chuzzlewit** until Florence Nightingale reformed the profession.

Wives and their property were entirely in the power of their husbands according to the law, though in practice they might take the management of both into their own hands, like the Wife of Bath. Shakespeare's *The Taming of the Shrew** is hard to appreciate in our society with its comparatively relaxed relationship between the sexes. A Dutch observer (1575) stated that England was called the 'Paradise of married women' because they took their lives more easily than continental wives. Nonetheless, a middle-class wife worked hard, as her husband's assistant (probably his accountant) in his business, and as a mistress of baking, brewing, household management and amateur medicine for the treatment of her family and servants.

19th C was the heroic age for women in Britain. No other nation before 20th C has produced such a distinguished line of women writers as the novelists Jane Austen*, Elizabeth Gaskell*, Charlotte and Emily Brontë* and George Eliot* (Mary Ann Evans). In addition there was the prison reformer, Elizabeth Fry; the reformer of the nursing profession, Florence Nightingale; the explorer, Mary Kingsley; the sociologist, Beatrice Webb*, pioneers in education, and the first women doctors. The Married Women's Property Act of 1882 for the first time gave wives rights to their own property which had hitherto been merged with their husbands'. Political rights came more slowly, and were preceded by an active and sometimes violent movement, led by the Suffragettes, who fought for them. Women over 30 were given the vote in 1918 as a natural consequence of their success in taking over men's work during Word War I, but women over 21 (the age at which men were entitled to vote or stand for Parliament) had to wait until 1928. Now most professions are open to women, including the law; a notable exception is the priesthood of the Church of England* and some other religious denominations. Indeed, at the present time of shortage of labour, there is pressure on married women to take up professions. However, there are still some examples of discrimination against women, especially in salary.

* **2.1**.3; *Nuns and Nunneries.*

Women in Love (1921)

A novel by D. H. Lawrence*. It continues the lives of two of the characters in *The Rainbow**, but it is not a sequel to the earlier book. Ursula Brangwen is a school-teacher, and her sister Gudrun is an artist. The other two main characters are Gerald Crich, a mine-owner and manager, and Rupert Birkin, a school-inspector. The main narrative is about the relationships of these four: the union of Rupert and Ursula after conflict, the union of Gerald and Gudrun ending in conflict and Gerald's death, the affinities and antagonisms between the sisters and between the men. The settings include Shortlands, the mansion of the mine-owning Crich family; Breadalby, the mansion of Lady Hermione Roddice, a meeting-place of the leading intellectuals of the day; the Café Pompadour in London, a centre for the artists, and a winter resort in the Austrian Tyrol. The theme is human relationship in the modern world, where intelligence has become the prisoner of self-consciousness, and spontaneous life-forces are perverted into violence, notably in Gerald, Hermione, and the German sculptor Loerke. Symbolic episodes centred on animals and other natural imagery are used to present those forces of the consciousness that lie outside rational articulation, and personal relationship is so investigated as to illuminate crucial aspects of modern culture: the life of industry, the life of art, the use and misuse of reason, and what is intimate considered as the nucleus of what is public. Rupert Birkin is a projection of Lawrence himself, but he is objectified sufficiently to be exposed to criticism.

* 4.5.3.

Woodlanders, The (1887)

A novel by Thomas Hardy*. The setting is Dorset in the south-west of England, and the human relationships are a kind of movement upwards, downwards, and upwards again from the primitive rural base. The primitive peasant girl, Marty South, is in love with the young cider-maker, Giles Winterbourne, who is as simple in his background as she is herself, but has great natural delicacy of feeling. Giles is himself in love with Grace Melbury, the daughter of a local timber merchant, who has had a 'lady's' education. She has not been spoiled by this, but her sensibilities have spoiled her for the primitive environment to which Giles belongs. Her parents marry her to the young doctor, Edred Fitzpiers, who, however, is enticed away by the great lady of the district, Felice Charmond. Grace takes refuge in the woods with Giles, who, though a sick man, abandons his cottage to her and lives in a hut nearby, where he dies. Grace and Marty South mourn together over his grave, but Grace becomes reconciled to Fitzpiers, and Marty is left to mourn alone. Neither Fitzpiers nor Mrs Charmond belongs to the rural background, and their intrusion into it is disruptive of its values, embodied above all in Giles Winterbourne.

Wool

* *Cloth Manufacture.*

Woolf, Virginia (1882–1941) /wulf/

Novelist and critic. She was the daughter of Leslie Stephen*, the literary critic; after his death in 1904, her house in the Bloomsbury district of London became the centre of the Bloomsbury Group* of intellectuals, one of whom, the socialist thinker Leonard Woolf, she married in 1912. Together they established the Hogarth Press which published much of the most memorable imaginative writing of the 1920s.

Her first two novels, *The Voyage Out* (1915) and *Night and Day* (1919), are usual in their technique, but in the next four – *Jacob's Room* (1922), *Mrs Dalloway* (1925), *To the Lighthouse** (1927) and *The Waves** (1931) – she became increasingly experimental and innovatory. Her attitude was formed by three influences: the negative one of dissatisfaction with the methods and outlook of the three novelists who, in the first 20 years of this century, dominated the contemporary public, H. G. Wells*, Arnold Bennett*, and John Galsworthy*; the outlook of the Bloomsbury circle with their strong emphasis on the value of personal relations and the cultivation of the sensibility; the sense of tragedy in the 19th-C Russian novelists, Tolstoy* and Dostoievsky, and the story-writer Chekhov*. She sought to develop a technique of expression which would capture the essence of the sensibility – the experiencing self – and to do this, she reduced the plot-and-story element of novel-writing as far as she could. The last two of the four experimental novels mentioned are usually considered to be her most successful achievements, especially *To the Lighthouse.* In her later novels, *The Years* (1937) and *Between the Acts* (1941), she again used a more customary technique, though with stress on symbolism and bringing out the slight incident as possibly that which is most revelatory.

*Orlando** (1928) is a composite work, ostensibly a biography of a woman poet (Victoria Sackville-West), but in part a brilliantly vivid historical novel (though her subject was her contemporary) and in part literary criticism. Her more formal literary criticism was published in two volumes *The Common Reader* (1925) and *The Common Reader, 2nd Series* (1932). In these she expressed her

philosophy of creative writing (for instance in the essay *Modern Fiction*, 1925) and her response to the writers and writings of the past that most interested her. She had a partly fictional way of re-creating the personalities of past writers which is sensitive and vivid. In her social and political attitude she was feminist, *ie* she was much concerned with the rights of women and especially of women writers. This is one of the basic themes of *Orlando* but it comes out most clearly in *A Room of One's Own* (1931). *Flush* (1933) is another experiment in fictional biography (of the Brownings) and she wrote a straight biography of her friend the art critic Roger Fry (1940). Her *Diary* was published by her husband in 1953.
Bib: Woolf, L., *Autobiography*; critical studies by Bennet, J., Daiches, D., Blackstone, B., and Brewster, D.; Johnstone, J. K., *The Bloomsbury Group*.

Woolwich /ˈwulidʒ/
A town at the mouth of the River Thames, now part of London. It was a naval station in 16th C, and was the site of the Royal Military Academy from 1741 to 1946; cadets were trained there for the Royal Artillery and the Royal Engineers.

Worcester, Battle of (1651) /ˈwustə/
The Battle that concluded the second Civil War*. The Scottish Presbyterians* had been allied to the English Parliament* against Charles I* in the first Civil War (1642–46) but in 1648 they changed sides on the king consenting to favour Presbyterianism, and on his death in 1649 they supported his son Charles II*. Cromwell* defeated their army, and Charles made his escape overseas.

Wordsworth, William (1770–1850) /ˈwəːdzwəθ/
Poet. He was born in Cumberland, the son of a law-agent. His mother, with whom his relationship was peculiarly happy, died when he was 8, and his father died, leaving the family rather poor, 5 years later. He was sent to school at Hawkshead, near his birthplace, and there he had time to lead a life of delighted freedom in the surrounding hills. In 1787 he went to Cambridge University, but more important as an influence on his life were his two visits to France, the first in 1790, and the second, lasting a year, from November 1791. On the second visit he had a love affair with Annette Vallon, who bore him a daughter. His relatives intended him for the Church, but his religious views at this time were disturbed by his early experiences in wild nature, his enthusiasm for the French Revolution* (in full course during his visits), and his reading of the French thinker, Rousseau*. In 1793, Britain went to war against France, and Wordsworth's sympathies were on the French side; in this mood the writings of the extreme rationalist* philosopher William Godwin* were congenial to him, and rationalist ideas removed him still further from the possibility of a career in the Church of England. In 1795 he received a legacy sufficient to keep him independent, and he settled down with his sister Dorothy, one of the most sustaining personal influences of his life. By 1797 he had made the friendship of Coleridge*, a personal influence of at least equal importance, and in 1798 the two poets collaborated in their famous volume, *Lyrical Ballads**. By this time, he was disillusioned with France, now under dictatorship, and had outgrown Godwinism. The formative influences of his early experience of wild nature and of Rousseau remained; Wordsworth had become the poet whose theme was the growth of the human spirit through communion with the natural environment, and this theme proved to be increasingly in accord with traditional religion, to which by degrees he returned. He likewise became more conservative in politics, to the disgust of younger men such as Byron* and Shelley*. The great decade of his poetry ran from 1797 to 1807; thereafter it slowly declined in merit while his reputation slowly grew. By 1830 his poetic eminence was generally acknowledged, and in 1843 he was made Poet Laureate*. He married Mary Hutchinson in 1802.

Wordsworth's first volumes (*Descriptive Sketches*, *An Evening Walk*, 1793) were in the tradition of 18th-C feeling for natural description. He then wrote a tragedy, *The Borderers*. From these, *Lyrical Ballads* (1798 – expanded in 1800) differs in marked ways, notably the uncompromising simplicity of much of the language, the strong sympathy not merely with the poor in general but with particular, dramatized examples of them, and the fusion of natural description with expressions of inward states of mind. With the encouragement of Coleridge, he now planned a long philosophical poem to be called *The Recluse*, and in preparation for it, wrote *The Prelude**. This was completed by 1805, but not published until 1850, and then in a revised form.

In 1807 Wordsworth published what is perhaps his richest book, *Poems in Two Volumes*, and in 1814 *The Excursion**, the only part of *The Recluse* to be completed besides the *Prelude*. These were followed by *The White Doe of Rylstone* (1815); *Peter Bell* (1819); *The River Duddon* (1820); *Ecclesiastical Sketches* (1822); *Sonnets* (1838).

Wordsworth expressed his theory of poetic diction in his Preface to the 1800 edition of the *Lyrical Ballads*. Seeking to reach and refresh the deepest, purest, and simplest feelings in the human personality, he considered that to do so the poet should use a diction as natural and direct as that of the most natural speech, and further, that men of the simplest kind like the peasants of the Lake District (*Michael**), best showed in their lives and in their language what it is to live at this level of feeling. Part of this theory was mistaken, as Coleridge was to show in *Biographia Literaria**, but when his own feelings had genuine life, Wordsworth's deliberate simplicity and refusal to decorate the truth of experience produced a kind of pure and profound poetry which no other poet has ever equalled. Examples of his achievement at the extreme of simplicity are the Lucy* poems (1807), and among his masterpieces are his verse tales of peasant life, especially *The Ruined Cottage** (written 1797, but published as the first book of

The Excursion, 1814). The first two books of *The Prelude* (especially the second) are other examples of his poetry at its height. The *Intimations of Immortality** Ode (1807) is often considered to be a recognition that his unique inspiration was leaving him, and also to show that he was not able to face this truth quite fully; but it is a mistake to suppose that Wordsworth wrote no good poetry after 1807. His achievement was to express the growth of the personality from its creative sources by assimilation of experience, both tragic and happy, and at the same time to present the human consciousness as continuous with environment and not differentiated from it, as in the 18th-C rationalist tradition.

* 6.3.2–4; 7.3; *Lake Poets*.

Bib: Moorman, M., *Life*; Legouis, E., *Wordsworth and Annette Vallon*; Margoliouth, H. M., *Wordsworth and Coleridge*; Bateson, F. W., *Wordsworth, a Reinterpretation*; Bradley, A. C., in *Oxford Lectures on Poetry*; Darbishire, H., *The Poet Wordsworth*; Grierson, H. J. C., *Wordsworth and Milton*; Knight, G. Wilson, in *The Starlit Dome*; Smith, J. C., *A Study of Wordsworth*; King, A., *Wordsworth and the Artist's Vision*; Havens, R. D., *The Mind of a Poet*; Todd, F. M., a study of Wordsworth's political development.

Workhouses

Institutions to accommodate the destitute at public expense, and to provide them with work to ensure that they were socially useful. They were first established under the Poor Law* of 1576; they increased in number, but by 18th C the administration of them, the responsibility of the parish, had become seriously inefficient, and magistrates* were more inclined to administer financial relief to the paupers in their homes. This 'outdoor relief' – the 'Speenhamland System', so called from the parish in which it was first used – tended to be demoralizing to the working poor, who earned very little more than the workless paupers. The whole system was remodelled by the New Poor Law of 1834, by which workhouses were established regionally and administered by Boards of Guardians. The philosophy behind the Poor Law was that most destitution was due to laziness and vice, so that workhouses ought to be practically penal institutions. Consequently, though they ceased to be places of brutality and vice as they had been in 18th C, they became coldly inhuman, providing only the barest necessities of existence. Their inhumanity aroused Dickens to his indignantly satirical picture of them in *Oliver Twist**; in his last complete novel, *Our Mutual Friend**, Dickens returned to the theme by portraying the old woman, Betty Higden, as dying by the roadside sooner than enter a workhouse. Workhouses were indeed bitterly hated by the poor, and in 20th C they have been gradually eliminated, partly by the reinstitution of assistance in the home, and partly by gradual modification into humane institutions chiefly for the aged poor.

Wreck of the Deutschland, The

A poem by Gerard Manley Hopkins*, written in 1875, but not printed until the first edition of his collected poems (edited by Robert Bridges*) was published in 1918, apart from a short extract in Bridges's anthology *The Spirit of Man* (1918). Hopkins had ceased writing poetry when he entered the Jesuit Order in 1868. He broke this silence in consequence of being deeply moved at the news of the loss of the ship *Deutschland* at the mouth of the Thames in the winter of 1875, and of the drowning of five German nuns, who were passengers and exiles on account of Bismarck's anti-Catholic legislation (the Falk Laws).

The poem has 35 8-line stanzas, and is in two parts. The first part (1–10) is concerned with the Passion of Jesus Christ and its power to draw the soul to God; the second part (11–35) describes the storm, a nun calling on Christ at the storm's crisis, and ends (30–35) in a tone of majestic calm and thanksgiving for God's redemption of the soul through suffering. It is the first of Hopkins's important poems to be written in what he called Sprung Rhythm*, which he employed for most of his subsequent poetry; the lines have a regular count of rhythmic stresses but a varying count of syllables. This rhythm enabled Hopkins to combine the emphasis and syntax of the spoken language with the musical devices of the verse, and his use of it illustrates his statement that the language of poetry is 'that of current speech heightened'. The technique was not really novel; it resembles that of Shakespeare's mature blank verse*, just as Hopkins's images, by the thoroughness with which he develops them to display the emotional content of this thought, recall the 17th-C Metaphysical* school, especially Donne*. Nonetheless it was a technique very foreign to later 19th-C ideas of poetic decorum, and explains why the poem was not published until much later: Hopkins offered it to the Jesuit journal *The Month*, but the editor declared that he dared not publish it. Hopkins's technique became acceptable only when 20th-C poets, especially Eliot*, had published their own work, based on comparable principles.

Wren, Sir Christopher (1632–1723) /ren/

Architect. He was also a distinguished mathematician and astronomer, a member of the circle which in 1662 became the Royal Society*. He was in fact a representative of his age, which regarded the great cultural tradition of Europe as descending from ancient Rome and Greece and immensely valued the scope and power of the human reason. His masterpiece is St Paul's Cathedral in London; even before the old Cathedral was burnt down in 1666, he proposed to remodel it 'after a good Roman manner' not following 'the Gothic* rudeness of the old design'. Wren's cathedral shows the dignity of proportion and the splendour of display which is an English version of the classical style known as Baroque elsewhere in contemporary Europe. He also proposed a replanning of the City of London, in an arrangement of wide streets radiating from a central space, but difficulties in agreeing about property valuations with the existing landowners prevented this. He did, however, rebuild 52 London churches after the Fire* of 1666, giving them towers and spires of ingeniously varied and graceful designs in white stone that stood out against the black dome of the cathedral – an effect now entirely ruined by the alteration of the skyline by commercial buildings. Wren also contributed fine buildings to Oxford and Cambridge. His conception of architectural value was characteristically Augustan* and social, and his buildings express in stone the values of contemporary writers such as Dryden*, Pope* and Swift*.

* 2.3.

Wriothesley, Henry

* *Southampton.*

Wuthering Heights (1847)

/ˈwʌðəriŋ ˈhaits/

The sole novel by Emily Brontë*. The title of the book is the name of an old house, high up on the Yorkshire moors, occupied by the Earnshaw family. The period is the very end of 18th C. Because of their remoteness, the Earnshaws live in a style more traditional than that characteristic of households in more domesticated parts of England; the family and the servants have a kind of democratic equality with each other which accounts for the independent judgement of the housekeeper (Nelly Dean, who tells most of the story) and her freedom of intimacy with her employers. Into this house Mr Earnshaw brings a child who has been living the life of a wild animal in the slums of Liverpool. His parents are quite unknown, and Earnshaw adopts him, giving him the single name of Heathcliff. However, Mr Earnshaw treats him less like a human being than like an over-indulged pet animal; this arouses the fierce resentment of his son Hindley, and it is only with the daughter Catherine (Cathy) that Heathcliff has a human relationship, and then only on the moors outside the house. After Mr Earnshaw's death, Heathcliff is maltreated by Hindley, now master of the house, and lives like a despised animal instead of a spoilt one; his strong bond with Cathy, however, remains. But Cathy marries Edgar Linton from the 'civilized' household of Thrushcross Grange in the valley. Heathcliff runs away, and is heard of no more for three years. During this period Cathy and Edgar are contented together, though she has fits of depression. When Heathcliff returns, he has become a rich man, but is as socially excluded as ever, as deeply identified with Cathy, and full of hatred for the Linton and the Earnshaw families, which he sets about to destroy, especially after the death of Cathy in giving birth to a daughter. He nearly succeeds in doing so, but has to withhold harm from Hareton Earnshaw, the son of Hindley, and Catherine Linton, the daughter of Cathy, who are deeply in love. Heathcliff becomes detached from external reality and lives only for his union with Cathy in death. On the last page a weeping little boy declares that he has seen the ghosts of the dead Heathcliff and Cathy walking on the moor.

Emily Brontë's aim seems to have been to present an image of the feminine personality under the social constrictions of the civilization of the time: Cathy rather than Heathcliff is the central character. Women were not supposed to possess the wilder, instinctive feelings which were acknowledged in men; and girls' training, among the middle and upper classes, was a systematic inhibition of anything of the sort. Cathy, however, has this element in herself awakened by her early association with Heathcliff, and though her marriage with Edgar Linton is in many ways ideal both personally and socially, she can never afterwards be fully herself: 'Nelly, I *am* Heathcliff.' Heathcliff, on the other hand, represents the savage forces in human beings which civilization attempts vainly to eliminate, whereas it should somehow assimilate them. A peculiarity of the book is that it is narrated entirely through two of the characters, Nelly, and Lockwood the 'gentleman' from the 'civilized' south of England.

* 4.4.2.

Wyatt, Sir Thomas (1503?–42) /ˈwaiət/

Poet. He was widely used by Henry VIII* on diplomatic missions, but was imprisoned several times, once perhaps because he had been the lover of Henry's second queen, Anne Boleyn. As a poet, he is quite the most important of the first half of 16th C. He wrote satires and versions of some of the Biblical Psalms, but he is memorable for his love poems, some of which were written in verse forms fashionable in France and Italy, such as the sonnet*, which he was the first to use in England. His best poetry, however, is in the more native idiom of English verse, in a somewhat irregular rhythm which recalls old English alliterative* verse. The irregularities bothered his first publisher (Tottel*, 1557) who edited the poems so as to make them smoother; modern critics, however, prefer Wyatt's original rhythms, with their inflexions that give the emphasis natural to the speaking voice. His diction, in his best poetry, is simple and poignant, so that poems which in other respects resemble the conventional love lyrics for music common at the time, have an unusual convincingness of personal feeling. Wyatt's diplomatic dispatches have the same vivid rhythms and diction.

It was Wyatt who first used a couplet* for the conclusion of sonnets – a practice followed by Shakespeare*, but not found in Italian and French sonneteers. Among his famous poems are: *They flee from me*; *Forget not yet*; *To his Lute*; *Is it possible.*

* 6.1.2.

Bib: Muir, K., *Life and Letters*; Mason, H. A., *Humanism and Poetry in the Early Tudor Period*; Southall, R., *The Courtly Maker*; Thomson, P., *Sir Thomas Wyatt and his Background*; Tillyard, E. M. W., *The Poetry of Sir Thomas Wyatt*; Harding, D. W., in The Pelican Guide I: *The Age of Chaucer*.

Wycherley, William (1640–1716)

/ˈwitʃəli/

Dramatist. He wrote four satirical comedies: *Love in a Wood* (1671); *The Gentleman Dancing-Master*

(1671–72); *The Country Wife** (1672–73); *The Plain Dealer* (1674). His reputation rests on the last two for their vigour, management of situation, and incisive dialogue. Dryden* praised 'the satire, strength and wit of Manly Wycherley'; the 19th C found him indecent. Modern critics are inclined to praise his liveliness but blame his shallowness and confusion of values.

* 5.2.2; *Manners, Comedy of.*

Bib: Connely, W., *Life*; critical study by Zimbardo, R. D.; Dobrée, B., in *Restoration Comedy*; Palmer, J., in *The Comedy of Manners*; Perry, H. T. E., in *The Comic Spirit in Restoration Drama.*

Wycliffe, John (1320?–84) /ˈwiklif/

Religious reformer. He was distinguished at Oxford for his ability in disputes; in 1374, he became Rector of Lutterworth, and soon afterwards he started attacking the Pope and the papal court, at first chiefly on political grounds. He attacked the wealth of the senior clergy, and contrasted it with the poverty of the parish priests. This suited a party of the nobility headed by John of Gaunt who became Wycliffe's patron and protector; they hated the rivalry of the upper clergy, and the powers possessed by the Pope to interfere in national affairs. His opposition to the Papacy grew and was accompanied by opposition to the international religious orders such as those of the friars; this divided Oxford into rival camps. He then went on to attack some of the central doctrines of the Church such as Transubstantiation, *ie* the conversion of the bread and wine of the Sacrament into the actual body and blood of Christ. He also preached direct communion between the individual and God, and wanted an English translation of the Bible; in fact he made one, which is regarded as one of the foundation works of English prose. In all this he anticipated the Reformation* which divided the Church across Europe in 16th C; yet such was the power of his protectors that he died safely in his bed. Although Wycliffe thus anticipated the 16th-C reformers, no independence

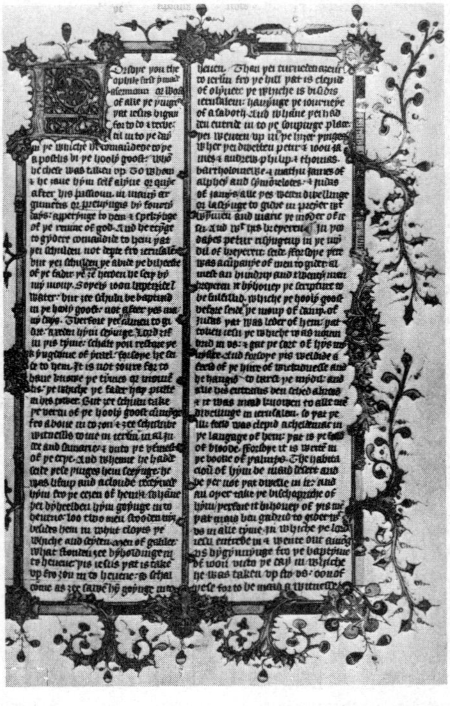

could come to the Church of England* until it suited the interests of the kings; the cause of Wycliffe's success was partly that Richard II* was little more than a boy, and unable to decide on religious policy.

* *Bible in England.*

Wykehamist /ˈwikəmist/

A boy, or former boy at the public school* called Winchester* College, founded by William of Wykeham (14th C).

X

Xanadu /ˈzanədu:/

A city mentioned in the opening lines of *Kubla Khan* (1797), one of the most famous poems by S. T. Coleridge*. Kubla (Kublai) was a 13th-C Mongol ruler who completed the conquest of China begun by his grandfather Genghis Khan, and acquired legendary grandeur in the minds of Western Europeans. In a preface to the poem, Coleridge describes how he fell asleep while reading a 17th-C travel book, *Purchas his Pilgrims.* He had reached the point where Purchas mentioned the city of Xandu, built by Kublai: 'Here the Khan Kubla commanded a palace to be built, and a stately garden thereunto. And thus ten miles of fertile ground were inclosed with a wall.' Coleridge declares that the poem then arose in his mind while he slept, and when he awoke he immediately started writing. The poem begins:

In Xanadu did Kubla Khan
A stately pleasure-dome decree:
Where Alph, the sacred river, ran
Through caverns measureless to man
Down to a sunless sea.
So twice five miles of fertile ground
With walls and towers were girdled round.

Unfortunately, when he had written 54 lines, Coleridge was interrupted by 'a person from Porlock', and the rest of the poem was lost. In a famous work of analytical deduction, *The Road to Xanadu*, J. Livingston Lowes uses Coleridge's note as a starting-point for an elaborate investigation of the working of the poet's mind. (Humphry House, in *Coleridge*, maintains that *Kubla Khan* is an artistically complete poem.)

Xenophon /ˈzenəfən/

Ancient Greek (Athenian) historian and philosopher, born about 430 BC. He was a disciple of Socrates*, and greatly embittered against Athens*, which had put his master to death. Because of this, although he had been an Athenian general, he left the city and served the Spartans*. His writings on Socrates, the *Memorabilia* and the *Symposium*, are the principal records we possess of Socrates besides those of Plato*. Xenophon's *Anabasis* is an account of the war against Artaxerxes; his *Hellenica* is a continuation of the history by Thucydides* down to 362 BC. He wrote other works on household management, hunting, the duties of a cavalry officer, and on the elder Cyrus, founder of the Persian monarchy.

Xerxes (5th C BC) /ˈzɜːksiːz/

King of Persia. He invaded Greece in 480 BC, crossing the Hellespont* between Asia Minor and Greece by a bridge of boats, and at first had great success. He captured the Pass of Thermopylae*, and drove the Greeks allied against him to the Isthmus of Corinth. Fortunately for the future of Europe, he was induced to fight on disadvantageous terms at sea, and was defeated at Salamis (480 BC). Xerxes also occurs in the ancient Jewish romance of *Esther* (Old Testament of the Bible) where he bears the name of Ahasuerus.

Y

Yankee

A slang term used by the British for an American from any part of the United States. In America, it was originally used for an American from the east coast region known as New England. The term arose in 18th C, perhaps from an American Indian word for English colonists, perhaps from an American Indian corruption of the French 'Anglais' = 'English'.

Yeats, W. B. (1865–1939) /jeits/

Anglo-Irish poet. He was of Protestant* family, a fact of importance in 19th-C Ireland where patriotism was so bound up with Roman Catholicism. His father was an eminent painter. He spent his boyhood between school in London and his mother's native county of Sligo, a wild and beautiful county in north-western Ireland which is a background to much of his poetry. His youth was passed during the upsurge of Irish political nationalism represented by the Home Rule* movement led by Parnell*. He shared the antagonism felt by English writers of Pre-Raphaelite background – notably William Morris* – to the urban and industrial harshness and materialism of contemporary English culture. He sought a basis for resistance to it in Irish peasant folk traditions and ancient Celtic myth. His first work was on a theme from this mythology – *The Wanderings of Oisin* (* Oisin). Yeats was indeed fortunate in having such a cultural basis at hand for his anti-materialist poetry, while his English contemporaries had further to look. His career divides naturally into four phases.

[1] *1889–99*. During this period he was a leading member of the Aesthetic* Movement in London, an outcome of Pre-Raphaelitism, but especially indebted to the Oxford scholar, Walter Pater*. In its revolt against Victorian materialism, it tended to Catholicism and to mysticism. Its meeting-place was the Rhymers' Club, and its public voice the Yellow Books*. Yeats shared its mystical sympathies, which in his case brought together Celtic and Indian mythology; these come out in his works of the period: prose – *The Celtic Twilight** (1893), *The Secret Rose*, *The Tables of the Law*, *The Adoration of the Magi* (1897); verse – *Crossways* (1889), *The Rose* (1893), *The Wind Among the Reeds* (1899); verse plays – *The Countess Cathleen* (1892) and *The Land of Heart's Desire* (1894).

[2] *1899–1909*. Yeats, with the help of Lady Gregory, built up the Irish National Theatre, which found a home in the Abbey Theatre*, Dublin. Until 1909, he was its manager, and he wrote plays for it, predominantly based on Irish myth. The period was disillusioning for him so far as his hopes for Irish culture went, but it was formative in his development as a major poet. He hoped to make the theatre the voice of a distinctively Irish modern culture, and at least he succeeded in creating one of the most interesting dramatic movements in contemporary Europe. In personal terms, the theatre business brought out new strength and realism in his character and in his writing; he was the first poet writing in English since 17th C to seek intelligently and purposefully for an effective dramatic idiom and for new methods of dramatic production. His only volume of verse during these 10 years was *In the Seven Woods* (1904); amongst his plays are *Cathleen ni Houlihan* (1902), *The King's Threshold* (1904), *Deirdre* (1907).

[3] *1910–1918 – the Period of Transition*. He had begun his career in the tradition of Spenser*, Shelley*, and the Pre-Raphaelites, and he had always been interested in the mysticism of Blake*, but he now became one of the poets, including Pound* (whom he met at this time) and T. S. Eliot*, drawn to the intellectually more vigorous tradition associated with the 17th-C Metaphysicals*, especially Donne*. He was no longer a Romantic, at least in the decadent sense of a dreamer, but though his mood was harsher and he had lost some of his faith, he searched no less assiduously for symbols which could give meaning to history and life. At first he turned away from Ireland, but the Irish Rebellion of 1916 turned him back to the country which was after all the human context of his emotions. His books *The Green Helmet* (1910) and *Responsibilities* (1914) represent the new austerity of his poetry.

[4] *1919–39 – the Great Period*. It is in this that Yeats grows into one of the very finest poets in English literature. The great books are *The Wild Swans at Coole* (1919), *Michael Robartes and the Dancer* (1921), *The Tower* (1928) and *The Winding Stair* (1933). This work is marked by strong rhythms, by stanza and rhyme patterns which enforce thought, by severe diction with few adjectives, and by a range of symbols each of which is a nucleus of meanings. The symbols are part of an elaborate theory of history (explained in the prose *A Vision*, 1925) derived from the Italian philosopher Vico (1668–1744) and the neo-Platonism of Plotinus (3rd C AD). Whatever the faultiness of the system considered apart from the poetry, it constituted for Yeats a mythology which he could use poetically to embody human experience widely and deeply. It is scarcely helpful to try to 'learn' this mythology in order to understand Yeats's poetry; it is elucidated by the poetry itself, if it is read in bulk. With these symbols (the tower, the moon, etc.) Yeats had a wide mythology of persons, some drawn from his own friends, some from history and myth, and some invented, *eg* Crazy Jane in *Words for Music Perhaps*. This, like *A Woman Young and Old*, *A Full Moon in March* (1935) and *Last Poems* (1936–39), has more bitterness and less richness than the previous volumes of his great period. Yeats continued to write plays and to improve his dramatic idiom, partly under the influence of the Japanese Noh* drama; his best play is nearly his last – *Purgatory* (1939). After 1910, Yeats's prose is also distinguished, notably his *Autobiographies* (1915 and 1922), some of his critical essays, *eg Per Amica Silentia* (1918) and his essays on drama, *Plays and Controversies* (1923).

* 5.3.2; 6.4.2.

Bib: Hone, J. M., *Life*; Ellmann, R., *Yeats, the Man and the Masks; The Identity of Yeats*; Henn, T. R., *The Lonely Tower*; Stock, *W. B. Yeats*; Rudd, M., *Divided Image: a Study of Blake and Yeats*; Unterecker, J., *A Reader's Guide to Yeats*; Kermode, F., *Romantic Image*; Hall and Steinmann (ed.) a collection of essays; Leavis, F. R., *New Bearings in English Poetry*.

Yellow Book

An illustrated quarterly review, 1894–97. It was a main organ of the arts during the period, and though it was especially the voice of the Aesthetic* Movement, it also published writers who did not belong to this movement, *eg* Henry James*.

Yellow Peril

A phrase used at the end of 19th C, expressing the fear that the Mongolian races might sweep across Asia and destroy the European ones. The fear is partly based on previous events, such as the invasion of the West by the Huns*, and that of eastern Europe by the Tartars*, and partly because of the rise of Japan and hostility to Europeans among the Chinese at the end of 19th C.

Yellow Press

A term for popular, sensational, and irresponsible journalism such as became prominent after 1880 (and has not declined). It originated in the U.S.A. as a term for experiments in colour printing in a similar sort of newspaper.

Yeoman

Originally the word probably meant 'countryman', but by 14th C it was used for a peasant freeholder, *ie* a man below the class of gentry, but an independent owner of land, or at least 'a tenant at will', *ie* a man who owed rent for his land but who could abandon his tenancy when he pleased. Yeomen thus formed a class between the gentry and the hired labourers or serfs (who were few after 14th C). The younger sons of yeomen would be landless, and commonly took service with the gentry, often bearing arms for them, like the Yeoman who follows the Squire in Chaucer's *Canterbury Tales**. As a class they were substantial and independent; their skill as archers caused them to be invaluable to the 14th- and 15th-C kings (especially Edward III* and Henry V*) engaged in wars with the French, who relied on cavalry. The success of the yeoman archers at the battles of Crécy* (1346), Poitiers (1356) and Agincourt* (1415) indeed brought about a military revolution; from 15th C the cavalryman declined in importance and the importance of the infantryman increased.

The Wars of the Roses* and the policy of the Tudor* sovereigns reduced the greatness of the old nobility and encouraged the prosperity of the yeomen, who flourished throughout 16th and 17th C, and often improved their condition so as to rise into the class of the gentry. In 18th C the tide ran the other way; the richer landowners were anxious to enclose land into large farms, and to buy out the freeholding yeomen whose small farms stood in the way. This freeholding class thus declined, or joined the ranks of the tenant farmers under the big land-owners. Often they went to work in the rapidly growing industrial towns. By mid-19th C, the term 'yeoman' practically disappeared.

The Yeomen of the Guard were established in 1485, and now guard the Tower of London*; they are popularly known as Beefeaters*. Yeomanry Regiments were regiments of volunteers who in peacetime trained as soldiers in their spare time; after 1920 they were known as the Territorials.

Yeoman's Tale, The Canon's

One of the *Canterbury Tales** by Geoffrey Chaucer. There are two yeomen among the Pilgrims, but the one attached to the Squire does not tell a tale. The Canon and his yeoman, *ie* servant, join the Pilgrims during their journey. The Canon is an alchemist, and his yeoman gives a spirited account of the follies of his master.

* *Alchemy*.

Yggdrasil /ˈigdrasil/

In ancient Scandinavian myth, a tree whose roots are in hell and whose summit is in heaven; its boughs overshadow the earth. It also contains the secrets of life, death, knowledge, fate, time and space.

Yonge, Charlotte Mary (1823–1901)

Novelist. She was a prolific writer with strong High Church beliefs which permeate her writing. Religiously she was influenced by the Oxford Movement* and artistically, to some extent, Pre-Raphaelitism. John Keble, one of the leaders of the former, first induced her to express her religious feelings in fiction. Among the novels which brought her fame, perhaps the best known were *The Heir of Redclyffe* (1853) and *The Daisy Chain* (1856). She wrote a number of historical romances, of which at least one, *The Little Duke* (1854), became a famous children's book.

Bib: Battiscombe, G., *Charlotte Mary Yonge*; Battiscombe, G. and Laski, M., (eds) *A Chaplet for Charlotte Yonge*.

Yorick /ˈjorik/

In Shakespeare's *Hamlet**, the former king's jester whose skull the gravedigger throws up in V. i, giving Hamlet a subject for meditation. It has been conjectured that Shakespeare may have been alluding to Tarlton*, or some other famous jester of the time.

In Sterne's novel *Tristram Shandy** the witty parson who, Sterne suggests, is probably a descendant of Shakespeare's Yorick. Sterne also used Yorick as the pen-name under which he published his sermons*, and as his pen-name in his *Sentimental Journey**.

York Mystery Plays

A cycle of medieval mystery* plays, numbering 48, starting with the Creation, and ending with the last Judgement. A list has survived of the craft guilds* performing the individual plays, showing that, where possible, some appropriate relationship existed between the subject and the trade of the guild, *eg* viii Shipwrights – the instructions of God to Noah for the building of the ark; xvi Goldsmiths – the three kings from the east inquiring for the Child Jesus; Pinners and Painters – the Crucifixion. The York Cycle, like the Wakefield* one, bears evidence of a master at work, commonly known as 'the York Realist'. The play of the Crucifixion is particularly impressive. The cycle was performed throughout 14th and 15th C and continued till 1580, when the antagonism of the Reformation* proved too strong. Annual performance in York has recently been revived.

* 5.1.1.2.

Yorkshire Tragedy, A

A domestic tragedy published in 1608, and based on actual murders occurring in 1605. The play was ascribed to Shakespeare* on its publication but he is not now thought to have had any hand in it. It is, however, a forceful work, in a tradition of domestic tragedy that is an important subordinate line of the drama of Shakespeare's time: *Arden of Feversham* (Anon., 1587); *Warning for Fair Women* (Anon., 1599), and Heywood's* *A Woman Killed with Kindness* (1603). They have in common that they deal with men and women of the middle classes (not, like the grand tragedy of the age, with the courts of princes), that they are realistic, and that they convey a strong moral warning.

Yorktown

The town on the east coast of the United States where General Cornwallis and the British army surrendered to the American rebels in 1781, thus ending the American War of Independence. Yorktown was blockaded by a French fleet, thus preventing relief from Britain.

Young, Edward

* *Night Thoughts.*

Yule, Yuletide

An old synonym for Christmas*. The word derives from the Norse name for a pagan feast to mark the turning of the year – compare Easter*.

Z

Zany /ˈzeini/

A court fool* or jester, from the Italian 'zani' for actors or clowns in the Commedia dell'Arte*.

Zeal-of-the-land Busy

A hypocritical Puritan* in Ben Jonson's comedy *Bartholomew Fair**. It was common for Puritans of the period to give themselves names that were phrases derived from Biblical texts.

Zeno /ˈziːnəu/

The name of two ancient Greek philosophers. Zeno of Citium (end of 4th C BC) was the founder of the Stoic* moral philosophy. Zeno of Elea (5th C BC) was a follower of Parmenides*; he sought to prove by a series of paradoxes that reality is basically unitary, not multiple. He is reputed to be the founder of the use of disputation for the investigation of truth, not for argumentative victory, *ie* he disputed as Socrates* was to dispute.

Zephyrus /ˈzefərəs/

In Greek myth, the west wind. Originally, like Boreas*, he was conceived as stormy and destructive, but later as soft and mild, the wind of Elysium*; his wife was Chloris, goddess of flowers, and his son, Carpus, the god of fruit. A zephyr is always a mild wind in English poetry, associated with the spring, as in the opening to Chaucer's Prologue* to the *Canterbury Tales*.

* *Figures of Speech.*

Zeugma /ˈzjuːgmə/

Figures of Speech

Zeus /zjuːs/

In Greek myth, the King of the gods, identified with the Roman Jupiter (Jove). He was first of all associated with day and sky; his weapons were thunder and the thunderbolts. Zeus was all-powerful and all-knowing, and gradually developed qualities of compassion. He was worshipped on mountain tops, and the oak tree was sacred to him. His most ancient sanctuary was Dodona, but his most famous was the temple of Olympia containing the great statue of him by Pheidias, one of the Seven Wonders*; this showed him crowned with olive leaves, carrying an eagle-topped sceptre in his left hand and the goddess of victory in his right. His queen was Hera*, a goddess specially associated with womanhood, but also originally a sky deity; she was constantly jealous and with good reason – their frequent quarrels were possibly a way of accounting for bad weather.

Before his union with Hera, his wives were Metis = wisdom; Themis = law, mother of Dike (Justice), Eirene (Peace) and the Fates; Mnemosyne*, mother of the Muses; Eurynome, mother of the three graces or charities – Aglaia, Euphrosyne, Thalia. He violated Demeter* (the fertile earth), who thus gave birth to Persephone*.

After union with Hera, Zeus had affairs with various Titanesses and Nymphs, including Leto, mother of Apollo and Artemis; Maia, mother of Hermes. By other relationships, Zeus was made the ancestor of various Greek races, including the Arcadians and the Lacedaemonians (Spartans).

In his affairs with mortal women, he frequently disguised himself to gain access to them: thus to Europa* he came as a bull, to Leda as a swan, to Danae* as a shower of gold, and to Alcmene he assumed the most effective disguise of all – that of her own husband. All such unions were in some way attempts to symbolize truths of nature, or attempts to find divine ancestry for human races. Thus the legend of Danae is thought to be an image of the fertilizing rays of the setting sun. The union with Hera remained, and Zeus was the protector of monogamous marriage and of the home.

The Roman Jupiter has many of the same characteristics as Zeus, but is perhaps more civic and political; he is the protector of the City and stands for the power of Empire.

Zimri /'zimrai/

In the Bible (*1 Kings* 16), he is a captain of chariots to Asa, king of Judah. He conspires against the king, and eventually kills him.

In Dryden's satirical fable, *Absalom and Achitophel**, Zimri stands for the 2nd Duke of Buckingham. The satire was directed against the movement led by Lord Shaftesbury* (Achitophel) to make Charles II's illegitimate son the Duke of Monmouth* (Absalom) heir to the throne in place of the King's brother, James, Duke of York. Buckingham figures in the poem ostensibly because he had also taken a line hostile to the King, though he was in fact also opposed to Monmouth and Shaftesbury. Dryden's real reason for including him was probably personal: Buckingham had satirized Dryden's tragedies in his comedy, *The Rehearsal* (1672).

Zionism

A Jewish nationalistic movement for the return of the Jews to Palestine. The Jews of Europe preserved their sense of national identity throughout the Middle Ages*, and in 16th and 17th C there was a succession of movements among them for a return to Zion – a synonym for Jerusalem. In 19th C the increase of anti-Semitism in various countries of Europe intensified the longing, and the movement received more coherent organization. George Eliot's* novel *Daniel Deronda* (1876) was an inspiration to the movement. During World War I, an English Jew, Chaim Weismann, proposed that Britain should provide for a home for the Jews in Palestine. In February 1918 Britain in association with France issued the Balfour Declaration (Balfour was British foreign secretary) declaring their support for the policy. In 1920 Palestine became a British mandate, and the policy was carried out. It was not originally intended that the Jewish community should turn itself into a Jewish state, nor that the rights of Arabs in Palestine should suffer.

Zola, Emile Edouard Charles Antoine (1840–1902) /'zeulə/

French novelist. He carried the realism of Flaubert* a stage further into the doctrine of naturalism*. He believed that the biological sciences (notably the discoveries of Darwin*) had changed the conditions under which the human character should be presented and interpreted, and that in future the novelist should present his characters in relation to the influences of heredity and environment, shown in fearless detail. This he carried out in the succession of novels about the Rougon and Macquart families, 1871–93 including *La Fortune des Rougon* (1871), *La Curée* (1874), *Le Ventre de Paris* (1874), *La Conquête de Plassans* (1875), *La Faute de l'Abbé Mouret* (1875), *Son Excellence Eugène Rougon* (1876), *L'Assommoir* – his most famous – (1878), *Nana* (1880), *Germinal* (1885), *La Terre* (1888), *La Débâcle* (1892) and *Docteur Pascal* (1893). Scientifically and in literary terms, Zola's naturalistic theory was ingenuous, but his creative imagination in presenting environment was genuine, and his influence was healthy in England inasmuch as the doctrine counteracted an English prejudice against the ugly, the 'indecent' and the horrible in art. He had English imitators, *eg* George Moore*, and he influenced such realists as Gissing*, Wells* and Bennett*; James Joyce's *Ulysses** takes Zola's art (but not his pesudo-scientific theory) to the furthest limit.

Zoroaster /zorəu'astə/

The Greek form of the Persian name Zarathustra. A Persian philosopher of 6th C BC, about whom there are many legends. He preached twin deities – Ormazd, who is light and good, and Ahriman, who is darkness and evil. They are in conflict, and their conflict is the history of the world; it centres on man, created by Ormazd, but brought to grief by Ahriman. Zoroastrianism has kinship with the dualistic religions of Mithraism and Manichaeism, rivals to Christianity in its early centuries. He originated the Magi (* *Magi* [1]).

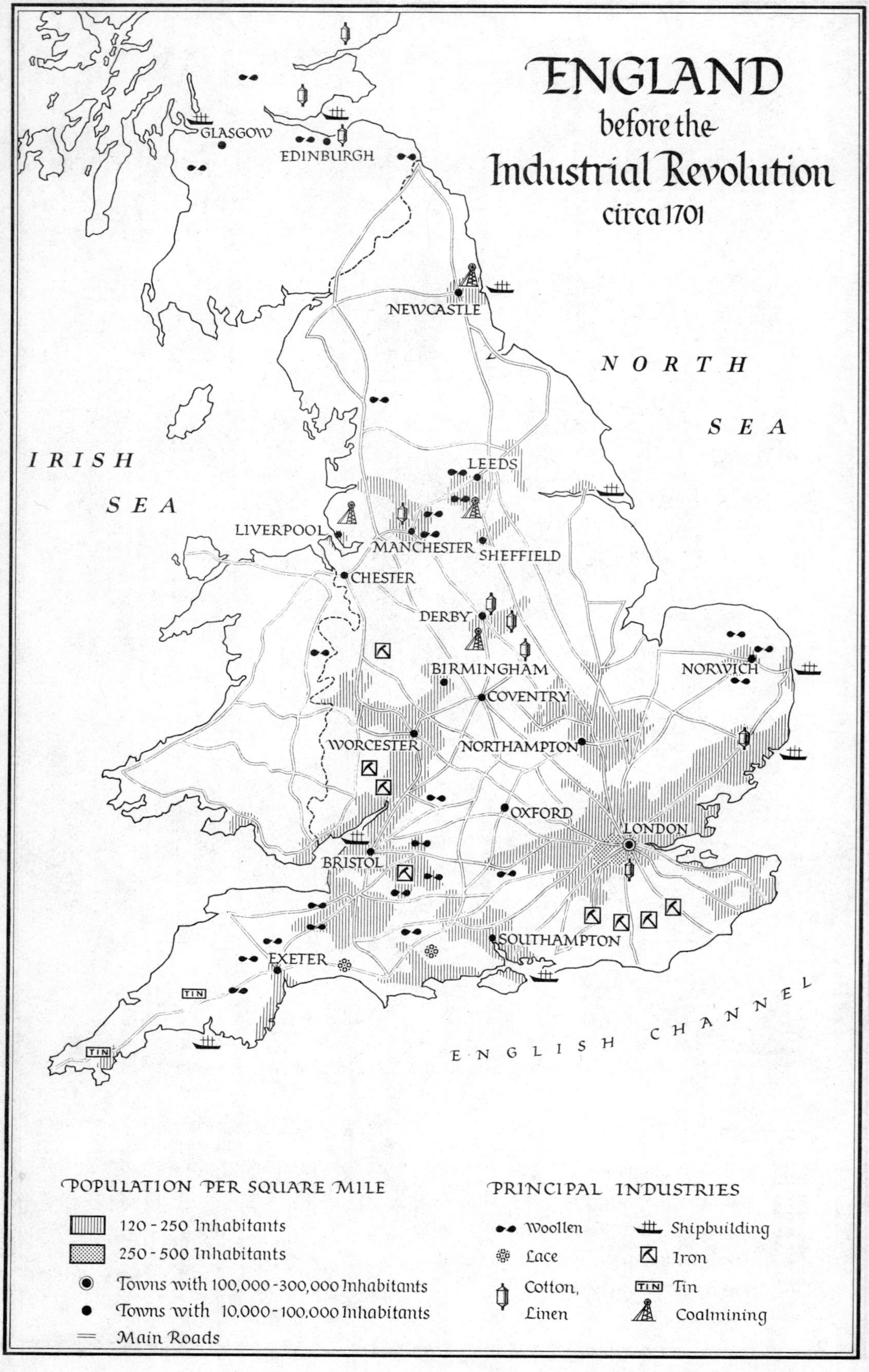
ENGLAND
before the
Industrial Revolution
circa 1701
NORTH
SEA
IRISH
SEA
ENGLISH CHANNEL
GLASGOW
EDINBURGH
NEWCASTLE
LEEDS
LIVERPOOL
MANCHESTER
SHEFFIELD
CHESTER
DERBY
BIRMINGHAM
COVENTRY
NORWICH
WORCESTER
NORTHAMPTON
OXFORD
LONDON
BRISTOL
SOUTHAMPTON
EXETER
TIN
TIN
POPULATION PER SQUARE MILE
120 - 250 Inhabitants
250 - 500 Inhabitants
Towns with 100,000 - 300,000 Inhabitants
Towns with 10,000 - 100,000 Inhabitants
Main Roads
PRINCIPAL INDUSTRIES
Woollen
Lace
Cotton, Linen
Shipbuilding
Iron
TIN Tin
Coalmining

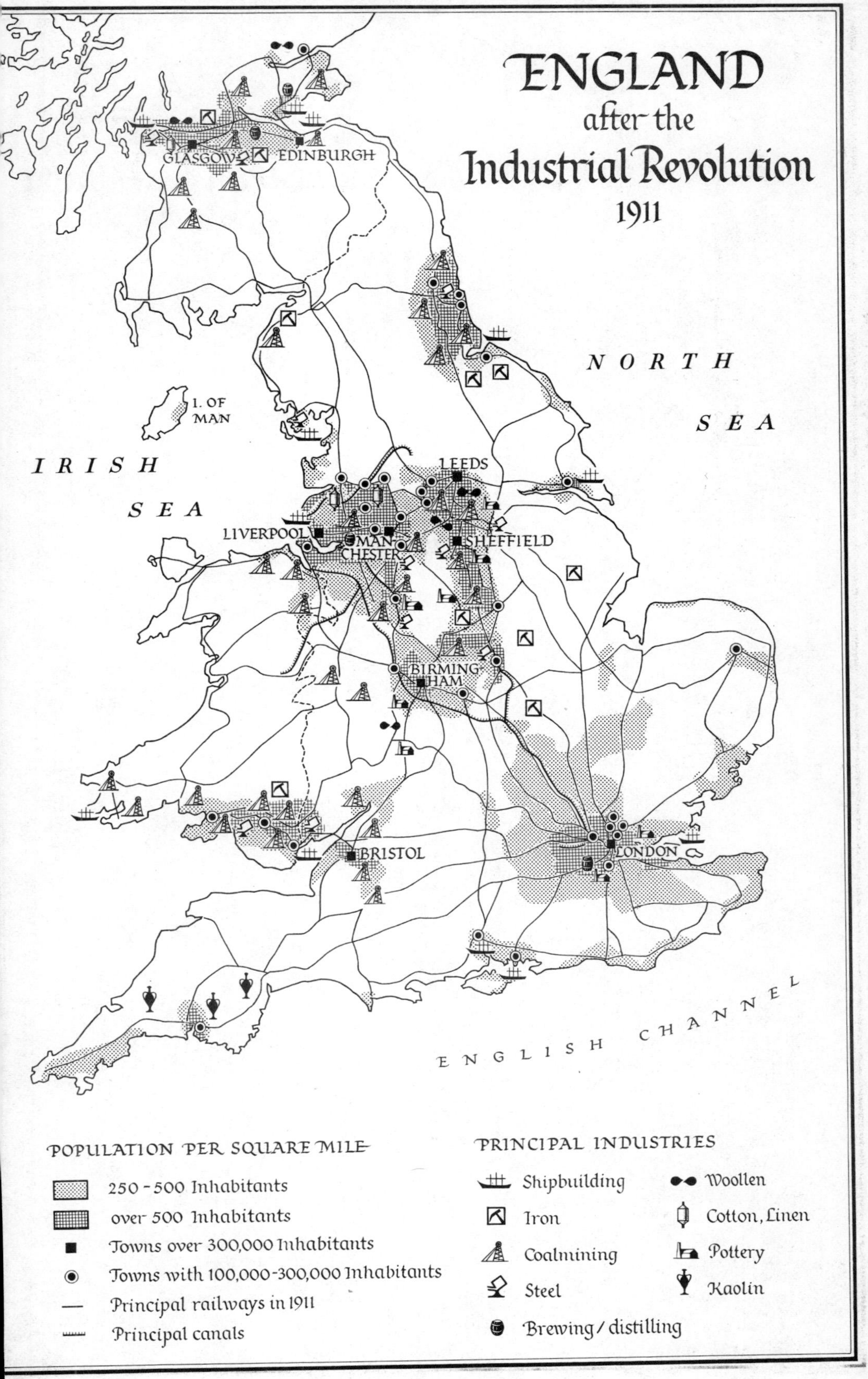

ENGLAND
after the
Industrial Revolution
1911
GLASGOW
EDINBURGH
NORTH
SEA
I. OF
MAN
IRISH
SEA
LEEDS
LIVERPOOL
MAN-
CHESTER
SHEFFIELD
BIRMING-
HAM
BRISTOL
LONDON
ENGLISH CHANNEL
POPULATION PER SQUARE MILE
250 - 500 Inhabitants
over 500 Inhabitants
Towns over 300,000 Inhabitants
Towns with 100,000-300,000 Inhabitants
Principal railways in 1911
Principal canals
PRINCIPAL INDUSTRIES
Shipbuilding
Iron
Coalmining
Steel
Brewing / distilling
Woollen
Cotton, Linen
Pottery
Kaolin